HOOVER'S MASTERLIST OF MAJOR U.S. COMPANIES 1993

Hoover's MasterList of Major U.S. Companies is intended to provide its readers with accurate and authoritative information about the enterprises covered in it. The information contained herein is as accurate as we could reasonably make it. However, we do not warrant that the book is absolutely accurate or without any errors. Readers should not rely on any information contained herein in instances where such reliance might cause loss or damage. The editors and publishers specifically disclaim all warranties, including the implied warranties of merchantability and fitness for a specific purpose. This book is sold with the understanding that neither the editors nor the publisher is engaged in providing investment, financial, accounting, legal, or other professional advice.

THE REFERENCE PRESS, INC.

10 9 8 7 6 5 4 3 2

Publisher Cataloging-In-Publication Data

Hoover's MasterList of Major U.S. Companies 1993. Edited by The Reference Press, Inc.

Includes indexes.
1. Business enterprises — Directories. 2. Corporations — Directories.
HF3010 338.7

ISBN 1-878753-14-2 clothbound
ISSN 1066-291X

This book was produced by The Reference Press on Apple Macintosh computers using Claris Corporation's FileMaker Pro 2.0, Quark, Inc.'s Quark XPress 3.1, EM Software, Inc.'s Xdata 2.0, and Adobe Systems Incorporated's fonts from the Palatino and Futura families. Cover design is by Kristin M. Jackson, of Austin, Texas. Electronic prepress was done by The Courier Connection in San Mateo, California, and the book was printed by Courier Corporation in Westford, Massachusetts. Text paper is 60# Postmark Bright White (manufactured by Union Camp). Cover stock is Kivar #5 cloth.

Hoover's MasterList of Major U.S. Companies and other Reference Press books are available from:

THE REFERENCE PRESS
6448 Highway 290 E., Suite E-104
Austin, Texas 78723
Phone: 512-454-7778
Fax: 512-454-9401

WILLIAM SNYDER PUBLISHING ASSOCIATES
5, Five Mile Drive,
Oxford OX2 8HT,
England
Phone & fax: +44 (0)865-513186

ACCESS NIPPON, INC.
Yamaguchi Bldg., 2-8-5,
Uchikanda,
Chiyada-ku, Tokyo, 101
Japan
Phone: +81-3-5256-1541
Fax: +81-3-3258-1487

CONTENTS

THE STAFF

Chairman: Gary Hoover
CEO, President, and Senior Editor: Patrick J. Spain
Senior Vice-President and Editor-in-Chief: Alta Campbell
Vice-President, Acting CFO, and Senior Writer: Alan Chai
Information Systems and Electronic Publishing Manager: Wendy Weigant
Director of Sales and Marketing: Dana L. Smith
Customer Service Manager: Andrea Avery
Office Manager: Tammy Fisher

ACKNOWLEDGMENTS

Editors
Roy W. Bernstein, Alta Campbell, Britton E. Jackson, Patrick J. Spain, Deborah Stratton

Database Designer
Wendy Weigant

Graphic Designer
Kristin M. Jackson

Desktop Publishers/Page Designers
Kristin M. Jackson, Wendy Weigant

Researchers
Mary L. Davidson, Ginger Dixon, Nancy C. Gravley, Britton E. Jackson, Diane Lee, Jeanne Minnich, Joel Nitz, Jennifer A. Sherman, Teri C. Sperry, Amanda Woods

Data Entry
Cherise Budwit, Ginger Dixon, Nancy C. Gravley, Denise Haney, Kyna Horton, Diane Lee, Tammy Robinson, Teri C. Sperry, Lora Watson

Proofreaders
Denise Haney, Britton E. Jackson, Diane Lee, Jeanne Minnich, Teri C. Sperry, Amanda Woods

Other Contributors
Andrea Avery

THE REFERENCE PRESS MISSION STATEMENT

1. To produce business information products and services of the highest quality, accuracy, and readability.
2. To make that information available whenever, wherever, and however our customers want it through mass distribution at affordable prices.
3. To continually expand our range of products and services and our markets for those products and services.
4. To reward our employees, suppliers, and shareholders based on their contributions to the success of our enterprise.
5. To hold to the highest ethical business standards, erring on the side of generosity when in doubt.

ABOUT HOOVER'S MASTERLIST OF MAJOR U.S. COMPANIES

Hoover's MasterList of Major U.S. Companies 1993 was created in response to requests from the readers of *Hoover's Handbooks* — the first widely distributed, reasonably priced, easy-to-use annual reference books on major companies. Readers of *Hoover's Handbooks* asked for a more comprehensive, but still affordable, source for company information. The Reference Press created *Hoover's MasterList* to meet that need.

While there are directories with more entries than *Hoover's MasterList*, there are none that are as focused and none that deliver better value for the money. The nearly 6,000 companies in the *MasterList* are the companies you need to know about: every major publicly listed U.S. company, the 500 largest private companies, nearly 500 of the fastest-growing private companies, and nearly 200 of the most important foreign companies with operations in the U.S. Making the basic information on these companies available for under $50 is a first in business reference publishing.

We recommend *Hoover's MasterList of Major U.S. Companies 1993* to anyone (particularly librarians, executives, salespeople, investors, job seekers, fund raisers, and students) needing the basic facts about the companies that are the backbone of American business.

SELECTION OF THE COMPANIES

The Reference Press selected the companies for *Hoover's MasterList of Major U.S. Companies* using the following criteria:

PUBLIC COMPANIES (4,812)

We included **every** public U.S. company traded on the New York Stock Exchange (NYSE), American Stock Exchange (AMEX), and NASDAQ National Market (NASDAQ). In addition, we included all large public companies still in business that used to trade on these exchanges but whose trading has been suspended because they are in bankruptcy reorganization (e.g., Continental Airlines and Southland).

While the companies traded on the NYSE and AMEX do not move on and off those exchanges frequently, companies listed on the NASDAQ are somewhat more volatile. Depending on market capitalization and trading volume, smaller companies move on and off the NASDAQ. We have used *Barron's* as our arbiter of what is and what is not a NASDAQ National Market company. We plan to add all over-the-counter (OTC) companies to the *MasterList* in a future edition.

PRIVATE COMPANIES (1,001)

Our customers told us that they were interested in the largest private companies in the U.S. We consulted the *Forbes* list of the largest 400 private companies in the U.S. and included **all** of them. We added some large private companies *Forbes* does not cover (e.g., Barnes & Noble and Hertz), some smaller private companies that just missed making the *Forbes* list, and nearly 100 of the largest mutual insurance companies, agricultural co-ops, sports teams, labor organizations, and not-for-profits, all of which appear in *Hoover's Handbook of American Business 1993.*

Our readers also asked us to include rapidly growing private companies — the ones that are hiring, buying products, and most likely to go public in the future. We looked at *Inc.* magazine's list, published in October 1992, of the 500 fastest-growing companies and included **all** but about 40 companies for which we were unable (after vigorous effort) to obtain enough information to allow inclusion in the *MasterList.* We then added most of the rapidly growing and well-known private companies that are included in *Hoover's Handbook of Emerging Companies* (e.g., NeXT and Kendall-Jackson Winery). We also included Demand Research Corporation (which contributed to the information in this book) and The Reference Press, Inc.

FOREIGN COMPANIES (181)

Finally, we believe that many people in the U.S. have not been made sufficiently aware of the business and employment opportunities at foreign companies with large U.S. operations. All of the companies we included are from *Hoover's Handbook of World Business 1993.*

SUMMARY

In total, there are 5,813 entries in the book you hold in your hands. Each company listed met the inclusion criteria detailed above. No company was omitted, even if it requested to be. We will be constantly adding companies to the *MasterList*, and when we do so, we will use objective criteria. For example, if we add law firms, we will add the top 25, 50, or 100, not just those who choose to respond to our inquiries.

INFORMATION PROVIDED ABOUT THE COMPANIES

Each capsule profile in the *MasterList* contains the basic information that most people need to locate, communicate with, and evaluate the companies listed in this book. We have included each company's name, street address, phone number, fax number, names of the chief executive officer (CEO) and chief financial officer (CFO), most recently available annual sales figure, number of employees, a description of what the company does, and status (private or public company). In the latter case, we have provided its trading symbol and exchange.

Some companies did not have (or would not provide) fax numbers. The sales figures for some private companies are estimated or approximate, as the companies would not divulge exact figures. For foreign companies we have provided the sales and employment information for the parent company. For companies with sales of under $11 million, we rounded to the nearest hundred thousand. For larger companies all sales figures are rounded to the nearest million. Most sales figures correspond to the companies' sales as of the most recently available fiscal years; however, so we could provide more updated information, many companies that are identified as having 1992 sales information, have information for the most recently available 12 months at the time we went to press. Sometimes this corresponded to the fiscal year; sometimes it did not. For fiscal years ending between January 1, 1992, and early February 1992, we have called the sales figures 1991. The same convention was also used in the subsequent year.

A few companies have joint CEOs or a chairman and a president, neither of whom has the title of CEO. In these cases, we have listed after the CEO heading the name of the person who appears first in the company's materials. In smaller companies, there is sometimes no one with the official title of CFO. In those cases, we have listed after the CFO heading the name of the person responsible for the finance and accounting function in the company — frequently a treasurer, controller, or accounting manager. For most U.S. operations of foreign companies and some smaller U.S. companies, we were unable by press time to obtain the names of their CFOs.

Companies in the *MasterList* that have in-depth profiles in *Hoover's Handbook of American Business 1993* are indicated by the symbol ✪ and those with profiles in *Hoover's Handbook of World Business 1993* are indicated by the symbol ✪. Readers who do not have *Hoover's Handbooks* may obtain information about purchasing them from The Reference Press (800-486-8666).

SOURCES OF INFORMATION

This book was developed from an internal database of company information developed by The Reference Press. We supplemented and expanded that database by obtaining additional information on U.S. public companies from Demand Research Corporation (Chicago, Illinois) and Standard & Poor's Compustat (Englewood, Colorado). While information for publicly traded companies could be verified from public sources, information on private companies was verified directly with those companies. We used a combination of telephone, fax, and mailed communications to verify information. All information is current through November 30, 1992, for public companies and through February 10, 1993, for private companies. In the case of personnel changes at the larger companies, we updated changes through February 27, 1993.

INDEXES

To help readers easily locate information, we have included three indexes in the *MasterList*. The companies are indexed by headquarters location, industry, and stock exchange symbol.

UPDATES

Hoover's MasterList of Major U.S. Companies will be updated annually. As well as adding new companies, we plan to expand coverage on existing ones. For example, next year we intend to include the names of the Human Resources Managers.

ELECTRONIC EDITION

For the first time The Reference Press is making the entire contents of a book, *Hoover's MasterList of Major U.S. Companies*, available in magnetic media. Users of the magnetic version of the *MasterList* will be able to use their own software to create mailing lists, send personalized letters, or search for companies by industry, revenue, number of employees, geographic location, etc. The magnetic version of the *MasterList* may be ordered from The Reference Press for $129.95. It is available on IBM-compatible and Macintosh disks and can be formatted in tab-separated text, spreadsheet, or database format. More information on this product is included at the back of this book.

PRICING

The mission of The Reference Press is to produce high-quality business reference products at affordable prices. Each entry in this book and each name in the magnetic version of the *MasterList* costs the purchaser less than a penny apiece. This is far below the price of other providers of such information. The Reference Press believes that basic information about companies should be reasonably priced and widely available. We are leading the movement to make this a reality, and we appreciate the support that you, our readers and customers, are providing to this effort.

SUGGESTIONS

The best suggestions we receive come from our readers. We welcome your suggestions and comments and encourage you to use the postcards in the back of this book to share your thoughts with us about additional information you would like to see included in future editions of the *MasterList*. If you believe there is a need for other reasonably priced business reference books, let us know.

COMPANY LISTINGS

1993

20th Century Industries
6301 Owensmouth Ave., Ste. 700
Woodland Hills, CA 91367
Phone: 818-704-3700 Fax: 818-704-3056
CEO: Louis W. Foster
CFO: James O. Curley
1992 Sales: $991 million Employees: —
Symbol: TW Exchange: NYSE
Industry: Insurance - property & casualty

21 International Holdings
153 E. 53rd St.
New York, NY 10022
Phone: 212-230-0400 Fax: 212-593-1363
CEO: Marshall S. Cogan
CFO: Robert Nelson
1991 Sales: $1,000 million Employees: 3,700
Ownership: Privately held
Industry: Diversified operations - restaurants, foam rubber & auto dealerships

3COM Corp.
5400 Bayfront Plaza
Santa Clara, CA 95054
Phone: 408-764-5000 Fax: 408-970-1112
CEO: Eric Benhamou
CFO: Christopher Paisley
1992 Sales: $408 million Employees: 1,896
Symbol: COMS Exchange: NASDAQ
Industry: Computers - local area networks

50-Off Stores, Inc.
8750 Tesoro Dr.
San Antonio, TX 78217
Phone: 210-805-9300 Fax: 210-805-0067
CEO: Charles M. Siegel
CFO: Pat L. Ross
1991 Sales: $130 million Employees: 1,984
Symbol: FOFF Exchange: NASDAQ
Industry: Retail - discount & variety

84 Lumber Co.
Rt. 519
Eighty Four, PA 15384
Phone: 412-228-8820 Fax: 412-225-2530
CEO: Joseph A. Hardy, Sr.
CFO: Curt Stump
1992 Sales: $900 million Employees: 3,500
Ownership: Privately held
Industry: Building products - retail

A. B. Dick Company
5700 W. Touhy Ave.
Chicago, IL 60648
Phone: 708-647-8800 Fax: 708-647-0845
CEO: D. Powell
CFO: —
1992 Sales: $17,643 million Employees: 104,995
Parent: The General Electric Company PLC
Industry: Electronic & power systems, telecommunications, consumer goods

A.G. Edwards & Sons, Inc.
One N. Jefferson Ave.
St. Louis, MO 63103
Phone: 314-289-3000 Fax: 314-289-3565
CEO: Benjamin F. Edwards III
CFO: David W. Mesker
1992 Sales: $1,038 million Employees: 8,736
Symbol: AGE Exchange: NYSE
Industry: Financial - investment bankers

A. H. Belo Corp.
400 S. Record St.
Dallas, TX 75202
Phone: 214-977-6600 Fax: 214-977-6603
CEO: Robert W. Decherd
CFO: Michael D. Perry
1991 Sales: $432 million Employees: 2,627
Symbol: BLC Exchange: NYSE
Industry: Broadcasting - radio & TV; newspapers

A. L. Laboratories, Inc.
One Executive Dr.
Ft. Lee, NJ 07024
Phone: 201-947-7774 Fax: 201-947-5541
CEO: Einar W. Sissener
CFO: Robert A. Pudlak
1991 Sales: $290 million Employees: 1,700
Symbol: BMD Exchange: NYSE
Industry: Drugs - generic

A. L. Williams Life Insurance Co.
3120 Breckinridge Blvd.
Duluth, GA 30199
Phone: 404-381-1674 Fax: 404-279-9540
CEO: John Treacy Beyer
CFO: D. Richard Williams
1991 Sales: $167 million Employees: 2,371
Symbol: ALW Exchange: NYSE
Industry: Insurance - life

A.M. Castle & Co.
3400 N. Wolf Rd.
Franklin Park, IL 60131
Phone: 708-455-7111 Fax: 708-455-0587
CEO: Richard G. Mork
CFO: Edward F. Culliton
1991 Sales: $436 million Employees: 1,268
Symbol: CAS Exchange: AMEX
Industry: Metal products - distribution

A.M. Express Inc.
1401 N. 26th St.
Escanaba, MI 49829
Phone: 906-786-0645 Fax: 906-786-0066
CEO: Robert Garcia
CFO: Robert Garcia
1991 Sales: $1.8 million Employees: 24
Ownership: Privately held
Industry: Transportation - truck

indicates company is in *Hoover's Handbook of American Business.*

indicates company is in *Hoover's Handbook of World Business;* sales and employee numbers are for parent company.

A. O. Smith Corp.
11270 W. Park Place
Milwaukee, WI 53224
Phone: 414-359-4000 Fax: 414-359-4180
CEO: Robert J. O'Toole
CFO: Glen R. Bomberger
1992 Sales: $1,046 million Employees: 9,400
Symbol: SMCA Exchange: AMEX
Industry: Automotive & trucking - original equipment

A. P. Green Industries, Inc.
Green Blvd.
Mexico, MO 65265
Phone: 314-473-3626 Fax: 314-473-3330
CEO: Harry M. Stover
CFO: Gary L. Roberts
1991 Sales: $170 million Employees: 1,637
Symbol: APGI Exchange: NASDAQ
Industry: Building products

A. Schulman, Inc.
3550 W. Market St.
Akron, OH 44333
Phone: 216-666-3751 Fax: 216-668-7204
CEO: Terry L. Haines
CFO: Robert A. Stefanko
1992 Sales: $727 million Employees: 1,491
Symbol: SHLM Exchange: NASDAQ
Industry: Chemicals - plastics

A.T. CROSS
One Albion Rd.
Lincoln, RI 02865
Phone: 401-333-1200 Fax: 401-333-0253
CEO: Bradford R. Boss
CFO: Michael El-Hillow
1991 Sales: $217 million Employees: 1,800
Symbol: ATXA Exchange: AMEX
Industry: Office & art materials - writing instruments, luggage & gift items

A&W Brands, Inc.
709 Westchester Ave.
White Plains, NY 10604
Phone: 914-397-1700 Fax: 914-993-0538
CEO: M. L. Lowenkron
CFO: Ernest J. Cavallo
1991 Sales: $123 million Employees: 173
Symbol: SODA Exchange: NASDAQ
Industry: Beverages - soft drinks

A-Mark Precious Metals , Inc.
100 Wilshire Blvd., 3rd Fl.
Santa Monica, CA 90401
Phone: 310-319-0200 Fax: 310-319-0279
CEO: Steven C. Markoff
CFO: —
1990 Sales: $1,000 million Employees: 32
Ownership: Privately held
Industry: Precious metals wholesaling

Aames Financial Corp.
3731 Wilshire Blvd.
Los Angeles, CA 90010
Phone: 213-351-6100 Fax: 213-380-9365
CEO: Gary J. Judis
CFO: Gregory J. Witherspoon
1991 Sales: $18 million Employees: 165
Symbol: AAMS Exchange: NASDAQ
Industry: Financial - mortgages & related services

AAMP of America, Inc.
13160 56th Court, Ste. 502-508
Clearwater, FL 34620
Phone: 813-572-9255 Fax: 813-573-9326
CEO: Micah S. Ansley
CFO: Micah S. Ansley
1991 Sales: $6.7 million Employees: 29
Ownership: Privately held
Industry: Auto parts - wholesale auto stereo parts

AAR Corp.
1111 Nicholas Blvd.
Elk Grove Village, IL 60007
Phone: 708-439-3939 Fax: 708-439-3955
CEO: Ira A. Eichner
CFO: Joseph J. Dzurinko
1992 Sales: $423 million Employees: 1,840
Symbol: AIR Exchange: NYSE
Industry: Aerospace - aircraft equipment

Aaron Rents, Inc.
3001 N. Fulton Dr. NE
Atlanta, GA 30363
Phone: 404-231-0011 Fax: 404-240-6598
CEO: R. Charles Loudermilk, Sr.
CFO: Gilbert L. Danielson
1992 Sales: $143 million Employees: 1,400
Symbol: ARON Exchange: NASDAQ
Industry: Retail - home furnishings, household appliance & consumer electronics rental

Aarque Cos.
111 W. 2nd St.
Jamestown, NY 14701
Phone: 716-664-6014 Fax: 716-664-5057
CEO: R. Quintus Anderson
CFO: Donald Proctor
1991 Sales: $450 million Employees: 2,665
Ownership: Privately held
Industry: Metal products - fabrication

ABA Personnel Services
690 Market St., Ste. 800
San Francisco, CA 94104
Phone: 415-434-4222 Fax: 415-434-3958
CEO: Valli Farmaian
CFO: Valli Farmaian
1991 Sales: $4.4 million Employees: 12
Ownership: Privately held
Industry: Business services - employment search services

Abacus Inc.
514 Bryant St.
San Francisco, CA 94107
Phone: 415-974-7000 Fax: 415-974-7005
CEO: Shari Tresky
CFO: Dan King
1991 Sales: $30 million Employees: 103
Ownership: Privately held
Industry: Computers - PC retail

Abacus Technology
5454 Wisconsin Ave.
Chevy Chase, MD 20815
Phone: 301-907-8500 Fax: 301-907-8508
CEO: Dennis Yee
CFO: William Magro
1991 Sales: $12 million Employees: 104
Ownership: Privately held
Industry: Business services - consulting & information systems

Abaxis, Inc.
1320 Chesapeake Terrace
Sunnyvale, CA 94089
Phone: 408-734-0200 Fax: —
CEO: Gary H. Stroy
CFO: Kurt E. Amundson
1992 Sales: — Employees: 49
Symbol: ABAX Exchange: NASDAQ
Industry: Medical instruments

Abbey Healthcare Group, Inc.
3560 Hyland Ave.
Costa Mesa, CA 92626
Phone: 714-957-2000 Fax: —
CEO: Timothy M. Aitken
CFO: Richard J. Rapp
1991 Sales: $227 million Employees: —
Symbol: ABBY Exchange: NASDAQ
Industry: Healthcare - outpatient & home

Abbott Laboratories
1 Abbott Park Rd.
Abbott Park, IL 60064
Phone: 708-937-6100 Fax: 708-937-1511
CEO: Duane L. Burnham
CFO: Gary P. Coughlan
1992 Sales: $7,852 million Employees: 45,694
Symbol: ABT Exchange: NYSE
Industry: Drugs, hospital equipment & consumer health care products

ABCO Markets Inc.
3001 W. Indian School Rd.
Phoenix, AZ 85017
Phone: 602-222-1600 Fax: 602-222-1684
CEO: Edward G. Hill
CFO: William O. Walters
1991 Sales: $700 million Employees: 5,000
Ownership: Privately held
Industry: Retail - supermarkets

Abex, Inc.
Liberty Lane
Hampton, NH 03842
Phone: 603-926-5911 Fax: 603-926-5661
CEO: Michael D. Dingman
CFO: Michael D. Dingman
1992 Sales: $728 million Employees: 5,000
Symbol: ABE Exchange: NYSE
Industry: Engineering - R&D services

Abington Bancorp, Inc.
533 Washington St.
Abington, MA 02351
Phone: 617-878-0103 Fax: —
CEO: James P. McDonough
CFO: Edward J. Merritt
1991 Sales: $23 million Employees: —
Symbol: ABBK Exchange: NASDAQ
Industry: Banks - Northeast

ABIOMED, Inc.
33 Cherry Hill Dr.
Danvers, MA 01923
Phone: 508-777-5410 Fax: 508-777-8411
CEO: David M. Lederman
CFO: David M. Lederman
1992 Sales: $2.7 million Employees: 69
Symbol: ABMD Exchange: NASDAQ
Industry: Medical instruments - cardiac

ABL Electronics
10942 Beaver Dam Rd.
Hunt Valley, MD 21030
Phone: 410-584-2700 Fax: 410-584-2790
CEO: Randy Amon
CFO: Randy Amon
1991 Sales: $3.2 million Employees: 39
Ownership: Privately held
Industry: Computers - computer & networking cabling & accessories

Abrams Industries, Inc.
5775-A Glenridge Dr. NE
Atlanta, GA 30328
Phone: 404-256-9785 Fax: 404-252-3891
CEO: Bernard W. Abrams
CFO: Joseph H. Rubin
1992 Sales: $83 million Employees: 373
Symbol: ABRI Exchange: NASDAQ
Industry: Diversified operations - construction, store fixtures & real estate development

ABS Industries, Inc.
Interstate Square, Ste. 300
Willoughby, OH 44094
Phone: 216-946-2274 Fax: 216-946-8298
CEO: William J. McCarthy
CFO: William J. McCarthy
1991 Sales: $36 million Employees: 302
Symbol: ABSI Exchange: NASDAQ
Industry: Machine tools & related products

indicates company is in *Hoover's Handbook of American Business.*

indicates company is in *Hoover's Handbook of World Business;* sales and employee numbers are for parent company.

ACC Corp.
39 State St.
Rochester, NY 14614
Phone: 716-987-3000 Fax: 716-987-3499
CEO: Richard T. Aab
CFO: Michael R. Daley
1991 Sales: $52 million Employees: 185
Symbol: ACCC Exchange: NASDAQ
Industry: Telecommunications services

ACCEL International Corp.
475 Metro Place North
Dublin, OH 43017
Phone: 614-764-7000 Fax: —
CEO: R. Max Williamson
CFO: Richard W. Ballantine
1991 Sales: $102 million Employees: 225
Symbol: ACLE Exchange: NASDAQ
Industry: Insurance - multiline & misc.

Access Health Marketing, Inc.
11020 White Rock Rd.
Rancho Cordova, CA 95670
Phone: 916-851-4000 Fax: 916-852-3890
CEO: Kenneth B. Plumlee
CFO: John E. Gebhart III
1991 Sales: $10.1 million Employees: 126
Symbol: ACCS Exchange: NASDAQ
Industry: Medical services

Acclaim Entertainment, Inc.
71 Audrey Ave.
Oyster Bay, NY 11771
Phone: 516-624-8888 Fax: 516-624-2885
CEO: Gregory Fischbach
CFO: Anthony Williams
1992 Sales: $215 million Employees: 133
Symbol: AKLM Exchange: NASDAQ
Industry: Toys - video game cartridges

Accor North America Corp.
2 Overhill Rd., Ste. 420
Scarsdale, NY 10583
Phone: 914-725-5055 Fax: 914-725-5640
CEO: Patrick Bourguignon
CFO: —
1991 Sales: $2,710 million Employees: 45,743
Parent: Accor SA
Industry: Hotels, restaurants & tours

AccSys Technology Inc.
1177 A Quarry Lane
Pleasanton, CA 94566
Phone: 510-462-6949 Fax: 510-462-6993
CEO: Robert W. Hamm
CFO: Curt W. Mason
1991 Sales: $3.2 million Employees: 38
Ownership: Privately held
Industry: Instruments - linear accelerator systems

Aceto Corp.
126-02 Northern Blvd.
Flushing, NY 11368
Phone: 516-627-6000 Fax: 718-803-6372
CEO: Arnold Frankel
CFO: Donald Horowitz
1991 Sales: $133 million Employees: 200
Symbol: ACET Exchange: NASDAQ
Industry: Chemicals - specialty

Achen Contractors
1343 N. Alma School, Ste. 125
Chandler, AZ 85224
Phone: 602-258-3047 Fax: 602-821-0678
CEO: Douglass Gardner
CFO: Sanders Achen
1991 Sales: $8.5 million Employees: 55
Ownership: Privately held
Industry: Construction - general contracting

Ackerley Communications, Inc.
800 Fifth Ave., Ste. 3770
Seattle, WA 98104
Phone: 206-624-2888 Fax: 206-623-7853
CEO: Barry Ackerley
CFO: Denis Curley
1991 Sales: $159 million Employees: 1,030
Symbol: AK Exchange: AMEX
Industry: Diversified operations - advertising, broadcasting & professional basketball team

ACMAT Corp.
233 Main St.
New Britain, CT 06051
Phone: 203-229-9000 Fax: 203-229-1111
CEO: Henry W. Nozko, Sr.
CFO: Michael P. Cifone
1991 Sales: $34 million Employees: 100
Symbol: ACMT Exchange: NASDAQ
Industry: Building - maintenance & services

Acme Electric Corp.
400 Quaker Rd.
East Aurora, NY 14052
Phone: 716-655-3800 Fax: 716-655-3348
CEO: G. Wayne Hawk
CFO: Daniel K. Corwin
1992 Sales: $73 million Employees: 706
Symbol: ACE Exchange: NYSE
Industry: Electrical products - power conversion equipment

Acme Metals Co.
13500 S. Perry Ave.
Riverdale, IL 60627
Phone: 708-849-2500 Fax: 708-841-6010
CEO: Brian W. H. Marsden
CFO: Jerry F. Williams
1991 Sales: $377 million Employees: 2,885
Symbol: ACME Exchange: NASDAQ
Industry: Metal processing & fabrication

Acme United Corp.
75 Kings Hwy. Cut-Off
Fairfield, CT 06430
Phone: 203-332-7330 Fax: 203-254-0002
CEO: Henry C. Wheeler
CFO: Dwight C. Wheeler II
1991 Sales: $48 million Employees: 633
Symbol: ACU Exchange: AMEX
Industry: Medical instruments & scissors

Acme-Cleveland Corp.
30195 Chagrin Blvd., Ste. 300
Pepper Pike, OH 44124
Phone: 216-292-2100 Fax: 216-292-2101
CEO: David L. Swift
CFO: Francis R. Appeldorn
1991 Sales: $184 million Employees: 2,247
Symbol: AMT Exchange: NYSE
Industry: Diversified operations - metal working, telecommunications & electronics

Action Industries, Inc.
Action Industrial Park
Cheswick, PA 15024
Phone: 412-782-4800 Fax: 412-782-8606
CEO: R. Craig Kirsch
CFO: Kenneth L. Campbell
1992 Sales: $96 million Employees: 543
Symbol: ACX Exchange: AMEX
Industry: Housewares - light bulbs, closet accessories, glassware & gifts

Action Temporary Services
4004 E. Morgan Ave.
Evansville, IN 47714
Phone: 812-479-8373 Fax: 812-473-1006
CEO: Kimberly Devine
CFO: —
1991 Sales: $1.9 million Employees: 7
Ownership: Privately held
Industry: Business services - temporary personnel

Active Voice Corporation
2901 Third Ave.
Seattle, WA 98121
Phone: 206-441-4700 Fax: 206-441-4784
CEO: Robert L. Richmond
CFO: Jose David
1991 Sales: $12 million Employees: 115
Ownership: Privately held
Industry: Computers - voice processing software & equipment

Acton Corp.
200 Unicorn Park Dr.
Woburn, MA 01801
Phone: 617-935-3377 Fax: 617-932-8167
CEO: Clyde Wm. Engle
CFO: Glenn J. Kennedy
1991 Sales: $228 million Employees: 1,453
Symbol: ATN Exchange: AMEX
Industry: Insurance - property & casualty

Acuson Corp.
1220 Charleston Rd.
Mountain View, CA 94039
Phone: 415-969-9112 Fax: 415-962-8018
CEO: Samuel H. Maslak
CFO: Robert J. Gallagher
1991 Sales: $336 million Employees: 1,413
Symbol: ACN Exchange: NYSE
Industry: Medical diagnostic ultrasound imaging systems

Acxiom Corp.
301 Industrial Blvd.
Conway, AR 72032
Phone: 501-336-1000 Fax: 501-450-1414
CEO: Charles D. Morgan, Jr.
CFO: Robert S. Bloom
1992 Sales: $88 million Employees: 1,600
Symbol: ACXM Exchange: NASDAQ
Industry: Computers - services

ADAC Laboratories
540 Alder Dr.
Milpitas, CA 95035
Phone: 408-945-2990 Fax: 408-945-1516
CEO: Michael O. Preletz
CFO: Irvin R. Reuling
1991 Sales: $101 million Employees: 448
Symbol: ADAC Exchange: NASDAQ
Industry: Medical instruments

Adage, Inc.
615 Willowbrook Lane
West Chester, PA 19382
Phone: 215-430-3900 Fax: 215-431-9636
CEO: Robert H. Cahill
CFO: Robert T. Holland
1991 Sales: $75 million Employees: 568
Symbol: ADGE Exchange: NASDAQ
Industry: Diversified operations - door openers, recycled paperboard & title insurance

Adams Resources & Energy, Inc.
6910 Fannin
Houston, TX 77030
Phone: 713-797-9966 Fax: 713-795-4495
CEO: K. S. Adams, Jr.
CFO: Richard B. Abshire
1992 Sales: $550 million Employees: 291
Symbol: AE Exchange: AMEX
Industry: Oil & gas - production & pipeline

Adaptec, Inc.
691 S. Milpitas Blvd.
Milpitas, CA 95035
Phone: 408-945-8600 Fax: 408-262-2533
CEO: John G. Adler
CFO: Paul G. Hansen
1992 Sales: $150 million Employees: 927
Symbol: ADPT Exchange: NASDAQ
Industry: Computers - storage devices, laser printers, network file servers

 indicates company is in *Hoover's Handbook of American Business.*

indicates company is in *Hoover's Handbook of World Business;* sales and employee numbers are for parent company.

ADC Telecommunications, Inc.
4900 W. 78th St.
Minneapolis, MN 55435
Phone: 612-938-8080 Fax: 612-946-3292
CEO: William J. Cadogan
CFO: LeRoy J. Morgan
1991 Sales: $294 million Employees: 2,428
Symbol: ADCT Exchange: NASDAQ
Industry: Telecommunications equipment

Addington Resources, Inc.
Route 180 & Big Run Rd.
Ashland, KY 41101
Phone: 606-928-3433 Fax: 606-928-9527
CEO: Larry Addington
CFO: R. Douglas Striebel
1991 Sales: $275 million Employees: 1,090
Symbol: ADDR Exchange: NASDAQ
Industry: Coal

Adelphia Communications Corp.
5 W. Third St.
Coudersport, PA 16915
Phone: 814-274-9830 Fax: 814-274-8631
CEO: John J. Rigas
CFO: Timothy J. Rigas
1992 Sales: $277 million Employees: 1,546
Symbol: ADLAC Exchange: NASDAQ
Industry: Cable TV

Adesa Corp.
1919 S. Post Rd.
Indianapolis, IN 46239
Phone: 317-862-7220 Fax: —
CEO: D. Michael Hockett
CFO: Larry S. Wechter
1991 Sales: $48 million Employees: 925
Symbol: SOLD Exchange: NASDAQ
Industry: Business services - temporary personnel

Adia Personnel Services, Inc.
64 Willow Place
Menlo Park, CA 94025
Phone: 415-324-0696 Fax: 415-324-8885
CEO: Walter W. Macauley
CFO: Jon H. Rowberry
1992 Sales: $743 million Employees: 201,950
Symbol: ADIA Exchange: NASDAQ
Industry: Business services - temporary personnel

Administaff
19001 Crescent Springs Dr.
Kingwood, TX 77339
Phone: 713-358-8986 Fax: 713-358-3354
CEO: Paul Sarvadi
CFO: Richard Rawson
1991 Sales: $298 million Employees: 11,380
Ownership: Privately held
Industry: Business services - staff leasing

Adobe Systems Inc.
1585 Charleston Rd.
Mountain View, CA 94039
Phone: 415-961-4400 Fax: 415-961-3769
CEO: John E. Warnock
CFO: M. Bruce Nakao
1991 Sales: $230 million Employees: 701
Symbol: ADBE Exchange: NASDAQ
Industry: Computers - software

Adolph Coors Co.
311 Ford St.
Golden, CO 80401
Phone: 303-279-6565 Fax: 303-277-6564
CEO: William K. Coors
CFO: Harold R. Smethills
1992 Sales: $1,551 million Employees: 11,800
Symbol: ACCOB Exchange: NASDAQ
Industry: Beverages - beer

Adtran Inc.
901 Explorer Blvd.
Huntsville, AL 35806
Phone: 205-971-8000 Fax: 205-971-8699
CEO: Mark Smith
CFO: Irwin Goldstein
1991 Sales: $42 million Employees: 350
Ownership: Privately held
Industry: Telecommunications equipment

AdvaCare, Inc.
2 Walnut Grove Dr.
Horsham, PA 19044
Phone: 215-674-1800 Fax: —
CEO: Gregory S. Campbell
CFO: Gregory S. Campbell
1991 Sales: $55 million Employees: 1,436
Symbol: AVCR Exchange: NASDAQ
Industry: Business services

Advance Circuits, Inc.
15102 Minnetonka Industrial Rd.
Minnetonka, MN 55345
Phone: 612-935-3311 Fax: 612-935-4012
CEO: Robert W. Heller
CFO: Thomas I. Mueller
1991 Sales: $89 million Employees: 910
Symbol: ADVC Exchange: NASDAQ
Industry: Electrical components - semiconductors

Advance Publications, Inc.
350 Madison Ave.
New York, NY 10017
Phone: 718-981-1234 Fax: 718-981-5679
CEO: Samuel I. Newhouse, Jr.
CFO: Arthur Silverstein
1991 Sales: $4,579 million Employees: 19,000
Ownership: Privately held
Industry: Publishing - newspapers, books, magazines & cable TV

Advance Ross Corp.
111 W. Monroe St., Ste. 2100E
Chicago, IL 60603
Phone: 312-346-9126 Fax: —
CEO: Harve A. Ferrill
CFO: Harvey E. Campbell
1991 Sales: $5.9 million Employees: 31
Symbol: AROS Exchange: NASDAQ
Industry: Pollution control equipment & services

Advanced Cellular Systems
PO Box 367247
San Juan, PR 00936
Phone: 809-783-0510 Fax: 809-783-5446
CEO: Cesar Negrette
CFO: DeJesus Alicia
1992 Sales: $12 million Employees: 56
Ownership: Privately held
Industry: Telecommunications services - cellular telephones

Advanced Computer Systems Inc.
10530 Rosehaven St. #520
Fairfax, VA 22030
Phone: 703-591-4000 Fax: 703-591-5591
CEO: S.P. Shrivastava
CFO: S.P. Shrivastava
1991 Sales: $11 million Employees: 250
Ownership: Privately held
Industry: Computers - services

Advanced Computer Techniques Corp.
417 Fifth Ave.
New York, NY 10016
Phone: 212-696-3600 Fax: 212-696-3784
CEO: Oscar H. Schachter
CFO: Anthony F. Grisanti
1991 Sales: $5.2 million Employees: 63
Symbol: ACTP Exchange: NASDAQ
Industry: Computers - software for health organizations

Advanced Interventional Systems, Inc.
9 Parker
Irvine, CA 92718
Phone: 714-586-1342 Fax: 714-586-8515
CEO: Robert E. Wall
CFO: Richard B. Crosby
1991 Sales: $3.4 million Employees: 121
Symbol: LAIS Exchange: NASDAQ
Industry: Lasers - systems & components

Advanced Logic Research, Inc.
9401 Jeronimo Rd.
Irvine, CA 92718
Phone: 714-581-6770 Fax: 714-581-9240
CEO: Gene Lu
CFO: James T. Richardson
1991 Sales: $228 million Employees: 699
Symbol: AALR Exchange: NASDAQ
Industry: Computers - mini & micro

Advanced Magnetics, Inc.
61 Mooney St.
Cambridge, MA 02138
Phone: 617-497-2070 Fax: 617-547-2445
CEO: Jerome Goldstein
CFO: Anthony P. Annese
1991 Sales: $10.9 million Employees: 79
Symbol: AVM Exchange: AMEX
Industry: Medical products - diagnostic

Advanced Marketing Services, Inc.
5880 Oberlin Dr., Ste. 400
San Diego, CA 92121
Phone: 619-457-2500 Fax: 619-452-2237
CEO: Charles C. Tillinghast III
CFO: Jonathan S. Fish
1992 Sales: $218 million Employees: 301
Symbol: ADMS Exchange: NASDAQ
Industry: Wholesale distribution - books, audio cassettes & video cassettes

Advanced Medical Technologies, Inc.
One Technology Court
Malvern, PA 19355
Phone: 619-566-9000 Fax: —
CEO: Stanley S. Anders III
CFO: Stanley S. Anders III
1991 Sales: $127 million Employees: —
Symbol: AMA Exchange: AMEX
Industry: Drugs

Advanced Micro Devices, Inc.
901 Thompson Place
Sunnyvale, CA 94008
Phone: 408-732-2400 Fax: 408-982-6164
CEO: W. Jeremiah Sanders III
CFO: Marvin D. Burkett
1992 Sales: $1,515 million Employees: 11,254
Symbol: AMD Exchange: NYSE
Industry: Electrical components - semiconductors

Advanced Polymer Systems, Inc.
3696 Haven Ave.
Redwood City, CA 94063
Phone: 415-366-2626 Fax: 415-365-6490
CEO: John J. Meakem, Jr.
CFO: John J. Meakem, Jr.
1991 Sales: $1.8 million Employees: 63
Symbol: APOS Exchange: NASDAQ
Industry: Medical products

Advanced Promotion Technologies, Inc.
626 S. Military Trail
Deerfield Beach, FL 33442
Phone: 305-425-7800 Fax: 305-425-7837
CEO: David R. Humble
CFO: John Morton
1991 Sales: $1.4 million Employees: 84
Symbol: APTV Exchange: NASDAQ
Industry: Business services - point-of-sale marketing system

Advanced Systems Technology
3490 Piedmont Rd.
Atlanta, GA 30305
Phone: 404-240-2930 Fax: 404-240-2931
CEO: Wayne Knox
CFO: Wayne Knox
1991 Sales: $12 million Employees: 155
Ownership: Privately held
Industry: Engineering - R&D services

Advanced Technology Laboratories, Inc.
701 Fifth Ave.
Seattle, WA 98104
Phone: 206-682-6800 Fax: —
CEO: Dennis C. Fill
CFO: Robert T. deGavre
1991 Sales: $505 million Employees: 3,623
Symbol: ATLI Exchange: NASDAQ
Industry: Medical instruments

Advanced Telecommunications Corp.
945 E. Paces Ferry Rd. NE, Ste. 2100
Atlanta, GA 30326
Phone: 404-261-5885 Fax: 404-262-3146
CEO: Stephen E. Raville
CFO: Patrick E. Delaney
1992 Sales: $355 million Employees: 1,316
Symbol: ATEL Exchange: NASDAQ
Industry: Telecommunications services

ADVANTA Corp.
650 Naamans Rd.
Claymont, DE 19703
Phone: 302-791-4400 Fax: —
CEO: Dennis Alter
CFO: Warren Kantor
1991 Sales: $312 million Employees: 1,082
Symbol: ADVNA Exchange: NASDAQ
Industry: Financial - business services

Advantage Health Corp.
304 Cambridge Rd.
Woburn, MA 01801
Phone: 617-935-2500 Fax: —
CEO: R. J. Dun III
CFO: R. E. Spencer
1991 Sales: $68 million Employees: 2,500
Symbol: ADHC Exchange: NASDAQ
Industry: Healthcare - outpatient & home

Advantage Remodeling
1811 W. Park Row
Arlington, TX 76013
Phone: 817-261-8560 Fax: 817-265-8236
CEO: Paul Kanesky
CFO: Rollie Jones
1991 Sales: $2 million Employees: 21
Ownership: Privately held
Industry: Construction - residential remodeling

Advest Group, Inc.
280 Trumbull St.
Hartford, CT 06103
Phone: 203-525-1421 Fax: 800-243-8115
CEO: Allen Weintraub
CFO: Martin M. Lilienthal
1991 Sales: $211 million Employees: 1,605
Symbol: ADV Exchange: NYSE
Industry: Financial - investment bankers

Advo-System, Inc.
One Univac Lane
Windsor, CT 06095
Phone: 203-285-6100 Fax: 203-285-6393
CEO: Robert J. Kamerschen
CFO: Larry G. Morris
1992 Sales: $816 million Employees: 4,800
Symbol: ADVO Exchange: NASDAQ
Industry: Business services - direct marketing

AEL Industries, Inc.
305 Richardson Rd.
Lansdale, PA 19446
Phone: 215-822-2929 Fax: 215-822-9165
CEO: Leon Riebman
CFO: George King
1992 Sales: $140 million Employees: 1,308
Symbol: AELNA Exchange: NASDAQ
Industry: Electronics - military

AEP Industries Inc.
125 Phillips Ave.
South Hackensack, NJ 07606
Phone: 201-641-6600 Fax: 201-807-2490
CEO: J. Brendan Barba
CFO: Paul M. Feeney
1991 Sales: $133 million Employees: 780
Symbol: AEPI Exchange: NASDAQ
Industry: Chemicals - plastics

Aequitron Medical, Inc.
14800 28th Ave. North
Plymouth, MN 55447
Phone: 612-557-9200 Fax: 612-557-8200
CEO: Curtis J. Olson
CFO: William M. Milne
1992 Sales: $25 million Employees: 230
Symbol: AQTN Exchange: NASDAQ
Industry: Medical instruments - infant monitors

Aero Systems, Inc.
5415 NW 36th St.
Miami Springs, FL 33166
Phone: 305-871-1300 Fax: 305-884-1400
CEO: Robert G. Holmes, Jr.
CFO: David A. Wayne
1992 Sales: $23 million Employees: 162
Symbol: AESM Exchange: NASDAQ
Industry: Aerospace - aircraft equipment

Aerovox, Inc.
740 Belleville Ave.
New Bedford, MA 02745
Phone: 508-994-9661 Fax: 508-994-9635
CEO: Clifford H. Tuttle
CFO: Ronald F. Murphy
1991 Sales: $64 million Employees: 784
Symbol: ARVX Exchange: NASDAQ
Industry: Electrical components - capacitors

AES Corp.
1001 N. 19th St.
Arlington, VA 22209
Phone: 703-522-1315 Fax: 703-528-4510
CEO: Roger W. Sant
CFO: Barry J. Sharp
1991 Sales: $334 million Employees: 490
Symbol: AESC Exchange: NASDAQ
Industry: Energy - cogeneration

Aetna Life and Casualty Co.
151 Farmington Ave.
Hartford, CT 06156
Phone: 203-273-0123 Fax: 203-275-2677
CEO: Ronald E. Compton
CFO: Patrick W. Kenny
1992 Sales: $17,497 million Employees: 48,300
Symbol: AET Exchange: NYSE
Industry: Insurance - multiline & misc.

Affiliated Bankshares of Colorado, Inc.
1125 17th St., Ste. 1500
Denver, CO 80202
Phone: 303-296-7788 Fax: —
CEO: Ronald L. Moore
CFO: Gordon M. Pedersen
1991 Sales: $269 million Employees: 2,106
Symbol: AFBK Exchange: NASDAQ
Industry: Banks - West

Affiliated Publications, Inc.
135 Morrissey Blvd.
Boston, MA 02125
Phone: 617-929-3300 Fax: 617-929-3490
CEO: William O. Taylor
CFO: William B. Huff
1991 Sales: $393 million Employees: 3,444
Symbol: AFP Exchange: NYSE
Industry: Publishing - newspapers

Affinity Biotech, Inc.
305 Chelsea Pkwy.
Boothwyn, PA 19061
Phone: 215-497-0500 Fax: —
CEO: Alan F. Dickason
CFO: Joseph L. Jackson
1991 Sales: $0.2 million Employees: 16
Symbol: AFBI Exchange: NASDAQ
Industry: Biomedical & genetic products

AFG Industries Inc.
301 Commerce St., Ste. 3300
Ft. Worth, TX 76102
Phone: 817-332-5006 Fax: 817-870-2685
CEO: R. D. Hubbard
CFO: Gary G. Miller
1991 Sales: $516 million Employees: 4,054
Ownership: Privately held
Industry: Glass products - flat glass manufacturing

AFL–CIO
815 16th St. NW
Washington, DC 20006
Phone: 202-637-5010 Fax: 202-637-5058
CEO: Lane Kirkland
CFO: Thomas R. Donahue
1991 Sales: $58 million Employees: —
Ownership: Privately held
Industry: Labor federation

AFLAC
1932 Wynnton Rd.
Columbus, GA 31999
Phone: 706-323-3431 Fax: 706-596-3593
CEO: Daniel P. Amos
CFO: Norman Foster
1992 Sales: $3,987 million Employees: —
Symbol: AFL Exchange: NYSE
Industry: Insurance - health, life & medical

Ag Services of America, Inc.
2302 W. First St.
Cedar Falls, IA 50613
Phone: 319-277-0261 Fax: —
CEO: Gaylen D. Miller
CFO: Kevin D. Schipper
1992 Sales: $36 million Employees: 31
Symbol: AGSV Exchange: NASDAQ
Industry: Agricultural operations

AGCO Corp.
5295 Triangle Pkwy.
Norcross, GA 30092
Phone: 404-447-5546 Fax: —
CEO: Robert J. Ratliff
CFO: Allen W. Ritchie
1991 Sales: $274 million Employees: 1,165
Symbol: AGCO Exchange: NASDAQ
Industry: Machinery - farm

Agency Rent-A-Car, Inc.
30000 Aurora Rd.
Solon, OH 44139
Phone: 216-349-1000 Fax: 216-349-0203
CEO: Sam J. Frankino
CFO: Robert J. Bronchetti
1991 Sales: $269 million Employees: 2,900
Symbol: AGNC Exchange: NASDAQ
Industry: Leasing - autos

indicates company is in *Hoover's Handbook of American Business.*

indicates company is in *Hoover's Handbook of World Business*; sales and employee numbers are for parent company.

Agouron Pharmaceuticals, Inc.
3565 General Atomics Court
San Diego, CA 92121
Phone: 619-622-3000 Fax: —
CEO: Peter Johnson
CFO: Steven S. Cowell
1992 Sales: $5.3 million Employees: 130
Symbol: AGPH Exchange: NASDAQ
Industry: Drugs

Agricultural Minerals Co.
23302 E. 56th St. North
Verdigris, OK 74015
Phone: 918-266-1511 Fax: 918-266-6091
CEO: R. B. Gwyn
CFO: J. A. Molenaar
1991 Sales: $247 million Employees: —
Symbol: AMC Exchange: NYSE
Industry: Fertilizers

AgriDyne Technologies, Inc.
417 Wakara Way, Ste. 300
Salt Lake City, UT 84108
Phone: 801-583-3500 Fax: 801-583-2945
CEO: Eric B. Hale
CFO: Monty K. Allen
1991 Sales: $3.1 million Employees: —
Symbol: AGRI Exchange: NASDAQ
Industry: Chemicals - specialty

Aileen, Inc.
1411 Broadway
New York, NY 10018
Phone: 212-398-9770 Fax: 212-398-9154
CEO: Abe Oberlin
CFO: Robert W. Tarpley
1991 Sales: $65 million Employees: 2,000
Symbol: AEE Exchange: NYSE
Industry: Textiles - apparel

Air Express International Corp.
120 Tokeneke Rd.
Darien, CT 06820
Phone: 203-655-7900 Fax: 203-655-5779
CEO: Guenter Rohrmann
CFO: Dennis M. Dolan
1992 Sales: $672 million Employees: 3,570
Symbol: AEX Exchange: AMEX
Industry: Transportation - air freight

Air Products and Chemicals, Inc.
7201 Hamilton Blvd.
Allentown, PA 18195
Phone: 215-481-4911 Fax: 215-481-4184
CEO: Dexter F. Baker
CFO: Gerald A. White
1992 Sales: $3,270 million Employees: 14,600
Symbol: APD Exchange: NYSE
Industry: Chemicals - specialty

Air & Water Technologies Corp.
Hwy. 22 & Station Rd.
Branchburg, NJ 08876
Phone: 908-685-4600 Fax: 908-685-4587
CEO: Eckardt C. Beck
CFO: Harvey Goldman
1992 Sales: $719 million Employees: 3,930
Symbol: AWT Exchange: AMEX
Industry: Pollution control equipment & services

Airborne Freight Corp.
3101 Western Ave.
Seattle, WA 98111
Phone: 206-285-4600 Fax: 206-281-7615
CEO: Robert S. Cline
CFO: Roy C. Liljebeck
1992 Sales: $1,484 million Employees: 13,800
Symbol: ABF Exchange: NYSE
Industry: Transportation - air freight

Airbus Industrie of North America, Inc.
593 Herndon Pkwy., Ste. 300
Herndon, VA 22070
Phone: 703-834-3400 Fax: 703-834-3340
CEO: Jonathan M. Schofield
CFO: —
1991 Sales: $7,700 million Employees: —
Parent: Airbus Industrie
Industry: Aerospace - aircraft equipment

AIRCOA Hotel Partners, L.P.
4600 S. Ulster St., Ste. 1200
Denver, CO 80237
Phone: 303-220-2000 Fax: 303-799-6367
CEO: Peter T. K. Yu
CFO: Arno C. Zeyn
1991 Sales: $43 million Employees: 1,035
Symbol: AHT Exchange: AMEX
Industry: Hotels & motels

Airgas, Inc.
5 Radnor Corporate Ctr., Ste. 550
Radnor, PA 19087
Phone: 215-687-5253 Fax: 215-687-1052
CEO: Peter McCausland
CFO: Britt Murdoch
1992 Sales: $352 million Employees: 2,400
Symbol: ARG Exchange: NYSE
Industry: Chemicals - specialty

Airlease Ltd.
615 Battery St.
San Francisco, CA 94119
Phone: 415-627-9300 Fax: —
CEO: David B. Gebler
CFO: Robert A. Keyes, Jr.
1991 Sales: $14 million Employees: —
Symbol: FLY Exchange: NYSE
Industry: Leasing

AirTran Corp.
7501 26th Ave. South
Minneapolis, MN 55450
Phone: 612-726-5151 Fax: —
CEO: Robert D. Swenson
CFO: Kenneth P. Bronson
1992 Sales: $102 million Employees: 1,072
Symbol: ATCC Exchange: NASDAQ
Industry: Transportation - airline

Akorn, Inc.
100 Akorn Dr.
Abita Springs, LA 70420
Phone: 504-893-9300 Fax: 504-893-1257
CEO: Doyle S. Gaw
CFO: Eric M. Wingerter
1992 Sales: $19 million Employees: 238
Symbol: AKRN Exchange: NASDAQ
Industry: Medical products - ophthalmic

ALAFIRST Bancshares, Inc.
255 Grant St. SE
Decatur, AL 35602
Phone: 205-353-2530 Fax: —
CEO: William D. Powell
CFO: C. Raymond Duncan
1991 Sales: $22 million Employees: 94
Symbol: AFB Exchange: AMEX
Industry: Financial - savings and loans

Alamco, Inc.
200 W. Main St.
Clarksburg, WV 26301
Phone: 304-623-6671 Fax: 304-624-9265
CEO: John L. Schwager
CFO: Robert S. Wilkie, Jr.
1991 Sales: $9.7 million Employees: 80
Symbol: AXO Exchange: AMEX
Industry: Oil & gas - US exploration & production

Alamo Rent A Car Inc.
110 SE Sixth St.
Ft. Lauderdale, FL 33301
Phone: 305-522-0000 Fax: 305-527-6589
CEO: Michael S. Egan
CFO: Bob Pickup
1991 Sales: $740 million Employees: 6,000
Ownership: Privately held
Industry: Leasing - auto rental

Alaska Air Group, Inc.
19300 Pacific Hwy. South
Seattle, WA 98188
Phone: 206-431-7040 Fax: 206-433-3366
CEO: Raymond J. Vecci
CFO: J. Ray Vingo
1992 Sales: $1,115 million Employees: 8,740
Symbol: ALK Exchange: NYSE
Industry: Transportation - airline

AlaTenn Resources, Inc.
100 E. 2nd St.
Sheffield, AL 35660
Phone: 205-383-3631 Fax: 205-383-6123
CEO: Jerry A. Howard
CFO: George G. Petty
1991 Sales: $94 million Employees: 37
Symbol: ATNG Exchange: NASDAQ
Industry: Oil & gas - production & pipeline

Alba-Waldensian, Inc.
201 St. Germain Ave. SW
Valdese, NC 28690
Phone: 704-874-2191 Fax: 704-879-2615
CEO: William F. Marmion-Karnbach
CFO: Van C. Irwin
1991 Sales: $40 million Employees: 801
Symbol: AWS Exchange: AMEX
Industry: Textiles - apparel

Albany International Corp.
1373 Broadway
Albany, NY 12204
Phone: 518-445-2200 Fax: 518-445-2265
CEO: J. Spencer Standish
CFO: Michael C. Nahl
1991 Sales: $560 million Employees: 5,726
Symbol: AIN Exchange: NYSE
Industry: Paper & paper products

Alberto-Culver Co.
2525 Armitage Ave.
Melrose Park, IL 60160
Phone: 708-450-3000 Fax: 708-450-3354
CEO: Leonard H. Lavin
CFO: Howard B. Bernick
1992 Sales: $1,114 million Employees: 7,300
Symbol: ACV Exchange: NYSE
Industry: Cosmetics & toiletries

Albertson's, Inc.
250 E. Parkcenter Blvd.
Boise, ID 83726
Phone: 208-385-6200 Fax: 208-385-6349
CEO: Gary G. Michael
CFO: A. Craig Olsen
1992 Sales: $9,685 million Employees: 60,000
Symbol: ABS Exchange: NYSE
Industry: Retail - supermarkets

ALC Communications Corp.
30300 Telegraph Rd., Ste. 350
Bingham Farms, MI 48025
Phone: 313-647-4060 Fax: 313-433-4926
CEO: John M. Zrno
CFO: Marvin C. Moses
1991 Sales: $347 million Employees: 1,550
Symbol: ALC Exchange: AMEX
Industry: Telecommunications services

indicates company is in *Hoover's Handbook of American Business.*

indicates company is in *Hoover's Handbook of World Business;* sales and employee numbers are for parent company.

Alcatel North America Inc.
2512 Penny Rd.
Claremont, NC 28610
Phone: 704-459-9787 Fax: 704-459-9312
CEO: John Peterson
CFO: —
1991 Sales: $30,904 million Employees: 213,100
Parent: Alcatel Alsthom
Industry: Telecommunications equipment, energy & electrical engineeering

Alco Health Services
300 Chesterfield Pkwy.
Valley Forge, PA 19482
Phone: 215-296-4480 Fax: 215-647-0141
CEO: John F. McNamara
CFO: —
1992 Sales: $3,300 million Employees: 2,269
Ownership: Privately held
Industry: Drugs - wholesale distribution

Alco Standard Corp.
825 Duportail Rd.
Valley Forge, PA 19087
Phone: 215-296-8000 Fax: 215-296-8419
CEO: Ray B. Mundt
CFO: O. Gordon Brewer, Jr.
1992 Sales: $5,217 million Employees: 18,800
Symbol: ASN Exchange: NYSE
Industry: Diversified operations - paper products, office equipment & steel distribution

Alden Press Co.
2000 Arthur Ave.
Elk Grove Village, IL 60007
Phone: 708-640-6000 Fax: —
CEO: Jerome B. Spier
CFO: Gary M. Minnig
1991 Sales: $175 million Employees: 776
Symbol: ALDN Exchange: NASDAQ
Industry: Printing - commercial

Aldus Corp.
411 First Ave. South, Ste. 200
Seattle, WA 98104
Phone: 206-622-5500 Fax: 206-343-4240
CEO: Paul Brainerd
CFO: William H. McAleer
1991 Sales: $168 million Employees: 952
Symbol: ALDC Exchange: NASDAQ
Industry: Computers - desktop publishing software

Alex. Brown Inc.
135 E. Baltimore St.
Baltimore, MD 21202
Phone: 410-727-1700 Fax: 410-783-5313
CEO: Benjamin H. Griswold IV
CFO: Beverly L. Wright
1991 Sales: $411 million Employees: 1,800
Symbol: AB Exchange: NYSE
Industry: Financial - investment bankers

Alex Lee
120 4th St. SW
Hickory, NC 28602
Phone: 704-323-4424 Fax: 704-323-4435
CEO: Boyd L. George
CFO: Ron W. Knedlik
1991 Sales: $1,009 million Employees: 3,000
Ownership: Privately held
Industry: Food - wholesale

Alexander & Alexander Services Inc.
1211 Avenue of the Americas
New York, NY 10036
Phone: 212-840-8500 Fax: —
CEO: Tinsley H. Irvin
CFO: Paul E. Rohner
1992 Sales: $1,350 million Employees: 15,600
Symbol: AAL Exchange: NYSE
Industry: Insurance - brokerage

Alexander & Baldwin, Inc.
822 Bishop St.
Honolulu, HI 96801
Phone: 808-525-6611 Fax: 808-525-6652
CEO: R. J. Pfeiffer
CFO: G. Stephen Holaday
1992 Sales: $754 million Employees: 2,957
Symbol: ALEX Exchange: NASDAQ
Industry: Transportation - shipping

Alexander Energy Corp.
701 Cedar Lake Blvd.
Oklahoma City, OK 73114
Phone: 405-478-8686 Fax: —
CEO: Bob G. Alexander
CFO: David E. Grose
1991 Sales: $7 million Employees: 43
Symbol: AEOK Exchange: NASDAQ
Industry: Oil & gas - US exploration & production

Alexander's, Inc.
500 Seventh Ave.
New York, NY 10018
Phone: 212-560-2121 Fax: 212-869-0368
CEO: Robin L. Farkas
CFO: Thomas M. Coleman
1991 Sales: $430 million Employees: 7,200
Symbol: ALX Exchange: NYSE
Industry: Retail - regional department stores

Alfa Farmers Federation Corp.
2108 E. South Blvd.
Montgomery, AL 36116
Phone: 205-288-3900 Fax: 205-284-3957
CEO: Goodwin L. Myrick
CFO: J. Donald Price
1991 Sales: $2 million Employees: 8
Symbol: ALFA Exchange: NASDAQ
Industry: Insurance - life

Alfin, Inc.
720 Fifth Ave., 8th Fl.
New York, NY 10019
Phone: 212-333-7700 Fax: 212-246-7423
CEO: Stanley Kohlenberg
CFO: Joseph G. Salloum
1991 Sales: $45 million Employees: 347
Symbol: AFN Exchange: AMEX
Industry: Cosmetics & toiletries

Algorex Corp.
45 Adams Ave.
Hauppauge, NY 11788
Phone: 516-434-9400 Fax: 516-434-9566
CEO: Sheldon O. Newman
CFO: Sheldon O. Newman
1991 Sales: $4 million Employees: 36
Symbol: ALGO Exchange: NASDAQ
Industry: Engineering - R&D services

Alico, Inc.
640 S. Main St.
La Belle, FL 33935
Phone: 813-675-2966 Fax: 813-675-6928
CEO: Ben Hill Griffin III
CFO: Walter R. Howard
1991 Sales: $27 million Employees: 118
Symbol: ALCO Exchange: NASDAQ
Industry: Agricultural operations

Alkermes, Inc.
26 Landsdowne St.
Cambridge, MA 02139
Phone: 617-494-0171 Fax: —
CEO: Richard F. Pops
CFO: Michael J. Landine
1992 Sales: $0.2 million Employees: 60
Symbol: ALKS Exchange: NASDAQ
Industry: Drugs

All American Semiconductor, Inc.
16251 NW 54th Ave.
Miami, FL 33014
Phone: 305-621-8282 Fax: 305-620-7831
CEO: Paul Goldberg
CFO: Howard L. Flanders
1991 Sales: $45 million Employees: 158
Symbol: SEMI Exchange: NASDAQ
Industry: Electrical components - semiconductors

All For A Dollar, Inc.
3664 Main St.
Springfield, MA 01107
Phone: 413-733-1203 Fax: —
CEO: V. Martin Effron
CFO: Roger A. Slate
1991 Sales: $29 million Employees: 809
Symbol: ADLR Exchange: NASDAQ
Industry: Retail - discount & variety

All Green Corp.
1503 Johnson Ferry Rd.
Marietta, GA 30062
Phone: 404-973-1600 Fax: 404-973-2401
CEO: Paul Anderegg
CFO: Richard Flaherty
1991 Sales: $9.5 million Employees: 240
Ownership: Privately held
Industry: Building - lawn, tree & shrub care & indoor pest control

All Nippon Airways Co., Ltd.
630 Fifth Ave., Ste. 646
New York, NY 10111
Phone: 212-956-8200 Fax: 212-969-9022
CEO: Koji Yamashita
CFO: —
1992 Sales: $7,001 million Employees: 13,974
Parent: All Nippon Airways Co., Ltd.
Industry: Transportation - airline

Alleghany Corp.
Park Ave. Plaza, 55 E. 52nd St.
New York, NY 10055
Phone: 212-752-1356 Fax: 212-759-8149
CEO: F. M. Kirby
CFO: David B. Cuming
1992 Sales: $1,788 million Employees: —
Symbol: Y Exchange: NYSE
Industry: Financial - business services

Allegheny Ludlum Corp.
1000 Six PPG Place
Pittsburgh, PA 15222
Phone: 412-394-2800 Fax: 412-394-2805
CEO: Robert P. Bozzone
CFO: James L. Murdy
1992 Sales: $1,036 million Employees: 5,400
Symbol: ALS Exchange: NYSE
Industry: Steel - specialty alloys

Allegheny Power System, Inc.
12 E. 49th St.
New York, NY 10017
Phone: 212-752-2121 Fax: Ext. 326
CEO: Klaus Bergman
CFO: Stanley I. Garnett II
1992 Sales: $2,307 million Employees: 6,007
Symbol: AYP Exchange: NYSE
Industry: Utility - electric power

Allegheny & Western Energy Corp.
501 Brickell Key Dr., Ste. 201
Miami, FL 33131
Phone: 305-358-3448 Fax: —
CEO: John G. McMillian
CFO: John A. Bielun
1992 Sales: $181 million Employees: —
Symbol: ALGH Exchange: NASDAQ
Industry: Oil & gas - US exploration & production

indicates company is in *Hoover's Handbook of American Business.*

indicates company is in *Hoover's Handbook of World Business;* sales and employee numbers are for parent company.

Allen Group Inc.
534 Broad Hollow Rd.
Melville, NY 11747
Phone: 516-293-5500 Fax: 516-293-5485
CEO: Philip Wm. Colburn
CFO: Robert A. Youdelman
1991 Sales: $262 million Employees: 2,400
Symbol: ALN Exchange: NYSE
Industry: Automotive & trucking - original equipment

Allen Organ Co.
150 Locust St.
Macungie, PA 18062
Phone: 215-966-2200 Fax: 215-965-3098
CEO: Steven Markowitz
CFO: Leonard W. Helfrich
1991 Sales: $25 million Employees: 450
Symbol: AORGB Exchange: NASDAQ
Industry: Electronic keyboard instruments

Allen Systems Group Inc.
750 11th St.
Naples, FL 33940
Phone: 813-263-6700 Fax: 813-263-1952
CEO: A. Allen
CFO: A. Allen
1992 Sales: $12 million Employees: 200
Ownership: Privately held
Industry: Computers - software

Allergan, Inc.
2525 Dupont Dr.
Irvine, CA 92715
Phone: 714-752-4500 Fax: 714-253-5596
CEO: Gavin S. Herbert
CFO: Edgar J. Cummins
1992 Sales: $898 million Employees: 5,600
Symbol: AGN Exchange: NYSE
Industry: Medical products - eye care

Alliance Capital Management Corp.
1345 Avenue of the Americas, 38th Fl.
New York, NY 10105
Phone: 212-969-1000 Fax: 212-969-1255
CEO: Dave H. Williams
CFO: John D. Carifa
1991 Sales: $298 million Employees: 778
Symbol: AC Exchange: NYSE
Industry: Financial - investment management

Alliance Employee Leasing
2351 W. Northwest Hwy., Ste. 3100
Dallas, TX 75220
Phone: 214-902-9100 Fax: 214-353-0470
CEO: Tynes Hilderdrand
CFO: Valerie Duncan
1991 Sales: $175 million Employees: 37
Ownership: Privately held
Industry: Business services - employee leasing

Alliance Imaging, Inc.
3111 N. Tustin Ave., Ste. 150
Orange, CA 92665
Phone: 714-921-5656 Fax: 714-921-5678
CEO: Richard N. Zehner
CFO: Vincent S. Pino
1991 Sales: $52 million Employees: 249
Symbol: SCAN Exchange: NASDAQ
Industry: Medical services - magnetic resonance imaging

Alliance Pharmaceutical Corp.
3040 Science Park Rd.
San Diego, CA 92121
Phone: 619-558-4300 Fax: 619-558-3625
CEO: Duane J. Roth
CFO: Theodore D. Roth
1991 Sales: $1.6 million Employees: 129
Symbol: ALLP Exchange: NASDAQ
Industry: Biomedical & genetic products

Alliant Techsystems Inc.
5901 Lincoln Dr.
Edina, MN 55436
Phone: 612-939-2000 Fax: 612-939-2480
CEO: Toby G. Watson
CFO: Dean M. Fjelstul
1992 Sales: $1,207 million Employees: 6,700
Symbol: ATK Exchange: NYSE
Industry: Weapons & weapon systems

Allianz Insurance Co.
6435 Wilshire Blvd.
Los Angeles, CA 90048
Phone: 213-658-5000 Fax: 213-852-8366
CEO: Wolfgang Schlink
CFO: —
1991 Sales: $32,738 million Employees: 61,158
Parent: Allianz AG Holding
Industry: Insurance - multiline & misc.

Allied Clinical Laboratories, Inc.
2515 Park Plaza
Nashville, TN 37203
Phone: 615-320-2283 Fax: 615-320-2013
CEO: Haywood D. Cochrane, Jr.
CFO: Gerard M. Hayden, Jr.
1991 Sales: $102 million Employees: 2,200
Symbol: ACLB Exchange: NASDAQ
Industry: Medical services - clinical test labs

Allied Group, Inc.
701 Fifth Ave.
Des Moines, IA 50309
Phone: 515-280-4211 Fax: —
CEO: John E. Evans
CFO: Jamie H. Shaffer
1991 Sales: $354 million Employees: 1,934
Symbol: ALGR Exchange: NASDAQ
Industry: Insurance - multiline & misc.

Allied Healthcare Products, Inc.
1720 Sublette Ave.
St. Louis, MO 63110
Phone: 314-771-2400 Fax: 314-771-0650
CEO: Earl R. Refsland
CFO: David V. LaRusso
1992 Sales: $59 million Employees: 449
Symbol: AHPI Exchange: NASDAQ
Industry: Medical products - respiratory therapy equipment

Allied Products Corp.
10 S. Riverside Plaza, Ste. 1600
Chicago, IL 60606
Phone: 312-454-1020 Fax: 312-454-1511
CEO: Richard A. Drexler
CFO: James M. Voss
1991 Sales: $324 million Employees: 3,300
Symbol: ADP Exchange: NYSE
Industry: Diversified operations - farm equipment, tool & die equipment & insulation

Allied Research Corp.
111 S. Calvert St., Ste. 2270
Baltimore, MD 21202
Phone: 410-625-1888 Fax: 410-625-1995
CEO: Reinald W. Carter
CFO: Reinald W. Carter
1991 Sales: $175 million Employees: 541
Symbol: ALR Exchange: AMEX
Industry: Weapons & weapon systems

Allied Waste Industries, Inc.
6575 W. Loop South, Ste. 250
Bellaire, TX 77401
Phone: 713-664-1888 Fax: —
CEO: Roger A. Ramsey
CFO: Roger A. Ramsey
1991 Sales: $9.4 million Employees: 311
Symbol: AWIN Exchange: NASDAQ
Industry: Waste disposal

Allied-Signal Inc.
101 Columbia Rd.
Morristown, NJ 07962
Phone: 201-455-2000 Fax: 201-455-4807
CEO: Lawrence A. Bossidy
CFO: John W. Barter
1992 Sales: $12,042 million Employees: 98,300
Symbol: ALD Exchange: NYSE
Industry: Diversified operations - aerospace, automotive & engineered products

Alling & Cory Co.
25 Verona St.
Rochester, NY 14608
Phone: 716-454-1880 Fax: 716-454-6169
CEO: Samuel T. Hubbard, Jr.
CFO: John B. Henderson
1991 Sales: $500 million Employees: 1,150
Ownership: Privately held
Industry: Paper & paper products, packaging & business products

Allou Health & Beauty Care, Inc.
50 Emjay Blvd.
Brentwood, NY 11717
Phone: 516-273-4000 Fax: 516-273-5318
CEO: Herman Jacobs
CFO: David Shamilzadeh
1992 Sales: $125 million Employees: 172
Symbol: ALU Exchange: AMEX
Industry: Cosmetics & toiletries

Allstar Builders Corporation
4901 SW 75th Ave.
Miami, FL 33155
Phone: 305-665-3825 Fax: 305-665-0725
CEO: Claudio Martinez
CFO: Gus Veitia
1991 Sales: $5 million Employees: 20
Ownership: Privately held
Industry: Construction - commercial & industrial general contracting

Allstate Financial Corp.
2700 S. Quincy St., Ste. 540
Arlington, VA 22206
Phone: 703-931-2274 Fax: 703-998-5470
CEO: Leon Fishman
CFO: Lawrence M. Winkler
1991 Sales: $11 million Employees: 46
Symbol: ASFN Exchange: NASDAQ
Industry: Financial - business services

Allsup Inc.
300 Allsup Place
Belleville, IL 62223
Phone: 618-234-8434 Fax: 618-236-5778
CEO: James Allsup
CFO: Richard C. Smith
1991 Sales: $6 million Employees: 89
Ownership: Privately held
Industry: Business services - claims services to health care industry

ALLTEL Corp.
One Allied Dr.
Little Rock, AR 72202
Phone: 501-661-8000 Fax: 501-664-3469
CEO: Joe T. Ford
CFO: Max E. Bobbitt
1992 Sales: $2,092 million Employees: 11,916
Symbol: AT Exchange: NYSE
Industry: Utility - telephone

Allwaste, Inc.
3040 Post Oak Blvd., Ste. 1300
Houston, TX 77056
Phone: 713-623-8777 Fax: —
CEO: Raymond L. Nelson, Jr.
CFO: I. T. Corley
1991 Sales: $167 million Employees: 2,371
Symbol: ALW Exchange: NYSE
Industry: Pollution control equipment & services

 indicates company is in *Hoover's Handbook of American Business.*

indicates company is in *Hoover's Handbook of World Business;* sales and employee numbers are for parent company.

Almacs Supermarkets
One Noyes St.
East Providence, RI 02916
Phone: 401-438-2700 Fax: 401-438-4870
CEO: Greg Mays
CFO: Dexter W. Pike
1991 Sales: $542 million Employees: 1,217
Ownership: Privately held
Industry: Retail - supermarkets

Aloette Cosmetics, Inc.
1301 Wright's Lane East
West Chester, PA 19380
Phone: 215-692-0600 Fax: 215-692-2334
CEO: Patricia J. Defibaugh
CFO: Jean M. Lewis
1991 Sales: $24 million Employees: 125
Symbol: ALET Exchange: NASDAQ
Industry: Cosmetics & toiletries

Alpha Industries, Inc.
20 Sylvan Rd.
Woburn, MA 01801
Phone: 617-935-5150 Fax: 617-935-4939
CEO: George S. Kariotis
CFO: William A. Krein
1992 Sales: $71 million Employees: 840
Symbol: AHA Exchange: AMEX
Industry: Electronics - military

Alpha Microsystems
3501 W. Sunflower Ave.
Santa Ana, CA 92704
Phone: 714-957-8500 Fax: 714-957-8705
CEO: Clarke E. Reynolds
CFO: John S. Cain
1992 Sales: $49 million Employees: 370
Symbol: ALMI Exchange: NASDAQ
Industry: Computers - mini & micro

Alpharel, Inc.
3601 Calle Tecate
Camarillo, CA 93010
Phone: 805-482-9815 Fax: 805-482-9818
CEO: Roger H. Erickson
CFO: John W. Low
1991 Sales: $6.6 million Employees: 31
Symbol: AREL Exchange: NASDAQ
Industry: Computers - document management software

Alpine Group, Inc.
Three University Plaza
Hackensack, NJ 07601
Phone: 201-343-7600 Fax: —
CEO: Steven S. Elbaum
CFO: Alan J. Nickerson
1992 Sales: $10.3 million Employees: —
Symbol: AGI Exchange: AMEX
Industry: Chemicals - specialty

Alpine Lace Brands, Inc.
111 Dunnell Rd.
Maplewood, NJ 07040
Phone: 201-378-8600 Fax: 201-378-8887
CEO: Carl T. Wolf
CFO: Carl T. Wolf
1991 Sales: $156 million Employees: 301
Symbol: LACE Exchange: NASDAQ
Industry: Food - cheese products

Alta Gold Co.
2319 Foothill Dr., Ste. 140
Salt Lake City, UT 84109
Phone: 801-483-1116 Fax: —
CEO: Dan S. Bushnell
CFO: Duane W. Moss
1991 Sales: $14 million Employees: 49
Symbol: ALTA Exchange: NASDAQ
Industry: Gold mining & processing

Altai, Inc.
624 Six Flags Dr.
Arlington, TX 76011
Phone: 817-640-8911 Fax: —
CEO: James P. Williams
CFO: Gary E. Leslie
1991 Sales: $8.2 million Employees: 78
Symbol: ALTI Exchange: NASDAQ
Industry: Computers - software

Alteon, Inc.
165 Ludlow Ave.
Northvale, NJ 07647
Phone: 201-784-1010 Fax: —
CEO: Charles A. Faden
CFO: Charles A. Faden
1991 Sales: $5 million Employees: 35
Symbol: ALTN Exchange: NASDAQ
Industry: Drugs

Altera Corp.
2610 Orchard Pkwy.
San Jose, CA 95134
Phone: 408-894-7000 Fax: 408-296-3140
CEO: Rodney Smith
CFO: Paul Newhagen
1992 Sales: $101 million Employees: 480
Symbol: ALTR Exchange: NASDAQ
Industry: Electrical components - semiconductors

Altron Inc.
One Jewel Dr.
Wilmington, MA 01887
Phone: 508-658-5800 Fax: 508-657-8887
CEO: Samuel Altschuler
CFO: Burton Doo
1991 Sales: $62 million Employees: 775
Symbol: ALRN Exchange: NASDAQ
Industry: Electrical connectors

Aluminum Company of America
1501 Alcoa Bldg.
Pittsburgh, PA 15219
Phone: 412-553-4545 Fax: 412-553-4498
CEO: Paul H. O'Neill
CFO: Jan H. M. Hommen
1992 Sales: $9,492 million Employees: 65,600
Symbol: AA Exchange: NYSE
Industry: Metals - nonferrous

Alza Corp.
950 Page Mill Rd.
Palo Alto, CA 94303
Phone: 415-494-5000 Fax: 415-494-5129
CEO: Martin S. Gerstel
CFO: Martin S. Gerstel
1992 Sales: $229 million Employees: 1,036
Symbol: AZA Exchange: NYSE
Industry: Medical products - rate controlled delivery systems

AM International, Inc.
333 W. Wacker Dr., Ste. 900
Chicago, IL 60606
Phone: 312-558-1966 Fax: 312-558-7965
CEO: Merle H. Banta
CFO: Steven F. Kaplan
1991 Sales: $858 million Employees: 5,959
Symbol: AM Exchange: NYSE
Industry: Office equipment & supplies

Am-Pro Protective Agency
7499 Parklane Rd., Ste. 136
Columbia, SC 29223
Phone: 803-741-0287 Fax: 803-741-0009
CEO: John E. Brown
CFO: John E. Brown
1991 Sales: $34 million Employees: 1,193
Ownership: Privately held
Industry: Protection - security guard services

Amax Gold Inc.
350 Indiana St.
Golden, CO 80401
Phone: 303-273-0600 Fax: 303-273-0703
CEO: Timothy J. Haddon
CFO: Marvin K. Kaiser
1991 Sales: $128 million Employees: 536
Symbol: AU Exchange: NYSE
Industry: Gold mining & processing

AMAX Inc.
200 Park Ave.
New York, NY 10166
Phone: 212-856-4200 Fax: 212-856-6075
CEO: Allen Born
CFO: Stephen C. Knup
1992 Sales: $3,698 million Employees: 20,800
Symbol: AMX Exchange: NYSE
Industry: Metal ores

AMBAC Inc.
One State St. Plaza, 15th Fl.
New York, NY 10004
Phone: 212-668-0340 Fax: 212-509-9190
CEO: Phillip B. Lassiter
CFO: Frank J. Bivona
1991 Sales: $187 million Employees: —
Symbol: ABK Exchange: NYSE
Industry: Insurance - multiline & misc.

Ambar, Inc.
101 La Rue France Blvd., Ste. 201
Lafayette, LA 70508
Phone: 318-237-5300 Fax: —
CEO: Randolph M. Moity
CFO: Randolph M. Moity
1992 Sales: $19 million Employees: 174
Symbol: AMBR Exchange: NASDAQ
Industry: Diversified operations

AmBase Corp.
59 Maiden Lane
New York, NY 10038
Phone: 212-530-6800 Fax: 212-701-8935
CEO: Richard A. Bianco
CFO: Jack R. Plaxe
1991 Sales: $510 million Employees: 1,300
Symbol: ABC Exchange: NYSE
Industry: Insurance - property & casualty

AMC Entertainment Inc.
106 W. 14th St.
Kansas City, MO 64141
Phone: 816-221-4000 Fax: 816-421-5744
CEO: Stanley H. Durwood
CFO: Peter C. Brown
1992 Sales: $406 million Employees: 6,821
Symbol: AEN Exchange: AMEX
Industry: Motion pictures & services - theaters

Amcast Industrial Corp.
3931 S. Dixie Ave.
Dayton, OH 45439
Phone: 513-298-5251 Fax: 513-298-4025
CEO: Leo W. Ladehoff
CFO: John H. Shuey
1991 Sales: $271 million Employees: 2,700
Symbol: AIZ Exchange: NYSE
Industry: Metal processing & fabrication

AMCORE Financial, Inc.
501 Seventh St.
Rockford, IL 61104
Phone: 815-968-2241 Fax: —
CEO: Carl J. Dargene
CFO: F. Taylor Carlin
1991 Sales: $138 million Employees: 855
Symbol: AMFI Exchange: NASDAQ
Industry: Banks - Midwest

 indicates company is in *Hoover's Handbook of American Business.*

indicates company is in *Hoover's Handbook of World Business;* sales and employee numbers are for parent company.

Amdahl Corp.
1250 E. Arques Ave.
Sunnyvale, CA 94088
Phone: 408-746-6000 Fax: 408-746-6468
CEO: John C. Lewis
CFO: Edward F. Thompson
1992 Sales: $2,525 million Employees: 9,400
Symbol: AMH Exchange: AMEX
Industry: Computers - mainframe

AMDURA Corp.
501 S. Cherry St., Ste. 600
Denver, CO 80222
Phone: 303-394-4500 Fax: —
CEO: Wayne E. Waldeara
CFO: Edward J. Rand
1991 Sales: $144 million Employees: 1,300
Symbol: ADU Exchange: NYSE
Industry: Building products - retail & wholesale

Amerada Hess Corp.
1185 Avenue of the Americas
New York, NY 10036
Phone: 212-997-8500 Fax: 212-536-8396
CEO: Leon Hess
CFO: John Y. Schreyer
1992 Sales: $5,970 million Employees: 10,317
Symbol: AHC Exchange: NYSE
Industry: Oil & gas - US integrated

Amerco
1325 Airmotive Way, Ste. 100
Reno, NV 89502
Phone: 702-688-6300 Fax: 702-688-6338
CEO: Edward J. Shoen
CFO: Gary Horton
1991 Sales: $971 million Employees: 9,300
Ownership: Privately held
Industry: Leasing - U-Haul vehicles

America Online, Inc.
8619 Westwood Center Dr.
Vienna, VA 22182
Phone: 703-448-8700 Fax: 703-883-1514
CEO: James V. Kimsey
CFO: Lennert J. Leader
1992 Sales: $26 million Employees: —
Symbol: AMER Exchange: NASDAQ
Industry: Computers - on-line information

America Service Group, Inc.
101 Lukens Dr., Ste. A
New Castle, DE 19720
Phone: 302-888-0200 Fax: —
CEO: Jeffrey A. Reasons
CFO: Margaret O. Harrison
1991 Sales: $60 million Employees: 834
Symbol: ASGR Exchange: NASDAQ
Industry: Healthcare - outpatient & home

America West Airlines, Inc.
51 W. 3rd St.
Tempe, AZ 85281
Phone: 602-693-0800 Fax: 602-693-5546
CEO: Michael J. Conway
CFO: Alphonse E. Frei
1992 Sales: $1,294 million Employees: 12,142
Trading Status: Suspended
Industry: Transportation - airline

American Bank of Connecticut
Two W. Main St.
Waterbury, CT 06702
Phone: 203-757-9401 Fax: 203-753-8699
CEO: Gene C. Guilbert
CFO: Floyd G. Champagne
1991 Sales: $35 million Employees: 99
Symbol: BKC Exchange: AMEX
Industry: Financial - savings and loans

American Bankers Insurance Group, Inc.
11222 Quail Roost Dr.
Miami, FL 33157
Phone: 305-253-2244 Fax: 305-252-6987
CEO: R. Kirk Landon
CFO: Floyd G. Denison
1991 Sales: $764 million Employees: 1,622
Symbol: ABIG Exchange: NASDAQ
Industry: Insurance - life

American Biltrite Inc.
57 River St.
Wellesley, MA 02181
Phone: 617-237-6655 Fax: 617-237-6880
CEO: Roger S. Marcus
CFO: Gilbert K. Gailius
1991 Sales: $154 million Employees: 1,000
Symbol: ABL Exchange: AMEX
Industry: Building products

American Biodyne, Inc.
400 Oyster Point Blvd.
South San Francisco, CA 94080
Phone: 415-742-0980 Fax: 415-742-0988
CEO: Albert S. Waxman
CFO: Kenneth B. Zimmerman
1991 Sales: $51 million Employees: 350
Symbol: ABDN Exchange: NASDAQ
Industry: Healthcare - outpatient & home

American Biogenetic Sciences, Inc.
PO Box 1001
Notre Dame, IN 46556
Phone: 219-239-7755 Fax: —
CEO: Alfred J. Roach
CFO: Timothy J. Roach
1992 Sales: — Employees: 14
Symbol: MABXA Exchange: NASDAQ
Industry: Biomedical & genetic products

American Brands, Inc.
1700 E. Putnam Ave.
Old Greenwich, CT 06870
Phone: 203-698-5000 Fax: 203-637-2580
CEO: William J. Alley
CFO: Arnold Henson
1992 Sales: $8,840 million Employees: 47,600
Symbol: AMB Exchange: NYSE
Industry: Tobacco

American Building Maintenance Industries, Inc.
50 Fremont St., Ste. 2600
San Francisco, CA 94105
Phone: 415-597-4500 Fax: 415-597-7160
CEO: Sydney J. Rosenberg
CFO: David H. Hebble
1992 Sales: $758 million Employees: 34,000
Symbol: ABM Exchange: NYSE
Industry: Building - maintenance & services

American Business Information
5711 S. 86th Circle
Omaha, NE 68127
Phone: 402-593-4600 Fax: 402-331-5481
CEO: Vinod Gupta
CFO: Roger J. Jensen
1991 Sales: $42 million Employees: 422
Symbol: ABII Exchange: NASDAQ
Industry: Business services - mailing lists & directories

American Business Products, Inc.
2100 Riveredge Pkwy., Ste. 1200
Atlanta, GA 30328
Phone: 404-953-8300 Fax: 404-952-2343
CEO: Thomas R. Carmody
CFO: W. C. Downer
1991 Sales: $446 million Employees: 3,894
Symbol: ABP Exchange: NYSE
Industry: Paper - business forms

American Cargo Systems
11020 King St., Ste. 350
Overland Park, KS 66210
Phone: 913-345-2518 Fax: 913-345-2827
CEO: Chris Ellis
CFO: Chris Ellis
1991 Sales: $6 million Employees: 14
Ownership: Privately held
Industry: Transportation - brokerage services

American City Business Journals, Inc.
128 S. Tryon St., Ste. 2200
Charlotte, NC 28202
Phone: 704-375-7404 Fax: 704-371-3299
CEO: Ray Shaw
CFO: Grant L. Hamrick
1991 Sales: $69 million Employees: 882
Symbol: AMBJ Exchange: NASDAQ
Industry: Publishing - city business newspapers

American Claims Evaluation, Inc.
375 N. Broadway, Ste. 3300
Jericho, NY 11753
Phone: 516-938-0400 Fax: 516-938-0405
CEO: Gary Gelman
CFO: Gary Gelman
1992 Sales: $7.9 million Employees: 56
Symbol: AMCE Exchange: NASDAQ
Industry: Business services - insurance claim verification

American Colloid Co.
1500 W. Shure Dr.
Arlington Heights, IL 60004
Phone: 708-392-4600 Fax: 708-506-6199
CEO: John Hughes
CFO: Paul G. Shelton
1991 Sales: $149 million Employees: 879
Symbol: ACOL Exchange: NASDAQ
Industry: Metal ores

American Consumer Products, Inc.
31100 Solon Rd.
Solon, OH 44139
Phone: 216-248-7000 Fax: 216-248-8051
CEO: Stephan W. Cole
CFO: Stephan W. Cole
1991 Sales: $95 million Employees: 969
Symbol: ACPI Exchange: NASDAQ
Industry: Specialty hardware

American Cyanamid Co.
One Cyanamid Plaza
Wayne, NJ 07470
Phone: 201-831-2000 Fax: 201-831-3151
CEO: Albert J. Costello
CFO: Terence D. Martin
1992 Sales: $5,268 million Employees: 31,587
Symbol: ACY Exchange: NYSE
Industry: Drugs

American Dental Laser, Inc.
2600 W. Big Beaver Rd.
Troy, MI 48084
Phone: 313-649-0000 Fax: 313-649-5141
CEO: Daniel S. Goldsmith
CFO: Eric A. Fris, Jr.
1991 Sales: $28 million Employees: 90
Symbol: ADLI Exchange: NASDAQ
Industry: Medical & dental supplies

American Ecology Corp.
9200 Shelbyville Rd., Ste. 300
Louisville, KY 40222
Phone: 502-426-7160 Fax: 818-426-5010
CEO: Harry J. Phillips, Jr.
CFO: C. Clifford Wright, Jr.
1991 Sales: $55 million Employees: 225
Symbol: ECOL Exchange: NASDAQ
Industry: Hazardous waste disposal

[A] indicates company is in *Hoover's Handbook of American Business.*

[W] indicates company is in *Hoover's Handbook of World Business;* sales and employee numbers are for parent company.

American Electric Power Co., Inc.
1 Riverside Plaza
Columbus, OH 43215
Phone: 614-223-1000 Fax: 614-223-1823
CEO: E. Linn Draper, Jr.
CFO: Gerald P. Maloney
1992 Sales: $5,045 million Employees: 22,736
Symbol: AEP Exchange: NYSE
Industry: Utility - electric power

American Exploration Co.
1331 Lamar, Ste. 900
Houston, TX 77010
Phone: 713-756-6000 Fax: 713-659-5620
CEO: Mark Andrews
CFO: Ronald E. Long
1991 Sales: $76 million Employees: 363
Symbol: AX Exchange: AMEX
Industry: Oil & gas - US exploration & production

American Express Co.
World Financial Center
New York, NY 10285
Phone: 212-640-2000 Fax: 212-619-9802
CEO: Harvey Golub
CFO: Michael P. Monaco
1992 Sales: $26,962 million Employees: 110,728
Symbol: AXP Exchange: NYSE
Industry: Financial - business services

American Fashion Jewels
651 Gateway Blvd., Ste. 900
San Francisco, CA 94080
Phone: 415-588-1800 Fax: 415-588-1805
CEO: Tom Herman
CFO: Patrick Holwagner
1991 Sales: $24 million Employees: 145
Ownership: Privately held
Industry: Retail - jewelry

American Fastsigns
4951 Airport Pkwy., Ste. 530
Dallas, TX 75248
Phone: 214-702-0000 Fax: 214-991-6058
CEO: Gary Salomon
CFO: Mary Ryan
1991 Sales: $3.5 million Employees: 35
Ownership: Privately held
Industry: Computer-generated vinyl signs

American Film Technologies, Inc.
1265 Drummers Lane, Ste. 108
Wayne, PA 19087
Phone: 215-688-1322 Fax: 215-688-1753
CEO: George R. Jensen, Jr.
CFO: Patrick J. Brennan
1991 Sales: $9.8 million Employees: 481
Symbol: AFTI Exchange: NASDAQ
Industry: Motion pictures & services - production

American Filtrona Corp.
3951 Westerre Pkwy., Ste. 300
Richmond, VA 23233
Phone: 804-346-2400 Fax: 804-346-0164
CEO: John L. Morgan
CFO: John D. Barlow, Jr.
1991 Sales: $144 million Employees: 1,100
Symbol: AFIL Exchange: NASDAQ
Industry: Fiber filters

American Financial Corp.
One E. Fourth St.
Cincinnati, OH 45202
Phone: 513-579-2121 Fax: 513-579-2580
CEO: Carl H. Lindner
CFO: Fred J. Runk
1991 Sales: $5,232 million Employees: 54,000
Ownership: Privately held
Industry: Diversified operations - insurance, food products & media

American Foods Group Inc.
544 Acme St.
Green Bay, WI 54302
Phone: 414-437-6330 Fax: 414-436-6510
CEO: Carl Kuehne
CFO: Jim Coulombe
1991 Sales: $575 million Employees: 1,445
Ownership: Privately held
Industry: Food - meat products

American Freightways
2200 Forward Dr.
Harrison, AR 72601
Phone: 501-741-9000 Fax: 501-741-3003
CEO: F. S. Garrison
CFO: James R. Dodd
1991 Sales: $198 million Employees: 3,058
Symbol: AFWY Exchange: NASDAQ
Industry: Transportation - truck

American Fructose Corp.
250 Harbor Dr.
Stamford, CT 06902
Phone: 203-356-9000 Fax: —
CEO: William Ziegler III
CFO: Edward P. Norris
1991 Sales: $211 million Employees: 233
Symbol: AFCA Exchange: AMEX
Industry: Food - sugar & refining

American General Corp.
2727 Allen Pkwy.
Houston, TX 77019
Phone: 713-522-1111 Fax: 713-831-3028
CEO: Harold S. Hook
CFO: Austin P. Young
1992 Sales: $4,602 million Employees: —
Symbol: AGC Exchange: NYSE
Industry: Insurance - life

American Greetings Corp.
10500 American Rd.
Cleveland, OH 44144
Phone: 216-252-7300 Fax: 216-252-6519
CEO: Morry Weiss
CFO: Henry Lowenthal
1992 Sales: $1,646 million Employees: 31,200
Symbol: AGREA Exchange: NASDAQ
Industry: Greeting cards & gift items

American Health Services Corp.
4440 Von Karman, Ste. 320
Newport Beach, CA 92660
Phone: 714-476-0733 Fax: 714-851-5981
CEO: E. Larry Atkins
CFO: Thomas V. Croal
1991 Sales: $42 million Employees: 198
Symbol: AHTS Exchange: NASDAQ
Industry: Medical services - radiology & imaging

American Healthcare Management, Inc.
660 American Ave., Ste. 200
King of Prussia, PA 19406
Phone: 215-768-5900 Fax: —
CEO: Steven L. Volla
CFO: William S. Harrigan
1991 Sales: $290 million Employees: 3,600
Symbol: AHI Exchange: AMEX
Industry: Hospitals

American Healthcorp, Inc.
One Burton Hills Blvd.
Nashville, TN 37215
Phone: 615-665-1122 Fax: —
CEO: Thomas G. Cigarran
CFO: Henry D. Herr
1991 Sales: $31 million Employees: 379
Symbol: AMHC Exchange: NASDAQ
Industry: Healthcare - outpatient & home

American Heritage Life Investment Corp.
76 S. Laura St.
Jacksonville, FL 32202
Phone: 904-354-1776 Fax: 904-359-2694
CEO: T. O'Neal Douglas
CFO: C. Richard Morehead
1991 Sales: $250 million Employees: —
Symbol: AHL Exchange: NYSE
Industry: Insurance - life

American Holdings, Inc.
56 Pennbrook Rd.
Far Hills, NJ 07931
Phone: 908-234-9220 Fax: —
CEO: Paul O. Koether
CFO: John W. Galuchie, Jr.
1991 Sales: $1.3 million Employees: 6
Symbol: HOLD Exchange: NASDAQ
Industry: Financial - investment for own account

American Home Products Corp.
685 Third Ave.
New York, NY 10017
Phone: 212-878-5000 Fax: 212-878-5771
CEO: John R. Stafford
CFO: John R. Considine
1992 Sales: $7,874 million Employees: 47,938
Symbol: AHP Exchange: NYSE
Industry: Drugs & consumer healthcare products

American Income Life Insurance Co.
1200 Wooded Acres
Waco, TX 76797
Phone: 817-772-3050 Fax: 817-751-0728
CEO: Bernard Rapoport
CFO: Mark E. Pape
1991 Sales: $169 million Employees: —
Symbol: AIH Exchange: NYSE
Industry: Insurance - multiline & misc.

American Indemnity Financial Corp.
One American Indemnity Plaza
Galveston, TX 77550
Phone: 409-766-4600 Fax: —
CEO: J. F. Seinsheimer, Jr.
CFO: Synott L. McNeel
1991 Sales: $63 million Employees: 265
Symbol: AIFC Exchange: NASDAQ
Industry: Insurance - property & casualty

American Insurance Group, Inc.
6245 E. Broadway Blvd., Ste. 600
Tucson, AZ 85711
Phone: 602-747-5555 Fax: 602-748-3256
CEO: Don H. Pace
CFO: Greg S. Kaplan
1991 Sales: $25 million Employees: 66
Symbol: AMGP Exchange: NASDAQ
Industry: Insurance - multiline & misc.

American Insurance Managers, Inc.
300 Interstate North, Ste. 500
Atlanta, GA 30339
Phone: 404-980-0591 Fax: 404-980-1706
CEO: David Dennett-Smith
CFO: David Dennett-Smith
1991 Sales: $16 million Employees: 100
Ownership: Privately held
Industry: Business services - insurance brokerage

American Integrity Corp.
Two Penn Center Plaza, 11th Fl.
Philadelphia, PA 19102
Phone: 215-561-1400 Fax: —
CEO: J. William Bradner
CFO: Robert R. Board
1991 Sales: $96 million Employees: 170
Symbol: AIIC Exchange: NASDAQ
Industry: Insurance - accident & health

American International Construction
14603 Chrisman
Houston, TX 97039
Phone: 713-449-9000 Fax: 713-442-6351
CEO: John Wilson
CFO: John Wilson
1991 Sales: $20 million Employees: 200
Ownership: Privately held
Industry: Construction - metal structures & mini-warehouses

American International Group, Inc.
70 Pine St.
New York, NY 10270
Phone: 212-770-7000 Fax: 212-770-7821
CEO: Maurice R. Greenberg
CFO: Edward E. Matthews
1992 Sales: $18,389 million Employees: 32,000
Symbol: AIG Exchange: NYSE
Industry: Insurance - property & casualty

American International Petroleum Co.
640 Fifth Ave.
New York, NY 10019
Phone: 212-956-3333 Fax: 212-956-4917
CEO: George N. Faris
CFO: Gysle R. Shellum
1991 Sales: $2.4 million Employees: 95
Symbol: AIPN Exchange: NASDAQ
Industry: Oil & gas - US exploration & production

American Isuzu Motors Inc.
13181 Crossroads Pkwy. North, 4th Fl.
City of Industry, CA 91746
Phone: 310-699-0500 Fax: 310-723-2125
CEO: Kozo Sakaino
CFO: —
1991 Sales: $12,184 million Employees: 13,600
Parent: Isuzu Motors Ltd.
Industry: Automotive & truck manufacturing, engines & components

American List Corp.
330 Old Country Rd.
Mineold, NY 11501
Phone: 516-248-6100 Fax: 516-248-6364
CEO: Martin Lerner
CFO: Martin Lerner
1992 Sales: $8.8 million Employees: 21
Symbol: AMZ Exchange: AMEX
Industry: Business services - mailing lists

American Locker Group Inc.
15 W. Second St.
Jamestown, NY 14702
Phone: 716-664-9600 Fax: 716-664-2949
CEO: Harold J. Ruttenberg
CFO: Harold J. Ruttenberg
1991 Sales: $14 million Employees: 158
Symbol: ALGI Exchange: NASDAQ
Industry: Building products

American Maize-Products Co.
250 Harbor Plaza Dr.
Stamford, CT 06902
Phone: 203-356-9000 Fax: 203-359-1020
CEO: William Ziegler III
CFO: Edward P. Norris
1991 Sales: $534 million Employees: 2,009
Symbol: AZEA Exchange: AMEX
Industry: Food - flour & grain

American Management Systems, Inc.
1777 N. Kent St.
Arlington, VA 22209
Phone: 703-841-6000 Fax: 703-841-6242
CEO: Charles O. Rossotti
CFO: Frank A. Nicolai
1991 Sales: $285 million Employees: 3,200
Symbol: AMSY Exchange: NASDAQ
Industry: Computers - services

American Medical Electronics, Inc.
4125 Keller Springs Rd.
Dallas, TX 75244
Phone: 214-248-6000 Fax: —
CEO: Joseph Mooibroek
CFO: Wesley E. Johnson, Jr.
1991 Sales: $27 million Employees: 208
Symbol: AMEI Exchange: NASDAQ
Industry: Medical instruments

American Medical Holdings, Inc.
8201 Preston Rd., Ste. 300
Dallas, TX 75225
Phone: 214-360-6300 Fax: 214-360-6363
CEO: Harry J. Gray
CFO: Wendy L. Simpson
1992 Sales: $2,241 million Employees: 29,600
Symbol: AMI Exchange: AMEX
Industry: Hospitals

American Medical Response, Inc.
67 Batterymarch St., Ste. 300
Boston, MA 02110
Phone: 617-261-1600 Fax: —
CEO: Paul M. Verrochi
CFO: Dominic J. Puopolo
1992 Sales: — Employees: 1,533
Symbol: EMT Exchange: NYSE
Industry: Medical services

American Megatrends, Inc.
6145 North Belt Pkwy.
Norcross, GA 30071
Phone: 404-263-8181 Fax: 404-263-9381
CEO: Subramonian Shanker
CFO: Victor Kannan
1991 Sales: $70 million Employees: 114
Ownership: Privately held
Industry: Computers - motherboards

American Mobile Systems, Inc.
21160 Califa St.
Woodland Hills, CA 91367
Phone: 818-593-3000 Fax: —
CEO: Richard G. Somers
CFO: Richard G. Somers
1991 Sales: $5.4 million Employees: 27
Symbol: AMSEE Exchange: NASDAQ
Industry: Telecommunications services

American National Insurance Co.
One Moody Plaza
Galveston, TX 77550
Phone: 409-763-4661 Fax: 409-766-6589
CEO: Orson C. Clay
CFO: C. D. Thompson
1992 Sales: $1,318 million Employees: —
Symbol: ANAT Exchange: NASDAQ
Industry: Insurance - life

American Nuclear Corp.
550 N. Poplar
Casper, WY 82602
Phone: 307-265-7912 Fax: 307-265-3777
CEO: James Cornell
CFO: P. Arlen Agren
1991 Sales: $0.1 million Employees: 5
Symbol: ANUC Exchange: NASDAQ
Industry: Metals - nonferrous

American Nursery Products, Inc.
W. Hwy. 51
Tahlequah, OK 74464
Phone: 918-456-6185 Fax: 918-456-2661
CEO: Lester E. Cashmere
CFO: Lester E. Cashmere
1991 Sales: $51 million Employees: 1,795
Symbol: ANSY Exchange: NASDAQ
Industry: Agricultural operations

American Oil and Gas Corp.
333 Clay St., Ste. 2000
Houston, TX 77002
Phone: 713-739-2900 Fax: 713-739-2963
CEO: David M. Carmichael
CFO: William P. Conner
1991 Sales: $381 million Employees: 283
Symbol: AOG Exchange: NYSE
Industry: Oil & gas - production & pipeline

American Pacific Corp.
3770 Howard Hughes Pkwy., Ste. 300
Las Vegas, NV 89109
Phone: 702-735-2200 Fax: 702-735-4876
CEO: Fred D. Gibson, Jr.
CFO: David N. Keyes
1991 Sales: $62 million Employees: 208
Symbol: APFC Exchange: NASDAQ
Industry: Chemicals - specialty

American Packaging Corp.
777 Driving Park Ave.
Rochester, NY 14613
Phone: 716-254-9500 Fax: 716-254-8501
CEO: Peter Schottland
CFO: Don Huttlin
1991 Sales: $1.8 million Employees: 200
Ownership: Privately held
Industry: Business services - contract packaging

American Physicians Service Group, Inc.
1301 Capital of Texas Hwy. South
Austin, TX 78746
Phone: 512-328-0888 Fax: 512-329-4398
CEO: Kenneth Shifrin
CFO: William H. Hayes
1991 Sales: $17 million Employees: 152
Symbol: AMPH Exchange: NASDAQ
Industry: Medical - healthcare management services

American Playworld Inc.
1213 W. 2550th St. South
Ogden, UT 84401
Phone: 801-392-6373 Fax: 801-399-2608
CEO: Stephen Nye
CFO: Stephen Nye
1991 Sales: $14 million Employees: 157
Ownership: Privately held
Industry: Playground equipment

American Power Conversion Corp.
132 Fairgrounds Rd.
West Kingston, RI 02892
Phone: 401-789-5735 Fax: 401-789-3710
CEO: Rodger B. Dowdell, Jr.
CFO: Rodger B. Dowdell, Jr.
1991 Sales: $94 million Employees: 461
Symbol: APCC Exchange: NASDAQ
Industry: Electrical products - uninterruptible power supplies

American Precision Industries Inc.
2777 Walden Ave.
Buffalo, NY 14225
Phone: 716-684-6700 Fax: 716-684-2129
CEO: Robert J. Fierle
CFO: John M. Murray
1991 Sales: $51 million Employees: 640
Symbol: APR Exchange: NYSE
Industry: Electrical products

American President Companies, Ltd.
1111 Broadway
Oakland, CA 94607
Phone: 510-272-8000 Fax: 510-272-7941
CEO: John M. Lillie
CFO: Will M. Storey
1992 Sales: $2,505 million Employees: 5,232
Symbol: APS Exchange: NYSE
Industry: Transportation - shipping

indicates company is in *Hoover's Handbook of American Business.*

indicates company is in *Hoover's Handbook of World Business;* sales and employee numbers are for parent company.

American Protection Industries, Inc.
12233 W. Olympic Blvd., Ste. 380
Los Angeles, CA 90064
Phone: 310-442-5700 Fax: 310-207-1557
CEO: Stewart Resnick
CFO: Robert Savesky
1991 Sales: $925 million Employees: 7,200
Ownership: Privately held
Industry: Retail - mail order & direct; flowers & collectibles

American Real Estate Partners, L.P.
10 Union Square East
New York, NY 10003
Phone: 212-353-7000 Fax: —
CEO: Marvin D. Kenigsberg
CFO: Thomas M. Finn
1991 Sales: $57 million Employees: 17
Symbol: ACP Exchange: NYSE
Industry: Real estate operations

American Recreation Centers, Inc.
11171 Sun Center Dr., Ste. 120
Rancho Cordova, CA 95670
Phone: 916-852-8005 Fax: 916-852-8004
CEO: Robert A. Crist
CFO: Karen B. Wagner
1992 Sales: $65 million Employees: 1,200
Symbol: AMRC Exchange: NASDAQ
Industry: Diversified operations - bowling center & children's products

American Restaurant Partners, L.P.
555 N. Woodlawn, Ste. 3102
Wichita, KS 67208
Phone: 316-684-5119 Fax: 316-684-9780
CEO: Hal W. McCoy
CFO: Gene R. Baldwin
1991 Sales: $33 million Employees: —
Symbol: RMC Exchange: AMEX
Industry: Retail - food & restaurants

American Rice, Inc.
16825 Northchase Dr., Ste. 1500
Houston, TX 77060
Phone: 713-873-8800 Fax: 713-873-2823
CEO: John M. Howland
CFO: Larry Dylla
1992 Sales: $176 million Employees: 230
Symbol: RICE Exchange: NASDAQ
Industry: Agricultural operations

American Science and Engineering, Inc.
40 Erie St.
Cambridge, MA 02139
Phone: 617-868-1600 Fax: 617-354-1054
CEO: Martin Annis
CFO: Richard R. Sullivan, Jr.
1992 Sales: $18 million Employees: 136
Symbol: ASE Exchange: AMEX
Industry: Electronics - measuring instruments

American Shared Hospital Services
444 Market St., Ste. 2420
San Francisco, CA 94111
Phone: 415-788-5300 Fax: 415-788-5660
CEO: Ernest A. Bates
CFO: John F. Lowrey
1991 Sales: $59 million Employees: 694
Symbol: AMS Exchange: AMEX
Industry: Medical services - respiratory therapy & magnetic resonance imaging

American Ship Building Co.
6001 S. Westshore Blvd.
Tampa, FL 33616
Phone: 813-835-7000 Fax: 813-832-2113
CEO: Paul D. Butcher
CFO: Kenneth G. Myers
1991 Sales: $74 million Employees: 1,600
Symbol: ABG Exchange: NYSE
Industry: Boat building

American Software, Inc.
470 E. Paces Ferry Rd. NE
Atlanta, GA 30305
Phone: 404-261-4381 Fax: 404-364-0883
CEO: James C. Edenfield
CFO: Neal L. Miller
1992 Sales: $113 million Employees: 912
Symbol: AMSWA Exchange: NASDAQ
Industry: Computers - inventory management software

American Standard Inc.
1114 6th Ave., 19th Fl.
New York, NY 10036
Phone: 212-703-5100 Fax: 212-703-5177
CEO: Emmanuel A. Kampouris
CFO: Fred A. Allardyce
1991 Sales: $3,595 million Employees: 32,000
Ownership: Privately held
Industry: Building products, plumbing products, air conditioning, auto products

American Steel & Wire Corp.
4300 E. 49th St.
Cuyahoga Heights, OH 44125
Phone: 216-883-3800 Fax: 216-441-6555
CEO: Thomas N. Tyrrell
CFO: C. V. Meserole III
1992 Sales: $210 million Employees: 532
Symbol: RODS Exchange: NASDAQ
Industry: Wire & cable products

American Stock Exchange
86 Trinity Pl.
New York, NY 10006
Phone: 212-306-1000 Fax: 212-306-1644
CEO: James R. Jones
CFO: William D. Strauss
1991 Sales: $100 million Employees: 850
Ownership: Privately held
Industry: Stock exchange

American Stores Co.
709 E. South Temple
Salt Lake City, UT 84102
Phone: 801-539-0112 Fax: 801-531-0768
CEO: Victor L. Lund
CFO: Teresa Beck
1992 Sales: $19,418 million Employees: 148,000
Symbol: ASC Exchange: NYSE
Industry: Retail - supermarkets

American Superconductor Corp.
149 Grove St.
Watertown, MA 02172
Phone: 617-923-1122 Fax: —
CEO: Gregory J. Yurek
CFO: Edward P. Hamilton
1992 Sales: $2.9 million Employees: 51
Symbol: AMSC Exchange: NASDAQ
Industry: Electrical components

American Suzuki Motor Corp.
3251 E. Imperial Hwy.
Brea, CA 9262
Phone: 714-996-7040 Fax: 714-970-6005
CEO: Kenji Shimizu
CFO: —
1992 Sales: $9,989 million Employees: 12,757
Parent: Suzuki Motor Corporation
Industry: Automotive manufacturing

American Technical Ceramics Corp.
17 Stepar Place
Huntington Station, NY 11746
Phone: 516-547-5700 Fax: 516-547-5748
CEO: Victor Insetta
CFO: Joseph A. Marino
1992 Sales: $19 million Employees: 323
Symbol: AMK Exchange: AMEX
Industry: Electrical components

American Teleconferencing Svcs.
10955 Lowell Ave.
Overland Park, KS 66210
Phone: 913-661-0700 Fax: 913-661-9188
CEO: Robert A. Cowan
CFO: Robert A. Cowan
1991 Sales: $3.5 million Employees: 43
Ownership: Privately held
Industry: Telecommunications services - conference call services

American Telephone & Telegraph Co.
32 Avenue of the Americas
New York, NY 10013
Phone: 212-605-5500 Fax: 212-308-1820
CEO: Robert E. Allen
CFO: Alex J. Mandl
1992 Sales: $64,904 million Employees: 317,100
Symbol: T Exchange: NYSE
Industry: Telecommunications services

American Travellers Corp.
3220 Tillman Dr.
Bensalem, PA 19020
Phone: 215-244-1600 Fax: —
CEO: John A. Powell
CFO: Ted M. Blecharczyk
1991 Sales: $125 million Employees: 314
Symbol: ATVC Exchange: NASDAQ
Industry: Insurance - accident & health

American United Global, Inc.
11634 Patton Rd.
Downey, CA 90241
Phone: 310-862-8163 Fax: 310-861-4955
CEO: Robert M. Rubin
CFO: John M. Palumbo
1992 Sales: — Employees: —
Symbol: AUGI Exchange: NASDAQ
Industry: Pumps & seals - O-rings & bonded sealing devices

American Vanguard Corp.
4100 E. Washington Blvd.
Los Angeles, CA 90023
Phone: 213-264-3910 Fax: —
CEO: Herbert A. Kraft
CFO: James A. Barry
1991 Sales: $29 million Employees: 118
Symbol: AMGD Exchange: NASDAQ
Industry: Chemicals - specialty

American Waste Services, Inc.
One American Way
Warren, OH 44484
Phone: 216-856-8800 Fax: 216-856-6988
CEO: Ronald E. Klingle
CFO: Charles Boryenace
1991 Sales: $91 million Employees: 453
Symbol: AW Exchange: NYSE
Industry: Waste disposal

American Water Works Co., Inc.
1025 Laurel Oak Rd.
Voorhees, NJ 08043
Phone: 609-346-8200 Fax: 609-346-8360
CEO: George W. Johnstone
CFO: J. James Barr
1991 Sales: $633 million Employees: 4,044
Symbol: AWK Exchange: NYSE
Industry: Utility - water supply

American Woodmark Corp.
3102 Shawnee Dr.
Winchester, VA 22601
Phone: 703-665-9100 Fax: 703-665-9176
CEO: William F. Brandt, Jr.
CFO: Gene S. Morphis
1992 Sales: $137 million Employees: 2,090
Symbol: AMWD Exchange: NASDAQ
Industry: Building products - doors & trim

indicates company is in *Hoover's Handbook of American Business.*

indicates company is in *Hoover's Handbook of World Business;* sales and employee numbers are for parent company.

Americana Hotels and Realty Corp.
535 Boylston St.
Boston, MA 02116
Phone: 617-247-3358 Fax: 617-247-0263
CEO: John A. Cervieri Jr.
CFO: Morris W. Kellogg
1991 Sales: $1 million Employees: —
Symbol: AHR Exchange: NYSE
Industry: Hotels & motels

AmeriServ Food Co.
13355 Noel Rd., Ste. 2225
Dallas, TX 75240
Phone: 214-385-8595 Fax: 214-702-7391
CEO: John P. Lewis
CFO: Wesley Mayland
1991 Sales: $725 million Employees: 1,200
Ownership: Privately held
Industry: Food - wholesale

Ameritech Corp.
30 S. Wacker Dr.
Chicago, IL 60606
Phone: 312-750-5000 Fax: 312-207-1601
CEO: William L. Weiss
CFO: John A. Edwardson
1992 Sales: $11,153 million Employees: 73,967
Symbol: AIT Exchange: NYSE
Industry: Utility - telephone

Ameriwood Industries International Corp.
4301 Canal Ave. SW
Grandville, MI 49418
Phone: 616-530-6300 Fax: 616-530-3044
CEO: Joseph J. Miglore
CFO: Joseph J. Miglore
1991 Sales: $79 million Employees: 600
Symbol: AWII Exchange: NASDAQ
Industry: Diversified operations

Ameron, Inc.
4700 Ramona Blvd.
Monterey Park, CA 91754
Phone: 213-268-4111 Fax: 213-263-7690
CEO: Lawrence R. Tollenaere
CFO: Kenneth J. Kay
1991 Sales: $465 million Employees: 2,900
Symbol: AMN Exchange: NYSE
Industry: Building products

Ames Department Stores, Inc.
2418 Main St.
Rocky Hill, CT 06067
Phone: 203-257-2000 Fax: 203-257-7806
CEO: Peter Thorner
CFO: Peter Thorner
1991 Sales: $2.8 million Employees: 28,000
Trading Status: Suspended
Industry: Retail - discount & variety

AMETEK, Inc.
Station Square 2
Paoli, PA 19301
Phone: 215-647-2121 Fax: 215-296-3412
CEO: Walter E. Blankley
CFO: Allan Kornfeld
1992 Sales: $770 million Employees: 6,100
Symbol: AME Exchange: NYSE
Industry: Electrical products - electro-mechanical devices, process equipment & precision instruments

Amgen Inc.
1840 Dehavilland Dr.
Thousand Oaks, CA 91320
Phone: 805-499-5725 Fax: 805-499-9315
CEO: Gordon M. Binder
CFO: Lowell E. Sears
1992 Sales: $1,093 million Employees: 1,723
Symbol: AMGN Exchange: NASDAQ
Industry: Biomedical & genetic products

Amistar Corp.
237 Via Vera Cruz
San Marcos, CA 92069
Phone: 619-471-1700 Fax: 619-471-9065
CEO: Stuart C. Baker
CFO: William W. Holl
1991 Sales: $14 million Employees: 181
Symbol: AMTA Exchange: NASDAQ
Industry: Machinery - material handling

Amity Bancorp Inc.
160 Amity Rd.
New Haven, CT 06525
Phone: 203-389-2800 Fax: —
CEO: Joseph V. Ciaburri
CFO: William B. Laudano, Jr.
1991 Sales: $18 million Employees: 93
Symbol: AMTY Exchange: NASDAQ
Industry: Banks - Northeast

Amoco Corp.
200 E. Randolph Dr.
Chicago, IL 60601
Phone: 312-856-6111 Fax: 312-856-2460
CEO: H. Laurance Fuller
CFO: Frederick S. Addy
1992 Sales: $28,223 million Employees: 54,120
Symbol: AN Exchange: NYSE
Industry: Oil & gas - US integrated

Amoskeag Co.
4500 Prudential Center
Boston, MA 02199
Phone: 617-262-4000 Fax: —
CEO: Joseph B. Ely II
CFO: Gerard J. Sarnie
1992 Sales: $1,248 million Employees: 17,772
Symbol: AMOS Exchange: NASDAQ
Industry: Diversified operations - management services

AMP Inc.
PO Box 3608
Harrisburg, PA 17105
Phone: 717-564-0100 Fax: 717-986-7605
CEO: William J. Hudson
CFO: Benjamin Savidge
1992 Sales: $3,337 million Employees: 25,000
Symbol: AMP Exchange: NYSE
Industry: Electrical connectors

Ampal-American Israel Corp.
10 Rockefeller Plaza
New York, NY 10020
Phone: 212-586-3232 Fax: 212-649-1749
CEO: Lawrence Lefkowitz
CFO: Alan L. Schaffer
1991 Sales: $66 million Employees: —
Symbol: AISA Exchange: AMEX
Industry: Financial - SBIC & commercial

Ampco-Pittsburgh Corp.
600 Grant St., Ste. 4600
Pittsburgh, PA 15219
Phone: 412-456-4400 Fax: 412-456-4404
CEO: Marshall L. Berkman
CFO: Ernest G. Siddons
1991 Sales: $221 million Employees: 2,068
Symbol: AP Exchange: NYSE
Industry: Metal processing & fabrication

Ampex Inc.
65 E. 55th St.
New York, NY 10022
Phone: 212-759-6301 Fax: —
CEO: Edward J. Brawson
CFO: Craig L. McKibben
Sales: $527 million Employees: 3,200
Symbol: AMPX Exchange: NASDAQ
Industry: Radio & TV communications equipment

Amphenol Corp.
358 Hall Ave.
Wallingford, CT 06492
Phone: 203-265-8900 Fax: 203-265-8793
CEO: Lawrence J. DeGeorge
CFO: Edward G. Jepsen
1991 Sales: $489 million Employees: 5,646
Symbol: APH Exchange: NYSE
Industry: Fiber optics

Amplicon, Inc.
2020 E. First St., Ste. 401
Santa Ana, CA 92705
Phone: 714-834-0525 Fax: —
CEO: Patrick E. Paddon
CFO: Glen T. Tsuma
1992 Sales: $130 million Employees: 144
Symbol: AMPI Exchange: NASDAQ
Industry: Leasing

AMR Corp.
4333 Amon Carter Blvd.
Ft. Worth, TX 76155
Phone: 817-963-1234 Fax: 817-967-9641
CEO: Robert L. Crandall
CFO: Donald J. Carty
1992 Sales: $14,396 million Employees: 116,264
Symbol: AMR Exchange: NYSE
Industry: Transportation - airline

AMRE, Inc.
8585 N. Stemmons Fwy., Ste. 102
Irving, TX 75247
Phone: 214-819-7000 Fax: 214-929-4133
CEO: Ronald I. Wagner
CFO: John S. Vanecko
1992 Sales: — Employees: 2,100
Symbol: AMM Exchange: NYSE
Industry: Building products - doors & trim

AMREP Corp.
10 Columbus Circle
New York, NY 10019
Phone: 212-541-7300 Fax: —
CEO: Anthony B. Gliedman
CFO: Rudolph J. Skalka
1992 Sales: $73 million Employees: 840
Symbol: AXR Exchange: NYSE
Industry: Building - residential & commercial

Amsco International, Inc.
500 Grant St., Ste. 5000
Pittsburgh, PA 15219
Phone: 412-338-6500 Fax: 412-338-6501
CEO: David A. Nelson
CFO: Steven F. Kreger
1992 Sales: $498 million Employees: 3,188
Symbol: ASZ Exchange: NYSE
Industry: Medical products

Amserv Healthcare, Inc.
1201 Corporate Blvd.
Reno, NV 89502
Phone: 702-348-1000 Fax: —
CEO: Eugene J. Mora
CFO: Andrea Merryman
1992 Sales: $15 million Employees: 78
Symbol: AMSR Exchange: NASDAQ
Industry: Medical services - cardiographic & temporary nursing

AmSouth Bancorporation
1900 5th Ave. North, 14th Fl.
Birmingham, AL 35203
Phone: 205-320-7151 Fax: 205-326-4072
CEO: John W. Woods
CFO: C. Stanley Bailey
1991 Sales: $900 million Employees: 5,222
Symbol: ASO Exchange: NYSE
Industry: Banks - Southeast

indicates company is in *Hoover's Handbook of American Business.*

indicates company is in *Hoover's Handbook of World Business;* sales and employee numbers are for parent company.

Amsted Industries
205 N. Michigan Ave., 44th Fl.
Chicago, IL 60601
Phone: 312-645-1700 Fax: 312-819-8425
CEO: Gordon Lohman
CFO: Gerald K. Walter
1991 Sales: $827 million Employees: 7,900
Ownership: Privately held
Industry: Machinery - railroad & industrial equipment, building products

Amtech Corp.
17304 Preston Rd., Ste. E100
Dallas, TX 75252
Phone: 214-733-6600 Fax: 214-733-6699
CEO: G. Russell Mortenson
CFO: Steve M. York
1991 Sales: $19 million Employees: 193
Symbol: AMTC Exchange: NASDAQ
Industry: Computers - products & software

AmVestors Financial Corp.
415 SW 8th Ave.
Topeka, KS 66603
Phone: 913-232-6945 Fax: 913-232-3534
CEO: Ralph W. Laster, Jr.
CFO: Ralph W. Laster, Jr.
1991 Sales: $173 million Employees: 76
Symbol: AVFC Exchange: NASDAQ
Industry: Insurance - life

Amway Corporation
7575 Fulton St. East
Ada, MI 49355
Phone: 616-676-6000 Fax: 616-676-7102
CEO: Tom Eggleston
CFO: Larry Call
1992 Sales: $3,900 million Employees: 10,000
Ownership: Privately held
Industry: Retail - multi-tier seller of household, personal care, health & fitness products

Amwest Insurance Group, Inc.
6320 Canoga Ave., Ste. 300
Woodland Hills, CA 91367
Phone: 818-704-1111 Fax: 818-592-3660
CEO: Richard H. Savage
CFO: Steven R. Kay
1991 Sales: $56 million Employees: —
Symbol: AMW Exchange: AMEX
Industry: Insurance - property & casualty

Amylin Pharmaceuticals, Inc.
9373 Towne Center Dr.
San Diego, CA 92121
Phone: 619-552-2200 Fax: —
CEO: Howard E. Greene, Jr.
CFO: Marjorie H. Tillman
1991 Sales: $0.2 million Employees: 69
Symbol: AMLN Exchange: NASDAQ
Industry: Drugs

Anacomp, Inc.
11550 N. Meridian St.
Carmel, IN 46032
Phone: 317-844-9666 Fax: 317-848-1360
CEO: Louis P. Ferrero
CFO: Neil M. Bardach
1991 Sales: $635 million Employees: 4,600
Symbol: AAC Exchange: NYSE
Industry: Computers - data center services

Anadarko Petroleum Corp.
16855 Northchase Dr.
Houston, TX 77060
Phone: 713-875-1101 Fax: 713-874-3385
CEO: Robert J. Allison, Jr.
CFO: M. E. Rose
1991 Sales: $337 million Employees: 910
Symbol: APC Exchange: NYSE
Industry: Oil & gas - US exploration & production

Analog Devices, Inc.
One Technology Way
Norwood, MA 02062
Phone: 617-329-4700 Fax: 617-326-8703
CEO: Ray Stata
CFO: Joseph E. McDonough
1991 Sales: $538 million Employees: 5,200
Symbol: ADI Exchange: NYSE
Industry: Electrical components - semiconductors

Analogic Corp.
8 Centennial Dr.
Peabody, MA 01960
Phone: 508-531-0567 Fax: 508-532-6097
CEO: Bernard M. Gordon
CFO: John A. Tarello
1991 Sales: $137 million Employees: 1,290
Symbol: ALOG Exchange: NASDAQ
Industry: Computers - peripheral equipment

Analysis & Technology, Inc.
Technology Park, Route 2
North Stonington, CT 06359
Phone: 203-599-3910 Fax: 209-599-2171
CEO: A. T. Mollegen, Jr.
CFO: David M. Nolf
1992 Sales: $109 million Employees: 1,477
Symbol: AATI Exchange: NASDAQ
Industry: Engineering - R&D services

Analysts International Corp.
7615 Metro Blvd.
Minneapolis, MN 55439
Phone: 612-835-2330 Fax: 612-835-4924
CEO: Frederick W. Lang
CFO: Gerald M. McGrath
1992 Sales: $130 million Employees: 2,070
Symbol: ANLY Exchange: NASDAQ
Industry: Computers - services for credit/collection agencies

Anaren Microwave, Inc.
6635 Kirkville Rd.
East Syracuse, NY 13057
Phone: 315-432-8909 Fax: 315-432-9121
CEO: Hugh A. Hair
CFO: Michael G. Rowe
1992 Sales: $33 million Employees: 291
Symbol: ANEN Exchange: NASDAQ
Industry: Electronics - military

Anchor Bancorp, Inc.
1420 Broadway
Hewlett, NY 11557
Phone: 516-596-3900 Fax: —
CEO: James M. Large, Jr.
CFO: John V. Brull
1991 Sales: $888 million Employees: 1,731
Symbol: ABKR Exchange: NASDAQ
Industry: Financial - savings and loans

Andersen Corp.
100 Fourth Ave. North
Bayport, MN 55003
Phone: 612-439-5150 Fax: 612-430-5107
CEO: Jerold W. Wulf
CFO: L. Kedrowski
1991 Sales: $900 million Employees: 3,700
Ownership: Privately held
Industry: Building products - windows, patio doors

Andersen Group, Inc.
1280 Blue Hills Ave.
Bloomfield, CT 06002
Phone: 203-242-0761 Fax: 203-242-9876
CEO: Francis E. Baker
CFO: Daniel E. Geffken
1992 Sales: $44 million Employees: 362
Symbol: ANDR Exchange: NASDAQ
Industry: Diversified services - video equipment, dental alloys & management consulting

Andersons
1200 Dussel Dr.
Maumee, OH 43537
Phone: 419-893-5050 Fax: 419-891-6655
CEO: Richard P. Anderson
CFO: Tom Companas
1991 Sales: $667 million Employees: 896
Ownership: Privately held
Industry: Food - agribusiness, consumer products

Andover Togs, Inc.
One Penn Plaza, 46th Fl.
New York, NY 10119
Phone: 212-244-0700 Fax: 212-947-4650
CEO: William L. Cohen
CFO: Alan Kanis
1991 Sales: $92 million Employees: 1,525
Symbol: ATOG Exchange: NASDAQ
Industry: Textiles - apparel

Andrea Electronics Corp.
11-40 45th Rd.
Long Island City, NY 11101
Phone: 718-729-8500 Fax: —
CEO: Frank A. D. Andrea, Jr.
CFO: Frank A. D. Andrea, Jr.
1991 Sales: $2.4 million Employees: 80
Symbol: AND Exchange: AMEX
Industry: Telecommunications equipment

Andrew Corp.
10500 W. 153rd St.
Orland Park, IL 60462
Phone: 708-349-3300 Fax: 708-349-5943
CEO: Floyd L. English
CFO: Charles R. Nicholas
1992 Sales: $442 million Employees: 3,040
Symbol: ANDW Exchange: NASDAQ
Industry: Telecommunications equipment

Andros, Inc.
2332 Fourth St.
Berkeley, CA 94710
Phone: 510-849-5700 Fax: 510-849-5849
CEO: George A. Schapiro
CFO: Norman H. Ray
1991 Sales: $22 million Employees: 148
Symbol: ANDY Exchange: NASDAQ
Industry: Electronics - measuring instruments

Anergen, Inc.
301 Penobscot Dr.
Redwood City, CA 94063
Phone: 415-361-8901 Fax: —
CEO: John W. Fara
CFO: John W. Varian
1992 Sales: — Employees: 32
Symbol: ANRG Exchange: NASDAQ
Industry: Biomedical & genetic products

Angeles Corp.
10301 W. Pico Blvd.
Los Angeles, CA 90064
Phone: 310-277-4900 Fax: 310-277-5970
CEO: William H. Elliott
CFO: Robert S. Sedor
1992 Sales: $47 million Employees: 805
Symbol: ANG Exchange: AMEX
Industry: Financial - investment management

Angelica Corp.
10176 Corporate Square Dr., Ste. 100
St. Louis, MO 63132
Phone: 314-854-3800 Fax: 314-854-3890
CEO: Lawrence J. Young
CFO: Theodore M. Armstrong
1991 Sales: $434 million Employees: 9,100
Symbol: AGL Exchange: NYSE
Industry: Linen supply & related - uniforms

indicates company is in *Hoover's Handbook of American Business.*

indicates company is in *Hoover's Handbook of World Business;* sales and employee numbers are for parent company.

Anheuser-Busch Companies, Inc.
One Busch Place
St. Louis, MO 63118
Phone: 314-577-2000 Fax: 314-577-2900
CEO: August A. Busch III
CFO: Jerry E. Ritter
1992 Sales: $11,394 million Employees: 44,836
Symbol: BUD Exchange: NYSE
Industry: Beverages - beer

AnnTaylor Stores Corp.
142 W. 57th St.
New York, NY 10019
Phone: 212-541-3300 Fax: 212-541-3298
CEO: Sally Frame Kasaks
CFO: Bert A. Tieben
1991 Sales: $444 million Employees: —
Symbol: ANN Exchange: NYSE
Industry: Retail - apparel & shoes

Anschutz Corp.
555 17th St., Ste. 2400
Denver, CO 80202
Phone: 303-298-1000 Fax: 303-298-8881
CEO: Philip F. Anschutz
CFO: Douglas Polson
1992 Sales: $2,900 million Employees: 21,500
Ownership: Privately held
Industry: Diversified operations - oil, railroads, real estate, mining

Anthem Electronics, Inc.
1160 Ridder Park Dr.
San Jose, CA 95131
Phone: 408-453-1200 Fax: 408-441-4504
CEO: Robert S. Throop
CFO: Wayne B. Snyder
1991 Sales: $420 million Employees: 604
Symbol: ATM Exchange: NYSE
Industry: Electronics - parts distribution

Anthony Industries, Inc.
4900 S. Eastern Ave.
Los Angeles, CA 90040
Phone: 213-724-2800 Fax: —
CEO: Bernard I. Forester
CFO: John J. Rangel
1991 Sales: $370 million Employees: 3,300
Symbol: ANT Exchange: NYSE
Industry: Skis, fishing tackle & pool equipment

AOI Coal Co.
300 W. Texas St., Ste. 500
Midland, TX 79701
Phone: 915-684-3773 Fax: —
CEO: James R. Sartori
CFO: Eric Urbanowicz
1991 Sales: $50 million Employees: 307
Symbol: AOI Exchange: AMEX
Industry: Coal

Aon Corp.
123 N. Wacker Dr.
Chicago, IL 60606
Phone: 312-701-3000 Fax: 312-701-3100
CEO: Patrick G. Ryan
CFO: Harvey N. Medvin
1992 Sales: $3,337 million Employees: —
Symbol: AOC Exchange: NYSE
Industry: Insurance - accident & health

Apache Corp.
1700 Lincoln St., Ste. 1900
Denver, CO 80203
Phone: 303-837-5000 Fax: 303-837-5688
CEO: Raymond Plank
CFO: Wayne W. Murdy
1991 Sales: $342 million Employees: 875
Symbol: APA Exchange: NYSE
Industry: Oil & gas - US exploration & production

Apertus Technologies, Inc.
7275 Flying Cloud Dr.
Eden Prairie, MN 55344
Phone: 612-828-0300 Fax: 612-828-0723
CEO: Robert D. Gordon
CFO: Charles F. Karpinske
1992 Sales: $23 million Employees: 189
Symbol: APTS Exchange: NASDAQ
Industry: Computers - peripheral equipment

Apogee Enterprises, Inc.
7900 Xerxes Ave. South, Ste. 1944
Minneapolis, MN 55431
Phone: 612-835-1874 Fax: 612-835-3196
CEO: Donald W. Goldfus
CFO: William G. Gardner
1992 Sales: $596 million Employees: 5,136
Symbol: APOG Exchange: NASDAQ
Industry: Glass products - windows

Apogee Research Inc.
4350 E. West Hwy. Ste. 600
Bethesda, MD 20814
Phone: 301-652-8444 Fax: 301-654-9355
CEO: Richard Mudge
CFO: Kenneth Rubin
1991 Sales: $3.1 million Employees: 35
Ownership: Privately held
Industry: Business services - financial & economic consulting services

Apple Computer, Inc.
20525 Mariani Ave.
Cupertino, CA 95014
Phone: 408-996-1010 Fax: 408-996-0275
CEO: John Sculley
CFO: Joseph A. Graziano
1992 Sales: $7,224 million Employees: 14,432
Symbol: AAPL Exchange: NASDAQ
Industry: Computers - mini & micro

Apple South, Inc.
Hancock at Washington
Madison, GA 30650
Phone: 706-342-4552 Fax: 706-342-4057
CEO: Tom E. DuPree, Jr.
CFO: Erich J. Booth
1991 Sales: $68 million Employees: 3,287
Symbol: APSO Exchange: NASDAQ
Industry: Retail - food & restaurants

Applebee's International, Inc.
2300 Main St., Ste. 900
Kansas City, MO 64108
Phone: 816-421-2501 Fax: —
CEO: Abe J. Gustin, Jr.
CFO: Timothy M. O'Halloran
1991 Sales: $45 million Employees: 1,714
Symbol: APPB Exchange: NASDAQ
Industry: Retail - food & restaurants

AppleTree Markets Inc.
4301 Windfern Lane
Houston, TX 77041
Phone: 713-460-5000 Fax: 713-460-8262
CEO: Fred R. Lummis
CFO: R. T. Kubicek
1991 Sales: $850 million Employees: 2,569
Ownership: Privately held
Industry: Retail - supermarkets

Applied Bioscience International Inc.
Mettlers Rd.
East Millstone, NJ 08876
Phone: 908-873-2550 Fax: 908-873-3992
CEO: Kenneth H. Harper
CFO: John H. Timoney
1991 Sales: $153 million Employees: 1,500
Symbol: APBI Exchange: NASDAQ
Industry: Medical services

Applied Biosystems, Inc.
850 Lincoln Centre Dr.
Foster City, CA 94404
Phone: 415-570-6667 Fax: 415-572-2743
CEO: Andre F. Marion
CFO: G. Bradley Cole
1992 Sales: $183 million Employees: 1,259
Symbol: ABIO Exchange: NASDAQ
Industry: Biomedical & genetic products

Applied Computer Technology
2573 Midpoint Dr.
Ft. Collins, CO 80525
Phone: 303-490-1849 Fax: 303-490-1439
CEO: Bud Prentice
CFO: Cindy Koehler
1991 Sales: $5.4 million Employees: 25
Ownership: Privately held
Industry: Computers - retail computer products & services

Applied Extrusion Technologies, Inc.
Middletown Industrial Park Dr.
Middletown, DE 19709
Phone: 302-378-8888 Fax: —
CEO: Amin J. Khoury
CFO: Bruce A. Edge
1991 Sales: $31 million Employees: 232
Symbol: AETC Exchange: NASDAQ
Industry: Rubber & plastic products

Applied Immune Sciences, Inc.
200 Constitution Dr.
Menlo Park, CA 94025
Phone: 415-326-7302 Fax: 415-326-0923
CEO: Thomas B. Okarma
CFO: Craig J. Huffaker
1991 Sales: $0.6 million Employees: 88
Symbol: AISX Exchange: NASDAQ
Industry: Medical products

Applied Magnetics Corp.
75 Robin Hill Rd.
Goleta, CA 93117
Phone: 805-683-5353 Fax: 805-967-8227
CEO: William R. Anderson
CFO: Michael S. Noling
1991 Sales: $456 million Employees: 10,013
Symbol: APM Exchange: NYSE
Industry: Computers - peripheral equipment

Applied Materials, Inc.
3050 Bowers Ave.
Santa Clara, CA 95054
Phone: 408-727-5555 Fax: 408-748-9943
CEO: James C. Morgan
CFO: Gerald F. Taylor
1992 Sales: $751 million Employees: 3,909
Symbol: AMAT Exchange: NASDAQ
Industry: Electrical components - semiconductors

Applied Power Inc.
13000 W. Silver Spring Dr.
Butler, WI 53007
Phone: 414-781-6600 Fax: 414-781-1049
CEO: Richard G. Sim
CFO: Robert T. Foote, Jr.
1991 Sales: $434 million Employees: 3,220
Symbol: APW Exchange: NYSE
Industry: Machine tools & related products

Applied Utility Systems
1140 E. Chestnut Ave.
Santa Ana, CA 92701
Phone: 714-953-9922 Fax: 714-953-0931
CEO: Yolanda Mansour
CFO: Yolanda Mansour
1991 Sales: $6.8 million Employees: 27
Ownership: Privately held
Industry: Business services - engineering consulting

Aquarion Co.
835 Main St.
Bridgeport, CT 06601
Phone: 203-367-6621 Fax: —
CEO: Jack E. McGregor
CFO: William F. Emswiler
1991 Sales: $100 million Employees: 725
Symbol: WTR Exchange: NYSE
Industry: Utility - water supply

ARA Group, Inc., The
1101 Market St.
Philadelphia, PA 19107
Phone: 215-238-3000 Fax: 215-238-3333
CEO: Joseph Neubauer
CFO: James E. Ksansnak
1992 Sales: $4,900 million Employees: 124,000
Ownership: Privately held
Industry: Diversified operations - food services, uniform rentals, child care services & magazine distribution

Arabian Shield Development Co.
10830 N. Central Expressway
Dallas, TX 75231
Phone: 214-692-7872 Fax: —
CEO: John A. Crichton
CFO: Drew Wilson
1991 Sales: $19 million Employees: 75
Symbol: ARSD Exchange: NASDAQ
Industry: Oil & gas - international specialty

Arbor Drugs, Inc.
3331 W. Big Beaver Rd.
Troy, MI 48084
Phone: 313-643-9420 Fax: 313-637-1636
CEO: Eugene Applebaum
CFO: Gilbert C. Gerhard
1991 Sales: $406 million Employees: 3,900
Symbol: ARBR Exchange: NASDAQ
Industry: Retail - drug stores

Arbor Systems
1545 Capital Dr., Ste. 108
Carrollton, TX 75006
Phone: 214-245-3434 Fax: 214-245-7463
CEO: John Watters
CFO: John Watters
1991 Sales: $2.6 million Employees: 16
Ownership: Privately held
Industry: Computers - peripheral equipment

Arcadian Corp.
6750 Poplar Ave., Ste. 600
Memphis, TN 38138
Phone: 901-758-5200 Fax: 901-758-5206
CEO: J. D. Campbell
CFO: R. A. Ewert
1992 Sales: $650 million Employees: 1,064
Ownership: Privately held
Industry: Fertilizers & chemicals - agricultural & industrial

Arcadian Partners, L.P.
6750 Poplar Ave., Ste. 600
Memphis, TN 38138
Phone: 901-758-5200 Fax: 901-758-5206
CEO: R. James Comeaux
CFO: Richard A. Ewert
1991 Sales: $571 million Employees: —
Symbol: UAN Exchange: NYSE
Industry: Chemicals - specialty

Arcata Corp.
601 California St., Ste. 1800
San Francisco, CA 94108
Phone: 415-781-4200 Fax: 415-989-2413
CEO: Edward L. Scarff
CFO: C. G. Mumford
1991 Sales: $560 million Employees: 6,800
Ownership: Privately held
Industry: Printing - books & magazines

Arch Communications Group, Inc.
110 Turnpike Rd., Ste. 210
Westborough, MA 01581
Phone: 508-898-0962 Fax: —
CEO: C. Edward Baker, Jr.
CFO: William A. Wilson
1991 Sales: $30 million Employees: 338
Symbol: APGR Exchange: NASDAQ
Industry: Telecommunications services

Arch Petroleum, Inc.
777 Taylor St., Ste. II-A
Ft. Worth, TX 76102
Phone: 817-332-9209 Fax: —
CEO: L. V. Kalas
CFO: F. R. Cantu
1991 Sales: $6.8 million Employees: 28
Symbol: ARCH Exchange: NASDAQ
Industry: Oil & gas - US exploration & production

Archer-Daniels-Midland Co.
4666 Faries Pkwy.
Decatur, IL 62525
Phone: 217-424-5200 Fax: 217-424-5839
CEO: Dwayne O. Andreas
CFO: Douglas J. Schmalz
1992 Sales: $9,232 million Employees: 13,524
Symbol: ADM Exchange: NYSE
Industry: Food - flour & grain

Archive Corp.
1650 Sunflower Ave.
Costa Mesa, CA 92626
Phone: 714-641-0279 Fax: 714-641-2582
CEO: D. Howard Lewis
CFO: B. J. Rone
1991 Sales: $346 million Employees: 2,489
Symbol: ACHV Exchange: NASDAQ
Industry: Computers - tape drives

ARCO Chemical Co.
3801 W. Chester Pike
Newtown Square, PA 19073
Phone: 215-359-2000 Fax: 215-359-2722
CEO: Alan R. Hirsig
CFO: Marvin O. Schlanger
1992 Sales: $3,098 million Employees: 4,220
Symbol: RCM Exchange: NYSE
Industry: Chemicals - specialty

Arctco, Inc.
600 S. Brooks Ave.
Thief River Falls, MN 56701
Phone: 218-681-8558 Fax: 218-681-3162
CEO: Christopher Twomey
CFO: Timothy C. Delmore
1992 Sales: $148 million Employees: 850
Symbol: ACAT Exchange: NASDAQ
Industry: Snowmobiles & accessories

Arden Group, Inc.
2020 S. Central Ave.
Compton, CA 90220
Phone: 310-638-2842 Fax: 310-631-0950
CEO: Bernard Briskin
CFO: Ernest T. Klinger
1991 Sales: $316 million Employees: 2,350
Symbol: ARDNA Exchange: NASDAQ
Industry: Telecommunications equipment

Argonaut Group, Inc.
1800 Avenue of the Stars
Los Angeles, CA 90067
Phone: 310-553-0561 Fax: 310-553-4868
CEO: Charles E. Rinsch
CFO: James B. Halliday
1991 Sales: $517 million Employees: —
Symbol: AGII Exchange: NASDAQ
Industry: Insurance - property & casualty

Argus Pharmaceuticals, Inc.
3400 Research Forest Dr.
The Woodlands, TX 77838
Phone: 713-367-1666 Fax: —
CEO: David M. Leech
CFO: David M. Leech
1992 Sales: — Employees: 15
Symbol: ARGS Exchange: NASDAQ
Industry: Drugs

ARI Network Services, Inc.
330 E. Kilbourn Ave.
Milwaukee, WI 53202
Phone: 414-278-7676 Fax: —
CEO: Edward D. Markham
CFO: Michael R. Pelton
1991 Sales: $3 million Employees: 121
Symbol: ARIS Exchange: NASDAQ
Industry: Computers - electronic data interchange services

Aritech Corp.
25 Newbury St.
Framingham, MA 01701
Phone: 508-620-0800 Fax: 508-879-7595
CEO: James A. Synk
CFO: Michael J. O'Donnell
1991 Sales: $84 million Employees: 421
Symbol: ARIT Exchange: NASDAQ
Industry: Protection - safety equipment & services

ARIX Corp.
871 Fox Lane
San Jose, CA 95131
Phone: 408-432-1200 Fax: 408-432-0263
CEO: Eugene Manno
CFO: Carter C. McCorkle
1991 Sales: $24 million Employees: 145
Symbol: ARIX Exchange: NASDAQ
Industry: Computers - mini & micro

Arizona Instrument Corp.
1100 E. University Dr.
Tempe, AZ 85281
Phone: 602-731-3400 Fax: 602-731-3434
CEO: John P. Hudnall
CFO: John P. Hudnall
1991 Sales: $8.5 million Employees: 71
Symbol: AZIC Exchange: NASDAQ
Industry: Instruments - control

Ark Restaurants Corp.
158 W. 29th St.
New York, NY 10001
Phone: 212-760-0520 Fax: 212-629-4318
CEO: Michael Weinstein
CFO: Robert Towers
1991 Sales: $42 million Employees: 1,632
Symbol: RK Exchange: AMEX
Industry: Retail - food & restaurants

Arkansas Best Corp.
1000 S. 21st St.
Ft. Smith, AR 72901
Phone: 501-785-6000 Fax: 501-785-6009
CEO: Robert A. Young III
CFO: Donald L. Neal
1992 Sales: $960 million Employees: 11,000
Symbol: ABFS Exchange: NASDAQ
Industry: Transportation - truck

Arkla, Inc.
PO Box 21734
Shreveport, LA 71151
Phone: 318-429-2700 Fax: 318-429-3896
CEO: Thomas F. McLarty III
CFO: William H. Kelly
1991 Sales: $2,779 million Employees: 9,100
Symbol: ALG Exchange: NYSE
Industry: Utility - gas distribution

indicates company is in *Hoover's Handbook of American Business.*

indicates company is in *Hoover's Handbook of World Business;* sales and employee numbers are for parent company.

ARM Financial Corp.
4600 Campus Dr., Ste. 201
Newport Beach, CA 92660
Phone: 714-474-3000 Fax: 714-474-2200
CEO: M. L. Goldberg
CFO: M. L. Goldberg
1991 Sales: $2.7 million Employees: 173
Symbol: RXM Exchange: AMEX
Industry: Diversified operations - medical services & real estate

Armatron International, Inc.
2 Main St.
Melrose, MA 02176
Phone: 617-321-2300 Fax: 617-321-2309
CEO: Charles J. Housman
CFO: Charles J. Housman
1991 Sales: $24 million Employees: 195
Symbol: ART Exchange: AMEX
Industry: Diversified operations - garden equipment & car radios

Armco Inc.
300 Interpace Pkwy.
Parsippany, NJ 07054
Phone: 201-316-5200 Fax: 201-316-5203
CEO: Robert L. Purdum
CFO: Wallace B. Askins
1992 Sales: $2,074 million Employees: 9,200
Symbol: AS Exchange: NYSE
Industry: Steel - production

Armor All Products Corp.
6 Liberty Dr.
Aliso Viejo, CA 92656
Phone: 714-362-0600 Fax: —
CEO: Kenneth M. Evans
CFO: Mervyn J. McCulloch
1992 Sales: $146 million Employees: 112
Symbol: ARMR Exchange: NASDAQ
Industry: Soap & cleaning preparations

Armstrong Pharmaceuticals, Inc.
71 Elm St.
New Canaan, CT 06840
Phone: 203-966-4170 Fax: 203-966-4763
CEO: Herman R. Shepherd
CFO: Augustine Lawlor
1991 Sales: $14 million Employees: 140
Symbol: ATPH Exchange: NASDAQ
Industry: Drugs

Armstrong World Industries, Inc.
313 W. Liberty St.
Lancaster, PA 17604
Phone: 717-397-0611 Fax: 717-396-2126
CEO: William W. Adams
CFO: William J. Wimer
1992 Sales: $2,550 million Employees: 24,066
Symbol: ACK Exchange: NYSE
Industry: Building products

Arnold Industries Inc.
625 S. Fifth Ave.
Lebanon, PA 17042
Phone: 717-274-2521 Fax: 717-274-5593
CEO: Edward H. Arnold
CFO: Ronald E. Walborn
1991 Sales: $165 million Employees: 1,800
Symbol: AIND Exchange: NASDAQ
Industry: Transportation - truck

Arrhythmia Research Technology, Inc.
5910 Courtyard Dr., Ste. 300
Austin, TX 78731
Phone: 512-343-6912 Fax: 512-343-7312
CEO: David A. Jenkins
CFO: Wayne Schroeder
1991 Sales: $5.8 million Employees: 18
Symbol: HRT Exchange: AMEX
Industry: Medical products

Arrow Automotive Industries, Inc.
3 Speen St.
Framingham, MA 01701
Phone: 508-872-3711 Fax: Call co. operator
CEO: Harry A. Holzwasser
CFO: James F. Fagan
1992 Sales: $95 million Employees: 1,563
Symbol: AI Exchange: AMEX
Industry: Automotive & trucking - replacement parts

Arrow Electronics, Inc.
25 Hub Dr.
Melville, NY 11747
Phone: 516-391-1300 Fax: 516-391-1644
CEO: Stephen P. Kaufman
CFO: Robert E. Klatell
1992 Sales: $1,622 million Employees: 4,200
Symbol: ARW Exchange: NYSE
Industry: Electronics - parts distribution

Arrow International, Inc.
3000 Bernville Rd.
Reading, PA 19612
Phone: 215-378-0131 Fax: 215-378-0131
CEO: Marlin Miller, Jr.
CFO: John H. Broadbent, Jr.
1991 Sales: $111 million Employees: —
Symbol: ARRO Exchange: NASDAQ
Industry: Medical products

Art's-Way Manufacturing Co., Inc.
Hwy. 9 West
Armstrong, IA 50514
Phone: 712-864-3131 Fax: 712-864-3154
CEO: Ronald W. Hottes
CFO: William T. Green
1992 Sales: $19 million Employees: 241
Symbol: ARTW Exchange: NASDAQ
Industry: Machinery - farm

Artel Communications Corp.
22 Kane Industrial Dr.
Hudson, MA 01749
Phone: 508-562-2100 Fax: 508-562-6942
CEO: Robert L. Bowman
CFO: Gerald M. Schimmoeller
1991 Sales: $4.9 million Employees: 59
Symbol: AXXX Exchange: NASDAQ
Industry: Telecommunications equipment

Arthur Andersen & Co., SC
59 W. Washington St.
Chicago, IL 60602
Phone: 312-580-0069 Fax: 312-507-6748
CEO: Lawrence A. Weinbach
CFO: John D. Lewis
1992 Sales: $5,570 million Employees: 62,000
Ownership: Privately held
Industry: Business services - accounting & technical consulting

Arthur J. Gallagher & Co.
Two Pierce Place
Itasca, IL 60143
Phone: 708-773-3800 Fax: 708-285-4000
CEO: Robert E. Gallagher
CFO: Michael J. Cloherty
1991 Sales: $232 million Employees: 2,341
Symbol: AJG Exchange: NYSE
Industry: Insurance - brokerage

Artisoft, Inc.
691 E. River Rd.
Tucson, AZ 85704
Phone: 602-293-4000 Fax: 602-293-8056
CEO: C. John Schoof II
CFO: William D. Baker
1992 Sales: $73 million Employees: 499
Symbol: ASFT Exchange: NASDAQ
Industry: Computers - local area network software

Artistic Greetings, Inc.
409 William St.
Elmira, NY 14901
Phone: 607-733-5541 Fax: 607-733-4157
CEO: Stuart Komer
CFO: Stuart Komer
1991 Sales: $63 million Employees: 630
Symbol: ARTG Exchange: NASDAQ
Industry: Retail - mail order & direct; stationery & gift items

Artistic Impressions Inc.
240 Cortland Ave.
Lombard, IL 60148
Phone: 708-916-0050 Fax: 708-916-1478
CEO: Bart Breighner
CFO: Julie Lamoureaux
1992 Sales: $10.5 million Employees: 67
Ownership: Privately held
Industry: Retail - paintings & lithography through home parties

Artra Group Inc.
500 Central Ave.
Northfield, IL 60093
Phone: 708-441-6650 Fax: —
CEO: John J. Harvey
CFO: James D. Doering
1991 Sales: $231 million Employees: 3,100
Symbol: ATA Exchange: NYSE
Industry: Diversified operations - costume jewelry & packaging products

Arvin Industries, Inc.
One Noblitt Plaza
Columbus, IN 47202
Phone: 812-379-3000 Fax: 812-379-3688
CEO: James K. Baker
CFO: Richard A. Smith
1992 Sales: $1,890 million Employees: 16,152
Symbol: ARV Exchange: NYSE
Industry: Automotive & trucking - original equipment

ARX, Inc.
35 S. Service Rd.
Plainview, NY 11803
Phone: 516-694-6700 Fax: 516-694-6771
CEO: Harvey R. Blau
CFO: Michael Gorin
1992 Sales: $63 million Employees: 660
Symbol: ARX Exchange: NYSE
Industry: Machinery - general industrial

ASARCO Inc.
180 Maiden Lane
New York, NY 10038
Phone: 212-510-2000 Fax: 212-510-2271
CEO: Richard de J. Osborne
CFO: Francis R. McAllister
1992 Sales: $1,909 million Employees: 9,055
Symbol: AR Exchange: NYSE
Industry: Metals - nonferrous

Asea Brown Boveri Inc.
900 Long Ridge Rd.
Stamford, CT 06904
Phone: 203-328-2380 Fax: 203-328-2383
CEO: Gerhard Schulmeyer
CFO: —
1991 Sales: $28,883 million Employees: 214,399
Parent: ABB Asea Brown Boveri Ltd.
Industry: Diversified operations - control systems, electrical engineering & construction

Ashland Coal, Inc.
2205 Fifth Street Rd.
Huntington, WV 25771
Phone: 304-526-3333 Fax: 304-526-3539
CEO: William C. Payne
CFO: Marc R. Solochek
1992 Sales: $580 million Employees: 1,090
Symbol: ACI Exchange: NYSE
Industry: Coal

 indicates company is in *Hoover's Handbook of American Business.*

indicates company is in *Hoover's Handbook of World Business;* sales and employee numbers are for parent company.

Ashland Oil, Inc.
1000 Ashland Dr.
Russell, KY 41169
Phone: 606-329-3333 Fax: 606-329-5274
CEO: John R. Hall
CFO: J. Marvin Quin II
1992 Sales: $9,640 million Employees: 32,900
Symbol: ASH Exchange: NYSE
Industry: Oil refining & marketing

Asia Source, Inc.
46820 Fremont Blvd.
Fremont, CA 94538
Phone: 510-226-8000 Fax: 510-226-8858
CEO: Marcel Liang
CFO: Marcel Liang
1991 Sales: $67 million Employees: 50
Ownership: Privately held
Industry: Computers - wholesale parts & services

ASK Computer Systems, Inc.
2440 W. El Camino Real
Mountain View, CA 94039
Phone: 415-969-4442 Fax: 415-962-1974
CEO: Eric D. Carlson
CFO: Leslie E. Wright
1992 Sales: $432 million Employees: 2,270
Symbol: ASKI Exchange: NASDAQ
Industry: Computers - software

Asosa Personnel
1016 E. Broadway Blvd.
Tucson, AZ 85719
Phone: 602-792-0622 Fax: 602-792-0655
CEO: Paul Payne
CFO: Margie Chicoine
1991 Sales: $4.1 million Employees: 22
Ownership: Privately held
Industry: Business services - temporary employment & personnel recruiting

Aspect Telecommunications Corp.
1730 Fox Dr.
San Jose, CA 95131
Phone: 408-441-2200 Fax: 408-441-2260
CEO: James R. Carreker
CFO: Jan A. Praisner
1991 Sales: $44 million Employees: 325
Symbol: ASPT Exchange: NASDAQ
Industry: Telecommunications equipment

Aspen Bancshares, Inc.
534 E. Hyman Ave.
Aspen, CO 81612
Phone: 303-925-6700 Fax: —
CEO: Morton A. Heller
CFO: Morton A. Heller
1991 Sales: $9 million Employees: 37
Symbol: ASBK Exchange: NASDAQ
Industry: Banks - West

Aspen Imaging International, Inc.
555 Aspen Ridge Dr.
Lafayette, CO 80026
Phone: 303-666-5750 Fax: 303-665-2972
CEO: Peter C. Williams
CFO: Florine N. Nath
1991 Sales: $18 million Employees: 280
Symbol: ARIB Exchange: NASDAQ
Industry: Computers - ink cartridges & ribbons for printers

Asplundh Tree Expert Co.
708 Blair Mill Rd.
Willow Grove, PA 19090
Phone: 215-784-4200 Fax: 215-784-4493
CEO: Christopher B. Asplundh
CFO: Joseph P. Dwyer
1992 Sales: $625 million Employees: 13,500
Ownership: Privately held
Industry: Business services - tree trimming

Assix International, Inc.
505 E. Jackson St., Ste. 220
Tampa, FL 33602
Phone: 813-224-0228 Fax: 813-227-9056
CEO: R. Park Newton III
CFO: Douglas S. Gardner
1991 Sales: $8.3 million Employees: 73
Symbol: ASIXE Exchange: NASDAQ
Industry: Auto parts - retail & wholesale

Associated Banc-Corp
112 N. Adams St.
Green Bay, WI 54301
Phone: 414-433-3166 Fax: —
CEO: Harry B. Conlon
CFO: Joseph B. Selner
1991 Sales: $195 million Employees: 1,091
Symbol: ASBC Exchange: NASDAQ
Industry: Banks - Midwest

Associated Communications Corp.
200 Gateway Towers
Pittsburgh, PA 15222
Phone: 412-281-1907 Fax: 412-281-1914
CEO: Jack N. Berkman
CFO: Myles P. Berkman
1991 Sales: $46 million Employees: 89
Symbol: ACCMA Exchange: NASDAQ
Industry: Telecommunications services

Associated Family Photographers, Inc.
2929 S. 48th St. #4
Tempe, AZ 85282
Phone: 602-496-5100 Fax: 602-431-1332
CEO: James Kraxner
CFO: Norm Rosenstein
1992 Sales: $33 million Employees: 1,500
Ownership: Privately held
Industry: Retail - family portrait photography

Associated Metals & Minerals Corp.
Three N. Corporate Park Dr.
White Plains, NY 10604
Phone: 914-251-5400 Fax: 914-251-1073
CEO: Colin H. Benjamin
CFO: Neil Goldberg
1991 Sales: $600 million Employees: 200
Ownership: Privately held
Industry: Steel - production

Associated Milk Producers, Inc.
6609 Blanco Rd.
San Antonio, TX 78279
Phone: 512-340-9100 Fax: 512-340-9158
CEO: Irvin J. Elkin
CFO: William Lenschow
1991 Sales: $2,768 million Employees: 4,319
Ownership: Privately held
Industry: Food - dairy products

Associated Natural Gas Corp.
370 17th St.
Denver, CO 80202
Phone: 303-595-3331 Fax: 303-595-0480
CEO: Cortlandt S. Dietler
CFO: Harold R. Logan, Jr.
1992 Sales: $1,060 million Employees: 506
Symbol: NGA Exchange: NYSE
Industry: Oil & gas - production & pipeline

AST Research, Inc.
16215 Alton Pkwy.
Irvine, CA 92713
Phone: 714-727-4141 Fax: 714-727-8584
CEO: Safi U. Qureshey
CFO: Bruce C. Edwards
1992 Sales: $1,141 million Employees: 3,560
Symbol: ASTA Exchange: NASDAQ
Industry: Computers - mini & micro

Astec Industries, Inc.
4101 Jerome Ave.
Chattanooga, TN 37407
Phone: 615-867-4210 Fax: 615-867-4127
CEO: J. Don Brock
CFO: Albert E. Guth
1991 Sales: $134 million Employees: 988
Symbol: ASTE Exchange: NASDAQ
Industry: Machinery - material handling

Astro-Med, Inc.
600 E. Greenwich Ave.
West Warwick, RI 02893
Phone: 401-828-4000 Fax: 401-822-2430
CEO: Albert W. Ondis
CFO: Eugene S. Libby
1991 Sales: $30 million Employees: 240
Symbol: ALOT Exchange: NASDAQ
Industry: Computers - high-speed printer peripherals

Astronics Corp.
80 S. Davis St.
Orchard Park, NY 14127
Phone: 716-662-6640 Fax: 716-662-2844
CEO: Kevin T. Keane
CFO: John M. Yessa
1991 Sales: $26 million Employees: 384
Symbol: ATRO Exchange: NASDAQ
Industry: Diversified operations - packaging & paper products, keyboard entry

Astrosystems, Inc.
6 Nevada Dr.
New Hyde Park, NY 11042
Phone: 516-328-1600 Fax: 516-328-1658
CEO: Seymour Barth
CFO: Gilbert H. Steinberg
1992 Sales: $18 million Employees: 181
Symbol: ASTR Exchange: NASDAQ
Industry: Instruments - control

Astrotech International Corp.
Two Chatham Center, Ste. 240
Pittsburgh, PA 15219
Phone: 412-391-1896 Fax: 412-391-3347
CEO: S. Kent Rockwell
CFO: S. Kent Rockwell
1991 Sales: $42 million Employees: 411
Symbol: AIX Exchange: AMEX
Industry: Oil & gas - field services

Atalanta/Sosnoff Capital Corp.
101 Park Ave.
New York, NY 10178
Phone: 212-867-5000 Fax: 212-922-1820
CEO: Martin T. Sosnoff
CFO: Anthony G. Miller
1991 Sales: $17 million Employees: 37
Symbol: ATL Exchange: NYSE
Industry: Financial - investment management

Atari Corp.
1196 Borregas Ave.
Sunnyvale, CA 94089
Phone: 408-745-2000 Fax: 408-745-8800
CEO: Sam Tramiel
CFO: Gregory A. Pratt
1991 Sales: $258 million Employees: 507
Symbol: ATC Exchange: AMEX
Industry: Computers - mini & micro

Atek Metals Center, Inc.
10052 Commerce Park Dr.
Cincinnati, OH 45246
Phone: 513-874-3490 Fax: 513-874-6182
CEO: Barry F. Bucher
CFO: Thomas J. Dagenback
1991 Sales: $53 million Employees: 201
Symbol: ATKM Exchange: NASDAQ
Industry: Metals - nonferrous

indicates company is in *Hoover's Handbook of American Business.*
indicates company is in *Hoover's Handbook of World Business;* sales and employee numbers are for parent company.

Athena Neurosciences, Inc.
800F Gateway Blvd.
South San Francisco, CA 94080
Phone: 415-877-0900 Fax: —
CEO: John Groom
CFO: Matthew A. Megaro
1991 Sales: $4.8 million Employees: 80
Symbol: ATHN Exchange: NASDAQ
Industry: Drugs

Athey Products Corp.
Rt. 1-A South
Wake Forest, NC 27602
Phone: 919-556-5171 Fax: 919-556-7950
CEO: James D. Cloonan
CFO: Archie Spencer
1991 Sales: $23 million Employees: 283
Symbol: ATPC Exchange: NASDAQ
Industry: Machinery - general industrial

Athletic Fitters
10125 Crosstown Cir. #310
Eden Prairie, MN 55344
Phone: 612-942-6332 Fax: 612-942-1995
CEO: Paul Taunton
CFO: Paul Taunton
1991 Sales: $8.1 million Employees: 41
Ownership: Privately held
Industry: Shoes & related apparel - athletic

Athlone Industries, Inc.
200 Webro Rd.
Parsippany, NJ 07054
Phone: 201-887-9100 Fax: 201-887-3396
CEO: Harold J. Miller
CFO: Gary M. Cademartori
1991 Sales: $209 million Employees: 1,100
Symbol: ATH Exchange: NYSE
Industry: Steel - specialty alloys

Atkinson-Baker & Associates
1612 W. Olive Ave., 2nd Fl.
Burbank, CA 91506
Phone: 818-566-8840 Fax: 818-566-4462
CEO: Alan Atkinson-Baker
CFO: Alan Atkinson-Baker
1991 Sales: $5 million Employees: 40
Ownership: Privately held
Industry: Business services - court reporting

Atlanta Gas Light Co.
235 Peachtree St. NE
Atlanta, GA 30302
Phone: 404-584-4000 Fax: 404-584-3709
CEO: David R. Jones
CFO: B. Lloyd Fackler
1992 Sales: $1,029 million Employees: 3,820
Symbol: ATG Exchange: NYSE
Industry: Utility - gas distribution

Atlantic American Corp.
4370 Peachtree Rd. NE
Atlanta, GA 30319
Phone: 404-266-5500 Fax: —
CEO: J. Mack Robinson
CFO: John W. Hancock
1991 Sales: $92 million Employees: 675
Symbol: AAME Exchange: NASDAQ
Industry: Insurance - accident & health

Atlantic Coast Textiles
3132 Oakcliff Industrial St.
Atlanta, GA 30340
Phone: 404-458-0772 Fax: 404-451-4905
CEO: Warren Bearden
CFO: Warren Bearden
1991 Sales: $3.3 million Employees: 8
Ownership: Privately held
Industry: Textiles - wholesale mill products

Atlantic Energy, Inc.
1199 Black Horse Pike
Pleasantville, NJ 08232
Phone: 609-645-4500 Fax: —
CEO: Jerrold L. Jacobs
CFO: Joseph G. Salomone
1991 Sales: $778 million Employees: 2,053
Symbol: ATE Exchange: NYSE
Industry: Utility - electric power

Atlantic Gulf Communities Corp.
2601 S. Bayshore Dr.
Miami, FL 33133
Phone: 305-859-4000 Fax: 305-859-4360
CEO: J. Larry Rutherford
CFO: Charles M. Andolsek
1992 Sales: — Employees: —
Symbol: AGLF Exchange: NASDAQ
Industry: Real estate development

Atlantic Network Systems, Inc.
975 Walnut St. #104
Cary, NC 27511
Phone: 919-469-8155 Fax: 919-469-5085
CEO: Doug Roberson
CFO: Doug Roberson
1992 Sales: $6.5 million Employees: 16
Ownership: Privately held
Industry: Telecommunications equipment - data & voice communications

Atlantic Richfield Co.
515 S. Flower St.
Los Angeles, CA 90071
Phone: 213-486-3511 Fax: 213-486-2063
CEO: Lodwrick M. Cook
CFO: James S. Morrison
1992 Sales: $18,668 million Employees: 27,700
Symbol: ARC Exchange: NYSE
Industry: Oil & gas - US integrated

Atlantic Southeast Airlines, Inc.
100 Hartsfield Center Pkwy., Ste. 800
Atlanta, GA 30354
Phone: 404-766-1400 Fax: 404-209-0162
CEO: George F. Pickett, Jr.
CFO: Ronald V. Sapp
1991 Sales: $222 million Employees: 1,692
Symbol: ASAI Exchange: NASDAQ
Industry: Transportation - airline

Atlantis Group, Inc.
2665 S. Bayshore Dr., 8th Fl.
Miami, FL 33133
Phone: 305-858-2200 Fax: 305-285-0102
CEO: Earl W. Powell
CFO: Craig A. Brumfield
1991 Sales: $169 million Employees: 897
Symbol: AGH Exchange: AMEX
Industry: Plastic & seating products

Atlas Corp.
370 Seventeenth St., Ste. 3150
Denver, CO 80202
Phone: 303-825-1200 Fax: 303-892-8808
CEO: Richard R. Weaver
CFO: Robert A. Sherman
1991 Sales: $31 million Employees: 245
Symbol: AZ Exchange: NYSE
Industry: Gold mining & processing

Atmel Corp.
2125 O'Nel Dr.
San Jose, CA 95131
Phone: 408-441-0311 Fax: 408-436-4200
CEO: George Perlegos
CFO: Raymond K. Ostby
1991 Sales: $120 million Employees: 872
Symbol: ATML Exchange: NASDAQ
Industry: Electrical components - semiconductors

Atmos Energy Corp.
5430 LBJ Fwy., 3 Lincoln Ctr., Ste. 1800
Dallas, TX 75240
Phone: 214-934-9227 Fax: 214-991-5235
CEO: Charles K. Vaughan
CFO: James F. Purser
1991 Sales: $336 million Employees: 1,407
Symbol: ATO Exchange: NYSE
Industry: Utility - gas distribution

Atrix Laboratories, Inc.
1625 Sharp Point Dr.
Ft. Collins, CO 80522
Phone: 303-482-5868 Fax: —
CEO: G. Lee Southard
CFO: Dale R. Clift
1991 Sales: $2 million Employees: 41
Symbol: ATRX Exchange: NASDAQ
Industry: Medical - periodontic treatment therapies

ATS Medical
3905 Annapolis Lane
Minneapolis, MN 55447
Phone: 612-553-7736 Fax: 612-553-1492
CEO: Manuel A. Villafana
CFO: John H. Jungbauer
1992 Sales: — Employees: 26
Symbol: ATSI Exchange: NASDAQ
Industry: Medical products - mechanical heart valve, proteins

Atwood Oceanics, Inc.
15835 Park Ten Place Dr.
Houston, TX 77084
Phone: 713-492-2929 Fax: 713-492-0345
CEO: Robert E. Turrentine
CFO: James M. Holland
1991 Sales: $54 million Employees: 750
Symbol: ATWD Exchange: NASDAQ
Industry: Oil & gas - offshore drilling

Au Bon Pain Co., Inc.
19 Fid Kennedy Ave.
Boston, MA 02210
Phone: 617-423-2100 Fax: 617-423-7879
CEO: Louis I. Kane
CFO: Kevin J. Leary
1991 Sales: $68 million Employees: 2,550
Symbol: ABPCA Exchange: NASDAQ
Industry: Retail - food & restaurants

Audio Partners Inc.
1133 High St.
Auburn, CA 95603
Phone: 916-888-7803 Fax: 916-888-7805
CEO: Grady Hesters
CFO: Grady Hesters
1991 Sales: $1.6 million Employees: 15
Ownership: Privately held
Industry: Publishing - books on cassette

Audio/Video Affiliates, Inc.
2875 Needmore Rd.
Dayton, OH 45414
Phone: 513-276-3931 Fax: 513-276-2713
CEO: Stuart A. Rose
CFO: Douglas L. Bruggeman
1991 Sales: $202 million Employees: 599
Symbol: AVA Exchange: NYSE
Industry: Retail - consumer electronics

Audiovox Corp.
150 Marcus Blvd.
Hauppauge, NY 11788
Phone: 516-231-7750 Fax: 516-434-3995
CEO: John J. Shalam
CFO: Charles M. Stoehr
1991 Sales: $328 million Employees: 634
Symbol: VOX Exchange: AMEX
Industry: Auto parts - retail & wholesale

indicates company is in *Hoover's Handbook of American Business.*

indicates company is in *Hoover's Handbook of World Business;* sales and employee numbers are for parent company.

Augat Inc.
89 Forbes Blvd.
Mansfield, MA 02048
Phone: 508-543-4300 Fax: 508-543-7019
CEO: Marcel P. Joseph
CFO: Ronald D. Yancey
1991 Sales: $282 million Employees: 4,100
Symbol: AUG Exchange: NYSE
Industry: Electrical connectors

Aura Systems, Inc.
2335 Alaska Ave.
El Segundo, CA 90245
Phone: 310-643-5300 Fax: —
CEO: Zvi Kurtzman
CFO: Francis T. Phelan
1992 Sales: $11 million Employees: —
Symbol: AURA Exchange: NASDAQ
Industry: Electrical products

Austin Industries Inc.
3535 Travis St.
Dallas, TX 75204
Phone: 214-443-5500 Fax: 214-443-5581
CEO: William T. Solomon
CFO: John P. Olsson
1992 Sales: $510 million Employees: 5,500
Ownership: Privately held
Industry: Construction & contracting - heavy, commercial & industrial

Authentic Fitness Corp.
7911 Haskell Ave.
Van Nuys, CA 91410
Phone: 818-376-0300 Fax: —
CEO: Linda J. Wachner
CFO: Roger A. Williams
1991 Sales: $86 million Employees: —
Symbol: ASM Exchange: NYSE
Industry: Apparel

Authorized Cellular/Security One
16276 13 Mile Rd.
Roseville, MI 48066
Phone: 313-774-8612 Fax: 313-775-1714
CEO: David Gagnon
CFO: David Gagnon
1991 Sales: $1.8 million Employees: 20
Ownership: Privately held
Industry: Telecommunications equipment - cellular phones

Auto-Soft Corporation
563 West 500 South
Bountiful, UT 84010
Phone: 801-295-2069 Fax: 801-292-1846
CEO: Dean Jolley
CFO: Mark Elwood
1991 Sales: $5.5 million Employees: 45
Ownership: Privately held
Industry: Computers - inventory control software

Auto-trol Technology Corp.
12500 N. Washington St.
Denver, CO 80233
Phone: 303-452-4919 Fax: —
CEO: Howard H. Hillman
CFO: David Brents
1991 Sales: $64 million Employees: 660
Symbol: ATTC Exchange: NASDAQ
Industry: Computers - graphics

AutoAlliance International, Inc.
1 Mazda Dr.
Flat Rock, MI 48134
Phone: 313-782-7800 Fax: 313-782-2189
CEO: W. Wayne Booker
CFO: —
1992 Sales: $21,780 million Employees: 29,835
Parent: Mazda Motor Corporation
Industry: Automotive manufacturing

Autocam Corp.
4070 E. Paris Ave.
Kentwood, MI 49512
Phone: 616-698-0707 Fax: 616-698-6876
CEO: John C. Kennedy
CFO: Warren A. Veltman
1992 Sales: $27 million Employees: 125
Symbol: ACAM Exchange: NASDAQ
Industry: Metal products - fabrication

Autoclave Engineers, Inc.
2930 W. 22nd St.
Erie, PA 16506
Phone: 814-838-2071 Fax: 814-833-0145
CEO: William F. Schilling
CFO: Thomas C. Guelcher
1992 Sales: $80 million Employees: 730
Symbol: ACLV Exchange: NASDAQ
Industry: Instruments - control

Autodesk, Inc.
2320 Marinship Way
Sausalito, CA 94965
Phone: 415-332-2344 Fax: 415-331-8093
CEO: Carol Bartz
CFO: Eric B. Herr
1992 Sales: $285 million Employees: 1,272
Symbol: ACAD Exchange: NASDAQ
Industry: Computers - software

AutoInfo, Inc.
1600 Route 208
Fair Lawn, NJ 07410
Phone: 201-703-0500 Fax: 201-703-1777
CEO: Jason Bacher
CFO: Scott Zecher
1992 Sales: $13 million Employees: 100
Symbol: AUTO Exchange: NASDAQ
Industry: Business services

Automated Systems Design, Inc.
1050 Northfield Court, Ste. 100
Roswell, GA 30076
Phone: 404-740-2300 Fax: 404-740-2313
CEO: Robert Eskew
CFO: Warren R. Royal
1992 Sales: $6.2 million Employees: 75
Ownership: Privately held
Industry: Computers - networks

Automatic Data Processing, Inc.
One ADP Blvd.
Roseland, NJ 07068
Phone: 201-994-5000 Fax: 201-994-5387
CEO: Josh S. Weston
CFO: Arthur F. Weinbach
1992 Sales: $2,076 million Employees: 20,500
Symbol: AUD Exchange: NYSE
Industry: Computers - payroll & on-line information services

Automation Partners International
601 Montgomery St., Ste. 400
San Francisco, CA 94111
Phone: 415-772-9000 Fax: 415-772-9007
CEO: John Mickel
CFO: Dick Hyatt
1991 Sales: $22 million Employees: 120
Ownership: Privately held
Industry: Business services - technology products & services for law firms

Automotive Industries Holding, Inc.
4508 IDS Center
Minneapolis, MN 55402
Phone: 612-332-6828 Fax: —
CEO: W. H. Clement
CFO: Scott D. Rued
1991 Sales: $210 million Employees: 2,550
Symbol: AIHI Exchange: NASDAQ
Industry: Automotive & trucking - original equipment

Autotote Corp.
10115 Cabin Creek Rd.
Shepherd, MT 59079
Phone: 406-373-5507 Fax: 406-373-6615
CEO: Brian Wolfson
CFO: Linda K. Shelhamer
1991 Sales: $44 million Employees: 292
Symbol: TOTAC Exchange: NASDAQ
Industry: Leisure & recreational products

Autotrol Corp.
5730 N. Glen Park Rd.
Milwaukee, WI 53209
Phone: 414-228-9100 Fax: 414-228-8729
CEO: Charles W. Palmer
CFO: Charles W. Palmer
1991 Sales: $36 million Employees: 281
Symbol: AUTR Exchange: NASDAQ
Industry: Water treatment equipment

AutoZone, Inc.
3030 Poplar Ave.
Memphis, TN 38111
Phone: 901-325-4600 Fax: 901-325-4655
CEO: J. R. Hyde III
CFO: Charles T. Bell
1992 Sales: $1,039 million Employees: 11,600
Symbol: AZO Exchange: NYSE
Industry: Auto parts - retail & wholesale

Avalon Corp.
101 E. 52nd St.
New York, NY 10022
Phone: 212-751-8700 Fax: —
CEO: John M. Donovan
CFO: Philip B. Cleland
1991 Sales: $1.6 million Employees: —
Symbol: AVL Exchange: NYSE
Industry: Oil & gas - US exploration & production

Avatar Holdings, Inc.
201 Alhambra Circle
Coral Gables, FL 33134
Phone: 305-442-7000 Fax: 305-443-3844
CEO: Lawrence Wilkov
CFO: Peter S. Kleinerman
1991 Sales: $103 million Employees: 1,056
Symbol: AVTR Exchange: NASDAQ
Industry: Real estate development

AVEMCO Corp.
411 Aviation Way
Frederick, MD 21701
Phone: 301-694-5700 Fax: 301-694-4232
CEO: William P. Condon
CFO: John R. Yuska
1991 Sales: $84 million Employees: —
Symbol: AVE Exchange: NYSE
Industry: Insurance - property & casualty

Avery Dennison Corp.
150 N. Orange Grove Blvd.
Pasadena, CA 91103
Phone: 818-304-2000 Fax: 818-792-7312
CEO: Charles D. Miller
CFO: R. Gregory Jenkins
1992 Sales: $2,623 million Employees: 17,095
Symbol: AVY Exchange: NYSE
Industry: Office & art materials

Avis, Inc.
900 Old Country Rd.
Garden City, NY 11530
Phone: 516-222-3000 Fax: 516-222-4381
CEO: Joseph V. Vittoria
CFO: Lawrence Ferezy
1992 Sales: $1,234 million Employees: 14,350
Ownership: Privately held
Industry: Leasing - autos

 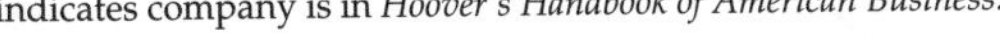
indicates company is in *Hoover's Handbook of American Business.*

indicates company is in *Hoover's Handbook of World Business;* sales and employee numbers are for parent company.

Avnet, Inc.
80 Cutter Mill Rd.
Great Neck, NY 11021
Phone: 516-466-7000 Fax: 516-466-1203
CEO: Leon Machiz
CFO: Raymond Sadowski
1992 Sales: $1,991 million Employees: 6,650
Symbol: AVT Exchange: NYSE
Industry: Electronics - parts distribution

Avon Products, Inc.
9 W. 57th St.
New York, NY 10019
Phone: 212-546-6015 Fax: 212-546-6136
CEO: James E. Preston
CFO: Edward J. Robinson
1992 Sales: $3,810 million Employees: 30,500
Symbol: AVP Exchange: NYSE
Industry: Cosmetics & toiletries

Avondale Industries, Inc.
5100 River Rd.
Avondale, LA 70094
Phone: 504-436-2121 Fax: 504-436-5375
CEO: Albert L. Bossier, Jr.
CFO: Thomas M. Kitchen
1991 Sales: $777 million Employees: 8,200
Symbol: AVDL Exchange: NASDAQ
Industry: Transportation - equipment & leasing

AW Computer Systems, Inc.
9000A Commerce Pkwy.
Mt. Laurel, NJ 08054
Phone: 609-234-3939 Fax: 609-234-9377
CEO: Nicholas Ambrus
CFO: Bradford Smith III
1991 Sales: $8.9 million Employees: 47
Symbol: AWCSA Exchange: NASDAQ
Industry: Computers - software for retailers

Aydin Corp.
700 Dresher Rd.
Horsham, PA 19044
Phone: 215-657-7510 Fax: 215-657-3830
CEO: Ayhan Hakimoglu
CFO: Jay L. Landis
1991 Sales: $158 million Employees: 1,400
Symbol: AYD Exchange: NYSE
Industry: Electronics - military

Aztar Corp.
2390 E. Camelback Rd.
Phoenix, AZ 85016
Phone: 602-381-4100 Fax: 602-381-4107
CEO: Paul E. Rubeli
CFO: Robert M. Haddock
1991 Sales: $481 million Employees: 7,200
Symbol: AZTR Exchange: NASDAQ
Industry: Casinos

Aztec Manufacturing Co., Inc.
PO Box 668
Crowley, TX 76036
Phone: 817-297-4361 Fax: 817-297-4621
CEO: L. C. Martin
CFO: Robert H. Johnson
1992 Sales: $30 million Employees: 282
Symbol: AZTC Exchange: NASDAQ
Industry: Oil field machinery & equipment

Aztech Controls, Inc.
2451 W. Birchwood Ave., Ste. 101
Mesa, AZ 85202
Phone: 602-966-4400 Fax: 602-966-5634
CEO: Pat Frazier
CFO: Pat Frazier
1991 Sales: $6.3 million Employees: 20
Ownership: Privately held
Industry: Valves & fittings

B. Green & Co. Inc.
3601 Washington Blvd.
Baltimore, MD 21227
Phone: 410-247-8300 Fax: 410-247-2839
CEO: Bernard Green
CFO: Jesse Swartz
1991 Sales: $525 million Employees: 1,000
Ownership: Privately held
Industry: Food - wholesale & grocery stores

B.M.J. Financial Corp.
243 Route 130
Bordentown, NJ 08505
Phone: 609-298-5500 Fax: —
CEO: Albert P. Mainka
CFO: Joseph M. Reardon
1991 Sales: $30 million Employees: 518
Symbol: BMJF Exchange: NASDAQ
Industry: Banks - Northeast

Babbage's Inc.
10741 King William Dr.
Dallas, TX 75220
Phone: 214-401-9000 Fax: 214-401-9002
CEO: James B. McCurry
CFO: Opal P. Ferraro
1991 Sales: $168 million Employees: 1,600
Symbol: BBGS Exchange: NASDAQ
Industry: Retail - personal computer software

Bacardi Imports Inc.
2100 Biscayne Blvd.
Miami, FL 33137
Phone: 305-573-8511 Fax: 305-573-0756
CEO: Juan Grau
CFO: Rodolfo Ruiz
1991 Sales: $580 million Employees: 288
Ownership: Privately held
Industry: Beverages - alcoholic; distilled spirits & wine

Bachman Information Systems, Inc.
8 New England Executive Park
Burlington, MA 01803
Phone: 617-273-9003 Fax: —
CEO: Arnold A. Kraft
CFO: Paul K. McGrath
1991 Sales: $32 million Employees: 287
Symbol: BACH Exchange: NASDAQ
Industry: Computers - software

Back Bay Restaurant Group, Inc.
855 Boylston St.
Boston, MA 02116
Phone: 617-536-2800 Fax: —
CEO: Charles F. Sarkis
CFO: Nabil N. El Hage
1991 Sales: $56 million Employees: 1,875
Symbol: PAPA Exchange: NASDAQ
Industry: Retail - food & restaurants

Badger Meter, Inc.
4545 W. Brown Deer Rd.
Milwaukee, WI 53223
Phone: 414-355-0400 Fax: 414-355-8096
CEO: James L. Forbes
CFO: R. Robert Howard
1991 Sales: $78 million Employees: 855
Symbol: BMI Exchange: AMEX
Industry: Electronics - measuring instruments

Badger Paper Mills, Inc.
200 W. Front St.
Peshtigo, WI 54157
Phone: 715-582-4551 Fax: 715-582-4853
CEO: Edwin A. Meyer, Jr.
CFO: Miles L. Kresl, Jr.
1991 Sales: $69 million Employees: 458
Symbol: BPMI Exchange: NASDAQ
Industry: Paper & paper products

Bailey Corp.
700 Lafayette Rd.
Seabrook, NH 03874
Phone: 603-474-3011 Fax: 603-474-8949
CEO: Roger R. Phillips
CFO: Leonard J. Heilman
1991 Sales: $24 million Employees: 366
Symbol: BAIB Exchange: NASDAQ
Industry: Automotive & trucking - original equipment

Bairnco Corp.
200 Park Ave.
New York, NY 10166
Phone: 212-490-8722 Fax: —
CEO: Luke Fichthorn
CFO: David C. Bevan Jr.
1991 Sales: $168 million Employees: 1,178
Symbol: BZ Exchange: NYSE
Industry: Diversified operations - adhesive tapes, meat cutting & electronic equipment

Baker Hughes Inc.
3900 Essex Lane
Houston, TX 77027
Phone: 713-439-8600 Fax: 713-439-8699
CEO: James D. Woods
CFO: Eric L. Mattson
1992 Sales: $2,620 million Employees: 21,300
Symbol: BHI Exchange: NYSE
Industry: Oil field machinery & equipment

Baker & McKenzie
One Prudential Plaza, 130 E. Randolph Dr.
Chicago, IL 60601
Phone: 312-861-8800 Fax: 312-861-8823
CEO: John V. McGuigan
CFO: Frank H. Wheeler
1992 Sales: $504 million Employees: 6,533
Ownership: Privately held
Industry: Business services - legal

Baker & Taylor
652 E. Main St.
Bridgewater, NJ 08807
Phone: 908-218-0400 Fax: 908-722-7420
CEO: Gerald G. Garbacz
CFO: David Finlon
1992 Sales: $850 million Employees: 2,500
Ownership: Privately held
Industry: Wholesale - books

Balchem Corp.
PO Box 175
Slate Hill, NY 10973
Phone: 914-355-2861 Fax: 914-355-6314
CEO: Herb Weiss
CFO: Herb Weiss
1991 Sales: $13 million Employees: 95
Symbol: BLCC Exchange: NASDAQ
Industry: Chemicals - specialty

Baldor Electric Co.
5711 S. 7th St.
Ft. Smith, AR 72902
Phone: 501-646-4711 Fax: 501-648-5792
CEO: Roland S. Boreham, Jr.
CFO: Gregory C. Kowert
1991 Sales: $286 million Employees: 2,976
Symbol: BEZ Exchange: NYSE
Industry: Machinery - electrical

Baldwin & Lyons, Inc.
1099 N. Meridian St.
Indianapolis, IN 46204
Phone: 317-636-9800 Fax: 317-632-9444
CEO: John C. Aldin
CFO: G. Patrick Corydon
1991 Sales: $120 million Employees: 204
Symbol: BWINA Exchange: NASDAQ
Industry: Insurance - property & casualty

indicates company is in *Hoover's Handbook of American Business.*

indicates company is in *Hoover's Handbook of World Business*; sales and employee numbers are for parent company.

Baldwin Piano & Organ Co.
422 Wards Corner Rd.
Loveland, OH 45140
Phone: 513-576-4500 Fax: 513-576-4546
CEO: R. S. Harrison
CFO: Charles R. Juengling
1991 Sales: $111 million Employees: 1,600
Symbol: BPAO Exchange: NASDAQ
Industry: Pianos

Baldwin Technology Co., Inc.
65 Rowayton Ave.
Rowayton, CT 06853
Phone: 203-838-7470 Fax: 203-852-7040
CEO: Wendell M. Smith
CFO: Kenneth W. Reynolds
1992 Sales: $222 million Employees: 1,130
Symbol: BLD Exchange: AMEX
Industry: Machinery - printing

Ball Corp.
345 S. High St.
Muncie, IN 47305
Phone: 317-747-6100 Fax: 317-747-6203
CEO: Delmont A. Davis
CFO: William L. Peterson
1992 Sales: $2,178 million Employees: 13,285
Symbol: BLL Exchange: NYSE
Industry: Glass products

Ballard Medical Products
12050 S. Lone Peak Pkwy.
Draper, UT 84020
Phone: 801-572-6800 Fax: 801-572-6999
CEO: Dale H. Ballard
CFO: Kenneth R. Sorenson
1992 Sales: $50 million Employees: 533
Symbol: BMED Exchange: NASDAQ
Industry: Medical & dental supplies

Bally Gaming International, Inc.
6601 S. Bermuda Rd.
Las Vegas, NV 89119
Phone: 702-896-7700 Fax: 702-896-7990
CEO: Richard Gillman
CFO: Gary J. Simpson
1991 Sales: $148 million Employees: 740
Symbol: BGII Exchange: NASDAQ
Industry: Gambling equipment

Bally Manufacturing Corp.
8700 W. Bryn Mawr Ave.
Chicago, IL 60631
Phone: 312-399-1300 Fax: 313-693-2982
CEO: Arthur M. Goldberg
CFO: Lee S. Hillman
1992 Sales: $1,297 million Employees: 32,540
Symbol: BLY Exchange: NYSE
Industry: Casinos & fitness centers

Baltek Corp.
10 Fairway Court
Northvale, NJ 07647
Phone: 201-767-1400 Fax: 201-387-6631
CEO: Jacques Kohn
CFO: Benson J. Zeikowitz
1991 Sales: $31 million Employees: 919
Symbol: BTEK Exchange: NASDAQ
Industry: Building products - wood

Baltimore Bancorp
120 E. Baltimore St., 25th Fl.
Baltimore, MD 21202
Phone: 410-244-3360 Fax: 410-576-0695
CEO: Charles H. Whittum, Jr.
CFO: Joseph A. Cicero
1991 Sales: $313 million Employees: 1,225
Symbol: BBB Exchange: NYSE
Industry: Banks - Southeast

Baltimore Gas and Electric Co.
39 W. Lexington St.
Baltimore, MD 21201
Phone: 410-234-5000 Fax: Call co. operator
CEO: George V. McGowan
CFO: Charles W. Shivery
1992 Sales: $2,491 million Employees: 9,405
Symbol: BGE Exchange: NYSE
Industry: Utility - electric

Bamberger Polymers, Inc.
1983 Marcus Ave.
Lake Success, NY 11042
Phone: 516-328-2772 Fax: 516-326-1005
CEO: Fred Garcia
CFO: Daniel T. Murphy
1991 Sales: $204 million Employees: 165
Symbol: BPI Exchange: AMEX
Industry: Rubber & plastic products

Banc One Corp.
100 E. Broad St.
Columbus, OH 43271
Phone: 614-248-5944 Fax: 614-248-5624
CEO: John B. McCoy
CFO: John W. Westman
1992 Sales: $5,999 million Employees: 27,500
Symbol: ONE Exchange: NYSE
Industry: Banks - Midwest

BancFlorida Financial Corp.
5801 Pelican Bay Blvd.
Naples, FL 33963
Phone: 813-597-1611 Fax: 813-597-8924
CEO: Mary Ellen Hawkins
CFO: J. Michael Holmes
1991 Sales: $156 million Employees: 692
Symbol: BFL Exchange: NYSE
Industry: Banks - Southeast

Bancorp Hawaii, Inc.
130 Merchant St.
Honolulu, HI 96813
Phone: 808-537-8111 Fax: 808-533-0175
CEO: H. Howard Stephenson
CFO: Richard J. Dahl
1992 Sales: $940 million Employees: 4,188
Symbol: BOH Exchange: NYSE
Industry: Banks - West

BancTec, Inc.
4435 Spring Valley Rd.
Dallas, TX 75244
Phone: 214-450-7700 Fax: 214-450-7867
CEO: Grahame N. Clark, Jr.
CFO: Gary T. Robinson
1992 Sales: $191 million Employees: 1,923
Symbol: BTEC Exchange: NASDAQ
Industry: Optical character recognition

BancTEXAS Group Inc.
13747 Montfort Dr., Ste. 350
Dallas, TX 75240
Phone: 214-701-4600 Fax: 214-701-4674
CEO: Nathan C. Collins
CFO: D. Kert Moore
1991 Sales: $24 million Employees: 159
Symbol: BTX Exchange: NYSE
Industry: Banks - Midwest

Bandag, Inc.
Bandag Center
Muscatine, IA 52761
Phone: 319-262-1400 Fax: 319-262-1377
CEO: Martin G. Carver
CFO: Thomas E. Dvorchak
1991 Sales: $583 million Employees: 2,477
Symbol: BDG Exchange: NYSE
Industry: Rubber tires

Bando McGlocklin Capital Corp.
13555 Bishops Court, Ste. 205
Brookfield, WI 53005
Phone: 414-784-9010 Fax: 414-784-3426
CEO: George R. Schonath
CFO: George R. Schonath
1992 Sales: $8.5 million Employees: —
Symbol: BMCC Exchange: NASDAQ
Industry: Financial - investment bankers

Bangor Hydro-Electric Co.
33 State St.
Bangor, ME 04402
Phone: 207-945-5621 Fax: 207-990-6990
CEO: Robert S. Briggs
CFO: John P. O'Sullivan
1991 Sales: $146 million Employees: 594
Symbol: BGR Exchange: NYSE
Industry: Utility - electric power

Bank of Boston Corp.
100 Federal St.
Boston, MA 02110
Phone: 617-434-2200 Fax: 617-575-2232
CEO: Ira Stepanian
CFO: Peter J. Manning
1992 Sales: $5,292 million Employees: 16,100
Symbol: BKB Exchange: NYSE
Industry: Banks - Northeast

Bank of New York Company, Inc.
48 Wall St.
New York, NY 10286
Phone: 212-495-1784 Fax: 212-495-1239
CEO: J. Carter Bacot
CFO: Deno D. Papageorge
1992 Sales: $3,583 million Employees: 13,226
Symbol: BK Exchange: NYSE
Industry: Banks - Northeast

Bank of San Francisco Holding Co.
550 Montgomery St.
San Francisco, CA 94111
Phone: 415-781-7810 Fax: 415-391-1468
CEO: Donald R. Stephens
CFO: William H. Adams
1991 Sales: $43 million Employees: 171
Symbol: BOF Exchange: AMEX
Industry: Banks - West

Bank of San Pedro
250 W. Fifth St.
San Pedro, CA 90731
Phone: 310-548-1281 Fax: 310-548-5708
CEO: Lance D. Oak
CFO: John Jenkins
1992 Sales: — Employees: —
Symbol: BOSP Exchange: NASDAQ
Industry: Banks - West

Bank South Corp.
55 Marietta St. NW
Atlanta, GA 30303
Phone: 404-529-4521 Fax: 404-521-7347
CEO: Patrick L. Flinn
CFO: Ralph E. Hutchins, Jr.
1991 Sales: $508 million Employees: 2,937
Symbol: BKSO Exchange: NASDAQ
Industry: Banks - Southeast

BankAmerica Corp.
Bank of America Center, 555 California St.
San Francisco, CA 94104
Phone: 415-622-3530 Fax: 415-622-7915
CEO: Richard M. Rosenberg
CFO: Frank N. Newman
1992 Sales: $15,262 million Employees: 62,609
Symbol: BAC Exchange: NYSE
Industry: Banks - West

indicates company is in *Hoover's Handbook of American Business.*

indicates company is in *Hoover's Handbook of World Business;* sales and employee numbers are for parent company.

BankAtlantic, F.S.B.
1750 E. Sunrise Blvd.
Ft. Lauderdale, FL 33304
Phone: 305-760-5000 Fax: —
CEO: Alan B. Levan
CFO: Jasper R. Eanes
1991 Sales: $47 million Employees: 813
Symbol: ASAL Exchange: NASDAQ
Industry: Banks - Northeast

Banker's Note, Inc.
4900 Highlands Pkwy.
Smyrna, GA 30082
Phone: 404-432-0636 Fax: 404-432-2499
CEO: Martin S. Suchik
CFO: Thomas J. Thirkell
1991 Sales: $26 million Employees: 325
Symbol: BKNTQ Exchange: NASDAQ
Industry: Retail - apparel & shoes

Bankers Corp.
210 Smith St.
Perth Amboy, NJ 08861
Phone: 908-442-4100 Fax: 908-442-9570
CEO: Joseph P. Gemmell
CFO: Howard S. Garfield II
1991 Sales: $125 million Employees: 369
Symbol: BKCO Exchange: NASDAQ
Industry: Banks - Northeast

Bankers First Corp.
945 Broad St.
Augusta, GA 30901
Phone: 404-823-3200 Fax: —
CEO: H. M. Osteen, Jr.
CFO: Glenn W. Peters
1991 Sales: $122 million Employees: 310
Symbol: BNKF Exchange: NASDAQ
Industry: Financial - savings and loans

Bankers Trust New York Corp.
280 Park Ave.
New York, NY 10017
Phone: 212-250-2500 Fax: 212-454-1704
CEO: Charles S. Sanford, Jr.
CFO: Timothy T. Yates
1992 Sales: $6,550 million Employees: 12,088
Symbol: BT Exchange: NYSE
Industry: Banks - money center

Banknorth Group, Inc.
300 Financial Plaza
Burlington, VT 05401
Phone: 802-658-2492 Fax: —
CEO: William H. Chadwick
CFO: Thomas J. Pruitt
1991 Sales: $174 million Employees: 1,008
Symbol: BKNG Exchange: NASDAQ
Industry: Banks - Northeast

BankWorcester Corp.
365 Main St.
Worcester, MA 01608
Phone: 508-831-4000 Fax: —
CEO: Harold Cabot
CFO: Anthony J. Keller
1991 Sales: $118 million Employees: 637
Symbol: BNKW Exchange: NASDAQ
Industry: Banks - Northeast

Banner Aerospace, Inc.
25700 Science Park Dr.
Cleveland, OH 44122
Phone: 216-464-3650 Fax: —
CEO: Samuel J. Krasney
CFO: Warren D. Persavich
1992 Sales: $262 million Employees: 795
Symbol: BAR Exchange: NYSE
Industry: Aerospace - aircraft equipment

Banta Corp.
225 Main St.
Menasha, WI 54952
Phone: 414-722-7777 Fax: 414-722-6495
CEO: Calvin W. Aurand, Jr.
CFO: Gerald A. Henseler
1992 Sales: $637 million Employees: 4,228
Symbol: BNTA Exchange: NASDAQ
Industry: Printing - commercial

Banyan Systems, Inc.
120 Flanders Rd.
Westborough, MA 01581
Phone: 508-898-1000 Fax: 508-898-1755
CEO: David C. Mahoney
CFO: Jeffrey D. Glidden
1991 Sales: $100 million Employees: 633
Symbol: BNYN Exchange: NASDAQ
Industry: Computers - networking software

Barclays Bank PLC
75 Wall St.
New York, NY 10265
Phone: 212-412-4000 Fax: 212-412-5600
CEO: J.A. Kerslake
CFO: —
1991 Sales: $26,110 million Employees: 111,400
Parent: Barclays PLC
Industry: Banks - money center

Barclays Law Publishers
400 Oyster Point Blvd.
San Francisco, CA 94080
Phone: 415-588-1155 Fax: 415-244-0408
CEO: R. Michael James
CFO: David C. Stegall
1991 Sales: $8.5 million Employees: 65
Ownership: Privately held
Industry: Business services - legal information services

Barclays Oxygen Homecare
8200 S. Akron, Ste. 119
Englewood, CO 80112
Phone: 303-799-8441 Fax: 303-799-8438
CEO: Stephen W. Gibson
CFO: Stephen W. Gibson
1992 Sales: $4.9 million Employees: 32
Ownership: Privately held
Industry: Health care - home oxygen services

Barefoot Inc.
1018 Proprietors Rd.
Worthington, OH 43085
Phone: 614-846-1800 Fax: —
CEO: Patrick J. Norton
CFO: Michael R. Goodrich
1992 Sales: $41 million Employees: 800
Symbol: BARE Exchange: NASDAQ
Industry: Agricultural operations

Barnes Group Inc.
123 Main St.
Bristol, CT 06010
Phone: 203-583-7070 Fax: —
CEO: William R. Fenoglio
CFO: A. Stanton Wells
1991 Sales: $203 million Employees: —
Symbol: B Exchange: NYSE
Industry: Wire & cable products

Barnes & Noble
122 Fifth Ave.
New York, NY 10011
Phone: 212-633-3300 Fax: 212-675-0413
CEO: Leonard Riggio
CFO: Mitchell S. Klipper
1992 Sales: $1,000 million Employees: 17,000
Ownership: Privately held
Industry: Retail - bookstores

Barnett Banks, Inc.
50 N. Laura St.
Jacksonville, FL 32202
Phone: 904-791-7720 Fax: 904-791-7166
CEO: Charles E. Rice
CFO: Charles W. Newman
1992 Sales: $3,457 million Employees: 18,752
Symbol: BBI Exchange: NYSE
Industry: Banks - Southeast

Barnwell Industries, Inc.
2828 Paa St., Ste. 2085
Honolulu, HI 96819
Phone: 808-836-0136 Fax: 808-833-5577
CEO: Morton H. Kinzler
CFO: Russell M. Gifford
1991 Sales: $19 million Employees: 58
Symbol: BRN Exchange: AMEX
Industry: Oil & gas - international specialty

Baroid Corp.
3000 N. Sam Houston Pkwy. East
Houston, TX 77032
Phone: 713-987-4000 Fax: 713-987-5742
CEO: J. Landis Martin
CFO: Joseph S. Campofelice
1992 Sales: $615 million Employees: 4,800
Symbol: BRC Exchange: NYSE
Industry: Oil field machinery & equipment

Barr Laboratories, Inc.
2 Quaker Rd.
Pomona, NY 10970
Phone: 914-362-1100 Fax: 914-362-1193
CEO: Edwin A. Cohen
CFO: Louis J. Guerci
1991 Sales: $94 million Employees: 531
Symbol: BRL Exchange: AMEX
Industry: Drugs - generic

Barra, Inc.
1995 University Ave., Ste. 400
Berkeley, CA 94704
Phone: 510-548-5442 Fax: —
CEO: Andrew Rudd
CFO: Ronald J. Lanstein
1992 Sales: $33 million Employees: 228
Symbol: BARZ Exchange: NASDAQ
Industry: Computers - portfolio-management software

Barrett Resources Corp.
1125 Seventeenth St.
Denver, CO 80202
Phone: 303-297-3900 Fax: 303-297-0807
CEO: William J. Barrett
CFO: Robert W. Howard
1991 Sales: $14 million Employees: 55
Symbol: BARC Exchange: NASDAQ
Industry: Oil & gas - US exploration & production

Barrister Information Systems Corp.
45 Oak St.
Buffalo, NY 14203
Phone: 716-845-5010 Fax: 716-845-0077
CEO: Henry P. Semmelhack
CFO: Richard P. Beyer
1992 Sales: $17 million Employees: 217
Symbol: BIS Exchange: AMEX
Industry: Computers - equipment & software for law offices

Barry T. Chouinard Inc.
12 North Main St.
Northfield, VT 05663
Phone: 802-485-8600 Fax: 802-485-6609
CEO: Barry T. Chouinard
CFO: Linda Hall
1991 Sales: $3.7 million Employees: 20
Ownership: Privately held
Industry: Textiles - apparel

indicates company is in *Hoover's Handbook of American Business.*

indicates company is in *Hoover's Handbook of World Business;* sales and employee numbers are for parent company.

Barry's Jewelers, Inc.
111 W. Lemon Ave.
Monrovia, CA 91016
Phone: 818-303-4741 Fax: 818-357-7596
CEO: David Blum
CFO: Thomas S. Liston
1992 Sales: $128 million Employees: 1,175
Symbol: BARY Exchange: NASDAQ
Industry: Retail - jewelry stores

Bartlett & Co.
4800 Main St., Ste. 600
Kansas City, MO 64112
Phone: 816-753-6300 Fax: 816-753-0062
CEO: Paul D. Bartlett, Jr.
CFO: Robert Berg
1991 Sales: $545 million Employees: 525
Ownership: Privately held
Industry: Food - flour & grain; cattle feed

Barton Malow Co.
27777 Franklin Rd., Ste. 800
Southfield, MI 48034
Phone: 313-351-4500 Fax: 313-351-4629
CEO: Ben Maibach III
CFO: Ed Jarchow
1991 Sales: $723 million Employees: 477
Ownership: Privately held
Industry: Construction - general contracting, construction management

Base Ten Systems, Inc.
One Electronics Dr.
Trenton, NJ 08619
Phone: 609-586-7010 Fax: 609-586-1593
CEO: Myles M. Kranzler
CFO: Edward J. Klinsport
1991 Sales: $26 million Employees: 301
Symbol: BASEA Exchange: NASDAQ
Industry: Computers - mini & micro

BASF Corporation
8 Campus Dr.
Parsippany, NJ 07054
Phone: 201-397-2700 Fax: 201-397-2737
CEO: Dieter Stein
CFO: —
1991 Sales: $29,473 million Employees: 129,434
Parent: BASF AG
Industry: Diversified operations - chemicals, consumer products, dyes & oil & gas

Bashas' Inc.
PO Box 488
Chandler, AZ 85244
Phone: 602-895-9350 Fax: 602-895-5292
CEO: Edward N. Basha, Jr.
CFO: Darl Anderson
1991 Sales: $553 million Employees: 4,500
Ownership: Privately held
Industry: Retail - supermarkets

Bassett Furniture Industries, Inc.
245 Main St.
Bassett, VA 24055
Phone: 703-629-6000 Fax: 703-629-6333
CEO: Robert H. Spilman
CFO: B. M. Brammer
1991 Sales: $402 million Employees: 7,460
Symbol: BSET Exchange: NASDAQ
Industry: Furniture

Bath Iron Works Corp.
700 Washington St.
Bath, ME 04530
Phone: 207-443-3311 Fax: 207-442-1567
CEO: Duane D. Fitzgerald
CFO: Howard J. Yates
1991 Sales: $825 million Employees: 10,500
Ownership: Privately held
Industry: Boat building

Battelle Memorial Institute
505 King Ave.
Columbus, OH 43201
Phone: 614-424-6424 Fax: 614-424-5263
CEO: Douglas E. Olesen
CFO: John H. Doster
1991 Sales: $860 million Employees: 8,300
Ownership: Privately held
Industry: Engineering - R&D services

Battle Mountain Gold Co.
333 Clay St., 42nd Fl.
Houston, TX 77002
Phone: 713-650-6400 Fax: 713-650-3636
CEO: Karl E. Elers
CFO: George W. Mitchell
1991 Sales: $170 million Employees: 1,517
Symbol: BMG Exchange: NYSE
Industry: Gold mining & processing

Bausch & Lomb Inc.
One Lincoln First Square
Rochester, NY 14601
Phone: 716-338-6000 Fax: 716-338-6007
CEO: Daniel E. Gill
CFO: Frank M. Stotz
1992 Sales: $1,709 million Employees: 13,700
Symbol: BOL Exchange: NYSE
Industry: Medical products - pharmaceuticals, contact lenses & optics

Baxter International Inc.
One Baxter Pkwy.
Deerfield, IL 60015
Phone: 708-948-2000 Fax: 708-948-3948
CEO: Vernon R. Loucks, Jr.
CFO: Robert J. Lambrix
1992 Sales: $8,471 million Employees: 65,900
Symbol: BAX Exchange: NYSE
Industry: Medical products & health services

Bay State Gas Co.
300 Friberg Pkwy.
Westborough, MA 01581
Phone: 508-836-7000 Fax: 508-836-7074
CEO: Roger A. Young
CFO: Thomas W. Sherman
1991 Sales: $338 million Employees: 1,145
Symbol: BGC Exchange: NYSE
Industry: Utility - gas distribution

Bay View Capital Corp.
2121 S. El Camino Real
San Mateo, CA 94403
Phone: 415-573-7300 Fax: —
CEO: Robert E. Barnes
CFO: Albert J. Thomson
1991 Sales: $283 million Employees: 343
Symbol: BVFS Exchange: NASDAQ
Industry: Financial - savings and loans

BayBanks, Inc.
175 Federal St.
Boston, MA 02110
Phone: 617-482-1040 Fax: —
CEO: William M. Crozier, Jr.
CFO: Michael W. Vasily
1992 Sales: $911 million Employees: 5,531
Symbol: BBNK Exchange: NASDAQ
Industry: Banks - Northeast

Bayou Steel Corp.
River Rd.
LaPlace, LA 70068
Phone: 504-652-4900 Fax: 504-652-8950
CEO: Howard M. Meyers
CFO: Howard M. Meyers
1991 Sales: $131 million Employees: 497
Symbol: BYX Exchange: AMEX
Industry: Steel - production

Bayport Restaurant Group, Inc.
10800 Biscayne Blvd., Ste. 500
Miami, FL 33161
Phone: 305-895-9505 Fax: 305-891-2271
CEO: William D. Korenbaum
CFO: Lawrence E. Smith
1991 Sales: $23 million Employees: 555
Symbol: PORT Exchange: NASDAQ
Industry: Retail - food & restaurants

BB&T Financial Corp.
223 W. Nash St.
Wilson, NC 27893
Phone: 919-399-4291 Fax: 919-399-4260
CEO: John A. Allison
CFO: Scott E. Reed
1991 Sales: $594 million Employees: 3,280
Symbol: BBTF Exchange: NASDAQ
Industry: Banks - Southeast

BE Aerospace, Inc.
1601 E. Chestnut Ave.
Santa Ana, CA 92701
Phone: 714-835-6575 Fax: 714-543-7790
CEO: Amin J. Khoury
CFO: Alex Hamid
1991 Sales: $24 million Employees: 155
Symbol: BEAV Exchange: NASDAQ
Industry: Aerospace - aircraft equipment

BE&K Inc.
2000 International Park Dr.
Birmingham, AL 35243
Phone: 205-969-3600 Fax: 205-972-6300
CEO: Theodore C. Kennedy
CFO: Clyde Smith
1991 Sales: $570 million Employees: 7,011
Ownership: Privately held
Industry: Construction - engineering & maintenance

Bear Stearns Companies Inc., The
245 Park Ave.
New York, NY 10167
Phone: 212-272-2000 Fax: 212-272-3105
CEO: Alan C. Greenberg
CFO: William J. Montgoris
1992 Sales: $2,617 million Employees: 5,873
Symbol: BSC Exchange: NYSE
Industry: Financial - investment bankers

Beard Oil Co.
5600 N. May Ave.
Oklahoma City, OK 73112
Phone: 405-842-2333 Fax: 405-842-9901
CEO: W. M. Beard
CFO: John A. Mason
1991 Sales: $64 million Employees: 476
Symbol: BOC Exchange: AMEX
Industry: Oil & gas - US exploration & production

Bearings, Inc.
3600 Euclid Ave.
Cleveland, OH 44115
Phone: 216-881-2838 Fax: 216-881-8988
CEO: John C. Dannemiller
CFO: Raymond E. Smiley
1992 Sales: $820 million Employees: 4,050
Symbol: BER Exchange: NYSE
Industry: Metal products - distribution

BeautiControl Cosmetics, Inc.
2121 Midway Rd.
Carrollton, TX 75006
Phone: 214-458-0601 Fax: 214-960-7923
CEO: Richard W. Heath
CFO: Vicki S. Miller
1991 Sales: $58 million Employees: 287
Symbol: BUTI Exchange: NASDAQ
Industry: Cosmetics & toiletries

indicates company is in *Hoover's Handbook of American Business.*

indicates company is in *Hoover's Handbook of World Business;* sales and employee numbers are for parent company.

Bechtel Group, Inc.
Fifty Beale St.
San Francisco, CA 94105
Phone: 415-768-1234 Fax: 415-768-9038
CEO: Riley P. Bechtel
CFO: V. Paul Unruh
1991 Sales: $7,526 million Employees: 20,479
Ownership: Privately held
Industry: Construction services - heavy, engineering, environmental

Beckman Instruments, Inc.
2500 Harbor Blvd.
Fullerton, CA 92635
Phone: 714-871-4848 Fax: 714-773-8283
CEO: Louis T. Rosso
CFO: George F. Kilmain
1992 Sales: $909 million Employees: 6,883
Symbol: BEC Exchange: NYSE
Industry: Medical instruments

Becton, Dickinson and Co.
1 Becton Dr.
Franklin Lakes, NJ 07417
Phone: 201-847-6800 Fax: 201-847-6475
CEO: Raymond V. Gilmartin
CFO: Robert A. Reynolds
1992 Sales: $2,425 million Employees: 18,600
Symbol: BDX Exchange: NYSE
Industry: Medical & dental supplies

Bed Bath & Beyond, Inc.
715 Morris Ave.
Springfield, NJ 07061
Phone: 201-379-1520 Fax: —
CEO: Warren Eisenberg
CFO: Richard D. Falcone
1992 Sales: $168 million Employees: 1,600
Symbol: BBBY Exchange: NASDAQ
Industry: Retail - home furnishings

Beeba's Creations, Inc.
9220 Activity Rd.
San Diego, CA 92126
Phone: 619-549-2922 Fax: 619-549-6857
CEO: Steven P. Wyandt
CFO: Thomas P. Baumann
1991 Sales: $132 million Employees: 404
Symbol: BEBA Exchange: NASDAQ
Industry: Textiles - apparel

BeefAmerica Inc.
5600 Harry Anderson Ave.
Omaha, NE 68137
Phone: 402-896-2400 Fax: 402-896-9074
CEO: Joseph Amore
CFO: Richard Grover
1991 Sales: $1,000 million Employees: 2,500
Ownership: Privately held
Industry: Food - meat products

BEI Electronics, Inc.
One Post St., Ste. 2500
San Francisco, CA 94104
Phone: 415-956-4477 Fax: 415-956-5564
CEO: Peter G. Paraskos
CFO: Lawrence W. Parrish
1992 Sales: $156 million Employees: 1,454
Symbol: BEII Exchange: NASDAQ
Industry: Electronics - military

BEI Holdings, Ltd.
2957 Clairmont Rd., Ste. 500
Atlanta, GA 30329
Phone: 404-315-6060 Fax: 404-762-1414
CEO: Gerald E. Eickhoff
CFO: Charles C. Ray, Jr.
1991 Sales: $41 million Employees: 432
Symbol: BEIH Exchange: NASDAQ
Industry: Business services - management consulting

Bel Fuse Inc.
198 Van Vorst St.
Jersey City, NJ 07302
Phone: 201-432-0463 Fax: 201-432-9542
CEO: Elliot Bernstein
CFO: Daniel Bernstein
1991 Sales: $37 million Employees: 676
Symbol: BELF Exchange: NASDAQ
Industry: Electrical components

Belding Heminway Co., Inc.
1430 Broadway
New York, NY 10018
Phone: 212-944-6040 Fax: 212-869-1029
CEO: Richard D. Hausman
CFO: Ronald V. Kaplan
1991 Sales: $141 million Employees: 1,375
Symbol: BHY Exchange: NYSE
Industry: Textiles - mill products

Belk Stores Services Inc.
2801 West Tyvola Rd.
Charlotte, NC 28217
Phone: 704-357-1000 Fax: 704-357-1876
CEO: John M. Belk
CFO: Russell Solt
1991 Sales: $1,700 million Employees: 19,200
Ownership: Privately held
Industry: Retail - regional department stores

Bell Atlantic Corp.
1717 Arch St.
Philadelphia, PA 19103
Phone: 215-963-6000 Fax: 215-963-6470
CEO: Raymond W. Smith
CFO: William O. Albertini
1992 Sales: $12,647 million Employees: 75,700
Symbol: BEL Exchange: NYSE
Industry: Utility - telephone

Bell Bancorp, Inc.
79 W. Monroe St.
Chicago, IL 60603
Phone: 312-346-1000 Fax: —
CEO: Edmond H. Shanahan
CFO: Kenneth C. Wagner
1992 Sales: $169 million Employees: 350
Symbol: BELL Exchange: NASDAQ
Industry: Banks - money center

Bell & Howell
5215 Old Orchard Rd.
Skokie, IL 60077
Phone: 708-470-7100 Fax: 708-470-9425
CEO: William J. White
CFO: Nils A. Johansson
1992 Sales: $670 million Employees: 5,670
Ownership: Privately held
Industry: Diversified operations - publishing, information systems, mail handling equipment

Bell Industries, Inc.
11812 San Vicente Blvd.
Los Angeles, CA 90049
Phone: 310-826-6778 Fax: 310-447-3265
CEO: Theodore Williams
CFO: Tracy A. Edwards
1992 Sales: $414 million Employees: 1,600
Symbol: BI Exchange: NYSE
Industry: Electronics - parts distribution

Bell Sports Corp.
Route 136 East
Rantoul, IL 61866
Phone: 217-893-9300 Fax: 217-892-8727
CEO: Terry G. Lee
CFO: Howard A. Kosick
1992 Sales: $64 million Employees: 637
Symbol: BSPT Exchange: NASDAQ
Industry: Leisure & recreational products

BellSouth Corp.
1155 Peachtree St. NE
Atlanta, GA 30367
Phone: 404-249-2000 Fax: 404-249-5599
CEO: John L. Clendenin
CFO: Harvey R. Holding
1992 Sales: $15,202 million Employees: 96,084
Symbol: BLS Exchange: NYSE
Industry: Utility - telephone

Belmac Corp.
4830 W. Kennedy Blvd.
Tampa, FL 33609
Phone: 813-286-4401 Fax: —
CEO: J. Rossignol
CFO: John P. Warnick
1992 Sales: — Employees: 24
Symbol: BLM Exchange: AMEX
Industry: Drugs

Bemis Co., Inc.
222 S. 9th St., Ste. 2300
Minneapolis, MN 55402
Phone: 612-375-3000 Fax: 612-376-3180
CEO: John H. Roe
CFO: Benjamin R. Field III
1992 Sales: $1,181 million Employees: 7,796
Symbol: BMS Exchange: NYSE
Industry: Containers - paper & plastic

Ben E. Keith
600 E. Ninth St.
Ft. Worth, TX 76102
Phone: 817-332-9171 Fax: 817-332-3471
CEO: Robert Hallam
CFO: Mel Cockrell
1991 Sales: $450 million Employees: 1,350
Ownership: Privately held
Industry: Food & beverage - wholesale

Ben Franklin Retail Stores, Inc.
500 E. North Ave.
Carol Stream, IL 60188
Phone: 708-462-6100 Fax: 708-462-6216
CEO: Dale D. Ward
CFO: John B. Menser
1992 Sales: $341 million Employees: 1,018
Symbol: BFRS Exchange: NASDAQ
Industry: Retail - discount & variety

Ben & Jerry's Homemade, Inc.
Route 100
Waterbury, VT 05676
Phone: 802-244-5641 Fax: 806-244-8018
CEO: Bennett R. Cohen
CFO: Frances Rathke
1991 Sales: $97 million Employees: 371
Symbol: BJICA Exchange: NASDAQ
Industry: Food - premium ice cream

Benchmark Electronics, Inc.
802 W. Brazos Park Dr.
Clute, TX 77531
Phone: 409-265-0991 Fax: —
CEO: Donald E. Nigbor
CFO: Cary T. Fu
1991 Sales: $33 million Employees: 307
Symbol: BHE Exchange: AMEX
Industry: Electical components - printed circuit boards

Bendco/Bending & Coiling Co., Inc.
801 Houston Ave.
Pasadena, TX 77502
Phone: 713-473-1557 Fax: 713-473-1882
CEO: Jim Friery
CFO: W. Jay Ward
1991 Sales: $4.3 million Employees: 53
Ownership: Privately held
Industry: Pipes & pressure vessels

indicates company is in *Hoover's Handbook of American Business.*

indicates company is in *Hoover's Handbook of World Business*; sales and employee numbers are for parent company.

Beneficial Corp.
400 Bellevue Pkwy.
Wilmington, DE 19809
Phone: 302-798-0800 Fax: 302-792-4747
CEO: Finn M. W. Caspersen
CFO: Andrew C. Halvorsen
1992 Sales: $1,819 million Employees: 8,100
Symbol: BNL Exchange: NYSE
Industry: Financial - consumer loans

Benetton USA Corp.
55 E. 59th St., 24th Fl.
New York, NY 10022
Phone: 212-593-0290 Fax: 212-371-1438
CEO: Carlo Tunioli
CFO: —
1991 Sales: $1,983 million Employees: 3,600
Parent: Benetton Group SpA
Industry: Apparel

Benihana National Corp.
8685 NW 53rd Terrace, Ste. 201
Miami, FL 33166
Phone: 305-593-0770 Fax: 305-592-6371
CEO: Rocky H. Aoki
CFO: Anthony J. Carvalho
1992 Sales: $37 million Employees: 906
Symbol: BNHN Exchange: NASDAQ
Industry: Retail - food & restaurants

Benjamin Moore & Co.
51 Chestnut Ridge Rd.
Montvale, NJ 07645
Phone: 201-573-9600 Fax: 201-573-0046
CEO: Richard Roob
CFO: William Fritz
1991 Sales: $463 million Employees: 1,925
Ownership: Privately held
Industry: Paints & allied products

Benson Eyecare Corp.
135 E. 57th St.
New York, NY 10022
Phone: 212-754-4849 Fax: 212-754-5806
CEO: Martin Franklin
CFO: Ian Ashken
1992 Sales: $0.1 million Employees: 2
Symbol: EB Exchange: AMEX
Industry: Retail - prescription eyecare products

Benton Oil and Gas Co.
2151 Alessandro Dr., Ste. 120
Ventura, CA 93001
Phone: 805-653-6061 Fax: 805-653-5684
CEO: Alex E. Benton
CFO: David H. Pratt
1991 Sales: $11 million Employees: 30
Symbol: BTN Exchange: AMEX
Industry: Oil & gas - US exploration & production

Bergen Brunswig Corp.
4000 Metropolitan Dr.
Orange, CA 92668
Phone: 714-385-4000 Fax: 714-385-1442
CEO: Robert E. Martini
CFO: George E. Reinhardt, Jr.
1992 Sales: $5,499 million Employees: 3,700
Symbol: BBC Exchange: AMEX
Industry: Drugs & sundries - wholesale

Bergstrom Capital Corp.
505 Madison St., Ste. 220
Seattle, WA 98104
Phone: 206-623-7302 Fax: —
CEO: William L. McQueen
CFO: William L. McQueen
1992 Sales: — Employees: —
Symbol: BEM Exchange: AMEX
Industry: Financial - investment management

Berkshire Gas Co.
115 Cheshire Rd.
Pittsfield, MA 01201
Phone: 413-442-1511 Fax: 413-443-0546
CEO: Scott S. Robinson
CFO: Michael J. Marrone
1992 Sales: $48 million Employees: 178
Symbol: BGAS Exchange: NASDAQ
Industry: Utility - gas distribution

Berkshire Hathaway Inc.
1440 Kiewit Plaza
Omaha, NE 68131
Phone: 402-346-1400 Fax: 402-536-3030
CEO: Warren E. Buffett
CFO: J. Verne McKenzie
1991 Sales: $3,106 million Employees: 22,000
Symbol: BRK Exchange: NYSE
Industry: Diversified operations - insurance, candy, home furnishings & cleaning systems

Berlitz International, Inc.
293 Wall St.
Princeton, NJ 08540
Phone: 609-924-8500 Fax: 609-924-1912
CEO: Robert Maxwell
CFO: Henry D. James
1991 Sales: $260 million Employees: 3,464
Symbol: BTZ Exchange: NYSE
Industry: Schools - language

Bernard Chaus, Inc.
1410 Broadway
New York, NY 10018
Phone: 212-354-1280 Fax: 212-302-8713
CEO: Josephine Chaus
CFO: Anthony M. Pisano
1991 Sales: $232 million Employees: 754
Symbol: CHS Exchange: NYSE
Industry: Textiles - apparel

Berry Petroleum Co.
28700 Hovey Hills Rd.
Taft, CA 93268
Phone: 805-769-8811 Fax: 805-769-8960
CEO: Harvey L. Bryant
CFO: Jerry V. Hoffman
1991 Sales: $77 million Employees: 119
Symbol: BRY Exchange: NYSE
Industry: Oil & gas - US exploration & production

Bertelsmann, Inc.
666 Fifth Ave.
New York, NY 10103
Phone: 212-391-0143 Fax: 212-391-1874
CEO: Peter Olson
CFO: —
1991 Sales: $9,528 million Employees: 45,110
Parent: Bertelsmann AG
Industry: Publishing - books; music video, broadcasting

Bertucci's, Inc.
60 Cummings Park
Woburn, MA 01801
Phone: 617-935-9700 Fax: 617-932-8173
CEO: Joseph Crugnale
CFO: Norman S. Mallett
1992 Sales: $51 million Employees: 1,628
Symbol: BERT Exchange: NASDAQ
Industry: Retail - food & restaurants

Best Buy Co., Inc.
4400 W. 78th St.
Minneapolis, MN 55435
Phone: 612-896-2300 Fax: 612-896-2422
CEO: Richard M. Schulze
CFO: Allen U. Lenzmeier
1992 Sales: $1,346 million Employees: 5,500
Symbol: BBY Exchange: NYSE
Industry: Retail - consumer electronics

Best Products Co. Inc.
1400 Best Plaza
Richmond, VA 23227
Phone: 804-261-2000 Fax: 804-261-2250
CEO: Stewart Kasen
CFO: Kevin McNamara
1991 Sales: $1,440 million Employees: 5,000
Ownership: Privately held
Industry: Retail - catalog showrooms; general merchandise & jewelry

Bestop, Inc.
2100 W. Midway Blvd.
Broomfield, CO 80038
Phone: 303-465-1755 Fax: —
CEO: Richard E. Sabourin
CFO: Ronald C. Fox
1991 Sales: $31 million Employees: 446
Symbol: BTOP Exchange: NASDAQ
Industry: Automotive & trucking - original equipment

BET Holdings, Inc.
1232 31st St. NW
Washington, DC 20007
Phone: 202-337-5260 Fax: 202-342-7882
CEO: Robert L. Johnson
CFO: Alan H. Nichols, Jr.
1992 Sales: $62 million Employees: 313
Symbol: BTV Exchange: NYSE
Industry: Broadcasting - radio & TV

Bethlehem Corp.
25th & Lennox Streets
Easton, PA 18044
Phone: 215-258-7111 Fax: —
CEO: James L. Leuthe
CFO: Niel C. Cavanaugh
1991 Sales: $13 million Employees: 151
Symbol: BET Exchange: AMEX
Industry: Machinery - general industrial

Bethlehem Steel Corp.
1170 8th Ave.
Bethlehem, PA 18016
Phone: 215-694-2424 Fax: 215-694-1509
CEO: Curtis H. Barnette
CFO: Gary L. Millenbruch
1992 Sales: $4,008 million Employees: 26,400
Symbol: BS Exchange: NYSE
Industry: Steel - production

Betz Laboratories, Inc.
4636 Somerton Rd.
Trevose, PA 19053
Phone: 215-355-3300 Fax: 215-355-2869
CEO: John F. McCaughan
CFO: R. Dale Voncanon
1992 Sales: $707 million Employees: 3,980
Symbol: BETZ Exchange: NASDAQ
Industry: Chemicals - specialty

Beverly Enterprises, Inc.
1200 S. Waldron Rd., Ste. 155
Ft. Smith, AR 72903
Phone: 501-452-6712 Fax: 501-452-5131
CEO: David R. Banks
CFO: Andre C. Dimitriadis
1992 Sales: $2,597 million Employees: 93,000
Symbol: BEV Exchange: NYSE
Industry: Nursing homes

BF Enterprises, Inc.
100 Bush St., Ste. 1700
San Francisco, CA 94104
Phone: 415-989-6580 Fax: 415-788-5756
CEO: Brian P. Burns
CFO: Paul Woodbury
1991 Sales: $0.6 million Employees: 9
Symbol: BFEN Exchange: NASDAQ
Industry: Real estate development

indicates company is in *Hoover's Handbook of American Business.*

indicates company is in *Hoover's Handbook of World Business;* sales and employee numbers are for parent company.

BF Goodrich Co.
3925 Embassy Pkwy.
Akron, OH 44333
Phone: 216-374-2000 Fax: 216-374-2333
CEO: John D. Ong
CFO: D. Lee Tobler
1992 Sales: $2,526 million Employees: 14,415
Symbol: GR Exchange: NYSE
Industry: Chemicals - diversified

BFS Bankorp, Inc.
110 William St.
New York, NY 10038
Phone: 212-227-4040 Fax: —
CEO: James A. Randall
CFO: Louis J. Orgera
1991 Sales: $46 million Employees: 133
Symbol: BFSI Exchange: NASDAQ
Industry: Banks - money center

BGS Systems, Inc.
128 Technology Center
Waltham, MA 02254
Phone: 617-891-0000 Fax: 617-890-0000
CEO: Harold S. Schwenk, Jr.
CFO: Jeffrey P. Buzen
1991 Sales: $25 million Employees: 160
Symbol: BGSS Exchange: NASDAQ
Industry: Computers - standard software

BHA Group, Inc.
8800 E. 63rd St.
Kansas City, MO 64133
Phone: 816-356-8400 Fax: 816-353-1873
CEO: Michael T. Zak
CFO: James C. King
1991 Sales: $70 million Employees: 541
Symbol: BHAGA Exchange: NASDAQ
Industry: Pollution control equipment & services

BHC Communications, Inc.
600 Madison Ave.
New York, NY 10022
Phone: 212-421-0200 Fax: 212-935-8462
CEO: Herbert J. Siegel
CFO: Laurence M. Kashdin
1991 Sales: $263 million Employees: 828
Symbol: BHC Exchange: AMEX
Industry: Broadcasting - radio & TV

BHP Minerals
550 California St.
San Francisco, CA 94104
Phone: 415-774-2030 Fax: 415-919-4746
CEO: Jerry Ellis
CFO: —
1991 Sales: $11,853 million Employees: 51,000
Parent: The Broken Hill Proprietary Co. Ltd.
Industry: Steel production, petroleum & minerals

BI Inc.
6400 Lookout Rd.
Boulder, CO 80301
Phone: 303-530-2911 Fax: —
CEO: David J. Hunter
CFO: Jeffrey J. Hiller
1992 Sales: $17 million Employees: 223
Symbol: BIAC Exchange: NASDAQ
Industry: Telecommunications equipment

BIC Corp.
500 BIC Dr.
Milford, CT 06460
Phone: 203-783-2000 Fax: 203-783-2081
CEO: Bruno Bich
CFO: Alexander Alexiades
1991 Sales: $369 million Employees: 2,300
Symbol: BIC Exchange: NYSE
Industry: Office & art materials

Big B, Inc.
2600 Morgan Rd.
Bessemer, AL 35023
Phone: 205-424-3421 Fax: 205-426-8748
CEO: Joseph S. Bruno
CFO: Michael J. Tortorice
1991 Sales: $488 million Employees: 4,000
Symbol: BIGB Exchange: NASDAQ
Industry: Retail - drug stores

Big O Tires, Inc.
11755 E. Peakview Ave.
Englewood, CO 80111
Phone: 303-790-2800 Fax: 303-790-0225
CEO: Steven P. Cloward
CFO: John A. Adams
1991 Sales: $114 million Employees: 277
Symbol: BIGO Exchange: NASDAQ
Industry: Retail - tires & automotive services

Big V Supermarkets Inc.
176 N. Main St.
Florida, NY 10921
Phone: 914-651-4411 Fax: 914-651-7048
CEO: David G. Bronstein
CFO: Gary Koppele
1991 Sales: $675 million Employees: 4,900
Ownership: Privately held
Industry: Retail - supermarkets

Big Y Foods
280 Chestnut St.
Springfield, MA 01102
Phone: 413-784-0600 Fax: 413-732-8475
CEO: Donald H. D'Amour
CFO: Robert B. Antrasian
1991 Sales: $460 million Employees: 4,000
Ownership: Privately held
Industry: Retail - supermarkets

Bike Pro USA
3701 W. Roanoke Ave., Ste. A
Phoenix, AZ 85009
Phone: 602-272-3588 Fax: 800-442-8900
CEO: John D. Alig
CFO: John D. Alig
1991 Sales: $1 million Employees: 26
Ownership: Privately held
Industry: Leisure & recreational products - bicycle packs & bags

Binary Arts Corporation
5601 Vine St.
Alexandria, VA 22310
Phone: 703-971-3401 Fax: 703-971-3403
CEO: Bill Ritchie
CFO: Jill Paul
1991 Sales: $1 million Employees: 5
Ownership: Privately held
Industry: Puzzles, mazes & games

Bindley Western Industries, Inc.
4212 W. 71st St.
Indianapolis, IN 46268
Phone: 317-298-9890 Fax: 317-297-5372
CEO: William E. Bindley
CFO: Thomas J. Salentine
1991 Sales: $2,393 million Employees: 464
Symbol: BIND Exchange: NASDAQ
Industry: Drugs & sundries - wholesale

Binks Manufacturing Co.
9201 W. Belmont Ave.
Franklin Park, IL 60131
Phone: 708-671-3000 Fax: 708-671-6489
CEO: Burke B. Roche
CFO: Burke B. Roche
1991 Sales: $222 million Employees: 1,660
Symbol: BIN Exchange: AMEX
Industry: Paints & allied products

Bio-logic Systems Corp.
One Bio-logic Plaza
Mundelein, IL 60060
Phone: 708-949-5200 Fax: —
CEO: Gabriel Raviv
CFO: Charles Z. Weingarten
1992 Sales: $10.1 million Employees: 86
Symbol: BLSC Exchange: NASDAQ
Industry: Medical instruments

Bio-Rad Laboratories, Inc.
1000 Alfred Nobel Dr.
Hercules, CA 94547
Phone: 510-724-7000 Fax: 510-724-3167
CEO: David Schwartz
CFO: James L. Viglienzone
1991 Sales: $311 million Employees: 2,400
Symbol: BIOA Exchange: AMEX
Industry: Biomedical & genetic products

Bio-Technology General Corp.
1250 Broadway
New York, NY 10001
Phone: 212-239-0450 Fax: —
CEO: Sim Fass
CFO: Ron Bendavid
1991 Sales: $4.7 million Employees: 129
Symbol: BTGC Exchange: NASDAQ
Industry: Biomedical & genetic products

Biocircuits Corp.
1450 Rollins Rd.
Burlingame, CA 94010
Phone: 415-343-1961 Fax: —
CEO: John Kaiser
CFO: Donald Hawthorne
1992 Sales: — Employees: 39
Symbol: BIOC Exchange: NASDAQ
Industry: Biomedical & genetic products

Biocraft Laboratories, Inc.
92 Rt. 46
Elmwood Park, NJ 07407
Phone: 201-796-3434 Fax: 201-796-1434
CEO: Harold Snyder
CFO: Steven J. Sklar
1992 Sales: $92 million Employees: 725
Symbol: BCL Exchange: NYSE
Industry: Drugs - generic

Biogen, Inc.
14 Cambridge Center
Cambridge, MA 02142
Phone: 617-252-9200 Fax: 617-252-9296
CEO: James L. Vincent
CFO: Kenneth M. Bate
1991 Sales: $70 million Employees: 331
Symbol: BGEN Exchange: NASDAQ
Industry: Biomedical & genetic products

Biomagnetic Technologies, Inc.
9727 Pacific Heights Blvd.
San Diego, CA 92121
Phone: 619-453-6300 Fax: 619-453-4913
CEO: Stephen O. James
CFO: William L. Stephan
1991 Sales: $9.2 million Employees: 136
Symbol: BTIX Exchange: NASDAQ
Industry: Medical instruments

Biomatrix, Inc.
65 Railroad Ave.
Ridgefield, NJ 07657
Phone: 201-945-9550 Fax: 201-945-0363
CEO: Endre A. Balazs
CFO: George A. Oram, Jr.
1991 Sales: $2.7 million Employees: 60
Symbol: BIOX Exchange: NASDAQ
Industry: Biomedical & genetic products

BioMedical Waste Systems, Inc.
200 High St.
Boston, MA 02110
Phone: 617-556-4033 Fax: —
CEO: Gene J. Frisco
CFO: R. Michael Rodgers
1992 Sales: $12 million Employees: 220
Symbol: BWSI Exchange: NASDAQ
Industry: Medical waste disposal

Biomet, Inc.
Airport Industrial Park
Warsaw, IN 46580
Phone: 219-267-6639 Fax: 219-267-8137
CEO: Dane A. Miller
CFO: Gregory D. Hartman
1992 Sales: $275 million Employees: 1,606
Symbol: BMET Exchange: NASDAQ
Industry: Medical products - orthopedic

Biopharmaceutics, Inc.
990 Station Rd.
Bellport, NY 11713
Phone: 516-286-5900 Fax: 516-286-5803
CEO: Edward Fine
CFO: Marc Feldman
1991 Sales: $6.2 million Employees: —
Symbol: BPH Exchange: AMEX
Industry: Drugs

Bioplasty, Inc.
1385 Centennial Dr.
St. Paul, MN 55113
Phone: 612-636-4112 Fax: 612-633-3204
CEO: Arthur A. Beisang
CFO: Donald A. Major
1991 Sales: $12 million Employees: 82
Symbol: BIOP Exchange: NASDAQ
Industry: Medical products for plastic surgery

BioSpecifics Technologies Corp.
35 Wilbur St.
Lynbrook, NY 11563
Phone: 516-593-7000 Fax: —
CEO: Edwin H. Wegman
CFO: Thomas L. Wegman
1991 Sales: $4.5 million Employees: 44
Symbol: BSTC Exchange: NASDAQ
Industry: Drugs

Biospherics Inc.
12051 Indian Creek Court
Beltsville, MD 20705
Phone: 301-369-3900 Fax: 301-725-4908
CEO: Gilbert V. Levin
CFO: Gilbert V. Levin
1991 Sales: $15 million Employees: 492
Symbol: BINC Exchange: NASDAQ
Industry: Environmental engineering services

Biosym Technologies, Inc.
9685 Scranton Rd.
San Diego, CA 92121
Phone: 619-458-9990 Fax: 619-458-0136
CEO: Kevin Roberts
CFO: Todd Schmidt
1991 Sales: $30 million Employees: 240
Ownership: Privately held
Industry: Computers - molecular-modeling software

Biosys
1057 E. Meadow Circle
Palo Alto, CA 94303
Phone: 415-856-9500 Fax: —
CEO: Venkatrao S. Sohoni
CFO: Bruce G. Fielding, Jr.
1991 Sales: $1.1 million Employees: 50
Symbol: BIOS Exchange: NASDAQ
Industry: Chemicals - specialty

BioTechnica International, Inc.
7300 W. 110th St., Ste. 540
Overland Park, KS 66210
Phone: 913-661-0611 Fax: —
CEO: Charles H. Baker
CFO: Stephen P. Hall
1991 Sales: $15 million Employees: 176
Symbol: BIOT Exchange: NASDAQ
Industry: Biomedical & genetic products

BioWhittaker, Inc.
8830 Biggs Ford Rd.
Walkersville, MD 21793
Phone: 301-898-7025 Fax: 301-845-8291
CEO: J. F. Alibrandi
CFO: Philip L. Rohrer, Jr.
1991 Sales: $41 million Employees: 400
Symbol: BWI Exchange: NYSE
Industry: Medical products - diagnostic products

Bird Corp.
One Dedham Place, Ste. 1
Dedham, MA 02026
Phone: 617-461-1414 Fax: 617-461-1618
CEO: George J. Haufler
CFO: William A. Krivsky
1991 Sales: $151 million Employees: 804
Symbol: BIRD Exchange: NASDAQ
Industry: Building products - misc.

Bird Medical Technologies, Inc.
3101 E. Allejo Rd.
Palm Springs, CA 92262
Phone: 619-778-7200 Fax: 619-778-7269
CEO: Thomas E. Winter
CFO: Patrick E. Thomas
1991 Sales: $37 million Employees: 443
Symbol: BMTI Exchange: NASDAQ
Industry: Medical products - respiratory care & infection control products

Birmingham Steel Corp.
3000 Riverchase Galleria
Birmingham, AL 35244
Phone: 619-778-7200 Fax: —
CEO: James A. Todd, Jr.
CFO: Dennis R. Plyler
1992 Sales: $418 million Employees: —
Symbol: BIR Exchange: NYSE
Industry: Steel - production

Birtcher Medical Systems, Inc.
4501 N. Arden Dr.
El Monte, CA 91731
Phone: 714-753-9400 Fax: 714-753-9171
CEO: William E. Maya
CFO: Daniel P. Whelan
1992 Sales: $52 million Employees: 185
Symbol: BIRT Exchange: NASDAQ
Industry: Medical instruments

Biscayne Holdings, Inc.
2665 S. Bayshore Dr., Ste. 801
Coconut Grove, FL 33133
Phone: 305-858-2200 Fax: 305-285-0102
CEO: John W. Partridge
CFO: Peter Vandenberg, Jr.
1991 Sales: $53 million Employees: 490
Symbol: BHA Exchange: AMEX
Industry: Textiles - apparel

BISYS Group, Inc.
150 Clove Rd.
Little Falls, NJ 07424
Phone: 201-812-8600 Fax: —
CEO: L. J. Mangum
CFO: R. J. McMullan
1992 Sales: $74 million Employees: 625
Symbol: BSYS Exchange: NASDAQ
Industry: Business services

BitWise Designs Inc.
Rotterdam Industrial Park, Bldg. 50
Schenectady, NY 12306
Phone: 518-356-9750 Fax: 518-356-9749
CEO: John Botti
CFO: Dennis Bunt
1991 Sales: $2.9 million Employees: 10
Ownership: Privately held
Industry: Computers - workstations for imaging marketplace

BJ Services Co.
5500 NW Central Dr.
Houston, TX 77092
Phone: 713-462-4239 Fax: 713-895-5851
CEO: J. W. Stewart
CFO: Michael McShane
1991 Sales: $390 million Employees: 2,632
Symbol: BJS Exchange: NYSE
Industry: Oil & gas - field services

Black & Decker Corp., The
701 E. Joppa Rd.
Towson, MD 21204
Phone: 410-716-3900 Fax: 410-716-2933
CEO: Nolan D. Archibald
CFO: Stephen F. Page
1992 Sales: $4,780 million Employees: 38,600
Symbol: BDK Exchange: NYSE
Industry: Diversified operations - power tools, small appliances & hardware

Black Hills Corp.
625 Ninth St.
Rapid City, SD 57701
Phone: 605-348-1700 Fax: 605-342-2464
CEO: Daniel P. Landguth
CFO: Dale E. Clement
1991 Sales: $133 million Employees: 460
Symbol: BKH Exchange: NYSE
Industry: Utility - electric power

Blair Corp.
220 Hickory St.
Warren, PA 16366
Phone: 814-723-3600 Fax: —
CEO: Murray K. McComas
CFO: Giles W. Schutte
1991 Sales: $509 million Employees: 2,200
Symbol: BL Exchange: AMEX
Industry: Retail - mail order & direct; apparel & home furnishings

Blessings Corp.
1 Crossroads Dr.
Bedminster, NJ 07921
Phone: 908-719-2300 Fax: 908-719-2060
CEO: Ivan E. Becker
CFO: James P. Luke
1991 Sales: $112 million Employees: 650
Symbol: BCO Exchange: AMEX
Industry: Diversified operations - plastic films, resin products, geriatric products

Bliss & Laughlin Industries Inc.
281 E. 155th St.
Harvey, IL 60426
Phone: 708-264-1800 Fax: —
CEO: Gregory H. Parker
CFO: George W. Fleck
1991 Sales: $114 million Employees: 419
Symbol: BLIS Exchange: NASDAQ
Industry: Steel - production

BLOC Development Corp.
800 Douglas Entrance
Coral Gables, FL 33134
Phone: 305-567-9931 Fax: 305-445-8370
CEO: Frank Millman
CFO: Samuel M. Waksman
1991 Sales: $43 million Employees: 290
Symbol: BDEV Exchange: NASDAQ
Industry: Computers - productivity & information management software

Block Drug Co., Inc.
257 Cornelison Ave.
Jersey City, NJ 07302
Phone: 201-434-3000 Fax: Ext. 357
CEO: Leonard Block
CFO: Thomas R. Block
1992 Sales: $563 million Employees: 3,301
Symbol: BLOCA Exchange: NASDAQ
Industry: Drugs

Blockbuster Entertainment Corp.
901 E. Las Olas Blvd.
Ft. Lauderdale, FL 33301
Phone: 305-524-8200 Fax: 305-462-4139
CEO: H. Wayne Huizenga
CFO: Steven R. Berrard
1992 Sales: $1,201 million Employees: 14,570
Symbol: BV Exchange: NYSE
Industry: Retail - video rentals

Bloomberg L. P.
499 Park Ave.
New York, NY 10022
Phone: 212-318-2000 Fax: 212-980-4585
CEO: Michael Bloomberg
CFO: —
1992 Sales: $240 million Employees: 860
Ownership: Privately held
Industry: On-line financial information

Blount, Inc.
4520 Executive Park Dr.
Montgomery, Al 36116
Phone: 205-244-4000 Fax: 205-271-8185
CEO: Winton M. Blount
CFO: Rodney W. Blakenship
1992 Sales: $709 million Employees: 4,700
Symbol: BLTA Exchange: AMEX
Industry: Machinery - general industrial

Blue Cross and Blue Shield Association
676 N. St. Clair St.
Chicago, IL 60611
Phone: 312-440-6000 Fax: 312-440-6609
CEO: Bernard R. Tresnowski
CFO: Frederick C. Cue
1991 Sales: $67,068 million Employees: 138,000
Ownership: Privately held
Industry: Insurance - accident & health

Blue Ridge Real Estate Co.
PO Box 707
Blakeslee, PA 18610
Phone: 717-443-8433 Fax: —
CEO: Robert J. Sule
CFO: Gary A. Smith
1992 Sales: $14 million Employees: 970
Symbol: BLRGZ Exchange: NASDAQ
Industry: Real estate operations

BMC Industries, Inc.
Two Appletree Square, 8011 34th Ave., Ste. 400
Minneapolis, MN 55425
Phone: 612-851-6000 Fax: 612-851-6050
CEO: Paul B. Burke
CFO: Merle D. Kerr
1991 Sales: $203 million Employees: 1,983
Symbol: BMC Exchange: NYSE
Industry: Medical & dental supplies

BMC Software, Inc.
One Sugar Creek Center Blvd., Ste. 320
Sugar Land, TX 77478
Phone: 713-240-8800 Fax: 713-242-6523
CEO: Max P. Watson, Jr.
CFO: David A. Farley
1992 Sales: $184 million Employees: 782
Symbol: BMCS Exchange: NASDAQ
Industry: Computers - software

BMC West Corp.
1475 Tyrell Lane
Boise, ID 83706
Phone: 208-338-1750 Fax: 208-338-4367
CEO: Donald S. Hendrickson
CFO: Ellis C. Goebel
1991 Sales: $219 million Employees: 1,125
Symbol: BMCW Exchange: NASDAQ
Industry: Building products - retail & wholesale

BMR Financial Group, Inc.
2302 Parklake Dr. NE
Atlanta, GA 30345
Phone: 404-938-8050 Fax: —
CEO: James L. Greene
CFO: Douglas G. Greene
1991 Sales: $30 million Employees: 197
Symbol: BMRG Exchange: NASDAQ
Industry: Financial - business services

BMW of North America, Inc.
PO Box 1227
Westwood, NJ 07675
Phone: 201-307-4000 Fax: 201-307-4004
CEO: Karl Gerlinger
CFO: —
1991 Sales: $19,631 million Employees: 74,385
Parent: Bayerische Motoren Werke AG
Industry: Automotive manufacturing

BNH Bancshares, Inc.
209 Church St.
New Haven, CT 06510
Phone: 203-498-3500 Fax: —
CEO: F. Patrick McFadden, Jr.
CFO: John F. Trentacosta
1991 Sales: $12 million Employees: 151
Symbol: BNHB Exchange: NASDAQ
Industry: Banks - Northeast

Boatmen's Bancshares, Inc.
800 Market St.
St. Louis, MO 63101
Phone: 314-466-6000 Fax: 314-466-4235
CEO: Andrew B. Craig III
CFO: James W. Kienker
1992 Sales: $2,001 million Employees: 9,124
Symbol: BOAT Exchange: NASDAQ
Industry: Banks - Midwest

Bob Evans Farms, Inc.
3776 S. High St.
Columbus, OH 43207
Phone: 614-491-2225 Fax: 614-492-4949
CEO: Daniel E. Evans
CFO: Keith P. Bradbury
1992 Sales: $606 million Employees: 18,000
Symbol: BOBE Exchange: NASDAQ
Industry: Retail - food & restaurants

Body Drama, Inc.
110 E. 9th St., Ste. B765
Los Angeles, CA 90079
Phone: 213-891-1214 Fax: —
CEO: Steven P. Wyandt
CFO: Thomas P. Baumann
1991 Sales: $27 million Employees: —
Symbol: BDRM Exchange: NASDAQ
Industry: Apparel

Boeing Co., The
7755 E. Marginal Way South
Seattle, WA 98108
Phone: 206-655-2121 Fax: 206-655-7004
CEO: Frank A. Shrontz
CFO: Boyd E. Givan
1992 Sales: $30,184 million Employees: 155,700
Symbol: BA Exchange: NYSE
Industry: Aerospace - aircraft equipment

Boise Cascade Corp.
One Jefferson Square
Boise, ID 83728
Phone: 208-384-6161 Fax: 208-384-7298
CEO: John B. Fery
CFO: Rex L. Dorman
1992 Sales: $3,716 million Employees: 19,619
Symbol: BCC Exchange: NYSE
Industry: Paper & paper products

Bolar Pharmaceutical Co., Inc.
33 Ralph Ave.
Copiague, NY 11726
Phone: 516-842-8383 Fax: 516-842-8630
CEO: Lawrence Raisfeld
CFO: David Genzler
1991 Sales: $7.3 million Employees: 106
Symbol: BLR Exchange: AMEX
Industry: Drugs - generic

Bolsa Chica Co.
Liberty Lane
Hampton, NH 03842
Phone: 603-926-5911 Fax: 603-929-2449
CEO: Michael D. Dingman
CFO: Paul M. Meister
1992 Sales: $37 million Employees: 30
Symbol: BLSA Exchange: NASDAQ
Industry: Real estate development

Bolt Beranek and Newman Inc.
70 Fawcett St.
Cambridge, MA 02138
Phone: 617-873-2000 Fax: 617-491-1496
CEO: Stephen R. Levy
CFO: Ralph A. Goldwasser
1992 Sales: $258 million Employees: 2,086
Symbol: BBN Exchange: NYSE
Industry: Engineering - R&D services

Bombay Company, Inc., The
550 Bailey, Ste. 700
Ft. Worth, TX 76107
Phone: 817-347-8200 Fax: 817-332-7066
CEO: Robert E. M. Nourse
CFO: James E. Herlihy
1992 Sales: $176 million Employees: 2,100
Symbol: BBA Exchange: AMEX
Industry: Retail - home furnishings

Bon-Ton Stores, Inc.
2801 E. Market St.
York, PA 17402
Phone: 717-757-7660 Fax: 717-751-3198
CEO: M. Thomas Grumbacher
CFO: Carlos E. Alberini
1991 Sales: $308 million Employees: 4,700
Symbol: BONT Exchange: NASDAQ
Industry: Retail - regional department stores

Boole & Babbage, Inc.
510 Oakmead Pkwy.
Sunnyvale, CA 94086
Phone: 408-735-9550 Fax: 408-730-0558
CEO: Paul E. Newton
CFO: Arthur F. Knapp
1991 Sales: $99 million Employees: 643
Symbol: BOOL Exchange: NASDAQ
Industry: Computers - standard, modular software

Boonton Electronics Corp.
791 Route 10
Randolph, NJ 07869
Phone: 201-584-1077 Fax: 201-584-3037
CEO: Joseph G. Gillespie
CFO: John E. Titterton
1991 Sales: $7.7 million Employees: 92
Symbol: BOON Exchange: NASDAQ
Industry: Electronics - measuring instruments

Booz, Allen & Hamilton
101 Park Ave.
New York, NY 10178
Phone: 212-697-1900 Fax: 212-697-2628
CEO: William Stasior
CFO: Edward H. Schwallie
1991 Sales: $530 million Employees: 3,200
Ownership: Privately held
Industry: Business services - management & technology consulting

Borden Chemicals and Plastics L.P.
Hwy. 73
Geismar, LA 70734
Phone: 504-387-5101 Fax: —
CEO: Joseph M. Saggese
CFO: David A. Kelly
1991 Sales: $410 million Employees: 700
Symbol: BCP Exchange: NYSE
Industry: Chemicals - diversified

Borden, Inc.
277 Park Ave.
New York, NY 10172
Phone: 212-573-4000 Fax: 212-371-2659
CEO: Anthony S. D'Amato
CFO: Lawrence O. Doza
1992 Sales: $7,143 million Employees: 44,400
Symbol: BN Exchange: NYSE
Industry: Food - dairy products, pasta & snacks

Border Fuel Supply
6400 S. Fiddler's Green Circle, Ste. 800
Englewood, CO 80111
Phone: 303-770-1600 Fax: 303-770-1604
CEO: Steve Arrington
CFO: Steve Arrington
1990 Sales: $700 million Employees: 25
Ownership: Privately held
Industry: Oil & marketing

Borg-Warner Automotive, Inc.
200 S. Michigan Ave.
Chicago, IL 60604
Phone: 312-322-8500 Fax: 312-322-8849
CEO: Siegfried P. Adler
CFO: —
1992 Sales: — Employees: —
Ownership: Privately held
Industry: Automotive components & systems

Borg-Warner Security Corporation
200 S. Michigan Ave.
Chicago, IL 60604
Phone: 312-322-8500 Fax: 312-322-8849
CEO: Donald C. Truscht
CFO: Neal F. Farrell
1992 Sales: $1,621 million Employees: 85,500
Symbol: BOR Exchange: NYSE
Industry: Guard, alarm, armored transportation & courier services

Borland International, Inc.
1800 Green Hills Rd.
Scotts Valley, CA 95066
Phone: 408-438-8400 Fax: 408-438-3623
CEO: Philippe R. Kahn
CFO: Alan S. Hendricks
1992 Sales: $482 million Employees: 1,331
Symbol: BORL Exchange: NASDAQ
Industry: Computers - software

Boston Acoustics, Inc.
70 Broadway
Lynnfield, MA 01940
Phone: 617-592-9000 Fax: 617-592-6148
CEO: Francis L. Reed
CFO: Francis L. Reed
1992 Sales: $33 million Employees: 172
Symbol: BOSA Exchange: NASDAQ
Industry: Audio & video home products

Boston Bancorp
460 W. Broadway
South Boston, MA 02127
Phone: 617-268-2500 Fax: —
CEO: Richard R. Laine
CFO: David L. Smart
1991 Sales: $149 million Employees: 186
Symbol: SBOS Exchange: NASDAQ
Industry: Banks - Northeast

Boston Beer Co.
30 Germania St.
Boston, MA 02130
Phone: 617-522-3400 Fax: 617-482-5527
CEO: Jim Koch
CFO: Alfred W. Rossow, Jr.
1992 Sales: — Employees: 65
Ownership: Privately held
Industry: Beverages - beer

Boston Celtics LP
151 Merrimac St.
Boston, MA 02114
Phone: 617-523-6050 Fax: 617-523-5949
CEO: Arnold Auerbach
CFO: Joseph G. DiLorenzo
1992 Sales: $46 million Employees: 42
Symbol: BOS Exchange: NYSE
Industry: Professional basketball team

Boston Digital Corp.
Granite Park
Milford, MA 01757
Phone: 508-473-4561 Fax: 508-478-7224
CEO: Ara Aykanian
CFO: Joseph F. Banafato
1992 Sales: $19 million Employees: 131
Symbol: BOST Exchange: NASDAQ
Industry: Machine tools & related products

Boston Edison Co.
800 Boylston St.
Boston, MA 02199
Phone: 617-424-2000 Fax: 617-424-2929
CEO: Bernard W. Reznicek
CFO: Thomas J. May
1992 Sales: $1,412 million Employees: 4,654
Symbol: BSE Exchange: NYSE
Industry: Utility - electric power

Boston Five Bancorp, Inc.
10 School St.
Boston, MA 02108
Phone: 617-742-6000 Fax: —
CEO: Peter J. Blampied
CFO: Karen Hammond
1991 Sales: $43 million Employees: 807
Symbol: BFCS Exchange: NASDAQ
Industry: Banks - Northeast

Boston Prepatory Co.
101 W. 55th St., Ste. 7A-A
New York, NY 10019
Phone: 212-247-8715 Fax: 212-247-8712
CEO: Ben Narasin
CFO: Ben Narasin
1991 Sales: $4 million Employees: 4
Ownership: Privately held
Industry: Apparel - sportswear

Boston Scientific Corp.
480 Pleasant St.
Watertown, MA 02172
Phone: 617-926-5026 Fax: 617-923-0677
CEO: Peter M. Nicholas
CFO: John H. Chiricotti
1991 Sales: $230 million Employees: 1,738
Symbol: BSX Exchange: NYSE
Industry: Medical products

Boston Technology, Inc.
100 Quannapowitt Pkwy.
Wakefield, MA 01880
Phone: 617-246-9000 Fax: —
CEO: John C. Taylor
CFO: William J. Burke
1991 Sales: $36 million Employees: 206
Symbol: BSTN Exchange: NASDAQ
Industry: Telecommunications equipment

Boulevard Bancorp, Inc.
410 N. Michigan Ave.
Chicago, IL 60611
Phone: 312-836-6500 Fax: —
CEO: Richard T. Schroeder
CFO: George H. Cook, Jr.
1991 Sales: $147 million Employees: 510
Symbol: BLVD Exchange: NASDAQ
Industry: Banks - Midwest

Bowater Inc.
One Parklands Dr.
Darien, CT 06820
Phone: 203-656-7200 Fax: 203-656-7273
CEO: Anthony P. Gammie
CFO: Richard D. McDonough
1992 Sales: $1,494 million Employees: 7,200
Symbol: BOW Exchange: NYSE
Industry: Paper & paper products

Bowl America Inc.
6446 Edsall Rd.
Alexandria, VA 22312
Phone: 703-941-6300 Fax: 703-256-2430
CEO: Leslie H. Goldberg
CFO: Ruth E. Macklin
1992 Sales: $26 million Employees: 750
Symbol: BWLA Exchange: AMEX
Industry: Leisure & recreational services

Bowmar Instrument Corp.
5080 N. 40th St., Ste. 175
Phoenix, AZ 85018
Phone: 602-957-0271 Fax: 602-381-1314
CEO: Edward A. White
CFO: Thomas K. Lanin
1991 Sales: $28 million Employees: 362
Symbol: BOM Exchange: AMEX
Industry: Electrical products

Bowne & Co., Inc.
345 Hudson St., 10th Fl.
New York, NY 10014
Phone: 212-924-5500 Fax: 212-229-3400
CEO: Richard H. Koontz
CFO: James P. O'Neil
1991 Sales: $236 million Employees: 1,805
Symbol: BNE Exchange: AMEX
Industry: Printing - commercial

BP America Inc.
200 Public Square
Cleveland, OH 44114
Phone: 216-586-4141 Fax: 216-586-8066
CEO: Rodney F. Chase
CFO: —
1991 Sales: $57,725 million Employees: 111,900
Parent: The British Petroleum Company PLC
Industry: Oil & gas - international integrated

Brad Ragan, Inc.
600 Oak Ave.
Spruce Pine, NC 28777
Phone: 704-765-6791 Fax: —
CEO: W. P. Brophey
CFO: Daniel J. Patrick
1991 Sales: $205 million Employees: 1,670
Symbol: BRD Exchange: AMEX
Industry: Rubber tires

indicates company is in *Hoover's Handbook of American Business.*

indicates company is in *Hoover's Handbook of World Business;* sales and employee numbers are for parent company.

Bradlees, Inc.
1 Bradlees Circle
Braintree, MA 02184
Phone: 617-380-8000 Fax: —
CEO: Barry A. Berman
CFO: Barry A. Berman
1992 Sales: $1.8 million Employees: 16,000
Symbol: BLE Exchange: NYSE
Industry: Retail - discount & variety

Braman Enterprises
1 SE 3rd Ave., Ste. 2130
Miami, FL 33131
Phone: 305-358-1889 Fax: 305-358-5811
CEO: Norman Braman
CFO: Robert E. Bernstein
1991 Sales: $650 million Employees: 830
Ownership: Privately held
Industry: Retail - auto dealerships

Brand Companies, Inc.
5 Westbrook Corporate Ctr., Ste. 800
Westchester, IL 60154
Phone: 708-298-1200 Fax: 708-298-1208
CEO: Victor J. Barnhart
CFO: Harold W. Ingalls
1991 Sales: $409 million Employees: 4,750
Symbol: BRAN Exchange: NASDAQ
Industry: Construction - heavy

Brandon Systems Corp.
One Harmon Plaza
Secaucus, NJ 07094
Phone: 201-392-0800 Fax: 201-392-0405
CEO: Ira B. Brown
CFO: Peter Lordi
1991 Sales: $38 million Employees: 6,214
Symbol: BRDN Exchange: NASDAQ
Industry: Business services - temporary computer personnel services

Branford Savings Bank
45 S. Main St.
Branford, CT 06405
Phone: 203-481-3471 Fax: —
CEO: Raymond J. Ryan
CFO: Bernard P. Isabelle
1992 Sales: — Employees: —
Symbol: BSBC Exchange: NASDAQ
Industry: Financial - savings and loans

Braun's Women's Apparel
10000 Valley View Rd.
Eden Prairie, MN 55344
Phone: 612-941-9590 Fax: 612-941-9336
CEO: Nicholas H. Cook
CFO: Herbert D. Froemming
1992 Sales: $71 million Employees: 1,200
Symbol: BFCI Exchange: NASDAQ
Industry: Retail - apparel & shoes

Brenco, Inc.
Petersburg Industrial Park
Petersburg, VA 23804
Phone: 804-794-1436 Fax: 804-732-2531
CEO: Needham B. Whitfield
CFO: Jacob M. Feichtner
1991 Sales: $79 million Employees: 821
Symbol: BREN Exchange: NASDAQ
Industry: Metal processing & fabrication

Brendle's Inc.
1919 N. Bridge St.
Elkin, NC 28621
Phone: 919-526-5600 Fax: 919-526-6578
CEO: Douglas D. Brendle
CFO: Jeffrey D. Mick
1991 Sales: $300 million Employees: 3,000
Symbol: BRDL Exchange: NASDAQ
Industry: Retail - discount & variety

Brenlin Group
670 W. Market St.
Akron, OH 44303
Phone: 216-762-2420 Fax: 216-762-4604
CEO: David L. Brennan
CFO: Jim Gaul
1991 Sales: $617 million Employees: 4,200
Ownership: Privately held
Industry: Metal processing & fabrication, steel & plastics

Bridgestone/Firestone, Inc.
One Bridgestone Park
Nashville, TN 37214
Phone: 615-391-0088 Fax: 615-872-2621
CEO: Yoichiro Kaizaki
CFO: —
1991 Sales: $14,111 million Employees: 83,081
Parent: Bridgestone Corporation
Industry: Rubber tires, bicycles, rubber products & batteries

Bridgford Foods Corp.
1308 N. Patt St.
Anaheim, CA 92801
Phone: 714-526-5533 Fax: Call co. operator
CEO: H. Wm. Bridgford
CFO: Robert E. Schulze
1991 Sales: $93 million Employees: 550
Symbol: BRID Exchange: NASDAQ
Industry: Food - refrigerated, frozen & fast food

Briggs & Stratton Corp.
PO Box 702
Milwaukee, WI 53201
Phone: 414-259-5622 Fax: 414-259-5338
CEO: Frederick P. Stratton, Jr.
CFO: Robert H. Eldridge
1992 Sales: $1,094 million Employees: 7,799
Symbol: BGG Exchange: NYSE
Industry: Engines - internal combustion

Brinker International, Inc.
6820 LBJ Fwy.
Dallas, TX 75240
Phone: 214-980-9917 Fax: 214-770-9593
CEO: Ron McDougall
CFO: Debra L. Smithart-Weitzman
1992 Sales: $519 million Employees: 28,000
Symbol: EAT Exchange: NYSE
Industry: Retail - food & restaurants

Bristol-Myers Squibb Co.
345 Park Ave.
New York, NY 10154
Phone: 212-546-4000 Fax: 212-546-4020
CEO: Richard L. Gelb
CFO: Michael E. Autera
1992 Sales: $11,156 million Employees: 53,500
Symbol: BMY Exchange: NYSE
Industry: Drugs & medical devices

Brite Voice Systems, Inc.
7309 E. 21st St.
Wichita, KS 67206
Phone: 316-652-6500 Fax: 316-652-6800
CEO: Stanley G. Brannan
CFO: Glenn A. Etherington
1991 Sales: $19 million Employees: 222
Symbol: BVSI Exchange: NASDAQ
Industry: Telecommunications equipment

British Aerospace, Inc.
13873 Park Center Rd., Ste. 500
Herndon, VA 22071
Phone: 703-478-9420 Fax: 703-478-9436
CEO: Robert L. Kirk
CFO: —
1991 Sales: $19,751 million Employees: 115,700
Parent: British Aerospace PLC
Industry: Aerospace - aircraft & defense equipment, motor vehicles

British Airways
75-20 Astoria Blvd.
Jackson Heights, NY 11370
Phone: 718-397-4000 Fax: 718-397-4364
CEO: John Story
CFO: —
1992 Sales: $9,069 million Employees: 50,409
Parent: British Airways PLC
Industry: Transportation - airline

Broad Inc.
11601 Wilshire Blvd., 12th Fl.
Los Angeles, CA 90025
Phone: 310-312-5000 Fax: —
CEO: Eli Broad
CFO: Eli Broad
1992 Sales: $840 million Employees: —
Symbol: BRO Exchange: NYSE
Industry: Insurance - life

Broad National Bancorporation
905 Broad St.
Newark, NJ 07102
Phone: 201-624-2300 Fax: —
CEO: Donald M. Karp
CFO: James Boyle
1991 Sales: $19 million Employees: 297
Symbol: BNBC Exchange: NASDAQ
Industry: Banks - Northeast

Broadcast International, Inc.
7050 Union Park Center
Midvale, UT 84047
Phone: 801-562-2252 Fax: —
CEO: Dwight H. Egan
CFO: E. Reese Davis, Jr.
1991 Sales: $31 million Employees: 434
Symbol: BRIN Exchange: NASDAQ
Industry: Telecommunications equipment

Broadcast Plus Productions
4133 Lamkershim Blvd.
Universal City, CA 91602
Phone: 818-760-7000 Fax: 818-985-8160
CEO: Bob Da Silva
CFO: Bob Da Silva
1991 Sales: $1.6 million Employees: 5
Ownership: Privately held
Industry: Video equipment

Brøderbund Software, Inc.
500 Redwood Blvd.
Novato, CA 94948
Phone: 415-382-4400 Fax: 415-382-4582
CEO: Douglas G. Carlston
CFO: William M. McDonagh
1992 Sales: $75 million Employees: 338
Symbol: BROD Exchange: NASDAQ
Industry: Computers - educational & game software

Brooke Group Ltd.
65 E. 55th St.
New York, NY 10022
Phone: 212-486-6100 Fax: —
CEO: Bennett S. LeBow
CFO: John A. Sarto
1991 Sales: $999 million Employees: —
Symbol: BGL Exchange: NYSE
Industry: Tobacco

Brooklyn Union Gas Co.
One MetroTech Center
Brooklyn, NY 11201
Phone: 718-403-2000 Fax: —
CEO: Robert B. Catell
CFO: Craig G. Matthews
1992 Sales: $1,115 million Employees: 3,594
Symbol: BU Exchange: NYSE
Industry: Utility - gas distribution

indicates company is in *Hoover's Handbook of American Business.*

indicates company is in *Hoover's Handbook of World Business;* sales and employee numbers are for parent company.

Brookshire Grocery Co.
PO Box 1411
Tyler, TX 75710
Phone: 903-534-3000 Fax: 903-534-3272
CEO: Bruce G. Brookshire
CFO: Harvey B. King
1991 Sales: $660 million Employees: 3,500
Ownership: Privately held
Industry: Retail - supermarkets

Brooktree Corp.
9950 Barnes Canyon Rd.
San Diego, CA 92121
Phone: 619-452-7580 Fax: 619-452-1249
CEO: James A. Bixby
CFO: William R. Peavey
1992 Sales: $92 million Employees: 544
Symbol: BTRE Exchange: NASDAQ
Industry: Electrical components - semiconductor

Brown Group, Inc.
8400 Maryland Ave.
St. Louis, MO 63166
Phone: 314-854-4000 Fax: 314-854-4274
CEO: B. A. Bridgewater, Jr.
CFO: Harry E. Rich
1992 Sales: $1,775 million Employees: 25,500
Symbol: BG Exchange: NYSE
Industry: Shoes & related apparel

Brown & Sharpe Manufacturing Co.
Precision Park
North Kingstown, RI 02852
Phone: 401-886-2000 Fax: 401-886-2762
CEO: Fred M. Stuber
CFO: Richard J. Duncan
1991 Sales: $176 million Employees: 2,000
Symbol: BNS Exchange: NYSE
Industry: Electronics - measuring instruments

Brown & Williamson Tobacco Corp.
PO Box 35090
Louisville, KY 40232
Phone: 502-568-5000 Fax: 502-568-7107
CEO: Ray Pritchard
CFO: —
1991 Sales: $22,137 million Employees: 212,316
Parent: B.A.T Industries PLC
Industry: Diversified operations - tobacco, insurance & financial services

Brown-Forman Corp.
PO Box 1080
Louisville, KY 40201
Phone: 502-585-1100 Fax: 502-774-7876
CEO: W. L. Lyons Brown, Jr.
CFO: Clifford G. Rompf, Jr.
1992 Sales: $1,339 million Employees: 6,900
Symbol: BFB Exchange: NYSE
Industry: Beverages - alcoholic

Browning-Ferris Industries, Inc.
757 N. Eldridge
Houston, TX 77253
Phone: 713-870-8100 Fax: 713-870-7844
CEO: William D. Ruckelshaus
CFO: Jeffrey E. Curtiss
1992 Sales: $3,334 million Employees: 27,000
Symbol: BFI Exchange: NYSE
Industry: Waste disposal

Bruce Co.
501 Third St. NW
Washington, DC 20001
Phone: 202-783-7100 Fax: 202-783-1105
CEO: John B. Wells
CFO: —
1992 Sales: $3.5 million Employees: 66
Ownership: Privately held
Industry: Environmental consulting

Bruno's, Inc.
800 Lakeshore Pkwy.
Birmingham, AL 35201
Phone: 205-940-9400 Fax: 205-940-9568
CEO: Ronald G. Bruno
CFO: Glenn J. Griffin
1992 Sales: $2,726 million Employees: 23,454
Symbol: BRNO Exchange: NASDAQ
Industry: Retail - supermarkets

Brunswick Corp.
One Brunswick Plaza
Skokie, IL 60077
Phone: 708-470-4700 Fax: 708-470-4765
CEO: Jack F. Reichert
CFO: William R. McManaman
1992 Sales: $2,059 million Employees: 19,500
Symbol: BC Exchange: NYSE
Industry: Boats, sporting goods & bowling center

Brush Wellman Inc.
Hanna Bldg., Ste. 1200
Cleveland, OH 44115
Phone: 216-443-1000 Fax: 216-443-1161
CEO: Gordon D. Harnett
CFO: Clark G. Waite
1991 Sales: $268 million Employees: 1,943
Symbol: BW Exchange: NYSE
Industry: Metals - nonferrous

BSB Bancorp, Inc.
58-68 Exchange St.
Binghamton, NY 13902
Phone: 607-779-2525 Fax: —
CEO: William H. Rincker
CFO: Edward R. Andrejko
1991 Sales: $35 million Employees: 388
Symbol: BSBN Exchange: NASDAQ
Industry: Financial - savings and loans

BSD Bancorp, Inc.
225 Broadway, Ste. 1309
San Diego, CA 92101
Phone: 619-237-5365 Fax: 619-237-5499
CEO: James S. Brown
CFO: Marilyn C. Jones
1991 Sales: $52 million Employees: 282
Symbol: BSD Exchange: AMEX
Industry: Banks - West

BSN Corp.
1901 Diplomat
Dallas, TX 75234
Phone: 214-484-9484 Fax: —
CEO: Michael J. Blumenfeld
CFO: Randy S. Kercho
1991 Sales: $8.4 million Employees: 230
Symbol: BSN Exchange: AMEX
Industry: Athletic equipment & trophies

BT Financial Corp.
532-534 Main St.
Johnstown, PA 15907
Phone: 814-536-7801 Fax: —
CEO: Gerald W. Swatsworth
CFO: Carl J. Motter, Jr.
1991 Sales: $76 million Employees: 558
Symbol: BTFC Exchange: NASDAQ
Industry: Banks - Northeast

BT North America
100 Park Ave.
New York, NY 10017
Phone: 212-297-2711 Fax: 212-297-2713
CEO: Laurie Huntley
CFO: —
1992 Sales: $23,206 million Employees: 210,500
Parent: British Telecommunications PLC
Industry: Telecommunications services

BTR Realty, Inc.
1302 Concourse Dr., Ste. 202
Linthicum, MD 21090
Phone: 410-684-2000 Fax: 410-859-5685
CEO: Archibald E. MacKay
CFO: Eugene T. Grady
1991 Sales: $23 million Employees: 65
Symbol: BTRI Exchange: NASDAQ
Industry: Real estate operations

BTU International, Inc.
23 Esquire Rd.
North Billerica, MA 01862
Phone: 508-667-4111 Fax: 508-667-9068
CEO: Paul van der Wansem
CFO: Paul van der Wansem
1991 Sales: $22 million Employees: 321
Symbol: BTUI Exchange: NASDAQ
Industry: Electrical components - semiconductors

Buckeye Partners, L.P.
5002 Buckeye Rd.
Emmaus, PA 18049
Phone: 215-820-8300 Fax: —
CEO: Alfred W. Martinelli
CFO: Ernest R. Varalli
1991 Sales: $152 million Employees: —
Symbol: BPL Exchange: NYSE
Industry: Oil & gas - production & pipeline

Buckle, Inc., The
2407 W. 24th St.
Kearney, NE 68847
Phone: 308-236-8491 Fax: —
CEO: Daniel J. Hirschfeld
CFO: Karen B. Rhoads
1992 Sales: $87 million Employees: 1,500
Symbol: BKLE Exchange: NASDAQ
Industry: Retail - apparel & shoes

Budd Company, The
3155 W. Big Beaver Rd.
Troy, MI 48007
Phone: 313-643-3500 Fax: 313-643-3593
CEO: David P. Williams
CFO: —
1991 Sales: $24,054 million Employees: 148,250
Parent: Thyssen AG
Industry: Steel - production; trading & services, capital goods & manufactured products

Budget Rent a Car Corp.
4225 Naperville Rd.
Lisle, IL 60532
Phone: 708-955-1900 Fax: 708-955-7799
CEO: William N. Plamondon
CFO: Kevin M. McShea
1991 Sales: $1,144 million Employees: 10,000
Ownership: Privately held
Industry: International car and truck rental

Buffets, Inc.
10260 Viking Dr., Ste. 100
Eden Prairie, MN 55344
Phone: 612-942-9760 Fax: 612-942-9658
CEO: Roe H. Hatlen
CFO: Clark C. Grant
1991 Sales: $196 million Employees: 7,500
Symbol: BOCB Exchange: NASDAQ
Industry: Retail - food & restaurants

Buffton Corp.
201 Main St., Ste. 501
Ft. Worth, TX 76102
Phone: 817-332-4761 Fax: 817-877-0420
CEO: Robert H. McLean
CFO: Robert Korman
1991 Sales: $69 million Employees: 720
Symbol: BFX Exchange: AMEX
Industry: Avionics & PVC pipes

indicates company is in *Hoover's Handbook of American Business.*

indicates company is in *Hoover's Handbook of World Business;* sales and employee numbers are for parent company.

Bugle Boy Industries
2900 Madera Rd.
Simi Valley, CA 93065
Phone: 805-582-1010 Fax: 805-522-1212
CEO: William Mow
CFO: Robert Miller
1991 Sales: $495 million Employees: 1,830
Ownership: Privately held
Industry: Apparel

Builders Transport, Inc.
2029 W. DeKalb St.
Camden, SC 29020
Phone: 803-432-1400 Fax: 803-425-1721
CEO: John R. Morris
CFO: George L. Corbin
1991 Sales: $212 million Employees: 3,287
Symbol: TRUK Exchange: NASDAQ
Industry: Transportation - truck

Bull & Bear Group, Inc.
11 Hanover Square
New York, NY 10005
Phone: 212-785-0900 Fax: 212-785-0908
CEO: Bassett S. Winmill
CFO: Mark C. Winmill
1991 Sales: $5.3 million Employees: 28
Symbol: BNBGA Exchange: NASDAQ
Industry: Financial - investment management

Bull HN Information Systems Inc.
300 Concord Rd.
Billerica, MA 01821
Phone: 508-294-6000 Fax: 508-294-4470
CEO: Axel Lebois
CFO: —
1991 Sales: $6,458 million Employees: 39,878
Parent: Compagnie des Machines Bull
Industry: Computers - mainframe, microcomputers, peripherals

Bull Run Gold Mines, Ltd.
4370 Peachtree Rd.
Atlanta, GA 30319
Phone: 404-266-8333 Fax: —
CEO: Robert S. Prather, Jr.
CFO: Samuel P. Davis, Jr.
1991 Sales: $0.1 million Employees: 3
Symbol: BULL Exchange: NASDAQ
Industry: Gold mining & processing

Burger King Investors Master L.P.
200 S. Sixth St.
Minneapolis, MN 55402
Phone: 612-330-8345 Fax: —
CEO: David F. Smith
CFO: David F. Smith
1991 Sales: $8.8 million Employees: —
Symbol: BKP Exchange: NYSE
Industry: Real estate operations

Burlington Coat Factory Warehouse Corp.
1830 Route 130 North
Burlington, NJ 08016
Phone: 609-387-7800 Fax: 609-387-7071
CEO: Monroe G. Milstein
CFO: Elisabeth Stout
1992 Sales: $1,120 million Employees: —
Symbol: BCF Exchange: NYSE
Industry: Retail - apparel & shoes

Burlington Industries Equity Inc.
3330 W. Friendly Ave.
Greensboro, NC 27420
Phone: 919-379-2000 Fax: 919-379-4504
CEO: Frank S. Greenberg
CFO: Donald R. Hughes
1992 Sales: $2,054 million Employees: 24,000
Symbol: BUR Exchange: NYSE
Industry: Textiles - mill products

Burlington Northern Inc.
3800 Continental Plaza, 777 Main St.
Ft. Worth, TX 76102
Phone: 817-878-2000 Fax: 817-878-2377
CEO: Gerald Grinstein
CFO: David C. Anderson
1992 Sales: $4,630 million Employees: 31,760
Symbol: BNI Exchange: NYSE
Industry: Transportation - rail

Burlington Resources Inc.
999 Third Ave.
Seattle, WA 98104
Phone: 206-467-3838 Fax: 206-467-3960
CEO: Thomas H. O'Leary
CFO: George E. Howison
1992 Sales: $1,141 million Employees: 4,347
Symbol: BR Exchange: NYSE
Industry: Oil & gas - US exploration & production

Burnup & Sims Inc.
One N. University Dr.
Ft. Lauderdale, FL 33324
Phone: 305-587-4512 Fax: 305-475-8780
CEO: Nick A. Caporella
CFO: George R. Bracken
1992 Sales: $154 million Employees: 2,250
Symbol: BSIM Exchange: NASDAQ
Industry: Telecommunications equipment

Burr-Brown Corp.
6730 S. Tucson Blvd.
Tucson, AZ 85706
Phone: 602-746-1111 Fax: 602-746-7752
CEO: James J. Burns
CFO: Robert E. Switz
1991 Sales: $179 million Employees: 1,650
Symbol: BBRC Exchange: NASDAQ
Industry: Electrical components - semiconductors

Burritt InterFinancial Bancorporation
267 Main St.
New Britain, CT 06050
Phone: 203-225-7601 Fax: —
CEO: Patrick W. Wisman
CFO: Barbara J. Bennett
1992 Sales: — Employees: —
Symbol: BANQ Exchange: NASDAQ
Industry: Financial - savings and loans

Buschman Corp.
4100 Payne Ave.
Cleveland, OH 44103
Phone: 216-431-6633 Fax: 216-431-5037
CEO: Tom Buschman
CFO: Ross DeFelice
1992 Sales: $2 million Employees: 17
Ownership: Privately held
Industry: Paper & paper products

Bush Industries, Inc.
One Mason Dr.
Jamestown, NY 14701
Phone: 716-665-2000 Fax: 716-665-2074
CEO: Paul S. Bush
CFO: Robert L. Ayres
1991 Sales: $126 million Employees: 1,285
Symbol: BSH Exchange: AMEX
Industry: Furniture

Business Computer Training Institute
6695 Kimball Dr., Bldg. A
Gig Harbor, WA 98335
Phone: 206-851-8876 Fax: 206-851-7917
CEO: Tom Jonez
CFO: Jack Day
1991 Sales: $8.8 million Employees: 300
Ownership: Privately held
Industry: Computers - training services

Business Records Corporation Holding Co.
1111 W. Mockingbird, Ste. 1400
Dallas, TX 75247
Phone: 214-688-1800 Fax: 214-905-2303
CEO: Perry E. Esping
CFO: Thomas E. Kiraly
1991 Sales: $76 million Employees: 804
Symbol: BRCP Exchange: NASDAQ
Industry: Office automation

Butler International, Inc.
110 Summit Ave.
Montvale, NJ 07645
Phone: 201-573-8000 Fax: —
CEO: Edward M. Kopko
CFO: Warren F. Brecht
1991 Sales: $250 million Employees: —
Symbol: BUTL Exchange: NASDAQ
Industry: Financial - SBIC & commercial

Butler Manufacturing Co.
BMA Tower, Penn Valley Park
Kansas City, MO 64141
Phone: 816-968-3000 Fax: 816-968-3279
CEO: Robert H. West
CFO: John J. Holland
1991 Sales: $461 million Employees: 3,040
Symbol: BTLR Exchange: NASDAQ
Industry: Building products

Buttrey Food and Drug Stores Co.
601 6th St. SW
Great Falls, MT 59404
Phone: 406-761-3401 Fax: 406-761-1295
CEO: Edward C. Agnew
CFO: Wayne S. Peterson
1991 Sales: $490 million Employees: 4,270
Symbol: BTRY Exchange: NASDAQ
Industry: Retail - convenience stores

BWIP International, Inc.
200 Oceangate Blvd., Ste. 900
Long Beach, CA 90802
Phone: 310-435-3700 Fax: 310-436-7203
CEO: Peter C. Valli
CFO: Eugene P. Cross
1991 Sales: $430 million Employees: 3,100
Symbol: BWIP Exchange: NASDAQ
Industry: Pumps and seals

Bytex Corp.
Four Technology Dr.
Westborough, MA 01581
Phone: 508-366-8000 Fax: 508-460-0098
CEO: Arthur Carr
CFO: Cynthia M. Deysher
1991 Sales: $45 million Employees: 299
Symbol: BYTX Exchange: NASDAQ
Industry: Computers - matrix switching systems

C.A. Short International, Inc.
5720 Avery Rd.
Amlin, OH 43002
Phone: 614-793-8749 Fax: —
CEO: S. Robert Davis
CFO: Richard A. Stimmel
1992 Sales: $22 million Employees: 137
Symbol: CASH Exchange: NASDAQ
Industry: Business services - incentive programs

C. H. Heist Corp.
810 N. Belcher Rd.
Clearwater, FL 34625
Phone: 813-461-5656 Fax: 813-447-1146
CEO: Charles H. Heist
CFO: Richard J. O'Neil
1991 Sales: $70 million Employees: 2,600
Symbol: HST Exchange: AMEX
Industry: Industrial maintenance

indicates company is in *Hoover's Handbook of American Business.*
indicates company is in *Hoover's Handbook of World Business;* sales and employee numbers are for parent company.

C.I.S. Technologies, Inc.
6100 S. Yale, Ste. 1901
Tulsa, OK 74136
Phone: 918-496-2451 Fax: 918-481-4275
CEO: Philip D. Kurtz
CFO: Richard A. Evans
1991 Sales: $18 million Employees: 313
Symbol: CISI Exchange: NASDAQ
Industry: Business services - health care management services

C. R. Bard, Inc.
730 Central Ave.
Murray Hill, NJ 07974
Phone: 908-277-8000 Fax: 908-277-8240
CEO: George T. Maloney
CFO: George A. Davis
1992 Sales: $990 million Employees: 9,100
Symbol: BCR Exchange: NYSE
Industry: Medical & dental supplies

C.R. Gibson Co.
32 Knight St.
Norwalk, CT 06851
Phone: 203-847-4543 Fax: 203-847-7613
CEO: Frank A. Rosenberry
CFO: James M. Harrison
1991 Sales: $63 million Employees: 600
Symbol: GIB Exchange: AMEX
Industry: Office & art materials

C&S Wholesale Grocers Inc.
Old Ferry Rd.
Brattleboro, VT 05301
Phone: 802-257-4371 Fax: 802-257-6727
CEO: Richard B. Cohen
CFO: Bill Hamlin
1991 Sales: $1,335 million Employees: 1,100
Ownership: Privately held
Industry: Food - wholesale

C-COR Electronics, Inc.
60 Decibel Rd.
State College, PA 16801
Phone: 814-238-2461 Fax: 814-238-4065
CEO: Richard E. Perry
CFO: Jack B. Andrews
1992 Sales: $52 million Employees: 531
Symbol: CCBL Exchange: NASDAQ
Industry: Telecommunications equipment

C-TEC Corp.
46 Public Square
Wilkes-Barre, PA 18703
Phone: 717-825-1100 Fax: —
CEO: Charles E. Parente
CFO: James E. Bogdan
1991 Sales: $233 million Employees: 1,324
Symbol: CTEX Exchange: NASDAQ
Industry: Utility - telephone

Cable Car Beverage Corp.
1700 E. 68th Ave.
Denver, CO 80229
Phone: 303-288-2212 Fax: 303-288-0901
CEO: Samuel Simpson
CFO: Arnold E. Bjork
1991 Sales: $12 million Employees: 56
Symbol: DRNK Exchange: NASDAQ
Industry: Beverages - soft drinks

Cable & Wireless Communications, Inc.
1919 Gallows Rd.
Vienna, VA 22182
Phone: 703-790-5300 Fax: 703-556-9687
CEO: Keith Bernard
CFO: —
1992 Sales: $5,939 million Employees: 38,835
Parent: Cable and Wireless PLC
Industry: Telecommunications services

Cabletron Systems, Inc.
35 Industrial Way
Rochester, NH 03867
Phone: 603-332-9400 Fax: 603-332-4616
CEO: S. Robert Levine
CFO: David Kirkpatrick
1992 Sales: $290 million Employees: 2,032
Symbol: CS Exchange: NYSE
Industry: Computers - local area networks

Cablevision Systems Corp.
One Media Crossways
Woodbury, NY 11797
Phone: 516-364-8450 Fax: 516-496-1780
CEO: Charles F. Dolan
CFO: Barry J. O'Leary
1991 Sales: $603 million Employees: 3,444
Symbol: CVC Exchange: AMEX
Industry: Cable TV

Cabot Corp.
75 State St.
Boston, MA 02109
Phone: 617-345-0100 Fax: 617-342-6103
CEO: Samuel W. Bodman
CFO: John D. Curtin, Jr.
1992 Sales: $1,568 million Employees: 5,300
Symbol: CBT Exchange: NYSE
Industry: Chemicals - specialty

Cabot Medical Corp.
2021 Cabot Blvd. West
Langhorne, PA 19047
Phone: 215-752-8300 Fax: 215-750-0161
CEO: Warren G. Wood
CFO: Marvin B. Sharfstein
1991 Sales: $41 million Employees: 196
Symbol: CBOT Exchange: NASDAQ
Industry: Medical products - gynecological & surgery devices

Cabot Oil & Gas Corp.
15375 Memorial Dr.
Houston, TX 77079
Phone: 713-589-4600 Fax: —
CEO: Charles P. Siess, Jr.
CFO: Roger J. Klatt
1991 Sales: $140 million Employees: 442
Symbol: COG Exchange: NYSE
Industry: Oil & gas - US exploration & production

Cache, Inc.
1460 Broadway
New York, NY 10036
Phone: 212-840-4242 Fax: Ext. 4225
CEO: Roy C. Chapman
CFO: Thomas E. Reinckens
1991 Sales: $55 million Employees: 507
Symbol: CACH Exchange: NASDAQ
Industry: Retail - apparel & shoes

CACI International Inc.
1700 N. Moore St.
Arlington, VA 22201
Phone: 703-841-7800 Fax: 703-841-7882
CEO: J. P. London
CFO: Samuel R. Strickland
1992 Sales: $140 million Employees: 2,180
Symbol: CACI Exchange: NASDAQ
Industry: Computers - services

Cadapult Graphic Systems Inc.
17 Arcadian Way
Paramus, NJ 07652
Phone: 201-368-1313 Fax: 201-368-1656
CEO: Michael Levin
CFO: Michael Levin
1991 Sales: $4.1 million Employees: 8
Ownership: Privately held
Industry: Computers - graphics

Cadbury Schweppes Inc.
High Ridge Park
Stamford, CT 06905
Phone: 203-329-0911 Fax: 203-968-7854
CEO: John Carson
CFO: —
1991 Sales: $6,025 million Employees: 35,372
Parent: Cadbury Schweppes PLC
Industry: Beverages - soft drinks; confectionery

Cade Industries, Inc.
5640 Enterprise Dr.
Lansing, MI 48911
Phone: 517-394-1333 Fax: 517-394-1404
CEO: Terrell L. Ruhlman
CFO: Edward B. Stephens
1991 Sales: $30 million Employees: 278
Symbol: CADE Exchange: NASDAQ
Industry: Aerospace - aircraft equipment

Cadence Design Systems, Inc.
555 River Oaks Pkwy.
San Jose, CA 95134
Phone: 408-943-1234 Fax: 408-943-0513
CEO: Joseph B. Costello
CFO: Leonard J. LeBlanc
1991 Sales: $392 million Employees: 2,588
Symbol: CDN Exchange: NYSE
Industry: Computers - computer automated design software

Cadmus Communications Corp.
5516 Falmouth St., Ste. 301
Richmond, VA 23230
Phone: 804-287-5680 Fax: 804-288-3436
CEO: Wallace Stettinius
CFO: David E. Bosher
1992 Sales: $188 million Employees: 1,895
Symbol: CDMS Exchange: NASDAQ
Industry: Printing - commercial

Cadmus Group Inc.
135 Beaver St.
Waltham, MA 02154
Phone: 617-894-9830 Fax: 617-894-7238
CEO: David J. Alexander
CFO: —
1992 Sales: $9.5 million Employees: 110
Ownership: Privately held
Industry: Environmental consulting

Caere Corp.
100 Cooper Court
Los Gatos, CA 95030
Phone: 408-395-7000 Fax: 408-354-2743
CEO: Robert G. Teresi
CFO: Blanche M. Sutter
1991 Sales: $32 million Employees: 155
Symbol: CAER Exchange: NASDAQ
Industry: Computers - optical character- recognition software

Caesars World, Inc.
1801 Century Park East, Ste. 2600
Los Angeles, CA 90067
Phone: 310-552-2711 Fax: 310-552-9446
CEO: Henry Gluck
CFO: Roger Lee
1992 Sales: $927 million Employees: 9,566
Symbol: CAW Exchange: NYSE
Industry: Casinos

Cagle's, Inc.
2000 Hills Ave. NW
Atlanta, GA 30318
Phone: 404-355-2820 Fax: 404-355-9326
CEO: J. Douglas Cagle
CFO: Kenneth R. Barkley
1992 Sales: $209 million Employees: 3,000
Symbol: CGLA Exchange: AMEX
Industry: Food - meat products

indicates company is in *Hoover's Handbook of American Business.*

indicates company is in *Hoover's Handbook of World Business;* sales and employee numbers are for parent company.

Calais Home Corp.
15957 Kuykendahl Rd.
Houston, TX 77068
Phone: 713-444-9300 Fax: 713-444-9576
CEO: Mike Barrineau
CFO: Mike Barrineau
1991 Sales: $9.5 million Employees: 20
Ownership: Privately held
Industry: Building - single-family homes

Caldor Corp.
20 Glover Ave.
Norwalk, CT 06850
Phone: 203-846-1641 Fax: 203-849-2019
CEO: Don R. Clarke
CFO: Robert S. Schauman
1992 Sales: $2,016 million Employees: 15,500
Symbol: CLD Exchange: NYSE
Industry: Retail - discount & variety

CalFed Inc.
5700 Wilshire Blvd.
Los Angeles, CA 90036
Phone: 213-932-4321 Fax: 213-930-7950
CEO: Jerry St. Dennis
CFO: Richard M. Greenwood
1992 Sales: $1,413 million Employees: 3,801
Symbol: CAL Exchange: NYSE
Industry: Financial - savings and loans

Calgene, Inc.
1920 Fifth St.
Davis, CA 95616
Phone: 916-753-6313 Fax: 916-753-1510
CEO: Roger H. Salquist
CFO: Daniel O. Wagster II
1992 Sales: $22 million Employees: 282
Symbol: CGNE Exchange: NASDAQ
Industry: Biomedical & genetic products

Calgon Carbon Corp.
400 Calgon Carbon Dr.
Pittsburgh, PA 15205
Phone: 412-787-6700 Fax: 412-787-6713
CEO: Thomas A. McConomy
CFO: C. P. Shannon
1991 Sales: $308 million Employees: 1,513
Symbol: CCC Exchange: NYSE
Industry: Carbon powder & filters

California Amplifier, Inc.
460 Calle San Pablo
Camarillo, CA 93012
Phone: 805-987-9000 Fax: 805-482-5842
CEO: Barry W. Hall
CFO: Barry W. Hall
1992 Sales: $21 million Employees: 235
Symbol: CAMP Exchange: NASDAQ
Industry: Telecommunications equipment

California Bancshares, Inc.
2320 Blanding Ave.
Alameda, CA 94501
Phone: 510-814-3400 Fax: —
CEO: Joseph P. Colmery
CFO: Vincent M. Leveroni
1991 Sales: $79 million Employees: 522
Symbol: CABI Exchange: NASDAQ
Industry: Banks - West

California Energy Co., Inc.
10831 Old Mill Rd.
Omaha, NE 94108
Phone: 402-330-8900 Fax: 402-330-9888
CEO: Walter Scott, Jr.
CFO: John G. Sylvia
1991 Sales: $104 million Employees: 200
Symbol: CE Exchange: AMEX
Industry: Energy - geothermal

California Financial Holding Co.
212 N. San Joaquin St.
Stockton, CA 95202
Phone: 209-948-6870 Fax: —
CEO: David K. Rea
CFO: Robert V. Kavanaugh
1991 Sales: $107 million Employees: 331
Symbol: CFHC Exchange: NASDAQ
Industry: Financial - savings and loans

California Micro Devices Corp.
215 Topaz St.
Milpitas, CA 95035
Phone: 408-263-3214 Fax: 408-263-7846
CEO: Chan M. Desaigoudar
CFO: Steven J. Henke
1992 Sales: $23 million Employees: 204
Symbol: CAMD Exchange: NASDAQ
Industry: Electrical components

California Microwave, Inc.
985 Almanor Ave.
Sunnyvale, CA 94086
Phone: 408-732-4000 Fax: 408-732-4244
CEO: Philip F. Otto
CFO: George L. Spillane
1992 Sales: $199 million Employees: 1,313
Symbol: CMIC Exchange: NASDAQ
Industry: Telecommunications equipment

California State Bank
100 N. Barranca St.
West Covina, CA 91791
Phone: 818-915-4424 Fax: —
CEO: Thomas A. Bishop
CFO: Paul E. Brandt
1992 Sales: — Employees: —
Symbol: CSTB Exchange: NASDAQ
Industry: Banks - West

California Water Service Co.
1720 N. First St.
San Jose, CA 95112
Phone: 408-453-8414 Fax: 408-437-9185
CEO: C. H. Stump
CFO: Harold C. Ulrich
1991 Sales: $127 million Employees: 593
Symbol: CWTR Exchange: NASDAQ
Industry: Utility - water supply

Callaway Golf Co.
2285 Rutherford Rd.
Carlsbad, CA 92008
Phone: 619-931-1771 Fax: 619-931-9539
CEO: E. Callaway
CFO: C. A. Kerley
1991 Sales: $55 million Employees: 376
Symbol: ELY Exchange: NYSE
Industry: Leisure & recreational products - golf supplies

Callon Consolidated Partners, L.P.
200 N. Canal St.
Natchez, MS 39120
Phone: 601-442-1601 Fax: 601-445-8319
CEO: John S. Callon
CFO: John S. Weatherly
1991 Sales: $8.8 million Employees: —
Symbol: CCLPZ Exchange: NASDAQ
Industry: Oil & gas - US exploration & production

Calloway's Nursery, Inc.
9003 Airport Fwy., Ste. 260
Ft. Worth, TX 76180
Phone: 817-656-1122 Fax: —
CEO: James C. Estill
CFO: James C. Estill
1992 Sales: $23 million Employees: 183
Symbol: CLWY Exchange: NASDAQ
Industry: Retail - garden centers

CalMat Co.
3200 N. San Fernando Rd.
Los Angeles, CA 90065
Phone: 213-258-2777 Fax: 213-258-1583
CEO: A. Frederick Gerstell
CFO: Ronald C. Hadfield
1991 Sales: $369 million Employees: 1,632
Symbol: CZM Exchange: NYSE
Industry: Construction - cement & concrete

Calprop Corp.
5456 McConnell Ave., Ste. 245
Los Angeles, CA 90066
Phone: 213-306-4314 Fax: 213-301-0435
CEO: Victor Zaccaglin
CFO: Scott W. Barnes
1991 Sales: $26 million Employees: 31
Symbol: CPP Exchange: AMEX
Industry: Real estate development

Calton Homes Inc.
500 Craig Rd.
Freehold, NJ 07728
Phone: 908-780-1800 Fax: 908-780-7257
CEO: Anthony J. Caldarone
CFO: Peter M. Pizza
1991 Sales: $118 million Employees: 215
Symbol: CN Exchange: NYSE
Industry: Real estate development

Calumet Bancorp, Inc.
1350 E. Sibley Blvd.
Dolton, IL 60419
Phone: 708-841-9010 Fax: —
CEO: Thaddeus Walczak
CFO: John L. Garlanger
1991 Sales: $42 million Employees: 170
Symbol: CBCI Exchange: NASDAQ
Industry: Banks - Midwest

Cambex Corp.
360 Second Ave.
Waltham, MA 02154
Phone: 617-890-6000 Fax: 617-890-2899
CEO: Joseph F. Kruy
CFO: Sheldon M. Schenkler
1992 Sales: $52 million Employees: 180
Symbol: CBEX Exchange: NASDAQ
Industry: Computers - add-on memory products

Cambrex Corp.
One Meadowlands Plaza
East Rutherford, NJ 07073
Phone: 201-804-3000 Fax: 201-804-9852
CEO: Cyril C. Baldwin, Jr.
CFO: John P. Lynch
1991 Sales: $144 million Employees: 583
Symbol: CBM Exchange: AMEX
Industry: Chemicals - diversified

Cambridge Biotech Corp.
365 Plantation St.
Worcester, MA 01605
Phone: 508-797-5777 Fax: —
CEO: Patrick J. Leonard
CFO: Peter P. Hartman
1991 Sales: $29 million Employees: 368
Symbol: CBCX Exchange: NASDAQ
Industry: Biomedical & genetic products

Cambridge NeuroScience, Inc.
One Kendall Square, Bldg. 700
Cambridge, MA 02139
Phone: 617-225-0600 Fax: 617-225-2741
CEO: Alan J. Dalby
CFO: Philip V. Holberton
1991 Sales: $1.1 million Employees: 52
Symbol: CNSI Exchange: NASDAQ
Industry: Drugs

indicates company is in *Hoover's Handbook of American Business.*

indicates company is in *Hoover's Handbook of World Business;* sales and employee numbers are for parent company.

Camelot Systems Inc.
216 River St.
Haverhill, MA 01832
Phone: 508-373-3742 Fax: 508-521-2105
CEO: Paul Cavallaro
CFO: Patti Cavallaro
1991 Sales: $4.7 million Employees: 35
Ownership: Privately held
Industry: Instruments - automated liquid dispensing

Campbell Soup Co.
Campbell Place
Camden, NJ 08103
Phone: 609-342-4800 Fax: 609-342-3878
CEO: David W. Johnson
CFO: Frank E. Weise III
1992 Sales: $6,412 million Employees: 43,256
Symbol: CPB Exchange: NYSE
Industry: Food - canned soups, cookies & candy

Canadian Imperial Holdings Inc.
425 Lexington Ave.
New York, NY 10017
Phone: 212-856-4000 Fax: 212-856-4178
CEO: Al Keiser
CFO: —
1991 Sales: $9,768 million Employees: 34,593
Parent: Canadian Imperial Bank of Commerce
Industry: Banks - money center

Canandaigua Wine Co., Inc.
116 Buffalo St.
Canandaigua, NY 14424
Phone: 716-394-7900 Fax: 716-394-2027
CEO: Marvin Sands
CFO: Lynn K. Fetterman
1991 Sales: $177 million Employees: 600
Symbol: WINEA Exchange: NASDAQ
Industry: Beverages - wine

Candela Laser Corp.
530 Boston Post Rd.
Wayland, MA 01778
Phone: 508-358-7637 Fax: 508-358-5602
CEO: John T. Pavlic
CFO: Gerard E. Puorro
1992 Sales: $35 million Employees: 197
Symbol: CLZR Exchange: NASDAQ
Industry: Lasers - systems & components

Cannon Express, Inc.
1901 Robinson
Springdale, AR 72764
Phone: 501-751-9209 Fax: —
CEO: Dean G. Cannon
CFO: Rose Marie Cannon
1992 Sales: $33 million Employees: 470
Symbol: CANX Exchange: NASDAQ
Industry: Transportation - trucks

Canon U.S.A., Inc.
One Canon Plaza
Lake Success, NY 11042
Phone: 516-488-6700 Fax: 516-488-3623
CEO: H. Takamoto
CFO: Keishi Fukuda
1991 Sales: $14,951 million Employees: 62,700
Parent: Canon Inc.
Industry: Office equipment - copiers, peripherals; cameras

Canonie Environmental Services Corp.
800 Canonie Dr.
Porter, IN 46304
Phone: 219-926-8651 Fax: 219-926-7169
CEO: Thomas A. Donovan
CFO: Leo G. MacKeller
1992 Sales: $66 million Employees: 348
Symbol: CANO Exchange: NASDAQ
Industry: Hazardous site clean-up services

Canvasbacks Inc.
224 W. Washington St.
Milwaukee, WI 53204
Phone: 414-384-4484 Fax: 414-384-4549
CEO: Janice Lutton
CFO: Jim Peters
1991 Sales: $6.7 million Employees: 50
Ownership: Privately held
Industry: Apparel - women's sportswear

Canyon Resources Corp.
14142 Denver West Pkwy.
Golden, CO 80401
Phone: 303-278-8464 Fax: 303-279-3772
CEO: Richard H. De Voto
CFO: Gary C. Huber
1991 Sales: $22 million Employees: 113
Symbol: CYNR Exchange: NASDAQ
Industry: Metals - nonferrous

Cap Toys
26201 Richmond Rd.
Bedford Heights, OH 44146
Phone: 216-292-6363 Fax: 216-292-4815
CEO: John Osher
CFO: Alan Pearlman
1992 Sales: $2.5 million Employees: 40
Ownership: Privately held
Industry: Toys

Cape Cod Bank & Trust Co.
307 Main St.
Hyannis, MA 02601
Phone: 508-394-1300 Fax: —
CEO: James H. Rice
CFO: Noal D. Reid
1992 Sales: — Employees: —
Symbol: CCBT Exchange: NASDAQ
Industry: Banks - Northeast

Capital Associates, Inc.
7175 W. Jefferson Ave.
Lakewood, CO 80235
Phone: 303-980-1000 Fax: —
CEO: Richard Kazan
CFO: Ronald Larson
1992 Sales: $153 million Employees: 162
Symbol: CAII Exchange: NASDAQ
Industry: Leasing

Capital Bancorporation, Inc.
407 N. Kingshighway, 4th Fl.
Cape Girardeau, MO 63701
Phone: 314-334-0700 Fax: —
CEO: Van H. Puls
CFO: David G. Collier
1991 Sales: $57 million Employees: 339
Symbol: CABK Exchange: NASDAQ
Industry: Banks - Midwest

Capital Cities/ABC, Inc.
77 W. 66th St.
New York, NY 10023
Phone: 212-456-7777 Fax: 212-456-6850
CEO: Daniel B. Burke
CFO: Ronald J. Doerfler
1992 Sales: $5,344 million Employees: 19,650
Symbol: CCB Exchange: NYSE
Industry: Broadcasting - radio & TV, publishing

Capital Holding Corp.
680 S. Fourth Ave.
Louisville, KY 40202
Phone: 502-560-2000 Fax: 502-560-2550
CEO: Irving W. Bailey II
CFO: Lee Adrean
1992 Sales: $2,853 million Employees: —
Symbol: CPH Exchange: NYSE
Industry: Insurance - life

Capital Re Corp.
787 Seventh Ave., 27th Fl.
New York, NY 10019
Phone: 212-974-0100 Fax: —
CEO: Michael E. Satz
CFO: David A. Buzen
1991 Sales: $41 million Employees: —
Symbol: KRE Exchange: NYSE
Industry: Insurance - property & casualty

Capital Southwest Corp.
12900 Preston Rd., Ste. 700
Dallas, TX 75230
Phone: 214-233-8242 Fax: —
CEO: William R. Thomas
CFO: Tim Smith
1991 Sales: $2.4 million Employees: 7
Symbol: CSWC Exchange: NASDAQ
Industry: Financial - investment bankers

Capitol Bancorp Ltd.
200 Washington Square North
Lansing, MI 48933
Phone: 517-487-6555 Fax: —
CEO: Joseph D. Reid
CFO: Robert C. Carr
1991 Sales: $12 million Employees: 59
Symbol: CBCL Exchange: NASDAQ
Industry: Banks - Midwest

Capitol Industries–EMI
1750 N. Vine St.
Hollywood, CA 90028
Phone: 213-462-6252 Fax: 213-467-6550
CEO: Joe Smith
CFO: —
1992 Sales: $7,394 million Employees: 53,757
Parent: Thorn EMI PLC
Industry: Diversified operations - music & TV, rentals, technology

Capitol Transamerica Corp.
4610 University Pl., Ste. 1400
Madison, WI 53705
Phone: 608-231-4450 Fax: 608-231-3125
CEO: George A. Fait
CFO: Paul J. Breitnauer
1992 Sales: — Employees: —
Symbol: CATA Exchange: NASDAQ
Industry: Insurance - property & casualty

Capucci Creations Internationale
9565 Santa Monica Blvd.
Beverly Hills, CA 90210
Phone: 310-275-0700 Fax: —
CEO: Albert J. Fenster
CFO: Jason Fields
1991 Sales: $461 million Employees: 505
Ownership: Privately held
Industry: Apparel

Cardboard Gold
1938 E. Pomona St.
Santa Ana, CA 92705
Phone: 714-259-0550 Fax: 714-259-1460
CEO: Jack Mayes
CFO: Jack Mayes
1991 Sales: $11 million Employees: 16
Ownership: Privately held
Industry: Sports - collectible supplies & accessories

Cardinal Distribution, Inc.
655 Metro Place South, Ste. 925
Dublin, OH 43017
Phone: 614-761-8700 Fax: 614-761-8919
CEO: Robert D. Walter
CFO: David Bearman
1992 Sales: $1,951 million Employees: 1,400
Symbol: CDIC Exchange: NASDAQ
Industry: Drugs & sundries - wholesale

indicates company is in *Hoover's Handbook of American Business.*

indicates company is in *Hoover's Handbook of World Business;* sales and employee numbers are for parent company.

Cardinal Financial Group, Inc.
700 Frederica St.
Owensboro, KY 42301
Phone: 502-684-9661 Fax: —
CEO: William R. Spurrier
CFO: Wayne Milligan
1991 Sales: $25 million Employees: 91
Symbol: CAFS Exchange: NASDAQ
Industry: Financial - savings and loans

CardioPulmonics, Inc.
5060 W. Amelia Earhart Dr.
Salt Lake City, UT 84116
Phone: 801-350-3600 Fax: —
CEO: George M. Sims
CFO: William S. Barth
1991 Sales: $0.4 million Employees: 43
Symbol: CRDS Exchange: NASDAQ
Industry: Medical products

Cardiovascular Imaging Systems, Inc.
595 N. Pastoria Ave.
Sunnyvale, CA 94086
Phone: 408-749-9088 Fax: —
CEO: Richard M. Ferrari
CFO: John M. Harland
1991 Sales: $6.8 million Employees: 83
Symbol: CVIS Exchange: NASDAQ
Industry: Medical instruments - ultrasound imaging catheters

Care Group, Inc.
One Hollow Lane
Lake Success, NY 11042
Phone: 516-869-8383 Fax: 516-869-8401
CEO: Ann T. Mittasch
CFO: Pat H. Celli
1991 Sales: $22 million Employees: 1,852
Symbol: CARE Exchange: NASDAQ
Industry: Healthcare - outpatient & home

CareerCom Corp.
1801 Oberlin Rd.
Middletown, PA 17057
Phone: 215-851-8900 Fax: 215-939-7549
CEO: Robert A. Smith
CFO: Robert N. Belcher
1991 Sales: $130 million Employees: 2,350
Symbol: CCM Exchange: NYSE
Industry: Schools - trade & childcare

CareFlorida Inc.
7950 NW 53rd, Ste. 300
Miami, FL 33166
Phone: 305-591-3311 Fax: 305-470-1996
CEO: Paul Cejas
CFO: David Wester
1991 Sales: $111 million Employees: 194
Ownership: Privately held
Industry: Health maintenance organization

CareNetwork, Inc.
111 W. Pleasant St.
Milwaukee, WI 53212
Phone: 414-223-3300 Fax: —
CEO: Kipton Kaplan
CFO: Craig R. Kasten
1991 Sales: $160 million Employees: 247
Symbol: CRNT Exchange: NASDAQ
Industry: Health maintenance organization

Cargill, Incorporated
15407 McGinty Rd.
Minnetonka, MN 55440
Phone: 612-475-7575 Fax: 612-475-6208
CEO: Whitney MacMillan
CFO: —
1992 Sales: $46,800 million Employees: 63,500
Ownership: Privately held
Industry: Food - trading & processing

Carl Karcher Enterprises, Inc.
1200 N. Harbor Blvd.
Anaheim, CA 92801
Phone: 714-774-5796 Fax: 714-778-7183
CEO: Donald E. Doyle
CFO: Loren C. Pannier
1991 Sales: $534 million Employees: 14,000
Symbol: CARL Exchange: NASDAQ
Industry: Retail - food & restaurants

Carlisle Companies Inc.
101 S. Salina St., Ste. 800
Syracuse, NY 13202
Phone: 315-474-2500 Fax: 315-474-2008
CEO: Stephen P. Munn
CFO: Dennis J. Hall
1991 Sales: $501 million Employees: 4,876
Symbol: CSL Exchange: NYSE
Industry: Rubber & plastic products

Carlisle Plastics, Inc.
One Union St.
Boston, MA 02108
Phone: 617-557-2600 Fax: 617-523-5428
CEO: William H. Binnie
CFO: Rajiv P. Bhatt
1991 Sales: $344 million Employees: 2,700
Symbol: CPA Exchange: NYSE
Industry: Rubber & plastic products

Carlsberg Brand Team
One Busch Place
St. Louis, MO 63118
Phone: 314-577-2000 Fax: 314-577-9749
CEO: Brian Porter
CFO: —
1991 Sales: $1,736 million Employees: 11,494
Parent: Carlsberg AS
Industry: Beverages - beer

Carlson Co.
3 Corporate Plaza, Ste. 100
Newport Beach, CA 92660
Phone: 714-640-1922 Fax: 714-640-2043
CEO: Paul Carlson
CFO: Nathan Aronstein
1991 Sales: $2.2 million Employees: 57
Ownership: Privately held
Industry: Real estate operations - commercial property management

Carlson Companies, Inc.
Carlson Pkwy.
Minneapolis, MN 55459
Phone: 612-540-5000 Fax: 615-540-5832
CEO: Curtis L. Carlson
CFO: Bruce L. Paulsen
1992 Sales: $9,900 million Employees: 98,000
Ownership: Privately held
Industry: Business services - travel, hospitality & restaurants

Carmike Cinemas, Inc.
1301 First Ave.
Columbus, GA 31901
Phone: 706-576-3400 Fax: 706-576-3441
CEO: Michael W. Patrick
CFO: John O. Barwick III
1991 Sales: $146 million Employees: 5,440
Symbol: CKE Exchange: NASDAQ
Industry: Motion pictures & services - theaters

Carnival Cruise Lines, Inc.
Carnival Place, 3655 NW 87th Ave.
Miami, FL 33178
Phone: 305-599-2600 Fax: 305-594-7598
CEO: Micky Arison
CFO: Howard S. Frank
1992 Sales: $1,474 million Employees: 16,000
Symbol: CCL Exchange: NYSE
Industry: Automotive manufacturing - recreational vehicles

Carolco Pictures Inc.
8800 Sunset Blvd.
Los Angeles, CA 90069
Phone: 213-850-8800 Fax: 310-657-1629
CEO: Mario F. Kassar
CFO: Louis Weiss
1991 Sales: $596 million Employees: —
Symbol: CRC Exchange: NYSE
Industry: Motion pictures & services - production

Carolina Financial Corp.
158 Meeting St.
Charleston, SC 29401
Phone: 803-577-4510 Fax: —
CEO: Lary R. Scott
CFO: Frank J. Cole
1991 Sales: $16 million Employees: —
Symbol: CF Exchange: AMEX
Industry: Financial - savings and loans

Carolina Freight Corp.
North Carolina Hwy.150 E.
Cherryville, NC 28021
Phone: 704-435-6811 Fax: —
CEO: Lary R. Scott
CFO: Shawn W. Poole
1992 Sales: $801 million Employees: 10,821
Symbol: CAO Exchange: NYSE
Industry: Transportation - trucks

Carolina Power & Light Co.
411 Fayetteville St.
Raleigh, NC 27601
Phone: 919-546-6111 Fax: —
CEO: Sherwood H. Smith, Jr.
CFO: Charles D. Barham, Jr.
1992 Sales: $2,767 million Employees: 8,149
Symbol: CPL Exchange: NYSE
Industry: Utility - electric power

Carpenter Technology Corp.
101 W. Bern St.
Reading, PA 19612
Phone: 215-371-2000 Fax: —
CEO: Robert W. Cardy
CFO: G. Walton Cottrell
1992 Sales: $570 million Employees: 3,534
Symbol: CRS Exchange: NYSE
Industry: Steel - specialty alloys

Carr Gottstein Foods Inc.
6411 A St.
Anchorage, AK 99518
Phone: 907-561-1944 Fax: 907-564-2218
CEO: John J. Cairns
CFO: Bill Kretschmer
1991 Sales: $521 million Employees: 2,400
Ownership: Privately held
Industry: Retail - supermarkets & liquor, food distribution

Carrefour (USA) Inc.
1 Franklin Blvd.
Philadelphia, PA 19154
Phone: 215-632-8201 Fax: 215-632-8392
CEO: Jean Quantin
CFO: —
1991 Sales: $19,378 million Employees: 76,200
Parent: Carrefour SA
Industry: Retail - hypermarkets

Carretas Inc.
1900 7th St. NW
Albuquerque, NM 87102
Phone: 505-764-0047 Fax: 505-764-9245
CEO: Alfredo Garcia
CFO: Diana Bunnell
1991 Sales: $1.9 million Employees: 30
Ownership: Privately held
Industry: Building products - kiosks, pushcarts & store fixtures

A indicates company is in *Hoover's Handbook of American Business.*

W indicates company is in *Hoover's Handbook of World Business;* sales and employee numbers are for parent company.

Carriage Industries, Inc.
PO Box 12542
Calhoun, GA 30703
Phone: 404-629-9234 Fax: —
CEO: Stephen R. Dickinson
CFO: Steven G. Jones
1992 Sales: $120 million Employees: 845
Symbol: CGE Exchange: NYSE
Industry: Textiles - home furnishings

Carrington Laboratories, Inc.
2001 Walnut Hill Lane
Irving, TX 75038
Phone: 214-518-1300 Fax: 214-518-1020
CEO: Karl H. Meister
CFO: Steven E. Brown
1991 Sales: $15 million Employees: 125
Symbol: CRN Exchange: AMEX
Industry: Biomedical & genetic products

Carter Hawley Hale Stores, Inc.
444 S. Flower St.
Los Angeles, CA 90071
Phone: 213-620-0150 Fax: 213-620-0555
CEO: David Dworkin
CFO: Larry G. Petersen
1992 Sales: $2,184 million Employees: 24,000
Symbol: CHH Exchange: NYSE
Industry: Retail - major department stores

Carter-Wallace, Inc.
1345 Avenue of the Americas
New York, NY 10105
Phone: 212-339-5000 Fax: 212-339-5100
CEO: Henry H. Hoyt, Jr.
CFO: Paul A. Veteri
1992 Sales: $673 million Employees: 4,170
Symbol: CAR Exchange: NYSE
Industry: Drugs & personal care products

Carver Corp.
20121 48th Ave. West
Lynnwood, WA 98036
Phone: 206-775-1202 Fax: 206-778-9453
CEO: Robert R. Dougherty
CFO: Sandra L. Jenkins
1991 Sales: $28 million Employees: 170
Symbol: CAVR Exchange: NASDAQ
Industry: Audio & video home products

Cascade Corp.
2020 SW 4th Ave.
Portland, OR 97201
Phone: 503-227-0024 Fax: —
CEO: Joseph J. Barclay
CFO: Gerald M. Bitz
1991 Sales: $154 million Employees: 875
Symbol: CASC Exchange: NASDAQ
Industry: Machinery - material handling

Cascade Natural Gas Co.
222 Fairview Ave. North
Seattle, WA 98109
Phone: 206-624-3900 Fax: 206-624-7215
CEO: Melvin C. Clapp
CFO: Donald E. Bennett
1991 Sales: $154 million Employees: 455
Symbol: CGC Exchange: NYSE
Industry: Utility - gas distribution

Casey's General Stores, Inc.
One Convenience Blvd.
Ankeny, IA 50021
Phone: 515-965-6100 Fax: 515-965-6160
CEO: Donald F. Lamberti
CFO: Douglas K. Shull
1992 Sales: $644 million Employees: 6,192
Symbol: CASY Exchange: NASDAQ
Industry: Retail - convenience stores

Cash America Investments, Inc.
306 W. 7th St., Ste. 1000
Ft. Worth, TX 76102
Phone: 817-335-1100 Fax: 817-335-1119
CEO: Jack R. Daugherty
CFO: Dale R. Westerfeld
1991 Sales: $138 million Employees: 1,300
Symbol: PWN Exchange: NYSE
Industry: Retail - pawn shops

Casio, Inc.
570 Mount Pleasant Ave.
Dover, NJ 07801
Phone: 201-361-5400 Fax: 201-361-3819
CEO: John J. McDonald
CFO: —
1992 Sales: $3,067 million Employees: 4,412
Parent: Casio Computer Co., Ltd.
Industry: Office equipment, calculators & timepieces

Caspen Oil, Inc.
777 S. Wadsworth Blvd.
Lakewood, CO 80226
Phone: 303-987-0925 Fax: 303-987-0464
CEO: Anthony J. Carroll
CFO: Gary N. Davis
1991 Sales: $3.5 million Employees: 3
Symbol: CNO Exchange: AMEX
Industry: Oil & gas - US exploration & production

Catalina Lighting, Inc.
6073 NW 167th St. C-16
Hialeah, FL 33015
Phone: 305-558-4777 Fax: 305-584-4927
CEO: Robert Hersh
CFO: Dean S. Rappaport
1991 Sales: $88 million Employees: 166
Symbol: LTG Exchange: AMEX
Industry: Building products - lighting fixtures

Catalina Marketing Corp.
721 E. Ball Rd.
Anaheim, CA 92805
Phone: 714-956-6600 Fax: 714-956-5592
CEO: Tommy D. Greer
CFO: Joseph P. Proctor
1992 Sales: $52 million Employees: 251
Symbol: POS Exchange: NYSE
Industry: Business services - market research

Catalyst Energy
535 Madison Ave., 18th Fl.
New York, NY 10022
Phone: 212-826-8600 Fax: 212-826-8740
CEO: Tom B. Pickens III
CFO: —
1991 Sales: $705 million Employees: 1,406
Ownership: Privately held
Industry: Energy - alternative sources

Catellus Development Corp.
201 Mission St., 30th Fl.
San Francisco, CA 94105
Phone: 415-974-4500 Fax: 415-974-4613
CEO: Vernon B. Schwartz
CFO: David A. Smith
1991 Sales: $145 million Employees: 286
Symbol: CDX Exchange: NYSE
Industry: Real estate development

Caterair International Corp.
7811 Montrose Rd., Ste. 400
Potomac, MD 20854
Phone: 301-309-2800 Fax: 301-309-2893
CEO: Daniel J. Altobello
CFO: Harry D'Andrea
1991 Sales: $1,100 million Employees: 22,000
Ownership: Privately held
Industry: Food - preparation & distribution of airline meals

Caterpillar Inc.
100 NE Adams St.
Peoria, IL 61629
Phone: 309-675-1000 Fax: 309-675-5948
CEO: Donald V. Fites
CFO: Charles E. Rager
1992 Sales: $10,194 million Employees: 53,636
Symbol: CAT Exchange: NYSE
Industry: Machinery - construction & mining

Catherines Inc.
1878 Brooks Rd. East
Memphis, TN 38116
Phone: 901-398-9500 Fax: Ext. 279
CEO: Bernard J. Wein
CFO: David C. Forell
1991 Sales: $133 million Employees: 1,235
Symbol: CATH Exchange: NASDAQ
Industry: Retail - apparel & shoes

Cato Corp.
8100 Denmark Rd.
Charlotte, NC 28273
Phone: 704-554-8510 Fax: 704-551-7200
CEO: Wayland H. Cato, Jr.
CFO: Thomas H. Hicks
1991 Sales: $274 million Employees: 5,300
Symbol: CACOA Exchange: NASDAQ
Industry: Retail - apparel & shoes

Cavalier Homes of Alabama, Inc.
Hwy. 41 North & Cavalier Rd.
Addison, AL 35540
Phone: 205-747-1575 Fax: 205-747-2107
CEO: Jerry F. Wilson
CFO: David A. Roberson
1991 Sales: $68 million Employees: 799
Symbol: CXV Exchange: AMEX
Industry: Building - residential & commercial

CB&T Financial Corp.
103 Adams St.
Fairmont, WV 26554
Phone: 304-363-5800 Fax: —
CEO: William T. McLaughlin II
CFO: William M. Sutton
1991 Sales: $26 million Employees: 461
Symbol: CBTF Exchange: NASDAQ
Industry: Banks - Southeast

CBI Industries, Inc.
800 Jorie Blvd.
Oak Brook, IL 60522
Phone: 708-572-7000 Fax: 708-572-7405
CEO: John E. Jones
CFO: George L. Schueppert
1992 Sales: $1,673 million Employees: 12,480
Symbol: CBH Exchange: NYSE
Industry: Construction - heavy

CBL Medical, Inc.
2029 Century Park East
Los Angeles, CA 90067
Phone: 213-788-5845 Fax: 213-788-5880
CEO: Robert B. Mishkin
CFO: Robert B. Bunker
1991 Sales: $8 million Employees: 126
Symbol: CBLM Exchange: NASDAQ
Industry: Healthcare - outpatient & home

CBS Inc.
51 W. 52nd St.
New York, NY 10019
Phone: 212-975-4321 Fax: 212-975-7133
CEO: Laurence A. Tisch
CFO: Peter W. Keegan
1991 Sales: $3,035 million Employees: 6,160
Symbol: CBS Exchange: NYSE
Industry: Broadcasting - radio & TV

indicates company is in *Hoover's Handbook of American Business.*

indicates company is in *Hoover's Handbook of World Business;* sales and employee numbers are for parent company.

CC Industries Inc.
222 N. LaSalle St., Ste. 1000
Chicago, IL 60601
Phone: 312-855-4000 Fax: 312-984-1456
CEO: Neele E. Stearns
CFO: D. Scott Bradley
1991 Sales: $500 million Employees: 5,100
Ownership: Privately held
Industry: Diversified operations - home furnishings, paper & real estate

CCA Industries, Inc.
200 Murray Hill Pkwy.
East Rutherford, NJ 07073
Phone: 201-330-1400 Fax: 201-935-0675
CEO: David Edell
CFO: David Edell
1991 Sales: $27 million Employees: 82
Symbol: CCAM Exchange: NASDAQ
Industry: Wholesale distribution - consumer products

CCAIR, Inc.
100 Terminal Rd., 2nd Fl.
Charlotte, NC 28208
Phone: 704-359-8990 Fax: 704-359-8997
CEO: Kenneth W. Gann
CFO: Virginia V. Bennett
1992 Sales: $53 million Employees: 482
Symbol: CCAR Exchange: NASDAQ
Industry: Transportation - airline

CCB Financial Corp.
PO Box 931
Durham, NC 27702
Phone: 919-683-7777 Fax: —
CEO: W. L. Burns, Jr.
CFO: Ernest C. Roessler
1991 Sales: $221 million Employees: 1,580
Symbol: CCBF Exchange: NASDAQ
Industry: Banks - Southeast

CCC Franchising Corp.
61 Broadway
New York, NY 10006
Phone: 212-732-4974 Fax: —
CEO: Roger A. Bodman
CFO: Roger Barnett
1992 Sales: — Employees: 250
Symbol: CCFR Exchange: NASDAQ
Industry: Business services - business acquisitions & combinations

CCNB Corp.
4242 Carlisle Pike
Camp Hill, PA 17011
Phone: 717-730-2262 Fax: —
CEO: John V. Petrycki
CFO: Michael S. Borocz
1991 Sales: $47 million Employees: 729
Symbol: CCNC Exchange: NASDAQ
Industry: Banks - Northeast

CCX, Inc.
1200 Route 22
Bridgewater, NJ 08807
Phone: 908-231-8888 Fax: 908-231-8848
CEO: Barry Silverstein
CFO: Francis X. Feeney
1991 Sales: $57 million Employees: 646
Symbol: CCX Exchange: NYSE
Industry: Diversified operations - wire & fiberglass screens; specialty steel conversion

CDI Corp.
Ten Penn Center (18th & Market), 12th Fl.
Philadelphia, PA 19103
Phone: 215-569-2200 Fax: 215-569-1750
CEO: Walter R. Garrison
CFO: Edgar D. Landis
1992 Sales: $855 million Employees: 1,500
Symbol: CDI Exchange: NYSE
Industry: Engineering - R&D services

CE Software Holdings, Inc.
1801 Industrial Circle
West Des Moines, IA 50265
Phone: 515-224-1995 Fax: 515-224-4534
CEO: Richard A. Skeie
CFO: John S. Kirk
1991 Sales: $8.6 million Employees: 80
Symbol: CESH Exchange: NASDAQ
Industry: Computers - personal computer software

Cedar Fair, L.P.
PO Box 5006
Sandusky, OH 44871
Phone: 419-626-0830 Fax: —
CEO: Richard L. Kinzel
CFO: Bruce A. Jackson
1991 Sales: $128 million Employees: 4,700
Symbol: FUN Exchange: NYSE
Industry: Leisure & recreational services

Cedar Group, Inc.
4700 Wissahickon Ave.
Philadelphia, PA 19144
Phone: 215-843-1000 Fax: —
CEO: Stephen S. Simyak
CFO: Stephen S. Simyak
1991 Sales: $15 million Employees: 28
Symbol: CDRGQ Exchange: NASDAQ
Industry: Metal products - fasteners

Celgene Corp.
7 Powder Horn Dr.
Warren, NJ 07059
Phone: 908-271-1001 Fax: 908-271-4184
CEO: John L. Ufheil
CFO: Richard G. Holmes
1991 Sales: $1.3 million Employees: 46
Symbol: CELG Exchange: NASDAQ
Industry: Chemicals - specialty

Cellcor, Inc.
200 Wells Ave.
Newton, MA 02159
Phone: 617-332-2500 Fax: —
CEO: Richard R. D'Antoni
CFO: Harry W. Wilcox III
1991 Sales: $1.5 million Employees: 90
Symbol: CLTX Exchange: NASDAQ
Industry: Biomedical & genetic products

CellPro, Inc.
22322 20th Ave. SE
Bothell, WA 98021
Phone: 206-485-7644 Fax: —
CEO: Christopher Porter
CFO: Larry G. Culver
1992 Sales: $0.1 million Employees: 75
Symbol: CPRO Exchange: NASDAQ
Industry: Medical products - monoclonal antibody separators

Cellular, Inc.
5990 Greenwood Plaza Blvd.
Englewood, CO 80111
Phone: 303-694-3234 Fax: —
CEO: Arnold C. Pohs
CFO: Daniel P. Dwyer
1991 Sales: $4.9 million Employees: 292
Symbol: CELS Exchange: NASDAQ
Industry: Telecommunications services

Celtrix Laboratories, Inc.
2500 Faber Place
Palo Alto, CA 94303
Phone: 415-494-2500 Fax: 415-856-0533
CEO: Bruce B. Pharriss
CFO: Sandra McNamara
1992 Sales: $0.8 million Employees: 102
Symbol: CTRX Exchange: NASDAQ
Industry: Drugs

Celutel, Inc.
900 Bestgate Rd., Ste. 400
Annapolis, MD 21401
Phone: 410-573-5200 Fax: —
CEO: Frank S. Scarpa
CFO: Richard J. Donnelly
1992 Sales: $14 million Employees: 125
Symbol: CLU Exchange: AMEX
Industry: Telecommunications services

CEM Corp.
3100 Smith Farm Rd.
Matthews, NC 28105
Phone: 704-821-7015 Fax: 704-821-7894
CEO: Michael J. Collins
CFO: C. Phillip Brown
1992 Sales: $24 million Employees: 171
Symbol: CEMX Exchange: NASDAQ
Industry: Instruments - scientific

CenCor, Inc.
12th & Baltimore
Kansas City, MO 64196
Phone: 816-474-4750 Fax: —
CEO: Robert F. Brozman
CFO: Nora K. Gosney
1991 Sales: $65 million Employees: —
Symbol: CNCR Exchange: NASDAQ
Industry: Financial - consumer loans

CENFED Financial Corp.
199 N. Lake Ave.
Pasadena, CA 91101
Phone: 818-577-0500 Fax: —
CEO: D. Tad Lowery
CFO: Patrick Hartman
1991 Sales: $105 million Employees: 394
Symbol: CENF Exchange: NASDAQ
Industry: Banks - West

Centel Corp.
311 S. Wacker Dr., Ste. 5200
Chicago, IL 60606
Phone: 312-399-2500 Fax: 312-399-4795
CEO: John P. Frazee, Jr.
CFO: Eugene H. Irminger
1992 Sales: $1,191 million Employees: 9,291
Symbol: CNT Exchange: NYSE
Industry: Utility - telephone

Centennial Bancorp
96 E. Broadway
Eugene, OR 97401
Phone: 503-342-3970 Fax: —
CEO: Richard C. Williams
CFO: Michael J. Nysingh
1991 Sales: $12 million Employees: 93
Symbol: CEBC Exchange: NASDAQ
Industry: Banks - Midwest

Centennial Cellular Corp.
50 Locust Ave.
New Canaan, CT 06840
Phone: 203-972-2000 Fax: —
CEO: Bernard P. Gallagher
CFO: Scott N. Schneider
1992 Sales: $31 million Employees: 275
Symbol: CYCL Exchange: NASDAQ
Industry: Telecommunications services

Centennial Group, Inc.
282 S. Anita Dr.
Orange, CA 92668
Phone: 714-634-9200 Fax: —
CEO: Ronald R. White
CFO: J. David Cheshier
1992 Sales: $3.6 million Employees: 42
Symbol: QCEQ Exchange: AMEX
Industry: Real estate development

indicates company is in *Hoover's Handbook of American Business.*

indicates company is in *Hoover's Handbook of World Business;* sales and employee numbers are for parent company.

Center for Applied Psychology
307 E. Church Rd.
King of Prussia, PA 19406
Phone: 215-592-1141 Fax: 215-277-4556
CEO: Larry Shapiro
CFO: Rosa Rossello
1991 Sales: $4.4 million Employees: 18
Ownership: Privately held
Industry: Toys, children's games & books

Centerbank
60 N. Main St.
Waterbury, CT 06702
Phone: 203-573-7400 Fax: —
CEO: Robert J. Narkis
CFO: Joseph Carlson II
1992 Sales: — Employees: —
Symbol: CTBX Exchange: NASDAQ
Industry: Banks - Northeast

Centerior Energy Corp.
6200 Oak Tree Blvd.
Independence, OH 44131
Phone: 216-447-3100 Fax: 216-447-3240
CEO: Robert J. Farling
CFO: Edgar H. Maugans
1992 Sales: $2,438 million Employees: 8,591
Symbol: CX Exchange: NYSE
Industry: Utility - electric power

Centex Corp.
3333 Lee Pkwy., Ste. 1200
Dallas, TX 75219
Phone: 214-559-6500 Fax: 214-522-7625
CEO: Laurence E. Hirsch
CFO: David W. Quinn
1992 Sales: $2,374 million Employees: 5,500
Symbol: CTX Exchange: NYSE
Industry: Building - residential & commercial

Centex Telemanagement, Inc.
185 Berry St., Bldg. 1, Ste. 5100
San Francisco, CA 94107
Phone: 415-777-0477 Fax: 415-394-5838
CEO: Peter A. Howley
CFO: Henry P. Huff III
1991 Sales: $147 million Employees: 435
Symbol: CNTX Exchange: NASDAQ
Industry: Telecommunications services

Centigram Communications Corp.
91 E. Tasman Dr.
San Jose, CA 95134
Phone: 408-944-0250 Fax: 408-942-3560
CEO: George H. Sollman
CFO: Anthony R. Muller
1991 Sales: $36 million Employees: 227
Symbol: CGRM Exchange: NASDAQ
Industry: Telecommunications equipment

Centocor, Inc.
200 Great Valley Pkwy.
Malvern, PA 19355
Phone: 215-651-6000 Fax: 215-651-6100
CEO: David P. Holveck
CFO: Michael R. Dougherty
1991 Sales: $53 million Employees: —
Symbol: CNTO Exchange: NASDAQ
Industry: Biomedical & genetic products

Central and South West Services Corp.
1616 Woodall Rodgers Fwy.
Dallas, TX 75266
Phone: 214-754-1000 Fax: 214-754-1033
CEO: E. R. Brooks
CFO: Glenn D. Rosilier
1992 Sales: $3,311 million Employees: 8,434
Symbol: CSR Exchange: NYSE
Industry: Utility - electric power

Central and Southern Holding Co.
150 W. Green St.
Milledgeville, GA 31061
Phone: 912-452-5541 Fax: —
CEO: Robert C. Oliver
CFO: Peggy E. Hunter
1991 Sales: $11 million Employees: 120
Symbol: CSBC Exchange: NASDAQ
Industry: Banks - Southeast

Central Bancshares of the South, Inc.
701 S. 20th St.
Birmingham, AL 35233
Phone: 205-933-3000 Fax: —
CEO: D. Paul Jones, Jr.
CFO: Garrett R. Hegel
1991 Sales: $572 million Employees: 3,000
Symbol: CBSS Exchange: NASDAQ
Industry: Banks - Southeast

Central Co-operative Bank
399 Highland Ave.
Somerville, MA 02144
Phone: 617-628-4000 Fax: —
CEO: John D. Doherty
CFO: John D. Doherty
1992 Sales: — Employees: —
Symbol: CEBK Exchange: NASDAQ
Industry: Banks - Northeast

Central Fidelity Banks, Inc.
1021 E. Cary St.
Richmond, VA 23261
Phone: 804-697-6700 Fax: 804-697-7260
CEO: Carroll L. Saine
CFO: Charles W. Tysinger
1991 Sales: $639 million Employees: 3,000
Symbol: CFBS Exchange: NASDAQ
Industry: Banks - Southeast

Central Holding Co.
22500 Metropolitan Pkwy.
Mt. Clemens, MI 48043
Phone: 313-792-7000 Fax: —
CEO: Dominic Moceri
CFO: Carlo J. Catenacci
1991 Sales: $44 million Employees: 367
Symbol: CHOL Exchange: NASDAQ
Industry: Banks - Midwest

Central Hudson Gas & Electric Corp.
284 South Ave.
Poughkeepsie, NY 12601
Phone: 914-452-2000 Fax: 914-486-5894
CEO: John E. Mack III
CFO: John F. Drain
1991 Sales: $495 million Employees: 1,393
Symbol: CNH Exchange: NYSE
Industry: Utility - electric power

Central Indiana Bancorp
200 W. Mulberry St.
Kokomo, IN 46903
Phone: 317-457-5551 Fax: —
CEO: Robert J. Heltzel
CFO: Ralph A. Grotrian
1991 Sales: $16 million Employees: 63
Symbol: KOKO Exchange: NASDAQ
Industry: Banks - Midwest

Central Jersey Bancorp
PO Box 30
Freehold, NJ 07728
Phone: 908-462-0011 Fax: —
CEO: Elsie Sokol
CFO: James S. Vaccaro
1991 Sales: $143 million Employees: 730
Symbol: CJER Exchange: NASDAQ
Industry: Banks - Northeast

Central Louisiana Electric Co., Inc.
2030 Donahue Ferry Rd.
Pineville, LA 71360
Phone: 318-484-7400 Fax: 318-484-7465
CEO: Scott O. Brame
CFO: David M. Eppler
1991 Sales: $342 million Employees: 1,304
Symbol: CNL Exchange: NYSE
Industry: Utility - electric power

Central Maine Power Co.
Edison Dr.
Augusta, ME 04336
Phone: 207-623-3521 Fax: 207-626-9586
CEO: Matthew Hunter
CFO: David E. Marsh
1991 Sales: $866 million Employees: 2,436
Symbol: CTP Exchange: NYSE
Industry: Utility - electric power

Central Newspapers, Inc.
135 N. Pennsylvania St.
Indianapolis, IN 46204
Phone: 317-231-9200 Fax: 317-231-9208
CEO: Frank E. Russell
CFO: Wayne D. Wallace
1991 Sales: $420 million Employees: 4,973
Symbol: ECP Exchange: NYSE
Industry: Publishing - newspapers

Central Pennsylvania Financial Corp.
100 W. Independence St.
Shamokin, PA 17872
Phone: 717-644-0861 Fax: —
CEO: John M. O'Brien
CFO: Florian J. Gutkowski
1992 Sales: $42 million Employees: 187
Symbol: CPSA Exchange: NASDAQ
Industry: Financial - savings and loans

Central Reserve Life Corp.
17800 Royalton Rd.
Strongsville, OH 44136
Phone: 216-572-2400 Fax: —
CEO: Fred Lick, Jr.
CFO: Frank W. Grimone
1991 Sales: $147 million Employees: —
Symbol: CRLC Exchange: NASDAQ
Industry: Insurance - accident & health

Central Securities Corp.
375 Park Ave.
New York, NY 10152
Phone: 212-688-3011 Fax: —
CEO: Wilmot H. Kidd
CFO: Charles N. Edgerton
1992 Sales: — Employees: —
Symbol: CET Exchange: AMEX
Industry: Financial - investment management

Central Sprinkler Corp.
451 N. Cannon Ave.
Lansdale, PA 19446
Phone: 215-362-0700 Fax: 215-362-5385
CEO: George G. Meyer
CFO: Albert T. Sabol
1991 Sales: $62 million Employees: 410
Symbol: CNSP Exchange: NASDAQ
Industry: Sprinkler heads

Central Vermont Public Service Corp.
77 Grove St.
Rutland, VT 05701
Phone: 802-773-2711 Fax: 802-747-2199
CEO: Thomas C. Webb
CFO: Robert H. Young
1991 Sales: $234 million Employees: 784
Symbol: CV Exchange: NYSE
Industry: Utility - electric power

Centura Banks, Inc.
131 N. Church St.
Rocky Mount, NC 27804
Phone: 919-977-4811 Fax: —
CEO: J. Richard Futrell, Jr.
CFO: Frank J. Pattillo
1991 Sales: $257 million Employees: 1,585
Symbol: CBC Exchange: NYSE
Industry: Banks - Southeast

Century Bancorp, Inc.
400 Mystic Ave.
Medford, MA 02145
Phone: 617-391-4000 Fax: —
CEO: Marshall M. Sloane
CFO: Paul V. Cusick, Jr.
1991 Sales: $45 million Employees: 291
Symbol: CNBKA Exchange: NASDAQ
Industry: Banks - Northeast

Century Communications Corp.
50 Locust Ave.
New Canaan, CT 06840
Phone: 203-972-2000 Fax: 203-966-9228
CEO: Leonard Tow
CFO: Scott N. Schneider
1992 Sales: $312 million Employees: 2,000
Symbol: CTY Exchange: AMEX
Industry: Cable TV

Century South Banks, Inc.
PO Box 780
Dahlonega, GA 30533
Phone: 404-864-1111 Fax: —
CEO: J. Russell Ivie
CFO: Susan J. Anderson
1991 Sales: $14 million Employees: 246
Symbol: CSBI Exchange: NASDAQ
Industry: Banks - Southeast

Century Telephone Enterprises, Inc.
1900 N. 18th St., Ste. 700
Monroe, LA 71201
Phone: 318-388-9600 Fax: 318-388-9562
CEO: Glen F. Post III
CFO: R. Stewart Ewing, Jr.
1991 Sales: $281 million Employees: 2,020
Symbol: CTL Exchange: NYSE
Industry: Utility - telephone

Cenvill Development Corp.
2601-24 S. Military Trail
West Palm Beach, FL 33415
Phone: 407-641-5900 Fax: —
CEO: Richard Siemens
CFO: James A. Paul
1990 Sales: $129 million Employees: 303
Symbol: CVL Exchange: AMEX
Industry: Real estate development

Cephalon, Inc.
145 Brandywine Pkwy.
West Chester, PA 19380
Phone: 215-344-0200 Fax: 215-344-0065
CEO: Frank J. Baldino, Jr.
CFO: Kenneth F. Bonney
1991 Sales: $5 million Employees: 73
Symbol: CEPH Exchange: NASDAQ
Industry: Medical products

Ceradyne, Inc.
3169 Redhill Ave.
Costa Mesa, CA 92626
Phone: 714-549-0421 Fax: 714-549-5787
CEO: Joel P. Moskowitz
CFO: James F. Gardner
1991 Sales: $22 million Employees: 260
Symbol: CRDN Exchange: NASDAQ
Industry: Ceramics & ceramic products

CERBCO, Inc.
3421 Pennsy Dr.
Landover, MD 20785
Phone: 301-773-1784 Fax: 301-322-3041
CEO: Robert W. Erikson
CFO: Robert W. Erikson
1992 Sales: $30 million Employees: 233
Symbol: CERB Exchange: NASDAQ
Industry: Pipeline rehabilitation & copier products

Ceridian Corp.
8100 34th Ave. South
Minneapolis, MN 55440
Phone: 612-853-8100 Fax: —
CEO: Lawrence Perlman
CFO: John R. Eickhoff
1992 Sales: $830 million Employees: 13,000
Symbol: CEN Exchange: NYSE
Industry: Computers - mainframe

Cerner Corp.
2800 Rockcreek Pkwy.
Kansas City, MO 64117
Phone: 816-221-1024 Fax: 816-474-1742
CEO: Neal L. Patterson
CFO: Maureen M. Evans
1991 Sales: $77 million Employees: 505
Symbol: CERN Exchange: NASDAQ
Industry: Computers - software for health care providers

CertainTeed Corporation
750 E. Swedesford Rd.
Valley Forge, PA 19482
Phone: 215-341-7000 Fax: 215-341-7797
CEO: Michel Besson
CFO: —
1991 Sales: $14,491 million Employees: 104,653
Parent: Compagnie de Saint-Gobain SA
Industry: Diversified operations - flat glass, insulation, building materials & pipe

Certified Abatement Systems
10500 Telephone Rd.
Houston, TX 77075
Phone: 713-991-0480 Fax: 713-991-2814
CEO: William F. Wallace, Jr.
CFO: William F. Wallace III
1991 Sales: $4 million Employees: 25
Ownership: Privately held
Industry: Asbestos & lead abatement

CF Income Partners L.P.
10960 Wilshire Blvd.
Los Angeles, CA 90024
Phone: 213-444-3900 Fax: —
CEO: Dennis A. Sondker
CFO: Leeann Morein
1991 Sales: $37 million Employees: —
Symbol: CFI Exchange: NYSE
Industry: Real estate development

CFS Financial Corp.
4020 University Dr.
Fairfax, VA 22030
Phone: 703-691-4400 Fax: —
CEO: Allan R. Plumley, Jr.
CFO: Craig W. Anderson
1991 Sales: $108 million Employees: 413
Symbol: CFSC Exchange: NASDAQ
Industry: Financial - savings and loans

CFSB Bancorp, Inc.
112 E. Allegan St.
Lansing, MI 48933
Phone: 517-371-2911 Fax: 517-374-3557
CEO: Robert H. Becker
CFO: John W. Abbott
1991 Sales: $65 million Employees: 304
Symbol: CFSB Exchange: NASDAQ
Industry: Financial - savings and loans

CH Robinson Co.
8100 Mitchell Rd., Ste. 200
Eden Prairie, MN 55344
Phone: 612-937-8500 Fax: 612-937-7889
CEO: D. R. Verdoorn
CFO: Dale Hanson
1992 Sales: $965 million Employees: 941
Ownership: Privately held
Industry: Food-distribution & procurement services, third-party transportation

CH2M Hill Cos.
6060 S. Willow Dr.
Denver, CO 80111
Phone: 303-771-0900 Fax: 303-220-5106
CEO: Ralph R. Peterson
CFO: Vern Nelson
1991 Sales: $525 million Employees: 5,336
Ownership: Privately held
Industry: Engineering design & consulting

Chalone Wine Group, Ltd.
301 Howard St.
San Francisco, CA 94105
Phone: 415-546-7755 Fax: 415-546-9473
CEO: W. Philip Woodward
CFO: William L. Hamilton
1991 Sales: $15 million Employees: 260
Symbol: CHLN Exchange: NASDAQ
Industry: Beverages - wine

Chambers Development Co., Inc.
10700 Frankstown Rd.
Pittsburgh, PA 15235
Phone: 412-242-6237 Fax: 412-244-6139
CEO: John G. Rangos, Sr.
CFO: Richard A. Knight
1990 Sales: $258 million Employees: 5,350
Symbol: CDVA Exchange: AMEX
Industry: Waste disposal

Champion Enterprises, Inc.
2701 University Dr., Ste. 320
Auburn Hills, MI 48326
Phone: 313-340-9090 Fax: 313-340-9345
CEO: Walter R. Young, Jr.
CFO: Gerald W. Paga
1992 Sales: $270 million Employees: 2,200
Symbol: CHB Exchange: AMEX
Industry: Building - mobile homes & RVs

Champion International Corp.
One Champion Plaza
Stamford, CT 06921
Phone: 203-358-7000 Fax: 203-358-2975
CEO: Andrew C. Sigler
CFO: Gerald J. Beiser
1992 Sales: $4,927 million Employees: 27,500
Symbol: CHA Exchange: NYSE
Industry: Paper & paper products

Champion Parts, Inc.
2525 22nd St.
Oak Brook, IL 60521
Phone: 708-573-6600 Fax: 708-573-0348
CEO: Charles P. Schwartz, Jr.
CFO: Leonard D. O'Brien
1991 Sales: $112 million Employees: 1,760
Symbol: CREB Exchange: NASDAQ
Industry: Automotive & trucking - replacement parts

Chancellor Corp.
745 Atlantic Ave.
Boston, MA 02111
Phone: 617-728-8500 Fax: 617-728-8550
CEO: Stephen G. Morison
CFO: W. Barry Tanner
1991 Sales: $28 million Employees: 54
Symbol: CHCR Exchange: NASDAQ
Industry: Leasing - equipment

indicates company is in *Hoover's Handbook of American Business.*

indicates company is in *Hoover's Handbook of World Business;* sales and employee numbers are for parent company.

Chaparral Steel Co.
300 Ward Rd.
Midlothian, TX 76065
Phone: 214-775-8241 Fax: 214-775-1037
CEO: Gordon E. Forward
CFO: Richard M. Fowler
1992 Sales: $417 million Employees: 985
Symbol: CSM Exchange: NYSE
Industry: Steel - production

Charles Pankow Builders Ltd.
2476 N. Lake Ave.
Altadena, CA 91001
Phone: 213-684-2320 Fax: —
CEO: Charles Pankow
CFO: Tim Murphy
1991 Sales: $457 million Employees: 132
Ownership: Privately held
Industry: Construction - general contracting

Charles Schwab Corp., The
101 Montgomery St.
San Francisco, CA 94104
Phone: 415-627-7000 Fax: 415-627-8538
CEO: Charles R. Schwab
CFO: A. John Gambs
1992 Sales: $909 million Employees: 3,800
Symbol: SCH Exchange: NYSE
Industry: Financial - investment bankers

Charming Shoppes, Inc.
450 Winks Lane
Bensalem, PA 19020
Phone: 215-245-9100 Fax: 215-638-6873
CEO: David V. Wachs
CFO: Ivan Szeftel
1992 Sales: $1,137 million Employees: 14,500
Symbol: CHRS Exchange: NASDAQ
Industry: Retail - apparel & shoes

Chart House Enterprises, Inc.
115 S. Acacia Ave.
Solana Beach, CA 92075
Phone: 619-755-8281 Fax: 619-481-2579
CEO: John M. Creed
CFO: Harold E. Gaubert, Jr.
1991 Sales: $162 million Employees: 6,000
Symbol: CHT Exchange: NYSE
Industry: Retail - food & restaurants

Charter Federal Savings Bank
110 Piedmont Ave.
Bristol, VA 24201
Phone: 703-669-5101 Fax: —
CEO: E. L. Byington, Jr.
CFO: Douglas D. Deppen
1992 Sales: — Employees: —
Symbol: CHFD Exchange: NASDAQ
Industry: Financial - savings and loans

Charter FSB Bancorp, Inc.
430 Route 10
Randolph, NJ 07869
Phone: 201-366-3300 Fax: —
CEO: Richard McAloon
CFO: Richard McAloon
1991 Sales: $30 million Employees: 86
Symbol: CFED Exchange: NASDAQ
Industry: Financial - savings and loans

Charter Golf, Inc.
2791 Loker Ave. West
Carlsbad, CA 92008
Phone: 619-438-6610 Fax: 619-438-6657
CEO: Gerald W. Montiel
CFO: Gerald W. Montiel
1991 Sales: $17 million Employees: 127
Symbol: CGOL Exchange: NASDAQ
Industry: Apparel

Charter Medical Corp.
577 Mulberry St.
Macon, GA 31298
Phone: 912-742-1161 Fax: 912-751-2909
CEO: William A. Fickling, Jr.
CFO: Lawrence W. Drinkard
1992 Sales: $1,283 million Employees: 14,700
Symbol: CMD Exchange: AMEX
Industry: Hospitals - general, psychiatric & acute care

Charter Oak Consulting Group
10 State House Sq.
Hartford, CT 06103
Phone: 203-987-5280 Fax: 203-987-8115
CEO: Jim Hassinger
CFO: Jim Hassinger
1991 Sales: $3.7 million Employees: 10
Ownership: Privately held
Industry: Business services - management & consulting

Charter One Financial, Inc.
1215 Superior Ave.
Cleveland, OH 44114
Phone: 216-589-8320 Fax: —
CEO: Charles John Koch
CFO: Leonard A. Krysinski
1991 Sales: $328 million Employees: 1,278
Symbol: COFI Exchange: NASDAQ
Industry: Financial - savings and loans

Charter Power Systems, Inc.
3043 Walton Rd.
Plymouth Meeting, PA 19462
Phone: 215-828-9000 Fax: 215-834-7307
CEO: Alfred Weber
CFO: Gary M. Cademartori
1991 Sales: $151 million Employees: 1,034
Symbol: CHP Exchange: AMEX
Industry: Electrical components - battery power systems

Chase Enterprises
One Commercial Plaza
Hartford, CT 06103
Phone: 203-549-1674 Fax: 203-293-4289
CEO: David T. Chase
CFO: Richard B. Steele
1991 Sales: $550 million Employees: 8,000
Ownership: Privately held
Industry: Diversified operations - real estate, media, investments & insurance

Chase Manhattan Corp., The
1 Chase Manhattan Plaza
New York, NY 10081
Phone: 212-552-2222 Fax: 212-552-5005
CEO: Thomas G. Labrecque
CFO: E. Michael Kruse
1992 Sales: $11,125 million Employees: 36,210
Symbol: CMB Exchange: NYSE
Industry: Banks - money center

Chattem, Inc.
1715 W. 38th St.
Chattanooga, TN 37409
Phone: 615-821-4571 Fax: 615-821-0395
CEO: Zan Guerry
CFO: Robert E. Bosworth
1992 Sales: $108 million Employees: 357
Symbol: CHTT Exchange: NASDAQ
Industry: Cosmetics & toiletries

Check Technology Corp.
1284 Corporate Center Dr.
St. Paul, MN 55121
Phone: 612-454-9300 Fax: 612-454-0367
CEO: Jay A. Herman
CFO: Jay A. Herman
1991 Sales: $22 million Employees: 162
Symbol: CTCQ Exchange: NASDAQ
Industry: Machinery - printing

Checkers Drive-In Restaurants, Inc.
600 Cleveland St., Ste. 1050
Clearwater, FL 34615
Phone: 813-441-3500 Fax: 813-443-7047
CEO: James E. Mattei
CFO: N. John Simmons, Jr.
1992 Sales: $89 million Employees: 2,170
Symbol: CHKR Exchange: NASDAQ
Industry: Retail - food & restaurants

Checkpoint Systems, Inc.
550 Grove Rd.
Thorofare, NJ 08086
Phone: 609-848-1800 Fax: 609-848-0937
CEO: A. E. Wolf
CFO: Steven G. Selfridge
1991 Sales: $53 million Employees: 809
Symbol: CHEK Exchange: NASDAQ
Industry: Protection - access control & article surveillance systems

Chemcentral Corp.
7050 W. 71st St.
Bedford Park, IL 60638
Phone: 708-594-7000 Fax: 708-594-7022
CEO: H. Daniel Wenstrup
CFO: A. L. Haines
1991 Sales: $575 million Employees: 780
Ownership: Privately held
Industry: Chemical distribution

ChemDesign Corp.
99 Development Rd.
Fitchburg, MA 01420
Phone: 508-345-9999 Fax: 508-342-9769
CEO: Richard E.T. Brooks
CFO: Jay R. LaMarche
1991 Sales: $40 million Employees: 304
Symbol: CDCC Exchange: NASDAQ
Industry: Chemicals - specialty

Chemed Corp.
255 E. Fifth St., 2600 Chemed Ctr.
Cincinnati, OH 45202
Phone: 513-762-6900 Fax: —
CEO: Edward L. Hutton
CFO: Timothy S. O'Toole
1991 Sales: $352 million Employees: 3,325
Symbol: CHE Exchange: NYSE
Industry: Chemicals - specialty

Chemex Pharmaceuticals, Inc.
One Executive Dr.
Ft. Lee, NJ 07024
Phone: 201-944-1449 Fax: 201-944-9474
CEO: Herbert H. McDade, Jr.
CFO: Leonard F. Stigliano
1991 Sales: $3 million Employees: 13
Symbol: CHMX Exchange: NASDAQ
Industry: Drugs

Chemfab Corp.
701 Daniel Webster Hwy.
Merrimack, NH 03054
Phone: 603-424-9000 Fax: 603-424-9028
CEO: Duane C. Montopoli
CFO: William H. Everett
1992 Sales: $50 million Employees: 381
Symbol: CMFB Exchange: NASDAQ
Industry: Chemicals - fibers

Chemfix Technologies, Inc.
3838 N. Causeway Blvd., Ste. 2500
Metairie, LA 70002
Phone: 504-835-4784 Fax: 504-833-4615
CEO: Daniel N. Silverman III
CFO: Michael E. McGoey
1991 Sales: $25 million Employees: 170
Symbol: CFIX Exchange: NASDAQ
Industry: Pollution control equipment & services

Chemical Banking Corp.
270 Park Ave.
New York, NY 10017
Phone: 212-270-6000 Fax: 212-270-2613
CEO: John F. McGillicuddy
CFO: Peter J. Tobin
1992 Sales: $12,174 million Employees: 43,169
Symbol: CHL Exchange: NYSE
Industry: Banks - money center

Chemical Financial Corp.
333 E. Main St.
Midland, MI 48640
Phone: 517-631-3310 Fax: —
CEO: Alan W. Ott
CFO: Lori A. Gwizdala
1991 Sales: $48 million Employees: 843
Symbol: CHFC Exchange: NASDAQ
Industry: Banks - Midwest

Chemical Leaman Corp.
102 Pickering Way
Exton, PA 19341
Phone: 215-363-4200 Fax: 215-363-4251
CEO: David R. Hamilton
CFO: Charles E. Fernald
1991 Sales: $223 million Employees: 1,852
Symbol: CLEA Exchange: NASDAQ
Industry: Transportation - truck

Chemical Waste Management, Inc.
3003 Butterfield Rd.
Oak Brook, IL 60521
Phone: 708-218-1500 Fax: 708-572-3094
CEO: David P. Payne
CFO: Bruce D. Tobecksen
1992 Sales: $1,519 million Employees: 11,425
Symbol: CHW Exchange: NYSE
Industry: Pollution control equipment & services

Chemoil Corp.
750 Battery St., 6th Fl.
San Francisco, CA 94111
Phone: 415-956-3834 Fax: 415-956-4877
CEO: Robert V. Chandran
CFO: Lucius Conrad
1990 Sales: $482 million Employees: 120
Ownership: Privately held
Industry: Oil marketing

Chempower, Inc.
807 E. Turkeyfoot Lake Rd.
Akron, OH 44319
Phone: 216-896-4202 Fax: 216-896-1866
CEO: Toomas J. Kukk
CFO: Robert E. Rohr
1991 Sales: $56 million Employees: 562
Symbol: CHEM Exchange: NASDAQ
Industry: Pollution control equipment & services - asbestos abatement

ChemTrak, Inc.
484 Oakmead Pkwy.
Sunnyvale, CA 94086
Phone: 408-773-8156 Fax: —
CEO: P. Singh
CFO: R. Terry Duryea
1991 Sales: $1.8 million Employees: 84
Symbol: CMTR Exchange: NASDAQ
Industry: Medical services

Cherokee Group, Inc.
9545 Wentworth St.
Sunland, CA 91040
Phone: 818-951-1002 Fax: 818-352-1851
CEO: Robert Margolis
CFO: Cary D. Cooper
1992 Sales: $195 million Employees: 640
Symbol: CHKE Exchange: NASDAQ
Industry: Apparel & shoes

Cherry Electrical Products
3600 Sunset Ave.
Waukegan, IL 60087
Phone: 708-662-9200 Fax: 708-360-3566
CEO: Peter B. Cherry
CFO: Edward R. Mass
1992 Sales: $229 million Employees: 2,682
Symbol: CHER Exchange: NASDAQ
Industry: Electrical components - misc.

Chesapeake Corp.
1021 E. Cary St.
Richmond, VA 23218
Phone: 804-697-1000 Fax: 804-697-1199
CEO: J. Carter Fox
CFO: Andrew J. Kohut
1992 Sales: $888 million Employees: 5,039
Symbol: CSK Exchange: NYSE
Industry: Paper & paper products

Chesapeake Utilities Corp.
350 S. Queen St.
Dover, DE 19901
Phone: 302-734-6700 Fax: 302-734-6787
CEO: Ralph J. Adkins
CFO: John R. Schimkaitis
1991 Sales: $70 million Employees: 311
Symbol: CHPK Exchange: NASDAQ
Industry: Utility - gas distribution

Cheshire Financial Corp.
194 West St.
Keene, NH 03431
Phone: 603-352-2502 Fax: 603-352-9310
CEO: Peter J. Baxter
CFO: Mark A. Gavin
1991 Sales: $60 million Employees: 320
Symbol: CFX Exchange: AMEX
Industry: Banks - Northeast

Chester Valley Bancorp Inc.
100 E. Lancaster Ave.
Downingtown, PA 19335
Phone: 215-269-9700 Fax: —
CEO: Ellen Ann Roberts
CFO: Anthony J. Biondi
1991 Sales: $16 million Employees: 75
Symbol: CVAL Exchange: NASDAQ
Industry: Financial - savings and loans

Chevron Corp.
225 Bush St.
San Francisco, CA 94104
Phone: 415-894-7700 Fax: 415-894-0593
CEO: Kenneth T. Derr
CFO: Martin R. Klitten
1992 Sales: $42,900 million Employees: 55,123
Symbol: CHV Exchange: NYSE
Industry: Oil & gas - international integrated

Cheyenne Software, Inc.
55 Bryant Ave.
Roslyn, NY 11576
Phone: 516-484-5110 Fax: 516-484-3446
CEO: Eli Oxenhorn
CFO: Elliot Levine
1992 Sales: $18 million Employees: 107
Symbol: CYE Exchange: AMEX
Industry: Computers - software

Chicago and North Western Holdings Corp.
One North Western Center
Chicago, IL 60606
Phone: 312-559-7000 Fax: 312-559-7072
CEO: Robert Schmiege
CFO: Thomas A. Tingleff
1992 Sales: $985 million Employees: 5,910
Symbol: CNW Exchange: NYSE
Industry: Transportation - rail

Chicago Rivet & Machine Co.
901 Frontenac Rd.
Naperville, IL 60563
Phone: 708-357-8500 Fax: 708-983-9314
CEO: John A. Morrissey
CFO: John C. Osterman
1991 Sales: $15 million Employees: 262
Symbol: CVR Exchange: AMEX
Industry: Metal products - fasteners

Chico's
15550 McGregor Blvd.
Ft. Myers, FL 33908
Phone: 813-433-5505 Fax: 813-433-5439
CEO: Marvin Gralinick
CFO: Jeff Zwick
1991 Sales: $23 million Employees: 240
Ownership: Privately held
Industry: Apparel - women's

Children's Discovery Centers of America, Inc.
1210 Fifth Ave.
San Rafael, CA 94901
Phone: 415-459-1291 Fax: 415-459-1374
CEO: Richard A. Niglio
CFO: Randall J. Truelove
1991 Sales: $20 million Employees: 1,700
Symbol: CDCRA Exchange: NASDAQ
Industry: Schools - preschool & child care

Chiles Offshore Corp.
1900 West Loop South, Ste. 1400
Houston, TX 77027
Phone: 713-621-4991 Fax: 713-621-7489
CEO: William E. Chiles
CFO: Jerry M. Brooks
1991 Sales: $53 million Employees: 580
Symbol: CHC Exchange: AMEX
Industry: Oil & gas - offshore drilling

Chilewich Sons
Twelve Water St.
White Plains, NY 10601
Phone: 914-997-2000 Fax: 914-997-2122
CEO: Simon Chilewich
CFO: Peter Bellig
1991 Sales: $500 million Employees: 850
Ownership: Privately held
Industry: Diversified operations - commodity trading, cattle, meatpacking

Chipcom Corp.
118 Turnpike Rd.
Southborough, MA 01772
Phone: 508-460-8900 Fax: 508-460-8950
CEO: John Robert Held
CFO: Robert P. Badavas
1992 Sales: $87 million Employees: 272
Symbol: CHPM Exchange: NASDAQ
Industry: Computers - network products

Chippewa Resources Corp.
555 Seventeenth St., Ste. 3310
Denver, CO 80202
Phone: 303-298-7425 Fax: 303-298-8251
CEO: Aleron H. Larson, Jr.
CFO: Aleron H. Larson, Jr.
1991 Sales: $3.4 million Employees: 12
Symbol: CWA Exchange: AMEX
Industry: Oil & gas - US exploration & production

Chips and Technologies, Inc.
3050 Zanker Rd.
San Jose, CA 95134
Phone: 408-434-0600 Fax: 408-434-9315
CEO: Gordon A. Campbell
CFO: Gary P. Martin
1992 Sales: $141 million Employees: 531
Symbol: CHPS Exchange: NASDAQ
Industry: Electrical components - semiconductors

ChipSoft, Inc.
6256 Greenwich Dr., Ste. 103
San Diego, CA 92122
Phone: 619-453-4446 Fax: 619-453-4440
CEO: Charles H. Gaylord, Jr.
CFO: William H. Lane III
1992 Sales: $50 million Employees: 314
Symbol: CSFT Exchange: NASDAQ
Industry: Computers - software

Chiquita Brands International, Inc.
250 E. 5th St.
Cincinnati, OH 45202
Phone: 513-784-8011 Fax: 513-784-8030
CEO: Carl H. Lindner
CFO: Fred J. Runk
1991 Sales: $4,627 million Employees: 50,000
Symbol: CQB Exchange: NYSE
Industry: Food - fruit, meats & prepared foods

Chiron Corp.
4560 Horton St.
Emeryville, CA 94608
Phone: 510-655-8730 Fax: 510-655-9910
CEO: Edward E. Penhoet
CFO: Dennis L. Winger
1991 Sales: $69 million Employees: 1,510
Symbol: CHIR Exchange: NASDAQ
Industry: Biomedical & genetic products

Chittenden Corp.
Two Burlington Square
Burlington, VT 05402
Phone: 802-658-4000 Fax: —
CEO: Paul A. Perrault
CFO: Nancy Rowden Brock
1991 Sales: $110 million Employees: 684
Symbol: CNDN Exchange: NASDAQ
Industry: Banks - Northeast

Chock Full O'Nuts Corp.
370 Lexington Ave.
New York, NY 10017
Phone: 212-532-0300 Fax: 212-679-9737
CEO: Joseph A. Breslin
CFO: Howard M. Leitner
1991 Sales: $270 million Employees: 1,300
Symbol: CHF Exchange: NYSE
Industry: Food - coffee & tea

Choice Drug Systems, Inc.
457 Doughty Blvd.
Inwood, NY 11696
Phone: 516-239-3673 Fax: —
CEO: Marvin Sirota
CFO: Frank Mandelbaum
1992 Sales: $27 million Employees: 129
Symbol: DOSE Exchange: NASDAQ
Industry: Medical services

Cholestech Corp.
3347 Investment Blvd.
Hayward, CA 94545
Phone: 510-732-7200 Fax: —
CEO: Edward L. Erickson
CFO: Warren E. Pinckert II
1992 Sales: $1.5 million Employees: 85
Symbol: CTEC Exchange: NASDAQ
Industry: Medical services

Chris-Craft Industries, Inc.
600 Madison Ave.
New York, NY 10022
Phone: 212-421-0200 Fax: 212-935-8462
CEO: Herbert J. Siegel
CFO: Laurence M. Kashdin
1991 Sales: $284 million Employees: 1,030
Symbol: CCN Exchange: NYSE
Industry: Broadcasting - radio & TV

Christiana Companies, Inc.
777 E. Wisconsin Ave.
Milwaukee, WI 53202
Phone: 414-291-9000 Fax: 414-291-9061
CEO: Sheldon B. Lubar
CFO: James C. Rowe
1992 Sales: $39 million Employees: 218
Symbol: CST Exchange: NYSE
Industry: Real estate development

Chromcraft Revington, Inc.
1100 N. Washington St.
Delphi, IN 46923
Phone: 317-564-3500 Fax: —
CEO: Michael E. Thomas
CFO: Frank T. Kane
1992 Sales: — Employees: 1,300
Symbol: CROM Exchange: NASDAQ
Industry: Furniture

Chronimed, Inc.
13911 Ridgedale Dr.
Minnetonka, MN 55343
Phone: 612-541-0239 Fax: —
CEO: Maurice R. Taylor II
CFO: Mary M. Lach
1991 Sales: $13 million Employees: —
Symbol: CHMD Exchange: NASDAQ
Industry: Medical products

Chrysler Corp.
12000 Chrysler Dr.
Highland Park, MI 48288
Phone: 313-956-5741 Fax: 313-956-3747
CEO: Lee A. Iacocca
CFO: Jerome B. York
1992 Sales: $36,900 million Employees: 124,000
Symbol: C Exchange: NYSE
Industry: Automotive manufacturing

Chubb Corp., The
15 Mountain View Rd.
Warren, NJ 07061
Phone: 908-580-2000 Fax: 908-580-2027
CEO: Dean R. O'Hare
CFO: Dean R. O'Hare
1992 Sales: $4,941 million Employees: —
Symbol: CB Exchange: NYSE
Industry: Insurance - property & casualty

Church & Dwight Co., Inc.
469 N. Harrison St.
Princeton, NJ 08540
Phone: 609-683-5900 Fax: 609-683-5092
CEO: Dwight C. Minton
CFO: Anthony P. Deasey
1991 Sales: $487 million Employees: 1,081
Symbol: CHD Exchange: NYSE
Industry: Soap & cleaning preparations

Chyron Corp.
265 Spagnoli Rd.
Melville, NY 11747
Phone: 516-845-2000 Fax: 516-249-3342
CEO: Alfred O.P. Leubert
CFO: John A. Poserina
1991 Sales: $24 million Employees: 257
Symbol: CHY Exchange: NYSE
Industry: Video equipment

Ciba-Geigy Corporation
444 Saw Mill River Rd.
Ardsley, NY 10502
Phone: 914-479-5000 Fax: 914-478-1201
CEO: Richard Barth
CFO: —
1991 Sales: $15,498 million Employees: 91,665
Parent: Ciba-Geigy Ltd.
Industry: Chemicals - diversified

CIGNA Corp.
One Liberty Place
Philadelphia, PA 19192
Phone: 215-761-1000 Fax: 215-761-5515
CEO: Wilson H. Taylor
CFO: James G. Stewart
1991 Sales: $18,750 million Employees: 53,250
Symbol: CI Exchange: NYSE
Industry: Insurance - multiline & misc.

CII Financial, Inc.
4001 W. Alameda Ave.
Burbank, CA 91505
Phone: 818-846-5297 Fax: —
CEO: Joseph G. Havlick
CFO: Thomas G. Bernard
1991 Sales: $112 million Employees: —
Symbol: CII Exchange: AMEX
Industry: Insurance - accident & health

CILCORP Inc.
300 Hamilton Blvd., Ste. 300
Peoria, IL 61602
Phone: 309-675-8850 Fax: 309-677-7579
CEO: R. O. Viets
CFO: W. M. Shay
1991 Sales: $590 million Employees: 3,060
Symbol: CER Exchange: NYSE
Industry: Utility - electric power

CIMCO, Inc.
265 Briggs Ave.
Costa Mesa, CA 92626
Phone: 714-546-4460 Fax: 714-556-6955
CEO: Russell T. Gilbert
CFO: Laurance W. Simmons
1992 Sales: $70 million Employees: 802
Symbol: CIMC Exchange: NASDAQ
Industry: Thermoplastic components

Cimflex Teknowledge Corp.
1195 Washington Pike, Corporate 1 West
Bridgeville, PA 15017
Phone: 412-787-3000 Fax: 412-787-0350
CEO: Rick Hayes-Roth
CFO: Thomas J. Gill
1991 Sales: $15 million Employees: 135
Symbol: CMTK Exchange: NASDAQ
Industry: Computers - software

Cincinnati Bell Inc.
201 E. Fourth St.
Cincinnati, OH 45202
Phone: 513-397-9900 Fax: 513-421-5973
CEO: Dwight H. Hibbard
CFO: Dennis J. Sullivan, Jr.
1992 Sales: $1,136 million Employees: 12,100
Symbol: CSN Exchange: NYSE
Industry: Utility - telephone

Cincinnati Financial Corp.
6200 S. Gilmore Rd.
Fairfield, OH 45014
Phone: 513-870-2000 Fax: 513-870-2088
CEO: John J. Schiff
CFO: Robert J. Driehaus
1992 Sales: $1,304 million Employees: —
Symbol: CINF Exchange: NASDAQ
Industry: Insurance - property & casualty

Cincinnati Gas & Electric Co.
139 E. Fourth St.
Cincinnati, OH 45202
Phone: 513-381-2000 Fax: 513-287-3698
CEO: Jackson H. Randolph
CFO: C. Robert Everman
1992 Sales: $1,553 million Employees: 5,472
Symbol: CIN Exchange: NYSE
Industry: Utility - electric power

indicates company is in *Hoover's Handbook of American Business.*

indicates company is in *Hoover's Handbook of World Business;* sales and employee numbers are for parent company.

Cincinnati Microwave, Inc.
One Microwave Plaza
Cincinnati, OH 45249
Phone: 513-489-5400 Fax: 512-489-8036
CEO: John L. Jaeger
CFO: Michael C. Koetters
1991 Sales: $54 million Employees: 400
Symbol: CNMW Exchange: NASDAQ
Industry: Electrical products - radar detectors

Cincinnati Milacron Inc.
4701 Marburg Ave.
Cincinnati, OH 45209
Phone: 513-841-8100 Fax: 513-841-8991
CEO: Daniel J. Meyer
CFO: William E. Buchholz
1992 Sales: $789 million Employees: 6,559
Symbol: CMZ Exchange: NYSE
Industry: Machine tools & related products

Cintas Corp.
6800 Cintas Blvd.
Mason, OH 45040
Phone: 513-459-1200 Fax: —
CEO: Richard T. Farmer
CFO: David T. Jeanmougin
1992 Sales: $402 million Employees: 7,088
Symbol: CTAS Exchange: NASDAQ
Industry: Linen supply & related - uniform rental and sale

Ciprico Inc.
2800 Campus Dr.
Plymouth, MN 55441
Phone: 612-559-2034 Fax: 612-559-8799
CEO: Robert H. Kill
CFO: Robert H. Kill
1991 Sales: $10.7 million Employees: 83
Symbol: CPCI Exchange: NASDAQ
Industry: Computers - peripheral equipment

CIPSCO Inc.
607 E. Adams St.
Springfield, IL 62739
Phone: 217-523-3600 Fax: 217-525-5825
CEO: Clifford L. Greenwalt
CFO: Robert W. Jackson
1991 Sales: $722 million Employees: 2,712
Symbol: CIP Exchange: NYSE
Industry: Utility - electric power

Circle Financial Corp.
11100 Reading Rd.
Sharonville, OH 45241
Phone: 513-563-1245 Fax: —
CEO: Donald H. Rolf, Jr.
CFO: David C. Greis
1992 Sales: — Employees: —
Symbol: CRCL Exchange: NASDAQ
Industry: Banks - Midwest

Circle Fine Art Corp.
303 E. Wacker Dr., Ste. 830
Chicago, IL 60601
Phone: 312-616-1300 Fax: 312-616-1301
CEO: Jack Solomon
CFO: Joseph R. Atkin
1991 Sales: $36 million Employees: 385
Trading Status: Suspended
Industry: Retail - art galleries

Circle K Corp., The
1601 N. 7th St.
Phoenix, AZ 85072
Phone: 602-253-9600 Fax: 602-257-4468
CEO: Bart A. Brown, Jr.
CFO: Larry J. Zine
1992 Sales: $2,904 million Employees: 21,487
Trading Status: Suspended
Industry: Retail - convenience stores

Circon Corp.
460 Ward Dr.
Santa Barbara, CA 93111
Phone: 805-967-0404 Fax: 805-967-5035
CEO: Richard A. Auhll
CFO: R. Bruce Thompson
1991 Sales: $69 million Employees: 694
Symbol: CCON Exchange: NASDAQ
Industry: Medical instruments - endoscopes

Circuit City Stores, Inc.
9950 Mayland Dr.
Richmond, VA 23233
Phone: 804-527-4000 Fax: 804-527-4164
CEO: Richard L. Sharp
CFO: Michael T. Chalifoux
1992 Sales: $3,075 million Employees: 16,635
Symbol: CC Exchange: NYSE
Industry: Retail - consumer electronics

Circuit Systems, Inc.
2350 E. Lunt Ave.
Elk Grove Village, IL 60007
Phone: 708-439-1999 Fax: —
CEO: D. S. Patel
CFO: Dilip S. Vyas
1992 Sales: $47 million Employees: 500
Symbol: CSYI Exchange: NASDAQ
Industry: Electrical components - printed circuit boards

Circus Circus Enterprises, Inc.
2880 Las Vegas Blvd. South
Las Vegas, NV 89109
Phone: 702-734-0410 Fax: 702-734-2268
CEO: William G. Bennett
CFO: Clyde T. Turner
1992 Sales: $840 million Employees: 13,464
Symbol: CIR Exchange: NYSE
Industry: Leisure & recreational services - casinos

Cirrus Logic, Inc.
3700 W. Warren Ave.
Fremont, CA 95035
Phone: 510-623-8300 Fax: 510-226-2240
CEO: Michael L. Hackworth
CFO: Sam S. Srinivasan
1992 Sales: $202 million Employees: 748
Symbol: CRUS Exchange: NASDAQ
Industry: Electrical components - semiconductors

Cisco Systems, Inc.
1525 O'Brien Dr.
Menlo Park, CA 94025
Phone: 415-326-1941 Fax: 415-326-1989
CEO: John P. Morgridge
CFO: John M. Russell
1992 Sales: $340 million Employees: 882
Symbol: CSCO Exchange: NASDAQ
Industry: Computers - internetworking hardware

Citadel Holding Corp.
600 N. Brand Blvd.
Glendale, CA 91203
Phone: 818-956-7100 Fax: 818-246-6162
CEO: William C. Walbrecher
CFO: Philip R. Sherringham
1991 Sales: $533 million Employees: 887
Symbol: CDL Exchange: AMEX
Industry: Financial - savings and loans

Citation Insurance Group
One Almaden Blvd.
San Jose, CA 95113
Phone: 408-292-0222 Fax: —
CEO: Donald D. Young
CFO: Dennis J. Pastirik
1991 Sales: $73 million Employees: 150
Symbol: CITN Exchange: NASDAQ
Industry: Insurance - accident & health

CitFed Bancorp, Inc.
One Citizens Federal Centre
Dayton, OH 45402
Phone: 513-223-4234 Fax: —
CEO: Jerry L. Kirby
CFO: William M. Vichich
1992 Sales: $156 million Employees: 577
Symbol: CTZN Exchange: NASDAQ
Industry: Banks - Midwest

Citicorp
399 Park Ave.
New York, NY 10043
Phone: 212-559-1000 Fax: 212-527-3277
CEO: John S. Reed
CFO: Thomas E. Jones
1992 Sales: $31,948 million Employees: 86,000
Symbol: CCI Exchange: NYSE
Industry: Banks - money center

Citizens Bancorp
14401 Sweitzer Lane
Laurel, MD 20707
Phone: 301-206-6080 Fax: —
CEO: Alfred H. Smith, Jr.
CFO: D. Kaye Arnold
1991 Sales: $102 million Employees: 1,664
Symbol: CIBC Exchange: NASDAQ
Industry: Banks - Northeast

Citizens Banking Corp.
One Citizens Banking Center
Flint, MI 48502
Phone: 313-766-7500 Fax: —
CEO: Charles R. Weeks
CFO: Wayne G. Schaeffer
1991 Sales: $99 million Employees: 1,684
Symbol: CBCF Exchange: NASDAQ
Industry: Financial - savings and loans

Citizens First Bancorp, Inc.
208 Harristown Rd.
Glen Rock, NJ 07452
Phone: 201-445-3400 Fax: —
CEO: Allan D. Nichols
CFO: Jack M. Blackin
1991 Sales: $236 million Employees: 921
Symbol: CFB Exchange: AMEX
Industry: Banks - Northeast

Citizens, Inc.
7801 N. IH-35
Austin, TX 78753
Phone: 512-836-9730 Fax: —
CEO: Harold E. Riley
CFO: Mark A. Oliver
1991 Sales: $27 million Employees: 43
Symbol: CINNA Exchange: NASDAQ
Industry: Insurance - life

Citizens Utilities Co.
High Ridge Park
Stamford, CT 06905
Phone: 203-329-8800 Fax: 203-322-7186
CEO: Leonard Tow
CFO: Hampton D. Graham, Jr.
1991 Sales: $548 million Employees: 2,374
Symbol: CZNB Exchange: NYSE
Industry: Utility - telephone

City Holding Co.
3601 MacCorkle Ave. SE
Charleston, WV 25304
Phone: 304-925-6611 Fax: 304-925-8073
CEO: Steven J. Day
CFO: Robert A. Henson
1991 Sales: $33 million Employees: 225
Symbol: CHCO Exchange: NASDAQ
Industry: Banks - Northeast

indicates company is in *Hoover's Handbook of American Business.*

indicates company is in *Hoover's Handbook of World Business;* sales and employee numbers are for parent company.

City National Corp.
400 N. Roxbury Dr.
Beverly Hills, CA 90210
Phone: 310-550-5400 Fax: 310-550-5875
CEO: Bram Goldsmith
CFO: J. F. Schulte
1991 Sales: $437 million Employees: 2,000
Symbol: CYN Exchange: NYSE
Industry: Banks - West

Civic BanCorp
2101 Webster St., 14th Fl.
Oakland, CA 94612
Phone: 510-836-6500 Fax: 510-835-1072
CEO: Herbert C. Foster
CFO: Martha Perry
1991 Sales: $34 million Employees: 188
Symbol: CIVC Exchange: NASDAQ
Industry: Banks - West

CK Federal Savings Bank
40 Cabarrus Ave. East
Concord, NC 28025
Phone: 704-788-3193 Fax: 704-784-1912
CEO: Gabe S. Stewart
CFO: Benjamin M. Guion
1992 Sales: — Employees: —
Symbol: CKSB Exchange: NASDAQ
Industry: Financial - savings and loans

Claire's Stores, Inc.
3 SW 129th Ave.
Pembroke Pines, FL 33027
Phone: 305-433-3900 Fax: 305-433-3999
CEO: Rowland Schaefer
CFO: Ira D. Kaplan
1991 Sales: $234 million Employees: 5,150
Symbol: CLE Exchange: NYSE
Industry: Retail - jewelry stores

CLARCOR Inc.
2323 S. Sixth St.
Rockford, IL 61125
Phone: 815-962-8867 Fax: 815-962-0417
CEO: Lawrence E. Gloyd
CFO: L. Paul Harnois
1991 Sales: $180 million Employees: 2,220
Symbol: CLC Exchange: NYSE
Industry: Diversified operations - filtration products

Clark Enterprises, Inc.
7500 Old Georgetown Rd.
Bethesda, MD 20814
Phone: 301-657-7100 Fax: 301-657-7263
CEO: A. James Clark
CFO: —
1991 Sales: $966 million Employees: 5,000
Ownership: Privately held
Industry: Diversified operations - construction, communications, real estate

Clark Equipment Co.
100 N. Michigan St.
South Bend, IN 46634
Phone: 219-239-0100 Fax: 219-239-0236
CEO: Leo J. McKernan
CFO: William N. Harper
1992 Sales: $803 million Employees: 8,033
Symbol: CKL Exchange: NYSE
Industry: Machinery - material handling

Clayton Homes, Inc.
4726 Airport Hwy.
Louisville, TN 37777
Phone: 615-970-7200 Fax: 615-970-1238
CEO: James L. Clayton
CFO: Richard B. Ray
1992 Sales: $371 million Employees: 2,679
Symbol: CMH Exchange: NYSE
Industry: Building - mobile homes & RVs

Clean Harbors, Inc.
1200 Crown Colony Dr.
Quincy, MA 02169
Phone: 617-849-1800 Fax: 617-786-8589
CEO: Alan S. McKim
CFO: Edward T. Sheehan
1991 Sales: $128 million Employees: 1,175
Symbol: CLHB Exchange: NASDAQ
Industry: Pollution control services

Clear Channel Communications, Inc.
7710 Jones Maltsberger Rd.
San Antonio, TX 78216
Phone: 210-822-2828 Fax: —
CEO: L. Lowry Mays
CFO: Thomas F. Klein
1991 Sales: $64 million Employees: 713
Symbol: CCU Exchange: AMEX
Industry: Broadcasting - radio & TV

Cleveland Electric Illuminating Co.
55 Public Square
Cleveland, OH 44113
Phone: 216-622-9800 Fax: —
CEO: Robert J. Farling
CFO: Edgar H. Maugans
1991 Sales: $1.8 million Employees: 4,531
Symbol: CVX Exchange: NYSE
Industry: Utility - electric power

Cleveland-Cliffs Inc.
1100 Superior Ave.
Cleveland, OH 44114
Phone: 216-694-5700 Fax: —
CEO: M. Thomas Moore
CFO: John S. Brinzo
1991 Sales: $317 million Employees: 6,500
Symbol: CLF Exchange: NYSE
Industry: Iron ores

Cliffs Drilling Co.
1200 Smith St.
Houston, TX 77002
Phone: 713-651-9426 Fax: 713-651-9466
CEO: Douglas E. Swanson
CFO: James E. Mitchell, Jr.
1991 Sales: $84 million Employees: 310
Symbol: CLDR Exchange: NASDAQ
Industry: Oil & gas - offshore drilling

Clinical Data, Inc.
1172 Commonwealth Ave.
Boston, MA 02134
Phone: 617-734-3700 Fax: 617-734-3903
CEO: Israel M. Stein
CFO: Israel M. Stein
1992 Sales: $10.9 million Employees: 91
Symbol: CLDA Exchange: NASDAQ
Industry: Medical instruments - clinical test equipment

Clinton Gas Systems, Inc.
4770 Indianola Ave.
Columbus, OH 43214
Phone: 614-888-9588 Fax: 614-888-6287
CEO: Jerry D. Jordan
CFO: Donald A. Nay
1991 Sales: $68 million Employees: 119
Symbol: CGAS Exchange: NASDAQ
Industry: Oil & gas - US exploration & production

Clorox Co., The
1221 Broadway
Oakland, CA 94612
Phone: 510-271-7000 Fax: 510-465-8875
CEO: G. Craig Sullivan
CFO: William F. Ausfahl
1992 Sales: $1,758 million Employees: 5,800
Symbol: CLX Exchange: NYSE
Industry: Soap & cleaning preparations & consumer products

Clothestime, Inc., The
5325 E. Hunter Ave.
Anaheim, CA 92807
Phone: 714-779-5881 Fax: 714-779-2032
CEO: Michael P. DeAngelo
CFO: David A. Sejpal
1991 Sales: $259 million Employees: 3,442
Symbol: CTME Exchange: NASDAQ
Industry: Retail - apparel & shoes

Club Med, Inc.
40 W. 57th St., 34th Fl.
New York, NY 10019
Phone: 212-977-2150 Fax: 212-315-5392
CEO: Serge Trigano
CFO: Jean-Luc Oizan-Chapon
1991 Sales: $519 million Employees: —
Symbol: CMI Exchange: NYSE
Industry: Leisure & recreational services

ClubCorp International
3030 LBJ Fwy.
Dallas, TX 75234
Phone: 214-243-6191 Fax: 214-888-7721
CEO: Robert H. Dedman
CFO: James P. McCoy
1991 Sales: $751 million Employees: 15,000
Ownership: Privately held
Industry: Leisure & recreational services - private clubs, resorts

CMG Health
25 Crossroads Dr.
Owings Mills, MD 21117
Phone: 410-581-5000 Fax: 410-581-5007
CEO: Alan Shusterman
CFO: Curt A.H. Jeschke, Jr.
1992 Sales: $27 million Employees: 150
Ownership: Privately held
Industry: Medical services - managed behavioral healthcare

CMI Corp.
I-40 & Morgan Rd.
Oklahoma City, OK 73101
Phone: 405-787-6020 Fax: 405-491-2417
CEO: Bill Swisher
CFO: Jim D. Holland
1991 Sales: $66 million Employees: 655
Symbol: CMX Exchange: AMEX
Industry: Machinery - material handling

CML Group, Inc.
524 Main St.
Acton, MA 01720
Phone: 508-264-4155 Fax: 508-264-4073
CEO: Charles M. Leighton
CFO: Robert J. Samuelson
1992 Sales: $494 million Employees: 4,500
Symbol: CML Exchange: NYSE
Industry: Retail - apparel, gardening equipment & nature stores

CMS Communications
715 Goddard Ave.
Chesterfield, MO 63005
Phone: 314-530-1320 Fax: 314-530-1316
CEO: Brent Bowman
CFO: Brent Bowman
1991 Sales: $18 million Employees: 152
Ownership: Privately held
Industry: Telecommunications services - equipment sales & repair

CMS Energy Corp.
330 Town Center Dr., Ste. 1100
Dearborn, MI 48126
Phone: 313-436-9200 Fax: 313-436-9225
CEO: William T. McCormick, Jr.
CFO: Alan M. Wright
1991 Sales: $2,941 million Employees: 9,347
Symbol: CMS Exchange: NYSE
Industry: Utility - electric power

indicates company is in *Hoover's Handbook of American Business.*

indicates company is in *Hoover's Handbook of World Business;* sales and employee numbers are for parent company.

CMS Enhancements, Inc.
2722 Michelson Dr.
Irvine, CA 92715
Phone: 714-222-6000 Fax: —
CEO: Jim Farooquee
CFO: Stephen G. Holmes
1991 Sales: $130 million Employees: 549
Symbol: CME Exchange: NYSE
Industry: Computers - hard disk drive peripheral equipment

CMS/Data Corp.
124 Marriott Dr.
Tallahassee, FL 32301
Phone: 904-878-5155 Fax: 904-656-4093
CEO: Rubin I. Osten
CFO: Walter K. Himelsbaugh
1992 Sales: $13 million Employees: 180
Symbol: LAWR Exchange: NASDAQ
Industry: Computers - software for law offices

CNA Financial Corp.
333 S. Wabash Ave.
Chicago, IL 60685
Phone: 312-822-5000 Fax: 312-822-6419
CEO: Laurence A. Tisch
CFO: Peter E. Jokiel
1991 Sales: $11,131 million Employees: —
Symbol: CNA Exchange: NYSE
Industry: Insurance - property & casualty

CNB Bancshares, Inc.
20 NW Third St.
Evansville, IN 47739
Phone: 812-464-3400 Fax: —
CEO: H. Lee Cooper
CFO: David L. Knapp
1991 Sales: $59 million Employees: 937
Symbol: CNBE Exchange: NASDAQ
Industry: Banks - Midwest

CNL Financial Corp.
2960 Riverside Dr.
Macon, GA 31204
Phone: 912-477-0400 Fax: —
CEO: Don K. Miller
CFO: B. W. Brown
1991 Sales: $25 million Employees: 60
Symbol: CNLF Exchange: NASDAQ
Industry: Insurance - multiline & misc.

Co-operative Bank of Concord, The
125 Nagog Park
Acton, MA 01720
Phone: 508-635-5000 Fax: —
CEO: David E. Bradbury
CFO: Paul S. Feeley
1990 Sales: $11 million Employees: 252
Symbol: COBK Exchange: NASDAQ
Industry: Banks - Northeast

Coachmen Industries, Inc.
601 E. Beardsley Ave.
Elkhart, IN 46514
Phone: 219-262-0123 Fax: 219-262-8823
CEO: Thomas H. Corson
CFO: Gary L. Groom
1991 Sales: $231 million Employees: 2,050
Symbol: COA Exchange: NYSE
Industry: Building - mobile homes & RVs

Coast Distribution System
1982 Zanker Rd.
San Jose, CA 95112
Phone: 408-436-0877 Fax: 408-436-0670
CEO: Thomas R. McGuire
CFO: Sandra A. Knell
1991 Sales: $115 million Employees: 380
Symbol: CRV Exchange: AMEX
Industry: Auto parts - retail & wholesale

Coast Savings Financial, Inc.
1000 Wilshire Blvd.
Los Angeles, CA 90017
Phone: 213-362-2222 Fax: 213-688-0837
CEO: Ray Martin
CFO: Robert L. Hunt II
1991 Sales: $935 million Employees: 1,717
Symbol: CSA Exchange: NYSE
Industry: Financial - savings and loans

Coastal Corp., The
Coastal Tower, Nine Greenway Plaza
Houston, TX 77046
Phone: 713-877-1400 Fax: 713-877-6754
CEO: James R. Paul
CFO: David A. Arledge
1992 Sales: $10,063 million Employees: 16,500
Symbol: CGP Exchange: NYSE
Industry: Oil & gas - production & pipeline

Coastal Environmental Services
1099 Winterson Rd., Ste. 130
Linthicum, MD 21090
Phone: 410-684-3324 Fax: 410-684-3326
CEO: Fred Jacobs
CFO: Fred Jacobs
1991 Sales: $2.8 million Employees: 33
Ownership: Privately held
Industry: Environmental consulting

Coastal Healthcare Group, Inc.
2828 Croasdaile Dr.
Durham, NC 27705
Phone: 919-383-0355 Fax: —
CEO: Steven M. Scott
CFO: Barry E. Snipes
1991 Sales: $214 million Employees: 1,326
Symbol: CGRP Exchange: NASDAQ
Industry: Medical hospital management services

Coca-Cola Bottling Co. Consolidated
1900 Rexford Rd.
Charlotte, NC 28211
Phone: 704-551-4400 Fax: 704-551-4646
CEO: James L. Moore, Jr.
CFO: David V. Singer
1991 Sales: $465 million Employees: 4,100
Symbol: COKE Exchange: NASDAQ
Industry: Beverages - soft drink bottling

Coca-Cola Bottling Co. of Chicago
7400 N. Oak Park Ave.
Niles, IL 60714
Phone: 312-775-0900 Fax: 708-647-7104
CEO: Marvin J. Herb
CFO: Jerry Moza
1991 Sales: $781 million Employees: 4,000
Ownership: Privately held
Industry: Beverages - soft drinks

Coca-Cola Co., The
One Coca-Cola Plaza NW
Atlanta, GA 30313
Phone: 404-676-2121 Fax: 404-676-6792
CEO: Roberto C. Goizueta
CFO: Jack L. Stahl
1992 Sales: $13,074 million Employees: 28,900
Symbol: KO Exchange: NYSE
Industry: Beverages - soft drinks

Coca-Cola Enterprises Inc.
Coca-Cola Plaza NW
Atlanta, GA 30313
Phone: 404-676-2100 Fax: 404-676-6792
CEO: Summerfield Johnston, Jr.
CFO: John R. Alm
1992 Sales: $5,127 million Employees: 25,000
Symbol: CCE Exchange: NYSE
Industry: Beverages - soft drink bottling

Coda Energy, Inc.
9400 N. Central Expressway, Ste. 500
Dallas, TX 75231
Phone: 214-692-1800 Fax: 214-692-7171
CEO: Douglas H. Miller
CFO: T. W. Eubank
1991 Sales: $22 million Employees: 31
Symbol: CODA Exchange: NASDAQ
Industry: Oil & gas - US exploration & production

Code-Alarm, Inc.
950 W. Whitcomb Ave.
Madison Heights, MI 48071
Phone: 313-583-9620 Fax: 313-585-4799
CEO: Rand W. Mueller
CFO: Richard Wierzbicki
1991 Sales: $44 million Employees: 448
Symbol: CODL Exchange: NASDAQ
Industry: Protection - safety equipment & systems for cars & homes

Codenoll Technology Corp.
1086 N. Broadway
Yonkers, NY 10701
Phone: 914-965-6300 Fax: —
CEO: Michael F. Coden
CFO: John F. Logan
1991 Sales: $9.7 million Employees: 71
Symbol: CODN Exchange: NASDAQ
Industry: Fiber optics

Coeur d'Alene Mines Corp.
505 Front Ave.
Coeur d'Alene, ID 83814
Phone: 208-667-3511 Fax: 208-765-0324
CEO: Dennis E. Wheeler
CFO: James A. Sabala
1991 Sales: $59 million Employees: 424
Symbol: CDE Exchange: NYSE
Industry: Silver mining & processing

Cognex Corp.
15 Crawford St.
Needham, MA 02194
Phone: 617-449-6030 Fax: 617-449-4013
CEO: Robert J. Shillman
CFO: Neil R. Bonke
1991 Sales: $32 million Employees: 138
Symbol: CGNX Exchange: NASDAQ
Industry: Computers - machine vision systems

Cognitronics Corp.
25 Crescent St.
Stamford, CT 06906
Phone: 203-327-5307 Fax: 203-327-2002
CEO: Matthew J. Flanigan
CFO: Garrett Sullivan
1991 Sales: $18 million Employees: 109
Symbol: CGN Exchange: AMEX
Industry: Computers - peripheral equipment

Cohasset Savings Bank
13 Elm St.
Cohasset, MA 02025
Phone: 617-383-1882 Fax: —
CEO: Donald E. Bates
CFO: William K. Brothers
1992 Sales: — Employees: —
Symbol: CHTB Exchange: NASDAQ
Industry: Financial - savings and loans

Coherent, Inc.
3210 Porter Dr.
Palo Alto, CA 94304
Phone: 415-493-2111 Fax: 415-858-7631
CEO: James L. Hobart
CFO: Robert J. Quillinan
1991 Sales: $208 million Employees: 1,594
Symbol: COHR Exchange: NASDAQ
Industry: Lasers - systems & components

indicates company is in *Hoover's Handbook of American Business.*

indicates company is in *Hoover's Handbook of World Business;* sales and employee numbers are for parent company.

Coho Resources, Inc.
14785 Preston Rd., Ste. 860
Dallas, TX 75240
Phone: 214-991-9493 Fax: —
CEO: Jeffrey Clarke
CFO: Jeffrey Clarke
1991 Sales: $24 million Employees: 50
Symbol: COHO Exchange: NASDAQ
Industry: Oil & gas - field services

Cohu, Inc. Electronics Div.
5755 Kearny Villa Rd.
San Diego, CA 92123
Phone: 619-277-6700 Fax: 619-277-0221
CEO: James W. Barnes
CFO: Charles A. Schwan
1991 Sales: $48 million Employees: 521
Symbol: COH Exchange: AMEX
Industry: Television & electronic test equipment

Coldwater Creek
1123 Lake St.
Sand Point, ID 83864
Phone: 208-263-2266 Fax: 208-263-1582
CEO: Dennis Pence
CFO: Marvin Harms
1992 Sales: $18 million Employees: 76
Ownership: Privately held
Industry: Retail - nature-related gifts

Coleman Co., Inc.
250 N. St. Francis
Wichita, KS 67202
Phone: 316-261-3211 Fax: 316-261-3400
CEO: Lawrence M. Jones
CFO: George Mileusnic
1991 Sales: $353 million Employees: 2,513
Symbol: CLN Exchange: NYSE
Industry: Leisure & recreational products

Colgate-Palmolive Co.
300 Park Ave.
New York, NY 10022
Phone: 212-310-2000 Fax: 212-310-3284
CEO: Reuben Mark
CFO: Robert M. Agate
1992 Sales: $7,007 million Employees: 24,900
Symbol: CL Exchange: NYSE
Industry: Soap & cleaning preparations & personal care products

Collaborative Research, Inc.
2 Oak Park
Bedford, MA 01730
Phone: 617-275-0004 Fax: 617-275-0043
CEO: Robert J. Hennessey
CFO: Fenel M. Eloi
1991 Sales: $9 million Employees: 49
Symbol: CRIC Exchange: NASDAQ
Industry: Biomedical & genetic products

Collagen Corp.
1850 Embarcadero Rd.
Palo Alto, CA 94303
Phone: 415-856-0200 Fax: 415-856-1430
CEO: Howard D. Palefsky
CFO: James T. McKinley
1992 Sales: $67 million Employees: 512
Symbol: CGEN Exchange: NASDAQ
Industry: Biomedical & genetic products

Collective Bancorp, Inc.
158 Philadelphia Ave.
Egg Harbor, NJ 08215
Phone: 609-625-1110 Fax: —
CEO: Thomas H. Hamilton
CFO: Edward J. McColgan
1991 Sales: $240 million Employees: 696
Symbol: COFD Exchange: NASDAQ
Industry: Financial - savings and loans

Collegiate Sports Design
Hwy. 75, PO Box 908
New Strawn, KS 66839
Phone: 316-364-8051 Fax: 316-364-8770
CEO: Greg Schuh
CFO: Greg Schuh
1991 Sales: $4.3 million Employees: 6
Ownership: Privately held
Industry: Leisure & recreational products - collegiate championship souvenirs

Collins & Aikman Group, Inc.
3340 Ocean Park Blvd.
Santa Monica, CA 90405
Phone: 310-452-0161 Fax: 310-452-9509
CEO: James R. Birle
CFO: Michael A. Jamieson
1992 Sales: — Employees: —
Symbol: CKGpA Exchange: AMEX
Industry: Textiles - carpets & fabrics

Collins Industries, Inc.
421 E. 30th Ave.
Hutchinson, KS 67502
Phone: 316-663-5551 Fax: 316-663-1630
CEO: Don L. Collins
CFO: Joseph S. Hebb
1991 Sales: $146 million Employees: 1,050
Symbol: COLL Exchange: NASDAQ
Industry: Automotive & trucking - original equipment

Colonial BancGroup, Inc.
One Commerce St.
Montgomery, AL 36104
Phone: 205-240-5000 Fax: —
CEO: Robert E. Lowder
CFO: W. Flake Oakley IV
1991 Sales: $151 million Employees: 1,045
Symbol: CLBGA Exchange: NASDAQ
Industry: Banks - Southeast

Colonial Companies, Inc.
1200 Colonial Life Blvd.
Columbia, SC 29210
Phone: 803-798-7000 Fax: —
CEO: Stephen G. Hall
CFO: David A. Halmrast
1991 Sales: $364 million Employees: —
Symbol: CLACB Exchange: NASDAQ
Industry: Insurance - accident & health

Colonial Gas Co.
40 Market St.
Lowell, MA 01853
Phone: 508-458-3171 Fax: 508-459-2314
CEO: Frederic L. Putnam, Jr.
CFO: Nickolas Stavropoulos
1991 Sales: $138 million Employees: 661
Symbol: CGES Exchange: NASDAQ
Industry: Utility - gas distribution

Colonial Group, Inc.
One Financial Center
Boston, MA 02111
Phone: 617-426-3750 Fax: —
CEO: John A. McNeice, Jr.
CFO: Davey S. Scoon
1991 Sales: $91 million Employees: 542
Symbol: COGRA Exchange: NASDAQ
Industry: Financial - investment management

Color Age, Inc.
900 Technology Park Dr., Bldg. 8
Billerica, MA 01821
Phone: 508-667-8585 Fax: 508-667-8821
CEO: Jeff Moore
CFO: Frank Finneran
1991 Sales: $5.2 million Employees: 38
Ownership: Privately held
Industry: Computers - desktop publishing software

Colorado National Bancshares, Inc.
950 Seventeenth St.
Denver, CO 80202
Phone: 303-629-1968 Fax: —
CEO: Will F. Nicholson, Jr.
CFO: James L. Basey
1991 Sales: $395 million Employees: 2,665
Symbol: COLC Exchange: NASDAQ
Industry: Banks - West

Colorado Prime Corp.
1 Michael Ave.
Farmingdale, NY 11735
Phone: 516-694-1111 Fax: —
CEO: John B. Masciandaro
CFO: Daniel Benjamin
1992 Sales: — Employees: —
Symbol: CPE Exchange: AMEX
Industry: Retail - food; wholesale refrigerators & grills

Coltec Industries Inc.
430 Park Ave.
New York, NY 10022
Phone: 212-940-0400 Fax: 212-319-8345
CEO: David L. Margolis
CFO: Paul G. Schoen
1992 Sales: $1,369 million Employees: 11,400
Symbol: COT Exchange: NYSE
Industry: Diversified operations - aerospace, automotive & industrial components

Columbia First Bank, F.S.B.
1560 Wilson Blvd.
Arlington, VA 22209
Phone: 703-247-5000 Fax: —
CEO: Thomas J. Schaefer
CFO: Robert J. Creighton
1992 Sales: — Employees: —
Symbol: CFFS Exchange: NASDAQ
Industry: Financial - savings and loans

Columbia Gas System, Inc., The
20 Montchanin Rd.
Wilmington, DE 19807
Phone: 302-429-5000 Fax: 302-429-5430
CEO: John H. Croom
CFO: Robert A. Oswald
1992 Sales: $2,922 million Employees: 10,715
Symbol: CG Exchange: NYSE
Industry: Oil & gas - production & pipeline

Columbia Hospital Corp.
777 Main St., Ste. 2100
Ft. Worth, TX 76102
Phone: 817-877-4621 Fax: —
CEO: Richard L. Scott
CFO: David C. Colby
1991 Sales: $499 million Employees: 6,300
Symbol: CHOS Exchange: NASDAQ
Industry: Hospitals

Columbia Laboratories, Inc.
4000 Hollywood Blvd.
Miami, FL 33021
Phone: 305-964-6666 Fax: 305-964-8476
CEO: Norman M. Meier
CFO: Margaret J. Roell
1991 Sales: $10.7 million Employees: 34
Symbol: COB Exchange: AMEX
Industry: Drugs

Comair Holdings, Inc.
PO Box 75021
Cincinnati, OH 45275
Phone: 606-525-2550 Fax: 606-525-3420
CEO: David R. Mueller
CFO: Randy D. Rademacher
1992 Sales: $217 million Employees: 2,248
Symbol: COMR Exchange: NASDAQ
Industry: Transportation - airline

indicates company is in *Hoover's Handbook of American Business.*

indicates company is in *Hoover's Handbook of World Business;* sales and employee numbers are for parent company.

COMARCO, Inc.
160 S. Old Springs Rd.
Anaheim, CA 92808
Phone: 714-282-3800 Fax: 714-283-0604
CEO: Don M. Bailey
CFO: C. Bruce Fitzgerald
1991 Sales: $80 million Employees: 1,400
Symbol: CMRO Exchange: NASDAQ
Industry: Engineering - R&D services

Combined Resource Technology
5555 Hilton Ave., Ste. 555
Baton Rouge, LA 70808
Phone: 504-927-0176 Fax: 504-927-0177
CEO: Chris B. Moran
CFO: Darwyn W. Williams
1991 Sales: $1.5 million Employees: 13
Ownership: Privately held
Industry: Business services - cost-reduction services

Comcast Corp.
1234 Market St., 16th Fl.
Philadelphia, PA 19107
Phone: 215-665-1700 Fax: 215-981-7790
CEO: Brian L. Roberts
CFO: John R. Alchin
1991 Sales: $721 million Employees: 3,722
Symbol: CMCSA Exchange: NASDAQ
Industry: Cable TV

COMCOA, Inc.
411 N. Webb Rd., Ste. 200
Wichita, KS 67206
Phone: 316-683-4411 Fax: —
CEO: Daniel J. Taylor
CFO: Gary L. Simmons
1991 Sales: $53 million Employees: 548
Symbol: CCOA Exchange: NASDAQ
Industry: Retail - consumer electronics rentals

Comdata Holdings Corp.
5301 Maryland Way
Brentwood, TN 37027
Phone: 615-370-7000 Fax: 615-370-7325
CEO: George L. McTavish
CFO: Dennis R. Hanson
1991 Sales: $184 million Employees: 1,696
Symbol: CMDT Exchange: NASDAQ
Industry: Financial - electronic funds transfers

Comdial Corp.
1180 Seminole Trail
Charlottesville, VA 22901
Phone: 804-978-2200 Fax: 804-978-2293
CEO: William G. Mustain
CFO: Wayne R. Wilver
1991 Sales: $63 million Employees: 905
Symbol: CMDL Exchange: NASDAQ
Industry: Telecommunications equipment

Comdisco, Inc.
6111 N. River Rd.
Rosemont, IL 60018
Phone: 708-698-3000 Fax: 708-518-5440
CEO: Kenneth N. Pontikes
CFO: John J. Vosicky
1992 Sales: $2,223 million Employees: 2,179
Symbol: CDO Exchange: NYSE
Industry: Computers - leasing

Comerica Inc.
211 W. Fort St.
Detroit, MI 48275
Phone: 313-222-3300 Fax: 313-222-6067
CEO: Eugene A. Miller
CFO: Eugene A. Miller
1992 Sales: $2,270 million Employees: 7,884
Symbol: CMA Exchange: NYSE
Industry: Banks - Midwest

Command Medical Products
15 Signal Ave
Ormond Beach, FL 32174
Phone: 904-672-8116 Fax: 904-677-7781
CEO: David Slick
CFO: Erin Cejka
1991 Sales: $3.1 million Employees: 130
Ownership: Privately held
Industry: Medical products - disposable

Commerce Bancorp, Inc.
1701 Route 70 East
Cherry Hill, NJ 08034
Phone: 609-751-9000 Fax: —
CEO: Vernon W. Hill II
CFO: C. Edward Jordan, Jr.
1991 Sales: $38 million Employees: 692
Symbol: COBA Exchange: NASDAQ
Industry: Banks - Northeast

Commerce Bancshares, Inc.
1000 Walnut St.
Kansas City, MO 64106
Phone: 816-234-2000 Fax: 816-234-2019
CEO: David W. Kemper
CFO: Charles E. Templer
1991 Sales: $594 million Employees: 3,473
Symbol: CBSH Exchange: NASDAQ
Industry: Banks - Midwest

Commerce Clearing House, Inc.
2700 Lake Cook Rd.
Riverwoods, IL 60015
Phone: 708-940-4600 Fax: 708-940-0113
CEO: Edward L. Massie
CFO: John I. Abernethy
1991 Sales: $704 million Employees: 7,180
Symbol: CCLR Exchange: NASDAQ
Industry: Financial - publishing, legal information & data processing services

CommerceBancorp
1201 Dove St.
Newport Beach, CA 92660
Phone: 714-851-9900 Fax: —
CEO: Raymond E. Dellerba
CFO: Roberta E. Masters
1991 Sales: $30 million Employees: 135
Symbol: CBNB Exchange: NASDAQ
Industry: Banks - West

Commercial Bancorporation of Colorado
3300 E. First Ave., Ste. 220
Denver, CO 80206
Phone: 303-321-1234 Fax: —
CEO: Jon P. Coates
CFO: George Mata
1991 Sales: $25 million Employees: 173
Symbol: CBOCA Exchange: NASDAQ
Industry: Banks - West

Commercial Benefits
21300 Califa St.
Woodland Hills, CA 91367
Phone: 818-704-1416 Fax: 818-704-0529
CEO: Bob Berns
CFO: Michael Rosenthal
1991 Sales: $2.6 million Employees: 20
Ownership: Privately held
Industry: Insurance - multiline & employee benefits services

Commercial Federal Corp.
2120 S. 72nd St.
Omaha, NE 68124
Phone: 402-554-9200 Fax: —
CEO: William A. Fitzgerald
CFO: James A. Laphen
1991 Sales: $483 million Employees: 880
Symbol: CFCN Exchange: NASDAQ
Industry: Financial - savings and loans

Commercial Intertech Corp.
1775 Logan Ave.
Youngstown, OH 44505
Phone: 216-746-8011 Fax: 216-746-1148
CEO: Paul J. Powers
CFO: Philip N. Winkelstern
1991 Sales: $437 million Employees: 3,860
Symbol: TEC Exchange: NYSE
Industry: Machinery - construction & mining

Commercial Metals Co.
7800 N. Stemmons Fwy.
Dallas, TX 75247
Phone: 214-689-4300 Fax: 214-689-4320
CEO: Stanley A. Rabin
CFO: Lawrence A. Engels
1992 Sales: $1,231 million Employees: 3,709
Symbol: CMC Exchange: NYSE
Industry: Metal processing & fabrication

Commodore International Ltd.
1200 Wilson Dr.
West Chester, PA 19380
Phone: 215-431-9100 Fax: 215-431-9156
CEO: Irving Gould
CFO: Ronald B. Alexander
1992 Sales: $732 million Employees: 2,890
Symbol: CBU Exchange: NYSE
Industry: Computers - mini & micro

Commonwealth Bancshares Corp.
101 W. Third St.
Williamsport, PA 17701
Phone: 717-327-5011 Fax: —
CEO: William D. Davis
CFO: John H. Turpish
1991 Sales: $71 million Employees: 890
Symbol: CBKS Exchange: NASDAQ
Industry: Banks - Northeast

Commonwealth Edison Co.
37th Fl., One First National Plaza
Chicago, IL 60690
Phone: 312-294-4321 Fax: 312-294-3110
CEO: James J. O'Connor
CFO: John C. Bukovski
1992 Sales: $6,026 million Employees: 19,727
Symbol: CWE Exchange: NYSE
Industry: Utility - electric power

Commonwealth Energy System
One Main St.
Cambridge, MA 02142
Phone: 617-225-4000 Fax: 617-225-4481
CEO: William G. Poist
CFO: Russell D. Wright
1991 Sales: $850 million Employees: 2,562
Symbol: CES Exchange: NYSE
Industry: Utility - electric power

Commonwealth Inc
11013 Kenwood Rd.
Cincinnati, OH 45242
Phone: 513-791-1966 Fax: 513-791-0880
CEO: Brian Collins
CFO: Brian Collins
1991 Sales: $4.2 million Employees: 30
Ownership: Privately held
Industry: Business services - contract warehousing

Communication Cable, Inc.
N. 2nd Ave. West
Siler City, NC 27344
Phone: 919-663-2629 Fax: 919-663-2297
CEO: James R. Fore
CFO: William B. Cooper
1991 Sales: $33 million Employees: 250
Symbol: CABL Exchange: NASDAQ
Industry: Wire & cable products

indicates company is in *Hoover's Handbook of American Business.*

indicates company is in *Hoover's Handbook of World Business;* sales and employee numbers are for parent company.

Communications and Entertainment Corp.
800 Third Ave.
New York, NY 10022
Phone: 212-486-3999 Fax: —
CEO: N. Norman Muller
CFO: Thomas Smith
1992 Sales: $30 million Employees: 30
Symbol: CECO Exchange: NASDAQ
Industry: Motion pictures & services - production

Communications, Marketing & Distr. Svcs.
2684 Peachtree Square
Atlanta, GA 30360
Phone: 404-455-1470 Fax: 404-458-8349
CEO: Mark Nedza
CFO: David Jacobson
1991 Sales: $2.1 million Employees: 43
Ownership: Privately held
Industry: Printing - commercial corporate literature

Communications Satellite Corp.
950 L'Enfant Plaza SW
Washington, DC 20024
Phone: 202-863-6000 Fax: —
CEO: Bruce L. Crockett
CFO: C. Thomas Faulders III
1991 Sales: $523 million Employees: 1,645
Symbol: CQ Exchange: NYSE
Industry: Telecommunications services

Communications Systems, Inc.
213 S. Main St.
Hector, MN 55342
Phone: 612-848-6231 Fax: 612-848-2702
CEO: Curtis A. Sampson
CFO: Paul N. Hanson
1991 Sales: $38 million Employees: 880
Symbol: CSII Exchange: NASDAQ
Industry: Telecommunications equipment

Communique Telecommunications, Inc.
4015 E. Guasti Rd.
Ontario, CA 91761
Phone: 714-391-3411 Fax: 714-988-5415
CEO: Vincent P. Murone
CFO: Richard Crouch
1992 Sales: $26 million Employees: 75
Ownership: Privately held
Industry: Telecommunications services

Community Banks, Inc.
150 Market Square
Millersburg, PA 17061
Phone: 717-692-4781 Fax: —
CEO: Thomas L. Miller
CFO: Terry L. Burrows
1991 Sales: $9.8 million Employees: 150
Symbol: CBKI Exchange: NASDAQ
Industry: Banks - Northeast

Community First Bankshares, Inc.
1112 Nodak Dr.
Fargo, ND 58103
Phone: 701-235-1600 Fax: —
CEO: Donald R. Mengedoth
CFO: Mark A. Anderson
1991 Sales: $76 million Employees: 391
Symbol: CFBX Exchange: NASDAQ
Industry: Banks - Midwest

Community Health Systems, Inc.
3707 FM 1960 West, Ste. 500
Houston, TX 77068
Phone: 713-537-5230 Fax: —
CEO: E. Thomas Chaney
CFO: Deborah G. Moffett
1991 Sales: $138 million Employees: 2,029
Symbol: CHSI Exchange: NASDAQ
Industry: Hospitals

Community Psychiatric Centers
24502 Pacific Park Dr.
Laguna Hills, CA 92656
Phone: 714-831-1166 Fax: 714-831-2202
CEO: James W. Conte
CFO: Steven S. Weis
1991 Sales: $393 million Employees: 6,586
Symbol: CMY Exchange: NYSE
Industry: Hospitals

COMNET Corp.
6404 Ivy Lane, Ste. 500
Greenbelt, MD 20770
Phone: 301-982-2000 Fax: 301-982-4069
CEO: Robert S. Bowen
CFO: Charles A. Crew
1992 Sales: $34 million Employees: 232
Symbol: CNET Exchange: NASDAQ
Industry: Computers - software

Compaq Computer Corp.
20555 Texas 249
Houston, TX 77070
Phone: 713-370-0670 Fax: 713-374-1740
CEO: Eckhard Pfeiffer
CFO: Daryl J. White
1992 Sales: $4,100 million Employees: 10,000
Symbol: CPQ Exchange: NYSE
Industry: Computers - mini & micro

Complete Health Services
2160 Highland Ave., Ste. 100
Birmingham, AL 35205
Phone: 205-933-7748 Fax: 205-933-0083
CEO: William Seatheringill
CFO: Joe McSorley
1991 Sales: $160 million Employees: 410
Ownership: Privately held
Industry: Healthcare - managed care services

Complete Property Services, Inc.
140 Pine Ave.
Oldsmar, FL 34677
Phone: 813-854-4201 Fax: 813-855-0640
CEO: Rick Krueger
CFO: Angela Krueger
1991 Sales: $2.4 million Employees: 25
Ownership: Privately held
Industry: Building - general contractors

Comprehensive Care Corp.
16305 Swingley Ridge Dr.
Chesterfield, MO 63017
Phone: 314-537-1288 Fax: 314-537-3079
CEO: James P. Carmany
CFO: Dennis C. Dickey
1992 Sales: $60 million Employees: 1,223
Symbol: CMP Exchange: NYSE
Industry: Healthcare - outpatient & home

Comprehensive Technologies International Inc.
14500 Avion Pkwy., Ste. 250
Chantilly, VA 22021
Phone: 703-263-1000 Fax: 703-263-1865
CEO: Cel Beltran
CFO: Michael Maraghy
1991 Sales: $33 million Employees: 547
Ownership: Privately held
Industry: Computers - software development, systems integration & networking services

Compression Labs, Inc.
2860 Junction Ave.
San Jose, CA 95134
Phone: 408-435-3000 Fax: 408-922-5429
CEO: John E. Tyson
CFO: William A. Berry
1991 Sales: $73 million Employees: 331
Symbol: CLIX Exchange: NASDAQ
Industry: Telecommunications equipment - video conferencing

Comptek Research, Inc.
110 Broadway
Buffalo, NY 14203
Phone: 716-842-2700 Fax: 716-842-2687
CEO: John R. Cummings
CFO: Kenneth E. Lanham
1992 Sales: $65 million Employees: 625
Symbol: CTK Exchange: AMEX
Industry: Electronics - military

Comptronix Corp.
1800 Gunter Ave.
Guntersville, AL 35976
Phone: 205-582-1800 Fax: 205-582-1856
CEO: Townes Duncan
CFO: —
1991 Sales: $102 million Employees: 1,034
Symbol: CMPX Exchange: NASDAQ
Industry: Electrical components - printed circuit boards

Compu-Call Inc.
252 John Dietsch Blvd.
Attleboro, MA 02763
Phone: 508-699-0400 Fax: 508-699-0410
CEO: Susan Quinn
CFO: Susan Quinn
1991 Sales: $5.2 million Employees: 9
Ownership: Privately held
Industry: Computers - computer hardware in the IBM marketplace

CompuAdd, Inc.
12303 Technology Blvd.
Austin, TX 78727
Phone: 512-250-2000 Fax: 512-331-2794
CEO: Bill H. Hayden
CFO: Donald Amicucci
1992 Sales: $525 million Employees: 1,300
Ownership: Privately held
Industry: Computers - micro & equipment

CompuCom Systems, Inc.
9333 Forest Lane
Dallas, TX 75243
Phone: 214-783-1252 Fax: 214-497-8470
CEO: Avery More
CFO: Robert J. Boutin
1992 Sales: $713 million Employees: 1,061
Symbol: BYTE Exchange: NASDAQ
Industry: Computers - retail & wholesale

CompUSA, Inc.
15160 Marsh Lane
Dallas, TX 75234
Phone: 214-406-4734 Fax: 214-484-4276
CEO: Nathan P. Morton
CFO: Mervyn Benjet
1992 Sales: $1,041 million Employees: 2,767
Symbol: CPU Exchange: NYSE
Industry: Retail - computer hardware & software

Compusense, Inc.
55 Constitution Dr. #101
Bedford, NH 03110
Phone: 603-472-2088 Fax: 603-472-8167
CEO: Wayne Williams
CFO: Wayne Williams
1991 Sales: $1.6 million Employees: 18
Ownership: Privately held
Industry: Computers - computer software & hardware integration & development

Computer Associates International, Inc.
One Computer Associates Plaza
Islandia, NY 11788
Phone: 516-342-5224 Fax: 516-342-5329
CEO: Charles B. Wang
CFO: Peter A. Schwartz
1992 Sales: $1,771 million Employees: 7,400
Symbol: CA Exchange: NYSE
Industry: Computers - software

indicates company is in *Hoover's Handbook of American Business.*

indicates company is in *Hoover's Handbook of World Business;* sales and employee numbers are for parent company.

Computer Communication Co.
27-A S. Commons Rd.
Waterbury, CT 06704
Phone: 203-573-8366 Fax: 203-574-0594
CEO: Weston C. Pullen III
CFO: Weston C. Pullen III
1992 Sales: $13 million Employees: 18
Ownership: Privately held
Industry: Computers - sales & support of local area and wide area networks

Computer Data Systems, Inc.
One Curie Court
Rockville, MD 20850
Phone: 301-921-7000 Fax: 301-948-9328
CEO: Gordon S. Glenn
CFO: Wyatt D. Tinsley
1992 Sales: $142 million Employees: 3,300
Symbol: CPTD Exchange: NASDAQ
Industry: Computers - services

Computer Horizons Corp.
747 Third Ave.
New York, NY 10017
Phone: 212-371-9600 Fax: 212-980-4676
CEO: John J. Cassese
CFO: Bernhard Hubert
1991 Sales: $94 million Employees: 1,251
Symbol: CHRZ Exchange: NASDAQ
Industry: Computers - systems integration services

Computer Identics Corp.
5 Shawmut Rd.
Canton, MA 02021
Phone: 617-821-0830 Fax: 617-828-8942
CEO: Frank J. Wezniak
CFO: Stephen D. Prendergast
1991 Sales: $21 million Employees: 161
Symbol: CIDN Exchange: NASDAQ
Industry: Computers - bar code systems

Computer Language Research, Inc.
2395 Midway Rd.
Carrollton, TX 75006
Phone: 214-250-7000 Fax: 214-250-8181
CEO: Stephen T. Winn
CFO: M. Brian Healy
1991 Sales: $116 million Employees: 1,210
Symbol: CLRI Exchange: NASDAQ
Industry: Computers - tax processing services

Computer Network Technology Corp.
6500 Wedgwood Rd.
Maple Grove, MN 55369
Phone: 612-550-8000 Fax: 612-550-8800
CEO: C. McKenzie Lewis III
CFO: John R. Brintnall
1991 Sales: $22 million Employees: 174
Symbol: CMNT Exchange: NASDAQ
Industry: Computers - services

Computer One
3401 Candelaria Rd. NE
Albuquerque, NM 87107
Phone: 505-884-6610 Fax: 505-884-6674
CEO: Carrie Roberts
CFO: Carrie Roberts
1991 Sales: $7.5 million Employees: 16
Ownership: Privately held
Industry: Computers - Macintosh support & third-party products

Computer Products, Inc.
7900 Glades Rd., Ste. 500
Boca Raton, FL 33434
Phone: 407-451-1000 Fax: 407-451-1050
CEO: John N. Lemasters
CFO: Richard J. Thompson
1991 Sales: $83 million Employees: 1,432
Symbol: CPRD Exchange: NASDAQ
Industry: Electrical components - power supplies

Computer Sciences Corp.
2100 E. Grand Ave.
El Segundo, CA 90245
Phone: 310-615-0311 Fax: 310-640-2648
CEO: William R. Hoover
CFO: Leon J. Level
1992 Sales: $2,474 million Employees: 26,500
Symbol: CSC Exchange: NYSE
Industry: Computers - services

Computer Service Supply Corp.
136 Harvey Rd.
Londonderry, NH 03053
Phone: 603-644-5005 Fax: 603-622-0128
CEO: Thomas Barnes
CFO: James Rowntree
1992 Sales: $6 million Employees: 40
Ownership: Privately held
Industry: Computers - parts advance exchange, repair & refurbishing

Computer Task Group, Inc.
800 Delaware Ave.
Buffalo, NY 14209
Phone: 716-882-8000 Fax: 716-887-7272
CEO: David N. Campbell
CFO: Samuel D. Horgan
1991 Sales: $285 million Employees: 4,143
Symbol: TSK Exchange: NYSE
Industry: Computers - services

Computerized Diagnostic Imaging Centers
1660 Chicago Ave., Ste. N-15
Riverside, CA 92507
Phone: 909-781-2270 Fax: 909-781-2293
CEO: Barbara Pudinski
CFO: Douglas Gascay
1991 Sales: $10.4 million Employees: 60
Ownership: Privately held
Industry: Medical services - radiology imaging centers

Computervision Corp.
100 Crosby Dr.
Bedford, MA 01730
Phone: 617-275-1800 Fax: 617-275-2670
CEO: John J. Shields
CFO: Harvey A. Wagner
1992 Sales: $1.1 million Employees: 5,900
Symbol: CVN Exchange: NYSE
Industry: Computers - software

CompuTrac, Inc.
222 Municipal Dr.
Richardson, TX 75080
Phone: 214-234-4241 Fax: 214-234-6280
CEO: Harry W. Margolis
CFO: Steven M. Crane
1991 Sales: $12 million Employees: 107
Symbol: LLB Exchange: AMEX
Industry: Computers - software for law offices

Comshare, Inc.
3001 S. State St.
Ann Arbor, MI 48108
Phone: 313-994-4800 Fax: 313-994-5895
CEO: Richard L. Crandall
CFO: T. Wallace Wrathall
1992 Sales: $119 million Employees: 999
Symbol: CSRE Exchange: NASDAQ
Industry: Computers - decision-support software

Comstock Resources, Inc.
5005 LBJ Fwy., Ste. 1150
Dallas, TX 75244
Phone: 214-701-2100 Fax: —
CEO: M. Jay Allison
CFO: Roland O. Burns
1991 Sales: $3 million Employees: 30
Symbol: CMRE Exchange: NASDAQ
Industry: Oil & gas - US exploration & production

Comtech Telecommunications Corp.
63 Oser Ave.
Hauppauge, NY 11788
Phone: 516-435-4646 Fax: —
CEO: F. Kornberg
CFO: G. Nocita
1991 Sales: $18 million Employees: 152
Symbol: CMTL Exchange: NASDAQ
Industry: Telecommunications equipment

ConAgra, Inc.
One ConAgra Dr.
Omaha, NE 68102
Phone: 402-595-4000 Fax: 402-595-4595
CEO: Philip B. Fletcher
CFO: Stephen L. Key
1992 Sales: $21,504 million Employees: 80,787
Symbol: CAG Exchange: NYSE
Industry: Food - meat products

Concord Camera Corp.
35 Mileed Way
Avenel, NJ 07001
Phone: 908-499-8280 Fax: —
CEO: Jack C. Benun
CFO: Jack C. Benun
1991 Sales: $48 million Employees: 178
Symbol: LENS Exchange: NASDAQ
Industry: Photographic equipment

Concord EFS, Inc.
2525 Horizon Lake Dr., Ste. 120
Memphis, TN 38133
Phone: 901-371-8000 Fax: 901-371-8093
CEO: Dan M. Palmer
CFO: Vickie L. Lutzy
1991 Sales: $48 million Employees: 392
Symbol: CEFT Exchange: NASDAQ
Industry: Financial - business services

Concord Fabrics Inc.
1359 Broadway, 4th Fl.
New York, NY 10018
Phone: 212-760-0300 Fax: 212-967-7025
CEO: Earl Kramer
CFO: Martin Wolfson
1991 Sales: $198 million Employees: 770
Symbol: CIS Exchange: AMEX
Industry: Textiles - mill products

Concord Financial Group Inc.
125 W. 55th St.
New York, NY 10019
Phone: 212-492-1600 Fax: 212-586-3174
CEO: Richard E. Stierwalt
CFO: Richard A. Fabietti
1991 Sales: $14 million Employees: 56
Ownership: Privately held
Industry: Financial - mutual funds

Concorde Career Colleges, Inc.
1100 Main St., Ste. 1050
Kansas City, MO 64105
Phone: 816-474-4750 Fax: 816-471-0398
CEO: Robert F. Brozman
CFO: Paul J. Vadovicky
1991 Sales: $53 million Employees: 775
Symbol: CNCD Exchange: NASDAQ
Industry: Schools

Concurrent Computer Corp.
2 Crescent Place
Oceanport, NJ 07757
Phone: 908-870-4500 Fax: 908-870-4249
CEO: Denis R. Brown
CFO: James P. McCloskey
1992 Sales: $222 million Employees: 1,800
Symbol: CCUR Exchange: NASDAQ
Industry: Computers - mini & micro

indicates company is in *Hoover's Handbook of American Business.*

indicates company is in *Hoover's Handbook of World Business;* sales and employee numbers are for parent company.

Cone Mills Corp.
1201 Maple St.
Greensboro, NC 27405
Phone: 919-379-6220 Fax: 919-379-6287
CEO: J. Patrick Danahy
CFO: John L. Bakane
1992 Sales: $705 million Employees: 7,800
Symbol: COE Exchange: NYSE
Industry: Textiles - mill products

ConferTech International, Inc.
2801 Youngfield, Ste. 240
Golden, CO 80401
Phone: 303-237-5151 Fax: 303-233-9051
CEO: H. Robert Gill
CFO: James R. Downs
1991 Sales: $19 million Employees: 188
Symbol: CFER Exchange: NASDAQ
Industry: Telecommunications services

Congress Street Properties, Inc.
188 E. Capitol St.
Jackson, MS 39201
Phone: 601-948-4091 Fax: —
CEO: Leland R. Speed
CFO: N. Keith McKey
1992 Sales: — Employees: 23
Symbol: CSTP Exchange: NASDAQ
Industry: Real estate operations

Conmec, Inc.
1480 Valley Center Pkwy.
Bethlehem, PA 18017
Phone: 215-758-7500 Fax: 215-758-7501
CEO: John Mirro
CFO: Ruth Jones
1992 Sales: $23 million Employees: 113
Ownership: Privately held
Industry: Machinery - rotating equipment

CONMED Corp.
310 Broad St.
Utica, NY 13501
Phone: 315-797-8375 Fax: 315-797-0321
CEO: Eugene R. Corasanti
CFO: Robert D. Shallish, Jr.
1991 Sales: $38 million Employees: 410
Symbol: CNMD Exchange: NASDAQ
Industry: Medical products - disposable devices

Connecticut Energy Corp.
880 Broad St.
Bridgeport, CT 06604
Phone: 203-382-8111 Fax: 203-382-8120
CEO: J. R. Crespo
CFO: Carol A. Forest
1991 Sales: $179 million Employees: 626
Symbol: CNE Exchange: NYSE
Industry: Utility - gas distribution

Connecticut Natural Gas Corp.
100 Columbus Blvd.
Hartford, CT 06103
Phone: 203-727-3000 Fax: 203-727-3064
CEO: Victor H. Frauenhofer
CFO: A. Mark Abramovic
1991 Sales: $214 million Employees: 678
Symbol: CTG Exchange: NYSE
Industry: Utility - gas distribution

Connecticut Water Service, Inc.
93 W. Main St.
Clinton, CT 06413
Phone: 203-669-8636 Fax: 203-669-9326
CEO: William C. Stewart
CFO: Bertram L. Lenz
1991 Sales: $37 million Employees: 176
Symbol: CTWS Exchange: NASDAQ
Industry: Utility - water supply

Connell Co.
45 Cardinal Dr.
Westfield, NJ 07090
Phone: 908-233-0700 Fax: 908-233-1070
CEO: Grover Connell
CFO: Terry Connell
1991 Sales: $1,050 million Employees: 200
Ownership: Privately held
Industry: Leasing - heavy equipment; food export & import

Connell Limited Partnership
One International Place, 31st Fl.
Boston, MA 02110
Phone: 617-737-2700 Fax: 617-737-1617
CEO: William F. Connell
CFO: Kathleen Murphy
1991 Sales: $732 million Employees: 3,358
Ownership: Privately held
Industry: Metal products - fabrication, industrial equipment

Conner Peripherals, Inc.
3081 Zanker Rd.
San Jose, CA 95134
Phone: 408-456-4500 Fax: 408-456-4501
CEO: Finis F. Conner
CFO: Carl W. Neun
1992 Sales: $2,238 million Employees: 8,284
Symbol: CNR Exchange: NYSE
Industry: Computers - disk drive peripherals

Conseco, Inc.
11825 N. Pennsylvania St.
Carmel, IN 46032
Phone: 317-573-6100 Fax: 317-573-2847
CEO: Stephen C. Hilbert
CFO: Rollin M. Dick
1992 Sales: $1,526 million Employees: 1,100
Symbol: CNC Exchange: NYSE
Industry: Insurance - life

Conservative Savings Corp.
11207 W. Dodge Rd.
Omaha, NE 68154
Phone: 402-334-8475 Fax: —
CEO: Robert P. Delay
CFO: Craig S. Allen
1991 Sales: $19 million Employees: 85
Symbol: CONS Exchange: NASDAQ
Industry: Banks - Midwest

Consilium, Inc.
640 Clyde Court
Mountain View, CA 94043
Phone: 415-940-1400 Fax: 415-691-6130
CEO: Thomas Tomasetti
CFO: Mark S. Finkel
1991 Sales: $27 million Employees: 262
Symbol: CSIM Exchange: NASDAQ
Industry: Computers - factory floor management software

Consolidated Edison Co. of New York, Inc.
4 Irving Place
New York, NY 10003
Phone: 212-460-4600 Fax: 212-982-7816
CEO: Eugene R. McGrath
CFO: Raymond J. McCann
1992 Sales: $5,933 million Employees: 19,480
Symbol: ED Exchange: NYSE
Industry: Utility - electric power

Consolidated Fibres Inc.
Two N. Riverside Plaza
Chicago, IL 60606
Phone: 312-454-0100 Fax: 312-454-9946
CEO: Donald W. Phillips
CFO: Susan Obuchowski
1992 Sales: $30 million Employees: 340
Symbol: CFIB Exchange: NASDAQ
Industry: Paper & paper products

Consolidated Freightways, Inc.
3240 Hillview Ave.
Palo Alto, CA 94303
Phone: 415-494-2900 Fax: 415-813-0160
CEO: Donald E. Moffitt
CFO: Gregory L. Quesnel
1992 Sales: $4,056 million Employees: 37,700
Symbol: CNF Exchange: NYSE
Industry: Transportation - truck

Consolidated Natural Gas Co.
625 Liberty Ave., CNG Tower
Pittsburgh, PA 15222
Phone: 412-227-1000 Fax: 412-227-1304
CEO: George A. Davidson, Jr.
CFO: Lester D. Johnson
1992 Sales: $2,521 million Employees: 7,726
Symbol: CNG Exchange: NYSE
Industry: Utility - gas distribution

Consolidated Papers, Inc.
231 1st. Ave. North
Wisconsin Rapids, WI 54494
Phone: 715-422-3111 Fax: 715-422-3469
CEO: George W. Mead
CFO: Richard J. Kenney
1992 Sales: $904 million Employees: 4,792
Symbol: CPER Exchange: NASDAQ
Industry: Paper & paper products

Consolidated Products, Inc.
36 S. Pennsylvania St.
Indianapolis, IN 46204
Phone: 317-633-4100 Fax: 317-633-4105
CEO: E. W. Kelley
CFO: James W. Bear
1991 Sales: $116 million Employees: 5,892
Symbol: COPIC Exchange: NASDAQ
Industry: Retail - food & restaurants

Consolidated Rail Corp.
Six Penn Center Plaza
Philadelphia, PA 19103
Phone: 215-977-4000 Fax: 215-977-5567
CEO: James A. Hagen
CFO: H. William Brown
1992 Sales: $3,345 million Employees: 25,852
Symbol: CRR Exchange: NYSE
Industry: Transportation - rail

Consolidated Stores Corp.
1105 N. Market St., Ste. 1300
Wilmington, DE 19899
Phone: 302-478-4896 Fax: —
CEO: William G. Kelley
CFO: William B. Snow
1992 Sales: $875 million Employees: 12,293
Symbol: CNS Exchange: NYSE
Industry: Retail - discount & variety

Consolidated-Tomoka Land Co.
149 S. Ridgewood Ave.
Daytona Beach, FL 32114
Phone: 904-255-7558 Fax: 904-239-0555
CEO: Bob D. Allen
CFO: Bruce W. Teeters
1991 Sales: $47 million Employees: 400
Symbol: CTO Exchange: AMEX
Industry: Real estate development

CONSTAR International Inc.
PO Box 6339
Chattanooga, TN 37401
Phone: 615-267-2973 Fax: 615-267-9978
CEO: Charles F. Casey
CFO: James J. Goldman
1991 Sales: $548 million Employees: 3,600
Symbol: CTR Exchange: NYSE
Industry: Containers - paper & plastic

indicates company is in *Hoover's Handbook of American Business.*

indicates company is in *Hoover's Handbook of World Business;* sales and employee numbers are for parent company.

Constellation Bancorp
68 Broad St.
Elizabeth, NJ 07207
Phone: 908-354-4080 Fax: —
CEO: George R. Zoffinger
CFO: Emile A. NeJame
1991 Sales: $283 million Employees: 1,179
Symbol: CSTL Exchange: NASDAQ
Industry: Banks - Northeast

Consumers Financial Corp.
1200 Camp Hill Bypass
Camp Hill, PA 17011
Phone: 717-761-4230 Fax: —
CEO: James C. Robertson
CFO: R. Fredric Zullinger
1991 Sales: $55 million Employees: 185
Symbol: CFIN Exchange: NASDAQ
Industry: Insurance - multiline & misc.

Consumers Power Co.
212 W. Michigan Ave.
Jackson, MI 49201
Phone: 517-788-0550 Fax: 517-788-0045
CEO: Frederick W. Buckman
CFO: Alan M. Wright
1991 Sales: $2,941 million Employees: 9,347
Symbol: CMS Exchange: NYSE
Industry: Utility - electric power

Consumers Water Co.
Three Canal Plaza
Portland, ME 04101
Phone: 207-773-6438 Fax: 207-761-7903
CEO: John van C. Parker
CFO: Robert W. Phelps
1991 Sales: $85 million Employees: 704
Symbol: CONW Exchange: NASDAQ
Industry: Utility - water supply

Contel Cellular Inc.
245 Perimeter Center Pkwy. NE
Atlanta, GA 30346
Phone: 404-391-8000 Fax: 404-391-1876
CEO: Dennis L. Whipple
CFO: Theodore J. Carrier
1992 Sales: $287 million Employees: 1,049
Symbol: CCXLA Exchange: NASDAQ
Industry: Telecommunications services

Continental Airlines Holdings, Inc.
2929 Allen Pkwy., Ste. 2010
Houston, TX 77019
Phone: 713-834-5000 Fax: 713-834-2087
CEO: Robert R. Ferguson III
CFO: John E. Luth
1991 Sales: $5,551 million Employees: 42,450
Trading Status: Suspended
Industry: Transportation - airline

Continental Bank Corp.
231 S. LaSalle St.
Chicago, IL 60697
Phone: 312-828-2345 Fax: 312-828-7150
CEO: Thomas C. Theobald
CFO: Hollis W. Rademacher
1992 Sales: $1,765 million Employees: 5,054
Symbol: CBK Exchange: NYSE
Industry: Banks - money center

Continental Cablevision
The Pilot House, Lewis Wharf
Boston, MA 02110
Phone: 617-742-9500 Fax: 617-742-0530
CEO: Amos B. Hostetter, Jr.
CFO: Nancy Hawthorne
1991 Sales: $1,039 million Employees: 8,000
Ownership: Privately held
Industry: Cable TV, multiple system operator

Continental Can Co.
One Aerial Way
Syosset, NY 11791
Phone: 516-822-4940 Fax: 516-931-6344
CEO: Donald J. Bainton
CFO: Marcial L'Hommedieu
1991 Sales: $294 million Employees: 1,693
Symbol: CAN Exchange: NYSE
Industry: Containers - paper & plastic

Continental Corp.
180 Maiden Lane
New York, NY 10038
Phone: 212-440-3000 Fax: 212-440-7130
CEO: John P. Mascotte
CFO: J. Heath Fitzsimmons
1991 Sales: $5,413 million Employees: —
Symbol: CIC Exchange: NYSE
Industry: Insurance - property & casualty

Continental General Corp.
8901 Indian Hills Dr.
Omaha, NE 68114
Phone: 402-397-3200 Fax: —
CEO: Herman E. Myers, Jr.
CFO: Carl A. Ramsey
1992 Sales: — Employees: —
Symbol: CGIC Exchange: NASDAQ
Industry: Insurance - accident & health

Continental Grain Company
277 Park Ave.
New York, NY 10172
Phone: 212-207-5100 Fax: 212-207-5181
CEO: Donald L. Staheli
CFO: James J. Bigham
1992 Sales: $15,000 million Employees: 14,750
Ownership: Privately held
Industry: Food - commodity merchandising & processing

Continental Homes Holding Corp.
7001 N. Scottsdale Rd., Ste. 2050
Scottsdale, AZ 85253
Phone: 602-483-0006 Fax: 602-951-7199
CEO: Donald R. Loback
CFO: Kenda B. Gonzales
1992 Sales: $170 million Employees: 177
Symbol: CON Exchange: AMEX
Industry: Building - residential & commercial

Continental Information Systems Corp.
One CIS Pkwy.
Syracuse, NY 13221
Phone: 315-437-1900 Fax: —
CEO: James P. Hassett
CFO: Thomas J. Prinzing
1992 Sales: — Employees: —
Symbol: CNY Exchange: NYSE
Industry: Computers - services

Continental Materials Corp.
325 N. Wells St.
Chicago, IL 60610
Phone: 312-661-7200 Fax: 312-822-0621
CEO: James G. Gidwitz
CFO: Joseph J. Sum
1991 Sales: $74 million Employees: 665
Symbol: CUO Exchange: AMEX
Industry: Building products - a/c & heating

Continental Medical Systems, Inc.
600 Wilson Lane
Mechanicsburg, PA 17055
Phone: 717-790-8300 Fax: 717-766-8277
CEO: Rocco A. Ortenzio
CFO: Dennis L. Lehman
1992 Sales: $778 million Employees: 2,100
Symbol: CNM Exchange: NYSE
Industry: Nursing homes

Continental Savings of America
250 Montgomery St.
San Francisco, CA 94104
Phone: 415-274-3000 Fax: —
CEO: Charles A. Chenes
CFO: Ernest J. Jurdana
1992 Sales: — Employees: —
Symbol: CSAV Exchange: NASDAQ
Industry: Financial - savings and loans

Continuum Company, Inc., The
9500 Arboretum Blvd.
Austin, TX 78759
Phone: 512-345-5700 Fax: 512-338-7041
CEO: W. Michael Long
CFO: John L. Westermann III
1992 Sales: $127 million Employees: 1,080
Symbol: CNU Exchange: NYSE
Industry: Computers - insurance industry software & services

Contract Manufacturer Inc.
300 Industrial Rd.
Madill, OK 73446
Phone: 405-795-5536 Fax: 405-795-7263
CEO: Ronald Jackson
CFO: Kay Jackson
1992 Sales: $10 million Employees: 150
Ownership: Privately held
Industry: Transportation - horse, stock, flatbed & cargo trailers

Control Data Corp.
8100 34th Ave. South
Minneapolis, MN 55440
Phone: 612-853-8100 Fax: 612-853-7173
CEO: Lawrence Perlman
CFO: Jerry J. Johnson
1991 Sales: $328 million Employees: 3,700
Symbol: CDA Exchange: NYSE
Industry: Computers - software

Control Resource Industries, Inc.
670 Mariner Dr.
Michigan City, IN 46360
Phone: 219-872-5591 Fax: 219-872-0070
CEO: John M. Wojcik
CFO: Timothy M. Cavanaugh
1991 Sales: $32 million Employees: 111
Symbol: CRIX Exchange: NASDAQ
Industry: Pollution control equipment & services

Convergent Solutions, Inc.
100 Metro Park South
Laurence Harbor, NJ 08878
Phone: 908-290-0090 Fax: 908-290-1494
CEO: Ralph Reda
CFO: Vincent Galano
1991 Sales: $6.1 million Employees: 75
Symbol: CSOL Exchange: NASDAQ
Industry: Computers - software

Conversion Industries Inc.
101 E. Green St., Ste. 14
Pasadena, CA 91105
Phone: 818-793-7526 Fax: —
CEO: John P. McGrain
CFO: Randall M. Gates
1992 Sales: $3.6 million Employees: 12
Symbol: CVD Exchange: AMEX
Industry: Energy - alternative sources

Convertible Holdings, Inc.
PO Box 9011
Princeton, NJ 08543
Phone: 609-282-3200 Fax: —
CEO: Arthur Zeikel
CFO: Gerald M. Richard
1992 Sales: — Employees: —
Symbol: CNV Exchange: NYSE
Industry: Financial - investment management

indicates company is in *Hoover's Handbook of American Business.*

indicates company is in *Hoover's Handbook of World Business;* sales and employee numbers are for parent company.

ConVest Energy Corp.
2401 Fountain View Dr.
Houston, TX 77057
Phone: 713-780-1952 Fax: —
CEO: Richard T. Howell
CFO: T. Scott O'Keefe
1991 Sales: $18 million Employees: 33
Symbol: COV Exchange: AMEX
Industry: Oil & gas - US exploration & production

CONVEX Computer Corp.
3000 Waterview Pkwy.
Richardson, TX 75080
Phone: 214-497-4000 Fax: 214-497-4441
CEO: Robert J. Paluck
CFO: William G. Bock
1991 Sales: $198 million Employees: 1,185
Symbol: CNX Exchange: NYSE
Industry: Computers - mini & micro

Cooker Restaurant Corp.
1530 Bethel Rd.
Columbus, OH 43220
Phone: 614-457-8500 Fax: —
CEO: G. Arthur Seelbinder
CFO: William Z. Esch
1991 Sales: $40 million Employees: 1,625
Symbol: COKR Exchange: NASDAQ
Industry: Retail - food & restaurants

Cooper Companies, Inc.
250 Park Ave.
New York, NY 10177
Phone: 212-557-2690 Fax: —
CEO: Gary A. Singer
CFO: Robert S. Weiss
1991 Sales: $36 million Employees: 422
Symbol: COO Exchange: NYSE
Industry: Medical & dental supplies

Cooper Development Co.
455 E. Middlefield Rd.
Mountain View, CA 94043
Phone: 415-856-5000 Fax: —
CEO: Parker G. Montgomery
CFO: Michael J. Braden
1991 Sales: $16 million Employees: 145
Symbol: COOL Exchange: NASDAQ
Industry: Diversified operations - skin care products & sunglasses

Cooper Industries, Inc.
First City Tower, 1001 Fannin St., Ste. 4000
Houston, TX 77002
Phone: 713-739-5400 Fax: 713-739-5555
CEO: Robert Cizik
CFO: Dewain K. Cross
1992 Sales: $6,159 million Employees: 53,900
Symbol: CBE Exchange: NYSE
Industry: Diversified operations - electrical, automotive & industrial equipment

Cooper Life Sciences, Inc.
160 Broadway
New York, NY 10038
Phone: 212-791-5362 Fax: 212-791-5367
CEO: Mel Schnell
CFO: Steven Rosenberg
1992 Sales: — Employees: 7
Symbol: ZAPS Exchange: NASDAQ
Industry: Wholesale - products for professional althletes

Cooper Tire & Rubber Co.
701 Lima Ave.
Findlay, OH 45840
Phone: 419-423-1321 Fax: 419-424-4108
CEO: Ivan W. Gorr
CFO: J. Alec Reinhardt
1992 Sales: $1,175 million Employees: 6,545
Symbol: CTB Exchange: NYSE
Industry: Rubber tires

Coopers & Lybrand
1251 Sixth Ave.
New York, NY 10019
Phone: 212-536-2000 Fax: 212-642-7328
CEO: Eugene M. Freedman
CFO: Frank Scalia
1992 Sales: $5,300 million Employees: 65,000
Ownership: Privately held
Industry: Business services - accounting & consulting

Copifax Inc.
411 Commerce Ln.
Berlin, NJ 08009
Phone: 609-753-8800 Fax: 609-753-8700
CEO: Tom Callinan
CFO: Tom Callinan
1991 Sales: $4.3 million Employees: 42
Ownership: Privately held
Industry: Office equipment & supplies - copiers, faxes & digital computers

Copyco Inc.
1011 SW 30th Ave.
Deerfield Beach, FL 33442
Phone: 305-428-1300 Fax: 305-429-9083
CEO: Steven Staller
CFO: Richard Staller
1991 Sales: $6.7 million Employees: 89
Ownership: Privately held
Industry: Office equipment - wholesale copiers, faxes & digital duplicators

CopyTele, Inc.
900 Walt Whitman Rd.
Huntington Station, NY 11746
Phone: 516-549-5900 Fax: 516-549-5974
CEO: Denis A. Krusos
CFO: Frank J. DiSanto, Jr.
1992 Sales: — Employees: 13
Symbol: COPY Exchange: NASDAQ
Industry: Electrical products

COR Therapeutics, Inc.
256 E. Grand Ave.
South San Francisco, CA 94080
Phone: 415-244-6800 Fax: 415-244-9208
CEO: Vaughn M. Kailian
CFO: Laura A. Brege
1991 Sales: $2.4 million Employees: 50
Symbol: CORR Exchange: NASDAQ
Industry: Drugs

Corcap, Inc.
90 State House Square
Hartford, CT 06103
Phone: 203-240-2900 Fax: 203-549-2345
CEO: Millard H. Pryor, Jr.
CFO: John E. Sundman
1991 Sales: $539 million Employees: —
Symbol: CCP Exchange: AMEX
Industry: Rubber & plastic products

Corcom, Inc.
1600 Winchester Rd.
Libertyville, IL 60048
Phone: 708-680-7400 Fax: 708-680-8169
CEO: Werner E. Neuman
CFO: Thomas J. Buns
1991 Sales: $27 million Employees: 834
Symbol: CORC Exchange: NASDAQ
Industry: Electrical components - frequency interference filters & power entry devices

Cordis Corp.
14201 NW 60th Ave.
Miami Lakes, FL 33014
Phone: 305-824-2000 Fax: 305-824-2080
CEO: Robert C. Strauss
CFO: Alfred J. Novak
1992 Sales: $223 million Employees: 2,300
Symbol: CORD Exchange: NASDAQ
Industry: Medical instruments

Core Industries Inc.
500 N. Woodward Ave.
Bloomfield Hills, MI 48304
Phone: 313-642-3400 Fax: 313-642-6816
CEO: Richard T. Walsh
CFO: Neil C. Wester
1991 Sales: $244 million Employees: 2,750
Symbol: CRI Exchange: NYSE
Industry: Diversified operations - electronics, farm machinery, valves, fittings

CoreStates Financial Corp.
15th & Market St.
Philadelphia, PA 19102
Phone: 215-973-3512 Fax: 215-973-3578
CEO: Terrence A. Larsen
CFO: David C. Carney
1992 Sales: $2,134 million Employees: 13,479
Symbol: CSFN Exchange: NASDAQ
Industry: Banks - Northeast

Cornerstone Financial Corp.
15 E. Broadway
Derry, NH 03038
Phone: 603-432-9517 Fax: —
CEO: John M. Terravecchia
CFO: Robert E. Benoit
1991 Sales: $14 million Employees: 103
Symbol: CSTN Exchange: NASDAQ
Industry: Banks - Northeast

Corning Inc.
Houghton Park
Corning, NY 14831
Phone: 607-974-9000 Fax: 607-974-8551
CEO: James R. Houghton
CFO: Van C. Campbell
1992 Sales: $3,744 million Employees: 30,700
Symbol: GLW Exchange: NYSE
Industry: Glass products & laboratory services

Corporate Child Care Management Services
631 2nd Ave. South
Nashville, TN 37210
Phone: 615-256-9915 Fax: 615-254-3766
CEO: Marguerite W. Sallee
CFO: Robert T. Brady
1991 Sales: $6.3 million Employees: 850
Ownership: Privately held
Industry: Employer-sponsored child development centers

Corporate Express
13800 East 39th Ave.
Aurora, CO 80011
Phone: 303-373-2800 Fax: 303-373-4739
CEO: Jirka Rysavy
CFO: Gary Jacobs
1991 Sales: $36 million Employees: 167
Ownership: Privately held
Industry: Office & computer supplies

Corporate Software Inc.
275 Dan Rd.
Canton, MA 02021
Phone: 617-821-4500 Fax: 617-821-5688
CEO: Morton H. Rosenthal
CFO: Donald F. Boudreau
1991 Sales: $227 million Employees: 487
Symbol: CSOF Exchange: NASDAQ
Industry: Computers - software

Corporate Staffing Resources
100 E. Wayne St., Ste 100
South Bend, IN 46516
Phone: 219-233-8209 Fax: 219-233-8155
CEO: William W. Wilkinson
CFO: William J. Wilkinson
1991 Sales: $13 million Employees: 60
Ownership: Privately held
Industry: Business services - temporary contract technical & executive search services

indicates company is in *Hoover's Handbook of American Business.*

indicates company is in *Hoover's Handbook of World Business;* sales and employee numbers are for parent company.

Corrections Corporation of America
102 Woodmont Blvd.
Nashville, TN 37205
Phone: 615-292-3100 Fax: 615-269-8635
CEO: R. Crants
CFO: Darrell K. Massengale
1991 Sales: $68 million Employees: 1,513
Symbol: CCAX Exchange: NASDAQ
Industry: Constructs & operates prisons

Corvas International, Inc.
3030 Science Park Rd.
San Diego, CA 92121
Phone: 619-455-9800 Fax: —
CEO: David S. Kabakoff
CFO: John E. Crawford
1991 Sales: $1.3 million Employees: 63
Symbol: CVAS Exchange: NASDAQ
Industry: Drugs

CorVel Corp.
1920 Main St., Ste. 1090
Irvine, CA 92714
Phone: 714-851-1473 Fax: 714-851-1469
CEO: V. Gordon Clemons
CFO: Richard J. Schweppe
1992 Sales: $47 million Employees: 1,020
Symbol: CRVL Exchange: NASDAQ
Industry: Medical services

Cosmair Inc.
575 Fifth Ave.
New York, NY 10017
Phone: 212-818-1500 Fax: 212-984-4128
CEO: Guy Peyrelongue
CFO: —
1991 Sales: $6,457 million Employees: 29,877
Parent: L'Oréal SA
Industry: Cosmetics & toiletries

Cosmetic Center, Inc.
8839 Greenwood Place
Savage, MD 20763
Phone: 301-497-6800 Fax: 301-497-6632
CEO: Mark S. Weinstein
CFO: Bruce E. Strohl
1991 Sales: $88 million Employees: 860
Symbol: COSCA Exchange: NASDAQ
Industry: Cosmetics & toiletries

Cosmo Communications Corp.
16501 NW 16th Court
Miami, FL 33169
Phone: 305-621-4227 Fax: 305-620-4559
CEO: Amancio V. Suarez
CFO: Amancio V. Suarez
1991 Sales: $11 million Employees: 50
Symbol: CSMO Exchange: NASDAQ
Industry: Digital clocks & radios

Costar Corp.
One Alewife Center
Cambridge, MA 02140
Phone: 617-868-6200 Fax: 617-868-2076
CEO: Richard L. Morningstar
CFO: Francis H. Murphy
1991 Sales: $63 million Employees: 561
Symbol: CSTR Exchange: NASDAQ
Industry: Rubber & plastic products

Costco Wholesale Corp.
10809 120th Ave. NE
Kirkland, WA 98033
Phone: 206-828-8100 Fax: 206-828-8103
CEO: James D. Sinegal
CFO: Richard A. Galanti
1992 Sales: $6,895 million Employees: 15,700
Symbol: COST Exchange: NASDAQ
Industry: Retail - discount & variety warehouse clubs

Cotton States Life and Health Insurance Co.
244 Perimeter Ctr. Pkwy. NE
Atlanta, GA 30348
Phone: 404-391-8600 Fax: —
CEO: J. Ridley Howard
CFO: Gary W. Meader
1991 Sales: $21 million Employees: 140
Symbol: CSLH Exchange: NASDAQ
Industry: Insurance - accident & health

Coulter Corp.
11800 SW 147th Ave.
Miami, FL 33010
Phone: 305-380-3800 Fax: 305-380-8312
CEO: Joe Coulter, Jr.
CFO: Sue Van
1991 Sales: $605 million Employees: 5,000
Ownership: Privately held
Industry: Medical products - medical equipment & electronic equipment

Country Originals, Inc.
3844 W. Northside Dr.
Jackson, MS 39209
Phone: 601-366-4229 Fax: 601-366-4294
CEO: Doug Williams
CFO: Doug Williams
1992 Sales: $3.5 million Employees: 22
Ownership: Privately held
Industry: Wholesale distribution - gifts & decorative products

Countrywide Credit Industries, Inc.
155 N. Lake Ave.
Pasadena, CA 91101
Phone: 818-304-8400 Fax: 818-584-2247
CEO: David S. Loeb
CFO: Stanford L. Kurland
1992 Sales: $573 million Employees: 3,000
Symbol: CCR Exchange: NYSE
Industry: Financial - mortgages & related services

Courier Corp.
165 Jackson St.
Lowell, MA 01852
Phone: 508-458-6351 Fax: 508-453-0344
CEO: James F. Conway, Jr.
CFO: Robert P. Story, Jr.
1991 Sales: $124 million Employees: 1,396
Symbol: CRRC Exchange: NASDAQ
Industry: Printing - commercial

Coventry Corp.
424 Church St., Ste. 2600
Nashville, TN 37219
Phone: 615-251-5500 Fax: —
CEO: Joseph P. Williams
CFO: Richard H. Jones
1991 Sales: $340 million Employees: 1,566
Symbol: CVTY Exchange: NASDAQ
Industry: Health maintenance organization

Coverall North America of San Diego Inc.
3111 Camino Del Rio North, Ste. 950
San Diego, CA 92108
Phone: 619-584-1911 Fax: 619-584-4923
CEO: Alex Roudi
CFO: Kathy Bilan
1992 Sales: $23 million Employees: 150
Ownership: Privately held
Industry: Building maintenance - commercial cleaning service franchise

Cox Enterprises, Inc.
1400 Lake Hearn Dr.
Atlanta, GA 30319
Phone: 404-843-5000 Fax: 404-843-5142
CEO: James C. Kennedy
CFO: John R. Dillon
1991 Sales: $2,323 million Employees: 31,000
Ownership: Privately held
Industry: Publishing - newspapers, TV & radio broadcasting, cable TV, auto auctions

CPAC, Inc.
2364 Leicester Rd.
Leicester, NY 14481
Phone: 716-382-3223 Fax: 716-382-3031
CEO: Thomas N. Hendrickson
CFO: Ian S. Ferdinands
1992 Sales: $32 million Employees: 191
Symbol: CPAK Exchange: NASDAQ
Industry: Chemicals - specialty

CPB Inc.
220 S. King St.
Honolulu, HI 96813
Phone: 808-544-0500 Fax: 808-531-2875
CEO: Yoshiharu Satoh
CFO: Donald Y. Kamemoto
1991 Sales: $98 million Employees: 523
Symbol: CPBI Exchange: NASDAQ
Industry: Banks - West

CPC International Inc.
700 Sylvan Ave.
Englewood Cliffs, NJ 07632
Phone: 201-894-4000 Fax: 201-894-0297
CEO: Charles R. Shoemate
CFO: Konrad Schlatter
1992 Sales: $6,599 million Employees: 35,000
Symbol: CPC Exchange: NYSE
Industry: Food - soup, pastas, baked goods

CPC-Rexcel, Inc.
625 W. Columbian Blvd.
Litchfield, IL 62056
Phone: 217-324-3586 Fax: 217-324-3536
CEO: Mitchell P. Rales
CFO: Richard A. Colletta
1991 Sales: $50 million Employees: 445
Symbol: CPST Exchange: NASDAQ
Industry: Rubber & plastic products

CPI Corp.
1706 Washington Ave.
St. Louis, MO 63103
Phone: 314-231-1575 Fax: —
CEO: Alyn V. Essman
CFO: Russell Isaak
1991 Sales: $414 million Employees: 10,100
Symbol: CPY Exchange: NYSE
Industry: Photographic equipment & supplies

Cracker Barrel Old Country Store, Inc.
Hartmann Drive
Lebanon, TN 37087
Phone: 615-444-5533 Fax: 615-443-6780
CEO: Dan W. Evins
CFO: Jimmie D. White
1992 Sales: $401 million Employees: 11,388
Symbol: CBRL Exchange: NASDAQ
Industry: Retail - food & restaurants

Craftmade International, Inc.
2700 112th St.
Grand Prairie, TX 75050
Phone: 214-647-8099 Fax: —
CEO: James Ridings
CFO: Kenneth Cancienne
1992 Sales: $23 million Employees: 63
Symbol: CRFT Exchange: NASDAQ
Industry: Housewares - ceiling fans & lights

Craftmatic/Contour Industries, Inc.
2500 Interplex Dr.
Trevose, PA 19053
Phone: 215-639-1310 Fax: 215-639-9941
CEO: Stanley A. Kraftsow
CFO: Nate Cooper
1991 Sales: $56 million Employees: 423
Symbol: CRCC Exchange: NASDAQ
Industry: Retail - adjustable beds, chairs, security shutters & filtration systems

indicates company is in *Hoover's Handbook of American Business.*

indicates company is in *Hoover's Handbook of World Business;* sales and employee numbers are for parent company.

Cragin Financial Corp.
5200 W. Fullerton Ave.
Chicago, IL 60639
Phone: 312-889-1000 Fax: —
CEO: Adam A. Jahns
CFO: Stanley E. Magiera
1991 Sales: $243 million Employees: 635
Symbol: CRGN Exchange: NASDAQ
Industry: Financial - savings and loans

Craig Corp.
116 N. Robertson Blvd.
Los Angeles, CA 90048
Phone: 213-659-6641 Fax: —
CEO: Edward L. Kane
CFO: Robert L. Woolheater
1991 Sales: $4 million Employees: —
Symbol: CRG Exchange: NYSE
Industry: Retail - supermarkets

Crane Co.
757 Third Ave.
New York, NY 10017
Phone: 212-415-7300 Fax: —
CEO: Robert S. Evans
CFO: Jeremiah P. Cronin
1992 Sales: $1,307 million Employees: 9,000
Symbol: CR Exchange: NYSE
Industry: Diversified operations - aerospace & defense products & millwork wholesales

Crawford & Co. Risk Management Services
5620 Glenridge Dr. NE
Atlanta, GA 30342
Phone: 404-256-0830 Fax: 404-847-4028
CEO: F. L. Minix
CFO: D. R. Chapman
1992 Sales: $598 million Employees: 7,907
Symbol: CRDA Exchange: NYSE
Industry: Insurance - property & casualty

Crawford Fittings Co.
29500 Solon Rd.
Solon, OH 44139
Phone: 216-248-4600 Fax: 216-349-5970
CEO: F. J. Callahan
CFO: Norge Tobbe
1991 Sales: $600 million Employees: 5,000
Ownership: Privately held
Industry: Metal products - valves, pipe fittings

Cray Computer Corp.
1110 Bayfield Dr.
Colorado Springs, CO 80906
Phone: 719-579-6464 Fax: 719-540-4028
CEO: Neil Davenport
CFO: Gregory T. Barnum
1991 Sales: $0.3 million Employees: 384
Symbol: CRAY Exchange: NASDAQ
Industry: Computers - supercomputers

Cray Research, Inc.
655-A Lone Oak Dr.
Eagan, MN 55121
Phone: 612-683-7100 Fax: 612-683-7299
CEO: John F. Carlson
CFO: Michael J. Lindseth
1992 Sales: $798 million Employees: 5,395
Symbol: CYR Exchange: NYSE
Industry: Computers - supercomputers

Creative Producers Group Inc.
4814 Washington Blvd.
St. Louis, MO 63108
Phone: 314-367-2255 Fax: 314-367-5510
CEO: Keith Alper
CFO: Keith Alper
1991 Sales: $1.5 million Employees: 12
Ownership: Privately held
Industry: Video production, event planning & training services, meetings, special events

Creative Products Inc.
4630 Coates Dr.
Fairburn, GA 30213
Phone: 404-969-8803 Fax: 404-969-9303
CEO: Dave Williams
CFO: Steve Munson
1991 Sales: $4.7 million Employees: 109
Ownership: Privately held
Industry: Business services - contract packaging

Creative Staffing
7700 N. Kendall Dr. #406
Miami, FL 33156
Phone: 305-279-7799 Fax: 305-598-9692
CEO: Ann Machado
CFO: Anna Barton
1991 Sales: $7.1 million Employees: 24
Ownership: Privately held
Industry: Business services - temporary & permanent employment services

Creative Technologies Corp.
170 53rd St.
Brooklyn, NY 11232
Phone: 718-492-8400 Fax: 718-492-3878
CEO: Richard Helfman
CFO: Richard Helfman
1991 Sales: $5.5 million Employees: 23
Symbol: CRTV Exchange: NASDAQ
Industry: Manufacturing - kitchen electronics

Credit Acceptance Corp.
21301 Civic Center Dr.
Southfield, MI 48076
Phone: 313-353-2700 Fax: —
CEO: Donald A. Foss
CFO: Richard E. Beckman
1991 Sales: $13 million Employees: 69
Symbol: CACC Exchange: NASDAQ
Industry: Business services

Crédit Lyonnais
1301 Avenue of the Americas
New York, NY 10019
Phone: 212-261-7000 Fax: 212-459-3170
CEO: Robert Cohen
CFO: —
1991 Sales: $29,446 million Employees: 70,567
Parent: Crédit Lyonnais
Industry: Banks - money center

Crest Industries, Inc.
8899 NW 18th Terr.
Miami, FL 33172
Phone: 305-592-5699 Fax: 305-594-9281
CEO: Ronald S. Kepes
CFO: Gary L. Rodney
1992 Sales: $44 million Employees: 124
Symbol: CRII Exchange: NASDAQ
Industry: Building products - retail & wholesale

Crestar Financial Corp.
919 E. Main St.
Richmond, VA 23261
Phone: 804-782-5000 Fax: 804-782-5815
CEO: Richard G. Tilghman
CFO: Patrick D. Giblin
1992 Sales: $1,082 million Employees: 5,771
Symbol: CRFC Exchange: NASDAQ
Industry: Banks - Southeast

Crestmont Financial Corp.
2035 Lincoln Hwy.
Edison, NJ 08817
Phone: 908-287-3838 Fax: —
CEO: Lawrence B. Seidman
CFO: Eric P. Graap
1992 Sales: $30 million Employees: 302
Symbol: CRES Exchange: NASDAQ
Industry: Financial - savings and loans

CRI Liquidating REIT, Inc.
11200 Rockville Pike
Rockville, MD 20852
Phone: 301-468-9200 Fax: —
CEO: William B. Dockser
CFO: Jay R. Cohen
1991 Sales: $31 million Employees: —
Symbol: CFR Exchange: NYSE
Industry: Financial - investment management

Criticare Systems, Inc.
20900 Swenson Dr., Ste. 398
Waukesha, WI 53186
Phone: 414-797-8282 Fax: 414-797-8104
CEO: Gerhard J. Von der Ruhr
CFO: Richard J. Osowski
1992 Sales: $26 million Employees: 144
Symbol: CXIM Exchange: NASDAQ
Industry: Medical instruments - portable patient-monitoring systems

Crompton & Knowles Corp.
One Station Place, Metro Circle
Stamford, CT 06902
Phone: 203-353-5400 Fax: 203-353-5424
CEO: Vincent A. Calarco
CFO: Charles J. Marsden
1991 Sales: $450 million Employees: 2,043
Symbol: CNK Exchange: NYSE
Industry: Chemicals - specialty

Crop Genetics International Corp.
7170 Standard Dr.
Hanover, MD 21076
Phone: 410-712-7170 Fax: 410-712-0104
CEO: Joseph W. Kelly
CFO: Joseph W. Kelly
1991 Sales: $1.4 million Employees: 100
Symbol: CROP Exchange: NASDAQ
Industry: Agricultural operations

Crowley Maritime Corp.
155 Grand Ave.
Oakland, CA 94612
Phone: 510-251-7500 Fax: 510-251-7625
CEO: Thomas B. Crowley, Sr.
CFO: Robert C. Hood
1991 Sales: $1,100 million Employees: 5,000
Ownership: Privately held
Industry: Transportation - shipping

Crowley, Milner and Co.
2301 W. Lafayette Blvd.
Detroit, MI 48216
Phone: 313-962-2400 Fax: 313-962-2529
CEO: Andrew J. Soffel
CFO: Mark A. VandenBerg
1991 Sales: $104 million Employees: 1,400
Symbol: COM Exchange: AMEX
Industry: Retail - regional department stores

Crown American Corp.
Pasquerilla Plaza
Johnstown, PA 15907
Phone: 814-536-4441 Fax: 814-535-9486
CEO: Frank J. Pasquerilla
CFO: Thomas Fetsko
1991 Sales: $730 million Employees: 9,500
Ownership: Privately held
Industry: Real estate operations - department stores, shopping malls, motels

Crown Andersen Inc.
306 Dividend Dr.
Peachtree City, GA 30269
Phone: 404-997-2000 Fax: 404-487-5066
CEO: Jack D. Brady
CFO: Randall H. Morgan
1991 Sales: $23 million Employees: 167
Symbol: CRAN Exchange: NASDAQ
Industry: Industrial control systems

indicates company is in *Hoover's Handbook of American Business.*

indicates company is in *Hoover's Handbook of World Business;* sales and employee numbers are for parent company.

Crown Books Corp.
3300 75th Ave.
Landover, MD 20785
Phone: 301-731-1200 Fax: 301-731-1340
CEO: Robert M. Haft
CFO: Richard J. Koll
1991 Sales: $232 million Employees: 2,376
Symbol: CRWN Exchange: NASDAQ
Industry: Retail - bookstores

Crown Central Petroleum Corp.
One N. Charles St.
Baltimore, MD 21201
Phone: 410-539-7400 Fax: 410-659-4880
CEO: Henry A. Rosenberg, Jr.
CFO: Edward L. Rosenberg
1991 Sales: $1,765 million Employees: 3,894
Symbol: CNPB Exchange: AMEX
Industry: Oil refining & marketing

Crown Cork & Seal Co., Inc.
9300 Ashton Rd.
Philadelphia, PA 19114
Phone: 215-698-5100 Fax: 215-698-5201
CEO: William J. Avery
CFO: Alan W. Rutherford
1992 Sales: $3,781 million Employees: 17,763
Symbol: CCK Exchange: NYSE
Industry: Containers - metal

Crown Crafts, Inc.
Edmond St.
Calhoun, GA 30703
Phone: 706-629-7941 Fax: 706-629-7754
CEO: Michael H. Bernstein
CFO: Paul A. Criscillis, Jr.
1992 Sales: $123 million Employees: 1,600
Symbol: CRW Exchange: AMEX
Industry: Textiles - home furnishings

Crown Resources Corp.
1225 17th St., Ste. 1500
Denver, CO 80202
Phone: 303-295-2171 Fax: 303-295-2249
CEO: Mark E. Jones III
CFO: John A. Labate
1991 Sales: $9.7 million Employees: 24
Symbol: CRRS Exchange: NASDAQ
Industry: Gold mining & processing

CRSS, Inc.
1177 West Loop South, Ste. 800
Houston, TX 77027
Phone: 713-552-2000 Fax: 713-552-2538
CEO: Bruce W. Wilkinson
CFO: William J. Gardiner
1992 Sales: $456 million Employees: 2,234
Symbol: CRX Exchange: NYSE
Industry: Construction - heavy

Cruise America, Inc.
5959 Blue Lagoon Dr., Ste. 205
Miami, FL 33126
Phone: 305-262-9611 Fax: 305-261-5293
CEO: Robert A. Smalley
CFO: Eric R. Bensen
1992 Sales: $76 million Employees: 287
Symbol: RVR Exchange: AMEX
Industry: Leisure & recreational services

Cryenco Sciences, Inc.
5995 N. Washington St.
Denver, CO 80216
Phone: 303-295-1161 Fax: —
CEO: Alfred Schechter
CFO: Jill N. Manaly
1992 Sales: — Employees: —
Symbol: CSCID Exchange: NASDAQ
Industry: Metal processing & fabrication - vacuum-jacketed containment systems

Cryomedical Sciences, Inc.
1300 Piccard Dr., Ste. 102
Rockville, MD 20850
Phone: 301-417-7070 Fax: 301-417-7077
CEO: J. J. Finkelstein
CFO: Theodore D. Pennington
1992 Sales: — Employees: 34
Symbol: CMSI Exchange: NASDAQ
Industry: Medical products - synthetic blood substitute solutions

Crystal Brands, Inc.
30 Crystal Brands Rd.
Southport, CT 06490
Phone: 203-254-6200 Fax: 203-254-6252
CEO: Gordon E. Allen
CFO: Gerald M. Chaney
1991 Sales: $827 million Employees: 9,800
Symbol: CBR Exchange: NYSE
Industry: Textiles - apparel

Crystal Oil Co.
229 Milam St.
Shreveport, LA 71101
Phone: 318-222-7791 Fax: Call co. operator
CEO: Joe N. Averett, Jr.
CFO: Jeffery A. Ballew
1991 Sales: $27 million Employees: 91
Symbol: COR Exchange: AMEX
Industry: Oil & gas - US exploration & production

CS First Boston, Inc.
Park Ave. Plaza, 55 E. 52nd St.
New York, NY 10005
Phone: 212-909-2000 Fax: 212-318-1187
CEO: John M. Hennessy
CFO: —
1992 Sales: $5,701 million Employees: 44,323
Parent: CS Holding
Industry: Financial - diversified services

CSF Holdings, Inc.
999 Brickell Ave.
Miami, FL 33131
Phone: 305-577-0400 Fax: —
CEO: Charles B. Stuzin
CFO: Morton Trilling
1991 Sales: $381 million Employees: 881
Symbol: CSFCB Exchange: NASDAQ
Industry: Financial - savings and loans

CSP Inc.
40 Linnell Circle
Billerica, MA 01821
Phone: 617-272-6020 Fax: 508-663-0150
CEO: David S. Botten
CFO: Gary W. Levine
1991 Sales: $13 million Employees: 105
Symbol: CSPI Exchange: NASDAQ
Industry: Computers - peripheral equipment

CSS Industries, Inc.
1401 Walnut St., 2nd Fl.
Philadelphia, PA 19102
Phone: 215-569-9900 Fax: Ext. 32
CEO: Jack Farber
CFO: James G. Baxter
1991 Sales: $171 million Employees: 2,020
Symbol: CSS Exchange: AMEX
Industry: Paper - business forms

CST Entertainment Imaging, Inc.
6171 W. Century Blvd., 2nd Fl.
Los Angeles, CA 90045
Phone: 213-417-3444 Fax: 213-417-3500
CEO: Gerald Shefsky
CFO: Gerald Shefsky
1991 Sales: $3.6 million Employees: 93
Symbol: CLR Exchange: AMEX
Industry: Leisure & recreational services

CSX Corp.
One James Ctr., 901 E. Cary St.
Richmond, VA 23219
Phone: 804-782-1400 Fax: 804-782-1409
CEO: John W. Snow
CFO: James Ermer
1992 Sales: $8,734 million Employees: 49,937
Symbol: CSX Exchange: NYSE
Industry: Transportation - rail

CTS Corp.
905 West Blvd. North
Elkhart, IN 46514
Phone: 219-293-7511 Fax: 219-293-6146
CEO: Joseph P. Walker
CFO: Gary N. Hoipkemier
1991 Sales: $230 million Employees: 4,847
Symbol: CTS Exchange: NYSE
Industry: Electrical components

CU Bancorp
16030 Ventura Blvd.
Encino, CA 91436
Phone: 818-907-9122 Fax: —
CEO: Steve Carpenter
CFO: Robert J. Vecci
1991 Sales: $32 million Employees: 144
Symbol: CUBN Exchange: NASDAQ
Industry: Banks - West

Cubic Corp.
9333 Balboa Ave.
San Diego, CA 92123
Phone: 619-277-6780 Fax: 619-277-1878
CEO: Walter J. Zable
CFO: William W. Boyle
1991 Sales: $308 million Employees: 3,100
Symbol: CUB Exchange: AMEX
Industry: Electronics - military

CUC International Inc.
707 Summer St.
Stamford, CT 06901
Phone: 203-324-9261 Fax: 203-348-4528
CEO: Walter A. Forbes
CFO: Stuart L. Bell
1992 Sales: $714 million Employees: 4,500
Symbol: CU Exchange: NYSE
Industry: Retail - mail order & direct via computer

Cucci International, Inc.
1901 Del Amo Blvd.
Torrance, CA 90501
Phone: 310-212-0802 Fax: 310-212-7634
CEO: Yvonne M. Cucci
CFO: Yvonne M. Cucci
1991 Sales: $2.9 million Employees: 34
Ownership: Privately held
Industry: Apparel - screen printed & embroidered custom corporate identity apparel

Culbro Corp.
387 Park Ave. South, 6th Fl.
New York, NY 10016
Phone: 212-561-8700 Fax: 212-561-8794
CEO: Edgar M. Cullman
CFO: Jay M. Green
1992 Sales: $1,149 million Employees: 3,750
Symbol: CUC Exchange: NYSE
Industry: Tobacco

Cullen/Frost Bankers, Inc.
100 W. Houston St.
San Antonio, TX 78205
Phone: 210-220-4605 Fax: 210-220-5557
CEO: T. C. Frost
CFO: Phillip D. Green
1991 Sales: $289 million Employees: 1,737
Symbol: CFBI Exchange: NASDAQ
Industry: Banks - Southwest

A indicates company is in *Hoover's Handbook of American Business.*

W indicates company is in *Hoover's Handbook of World Business;* sales and employee numbers are for parent company.

Cullum Cos. Inc.
14303 Inwood Rd.
Dallas, TX 75244
Phone: 214-661-9700 Fax: 214-661-3866
CEO: Jack W. Evans, Jr.
CFO: James T. Stiles
1991 Sales: $1,123 million Employees: 6,000
Ownership: Privately held
Industry: Retail - supermarkets & drug stores

Culp, Inc.
101 S. Main St.
High Point, NC 27261
Phone: 919-889-5161 Fax: 919-889-8339
CEO: Robert G. Culp III
CFO: Franklin N. Saxon
1992 Sales: $191 million Employees: 1,828
Symbol: CULP Exchange: NASDAQ
Industry: Textiles - home furnishings

Cumberland Farms Inc.
777 Dedham St.
Canton, MA 02021
Phone: 617-828-4900 Fax: 617-828-8137
CEO: Lily H. Bentas
CFO: Arthur Koumantzils
1991 Sales: $1,111 million Employees: 3,800
Ownership: Privately held
Industry: Retail - convenience stores & gas distribution

Cumberland Federal Bancorporation, Inc.
200 W. Broadway
Louisville, KY 40202
Phone: 502-562-5320 Fax: —
CEO: H. David Hale
CFO: P. Norris Shockley, Jr.
1991 Sales: $31 million Employees: 443
Symbol: CMBK Exchange: NASDAQ
Industry: Banks - Midwest

Cummins Engine Co., Inc.
500 Jackson St.
Columbus, IN 47202
Phone: 812-377-5000 Fax: 812-377-3334
CEO: Henry B. Schacht
CFO: Peter B. Hamilton
1992 Sales: $3,749 million Employees: 22,900
Symbol: CUM Exchange: NYSE
Industry: Engines - internal combustion

Cupertino National Bancorp
20230 Stevens Creek Blvd.
Cupertino, CA 95014
Phone: 408-996-1144 Fax: 408-996-0657
CEO: C. Donald Allen
CFO: Kenneth L. Brown
1991 Sales: $14 million Employees: 55
Symbol: CUNB Exchange: NASDAQ
Industry: Banks - West

Curaflex Health Services, Inc.
3281 Guasti Rd., Ste. 700
Ontario, CA 91761
Phone: 909-460-2400 Fax: 909-460-2466
CEO: Charles A. Laverty
CFO: Ralph B. Strong
1991 Sales: $39 million Employees: 380
Symbol: CFLX Exchange: NASDAQ
Industry: Healthcare - outpatient & home

Curative Technologies, Inc.
14 Research Way
East Setauket, NY 11733
Phone: 516-689-7000 Fax: —
CEO: Russell B. Whitman
CFO: John C. Prior
1991 Sales: $20 million Employees: 197
Symbol: CURE Exchange: NASDAQ
Industry: Drugs - human growth factors

Curtice Burns Foods, Inc.
90 Linden Place
Rochester, NY 14625
Phone: 716-383-1850 Fax: 716-383-1281
CEO: J. William Petty
CFO: William D. Rice
1992 Sales: $894 million Employees: 6,539
Symbol: CBI Exchange: AMEX
Industry: Food - canned vegetables & fruits

Curtiss-Wright Corp.
1200 Wall St. West
Lyndhurst, NJ 07071
Phone: 201-896-8400 Fax: 201-438-5680
CEO: Shirley D. Brinsfield
CFO: Robert A. Bosi
1991 Sales: $191 million Employees: 1,842
Symbol: CW Exchange: NYSE
Industry: Aerospace - aircraft equipment

Custom Chrome, Inc.
16100 Jacqueline Court
Morgan Hill, CA 95037
Phone: 408-778-0500 Fax: 408-778-0520
CEO: Ignatius J. Panzica
CFO: Robert T. Lanz
1991 Sales: $44 million Employees: 218
Symbol: CSTM Exchange: NASDAQ
Industry: Automotive & trucking - replacement parts

Customedix Corp.
40 Industrial Rd.
Berkeley Heights, NJ 07922
Phone: 908-464-2214 Fax: —
CEO: Gordon S. Cohen
CFO: Andrew A. Miller
1992 Sales: $37 million Employees: 143
Symbol: CUS Exchange: AMEX
Industry: Dental health care products & supplies

Cutchall Management Co.
4524 Farnam
Omaha, NE 68132
Phone: 402-558-3333 Fax: 402-558-1512
CEO: Greg Cutchall
CFO: Greg Cutchall
1992 Sales: $3.7 million Employees: 200
Ownership: Privately held
Industry: Retail - food & restaurants

CVB Financial Corp.
701 N. Haven Ave., Ste. 350
Ontario, CA 91764
Phone: 909-980-4030 Fax: 909-980-5232
CEO: D. Lynn Wiley
CFO: Robert J. Schurheck
1991 Sales: $56 million Employees: 331
Symbol: CVB Exchange: AMEX
Industry: Banks - West

CXR Corp.
2332 McGaw Ave.
Irvine, CA 92714
Phone: 714-756-7150 Fax: 714-756-7129
CEO: F. Jack Gorry
CFO: Kent M. Wilkins
1992 Sales: $32 million Employees: 244
Symbol: CXR Exchange: AMEX
Industry: Telecommunications equipment

CyberOptics Corp.
2505 Kennedy St. NE
Minneapolis, MN 55413
Phone: 612-331-5702 Fax: 612-331-3826
CEO: Stephen K. Case
CFO: Kent O. Lillemoe
1991 Sales: $7.8 million Employees: 65
Symbol: CYBE Exchange: NASDAQ
Industry: Lasers - systems & components

Cybertek Computer Products Inc.
7800 N. Stemmons Fwy., Ste. 600
Dallas, TX 75247
Phone: 214-637-1540 Fax: 214-638-2810
CEO: Vaughn W. Morgan
CFO: David R. Bankhead
1992 Sales: $29 million Employees: 248
Symbol: CKCP Exchange: NASDAQ
Industry: Computers - software

CyCare Systems, Inc.
7001 N. Scottsdale Rd., Ste. 1000
Scottsdale, AZ 85253
Phone: 602-596-4300 Fax: 602-596-4466
CEO: Jim H. Houtz
CFO: Mark R. Schonau
1991 Sales: $74 million Employees: 1,131
Symbol: CYS Exchange: NYSE
Industry: Computers - services

Cygnus Therapeutic Systems
400 Penobscot Dr.
Redwood City, CA 94063
Phone: 415-369-4300 Fax: —
CEO: David H. de Weese
CFO: Shirley L. Clayton
1991 Sales: $5.1 million Employees: 154
Symbol: CYGN Exchange: NASDAQ
Industry: Medical products - transdermal drug delivery systems

Cypress Semiconductor Corp.
3901 N. First St.
San Jose, CA 95134
Phone: 408-943-2600 Fax: 408-943-2741
CEO: T. J. Rodgers
CFO: Kenneth A. Goldman
1991 Sales: $287 million Employees: 1,945
Symbol: CY Exchange: NYSE
Industry: Electrical components - semiconductors

Cyprus Minerals Co.
9100 E. Mineral Circle
Englewood, CO 80112
Phone: 303-643-5000 Fax: 303-643-5049
CEO: Milton H. Ward
CFO: Gerald J. Malys
1992 Sales: $1,641 million Employees: 8,100
Symbol: CYM Exchange: NYSE
Industry: Metal ores

Cyrix Corp.
2703 N. Central Expwy.
Richardson, TX 75080
Phone: 214-994-8388 Fax: 214-699-9857
CEO: Jerry Rogers
CFO: —
1991 Sales: $26 million Employees: 85
Ownership: Privately held
Industry: Electrical components - semiconductors

Cytel Corp.
3525 John Hopkins Court
San Diego, CA 92121
Phone: 619-552-3000 Fax: 619-552-8801
CEO: Jay D. Kranzler
CFO: Jay D. Kranzler
1991 Sales: $6.4 million Employees: 125
Symbol: CYTL Exchange: NASDAQ
Industry: Biomedical & genetic products

Cytocare, Inc.
9975 Toledo Way
Irvine, CA 92718
Phone: 714-587-0500 Fax: 714-587-1133
CEO: Errol Payne
CFO: David V. Radlinski
1991 Sales: $9.1 million Employees: 50
Symbol: CYTI Exchange: NASDAQ
Industry: Medical services

indicates company is in *Hoover's Handbook of American Business.*

indicates company is in *Hoover's Handbook of World Business;* sales and employee numbers are for parent company.

CYTOGEN Corp.
600 College Rd. East
Princeton, NJ 08540
Phone: 609-987-8200 Fax: —
CEO: George W. Ebright
CFO: Martin D. Cleary
1991 Sales: $7 million Employees: 189
Symbol: CYTO Exchange: NASDAQ
Industry: Biomedical & genetic products

CytoTherapeutics, Inc.
2 Richmond Square
Providence, RI 02906
Phone: 401-272-3310 Fax: —
CEO: Seth A. Rudnick
CFO: Thomas G. Wiggans
1991 Sales: $0.5 million Employees: 50
Symbol: CTII Exchange: NASDAQ
Industry: Medical services

D. J. King Trucking & Excavating
63 Newberry Rd.
East Windsor, CT 06088
Phone: 203-623-4649 Fax: 203-623-9983
CEO: Marilyn King
CFO: Douglas King, Jr.
1991 Sales: $2.6 million Employees: 28
Ownership: Privately held
Industry: Construction - site contracting

D & N Financial Corp.
400 Quincy St.
Hancock, MI 49930
Phone: 906-482-2700 Fax: —
CEO: Kenneth D. Seaton
CFO: Kenneth R. Janson
1991 Sales: $30 million Employees: 536
Symbol: DNFC Exchange: NASDAQ
Industry: Financial - savings and loans

D. R. Horton, Inc.
2221 E. Lamar Blvd., Ste. 950
Arlington, TX 76006
Phone: 817-640-8200 Fax: 817-633-6801
CEO: Donald R. Horton
CFO: David J. Keller
1991 Sales: $124 million Employees: 185
Symbol: DRHI Exchange: NASDAQ
Industry: Building - residential & commercial

D&K Enterprises Inc.
3216 Commander Dr. #101
Carrollton, TX 75006
Phone: 214-353-9999 Fax: 214-248-9750
CEO: Tom Mosey
CFO: Tom Mosey
1991 Sales: $2.1 million Employees: 25
Ownership: Privately held
Industry: Diversified operations - personalized books, child IDs & signature analysis

D'Arcy Masius Benton & Bowles Inc.
1675 Broadway
New York, NY 10019
Phone: 212-468-3622 Fax: 212-468-4385
CEO: Roy Bostock
CFO: Craig D. Brown
1992 Sales: $550 million Employees: 5,000
Ownership: Privately held
Industry: Advertising

Daewoo International (America) Corp.
100 Daewoo Place
Carlstadt, NJ 07072
Phone: 201-935-8700 Fax: 201-935-6491
CEO: Ki Bum Yoo
CFO: —
1991 Sales: $8,430 million Employees: 8,983
Parent: Daewoo Group
Industry: Diversified operations - electronics, ships, textiles & steel

Dahlberg, Inc.
4101 Dahlberg Dr.
Golden Valley, MN 55422
Phone: 612-520-9500 Fax: 612-520-9520
CEO: K. Jeffrey Dahlberg
CFO: Sally J. Smith
1991 Sales: $92 million Employees: 1,040
Symbol: DAHL Exchange: NASDAQ
Industry: Medical instruments

Dai-Ichi Kangyo Bank
One World Trade Ctr., Ste. 4911
New York, NY 10048
Phone: 212-466-5200 Fax: 212-524-0579
CEO: Hideo Kitahara
CFO: —
1992 Sales: $34,531 million Employees: 18,703
Parent: Dai-Ichi Kangyo Bank, Ltd., The
Industry: Banks - money center

Daily Journal Corp.
355 S. Grand Ave., 34th Fl.
Los Angeles, CA 90071
Phone: 213-625-2141 Fax: —
CEO: Charles T. Munger
CFO: Gerald L. Salzman
1991 Sales: $29 million Employees: 320
Symbol: DJCO Exchange: NASDAQ
Industry: Publishing - newspapers

Dairy Mart Convenience Stores, Inc.
240 South Rd.
Enfield, CT 06082
Phone: 203-741-3611 Fax: 203-741-3072
CEO: Frank Colaccino
CFO: Gregory G. Landry
1991 Sales: $551 million Employees: 5,500
Symbol: DMCVA Exchange: NASDAQ
Industry: Retail - convenience stores

DAKA International, Inc.
55 Ferncroft Rd., 1 Corporate Pl.
Danvers, MA 01923
Phone: 508-774-9115 Fax: 508-750-1414
CEO: William H. Baumhauer
CFO: David N. Terhune
1992 Sales: $164 million Employees: 8,135
Symbol: DKAI Exchange: NASDAQ
Industry: Diversified operations

Dallas Semiconductor Corp.
4401 S. Beltwood Pkwy.
Dallas, TX 75244
Phone: 214-450-0470 Fax: 214-450-0470
CEO: Charles V. Prothro
CFO: Michael G. Pate
1991 Sales: $104 million Employees: 662
Symbol: DS Exchange: NYSE
Industry: Electrical components - semiconductors

Damark International, Inc.
7101 Winnetka Ave. North
Minneapolis, MN 55428
Phone: 612-531-0066 Fax: 612-531-0180
CEO: Mark A. Cohn
CFO: James E. Tuller
1991 Sales: $216 million Employees: 770
Symbol: DMRK Exchange: NASDAQ
Industry: Retail - mail order & direct

Dames & Moore, Inc.
911 Wilshire Blvd., Ste. 700
Los Angeles, CA 90017
Phone: 213-683-1560 Fax: 213-628-0015
CEO: George D. Leal
CFO: Robert M. Perry
1992 Sales: $260 million Employees: 3,300
Symbol: DM Exchange: NYSE
Industry: Engineering - R&D services

Damon Corp.
115 Fourth Ave.
Needham Heights, MA 02194
Phone: 617-449-0800 Fax: —
CEO: Robert L. Rosen
CFO: Glen M. Kassan
1991 Sales: $262 million Employees: 3,200
Symbol: DCL Exchange: NYSE
Industry: Medical services - clinical laboratory testing service

Dana Corp.
4500 Dorr St.
Toledo, OH 43615
Phone: 419-535-4500 Fax: 419-535-4643
CEO: Southwood J. Morcott
CFO: James E. Ayers
1992 Sales: $4,872 million Employees: 35,000
Symbol: DCN Exchange: NYSE
Industry: Automotive & trucking - original equipment

Danaher Corp.
1250 24th St. NW, Ste. 800
Washington, DC 20037
Phone: 202-828-0850 Fax: 202-828-0860
CEO: George M. Sherman
CFO: Patrick W. Allender
1992 Sales: $956 million Employees: 7,133
Symbol: DHR Exchange: NYSE
Industry: Automotive & trucking - original equipment

Danek Group, Inc.
3092 Directors Row
Memphis, TN 38131
Phone: 901-396-2695 Fax: 901-396-2699
CEO: E. R. Pickard
CFO: Laurence Y. Fairey
1992 Sales: $76 million Employees: 260
Symbol: DNKG Exchange: NASDAQ
Industry: Medical products

Daniel Industries, Inc.
9753 Pine Lake Dr.
Houston, TX 77055
Phone: 713-467-6000 Fax: 713-827-3889
CEO: W. A. Griffin
CFO: Henry G. Schopfer III
1991 Sales: $202 million Employees: 1,800
Symbol: DAN Exchange: NYSE
Industry: Oil field machinery & equipment

Danielson Holding Corp.
767 Third Ave., 5th Fl.
New York, NY 10017
Phone: 212-888-0347 Fax: 212-888-6704
CEO: C. Kirk Rhein, Jr.
CFO: Michael T. Carney
1991 Sales: $74 million Employees: —
Symbol: DHC Exchange: AMEX
Industry: Insurance underwriting - property, casualty & workers compensation

Dannon Company, The
1111 Westchester Ave.
White Plains, NY 10604
Phone: 914-697-9700 Fax: 914-934-2805
CEO: P. Gournay
CFO: —
1991 Sales: $12,755 million Employees: 59,158
Parent: BSN Groupe
Industry: Food - dairy, beer, mineral water, biscuits

Danskin, Inc.
111 W. 40th St.
New York, NY 10018
Phone: 212-764-4630 Fax: —
CEO: Byron A. Hero, Jr.
CFO: Beverly Eichel
1992 Sales: $130 million Employees: 1,855
Symbol: DANS Exchange: NASDAQ
Industry: Apparel

Dart Container Corporation
500 Hogsback Rd.
Mason, MI 48864
Phone: 517-676-3800 Fax: 517-676-3883
CEO: Kenneth Dart
CFO: William Myers
1991 Sales: $464 million Employees: 3,000
Ownership: Privately held
Industry: Containers - plastic & foam cups & food containers

Dart Group Corp.
3300 75th Ave.
Landover, MD 20785
Phone: 301-731-1200 Fax: 301-731-1340
CEO: Herbert H. Haft
CFO: Richard J. Koll
1992 Sales: $1,246 million Employees: 9,300
Symbol: DARTA Exchange: NASDAQ
Industry: Retail - discount auto parts, book stores & grocery stores

Data General Corp.
4400 Computer Dr.
Westborough, MA 01580
Phone: 508-366-8911 Fax: 508-366-1319
CEO: Ronald L. Skates
CFO: Robert C. McBride
1992 Sales: $1,101 million Employees: 8,500
Symbol: DGN Exchange: NYSE
Industry: Computers - mini & micro

Data I/O Corp.
10525 Willows Rd. NE
Redmond, WA 98052
Phone: 206-881-6444 Fax: 206-882-1043
CEO: Thomas R. Clark
CFO: John J. Hagedorn
1991 Sales: $67 million Employees: 487
Symbol: DAIO Exchange: NASDAQ
Industry: Electronics - measuring instruments

Data Measurement Corp.
15884 Gaither Dr.
Gaithersburg, MD 20877
Phone: 301-948-2450 Fax: 301-670-0506
CEO: Dominique Gignoux
CFO: Sam Clatworthy
1991 Sales: $20 million Employees: 177
Symbol: DMCB Exchange: NASDAQ
Industry: Electronics - measuring instruments

Data Research Associates, Inc.
1276 N. Warson Rd.
St. Louis, MO 63132
Phone: 314-432-1100 Fax: 314-993-8927
CEO: Michael J. Mellinger
CFO: Michael J. Mellinger
1991 Sales: $21 million Employees: —
Symbol: DRAI Exchange: NASDAQ
Industry: Computers - software

Data Sciences
2678 Patton Rd.
Roseville, MN 55113
Phone: 612-636-0461 Fax: 612-636-1095
CEO: Brian Brockway
CFO: Charles Coggin
1991 Sales: $2 million Employees: 33
Ownership: Privately held
Industry: Instruments - biological research

Data Storage Marketing, Inc.
5718 Central Ave.
Boulder, CO 80301
Phone: 303-442-4747 Fax: 303-442-7985
CEO: Thomas Ward
CFO: Steve Yoder
1992 Sales: $85 million Employees: 145
Ownership: Privately held
Industry: Computers - components & peripheral equipment; microcomputer manufacturing

Data Switch Corp.
One Enterprise Dr.
Shelton, CT 06484
Phone: 203-926-1801 Fax: 203-929-6408
CEO: Robert G. Gilbertson
CFO: Michael Stashower
1991 Sales: $103 million Employees: 645
Symbol: DASW Exchange: NASDAQ
Industry: Electrical components

Data Translation, Inc.
100 Locke Dr.
Marlborough, MA 01752
Phone: 508-481-3700 Fax: 508-481-8620
CEO: Alfred A. Molinari, Jr.
CFO: Mark S. Santangelo
1991 Sales: $34 million Employees: 230
Symbol: DATX Exchange: NASDAQ
Industry: Computers - graphics

Data Transmission Network Corp.
9110 W. Dodge Rd., Ste. 200
Omaha, NE 68114
Phone: 402-390-2328 Fax: 402-390-7188
CEO: Roger R. Brodersen
CFO: Dean L. Giesselmann
1991 Sales: $22 million Employees: 175
Symbol: DTLN Exchange: NASDAQ
Industry: Business services - on-line business information

Data-Design Laboratories, Inc.
7925 Center Ave.
Rancho Cucamonga, CA 91730
Phone: 714-987-2511 Fax: —
CEO: William E. Cook
CFO: Alan R. Steel
1992 Sales: $58 million Employees: —
Symbol: DDL Exchange: NYSE
Industry: Electrical products - printed circuit boards & signal transmission equipment

Dataflex Corp.
3920 Park Ave.
Edison, NJ 08820
Phone: 908-321-1100 Fax: 908-321-6590
CEO: Richard C. Rose
CFO: Gordon J. McLenithan
1992 Sales: $90 million Employees: 197
Symbol: DFLX Exchange: NASDAQ
Industry: Computers - mini & micro

Datakey, Inc.
407 W. Travelers Trail
Burnsville, MN 55337
Phone: 612-890-6850 Fax: 612-890-2726
CEO: John H. Underwood
CFO: Alan G. Shuler
1991 Sales: $7.9 million Employees: 49
Symbol: DKEY Exchange: NASDAQ
Industry: Instruments - control

DataLOK
5990 Malburg Way
Los Angeles, CA 90058
Phone: 213-269-0700 Fax: 213-581-8285
CEO: Jeff Anthony
CFO: Newton Anthony
1991 Sales: $3.2 million Employees: 41
Ownership: Privately held
Industry: Computers - document storage, retrieval & delivery services

Datamarine International, Inc.
53 Portside Dr.
Pocasset, MA 02559
Phone: 508-563-7151 Fax: 508-564-4707
CEO: Peter D. Brown
CFO: Geoffrey W. Kreiger
1991 Sales: $15 million Employees: 129
Symbol: DMAR Exchange: NASDAQ
Industry: Electrical products - marine electronics

Datametrics Corp.
8966 Comanche Ave.
Chatsworth, CA 91311
Phone: 818-341-2901 Fax: 818-718-1503
CEO: Sidney E. Wing
CFO: John J. Van Buren
1991 Sales: $21 million Employees: 172
Symbol: DC Exchange: AMEX
Industry: Electronics - military

DATAPHAZ, Inc.
15002 N. 25th Dr., Ste. 1
Phoenix, AZ 85023
Phone: 602-351-2800 Fax: —
CEO: Edward E. Faber
CFO: Thomas M. Proud
1990 Sales: $72 million Employees: 228
Symbol: DPHZ Exchange: NASDAQ
Industry: Computers - retail & wholesale

Datapoint Corp.
9725 Datapoint Dr.
San Antonio, TX 78229
Phone: 210-593-7000 Fax: 210-699-7184
CEO: Asher B. Edelman
CFO: Kenneth R. Kamp
1991 Sales: $266 million Employees: 1,741
Symbol: DPT Exchange: NYSE
Industry: Computers - mini & micro

Dataram Corp.
PO Box 7528
Princeton, NJ 08543
Phone: 609-799-0071 Fax: 609-799-6734
CEO: Robert V. Tarantino
CFO: Frank Kardashian
1992 Sales: $40 million Employees: 132
Symbol: DTM Exchange: AMEX
Industry: Computers - peripheral equipment

Datascope Corp.
580 Winters Ave.
Paramus, NJ 07652
Phone: 201-265-8800 Fax: 201-265-8562
CEO: Lawrence Saper
CFO: Richard L. Smernoff
1992 Sales: $156 million Employees: 1,100
Symbol: DSCP Exchange: NASDAQ
Industry: Medical instruments

DataServ Inc.
37562 Hills Tech Dr.
Farmington Hills, MI 48331
Phone: 313-489-8400 Fax: 313-489-8403
CEO: Marvin Saver
CFO: Marvin Saver
1991 Sales: $4.2 million Employees: 25
Ownership: Privately held
Industry: Computers - integration services

Datasouth Computer Corp.
4216 Stuart Andrew Blvd.
Charlotte, NC 28217
Phone: 704-523-8500 Fax: 704-523-9298
CEO: James W. Busby
CFO: Gordon W. Friedrich
1991 Sales: $16 million Employees: 122
Symbol: DSCC Exchange: NASDAQ
Industry: Computers - peripheral equipment

Datastorm Technologies Inc.
3212 Lemone Industrial Blvd.
Columbia, MO 65201
Phone: 314-443-3282 Fax: 314-875-0595
CEO: Bruce Barkelew
CFO: Chris Force
1992 Sales: $25 million Employees: 130
Ownership: Privately held
Industry: Computers - software

indicates company is in *Hoover's Handbook of American Business.*

indicates company is in *Hoover's Handbook of World Business*; sales and employee numbers are for parent company.

Datawatch Corp.
234 Ballardvale St.
Wilmington, MA 01887
Phone: 508-988-9700 Fax: 508-988-9295
CEO: Thomas R. Foley
CFO: Bruce R. Gardner
1991 Sales: $17 million Employees: —
Symbol: DWCH Exchange: NASDAQ
Industry: Computers - mini & micro

Datron Systems, Inc.
200 W. Los Angeles Ave.
Simi Valley, CA 93065
Phone: 805-584-1717 Fax: —
CEO: David A. Derby
CFO: Thomas V. Baker
1992 Sales: $73 million Employees: 573
Symbol: DTSI Exchange: NASDAQ
Industry: Telecommunications equipment

Datum Inc.
1363 S. State College Blvd.
Anaheim, CA 92806
Phone: 714-533-6333 Fax: 714-533-6345
CEO: Louis B. Horwitz
CFO: Benjamin F. Tarver
1991 Sales: $32 million Employees: 337
Symbol: DATM Exchange: NASDAQ
Industry: Fiber optics

Dauphin Deposit Bank & Trust Co.
213 Market St.
Harrisburg, PA 17101
Phone: 717-255-2121 Fax: 717-237-6153
CEO: William J. King
CFO: Dennis L. Dinger
1991 Sales: $334 million Employees: 1,894
Symbol: DAPN Exchange: NASDAQ
Industry: Banks - Northeast

David Mitchell & Associates
2345 Rice St., Ste. 205
St. Paul, MN 55113
Phone: 612-482-0071 Fax: 612-482-0976
CEO: David Mitchell
CFO: David Mitchell
1992 Sales: $10 million Employees: 125
Ownership: Privately held
Industry: Computers - consulting services

Davis Water & Waste Industries, Inc.
1820 Metcalf Ave.
Thomasville, GA 31792
Phone: 912-226-5733 Fax: 912-226-8337
CEO: R. Doyle White
CFO: Stanley White
1992 Sales: $187 million Employees: 780
Symbol: DWW Exchange: NYSE
Industry: Pollution control equipment & services

Davox Corp.
3 Federal St.
Billerica, MA 01821
Phone: 508-667-4455 Fax: —
CEO: Daniel A. Hosage
CFO: J. Lawrence Doherty
1991 Sales: $32 million Employees: 203
Symbol: DAVX Exchange: NASDAQ
Industry: Telecommunications equipment

Davstar Industries, Ltd.
1301 Dove St., Ste. 360
Newport Beach, CA 92660
Phone: 714-852-8492 Fax: —
CEO: Jerry B. Silver
CFO: Robert Butnik
1991 Sales: $4.5 million Employees: 75
Symbol: DVS Exchange: NASDAQ
Industry: Medical products

Dawson Geophysical Co.
208 S. Marienfeld St.
Midland, TX 79701
Phone: 915-682-7356 Fax: 915-683-4298
CEO: L. Decker Dawson
CFO: L. Decker Dawson
1991 Sales: $8.5 million Employees: —
Symbol: DWSN Exchange: NASDAQ
Industry: Oil & gas - field services

Daxor Corp.
645 Madison Ave.
New York, NY 10022
Phone: 212-935-1430 Fax: —
CEO: Joseph Feldschuh
CFO: Alvin M. Petersen
1991 Sales: $2 million Employees: 48
Symbol: DXR Exchange: AMEX
Industry: Medical services

Day Runner, Inc.
2750 W. Moore Ave.
Fullerton, CA 92633
Phone: 714-680-3500 Fax: 714-680-0540
CEO: Mark A. Vidovich
CFO: Dennis K. Marquardt
1992 Sales: $71 million Employees: 515
Symbol: DAYR Exchange: NASDAQ
Industry: Paper & paper products

Day & Zimmermann Inc.
280 King of Prussia Rd.
Radnor, PA 19087
Phone: 215-975-6875 Fax: 215-975-6969
CEO: Harold L. Yoh, Jr.
CFO: John P. Follman
1991 Sales: $650 million Employees: 12,800
Ownership: Privately held
Industry: Business services - engineering, consulting

Dayton Hudson Corp.
777 Nicollet Mall
Minneapolis, MN 55402
Phone: 612-370-6948 Fax: 612-370-5502
CEO: Karol D, Emmerich
CFO: Willard C. Shull III
1992 Sales: $17,275 million Employees: 168,000
Symbol: DH Exchange: NYSE
Industry: Retail - major department stores

DAZSER Corp.
5421 Beaumont Center Blvd., Ste. 685
Tampa, FL 33634
Phone: 813-881-0440 Fax: 813-881-0582
CEO: Dave Zillig
CFO: Steve Roesch
1991 Sales: $5.2 million Employees: 16
Ownership: Privately held
Industry: Building maintenance - commercial cleaning franchise

DBA Systems, Inc.
1200 S. Woody Burke Rd.
Melbourne, FL 32902
Phone: 407-727-0660 Fax: Ext. 2571
CEO: John L. Slack
CFO: Jon D. Guess
1992 Sales: $39 million Employees: 350
Symbol: DBAS Exchange: NASDAQ
Industry: Electronics - military

DCS Software & Consulting
997 Hampshire Lane
Richardson, TX 75080
Phone: 214-705-8200 Fax: 214-690-9869
CEO: Henry Garland
CFO: Jeff Hurt
1991 Sales: $4.4 million Employees: 90
Ownership: Privately held
Industry: Computers - IBM computer consulting

DDI Pharmaceuticals, Inc.
518 Logue Ave.
Mountain View, CA 94043
Phone: 415-964-7676 Fax: 415-967-5243
CEO: Henry Lerman
CFO: Henry Lerman
1991 Sales: $2.7 million Employees: 25
Symbol: DDIX Exchange: NASDAQ
Industry: Drugs

De-Mar Plumbing, Heating & Air Conditioning
205 W. Pontiac Way
Clovis, CA 93612
Phone: 209-251-4322 Fax: 209-292-0269
CEO: Larry Harmon
CFO: Larry Harmon
1991 Sales: $3.1 million Employees: 35
Ownership: Privately held
Industry: Building products - a/c, heating & plumbing

Dean Foods Co.
3600 N. River Rd.
Franklin Park, IL 60131
Phone: 708-678-1680 Fax: 708-678-2779
CEO: Howard M. Dean
CFO: Timothy J. Bondy
1992 Sales: $2,322 million Employees: 10,100
Symbol: DF Exchange: NYSE
Industry: Food - dairy products

Deb Shops, Inc.
9401 Blue Grass Rd.
Philadelphia, PA 19114
Phone: 215-676-6000 Fax: —
CEO: Marvin Rounick
CFO: Warren Weiner
1991 Sales: $220 million Employees: 3,300
Symbol: DEBS Exchange: NASDAQ
Industry: Retail - apparel & shoes

Decorator Industries, Inc.
10011 Pines Blvd., Ste. 201
Pembroke Pines, FL 33024
Phone: 305-436-8909 Fax: 305-436-1778
CEO: William A. Bassett
CFO: Michael K. Solomon
1991 Sales: $18 million Employees: 325
Symbol: DII Exchange: AMEX
Industry: Textiles - home furnishings

Deerbank Corp.
745 Deerfield Rd.
Deerfield, IL 60015
Phone: 708-945-2550 Fax: 708-945-2620
CEO: Wayne V. Ecklund
CFO: David Mullins
1991 Sales: $16 million Employees: 145
Symbol: DEER Exchange: NASDAQ
Industry: Financial - savings and loans

Deere & Co.
John Deere Rd.
Moline, IL 61265
Phone: 309-765-8000 Fax: 309-765-5772
CEO: Hans W. Becherer
CFO: Eugene L. Schotanus
1992 Sales: $6,961 million Employees: 36,469
Symbol: DE Exchange: NYSE
Industry: Machinery - farm & construction

Defense Software & Systems, Inc.
200 Route 17
Mahwah, NJ 07430
Phone: 201-529-2026 Fax: —
CEO: George Morgenstern
CFO: George Morgenstern
1991 Sales: $11 million Employees: 224
Symbol: DSSI Exchange: NASDAQ
Industry: Computers - software

indicates company is in *Hoover's Handbook of American Business.*

indicates company is in *Hoover's Handbook of World Business;* sales and employee numbers are for parent company.

Defiance, Inc.
1125 Precision Way
Defiance, OH 43512
Phone: 419-782-3334 Fax: 419-782-8162
CEO: Jerry A. Cooper
CFO: Michael J. Meier
1992 Sales: $70 million Employees: 807
Symbol: DEFI Exchange: NASDAQ
Industry: Automotive & trucking - original equipment

DEKALB Energy Co.
1625 Broadway
Denver, CO 80202
Phone: 303-595-0707 Fax: 303-592-5901
CEO: Bruce P. Bickner
CFO: Thomas R. Rauman
1991 Sales: $95 million Employees: 255
Symbol: ENRGB Exchange: NASDAQ
Industry: Oil & gas - US exploration & production

DEKALB Genetics Corp.
3100 Sycamore Rd.
DeKalb, IL 60115
Phone: 815-758-3461 Fax: 815-758-3711
CEO: Bruce P. Bickner
CFO: Alan D. Skouby
1991 Sales: $276 million Employees: 2,361
Symbol: SEEDB Exchange: NASDAQ
Industry: Agricultural operations

Del Electronics Corp.
1 Commerce Park
Valhalla, NY 10595
Phone: 914-686-3600 Fax: 914-686-5425
CEO: Leonard A. Trugman
CFO: Leonard A. Trugman
1991 Sales: $17 million Employees: 226
Symbol: DEL Exchange: AMEX
Industry: Electrical products - high voltage power conversion systems

Del Laboratories, Inc.
565 Broad Hollow Rd.
Farmingdale, NY 11735
Phone: 516-293-7070 Fax: 516-293-1515
CEO: Dan K. Wassong
CFO: Melvyn C. Goldstein
1991 Sales: $128 million Employees: 970
Symbol: DLI Exchange: AMEX
Industry: Cosmetics & toiletries

Del Monte Foods U.S.A.
One Market Plaza
San Francisco, CA 94105
Phone: 415-442-4000 Fax: 415-442-4894
CEO: A. Ewan Macdonald
CFO: Allan Sweeny
1991 Sales: $1,431 million Employees: 14,500
Ownership: Privately held
Industry: Food - canned

Del Webb Corp.
2231 E. Camelback Rd.
Phoenix, AZ 85016
Phone: 602-468-6800 Fax: —
CEO: Philip J. Dion
CFO: John A. Spencer
1992 Sales: $261 million Employees: 750
Symbol: WBB Exchange: NYSE
Industry: Real estate operations

Delaware North Cos. Inc.
438 Main St.
Buffalo, NY 14202
Phone: 716-858-5000 Fax: 716-858-5479
CEO: Jeremy M. Jacobs
CFO: Richard T. Stephens
1992 Sales: $1,300 million Employees: 17,000
Ownership: Privately held
Industry: Diversified operations - food services, pari-mutuels, metals & typography

Delaware Otsego Corp.
1 Railroad Ave.
Cooperstown, NY 13326
Phone: 607-547-2555 Fax: Call co. operator
CEO: Walter G. Rich
CFO: William B. Blatter
1991 Sales: $28 million Employees: 165
Symbol: DOCP Exchange: NASDAQ
Industry: Transportation - rail

Delchamps, Inc.
305 Delchamps Dr.
Mobile, AL 36602
Phone: 205-433-0431 Fax: 205-433-0437
CEO: Randy Delchamps
CFO: Roy W. Henderson
1992 Sales: $987 million Employees: 8,148
Symbol: DLCH Exchange: NASDAQ
Industry: Retail - supermarkets

Dell Computer Corp.
9505 Arboretum Blvd.
Austin, TX 78759
Phone: 512-338-4400 Fax: 512-338-8700
CEO: Michael S. Dell
CFO: Thomas J. Meredith
1992 Sales: $1,679 million Employees: 2,970
Symbol: DELL Exchange: NASDAQ
Industry: Computers - mini & micro

Delmarva Power & Light Co.
800 King St.
Wilmington, DE 19899
Phone: 302-429-3011 Fax: 302-429-3665
CEO: Nevius M. Curtis
CFO: Paul S. Gerritsen
1991 Sales: $845 million Employees: 2,817
Symbol: DEW Exchange: NYSE
Industry: Utility - electric power

Deloitte & Touche
10 Westport Rd.
Wilton, CT 06897
Phone: 203-761-3000 Fax: 203-834-2231
CEO: J. Michael Cook
CFO: —
1991 Sales: $4,500 million Employees: 16,500
Ownership: Privately held
Industry: Business services - accounting & consulting

Delphi Financial Group, Inc.
1105 N. Market St., Ste. 1230
Wilmington, DE 19899
Phone: 302-478-5142 Fax: —
CEO: Robert Rosenkranz
CFO: Jane R. Dunlap
1991 Sales: $333 million Employees: —
Symbol: DLFI Exchange: NASDAQ
Industry: Insurance - multiline & misc.

Delphi Information Systems, Inc.
31416 Agoura Rd.
Westlake Village, CA 91361
Phone: 818-706-8989 Fax: 818-991-6469
CEO: Richard R. Janssen
CFO: Terance A. Kinninger
1992 Sales: $42 million Employees: 368
Symbol: DLPH Exchange: NASDAQ
Industry: Computers - software for insurance industry

Delta Air Lines, Inc.
Hartsfield Atlanta Int'l Airport, 1030 Delta Blvd.
Atlanta, GA 30320
Phone: 404-765-2600 Fax: 404-765-2233
CEO: Ronald W. Allen
CFO: Thomas J. Roeck, Jr.
1992 Sales: $11,579 million Employees: 77,907
Symbol: DAL Exchange: NYSE
Industry: Transportation - airline

Delta Environmental Consultants
3900 N. Woods Dr., Ste. 200
St. Paul, MN 51112
Phone: 612-486-8022 Fax: 612-486-0769
CEO: Jerry Rick
CFO: Jerry Rick
1992 Sales: $43 million Employees: 445
Ownership: Privately held
Industry: Environmental consulting

Delta Natural Gas Co., Inc.
3617 Lexington Rd.
Winchester, KY 40391
Phone: 606-744-6171 Fax: Call co. operator
CEO: Glenn R. Jennings
CFO: John F. Hall
1992 Sales: $29 million Employees: 182
Symbol: DGAS Exchange: NASDAQ
Industry: Utility - gas distribution

Delta Queen Steamboat Co.
30 Robin St. Wharf
New Orleans, LA 70130
Phone: 504-586-0631 Fax: 504-585-0630
CEO: S. Cody Engle
CFO: S. M. Isaacson
1992 Sales: $62 million Employees: 574
Symbol: DQSB Exchange: NASDAQ
Industry: Leisure & recreational services

Delta Woodside Industries, Inc.
233 N. Main St., Ste. 200
Greenville, SC 29601
Phone: 803-232-8301 Fax: 803-232-6164
CEO: E. Erwin Maddrey II
CFO: Bettis C. Rainsford
1992 Sales: $685 million Employees: 8,300
Symbol: DLW Exchange: NYSE
Industry: Textiles - apparel

Deltona Corp.
3250 SW Third Ave.
Miami, FL 33129
Phone: 305-854-1111 Fax: 305-856-9475
CEO: William R. Avella
CFO: Donald O. McNelley
1991 Sales: $10.8 million Employees: 163
Symbol: DLT Exchange: NYSE
Industry: Real estate development

Deluxe Corp.
1080 W. County Rd. F
St. Paul, MN 55126
Phone: 612-483-7111 Fax: 612-481-4163
CEO: Harold V. Haverty
CFO: Charles M. Osborne
1992 Sales: $1,534 million Employees: 17,563
Symbol: DLX Exchange: NYSE
Industry: Paper - business forms, check printing, electronic funds transfer software

Demand Research Corporation
625 N. Michigan Ave.
Chicago, IL 60611
Phone: 312-664-6500 Fax: 312-266-2016
CEO: Roy W. Bernstein
CFO: —
1992 Sales: $1 million Employees: 4
Ownership: Privately held
Industry: Business services - company database information & market research

DeMoulas Super Markets Inc.
875 East St.
Tewksbury, MA 01876
Phone: 508-851-8000 Fax: 505-851-3942
CEO: T. A. DeMoulas
CFO: D. Harold Sullivan
1991 Sales: $1,200 million Employees: 3,500
Ownership: Privately held
Industry: Retail - supermarkets

Deneba Systems, Inc.
7400 SW 87th Ave.
Miami, FL 33173
Phone: 305-596-5644 Fax: 305-273-9069
CEO: Manny Menendez
CFO: Joaquin DeSoto
1991 Sales: $8.4 million Employees: 60
Ownership: Privately held
Industry: Computers - microcomputer software

Dento-Med Industries, Inc.
941 Clint Moore Rd.
Boca Raton, FL 33487
Phone: 407-994-6191 Fax: 407-994-6598
CEO: Harvey Tauman
CFO: Harvey Tauman
1991 Sales: $0.2 million Employees: 4
Symbol: DTMD Exchange: NASDAQ
Industry: Medical & dental supplies

Dentsu Inc.
30th Fl., Grace Bldg., 1114 Avenue of the Americas
New York, NY 10036
Phone: 212-869-8318 Fax: 212-719-5028
CEO: Koichi Arai
CFO: —
1992 Sales: $1,481 million Employees: 6,000
Parent: Densu Inc.
Industry: Advertising

Dep Corp.
2101 E. Via Arado
Rancho Dominguez, CA 90220
Phone: 310-604-0777 Fax: 310-537-8438
CEO: Robert Berglass
CFO: Grant W. Johnson
1991 Sales: $106 million Employees: 387
Symbol: DEPC Exchange: NASDAQ
Industry: Cosmetics & toiletries

Deposit Guaranty Corp.
210 E. Capitol St.
Jackson, MS 39201
Phone: 601-354-8564 Fax: 601-354-8192
CEO: E. B. Robinson, Jr.
CFO: Arlen L. McDonald
1991 Sales: $446 million Employees: 2,527
Symbol: DEPS Exchange: NASDAQ
Industry: Banks - Southeast

Design Automation Systems, Inc.
6100 Corporate Dr., Ste. 380
Houston, TX 77036
Phone: 713-981-7766 Fax: 713-981-9415
CEO: Carl Rose
CFO: Jim Fitzwater
1992 Sales: $5.3 million Employees: 14
Ownership: Privately held
Industry: Computers - systems integration

Design Basics Inc.
11112 John Galt Blvd.
Omaha, NE 68137
Phone: 402-331-9223 Fax: 402-331-5507
CEO: Dennis Brozak
CFO: Dennis Brozak
1991 Sales: $2.1 million Employees: 50
Ownership: Privately held
Industry: Publishing - home plans magazine

Design Fabricators Inc.
6930 Winchester Circle
Boulder, CO 80301
Phone: 303-530-4900 Fax: 303-530-4949
CEO: Bob Coleman
CFO: Steve Boas
1991 Sales: $3.3 million Employees: 53
Ownership: Privately held
Industry: Building products - custom commercial fixtures & furniture

Designatronics Inc.
2101 Jericho Tnpk.
New Hyde Park, NY 11040
Phone: 516-328-3300 Fax: 516-326-8827
CEO: Sol Schwartz
CFO: Martin Hoffman
1991 Sales: $25 million Employees: 561
Symbol: DSG Exchange: AMEX
Industry: Machinery - material handling

Designcraft Industries, Inc.
823 Eleventh Ave.
New York, NY 10019
Phone: 212-541-5534 Fax: 212-541-6051
CEO: John Catsimatidis
CFO: Frank Sebastiano
1992 Sales: — Employees: 2
Symbol: DJI Exchange: AMEX
Industry: Metal processing & fabrication

Designs, Inc.
1244 Boylston St.
Chestnut Hill, MA 01267
Phone: 617-739-6722 Fax: 617-277-3516
CEO: Calvin Margolis
CFO: Geoffrey M. Holczer
1991 Sales: $151 million Employees: 1,750
Symbol: DESI Exchange: NASDAQ
Industry: Retail - apparel & shoes

DeSoto, Inc.
1471 Business Center Dr., Ste. 800
Mt. Prospect, IL 60056
Phone: 708-391-9000 Fax: 708-391-9304
CEO: William Spier
CFO: William Spier
1991 Sales: $59 million Employees: 264
Symbol: DSO Exchange: NYSE
Industry: Paints & allied products

Destec Energy, Inc.
2500 CityWest Blvd., Ste. 150
Houston, TX 77210
Phone: 713-735-4000 Fax: 713-974-8201
CEO: Robert McFedries
CFO: Diane K. Mott
1991 Sales: $437 million Employees: 568
Symbol: ENG Exchange: NYSE
Industry: Energy - cogeneration

Detection Systems, Inc.
130 Perinton Pkwy.
Fairport, NY 14450
Phone: 716-223-4060 Fax: 716-223-9180
CEO: Karl H. Kostusiak
CFO: Frank J. Ryan
1992 Sales: $27 million Employees: 301
Symbol: DETC Exchange: NASDAQ
Industry: Electrical products

Detrex Corp.
4000 Town Center, Ste. 1100
Southfield, MI 48075
Phone: 313-358-5800 Fax: 313-358-5803
CEO: Joseph L. Wenzler
CFO: R. M. Potter
1991 Sales: $78 million Employees: 447
Symbol: DTRX Exchange: NASDAQ
Industry: Chemicals - specialty

Detroit Edison Co.
2000 Second Ave.
Detroit, MI 48226
Phone: 313-237-8000 Fax: 313-237-8828
CEO: John E. Lobbia
CFO: Larry G. Garberding
1992 Sales: $3,558 million Employees: 9,392
Symbol: DTE Exchange: NYSE
Industry: Utility - electric power

Deutsche Bank AG (New York Branch)
31 W. 52nd St.
New York, NY 10019
Phone: 212-474-8000 Fax: 212-355-5655
CEO: John A. Rolls
CFO: —
1991 Sales: $28,223 million Employees: 71,400
Parent: Deutsche Bank AG
Industry: Banks - money center

Devcon International Corp.
1350 E. Newport Center Dr., Ste. 201
Deerfield Beach, FL 33442
Phone: 305-429-1500 Fax: 305-429-1506
CEO: Donald L. Smith, Jr.
CFO: Walter B. Barrett
1991 Sales: $90 million Employees: 663
Symbol: DEVC Exchange: NASDAQ
Industry: Construction - cement & concrete

DeVlieg-Bullard, Inc.
3100 West End Ave., Ste. 880
Nashville, TN 37203
Phone: 615-383-7892 Fax: 615-383-8027
CEO: Laurence DeFrance
CFO: Arthur B. Hammond
1991 Sales: $94 million Employees: 760
Symbol: DVLG Exchange: NASDAQ
Industry: Machine tools & related products

Devon Energy Corp.
20 N. Broadway Ave., Ste. 1500
Oklahoma City, OK 73102
Phone: 405-235-3611 Fax: 405-236-4258
CEO: J. Larry Nichols
CFO: William T. Vaughn
1991 Sales: $30 million Employees: 116
Symbol: DVN Exchange: AMEX
Industry: Oil & gas - US exploration & production

Devon Group, Inc.
Six Stamford Forum, Ste. 501
Stamford, CT 06901
Phone: 203-964-1444 Fax: 203-964-1036
CEO: Marne Obernauer, Jr.
CFO: Bruce K. Koch
1992 Sales: $143 million Employees: 1,600
Symbol: DEVN Exchange: NASDAQ
Industry: Printing - commercial

DeVRY Inc.
1 Tower Lane
Oakbrook Terrace, IL 60181
Phone: 708-571-7700 Fax: 708-571-0317
CEO: Dennis J. Keller
CFO: Norman M. Levine
1992 Sales: $179 million Employees: 1,900
Symbol: DVRY Exchange: NASDAQ
Industry: Schools - trade & business

Dexter Corp.
One Elm St.
Windsor Locks, CT 06096
Phone: 203-627-9051 Fax: 203-627-9713
CEO: K. Grahame Walker
CFO: Robert E. McGill III
1992 Sales: $951 million Employees: 5,600
Symbol: DEX Exchange: NYSE
Industry: Chemicals - specialty

DFSoutheastern, Inc.
250 E. Ponce De Leon Ave.
Decatur, GA 30030
Phone: 404-371-4000 Fax: —
CEO: Robert C. McMahan
CFO: James R. Wallis
1991 Sales: $259 million Employees: 872
Symbol: DFSE Exchange: NASDAQ
Industry: Financial - savings and loans

indicates company is in *Hoover's Handbook of American Business.*

indicates company is in *Hoover's Handbook of World Business;* sales and employee numbers are for parent company.

DH Technology, Inc.
15070 Avenue of Science
San Diego, CA 92128
Phone: 619-451-3485 Fax: 619-451-3573
CEO: William H. Gibbs
CFO: M. Dean Gilliam
1991 Sales: $46 million Employees: 611
Symbol: DHTK Exchange: NASDAQ
Industry: Computers - peripheral equipment

DHL Worldwide Express
333 Twin Dolphin Dr.
Redwood City, CA 94065
Phone: 415-593-7474 Fax: 415-593-1689
CEO: Patrick Foley
CFO: William Smartt
1991 Sales: $2,300 million Employees: 25,000
Ownership: Privately held
Industry: Transportation - air express

DI Industries, Inc.
450 Gears Rd., Ste. 625
Houston, TX 77067
Phone: 713-874-0202 Fax: —
CEO: Max M. Dillard
CFO: David J. Cone
1992 Sales: $65 million Employees: 760
Symbol: DRL Exchange: AMEX
Industry: Oil & gas - field services

Diagnostek, Inc.
4500 Alexander Blvd. NE
Albuquerque, NM 87107
Phone: 505-345-8080 Fax: 505-345-1455
CEO: Nunzio P. DeSantis
CFO: Dennis E. Evans
1992 Sales: $290 million Employees: 1,100
Symbol: DXK Exchange: NYSE
Industry: Healthcare - outpatient & home

Diagnostic Products Corp.
5700 W. 96th St.
Los Angeles, CA 90045
Phone: 213-776-0180 Fax: 213-776-0204
CEO: Sigi Ziering
CFO: Julian R. Bockserman
1991 Sales: $90 million Employees: 724
Symbol: DP Exchange: NYSE
Industry: Medical services - immunodiagnostic test kits

Diagnostic/Retrieval Systems, Inc.
16 Thornton Rd.
Oakland, NJ 07436
Phone: 201-337-3314 Fax: 201-337-3314
CEO: Leonard Newman
CFO: Mark S. Newman
1992 Sales: $29 million Employees: 294
Symbol: DRSA Exchange: AMEX
Industry: Electronics - military

Dial Corp.,The
Dial Tower
Phoenix, AZ 85077
Phone: 602-207-4000 Fax: 602-207-5473
CEO: John W. Teets
CFO: F. Edward Lake
1992 Sales: $3,389 million Employees: 32,746
Symbol: DL Exchange: NYSE
Industry: Diversified operations - consumer, personal care & cleaning products

Dial REIT, Inc.
11506 Nicholas St., Ste. 205
Omaha, NE 68154
Phone: 402-496-7184 Fax: —
CEO: Joseph H. Carter
CFO: Joseph H. Carter
1991 Sales: $15 million Employees: 170
Symbol: DR Exchange: NYSE
Industry: Real estate operations

Diamond Shamrock, Inc.
9830 Colonnade Blvd.
San Antonio, TX 78230
Phone: 210-641-6800 Fax: 512-641-8687
CEO: Roger R. Hemminghaus
CFO: Robert C. Becker
1992 Sales: $2,603 million Employees: 5,925
Symbol: DRM Exchange: NYSE
Industry: Oil refining & marketing

Diamond Shamrock Offshore Partners L.P.
717 N. Harwood St.
Dallas, TX 75201
Phone: 214-953-2978 Fax: 214-953-2906
CEO: Steven G. Crowell
CFO: Michael J. Barron
1991 Sales: $105 million Employees: —
Symbol: DSP Exchange: NYSE
Industry: Oil & gas - US exploration & production

Diana Corp.
111 E. Wisconsin Ave.
Milwaukee, WI 53202
Phone: 414-289-9797 Fax: —
CEO: Richard Y. Fisher
CFO: R. Scott Miswald
1992 Sales: $162 million Employees: 233
Symbol: DNA Exchange: NYSE
Industry: Food - wholesale

DIANON Systems, Inc.
200 Watson Blvd.
Stratford, CT 06497
Phone: 203-381-4000 Fax: —
CEO: Richard A. Sandberg
CFO: Richard A. Sandberg
1991 Sales: $28 million Employees: 249
Symbol: DIAN Exchange: NASDAQ
Industry: Medical services

Diasonics, Inc.
1565 Barber Lane
Milpitas, CA 95035
Phone: 408-432-9000 Fax: 408-432-0656
CEO: Stewart Carrell
CFO: James R. Higdon
1991 Sales: $286 million Employees: 1,635
Symbol: DIA Exchange: NYSE
Industry: Medical instruments

Dibrell Brothers, Inc.
512 Bridge St.
Danville, VA 24541
Phone: 804-792-7511 Fax: 804-791-0378
CEO: Claude B. Owen, Jr.
CFO: Thomas H. Faucett
1992 Sales: $1,108 million Employees: 8,050
Symbol: DBRL Exchange: NASDAQ
Industry: Tobacco

Diceon Electronics, Inc.
18522 Von Karman Ave.
Irvine, CA 92715
Phone: 714-833-0870 Fax: 714-752-4014
CEO: Roland G. Matthews
CFO: Peter S. Jonas
1991 Sales: $106 million Employees: 1,090
Symbol: DICN Exchange: NASDAQ
Industry: Electrical components

Dick Clark Productions, Inc.
3003 W. Olive Ave.
Burbank, CA 91510
Phone: 818-841-3003 Fax: —
CEO: Richard W. Clark
CFO: Kenneth H. Ferguson
1992 Sales: $37 million Employees: 150
Symbol: DCPI Exchange: NASDAQ
Industry: Leisure & recreational services

Dick Corp.
PO Box 10896
Pittsburgh, PA 15236
Phone: 412-384-1000 Fax: 412-384-1150
CEO: David Dick
CFO: Stephen K. Peary
1991 Sales: $510 million Employees: 2,500
Ownership: Privately held
Industry: Construction - commercial & industrial

Dickens Data Systems, Inc.
1175 North Meadow Pkwy., Ste. 150
Roswell, GA 30076
Phone: 404-475-8860 Fax: 404-442-7525
CEO: Gordon Dickens
CFO: Norman Wicks
1991 Sales: $36 million Employees: 85
Ownership: Privately held
Industry: Computers - systems integration, software publishing & peripheral manufacturing

Diebold, Inc.
818 Mulberry Rd. SE
Canton, OH 44711
Phone: 216-489-4000 Fax: 216-489-4104
CEO: Robert W. Mahoney
CFO: Gerald F. Morris
1991 Sales: $506 million Employees: 3,858
Symbol: DBD Exchange: NYSE
Industry: Automated banking transaction machines & protection - safety equipment & services

DiFeo Automotive Network
585 Route 440
Jersey City, NJ 07034
Phone: 201-433-9297 Fax: 201-433-9743
CEO: Sam DiFeo
CFO: Donald Betson
1990 Sales: $527 million Employees: 1,067
Ownership: Privately held
Industry: Retail - auto dealership

Digi International, Inc.
6400 Flying Cloud Dr.
Eden Prairie, MN 55426
Phone: 612-943-9020 Fax: 612-943-5330
CEO: Mykola Moroz
CFO: Gerald A. Wall
1992 Sales: $58 million Employees: 204
Symbol: DGII Exchange: NASDAQ
Industry: Computers - peripheral equipment

Digicon, Inc.
3701 Kirby Dr., Ste. 112
Houston, TX 77098
Phone: 713-526-5611 Fax: 713-630-4456
CEO: Edward R. Prince, Jr.
CFO: Allan C. Pogach
1991 Sales: $94 million Employees: 1,077
Symbol: DGC Exchange: AMEX
Industry: Oil & gas - field services

Digidesign Inc.
1360 Willow Rd., Ste. 101
Menlo Park, CA 94025
Phone: 415-688-0600 Fax: 415-327-0777
CEO: Peter Gotcher
CFO: Joy Covey
1991 Sales: $14 million Employees: 120
Ownership: Privately held
Industry: Electrical products - digital audio recording systems

DiGiorgio
Two Executive Dr.
Somerset, NJ 08873
Phone: 908-469-4444 Fax: 908-469-3876
CEO: Arthur M. Goldberg
CFO: Richard Neff
1991 Sales: $1,100 million Employees: 2,300
Ownership: Privately held
Industry: Food distribution, lumber

Digital Communications Associates, Inc.
1000 Alderman Dr.
Alpharetta, GA 30202
Phone: 404-442-4268 Fax: 404-442-4346
CEO: Charles G. Betty
CFO: Charles G. Betty
1992 Sales: $209 million Employees: 1,256
Symbol: DCA Exchange: NYSE
Industry: Computers - software

Digital Equipment Corp.
146 Main St.
Maynard, MA 01754
Phone: 508-493-5111 Fax: 508-493-8780
CEO: Robert B. Palmer
CFO: William M. Steul
1992 Sales: $14,162 million Employees: 113,800
Symbol: DEC Exchange: NYSE
Industry: Computers - mini & micro

Digital Instruments Inc.
520 E. Montecito St.
Santa Barbara, CA 93103
Phone: 805-899-3380 Fax: 805-899-3392
CEO: Virgil Elings
CFO: Mark Lien
1991 Sales: $17 million Employees: 65
Ownership: Privately held
Industry: Medical instruments - high-resolution scanning probe microscopes

Digital Microwave Corp.
170 Rose Orchard Way
San Jose, CA 95134
Phone: 408-943-0777 Fax: 408-432-8001
CEO: William E. Gibson
CFO: P. Michael Friedenbach
1992 Sales: $90 million Employees: 490
Symbol: DMIC Exchange: NASDAQ
Industry: Fiber optics

Digital Network Associates
110 Wall St., 25th Fl.
New York, NY 10005
Phone: 212-425-8000 Fax: 212-425-0809
CEO: Eric B. Schwartz
CFO: Joseph B. Goeller
1991 Sales: $5.6 million Employees: 22
Ownership: Privately held
Industry: Computers - systems integrator

Digital Sound Corp.
2030 Alameda Padre Serra
Santa Barbara, CA 91303
Phone: 805-569-0700 Fax: 805-682-0098
CEO: Bryan R. Gummon
CFO: Eugene F. Hovanec
1991 Sales: $34 million Employees: 182
Symbol: DGSD Exchange: NASDAQ
Industry: Telecommunications equipment

Digital Systems International, Inc.
6464 185th Ave. NE
Redmond, WA 98052
Phone: 206-881-7544 Fax: 206-869-4530
CEO: Michael L. Darland
CFO: Michael T. Osborn
1991 Sales: $52 million Employees: 380
Symbol: DGTL Exchange: NASDAQ
Industry: Telecommunications equipment

Digitran Systems, Inc.
90 North 100 East
Logan, UT 84321
Phone: 801-752-9067 Fax: 801-752-5888
CEO: Donald G. Gallent
CFO: James R. Bryan
1992 Sales: $6.6 million Employees: 31
Symbol: DGT Exchange: AMEX
Industry: Machinery - material handling

Dillard Department Stores, Inc.
1600 Cantrell Rd.
Little Rock, AR 72201
Phone: 501-376-5200 Fax: 501-376-5917
CEO: William Dillard
CFO: James I. Freeman
1992 Sales: $4,662 million Employees: 32,132
Symbol: DDS Exchange: NYSE
Industry: Retail - major department stores

Dillingham Construction Corp.
5960 Inglewood Dr.
Pleasanton, CA 94588
Phone: 510-463-3300 Fax: 510-463-9469
CEO: Donald K. Stager
CFO: Larry Magelitz
1991 Sales: $770 million Employees: 1,050
Ownership: Privately held
Industry: Construction - contracting & construction management & design building services

Dimark, Inc.
One Deadline Dr.
Westville, NJ 08093
Phone: 609-456-8666 Fax: 609-456-9271
CEO: Stephen C. Marcus
CFO: Lesley A. Bachman
1992 Sales: $38 million Employees: 180
Symbol: DMK Exchange: AMEX
Industry: Printing - commercial

Dime Financial Corp.
95 Barnes Rd.
Wallingford, CT 06492
Phone: 203-269-8881 Fax: —
CEO: John C. Shortell
CFO: Marie L. Buno
1991 Sales: $75 million Employees: 223
Symbol: DIBK Exchange: NASDAQ
Industry: Banks - Northeast

Dime Savings Bank of New York, FSB
975 Franklin Ave.
Garden City, NY 11530
Phone: 516-873-5293 Fax: 516-741-8372
CEO: Richard D. Parsons
CFO: Richard D. Parsons
1991 Sales: $993 million Employees: 2,345
Symbol: DME Exchange: NYSE
Industry: Financial - savings and loans

Diodes Inc.
9957 Canoga Ave.
Chatsworth, CA 91311
Phone: 818-882-4920 Fax: 818-341-1736
CEO: Thomas Hurley
CFO: Joseph Liu
1991 Sales: $15 million Employees: —
Symbol: DIO Exchange: AMEX
Industry: Electrical components - semiconductors

Dionex Corp.
501 Mercury Dr.
Sunnyvale, CA 94086
Phone: 408-737-0700 Fax: 408-730-9403
CEO: A. Blaine Bowman
CFO: A. Blaine Bowman
1992 Sales: $96 million Employees: —
Symbol: DNEX Exchange: NASDAQ
Industry: Instruments - scientific

Diplomatic Language Services, Inc.
1117 N. 19th St., Ste. 800
Arlington, VA 22209
Phone: 703-243-4855 Fax: 703-351-7426
CEO: John Ratliff III
CFO: John Ratliff IV
1991 Sales: $2.8 million Employees: 122
Ownership: Privately held
Industry: Business services - language training, translation & interpreting services

Directed Electronics, Inc.
2560 Progress St.
Vista, CA 92083
Phone: 619-598-6200 Fax: 619-598-6400
CEO: Darrell Issa
CFO: Darrell Issa
1992 Sales: $47 million Employees: 125
Ownership: Privately held
Industry: Protection - electronic automotive-security products

Discount Auto Parts, Inc.
4900 Frontage Rd. South
Lakeland, FL 33801
Phone: 813-687-9226 Fax: —
CEO: Denis L. Fontaine
CFO: William C. Perkins
1992 Sales: $141 million Employees: 1,526
Symbol: DAP Exchange: NYSE
Industry: Retail - auto parts

Discount Corporation of New York
58 Pine St.
New York, NY 10005
Phone: 212-248-8900 Fax: 212-509-2483
CEO: R. de la Gueronniere
CFO: Richard A. Pregiato
1991 Sales: $266 million Employees: 389
Symbol: DCY Exchange: NYSE
Industry: Financial - investment bankers

Diversco, Inc.
105 Diversco Dr.
Spartanburg, SC 29304
Phone: 803-579-3420 Fax: 803-579-7366
CEO: William A. Hudson
CFO: Don R. Bain
1992 Sales: $41 million Employees: 3,000
Symbol: DVRS Exchange: NASDAQ
Industry: Business services - industrial temporary personnel

Diversicare Corp. of America
105 Reynolds Dr.
Franklin, TN 37064
Phone: 615-794-3313 Fax: 615-790-7465
CEO: Charles W. Birkett
CFO: Mary M. Hamlett
1991 Sales: $26 million Employees: 650
Symbol: DVCR Exchange: NASDAQ
Industry: Healthcare - outpatient & home

Diversified Communications Industries, Ltd.
777 S. Flagler Dr., Ste. 700
West Palm Beach, FL 33401
Phone: 407-655-9101 Fax: —
CEO: Joseph F. Bradway, Jr.
CFO: Joseph F. Bradway, Jr.
1991 Sales: $4.7 million Employees: 20
Symbol: DVC Exchange: AMEX
Industry: Electrical components - power supplies

Diversified Industries, Inc.
101 S. Hanley Rd., Ste. 1450
Clayton, MO 63105
Phone: 314-862-8200 Fax: 314-862-0109
CEO: John B. von Echt
CFO: Darrell P. Stoecklin
1991 Sales: $199 million Employees: 160
Symbol: DMC Exchange: NYSE
Industry: Metal processing & fabrication

Diversified Pacific Construction
2301 DuPont Dr., Ste. 400
Irvine, CA 92715
Phone: 714-833-9070 Fax: 714-833-7531
CEO: David Jones
CFO: David Jones
1991 Sales: $12 million Employees: 16
Ownership: Privately held
Industry: Construction - general contracting & construction management services

indicates company is in *Hoover's Handbook of American Business.*

indicates company is in *Hoover's Handbook of World Business;* sales and employee numbers are for parent company.

Dixie Yarns, Inc.
1100 S. Watkins St.
Chattanooga, TN 37404
Phone: 615-698-2501 Fax: 615-493-7353
CEO: Daniel K. Frierson
CFO: Morgan M. Schuessler
1991 Sales: $492 million Employees: 6,600
Symbol: DXYN Exchange: NASDAQ
Industry: Textiles - mill products

Dixon Ticonderoga Co.
2600 Maitland Center Pkwy., Ste. 200
Maitland, FL 32751
Phone: 407-875-9000 Fax: 407-875-2574
CEO: Gino N. Pala
CFO: Richard A. Asta
1991 Sales: $71 million Employees: 1,320
Symbol: DXT Exchange: AMEX
Industry: Office & art materials

DNA Plant Technology Corp.
2611 Branch Pike
Cinnaminson, NJ 08077
Phone: 609-829-0110 Fax: 609-829-5087
CEO: Richard Laster
CFO: Richard M. Sykes
1991 Sales: $9.1 million Employees: 144
Symbol: DNAP Exchange: NASDAQ
Industry: Agricultural operations

DNX Corp.
303B College Rd. East
Princeton, NJ 08540
Phone: 216-520-0300 Fax: —
CEO: Paul J. Schmitt
CFO: John G. Cooper
1991 Sales: $3.1 million Employees: —
Symbol: DNXX Exchange: NASDAQ
Industry: Medical products & testing services

Dobbs Brothers Management
5170 Sanderlin Ave., Ste. 102
Memphis, TN 38117
Phone: 901-685-8881 Fax: 901-685-9053
CEO: Jimmy Dobbs III
CFO: Marge Green
1991 Sales: $527 million Employees: 1,300
Ownership: Privately held
Industry: Retail - auto dealerships

Dole Food Company, Inc.
31355 Oak Crest Dr.
Westlake Village, CA 91361
Phone: 818-879-6600 Fax: 818-879-6618
CEO: David H. Murdock
CFO: William J. Hain, Jr.
1992 Sales: $3,376 million Employees: 50,000
Symbol: DOL Exchange: NYSE
Industry: Food - canned fruits & juices

Dollar General Corp.
427 Beech St.
Scottsville, KY 42164
Phone: 502-237-5444 Fax: 502-237-3213
CEO: Cal Turner, Jr.
CFO: Bruce A. Quinnell
1992 Sales: $872 million Employees: 10,000
Symbol: DOLR Exchange: NASDAQ
Industry: Retail - discount & variety

Dominant Systems Corp.
3950 Varsity Dr.
Ann Arbor, MI 48108
Phone: 313-971-1210 Fax: 313-677-3321
CEO: Terry Weadock
CFO: Terry Weadock
1991 Sales: $1.6 million Employees: 10
Ownership: Privately held
Industry: Computers - computer services integration

Dominguez Water Corp.
21718 S. Alameda St.
Long Beach, CA 90810
Phone: 213-775-2301 Fax: 310-834-8471
CEO: Charles W. Porter
CFO: John S. Tootle
1991 Sales: $19 million Employees: 82
Symbol: DOMZ Exchange: NASDAQ
Industry: Utility - water supply

Dominicks Finer Foods Inc.
505 Railroad Ave.
Northlake, IL 60164
Phone: 708-562-1000 Fax: 708-409-6032
CEO: James DiMatteo
CFO: Rick Weber
1991 Sales: $2,050 million Employees: 7,500
Ownership: Privately held
Industry: Retail - supermarkets

Dominion Bankshares Corp.
213 S. Jefferson St.
Roanoke, VA 24011
Phone: 703-563-7000 Fax: 703-563-6300
CEO: Warner N. Dalhouse
CFO: James E. Adams
1991 Sales: $1,030 million Employees: 5,349
Symbol: DMBK Exchange: NASDAQ
Industry: Banks - Southeast

Dominion Resources, Inc.
701 E. Byrd St., West Tower, 17th Fl.
Richmond, VA 23219
Phone: 804-775-5700 Fax: 804-775-5819
CEO: Thos. E. Capps
CFO: O. James Peterson III
1992 Sales: $3,789 million Employees: 12,728
Symbol: D Exchange: NYSE
Industry: Utility - electric power

Domino's Pizza, Inc.
30 Frank Lloyd Wright Dr.
Ann Arbor, MI 48106
Phone: 313-930-3030 Fax: 313-668-4614
CEO: Thomas S. Monaghan
CFO: Tim Carr
1991 Sales: $2,400 million Employees: 115,000
Ownership: Privately held
Industry: Retail - food; pizza delivery & carryout

Donaldson Co., Inc.
1400 W. 94th St.
Minneapolis, MN 55431
Phone: 612-887-3131 Fax: 612-887-3155
CEO: William A. Hodder
CFO: John R. Schweers
1991 Sales: $458 million Employees: 3,688
Symbol: DCI Exchange: NYSE
Industry: Pollution control equipment & services

Donegal Group Inc.
Route 441
Marietta, PA 17547
Phone: 717-426-1931 Fax: —
CEO: Donald H. Nikolaus
CFO: Ralph G. Spontak
1991 Sales: $58 million Employees: 257
Symbol: DGIC Exchange: NASDAQ
Industry: Insurance - multiline & misc.

Donnelly Corp.
414 E. Fortieth St.
Holland, MI 49423
Phone: 616-786-7000 Fax: 616-786-6034
CEO: J. Dwane Baumgardner
CFO: James A. Knister
1992 Sales: $271 million Employees: 2,582
Symbol: DON Exchange: AMEX
Industry: Automotive & trucking - original equipment

Dorchester Hugoton, Ltd.
9696 Skillman St.
Dallas, TX 75243
Phone: 214-739-2002 Fax: —
CEO: Howard C. Wadsworth
CFO: Howard C. Wadsworth
1991 Sales: $5.1 million Employees: —
Symbol: DHULZ Exchange: NASDAQ
Industry: Oil & gas - U.S. exploration

Doskocil Foods Group
321 N. Main St.
South Hutchinson, KS 67504
Phone: 316-663-6141 Fax: Ext. 2818
CEO: John T. Hanes
CFO: Theodore A. Myers
1992 Sales: $771 million Employees: 3,400
Symbol: DOSK Exchange: NASDAQ
Industry: Food - meat products

Dotronix, Inc.
160 First St. SE
New Brighton, MN 55112
Phone: 612-633-1742 Fax: 612-633-7025
CEO: William S. Sadler
CFO: Warren M. White
1992 Sales: $22 million Employees: 264
Symbol: DOTX Exchange: NASDAQ
Industry: Video equipment

Douglas & Lomason Co.
24600 Hollywood Court
Farmington Hills, MI 48335
Phone: 313-478-7800 Fax: 313-478-5189
CEO: Harry A. Lomason II
CFO: James J. Hoey
1991 Sales: $376 million Employees: 5,562
Symbol: DOUG Exchange: NASDAQ
Industry: Automotive & trucking - original equipment

Dover Corp.
280 Park Ave.
New York, NY 10017
Phone: 212-922-1640 Fax: 212-922-1656
CEO: Gary L. Roubos
CFO: John F. McNiff
1992 Sales: $2,272 million Employees: 18,898
Symbol: DOV Exchange: NYSE
Industry: Machinery - general industrial

Dow Chemical Co., The
2030 Willard H. Dow Center, Ste. 2030
Midland, MI 48674
Phone: 517-636-1000 Fax: 517-636-0922
CEO: Frank P. Popoff
CFO: Enrique C. Falla
1992 Sales: $18,971 million Employees: 62,219
Symbol: DOW Exchange: NYSE
Industry: Chemicals - diversified

Dow Jones & Co., Inc.
World Financial Center, 200 Liberty St.
New York, NY 10281
Phone: 212-416-2000 Fax: 212-416-3299
CEO: Peter R. Kann
CFO: Kevin J. Roche
1992 Sales: $1,818 million Employees: 9,459
Symbol: DJ Exchange: NYSE
Industry: Publishing - newspapers & on-line business information

Downey Savings and Loan Association
3501 Jamboree Rd.
Newport Beach, CA 92660
Phone: 714-854-3100 Fax: 714-725-0921
CEO: Robert L. Kemper
CFO: David T. Hansen
1991 Sales: $354 million Employees: 1,010
Symbol: DSL Exchange: NYSE
Industry: Financial - savings and loans

indicates company is in *Hoover's Handbook of American Business.*

indicates company is in *Hoover's Handbook of World Business;* sales and employee numbers are for parent company.

DPL Inc.
1065 Woodman Dr.
Dayton, OH 45432
Phone: 513-224-6000 Fax: 513-259-7385
CEO: Peter H. Forster
CFO: Thomas M. Jenkins
1992 Sales: $1,034 million Employees: 3,073
Symbol: DPL Exchange: NYSE
Industry: Utility - electric power

DQE, Inc.
301 Grant St., 1 Oxford Circle
Pittsburgh, PA 15279
Phone: 412-393-6000 Fax: 412-393-6448
CEO: Wesley W. von Shack
CFO: Gary L. Schwass
1992 Sales: $1,185 million Employees: 4,237
Symbol: DQE Exchange: NYSE
Industry: Utility - electric power

Dr Pepper/Seven-Up Companies, Inc.
8144 Walnut Hill Ln.
Dallas, TX 75231
Phone: 214-360-7000 Fax: 214-360-7981
CEO: John R. Albers
CFO: Ira M. Rosenstein
1991 Sales: $601 million Employees: 905
Symbol: DRP Exchange: NYSE
Industry: Beverages - soft drinks

Dravo Corp.
One Oliver Plaza, Ste. 3600
Pittsburgh, PA 15222
Phone: 412-566-3000 Fax: 412-566-3116
CEO: Carl A. Torbert, Jr.
CFO: Ernest F. Ladd III
1991 Sales: $296 million Employees: 1,556
Symbol: DRV Exchange: NYSE
Industry: Construction - cement & concrete

DRCA Medical Corp.
3 Riverway, Ste. 1430
Houston, TX 77056
Phone: 713-439-7511 Fax: —
CEO: Jose E. Kauachi
CFO: Marvin R. Lewis
1991 Sales: $9 million Employees: 144
Symbol: DRC Exchange: AMEX
Industry: Medical services

Dress Barn, Inc.
88 Hamilton Ave.
Stamford, CT 06902
Phone: 203-327-4242 Fax: 203-359-4458
CEO: Elliot S. Jaffe
CFO: Armand Correia
1991 Sales: $325 million Employees: 4,800
Symbol: DBRN Exchange: NASDAQ
Industry: Retail - apparel & shoes

Dresser Industries, Inc.
1600 Pacific Bldg.
Dallas, TX 75201
Phone: 214-740-6000 Fax: 214-740-6584
CEO: John J. Murphy
CFO: David P. McElvain
1992 Sales: $3,797 million Employees: 31,800
Symbol: DI Exchange: NYSE
Industry: Oil field machinery & equipment

Drew Industries Inc.
200 Mamaroneck Ave.
White Plains, NY 10601
Phone: 914-428-9098 Fax: 914-428-4581
CEO: Leigh J. Abrams
CFO: Fredric M. Zinn
1991 Sales: $93 million Employees: 1,079
Symbol: DREW Exchange: NASDAQ
Industry: Building products - aluminum windows & skylights

Drexler Technology Corp.
2557 Charleston Rd.
Mountain View, CA 94043
Phone: 415-969-7277 Fax: 415-969-6121
CEO: Jerome Drexler
CFO: Steven G. Larson
1992 Sales: $1.9 million Employees: 40
Symbol: DRXR Exchange: NASDAQ
Industry: Computers - optical memory cards

Dreyer's Grand Ice Cream, Inc.
5929 College Ave.
Oakland, CA 94618
Phone: 510-652-8187 Fax: 510-601-4405
CEO: T. Gary Rogers
CFO: Paul R. Woodland
1991 Sales: $355 million Employees: 1,259
Symbol: DRYR Exchange: NASDAQ
Industry: Food - dairy products

Dreyfus Corp.
200 Park Ave.
New York, NY 10166
Phone: 212-922-6000 Fax: —
CEO: Howard Stein
CFO: Alan M. Eisner
1991 Sales: $282 million Employees: 1,500
Symbol: DRY Exchange: NYSE
Industry: Financial - investment management

Driver-Harris Co.
308 Middlesex St.
Harrison, NJ 07029
Phone: 201-483-4800 Fax: 201-483-7100
CEO: Frank L. Driver III
CFO: Henry Hirschmann
1991 Sales: $88 million Employees: 444
Symbol: DRH Exchange: AMEX
Industry: Metals - nonferrous

Drug Emporium, Inc.
155 Hidden Ravine Dr.
Powell, OH 43065
Phone: 614-548-7080 Fax: 614-888-3689
CEO: Gary Wilber
CFO: Catherine K. Wilber
1992 Sales: $760 million Employees: 6,200
Symbol: DEMP Exchange: NASDAQ
Industry: Retail - drug stores

Drummond Co. Inc.
PO Box 1549
Jasper, AL 35501
Phone: 205-387-0501 Fax: 205-384-2456
CEO: Garry N. Drummond
CFO: Charles W. Adair
1991 Sales: $705 million Employees: 2,650
Ownership: Privately held
Industry: Coal

DS Bancor, Inc.
33 Elizabeth St.
Derby, CT 06418
Phone: 203-736-9921 Fax: —
CEO: Harry P. DiAdamo, Jr.
CFO: Alfred T. Santoro
1991 Sales: $58 million Employees: 167
Symbol: DSBC Exchange: NASDAQ
Industry: Financial - savings and loans

DSC Communications Corp.
1000 Coit Rd.
Plano, TX 75075
Phone: 214-519-3000 Fax: 214-519-2322
CEO: James L. Donald
CFO: Gerald F. Montry
1992 Sales: $536 million Employees: 3,262
Symbol: DIGI Exchange: NASDAQ
Industry: Telecommunications equipment

DSP Technology, Inc.
48500 Kato Rd.
Fremont, CA 94538
Phone: 510-657-7555 Fax: 510-657-7576
CEO: F. Gil Troutman, Jr.
CFO: Jose M. Millares, Jr.
1991 Sales: $8.2 million Employees: 71
Symbol: DSPT Exchange: NASDAQ
Industry: Electronics - measuring instruments

DSS, Inc.
27847 Berwick Dr.
Carmel, CA 93923
Phone: 408-375-5315 Fax: 408-626-8746
CEO: Bonney H. Smith
CFO: Fredrick Smith
1991 Sales: $4.4 million Employees: 180
Ownership: Privately held
Industry: Business services - government services contractor

Duchossois Industries Inc.
845 Larch Ave.
Elmhurst, IL 60126
Phone: 708-279-3600 Fax: 708-530-6091
CEO: Richard L. Duchossois
CFO: James Yerbic
1991 Sales: $750 million Employees: 6,000
Ownership: Privately held
Industry: Diversified operations - transportation, entertainment, defense, consumer products

Ducommun Inc.
23301 S. Wilmington Ave.
Carson, CA 90745
Phone: 310-513-7200 Fax: 310-518-0176
CEO: Norman A. Barkeley
CFO: Donald R. Schort
1991 Sales: $74 million Employees: 762
Symbol: DCO Exchange: AMEX
Industry: Aerospace - aircraft equipment

Duff & Phelps Corp.
55 E. Monroe
Chicago, IL 60603
Phone: 312-263-2610 Fax: —
CEO: F. E. Jeffries
CFO: L. P. Zogg
1991 Sales: $69 million Employees: 300
Symbol: DUF Exchange: NYSE
Industry: Financial - investment management

Duke Power Co.
422 S. Church St.
Charlotte, NC 28242
Phone: 704-373-4011 Fax: 704-373-8038
CEO: William S. Lee
CFO: Richard J. Osborne
1992 Sales: $3,962 million Employees: 19,689
Symbol: DUK Exchange: NYSE
Industry: Utility - electric power

Dun & Bradstreet Corp., The
299 Park Ave.
New York, NY 10171
Phone: 212-593-6800 Fax: 212-593-4143
CEO: Charles W. Moritz
CFO: Edwin A. Bescherer, Jr.
1992 Sales: $4,751 million Employees: 58,500
Symbol: DNB Exchange: NYSE
Industry: Financial - marketing & credit information, software & financial services

Dunavant Enterprises Inc.
3797 New Getwell Rd.
Memphis, TN 38118
Phone: 901-369-1500 Fax: 901-369-1608
CEO: William B. Dunavant, Jr.
CFO: Louis Baioni
1991 Sales: $1,400 million Employees: 2,500
Ownership: Privately held
Industry: Textiles - cotton

indicates company is in *Hoover's Handbook of American Business.*

indicates company is in *Hoover's Handbook of World Business;* sales and employee numbers are for parent company.

Dunsirn Industries Inc.
2415 Industrial Dr.
Neenah, WI 54957
Phone: 414-725-3814 Fax: 414-725-9643
CEO: Brian Dunsirn
CFO: Brian Dunsirn
1991 Sales: $9.8 million Employees: 62
Ownership: Privately held
Industry: Paper & film products

Duplex Products, Inc.
1947 Bethany Rd.
Sycamore, IL 60178
Phone: 815-895-2101 Fax: 815-895-6173
CEO: Carl L. Peterson
CFO: Andrew N. Peterson
1991 Sales: $285 million Employees: 2,553
Symbol: DPX Exchange: AMEX
Industry: Paper - business forms

Dura Pharmaceuticals, Inc.
11175 Flintkote Ave.
San Diego, CA 92121
Phone: 619-457-2553 Fax: 619-452-7524
CEO: Cam L. Garner
CFO: James W. Newman
1991 Sales: $5.5 million Employees: —
Symbol: DURA Exchange: NASDAQ
Industry: Drugs

Duracell International, Inc.
Berkshire Industrial Park
Bethel, CT 06801
Phone: 203-796-4000 Fax: 203-796-4187
CEO: C. Robert Kidder
CFO: G. Wade Lewis
1992 Sales: $1,682 million Employees: 8,000
Symbol: DUR Exchange: NYSE
Industry: Electrical products - batteries

Durakon Industries, Inc.
2101 N. Lapeer Rd.
Lapeer, MI 48446
Phone: 313-664-0850 Fax: 313-664-0231
CEO: William Webster
CFO: Thomas A. Gallas
1991 Sales: $68 million Employees: 412
Symbol: DRKN Exchange: NASDAQ
Industry: Automotive & trucking - replacement parts

Duriron Co., Inc.
3100 Research Blvd., Miami Valley Research Park
Dayton, OH 45420
Phone: 513-476-6100 Fax: 513-476-6232
CEO: John S. Haddick
CFO: Joe E. Johnson
1991 Sales: $296 million Employees: 2,450
Symbol: DURI Exchange: NASDAQ
Industry: Machinery - general industrial

Duty Free International, Inc.
19 Catoonah St.
Ridgefield, CT 06877
Phone: 203-431-6057 Fax: 203-438-1356
CEO: John A. Couri
CFO: Gerald F. Egan
1991 Sales: $190 million Employees: 1,100
Symbol: DFI Exchange: NYSE
Industry: Retail - discount & variety

DVI Health Services Corp.
One Park Plaza, Ste. 800
Irvine, CA 92714
Phone: 714-474-5800 Fax: —
CEO: David L. Higgins
CFO: Daniel Vogel
1991 Sales: $20 million Employees: —
Symbol: DVI Exchange: NYSE
Industry: Leasing medical equipment

DWG Inc.
6917 Collins Ave.
Miami Beach, FL 33141
Phone: 305-866-7771 Fax: 305-866-7771
CEO: Victor Posner
CFO: Jack Coppersmith
1992 Sales: $1,295 million Employees: 17,600
Symbol: DWG Exchange: AMEX
Industry: Diversified operations - liquefied petroleum gas, dyes & restaurants

Dycom Industries, Inc.
450 Australian Ave. South, Ste. 860
West Palm Beach, FL 33401
Phone: 407-659-6301 Fax: 407-659-5876
CEO: Thomas R. Pledger
CFO: Robert T. Owens
1991 Sales: $147 million Employees: 2,235
Symbol: DY Exchange: NYSE
Industry: Telecommunications equipment

Dyersburg Fabrics Inc.
1315 E. Philips St.
Dyersburg, TN 38024
Phone: 901-285-2323 Fax: 901-286-3474
CEO: T. Eugene McBride
CFO: Jerome M. Wiggins
1991 Sales: $135 million Employees: 1,189
Symbol: DBG Exchange: NYSE
Industry: Textiles - apparel

Dynamics Corporation of America
475 Steamboat Rd.
Greenwich, CT 06830
Phone: 203-869-3211 Fax: 203-869-8708
CEO: Andrew Lozyniak
CFO: Patrick J. Dorme
1991 Sales: $112 million Employees: 1,221
Symbol: DYA Exchange: NYSE
Industry: Diversified operations - appliances, metal & environmental systems

Dynamics Research Corp.
60 Concord St.
Wilmington, MA 01887
Phone: 508-658-6100 Fax: 508-657-7765
CEO: Albert Rand
CFO: Thomas P. Graham
1991 Sales: $98 million Employees: 1,195
Symbol: DRCO Exchange: NASDAQ
Industry: Engineering - R&D services

Dynascan Corp.
6460 W. Cortland St.
Chicago, IL 60635
Phone: 312-889-8870 Fax: 312-889-6343
CEO: Jerry Kalov
CFO: James J. Bode
1991 Sales: $136 million Employees: 280
Symbol: DYNA Exchange: NASDAQ
Industry: Electrical products - radar detectors, cordless phones & clock radios

Dynasty Classics Corp.
22333 S. Wilmington Ave.
Carson, CA 90745
Phone: 310-834-3637 Fax: 310-834-1710
CEO: Craig A. Winn
CFO: Michael J. Simmons
1991 Sales: $95 million Employees: 360
Symbol: DNST Exchange: NASDAQ
Industry: Building products - lighting fixtures

Dynatech Corp.
3 New England Executive Park
Burlington, MA 01803
Phone: 617-272-6100 Fax: 617-272-2304
CEO: John F. Reno
CFO: Robert H. Hertz
1992 Sales: $486 million Employees: 3,156
Symbol: DYTC Exchange: NASDAQ
Industry: Instruments - scientific

DynCorp
2000 Edmund Halley Dr.
Reston, VA 22091
Phone: 703-264-0330 Fax: 703-264-8600
CEO: Dan Bannister
CFO: T. E. Blanchard
1991 Sales: $807 million Employees: 17,600
Ownership: Privately held
Industry: Business services - technical & professional

Dyson-Kissner-Moran Corporation, The
230 Park Ave.
New York, NY 10169
Phone: 212-661-4600 Fax: 212-599-5105
CEO: Robert R. Dyson
CFO: Joseph L. Aurichio
1991 Sales: $3,000 million Employees: 12,000
Ownership: Privately held
Industry: Diversified operations

E.I. Du Pont de Nemours and Co.
1007 Market St.
Wilmington, DE 19898
Phone: 302-774-1000 Fax: 302-774-7322
CEO: Edgar S. Woolard, Jr.
CFO: John J. Quindlen
1992 Sales: $37,799 million Employees: 132,578
Symbol: DD Exchange: NYSE
Industry: Diversified operations - oil production, chemicals & consumer products

E. & J. Gallo Winery
PO Box 1130
Modesto, CA 95353
Phone: 209-579-3111 Fax: 209-579-3312
CEO: Ernest Gallo
CFO: Louis Freedman
1991 Sales: $1,000 million Employees: 3,000
Ownership: Privately held
Industry: Beverages - wine

E. W. Scripps Co., The
1105 N. Market St.
Wilmington, DE 19801
Phone: 302-478-4141 Fax: 302-427-7663
CEO: Lawrence A. Leser
CFO: Daniel J. Castellini
1992 Sales: $1,263 million Employees: 9,700
Symbol: SSP Exchange: NYSE
Industry: Publishing - newspapers

E'town Corp.
600 South Ave.
Westfield, NJ 07090
Phone: 908-654-1234 Fax: —
CEO: Robert W. Kean, Jr.
CFO: Andrew M. Chapman
1991 Sales: $86 million Employees: 374
Symbol: ETW Exchange: NYSE
Industry: Utility - water supply

E-II Holdings
370 Washington St., 3rd Fl.
Wellesley, MA 02181
Phone: 617-431-4400 Fax: 617-431-1007
CEO: Steven Green
CFO: Joseph Dempsey
1991 Sales: $885 million Employees: 10,000
Ownership: Privately held
Industry: Diversified operations - luggage, water & apparel

E-Systems, Inc.
6250 LBJ Fwy.
Dallas, TX 75240
Phone: 214-661-1000 Fax: 214-661-8508
CEO: E. Gene Keiffer
CFO: James W. Pope
1992 Sales: $2,095 million Employees: 18,622
Symbol: ESY Exchange: NYSE
Industry: Electronics - military

indicates company is in *Hoover's Handbook of American Business.*

indicates company is in *Hoover's Handbook of World Business;* sales and employee numbers are for parent company.

E-Z Serve Corp.
10700 N. Fwy., Ste. 500
Houston, TX 77037
Phone: 713-591-1111 Fax: —
CEO: Neil H. McLaurin
CFO: John T. Miller
1991 Sales: $164 million Employees: 395
Symbol: EZS Exchange: AMEX
Industry: Oil refining & marketing

E-Z-EM, Inc.
717 Main St.
Westbury, NY 11590
Phone: 516-333-8230 Fax: 516-333-8278
CEO: Howard S. Stern
CFO: Dennis J. Curtin
1992 Sales: $88 million Employees: 1,020
Symbol: EZEMA Exchange: NASDAQ
Industry: Medical instruments - diagnostic imaging systems

EA Engineering, Science, and Technology, Inc.
11019 McCormick Rd.
Hunt Valley, MD 21031
Phone: 410-584-7000 Fax: 410-771-1625
CEO: Loren D. Jensen
CFO: Joseph A. Spadaro
1991 Sales: $46 million Employees: 700
Symbol: EACO Exchange: NASDAQ
Industry: Environmental consulting

Eagle Bancorp, Inc.
227 Capitol St.
Charleston, WV 25301
Phone: 304-340-4600 Fax: —
CEO: William W. Wagner
CFO: A. Lawrence Crimmins, Jr.
1991 Sales: $20 million Employees: 104
Symbol: EBCI Exchange: NASDAQ
Industry: Banks - Southeast

Eagle Bancshares, Inc.
4305 Lynburn Dr.
Tucker, GA 30084
Phone: 404-270-1017 Fax: —
CEO: Conrad J. Sechler, Sr.
CFO: Zelma B. Martin
1992 Sales: $27 million Employees: 168
Symbol: EBSI Exchange: NASDAQ
Industry: Banks - Southeast

Eagle Financial Corp.
222 Main St.
Bristol, CT 06010
Phone: 203-589-4600 Fax: —
CEO: Ralph T. Linsley
CFO: Mark J. Blum
1991 Sales: $49 million Employees: 195
Symbol: EAG Exchange: AMEX
Industry: Financial - savings and loans

Eagle Food Centers, Inc.
Route 67 & Knoxville Rd.
Milan, IL 61264
Phone: 309-787-7700 Fax: 309-787-7895
CEO: Pasquale V. Petitti
CFO: Robert L. Van De Voorde
1992 Sales: $1,080 million Employees: 8,559
Symbol: EGLE Exchange: NASDAQ
Industry: Retail - supermarkets

Eagle Hardware & Garden, Inc.
101 Andover Park East
Tukwila, WA 98188
Phone: 206-431-5740 Fax: 206-241-7184
CEO: David J. Heerensperger
CFO: Myron E. Kirkpatrick
1991 Sales: $39 million Employees: 650
Symbol: EAGL Exchange: NASDAQ
Industry: Building products - retail & wholesale

Eagle-Picher Industries, Inc.
580 Walnut St.
Cincinnati, OH 45202
Phone: 513-721-7010 Fax: 513-721-2341
CEO: Thomas E. Petry
CFO: David N. Hall
1992 Sales: $612 million Employees: 6,300
Symbol: EPI Exchange: NYSE
Industry: Diversified operations

Earl Scheib, Inc.
8737 Wilshire Blvd.
Beverly Hills, CA 90211
Phone: 310-652-4880 Fax: 310-659-8150
CEO: Erwin Buchalter
CFO: John K. Minnihan
1992 Sales: $58 million Employees: 1,435
Symbol: ESH Exchange: AMEX
Industry: Auto repair

Earle M. Jorgensen Co.
3050 E. Birch St.
Brea, CA 92621
Phone: 714-579-8823 Fax: 714-524-1072
CEO: Neven Hulsey
CFO: Will Dale
1991 Sales: $875 million Employees: 2,400
Ownership: Privately held
Industry: Steel - production; aluminum product distribution

Earth Care Paper
PO Box 14140
Madison, WI 53714
Phone: 608-223-4000 Fax: 608-223-4040
CEO: John Magee
CFO: John Magee
1991 Sales: $5.1 million Employees: 45
Ownership: Privately held
Industry: Paper & paper products - recycled

Earth Technology Corp. (USA)
100 W. Broadway, Ste. 5000
Long Beach, CA 90802
Phone: 310-495-4449 Fax: 310-426-0666
CEO: Diane C. Creel
CFO: Creighton K. Early
1991 Sales: $38 million Employees: 400
Symbol: ETCO Exchange: NASDAQ
Industry: Engineering - R&D services

Easel Corp.
25 Corporate Dr.
Burlington, MA 01803
Phone: 617-221-2100 Fax: 617-221-3099
CEO: R. Douglas Kahn
CFO: John P. McDonough
1991 Sales: $28 million Employees: 212
Symbol: EASL Exchange: NASDAQ
Industry: Computers - graphical user interface design software

Eastco Industrial Safety Corp.
130 W. 10th St.
Huntington Station, NY 11746
Phone: 516-427-1802 Fax: 516-427-1840
CEO: Alan E. Densen
CFO: Vincent Pomarico
1991 Sales: $30 million Employees: 257
Symbol: ESTO Exchange: NASDAQ
Industry: Textiles - apparel

Eastern Bancorp, Inc.
282 Williston Rd.
Williston, VT 05495
Phone: 802-879-9000 Fax: 203-723-8653
CEO: John A. Cobb
CFO: William H. Hill
1991 Sales: $64 million Employees: 317
Symbol: VFBK Exchange: NASDAQ
Industry: Banks - Northeast

Eastern Co.
112 Bridge St.
Naugatuck, CT 06770
Phone: 203-729-2255 Fax: 203-723-8653
CEO: Stedman G. Sweet
CFO: Donald E. Whitmore, Jr.
1991 Sales: $57 million Employees: 468
Symbol: EML Exchange: AMEX
Industry: Diversified operations

Eastern Enterprises
9 Riverside Rd.
Weston, MA 02193
Phone: 617-647-2300 Fax: 617-647-2344
CEO: J. Atwood Ives
CFO: J. Atwood Ives
1991 Sales: $993 million Employees: 4,400
Symbol: EFU Exchange: NYSE
Industry: Utility - gas distribution

Eastern Environmental Services, Inc.
1620 E. Adamo Dr.
Tampa, FL 33605
Phone: 813-248-2200 Fax: —
CEO: Randall Skuba
CFO: Randall Skuba
1991 Sales: $18 million Employees: 198
Symbol: EESI Exchange: NASDAQ
Industry: Environmental consulting, asbestos removal

Eastern Group, The
333 N. Fairfax St.
Alexandria, VA 22314
Phone: 703-684-1464 Fax: 703-684-7787
CEO: Ralph L. Bradley
CFO: Stevens V. Gillespie
1991 Sales: $53 million Employees: 60
Ownership: Privately held
Industry: Oil & gas - US integrated

Eastern Utilities Associates
One Liberty Square
Boston, MA 02109
Phone: 617-357-9590 Fax: 617-357-7320
CEO: Donald G. Pardus
CFO: John R. Stevens
1991 Sales: $524 million Employees: 1,376
Symbol: EUA Exchange: NYSE
Industry: Utility - electric power

Eastex Energy Inc.
1000 Louisiana St., Ste. 6400
Houston, TX 77002
Phone: 713-650-6255 Fax: 713-650-6703
CEO: Robert G. Phillips
CFO: Robert G. Phillips
1991 Sales: $134 million Employees: —
Symbol: ETEX Exchange: NASDAQ
Industry: Oil & gas - production & pipeline

Eastland Financial Corp.
25 Cummings Way
Woonsocket, RI 02895
Phone: 401-767-3900 Fax: —
CEO: Merrill W. Sherman
CFO: Frederick M. Fink
1991 Sales: $74 million Employees: 333
Symbol: EAFC Exchange: NASDAQ
Industry: Banks - Northeast

Eastman Kodak Co.
343 State St.
Rochester, NY 14650
Phone: 716-724-4000 Fax: 716-724-0663
CEO: Kay R. Whitmore
CFO: Christopher J. Steffen
1992 Sales: $20,183 million Employees: 133,200
Symbol: EK Exchange: NYSE
Industry: Diversified - photographic equipment, drugs, copiers & chemicals

indicates company is in *Hoover's Handbook of American Business.*

indicates company is in *Hoover's Handbook of World Business;* sales and employee numbers are for parent company.

Eaton Corp.
Eaton Center, 1111 Superior Ave. East
Cleveland, OH 44114
Phone: 216-523-5000 Fax: 216-523-4787
CEO: William E. Butler
CFO: Stephen R. Hardis
1992 Sales: $3,869 million Employees: 35,656
Symbol: ETN Exchange: NYSE
Industry: Automotive & trucking - original equipment

Eaton Vance Corp.
24 Federal St.
Boston, MA 02110
Phone: 617-482-8260 Fax: 617-482-2396
CEO: M. Dozier Gardner
CFO: Curtis H. Jones
1991 Sales: $120 million Employees: 726
Symbol: EAVN Exchange: NASDAQ
Industry: Financial - investment management

Eby-Brown Cos.
1001 Sullivan Rd.
Aurora, IL 60507
Phone: 708-897-8792 Fax: 708-897-9220
CEO: Richard Wake
CFO: Janice O'Connor
1991 Sales: $1,200 million Employees: 974
Ownership: Privately held
Industry: Food - candy; tobacco & merchandise distribution

ECC International Corp.
175 Strafford Ave.
Wayne, PA 19087
Phone: 215-687-2600 Fax: 215-254-9268
CEO: George W. Murphy
CFO: Richard F. Thompson
1992 Sales: $63 million Employees: 811
Symbol: ECC Exchange: NYSE
Industry: Electronics - military

Echlin Inc.
100 Double Beach Rd.
Branford, CT 06405
Phone: 203-481-5751 Fax: 203-488-0370
CEO: Frederick J. Mancheski
CFO: Joseph A. Onorato
1992 Sales: $1,824 million Employees: 17,800
Symbol: ECH Exchange: NYSE
Industry: Automotive & trucking - replacement parts

ECI Environmental, Inc.
5720 Shattuck Ave.
Oakland, CA 94609
Phone: 510-655-5855 Fax: —
CEO: Kurt P. Zimmerman
CFO: Richard G. Cleveland
1991 Sales: $17 million Employees: 237
Symbol: ECI Exchange: AMEX
Industry: Asbestos abatement supplies & services

ECI Systems and Engineering
5700 Cleveland St., Ste. 400
Virginia Beach, VA 23462
Phone: 804-671-8000 Fax: 804-497-2600
CEO: Richard Cheng
CFO: Dave Nanson
1991 Sales: $50 million Employees: 350
Ownership: Privately held
Industry: Electronic engineering & diversified systems

Ecogen Inc.
2005 Cabot Blvd. West
Langhorne, PA 19047
Phone: 215-757-1590 Fax: 215-757-2956
CEO: John E. Davies
CFO: Peter B. Stevens
1991 Sales: $6.2 million Employees: 80
Symbol: EECN Exchange: NASDAQ
Industry: Chemicals - agricultural pesticides

Ecolab Inc.
Ecolab Center, 370 Wabasha St. North
St. Paul, MN 55102
Phone: 612-293-2233 Fax: 612-225-3059
CEO: Pierson M. Grieve
CFO: Michael E. Shannon
1992 Sales: $1,005 million Employees: 7,263
Symbol: ECL Exchange: NYSE
Industry: Building - maintenance & services

Ecology and Environment, Inc.
368 Pleasantview Dr.
Lancaster, NY 14086
Phone: 716-684-8060 Fax: 716-684-0844
CEO: Gerhard J. Neumaier
CFO: Ronald L. Frank
1991 Sales: $87 million Employees: 1,200
Symbol: EEI Exchange: AMEX
Industry: Environmental consulting

EcoScience Corp.
One Innovation Dr.
Worcester, MA 01605
Phone: 508-754-0300 Fax: —
CEO: James A. Wylie, Jr.
CFO: James A. Wylie, Jr.
1992 Sales: $0.1 million Employees: 70
Symbol: ECSC Exchange: NASDAQ
Industry: Chemicals - specialty

EDECO Engineers
4500 S. Garnett Rd. #700
Tulsa, OK 74146
Phone: 918-663-7100 Fax: 918-663-7377
CEO: Harvey Green
CFO: Dave Robinson
1991 Sales: $7.1 million Employees: 170
Ownership: Privately held
Industry: Oil & gas - engineering consulting

Edison Brothers Stores, Inc.
501 N. Broadway
St. Louis, MO 63102
Phone: 314-331-6000 Fax: 314-331-7200
CEO: Andrew E. Newman
CFO: Lee G. Weeks
1992 Sales: $1,478 million Employees: 20,900
Symbol: EBS Exchange: NYSE
Industry: Retail - apparel & shoes

Edison Control Corp.
140 Ethyl Rd. West
Piscataway, NJ 08854
Phone: 908-819-8800 Fax: —
CEO: Taft B. Russell
CFO: Anthony Gagliardi
1991 Sales: $1.7 million Employees: 21
Symbol: EDCO Exchange: NASDAQ
Industry: Electrical products - fault indicators

Edisto Resources Corp.
2121 San Jacinto St., Ste. 2600
Dallas, TX 75201
Phone: 214-880-0243 Fax: 214-220-1054
CEO: James R. McNab, Jr.
CFO: David N. Broussard
1991 Sales: $345 million Employees: 226
Symbol: EDS Exchange: AMEX
Industry: Oil & gas - offshore drilling

EDO Corp.
14-04 111th St.
College Point, NY 11356
Phone: 718-321-4000 Fax: 718-939-0119
CEO: Gerald Albert
CFO: Michael J. Hegarty
1991 Sales: $146 million Employees: 1,439
Symbol: EDO Exchange: NYSE
Industry: Electronics - military

EduCare Community Living Corp. Texas
9171 Cap. of Tx. Hwy. North, Bowie Bldg., Ste. 100
Austin, TX 78759
Phone: 512-338-4182 Fax: 512-338-4449
CEO: Richard D. Relyea
CFO: Barbara Bowman
1991 Sales: $14 million Employees: 328
Ownership: Privately held
Industry: Healthcare - long-term healthcare for the disabled

Edward J. DeBartolo Corp.
7620 Market St.
Youngstown, OH 44513
Phone: 216-758-7292 Fax: 216-758-3598
CEO: Edward J. DeBartolo
CFO: Anthony W. Liberati
1991 Sales: $1,500 million Employees: 14,000
Ownership: Privately held
Industry: Real estate development & management

EFI Electronics Corp.
2415 South 2300 West
Salt Lake City, UT 84119
Phone: 801-977-9009 Fax: 801-977-0200
CEO: Scott H. Nelson
CFO: David K. Giles
1992 Sales: $12 million Employees: 115
Symbol: EFIC Exchange: NASDAQ
Industry: Electrical products - surge protectors

EG&G, Inc.
45 William St.
Wellesley, MA 02181
Phone: 617-237-5100 Fax: 617-431-4255
CEO: John M. Kucharski
CFO: Richard P. Delio
1992 Sales: $2,789 million Employees: 35,600
Symbol: EGG Exchange: NYSE
Industry: Instruments - scientific, military equipment

Egghead, Inc.
22011 SE 51st St.
Issaquah, WA 98027
Phone: 206-391-0800 Fax: 206-391-0880
CEO: Tim Turnpaugh
CFO: Carolyn J. Tobias
1992 Sales: $685 million Employees: 2,000
Symbol: EGGS Exchange: NASDAQ
Industry: Retail - personal computer software

EIP Microwave, Inc.
3991 MacArthur Blvd.
Newport Beach, CA 92660
Phone: 714-724-1666 Fax: 714-724-8985
CEO: John F. Bishop
CFO: John F. Bishop
1991 Sales: $7.8 million Employees: 65
Symbol: EIPM Exchange: NASDAQ
Industry: Electronics - measuring instruments

Ekco Group, Inc.
98 Spit Brook Rd., Ste. 102
Nashua, NH 03062
Phone: 603-888-1212 Fax: 603-888-1427
CEO: Robert Stein
CFO: Robert Stein
1991 Sales: $167 million Employees: 905
Symbol: EKO Exchange: NYSE
Industry: Appliances - household housewares; utensils & bakeware

El Chico Corp.
12200 Stemmons Fwy., Ste. 100
Dallas, TX 75234
Phone: 214-241-5500 Fax: —
CEO: Gilbert Cuellar, Jr.
CFO: Gary W. Coder
1992 Sales: $91 million Employees: 3,650
Symbol: ELCH Exchange: NASDAQ
Industry: Retail - food & restaurants

indicates company is in *Hoover's Handbook of American Business.*

indicates company is in *Hoover's Handbook of World Business;* sales and employee numbers are for parent company.

El Paso Electric Co.
303 N. Oregon St.
El Paso, TX 79901
Phone: 915-543-5711 Fax: 915-542-3905
CEO: David H. Wiggs, Jr.
CFO: William J. Johnson
1991 Sales: $462 million Employees: 1,077
Symbol: ELPAQ Exchange: NASDAQ
Industry: Utility - electric power

El Paso Natural Gas Co.
3300 N. A St.
Midland, TX 79705
Phone: 915-684-5701 Fax: Ext. 215
CEO: William A. Wise
CFO: H. Brent Austin
1991 Sales: $735 million Employees: 2,560
Symbol: EPG Exchange: NYSE
Industry: Utility - gas distribution

El Paso Refinery, L.P.
6500 Trowbridge
El Paso, TX 79905
Phone: 915-772-1433 Fax: 915-779-2198
CEO: David N. Jones
CFO: Ransom B. Jones
1992 Sales: — Employees: —
Symbol: ELP Exchange: NYSE
Industry: Oil refining & marketing

Elco Industries, Inc.
1111 Samuelson Rd.
Rockford, IL 61125
Phone: 815-397-5151 Fax: 815-398-4569
CEO: Jack W. Packard
CFO: August F. DeLuca
1992 Sales: $189 million Employees: 1,755
Symbol: ELCN Exchange: NASDAQ
Industry: Metal products - fasteners

Elcor Corp.
14643 Dallas Pkwy., Ste. 1000
Dallas, TX 75240
Phone: 214-851-0500 Fax: 214-851-0543
CEO: Roy E. Campbell
CFO: Richard J. Rosebery
1992 Sales: $149 million Employees: 773
Symbol: ELK Exchange: NYSE
Industry: Building products - roofing

ELDEC Corp.
16700 13th Ave. West
Lynnwood, WA 98037
Phone: 206-743-1313 Fax: 206-743-8234
CEO: Max E. Gellert
CFO: Phillip H. Lorenzen
1992 Sales: $110 million Employees: 1,326
Symbol: ELDC Exchange: NASDAQ
Industry: Electrical components

Elder-Beerman Stores Corp.
3155 El-Bee Rd.
Dayton, OH 45439
Phone: 513-296-2700 Fax: 513-296-2915
CEO: Milton E. Hartley
CFO: Bruce Macke
1991 Sales: $665 million Employees: 8,000
Ownership: Privately held
Industry: Retail - regional department stores

Eldorado Bancorp
24012 Calle de la Plata, Ste. 150
Laguna Hills, CA 92653
Phone: 714-830-8800 Fax: —
CEO: J. B. Crowell
CFO: David R. Brown
1991 Sales: $32 million Employees: 226
Symbol: ELB Exchange: AMEX
Industry: Banks - West

Electro Rent Corp.
6060 Sepulveda Blvd.
Van Nuys, CA 91411
Phone: 818-787-2100 Fax: 818-786-4354
CEO: Daniel Greenberg
CFO: Craig R. Jones
1992 Sales: $102 million Employees: 438
Symbol: ELRC Exchange: NASDAQ
Industry: Leasing - electronics

Electro Scientific Industries, Inc.
13900 NW Science Park Dr.
Portland, OR 97229
Phone: 503-641-4141 Fax: 503-643-4873
CEO: Michael J. Ellsworth
CFO: O. Dean Finley
1992 Sales: $58 million Employees: 550
Symbol: ESIO Exchange: NASDAQ
Industry: Lasers - systems & components

Electro-Catheter Corp.
2100 Felver Court
Rahway, NJ 07065
Phone: 908-382-5600 Fax: —
CEO: Robert I. Bernstein
CFO: Joseph P. Macaluso
1991 Sales: $7.9 million Employees: 124
Symbol: ECTH Exchange: NASDAQ
Industry: Medical products - catheters & cardiovascular diagnostic equipment

Electro-Sensors, Inc.
10365 W. 70th St.
Eden Prairie, MN 55344
Phone: 612-941-8171 Fax: —
CEO: James P. Slattery
CFO: James P. Slattery
1991 Sales: $4.7 million Employees: 39
Symbol: ELSE Exchange: NASDAQ
Industry: Diversified operations - process controls systems, small gas torches, investments

Electrocom Automation, Inc.
2910 Ave. F East
Arlington, TX 76011
Phone: 817-640-5690 Fax: 817-695-5599
CEO: R. S. Buzard
CFO: G. D. Thompson
1991 Sales: $306 million Employees: 1,425
Symbol: ECA Exchange: NYSE
Industry: Machinery - material handling

Electromagnetic Sciences, Inc.
660 Engineering Dr.
Norcross, GA 30092
Phone: 404-448-5770 Fax: 404-263-8130
CEO: John E. Pippin
CFO: Don T. Scartz
1991 Sales: $75 million Employees: 600
Symbol: ELMG Exchange: NASDAQ
Industry: Electronics - military

Electromedics, Inc.
7337 S. Revere Pkwy.
Englewood, CO 80112
Phone: 303-790-8700 Fax: 303-790-0619
CEO: F. James Lynch
CFO: Richard B. Carlock
1991 Sales: $35 million Employees: 294
Symbol: ELMD Exchange: NASDAQ
Industry: Medical products - instruments

Electronic Arts, Inc.
1450 Fashion Island Blvd.
San Mateo, CA 94404
Phone: 415-571-7171 Fax: 415-571-6375
CEO: Lawrence F. Probst III
CFO: E. Stanton McKee, Jr.
1992 Sales: $162 million Employees: 470
Symbol: ERTS Exchange: NASDAQ
Industry: Computers - games software

Electronic Associates, Inc.
185 Monmouth Park Hwy.
West Long Branch, NJ 07764
Phone: 908-229-1100 Fax: 908-229-1329
CEO: Robert G. Finney
CFO: Louis J. Tedeschi
1991 Sales: $42 million Employees: 368
Symbol: EA Exchange: NYSE
Industry: Computers - services

Electronic Ballast Technology
2510 W. 237th St.
Torrance, CA 90505
Phone: 310-784-2000 Fax: 310-534-8214
CEO: Peter Shen
CFO: Peter Shen
1991 Sales: $42 million Employees: 450
Ownership: Privately held
Industry: Electrical components - ballasts for fluorescent lamps

Electronic Information Systems, Inc.
1351 Washington Blvd.
Stamford, CT 06902
Phone: 203-351-4800 Fax: —
CEO: Joseph J. Porfeli
CFO: E. Kevin Dahill
1991 Sales: $21 million Employees: 102
Symbol: EISI Exchange: NASDAQ
Industry: Telecommunications equipment

Electronic Label Technology
9916-A E. 43rd St.
Tulsa, OK 74146
Phone: 918-622-6792 Fax: 918-664-8207
CEO: Tim Wright
CFO: Ted Morgan
1991 Sales: $15 million Employees: 63
Ownership: Privately held
Industry: Machinery - bar code printing

Electronic Tele-Communications, Inc.
1915 MacArthur Rd.
Waukesha, WI 53188
Phone: 414-542-5600 Fax: 414-542-1524
CEO: George W. Danner
CFO: Jeffrey M. Nigl
1991 Sales: $18 million Employees: 222
Symbol: ETCIA Exchange: NASDAQ
Industry: Telecommunications equipment

Elf Aquitaine, Inc.
280 Park Ave., 36th Fl.
New York, NY 10017
Phone: 212-922-3000 Fax: 212-922-3001
CEO: Michel Schneider-Maunoury
CFO: —
1991 Sales: $38,740 million Employees: 86,900
Parent: Société National Elf Aquitaine
Industry: Oil & gas - international integrated

Eli Lilly and Co.
Lilly Corporate Center
Indianapolis, IN 46285
Phone: 317-276-2000 Fax: 317-276-2095
CEO: Vaughn D. Bryson
CFO: James M. Cornelius
1992 Sales: $6,167 million Employees: 30,800
Symbol: LLY Exchange: NYSE
Industry: Drugs, diagnostic products, animal health products

Eljer Industries, Inc.
17120 Dallas Pkwy., Ste. 205
Plano, TX 75287
Phone: 214-407-2771 Fax: 214-407-2789
CEO: Scott G. Arbuckle
CFO: Carl Mudd
1991 Sales: $402 million Employees: 3,800
Symbol: ELJ Exchange: NYSE
Industry: Building products - plumbing & venting

indicates company is in *Hoover's Handbook of American Business.*

indicates company is in *Hoover's Handbook of World Business;* sales and employee numbers are for parent company.

Elm Financial Services, Inc.
100 Addison St.
Elmhurst, IL 60126
Phone: 708-833-8000 Fax: —
CEO: Charles H. Walsh
CFO: Ralph P. Pechanio
1991 Sales: $11 million Employees: 126
Symbol: ELMF Exchange: NASDAQ
Industry: Banks - Midwest

Elmwood Federal Savings Bank
112 Chesley Dr.
Media, PA 19063
Phone: 215-565-8200 Fax: 215-891-8774
CEO: Frank C. Freeman
CFO: Philip N. Travaglini
1992 Sales: — Employees: —
Symbol: EFSB Exchange: NASDAQ
Industry: Financial - savings and loans

Elsinore Corp.
202 E. Fremont St.
Las Vegas, NV 89101
Phone: 702-385-4011 Fax: 702-385-5580
CEO: Jeanne Hood
CFO: Jeanne Hood
1991 Sales: $63 million Employees: 1,258
Symbol: ELS Exchange: AMEX
Industry: Leisure & recreational services - casinos

ELXSI Corp.
115 E. Putnam Ave.
Greenwich, CT 06830
Phone: 203-661-9645 Fax: 203-661-1119
CEO: James K. Dutton
CFO: James K. Dutton
1991 Sales: $21 million Employees: 1,600
Symbol: ELXS Exchange: NASDAQ
Industry: Computers - mini & micro

Embrex, Inc.
1035 Swabia Court
Morrisville, NC 27560
Phone: 919-941-5185 Fax: —
CEO: Randall L. Marcuson
CFO: John A. Hagan
1991 Sales: $0.1 million Employees: 38
Symbol: EMBX Exchange: NASDAQ
Industry: Biomedical & genetic products

EMC Corp.
171 South St.
Hopkinton, MA 01748
Phone: 508-435-1000 Fax: 508-435-5222
CEO: Michael C. Ruettgers
CFO: W. Paul Fitzgerald
1991 Sales: $232 million Employees: 1,155
Symbol: EMC Exchange: NYSE
Industry: Computers - peripheral equipment

EMC Engineers, Inc.
2750 S. Wadsworth Blvd. #C200
Denver, CO 80227
Phone: 303-988-2951 Fax: 303-985-2527
CEO: Virgil Carrier
CFO: Stuart Ratzlaff
1991 Sales: $3.7 million Employees: 43
Ownership: Privately held
Industry: Engineering - facilities, utilities & environmental services

EMC Insurance Group Inc.
717 Mulberry St.
Des Moines, IA 50309
Phone: 515-280-2581 Fax: —
CEO: Robb B. Kelley
CFO: E. H. Creese
1991 Sales: $134 million Employees: 1,555
Symbol: EMCI Exchange: NASDAQ
Industry: Insurance - property & casualty

EMCON Associates
1921 Ringwood Ave.
San Jose, CA 95131
Phone: 408-453-7300 Fax: 408-453-7300
CEO: Thorley D. Briggs
CFO: Eugene M. Herson
1991 Sales: $69 million Employees: 879
Symbol: MCON Exchange: NASDAQ
Industry: Environmental consulting

Emerson Electric Co.
8000 W. Florissant Ave.
St. Louis, MO 63136
Phone: 314-553-2000 Fax: 314-553-3527
CEO: Charles F. Knight
CFO: W. J. Galvin
1992 Sales: $7,873 million Employees: 69,500
Symbol: EMR Exchange: NYSE
Industry: Machinery - electric motors, hand held tools & misc. electric equipment

Emerson Radio Corp.
One Emerson Lane
North Bergen, NJ 07047
Phone: 201-854-6600 Fax: 201-854-8357
CEO: Gerald Zarin
CFO: Harold N. Falik
1991 Sales: $790 million Employees: 850
Symbol: EME Exchange: NYSE
Industry: Audio & video home products

Empi, Inc.
1275 Grey Fox Rd.
St. Paul, MN 55112
Phone: 612-636-6600 Fax: 612-639-2405
CEO: Donald D. Maurer
CFO: Timothy E. Briggs
1991 Sales: $22 million Employees: 222
Symbol: EMPI Exchange: NASDAQ
Industry: Medical products - diagnostic equipment, biomedica devices

Empire District Electric Co.
602 Joplin St.
Joplin, MO 64801
Phone: 417-623-4700 Fax: 417-625-5155
CEO: R. L. Lamb
CFO: V. E. Brill
1991 Sales: $150 million Employees: 658
Symbol: EDE Exchange: NYSE
Industry: Utility - electric power

Empire of Carolina, Inc.
441 S. Federal Hwy.
Deerfield Beach, FL 33441
Phone: 305-428-9001 Fax: 305-480-2983
CEO: Maurice A. Halperin
CFO: J. Artie Rogers
1991 Sales: $243 million Employees: 1,190
Symbol: EMP Exchange: AMEX
Industry: Diversified operations - toys, frozen desserts & decorative items

Empire-Orr, Inc.
10 W. 33rd St.
New York, NY 10001
Phone: 212-564-9191 Fax: —
CEO: W. Lee Clark
CFO: W. Lee Clark
1992 Sales: — Employees: —
Symbol: EORR Exchange: NASDAQ
Industry: Leather & related products

Employee Benefit Plans, Inc.
435 Ford Ave., Ste. 500
Minneapolis, MN 55426
Phone: 612-546-4353 Fax: 612-546-6609
CEO: William E. Sagan
CFO: Mark A. Sorensen
1992 Sales: $219 million Employees: —
Symbol: EBP Exchange: NYSE
Industry: Health maintenance organization

Emulex Corp.
3545 Harbor Blvd.
Costa Mesa, CA 92626
Phone: 714-662-5600 Fax: 714-241-0792
CEO: Robert N. Stephens
CFO: Marshall A. Petersen
1992 Sales: $101 million Employees: 594
Symbol: EMLX Exchange: NASDAQ
Industry: Computers - peripheral equipment

EnClean, Inc.
6750 West Loop South, Ste. 1000
Bellaire, TX 77401
Phone: 713-661-4777 Fax: 713-661-0742
CEO: Malcolm Waddell
CFO: James R. O'Hare
1992 Sales: $108 million Employees: 1,750
Symbol: ENCL Exchange: NASDAQ
Industry: Environmental cleaning services

Encore Wire Corp.
1410 Millwood Rd.
McKinney, TX 75069
Phone: 214-548-9473 Fax: —
CEO: Donald M. Spurgin
CFO: Nicholas B. Vita
1991 Sales: $31 million Employees: 72
Symbol: WIRE Exchange: NASDAQ
Industry: Wire & cable products

Encyclopaedia Britannica Inc.
310 S. Michigan Ave.
Chicago, IL 60604
Phone: 312-347-7000 Fax: 312-347-7135
CEO: Robert P. Gwinn
CFO: Fred Figge
1992 Sales: $586 million Employees: 2,500
Ownership: Privately held
Industry: Publishing - reference books; educational services

Endevco, Inc.
8080 N. Central Expressway, Ste. 1200
Dallas, TX 75206
Phone: 214-691-5536 Fax: 214-691-5682
CEO: James W. Bryant
CFO: Jack W. Young
1991 Sales: $210 million Employees: 177
Symbol: EI Exchange: AMEX
Industry: Oil & gas - production & pipeline

Endosonics Corp.
6616 Owens Dr.
Pleasanton, CA 94588
Phone: 510-734-0464 Fax: —
CEO: Michael R. Henson
CFO: Dana P. Nickell
1991 Sales: $4.6 million Employees: 63
Symbol: ESON Exchange: NASDAQ
Industry: Medical products - catheters & imaging systems

EnecoTech Group
1580 Lincoln, Ste. 1000
Denver, CO 80203
Phone: 303-861-2200 Fax: 303-861-2201
CEO: Barry Stuart
CFO: Barry Stuart
1991 Sales: $15 million Employees: 200
Ownership: Privately held
Industry: Environmental consulting

Energen Corp.
2101 Sixth Ave. North
Birmingham, AL 35203
Phone: 205-326-8100 Fax: 205-322-6895
CEO: Rex J. Lysinger
CFO: Geoffrey C. Ketcham
1991 Sales: $326 million Employees: 1,569
Symbol: EGN Exchange: NYSE
Industry: Utility - gas distribution

A indicates company is in *Hoover's Handbook of American Business.*

W indicates company is in *Hoover's Handbook of World Business*; sales and employee numbers are for parent company.

Energy Dynamics Inc.
2817 S. 171st St.
New Berlin, WI 53151
Phone: 414-785-1711 Fax: 414-785-2774
CEO: Al Larson
CFO: Cameron Cook
1991 Sales: $15 million Employees: 35
Ownership: Privately held
Industry: Machinery - diesel electric generators

Energy North Natural Gas, Inc.
1260 Elm St.
Manchester, NH 03101
Phone: 603-625-4000 Fax: 603-624-6864
CEO: Robert R. Giordano
CFO: Michael J. Mancini, Jr.
1991 Sales: $73 million Employees: 280
Symbol: ENNI Exchange: NASDAQ
Industry: Utility - gas distribution

Energy Service Co., Inc.
1776 Yorktown St., Ste. 700
Houston, TX 77056
Phone: 713-961-7000 Fax: 713-961-7020
CEO: Carl F. Thorne
CFO: C. C. Gaut
1991 Sales: $207 million Employees: 1,000
Symbol: ESV Exchange: AMEX
Industry: Oil & gas - offshore drilling

Energy Ventures, Inc.
515 Post Oak Blvd., Ste. 1760
Houston, TX 77027
Phone: 713-297-8400 Fax: 713-963-9785
CEO: Mark R. Wellman
CFO: Frank R. Pierce
1991 Sales: $178 million Employees: 1,700
Symbol: ENGY Exchange: NASDAQ
Industry: Oil & gas - US exploration & production

ENEX Resources Corp.
3 Kingwood Pl., Ste. 200
Kingwood, TX 77339
Phone: 713-358-8401 Fax: 713-358-7895
CEO: Gerald B. Eckley
CFO: Robert E. Densford
1991 Sales: $5.7 million Employees: 33
Symbol: ENEX Exchange: NASDAQ
Industry: Oil & gas - US exploration & production

Engelhard Corp.
101 Wood Ave. South
Iselin, NJ 08830
Phone: 908-205-6000 Fax: 908-321-1161
CEO: Orin R. Smith
CFO: Robert L. Guyett
1992 Sales: $2,400 million Employees: —
Symbol: EC Exchange: NYSE
Industry: Chemicals - specialty

Engineered Support Systems, Inc.
1270 N. Price Rd.
St. Louis, MO 63132
Phone: 314-993-5880 Fax: 314-567-4052
CEO: Michael F. Shanahan, Sr.
CFO: James A. Zweifel
1991 Sales: $68 million Employees: 259
Symbol: EASI Exchange: NASDAQ
Industry: Military equipment

Engineering Management & Economics
51 Monroe St., Ste. 507
Rockville, MD 20850
Phone: 301-738-2266 Fax: 301-738-9284
CEO: Bruce J. Block
CFO: Sue Curry
1991 Sales: $1.2 million Employees: 15
Ownership: Privately held
Industry: Computers - services

Engineering Measurements Co.
600 Diagonal Hwy.
Longmont, CO 80501
Phone: 303-651-0550 Fax: 303-678-7152
CEO: Charles E. Miller
CFO: John P. Fay
1992 Sales: $7.4 million Employees: 64
Symbol: EMCO Exchange: NASDAQ
Industry: Electronics - measuring instruments

Engle Homes, Inc.
123 NW 13th St., Ste. 300
Boca Raton, FL 33432
Phone: 407-391-4012 Fax: —
CEO: Alec Englestein
CFO: David Shapiro
1991 Sales: $78 million Employees: 123
Symbol: ENGL Exchange: NASDAQ
Industry: Building - residential & commercial

Engraph, Inc.
2635 Century Pkwy. NE, Ste. 900
Atlanta, GA 30345
Phone: 404-329-0332 Fax: 404-320-7460
CEO: Leo Benatar
CFO: John H. Dykes
1991 Sales: $200 million Employees: 1,349
Symbol: ENGH Exchange: NASDAQ
Industry: Paper & paper products

Enhance Financial Services Group, Inc.
360 Madison Ave.
New York, NY 10017
Phone: 212-983-3100 Fax: —
CEO: W. O. Sellers
CFO: W. O. Sellers
1991 Sales: $70 million Employees: —
Symbol: EFS Exchange: NYSE
Industry: Insurance - multiline & misc.

Enhanced Imaging Technologies, Inc.
17601 Fitch Ave.
Irvine, CA 92714
Phone: 714-553-1084 Fax: —
CEO: Peter P. Tong
CFO: John W. Worley
1991 Sales: $30 million Employees: 145
Symbol: EITI Exchange: NASDAQ
Industry: Photographic equipment & supplies

ENI USA Representative Office
666 Fifth Ave.
New York, NY 10103
Phone: 212-887-0315 Fax: 212-246-0009
CEO: Enzo Viscusi
CFO: —
1991 Sales: $44,323 million Employees: 131,248
Parent: Ente Nazionale Idrocarburi
Industry: Diversified operations - energy, chemicals, engineering

Ennis Business Forms, Inc.
107 N. Sherman St.
Ennis, TX 75119
Phone: 214-875-6581 Fax: 214-875-4915
CEO: Kenneth A. McCrady
CFO: Harve Cathey
1992 Sales: $132 million Employees: 1,354
Symbol: EBF Exchange: NYSE
Industry: Paper - business forms

Enquirer/Star Group, Inc.
600 South East Coast Ave.
Lantana, FL 33462
Phone: 407-586-1111 Fax: 407-540-1018
CEO: Peter J. Callahan
CFO: David H. Galpern
1992 Sales: $284 million Employees: 1,330
Symbol: ENQ Exchange: NYSE
Industry: Publishing - periodicals

Enron Corp.
1400 Smith St.
Houston, TX 77002
Phone: 713-853-6161 Fax: 713-853-3129
CEO: Kenneth L. Lay
CFO: Jack I. Tompkins
1992 Sales: $6,325 million Employees: 7,400
Symbol: ENE Exchange: NYSE
Industry: Oil & gas - production & pipeline

Enron Oil & Gas Co.
1400 Smith St.
Houston, TX 77002
Phone: 713-853-6161 Fax: 713-853-3129
CEO: Forrest E. Hoglund
CFO: Walter C. Wilson
1991 Sales: $388 million Employees: 630
Symbol: EOG Exchange: NYSE
Industry: Oil & gas - US exploration & production

ENSERCH Corp.
300 South St. Paul St.
Dallas, TX 75201
Phone: 214-651-8700 Fax: 214-670-2520
CEO: William C. McCord
CFO: Sanford R. Singer
1992 Sales: $2,825 million Employees: 11,000
Symbol: ENS Exchange: NYSE
Industry: Oil & gas - production & pipeline

Enserch Exploration Partners, Ltd.
1817 Wood St.
Dallas, TX 75201
Phone: 214-748-1110 Fax: —
CEO: William C. McCord
CFO: James E. Niemeyer
1991 Sales: $174 million Employees: —
Symbol: EP Exchange: NYSE
Industry: Oil & gas - US exploration & production

Entergy Corp.
225 Baronne St.
New Orleans, LA 70112
Phone: 504-529-5262 Fax: 504-569-4265
CEO: Edwin Lupberger
CFO: Gerald D. McInvale
1992 Sales: $4,117 million Employees: 13,034
Symbol: ETR Exchange: NYSE
Industry: Utility - electric power

Enterprise Rent-A-Car Corp.
8850 Ladue Rd.
St. Louis, MO 63124
Phone: 314-863-7000 Fax: 314-863-7621
CEO: Andrew C. Taylor
CFO: John T. O'Connell
1991 Sales: $1,200 million Employees: 11,250
Ownership: Privately held
Industry: Leasing - autos

Enterra Corp.
13100 Northwest Fwy., Ste. 600
Houston, TX 77040
Phone: 713-462-7300 Fax: 713-462-7816
CEO: D. Dale Wood
CFO: Steven W. Krablin
1991 Sales: $175 million Employees: 1,200
Symbol: EN Exchange: NYSE
Industry: Oil & gas - field services

Entree Corp.
250 E. Wisconsin Ave., Ste. 1800
Milwaukee, WI 53202
Phone: 414-289-9797 Fax: 414-271-0557
CEO: Donald E. Runge
CFO: Donald E. Runge
1992 Sales: $24 million Employees: 220
Symbol: ETRC Exchange: NASDAQ
Industry: Food - meat products

A indicates company is in *Hoover's Handbook of American Business.*

W indicates company is in *Hoover's Handbook of World Business;* sales and employee numbers are for parent company.

Envirodyne Industries Inc.
701 Harger Rd., Ste. 121
Oak Brook, IL 60521
Phone: 708-575-2400 Fax: 708-571-0959
CEO: Donald P. Kelly
CFO: John S. Corcoran
1991 Sales: $544 million Employees: 4,600
Ownership: Privately held
Industry: Diversified operations - sausage casings & plastics

Envirogen, Inc.
4100 Quakerbridge Rd.
Lawrenceville, NJ 08648
Phone: 609-936-9300 Fax: —
CEO: Roger J. Colley
CFO: Ronald H. Spair
1991 Sales: $2 million Employees: 63
Symbol: ENVG Exchange: NASDAQ
Industry: Pollution control equipment & services

Environmental Elements Corp.
3700 Koppers St.
Baltimore, MD 21227
Phone: 410-368-7000 Fax: 410-368-6896
CEO: F. Bradford Smith
CFO: Thomas B. McCord
1992 Sales: $92 million Employees: 333
Symbol: EEC Exchange: NYSE
Industry: Air pollution control systems

Environmental Operations
2649 Pestalozzi St.
St. Louis, MO 63118
Phone: 314-231-8226 Fax: 314-771-5772
CEO: Roger Hopson
CFO: Roger Hopson
1991 Sales: $1.8 million Employees: 29
Ownership: Privately held
Industry: Environmental consulting

Environmental Services of America, Inc.
119 Paris St.
Newark, NJ 07105
Phone: 201-589-3850 Fax: 201-589-4289
CEO: Jon Colin
CFO: Jon Colin
1991 Sales: $21 million Employees: 186
Symbol: ENSA Exchange: NASDAQ
Industry: Waste disposal services, environmental consulting

Environmental Tectonics Corp.
County Line Industrial Park
Southampton, PA 18966
Phone: 215-355-9100 Fax: 215-357-4000
CEO: William F. Mitchell
CFO: John F. Schoenfelder
1992 Sales: $28 million Employees: 269
Symbol: ETC Exchange: AMEX
Industry: Instruments - control & measurement

Enviroq Corp.
801 5th Ave. North
Birmingham, AL 35203
Phone: 205-251-6261 Fax: 205-251-1409
CEO: James J. Baird, Jr.
CFO: Charles A. Long, Jr.
1992 Sales: $16 million Employees: 123
Symbol: EROQ Exchange: NASDAQ
Industry: Waste water systems repair

EnviroSearch International
844 South 200 East
Salt Lake City, UT 84111
Phone: 801-532-1717 Fax: 801-532-1777
CEO: David Nelson
CFO: J. D. Henrickson
1992 Sales: $3 million Employees: 45
Ownership: Privately held
Industry: Environmental consulting & engineering services

EnviroSource, Inc.
Five High Ridge Park
Stamford, CT 06905
Phone: 203-322-8333 Fax: 203-968-1039
CEO: Louis A. Guzzetti, Jr.
CFO: James C. Hull
1991 Sales: $224 million Employees: 1,900
Symbol: ENSO Exchange: NASDAQ
Industry: Waste disposal services

ENVOY Corp.
15 Century Blvd., Ste. 600
Nashville, TN 37214
Phone: 615-885-3700 Fax: —
CEO: Fred C. Goad, Jr.
CFO: Don R. Foutch
1991 Sales: $30 million Employees: 193
Symbol: ENVY Exchange: NASDAQ
Industry: Business services - electronic transaction processing

Envoy Global Inc.
919 SW Taylor St. #400
Portland, OR 97205
Phone: 503-224-6505 Fax: 503-224-6412
CEO: Bruce Frydenlund
CFO: Bruce Frydenlund
1991 Sales: $4 million Employees: 40
Ownership: Privately held
Industry: Telecommunications services - business

Enzo Biochem, Inc.
40 Oak Dr.
Syosset, NY 11791
Phone: 516-496-8080 Fax: 516-496-0830
CEO: Elazar Rabbani
CFO: Shahram K. Rabbani
1991 Sales: $20 million Employees: 280
Symbol: ENZ Exchange: AMEX
Industry: Biomedical & genetic products

Enzon, Inc.
16020 Industrial Dr.
Gaithersburg, MD 20877
Phone: 301-258-0552 Fax: 301-926-1221
CEO: Abraham Abuchowski
CFO: Gail E. Wasilewski
1992 Sales: $5.7 million Employees: 224
Symbol: ENZN Exchange: NASDAQ
Industry: Biomedical & genetic products

Enzymatics, Inc.
500 Enterprise Rd.
Horsham, PA 19044
Phone: 215-674-3288 Fax: —
CEO: S. Wayne Kay
CFO: S. Wayne Kay
1991 Sales: $0.4 million Employees: 54
Symbol: ENZY Exchange: NASDAQ
Industry: Medical products

Epic Healthcare Group
3333 Lee Pkwy.
Dallas, TX 75219
Phone: 214-443-3333 Fax: 214-443-3599
CEO: Kenn S. George
CFO: Tom Schleck
1991 Sales: $941 million Employees: 13,600
Ownership: Privately held
Industry: Hospitals

Epitope, Inc.
8505 SW Creekside Place
Beaverton, OR 97005
Phone: 503-641-6115 Fax: 503-643-2781
CEO: Adolph J. Ferro
CFO: Gilbert N. Miller
1991 Sales: $3.8 million Employees: 110
Symbol: EPT Exchange: AMEX
Industry: Medical products - diagnostics, pharmaceuticals, test kits

EQK Green Acres, L.P.
5775 Peachtree Dunwoody Rd.
Atlanta, GA 30342
Phone: 404-303-6100 Fax: —
CEO: Myles H. Tanenbaum
CFO: Phillip E. Stephens
1991 Sales: $17 million Employees: —
Symbol: EGA Exchange: NYSE
Industry: Real estate operations

Equifax Inc.
1600 Peachtree St. NW
Atlanta, GA 30302
Phone: 404-885-8000 Fax: 404-888-5043
CEO: C. B. Rogers, Jr.
CFO: D. V. Smith
1992 Sales: $1,134 million Employees: 13,400
Symbol: EFX Exchange: NYSE
Industry: Business services - credit reporting & insurance support services

Equimark Corp.
Two Oliver Plaza
Pittsburgh, PA 15222
Phone: 412-288-5000 Fax: —
CEO: Gary W. Fiedler
CFO: Joseph J. Whiteside
1991 Sales: $360 million Employees: 1,513
Symbol: EQK Exchange: NYSE
Industry: Banks - Northeast

Equitable Cos., Inc., The
787 Seventh Ave.
New York, NY 10019
Phone: 212-554-1234 Fax: 212-554-2320
CEO: Richard H. Jenrette
CFO: Jerry M. de St. Paer
1992 Sales: $6.3 million Employees: 5
Symbol: EQ Exchange: NYSE
Industry: Insurance - life, financial services

Equitable of Iowa Companies
699 Walnut St.
Des Moines, IA 50309
Phone: 515-282-1335 Fax: 515-282-9538
CEO: Frederick S. Hubbell
CFO: Paul E. Larson
1991 Sales: $730 million Employees: 17,854
Symbol: EQIC Exchange: NASDAQ
Industry: Insurance - life

Equitable Real Estate Shopping Centers L.P.
31 W. 52nd St., 10th Fl.
New York, NY 10019
Phone: 212-767-3400 Fax: —
CEO: Jeffrey C. Carter
CFO: Karen A. Cassidy
1991 Sales: $30 million Employees: —
Symbol: EQM Exchange: NYSE
Industry: Real estate operations

Equitable Resources, Inc.
420 Boulevard of the Allies
Pittsburgh, PA 15219
Phone: 412-261-3000 Fax: 412-553-5914
CEO: Donald I. Moritz
CFO: Robert E. Daley
1991 Sales: $680 million Employees: 2,223
Symbol: EQT Exchange: NYSE
Industry: Utility - gas distribution

Equitex, Inc.
7315 E. Peakview Ave.
Englewood, CO 80111
Phone: 303-796-8940 Fax: 303-796-9762
CEO: Henry Fong
CFO: Henry Fong
1991 Sales: $6.1 million Employees: 4
Symbol: EQTX Exchange: NASDAQ
Industry: Financial - SBIC & commercial

indicates company is in *Hoover's Handbook of American Business.*

indicates company is in *Hoover's Handbook of World Business;* sales and employee numbers are for parent company.

Equitrac Corp.
836 Ponce de Leon Blvd.
Coral Gables, FL 33134
Phone: 305-442-2060 Fax: 305-442-0687
CEO: George P. Wilson
CFO: Scott J. Modist
1992 Sales: $24 million Employees: 220
Symbol: ETRC Exchange: NASDAQ
Industry: Computers - services

Equity Oil Co.
10 W. Broadway, Ste. 806
Salt Lake City, UT 84101
Phone: 801-521-3515 Fax: 801-521-3534
CEO: Fred H. Evans
CFO: Clay Newton
1991 Sales: $15 million Employees: 18
Symbol: EQTY Exchange: NASDAQ
Industry: Oil & gas - US exploration & production

ER Carpenter Company, Inc.
PO Box 27205
Richmond, VA 23261
Phone: 804-359-0800 Fax: 804-353-0694
CEO: Stanley F. Pauley
CFO: Art Markey
1991 Sales: $549 million Employees: 8,250
Ownership: Privately held
Industry: Chemicals - specialty; polyurethane foam

Ergodyne Corp.
1410 Energy Park Dr. #1
St. Paul, MN 55108
Phone: 612-642-9889 Fax: 612-642-1882
CEO: Tom Votel
CFO: Tom Votel
1991 Sales: $12 million Employees: 27
Ownership: Privately held
Industry: Protection - safety equipment & technology

Ericsson North America, Inc.
730 International Pkwy.
Richardson, TX 75081
Phone: 214-669-9900 Fax: 214-669-1374
CEO: Leif Kallen
CFO: —
1991 Sales: $8,310 million Employees: 71,247
Parent: LM Ericsson Telephone Company
Industry: Telecommunications equipment

ERLY Industries Inc.
10990 Wilshire Blvd. #1800
Los Angeles, CA 90024
Phone: 213-879-1480 Fax: 213-473-8890
CEO: Gerald D. Murphy
CFO: Richard N. McCombs
1992 Sales: $352 million Employees: 1,014
Symbol: ERLY Exchange: NASDAQ
Industry: Food - flour & grain

ERM-Rocky Mountain Inc.
5950 S. Willow Dr. #200
Englewood, CO 80111
Phone: 303-741-5050 Fax: 303-773-2624
CEO: Robert Arnott
CFO: Robert Arnott
1991 Sales: $4.8 million Employees: 56
Ownership: Privately held
Industry: Environmental consulting

Ernst & Young
277 Park Ave., 23rd Fl.
New York, NY 10172
Phone: 212-773-3000 Fax: 212-773-2821
CEO: Ray J. Groves
CFO: Robert G. Streit
1991 Sales: $5,406 million Employees: 67,000
Ownership: Privately held
Industry: Business services - accounting & consulting

ESB Bancorp, Inc.
2301 Sheffield Rd.
Aliquippa, PA 15001
Phone: 412-378-4436 Fax: —
CEO: Charles Delman
CFO: Robert C. Hilliard
1991 Sales: $12 million Employees: 33
Symbol: ESBB Exchange: NASDAQ
Industry: Financial - savings and loans

ESCAgenetics Corp.
830 Bransten Rd.
San Carlos, CA 94070
Phone: 415-595-5335 Fax: 415-595-4332
CEO: Raymond J. Moshy
CFO: William J. Koenig
1992 Sales: $1.7 million Employees: 54
Symbol: ESN Exchange: AMEX
Industry: Biomedical & genetic products

Escalade, Inc.
817 Maxwell Ave.
Evansville, IN 47717
Phone: 812-426-2281 Fax: 812-425-1425
CEO: Robert E. Griffin
CFO: John R. Wilson
1991 Sales: $89 million Employees: 1,000
Symbol: ESCA Exchange: NASDAQ
Industry: Sporting goods, office & graphic arts products

ESCO Electronics Corp.
8100 W. Florissant Ave.
St. Louis, MO 63136
Phone: 314-553-7777 Fax: 314-553-3517
CEO: J. J. Adorjan
CFO: P. M. Ford
1991 Sales: $481 million Employees: 5,200
Symbol: ESE Exchange: NYSE
Industry: Electronics - military

ESE Inc.
3600 Downwind Dr.
Marshfield, WI 54449
Phone: 715-387-4778 Fax: 715-387-0125
CEO: Mark Weber
CFO: Mark Weber
1992 Sales: $4.2 million Employees: 39
Ownership: Privately held
Industry: Engineering services - process control & data acquisition engineering

ESELCO, Inc.
725 E. Portage Ave.
Sault Ste. Marie, MI 49783
Phone: 906-632-2221 Fax: —
CEO: Thomas S. Nurnberger
CFO: David R. Hubbard
1991 Sales: $29 million Employees: 96
Symbol: EDSE Exchange: NASDAQ
Industry: Utility - electric power

ESI Industries, Inc.
Stausser/Industrial Park
Taylor, NJ 18504
Phone: 717-562-0115 Fax: —
CEO: Herbert M. Gardner
CFO: Peter P. Borsuk
1991 Sales: $82 million Employees: 960
Symbol: ESI Exchange: AMEX
Industry: Automotive & trucking - original equipment

Eskimo Pie Corp.
7204 Glen Forest Dr.
Richmond, VA 23226
Phone: 804-560-8400 Fax: 804-330-3537
CEO: David V. Clark
CFO: William M. Fariss, Jr.
1991 Sales: $61 million Employees: 130
Symbol: EPIE Exchange: NASDAQ
Industry: Food - dairy products

Espey Manufacturing & Electronics Corp.
Congress & Ballston Avenues
Saratoga Springs, NY 12866
Phone: 518-584-4100 Fax: 518-584-4330
CEO: Sol Pinsley
CFO: Garry M. Jones
1992 Sales: $16 million Employees: 217
Symbol: ESP Exchange: AMEX
Industry: Electronics - military

Esprit de Corp.
900 Minnesota St.
San Francisco, CA 94107
Phone: 415-648-6900 Fax: 415-550-4890
CEO: Fritz Ammann
CFO: Jim Sulat
1991 Sales: $552 million Employees: 4,200
Ownership: Privately held
Industry: Apparel

Esquire Radio & Electronics, Inc.
4100 First Ave.
Brooklyn, NY 11232
Phone: 718-499-0020 Fax: 718-499-6494
CEO: A. Robert Lieberman
CFO: Harvey Lieberman
1991 Sales: $68 million Employees: 200
Symbol: EE Exchange: AMEX
Industry: Telecommunications equipment

Essef Corp.
220 Park Dr.
Chardon, OH 44024
Phone: 216-286-2200 Fax: 216-286-2206
CEO: James A. Horner
CFO: John B. Calfee, Jr.
1991 Sales: $96 million Employees: 630
Symbol: ESSF Exchange: NASDAQ
Industry: Machinery - general industrial

Essex Corp.
9170 Rumsey Rd.
Columbia, MD 21045
Phone: 410-730-1097 Fax: —
CEO: Harry L. Letaw, Jr.
CFO: Joseph R. Kurry, Jr.
1991 Sales: $17 million Employees: 170
Symbol: ESEX Exchange: NASDAQ
Industry: Engineering - R&D services

Essex County Gas Co.
7 N. Hunt Rd.
Amesbury, MA 01913
Phone: 508-388-4000 Fax: 508-388-4428
CEO: Charles E. Billups
CFO: L. David Vincola
1991 Sales: $38 million Employees: 123
Symbol: ECGC Exchange: NASDAQ
Industry: Utility - gas distribution

Essex Financial Partners L.P.
370 17th St., Ste. 4125
Denver, CO 80202
Phone: 800-477-8209 Fax: —
CEO: Gene D. Ross
CFO: Gene D. Ross
1991 Sales: $58 million Employees: 209
Symbol: ESX Exchange: AMEX
Industry: Financial - savings and loans

Essex Group Inc.
1601 Wall St.
Ft. Wayne, IN 46802
Phone: 219-461-4000 Fax: 219-461-4150
CEO: Stanley C. Craft
CFO: David C. Minzie
1991 Sales: $886 million Employees: 3,400
Ownership: Privately held
Industry: Wire & cable products & electrical insulation

Esstar Inc.
555 Long Wharf Dr., Ste. 12
New Haven, CT 06511
Phone: 203-777-2274 Fax: 203-785-8851
CEO: Robert A. Haversat, Sr.
CFO: Jeffrey A. Mereschuk
1990 Sales: $510 million Employees: 4,000
Ownership: Privately held
Industry: Metal products - hardware

Estée Lauder Inc.
767 Fifth Ave.
New York, NY 10153
Phone: 212-572-4200 Fax: 212-572-3941
CEO: Leonard A. Lauder
CFO: Robert J. Bigler
1991 Sales: $2,420 million Employees: 12,000
Ownership: Privately held
Industry: Cosmetics & toiletries

Esterline Corp.
10800 NE 8th St., Ste. 600
Bellevue, WA 98004
Phone: 206-453-6001 Fax: 206-453-2916
CEO: Wendell P. Hurlbut
CFO: Robert W. Stevenson
1991 Sales: $351 million Employees: 3,500
Symbol: ESL Exchange: NYSE
Industry: Instruments - control

ESW Inc. (Educational Systems Workshops)
1200 Sheffield Ave.
Dyer, IN 46311
Phone: 219-865-1318 Fax: 219-865-2775
CEO: James F. Razumich
CFO: Lawrence M. Caldwell
1991 Sales: $1.4 million Employees: 39
Ownership: Privately held
Industry: Business services - custom industrial training

Ethan Allen Inc.
Ethan Allen Dr.
Danbury, CT 06813
Phone: 203-743-8000 Fax: 203-743-8293
CEO: M. Farooq Kathwari
CFO: Ed Schade
1991 Sales: $675 million Employees: 9,000
Ownership: Privately held
Industry: Retail - home furnishings; furniture, accessories, rugs

Ethix Corp.
12655 SW Center St.
Beaverton, OR 97005
Phone: 503-643-8449 Fax: 503-626-4449
CEO: Stephen Gregg
CFO: Frederick J. Davidson
1992 Sales: $25 million Employees: 400
Ownership: Privately held
Industry: Healthcare - management services

Ethyl Corp.
330 S. Fourth St.
Richmond, VA 23217
Phone: 804-788-5000 Fax: 804-788-5688
CEO: Floyd D. Gottwald, Jr.
CFO: Charles B. Walker
1992 Sales: $2,975 million Employees: 6,000
Symbol: EY Exchange: NYSE
Industry: Chemicals - specialty

European Toy Collection
6643 Melton Rd.
Portage, IN 46368
Phone: 219-763-3234 Fax: 219-762-1740
CEO: Mel Brown
CFO: Mel Brown
1991 Sales: $2.3 million Employees: 9
Ownership: Privately held
Industry: Toys & gifts

Evans, Inc.
36 S. State St.
Chicago, IL 60603
Phone: 312-855-2000 Fax: 312-855-2128
CEO: David B. Meltzer
CFO: Patrick J. Regan
1992 Sales: $103 million Employees: 1,000
Symbol: EVAN Exchange: NASDAQ
Industry: Retail - apparel & furs

Evans & Sutherland Computer Corp.
600 Komas Dr.
Salt Lake City, UT 84108
Phone: 801-582-5847 Fax: —
CEO: Rodney S. Rougelot
CFO: J. Robert Driggs
1991 Sales: $145 million Employees: 1,300
Symbol: ESCC Exchange: NASDAQ
Industry: Computers - graphics

Evansville Federal Savings Bank
18 NW 4th St.
Evansville, IN 47706
Phone: 812-424-0921 Fax: 812-429-0542
CEO: Edward A. Newton
CFO: John O. Meeks
1992 Sales: — Employees: 37
Symbol: EVSB Exchange: NASDAQ
Industry: Financial - savings and loans

Everest & Jennings International Ltd.
1100 Corporate Square Dr.
St. Louis, MO 63132
Phone: 314-569-3515 Fax: 314-569-3808
CEO: Robert Sutherland
CFO: Warren J. Nelson III
1991 Sales: $119 million Employees: 1,221
Symbol: EJ.A Exchange: AMEX
Industry: Medical products - wheelchairs, hospital beds, oxygen therapy products

Everex Systems, Inc.
48431 Milmont Dr.
Fremont, CA 94538
Phone: 510-498-1111 Fax: 510-651-0728
CEO: Jack Kenny
CFO: Jack Kirby
1991 Sales: $425 million Employees: 2,285
Trading Status: Suspended
Industry: Computers - mini & micro

Evergreen Bancorp, Inc.
237 Glen St.
Glens Falls, NY 12801
Phone: 518-792-1151 Fax: —
CEO: William L. Bitner III
CFO: Daniel Pekrol
1991 Sales: $87 million Employees: 406
Symbol: EVGN Exchange: NASDAQ
Industry: Banks - Northeast

Evergreen Environmental Group, Inc.
7416 Hwy. 329
Crestwood, KY 40014
Phone: 502-241-4171 Fax: 502-241-4347
CEO: Jerry McCandless
CFO: Kendrick McCandless
1991 Sales: $4.2 million Employees: 29
Ownership: Privately held
Industry: Environmental engineering

Evergreen Healthcare/National Heritage Inc.
11350 N. Meridian, Ste. 200
Carmel, IN 75248
Phone: 317-580-8585 Fax: 317-580-8575
CEO: Robert M. Galecke
CFO: Joseph L. Rzepka
1992 Sales: $52 million Employees: 2,358
Symbol: NHR Exchange: NYSE
Industry: Nursing homes

Evergreen Resources, Inc.
1512 Larimer St.
Denver, CO 80202
Phone: 303-534-0400 Fax: 303-534-0420
CEO: James C. Ryan, Jr.
CFO: Timothy G. Corey
1992 Sales: $3 million Employees: 32
Symbol: EVER Exchange: NASDAQ
Industry: Oil & gas - US exploration & production

Exabyte Corp.
1685 38th St.
Boulder, CO 80301
Phone: 303-442-4333 Fax: 303-442-4269
CEO: Peter D. Behrendt
CFO: William L. Marriner
1992 Sales: $287 million Employees: 877
Symbol: EXBT Exchange: NASDAQ
Industry: Computers - peripheral equipment; cartridge tape subsystems

Exar Corp.
2222 Qume Dr.
San Jose, CA 95131
Phone: 408-434-6400 Fax: 408-943-8245
CEO: Kozo Sato
CFO: Ronald W. Guire
1992 Sales: $140 million Employees: 501
Symbol: EXAR Exchange: NASDAQ
Industry: Electrical components - semiconductors

Excalibur Technologies Corp.
2300 Buena Vista Dr. SE
Albuquerque, NM 87106
Phone: 505-764-0081 Fax: 505-764-0087
CEO: Richard H. Duddy
CFO: Douglas R. Johnson
1991 Sales: $4.9 million Employees: 78
Symbol: EXCA Exchange: NASDAQ
Industry: Computers - software

Excel Industries, Inc.
1120 N. Main St.
Elkhart, IN 46514
Phone: 219-264-2131 Fax: 219-264-2136
CEO: James J. Lohman
CFO: Joseph A. Robinson
1991 Sales: $352 million Employees: 2,940
Symbol: EXC Exchange: AMEX
Industry: Automotive & trucking - original equipment

Excel Technology, Inc.
101-2 Colin Dr.
Holbrook, NY 11741
Phone: 516-563-7067 Fax: —
CEO: C. R. Rao
CFO: C. R. Rao
1991 Sales: $0.3 million Employees: 10
Symbol: XLTC Exchange: NASDAQ
Industry: Lasers - systems & components

Executive Software
701 N. Brand Blvd., 6th Fl.
Glendale, CA 91203
Phone: 800-829-4357 Fax: 818-545-9241
CEO: Craig Jensen
CFO: Sally Jensen
1991 Sales: $15 million Employees: 95
Ownership: Privately held
Industry: Computers - VAX/VMS software

Executive TeleCard, Ltd.
8 Avenue C
Nanuet, NY 10954
Phone: 914-627-2060 Fax: —
CEO: William V. Moore
CFO: William V. Moore
1992 Sales: $3.2 million Employees: —
Symbol: EXTL Exchange: NASDAQ
Industry: Telecommunications services - telephone charge card

EXECUTONE Information Systems, Inc.
6 Thorndal Circle
Darien, CT 06820
Phone: 203-655-6500 Fax: 203-655-7872
CEO: Alan Kessman
CFO: Michael W. Yacenda
1991 Sales: $267 million Employees: 2,200
Symbol: XTON Exchange: NASDAQ
Industry: Telecommunications equipment - hospital, voice & data communications equipment

Exide Corp.
645 Penn St.
Reading, PA 19601
Phone: 215-378-0500 Fax: 215-378-0616
CEO: Arthur Hawkins
CFO: Richard Touve
1992 Sales: $600 million Employees: 4,500
Ownership: Privately held
Industry: Electrical products - auto & industrial batteries

Exide Electronics Corp.
3201 Spring Forest Rd.
Raleigh, NC 27604
Phone: 919-872-3020 Fax: 919-870-3250
CEO: James A. Risher
CFO: Marty R. Kittrell
1991 Sales: $192 million Employees: 1,300
Symbol: XUPS Exchange: NASDAQ
Industry: Electrical products - uninterruptible power supply products

Expeditors International of Washington, Inc.
19119 16th Ave. South
Seattle, WA 98188
Phone: 206-246-3711 Fax: 206-246-3197
CEO: Peter J. Rose
CFO: Gary E. Fowler
1991 Sales: $254 million Employees: 927
Symbol: EXPD Exchange: NASDAQ
Industry: Transportation - services

Exploration Company of Louisiana, Inc.
110 Rue Jean Lafitte
Lafayette, LA 70508
Phone: 318-237-0325 Fax: 318-237-3316
CEO: Marsden W. Miller, Jr.
CFO: William D. Crays
1991 Sales: $11 million Employees: 51
Symbol: XCL Exchange: AMEX
Industry: Oil & gas - US exploration & production

Express Scripts, Inc.
2369 Schuetz Rd.
St. Louis, MO 63146
Phone: 314-567-4661 Fax: —
CEO: Barrett A. Toan
CFO: Stuart I. Bascomb
1991 Sales: $47 million Employees: 222
Symbol: ESRX Exchange: NASDAQ
Industry: Medical services

Exxon Corp.
225 E. John W. Carpenter Fwy.
Irving, TX 75062
Phone: 214-444-1000 Fax: 214-444-1505
CEO: Lee R. Raymond
CFO: E. A. Robinson
1992 Sales: $104,111 million Employees: 101,000
Symbol: XON Exchange: NYSE
Industry: Oil & gas - international integrated

EZCORP, Inc.
1901 Capital Pkwy.
Austin, TX 78701
Phone: 512-314-3400 Fax: 512-314-3404
CEO: Courtland L. Logue, Jr.
CFO: Gary S. Kofnovec
1992 Sales: $49 million Employees: 919
Symbol: EZPW Exchange: NASDAQ
Industry: Retail - pawn shops

F.A. Tucker Group, Inc.
75 E. Wacker Dr., Ste. 1300
Chicago, IL 60601
Phone: 312-368-0653 Fax: —
CEO: Stephen P. Hayman
CFO: Alan J. Hayman
1991 Sales: $32 million Employees: 404
Symbol: TCK Exchange: AMEX
Industry: Construction - heavy

F & C Bancshares, Inc.
410 Taylor St.
Punta Gorda, FL 33950
Phone: 813-639-2141 Fax: —
CEO: D. R. Witter, Jr.
CFO: Ronald W. Miller
1992 Sales: — Employees: —
Symbol: FSCC Exchange: NASDAQ
Industry: Financial - savings and loans

F & C International, Inc.
11260 Chester Rd.
Cincinnati, OH 11237
Phone: 513-771-5904 Fax: 513-782-5145
CEO: Jon P. Fries
CFO: David E. Ziegler
1992 Sales: $58 million Employees: 435
Symbol: FCIN Exchange: NASDAQ
Industry: Food - flavors & fragrances

F.F.O. Financial Group, Inc.
2200 Live Oak Blvd.
St. Cloud, FL 34771
Phone: 407-892-1200 Fax: —
CEO: James B. Davis
CFO: James B. Davis
1992 Sales: $9.3 million Employees: 228
Symbol: FFFG Exchange: NASDAQ
Industry: Financial - savings and loans

F & M National Corp.
38 Rouss Ave.
Winchester, VA 22601
Phone: 703-665-4200 Fax: —
CEO: W. M. Feltner
CFO: Barbara H. Ward
1991 Sales: $88 million Employees: 144
Symbol: FMNT Exchange: NASDAQ
Industry: Banks - Southeast

F&M Bancorp
110 Thomas Johnson Dr.
Frederick, MD 21702
Phone: 301-694-4000 Fax: —
CEO: Charles W. Hoff III
CFO: Gordon M. Cooley
1991 Sales: $53 million Employees: 353
Symbol: FMBN Exchange: NASDAQ
Industry: Banks - Northeast

Fab Industries, Inc.
200 Madison Ave.
New York, NY 10016
Phone: 212-279-9000 Fax: 212-689-6929
CEO: Samson Bitensky
CFO: Howard Soren
1991 Sales: $186 million Employees: 1,900
Symbol: FIT Exchange: AMEX
Industry: Textiles - mill products

Fabri-Centers of America, Inc.
5555 Darrow Rd.
Hudson, OH 44236
Phone: 216-656-2600 Fax: 216-656-3057
CEO: Alan Rosskamm
CFO: Robert Norton
1991 Sales: $469 million Employees: 10,200
Symbol: FCA Exchange: NYSE
Industry: Retail - fabric & notions

Failure Analysis Assoc., Inc.
149 Commonwealth Dr.
Menlo Park, CA 94025
Phone: 415-326-9400 Fax: 415-326-8072
CEO: Roger L. McCarthy
CFO: Duane W. Bell
1992 Sales: $70 million Employees: 450
Symbol: FAIL Exchange: NASDAQ
Industry: Engineering - R&D services

Fair, Isaac and Co., Inc.
120 N. Redwood Dr.
San Rafael, CA 94903
Phone: 415-472-2211 Fax: 415-492-9381
CEO: Larry E. Rosenberger
CFO: Gerald de Kerchove
1991 Sales: $32 million Employees: 347
Symbol: FICI Exchange: NASDAQ
Industry: Business services

Fairchild Corp.
300 W. Service Rd.
Chantilly, VA 22021
Phone: 703-478-5800 Fax: 703-478-5915
CEO: Jeffrey J. Steiner
CFO: Michael T. Alcox
1992 Sales: $490 million Employees: 4,100
Symbol: FA Exchange: NYSE
Industry: Aerospace - aircraft equipment

Fairfield Communities, Inc.
2800 Cantrell Rd.
Little Rock, AR 72202
Phone: 501-664-6000 Fax: —
CEO: John W. McConnell
CFO: John W. McConnell
1991 Sales: $132 million Employees: 1,850
Symbol: FCI Exchange: NYSE
Industry: Building - residential & commercial

Falcon Cable Systems Co.
10866 Wilshire Blvd., Ste. 500
Los Angeles, CA 90024
Phone: 310-470-4884 Fax: 310-470-4497
CEO: Marc B. Nathanson
CFO: Michael K. Menerey
1991 Sales: $46 million Employees: 173
Symbol: FAL Exchange: AMEX
Industry: Cable TV

Falcon Microsystems Inc.
1100 Mercantile Ln.
Landover, MD 20785
Phone: 301-341-0100 Fax: 301-341-0187
CEO: Dendy Young
CFO: Bob Russell
1992 Sales: $170 million Employees: 290
Ownership: Privately held
Industry: Computers - Macintosh, networks & software

Falcon Oil & Gas Co., Inc.
4801 Woodway, Ste. 330-W
Houston, TX 77056
Phone: 713-623-0853 Fax: —
CEO: Spencer M. Murchison
CFO: Gary R. Jackson
1991 Sales: $3.4 million Employees: 8
Symbol: FLOG Exchange: NASDAQ
Industry: Oil & gas - US exploration & production

Falcon Products, Inc.
9387 Dielman Industrial Dr.
St. Louis, MO 63132
Phone: 314-991-9200 Fax: 314-991-9227
CEO: Franklin A. Jacobs
CFO: Stephen L. Clanton
1991 Sales: $39 million Employees: —
Symbol: FLCP Exchange: NASDAQ
Industry: Furniture - tables, booths, chairs, sheet metal kitchen equipment

Family Bancorp
153 Merrimack St.
Haverhill, MA 01830
Phone: 508-374-1911 Fax: —
CEO: Philip C. Hefner
CFO: George E. Fahey
1991 Sales: $52 million Employees: 239
Symbol: FMLY Exchange: NASDAQ
Industry: Banks - Northeast

Family Dollar Stores, Inc.
10401 Old Monroe Rd.
Matthews, NC 28105
Phone: 704-847-6961 Fax: 704-847-5534
CEO: Leon Levine
CFO: C. Scott Litten
1992 Sales: $1,199 million Employees: 13,400
Symbol: FDO Exchange: NYSE
Industry: Retail - discount & variety; soft goods

Family Steak Houses of Florida, Inc.
2113 Florida Blvd.
Neptune Beach, FL 32233
Phone: 904-249-4197 Fax: —
CEO: James W. Osborn
CFO: Edward B. Alexander
1991 Sales: $48 million Employees: 1,800
Symbol: RYFL Exchange: NASDAQ
Industry: Retail - food & restaurants

Fanamation
555 W. Victoria St.
Compton, CA 90220
Phone: 310-604-6041 Fax: 310-764-4847
CEO: Mark Towaalfhoven
CFO: Mark Towaalfhoven
1991 Sales: $5.6 million Employees: 48
Ownership: Privately held
Industry: Electronics - measuring instruments

Fansteel Inc.
Number One Tantalum Place
North Chicago, IL 60064
Phone: 708-689-4900 Fax: 708-689-0307
CEO: Keith R. Garrity
CFO: R. M. McEntee
1991 Sales: $135 million Employees: 1,190
Symbol: FNL Exchange: NYSE
Industry: Metal processing & fabrication

Farah Inc.
8889 Gateway West
El Paso, TX 79925
Phone: 915-593-4444 Fax: 915-593-4203
CEO: Richard C. Allender
CFO: James C. Swaim
1991 Sales: $151 million Employees: 4,600
Symbol: FRA Exchange: NYSE
Industry: Textiles - apparel for men & boys

Farley Industries Inc.
233 S. Wacker Dr., Ste. 5000
Chicago, IL 60606
Phone: 312-876-7000 Fax: 312-993-1749
CEO: William Farley
CFO: Paul M. O'Hara
1990 Sales: $893 million Employees: 33,000
Ownership: Privately held
Industry: Diversified operations - apparel, boots & auto parts

Farm Fresh Inc.
7530 Tidewater Dr.
Norfolk, VA 23505
Phone: 804-480-6700 Fax: 804-480-6399
CEO: Michael E. Julian
CFO: Keith E. Alessi
1991 Sales: $650 million Employees: 3,000
Ownership: Privately held
Industry: Retail - supermarkets

Farm & Home Financial Corp.
221 W. Cherry
Nevada, MO 64772
Phone: 417-667-3333 Fax: 417-667-5619
CEO: John Morton III
CFO: J. C. Alstrin
1991 Sales: $311 million Employees: 734
Symbol: FAHS Exchange: NASDAQ
Industry: Financial - savings and loans

Farmer Bros. Co.
20333 S. Normandie Ave.
Torrance, CA 90502
Phone: 310-320-1212 Fax: 310-320-2436
CEO: Roy F. Farmer
CFO: John Simmons
1991 Sales: $196 million Employees: 1,217
Symbol: FARM Exchange: NASDAQ
Industry: Food - wholesale coffee, spices, food

Farr Co.
2221 Park Place
El Segundo, CA 90245
Phone: 213-772-5221 Fax: 310-643-9086
CEO: Charles R. Wofford
CFO: Jack D. Carr
1991 Sales: $112 million Employees: 1,263
Symbol: FARC Exchange: NASDAQ
Industry: Filtration products

Farragut Mortgage Co., Inc.
21 Oxford Rd.
Mansfield, MA 02048
Phone: 508-337-8605 Fax: —
CEO: Edward D. LaGarde
CFO: Kenneth J. MacLeod
1991 Sales: $2.4 million Employees: 46
Symbol: FMS Exchange: AMEX
Industry: Financial - mortgages & related services

Farrel Corp.
25 Main St.
Ansonia, CT 06401
Phone: 203-736-5500 Fax: 203-735-6267
CEO: Rolf K. Liebergesell
CFO: Allan J. Williamson
1992 Sales: $96 million Employees: 624
Symbol: FARL Exchange: NASDAQ
Industry: Engineering - R&D services

Fastenal Co.
2001 Theurer Blvd.
Winona, MN 55987
Phone: 507-454-5374 Fax: 507-454-6542
CEO: Robert A. Kierlin
CFO: Stephen M. Slaggie
1991 Sales: $62 million Employees: 648
Symbol: FAST Exchange: NASDAQ
Industry: Building products - retail & wholesale

Faxon
15 Southwest Park
Westwood, MA 02090
Phone: 617-329-3350 Fax: 617-329-9875
CEO: Richard R. Rowe
CFO: Mark Zuroff
1991 Sales: $505 million Employees: 865
Ownership: Privately held
Industry: Periodical wholesale

Fay's, Inc.
7245 Henry Clay Blvd.
Liverpool, NY 13088
Phone: 315-451-8000 Fax: 315-451-2470
CEO: Henry A. Panasci, Jr.
CFO: James F. Poole, Jr.
1992 Sales: $884 million Employees: 8,800
Symbol: FAY Exchange: NYSE
Industry: Retail - drug stores

FDP Corp.
2140 S. Dixie Hwy.
Miami, FL 33133
Phone: 305-858-8200 Fax: 305-858-7282
CEO: Michael C. Goldberg
CFO: Michael C. Goldberg
1991 Sales: $16 million Employees: 192
Symbol: FDPC Exchange: NASDAQ
Industry: Computers - life insurance & employee benefit software

Fedders Corp.
158 Hwy. 206
Peapack, NJ 07977
Phone: 908-234-2100 Fax: 908-234-0906
CEO: Salvatore Giordano, Jr.
CFO: Robert L. Laurent, Jr.
1991 Sales: $196 million Employees: 1,900
Symbol: FJQ Exchange: NYSE
Industry: Building products - a/c & heating

Federal Express Corp.
2005 Corporate Ave.
Memphis, TN 38132
Phone: 901-369-3600 Fax: 901-795-1027
CEO: Frederick W. Smith
CFO: Alan B. Graf
1992 Sales: $7,611 million Employees: 95,000
Symbol: FDX Exchange: NYSE
Industry: Transportation - air freight

Federal Home Loan Mortgage Corp.
8200 Jones Branch Dr.
McLean, VA 22102
Phone: 800-336-3672 Fax: —
CEO: Leland C. Brendsel
CFO: Paul T. Peterson
1991 Sales: $4,219 million Employees: —
Symbol: FRE Exchange: NYSE
Industry: Financial - mortgages & related services

Federal Investment Co., Inc.
100 Amaral St.
East Providence, RI 02915
Phone: 401-435-4400 Fax: 401-431-0900
CEO: James S. Gladney
CFO: Roderick A. Mitchell
1991 Sales: $20 million Employees: 40
Ownership: Privately held
Industry: Real estate development & property-brokerage services

Federal National Mortgage Association
3900 Wisconsin Ave. NW
Washington, DC 20016
Phone: 202-752-7000 Fax: 202-752-6099
CEO: James A. Johnson
CFO: J. Timothy Howard
1992 Sales: $14,558 million Employees: 2,765
Symbol: FNM Exchange: NYSE
Industry: Financial - mortgages & related services

Federal Paper Board Co., Inc.
75 Chestnut Ridge Rd.
Montvale, NJ 07645
Phone: 201-391-1776 Fax: 201-307-6125
CEO: John R. Kennedy
CFO: Thomas L. Cox
1992 Sales: $1,461 million Employees: 7,000
Symbol: FBO Exchange: NYSE
Industry: Paper & paper products

Federal Savings Bank, The
94 W. Main St.
New Britain, CT 06050
Phone: 203-225-7707 Fax: —
CEO: Frank J. Borrelli, Jr.
CFO: John R. Smith
1992 Sales: — Employees: —
Symbol: TFSB Exchange: NASDAQ
Industry: Financial - savings and loans

Federal Screw Works
2400 Buhl Bldg.
Detroit, MI 48226
Phone: 313-963-2323 Fax: 313-963-0755
CEO: W. T. ZurSchmiede, Jr.
CFO: W. T. ZurSchmiede, Jr.
1992 Sales: $68 million Employees: 498
Symbol: FSCR Exchange: NASDAQ
Industry: Metal products - fabrication

Federal Signal Corp.
1415 W. 22nd St., Ste. 1100
Oak Brook, IL 60521
Phone: 708-954-2000 Fax: 708-954-2030
CEO: Joseph J. Ross
CFO: Charles R. Campbell
1991 Sales: $467 million Employees: 4,212
Symbol: FSS Exchange: NYSE
Industry: Diversified operations - emergency vehicles, cutting tools, communications equipment

Federal-Mogul Corp.
PO Box 1966
Detroit, MI 48235
Phone: 313-354-7700 Fax: 313-354-8950
CEO: Dennis J. Gormley
CFO: Martin E. Welch III
1992 Sales: $1,264 million Employees: 13,500
Symbol: FMO Exchange: NYSE
Industry: Automotive & trucking - replacement parts

Federated Bank, S.S.B.
2600 N. Mayfair Rd.
Wauwatosa, WI 53226
Phone: 414-257-2100 Fax: 414-475-9107
CEO: Robert B. Pieters
CFO: Brian B. Blank
1992 Sales: — Employees: —
Symbol: FEDF Exchange: NASDAQ
Industry: Financial - savings and loans

Federated Department Stores, Inc.
7 W. Seventh St.
Cincinnati, OH 45202
Phone: 513-579-7000 Fax: 513-579-7555
CEO: Allen I. Questrom
CFO: Ronald W. Tysoe
1992 Sales: $6,952 million Employees: 78,900
Symbol: FD Exchange: NYSE
Industry: Retail - major department stores

FedFirst Bancshares, Inc.
230 N. Cherry St.
Winston-Salem, NC 27101
Phone: 919-723-3604 Fax: —
CEO: William G. White, Jr.
CFO: Ted A. Boyer
1991 Sales: $35 million Employees: 79
Symbol: FFBS Exchange: NASDAQ
Industry: Financial - savings and loans

Fenders & More Inc.
85 Cleveland St.
Nashville, TN 37207
Phone: 615-226-9090 Fax: 615-226-9577
CEO: Dewey Morris, Jr.
CFO: Randall Matthews
1992 Sales: $13 million Employees: 100
Ownership: Privately held
Industry: Auto parts - wholesale parts & accessories

Ferrellgas
One Liberty Plaza
Liberty, MO 64068
Phone: 816-792-1600 Fax: 816-792-7985
CEO: James E. Ferrell
CFO: Geoffrey H. Ramsden
1991 Sales: $501 million Employees: 3,000
Ownership: Privately held
Industry: Energy - propane gas

Ferro Corp.
1000 Lakeside Ave. E
Cleveland, OH 44144
Phone: 216-641-8580 Fax: Ext. 6133
CEO: Adolph Posnick
CFO: Hector R. Ortino
1992 Sales: $1,098 million Employees: 7,306
Symbol: FOE Exchange: NYSE
Industry: Paints & allied products

Ferrofluidics Corp.
40 Simon St.
Nashua, NH 03060
Phone: 603-883-9800 Fax: 603-883-2308
CEO: Ronald Moskowitz
CFO: Jan R. Kirk
1992 Sales: $27 million Employees: 197
Symbol: FERO Exchange: NASDAQ
Industry: Electrical components - rotary sealing devices, crystal growing systems

FF Bancorp, Inc.
900 N. Dixie Fwy.
New Smyrna Beach, FL 32168
Phone: 904-428-2466 Fax: —
CEO: Frances R. Ford
CFO: Patricia J. Van Eck
1992 Sales: — Employees: —
Symbol: FFSB Exchange: NASDAQ
Industry: Financial - savings and loans

FFP Partners, L.P.
2801 Glenda Ave.
Ft. Worth, TX 76117
Phone: 817-838-4700 Fax: 817-831-3463
CEO: John Harvison
CFO: Steven B. Hawkins
1991 Sales: $211 million Employees: 1,404
Symbol: FFP Exchange: AMEX
Industry: Retail - convenience stores

FHP International Corp.
9900 Talbert Ave.
Fountain Valley, CA 92708
Phone: 714-963-7233 Fax: 714-964-5922
CEO: Westcott W. Price III
CFO: William R. Benz
1992 Sales: $1,756 million Employees: 9,900
Symbol: FHPC Exchange: NASDAQ
Industry: Health maintenance organization

Fiat USA, Inc.
375 Park Ave.
New York, NY 10152
Phone: 212-355-2600 Fax: 212-688-2848
CEO: Vittorio Vellano
CFO: —
1991 Sales: $49,206 million Employees: 287,957
Parent: Fiat SpA
Industry: Automotive manufacturing

Fiber Optic Technologies, Inc.
6555 S. Kenton St. #301
Englewood, CO 80111
Phone: 303-792-0770 Fax: 303-792-078
CEO: Keith Burge
CFO: Glenn Garvey
1991 Sales: $5.9 million Employees: 73
Ownership: Privately held
Industry: Fiber optics - voice & data network services

Fibreboard Corp.
1000 Burnett Ave., Ste. 410
Concord, CA 94520
Phone: 415-686-0700 Fax: 415-686-8751
CEO: John D. Roach
CFO: James P. Donohue
1991 Sales: $234 million Employees: 2,200
Symbol: FBD Exchange: AMEX
Industry: Building products - wood

Fibronics International Inc.
25 Communications Way
Hyannis, MA 02601
Phone: 508-778-0700 Fax: 508-778-0821
CEO: Gil Weiser
CFO: John T. Hislop
1991 Sales: $54 million Employees: 465
Symbol: FBRX Exchange: NASDAQ
Industry: Fiber optics

Fidelity Investments Inc.
82 Devonshire St.
Boston, MA 02109
Phone: 617-570-7000 Fax: 617-720-3836
CEO: Edward C. Johnson III
CFO: Ned Johnson
1991 Sales: $1,473 million Employees: 8,700
Ownership: Privately held
Industry: Financial - business services; mutual fund management, discount brokerage

Fidelity Medical, Inc.
6 Vreeland Rd.
Florham Park, NJ 07932
Phone: 201-377-0400 Fax: —
CEO: Werner J. Haas
CFO: Werner J. Haas
1991 Sales: $5.2 million Employees: 60
Symbol: FMSI Exchange: NASDAQ
Industry: Medical instruments - image-processing devices & electrocardiographs

Fidelity National Financial, Inc.
2100 SE Main St., Ste. 400
Irvine, CA 92714
Phone: 714-852-9770 Fax: —
CEO: William P. Foley II
CFO: Gary R. Nelson
1991 Sales: $221 million Employees: 2,800
Symbol: FNF Exchange: NYSE
Industry: Insurance - multiline & misc.

Fidelity Savings Bank
1009 Perry Hwy.
Pittsburgh, PA 15237
Phone: 412-367-3300 Fax: 919-627-3114
CEO: William L. Windisch
CFO: Richard G. Spencer
1992 Sales: — Employees: 63
Symbol: FSVA Exchange: NASDAQ
Industry: Financial - savings and loans

Field Brothers Construction
676 Bellefontaine
Marion, OH 43302
Phone: 614-382-1688 Fax: 614-382-9825
CEO: Joel A. Field
CFO: —
1991 Sales: $12 million Employees: 155
Ownership: Privately held
Industry: Construction - general contracting services

Fieldcrest Cannon, Inc.
326 E. Stadium Dr.
Eden, NC 27288
Phone: 919-627-3042 Fax: 919-627-3133
CEO: James M. Fitzgibbons
CFO: K. William Fraser, Jr.
1992 Sales: $1,217 million Employees: 17,407
Symbol: FLD Exchange: NYSE
Industry: Textiles - home furnishings; bed & bath products, carpets & rugs

Fiesta Mart Inc.
5235 Katy Fwy.
Houston, TX 77007
Phone: 713-869-5060 Fax: 713-869-6197
CEO: Donald L. Bonham
CFO: Robert Walker
1991 Sales: $600 million Employees: 5,000
Ownership: Privately held
Industry: Retail - supermarkets

indicates company is in *Hoover's Handbook of American Business.*

indicates company is in *Hoover's Handbook of World Business;* sales and employee numbers are for parent company.

Fifth Third Bank
38 Fountain Square Plaza
Cincinnati, OH 45263
Phone: 513-579-5300 Fax: 513-762-7577
CEO: George A. Schaefer, Jr.
CFO: P. Michael Brumm
1992 Sales: $895 million Employees: 4,159
Symbol: FITB Exchange: NASDAQ
Industry: Banks - Midwest

Figgie International Inc.
4420 Sherwin Rd.
Willoughby, OH 44094
Phone: 216-953-2700 Fax: 216-951-1724
CEO: Harry E. Figgie, Jr.
CFO: Joseph J. Skadra
1992 Sales: $1,173 million Employees: 13,700
Symbol: FIGI Exchange: NASDAQ
Industry: Diversified operations - vacuum cleaners, fire trucks, insurance, real estate

Filene's Basement Corp.
40 Walnut St.
Wellesley, MA 02181
Phone: 617-348-7000 Fax: —
CEO: Samuel J. Gerson
CFO: Peter D. Hughes
1991 Sales: $465 million Employees: 3,900
Symbol: BSMT Exchange: NASDAQ
Industry: Retail - discount & variety

FileNet Corp.
3565 Harbor Blvd.
Costa Mesa, CA 92626
Phone: 714-966-3400 Fax: 714-966-3440
CEO: Theodore J. Smith
CFO: Mark S. St. Clare
1991 Sales: $122 million Employees: 854
Symbol: FILE Exchange: NASDAQ
Industry: Computers - services

Filtertek, Inc.
11411 Price Rd.
Hebron, IL 60034
Phone: 815-648-2416 Fax: 815-648-2929
CEO: Michael H. Leason
CFO: Stephen P. Soltwedel
1991 Sales: $44 million Employees: 785
Symbol: FTK Exchange: NYSE
Industry: Chemicals - fibers

FINA, Inc.
FINA Plaza, 8350 N. Central Expwy.
Dallas, TX 75206
Phone: 214-750-2400 Fax: 214-750-2508
CEO: Ron W. Haddock
CFO: —
1992 Sales: $3,398 million Employees: 17,069
Parent: Petrofina SA
Industry: Oil & gas - international integrated; chemicals & paints

Financial Federal Corp.
745 Fifth Ave.
New York, NY 10151
Phone: 212-888-3344 Fax: —
CEO: Clarence Y. Palitz, Jr.
CFO: Michael C. Palitz
1991 Sales: $17 million Employees: 67
Symbol: FINF Exchange: NASDAQ
Industry: Financial - business services

Fingerhut Companies, Inc.
4400 Baker Rd.
Minnetonka, MN 55343
Phone: 612-932-3100 Fax: 612-932-3292
CEO: Theodore Deikel
CFO: Michael A. Qualen
1992 Sales: $1,606 million Employees: 10,700
Symbol: FHT Exchange: NYSE
Industry: Retail - mail order & direct

Fingermatrix, Inc.
30 Virginia Rd.
North White Plains, NY 10603
Phone: 914-428-5441 Fax: 914-428-0971
CEO: Michael Schiller
CFO: Michael Schiller
1991 Sales: $0.9 million Employees: —
Symbol: FINX Exchange: NASDAQ
Industry: Electro-optical fingerprint verification systems

Finish Line, Inc.
3308 N. Mitthoeffer Rd.
Indianapolis, IN 46236
Phone: 317-899-1022 Fax: —
CEO: Alan H. Cohen
CFO: Steven J. Schneider
1992 Sales: $98 million Employees: 1,570
Symbol: FINL Exchange: NASDAQ
Industry: Retail - apparel & shoes

First Alabama Bancshares, Inc.
417 N. 20th St.
Birmingham, AL 35203
Phone: 205-326-7167 Fax: 205-326-7571
CEO: J. Stanley Mackin
CFO: Richard D. Horsley
1991 Sales: $658 million Employees: 4,465
Symbol: FABC Exchange: NASDAQ
Industry: Banks - Southeast

First Albany Corp.
41 State St., 9th Fl.
Albany, NY 12207
Phone: 518-447-8500 Fax: 518-447-7979
CEO: George C. McNamee
CFO: David J. Cunningham
1991 Sales: $73 million Employees: 511
Symbol: FACT Exchange: NASDAQ
Industry: Financial - business services

First Amarillo Bancorporation, Inc.
PO Box 1331
Amarillo, TX 79180
Phone: 806-379-5321 Fax: —
CEO: Don Powell
CFO: H. Joe Horn
1991 Sales: $56 million Employees: 354
Symbol: FAMA Exchange: NASDAQ
Industry: Banks - Southwest

First American Corp.
First American Center, 300 Union St.
Nashville, TN 37237
Phone: 615-748-2000 Fax: 615-781-7851
CEO: Dennis C. Bottorff
CFO: John C. Fox
1991 Sales: $588 million Employees: 3,126
Symbol: FATN Exchange: NASDAQ
Industry: Banks - Southeast

First AmFed Corp.
1900 Memorial Pkwy.
Huntsville, AL 35801
Phone: 205-539-5761 Fax: —
CEO: Morris W. Anderson
CFO: William F. Childress
1991 Sales: $40 million Employees: 152
Symbol: FAMF Exchange: NASDAQ
Industry: Financial - savings and loans

First Bancorp
341 N. Main St.
Troy, NC 27371
Phone: 919-576-6171 Fax: 919-576-1070
CEO: John C. Wallace
CFO: Kirby A. Tyndall
1991 Sales: $23 million Employees: 205
Symbol: FBNC Exchange: NASDAQ
Industry: Banks - Southeast

First Bancorp Indiana Inc.
101 N. Fourth St.
Lafayette, IN 47902
Phone: 317-423-2525 Fax: —
CEO: Elbert R. Strain
CFO: Eric D. Carlson
1991 Sales: $22 million Employees: 79
Symbol: FBII Exchange: NASDAQ
Industry: Financial - savings and loans

First Bancorporation of Ohio
First National Tower
Akron, OH 44308
Phone: 216-384-8000 Fax: —
CEO: Howard L. Flood
CFO: Gary J. Elek
1991 Sales: $360 million Employees: 2,670
Symbol: FBOH Exchange: NASDAQ
Industry: Banks - Midwest

First Bank System, Inc.
200 S. 6th St.
Minneapolis, MN 55480
Phone: 612-370-5100 Fax: 612-370-4047
CEO: John F. Grundhofer
CFO: Richard A. Zona
1992 Sales: $1,864 million Employees: 8,900
Symbol: FBS Exchange: NYSE
Industry: Banks - Midwest

First Benefit Corp
1724 E. 53rd St. #B
Anderson, IN 46013
Phone: 317-642-5599 Fax: 317-642-0273
CEO: Greg Bell
CFO: Greg Bell
1991 Sales: $5.3 million Employees: 98
Ownership: Privately held
Industry: Healthcare management for employee health benefit plans

First Brands Corp.
83 Wooster Heights Rd., Bldg. 301
Danbury, CT 06813
Phone: 203-731-2300 Fax: 203-731-2518
CEO: Alfred E. Dudley
CFO: Donald A. DeSantis
1992 Sales: $1,021 million Employees: 3,800
Symbol: FBR Exchange: NYSE
Industry: Diversified operations - consumer products

First Central Financial Corp.
266 Merrick Rd.
Lynbrook, NY 11563
Phone: 516-593-7070 Fax: 516-593-8880
CEO: Martin J. Simon
CFO: Joan Locasio
1991 Sales: $33 million Employees: —
Symbol: FCC Exchange: AMEX
Industry: Insurance - property & casualty

First Charter Corp.
22 Union St. North
Concord, NC 28025
Phone: 704-786-3300 Fax: —
CEO: Lawrence M. Kimbrough
CFO: Lawrence M. Kimbrough
1991 Sales: $24 million Employees: 179
Symbol: FCTR Exchange: NASDAQ
Industry: Banks - Southeast

First Chattanooga Financial Corp.
601 Market Center
Chattanooga, TN 37402
Phone: 615-756-4600 Fax: —
CEO: Spencer H. Wright
CFO: William R. McCamy
1991 Sales: $61 million Employees: 241
Symbol: FCHT Exchange: NASDAQ
Industry: Financial - savings and loans

indicates company is in *Hoover's Handbook of American Business.*

indicates company is in *Hoover's Handbook of World Business;* sales and employee numbers are for parent company.

First Chicago Corp.
One First National Plaza
Chicago, IL 60670
Phone: 312-732-4000 Fax: 312-732-5976
CEO: Richard L. Thomas
CFO: W. G. Jurgensen
1992 Sales: $4,358 million Employees: 18,549
Symbol: FNB Exchange: NYSE
Industry: Banks - money center

First Citizens Bank & Trust
239 Fayetteville St.
Raleigh, NC 27602
Phone: 919-755-7000 Fax: 919-755-7277
CEO: Lewis R. Holding
CFO: Kenneth A. Black
1991 Sales: $492 million Employees: 3,832
Symbol: FCNCA Exchange: NASDAQ
Industry: Banks - Southeast

First Citizens Financial Corp.
8485 Fenton St.
Silver Spring, MD 20910
Phone: 301-565-8900 Fax: —
CEO: Stanley Betts
CFO: Robert E. Wolpert
1991 Sales: $52 million Employees: 182
Symbol: FCIT Exchange: NASDAQ
Industry: Financial - savings and loans

First City Bancorp, Inc.
201 S. Church St.
Murfreesboro, TN 37130
Phone: 615-898-1111 Fax: —
CEO: William E. Rowland
CFO: Robert B. Murfree
1991 Sales: $17 million Employees: 100
Symbol: FCT Exchange: AMEX
Industry: Banks - Southeast

First City Bancorporation of Texas, Inc.
1001 Main St.
Houston, TX 77002
Phone: 713-658-6011 Fax: 713-658-6879
CEO: C. Ivan Wilson
CFO: Robert W. Brown
1991 Sales: $1,144 million Employees: 6,143
Symbol: FBT Exchange: NYSE
Industry: Banks - Southwest

First Colonial Group, Inc.
76 S. Main St.
Nazareth, PA 18064
Phone: 215-746-7300 Fax: —
CEO: S. Eric Beattie
CFO: Reid L. Heeren
1991 Sales: $29 million Employees: 148
Symbol: FCOLA Exchange: NASDAQ
Industry: Banks - Midwest

First Commerce Bankshares, Inc.
13th & "O" Sts.
Lincoln, NE 68508
Phone: 402-434-4110 Fax: —
CEO: James Stuart, Jr.
CFO: John E. Sable
1991 Sales: $48 million Employees: 893
Symbol: FCBI Exchange: NASDAQ
Industry: Banks - Midwest

First Commerce Corp.
210 Baronne St.
New Orleans, LA 70112
Phone: 504-561-1371 Fax: 504-582-7405
CEO: Ian Arnof
CFO: Michael A. Flick
1991 Sales: $478 million Employees: 2,695
Symbol: FCOM Exchange: NASDAQ
Industry: Banks - Southeast

First Commercial Bancorp, Inc.
2450 Venture Oaks Way
Sacramento, CA 95833
Phone: 916-646-0554 Fax: —
CEO: W. Greg Karr
CFO: Anne H. Long
1991 Sales: $40 million Employees: 197
Symbol: FCOB Exchange: NASDAQ
Industry: Banks - West

First Commercial Bancshares, Inc.
2000 SouthBridge Pkwy.
Birmingham, AL 35209
Phone: 205-879-2800 Fax: —
CEO: John T. Oliver, Jr.
CFO: Robert M. Couch
1992 Sales: $842 million Employees: 82
Symbol: FSCB Exchange: NASDAQ
Industry: Banks - Southeast

First Commercial Corp.
400 W. Capitol Ave.
Little Rock, AR 72201
Phone: 501-371-7000 Fax: —
CEO: William H. Bowen
CFO: Thomas R. Hill
1991 Sales: $231 million Employees: 1,580
Symbol: FCLR Exchange: NASDAQ
Industry: Banks - Southeast

First Commonwealth Financial Corp.
22 N. Sixth St.
Indiana, PA 15701
Phone: 412-349-7220 Fax: —
CEO: E. James Trimarchi
CFO: John J. Dolan
1991 Sales: $119 million Employees: 693
Symbol: FCF Exchange: NYSE
Industry: Banks - Midwest

First Community Bancorp, Inc.
6000 E. State St.
Rockford, IL 61110
Phone: 815-962-3771 Fax: 815-229-1027
CEO: R. Richard Bastian III
CFO: Jerry A. Lecklider
1991 Sales: $65 million Employees: 400
Symbol: FRFD Exchange: NASDAQ
Industry: Banks - Midwest

First Constitution Financial Corp.
80 Elm St.
New Haven, CT 06510
Phone: 203-782-4570 Fax: —
CEO: John J. Crawford
CFO: George H. Brooks-Gonyer
1991 Sales: $182 million Employees: —
Symbol: FCON Exchange: NASDAQ
Industry: Financial - savings and loans

First Data Corp.
World Financial Center
New York, NY 10285
Phone: 212-640-2000 Fax: —
CEO: Henry C. Duques
CFO: Robert A. Minicucci
1992 Sales: $1,205 million Employees: 18,300
Symbol: FDC Exchange: NYSE
Industry: Business services - information processing

First Eastern Corp.
Public Square
Wilkes-Barre, PA 18768
Phone: 717-821-4420 Fax: —
CEO: Richard M. Ross, Jr.
CFO: John W. Adonizio
1991 Sales: $281 million Employees: 1,370
Symbol: FEBC Exchange: NASDAQ
Industry: Banks - Northeast

First Empire State Corp.
One M&T Plaza, 5th Fl.
Buffalo, NY 14203
Phone: 716-842-5445 Fax: 716-842-5177
CEO: Robert G. Wilmers
CFO: James L. Vardon
1992 Sales: $890 million Employees: 3,338
Symbol: FES Exchange: AMEX
Industry: Banks - Northeast

First Essex Bancorp, Inc.
296 Essex St.
Lawrence, MA 01840
Phone: 508-681-7500 Fax: —
CEO: Leonard A. Wilson
CFO: David W. Dailey
1991 Sales: $48 million Employees: 227
Symbol: FESX Exchange: NASDAQ
Industry: Banks - Northeast

First Federal Capital Corp.
605 State St.
LaCrosse, WI 54601
Phone: 608-784-8000 Fax: —
CEO: Thomas W. Schini
CFO: Jack C. Rusch
1991 Sales: $83 million Employees: 423
Symbol: FTFC Exchange: NASDAQ
Industry: Financial - savings and loans

First Federal Financial Corp. of Kentucky
202 W. Dixie Ave.
Elizabethtown, KY 42701
Phone: 502-765-2131 Fax: —
CEO: Wayne G. Overall, Jr.
CFO: Dennis Young
1991 Sales: $21 million Employees: 59
Symbol: FFKY Exchange: NASDAQ
Industry: Financial - savings and loans

First Federal Savings Bank
505 East 200 South
Salt Lake City, UT 84102
Phone: 801-366-2265 Fax: —
CEO: Gerald R. Christensen
CFO: M. Keith Midgley
1990 Sales: $10.5 million Employees: 40
Symbol: FFUT Exchange: NASDAQ
Industry: Financial - savings and loans

First Federal Savings Bank of LaGrange
101 N. Greenwood St.
LaGrange, GA 30240
Phone: 404-845-5000 Fax: —
CEO: John S. Holle
CFO: Ellison C. Rudd
1992 Sales: — Employees: —
Symbol: FLAG Exchange: NASDAQ
Industry: Financial - savings and loans

First Federal Savings & Loan Assn. of Ft. Myers
2201 Second St.
Ft. Myers, FL 33901
Phone: 813-334-4106 Fax: —
CEO: Thomas F. Orthman
CFO: Thomas F. Orthman
1992 Sales: — Employees: —
Symbol: FFMY Exchange: NASDAQ
Industry: Financial - savings and loans

First Federal Savings & Loan of E. Hartford
1137 Main St.
East Hartford, CT 06108
Phone: 203-289-6401 Fax: —
CEO: James D. Shelton
CFO: Robert F. Felix
1992 Sales: — Employees: —
Symbol: FFES Exchange: NASDAQ
Industry: Financial - savings and loans

indicates company is in *Hoover's Handbook of American Business.*

indicates company is in *Hoover's Handbook of World Business;* sales and employee numbers are for parent company.

First Fidelity Bancorp, Inc.
301 Adams St.
Fairmont, WV 26554
Phone: 304-363-1300 Fax: —
CEO: Patrick L. Schulte
CFO: Frank R. Kerekes
1991 Sales: $28 million Employees: 87
Symbol: FFWV Exchange: NASDAQ
Industry: Banks - Southeast

First Fidelity Bancorporation
1009 Lenox Dr., Bldg. 4
Lawrenceville, NJ 08648
Phone: 609-895-6800 Fax: 609-895-6863
CEO: Anthony P. Terracciano
CFO: Wolfgang Schoellkopf
1992 Sales: $2,462 million Employees: 10,600
Symbol: FFB Exchange: NYSE
Industry: Banks, insurance & stock brokerage, automobile & equipment leasing

First Financial Bancorp
300 High St.
Hamilton, OH 45011
Phone: 513-867-4700 Fax: 513-867-4995
CEO: Richard J. Fitton
CFO: Richard E. Weinman
1991 Sales: $9.1 million Employees: 61
Symbol: FFBC Exchange: NASDAQ
Industry: Banks - Midwest

First Financial Corp.
1305 Main St.
Stevens Point, WI 54481
Phone: 715-341-0400 Fax: —
CEO: John C. Seramur
CFO: Walter T. Koziol
1992 Sales: $334 million Employees: 1,409
Symbol: FFHC Exchange: NASDAQ
Industry: Financial - savings and loans

First Financial Corp.
PO Box 540
Terre Haute, IN
Phone: 812-238-6000 Fax: —
CEO: Donald E. Smith
CFO: Michael A. Carty
1991 Sales: $87 million Employees: 481
Symbol: THFF Exchange: NASDAQ
Industry: Banks - Midwest

First Financial Corp. of Western Maryland
118 Baltimore St.
Cumberland, MD 21502
Phone: 301-724-3363 Fax: —
CEO: Richard C. Deckerhoff
CFO: M. Ray Kiddy
1990 Sales: $32 million Employees: 126
Symbol: FFWM Exchange: NASDAQ
Industry: Banks - Northeast

First Financial Holdings, Inc.
34 Broad St.
Charleston, SC 29401
Phone: 803-724-0800 Fax: —
CEO: A. L. Hutchinson, Jr.
CFO: A. Thomas Hood
1991 Sales: $97 million Employees: 379
Symbol: FFCH Exchange: NASDAQ
Industry: Financial - savings and loans

First Financial Management Corp.
3 Corporate Square, Ste. 700
Atlanta, GA 30329
Phone: 404-321-0120 Fax: 404-633-2412
CEO: Patrick H. Thomas
CFO: E. D. M. Schachner
1992 Sales: $1,405 million Employees: 9,300
Symbol: FFM Exchange: NYSE
Industry: Financial - data processing, banking services

First Florida Banks, Inc.
111 Madison St.
Tampa, FL 33651
Phone: 813-224-1455 Fax: 813-832-0145
CEO: Paul M. Homan
CFO: William G. Foster
1991 Sales: $561 million Employees: 3,933
Symbol: FFBK Exchange: NASDAQ
Industry: Banks - Southeast

First Franklin Corp.
One Bowen Place
Cincinnati, OH 45202
Phone: 513-721-0808 Fax: —
CEO: Thomas H. Siemers
CFO: Daniel T. Voelpel
1991 Sales: $19 million Employees: 58
Symbol: FFHS Exchange: NASDAQ
Industry: Financial - savings and loans

First Georgia Holding, Inc.
1703 Gloucester St.
Brunswick, GA 31520
Phone: 912-267-7283 Fax: —
CEO: Amanda Thomson
CFO: Robert Bennett
1991 Sales: $17 million Employees: 82
Symbol: FGHC Exchange: NASDAQ
Industry: Banks - Southeast

First Golden Bancorporation
1301 Jackson St.
Golden, CO 80401
Phone: 303-279-4563 Fax: —
CEO: William J. Fortune
CFO: G. Scott Gagon
1991 Sales: $9.5 million Employees: 175
Symbol: FGBC Exchange: NASDAQ
Industry: Banks - West

First Harrisburg Bancor, Inc.
234 N. Second St.
Harrisburg, PA 17101
Phone: 717-232-6661 Fax: —
CEO: Robert H. Trewhella
CFO: J. Frederic Redslob
1991 Sales: $25 million Employees: 132
Symbol: FFHP Exchange: NASDAQ
Industry: Banks - Northeast

First Hawaiian, Inc.
165 S. King St.
Honolulu, HI 96813
Phone: 808-525-7000 Fax: —
CEO: Walter A. Dods, Jr.
CFO: Howard H. Karr
1991 Sales: $578 million Employees: 2,816
Symbol: FHWN Exchange: NASDAQ
Industry: Banks - West

First Home Savings Bank, S.L.A.
125 S. Broadway
Pennsville, NJ 08070
Phone: 609-678-4400 Fax: —
CEO: Stephen D. Miller
CFO: Robert A. DiValerio
1992 Sales: $17 million Employees: —
Symbol: FSPG Exchange: NASDAQ
Industry: Financial - savings and loans

First Illinois Corp.
800 Davis St.
Evanston, IL 60204
Phone: 708-866-6000 Fax: —
CEO: William C. Croft
CFO: James A. Doyle
1990 Sales: $165 million Employees: 752
Symbol: FTIL Exchange: NASDAQ
Industry: Banks - Midwest

First Indiana Corp.
135 N. Pennsylvania St.
Indianapolis, IN 46204
Phone: 317-269-1200 Fax: —
CEO: Robert H. McKinney
CFO: David L. Gray
1991 Sales: $105 million Employees: 463
Symbol: FISB Exchange: NASDAQ
Industry: Financial - savings and loans

First Inter-Bancorp Inc.
One Summit Court, Route 52
Fishkill, NY 12524
Phone: 914-897-2800 Fax: 914-896-4228
CEO: Robert M. Chambers
CFO: Joseph V. DiCarlo
1991 Sales: $14 million Employees: 1,376
Symbol: FIBI Exchange: NASDAQ
Industry: Banks - Northeast

First Interstate Bancorp
633 W. Fifth St., 72nd Fl.
Los Angeles, CA 90071
Phone: 213-614-3001 Fax: 213-614-3741
CEO: Edward M. Carson
CFO: Thomas P. Marrie
1992 Sales: $4,102 million Employees: 30,281
Symbol: I Exchange: NYSE
Industry: Banks - money center

First Liberty Financial Corp.
201 Second St.
Macon, GA 31297
Phone: 912-743-0911 Fax: —
CEO: Robert F. Hatcher
CFO: David L. Hall
1991 Sales: $74 million Employees: 342
Symbol: FLFC Exchange: NASDAQ
Industry: Financial - savings and loans

First Merchants Corp.
200 E. Jackson St.
Muncie, IN 47305
Phone: 317-747-1500 Fax: —
CEO: Stefan S. Anderson
CFO: James L. Thrash
1991 Sales: $22 million Employees: 350
Symbol: FRME Exchange: NASDAQ
Industry: Banks - Midwest

First Michigan Bank Corp.
115 Clover Ave.
Holland, MI 49423
Phone: 616-396-9000 Fax: —
CEO: David M. Ondersma
CFO: David M. Ondersma
1991 Sales: $188 million Employees: 1,214
Symbol: FMBC Exchange: NASDAQ
Industry: Banks - Midwest

First Midwest Bancorp, Inc.
50 E. Shuman Blvd., Ste. 310
Naperville, IL 60566
Phone: 708-778-8700 Fax: —
CEO: Robert P. O'Meara
CFO: Donald J. Swistowicz
1991 Sales: $230 million Employees: 1,250
Symbol: FMBI Exchange: NASDAQ
Industry: Banks - Midwest

First Mississippi Corp.
700 North St.
Jackson, MS 39202
Phone: 601-948-7550 Fax: 601-949-0228
CEO: J. Kelley Williams
CFO: R. Michael Summerford
1992 Sales: $525 million Employees: —
Symbol: FRM Exchange: NYSE
Industry: Chemicals - specialty

indicates company is in *Hoover's Handbook of American Business.*

indicates company is in *Hoover's Handbook of World Business*; sales and employee numbers are for parent company.

First Mortgage Corp.
3230 Fallowfield Dr.
Diamond Bar, CA 91765
Phone: 714-595-1996 Fax: —
CEO: Clement Ziroli
CFO: Pac W. Dong
1992 Sales: $0.2 million Employees: —
Symbol: FMOR Exchange: NASDAQ
Industry: Financial - mortgages & related services

First Mutual Savings Bank
400 108th NE
Bellevue, WA 98004
Phone: 206-455-7300 Fax: —
CEO: John R. Valaas
CFO: Robert A. Mandery
1992 Sales: — Employees: —
Symbol: FMSB Exchange: NASDAQ
Industry: Financial - savings and loans

First National Bancorp
111 Green St. SE
Gainesville, GA 30501
Phone: 404-503-2000 Fax: —
CEO: J. M. McRae
CFO: Peter D. Miller
1991 Sales: $176 million Employees: 917
Symbol: FBAC Exchange: NASDAQ
Industry: Banks - Southeast

First National Bank Corp.
18800 Hall Rd.
Mt. Clemens, MI 48046
Phone: 313-465-2400 Fax: —
CEO: Harold W. Allmacher
CFO: Richard J. Miller
1991 Sales: $44 million Employees: 246
Symbol: MTCL Exchange: NASDAQ
Industry: Banks - Midwest

First National Corp.
401 W. "A" St.
San Diego, CA 92101
Phone: 619-233-5588 Fax: —
CEO: Robert D. Richley
CFO: Nancy D. Celick
1991 Sales: $58 million Employees: 351
Symbol: FN Exchange: AMEX
Industry: Banks - West

First New York Bank for Business
28 W. 23rd St.
New York, NY 10010
Phone: 212-886-9700 Fax: —
CEO: Martin A. Simon
CFO: Louis P. Palermo
1992 Sales: $19 million Employees: 171
Symbol: FNYB Exchange: NASDAQ
Industry: Banks - Northeast

First Northern Savings Bank S.A.
201 N. Monroe Ave.
Green Bay, WI 54301
Phone: 414-437-7101 Fax: —
CEO: Michael D. Meeuwsen
CFO: Rick B. Colberg
1992 Sales: — Employees: —
Symbol: FNGB Exchange: NASDAQ
Industry: Financial - savings and loans

First Oak Brook Bancshares, Inc.
2015 Spring Rd.
Oak Brook, IL 60521
Phone: 708-571-1050 Fax: —
CEO: Eugene P. Heytow
CFO: Rosemarie Burget
1991 Sales: $40 million Employees: 247
Symbol: FOBBA Exchange: NASDAQ
Industry: Banks - Midwest

First of America Bank Corp.
108 E. Michigan Ave.
Kalamazoo, MI 49007
Phone: 616-376-9000 Fax: 616-376-6020
CEO: Daniel R. Smith
CFO: Thomas W. Lambert
1992 Sales: $1,857 million Employees: 11,405
Symbol: FOA Exchange: NYSE
Industry: Banks - Midwest

First Pacific Networks, Inc.
601 W. California Ave.
Sunnyvale, CA 94086
Phone: 408-730-6600 Fax: —
CEO: James K. Gibby
CFO: Kennth Schneider
1991 Sales: $9.5 million Employees: 64
Symbol: FPNX Exchange: NASDAQ
Industry: Telecommunications services

First Republic Bancorp Inc.
388 Market St.
San Francisco, CA 94111
Phone: 415-392-1400 Fax: 415-392-1413
CEO: James H. Herbert II
CFO: Willis H. Newton, Jr.
1991 Sales: $86 million Employees: 103
Symbol: FRC Exchange: NYSE
Industry: Banks - West

First Savings Bank, FSB
301 College St.
Greenville, SC 29601
Phone: 803-458-2000 Fax: —
CEO: Luther C. Boliek
CFO: Milton E. Futch
1992 Sales: — Employees: —
Symbol: FTSC Exchange: NASDAQ
Industry: Financial - savings and loans

First Security Corp.
79 S. Main St.
Salt Lake City, UT 84111
Phone: 801-350-6000 Fax: 801-350-5262
CEO: Spencer F. Eccles
CFO: Scott C. Ulbrich
1991 Sales: $707 million Employees: 4,736
Symbol: FSCO Exchange: NASDAQ
Industry: Banks - West

First Security Financial Corp.
215-217 S. Main St.
Salisbury, NC 28144
Phone: 704-633-7800 Fax: —
CEO: Lloyd G. Gurley
CFO: Carl L. Dean
1991 Sales: $36 million Employees: —
Symbol: FSFC Exchange: NASDAQ
Industry: Banks - Southeast

First Seismic Corp.
600 17th St., Ste. 400
Denver, CO 80202
Phone: 303-573-0200 Fax: —
CEO: Rogers E. Beall
CFO: Michael J. Smith
1991 Sales: $24 million Employees: 89
Symbol: FSEI Exchange: NASDAQ
Industry: Oil & gas - field services

First State Financial Services, Inc.
1120 Bloomfield Ave., CN 2449
West Caldwell, NJ 07007
Phone: 201-575-5800 Fax: —
CEO: Michael J. Quigley III
CFO: Emil J. Butchko
1991 Sales: $41 million Employees: 155
Symbol: FSFI Exchange: NASDAQ
Industry: Financial - savings and loans

First Team Sports, Inc.
2274 Woodale Dr.
Mounds View, MN 55112
Phone: 612-780-4454 Fax: 612-780-8908
CEO: David G. Soderquist
CFO: Ronald W. Berg
1992 Sales: $27 million Employees: 39
Symbol: FTSP Exchange: NASDAQ
Industry: Leisure & recreational products - roller skates & related accessories

First Tennessee National Corp.
165 Madison Ave.
Memphis, TN 38103
Phone: 901-523-5630 Fax: 901-523-4354
CEO: Ronald Terry
CFO: Susan S. Bies
1991 Sales: $756 million Employees: 4,209
Symbol: FTEN Exchange: NASDAQ
Industry: Banks - Southeast

First Union Corp.
One First Union Ctr., 301 S. Tyron St.
Charlotte, NC 28288
Phone: 704-374-6161 Fax: 704-374-2407
CEO: Edward E. Crutchfield, Jr.
CFO: Robert T. Atwood
1992 Sales: $4,355 million Employees: 24,203
Symbol: FTU Exchange: NYSE
Industry: Banks - Southeast

First United Bancshares, Inc.
Main St. at Washington St.
El Dorado, AR 71730
Phone: 501-863-3181 Fax: —
CEO: James V. Kelley
CFO: James V. Kelley
1991 Sales: $69 million Employees: 365
Symbol: UNTD Exchange: NASDAQ
Industry: Banks - Southeast

First United Corp.
19 S. Second St.
Oakland, MD 21550
Phone: 301-334-9471 Fax: —
CEO: Richard G. Stanton
CFO: Robert W. Kurtz
1991 Sales: $36 million Employees: 274
Symbol: FUNC Exchange: NASDAQ
Industry: Banks - Northeast

First USA, Inc.
2001 Bryan Tower, 38th Fl.
Dallas, TX 75201
Phone: 214-746-8700 Fax: —
CEO: John C. Tolleson
CFO: Pamela H. Patsley
1992 Sales: $422 million Employees: —
Symbol: FUS Exchange: NYSE
Industry: Financial - business services

First Virginia Banks, Inc.
6400 Arlington Blvd.
Falls Church, VA 22042
Phone: 703-241-4866 Fax: 703-241-3464
CEO: Robert H. Zalokar
CFO: Richard F. Bowman
1991 Sales: $588 million Employees: 5,075
Symbol: FVB Exchange: NYSE
Industry: Banks - Southeast

First Western Bancorp, Inc.
101 E. Washington St.
New Castle, PA 16103
Phone: 412-652-8550 Fax: —
CEO: Thomas J. O'Shane
CFO: Robert H. Young
1991 Sales: $93 million Employees: 548
Symbol: FWBI Exchange: NASDAQ
Industry: Banks - Northeast

First Western Corp.
9060 E. Via Linda St.
Scottsdale, AZ 85258
Phone: 602-661-3577 Fax: —
CEO: Robert W. Stallings
CFO: James R. Reis
1991 Sales: $6.9 million Employees: 115
Symbol: FWCO Exchange: NASDAQ
Industry: Financial - mortgages & related services

First Western Financial Corp.
2700 W. Sahara Ave.
Las Vegas, NV 89102
Phone: 702-871-2000 Fax: —
CEO: Anne Bacon
CFO: Catherine A. Sourk
1991 Sales: $14 million Employees: 268
Symbol: FWES Exchange: NASDAQ
Industry: Financial - savings and loans

Firstar Corp.
777 E. Wisconsin Ave.
Milwaukee, WI 53202
Phone: 414-765-4321 Fax: 414-765-4349
CEO: John H. Hendee, Jr.
CFO: William H. Risch
1992 Sales: $1,199 million Employees: 8,671
Symbol: FSR Exchange: NYSE
Industry: Banks - Midwest

Firstbank of Illinois Co.
205 S. Fifth St.
Springfield, IL 62701
Phone: 217-753-7543 Fax: —
CEO: Mark H. Ferguson
CFO: Chris R. Zettek
1991 Sales: $119 million Employees: 706
Symbol: FBIC Exchange: NASDAQ
Industry: Banks - Midwest

FirstFed Financial Corp.
401 Wilshire Blvd.
Santa Monica, CA 90401
Phone: 310-319-6000 Fax: 310-319-5899
CEO: William S. Mortensen
CFO: Babette E. Heimbush
1991 Sales: $304 million Employees: 426
Symbol: FED Exchange: NYSE
Industry: Financial - savings and loans

FirstFed Michigan Corp.
1001 Woodward Ave.
Detroit, MI 48226
Phone: 313-965-1400 Fax: —
CEO: James A. Aliber
CFO: Richard W. Neu
1991 Sales: $102 million Employees: 1,234
Symbol: FFOM Exchange: NASDAQ
Industry: Financial - savings and loans

FirstFederal Financial Services Corp.
135 E. Liberty St.
Wooster, OH 44691
Phone: 216-264-8001 Fax: —
CEO: Richard E. Herald
CFO: L. Dwight Douce
1991 Sales: $9.6 million Employees: 231
Symbol: FFSW Exchange: NASDAQ
Industry: Financial - savings and loans

FirsTier Financial, Inc.
1700 Farnam St.
Omaha, NE 68102
Phone: 402-348-6299 Fax: —
CEO: David A. Rismiller
CFO: Aaron C. Hilkemann
1991 Sales: $293 million Employees: 1,509
Symbol: FRST Exchange: NASDAQ
Industry: Banks - Midwest

FirstMiss Gold Inc.
5190 Neil Rd., Ste. 310
Reno, NV 89502
Phone: 702-827-0211 Fax: 702-827-0541
CEO: Cecil Alvarez
CFO: Larry Bigler
1992 Sales: $83 million Employees: 167
Symbol: FRMG Exchange: NASDAQ
Industry: Gold mining & processing

Fischer Imaging Corp.
12300 N. Grant St.
Denver, CO 80241
Phone: 303-452-6800 Fax: 303-450-4335
CEO: Morgan W. Nields
CFO: Roberto A. Cascella
1991 Sales: $58 million Employees: 532
Symbol: FIMG Exchange: NASDAQ
Industry: Medical products - X-ray imaging systems

Fischer & Porter Co.
125 E. County Line Rd.
Warminster, PA 18974
Phone: 215-674-6000 Fax: 215-674-7183
CEO: Jay H. Tolson
CFO: Laurence P. Finnegan, Jr.
1991 Sales: $237 million Employees: 2,413
Symbol: FP Exchange: AMEX
Industry: Instruments - control

FIserv, Inc.
2152 S. 114th St.
West Allis, WI 53227
Phone: 414-546-5000 Fax: 414-546-5275
CEO: George D. Dalton
CFO: Kenneth R. Jensen
1991 Sales: $281 million Employees: 3,700
Symbol: FISV Exchange: NASDAQ
Industry: Business services - data processing systems & information management

Fisher Industrial Services, Inc.
402 Webster Chapel Rd.
Glencoe, AL 35905
Phone: 205-492-8340 Fax: 205-492-8395
CEO: Marvin Fisher
CFO: Marvin Fisher
1991 Sales: $6.5 million Employees: 105
Ownership: Privately held
Industry: Hazardous waste management facility

Fisher Scientific International, Inc.
1410 Wayne Ave.
Indiana, PA 15701
Phone: 412-357-1000 Fax: 412-357-1107
CEO: P. M. Montrone
CFO: P. M. Meister
1992 Sales: $814 million Employees: 3,200
Symbol: FSH Exchange: NYSE
Industry: Instruments - scientific

Fisher-Price Toys, Inc.
636 Girard Ave.
East Aurora, NY 14052
Phone: 716-687-3000 Fax: 716-687-3476
CEO: Ronald J. Jackson
CFO: William Bingham
1992 Sales: $694 million Employees: 5,800
Symbol: FPP Exchange: NYSE
Industry: Toys - games & hobby products; infant and preschool

Fitec International, Inc.
3533 Ridge Meadow Pkwy.
Memphis, TN 38115
Phone: 901-366-9144 Fax: 901-366-9446
CEO: Josepf Amore
CFO: Thomas Feeney
1991 Sales: $34 million Employees: 480
Ownership: Privately held
Industry: Commercial fishing products

Flagler Bank Corp.
501 S. Flagler Dr.
West Palm Beach, FL 33401
Phone: 407-659-2265 Fax: —
CEO: Thomas E. Rossin
CFO: Glenn G. Schanel
1991 Sales: $41 million Employees: 283
Symbol: FLGLA Exchange: NASDAQ
Industry: Banks - Southeast

Flagship Financial Corp.
500 Old York Rd.
Jenkintown, PA 19046
Phone: 215-576-5900 Fax: —
CEO: John M. Mason
CFO: John M. Mason
1991 Sales: $28 million Employees: 310
Symbol: FLGF Exchange: NASDAQ
Industry: Financial - savings and loans

Flamemaster Corp.
11120 Sherman Way
Sun Valley, CA 91352
Phone: 818-982-1650 Fax: 818-765-5603
CEO: Joseph Mazin
CFO: Barbara E. Waite
1991 Sales: $5 million Employees: 31
Symbol: FAME Exchange: NASDAQ
Industry: Specialty chemicals - coatings & sealants

Flanigan's Enterprises, Inc.
2841 W. Cypress Creek Rd.
Ft. Lauderdale, FL 33309
Phone: 305-624-9681 Fax: 305-974-2940
CEO: Joseph G. Flanigan
CFO: Mary C. Reymann
1991 Sales: $22 million Employees: 321
Symbol: BDL Exchange: AMEX
Industry: Beverages - alcoholic; cocktail lounges

Fleet Aerospace, Inc.
310 Euclid Ave.
San Diego, CA 92114
Phone: 619-264-3181 Fax: 619-264-4329
CEO: A. George Dragone
CFO: B. W. McGowan
1991 Sales: $48 million Employees: 552
Symbol: FLAI Exchange: NASDAQ
Industry: Aerospace - aircraft equipment

Fleet Call, Inc.
201 Route 17 North
Rutherford, NJ 07070
Phone: 201-438-1400 Fax: —
CEO: B. D. McAuley
CFO: E. G. Long
1992 Sales: $52 million Employees: 343
Symbol: CALL Exchange: NASDAQ
Industry: Telecommunications services - mobile radio wireless communication services

Fleet Financial Group, Inc.
50 Kennedy Plaza, 18th Fl.
Providence, RI 02903
Phone: 401-278-5800 Fax: 401-278-5801
CEO: J. Terrence Murray
CFO: John W. Flynn
1992 Sales: $4,852 million Employees: 25,200
Symbol: FLT Exchange: NYSE
Industry: Banks - Northeast

Fleetwood Enterprises, Inc.
3125 Myers St.
Riverside, CA 92503
Phone: 909-351-3500 Fax: 909-351-3690
CEO: John C. Crean
CFO: Paul M. Bingham
1992 Sales: $1,743 million Employees: 12,000
Symbol: FLE Exchange: NYSE
Industry: Diversified operations - manufactured housing & recreational vehicles

indicates company is in *Hoover's Handbook of American Business.*
indicates company is in *Hoover's Handbook of World Business*; sales and employee numbers are for parent company.

Fleming Companies, Inc.
6301 Waterford Blvd.
Oklahoma City, OK 73118
Phone: 405-840-7200 Fax: 405-841-8149
CEO: E. Dean Werries
CFO: R. Randolph Devening
1992 Sales: $12,931 million Employees: 22,800
Symbol: FLM Exchange: NYSE
Industry: Food - wholesale

Flexible Personnel
1010 Coliseum Blvd. West, Ste. E
Ft. Wayne, IN 46808
Phone: 219-482-3532 Fax: 219-471-1728
CEO: Doug Curtis
CFO: Doug Curtis
1991 Sales: $8 million Employees: 29
Ownership: Privately held
Industry: Business services - temporary employment service

Flexsteel Industries, Inc.
3400 Jackson Brunswick Industrial Block
Dubuque, IA 52001
Phone: 319-556-7730 Fax: 319-556-8345
CEO: Jack B. Crahan
CFO: Marvin O. Becker
1992 Sales: $158 million Employees: 2,040
Symbol: FLXS Exchange: NASDAQ
Industry: Furniture

FlightSafety International, Inc.
Marine Air Terminal, LaGuardia Airport
Flushing, NY 11371
Phone: 718-565-4100 Fax: 718-565-4134
CEO: Albert L. Ueltschi
CFO: Kenneth W. Motschwiller
1991 Sales: $268 million Employees: 2,259
Symbol: FSI Exchange: NYSE
Industry: Schools - aircraft operator training

Flint Ink Corp.
25111 Glendale Ave.
Detroit, MI 48239
Phone: 313-538-6800 Fax: 313-538-1828
CEO: Howard Flint II
CFO: Leonard D. Frescoln
1991 Sales: $510 million Employees: 2,650
Ownership: Privately held
Industry: Chemicals - specialty; printing ink

Florida Bank, F.S.B.
6320 St. Augustine Rd.
Jacksonville, FL 32217
Phone: 904-731-3822 Fax: —
CEO: J. Malcolm Jones, Jr.
CFO: Kerry P. Charlet
1992 Sales: — Employees: —
Symbol: FLBK Exchange: NASDAQ
Industry: Financial - savings and loans

Florida East Coast Industries, Inc.
One Malaga St.
St. Augustine, FL 32084
Phone: 904-829-3421 Fax: 904-826-2352
CEO: W. L. Thornton
CFO: T. N. Smith
1991 Sales: $167 million Employees: 1,507
Symbol: FLA Exchange: NYSE
Industry: Transportation - rail; real estate operations

Florida First Federal Savings Bank
144 Harrison Ave.
Panama City, FL 32401
Phone: 904-872-7000 Fax: —
CEO: Andrew W. Stein
CFO: Barbara L. Haag
1992 Sales: — Employees: —
Symbol: FFPC Exchange: NASDAQ
Industry: Financial - savings and loans

Florida Infusion
1053 Progress Court
Palm Harbor, FL 34683
Phone: 813-942-1829 Fax: 813-942-6165
CEO: Rudy Ciccarello
CFO: Rudy Ciccarello
1992 Sales: $37 million Employees: 19
Ownership: Privately held
Industry: Drugs & medical supplies - wholesale

Florida Marketing International (Mac Academy)
477 South Nova Rd.
Ormond Beach, FL 32174
Phone: 904-677-1918 Fax: 904-677-6717
CEO: Randall Smith
CFO: Jun Lalog
1991 Sales: $7.6 million Employees: 30
Ownership: Privately held
Industry: Computers - Macintosh training sessions & tutorials

Florida Progress Corp.
One Progress Plaza
St. Petersburg, FL 33701
Phone: 813-824-6400 Fax: 813-824-6751
CEO: Jack B. Critchfield
CFO: David R. Kuzma
1992 Sales: $2,095 million Employees: 7,350
Symbol: FPC Exchange: NYSE
Industry: Utility - electric power

Florida Public Utilities Co.
401 S. Dixie Hwy.
West Palm Beach, FL 33401
Phone: 407-832-2461 Fax: 407-833-0151
CEO: Franklin C. Cressman
CFO: Jack R. Brown
1991 Sales: $63 million Employees: 288
Symbol: FPU Exchange: AMEX
Industry: Utility - gas distribution

Florida Rock Industries, Inc.
155 E. 21st St.
Jacksonville, FL 32206
Phone: 904-355-1781 Fax: 904-355-0817
CEO: Edward L. Baker
CFO: Ruggles B. Carlson
1991 Sales: $296 million Employees: 2,385
Symbol: FRK Exchange: AMEX
Industry: Construction - cement & concrete

Florida Steel
PO Box 31328
Tampa, FL 33631
Phone: 813-251-8811 Fax: 813-251-5677
CEO: Edward Flom
CFO: Marvin Hill
1991 Sales: $453 million Employees: 2,100
Ownership: Privately held
Industry: Steel manufacturing & marketing

Flow International Corp.
21440 68th Ave. South
Kent, WA 98032
Phone: 206-872-4900 Fax: 206-872-3283
CEO: Ronald W. Tarrant
CFO: Thomas A. Cross
1992 Sales: $48 million Employees: 320
Symbol: FLOW Exchange: NASDAQ
Industry: Machine tools & related products

Flowers Industries, Inc.
PO Box 1338
Thomasville, GA 31799
Phone: 912-226-9110 Fax: 912-226-9231
CEO: Amos R. McMullian
CFO: C. Martin Wood III
1992 Sales: $912 million Employees: 8,200
Symbol: FLO Exchange: NYSE
Industry: Food - breads, snacks, vegetable & convenience food products

FLS Holdings Inc.
1715 Cleveland St.
Tampa, FL 33606
Phone: 813-251-8811 Fax: —
CEO: Edward L. Flom
CFO: Alfred D. Gres
1991 Sales: $463 million Employees: 2,200
Symbol: FLSH Exchange: NASDAQ
Industry: Steel - production

Fluor Corp.
3333 Michelson Dr.
Irvine, CA 92730
Phone: 714-975-2000 Fax: 714-975-5271
CEO: Leslie G. McCraw
CFO: James O. Rollans
1992 Sales: $6,601 million Employees: 40,593
Symbol: FLR Exchange: NYSE
Industry: Construction - heavy

Flying J Inc.
50 West 990 South
Brigham City, UT 84302
Phone: 801-734-6400 Fax: 801-734-6556
CEO: J. Phillip Adams
CFO: R. W. Anderson
1991 Sales: $624 million Employees: 4,600
Ownership: Privately held
Industry: Oil & gas - US integrated

FM Properties Inc.
1615 Poydras St.
New Orleans, LA 70112
Phone: 504-582-4000 Fax: —
CEO: Richard C. Adkerson
CFO: Richard C. Adkerson
1992 Sales: — Employees: —
Symbol: FMPO Exchange: NASDAQ
Industry: Oil & gas - US exploration & production

FMC Corp.
200 E. Randolph Dr.
Chicago, IL 60601
Phone: 312-861-6000 Fax: 312-861-6176
CEO: Robert N. Burt
CFO: Arthur D. Lyons
1992 Sales: $3,974 million Employees: 23,150
Symbol: FMC Exchange: NYSE
Industry: Diversified operations - chemicals, defense systems, machinery & equipment

FMC Gold Co.
5011 Meadowood Way
Reno, NV 89502
Phone: 702-827-3777 Fax: 702-827-7133
CEO: Larry D. Brady
CFO: Stephanie K. Kushner
1991 Sales: $139 million Employees: 473
Symbol: FGL Exchange: NYSE
Industry: Gold & silver mining & processing

FMS Financial Corp.
Sunset & Salem Roads
Burlington, NJ 08016
Phone: 609-386-2400 Fax: —
CEO: Craig W. Yates
CFO: David L. Gordon
1991 Sales: $33 million Employees: 148
Symbol: FMCO Exchange: NASDAQ
Industry: Financial - savings and loans

FNB Rochester Corp.
35 State St.
Rochester, NY 14614
Phone: 716-546-3300 Fax: —
CEO: R. Carlos Carballada
CFO: Stacy C. Campbell
1991 Sales: $31 million Employees: 204
Symbol: FNBR Exchange: NASDAQ
Industry: Banks - Northeast

indicates company is in *Hoover's Handbook of American Business.*

indicates company is in *Hoover's Handbook of World Business;* sales and employee numbers are for parent company.

Focus Healthcare Management
7101 Executive Center Dr. #375
Brentwood, TN 37027
Phone: 615-377-9936 Fax: 615-377-6098
CEO: Stryker Warren
CFO: David Iskowe
1991 Sales: $12 million Employees: 200
Ownership: Privately held
Industry: Business services - workers' compensation medical-cost-management services

Follett Corp.
1000 W. Washington Blvd.
Chicago, IL 60607
Phone: 312-666-4300 Fax: 312-829-8435
CEO: Robert Follett
CFO: Kenneth Hull
1991 Sales: $549 million Employees: 4,700
Ownership: Privately held
Industry: Diversified operations - college bookstores, educational software & publishing

Food 4 Less Supermarkets
777 S. Harbor Blvd.
LaHabra, CA 90631
Phone: 714-738-2000 Fax: 714-738-2134
CEO: Ronald W. Burkle
CFO: Greg Mays
1991 Sales: $2,900 million Employees: 12,900
Ownership: Privately held
Industry: Retail - supermarkets

Food Lion, Inc.
2110 Executive Dr.
Salisbury, NC 28144
Phone: 704-633-8250 Fax: 704-636-5024
CEO: Tom E. Smith
CFO: Dan A. Boone
1992 Sales: $7,196 million Employees: 53,583
Symbol: FDLNA & FDLNB Exchange: NASDAQ
Industry: Retail - supermarkets

Foodarama Supermarkets, Inc.
303 W. Main St.
Freehold, NJ 07728
Phone: 908-462-4700 Fax: 908-409-0175
CEO: Joseph J. Saker
CFO: Joseph C. Troilo
1992 Sales: $695 million Employees: 4,600
Symbol: FSM Exchange: AMEX
Industry: Retail - supermarkets

Foodmaker, Inc.
9330 Balboa Ave.
San Diego, CA 92123
Phone: 619-571-2121 Fax: 619-571-2101
CEO: J. W. Goodall Jr.
CFO: Charles W. Duddles
1992 Sales: $1,256 million Employees: 22,730
Symbol: FM Exchange: NYSE
Industry: Retail - food & restaurants: Jack- in-the-Box, Chi-Chi's

Foote, Cone & Belding Communications, Inc.
101 E. Erie St.
Chicago, IL 60611
Phone: 312-751-7000 Fax: 312-751-3501
CEO: Bruce Mason
CFO: Terry M. Ashwill
1991 Sales: $342 million Employees: 3,696
Symbol: FCB Exchange: NYSE
Industry: Advertising - direct marketing, PR, sales promotions

Foothill Group, Inc.
11111 Santa Monica Blvd., Ste. 1500
Los Angeles, CA 90025
Phone: 310-478-8383 Fax: 310-478-2961
CEO: Don L. Gevirtz
CFO: Henry K. Jordan
1991 Sales: $90 million Employees: 159
Symbol: FGI Exchange: NYSE
Industry: Financial - SBIC & commercial

Foothill Independent Bancorp
510 S. Grand Ave.
Glendora, CA 91740
Phone: 818-963-8551 Fax: —
CEO: J. T. Waller
CFO: George E. Langley
1991 Sales: $29 million Employees: 216
Symbol: FOOT Exchange: NASDAQ
Industry: Banks - West

Forcum/Mackey Construction Inc.
15695 Jasmine Ave.
Ivanhoe, CA 93235
Phone: 209-798-1837 Fax: 209-798-1412
CEO: Renae Mackey
CFO: Joe Mackey
1991 Sales: $8 million Employees: 18
Ownership: Privately held
Industry: Construction - commercial & industrial

Ford Motor Co.
The American Rd.
Dearborn, MI 48121
Phone: 313-322-3000 Fax: 313-322-7896
CEO: Harold A. Poling
CFO: Stanley A. Seneker
1992 Sales: $100,132 million Employees: 332,700
Symbol: F Exchange: NYSE
Industry: Automotive manufacturing & financial services

Foremost Corporation of America
5600 Beach Tree Lane
Caledonia, MI 49316
Phone: 616-942-3000 Fax: —
CEO: Richard L. Antonini
CFO: F. Robert Woudstra
1991 Sales: $449 million Employees: 1,307
Symbol: FCOA Exchange: NASDAQ
Industry: Insurance - property & casualty

Forest City Enterprises, Inc.
10800 Brookpark Rd.
Cleveland, OH 44130
Phone: 216-267-1200 Fax: 216-362-2618
CEO: Albert B. Ratner
CFO: Thomas G. Smith
1991 Sales: $451 million Employees: 2,764
Symbol: FCEA Exchange: AMEX
Industry: Real estate development

Forest Laboratories, Inc.
150 E. 58th St.
New York, NY 10155
Phone: 212-421-7850 Fax: 212-750-9152
CEO: Howard Solomon
CFO: Kenneth E. Goodman
1992 Sales: $240 million Employees: 1,141
Symbol: FRX Exchange: AMEX
Industry: Drugs

Forest Oil Corp.
950 17th St., Ste. 1500
Denver, CO 80202
Phone: 303-592-2400 Fax: 303-592-2602
CEO: William L. Dorn
CFO: Robert S. Boswell
1991 Sales: $69 million Employees: 182
Symbol: FOIL Exchange: NASDAQ
Industry: Oil & gas - US exploration & production

Formosa Plastics Corp., U.S.A.
9 Peach Tree Hill Rd.
Livingston, NJ 07039
Phone: 201-992-2090 Fax: 201-992-9627
CEO: C.T. Lee
CFO: —
1991 Sales: $1,243 million Employees: 4,767
Parent: Formosa Plastics Group
Industry: Chemicals - plastics & fibers

Forschner Group, Inc.
151 Long Hill Cross Rds.
Shelton, CT 06484
Phone: 203-929-6391 Fax: 203-929-3786
CEO: James W. Kennedy
CFO: Thomas M. Lupinski
1991 Sales: $60 million Employees: 100
Symbol: FSNR Exchange: NASDAQ
Industry: Housewares - cutlery

Forstmann & Co., Inc.
1185 Avenue of the Americas
New York, NY 10036
Phone: 212-642-6900 Fax: —
CEO: Christopher Schaller
CFO: William B. Towne
1991 Sales: $195 million Employees: 2,889
Symbol: FSTM Exchange: NASDAQ
Industry: Textiles - wool & wool-blend fabrics

Fort Howard Corp.
1919 S. Broadway
Green Bay, WI 54304
Phone: 414-435-8821 Fax: 414-435-3703
CEO: Donald H. DeMeuse
CFO: Kathleen J. Hampel
1992 Sales: $1,151 million Employees: 6,200
Ownership: Privately held
Industry: Paper & products

Fort Wayne National Corp.
110 W. Berry St.
Ft. Wayne, IN 46801
Phone: 219-426-0555 Fax: —
CEO: Jackson R. Lehman
CFO: Stephen R. Gillig
1991 Sales: $179 million Employees: 1,014
Symbol: FWNC Exchange: NASDAQ
Industry: Banks - Midwest

Fortitech Inc.
Rotterdam Ind. Park, Bldg. #1
Schenectady, NY 12306
Phone: 518-356-5155 Fax: 518-356-2729
CEO: Walter F. Borisenok
CFO: Walter F. Borisenok
1991 Sales: $5.2 million Employees: 18
Ownership: Privately held
Industry: Vitamins & nutritional products

Fortune Bancorp
16120 US 19 North
Clearwater, FL 34624
Phone: 813-538-1000 Fax: —
CEO: John R. Torell III
CFO: Martin W. Gladysz
1992 Sales: — Employees: —
Symbol: FORB Exchange: NASDAQ
Industry: Financial - savings and loans

Forum Group, Inc.
8900 Keystone Crossing, Ste. 200
Indianapolis, IN 46240
Phone: 317-846-0700 Fax: 317-575-1246
CEO: O. U. Mutz
CFO: Paul A. Shively
1991 Sales: $42 million Employees: —
Symbol: FRL Exchange: AMEX
Industry: Real estate operations

Fostec, Inc.
273 Genesee St.
Auburn, NY 13021
Phone: 315-255-2791 Fax: 315-255-2695
CEO: Rolf Mueller
CFO: Susan Hawley
1991 Sales: $3 million Employees: 40
Ownership: Privately held
Industry: Fiber optics for illumination

indicates company is in *Hoover's Handbook of American Business.*

indicates company is in *Hoover's Handbook of World Business;* sales and employee numbers are for parent company.

Foster Wheeler USA
Perryville Corporate Park
Clinton, NJ 08809
Phone: 908-730-4000 Fax: 908-730-4959
CEO: Louis E. Azzato
CFO: David J. Roberts
1992 Sales: $2,495 million Employees: 9,335
Symbol: FWC Exchange: NYSE
Industry: Machinery - electric utility

Foundation Health Corp.
3400 Data Dr.
Rancho Cordova, CA 95670
Phone: 916-631-5000 Fax: 916-631-5149
CEO: Daniel D. Crowley
CFO: Jeffrey L. Elder
1992 Sales: $1,285 million Employees: 1,940
Symbol: FH Exchange: NYSE
Industry: Healthcare - outpatient & home

Fountain Powerboat Industries, Inc.
Wichards Beach Rd.
Washington, NC 27889
Phone: 919-975-2000 Fax: 919-975-6793
CEO: Reginald M. Fountain, Jr.
CFO: Allan L. Krehbiel
1991 Sales: $19 million Employees: 289
Symbol: FPI Exchange: AMEX
Industry: Leisure & recreational products - sport-fishing & deep-water sports boats

FourGen Software Inc.
115 NE 100th St.
Seattle, WA 98125
Phone: 206-522-0055 Fax: 206-522-0053
CEO: Gary Gagliardi
CFO: Todd Steben
1992 Sales: $7 million Employees: 84
Ownership: Privately held
Industry: Computers - accounting software & CASE tools

Fourth Financial Corp.
100 N. Broadway
Wichita, KS 67202
Phone: 316-261-4444 Fax: 316-261-2111
CEO: Darrell G. Knudson
CFO: Michael J. Shonka
1991 Sales: $416 million Employees: 2,055
Symbol: FRTH Exchange: NASDAQ
Industry: Banks - Midwest

FoxMeyer Drug Co.
1220 Senlac Dr.
Carrollton, TX 75006
Phone: 214-446-4800 Fax: 214-446-4499
CEO: Robert L. King
CFO: Dennis J. Letham
1992 Sales: $4,095 million Employees: 2,107
Symbol: FOX Exchange: NYSE
Industry: Drugs & sundries - wholesale

FPA Corp.
2507 Philmont Ave.
Huntingdon Valley, PA 19006
Phone: 215-947-8900 Fax: —
CEO: Jeffrey P. Orleans
CFO: Lawrence Abrams
1992 Sales: $38 million Employees: 88
Symbol: FPO Exchange: AMEX
Industry: Real estate development

FPL Group, Inc.
700 Universe Blvd.
Juno Beach, FL 33408
Phone: 407-694-4000 Fax: 407-694-6490
CEO: James L. Broadhead
CFO: Joe L. Howard
1992 Sales: $5,193 million Employees: 15,144
Symbol: FPL Exchange: NYSE
Industry: Utility - electric power

Frame Technology Corp.
1010 Rincon Circle
San Jose, CA 95131
Phone: 408-433-3311 Fax: 408-433-1928
CEO: Paul R. Robichaux
CFO: Donald E. Lundgren
1992 Sales: $77 million Employees: 303
Symbol: FRAM Exchange: NASDAQ
Industry: Computers - publishing software

Framingham Savings Bank
600 Worcester Rd.
Framingham, MA 01701
Phone: 508-620-0300 Fax: —
CEO: Walter H. Braillard II
CFO: Walter H. Braillard II
1992 Sales: — Employees: —
Symbol: FSBX Exchange: NASDAQ
Industry: Financial - savings and loans

Frank B. Hall & Co. Inc.
261 Madison Ave.
New York, NY 10016
Phone: 212-922-1300 Fax: —
CEO: Donald R. Bell
CFO: John A. Addeo
1991 Sales: $462 million Employees: 4,775
Symbol: FBH Exchange: NYSE
Industry: Insurance - brokerage

Frank Consolidated Enterprises, Inc.
666 Garland Place
Des Plaines, IL 60016
Phone: 708-699-7000 Fax: 708-699-0681
CEO: James S. Frank
CFO: Ford Pearson
1991 Sales: $1,560 million Employees: 2,020
Ownership: Privately held
Industry: Retail - auto dealerships, travel services & fleet management

Frankford Corp.
601 Dresher Rd.
Horsham, PA 19044
Phone: 215-956-7000 Fax: —
CEO: Leon H. Layton
CFO: Donald G. Mihok
1991 Sales: $24 million Employees: 300
Symbol: FKFD Exchange: NASDAQ
Industry: Banks - Northeast

Franklin Bank, N.A.
26400 W. Twelve Mile Rd.
Southfield, MI 48034
Phone: 313-358-4710 Fax: —
CEO: Read P. Dunn
CFO: Edward J. Shehab
1992 Sales: — Employees: —
Symbol: FSVB Exchange: NASDAQ
Industry: Financial - savings and loans

Franklin Electric Co., Inc.
400 E. Spring St.
Bluffton, IN 46714
Phone: 219-824-2900 Fax: 219-824-2909
CEO: William H. Lawson
CFO: Dean W. Pfister
1991 Sales: $184 million Employees: 2,049
Symbol: FELE Exchange: NASDAQ
Industry: Machinery - electrical

Franklin Electronic Publishers, Inc.
122 Burrs Rd.
Mt. Holly, NJ 08060
Phone: 609-261-4800 Fax: 609-261-2984
CEO: Morton E. David
CFO: Kenneth H. Lind
1992 Sales: $54 million Employees: 156
Symbol: FPUB Exchange: NASDAQ
Industry: Electrical products - electronic books

Franklin First Financial Corp.
44 W. Market St.
Wilkes-Barre, PA 18773
Phone: 717-821-7100 Fax: —
CEO: Thomas H. van Arsdale
CFO: Richard F. Mebane
1991 Sales: $30 million Employees: —
Symbol: FFFC Exchange: NASDAQ
Industry: Financial - savings and loans

Franklin Holding Corp.
767 Fifth Ave.
New York, NY 10153
Phone: 212-486-2323 Fax: 212-755-5451
CEO: Stephen L. Brown
CFO: Stephen L. Brown
1992 Sales: — Employees: —
Symbol: FKL Exchange: AMEX
Industry: Financial - SBIC & commercial

Franklin Quest Co.
2200 W. Parkway Blvd.
Salt Lake City, UT 84119
Phone: 801-975-1776 Fax: 801-977-1431
CEO: Hyrum W. Smith
CFO: Jay L. Atwood
1991 Sales: $82 million Employees: 1,011
Symbol: FNQ Exchange: NYSE
Industry: Business services - productivity seminars, business calendars & planners

Franklin Resources, Inc.
777 Mariners Island Blvd.
San Mateo, CA 94404
Phone: 415-312-2000 Fax: 415-378-5755
CEO: Charles B. Johnson
CFO: Kenneth V. Domingues
1991 Sales: $318 million Employees: 2,128
Symbol: BEN Exchange: NYSE
Industry: Financial - investment management

Fred Meyer, Inc.
3800 SE 22nd Ave.
Portland, OR 97202
Phone: 503-232-8844 Fax: 503-233-4535
CEO: Robert G. Miller
CFO: Kenneth Thrasher
1992 Sales: $2,812 million Employees: 24,156
Symbol: FMY Exchange: NYSE
Industry: Retail - regional department stores

Fred W. Albrecht Grocery
2700 Gilchrist Rd.
Akron, OH 44305
Phone: 216-733-2861 Fax: 216-733-8782
CEO: F. Steven Albrecht
CFO: Jim Nilsen
1991 Sales: $475 million Employees: 3,105
Ownership: Privately held
Industry: Retail - supermarkets

Fred's, Inc.
4300 New Getwell Rd.
Memphis, TN 38118
Phone: 901-365-8880 Fax: —
CEO: Michael J. Hayes
CFO: Michael J. Hayes
1991 Sales: $292 million Employees: 3,350
Symbol: FRED Exchange: NASDAQ
Industry: Retail - discount & variety

Frederick's of Hollywood, Inc.
6608 Hollywood Blvd.
Los Angeles, CA 90028
Phone: 213-466-5151 Fax: —
CEO: George W. Townson
CFO: John B. Hatfield
1991 Sales: $114 million Employees: 1,500
Symbol: FHO Exchange: NYSE
Industry: Retail - women's apparel

indicates company is in *Hoover's Handbook of American Business.*

indicates company is in *Hoover's Handbook of World Business;* sales and employee numbers are for parent company.

Freedom Newspapers Inc.
PO Box 19549
Irvine, CA 92713
Phone: 714-553-9292 Fax: 714-474-4943
CEO: James N. Rosse
CFO: Richard K. Walker
1991 Sales: $464 million Employees: 4,928
Ownership: Privately held
Industry: Publishing - newspapers & TV

Freeport-McMoRan Copper & Gold Inc.
1615 Poydras St.
New Orleans, LA 70112
Phone: 504-582-4000 Fax: 504-585-3265
CEO: Milton H. Ward
CFO: James L. Shea
1992 Sales: $714 million Employees: 4,486
Symbol: FCX Exchange: NYSE
Industry: Metals - nonferrous

Freeport-McMoRan Global Resource Co.
1615 Poydras St.
New Orleans, LA 70112
Phone: 504-582-4000 Fax: 504-582-1847
CEO: Rene L. Latiolais
CFO: Charles W. Goodyear
1991 Sales: $904 million Employees: —
Symbol: FRP Exchange: NYSE
Industry: Fertilizers

Freeport-McMoRan Inc.
1615 Poydras St.
New Orleans, LA 70112
Phone: 504-582-4000 Fax: 504-582-1847
CEO: James R. Moffett
CFO: Ronald Grossman
1992 Sales: $1,655 million Employees: 7,253
Symbol: FTX Exchange: NYSE
Industry: Fertilizers

Fremont General Corp.
2020 Santa Monica Blvd.
Santa Monica, CA 90404
Phone: 310-315-5500 Fax: —
CEO: James A. McIntyre
CFO: William R. Bailey
1991 Sales: $581 million Employees: 1,468
Symbol: FRMT Exchange: NASDAQ
Industry: Insurance - property & casualty

Frequency Electronics, Inc.
55 Charles Lindbergh Blvd.
Uniondale, NY 11553
Phone: 516-794-4500 Fax: 516-794-4340
CEO: Martin B. Bloch
CFO: Joseph B. Kastenholz
1992 Sales: $53 million Employees: 587
Symbol: FEI Exchange: AMEX
Industry: Electronics - military

Fretter, Inc.
35901 Schoolcraft Rd.
Livonia, MI 48150
Phone: 313-591-0600 Fax: 313-591-8139
CEO: Oliver L. Fretter
CFO: John B. Hurley
1991 Sales: $293 million Employees: 1,664
Symbol: FTTR Exchange: NASDAQ
Industry: Retail - consumer electronics

Freymiller Trucking, Inc.
1400 S. Union Ave.
Bakersfield, CA 93307
Phone: 805-397-4151 Fax: —
CEO: Jerry K. Stanners
CFO: Richard E. Kuehn
1991 Sales: $92 million Employees: 1,192
Symbol: FRML Exchange: NASDAQ
Industry: Transportation - truck

Friedman Industries, Inc.
4001 Homestead Rd.
Houston, TX 77028
Phone: 713-672-9433 Fax: 713-672-7043
CEO: Jack Friedman
CFO: Harold Friedman
1992 Sales: $43 million Employees: 85
Symbol: FRD Exchange: AMEX
Industry: Steel - production

Frigidaire Co.
11770 Berea Rd.
Cleveland, OH 44111
Phone: 216-252-3700 Fax: 216-252-8073
CEO: Hans G. Bäckman
CFO: —
1991 Sales: $13,308 million Employees: 130,300
Parent: AB Electrolux
Industry: Appliances - household; industrial products

Frisch's Restaurants, Inc.
2800 Gilbert Ave.
Cincinnati, OH 45206
Phone: 513-961-2660 Fax: 513-559-5160
CEO: Craig F. Maier
CFO: Louis J. Ullman
1992 Sales: $138 million Employees: 5,700
Symbol: FRS Exchange: AMEX
Industry: Retail - food & restaurants

Frontier Adjusters of America, Inc.
45 E. Monterey Way
Phoenix, AZ 85012
Phone: 602-264-1061 Fax: —
CEO: William J. Rocke
CFO: Jean E. Ryberg
1992 Sales: $4.3 million Employees: —
Symbol: FRON Exchange: NASDAQ
Industry: Insurance - brokerage

Frontier Insurance Group, Inc.
196 Broadway
Monticello, NY 12701
Phone: 914-796-2100 Fax: —
CEO: Walter A. Rhulen
CFO: Dennis F. Plante
1991 Sales: $96 million Employees: —
Symbol: FTR Exchange: NYSE
Industry: Insurance - property & casualty

Frozen Food Express Industries, Inc.
318 Cadiz St.
Dallas, TX 75207
Phone: 214-428-7661 Fax: —
CEO: Stoney M. Stubbs, Jr.
CFO: Burl G. Cott
1991 Sales: $177 million Employees: 1,534
Symbol: JIT Exchange: AMEX
Industry: Transportation - truck

FRP Properties, Inc.
155 E. 21st St.
Jacksonville, FL 32201
Phone: 904-355-1781 Fax: —
CEO: John E. Anderson
CFO: John D. Baker II
1991 Sales: $43 million Employees: 478
Symbol: FRPP Exchange: NASDAQ
Industry: Transportation - truck

Fruehauf Trailer Corp.
26999 Central Park Blvd.
Southfield, MI 48076
Phone: 313-267-1000 Fax: 313-746-9935
CEO: Thomas B. Roller
CFO: John F. Liechty
1991 Sales: $513 million Employees: 5,200
Symbol: FTC Exchange: NYSE
Industry: Automotive & trucking - original equipment

Fruit of the Loom, Inc.
5000 Sears Tower, 233 S. Wacker Dr.
Chicago, IL 60606
Phone: 312-876-1724 Fax: 312-993-1749
CEO: William Farley
CFO: Paul M. O'Hara
1992 Sales: $1,855 million Employees: 26,700
Symbol: FTL Exchange: AMEX
Industry: Textiles - apparel: underwear, T-shirts, infant & toddler clothing, sweatshirts

FSI International, Inc.
322 Lake Hazeltine Dr.
Chaska, MN 55318
Phone: 612-448-5440 Fax: 612-448-2825
CEO: Joel A. Elftmann
CFO: Benno G. Sand
1991 Sales: $45 million Employees: 309
Symbol: FSII Exchange: NASDAQ
Industry: Electrical components - automated wafer-processing equipment

Fuji Photo Film U.S.A., Inc.
555 Taxter Rd.
Elmsford, NY 10523
Phone: 914-789-8100 Fax: 914-682-4955
CEO: Sam Inoue
CFO: —
1991 Sales: $8,662 million Employees: 23,690
Parent: Fuji Photo Film Co., Ltd.
Industry: Photographic equipment & supplies, magnetic products

Fujitsu Computer Products of America, Inc.
2904 Orchard Pkwy.
San Jose, CA 95134
Phone: 408-432-6333 Fax: 408-894-1709
CEO: Lewis Frauenfelder
CFO: —
1992 Sales: $27,536 million Employees: 155,779
Parent: Fujitsu Ltd.
Industry: Computers - mini & micro

Fulton Computer Products
212 Merrick Rd.
Rockville Centre, NY 11570
Phone: 516-764-2822 Fax: 516-764-3873
CEO: Barry Weinstein
CFO: Barry Weinstein
1992 Sales: $19 million Employees: 24
Ownership: Privately held
Industry: Computers - computer hardware, software & peripheral equipment

Fulton Financial Corp.
One Penn Square
Lancaster, PA 17604
Phone: 717-291-2411 Fax: —
CEO: Robert D. Garner
CFO: Robert D. Garner
1991 Sales: $188 million Employees: 1,184
Symbol: FULT Exchange: NASDAQ
Industry: Banks - Northeast

Fuqua Industries, Inc.
4900 Georgia-Pacific Center
Atlanta, GA 30303
Phone: 404-658-9000 Fax: 404-577-6142
CEO: Charles R. Scott
CFO: Frederick B. Beilstein III
1992 Sales: $1,149 million Employees: 10,675
Symbol: FQA Exchange: NYSE
Industry: Diversified operations - photofinishing, lawn & garden equipment, sporting goods

Furon Co.
29982 Ivy Glenn Dr.
Laguna Niguel, CA 92677
Phone: 714-831-5350 Fax: 714-643-1548
CEO: J. Michael Hagan
CFO: Monty A. Houdeshell
1991 Sales: $306 million Employees: 2,637
Symbol: FCBN Exchange: NASDAQ
Industry: Rubber & plastic products

indicates company is in *Hoover's Handbook of American Business.*

indicates company is in *Hoover's Handbook of World Business;* sales and employee numbers are for parent company.

Furr's Supermarkets, Inc.
1730 Montano Rd. NW
Albuquerque, NM 87107
Phone: 505-344-6525 Fax: 505-344-1118
CEO: Jan Friederich
CFO: Mike Daly
1991 Sales: $900 million Employees: 6,000
Ownership: Privately held
Industry: Retail - supermarkets

Furr's/Bishop's Cafeterias, L.P.
6901 Quaker Ave.
Lubbock, TX 79413
Phone: 806-792-7151 Fax: 806-792-8277
CEO: Michael J. Levenson
CFO: Alton R. Smith
1991 Sales: $268 million Employees: 9,925
Symbol: CHI Exchange: NYSE
Industry: Retail - food & restaurants

Future Communications, Inc.
11407 Emerald Rd., Ste. 109
Dallas, TX 75229
Phone: 214-243-2267 Fax: —
CEO: Sergio Bosco
CFO: Sergio Bosco
1991 Sales: $1.7 million Employees: 7
Symbol: FCMI Exchange: NASDAQ
Industry: Broadcasting - radio & TV

Future Now, Inc.
2722 E. Kemper Rd.
Cincinnati, OH 45241
Phone: 513-771-7110 Fax: —
CEO: Terry L. Theye
CFO: David L. Durham
1991 Sales: $139 million Employees: 510
Symbol: FNOW Exchange: NASDAQ
Industry: Computers - turnkey microcomputer systems services

G&K Services, Inc.
505 Hwy. 169 North, Ste. 455
Plymouth, MN 55441
Phone: 612-546-7440 Fax: 612-549-7872
CEO: Richard Fink
CFO: Stephen F. LaBelle
1991 Sales: $176 million Employees: 3,532
Symbol: GKSRA Exchange: NASDAQ
Industry: Linen supply & laundering - uniforms

G-III Apparel Group, Ltd.
345 W. 37th St.
New York, NY 10018
Phone: 212-629-8830 Fax: 212-967-1487
CEO: Morris Goldfarb
CFO: Alan Feller
1991 Sales: $142 million Employees: 197
Symbol: GIII Exchange: NASDAQ
Industry: Leather & related products

GAF
1361 Alps Rd.
Wayne, NJ 07470
Phone: 201-628-3000 Fax: 201-628-3311
CEO: Samuel J. Heyman
CFO: Raymond J. Lacroix
1991 Sales: $926 million Employees: 4,075
Ownership: Privately held
Industry: Building products & chemicals

GAINSCO, INC.
5701 E. Loop 820 South
Ft. Worth, TX 76119
Phone: 817-483-0007 Fax: 817-483-1572
CEO: Joseph D. Macchia
CFO: Daniel J. Coots
1991 Sales: $60 million Employees: —
Symbol: GNA Exchange: AMEX
Industry: Insurance - property & casualty

Galaxy Cablevision, L.P.
1100 N. Main
Sikeston, MO 63801
Phone: 314-471-3080 Fax: —
CEO: Tommy L. Gleason
CFO: J. Keith Davidson
1991 Sales: $17 million Employees: 151
Symbol: GTV Exchange: AMEX
Industry: Cable TV

Gale Group
111 N. Orlando Ave.
Winter Park, FL 32789
Phone: 407-621-4253 Fax: 407-621-2505
CEO: Gary Gale
CFO: Mark Lowery
1991 Sales: $58 million Employees: 300
Ownership: Privately held
Industry: Retail - lawn & garden products

Galey & Lord, Inc.
7736 McCloud Rd., Ste. 300
Greensboro, NC 27409
Phone: 919-665-3000 Fax: 919-665-3106
CEO: Arthur C. Wiener
CFO: Michael R. Harmon
1991 Sales: $329 million Employees: 3,108
Symbol: GANL Exchange: NASDAQ
Industry: Textiles - mill products

Galileo Electro-Optics Corp.
Galileo Park
Sturbridge, MA 01566
Phone: 508-347-9191 Fax: 508-347-3849
CEO: William T. Hanley
CFO: Josef W. Rokus
1991 Sales: $36 million Employees: 329
Symbol: GAEO Exchange: NASDAQ
Industry: Fiber optics

Galveston-Houston Co.
4900 Woodway, Ste. 1200
Houston, TX 77056
Phone: 713-966-2500 Fax: 713-966-2575
CEO: Nathan M. Avery
CFO: Pamela L. Reiland
1991 Sales: $99 million Employees: 924
Symbol: GHX Exchange: NYSE
Industry: Oil field machinery & equipment

Gamma Biologicals, Inc.
3700 Mangum Rd.
Houston, TX 77092
Phone: 713-681-8481 Fax: 713-956-3333
CEO: David E. Hatcher
CFO: Margaret J. O'Bannion
1992 Sales: $17 million Employees: 137
Symbol: GBL Exchange: AMEX
Industry: Biomedical & genetic products

Gander Mountain, Inc.
Hwy. West
Wilmot, WI 53192
Phone: 414-862-2331 Fax: 414-862-2330
CEO: Ralph L. Freitag
CFO: Theodore E. Schultz
1992 Sales: $152 million Employees: 922
Symbol: GNDR Exchange: NASDAQ
Industry: Retail - mail order & direct

Gannett Co., Inc.
1100 Wilson Blvd.
Arlington, VA 22234
Phone: 703-284-6000 Fax: 703-558-4697
CEO: John J. Curley
CFO: Douglas H. McCorkindale
1992 Sales: $3,469 million Employees: 36,700
Symbol: GCI Exchange: NYSE
Industry: Publishing - newspapers; radio & TV broadcasting

Gantos, Inc.
3260 Patterson SE
Grand Rapids, MI 49508
Phone: 616-949-7000 Fax: 616-949-5884
CEO: L. Douglas Gantos
CFO: James P. Curley
1992 Sales: $267 million Employees: 2,955
Symbol: GTOS Exchange: NASDAQ
Industry: Retail - apparel & shoes

Gap, Inc., The
One Harrison St.
San Francisco, CA 94105
Phone: 415-952-4400 Fax: 415-896-0322
CEO: Donald G. Fisher
CFO: David M. DeMattei
1992 Sales: $2,834 million Employees: 32,000
Symbol: GPS Exchange: NYSE
Industry: Retail - apparel & shoes

Garan, Inc.
350 Fifth Ave.
New York, NY 10118
Phone: 212-563-2000 Fax: 212-564-7994
CEO: Seymour Lichtenstein
CFO: William J. Wilson
1991 Sales: $146 million Employees: 3,100
Symbol: GAN Exchange: AMEX
Industry: Textiles - apparel

Gardner/Fox Associates, Inc.
919 Glenbrook Ave.
Bryn Mawr, PA 19010
Phone: 215-525-8305 Fax: 215-525-8977
CEO: Brook Gardner
CFO: Mark Pennington
1991 Sales: $5.1 million Employees: 45
Ownership: Privately held
Industry: Construction - general contracting

Garnet Resources Corp.
333 Clay St., Ste. 4500
Houston, TX 77002
Phone: 713-759-1692 Fax: 713-759-9122
CEO: Albert E. Whitehead
CFO: W. Kirk Bosche
1991 Sales: $0.8 million Employees: 7
Symbol: GARN Exchange: NASDAQ
Industry: Oil & gas - international specialty

Gates Rubber Co.
900 S. Broadway
Denver, CO 80209
Phone: 303-744-1911 Fax: 303-744-4000
CEO: Charles C. Gates
CFO: R. L. Stamp
1991 Sales: $1,380 million Employees: 16,950
Ownership: Privately held
Industry: Rubber & formed fiber products, rechargeable batteries

Gates/FA Distributing, Inc.
121 Interstate Blvd.
Greenville, SC 29615
Phone: 803-234-0736 Fax: 803-627-2184
CEO: Philip D. Ellett
CFO: William T. Mauldin
1992 Sales: $232 million Employees: 295
Symbol: GAFA Exchange: NASDAQ
Industry: Computers - micro; peripheral equipment; networking software

Gateway 2000
610 Gateway Dr.
North Sioux City, SD 57049
Phone: 605-232-2000 Fax: 605-232-2023
CEO: Ted Waitt
CFO: John Morrisey
1992 Sales: $1,100 million Employees: 1,847
Ownership: Privately held
Industry: Computers - mail-order microcomputers

indicates company is in *Hoover's Handbook of American Business.*

indicates company is in *Hoover's Handbook of World Business*; sales and employee numbers are for parent company.

Gateway Bancorp, Inc.
1630 Richmond Rd.
Staten Island, NY 10304
Phone: 718-979-4000 Fax: —
CEO: Merton Corn
CFO: Mark D. Curtis
1991 Sales: $27 million Employees: 196
Symbol: GBAN Exchange: NASDAQ
Industry: Banks - Northeast

Gateway Communications, Inc.
1 Bala Plaza, Ste. 237
Bala Cynwyd, PA 19004
Phone: 215-664-4400 Fax: —
CEO: Patrick F. Cadigan
CFO: Kirk E. Andrews
1991 Sales: $24 million Employees: 105
Symbol: GWAY Exchange: NASDAQ
Industry: Computers - local area networks & wide area networks

Gateway Fed Corp.
128 E. Fourth St.
Cincinnati, OH 45202
Phone: 513-621-9600 Fax: 513-723-8319
CEO: Robert M. McLaughlin
CFO: Joseph T. Powell
1991 Sales: $60 million Employees: 154
Symbol: GATW Exchange: NASDAQ
Industry: Financial - savings and loans

Gateway Financial Corp.
383 Main Ave.
Norwalk, CT 06851
Phone: 203-845-7700 Fax: —
CEO: Reginald DeKoven III
CFO: Richard A. Martin
1991 Sales: $103 million Employees: 399
Symbol: GTWY Exchange: NASDAQ
Industry: Banks - Northeast

GATX Corp.
120 S. Riverside Plaza
Chicago, IL 60606
Phone: 312-621-6200 Fax: 312-621-6646
CEO: James J. Glasser
CFO: John F. Chlebowski, Jr.
1992 Sales: $1,019 million Employees: 5,100
Symbol: GMT Exchange: NYSE
Industry: Transportation - equipment & leasing

Gaylord Container Corp.
500 Lake Cook Rd., Ste. 400
Deerfield, IL 60015
Phone: 708-405-5500 Fax: 708-405-5585
CEO: Marvin A. Pomerantz
CFO: Daniel P. Casey
1992 Sales: $731 million Employees: 4,150
Symbol: GCR Exchange: AMEX
Industry: Paper & paper products

Gaylord Entertainment Co.
2806 Opryland Dr.
Nashville, TN 37214
Phone: 615-889-6611 Fax: 615-871-5787
CEO: Earl W. Wendell
CFO: Terry E. London
1991 Sales: $601 million Employees: 8,700
Symbol: GET Exchange: NYSE
Industry: Musical show park, convention/resort complex; TV stations & cable networks

GBC Bancorp
201 S. Figueroa St.
Los Angeles, CA 90012
Phone: 213-972-4170 Fax: —
CEO: Li-Pei Wu
CFO: Philip J. Gitzinger
1991 Sales: $78 million Employees: 193
Symbol: GBCB Exchange: NASDAQ
Industry: Banks - West

Geerlings & Wade
960 T-Pik St.
Canton, MA 02021
Phone: 617-821-4152 Fax: 617-821-4153
CEO: Phillip Wade
CFO: Huib Geerlings
1991 Sales: $3.1 million Employees: 13
Ownership: Privately held
Industry: Beverages - premium wines

Gehl Co.
143 Water St.
West Bend, WI 53095
Phone: 414-334-9461 Fax: 414-334-1565
CEO: Bernard L. Nielsen
CFO: Kenneth F. Kaplan
1991 Sales: $127 million Employees: 1,150
Symbol: GEHL Exchange: NASDAQ
Industry: Machinery - farm

GEICO Corp.
One GEICO Plaza
Washington, DC 20076
Phone: 301-986-3000 Fax: 301-986-2113
CEO: William B. Snyder
CFO: W. Alvon Sparks, Jr.
1992 Sales: $2,420 million Employees: 7,374
Symbol: GEC Exchange: NYSE
Industry: Insurance - property & casualty

Gelman Sciences, Inc.
600 S. Wagner Rd.
Ann Arbor, MI 48106
Phone: 313-665-0651 Fax: 313-761-1114
CEO: Charles Gelman
CFO: Craig S. Camalo
1991 Sales: $76 million Employees: 765
Symbol: GSC Exchange: AMEX
Industry: Filtration products

Gemco National, Inc.
7200 W. Camino Real
Boca Raton, FL 33433
Phone: 407-391-5043 Fax: 407-391-0316
CEO: Melvin C. Parker
CFO: Richard T. Magsam
1991 Sales: $13 million Employees: 19
Symbol: GNL Exchange: AMEX
Industry: Insurance - life

GenCare Health Systems, Inc.
969 Executive Pkwy.
St. Louis, MO 63141
Phone: 314-434-6114 Fax: 314-434-6328
CEO: H. Edwin Trusheim
CFO: Leonard M. Rubenstein
1991 Sales: $130 million Employees: —
Symbol: GNCR Exchange: NASDAQ
Industry: Health maintenance organization

Gencor Industries, Inc.
5201 N. Orange Blossom Trail
Orlando, FL 32810
Phone: 407-290-6000 Fax: 407-578-0577
CEO: E. J. Elliott
CFO: R. Victor Taglia
1991 Sales: $38 million Employees: 414
Symbol: GCOR Exchange: NASDAQ
Industry: Diversified operations - asphalt, combustion & fluid heat transfer systems

GenCorp Inc.
175 Ghent Rd.
Fairlawn, OH 44333
Phone: 216-869-4200 Fax: 216-869-4211
CEO: A. William Reynolds
CFO: D. Michael Steuert
1992 Sales: $1,937 million Employees: 14,500
Symbol: GY Exchange: NYSE
Industry: Diversified operations - defense products, polymer products for the auto industry

GENDEX Corp.
901 W. Oakton St.
Des Plaines, IL 60018
Phone: 708-640-4800 Fax: 708-640-6165
CEO: John J. McDonough
CFO: Arthur L. Herbst, Jr.
1992 Sales: $85 million Employees: 700
Symbol: XRAY Exchange: NASDAQ
Industry: Medical & dental supplies - X-ray equipment

Genelabs Technologies, Inc.
505 Penobscot Dr.
Redwood City, CA 94063
Phone: 415-369-9500 Fax: 415-368-0709
CEO: Frank F. C. Kung
CFO: Linda P. O'Keefe
1991 Sales: $4.3 million Employees: 121
Symbol: GNLB Exchange: NASDAQ
Industry: Biomedical & genetic products

Genentech, Inc.
460 Point San Bruno Blvd.
South San Francisco, CA 94080
Phone: 415-266-1000 Fax: 415-588-3255
CEO: G. Kirk Raab
CFO: Louis J. Lavigne, Jr.
1991 Sales: $460 million Employees: 2,202
Symbol: GNE Exchange: NYSE
Industry: Biomedical & genetic products

General American Investors Co., Inc.
330 Madison Ave.
New York, NY 10017
Phone: 212-916-8400 Fax: —
CEO: William J. Gedale
CFO: Diane G. Radosti
1992 Sales: — Employees: —
Symbol: GAM Exchange: NYSE
Industry: Financial - investment management

General Automation, Inc.
1055 S. East St.
Anaheim, CA 92805
Phone: 714-778-4800 Fax: 714-535-7092
CEO: Paul Thompson
CFO: Donald W.S. Rutherford
1991 Sales: $49 million Employees: 380
Symbol: GA Exchange: AMEX
Industry: Computers - mini & micro

General Binding Corp.
One GBC Plaza
Northbrook, IL 60062
Phone: 708-272-3700 Fax: 708-272-1389
CEO: Rudolph Grua
CFO: Edward J. McNulty
1991 Sales: $311 million Employees: 3,537
Symbol: GBND Exchange: NASDAQ
Industry: Office equipment & supplies

General Building Products Corp.
2577 Route 112
Medford, NY 11763
Phone: 516-654-3500 Fax: 516-654-9204
CEO: Bruce G. Meltzer
CFO: Thomas S. Kiritsis
1991 Sales: $45 million Employees: 241
Symbol: GBLD Exchange: NASDAQ
Industry: Building products - retail & wholesale

General Cable Corp.
One East Fourth St.
Cincinnati, OH 45202
Phone: 513-579-6690 Fax: —
CEO: Ronald F. Walker
CFO: James E. Schwab
1991 Sales: $1,024 million Employees: 6,339
Symbol: GENC Exchange: NASDAQ
Industry: Wire & cable products

General Cinema Corp.
27 Boylston St.
Chestnut Hill, MA 02167
Phone: 617-232-8200 Fax: 617-232-4808
CEO: Robert J. Tarr, Jr.
CFO: John R. Cook
1992 Sales: $3,717 million Employees: 32,641
Symbol: GCN Exchange: NYSE
Industry: Diversified operations - retail apparel, theaters, publishing

General Computer Corp.
2045 Midway Dr.
Twinsburg, OH 44087
Phone: 216-425-3241 Fax: 216-425-3249
CEO: Richard R. Pilarczyk
CFO: David R. Stitt
1992 Sales: $13 million Employees: 183
Symbol: GCCC Exchange: NASDAQ
Industry: Computers - data processing services for health care market

General DataComm Industries, Inc.
1579 Straits Tnpk.
Middlebury, CT 06762
Phone: 203-574-1118 Fax: 203-758-8507
CEO: Charles P. Johnson
CFO: William S. Lawrence
1991 Sales: $192 million Employees: 1,737
Symbol: GDC Exchange: NYSE
Industry: Computers - data communications equipment & networks

General Dynamics Corp.
3190 Fairview Park Dr.
Falls Church, VA 22042
Phone: 703-876-3000 Fax: 703-876-3125
CEO: William A. Anders
CFO: James J. Cunnane
1992 Sales: $3,472 million Employees: 75,300
Symbol: GD Exchange: NYSE
Industry: Military equipment - tactical aircraft, nuclear submarines, armored vehicles

General Electric Co.
3135 Easton Tnpk.
Fairfield, CT 06431
Phone: 203-373-2259 Fax: 203-373-3131
CEO: John F. Welch, Jr.
CFO: Dennis D. Dammerman
1992 Sales: $62,200 million Employees: 284,000
Symbol: GE Exchange: NYSE
Industry: Diversified operations - financing, aircraft engines, industrial products

General Employment Enterprises, Inc.
One Tower Lane, Ste. 2100
Oakbrook Terrace, IL 60181
Phone: 708-954-0400 Fax: 708-572-1283
CEO: Herbert F. Imhoff
CFO: Herbert F. Imhoff, Jr.
1991 Sales: $13 million Employees: 330
Symbol: JOB Exchange: AMEX
Industry: Business services - personnel services

General Host Corp.
1 Station Place
Stamford, CT 06902
Phone: 203-357-9900 Fax: 203-357-0148
CEO: Harris J. Ashton
CFO: Robert M. Lovejoy
1991 Sales: $520 million Employees: —
Symbol: GH Exchange: NYSE
Industry: Retail - gardening, crafts, Christmas merchandise

General Housewares Corp.
6 Suburban Ave.
Stamford, CT 06904
Phone: 203-325-4141 Fax: 203-348-5247
CEO: Paul A. Saxton
CFO: Robert L. Gray
1991 Sales: $74 million Employees: 640
Symbol: GHW Exchange: NYSE
Industry: Housewares - gardening, crafts, Christmas merchandise

General Instrument Corp.
181 W. Madison, 49th Fl.
Chicago, IL 60602
Phone: 312-541-5000 Fax: 312-541-8038
CEO: Donald H. Rumsfeld
CFO: Richard S. Friedland
1992 Sales: $1,075 million Employees: 8,600
Symbol: GIC Exchange: NYSE
Industry: Electrical components - semiconductors; broad-band communications equipment

General Kinetics Inc.
12300 Parklawn Dr.
Rockville, MD 20852
Phone: 301-881-2044 Fax: 301-881-3109
CEO: Louis R. Schap
CFO: Stanley J. Sarnowski
1991 Sales: $19 million Employees: 220
Symbol: GKI Exchange: AMEX
Industry: Diversified operations - fax machines, electronic enclosure products

General Magnaplate Corp.
1331 U.S. Route 1
Linden, NJ 07036
Phone: 908-862-6200 Fax: 908-862-6110
CEO: Charles P. Covino
CFO: Charles P. Covino
1991 Sales: $10.5 million Employees: 136
Symbol: GMCC Exchange: NASDAQ
Industry: Metal processing & fabrication

General Microwave Corp.
5500 New Horizons Blvd.
Amityville, NY 11701
Phone: 516-226-8900 Fax: 516-226-8966
CEO: Sherman A. Rinkel
CFO: Sherman A. Rinkel
1992 Sales: $23 million Employees: 275
Symbol: GMW Exchange: AMEX
Industry: Electrical components - microwave components & subsystems

General Mills, Inc.
1 General Mills Blvd.
Minneapolis, MN 55426
Phone: 612-540-2311 Fax: 612-540-4925
CEO: H. Brewster Atwater, Jr.
CFO: Joe R. Lee
1992 Sales: $7,985 million Employees: 111,501
Symbol: GIS Exchange: NYSE
Industry: Food - cereals, snack foods, prepared mixes & frostings; restaurants

General Motors Corp.
3044 W. Grand Blvd.
Detroit, MI 48202
Phone: 313-556-5000 Fax: 313-556-5108
CEO: John F. Smith, Jr.
CFO: G. Richard Wagoner, Jr.
1992 Sales: $132,429 million Employees: 756,300
Symbol: GM Exchange: NYSE
Industry: Diversified operations - automotive manufacturing, finance & insurance

General Parametrics Corp.
1250 Ninth St.
Berkeley, CA 94710
Phone: 510-524-3950 Fax: 510-524-9954
CEO: Herbert B. Baskin
CFO: William A. Spazante
1991 Sales: $14 million Employees: 81
Symbol: GPAR Exchange: NASDAQ
Industry: Computers - desktop graphics

General Physics Corp.
6700 Alexander Bell Dr.
Columbia, MD 21046
Phone: 410-290-2300 Fax: 410-290-2600
CEO: R. Eugene Klose
CFO: John C. McAuliffe
1991 Sales: $85 million Employees: 849
Symbol: GPH Exchange: NYSE
Industry: Business services - technical support & staff training; environmental engineering

General Public Utilities Corp.
100 Interpace Pkwy.
Parsippany, NJ 07054
Phone: 201-263-6500 Fax: 201-263-6822
CEO: James R. Leva
CFO: John G. Graham
1992 Sales: $3,434 million Employees: 12,152
Symbol: GPU Exchange: NYSE
Industry: Utility - electric power

General Re Corp.
695 E. Main St.
Stamford, CT 06904
Phone: 203-328-5000 Fax: 203-328-5329
CEO: Ronald E. Ferguson
CFO: Joseph P. Brandon
1992 Sales: $3,387 million Employees: 2,513
Symbol: GRN Exchange: NYSE
Industry: Insurance - property & casualty; reinsurance

General Signal Corp.
1 High Ridge Park
Stamford, CT 06904
Phone: 203-357-8800 Fax: 203-329-4159
CEO: Edmund M. Carpenter
CFO: Stephen W. Nagy
1992 Sales: $1,618 million Employees: 14,738
Symbol: GSX Exchange: NYSE
Industry: Instruments - control

Genesco Inc.
Genesco Park, 1415 Murfreesboro Rd.
Nashville, TN 37217
Phone: 615-367-7000 Fax: 615-367-8179
CEO: E. Douglas Grindstaff
CFO: James S. Gulmi
1991 Sales: $472 million Employees: 6,150
Symbol: GCO Exchange: NYSE
Industry: Shoes & related apparel

Genesee Corp.
445 St. Paul St.
Rochester, NY 14605
Phone: 716-546-1030 Fax: —
CEO: John L. Wehle, Jr.
CFO: Edward J. Rompala
1992 Sales: $145 million Employees: 844
Symbol: GENBB Exchange: NASDAQ
Industry: Beverages - beers & ales

Genesis Automation Inc.
2 Research Dr.
Shelton, CT 06484
Phone: 203-929-3555 Fax: 203-926-8830
CEO: Sal Brogna
CFO: Sal Brogna
1991 Sales: $2.1 million Employees: 13
Ownership: Privately held
Industry: Industrial automation & robotics for fast food industry

Genesis Health Ventures, Inc.
148 W. State St., Ste. 100
Kennett Square, PA 19348
Phone: 215-444-6350 Fax: —
CEO: Michael R. Walker
CFO: Gregory M. Stevens
1991 Sales: $171 million Employees: 7,000
Symbol: GHVI Exchange: NASDAQ
Industry: Healthcare - outpatient & home

Genetic Therapy, Inc.
19 Firstfield Rd.
Gaithersburg, MD 20878
Phone: 301-590-2626 Fax: —
CEO: M. James Barrett
CFO: Marc R. Schneebaum
1991 Sales: $0.1 million Employees: 52
Symbol: GTII Exchange: NASDAQ
Industry: Biomedical & genetic products

indicates company is in *Hoover's Handbook of American Business.*

indicates company is in *Hoover's Handbook of World Business;* sales and employee numbers are for parent company.

Genetics Institute, Inc.
87 Cambridge Park Dr.
Cambridge, MA 02140
Phone: 617-876-1170 Fax: 617-876-1504
CEO: Gabriel Schmergel
CFO: Joseph Grimm
1991 Sales: $83 million Employees: 591
Symbol: GENIZ Exchange: NASDAQ
Industry: Biomedical & genetic products

Geneva Steel
1600 W. Center St.
Vineyard, UT 84058
Phone: 801-227-9000 Fax: 801-227-9090
CEO: Joseph A. Cannon
CFO: Dennis L. Wanlass
1991 Sales: $446 million Employees: 2,750
Symbol: GNV Exchange: NYSE
Industry: Steel - production

GENICOM Corp.
RR 2 Box 80, Fort Herkimer Rd.
Mohawk, NY 13407
Phone: 315-866-6900 Fax: —
CEO: Paul T. Winn
CFO: James C. Gale
1991 Sales: $217 million Employees: 2,512
Symbol: GECM Exchange: NASDAQ
Industry: Computers - printers

Genisco Technology Corp.
1657 Pacific Rim Ct.
San Diego, CA 92173
Phone: 619-661-5100 Fax: 619-661-5120
CEO: Phillip C. Friedman
CFO: John J. Gallogly
1991 Sales: $24 million Employees: 273
Symbol: GES Exchange: AMEX
Industry: Computers - peripheral equipment, printers

Genlyte Group Inc.
100 Lighting Way
Secaucus, NJ 07096
Phone: 201-864-3000 Fax: 201-392-3784
CEO: Fred Heller
CFO: Fred Heller
1991 Sales: $428 million Employees: 3,189
Symbol: GLYT Exchange: NASDAQ
Industry: Building products - lighting fixtures

Genovese Drug Stores, Inc.
80 Marcus Dr.
Melville, NY 11747
Phone: 516-420-1900 Fax: 516-420-1807
CEO: Leonard Genovese
CFO: Jerome Stengel
1991 Sales: $447 million Employees: 3,575
Symbol: GDXA Exchange: AMEX
Industry: Retail - drug stores

Genpack USA Inc.
8300 Boettner Rd.
Bridgewater, MI 48115
Phone: 313-429-7647 Fax: 313-429-4714
CEO: Al Gentile
CFO: Al Gentile
1991 Sales: $3.4 million Employees: 20
Ownership: Privately held
Industry: Business services - contract packaging

GenRad, Inc.
300 Baker Ave.
Concord, MA 01742
Phone: 508-369-4400 Fax: 508-369-6974
CEO: Robert E. Anderson
CFO: Robert C. Aldworth
1991 Sales: $156 million Employees: 1,370
Symbol: GEN Exchange: NYSE
Industry: Electronics - measuring instruments

Gensia Pharmaceuticals, Inc.
110275 Roselle St.
San Diego, CA 92121
Phone: 619-546-8300 Fax: 619-453-0095
CEO: David F. Hale
CFO: Arthur C. Johnson
1991 Sales: $8.6 million Employees: 286
Symbol: GNSA Exchange: NASDAQ
Industry: Drugs

Gensym
125 Cambridge Park Dr., 5th Fl.
Cambridge, MA 02140
Phone: 617-547-2500 Fax: 617-547-1962
CEO: Lowell Hawkinson
CFO: Stephen Gregorio
1991 Sales: $14 million Employees: 115
Ownership: Privately held
Industry: Computers - expert systems software & services

Genta, Inc.
3550 General Atomics Court
San Diego, CA 92121
Phone: 619-455-2700 Fax: —
CEO: Thomas H. Adams
CFO: Howard Sampson
1991 Sales: $2.6 million Employees: 71
Symbol: GNTA Exchange: NASDAQ
Industry: Drugs

Gentex Corp.
600 N. Centennial St.
Zeeland, MI 49464
Phone: 616-772-1800 Fax: 616-772-7348
CEO: Fred Bauer
CFO: Enoch Jen
1991 Sales: $27 million Employees: 343
Symbol: GNTX Exchange: NASDAQ
Industry: Automotive & trucking - original equipment

Genuine Parts Co.
2999 Circle 75 Pkwy. NW
Atlanta, GA 30339
Phone: 404-953-1700 Fax: 404-956-2211
CEO: Larry L. Prince
CFO: George W. Kalafut
1992 Sales: $3,669 million Employees: 17,107
Symbol: GPC Exchange: NYSE
Industry: Auto parts - retail & wholesale

Genus, Inc.
555 Ellis St.
Mountain View, CA 94043
Phone: 415-960-1120 Fax: 415-969-9657
CEO: William W.R. Elder
CFO: Richard D. Hannigan
1991 Sales: $52 million Employees: 259
Symbol: GGNS Exchange: NASDAQ
Industry: Electrical components - semiconductors

Genzyme Corp.
1 Kendall Sq.
Cambridge, MA 02139
Phone: 617-252-7500 Fax: 617-252-7600
CEO: Henri A. Termeer
CFO: David J. McLachlan
1991 Sales: $112 million Employees: 789
Symbol: GENZ Exchange: NASDAQ
Industry: Biomedical & genetic products

Geo. A. Hormel & Co.
501 16th Ave. NE
Austin, MN 55912
Phone: 507-437-5737 Fax: 507-437-5489
CEO: Richard L. Knowlton
CFO: Don J. Hodapp
1992 Sales: $2,814 million Employees: 8,300
Symbol: HRL Exchange: NYSE
Industry: Food - meat products

GEO International Corp.
4 Landmark Square
Stamford, CT 06901
Phone: 203-977-1510 Fax: 203-977-1514
CEO: John E. McConnaughy, Jr
CFO: William J. Garry
1991 Sales: $85 million Employees: 519
Symbol: GX Exchange: NYSE
Industry: Diversified operations - screen printing equipment, laboratories, oil & gas services

Geodynamics Corp.
5520 Ekwill St., Ste. A
Santa Barbara, CA 93111
Phone: 805-964-9905 Fax: 805-967-0433
CEO: Robert L. Paulson
CFO: David P. Nelson
1992 Sales: $58 million Employees: 469
Symbol: GDYN Exchange: NASDAQ
Industry: Computers - US government intelligence & military software

Geodyne Resources, Inc.
320 S. Boston Ave.
Tulsa, OK 74103
Phone: 918-583-5525 Fax: 918-583-6023
CEO: Michael W. Tomasso
CFO: Michael E. Luttrell
1992 Sales: $9.1 million Employees: 160
Symbol: GDR Exchange: AMEX
Industry: Financial - investment management

Geonex Corp.
150 Second Ave. North, 12th Fl.
St. Petersburg, FL 33701
Phone: 813-823-3300 Fax: 813-894-7143
CEO: Harold F. Flynn
CFO: Douglas R. Saporta
1991 Sales: $68 million Employees: 1,457
Symbol: GEOX Exchange: NASDAQ
Industry: Engineering - R&D services

George E. Warren Corp.
605 17th St.
Vero Beach, FL 32960
Phone: 407-778-7100 Fax: 407-778-7171
CEO: Thomas L. Corr
CFO: Jon Taylor
1990 Sales: $1,568 million Employees: 30
Ownership: Privately held
Industry: Oil marketing

Georgetown Industries Inc.
1901 Roxborough Rd., Ste. 200
Charlotte, NC 28211
Phone: 704-366-6901 Fax: 704-365-4340
CEO: Roger R. Regelbrugge
CFO: Gerald L. Anderson
1992 Sales: $560 million Employees: 3,873
Ownership: Privately held
Industry: Diversified operations - home furnishings, steel manufacturing, lumber distribution

Georgia Bonded Fibers, Inc.
15 Nuttman St.
Newark, NJ 07103
Phone: 201-642-3547 Fax: 201-642-1961
CEO: Hugo N. Surmonte
CFO: Hugo N. Surmonte
1992 Sales: $46 million Employees: 208
Symbol: GBFH Exchange: NASDAQ
Industry: Rubber & plastic products

Georgia Crown Distributing
7 Crown Circle
Columbus, GA 31907
Phone: 706-568-4580 Fax: 706-561-4167
CEO: Donald M. Leebern, Jr.
CFO: Orlene Boviard
1991 Sales: $590 million Employees: 1,700
Ownership: Privately held
Industry: Beverages - wholesale distribution

indicates company is in *Hoover's Handbook of American Business.*

indicates company is in *Hoover's Handbook of World Business;* sales and employee numbers are for parent company.

Georgia Gulf Corp.
400 Perimeter Center Terrace NE, Ste. 595
Atlanta, GA 30346
Phone: 404-395-4500 Fax: 404-395-4529
CEO: James R. Kuse
CFO: Richard B. Marchese
1992 Sales: $780 million Employees: 1,103
Symbol: GGC Exchange: NYSE
Industry: Chemicals - specialty

Georgia Power Co.
333 Piedmont Ave. NE
Atlanta, GA 30308
Phone: 404-526-6526 Fax: —
CEO: A. W. Dahlberg
CFO: Warren Y. Jobe
1991 Sales: $4.3 million Employees: 13,700
Symbol: GPE Exchange: NYSE
Industry: Utility - electric power

Georgia-Pacific Corp.
133 Peachtree St. NE
Atlanta, GA 30303
Phone: 404-521-4000 Fax: 404-521-4422
CEO: A.D. Correll
CFO: James C. Van Meter
1992 Sales: $11,847 million Employees: 57,000
Symbol: GP Exchange: NYSE
Industry: Building products - wood; paper & paper products

Geraghty & Miller, Inc.
125 E. Bethpage Rd.
Plainview, NY 11803
Phone: 516-249-7600 Fax: 516-249-7610
CEO: David W. Miller
CFO: John McCusker
1991 Sales: $88 million Employees: 1,109
Symbol: GMGW Exchange: NASDAQ
Industry: Pollution control equipment & services - water protection & clean up

Gerber Products Co.
445 State St.
Fremont, MI 49413
Phone: 616-928-2000 Fax: 616-928-2723
CEO: Alfred A. Piergallini
CFO: Fred K. Schomer
1992 Sales: $1,299 million Employees: 12,871
Symbol: GEB Exchange: NYSE
Industry: Food - baby food & formulas; apparel

Gerber Scientific, Inc.
83 Gerber Rd. West
South Windsor, CT 06074
Phone: 203-644-1551 Fax: 203-649-7157
CEO: H. Joseph Gerber
CFO: George M. Gentile
1992 Sales: $250 million Employees: 1,550
Symbol: GRB Exchange: NYSE
Industry: Industrial automation & robotics

Geriatric & Medical Centers, Inc.
5601 Chestnut St.
Philadelphia, PA 19139
Phone: 215-476-2250 Fax: 215-748-8862
CEO: Daniel Veloric
CFO: Robert F. Carfagno
1992 Sales: $165 million Employees: 4,018
Symbol: GEMC Exchange: NASDAQ
Industry: Nursing homes

Germantown Savings Bank
One Belmont Ave.
Bala Cynwyd, PA 19004
Phone: 215-667-9300 Fax: —
CEO: Martin I. Kleppe
CFO: John M. Junkin, Jr.
1992 Sales: — Employees: —
Symbol: GSBK Exchange: NASDAQ
Industry: Financial - savings and loans

Gerrity Oil & Gas Corp.
4100 E. Mississippi Ave.
Denver, CO 80222
Phone: 303-757-1110 Fax: 303-757-1197
CEO: Robert W. Gerrity
CFO: Diana K. Ten Eyck
1991 Sales: $16 million Employees: 60
Symbol: GOIL Exchange: NASDAQ
Industry: Oil & gas - US exploration & production

GET Travel Holidays
675 Yanacio Valley Rd., Ste. 211
Walnut Creek, CA 94596
Phone: 510-944-5844 Fax: 510-946-5214
CEO: Ripley Hunter
CFO: M. David Hunter
1991 Sales: $5.5 million Employees: 20
Ownership: Privately held
Industry: Business services - group & individual travel arrangements

Getty Petroleum Corp.
125 Jericho Tnpk.
Jericho, NY 11753
Phone: 516-338-6000 Fax: 516-338-6051
CEO: Leo Liebowitz
CFO: John J. Fitteron
1992 Sales: $974 million Employees: 1,096
Symbol: GTY Exchange: NYSE
Industry: Oil refining & marketing

GF Industries Inc.
930 98th Ave.
Oakland, CA 94603
Phone: 510-568-0711 Fax: 510-568-9210
CEO: Wilfred Uytengsu
CFO: —
1991 Sales: $645 million Employees: 5,000
Ownership: Privately held
Industry: Food - snacks & biscuits

GFC Financial Corp.
1850 N. Central Ave.
Phoenix, AZ 85004
Phone: 602-207-4900 Fax: —
CEO: Samuel L. Eichenfield
CFO: Robert J. Fitzsimmons
1991 Sales: $258 million Employees: —
Symbol: GFC Exchange: NYSE
Industry: Financial - business services

Giant Eagle, Inc.
101 Kappa Dr.
Pittsburgh, PA 15238
Phone: 412-963-6200 Fax: 412-963-0374
CEO: David S. Shapira
CFO: Fred Nimtz
1991 Sales: $1,950 million Employees: 9,000
Ownership: Privately held
Industry: Retail - supermarkets

Giant Food Inc.
6300 Sheriff Rd.
Landover, MD 20785
Phone: 301-341-4100 Fax: 301-341-4804
CEO: Israel Cohen
CFO: David B. Sykes
1992 Sales: $3,512 million Employees: 24,800
Symbol: GFSA Exchange: AMEX
Industry: Retail - supermarkets

Giant Group, Ltd.
Hwy.453
Harleyville, SC 29448
Phone: 803-496-7880 Fax: 803-496-5071
CEO: Burt Sugarman
CFO: Terry L. Kinder
1991 Sales: $66 million Employees: 550
Symbol: GPO Exchange: NYSE
Industry: Construction - cement & concrete

Giant Industries, Inc.
23733 N. Scottsdale Rd.
Scottsdale, AZ 85255
Phone: 602-585-8888 Fax: 602-585-8894
CEO: James E. Acridge
CFO: Robert L. Harvey
1991 Sales: $268 million Employees: 1,170
Symbol: GI Exchange: NYSE
Industry: Oil refining & marketing

Gibraltar Packaging Group, Inc.
2000 Summit Ave.
Hastings, NE 68901
Phone: 402-463-1366 Fax: —
CEO: Deke C. Abbott, Jr.
CFO: Deke C. Abbott, Jr.
1992 Sales: $26 million Employees: 355
Symbol: PACK Exchange: NASDAQ
Industry: Containers - paper & plastic

Gibson Greetings, Inc.
2100 Section Rd.
Cincinnati, OH 45237
Phone: 513-841-6600 Fax: 513-841-6739
CEO: Benjamin J. Sottile
CFO: Ward A. Cavanaugh
1992 Sales: $486 million Employees: 9,500
Symbol: GIBG Exchange: NASDAQ
Industry: Office & art materials

Giddings & Lewis, Inc.
142 Doty St.
Fond du Lac, WI 54935
Phone: 414-921-9400 Fax: 414-929-4537
CEO: William J. Fife, Jr.
CFO: Richard C. Kleinfeldt
1991 Sales: $327 million Employees: 4,813
Symbol: GIDL Exchange: NASDAQ
Industry: Machine tools & related products

Giga-tronics, Inc.
2495 Estand Way
Pleasant Hill, CA 94523
Phone: 415-680-8160 Fax: 415-680-7736
CEO: Donald F. Bogue
CFO: Cherrie L. Jurado
1992 Sales: $16 million Employees: 159
Symbol: GIGA Exchange: NASDAQ
Industry: Electronics - military

Gilbane Building Co.
Seven Jackson Walkway
Providence, RI 02940
Phone: 401-456-5800 Fax: 401-456-5936
CEO: Paul J. Choquette, Jr.
CFO: Norman E. Roy
1991 Sales: $1,157 million Employees: 865
Ownership: Privately held
Industry: Construction - heavy commercial & industrial

Gilbert Associates, Inc.
PO Box 1498
Reading, PA 19603
Phone: 215-775-5900 Fax: —
CEO: Alexander F. Smith
CFO: James R. Itin
1991 Sales: $271 million Employees: 3,398
Symbol: GILBA Exchange: NASDAQ
Industry: Engineering - R&D services

Gilead Sciences, Inc.
346 Lakeside Dr.
Foster City, CA 94404
Phone: 415-574-3000 Fax: —
CEO: Michael L. Riordan
CFO: Michael F. Bigham
1992 Sales: $2.8 million Employees: 69
Symbol: GILD Exchange: NASDAQ
Industry: Drugs

indicates company is in *Hoover's Handbook of American Business.*
indicates company is in *Hoover's Handbook of World Business;* sales and employee numbers are for parent company.

Gillett Holdings Inc.
555 17th St., Ste. 3300
Denver, CO 80202
Phone: 303-292-0045 Fax: 303-292-9603
CEO: George N. Gillett, Jr.
CFO: David A. Ramon
1991 Sales: $735 million Employees: 5,405
Ownership: Privately held
Industry: Diversified operations - broadcasting, meatpacking & resorts

Gillette Co., The
Prudential Tower Bldg., 800 Boylston St.
Boston, MA 02199
Phone: 617-421-7000 Fax: 617-421-7123
CEO: Alfred M. Zeien
CFO: Thomas F. Skelly
1992 Sales: $5,163 million Employees: 31,200
Symbol: G Exchange: NYSE
Industry: Cosmetics & toiletries, small appliances

Gish Biomedical, Inc.
2350 Pullman Ave.
Santa Ana, CA 92705
Phone: 714-261-1330 Fax: 714-261-6596
CEO: Jack W. Brown
CFO: Jeanne M. Miller
1992 Sales: $21 million Employees: 224
Symbol: GISH Exchange: NASDAQ
Industry: Biomedical & genetic products

Gitano Group, Inc.
1411 Broadway
New York, NY 10018
Phone: 212-819-0707 Fax: 212-730-0349
CEO: Morris Dabah
CFO: Stanley A. Greenstein
1991 Sales: $780 million Employees: 5,658
Symbol: GIT Exchange: NYSE
Industry: Textiles - apparel

Glacier Bancorp, Inc.
202 Main St.
Kalispell, MT 59901
Phone: 406-756-4200 Fax: —
CEO: F. Charles Mercord
CFO: Thomas E. Anderson
1991 Sales: $19 million Employees: 131
Symbol: GBCI Exchange: NASDAQ
Industry: Financial - savings and loans

Glacier Water Services, Inc.
3219 Roymar Rd.
Oceanside, CA 92054
Phone: 619-433-4072 Fax: —
CEO: Duke Bushong
CFO: Kathleen M. Fisher
1991 Sales: $23 million Employees: 164
Symbol: HOO Exchange: NASDAQ
Industry: Retail

Glaxo Inc.
5 Moore Dr.
Research Triangle Park, NC 27709
Phone: 919-248-2100 Fax: 919-248-2381
CEO: C.A. Sanders
CFO: —
1991 Sales: $5,496 million Employees: 35,640
Parent: Glaxo Holdings PLC
Industry: Drugs

Gleason Corp.
2999 Overland Ave., Ste. 210
Los Angeles, CA 90064
Phone: 310-559-4811 Fax: —
CEO: James S. Gleason
CFO: John C. Kobiliak
1991 Sales: $178 million Employees: 1,706
Symbol: GLE Exchange: NYSE
Industry: Machine tools & related products

Glenayre Technologies, Inc.
645 E. Missouri Ave.
Phoenix, AZ 85012
Phone: 602-263-9161 Fax: —
CEO: Clarke H. Bailey
CFO: Vickie M. Sixta
1992 Sales: — Employees: —
Ownership: Privately held
Industry: Telecommunications equipment - manufacturing

Glendale Bancorporation
1099 White Horse Rd.
Voorhees, NJ 08043
Phone: 609-346-8400 Fax: —
CEO: Constantinos Costalas
CFO: Constantinos Costalas
1991 Sales: $23 million Employees: 188
Symbol: GNBC Exchange: NASDAQ
Industry: Banks - Northeast

Glenfed Brokerage, Inc.
700 N. Brand Blvd.
Glendale, CA 91203
Phone: 818-500-2000 Fax: 818-409-5309
CEO: Norman M. Coulson
CFO: Stephen J. Trafton
1992 Sales: $1,358 million Employees: 3,761
Symbol: GLN Exchange: NYSE
Industry: Financial - savings and loans

Glitterwrap
40 Carver Ave.
Westwood, NJ 07675
Phone: 201-666-9700 Fax: 201-666-5444
CEO: Alfred Scott
CFO: Tom Orefice
1991 Sales: $10.4 million Employees: 75
Ownership: Privately held
Industry: Retail - metallic & iridescent gift wrap & tote bags

Global Mail, Ltd.
22455 Davis Dr., Ste. 110
Sterling, VA 22170
Phone: 703-790-8686 Fax: 703-356-4318
CEO: Harry Geller
CFO: Glenn Cafritz
1991 Sales: $9 million Employees: 45
Ownership: Privately held
Industry: Business services - international mailing services

Global Marine, Inc.
777 N. Eldridge Rd.
Houston, TX 77079
Phone: 713-596-5100 Fax: 713-531-1260
CEO: C. Russell Luigs
CFO: Jerry C. Martin
1991 Sales: $315 million Employees: 1,900
Symbol: GLM Exchange: NYSE
Industry: Oil & gas - offshore drilling

Global Natural Resources Inc.
5300 Memorial Dr., Ste. 800
Houston, TX 77007
Phone: 713-880-5464 Fax: 713-880-2106
CEO: James G. Niven
CFO: Eric Lynn Hill
1991 Sales: $60 million Employees: 82
Symbol: GNR Exchange: NYSE
Industry: Oil & gas - US exploration & production

Global Petroleum Corp.
800 South St.
Waltham, MA 02154
Phone: 617-894-8800 Fax: 617-893-7642
CEO: Alfred A. Slifka
CFO: Tom McManmon
1991 Sales: $2,560 million Employees: 150
Ownership: Privately held
Industry: Oil & gas - wholesaling & retailing

Glycomed Inc.
860 Atlantic Ave.
Alameda, CA 94501
Phone: 510-523-5555 Fax: 510-523-5815
CEO: Alan R. Timms
CFO: Raymond W. Anderson
1992 Sales: $3.6 million Employees: 76
Symbol: GLYC Exchange: NASDAQ
Industry: Drugs

GMIS Inc.
5 Country View Rd.
Malvern, PA 19355
Phone: 215-296-3838 Fax: —
CEO: Carl Witonsky
CFO: Jeffrey Stello
1991 Sales: $8.7 million Employees: 80
Symbol: GMIS Exchange: NASDAQ
Industry: Medical services - computer software for health care payers

GNI Group, Inc.
2525 Battleground Rd.
Deer Park, TX 77536
Phone: 713-930-0350 Fax: —
CEO: Carl V. Rush, Jr.
CFO: Titus H. Harris III
1991 Sales: $19 million Employees: 128
Symbol: GNUC Exchange: NASDAQ
Industry: Pollution control equipment & services - hazardous waste disposal

GNW Financial Corp.
500 Pacific Ave.
Bremerton, WA 98310
Phone: 206-479-1551 Fax: —
CEO: Raymond L. Soule
CFO: Ronald J. Moinette
1991 Sales: $69 million Employees: 237
Symbol: GNWF Exchange: NASDAQ
Industry: Financial - savings and loans

Go-Video, Inc.
14455 N. Hayden Rd., Ste. 219
Scottsdale, AZ 85260
Phone: 602-998-3400 Fax: 602-951-4404
CEO: R. Terren Dunlap
CFO: Robert J. Brilon
1991 Sales: $12 million Employees: 24
Symbol: VCR Exchange: AMEX
Industry: Audio & video home products

Goal Systems International, Inc.
7965 N. High St.
Columbus, OH 43235
Phone: 614-888-1775 Fax: 614-785-2702
CEO: David C. Wetmore
CFO: Thomas J. Kelley
1991 Sales: $128 million Employees: 880
Symbol: GOAL Exchange: NASDAQ
Industry: Computers - software

Golden Enterprises, Inc.
2101 Magnolia Ave. South, Ste. 212
Birmingham, AL 35205
Phone: 205-326-6101 Fax: 205-326-6148
CEO: John S. Stein
CFO: John S. Stein
1992 Sales: $132 million Employees: 1,444
Symbol: GLDC Exchange: NASDAQ
Industry: Diversified operations - snack food products, advertising, bolts & fasteners

Golden Poultry Co., Inc.
244 Perimeter Ctr. Pkwy. NE
Atlanta, GA 30346
Phone: 404-393-5000 Fax: 404-393-5421
CEO: D. W. Sands
CFO: Langley C. Thomas, Jr.
1992 Sales: $337 million Employees: 3,944
Symbol: CHIK Exchange: NASDAQ
Industry: Food - meat products

Golden State Foods Corp.
18301 Von Karman Ave., Ste. 1100
Irvine, CA 92715
Phone: 714-252-2000 Fax: 714-252-2080
CEO: James E. Williams
CFO: Gene Olson
1991 Sales: $1,032 million Employees: 1,700
Ownership: Privately held
Industry: Food processing & distribution for McDonald's

Golden West Financial Corp.
1901 Harrison St.
Oakland, CA 94612
Phone: 510-446-6000 Fax: 510-446-4259
CEO: Herbert M. Sandler
CFO: David C. Welch
1992 Sales: $2,026 million Employees: 3,798
Symbol: GDW Exchange: NYSE
Industry: Financial - savings and loans

Goldfield Corp.
100 Rialto Place, Ste. 500
Melbourne, FL 32901
Phone: 407-724-1700 Fax: 407-724-1703
CEO: John H. Sottile
CFO: Stephen R. Wherry
1991 Sales: $10.5 million Employees: 110
Symbol: GV Exchange: AMEX
Industry: Construction - heavy

Goldman Sachs Group, LP, The
85 Broad St.
New York, NY 10004
Phone: 212-902-1000 Fax: 212-902-3925
CEO: Stephen Friedman
CFO: Angelo DeCaro
1991 Sales: $8,500 million Employees: 6,750
Ownership: Privately held
Industry: Business services - investment banking & securities brokerage

Goldtex, Inc.
401 Patetown Rd.
Goldsboro, NC 27530
Phone: 919-736-7411 Fax: —
CEO: Wilbur O. Hopper
CFO: Wilbur O. Hopper
1991 Sales: $28 million Employees: 325
Symbol: GLTX Exchange: NASDAQ
Industry: Textiles - mill products

Golodetz Trading Corp.
666 Fifth Ave.
New York, NY 10103
Phone: 212-581-2400 Fax: 212-307-1002
CEO: Gavin J. Parfitt
CFO: —
1991 Sales: $750 million Employees: 800
Ownership: Privately held
Industry: Diversified operations - trading, agriculture, real estate, venture capital

Golub Corp.
501 Duanesburg Rd.
Schenectady, NY 12306
Phone: 518-355-5000 Fax: 518-355-0843
CEO: Lewis Golub
CFO: Lawrence G. Olsen
1991 Sales: $1,160 million Employees: 11,000
Ownership: Privately held
Industry: Retail - supermarkets

Good Guys, Inc., The
7000 Marina Blvd.
Brisbane, CA 94102
Phone: 415-615-5000 Fax: 415-615-6287
CEO: Ronald A. Unkefer
CFO: Robert A. Gunst
1992 Sales: $520 million Employees: 2,474
Symbol: GGUY Exchange: NASDAQ
Industry: Retail - consumer electronics

Goodheart-Willcox Co., Inc.
123 W. Taft Dr.
South Holland, IL 60473
Phone: 708-333-7200 Fax: 708-333-9130
CEO: John F. Flanagan
CFO: Donald A. Mussucci
1992 Sales: $11 million Employees: 47
Symbol: GWOX Exchange: NASDAQ
Industry: Publishing - books

Goodman Music
4024 S. Sepulveda
Culver City, CA 90230
Phone: 310-558-5500 Fax: 310-558-5505
CEO: Joseph Goodman
CFO: Joseph Goodman
1991 Sales: $11 million Employees: 40
Ownership: Privately held
Industry: Retail - musical instruments & recording equipment

GoodMark Foods, Inc.
6131 Falls of Neuse Rd.
Raleigh, NC 27609
Phone: 919-790-9940 Fax: 919-790-6535
CEO: Ron E. Doggett
CFO: Edward B. McLean
1992 Sales: $144 million Employees: 1,050
Symbol: GDMK Exchange: NASDAQ
Industry: Food - meat products

Goody Products, Inc.
969 Newark Tnpk.
Kearny, NJ 07032
Phone: 201-997-3000 Fax: 800-631-0421
CEO: Leonard Goodman
CFO: Kevin E. Walsh
1991 Sales: $216 million Employees: 2,830
Symbol: GOOD Exchange: NASDAQ
Industry: Cosmetics & toiletries

Goody's Family Clothing, Inc.
1605 Congress Pkwy., Store 13
Athens, TN 37303
Phone: 615-745-0198 Fax: —
CEO: Robert M. Goodfriend
CFO: Donald A. VandenBerg
1991 Sales: $362 million Employees: 3,290
Symbol: GDYS Exchange: NASDAQ
Industry: Retail - apparel & shoes

Goodyear Tire & Rubber Co., The
1144 E. Market St.
Akron, OH 44316
Phone: 216-796-2121 Fax: 216-796-2222
CEO: Stanley C. Gault
CFO: Samir F. Gibara
1992 Sales: $11,785 million Employees: 97,420
Symbol: GT Exchange: NYSE
Industry: Rubber tires, chemicals, film products

Gordon Food Service, Inc.
333 50th St. SW
Grand Rapids, MI 49548
Phone: 616-530-7000 Fax: 616-249-4165
CEO: Paul Gordon
CFO: Arthur Surowiec
1991 Sales: $830 million Employees: 2,000
Ownership: Privately held
Industry: Food - wholesale

Gorman-Rupp Co.
305 Bowman St.
Mansfield, OH 44903
Phone: 419-755-1011 Fax: 419-755-1251
CEO: James C. Gorman
CFO: Kenneth E. Dudley
1991 Sales: $123 million Employees: 1,029
Symbol: GRC Exchange: AMEX
Industry: Machinery - general industrial

Gottschalks Inc.
7 River Park Place East
Fresno, CA 93720
Phone: 209-434-8000 Fax: —
CEO: Joe Levy
CFO: James R. Clifford
1991 Sales: $324 million Employees: 4,200
Symbol: GOT Exchange: NYSE
Industry: Retail - apparel & shoes

Goulds Pumps, Inc.
240 Fall St.
Seneca Falls, NY 13148
Phone: 315-568-2811 Fax: 315-568-2418
CEO: Stephen V. Ardia
CFO: John Morphy
1991 Sales: $567 million Employees: 4,350
Symbol: GULD Exchange: NASDAQ
Industry: Machinery - general industrial

Government Technology Services, Inc.
4100 Lafayette Center Dr.
Chantilly, VA 22021
Phone: 703-631-1177 Fax: 703-222-5211
CEO: R. M. Rickenbach
CFO: George A. Barstis
1991 Sales: $359 million Employees: 465
Symbol: GTSI Exchange: NASDAQ
Industry: Computers - reselling services

Govind & Associates
541 McBride
Corpus Christi, TX 78469
Phone: 512-289-1385 Fax: 512-289-0712
CEO: Govind Nadkarni
CFO: Michael Stridde
1991 Sales: $7.5 million Employees: 170
Ownership: Privately held
Industry: Engineering - R&D services

Graco Inc.
60 11th Ave. NE
Minneapolis, MN 55413
Phone: 612-623-6000 Fax: 612-623-6233
CEO: David A. Koch
CFO: Roger L. King
1991 Sales: $312 million Employees: 2,150
Symbol: GGG Exchange: NYSE
Industry: Machinery - general industrial

Gradco Systems, Inc.
7 Morgan
Irvine, CA 92718
Phone: 714-770-1223 Fax: 714-768-6939
CEO: Martin E. Tash
CFO: Harland L. Mischler
1992 Sales: $53 million Employees: 100
Symbol: GRCO Exchange: NASDAQ
Industry: Office automation

Graham Corp.
20 Florence Ave.
Batavia, NY 14020
Phone: 716-343-2216 Fax: 716-343-1097
CEO: Frederick D. Berkeley
CFO: Alvin L. Snyder
1991 Sales: $71 million Employees: 683
Symbol: GHM Exchange: AMEX
Industry: Machinery - general industrial

Graham-Field Health Products, Inc.
400 Rabro Dr.
Hauppauge, NY 11788
Phone: 516-582-5900 Fax: 516-582-5608
CEO: Irwin Selinger
CFO: Donald J. Harnett
1991 Sales: $57 million Employees: 536
Symbol: GFI Exchange: NYSE
Industry: Medical products - diagnostic & surgical instruments, home healthcare products

indicates company is in *Hoover's Handbook of American Business.*

indicates company is in *Hoover's Handbook of World Business;* sales and employee numbers are for parent company.

GranCare, Inc.
300 Corporate Pointe, Ste. 300
Culver City, CA 90230
Phone: 310-645-1555 Fax: 310-645-1609
CEO: Gene E. Burleson
CFO: Kevin W. Pendergest
1992 Sales: $302 million Employees: 6,500
Symbol: GRNC Exchange: NASDAQ
Industry: Healthcare - outpatient & home

Grand Aire Express, Inc.
2800 N. Custer
Monroe, MI 48161
Phone: 313-457-1730 Fax: 313-457-1733
CEO: Tahir Cheema
CFO: Katrina Cheema
1991 Sales: $3.8 million Employees: 41
Ownership: Privately held
Industry: Transportation - on-demand charter airline & cargo

Grand Casinos, Inc.
13705 First Ave. North
Plymouth, MN 55441
Phone: 612-449-9206 Fax: —
CEO: Lyle Berman
CFO: James White
1991 Sales: $2.4 million Employees: 8
Symbol: GRND Exchange: NASDAQ
Industry: Leisure & recreational services - casinos

Grand Metropolitan, Inc.
712 Fifth Ave., Ste. 4600
New York, NY 10019
Phone: 212-554-9200 Fax: 212-554-9243
CEO: George J. Bull
CFO: —
1991 Sales: $16,359 million Employees: 122,178
Parent: Grand Metropolitan PLC
Industry: Food, beverages & retailing

Grand Union Co.
201 Willowbrook Blvd.
Wayne, NJ 07470
Phone: 201-890-6000 Fax: 201-890-6671
CEO: Joseph J. McCaig
CFO: R. Terrence Galvin
1991 Sales: $2,969 million Employees: 20,000
Ownership: Privately held
Industry: Retail - supermarkets

Grand Valley Gas Co.
50 W. Broadway, 10th Fl.
Salt Lake City, UT 84101
Phone: 801-532-7526 Fax: 801-364-7340
CEO: Jeff J. Fishman
CFO: Deanna F. Hadley
1992 Sales: $197 million Employees: 38
Symbol: GVGC Exchange: NASDAQ
Industry: Utility - gas distribution

Granite Broadcasting Corp.
One Dag Hammarskjold Plaza
New York, NY 10017
Phone: 212-826-2530 Fax: 212-826-2858
CEO: W. Don Cornwell
CFO: Lawrence I. Wills
1991 Sales: $33 million Employees: 345
Symbol: GBTVK Exchange: NASDAQ
Industry: Broadcasting - radio & TV

Granite Construction Inc.
585 W. Beach St.
Watsonville, CA 95076
Phone: 408-724-1011 Fax: 408-722-9657
CEO: David H. Watts
CFO: William E. Barton
1991 Sales: $564 million Employees: 2,748
Symbol: GCCO Exchange: NASDAQ
Industry: Construction - heavy

Granite State Bankshares, Inc.
122 West St.
Keene, NH 03431
Phone: 603-352-1600 Fax: —
CEO: Charles W. Smith
CFO: William G. Pike
1991 Sales: $24 million Employees: 171
Symbol: GSBI Exchange: NASDAQ
Industry: Banks - Northeast

Grant Tensor Corp.
10550 Richmond Ave.
Houston, TX 77042
Phone: 713-781-4000 Fax: 713-781-6934
CEO: Henry L. Grant
CFO: Derry D. Essary
1991 Sales: $103 million Employees: 3,909
Symbol: GRNT Exchange: NASDAQ
Industry: Oil & gas - field services

Graphic Industries, Inc.
2155 Monroe Dr. NE
Atlanta, GA 30324
Phone: 404-874-3327 Fax: 404-874-7589
CEO: Mark C. Pope III
CFO: J. Fred Johnson
1991 Sales: $311 million Employees: 2,715
Symbol: GRPH Exchange: NASDAQ
Industry: Printing - commercial

Gravity Graphics Inc.
26 Bridge St.
Brooklyn, NY 11201
Phone: 718-875-1170 Fax: 718-875-4875
CEO: Jeff Sharp
CFO: Jeff Sharp
1992 Sales: $3.5 million Employees: 42
Ownership: Privately held
Industry: Textiles & graphics - activewear silk-screening

Graybar Electric
PO Box 7231
St. Louis, MO 63177
Phone: 314-727-3900 Fax: 314-727-0788
CEO: Edward McGrath
CFO: John W. Wolf
1991 Sales: $1,744 million Employees: 4,729
Ownership: Privately held
Industry: Electrical products - wholesale

GRC International, Inc.
1900 Gallows Rd.
Vienna, VA 22182
Phone: 703-506-5000 Fax: 703-506-9241
CEO: Edward T. Jones
CFO: Philip R. Pietras
1992 Sales: $114 million Employees: 1,219
Symbol: GRH Exchange: NYSE
Industry: Electronics - military

Great American Communications Co.
One E. Fourth St.
Cincinnati, OH 45202
Phone: 513-562-8000 Fax: 513-721-8413
CEO: Carl H. Lindner
CFO: Gregory C. Thomas
1991 Sales: $196 million Employees: 1,500
Symbol: GACC Exchange: NASDAQ
Industry: Broadcasting - radio & TV

Great American Recreation, Inc.
Rt. 94
Vernon, NJ 07462
Phone: 201-827-2000 Fax: 201-827-3586
CEO: Gene W. Mulvihill
CFO: James Fleming
1992 Sales: $23 million Employees: 2,660
Symbol: GRARE Exchange: NASDAQ
Industry: Leisure & recreational services - ski area & summer action park

Great Atlantic & Pacific Tea Co., Inc., The
2 Paragon Dr.
Montvale, NJ 07645
Phone: 201-573-9700 Fax: 201-930-8106
CEO: James Wood
CFO: Fred Corrado
1992 Sales: $10,864 million Employees: 94,600
Symbol: GAP Exchange: NYSE
Industry: Retail - supermarkets

Great Bay Bankshares, Inc.
100 Main St.
Dover, NH 03820
Phone: 406-761-7100 Fax: 406-761-1053
CEO: Donald R. Hatt
CFO: Donald R. Hatt
1991 Sales: $31 million Employees: 143
Symbol: GBBS Exchange: NASDAQ
Industry: Banks - Northeast

Great Country Bank
211 Main St.
Ansonia, CT 06401
Phone: 203-734-2561 Fax: —
CEO: Frederick J. Quinn
CFO: Richard N. Morrison
1991 Sales: $37 million Employees: 175
Symbol: GCBK Exchange: NASDAQ
Industry: Banks - Northeast

Great Falls Gas Co.
No. 1 First Ave. South
Great Falls, MT 59401
Phone: 406-761-7100 Fax: 406-761-7560
CEO: Larry D. Geske
CFO: William J. Quast
1992 Sales: $23 million Employees: 106
Symbol: GFGC Exchange: NASDAQ
Industry: Utility - gas distribution

Great Lakes Bancorp, F.S.B.
401 E. Liberty St.
Ann Arbor, MI 48107
Phone: 313-769-8300 Fax: —
CEO: Roy E. Weber
CFO: Glenn J. Ohl
1992 Sales: — Employees: —
Symbol: GLBC Exchange: NASDAQ
Industry: Financial - savings and loans

Great Lakes Chemical Corp.
US Hwy. 52 NW
West Lafayette, IN 47906
Phone: 317-497-6100 Fax: 317-497-6234
CEO: Emerson Kampen
CFO: Robert T. Jeffares
1992 Sales: $1,497 million Employees: 5,700
Symbol: GLK Exchange: NYSE
Industry: Chemicals - specialty

Great Northern Iron Ore Properties
332 Minnesota St.
St. Paul, MN 55101
Phone: 612-224-2385 Fax: —
CEO: Harry L. Holtz
CFO: Harry L. Holtz
1991 Sales: $9.9 million Employees: 12
Symbol: GNI Exchange: NYSE
Industry: Iron ores

Great Southern Bancorp, Inc.
1451 E. Battlefield
Springfield, MO 65804
Phone: 417-887-4400 Fax: —
CEO: William V. Turner
CFO: Don M. Gibson
1991 Sales: $43 million Employees: 362
Symbol: GSBC Exchange: NASDAQ
Industry: Banks - Midwest

indicates company is in *Hoover's Handbook of American Business.*

indicates company is in *Hoover's Handbook of World Business;* sales and employee numbers are for parent company.

Great Western Financial Corp.
9200 Oakdale Ave.
Chatsworth, CA 91311
Phone: 818-775-3411 Fax: 818-775-3434
CEO: James F. Montgomery
CFO: Carl F. Geuther
1992 Sales: $3,154 million Employees: 14,786
Symbol: GWF Exchange: NYSE
Industry: Financial - savings and loans

Greater New York Savings Bank
One Penn Plaza
New York, NY 10119
Phone: 212-613-4000 Fax: —
CEO: Gerard C. Keegan
CFO: Philip T. Spies
1992 Sales: — Employees: —
Symbol: GRTR Exchange: NASDAQ
Industry: Financial - savings and loans

Green Bay Packers, Inc., The
1265 Lombardi Ave.
Green Bay, WI 54304
Phone: 414-496-5700 Fax: 414-496-5738
CEO: Robert E. Harlan
CFO: Michael R. Reinfeldt
1991 Sales: $45 million Employees: 62
Ownership: Privately held
Industry: Professional football team

Green Isle Environmental Services, Inc.
410 - 11th Ave. South
Hopkins, MN 55343
Phone: 612-935-6921 Fax: 612-933-5803
CEO: Edward J. Reuter
CFO: Jerome B. Misukanis
1991 Sales: $28 million Employees: 327
Symbol: GIES Exchange: NASDAQ
Industry: Rubber & plastic products

Green Mountain Power Corp.
25 Green Mountain Dr.
South Burlington, VT 05403
Phone: 802-864-5731 Fax: 802-865-9974
CEO: John V. Cleary, Jr.
CFO: Edwin M. Norse
1991 Sales: $144 million Employees: 465
Symbol: GMP Exchange: NYSE
Industry: Utility - electric power

Green Tree Acceptance, Inc.
345 Saint Peter St., Ste 600
St. Paul, MN 55102
Phone: 612-293-3500 Fax: 612-293-3503
CEO: Lawrence M. Coss
CFO: John W. Brink
1991 Sales: $215 million Employees: 1,206
Symbol: GNT Exchange: NYSE
Industry: Financial - mortgages & related services

Greenery Rehabilitation Group, Inc.
400 Center St.
Newton, MA 02158
Phone: 617-244-4744 Fax: 617-558-2588
CEO: Gerard M. Martin
CFO: Pelino Campea
1991 Sales: $102 million Employees: 2,345
Symbol: GRG Exchange: NYSE
Industry: Hospitals

Greenman Bros. Inc.
105 Price Pkwy.
Farmingdale, NY 11735
Phone: 516-293-5300 Fax: 516-293-7392
CEO: Stanley Greenman
CFO: William A. Johnson Jr.
1991 Sales: $165 million Employees: 721
Symbol: GMN Exchange: AMEX
Industry: Wholesale distribution - consumer products

Greenwich Financial Corp.
67 Mason St.
Greenwich, CT 06830
Phone: 203-661-9550 Fax: —
CEO: Joseph D. Gioffre
CFO: Mary G. Child
1991 Sales: $28 million Employees: 79
Symbol: GFCT Exchange: NASDAQ
Industry: Financial - savings and loans

Greenwich Pharmaceuticals Inc.
501 Office Center Dr.
Ft. Washington, PA 19034
Phone: 215-540-9500 Fax: 215-540-9696
CEO: Edwin R. Thompson
CFO: Lorin J. Randall
1991 Sales: $4.7 million Employees: 44
Symbol: GRPI Exchange: NASDAQ
Industry: Drugs

Greenwood Mills
PO Drawer 1017
Greenwood, SC 29648
Phone: 803-229-2571 Fax: 803-229-1111
CEO: James C. Self, Jr.
CFO: Paul E. Welder
1991 Sales: $450 million Employees: 7,000
Ownership: Privately held
Industry: Textiles - denim, other fabrics

Greiner Engineering, Inc.
909 E. Las Colinas Blvd., Ste 1900
Irving, TX 75039
Phone: 214-869-1001 Fax: 214-869-3111
CEO: Frank T. Callahan
CFO: Robert L. Costello
1991 Sales: $127 million Employees: 1,550
Symbol: GII Exchange: NYSE
Industry: Engineering - R&D services

Grenada Sunburst System Corp.
2000 Gateway
Grenada, MS 38901
Phone: 601-226-1100 Fax: —
CEO: Robert E. Kennington II
CFO: Daniel L. Holland
1991 Sales: $183 million Employees: 1,320
Symbol: GSSC Exchange: NASDAQ
Industry: Banks - Southeast

Grey Advertising Inc.
777 Third Ave.
New York, NY 10017
Phone: 212-546-2000 Fax: 212-546-1495
CEO: Edward H. Meyer
CFO: Steven G. Felsher
1992 Sales: $565 million Employees: 1,478
Symbol: GREY Exchange: NASDAQ
Industry: Advertising

Greyhound Lines, Inc.
15110 N. Dallas Pkwy.
Dallas, TX 75248
Phone: 214-744-6500 Fax: 214-419-3994
CEO: Frank J. Schmieder
CFO: J. Michael Doyle
1992 Sales: $682 million Employees: 9,200
Symbol: BUS Exchange: AMEX
Industry: Transportation - bus

Griffin Technology Inc.
6132 Victor-Manchester Rd.
Victor, NY 14564
Phone: 716-924-7121 Fax: 716-924-1553
CEO: Robert S. Urland
CFO: Joseph A. Murrer
1992 Sales: $17 million Employees: 259
Symbol: GRIF Exchange: NASDAQ
Industry: Protection - safety equipment & services

Griffis/Blessing Inc.
830 N. Tejon, Ste. 106
Colorado Springs, CO 80903
Phone: 719-520-1234 Fax: 719-520-1204
CEO: Buck Blessing
CFO: Gary Winegar
1991 Sales: $1.1 million Employees: 45
Ownership: Privately held
Industry: Real estate operations - management, investment & development

Grist Mill Co.
21340 Hayes Ave.
Lakeville, MN 55044
Phone: 612-469-4981 Fax: 612-469-5550
CEO: Ronald K. Zuckerman
CFO: Daniel J. Kinsella
1992 Sales: $66 million Employees: 435
Symbol: GRST Exchange: NASDAQ
Industry: Food - granola & cereal products

Grocers Supply Co.
3131 E. Holcombe Blvd.
Houston, TX 77021
Phone: 713-747-5000 Fax: 713-749-9320
CEO: Milton Levit
CFO: Max Levit
1991 Sales: $1,200 million Employees: 1,300
Ownership: Privately held
Industry: Food - wholesale

Grossman's Inc.
200 Union St.
Braintree, MA 02184
Phone: 617-848-0100 Fax: —
CEO: Thomas R. Schwarz
CFO: Sydney L. Katz
1992 Sales: $833 million Employees: 4,700
Symbol: GROS Exchange: NASDAQ
Industry: Building products - retail & wholesale

Ground Round Restaurants, Inc.
10 Woodbridge Center Dr.
Woodbridge, NJ 07095
Phone: 908-750-1122 Fax: —
CEO: J. Eric Hanson
CFO: Michael R. Jorgensen
1991 Sales: $162 million Employees: 9,200
Symbol: GRX Exchange: AMEX
Industry: Retail - food & restaurants

Groundwater & Environmental Svcs.
1340 Campus Pkwy.
Wall, NJ 07719
Phone: 908-919-1646 Fax: 908-919-1678
CEO: Anthony Kull
CFO: Anthony Kull
1991 Sales: $16 million Employees: 145
Ownership: Privately held
Industry: Environmental consulting services

Groundwater Protection Inc.
4315 SW 34th St.
Orlando, FL 32811
Phone: 407-426-7885 Fax: 407-426-7586
CEO: Kevin Barley
CFO: David Wigle
1991 Sales: $6.9 million Employees: 85
Ownership: Privately held
Industry: Environmental drilling & remedial construction services

Groundwater Technology, Inc.
100 River Ridge Dr.
Norwood, MA 02062
Phone: 617-769-7600 Fax: 617-769-7992
CEO: Walter C. Barber
CFO: Robert E. Sliney, Jr.
1992 Sales: $194 million Employees: 1,904
Symbol: GWTI Exchange: NASDAQ
Industry: Pollution control equipment & services - groundwater cleanup & restoration services

indicates company is in *Hoover's Handbook of American Business.*

indicates company is in *Hoover's Handbook of World Business;* sales and employee numbers are for parent company.

Group 1 Software, Inc.
6404 Ivy Lane, Ste. 500
Greenbelt, MD 20770
Phone: 301-982-2000 Fax: 301-982-4069
CEO: Robert S. Bowen
CFO: Martin T. Johnson
1992 Sales: $31 million Employees: 148
Symbol: GSOF Exchange: NASDAQ
Industry: Computers - mailing list/list management software

Grove Bank
35 Washington St.
Brighton, MA 02146
Phone: 617-731-1900 Fax: 617-734-0722
CEO: Thomas R. Venables
CFO: Daniel C. Calore
1992 Sales: — Employees: —
Symbol: GROV Exchange: NASDAQ
Industry: Financial - savings and loans

Grow Group, Inc.
200 Park Ave., 49th Fl.
New York, NY 10166
Phone: 212-599-4400 Fax: 212-286-0940
CEO: Russell Banks
CFO: Frank V. Esser
1992 Sales: $416 million Employees: 2,000
Symbol: GRO Exchange: NYSE
Industry: Paints & allied products

Grubb & Ellis Co.
One Montgomery St.
San Francisco, CA 94104
Phone: 415-956-1990 Fax: 415-274-9700
CEO: Wilbert F. Schwartz
CFO: Joseph F. Hamilton
1991 Sales: $266 million Employees: 2,400
Symbol: GBE Exchange: NYSE
Industry: Real estate operations

Grumman Corp.
1111 Stewart Ave.
Bethpage, NY 11714
Phone: 516-575-0574 Fax: 516-575-1411
CEO: Renso Caporali
CFO: J. Robert Anderson
1992 Sales: $3,504 million Employees: 23,600
Symbol: GQ Exchange: NYSE
Industry: Aerospace - aircraft equipment, electronics systems, information services

GS Industries
3223 Trebor St.
Pasadena, TX 77505
Phone: 713-487-7800 Fax: 713-487-5777
CEO: Jimmy Guillori
CFO: Byron Stillwell
1991 Sales: $2 million Employees: 10
Ownership: Privately held
Industry: Telecommunications - communication & navigation equipment for ships

GSC Enterprises, Inc.
130 Hillcrest St.
Sulphur Springs, TX 75482
Phone: 903-885-7621 Fax: 903-439-2349
CEO: Michael K. McKenzie
CFO: Mike Mize
1992 Sales: $699 million Employees: 1,250
Ownership: Privately held
Industry: Food - wholesale

GTE Corp.
One Stamford Forum
Stamford, CT 06904
Phone: 203-965-2000 Fax: 203-965-2277
CEO: Charles R. Lee
CFO: Nicholas L. Trivisonno
1992 Sales: $19,984 million Employees: 162,000
Symbol: GTE Exchange: NYSE
Industry: Utility - telephone, cellular communications, information services

GTECH Holdings Corp.
55 Technology Way
West Greenwich, RI 02816
Phone: 401-392-1000 Fax: 401-392-1234
CEO: Guy B. Snowden
CFO: Robert A. Breakstone
1992 Sales: $350 million Employees: 2,460
Symbol: GTK Exchange: NYSE
Industry: Telecommunications services

GTI Corp.
9171 Towne Centre Dr., Ste. 355
San Diego, CA 92122
Phone: 619-578-3111 Fax: 619-546-0568
CEO: Gary L. Luick
CFO: Douglas J. Downs
1991 Sales: $78 million Employees: 2,144
Symbol: GGTI Exchange: NASDAQ
Industry: Electrical components - circuit boards, electronic processing equipment

Guaranty National Corp.
100 Inverness Terrace East
Englewood, CO 80112
Phone: 303-790-8200 Fax: 303-790-7136
CEO: Roger B. Ware
CFO: Michael L. Pautler
1991 Sales: $211 million Employees: —
Symbol: GNC Exchange: NYSE
Industry: Insurance - multiline & misc.

Guardian Bancorp
800 S. Figueroa St.
Los Angeles, CA 90017
Phone: 213-239-0800 Fax: 213-239-0846
CEO: Paul M. Harris
CFO: Vincent A. Bell
1991 Sales: $51 million Employees: 157
Symbol: GB Exchange: AMEX
Industry: Banks - West

Guardian Industries Corp.
43043 W. Nine Mile Rd.
Northville, MI 48167
Phone: 313-347-0100 Fax: 313-349-5995
CEO: William Davidson
CFO: Jeffrey A. Knight
1991 Sales: $1,050 million Employees: 8,400
Ownership: Privately held
Industry: Glass products - flat glass, fiberglass insulation, plastics

Guardsman Products, Inc.
3033 Orchard Vista Dr. SE, Ste. 200
Grand Rapids, MI 49546
Phone: 616-957-2600 Fax: 616-957-1236
CEO: Keith C. Vander Hyde
CFO: Edward D. Corlett
1991 Sales: $141 million Employees: 757
Symbol: GPI Exchange: NYSE
Industry: Paints & allied products

Guess Inc.
1444 S. Alameda St.
Los Angeles, CA 90021
Phone: 213-765-3100 Fax: 213-765-3226
CEO: Georges Marciano
CFO: Roy Pierce
1991 Sales: $810 million Employees: 2,450
Ownership: Privately held
Industry: Apparel

Guest Supply, Inc.
720 U.S. Hwy. One
North Brunswick, NJ 08902
Phone: 908-246-3011 Fax: 908-828-2342
CEO: Clifford W. Stanley
CFO: Paul T. Xenis
1991 Sales: $78 million Employees: 550
Symbol: GEST Exchange: NASDAQ
Industry: Cosmetics & toiletries

Guilford Mills, Inc.
4925 W. Market St.
Greensboro, NC 27407
Phone: 919-316-4000 Fax: 919-316-4059
CEO: Charles A. Hayes
CFO: Donald L. Park
1992 Sales: $615 million Employees: 4,364
Symbol: GFD Exchange: NYSE
Industry: Textiles - mill products

Guinness Import Company, Inc.
6 Landmark Square
Stamford, CT 06901
Phone: 203-359-7100 Fax: 203-975-1820
CEO: William T. Olson
CFO: —
1991 Sales: $7,605 million Employees: 24,788
Parent: Guinness PLC
Industry: Beverages - beer & spirits

Gulf States Toyota
7701 Wilshire Place Dr.
Houston, TX 77240
Phone: 713-744-3300 Fax: 713-744-3332
CEO: Jerry Pyle
CFO: F. R. Mason
1991 Sales: $1,190 million Employees: 1,000
Ownership: Privately held
Industry: Retail - auto dealerships

Gulf States Utilities Co.
350 Pine St.
Beaumont, TX 77701
Phone: 409-838-6631 Fax: 409-839-3077
CEO: Joseph L. Donnelly
CFO: Jack L. Schenck
1992 Sales: $1,773 million Employees: 4,867
Symbol: GSU Exchange: NYSE
Industry: Utility - electric power

Gulf USA Corp.
99 High St., Ste. 1600
Boston, MA 02110
Phone: 617-482-2555 Fax: —
CEO: Graham F. Lacey
CFO: David J. Angelicchio
1991 Sales: $73 million Employees: 353
Symbol: GRE Exchange: NYSE
Industry: Coal

GulfMark International, Inc.
5 Post Oak Park, Ste. 1170
Houston, TX 77027
Phone: 713-963-9522 Fax: 713-963-9796
CEO: David J. Butters
CFO: Frank R. Pierce
1991 Sales: $17 million Employees: 211
Symbol: GMRK Exchange: NASDAQ
Industry: Oil & gas - field services

Gulfstream Aerospace Corp.
500 Gulfstream Rd.
Savannah, GA 31408
Phone: 912-964-3000 Fax: 912-964-3775
CEO: William C. Lowe
CFO: Craig Wills
1991 Sales: $887 million Employees: 4,800
Ownership: Privately held
Industry: Aerospace - corporate jets

Gull Laboratories, Inc.
1011 East 4800 South
Salt Lake City, UT 84117
Phone: 801-263-3524 Fax: 801-265-9268
CEO: Myron W. Wentz
CFO: Donald L. Hodges
1991 Sales: $7 million Employees: 127
Symbol: GULL Exchange: NASDAQ
Industry: Medical products - diagnostic test kits

indicates company is in *Hoover's Handbook of American Business.*

indicates company is in *Hoover's Handbook of World Business;* sales and employee numbers are for parent company.

Gundle Environmental Systems, Inc.
19103 Gundle Rd.
Houston, TX 77073
Phone: 713-443-8564 Fax: 713-875-6010
CEO: David S. Eakin
CFO: Daniel L. Shook
1991 Sales: $135 million Employees: 830
Symbol: GUN Exchange: AMEX
Industry: Pollution control equipment & services - hazardous waste disposal

Gupta Corporation
1060 Marsh Rd.
Menlo Park, CA 94025
Phone: 415-321-9500 Fax: 415-321-5471
CEO: Umang Gupta
CFO: Richard M. Noling
1992 Sales: $33 million Employees: 204
Ownership: Privately held
Industry: Computers - database management systems software

Guy F. Atkinson Co. of California
10 W. Orange Ave.
South San Francisco, CA 94080
Phone: 415-876-1000 Fax: 415-876-1143
CEO: Thomas J. Henderson
CFO: Richard K. Hoffman
1991 Sales: $684 million Employees: —
Symbol: ATKN Exchange: NASDAQ
Industry: Diversified operations - construction & engineering services, industrial pipe

GWC Corp.
2000 First State Blvd.
Wilmington, DE 19804
Phone: 302-633-5918 Fax: —
CEO: Frank J. Pizzitola
CFO: Joseph V. Boyle
1991 Sales: $112 million Employees: 760
Symbol: GWCC Exchange: NASDAQ
Industry: Utility - water supply

Gwinnett Bancshares, Inc.
750 Perry St.
Lawrenceville, GA 30245
Phone: 404-995-6000 Fax: —
CEO: James F. Pack
CFO: Robert F. Huttman
1991 Sales: $27 million Employees: —
Symbol: GBSI Exchange: NASDAQ
Industry: Banks - Southeast

Gym Masters
1025 Solano Ave.
Albany, CA 94706
Phone: 510-528-0231 Fax: 510-528-4628
CEO: Adam Shaw
CFO: Adam Shaw
1991 Sales: $6.2 million Employees: 60
Ownership: Privately held
Industry: Fitness centers

GZA GeoEnvironmental Technologies, Inc.
320 Needham St.
Newton Upper Falls, MA 02164
Phone: 617-969-0700 Fax: 617-965-7769
CEO: Donald T. Goldberg
CFO: Joseph P. Hehir
1992 Sales: $35 million Employees: 560
Symbol: GZEA Exchange: NASDAQ
Industry: Pollution control equipment & services - environmental consulting

H. B. Fuller Co.
2400 Energy Park Dr.
St. Paul, MN 55108
Phone: 612-645-3401 Fax: 612-645-6936
CEO: Anthony L. Andersen
CFO: Vartkes H. Ehramjian
1992 Sales: $934 million Employees: 5,600
Symbol: FULL Exchange: NASDAQ
Industry: Chemicals - specialty

H. D. Vest Financial Services
433 E. Las Colinas Blvd., 3rd Fl.
Irving, TX 75039
Phone: 214-556-1651 Fax: 214-556-1724
CEO: Herb D. Vest
CFO: Steven C. Hastings
1991 Sales: $20 million Employees: 99
Symbol: HDVS Exchange: NASDAQ
Industry: Financial - business services

H. F. Ahmanson & Co.
4900 Rivergrade Rd., 24th Fl.
Irwindale, CA 91706
Phone: 818-960-6311 Fax: 818-814-3675
CEO: Richard H. Deihl
CFO: Jack A. Frazee
1992 Sales: $3,638 million Employees: 10,292
Symbol: AHM Exchange: NYSE
Industry: Financial - savings and loans

H & H Oil Tool Co., Inc.
201 S. Hallock Dr.
Santa Paula, CA 93060
Phone: 805-525-6679 Fax: 805-933-0299
CEO: Henry H. Rushing
CFO: Robert K. Foote
1991 Sales: $23 million Employees: 184
Symbol: HHOT Exchange: NASDAQ
Industry: Oil field machinery & equipment

H.J. Ford Associates
1111 Jefferson Davis Hwy., Ste. 808
Arlington, VA 22202
Phone: 703-553-5580 Fax: 703-553-5587
CEO: Don Jorge Alducin
CFO: Edward R. Dieterle
1991 Sales: $9.5 million Employees: 123
Ownership: Privately held
Industry: Information systems and engineering sciences professional services

H. J. Heinz Co.
600 Grant St., 60th Fl.
Pittsburgh, PA 15219
Phone: 412-456-5700 Fax: 412-237-5377
CEO: Anthony J. F. O'Reilly
CFO: David R. Williams
1992 Sales: $6,792 million Employees: 35,500
Symbol: HNZ Exchange: NYSE
Industry: Food - ketchup, tuna, pet food, baby food

H. W. Kaufman Financial Group, Inc.
27777 Franklin Rd., 1650 American Ctr.
Southfield, MI 48034
Phone: 313-354-0400 Fax: —
CEO: Herbert W. Kaufman
CFO: Gerald F. Wesolowski
1991 Sales: $27 million Employees: 256
Symbol: HWK Exchange: AMEX
Industry: Insurance - property & casualty

H&R Block, Inc.
4410 Main St.
Kansas City, MO 64111
Phone: 816-753-6900 Fax: 816-753-5346
CEO: Thomas M. Bloch
CFO: William P. Anderson
1992 Sales: $1,363 million Employees: 89,400
Symbol: HRB Exchange: NYSE
Industry: Business services - tax preparation, on-line information network & temporary personnel services

Hach Co.
PO Box 389
Loveland, CO 80539
Phone: 303-669-3050 Fax: 303-669-2932
CEO: Kathryn C. Hach
CFO: Gary R. Dreher
1992 Sales: $85 million Employees: 860
Symbol: HACH Exchange: NASDAQ
Industry: Instruments - scientific

Hachette Magazines, Inc.
1633 Broadway
New York, NY 10019
Phone: 212-767-6000 Fax: 212-767-5600
CEO: David J. Pecker
CFO: —
1991 Sales: $5,871 million Employees: 28,460
Parent: Hachette SA
Industry: Publishing - magazines, newspapers, books; broadcasting

HADCO Corp.
10 Manor Pkwy.
Salem, NH 03079
Phone: 603-898-8000 Fax: 603-898-6227
CEO: Patrick Sweeney
CFO: Rodney P. DeRego
1991 Sales: $153 million Employees: 1,751
Symbol: HDCO Exchange: NASDAQ
Industry: Electrical components - printed circuit boards

Hadson Corp.
101 Park Ave.
Oklahoma City, OK 73102
Phone: 405-235-9531 Fax: 405-235-5044
CEO: T. K. Hendrick
CFO: Robert P. Capps
1991 Sales: $439 million Employees: 220
Symbol: HAD Exchange: NYSE
Industry: Oil & gas - US exploration & production

Haemonetics Corp.
400 Wood Rd.
Braintree, MA 02184
Phone: 617-848-7100 Fax: 617-848-5106
CEO: John F. White
CFO: J. Neal Armstrong
1992 Sales: $176 million Employees: 965
Symbol: HAE Exchange: NYSE
Industry: Medical products - blood processing systems

Hako Minuteman, Inc.
111 S. Route 53
Addison, IL 60101
Phone: 708-627-6900 Fax: 708-627-1130
CEO: Jerome E. Rau
CFO: Thomas J. Nolan
1991 Sales: $30 million Employees: 197
Symbol: HAKO Exchange: NASDAQ
Industry: Building - maintenance & services

HAL, Inc.
1164 Bishop St., Ste. 800
Honolulu, HI 96813
Phone: 808-835-3001 Fax: 808-835-3015
CEO: John A. Ueberroth
CFO: Edward S. Van Lier Ribbink
1991 Sales: $365 million Employees: 2,702
Symbol: HA Exchange: AMEX
Industry: Transportation - airline

Hale-Halsell Co. Inc.
PO Box 582898
Tulsa, OK 74158
Phone: 918-835-4484 Fax: 918-834-1347
CEO: Robert D. Hawk
CFO: Jim Lewis
1991 Sales: $608 million Employees: 3,651
Ownership: Privately held
Industry: Food - wholesale

Halifax Corp.
5250 Cherokee Ave.
Alexandria, VA 22312
Phone: 703-750-2202 Fax: 703-658-2411
CEO: Howard C. Mills
CFO: Richard J. Smithson
1992 Sales: $34 million Employees: 675
Symbol: HX Exchange: AMEX
Industry: Engineering - R&D services

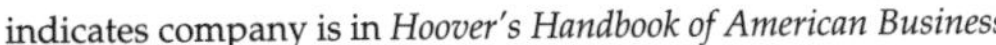
indicates company is in *Hoover's Handbook of American Business.*

indicates company is in *Hoover's Handbook of World Business;* sales and employee numbers are for parent company.

Hall-Mark Electronics Corp.
11333 Pagemill Rd.
Dallas, TX 75243
Phone: 214-343-5000 Fax: 214-343-5988
CEO: Joseph W. Semmer
CFO: Bruce Evashevski
1992 Sales: $695 million Employees: 1,491
Symbol: HMEC Exchange: NASDAQ
Industry: Electronics - parts distribution

Hallador Petroleum Co.
1660 Lincoln St., Ste. 2700
Denver, CO 80264
Phone: 303-839-5504 Fax: 303-832-3013
CEO: Victor P. Stabio
CFO: W. Anderson Bishop
1991 Sales: $5.4 million Employees: 28
Symbol: HPET Exchange: NASDAQ
Industry: Oil & gas - US exploration & production

Halliburton Co.
3600 Lincoln Plaza
Dallas, TX 75201
Phone: 214-978-2600 Fax: 214-978-2611
CEO: Thomas H. Cruikshank
CFO: Jerry H. Blurton
1992 Sales: $6,566 million Employees: 73,400
Symbol: HAL Exchange: NYSE
Industry: Oil & gas - field services

Hallmark Cards, Inc.
2501 McGee
Kansas City, MO 64141
Phone: 816-274-5111 Fax: 816-274-8513
CEO: Irvine O. Hockaday, Jr.
CFO: Henry F. Frigon
1991 Sales: $2,850 million Employees: 23,460
Ownership: Privately held
Industry: Retail - greeting cards & related products

Hallwood Energy Partners, L.P.
4582 S. Ulster St. Pkwy.
Denver, CO 80237
Phone: 303-850-7373 Fax: —
CEO: Anthony J. Gumbiner
CFO: Anthony J. Gumbiner
1991 Sales: $77 million Employees: —
Symbol: HEP Exchange: AMEX
Industry: Oil & gas - US exploration & production

Hallwood Group Inc.
3710 Rawlins St., Ste. 1500
Dallas, TX 75219
Phone: 214-528-5588 Fax: 214-528-8200
CEO: Anthony J. Gumbiner
CFO: Melvin J. Melle
1991 Sales: $80 million Employees: 652
Symbol: HWG Exchange: NYSE
Industry: Financial - business services

Halsey Drug Co., Inc.
1827 Pacific St.
Brooklyn, NY 11233
Phone: 718-467-7500 Fax: 718-493-1575
CEO: Jay Marcus
CFO: Rosendo Ferran
1991 Sales: $38 million Employees: 347
Symbol: HDG Exchange: AMEX
Industry: Drugs - generic

Hamburger Hamlets, Inc.
14156 Magnolia Blvd.
Sherman Oaks, CA 91423
Phone: 818-995-7333 Fax: 818-783-1525
CEO: Thomas A. McFall
CFO: Paul M. Brockman
1991 Sales: $53 million Employees: 1,500
Symbol: HAMB Exchange: NASDAQ
Industry: Retail - food & restaurants

Hammond Co.
4910 Campus Dr.
Newport Beach, CA 92660
Phone: 714-752-6671 Fax: 714-724-4477
CEO: Thomas T. Hammond
CFO: Jonathan T. Bastis
1992 Sales: $14 million Employees: 177
Symbol: THCO Exchange: NASDAQ
Industry: Financial - mortgages & related services

Hampshire Designers, Inc.
215 Commerce Blvd.
Anderson, SC 29625
Phone: 803-225-6232 Fax: 803-225-4421
CEO: Richard M. Owezarzak
CFO: Charles W. Clayton
1991 Sales: $87 million Employees: 2,000
Symbol: HAMP Exchange: NASDAQ
Industry: Apparel

Hampton Industries, Inc.
2000 Greenbelle Hwy.
Kinston, NC 28501
Phone: 919-527-8011 Fax: 919-527-3538
CEO: David Fuchs
CFO: Robert J. Stiehl, Jr.
1991 Sales: $162 million Employees: 2,400
Symbol: HAI Exchange: AMEX
Industry: Textiles - apparel

Hamptons Bancshares, Inc.
295 North Sea Rd.
Southampton, NY 11968
Phone: 516-287-3100 Fax: —
CEO: John F. Kidd
CFO: Ronald M. Krawczyk
1991 Sales: $15 million Employees: 141
Symbol: HBSI Exchange: NASDAQ
Industry: Banks - Northeast

Hancock Fabrics, Inc.
3406 W. Main St.
Tupelo, MS 38801
Phone: 601-842-2834 Fax: Ext. 100
CEO: Morris O. Jarvis
CFO: Larry G. Kirk
1991 Sales: $388 million Employees: 7,022
Symbol: HKF Exchange: NYSE
Industry: Retail - fabric & notions

Hancock Holding Co.
One Hancock Plaza
Gulfport, MS 39501
Phone: 601-868-4715 Fax: —
CEO: Leo W. Seal, Jr.
CFO: Leo W. Seal, Jr.
1991 Sales: $145 million Employees: 1,004
Symbol: HBHC Exchange: NASDAQ
Industry: Banks - Southeast

Handex Environmental Recovery, Inc.
500 Campus Dr.
Morganville, NJ 07751
Phone: 908-536-8500 Fax: 908-536-7751
CEO: Curtis Lee Smith, Jr.
CFO: John T. St. James
1991 Sales: $50 million Employees: 533
Symbol: HAND Exchange: NASDAQ
Industry: Pollution control equipment & services - groundwater clean up

Handleman Co.
500 Kirts Blvd.
Troy, MI 48084
Phone: 313-362-4400 Fax: 313-362-3615
CEO: Stephen Strome
CFO: Louis A. Kircos
1992 Sales: $1,109 million Employees: 3,947
Symbol: HDL Exchange: NYSE
Industry: Wholesale distribution - consumer products

Handy & Harman
850 Third Ave.
New York, NY 10022
Phone: 212-752-3400 Fax: 212-207-2614
CEO: Richard N. Daniel
CFO: Stephen B. Mudd
1991 Sales: $462 million Employees: 4,333
Symbol: HNH Exchange: NYSE
Industry: Precious metals & jewelry

Hanger Orthopedic Group, Inc.
8200 Wisconsin Ave.
Bethesda, MD 20814
Phone: 301-986-0701 Fax: —
CEO: Ronald J. Manganiello
CFO: Richard A. Stein
1991 Sales: $24 million Employees: 337
Symbol: HGR Exchange: AMEX
Industry: Medical products - prosthetic & orthotic products & services

Hannaford Bros. Co. Inc.
145 Pleasant Hill Rd.
Scarborough, ME 04074
Phone: 207-883-2911 Fax: Call co. operator
CEO: James L. Moody, Jr.
CFO: Robert F. Wade
1992 Sales: $2,066 million Employees: 16,000
Symbol: HRD Exchange: NYSE
Industry: Retail - supermarkets

Hanover Insurance Co.
100 North Pkwy.
Worcester, MA 01605
Phone: 508-853-7200 Fax: —
CEO: John F. O'Brien
CFO: Joseph C. Henry
1991 Sales: $1.6 million Employees: 5,530
Symbol: HINS Exchange: NASDAQ
Industry: Insurance - property & casualty

W **Hanson Industries**
99 Wood Ave. South
Iselin, NJ 08830
Phone: 908-603-6600 Fax: 908-603-6878
CEO: David H. Clarke
CFO: —
1991 Sales: $13,363 million Employees: 70,000
Parent: Hanson PLC
Industry: Diversified operations - consumer goods, industrial & building products

Harbert Corp.
1 Riverchase Pkwy. South
Birmingham, AL 35244
Phone: 205-987-5500 Fax: 205-987-5568
CEO: Raymond J. Harbert
CFO: Jerry M. Johnston
1991 Sales: $525 million Employees: 2,200
Ownership: Privately held
Industry: Construction - commercial & real estate development

Harbour Group Ltd.
7701 Forsyth Blvd., Ste. 600
St. Louis, MO 63105
Phone: 314-727-5550 Fax: 314-727-0941
CEO: Sam Fox
CFO: Francis M. Loveland
1992 Sales: $550 million Employees: 5,000
Ownership: Privately held
Industry: Diversified operations - cutting tools, polymers, pumps, special machinery

Harding Lawson Assoc. Inc.
7655 Redwood Blvd.
Novato, CA 94945
Phone: 415-892-0821 Fax: 415-892-0831
CEO: Richard P. Prezio
CFO: Herbert D. Montgomery
1992 Sales: $83 million Employees: 1,015
Symbol: HRDG Exchange: NASDAQ
Industry: Engineering - R&D services

A indicates company is in *Hoover's Handbook of American Business.*

W indicates company is in *Hoover's Handbook of World Business*; sales and employee numbers are for parent company.

Harken Energy Corp.
2505 N. Hwy. 360, Ste. 800
Grand Prairie, TX 75050
Phone: 817-695-4900 Fax: —
CEO: Mikel D. Faulkner
CFO: Bruce N. Huff
1991 Sales: $4.8 million Employees: 100
Symbol: HEC Exchange: AMEX
Industry: Oil & gas - US exploration & production

Harley-Davidson, Inc.
3700 W. Juneau Ave.
Milwaukee, WI 53208
Phone: 414-342-4680 Fax: 414-935-4977
CEO: Richard F. Teerlink
CFO: James L. Ziemer
1992 Sales: $1,105 million Employees: 5,300
Symbol: HDI Exchange: NYSE
Industry: Leisure & recreational products - motorcycles & related products

Harleysville Group Inc.
355 Maple Ave.
Harleysville, PA 19438
Phone: 215-256-5000 Fax: 215-256-5601
CEO: Bradford W. Mitchell
CFO: Michael G. McCarter
1991 Sales: $422 million Employees: 2,224
Symbol: HGIC Exchange: NASDAQ
Industry: Insurance - property & casualty

Harleysville National Corp.
483 Main St.
Harleysville, PA 19438
Phone: 215-256-8851 Fax: —
CEO: Walter E. Daller, Jr.
CFO: Earle H. Richmond
1991 Sales: $45 million Employees: 206
Symbol: HNBC Exchange: NASDAQ
Industry: Banks - Northeast

Harleysville Savings Bank
271 Main St.
Harleysville, PA 19438
Phone: 215-256-8828 Fax: 215-256-0510
CEO: Edward J. Molnar
CFO: Ronald B. Geib
1992 Sales: — Employees: —
Symbol: HARL Exchange: NASDAQ
Industry: Financial - savings and loans

Harlyn Products, Inc.
1515 S. Main St.
Los Angeles, CA 90015
Phone: 213-746-0745 Fax: 213-742-6701
CEO: William K. Hood
CFO: Edward Dudziak
1992 Sales: $28 million Employees: 469
Symbol: HRN Exchange: AMEX
Industry: Precious metals & jewelry

Harman International Industries, Inc.
1101 Pennsylvania Ave. NW
Washington, DC 20004
Phone: 202-393-1101 Fax: 202-393-3064
CEO: Sidney Harman
CFO: Bernard A. Girod
1992 Sales: $627 million Employees: 4,438
Symbol: HAR Exchange: NYSE
Industry: Audio & video home products

Harmon Industries, Inc.
1300 Jefferson Court
Blue Springs, MO 64015
Phone: 816-229-3345 Fax: 816-229-0556
CEO: Robert E. Harmon
CFO: Charles M. Foudree
1991 Sales: $71 million Employees: 776
Symbol: HRMN Exchange: NASDAQ
Industry: Transportation - equipment & leasing

Harmonia Bancorp, Inc.
1700 Galloping Hill Rd.
Kenilworth, NJ 07033
Phone: 908-241-8400 Fax: —
CEO: Walter D. Tombs
CFO: Walter D. Tombs
1991 Sales: $63 million Employees: 258
Symbol: HBCI Exchange: NASDAQ
Industry: Banks - Northeast

Harmony Schools
139 Village Blvd.
Princeton, NJ 08540
Phone: 609-799-4411 Fax: 609-243-0037
CEO: Lisa Forrester
CFO: Lisa Forrester
1991 Sales: $2.7 million Employees: 104
Ownership: Privately held
Industry: Schools - child care services

Harnischfeger Industries Corp.
16400 Bishops Lane
Brookfield, WI 53005
Phone: 414-671-4400 Fax: 414-671-7604
CEO: Jeffery T. Grade
CFO: Francis M. Corby, Jr.
1992 Sales: $1,390 million Employees: 11,600
Symbol: HPH Exchange: NYSE
Industry: Machinery - construction & mining

Harold's Stores, Inc.
765 Asp Ave.
Norman, OK 73069
Phone: 405-329-4045 Fax: 405-366-2588
CEO: Harold G. Powell
CFO: H. Rainey Powell
1991 Sales: $41 million Employees: 512
Symbol: HLD Exchange: AMEX
Industry: Retail - apparel & shoes

Harper Group, Inc.
260 Townsend St.
San Francisco, CA 94107
Phone: 415-978-0600 Fax: 415-978-0626
CEO: John H. Robinson
CFO: Stuart O. Keirle
1991 Sales: $454 million Employees: 3,279
Symbol: HARG Exchange: NASDAQ
Industry: Transportation - air freight

Harris Corp.
1025 W. NASA Blvd.
Melbourne, FL 32919
Phone: 407-727-9100 Fax: 407-727-5118
CEO: John T. Hartley
CFO: Bryan R. Roub
1992 Sales: $3,059 million Employees: 28,300
Symbol: HRS Exchange: NYSE
Industry: Telecommunications equipment, semiconductors, electronic systems

Harris & Harris Group, Inc.
620 Fifth Ave., Ste. 201
New York, NY 10020
Phone: 212-307-4380 Fax: 212-307-4384
CEO: Charles E. Harris
CFO: C. Richard Childress
1991 Sales: $4.6 million Employees: 63
Symbol: HHGP Exchange: NASDAQ
Industry: Insurance - brokerage

Harsco Corp.
350 Poplar Church Rd.
Camp Hill, PA 17011
Phone: 717-763-7064 Fax: 717-763-6424
CEO: Malcolm W. Gambill
CFO: George F. Rezich
1992 Sales: $1,625 million Employees: 10,500
Symbol: HSC Exchange: NYSE
Industry: Metal processing & fabrication

Hartford Steam Boiler Inspection and Ins. Co.
One State St.
Hartford, CT 06102
Phone: 203-722-1866 Fax: 203-722-5106
CEO: Wilson Wilde
CFO: Robert W. Trainer
1992 Sales: $682 million Employees: —
Symbol: HSB Exchange: NYSE
Industry: Insurance - property & casualty

Hartmarx Corp.
101 N. Wacker Dr.
Chicago, IL 60606
Phone: 312-372-6300 Fax: 312-444-2710
CEO: Elbert O. Hand
CFO: Wallace L. Rueckel
1992 Sales: $1,054 million Employees: 20,000
Symbol: HMX Exchange: NYSE
Industry: Apparel

Hartz Group
667 Madison Ave.
New York, NY 10021
Phone: 212-308-3336 Fax: 212-644-5987
CEO: Leonard N. Stern
CFO: Curtis Schwartz
1991 Sales: $846 million Employees: 3,500
Ownership: Privately held
Industry: Veterinary products & services - pet supplies, real estate, publishing

Harvard Industries Inc.
1 Central Ave.
Farmingdale, NJ 07727
Phone: 908-938-9000 Fax: 908-919-2482
CEO: William D. Hurley
CFO: Joseph Gagliardi
1991 Sales: $662 million Employees: 7,200
Ownership: Privately held
Industry: Aerospace - aircraft equipment & auto equipment

Harvey Group Inc.
3 Expressway Plaza
Roslyn Heights, NY 11577
Phone: 516-621-5550 Fax: 516-621-1617
CEO: Harvey E. Sampson
CFO: Dennis R. Wilson
1991 Sales: $28 million Employees: 116
Symbol: HRA Exchange: AMEX
Industry: Food - wholesale

Hasbro, Inc.
1027 Newport Ave.
Pawtucket, RI 02861
Phone: 401-431-8697 Fax: 401-727-5544
CEO: Alan G. Hassenfeld
CFO: John T. O'Neill
1992 Sales: $2,541 million Employees: 10,500
Symbol: HAS Exchange: AMEX
Industry: Toys - games & hobby products, infant products

Hastings Manufacturing Co.
325 N. Hanover St.
Hastings, MI 49058
Phone: 616-945-2491 Fax: 616-945-4667
CEO: Stephen I. Johnson
CFO: Thomas J. Bellgraph
1991 Sales: $61 million Employees: 660
Symbol: HMF Exchange: AMEX
Industry: Automotive & trucking - replacement parts

Hathaway Systems Corp.
8700 Turnpike Dr., Ste. 300
Westminster, CO 80030
Phone: 303-426-1600 Fax: 303-426-0932
CEO: Eugene E. Prince
CFO: Richard D. Smith
1992 Sales: $69 million Employees: 641
Symbol: HATH Exchange: NASDAQ
Industry: Computers - accounting software

indicates company is in *Hoover's Handbook of American Business.*

indicates company is in *Hoover's Handbook of World Business;* sales and employee numbers are for parent company.

Hauser Chemical Research, Inc.
5555 Airport Blvd.
Boulder, CO 80301
Phone: 303-443-4662 Fax: 303-441-5800
CEO: Dean P. Stull
CFO: William E. Paukert
1992 Sales: $26 million Employees: 230
Symbol: HAUS Exchange: NASDAQ
Industry: Chemicals - specialty; anti-cancer chemicals, bulk pharmaceuticals & natural flavor ingredients

Haverfield Corp.
14650 Detroit Ave.
Lakewood, OH 44107
Phone: 216-226-0510 Fax: —
CEO: William A. Valerian
CFO: Richard C. Ebner
1991 Sales: $30 million Employees: 149
Symbol: HVFD Exchange: NASDAQ
Industry: Financial - savings and loans

Haverty Furniture Companies, Inc.
866 W. Peachtree St. NW
Atlanta, GA 30308
Phone: 404-881-1911 Fax: 404-870-9424
CEO: Frank S. McGaughey, Jr.
CFO: Dennis L. Fink
1991 Sales: $258 million Employees: 2,212
Symbol: HAVT Exchange: NASDAQ
Industry: Retail - home furnishings

Hawaiian Electric Industries, Inc.
900 Richards St.
Honolulu, HI 96813
Phone: 808-543-5662 Fax: 808-543-7966
CEO: Robert F. Clarke
CFO: Robert F. Mougeot
1992 Sales: $1,031 million Employees: 3,395
Symbol: HE Exchange: NYSE
Industry: Utility - electric power

Hawkeye Bancorporation
604 Locust St.
Des Moines, IA 50309
Phone: 515-284-1930 Fax: 515-248-7570
CEO: Robert W. Murray
CFO: Robert W. Murray
1991 Sales: $129 million Employees: 703
Symbol: HWKB Exchange: NASDAQ
Industry: Banks - Midwest

Hawkins Chemical, Inc.
3100 E. Hennepin Ave.
Minneapolis, MN 55413
Phone: 612-331-6910 Fax: 612-331-5304
CEO: Howard J. Hawkins
CFO: Howard M. Hawkins
1991 Sales: $66 million Employees: 152
Symbol: HWKN Exchange: NASDAQ
Industry: Chemicals - specialty

Haworth, Inc.
One Haworth Center
Holland, MI 49423
Phone: 616-393-3000 Fax: 616-393-1570
CEO: Richard G. Haworth
CFO: Jim Lehmann
1991 Sales: $650 million Employees: 4,500
Ownership: Privately held
Industry: Furniture - office

Hawthorne Financial Corp.
13658 S. Hawthorne Blvd.
Hawthorne, CA 90250
Phone: 310-973-8964 Fax: —
CEO: Vernon D. Herbst
CFO: Douglas J. Herbst
1991 Sales: $107 million Employees: 197
Symbol: HTHR Exchange: NASDAQ
Industry: Financial - savings and loans

Hazco Services Inc.
2006 Springboro West
Dayton, OH 45439
Phone: 513-293-2700 Fax: 513-293-9227
CEO: Philip Sheridan
CFO: Ralph Miller
1991 Sales: $11 million Employees: 65
Ownership: Privately held
Industry: Hazardous waste safety equipment

HazWaste Industries Inc.
2104 W. Laburnum Ave. #104
Richmond, VA 23227
Phone: 804-358-5858 Fax: 804-358-5958
CEO: Michael J. Higgins
CFO: Richard H. Guilford
1992 Sales: $44 million Employees: 270
Ownership: Privately held
Industry: Environmental consulting, remediation & analytical laboratory services

HB Zachry Co.
527 Logwood Ave.
San Antonio, TX 78221
Phone: 210-922-1213 Fax: 210-927-8060
CEO: H. Bartell Zachry, Jr.
CFO: Charles Ebrom
1991 Sales: $783 million Employees: 8,800
Ownership: Privately held
Industry: Construction - general contracting

HBO & Co.
301 Perimeter Center North
Atlanta, GA 30346
Phone: 404-393-6000 Fax: 404-393-6092
CEO: Holcombe T. Green, Jr.
CFO: Thomas H. Muller, Jr.
1991 Sales: $171 million Employees: 1,603
Symbol: HBOC Exchange: NASDAQ
Industry: Computers - information systems services

HCA Hospital Corporation of America
One Park Plaza
Nashville, TN 37203
Phone: 615-327-9551 Fax: 615-320-2222
CEO: Thomas F. Frist, Jr.
CFO: Roger E. Mick
1992 Sales: $5,126 million Employees: 70,000
Symbol: HCA Exchange: NYSE
Industry: Hospitals

HCB Contractors
1400 Elm St., Ste. 4600
Dallas, TX 75202
Phone: 214-747-8541 Fax: 214-748-5063
CEO: Lawrence A. Wilson
CFO: James F. Russell
1990 Sales: $640 million Employees: 400
Ownership: Privately held
Industry: Construction - general contracting and management

HDR Power Systems, Inc.
4242 Reynolds Dr.
Hilliard, OH 43026
Phone: 614-771-5500 Fax: —
CEO: David R. Bratton
CFO: Richard J. Lippott
1992 Sales: $8.1 million Employees: 72
Symbol: HDRP Exchange: NASDAQ
Industry: Electrical products - uninterruptible power sources

He-Ro Group, Ltd.
550 Seventh Ave.
New York, NY 10018
Phone: 212-840-6047 Fax: 212-764-6108
CEO: Herbert Rounick
CFO: Paul Kittner
1992 Sales: $140 million Employees: 956
Symbol: HRG Exchange: NYSE
Industry: Apparel

Health Advancement Services, Inc.
1457 W. Alameda Dr., Ste. 10
Tempe, AZ 85282
Phone: 602-966-1599 Fax: —
CEO: Glenn M. Friedman
CFO: Marilyn Bagwell
1992 Sales: — Employees: 12
Symbol: HASI Exchange: NASDAQ
Industry: Medical services - worksite health evaluation & education programs

Health Care and Retirement Corp.
One Seagate
Toledo, OH 43666
Phone: 419-247-5000 Fax: 419-247-1364
CEO: Paul A. Ormand
CFO: Geoffrey G. Meyers
1991 Sales: $476 million Employees: 16,600
Symbol: HCR Exchange: NYSE
Industry: Healthcare - outpatient & home

Health Images, Inc.
8601 Dunwoody Place, Ste. 200
Atlanta, GA 30350
Phone: 404-587-5084 Fax: —
CEO: Robert D. Carl III
CFO: Robert D. Carl III
1991 Sales: $61 million Employees: 494
Symbol: HIMG Exchange: NASDAQ
Industry: Healthcare - outpatient & home

Health Management Associates, Inc.
5811 Pelican Bay Blvd., Ste. 500
Naples, FL 33963
Phone: 813-598-3131 Fax: 813-597-5794
CEO: William J. Schoen
CFO: William J. Schoen
1991 Sales: $226 million Employees: 4,100
Symbol: HMA Exchange: NYSE
Industry: Hospitals

Health O Meter Products, Inc.
7400 W. 100th Place
Bridgeview, IL 60455
Phone: 708-598-9100 Fax: 708-599-0150
CEO: Lawrence Zalusky
CFO: Donald E. Herbert
1991 Sales: $46 million Employees: 461
Symbol: SCAL Exchange: NASDAQ
Industry: Medical instruments

Health Risk Management, Inc.
8000 W. 78th St.
Minneapolis, MN 55439
Phone: 612-829-3500 Fax: —
CEO: Gary T. McIlroy
CFO: Thomas P. Clark
1992 Sales: $28 million Employees: 663
Symbol: HRMI Exchange: NASDAQ
Industry: Medical services - integrated health care management

Health-Chem Corp.
1212 Avenue of the Americas
New York, NY 10036
Phone: 212-398-0700 Fax: 212-398-0884
CEO: Marvin M. Speiser
CFO: Paul R. Moeller
1991 Sales: $37 million Employees: 220
Symbol: HCH Exchange: AMEX
Industry: Medical products - synthetic fabrics & health care products

Health-Mor Inc.
3500 Payne Ave
Cleveland, OH 44114
Phone: 216-432-1990 Fax: 216-432-0250
CEO: Kirk W. Foley
CFO: Gerald M. Burke
1991 Sales: $61 million Employees: 550
Symbol: HMI Exchange: AMEX
Industry: Appliances - household

HealthCare Compare Corp.
3200 Highland Ave.
Downers Grove, IL 60515
Phone: 708-719-9000 Fax: —
CEO: James C. Smith
CFO: Joseph E. Whitters
1991 Sales: $71 million Employees: 888
Symbol: HCCC Exchange: NASDAQ
Industry: Financial - business services

HealthCare Imaging Services, Inc.
59 Avenue at the Common
Shrewsbury, NJ 07702
Phone: 908-542-3311 Fax: —
CEO: Elliott H. Vernon
CFO: Elliott H. Vernon
1991 Sales: $6 million Employees: 28
Symbol: HISS Exchange: NASDAQ
Industry: Medical services

Healthcare International, Inc.
912 Capitol of Texas South
Austin, TX 78746
Phone: 512-346-4300 Fax: 512-314-5254
CEO: Jean P. Smith
CFO: J. Mack Nunn
1991 Sales: $212 million Employees: 4,100
Symbol: HII Exchange: AMEX
Industry: Healthcare - outpatient & home

Healthcare Services Group, Inc.
2643 Huntingdon Pike
Huntingdon Valley, PA 19006
Phone: 215-938-1661 Fax: 215-938-1590
CEO: Daniel P. McCartney
CFO: Thomas A. Cook
1991 Sales: $83 million Employees: 6,718
Symbol: HCSG Exchange: NASDAQ
Industry: Building - maintenance & services

Healthco International
470 Atlantic Ave.
Boston, MA 02110
Phone: 617-574-4200 Fax: 617-574-4552
CEO: Gary Cooper
CFO: James Moyle
1991 Sales: $500 million Employees: 2,699
Ownership: Privately held
Industry: Medical products - dental supplies

Healthdyne, Inc.
1850 Parkway Place
Marietta, GA 30067
Phone: 404-423-4500 Fax: 404-423-4640
CEO: Parker H. Petit
CFO: Donald R. Millard
1991 Sales: $191 million Employees: 2,550
Symbol: HDYN Exchange: NASDAQ
Industry: Healthcare - outpatient & home

HealthInfusion, Inc.
5200 Blue Lagoon Dr., Ste. 200
Miami, FL 33126
Phone: 305-267-1177 Fax: 305-263-9945
CEO: Miles E. Gilman
CFO: Jack T. Thompson
1991 Sales: $29 million Employees: 166
Symbol: HINF Exchange: NASDAQ
Industry: Healthcare - outpatient & home

Healthsource, Inc.
Donovan St. Extension
Concord, NH 03301
Phone: 603-225-5077 Fax: 603-225-7621
CEO: Norman C. Payson
CFO: Thomas M. Congoran
1991 Sales: $88 million Employees: 400
Symbol: HS Exchange: NYSE
Industry: Health maintenance organization

Healthsouth Rehabilitation Corp.
Two Perimeter Park South, Ste. 224W
Birmingham, AL 35243
Phone: 205-967-7116 Fax: Call co. operator
CEO: Richard M. Scrushy
CFO: Aaron Beam, Jr.
1991 Sales: $226 million Employees: 6,541
Symbol: HRC Exchange: NYSE
Industry: Healthcare - outpatient & home

HealthTrust, Inc., The Hospital Co.
4525 Harding Rd.
Nashville, TN 37205
Phone: 615-383-4444 Fax: 615-298-6377
CEO: R. C. McWhorter
CFO: M. A. Koban, Jr.
1992 Sales: $2,299 million Employees: 30,000
Symbol: HTI Exchange: NYSE
Industry: Hospitals

HealthWatch Technologies, Inc.
3400 Industrial Lane, Ste. A
Broomfield, CO 80020
Phone: 303-465-2000 Fax: 303-465-2242
CEO: Sanford L. Schwartz
CFO: John W. Erickson
1992 Sales: $8.1 million Employees: 72
Symbol: HEAL Exchange: NASDAQ
Industry: Medical products - cardiovascular diagnostic instruments

Hearst Corporation, The
959 8th Ave.
New York, NY 10019
Phone: 212-649-2000 Fax: 212-765-3528
CEO: Frank A. Bennack, Jr.
CFO: Victor F. Ganzi
1991 Sales: $1,947 million Employees: 14,000
Ownership: Privately held
Industry: Publishing - magazines, newspapers & books; broadcasting & cable

Heart Technology, Inc.
2515 140th Ave. NE
Bellevue, WA 98005
Phone: 206-869-6160 Fax: 206-867-5466
CEO: David C. Auth
CFO: William L. Scott
1991 Sales: $6.2 million Employees: 123
Symbol: HRTT Exchange: NASDAQ
Industry: Medical products

Heartland Express, Inc.
2777 Heartland Dr.
Coralville, IA 52241
Phone: 319-645-2728 Fax: 319-645-2338
CEO: Russell A. Gerdin
CFO: John P. Cosaert
1991 Sales: $74 million Employees: 428
Symbol: HTLD Exchange: NASDAQ
Industry: Transportation - truck

Heartland Partners, L.P.
547 W. Jackson Blvd.
Chicago, IL 60606
Phone: 312-822-0400 Fax: —
CEO: Edwin Jacobson
CFO: Leon F. Fiorentino
1991 Sales: $4.9 million Employees: 28
Symbol: HTL Exchange: AMEX
Industry: Real estate operations

HEB Grocery
646 S. Main Ave.
San Antonio, TX 78204
Phone: 210-246-8000 Fax: 210-246-8169
CEO: Charles C. Butt
CFO: John C. Brouillard
1992 Sales: $3,800 million Employees: 40,000
Ownership: Privately held
Industry: Retail - supermarkets

Hechinger Co.
1616 McCormick Dr.
Landover, MD 20785
Phone: 301-341-1000 Fax: 301-925-3906
CEO: John W. Hechinger, Jr.
CFO: W. Clark McClelland
1992 Sales: $1,811 million Employees: 17,000
Symbol: HECHA Exchange: NASDAQ
Industry: Building products - retail & wholesale

Hecla Mining Co.
6500 Mineral Dr.
Coeur d'Alene, ID 83814
Phone: 208-769-4100 Fax: 208-769-4107
CEO: Arthur Brown
CFO: John P. Stilwell
1991 Sales: $118 million Employees: 911
Symbol: HL Exchange: NYSE
Industry: Gold mining & processing

Hector Communications Corp.
211 S. Main St.
Hector, MN 55342
Phone: 612-848-6231 Fax: 612-848-2702
CEO: Curtis A. Sampson
CFO: Charles A. Braun
1991 Sales: $4.2 million Employees: 30
Symbol: HCCO Exchange: NASDAQ
Industry: Telecommunications services

Heekin Can, Inc.
11310 Cornell Park Dr.
Cincinnati, OH 45242
Phone: 513-489-3200 Fax: 513-530-1310
CEO: John A. Haas
CFO: Perry H. Schwartz
1991 Sales: $353 million Employees: 1,500
Symbol: HEKN Exchange: NASDAQ
Industry: Containers - metal

HEI, Inc.
1495 Steiger Lake Lane
Victoria, MN 55386
Phone: 612-443-2500 Fax: 612-443-2668
CEO: Eugene W. Courtney
CFO: Jerald H. Mortenson
1991 Sales: $9 million Employees: 130
Symbol: HEII Exchange: NASDAQ
Industry: Electrical components - optoelectronic components, optical card readers

HEICO Corp.
3000 Taft St.
Hollywood, FL 33021
Phone: 305-987-6101 Fax: 305-966-2169
CEO: Laurans A. Mendelson
CFO: Thomas S. Irwin
1991 Sales: $25 million Employees: 242
Symbol: HEI Exchange: AMEX
Industry: Aerospace - aircraft equipment

Heilig-Meyers Co.
2235 Staples Mill Rd.
Richmond, VA 23230
Phone: 804-359-9171 Fax: 804-254-1498
CEO: William C. DeRusha
CFO: Joseph R. Jenkins
1992 Sales: $623 million Employees: 6,700
Symbol: HMY Exchange: NYSE
Industry: Retail - home furnishings

Hein-Werner Corp.
2120 N. Pewaukee Rd.
Waukesha, WI 53187
Phone: 414-542-6611 Fax: 414-542-4884
CEO: Joseph L. Dindorf
CFO: Edward F. Duffy
1991 Sales: $85 million Employees: 667
Symbol: HNW Exchange: AMEX
Industry: Machine tools & related products

indicates company is in *Hoover's Handbook of American Business.*

indicates company is in *Hoover's Handbook of World Business*; sales and employee numbers are for parent company.

Helen of Troy Corp.
6827 Market Ave.
El Paso, TX 79915
Phone: 915-779-6363 Fax: 915-778-8242
CEO: Gerald J. Rubin
CFO: Sam L. Henry
1992 Sales: $120 million Employees: 348
Symbol: HELE Exchange: NASDAQ
Industry: Cosmetics & toiletries

Helene Curtis Industries, Inc.
325 N. Wells St.
Chicago, IL 60610
Phone: 312-661-0222 Fax: 312-836-0125
CEO: Ronald J. Gidwitz
CFO: Lewis D. Duberman
1992 Sales: $1,128 million Employees: 3,100
Symbol: HC Exchange: NYSE
Industry: Cosmetics & toiletries

Helian Health Group, Inc.
9600 Blue Larkspur
Monterey, CA 93940
Phone: 408-646-9000 Fax: —
CEO: Thomas D. Wilson
CFO: Donald C. Blanding
1991 Sales: $21 million Employees: 295
Symbol: HHGR Exchange: NASDAQ
Industry: Medical services - specialized ambulatory health care facilities

Helionetics Inc.
2300 Main St.
Irvine, CA 97214
Phone: 714-261-8313 Fax: 714-261-0413
CEO: E. Maxwell Malone
CFO: E. Maxwell Malone
1991 Sales: $10 million Employees: —
Symbol: ZAP Exchange: AMEX
Industry: Electrical products - electrical power conversion & laser equipment

Helix Technology Corp.
Nine Hampshire St.
Mansfield, MA 02048
Phone: 508-337-5454 Fax: 508-337-5175
CEO: Robert J. Lepofsky
CFO: Stanley D. Piekos
1991 Sales: $56 million Employees: 343
Symbol: HELX Exchange: NASDAQ
Industry: Instruments - scientific

Helm Resources, Inc.
66 Field Point Rd.
Greenwich, CT 06830
Phone: 203-629-1400 Fax: 203-629-1961
CEO: Herbert M. Pearlman
CFO: Daniel T. Murphy
1991 Sales: $224 million Employees: 394
Symbol: H Exchange: AMEX
Industry: Diversified operations - thermoplastic resins, seismic survey licensing

Helmerich & Payne, Inc.
1579 E. 21st. St.
Tulsa, OK 74114
Phone: 918-742-5531 Fax: 918-742-0237
CEO: Hans Helmerich
CFO: Douglas E. Fears
1991 Sales: $190 million Employees: 1,758
Symbol: HP Exchange: NYSE
Industry: Oil & gas - US exploration & production

Helmsley Enterprises Inc.
60 E. 42nd St.
New York, NY 10165
Phone: 212-687-6400 Fax: 212-687-6437
CEO: Harry B. Helmsley
CFO: Martin S. Stone
1991 Sales: $1,327 million Employees: 13,000
Ownership: Privately held
Industry: Real estate operations - brokerage & management

Helmstar Group, Inc.
Two World Trade Center
New York, NY 10048
Phone: 212-775-0400 Fax: —
CEO: George W. Benoit
CFO: Roger J. Burns
1991 Sales: $1.8 million Employees: 37
Symbol: HLM Exchange: AMEX
Industry: Financial - investment bankers

Hendrick Management Corp.
6000 Monroe Rd., Ste 100
Charlotte, NC 28212
Phone: 704-568-5550 Fax: 704-535-5592
CEO: J. R. Hendrick III
CFO: J. Huzi
1991 Sales: $687 million Employees: 1,537
Ownership: Privately held
Industry: Diversified oeprations - auto dealerships, sportswear, motorsports

Henkel Corporation
The Triad, Ste. 200, 2200 Renaissance Blvd.
Gulph Mills, PA 19406
Phone: 215-270-8100 Fax: 215-270-8102
CEO: Harald P. Wulff
CFO: —
1991 Sales: $8,490 million Employees: 41,475
Parent: Henkel KGaA
Industry: Chemicals - oleochemicals, adhesives, detergents

Henley International, Inc.
104 Industrial Blvd.
Sugar Land, TX 77478
Phone: 713-240-2442 Fax: —
CEO: Kenneth W. Davidson
CFO: Peter M. Graham
1991 Sales: $45 million Employees: 798
Symbol: HEN Exchange: AMEX
Industry: Medical products - physical therapy products, home pain management

Hensel Phelps Construction Co.
420 6th Ave.
Greeley, CO 80632
Phone: 303-352-6565 Fax: 303-352-9311
CEO: Jerry L. Morgensen
CFO: Steve Carrico
1991 Sales: $727 million Employees: 1,525
Ownership: Privately held
Industry: Building - commercial

Herbalife International, Inc.
9800 La Cienega Blvd.
Inglewood, CA 90301
Phone: 310-410-9600 Fax: 310-216-7255
CEO: Mark Hughes
CFO: T. Gerrity
1991 Sales: $103 million Employees: 294
Symbol: HERB Exchange: NASDAQ
Industry: Vitamins & nutritional products

Hercules Inc.
1313 N. Market St., Hercules Plaza
Wilmington, DE 19894
Phone: 302-594-5000 Fax: 302-594-5400
CEO: Thomas L. Gossage
CFO: R. Keith Elliott
1992 Sales: $2,865 million Employees: 17,324
Symbol: HPC Exchange: NYSE
Industry: Specialty chemicals - polymers, aerospace materials & food

Heritage Asset Management Group
6009 Belt Line Rd., Ste. 100
Dallas, TX 75240
Phone: 214-490-1776 Fax: 214-490-1770
CEO: Dennis Flynn
CFO: Terri Ferguson
1991 Sales: $2 million Employees: 72
Ownership: Privately held
Industry: Real estate operations & brokerage

Heritage Bancorp, Inc.
330 Whitney Ave.
Holyoke, MA 01040
Phone: 413-539-6000 Fax: —
CEO: Richard B. Covell
CFO: Charles D. Jeffrey
1991 Sales: $136 million Employees: 429
Symbol: HNIS Exchange: NASDAQ
Industry: Banks - Northeast

Heritage Bankcorp, Inc.
20600 Eureka Rd.
Taylor, MI 48180
Phone: 313-285-1010 Fax: —
CEO: E. G. Wilkinson, Jr.
CFO: Brian A. Barbuto
1991 Sales: $84 million Employees: 398
Symbol: HEBC Exchange: NASDAQ
Industry: Financial - savings and loans

Heritage Federal Bancshares, Inc.
110 E. Center St.
Kingsport, TN 37660
Phone: 615-378-8000 Fax: —
CEO: William E. Kreis
CFO: William F. Richmond
1992 Sales: — Employees: —
Symbol: HFBS Exchange: NASDAQ
Industry: Banks - Southeast

Heritage Financial Services, Inc.
17500 South Oak Park Ave.
Tinley Park, IL 60477
Phone: 708-532-8000 Fax: —
CEO: Richard T. Wojcik
CFO: Paul A. Eckroth
1991 Sales: $61 million Employees: 325
Symbol: HERS Exchange: NASDAQ
Industry: Banks - Midwest

Heritage Media Corp.
13555 Noel Rd., Ste. 1500
Dallas, TX 75240
Phone: 214-702-7380 Fax: 214-702-7382
CEO: David N. Walthall
CFO: Joseph D. Mahaffey
1991 Sales: $222 million Employees: 14,200
Symbol: HTG Exchange: AMEX
Industry: Broadcasting - radio & TV

Herley Industries, Inc.
10 Industry Dr.
Lancaster, PA 17603
Phone: 717-397-2777 Fax: 717-397-4475
CEO: Lee N. Blatt
CFO: Myron Levy
1991 Sales: $14 million Employees: 133
Symbol: HRLY Exchange: NASDAQ
Industry: Electronics - military

Herman Miller, Inc.
8500 Byron Rd.
Zeeland, MI 49464
Phone: 616-772-3300 Fax: 616-654-5385
CEO: Richard H. Ruch
CFO: James H. Bloem
1992 Sales: $819 million Employees: 6,001
Symbol: MLHR Exchange: NASDAQ
Industry: Furniture

Hernandez Engineering Inc.
17625 El Camino Real, Ste. 200
Houston, TX 77058
Phone: 713-280-5159 Fax: 713-480-7525
CEO: Mike Hernandez
CFO: Tery Hernandez
1991 Sales: $17 million Employees: 345
Ownership: Privately held
Industry: Engineering - training, technical & R&D services

indicates company is in *Hoover's Handbook of American Business.*

indicates company is in *Hoover's Handbook of World Business;* sales and employee numbers are for parent company.

Hershey Foods Corp.
100 Crystal A Dr.
Hershey, PA 17033
Phone: 717-534-4001 Fax: 717-534-4078
CEO: Richard A. Zimmerman
CFO: Michael F. Pasquale
1992 Sales: $3,220 million Employees: 14,000
Symbol: HSY Exchange: NYSE
Industry: Food - confectionery

Hertz Corp., The
225 Brae Blvd.
Park Ridge, NJ 07656
Phone: 201-307-2000 Fax: 201-307-2644
CEO: Frank A. Olson
CFO: William Sider
1991 Sales: $2,407 million Employees: 18,100
Ownership: Privately held
Industry: Leasing - cars

Hewlett-Packard Co.
3000 Hanover St.
Palo Alto, CA 94304
Phone: 415-857-1501 Fax: 415-857-7299
CEO: John A. Young
CFO: Robert P. Wayman
1992 Sales: $16,410 million Employees: 89,000
Symbol: HWP Exchange: NYSE
Industry: Computers - mini & micro, peripheral & network equipment

Hexcel Corp.
11555 Dublin Blvd.
Dublin, CA 94568
Phone: 510-828-4200 Fax: 510-828-2277
CEO: Robert L. Witt
CFO: David G. Schmidt
1991 Sales: $387 million Employees: 3,062
Symbol: HXL Exchange: NYSE
Industry: Aerospace - aircraft equipment

HF Financial Corp.
225 S. Main Ave.
Sioux Falls, SD 57102
Phone: 605-333-7556 Fax: —
CEO: Curtis L. Hage
CFO: Donald F. Bertsch
1992 Sales: — Employees: —
Symbol: HFFC Exchange: NASDAQ
Industry: Banks - Midwest

Hi-Lo Auto Supply, Inc.
8601 Tavenor Lane
Houston, TX 77075
Phone: 713-991-6052 Fax: 713-991-1132
CEO: T. Michael Young
CFO: Gary D. Walther
1991 Sales: $156 million Employees: 2,032
Symbol: HLO Exchange: NYSE
Industry: Auto parts - retail & wholesale

Hi-Shear Industries Inc.
3333 New Hyde Park Rd.
New Hyde Park, NY 11042
Phone: 516-627-8600 Fax: 516-365-8629
CEO: David A. Wingate
CFO: Victor J. Galgano
1992 Sales: $106 million Employees: 998
Symbol: HSI Exchange: NYSE
Industry: Metal products - fasteners

Hi-Tech Pharmacal Co.
362 Bayview Ave.
Amityville, NY 11701
Phone: 516-789-8228 Fax: —
CEO: Bernard Seltzer
CFO: Arthur S. Goldberg
1992 Sales: $7.5 million Employees: 139
Symbol: HITK Exchange: NASDAQ
Industry: Drugs

Hibernia Corp.
313 Carondelet St.
New Orleans, LA 70130
Phone: 504-586-5552 Fax: 504-586-2199
CEO: Stephen A. Hansel
CFO: Thomas A. Masilla, Jr.
1991 Sales: $690 million Employees: 3,238
Symbol: HIB Exchange: NYSE
Industry: Banks - Southeast

Hibernia Savings Bank
731 Hancock St.
Quincy, MA 02170
Phone: 617-479-2265 Fax: —
CEO: Mark A. Osborne
CFO: Gerard F. Linskey
1992 Sales: — Employees: —
Symbol: HSBK Exchange: NASDAQ
Industry: Financial - savings and loans

High Plains Corp.
333 N. Waco
Wichita, KS 67202
Phone: 316-269-4310 Fax: 316-269-4008
CEO: Stanley E. Larson
CFO: Raymond G. Friend
1991 Sales: $23 million Employees: 46
Symbol: HIPC Exchange: NASDAQ
Industry: Energy - alternative sources

Hilb, Rogal and Hamilton Co.
4235 Innslake Dr.
Glen Allen, VA 23060
Phone: 804-747-6500 Fax: 804-747-6046
CEO: Robert H. Hilb
CFO: Timothy J. Korman
1991 Sales: $115 million Employees: 1,600
Symbol: HRH Exchange: NYSE
Industry: Insurance - brokerage

Hillenbrand Industries, Inc.
700 Hwy. 46
Batesville, IN 47006
Phone: 812-934-7000 Fax: 812-934-7364
CEO: W. August Hillenbrand
CFO: Tom E. Brewer
1992 Sales: $1,430 million Employees: 10,500
Symbol: HB Exchange: NYSE
Industry: Diversified operations - hospital beds, caskets, luggage & security locks

Hillhaven Corp.
1148 Broadway Plaza, CS2264
Tacoma, WA 98401
Phone: 206-572-4901 Fax: 206-756-4745
CEO: Bruce L. Busby
CFO: Robert F. Pacquer
1992 Sales: $1,199 million Employees: 40,800
Symbol: HIL Exchange: AMEX
Industry: Nursing homes

Hillman Co.
2000 Grant Bldg., Ste. 1900
Pittsburgh, PA 15219
Phone: 412-281-2620 Fax: 412-338-3520
CEO: C. G. Grefenstette
CFO: Lawrence M. Wagner
1991 Sales: $1,600 million Employees: 1,900
Ownership: Privately held
Industry: Diversified operations - investment

Hills Department Stores, Inc.
15 Dan Rd.
Canton, MA 02021
Phone: 617-821-1000 Fax: 617-821-4379
CEO: Michael Bozic
CFO: John G. Reen
1992 Sales: $1,715 million Employees: 21,500
Symbol: HDS Exchange: NYSE
Industry: Retail - discount & variety

Hilton Hotels Corp.
9336 Civic Center Dr.
Beverly Hills, CA 90209
Phone: 310-278-4321 Fax: 310-205-4599
CEO: Barron Hilton
CFO: Maurice J. Scanlon
1992 Sales: $1,230 million Employees: 40,000
Symbol: HLT Exchange: NYSE
Industry: Hotels & motels, casinos

Hingham Institution for Savings
55 Main St.
Hingham, MA 02043
Phone: 617-749-2200 Fax: —
CEO: Paul E. Bulman
CFO: Robert F. Cass
1992 Sales: — Employees: —
Symbol: HIFS Exchange: NASDAQ
Industry: Financial - savings and loans

Hipotronics, Inc.
Route 22
Brewster, NY 10509
Phone: 914-279-8091 Fax: 914-279-2467
CEO: Stanley G. Peschel
CFO: Banning B. Howes
1991 Sales: $27 million Employees: 219
Symbol: HIP Exchange: AMEX
Industry: Machinery - electric utility

Hitachi America, Ltd.
50 Prospect Ave.
Tarrytown, NY 10591
Phone: 914-332-5800 Fax: 914-332-5555
CEO: Keishi Toda
CFO: —
1992 Sales: $58,388 million Employees: 324,292
Parent: Hitachi, Ltd.
Industry: Diversified operations - computers, heavy machinery, power plants & consumer products

Hitox Corporation of America
418 Peoples St.
Corpus Christi, TX 78401
Phone: 512-882-5175 Fax: 512-882-6948
CEO: Richard L. Bowers
CFO: Thomas L. Tao
1991 Sales: $12 million Employees: 61
Symbol: HTXA Exchange: NASDAQ
Industry: Metal ores

HMA Behavioral Health
225 Park Ave., Ste. 800
Worcester, MA 01609
Phone: 508-757-2290 Fax: 508-754-3616
CEO: John Healy
CFO: Linda Roth
1991 Sales: $2.4 million Employees: 22
Ownership: Privately held
Industry: Medical services - medical & mental health screening services

HMO America, Inc.
540 N. La Salle St.
Chicago, IL 60610
Phone: 312-751-7500 Fax: 312-751-7448
CEO: Robert J. Weinstein
CFO: Clement J. Horne
1991 Sales: $218 million Employees: 339
Symbol: HMO Exchange: NYSE
Industry: Health maintenance organization

Hodgson Houses, Inc.
600 Madison Ave.
New York, NY 10022
Phone: 212-355-0200 Fax: —
CEO: Robert B. Friedman
CFO: Ralph F. Laughlin
1990 Sales: $5.3 million Employees: 59
Symbol: HDGH Exchange: NASDAQ
Industry: Building products - sectional, modular & single family homes

indicates company is in *Hoover's Handbook of American Business.*

indicates company is in *Hoover's Handbook of World Business;* sales and employee numbers are for parent company.

Hoechst Celanese Corp.
PO Box 2500, Route 202-206 North
Somerville, NJ 08876
Phone: 908-231-2000 Fax: 908-231-3225
CEO: Ernest H. Drew
CFO: —
1991 Sales: $31,043 million Employees: 179,332
Parent: Hoechst AG
Industry: Chemicals - diversified

Hoenig & Co. Inc.
770 Lexington Ave., 13th Fl.
New York, NY 10021
Phone: 212-308-7000 Fax: 212-888-4806
CEO: Ronald H. Hoenig
CFO: Alan B. Herzog
1991 Sales: $49 million Employees: 71
Symbol: HOEN Exchange: NASDAQ
Industry: Business services

Hoffmann–La Roche, Inc.
340 Kingsland St.
Nutley, NJ 07110
Phone: 201-235-5000 Fax: 201-235-7606
CEO: Erwin Lerner
CFO: —
1991 Sales: $8,420 million Employees: 55,134
Parent: Roche Group
Industry: Drugs, vitamins & fine chemicals, diagnostics

Hofgard Benefit Plan Administrators
1871 Folsom St.
Boulder, CO 80302
Phone: 303-449-0054 Fax: 303-442-1505
CEO: Mark Hofgard
CFO: Mark Hofgard
1991 Sales: $1.4 million Employees: 28
Ownership: Privately held
Industry: Medical services - employee benefits plans

Hogan Systems, Inc.
5080 Spectrum Dr., Ste. 400E
Dallas, TX 75248
Phone: 214-386-0020 Fax: 214-386-0315
CEO: Patric J. Jerge
CFO: Richard C. Schwenk, Jr.
1992 Sales: $56 million Employees: 385
Symbol: HOGN Exchange: NASDAQ
Industry: Computers - banking software

Holiday Cos.
4567 W. 80th St.
Bloomington, MN 55437
Phone: 612-830-8700 Fax: 612-830-8864
CEO: Ronald A. Erickson
CFO: E. Mickelson
1991 Sales: $1,460 million Employees: 3,600
Ownership: Privately held
Industry: Retail - convenience stores & grocery wholesaling

Holiday Inn Worldwide
1100 Ashwood Pkwy., Ste. 200
Atlanta, GA 30338
Phone: 404-551-3500 Fax: 404-390-0123
CEO: Bryan D. Langton
CFO: —
1991 Sales: $8,196 million Employees: 90,104
Parent: Bass PLC
Industry: Hotels

Holiday RV Superstores, Inc.
5001 Sand Lake Rd.
Orlando, FL 32819
Phone: 407-351-3096 Fax: 407-351-5140
CEO: Newton C. Kindlund
CFO: W. Hardee McAlhaney
1991 Sales: $36 million Employees: 145
Symbol: RVEE Exchange: NASDAQ
Industry: Retail

Holly Corp.
100 Crescent Court, Ste. 1600
Dallas, TX 75201
Phone: 214-871-3555 Fax: 214-871-3566
CEO: Lamar Norsworthy
CFO: Henry A. Teichholz
1991 Sales: $489 million Employees: 452
Symbol: HOC Exchange: AMEX
Industry: Oil refining & marketing

Holman Enterprises
7411 Maple Ave.
Pennsauken, NJ 08109
Phone: 609-663-5200 Fax: 609-665-1419
CEO: Joseph S. Holman
CFO: Ken Coppola
1991 Sales: $922 million Employees: 2,093
Ownership: Privately held
Industry: Retail - auto dealership, parts remanufacturing, fleet leasing

Holnam Inc.
6211 N. Ann Arbor Rd.
Dundee, MI 48131
Phone: 313-529-2411 Fax: 313-529-5512
CEO: Marc R. von Wyss
CFO: Paul A. Yhouse
1991 Sales: $979 million Employees: 5,785
Symbol: HLN Exchange: NYSE
Industry: Construction - cement & concrete

Hologic, Inc.
590 Lincoln St.
Waltham, MA 02154
Phone: 617-890-2300 Fax: 617-890-8031
CEO: S. David Ellenbogen
CFO: S. David Ellenbogen
1991 Sales: $17 million Employees: 123
Symbol: HOLX Exchange: NASDAQ
Industry: Medical instruments - X-ray systems

HoloPak Technologies, Inc.
9 Cotters Lane
East Brunswick, NJ 08816
Phone: 908-238-2883 Fax: 908-613-1018
CEO: Harry Parker
CFO: David W. Jaffin
1992 Sales: $33 million Employees: 231
Symbol: HOLO Exchange: NASDAQ
Industry: Hot stamp foils

Holson-Burnis Group
582 Great Rd.
North Smithfield, RI 02895
Phone: 401-769-8000 Fax: 401-769-0240
CEO: Charles Gordon
CFO: Steven W. Barnes
1991 Sales: $112 million Employees: 790
Symbol: HBGI Exchange: NASDAQ
Industry: Photo albums & frames

Home Beneficial Life Insurance Co.
3901 W. Broad St.
Richmond, VA 23230
Phone: 804-358-8431 Fax: —
CEO: R. W. Wiltshire
CFO: D. M. Westerhouse, Jr.
1991 Sales: $197 million Employees: —
Symbol: HBENB Exchange: NASDAQ
Industry: Insurance - life

Home Care Affiliates Inc.
9100 Shelbyville Rd. #345
Louisville, KY 40222
Phone: 502-339-7025 Fax: 502-339-0204
CEO: Paul Gordon
CFO: Greg Hardt
1991 Sales: $31 million Employees: 436
Ownership: Privately held
Industry: Healthcare - home healthcare services

Home Depot, Inc., The
2727 Paces Ferry Rd. NW
Atlanta, GA 30339
Phone: 404-433-8211 Fax: 404-431-2709
CEO: Bernard Marcus
CFO: Ronald M. Brill
1992 Sales: $6,629 million Employees: 28,000
Symbol: HD Exchange: NYSE
Industry: Building products - retail & wholesale

Home Federal Corp.
122-128 W. Washington St.
Hagerstown, MD 21740
Phone: 301-733-6300 Fax: 301-733-5170
CEO: Richard W. Phoebus, Sr.
CFO: Salvatore M. Savino
1991 Sales: $27 million Employees: 159
Symbol: HFMD Exchange: NASDAQ
Industry: Financial - savings and loans

Home Federal Financial Corp.
20 O'Farrell St.
San Francisco, CA 94108
Phone: 415-982-4560 Fax: 415-982-4948
CEO: Stanley E. Bailey
CFO: David C. Woo
1991 Sales: $65 million Employees: 204
Symbol: HFSF Exchange: NASDAQ
Industry: Financial - savings and loans

Home Federal Savings Bank
300 W. Oak St.
Ft. Collins, CO 80521
Phone: 303-482-3216 Fax: 303-221-2811
CEO: Thomas J. Flanagan
CFO: Albert J. Litzau
1992 Sales: — Employees: 96
Symbol: HROK Exchange: NASDAQ
Industry: Financial - savings and loans

Home Federal Savings Bank
222 W. Second St.
Seymour, IN 47274
Phone: 812-522-1592 Fax: 812-522-1611
CEO: John K. Keach, Sr.
CFO: Lawrence E. Welker
1992 Sales: — Employees: —
Symbol: HOMF Exchange: NASDAQ
Industry: Financial - savings and loans

Home Federal Savings Bank of Missouri
12680 Olive St.
St. Louis, MO 63141
Phone: 314-576-4500 Fax: 314-576-5540
CEO: Bernard D. Benney
CFO: John D. Aton
1992 Sales: — Employees: —
Symbol: HFMO Exchange: NASDAQ
Industry: Financial - savings and loans

Home Financial Corp.
2112 N. Roan St.
Johnson City, TN 37601
Phone: 615-282-6311 Fax: —
CEO: Vance W. Cheek
CFO: Betty S. Shell
1991 Sales: $25 million Employees: 212
Symbol: HFET Exchange: NASDAQ
Industry: Financial - savings and loans

Home Intensive Care, Inc.
150 N.W. 168th St., 2nd Fl.
North Miami Beach, FL 33169
Phone: 305-653-0000 Fax: 305-651-2147
CEO: James P. Cefaratti
CFO: Joel Birnbaum
1991 Sales: $56 million Employees: 600
Symbol: HICI Exchange: NASDAQ
Industry: Healthcare - outpatient & home

indicates company is in *Hoover's Handbook of American Business.*

indicates company is in *Hoover's Handbook of World Business;* sales and employee numbers are for parent company.

Home Interiors & Gifts
4550 Spring Valley Rd.
Dallas, TX 75244
Phone: 214-386-1000 Fax: 214-233-8825
CEO: Donald J. Carter
CFO: Bill Hendrix
1991 Sales: $450 million Employees: 1,400
Ownership: Privately held
Industry: Wholesale distribution - decorative accessories

Home Nutritional Services, Inc.
600 Alandex Plaza
Parsippany, NJ 07054
Phone: 201-515-4900 Fax: 201-515-8629
CEO: Kent H. Kerkhof
CFO: Yvonne V. Scoggins
1991 Sales: $101 million Employees: 1,155
Symbol: HNSI Exchange: NASDAQ
Industry: Healthcare - outpatient & home

Home Office Reference Laboratory, Inc.
10310 W. 84th Terrace
Shawnee Mission, KS 66214
Phone: 913-888-1770 Fax: 913-888-1845
CEO: Kenneth A. Stelzer
CFO: Michael L. Shopmaker
1991 Sales: $76 million Employees: 591
Symbol: HORL Exchange: NASDAQ
Industry: Medical services - laboratory testing services for life insurance industry

Home Port Bancorp, Inc.
104 Pleasant St.
Nantucket, MA 02554
Phone: 508-228-0580 Fax: —
CEO: Robert G. Stover
CFO: John L. Silva
1991 Sales: $5 million Employees: 36
Symbol: HPBC Exchange: NASDAQ
Industry: Banks - Northeast

Home Shopping Network, Inc.
2501 118th Ave. North
St. Petersburg, FL 33716
Phone: 813-572-8585 Fax: Ext. 5356
CEO: Roy M. Speer
CFO: Les R. Wandler
1992 Sales: $1,072 million Employees: 5,966
Symbol: HSN Exchange: NYSE
Industry: Retail - mail order & direct

Homecare Management, Inc.
80 Air Park Dr.
Ronkonkoma, NY 11779
Phone: 516-981-0034 Fax: —
CEO: Clifford E. Hotte
CFO: Drew Bergman
1992 Sales: $15 million Employees: 50
Symbol: HMIS Exchange: NASDAQ
Industry: Healthcare - outpatient & home, pharmaceutical supplies

HomeCorp, Inc.
1107 E. State St.
Rockford, IL 61104
Phone: 815-987-2200 Fax: —
CEO: C. Steven Sjogren
CFO: C. Steven Sjogren
1991 Sales: $7.5 million Employees: 217
Symbol: HMCI Exchange: NASDAQ
Industry: Banks - Midwest

Homedco Group, Inc.
17650 Newhope St.
Fountain Valley, CA 92708
Phone: 714-755-5600 Fax: 714-755-5617
CEO: Jeremy M. Jones
CFO: Lawrence H. Smallen
1991 Sales: $222 million Employees: 2,760
Symbol: HOME Exchange: NASDAQ
Industry: Healthcare - outpatient & home

Homeland Stores Inc.
400 NE 36th St.
Oklahoma City, OK 73105
Phone: 405-557-5500 Fax: 405-557-5600
CEO: Max E. Raydon
CFO: Mark Sellers
1991 Sales: $787 million Employees: 6,600
Ownership: Privately held
Industry: Retail - supermarkets

Homeowners Group, Inc.
6365 Taft St., Ste. 2000
Hollywood, FL 33024
Phone: 305-983-0350 Fax: —
CEO: Carl Buccellato
CFO: C. Gregory Morris
1991 Sales: $42 million Employees: 201
Symbol: HOMG Exchange: NASDAQ
Industry: Business services to real estate brokerage firms

Homestake Mining Co.
650 California St., 9th Fl.
San Francisco, CA 94108
Phone: 415-981-8150 Fax: 415-397-5038
CEO: Harry M. Conger
CFO: Gene E. Elam
1991 Sales: $387 million Employees: 2,227
Symbol: HM Exchange: NYSE
Industry: Gold mining & processing

Homestyle Buffet, Inc.
35207 US 19 North
Palm Harbor, FL 34684
Phone: 813-785-1370 Fax: 813-798-5078
CEO: Barry M. Rowles
CFO: Ernest V. Trigilio
1991 Sales: $49 million Employees: 2,000
Symbol: HBUF Exchange: NASDAQ
Industry: Retail - food & restaurants

Hometown Bancorporation, Inc.
20 West Ave.
Darien, CT 06820
Phone: 203-656-2265 Fax: —
CEO: Douglas D. Milne III
CFO: Robert A. Foote, Jr.
1991 Sales: $9.4 million Employees: 47
Symbol: HTWN Exchange: NASDAQ
Industry: Banks - Northeast

Hon Industries Inc.
414 E. Third St.
Muscatine, IA 52761
Phone: 319-264-7400 Fax: 319-264-7217
CEO: Jack D. Michaels
CFO: John W. Axel
1992 Sales: $707 million Employees: 5,599
Symbol: HONI Exchange: NASDAQ
Industry: Office equipment & supplies

Honda North America, Inc.
1290 Avenue of the Americas, Ste. 3330
New York, NY 10104
Phone: 212-765-3804 Fax: 212-541-9855
CEO: Koichi Amemiya
CFO: —
1992 Sales: $33,059 million Employees: 90,500
Parent: Honda Motor Co., Ltd.
Industry: Automotive manufacturing

Hondo Oil & Gas Co.
410 E. College Blvd.
Roswell, NM 88201
Phone: 505-625-8700 Fax: 505-625-6876
CEO: Robert O. Anderson
CFO: A. Wayne Davenport
1991 Sales: $81 million Employees: 155
Symbol: HOG Exchange: AMEX
Industry: Oil & gas - US exploration & production

Honeywell Inc.
Honeywell Plaza, 2701 4th Ave. South
Minneapolis, MN 55408
Phone: 612-870-5200 Fax: 612-870-2086
CEO: Michael R. Bonsignore
CFO: —
1992 Sales: $6,223 million Employees: 58,182
Symbol: HON Exchange: NYSE
Industry: Diversified operations - industrial & environmental control systems, avionics

HongkongBank
140 Broadway
New York, NY 10015
Phone: 212-658-2888 Fax: 212-658-2929
CEO: Mike Geoghegan
CFO: —
1992 Sales: — Employees: 53,770
Parent: HSBC Holdings PLC
Industry: Banks - money center

Hook-SupeRx, Inc.
175 Tri-County Pkwy.
Cincinnati, OH 45246
Phone: 513-782-3000 Fax: 513-782-3000
CEO: Philip E. Beekman
CFO: Timothy M. Mooney
1992 Sales: $2,178 million Employees: 17,200
Symbol: HSX Exchange: NYSE
Industry: Retail - drug stores

Hooper Holmes, Inc.
170 Mt. Airy Rd.
Basking Ridge, NJ 07920
Phone: 908-766-5000 Fax: 908-766-5073
CEO: James M. McNamee
CFO: Fred Lash
1991 Sales: $132 million Employees: 7,189
Symbol: HH Exchange: AMEX
Industry: Business services

Horace Mann Educators Corporation
1 Horace Mann Plaza
Springfield, IL 62715
Phone: 217-789-2500 Fax: 217-788-5161
CEO: Paul J. Kardos
CFO: Larry K. Becker
1992 Sales: $706 million Employees: 2,469
Symbol: HMN Exchange: NYSE
Industry: Insurance - multiline & misc.

Horizon Bank
1500 Cornwall Ave.
Bellingham, WA 98225
Phone: 206-733-3050 Fax: 206-733-7019
CEO: V. Lawrence Evans
CFO: V. Lawrence Evans
1992 Sales: — Employees: —
Symbol: HRZB Exchange: NASDAQ
Industry: Financial - savings and loans

Horizon Data Corp.
10700 Parkridge Blvd. #250
Reston, VA 22091
Phone: 703-758-0531 Fax: 703-758-9713
CEO: José R. Rivera
CFO: C. T. Smith
1991 Sales: $10.4 million Employees: 50
Ownership: Privately held
Industry: Systems analysis integration, telecommunications & knowledge-based systems

Horizon Financial Services, Inc.
23175 Commerce Park Rd.
Beachwood, OH 44122
Phone: 216-765-1100 Fax: —
CEO: Lynn L. Fritzsche
CFO: Frank A. Hawkins
1991 Sales: $9.5 million Employees: 105
Symbol: HFIN Exchange: NASDAQ
Industry: Financial - savings and loans

Horizon Healthcare Corp.
6001 Indian School Rd. NE
Albuquerque, NM 87110
Phone: 505-881-4961 Fax: 505-881-5097
CEO: Neal M. Elliott
CFO: Klemett L. Belt, Jr.
1992 Sales: $159 million Employees: 6,500
Symbol: HHC Exchange: NYSE
Industry: Nursing homes

Horizon Industries, Inc.
S. Industrial Blvd.
Calhoun, GA 30701
Phone: 404-629-7721 Fax: Ext. 415
CEO: Peter R. Spirer
CFO: Dennis L. Fink
1991 Sales: $278 million Employees: 2,300
Symbol: HRZN Exchange: NASDAQ
Industry: Textiles - home furnishings

Horizon Resources Corp.
1536 Cole Blvd., Ste. 140
Golden, CO 80401
Phone: 303-239-8701 Fax: —
CEO: Charles E. Stott, Jr.
CFO: James A. Applegate
1992 Sales: $4.4 million Employees: 419
Symbol: HRIZ Exchange: NASDAQ
Industry: Gold mining & processing

Horn & Hardart Co.
1500 Harbor Blvd.
Weehawken, NJ 89109
Phone: 201-865-3800 Fax: 201-319-3468
CEO: Donald Schupak
CFO: Gerald Zarin
1992 Sales: $587 million Employees: 2,700
Symbol: HOR Exchange: AMEX
Industry: Retail - mail order & direct

Hornbeck Offshore Services, Inc.
2317 Broadway
Galveston, TX 77550
Phone: 409-762-8228 Fax: —
CEO: Larry D. Hornbeck
CFO: Robert W. Hampton
1991 Sales: $20 million Employees: 300
Symbol: HOSS Exchange: NASDAQ
Industry: Oil & gas - offshore drilling

Horsehead Industries
110 E. 59th St.
New York, NY 10022
Phone: 212-527-3000 Fax: 212-527-3008
CEO: William E. Flaherty
CFO: W. Flatley
1991 Sales: $636 million Employees: 2,600
Ownership: Privately held
Industry: Metals - zinc, carbon, graphite; environmental services

Horsehead Resource Development Co., Inc.
613 Third St.
Palmerton, PA 18071
Phone: 215-826-8608 Fax: —
CEO: James H. Davis
CFO: Robert L. Hoguet III
1991 Sales: $71 million Employees: 680
Symbol: HHRD Exchange: NASDAQ
Industry: Pollution control equipment & services - hazardous waste resource recovery

Hospital Staffing Services, Inc.
6245 N. Federal Hwy., Ste. 500
Ft. Lauderdale, FL 33308
Phone: 305-771-0500 Fax: 305-771-0899
CEO: Ronald A. Cass
CFO: Leonard J. Cass
1991 Sales: $90 million Employees: 2,540
Symbol: HSS Exchange: NYSE
Industry: Medical services - interim medical personnel

Hospitality Network
2625 Green Valley Pkwy., Ste. 200
Henderson, NV 89014
Phone: 702-435-4600 Fax: 702-435-4009
CEO: Jerry Hodge
CFO: Kelley Summerhill
1991 Sales: $15 million Employees: 65
Ownership: Privately held
Industry: Pay movies & cable TV for hotels

Hosposable Products, Inc.
Central Jersey Industrial Park
Bound Brook, NJ 08805
Phone: 908-469-8700 Fax: 908-469-0769
CEO: Leonard Schramm
CFO: Richard Cohan
1991 Sales: $27 million Employees: 210
Symbol: HOSP Exchange: NASDAQ
Industry: Medical & dental supplies

Hotelcopy, Inc.
17850 NE 5th Ave.
Miami, FL 33162
Phone: 305-651-5176 Fax: 305-651-8536
CEO: W. Edd Helms, Jr.
CFO: Philip Kabot
1992 Sales: $2.5 million Employees: 21
Symbol: FAXMC Exchange: NASDAQ
Industry: Telecommunications services

Houghton Mifflin Co.
One Beacon St.
Boston, MA 02108
Phone: 617-725-5000 Fax: 617-227-5409
CEO: Nader F. Darehshori
CFO: Stephen O. Jaeger
1991 Sales: $467 million Employees: 2,187
Symbol: HTN Exchange: NYSE
Industry: Publishing - books

House of Fabrics, Inc.
13400 Riverside Dr.
Sherman Oaks, CA 91423
Phone: 818-995-7000 Fax: 818-789-4378
CEO: Gary L. Larkins
CFO: Wm. James Heaton
1991 Sales: $493 million Employees: 16,411
Symbol: HF Exchange: NYSE
Industry: Retail - fabrics & notions

Household International, Inc.
2700 Sanders Rd.
Prospect Heights, IL 60070
Phone: 708-564-5000 Fax: 708-205-7452
CEO: Edwin P. Hoffman
CFO: Gaylen N. Larson
1992 Sales: $2,750 million Employees: 14,200
Symbol: HI Exchange: NYSE
Industry: Financial - consumer loans, life insurance

Houston Industries Inc.
4400 Post Oak Pkwy., Ste. 2700
Houston, TX 77027
Phone: 713-629-3000 Fax: 713-629-3129
CEO: Don D. Jordan
CFO: William A. Cropper
1992 Sales: $4,596 million Employees: 13,289
Symbol: HOU Exchange: NYSE
Industry: Utility - electric power

Hovnanian K Enterprises, Inc.
10 Hwy. 35
Red Bank, NJ 07701
Phone: 908-747-7800 Fax: 908-747-7159
CEO: Kevork S. Hovnanian
CFO: J. Larry Sorsby
1992 Sales: $318 million Employees: 550
Symbol: HOV Exchange: AMEX
Industry: Building - residential & commercial

Howard B. Wolf, Inc.
3809 Parry Ave.
Dallas, TX 75226
Phone: 214-823-9941 Fax: 214-828-0631
CEO: Robert D. Wolf
CFO: Eugene K. Friesen
1992 Sales: $10.8 million Employees: 87
Symbol: HBW Exchange: AMEX
Industry: Textiles - apparel

Howell Corp.
1010 Lamar, Ste. 1800
Houston, TX 77002
Phone: 713-658-4000 Fax: 713-658-4007
CEO: Paul W. Funkhouser
CFO: Allyn R. Skelton II
1991 Sales: $478 million Employees: 234
Symbol: HWL Exchange: NYSE
Industry: Oil & gas - US integrated

Howell Industries, Inc.
17515 W. Nine-Mile Rd.
Southfield, MI 48075
Phone: 313-424-8220 Fax: 313-424-8131
CEO: Morton Schiff
CFO: Morton Schiff
1991 Sales: $36 million Employees: 250
Symbol: HOW Exchange: AMEX
Industry: Automotive & trucking - original equipment

Howtek, Inc.
21 Park Ave.
Hudson, NH 03051
Phone: 603-882-5200 Fax: 603-880-3843
CEO: Robert Howard
CFO: David R. Bothwell
1991 Sales: $12 million Employees: 86
Symbol: HTK Exchange: AMEX
Industry: Computers - color monitors & related peripheral equipment

HPSC, Inc.
25 Stuart St.
Boston, MA 02116
Phone: 617-423-0643 Fax: 800-526-0259
CEO: Ray C. Davis
CFO: John P. Murgo
1991 Sales: $26 million Employees: 29
Symbol: HPSC Exchange: NASDAQ
Industry: Financial - mortgages & related services

Hub City Florida Terminals
2105 Park Ave.
Orange Park, FL 32073
Phone: 904-264-6551 Fax: 904-264-8588
CEO: Robert Maisch
CFO: Jan Maisch
1991 Sales: $22 million Employees: 14
Ownership: Privately held
Industry: Transportation - freight services

Hubbell Inc.
584 Derby Milford Rd.
Orange, CT 06477
Phone: 203-799-4100 Fax: 203-799-4223
CEO: G. J. Ratcliffe
CFO: James H. Biggart, Jr.
1992 Sales: $786 million Employees: 5,532
Symbol: HUBB Exchange: NYSE
Industry: Electrical products - electrical wiring devices, industrial controls

HUBCO, Inc.
3100 Bergenline Ave.
Union City, NJ 07087
Phone: 201-348-2300 Fax: 201-348-0689
CEO: James E. Schierloh
CFO: James E. Schierloh
1991 Sales: $57 million Employees: 343
Symbol: HCO Exchange: AMEX
Industry: Banks - Northeast

Huber Hunt & Nichols
2450 S. Tibbs Ave.
Indianapolis, IN 46241
Phone: 317-241-6301 Fax: 317-243-3461
CEO: Robert C. Hunt
CFO: M. V. Furlow, Jr.
1991 Sales: $720 million Employees: 2,316
Ownership: Privately held
Industry: Construction - general contracting & construction management

Huckell/Weinman Associates
205 Lake St. South, Ste. 202
Kirkland, WA 98033
Phone: 206-828-4463 Fax: 206-828-3861
CEO: Duane Huckell
CFO: Duane Huckell
1991 Sales: $1.2 million Employees: 9
Ownership: Privately held
Industry: Environmental planning & economic consulting services

Hudson Foods, Inc.
1225 W. Hudson Rd.
Rogers, AR 72756
Phone: 501-636-1100 Fax: 501-631-5192
CEO: James T. Hudson
CFO: Charles B. Jurgensmeyer
1992 Sales: $828 million Employees: 7,659
Symbol: HFI Exchange: NYSE
Industry: Food - meat products

Hudson General Corp.
111 Great Neck Rd.
Great Neck, NY 11021
Phone: 516-487-8610 Fax: 516-487-4855
CEO: Jay B. Langner
CFO: Michael Rubin
1992 Sales: $126 million Employees: 3,000
Symbol: HGC Exchange: AMEX
Industry: Transportation - services

Huffman Koos Inc.
Route 4 West & Main St.
River Edge, NJ 07661
Phone: 201-343-4300 Fax: 201-343-0575
CEO: Fred Berk
CFO: Joseph Albanese
1991 Sales: $83 million Employees: 460
Symbol: HUFK Exchange: NASDAQ
Industry: Retail - home furnishings

Huffy Corp.
7701 Byers Rd.
Miamisburg, OH 45342
Phone: 513-866-6251 Fax: 513-865-5470
CEO: Richard L. Mollen
CFO: Charlton L. George
1992 Sales: $703 million Employees: 6,330
Symbol: HUF Exchange: NYSE
Industry: Leisure & recreational products - bicycles, lawn & garden tools

Hughes Markets Inc.
14005 Live Oak Ave.
Irwindale, CA 91706
Phone: 818-856-6580 Fax: 818-856-6050
CEO: Roger K. Hughes
CFO: Al Brennan
1991 Sales: $1,100 million Employees: 5,050
Ownership: Privately held
Industry: Retail - supermarkets

Hughes Supply, Inc.
521 W. Central Blvd.
Orlando, FL 32801
Phone: 407-841-4710 Fax: 407-849-1281
CEO: David H. Hughes
CFO: J. Stephen Zepf
1991 Sales: $481 million Employees: 1,900
Symbol: HUG Exchange: NYSE
Industry: Building products - retail & wholesale

Humana Inc.
500 W. Main St.
Louisville, KY 40201
Phone: 502-580-1000 Fax: 502-580-3694
CEO: David A. Jones
CFO: W. Roger Drury
1992 Sales: $3,995 million Employees: 70,500
Symbol: HUM Exchange: NYSE
Industry: Hospitals & health benefit plans

Humanix Temporary Services
111 E. Magnesium Rd., Ste. F
Spokane, WA 99208
Phone: 509-467-0062 Fax: 509-467-0093
CEO: Julie Prafke
CFO: Julie Prafke
1992 Sales: $4 million Employees: 12
Ownership: Privately held
Industry: Business services - temporary employment

Humiston-Keeling Inc.
233 E. Erie St., Ste. 200
Chicago, IL 60611
Phone: 312-943-6066 Fax: 312-751-0473
CEO: Larry G. Olin
CFO: Louis Genesen
1991 Sales: $786 million Employees: 192
Ownership: Privately held
Industry: Drugs & sundries - wholesale

Hunt Manufacturing Co.
230 S. Broad St., 13th Fl.
Philadelphia, PA 19102
Phone: 215-732-7700 Fax: 215-875-5252
CEO: Ronald J. Naples
CFO: Rudolph M. Peins, Jr.
1991 Sales: $229 million Employees: 1,954
Symbol: HUN Exchange: NYSE
Industry: Office & art materials

Hunter Environmental Services, Inc.
2960 Post Rd.
Southport, CT 06490
Phone: 203-255-8777 Fax: 203-255-9137
CEO: Kirtland C. Gardner III
CFO: Dennis S. Oistacher
1992 Sales: $0.7 million Employees: 17
Symbol: HESI Exchange: NASDAQ
Industry: Pollution control equipment & services - hazardous waste disposal

Huntington Bancshares Inc.
41 S. High St.
Columbus, OH 43287
Phone: 614-463-4395 Fax: 614-476-8029
CEO: Frank Wobst
CFO: Gerald R. Williams
1992 Sales: $1,259 million Employees: 6,250
Symbol: HBAN Exchange: NASDAQ
Industry: Banks - Midwest

Huntsman Chemical Corp.
2000 Eagle Gate Tower
Salt Lake City, UT 84111
Phone: 801-532-5200 Fax: 801-355-6629
CEO: Jon M. Huntsman
CFO: Terry Parker
1992 Sales: $920 million Employees: 1,200
Ownership: Privately held
Industry: Chemicals

Huntway Partners, L.P.
23822 W. Valencia Blvd.
Valencia, CA 91355
Phone: 805-253-1799 Fax: —
CEO: Juan Y. Forster
CFO: Douglas C. Hansen
1991 Sales: $0.1 million Employees: 88
Symbol: HWY Exchange: NYSE
Industry: Oil refining & marketing

Hurco Mfg. Co., Inc.
1 Technology Way
Indianapolis, IN 46268
Phone: 317-293-5309 Fax: 317-298-2841
CEO: Brian D. McLaughlin
CFO: Roger J. Wolf
1991 Sales: $81 million Employees: 621
Symbol: HURC Exchange: NASDAQ
Industry: Machine tools & related products

Hutchinson Technology Inc.
40 W. Highland Park Dr.
Hutchinson, MN 55350
Phone: 612-587-3797 Fax: 612-587-1892
CEO: Jeffrey W. Green
CFO: John A. Ingleman
1991 Sales: $143 million Employees: 2,798
Symbol: HTCH Exchange: NASDAQ
Industry: Computers - peripheral equipment

Hy-Vee Food Stores Inc.
1801 Osceola Ave.
Chariton, IA 50049
Phone: 515-774-2121 Fax: 515-774-7211
CEO: Ronald D. Pearson
CFO: Michael D. Wheeler
1991 Sales: $2,200 million Employees: 28,000
Ownership: Privately held
Industry: Retail - supermarkets, drug & convenience stores

Hyatt Corporation
200 W. Madison St., 39th Fl.
Chicago, IL 60606
Phone: 312-750-1234 Fax: 312-750-8550
CEO: Jay Pritzker
CFO: Ken Posher
1991 Sales: $2,915 million Employees: 49,820
Ownership: Privately held
Industry: Hotels

Hycor Biomedical Inc.
7272 Chapman Ave.
Garden Grove, CA 92641
Phone: 714-895-9558 Fax: 714-895-6520
CEO: Richard D. Hamill
CFO: Reginald P. Jones
1991 Sales: $18 million Employees: 250
Symbol: HYBD Exchange: NASDAQ
Industry: Medical products - diagnostic instruments

Hyde Athletic Industries, Inc.
13 Centennial Dr.
Peabody, MA 01960
Phone: 508-532-9000 Fax: 508-532-6105
CEO: John H. Fisher
CFO: John H. Fisher
1991 Sales: $58 million Employees: 300
Symbol: HYDE Exchange: NASDAQ
Industry: Shoes & related apparel

Hyundai Corp. U.S.A.
300 Sylvan Ave.
Englewood Cliffs, NJ 07632
Phone: 201-816-4000 Fax: 201-816-4036
CEO: Y. D. Kim
CFO: —
1991 Sales: $12,334 million Employees: 814
Parent: Hyundai Group
Industry: Diversified operations - electronics & electrical, machinery & transportation, ships

I.C.H. Corp.
4211 Norbourne Blvd.
Louisville, KY 40207
Phone: 502-897-1861 Fax: 502-897-6470
CEO: Robert T. Shaw
CFO: Michael E. Sproule
1991 Sales: $1,888 million Employees: —
Symbol: ICH Exchange: AMEX
Industry: Insurance - life

 indicates company is in *Hoover's Handbook of American Business.*

indicates company is in *Hoover's Handbook of World Business;* sales and employee numbers are for parent company.

i-STAT Corp.
303 College Rd. East
Princeton, NJ 08540
Phone: 609-243-9300 Fax: 609-243-9311
CEO: William P. Moffitt
CFO: William P. Sarther
1992 Sales: — Employees: 115
Symbol: STAT Exchange: NASDAQ
Industry: Medical instruments

IBP, Inc.
IBP Ave.
Dakota City, NE 68731
Phone: 402-494-2061 Fax: 402-241-2068
CEO: Robert L. Peterson
CFO: Lonnie O. Grigsby
1992 Sales: $11,128 million Employees: 26,500
Symbol: IBP Exchange: NYSE
Industry: Food - meat products

ICC Industries Inc.
720 Fifth Ave.
New York, NY 10019
Phone: 212-903-1700 Fax: 212-903-1794
CEO: John J. Farber
CFO: Susan Bernstein
1991 Sales: $568 million Employees: 1,400
Ownership: Privately held
Industry: Chemicals

ICF International, Inc.
9300 Lee Hwy.
Fairfax, VA 22031
Phone: 703-934-3600 Fax: 703-934-9740
CEO: James O. Edwards
CFO: James D. Russo
1992 Sales: $711 million Employees: 4,500
Symbol: ICFI Exchange: NASDAQ
Industry: Business services - consulting, engineering & construction management

ICI American Holdings Inc.
Concord Pike & New Murphy Rd.
Wilmington, DE 19897
Phone: 302-886-3000 Fax: 302-886-2972
CEO: B. H. Lochtenberg
CFO: —
1991 Sales: $23,353 million Employees: 123,600
Parent: Imperial Chemical Industries PLC
Industry: Chemicals - diversified

ICN Biomedicals, Inc.
3300 Hyland Ave.
Costa Mesa, CA 92626
Phone: 714-545-0113 Fax: 714-641-7265
CEO: Milan Panic
CFO: John E. Giordani
1991 Sales: $96 million Employees: 775
Symbol: BIM Exchange: AMEX
Industry: Medical products - diagnostic testing chemicals & instruments

ICN Pharmaceuticals, Inc.
3300 Hyland Ave.
Costa Mesa, CA 92626
Phone: 714-545-0100 Fax: 714-556-0131
CEO: Milan Panic
CFO: John E. Giordani
1991 Sales: $460 million Employees: 6,300
Symbol: ICN Exchange: NYSE
Industry: Drugs

ICO, Inc
6500 W. Fwy., Ste. 220
Ft. Worth, TX 76116
Phone: 817-735-1331 Fax: 817-737-7031
CEO: James P. Shanahan, Jr.
CFO: Stephen D. Houk
1991 Sales: $38 million Employees: 500
Symbol: ICOC Exchange: NASDAQ
Industry: Oil field machinery & equipment

Iconics Inc.
100 Foxborough Blvd.
Foxborough, MA 02035
Phone: 508-543-8600 Fax: 508-543-1503
CEO: Russell Agrusa
CFO: Paula Agrusa
1991 Sales: $7.3 million Employees: 55
Ownership: Privately held
Industry: Computers - process-automation software development

ICOS Corp.
22021 20th Ave. SE
Bothell, WA 98021
Phone: 206-485-1900 Fax: —
CEO: Robert C. Nowinski
CFO: Janice M. LeCocq
1991 Sales: $0.8 million Employees: 91
Symbol: ICOS Exchange: NASDAQ
Industry: Drugs

ICOT Corp.
3801 Zanker Rd.
San Jose, CA 95134
Phone: 408-433-3300 Fax: 408-433-0260
CEO: Joel M. Becker
CFO: John E. Arnold
1991 Sales: $16 million Employees: 112
Symbol: ICOT Exchange: NASDAQ
Industry: Telecommunications equipment

ICU Medical, Inc.
142 Technology Dr.
Irvine, CA 92718
Phone: 714-753-1599 Fax: —
CEO: George A. Lopez
CFO: William C. Moore
1991 Sales: $7.5 million Employees: 11
Symbol: ICUI Exchange: NASDAQ
Industry: Medical products

Idaho Power Co.
1220 W. Idaho St.
Boise, ID 83702
Phone: 208-383-2200 Fax: 208-383-2336
CEO: Joseph W. Marshall
CFO: J. LaMont Keen
1991 Sales: $483 million Employees: 1,678
Symbol: IDA Exchange: NYSE
Industry: Utility - electric power

IDB Communications Group, Inc.
10525 W. Washington Blvd.
Culver City, CA 90232
Phone: 213-870-9000 Fax: 213-240-3901
CEO: Jeffrey P. Sudikoff
CFO: Edward R. Cheramy
1991 Sales: $104 million Employees: 340
Symbol: IDBX Exchange: NASDAQ
Industry: Telecommunications services

IDEC Pharmaceuticals Corp.
11099 N. Torrey Pines Rd.
La Jolla, CA 92037
Phone: 619-458-0600 Fax: —
CEO: William H. Rastetter
CFO: William H. Rastetter
1991 Sales: $5.2 million Employees: 107
Symbol: IDPH Exchange: NASDAQ
Industry: Drugs

Identix Inc.
510 N. Pastoria Ave.
Sunnyvale, CA 94086
Phone: 408-739-2000 Fax: 408-739-3308
CEO: Randall C. Fowler
CFO: James P. Scullion
1991 Sales: $2 million Employees: 38
Symbol: IDX Exchange: AMEX
Industry: Electronics - measuring instruments

IDEX Corp.
630 Dundee Rd., Ste. 400
Northbrook, IL 60065
Phone: 708-498-7070 Fax: 708-498-3940
CEO: Donald N. Boyce
CFO: Wayne P. Sayatovic
1991 Sales: $228 million Employees: 2,000
Symbol: IEX Exchange: NYSE
Industry: Machinery - general industrial

IDEXX Laboratories, Inc.
100 Fore St.
Portland, ME 04101
Phone: 207-774-4334 Fax: —
CEO: David E. Shaw
CFO: John P. Deckro
1991 Sales: $31 million Employees: 232
Symbol: IDXX Exchange: NASDAQ
Industry: Biomedical & genetic products

IEH Corp.
140 58th St., Ste. 8E
Brooklyn, NY 11220
Phone: 718-492-9673 Fax: —
CEO: Michael Offerman
CFO: Robert Knoth
1992 Sales: $6.2 million Employees: 150
Symbol: IEHC Exchange: NASDAQ
Industry: Electrical connectors

IES Industries Inc.
200 1st St. SE
Cedar Rapids, IA 52401
Phone: 319-398-4411 Fax: 319-398-4623
CEO: Lee Liu
CFO: Blake O. Fisher, Jr.
1991 Sales: $662 million Employees: 2,528
Symbol: IES Exchange: NYSE
Industry: Utility - electric power

IFR Systems, Inc.
10200 W. York St.
Wichita, KS 67215
Phone: 316-522-4981 Fax: 316-524-2623
CEO: Alfred H. Hunt III
CFO: Bruce C. Bingham
1992 Sales: $40 million Employees: 656
Symbol: IFRS Exchange: NASDAQ
Industry: Electronics - measuring instruments

IG Laboratories, Inc.
One Mountain Rd.
Framingham, MA 01701
Phone: 508-872-8400 Fax: —
CEO: Robert J. Carpenter
CFO: David J. McLachlan
1991 Sales: $12 million Employees: 177
Symbol: IGLI Exchange: NASDAQ
Industry: Medical services - genetic testing services

IGI, Inc
2285 E. Landis Ave.
Vineland, NJ 08360
Phone: 609-691-2411 Fax: 609-691-1177
CEO: Edward B. Hager
CFO: Donald J. MacPhee
1991 Sales: $22 million Employees: 177
Symbol: IG Exchange: AMEX
Industry: Drugs

IHOP Corp.
525 N. Brand Blvd.
Glendale, CA 91203
Phone: 818-240-6055 Fax: 818-247-0694
CEO: Richard K. Herzer
CFO: Frederick G. Silny
1991 Sales: $103 million Employees: 2,190
Symbol: IHOP Exchange: NASDAQ
Industry: Retail - food & restaurants

indicates company is in *Hoover's Handbook of American Business.*

indicates company is in *Hoover's Handbook of World Business;* sales and employee numbers are for parent company.

II VI Inc.
375 Saxonburg Blvd.
Saxonburg, PA 16056
Phone: 412-352-4455 Fax: 412-352-4980
CEO: Carl J. Johnson
CFO: John M. Sherbin II
1992 Sales: $17 million Employees: 223
Symbol: IIVI Exchange: NASDAQ
Industry: Electrical components - optical & electro-optical components

IKOS Systems, Inc.
145 N. Wolf Rd.
Sunnyvale, CA 94086
Phone: 408-245-1900 Fax: 408-245-6219
CEO: Gerald S. Casilli
CFO: Joseph W. Rockom
1991 Sales: $15 million Employees: 114
Symbol: IKOS Exchange: NASDAQ
Industry: Computers - software

ILC Technology, Inc.
399 W. Java Dr.
Sunnyvale, CA 94089
Phone: 408-745-7900 Fax: 408-744-0829
CEO: Henry C. Baumgartner
CFO: Ronald E. Fredianelli
1991 Sales: $40 million Employees: 280
Symbol: ILCT Exchange: NASDAQ
Industry: Instruments - control

Ilio, Inc.
20 Enterprise Ave.
Secaucus, NJ 07094
Phone: 201-392-8800 Fax: 201-392-0711
CEO: J. Ross
CFO: J. Ross
1992 Sales: $49 million Employees: 85
Symbol: ILIO Exchange: NASDAQ
Industry: Textiles - apparel

Illinois Central Corp.
233 N. Michigan Ave.
Chicago, IL 60601
Phone: 312-819-7500 Fax: 312-819-8064
CEO: E. Hunter Harrison
CFO: Dale W. Phillips
1991 Sales: $550 million Employees: 3,100
Symbol: IC Exchange: NYSE
Industry: Transportation - rail

Illinois Power Co.
500 S. 27th St.
Decatur, IL 62525
Phone: 217-424-6600 Fax: 217-424-6978
CEO: Larry D. Haab
CFO: Larry F. Altenbaumer
1992 Sales: $1,479 million Employees: 4,458
Symbol: IPC Exchange: NYSE
Industry: Utility - electric power

Illinois Tool Works Inc.
3600 W. Lake Ave.
Glenview, IL 60025
Phone: 708-724-7500 Fax: 708-657-4261
CEO: John D. Nichols
CFO: David Byron Smith
1992 Sales: $2,812 million Employees: 18,700
Symbol: ITW Exchange: NYSE
Industry: Metal products - fasteners; industrial fluids & adhesives

Image Entertainment, Inc.
9333 Oso Ave.
Chatsworth, CA 91311
Phone: 818-407-9100 Fax: 818-407-9151
CEO: Martin W. Greenwald
CFO: Jerome M. Smolar
1992 Sales: $59 million Employees: 104
Symbol: DISK Exchange: NASDAQ
Industry: Leisure & recreational products - video programming for laser discs

Imagine Films Entertainment, Inc.
1925 Century Park East, Ste. 2300
Los Angeles, CA 90067
Phone: 310-277-1665 Fax: 310-785-0107
CEO: Brian Grazer
CFO: Michael Meltzer
1991 Sales: $30 million Employees: 47
Symbol: IFEI Exchange: NASDAQ
Industry: Motion pictures & services

Imasco USA, Inc.
1233 Hardee's Blvd.
Rocky Mount, NC 27804
Phone: 919-977-2000 Fax: 919-977-4342
CEO: Robert F. Autry
CFO: —
1991 Sales: $13,412 million Employees: 180,005
Parent: Imasco Ltd.
Industry: Diversified operations - drug stores, tobacco, restaurants & financial

Imatron Inc.
389 Oyster Point Blvd.
South San Francisco, CA 94080
Phone: 415-583-9964 Fax: 415-871-0418
CEO: Rodney L. Derbyshire
CFO: Douglas P. Boyd
1991 Sales: $23 million Employees: 142
Symbol: IMAT Exchange: NASDAQ
Industry: Medical instruments - scanner for use in cardiac & radiological diagnostic procedures

IMC Fertilizer, Inc.
2100 Sanders Rd.
Northbrook, IL 60062
Phone: 708-272-9200 Fax: 708-205-4805
CEO: Wendell F. Bueche
CFO: Robert C. Brauneker
1992 Sales: $966 million Employees: 5,400
Symbol: IFL Exchange: NYSE
Industry: Fertilizers

IMCERA Group Inc.
2315 Sanders Rd.
Northbrook, IL 60062
Phone: 708-564-8600 Fax: 708-205-2243
CEO: C. Ray Holman
CFO: A. J. Dout
1992 Sales: $1,759 million Employees: 9,500
Symbol: IMA Exchange: NYSE
Industry: Diversified operations - radiology products, radiopharmaceuticals

ImClone Systems, Inc.
180 Varick St.
New York, NY 10014
Phone: 212-645-1405 Fax: —
CEO: Samuel D. Waksal
CFO: Brooks Boveroux
1992 Sales: $0.8 million Employees: 77
Symbol: IMCL Exchange: NASDAQ
Industry: Biomedical & genetic products

IMCO Recycling
1508 N. 8th St.
Sapulpa, OK 74066
Phone: 918-224-4746 Fax: 918-224-4849
CEO: Ralph L. Cheek
CFO: Paul V. Dufour
1991 Sales: $49 million Employees: 322
Symbol: IMR Exchange: NYSE
Industry: Metal processing & fabrication

Immucor, Inc.
3130 Gateway Dr.
Norcross, GA 30071
Phone: 404-441-2051 Fax: 404-441-3807
CEO: Edward L. Gallup
CFO: Richard J. Still
1992 Sales: $27 million Employees: 152
Symbol: BLUD Exchange: NASDAQ
Industry: Medical & dental supplies

ImmuLogic Pharmaceutical Corp.
One Kendall Square, Bldg. 600
Cambridge, MA 02139
Phone: 617-494-0060 Fax: 617-577-8686
CEO: Richard E. Bagley
CFO: Janet C. Bush
1991 Sales: $3.2 million Employees: 106
Symbol: IMUL Exchange: NASDAQ
Industry: Biomedical & genetic products

Immune Response Corp.
5935 Darwin Court
Carlsbad, CA 92008
Phone: 619-431-7080 Fax: 619-431-8636
CEO: James B. Glavin
CFO: Charles J. Cashion
1991 Sales: $4.3 million Employees: 62
Symbol: IMNR Exchange: NASDAQ
Industry: Biomedical & genetic products

Immunex Corp.
51 University St.
Seattle, WA 98101
Phone: 206-587-0430 Fax: 206-587-0606
CEO: Stephen A. Duzan
CFO: Douglas G. Southern
1991 Sales: $53 million Employees: 527
Symbol: IMNX Exchange: NASDAQ
Industry: Biomedical & genetic products

ImmunoGen, Inc.
60 Hamilton St.
Cambridge, MA 02139
Phone: 617-661-9312 Fax: —
CEO: Mitchell Sayare
CFO: Frank J. Pocher
1992 Sales: — Employees: 162
Symbol: IMGN Exchange: NASDAQ
Industry: Drugs

Immunomedics, Inc.
150 Mt. Bethel Rd.
Warren, NJ 07059
Phone: 908-647-5400 Fax: 908-647-5888
CEO: David M. Goldenberg
CFO: Amy Factor
1992 Sales: $7 million Employees: 75
Symbol: IMMU Exchange: NASDAQ
Industry: Biomedical & genetic products

IMNET, Inc.
100 Century Blvd.
West Palm Beach, FL 33417
Phone: 407-640-3120 Fax: 407-640-3160
CEO: Joseph D. Weingard
CFO: Jack Jaiven
1991 Sales: $3.5 million Employees: 26
Symbol: IMGE Exchange: NASDAQ
Industry: Computers - document image-processing systems

Imo Industries Inc.
3450 Princeton Pike
Lawrenceville, NJ 08648
Phone: 609-896-7600 Fax: 609-896-7688
CEO: William J. Holcombe
CFO: Leffert G. Carroll
1992 Sales: $928 million Employees: 8,600
Symbol: IMD Exchange: NYSE
Industry: Instruments - control

Impact
10435 Burnet Rd., Ste. 114
Austin, TX 78758
Phone: 512-832-9151 Fax: 512-832-9321
CEO: David Gillett
CFO: Dene Jacobson
1991 Sales: $6.7 million Employees: 104
Ownership: Privately held
Industry: Computers - dot-matrix print-head refurbishing, monitor & laser fuser repair & parts sales

indicates company is in *Hoover's Handbook of American Business.*

indicates company is in *Hoover's Handbook of World Business;* sales and employee numbers are for parent company.

Impact Systems, Inc.
1075 E. Brokaw Rd.
San Jose, CA 95131
Phone: 408-453-3700 Fax: 408-453-4115
CEO: Kenneth P. Ostrow
CFO: Robert M. Gorski
1992 Sales: $17 million Employees: 80
Symbol: MPAC Exchange: NASDAQ
Industry: Instruments - control

Imperial Bancorp
9920 S. La Cienega Blvd.
Inglewood, CA 90301
Phone: 310-417-5600 Fax: 310-417-5888
CEO: George L. Graziadio, Jr.
CFO: David A. Sklar
1991 Sales: $303 million Employees: —
Symbol: IBAN Exchange: NASDAQ
Industry: Banks - West

Imperial Credit Industries, Inc.
1401 Dove St., Ste. 600
Newport Beach, CA 92660
Phone: 714-752-2820 Fax: —
CEO: H. Wayne Snavely
CFO: Michele M. Perrin
1991 Sales: $21 million Employees: 203
Symbol: ICII Exchange: NASDAQ
Industry: Financial - mortgages & related services

Imperial Holly Corp.
8016 Hwy. 908
Sugar Land, TX 77478
Phone: 713-491-9181 Fax: 713-491-9198
CEO: Robert C. Hanna
CFO: James C. Kempner
1992 Sales: $636 million Employees: 4,570
Symbol: IHK Exchange: AMEX
Industry: Food - sugar & refining

IMRS Inc.
777 Long Ridge Rd., Bldg. A
Stamford, CT 06902
Phone: 203-321-3500 Fax: 203-322-3904
CEO: James A. Perakis
CFO: Lucy Rae Ricciardi
1992 Sales: $46 million Employees: 335
Symbol: IMRS Exchange: NASDAQ
Industry: Computers - executive information systems software

In Focus Systems, Inc.
7770 SW Mohawk St.
Tualtin, OR 97062
Phone: 503-692-4968 Fax: 503-692-4476
CEO: Steven R. Hix
CFO: Joseph I. Martin
1991 Sales: $50 million Employees: 156
Symbol: INFS Exchange: NASDAQ
Industry: Computers - video display peripherals

In Home Health, Inc.
601 Lakeshore Pkwy., Ste. 500
Minnetonka, MN 55305
Phone: 612-449-7500 Fax: 612-449-7599
CEO: Judy M. Figge
CFO: Kenneth J. Figge
1992 Sales: $75 million Employees: 4,000
Ownership: Privately held
Industry: Healthcare - outpatient & home

In-Store Advertising, Inc.
411 W. Putnam Ave.
Greenwich, CT 10022
Phone: 203-861-5700 Fax: 203-861-5878
CEO: Steve Kahler
CFO: John E. Capps
1991 Sales: $17 million Employees: 73
Symbol: ISAN Exchange: NASDAQ
Industry: Advertising

InaCom, Inc.
10810 Farnam
Omaha, NE 68154
Phone: 402-392-3900 Fax: 402-392-7209
CEO: Bill L. Fairfield
CFO: David C. Guenthner
1992 Sales: $1,015 million Employees: 1,380
Symbol: INAC Exchange: NASDAQ
Industry: Retail - computer hardware & software

INCSTAR Corp.
1990 Industrial Blvd. South
Stillwater, MN 55082
Phone: 612-439-9710 Fax: 612-779-7847
CEO: Orwin L. Carter
CFO: John J. Booth
1991 Sales: $38 million Employees: 382
Symbol: ISR Exchange: AMEX
Industry: Medical products - test reagents & test kits

Indeck Energy Services, Inc.
1130 Lake Cook Rd., Ste. 300
Buffalo Grove, IL 60089
Phone: 708-520-3212 Fax: 708-520-9883
CEO: Gerald Forsythe
CFO: Lawrence Lagowski
1991 Sales: $78 million Employees: 126
Ownership: Privately held
Industry: Energy - cogeneration

Independence Bancorp, Inc.
One Hillendale Rd.
Perkasie, PA 18944
Phone: 215-257-2402 Fax: —
CEO: John D. Harding
CFO: Philip H. Rinnander
1991 Sales: $231 million Employees: 1,513
Symbol: INBC Exchange: NASDAQ
Industry: Banks - Northeast

Independence Federal Savings Bank
1229 Connecticut Ave. NW
Washington, DC 20036
Phone: 202-628-5500 Fax: —
CEO: William B. Fitzgerald, Sr.
CFO: Marco J. Papa
1992 Sales: — Employees: —
Symbol: IFSB Exchange: NASDAQ
Industry: Financial - savings and loans

Independence Holding Co.
335 Madison Ave.
New York, NY 10017
Phone: 212-297-1400 Fax: —
CEO: Sheldon S. Gordon
CFO: John A. Slattery
1991 Sales: $94 million Employees: 305
Symbol: INHO Exchange: NASDAQ
Industry: Financial - business services

Independent Bank Corp.
230 W. Main St.
Ionia, MI 48846
Phone: 616-527-2400 Fax: —
CEO: Loren C. Adgate
CFO: William R. Kohls
1991 Sales: $19 million Employees: 285
Symbol: IBCP Exchange: NASDAQ
Industry: Banks - Midwest

Independent Bank Corp.
288 Union St.
Rockland, MA 02370
Phone: 617-878-6100 Fax: —
CEO: John F. Spence, Jr.
CFO: Gregory W. Dee
1992 Sales: — Employees: —
Symbol: INDB Exchange: NASDAQ
Industry: Banks - Midwest

Independent Insurance Group, Inc.
One Independent Dr.
Jacksonville, FL 32202
Phone: 904-358-5151 Fax: 904-355-9541
CEO: Wilford C. Lyon, Jr.
CFO: Boyd E. Lyon, Sr.
1991 Sales: $570 million Employees: —
Symbol: INDHK Exchange: NASDAQ
Industry: Insurance - life

Indiana Energy, Inc.
1630 N. Meridian St.
Indianapolis, IN 46202
Phone: 317-926-3351 Fax: 317-321-0499
CEO: Lawrence A. Ferger
CFO: Niel C. Ellerbrook
1991 Sales: $390 million Employees: 1,103
Symbol: IEI Exchange: NYSE
Industry: Utility - gas distribution

Indiana Federal Corp.
56 S. Washington St.
Valparaiso, IN 46383
Phone: 219-462-4131 Fax: —
CEO: Peter R. Candela
CFO: George J. Eberhardt
1991 Sales: $19 million Employees: 302
Symbol: IFSL Exchange: NASDAQ
Industry: Banks - Midwest

Indiana Michigan Power Co.
One Summit Square
Ft. Wayne, IN 46801
Phone: 219-425-2111 Fax: —
CEO: R. E. Disbrow
CFO: Gerald P. Maloney
1991 Sales: $1.2 million Employees: 3,894
Symbol: IMEpB Exchange: NYSE
Industry: Utility - electric power

Indiana United Bancorp
201 N. Broadway
Greenburg, IN 47240
Phone: 812-663-4711 Fax: —
CEO: Robert E. Hoptry
CFO: Howard R. Sanders
1992 Sales: — Employees: 188
Symbol: IUBC Exchange: NASDAQ
Industry: Banks - Midwest

Inductotherm Industries
Ten Indel Ave.
Rancocas, NJ 08073
Phone: 609-267-9000 Fax: 609-267-3537
CEO: Henry M. Rowan
CFO: Harold Zierau
1991 Sales: $468 million Employees: 4,278
Ownership: Privately held
Industry: Machinery - general industrial

Industrial Acoustics Co., Inc.
1160 Commerce Ave.
Bronx, NY 10462
Phone: 212-931-8000 Fax: 212-863-1138
CEO: Martin Hirschorn
CFO: Robert N. Bertrand
1991 Sales: $81 million Employees: 773
Symbol: IACI Exchange: NASDAQ
Industry: Building products - noise-suppression materials

Industrial Bank of Japan Trust Company, The
245 Park Ave.
New York, NY 10167
Phone: 212-557-3535 Fax: 212-557-3581
CEO: Yuji Suzuki
CFO: —
1992 Sales: $25,813 million Employees: 5,151
Parent: Industrial Bank of Japan, Ltd.
Industry: Banks - money center

indicates company is in *Hoover's Handbook of American Business.*

indicates company is in *Hoover's Handbook of World Business*; sales and employee numbers are for parent company.

Industrial Holdings, Inc.
1100 Milam, Ste. 2050
Houston, TX 77002
Phone: 713-650-6386 Fax: —
CEO: Robert E. Cone
CFO: James H. Brock, Jr.
1991 Sales: $17 million Employees: 80
Symbol: IHII Exchange: NASDAQ
Industry: Machinery - general industrial

Industrial Training Corp.
13515 Dulles Technology Dr.
Herndon, VA 22071
Phone: 703-713-3335 Fax: 703-471-0381
CEO: James H. Walton
CFO: Arthur Rosenberg
1991 Sales: $11 million Employees: 72
Symbol: ITCC Exchange: NASDAQ
Industry: Business services - videotape-based training services; consulting

Infinity Broadcasting Corp.
600 Madison Ave.
New York, NY 10022
Phone: 212-750-6400 Fax: 212-888-2959
CEO: Mel Karmazin
CFO: Farid Suleman
1991 Sales: $118 million Employees: 510
Symbol: INFTA Exchange: NASDAQ
Industry: Broadcasting - radio & TV

Infodata Systems Inc.
5205 Leesburg Pike, Ste. 700
Falls Church, VA 22041
Phone: 703-578-3430 Fax: 703-578-4516
CEO: Harry Kaplowitz
CFO: Harry Kaplowitz
1991 Sales: $12 million Employees: 116
Symbol: INFD Exchange: NASDAQ
Industry: Computers - text & database management software

Information America, Inc.
600 W. Peachtree St. NW
Atlanta, GA 30308
Phone: 404-892-1800 Fax: —
CEO: Burton B. Goldstein
CFO: Mary A. Madden
1991 Sales: $16 million Employees: 116
Symbol: INFO Exchange: NASDAQ
Industry: Business services - on-line service for lawyers

Information Display Technology, Inc.
1305 Grandview Ave.
Pittsburgh, PA 15211
Phone: 412-381-2600 Fax: 412-381-9120
CEO: Herbert T. Kerr
CFO: Willard M. Bellows
1991 Sales: $59 million Employees: 472
Symbol: IDT Exchange: AMEX
Industry: Video equipment

Information International, Inc.
5933 Slauson Ave.
Culver City, CA 90230
Phone: 310-390-8611 Fax: 310-391-7724
CEO: Charles Ying
CFO: Terry N. Taugner
1992 Sales: $23 million Employees: 279
Symbol: IINT Exchange: NASDAQ
Industry: Machinery - printing

Information Resources, Inc.
150 N. Clinton St.
Chicago, IL 60661
Phone: 312-726-1221 Fax: 312-726-8214
CEO: Gian M. Fulgoni
CFO: Thomas M. Walker
1992 Sales: $276 million Employees: 3,679
Symbol: IRIC Exchange: NASDAQ
Industry: Business services - market research

Informix Corp.
4100 Bohannon Dr.
Menlo Park, CA 94025
Phone: 415-926-6300 Fax: 415-926-6593
CEO: Phillip E. White
CFO: Howard H. Graham
1991 Sales: $180 million Employees: 1,121
Symbol: IFMX Exchange: NASDAQ
Industry: Computers - data-management software

Inforum, Inc.
53 Century Blvd., Ste. 250
Nashville, TN 37214
Phone: 615-885-3560 Fax: —
CEO: Harold L. Siebert
CFO: J. Edward Pearson, Jr.
1991 Sales: $6.7 million Employees: 45
Symbol: INFM Exchange: NASDAQ
Industry: Hospitals

InfoSource, Inc.
6903 University Blvd.
Winter Park, FL 32792
Phone: 407-677-0300 Fax: 407-677-9226
CEO: Michael Werner
CFO: Michael Werner
1991 Sales: $2 million Employees: 50
Ownership: Privately held
Industry: Computers - training software

Ingersoll-Rand Co.
200 Chestnut Ridge Rd.
Woodcliff Lake, NJ 07675
Phone: 201-573-0123 Fax: 201-573-3448
CEO: Theodore H. Black
CFO: Clyde H. Folley
1992 Sales: $3,784 million Employees: 31,117
Symbol: IR Exchange: NYSE
Industry: Machinery - general industrial, engineered equipment & bearings, locks & tools

Ingles Markets, Inc.
Hwy. 70 East
Black Mountain, NC 28711
Phone: 704-669-2941 Fax: 704-669-5159
CEO: Robert P. Ingle
CFO: Jack R. Ferguson
1992 Sales: $1,083 million Employees: 8,195
Symbol: IMKTA Exchange: NASDAQ
Industry: Retail - supermarkets

Ingram Industries
4400 Harding Rd.
Nashville, TN 37205
Phone: 615-298-8200 Fax: 615-298-8378
CEO: E. Bronson Ingram
CFO: Tom Lunn
1991 Sales: $3,422 million Employees: 6,526
Ownership: Privately held
Industry: Wholesale distribution - books & microcomputer software

Inland Group, Inc., The
2901 Butterfield Rd.
Oak Brook, IL 60521
Phone: 708-218-8000 Fax: 708-218-4957
CEO: Daniel L. Goodwin
CFO: Alan Kremin
1991 Sales: $556 million Employees: 750
Ownership: Privately held
Industry: Diversified operations - real estate investment, finance & brokerage

Inland Steel Industries, Inc.
30 W. Monroe St.
Chicago, IL 60603
Phone: 312-346-0300 Fax: 312-899-3672
CEO: Robert J. Darnall
CFO: Earl L. Mason
1992 Sales: $3,494 million Employees: 18,600
Symbol: IAD Exchange: NYSE
Industry: Steel - production & distribution

Inmac Corp.
2465 Augustine Dr.
Santa Clara, CA 95052
Phone: 408-727-1970 Fax: 408-727-4131
CEO: Kenneth A. Eldred
CFO: Michael J. Waide
1991 Sales: $303 million Employees: 1,275
Symbol: INMC Exchange: NASDAQ
Industry: Retail - mail order & direct

Innovex, Inc.
1313 5th St. South
Hopkins, MN 55343
Phone: 612-938-4155 Fax: 612-938-7718
CEO: Thomas W. Haley
CFO: Jeffrey L. Burnham
1991 Sales: $35 million Employees: 555
Symbol: INVX Exchange: NASDAQ
Industry: Photographic equipment & supplies

INOTEK Technologies Corp.
10509 Markison Rd.
Dallas, TX 75238
Phone: 214-341-1396 Fax: —
CEO: Neal E. Young
CFO: David L. White
1992 Sales: $24 million Employees: 126
Symbol: INTK Exchange: NASDAQ
Industry: Instruments - wholesale process control

Input/Output, Inc.
4235 Greenbriar Dr.
Stafford, TX 77477
Phone: 713-240-2200 Fax: 713-240-2419
CEO: Charles E. Selecman
CFO: Robert P. Brindley
1992 Sales: $46 million Employees: 197
Symbol: IPOP Exchange: NASDAQ
Industry: Electronics - measuring instruments

Inrad, Inc.
181 Legrand Ave.
Northvale, NJ 07647
Phone: 201-767-1910 Fax: 201-767-9644
CEO: Warren Ruderman
CFO: Ronald Tassello
1991 Sales: $6.2 million Employees: 86
Symbol: INRD Exchange: NASDAQ
Industry: Lasers - systems & components

Inserra Supermarkets
20 Ridge Rd.
Mahwah, NJ 07430
Phone: 201-529-5900 Fax: 201-529-1189
CEO: Lawrence R. Inserra
CFO: Frank Festa
1991 Sales: $456 million Employees: 2,100
Ownership: Privately held
Industry: Retail - supermarkets

Inside Communications
1830 N. 55th St.
Boulder, CO 80301
Phone: 303-440-0601 Fax: 303-444-6788
CEO: Felix Magowan
CFO: David Walls
1992 Sales: $4.2 million Employees: 26
Ownership: Privately held
Industry: Publishing - cycling books & magazines

Insight Distribution Network, Inc.
1912 W. Fourth St.
Tempe, AZ 85281
Phone: 800-927-7848 Fax: 602-350-1148
CEO: Eric Crown
CFO: Stan Layburne
1992 Sales: $150 million Employees: 375
Ownership: Privately held
Industry: Computers - personal computers

indicates company is in *Hoover's Handbook of American Business.*

indicates company is in *Hoover's Handbook of World Business;* sales and employee numbers are for parent company.

Insilco Corp.
300 N. Marienfeld, Ste. 400
Midland, TX 79701
Phone: 915-684-4411 Fax: 915-688-7327
CEO: Joel L. Reed
CFO: J. Randal Greaves
1992 Sales: $575 million Employees: 5,300
Ownership: Privately held
Industry: Diversified operations - metal fabricating, electronics & communications

Insituform East, Inc.
3421 Pennsy Dr.
Landover, MD 20785
Phone: 301-386-4100 Fax: 301-386-2444
CEO: Arthur G. Lang III
CFO: Raymond T. Verrey
1992 Sales: $20 million Employees: 154
Symbol: INEI Exchange: NASDAQ
Industry: Wastewater systems & pipeline repair

Insituform Mid-America, Inc.
17988 Edison Ave.
Chesterfield, MO 63005
Phone: 314-532-6137 Fax: 314-537-1214
CEO: Robert W. Affholder
CFO: Joseph F. Olson
1991 Sales: $50 million Employees: 264
Symbol: INSMA Exchange: NASDAQ
Industry: Wastewater systems repair

Insituform of North America, Inc.
3315 Democrat Rd.
Memphis, TN 38118
Phone: 901-363-2105 Fax: 901-365-3906
CEO: James D. Krugman
CFO: William A. Martin
1991 Sales: $30 million Employees: 189
Symbol: INSUA Exchange: NASDAQ
Industry: Building products

Insteel Industries, Inc.
1373 Boggs Dr.
Mt. Airy, NC 27030
Phone: 919-786-2141 Fax: 919-786-2144
CEO: H. O. Woltz III
CFO: Gary D. Kniskern
1991 Sales: $240 million Employees: 1,017
Symbol: III Exchange: NYSE
Industry: Wire & cable products

Instron Corp.
100 Royall St.
Canton, MA 02021
Phone: 617-828-2500 Fax: 617-828-2112
CEO: James M. McConnell
CFO: Linton A. Moulding
1991 Sales: $126 million Employees: 1,026
Symbol: ISN Exchange: AMEX
Industry: Electronics - measuring instruments

Instrument Systems Corp.
100 Jericho Quadrangle
Jericho, NY 11753
Phone: 516-938-5544 Fax: 516-938-5644
CEO: Harvey R. Blau
CFO: Patrick L. Alesia
1991 Sales: $494 million Employees: 5,700
Symbol: ISY Exchange: AMEX
Industry: Diversified operations - customized plastic films, garage doors

Insurance Auto Auctions, Inc.
7245 Laurel Canyon Blvd.
North Hollywood, CA 91605
Phone: 818-764-3200 Fax: —
CEO: Bradley S. Scott
CFO: Steven M. Johnson
1991 Sales: $42 million Employees: 101
Symbol: IAAI Exchange: NASDAQ
Industry: Insurance - property & casualty

Intech Inc.
2270 Martin Ave.
Santa Clara, CA 95050
Phone: 408-727-0500 Fax: 408-748-9489
CEO: Leroy M. Buckler
CFO: Thomas M. Hogan
1991 Sales: $12 million Employees: 127
Symbol: INTE Exchange: NASDAQ
Industry: Electrical components - electronic circuits, systems & instruments

Integon Corp.
500 W. Fifth St.
Winston-Salem, NC 27152
Phone: 919-770-2000 Fax: 919-770-2942
CEO: J. C. Head III
CFO: B. M. Emerson II
1991 Sales: $185 million Employees: —
Symbol: IN Exchange: NYSE
Industry: Insurance - property & casualty

Integra Financial Corp.
Four PPG Place, 300 4th Ave.
Pittsburgh, PA 15222
Phone: 412-644-7669 Fax: 412-261-7279
CEO: William F. Roemer
CFO: Gary E. Wolbert
1992 Sales: $890 million Employees: 3,905
Symbol: ITGR Exchange: NASDAQ
Industry: Banks - Northeast

Integrated Circuit Systems, Inc.
2626 Van Buren Ave.
Norristown, PA 19403
Phone: 215-666-1900 Fax: 215-666-1099
CEO: Edward H. Arnold
CFO: Keith D. Schneck
1992 Sales: $23 million Employees: 97
Symbol: ICST Exchange: NASDAQ
Industry: Electrical components - integrated circuits

Integrated Device Technology, Inc.
2975 Stender Way
Santa Clara, CA 95054
Phone: 408-727-6116 Fax: 408-492-8512
CEO: D. John Carey
CFO: Jay R. Zerfoss
1992 Sales: $203 million Employees: 2,159
Symbol: IDTI Exchange: NASDAQ
Industry: Electrical components - semiconductors

Integrated Health Services, Inc.
11011 McCormick Rd.
Hunt Valley, MD 21031
Phone: 410-584-7050 Fax: 410-584-7387
CEO: Robert N. Elkins
CFO: Stephen A. Drury
1991 Sales: $144 million Employees: 5,050
Symbol: IHSI Exchange: NASDAQ
Industry: Medical services - subacute care

Integrated Systems, Inc.
3260 Jay St.
Santa Clara, CA 95054
Phone: 408-980-1500 Fax: 408-980-0400
CEO: Narendra K. Gupta
CFO: Scott C. McDonald
1992 Sales: $25 million Employees: 196
Symbol: INTS Exchange: NASDAQ
Industry: Computers - CAE/CASE software

Integrated Waste Services, Inc.
201 Ganson St.
Buffalo, NY 14203
Phone: 716-852-2345 Fax: —
CEO: James H. Williams
CFO: Kevin McDonald
1991 Sales: $31 million Employees: 197
Symbol: IWSI Exchange: NASDAQ
Industry: Pollution control equipment & services - solid waste management

Integratrak
146 N. Canal St., Ste. 300
Seattle, WA 98103
Phone: 206-547-3390 Fax: 206-547-2502
CEO: Bill Wehrenberg
CFO: Rebecca Wehrenberg
1991 Sales: $2.2 million Employees: 33
Ownership: Privately held
Industry: Computers - telemanagement software

Integrity Industries-Blue
2710 E. Corral
Kingsville, TX 78363
Phone: 512-595-5561 Fax: 512-595-5588
CEO: Max Ducan
CFO: Todd Gaddie
1991 Sales: $6.3 million Employees: 16
Ownership: Privately held
Industry: Chemicals - specialty

Intel Corp.
2200 Mission College Blvd.
Santa Clara, CA 95052
Phone: 408-765-8080 Fax: 408-765-1402
CEO: Andrew S. Grove
CFO: Harold E. Hughes, Jr.
1992 Sales: $5,844 million Employees: 24,600
Symbol: INTC Exchange: NASDAQ
Industry: Electrical components - semiconductors; peripheral equipment, supercomputers

Intellicall, Inc.
2155 Chenault, Ste. 410
Carrollton, TX 75006
Phone: 214-416-0022 Fax: 214-416-7213
CEO: R. Stephen Polley
CFO: Thomas A. Floerchinger
1991 Sales: $220 million Employees: 294
Symbol: ICL Exchange: NYSE
Industry: Telecommunications equipment

IntelliCorp, Inc.
1975 El Camino Real West
Mountain View, CA 94040
Phone: 415-965-5500 Fax: 415-965-5647
CEO: Thomas P. Kehler
CFO: Kenneth H. Haas
1991 Sales: $14 million Employees: 147
Symbol: INAI Exchange: NASDAQ
Industry: Computers - artificial intelligence technology software

Intelligent Electronics, Inc.
411 Eagleview Blvd.
Exton, PA 19341
Phone: 215-458-5500 Fax: 215-458-8454
CEO: Richard D. Sanford
CFO: Garland P. Asher
1992 Sales: $2,583 million Employees: 2,669
Symbol: INEL Exchange: NASDAQ
Industry: Computers - retail & wholesale

Intelligent Systems Master LP
4355 Shackleford Rd.
Norcross, GA 30093
Phone: 404-381-2900 Fax: 404-381-2808
CEO: J. Leland Strange
CFO: John E. McCormick
1991 Sales: $49 million Employees: 181
Symbol: INS Exchange: AMEX
Industry: Computers - peripheral equipment

Intelogic Trace, Inc.
Turtle Creek Tower I, 8415 Datapoint Dr.
San Antonio, TX 78229
Phone: 210-593-5700 Fax: —
CEO: Asher B. Edelman
CFO: Richard E. Wilson
1991 Sales: $144 million Employees: 1,517
Symbol: IT Exchange: NYSE
Industry: Computers - services

indicates company is in *Hoover's Handbook of American Business.*

indicates company is in *Hoover's Handbook of World Business;* sales and employee numbers are for parent company.

Inter-Regional Financial Group, Inc.
60 S. Sixth St.
Minneapolis, MN 55402
Phone: 612-371-7750 Fax: 612-371-7755
CEO: Irving Weiser
CFO: John C. Appel
1991 Sales: $378 million Employees: 2,500
Symbol: IFG Exchange: NYSE
Industry: Financial - investment bankers

Inter-Tel, Inc.
6505 W. Chandler Blvd.
Chandler, AZ 85226
Phone: 602-961-9000 Fax: 602-961-1370
CEO: Steven G. Mihaylo
CFO: Ralph Marsh
1991 Sales: $66 million Employees: 565
Symbol: INTL Exchange: NASDAQ
Industry: Telecommunications equipment

Interactive Network, Inc.
1991 Landings Dr.
Mountain View, CA 94043
Phone: 415-903-4000 Fax: 415-960-3331
CEO: David B. Lockton
CFO: Frank E. Murnane
1991 Sales: $0.1 million Employees: 62
Symbol: INNN Exchange: NASDAQ
Industry: Leisure & recreational products - interactive TV entertainment system

Intercargo Corp.
1450 E. American Lane
Schaumburg, IL 60173
Phone: 708-517-2510 Fax: 708-517-2996
CEO: James R. Zuhlke
CFO: Kenneth J. Kranig
1991 Sales: $43 million Employees: 66
Symbol: ICAR Exchange: NASDAQ
Industry: Insurance - property & casualty

Interchange Financial Services Corp.
Park 80 West/Plaza Two
Saddle Brook, NJ 07662
Phone: 201-703-2265 Fax: —
CEO: Anthony S. Abbate
CFO: Robert N. Harris
1991 Sales: $32 million Employees: 160
Symbol: ISB Exchange: AMEX
Industry: Banks - Northeast

INTERCO Inc.
101 S. Hanley Rd.
St. Louis, MO 63105
Phone: 314-863-1100 Fax: 314-863-5306
CEO: Richard B. Loynd
CFO: Eugene F. Smith
1992 Sales: $1,520 million Employees: 19,800
Symbol: ISS Exchange: NYSE
Industry: Diversified operations - footwear & furniture

Intercontinental Bank
200 SE First St.
Miami, FL 33131
Phone: 305-377-6900 Fax: —
CEO: William H. Allen, Jr.
CFO: Thomas E. Beier
1992 Sales: — Employees: —
Symbol: ICBK Exchange: NASDAQ
Industry: Banks - Southeast

Interdigital Communications Corp.
2200 Renaissance Blvd.
King of Prussia, PA 19406
Phone: 215-278-7800 Fax: 215-278-6801
CEO: William J. Hilsman
CFO: Richard A. Guttendorf, Jr.
1991 Sales: $34 million Employees: 138
Symbol: IDC Exchange: AMEX
Industry: Telecommunications equipment

Interface, Inc.
1503 Orchard Hill Rd.
LaGrange, GA 30240
Phone: 404-882-1891 Fax: 404-882-0500
CEO: Ray C. Anderson
CFO: Daniel T. Hendrix
1991 Sales: $582 million Employees: 3,888
Symbol: IFSIA Exchange: NASDAQ
Industry: Textiles - home furnishings

Interface Systems, Inc.
5855 Interface Dr.
Ann Arbor, MI 48103
Phone: 313-769-5900 Fax: 313-769-1047
CEO: Carl L. Bixby
CFO: David O. Schupp
1991 Sales: $34 million Employees: 259
Symbol: INTF Exchange: NASDAQ
Industry: Computers - printers & interfaces

Interferon Sciences, Inc.
783 Jersey Ave.
New Brunswick, NJ 08901
Phone: 908-249-3232 Fax: 908-249-6895
CEO: Martin M. Pollak
CFO: Jerome I. Feldman
1991 Sales: $2.5 million Employees: 64
Symbol: IFSC Exchange: NASDAQ
Industry: Medical services - alpha-interferon pharmaceuticals production

Intergraph Corp.
289 Dunlop Blvd. SW
Huntsville, AL 35824
Phone: 205-730-2000 Fax: 205-730-2164
CEO: James W. Meadlock
CFO: Larry J. Laster
1992 Sales: $1,177 million Employees: 10,300
Symbol: INGR Exchange: NASDAQ
Industry: Computers - graphics; CAD/CAM systems, micro stations

Intergroup Corp.
2121 Avenue of the Stars
Los Angeles, CA 90067
Phone: 213-556-1999 Fax: —
CEO: John V. Winfield
CFO: Richard A. Fox
1992 Sales: $7.1 million Employees: —
Symbol: INTG Exchange: NASDAQ
Industry: Real estate operations

Intergroup Healthcare Corp.
1010 N. Finance Center Dr.
Tucson, AZ 85710
Phone: 602-721-4444 Fax: 602-290-7585
CEO: Charles F. Barrett
CFO: Carwin Y. Peterson
1991 Sales: $243 million Employees: 315
Symbol: IGHC Exchange: NASDAQ
Industry: Health maintenance organization

Interlake Conveyors Inc.
550 Warrenville Rd.
Lisle, IL 60532
Phone: 708-852-8800 Fax: 708-719-7152
CEO: W. Robert Reum
CFO: Richard I. Polanek
1992 Sales: $708 million Employees: 4,902
Symbol: IK Exchange: NYSE
Industry: Machinery - material handling

Interlaken Capital Inc.
165 Mason St.
Greenwich, CT 06830
Phone: 203-629-8750 Fax: 203-629-8554
CEO: William R. Berkley
CFO: Charlie Martin
1991 Sales: $2,900 million Employees: 12,900
Ownership: Privately held
Industry: Diversified operations - food processing, insurance & health care

Interleaf, Inc.
9 Hillside Ave., Prospect Pl.
Waltham, MA 02154
Phone: 617-290-0710 Fax: 617-290-4943
CEO: David A. Boucher
CFO: David J. Collard
1992 Sales: $100 million Employees: 850
Symbol: LEAF Exchange: NASDAQ
Industry: Computers - publishing software

Intermagnetics General Corp.
New Karner Rd.
Guilderland, NY 12084
Phone: 518-456-5456 Fax: 518-456-0028
CEO: Carl H. Rosner
CFO: Michael C. Zeigler
1992 Sales: $58 million Employees: 444
Symbol: IMG Exchange: AMEX
Industry: Magnets

Intermark, Inc.
1020 Prospect St., Ste. 210
La Jolla, CA 92037
Phone: 619-459-3842 Fax: 619-456-7897
CEO: Charles R. Scott
CFO: James V. Iaco, Jr.
1992 Sales: $295 million Employees: —
Symbol: IMI Exchange: AMEX
Industry: Diversified operations - liquor stores, turbine engines, real estate development

Intermedia Communications of Florida, Inc.
9280 Bay Plaza Blvd., Ste. 720
Tampa, FL 33619
Phone: 813-621-0011 Fax: —
CEO: Robert F. Benton
CFO: Daniel J. Montague
1991 Sales: $5.2 million Employees: 27
Symbol: ICIX Exchange: NASDAQ
Industry: Telecommunications services

Intermet Corp.
2859 Paces Ferry Rd., Ste. 1600
Atlanta, GA 30339
Phone: 404-431-6000 Fax: 404-431-6001
CEO: George W. Mathews, Jr.
CFO: John D. Ernst
1991 Sales: $320 million Employees: 3,496
Symbol: INMT Exchange: NASDAQ
Industry: Automotive & trucking - original equipment

Intermetrics, Inc.
733 Concord Ave.
Cambridge, MA 02138
Phone: 617-661-1840 Fax: 617-868-2843
CEO: Joseph A. Saponaro
CFO: Nicholas A. Pettinella
1992 Sales: $61 million Employees: 588
Symbol: IMET Exchange: NASDAQ
Industry: Computers - software

International Airline Support Group, Inc.
6915 NW 43rd St.
Miami, FL 33166
Phone: 305-593-2658 Fax: 305-593-1751
CEO: Richard Wellman
CFO: William Hartman
1992 Sales: $27 million Employees: 60
Symbol: IASG Exchange: NASDAQ
Industry: Aerospace - aircraft equipment

International Aluminum Corp.
767 Monterey Pass Rd.
Monterey Park, CA 91754
Phone: 213-264-1670 Fax: 213-266-3838
CEO: Cornelius C. Vanderstar
CFO: David C. Treinen
1992 Sales: $158 million Employees: 1,700
Symbol: IAL Exchange: NYSE
Industry: Building products - doors & trim

A indicates company is in *Hoover's Handbook of American Business.*

W indicates company is in *Hoover's Handbook of World Business;* sales and employee numbers are for parent company.

International Business Machines Corp.
1 Old Orchard Rd.
Armonk, NY 10504
Phone: 914-765-1900 Fax: 914-765-4190
CEO: John F. Akers
CFO: Frank A. Metz, Jr.
1992 Sales: $64,523 million Employees: 344,553
Symbol: IBM Exchange: NYSE
Industry: Computers - mainframe; processors, software & peripherals

International Cablecasting Technologies, Inc.
11400 W. Olympic Blvd.
Los Angeles, CA 90064
Phone: 310-444-1744 Fax: 310-444-1717
CEO: Jerold H. Rubinstein
CFO: Patti Dennis
1992 Sales: — Employees: 38
Symbol: TUNE Exchange: NASDAQ
Industry: Leisure & recreational services - cable audio services

International Computer Graphics
6090 Stewart Ave.
Fremont, CA 94538
Phone: 510-249-4300 Fax: 510-657-8879
CEO: Mike Ahmar
CFO: Mike Ahmar
1992 Sales: $45 million Employees: 30
Ownership: Privately held
Industry: Computers - computer-aided design peripherals distribution

International Container Systems, Inc.
5401 W. Kennedy Blvd., Ste. 760
Tampa, FL 33609
Phone: 813-287-8940 Fax: 813-286-2070
CEO: Van L. McNeel
CFO: Tom L. Irving
1991 Sales: $14 million Employees: 14
Symbol: ICSI Exchange: NASDAQ
Industry: Containers - paper & plastic

International Controls Corp.
2016 N. Pitcher St.
Kalamazoo, MI 49007
Phone: 616-343-6121 Fax: 616-343-2244
CEO: David R. Markin
CFO: Wilmer J. Thomas, Jr.
1991 Sales: $555 million Employees: 3,854
Ownership: Privately held
Industry: Diversified operations - truck trailer manufacturing, auto stamping & insurance

International Dairy Queen, Inc.
5701 Green Valley Dr.
Minneapolis, MN 55437
Phone: 612-830-0200 Fax: 612-830-0270
CEO: Michael P. Sullivan
CFO: Frank L. Heit
1991 Sales: $287 million Employees: 592
Symbol: INDQA Exchange: NASDAQ
Industry: Retail - food & restaurants; office placement services

International Data Group Inc.
One Exeter Plaza, 15th Fl.
Boston, MA 02116
Phone: 617-534-1200 Fax: 617-859-8642
CEO: Patrick J. McGovern
CFO: W. P. Murphy
1992 Sales: $800 million Employees: 5,000
Ownership: Privately held
Industry: Publishing - computer publications; market research, trade shows

International Family Entertainment, Inc.
1000 Centerville Tnpk.
Virginia Beach, VA 23463
Phone: 804-523-7301 Fax: 804-523-7878
CEO: Timothy B. Robertson
CFO: Larry W. Dantzler
1991 Sales: $114 million Employees: 260
Symbol: FAM Exchange: NYSE
Industry: Cable TV

International Flavors & Fragrances, Inc.
521 W. 57th St.
New York, NY 10019
Phone: 212-765-5500 Fax: 212-708-7132
CEO: Eugene P. Grisanti
CFO: Thomas H. Hoppel
1992 Sales: $1,126 million Employees: 4,218
Symbol: IFF Exchange: NYSE
Industry: Cosmetics & toiletries - fragrances; flavors

International Game Technology
520 S. Rock Blvd.
Reno, NV 89502
Phone: 702-688-0100 Fax: 702-688-0120
CEO: Charles N. Mathewson
CFO: G. Thomas Baker
1992 Sales: $399 million Employees: 2,240
Symbol: IGT Exchange: NYSE
Industry: Leisure & recreational products - gambling equipment & casinos

International Holding Capital Corp.
841 Bishop St., Ste. 222
Honolulu, HI 96813
Phone: 808-547-5110 Fax: 808-544-8552
CEO: Lionel Y. Tokioka
CFO: Paul C. Chun
1992 Sales: — Employees: —
Symbol: ISLH Exchange: NASDAQ
Industry: Financial - savings and loans

International Jensen, Inc.
25 Tri-State Intl. Off. Ctr., Ste. 400
Lincolnshire, IL 60069
Phone: 708-317-3700 Fax: 708-317-3842
CEO: Robert G. Shaw
CFO: Robert G. Shaw
1992 Sales: $153 million Employees: 1,550
Symbol: IJIN Exchange: NASDAQ
Industry: Audio & video home products

International Microelectronic Products, Inc.
2830 N. First St.
San Jose, CA 95134
Phone: 408-432-9100 Fax: 408-434-0335
CEO: Barry M. Carrington
CFO: Charles S. Isherwood
1992 Sales: $46 million Employees: 331
Symbol: IMPX Exchange: NASDAQ
Industry: Electrical components - integrated circuits

International Movie Group, Inc.
1900 Avenue of the Stars, Ste. 1425
Los Angeles, CA 90067
Phone: 310-556-2830 Fax: 310-277-1490
CEO: Peter E. Strauss
CFO: Ann Oliver
1991 Sales: $18 million Employees: 11
Symbol: IMV Exchange: AMEX
Industry: Motion pictures & services - foreign distribution of English-language feature films

International Multifoods Corp.
33 S. 6th St., 50th Fl.
Minneapolis, MN 55402
Phone: 612-340-3300 Fax: 612-340-3338
CEO: Anthony Luiso
CFO: Duncan H. Cocroft
1992 Sales: $2,239 million Employees: 8,231
Symbol: IMC Exchange: NYSE
Industry: Food - flour & grain

International Nickel Inc.
One New York Plaza
New York, NY 10004
Phone: 212-612-5500 Fax: 212-612-5770
CEO: David J. Anderson
CFO: —
1991 Sales: $2,999 million Employees: 18,369
Parent: Inco Ltd.
Industry: Metal ores - nickel

International Paper Co.
Two Manhattanville Rd.
Purchase, NY 10577
Phone: 914-397-1500 Fax: 914-397-1596
CEO: John A. Georges
CFO: Robert C. Butler
1992 Sales: $13,620 million Employees: 70,500
Symbol: IP Exchange: NYSE
Industry: Paper & paper products, distribution, specialty products, wood & timber

International Power Machines Corp.
2975 Miller Park North
Garland, TX 75042
Phone: 214-272-8000 Fax: 214-494-2690
CEO: Warren H. Haber
CFO: William L. Zang
1991 Sales: $30 million Employees: 207
Symbol: PWR Exchange: AMEX
Industry: Electrical products - uninterruptible power supply; cleanroom installation & service

International Recovery Corp.
700 S. Royal Poinciana Blvd., Ste. 800
Miami Springs, FL 33166
Phone: 305-884-2001 Fax: 305-883-0186
CEO: Ralph R. Weiser
CFO: Robert S. Tocci
1992 Sales: $206 million Employees: 268
Symbol: INT Exchange: NYSE
Industry: Oil refining & marketing

International Rectifier Corp.
233 Kansas St.
El Segundo, CA 90245
Phone: 310-322-3331 Fax: 310-322-3332
CEO: Eric Lidow
CFO: Roger Hay
1992 Sales: $266 million Employees: 3,000
Symbol: IRF Exchange: NYSE
Industry: Electrical components - semiconductors

International Research and Development Corp.
500 N. Main St.
Mattawan, MI 49071
Phone: 616-668-3336 Fax: 616-668-4151
CEO: Francis X. Wazeter
CFO: David A. Stover
1991 Sales: $35 million Employees: 375
Symbol: IRDV Exchange: NASDAQ
Industry: Medical services - safety evaluation of chemicals & drugs, data analysis

International Shipholding Corp.
650 Poydras St., Ste. 1700
New Orleans, LA 70130
Phone: 504-529-5461 Fax: 504-529-5745
CEO: Niels W. Johnsen
CFO: Gary L. Ferguson
1991 Sales: $328 million Employees: 775
Symbol: ISH Exchange: NYSE
Industry: Transportation - shipping

International Specialty Products Inc.
1361 Alps Rd.
Wayne, NJ 19801
Phone: 201-628-4000 Fax: 201-628-3311
CEO: Samuel J. Heyman
CFO: Irwin Engelman
1991 Sales: $526 million Employees: 2,265
Symbol: ISP Exchange: NYSE
Industry: Chemicals - specialty

International Technology Corp.
23456 Hawthorne Blvd.
Torrance, CA 90505
Phone: 310-378-9933 Fax: 310-791-2587
CEO: Murray H. Hutchison
CFO: Anthony J. DeLuca
1992 Sales: $420 million Employees: 3,865
Symbol: ITX Exchange: NYSE
Industry: Environmental management services, hazardous waste disposal

indicates company is in *Hoover's Handbook of American Business.*

indicates company is in *Hoover's Handbook of World Business;* sales and employee numbers are for parent company.

International Telecharge, Inc.
1412 Main St.
Dallas, TX 75202
Phone: 214-744-0240 Fax: 214-653-1427
CEO: Ronald J. Haan
CFO: Thomas M. Hyatt
1991 Sales: $178 million Employees: 1,536
Symbol: ITI Exchange: AMEX
Industry: Telecommunications services

International Testing Services, Inc.
363 N. Sam Houston Park East
Houston, TX 77060
Phone: 713-591-8880 Fax: —
CEO: William G. Flesner
CFO: John B. Connally III
1991 Sales: $5.6 million Employees: 256
Symbol: ITS Exchange: AMEX
Industry: Oil & gas - field services

International Thoroughbred Breeders, Inc.
525 Hwy. 33 East
Englishtown, NJ 07726
Phone: 908-446-0700 Fax: —
CEO: Robert E. Brennan
CFO: William H. Warner
1992 Sales: $40 million Employees: 677
Symbol: ITB Exchange: AMEX
Industry: Thoroughbred horse breeding & sales & horse racetrack operation

International Totalizator Systems, Inc.
2131 Faraday Ave.
Carlsbad, CA 92008
Phone: 619-931-4000 Fax: 619-931-1789
CEO: James T. Walters
CFO: Kenneth Hoitt
1991 Sales: $30 million Employees: 201
Symbol: ITSI Exchange: NASDAQ
Industry: Ticket processing for parimutuel wagering & lotteries

International Veronex Resources Ltd.
9701 Lakewood Blvd.
Downey, CA 90240
Phone: 310-861-0383 Fax: 310-861-1256
CEO: David A. Hite
CFO: David A. Hite
1992 Sales: — Employees: 7
Symbol: VX Exchange: AMEX
Industry: Diversified operations

Interneuron Pharmaceuticals, Inc.
99 Hayden Ave.
Lexington, MA 02173
Phone: 617-861-8444 Fax: —
CEO: Charles J. Casamento
CFO: Charles J. Casamento
1991 Sales: $0.1 million Employees: 19
Symbol: IPIC Exchange: NASDAQ
Industry: Drugs

Interphase Corp.
13800 Senlac Dr.
Dallas, TX 75234
Phone: 214-919-9000 Fax: 214-919-9200
CEO: Michael E. Cope
CFO: James L. May, Jr.
1991 Sales: $40 million Employees: 251
Symbol: INPH Exchange: NASDAQ
Industry: Computers - disk drive subsystems

Interpoint Corp.
10301 Willows Rd. NE
Redmond, WA 98073
Phone: 206-882-3100 Fax: 206-869-7402
CEO: Peter van Oppen
CFO: Leslie S. Rock
1991 Sales: $30 million Employees: 473
Symbol: INTP Exchange: NASDAQ
Industry: Electrical components - power converter microcircuits

Interpublic Group of Companies, Inc.
1271 Avenue of the Americas, 44th Fl.
New York, NY 10020
Phone: 212-399-8000 Fax: —
CEO: Philip H. Geier, Jr.
CFO: Eugene P. Beard
1992 Sales: $1,856 million Employees: 16,800
Symbol: IPG Exchange: NYSE
Industry: Advertising

INTERSOLV Inc.
3200 Tower Oaks Blvd.
Rockville, MD 20852
Phone: 301-230-3200 Fax: 301-231-7813
CEO: Kevin J. Burns
CFO: Melody S. Ranelli
1991 Sales: $72 million Employees: 450
Symbol: SGSI Exchange: NASDAQ
Industry: Computers - engineering software

Intersource Technologies, Inc.
1270 Oakmead Pkwy., Ste. 310
Sunnyvale, CA 94086
Phone: 408-732-6767 Fax: 408-732-6760
CEO: Stephen J. Britt
CFO: Nicholas A. Godley
1992 Sales: — Employees: —
Ownership: Privately held
Industry: Electrical products - light bulbs

Interspec, Inc.
110 W. Butler Ave.
Ambler, PA 19002
Phone: 215-540-9190 Fax: 215-540-9711
CEO: Edward Ray
CFO: Michael J. Wassil
1991 Sales: $62 million Employees: 577
Symbol: ISPC Exchange: NASDAQ
Industry: Medical instruments

Interstate Bakeries Corp.
12 E. Armour Blvd.
Kansas City, MO 64111
Phone: 816-561-6600 Fax: Ext. 255
CEO: Charles A. Sullivan
CFO: Paul E. Yarick
1992 Sales: $1,163 million Employees: 14,000
Symbol: IBC Exchange: NYSE
Industry: Food - bakery products

Interstate General Co. L.P.
222 Smallwood Village Center
St. Charles, MD 20602
Phone: 301-843-8600 Fax: —
CEO: James J. Wilson
CFO: Kimberly H. Carroll
1991 Sales: $47 million Employees: 337
Symbol: IGC Exchange: AMEX
Industry: Real estate development

Interstate Power Co.
1000 Main St.
Dubuque, IA 52004
Phone: 319-582-5421 Fax: 319-557-2202
CEO: Wayne H. Stoppelmoor
CFO: Wayne H. Stoppelmoor
1991 Sales: $290 million Employees: 970
Symbol: IPW Exchange: NYSE
Industry: Utility - electric power

Interstate/Johnson Lane, Inc.
121 W. Trade St., Ste. 1500
Charlotte, NC 28202
Phone: 704-379-9000 Fax: 704-379-9075
CEO: Parks H. Dalton
CFO: Edward C. Ruff
1991 Sales: $122 million Employees: 984
Symbol: IS Exchange: NYSE
Industry: Financial - investment bankers

Intertrans Corp.
125 E. Carpenter Fwy., Ste. 900
Irving, TX 75063
Phone: 214-830-8888 Fax: 214-830-7488
CEO: Keith McKinney
CFO: David M. Thomas
1991 Sales: $162 million Employees: 1,053
Symbol: ITRN Exchange: NASDAQ
Industry: Transportation - services

Intervisual Books, Inc.
2850 Ocean Park Blvd.
Santa Monica, CA 90405
Phone: 310-396-8708 Fax: 310-339-0419
CEO: Charles E. Gates
CFO: Charles E. Gates
1991 Sales: $16 million Employees: 31
Symbol: IBI Exchange: AMEX
Industry: Publishing - books

InterVoice, Inc.
17811 Waterview Pkwy.
Dallas, TX 75252
Phone: 214-669-3988 Fax: 214-907-1079
CEO: Daniel D. Hammond
CFO: Daniel D. Hammond
1992 Sales: $30 million Employees: 262
Symbol: INTV Exchange: NASDAQ
Industry: Telecommunications equipment

InterWest Savings Bank
1259 W. Pioneer Way
Oak Harbor, WA 98277
Phone: 206-679-4181 Fax: —
CEO: Stephen M. Walden
CFO: H. Glenn Mouw
1992 Sales: — Employees: —
Symbol: IWBK Exchange: NASDAQ
Industry: Financial - savings and loans

Intl. Computers & Telecommunications, Inc.
18310 Montgomery Village, Ste. 610
Rockville, MD 20879
Phone: 301-948-0200 Fax: 301-948-9851
CEO: David Sohn
CFO: Kay Buck
1991 Sales: $11 million Employees: 205
Ownership: Privately held
Industry: Computers - high-tech systems support

Intuit, Inc.
155 Linfield Dr.
Menlo Park, CA 94025
Phone: 415-322-0573 Fax: 415-322-1013
CEO: Scott Cook
CFO: Eric Dunn
1991 Sales: $45 million Employees: 242
Symbol: INTU Exchange: NASDAQ
Industry: Computers - financial software

Invacare Corp.
899 Cleveland St.
Elyria, OH 44036
Phone: 216-329-6000 Fax: 216-366-6160
CEO: A. Malachi Mixon III
CFO: Gerald B. Blouch
1991 Sales: $263 million Employees: 2,440
Symbol: IVCR Exchange: NASDAQ
Industry: Medical & dental supplies

Investors Savings Corp.
1817 Plymouth Rd. South
Minnetonka, MN 55343
Phone: 612-542-8000 Fax: —
CEO: James M. Burkholder
CFO: Lynn Bueltel
1991 Sales: $18 million Employees: 318
Symbol: INVS Exchange: NASDAQ
Industry: Financial - savings and loans

indicates company is in *Hoover's Handbook of American Business.*

indicates company is in *Hoover's Handbook of World Business;* sales and employee numbers are for parent company.

Investors Title Co.
121 N. Columbia St.
Chapel Hill, NC 27514
Phone: 919-968-2200 Fax: 919-942-4686
CEO: J. Allen Fine
CFO: James A. Fine, Jr.
1991 Sales: $10.4 million Employees: 29
Symbol: ITIC Exchange: NASDAQ
Industry: Insurance - multiline & misc.

INVG Mortgage Securities Corp.
55 Water St.
New York, NY 10041
Phone: 212-668-4000 Fax: —
CEO: Patrick M. Ahern
CFO: Edward J. O'Hara
1991 Sales: $106 million Employees: —
Symbol: INVG Exchange: NASDAQ
Industry: Financial - mortgages & related services

Iomega Corp.
1821 West 4000 South
Roy, UT 84067
Phone: 801-778-1000 Fax: 801-778-3190
CEO: Fred Wenninger
CFO: Phillip P. Krumb
1991 Sales: $137 million Employees: 1,153
Symbol: IOMG Exchange: NASDAQ
Industry: Computers - data storage products

Ionics, Inc.
65 Grove St.
Watertown, MA 02172
Phone: 617-926-2500 Fax: 617-926-4304
CEO: Arthur L. Goldstein
CFO: Theodore G. Papastavros
1991 Sales: $138 million Employees: 1,000
Symbol: ION Exchange: NYSE
Industry: Filtration products

Iowa National Bankshares Corp.
100 E. Park Ave.
Waterloo, IA 50703
Phone: 319-291-5200 Fax: —
CEO: Erl A. Schmiesing
CFO: Robert S. Kahler
1991 Sales: $81 million Employees: 439
Symbol: INBS Exchange: NASDAQ
Industry: Banks - Midwest

Iowa-Illinois Gas and Electric Co.
206 E. Second St.
Davenport, IA 52801
Phone: 319-326-7111 Fax: 319-326-7681
CEO: Stanley J. Bright
CFO: Lance E. Cooper
1991 Sales: $512 million Employees: 1,568
Symbol: IWG Exchange: NYSE
Industry: Utility - gas distribution

IP Timberlands
Two Manhattanville Rd.
Purchase, NY 10577
Phone: 914-397-1500 Fax: —
CEO: John A. Georges
CFO: Kenneth J. Waite
1991 Sales: $237 million Employees: —
Symbol: IPT Exchange: NYSE
Industry: Building products - wood

IPALCO Enterprises, Inc.
25 Monument Circle
Indianapolis, IN 46204
Phone: 317-261-8261 Fax: 317-261-8701
CEO: John R. Hodowal
CFO: John R. Brehm
1991 Sales: $648 million Employees: —
Symbol: IPL Exchange: NYSE
Industry: Utility - electric power

IPL Systems, Inc.
360 2nd St.
Waltham, MA 02154
Phone: 617-890-6620 Fax: 617-890-1405
CEO: Robert W. Norton
CFO: Eugene F. Tallone
1991 Sales: $60 million Employees: 133
Symbol: IPLSA Exchange: NASDAQ
Industry: Computers - add-in memory & storage subsystems

IQ Software Corp.
3295 River Exchange Dr. #550
Norcross, GA 30092
Phone: 404-446-8880 Fax: 404-448-4088
CEO: Rick Chitty
CFO: Michael Casey
1991 Sales: $7.8 million Employees: 70
Ownership: Privately held
Industry: Computers - software

IRI Holding
1101 15th St. NW, Ste. 612
Washington, DC 20005
Phone: 202-223-5804 Fax: 202-331-0560
CEO: Roberto Albisetti
CFO: —
1991 Sales: $69,600 million Employees: 408,066
Parent: IRI Holding
Industry: Diversified operations - telecommunications, steel, mechanical engineering

Iroquois Bancorp, Inc.
115 Genesee St.
Auburn, NY 13021
Phone: 315-252-9521 Fax: 315-255-3099
CEO: Robert J. Steigerwald
CFO: Marianne R. O'Connor
1991 Sales: $35 million Employees: 160
Symbol: IROQ Exchange: NASDAQ
Industry: Banks - Northeast

IRT Corp.
3030 Callan Rd.
San Diego, CA 92121
Phone: 619-450-4343 Fax: 619-450-9994
CEO: Clifford V. Brokaw III
CFO: Clifford V. Brokaw III
1992 Sales: $17 million Employees: 135
Symbol: IX Exchange: AMEX
Industry: Electronics - measuring instruments

Irvine Company, The
550 Newport Center Dr.
Newport Beach, CA 92660
Phone: 714-720-2000 Fax: 714-720-9453
CEO: Donald Bren
CFO: Norman Metcalfe
1991 Sales: $700 million Employees: 300
Ownership: Privately held
Industry: Real estate & community development & investment

Irwin Financial Corp.
500 Washington St.
Columbus, IN 47201
Phone: 812-376-1020 Fax: —
CEO: John A. Nash
CFO: Thomas D. Washburn
1991 Sales: $20 million Employees: 872
Symbol: IRWN Exchange: NASDAQ
Industry: Financial - business services

Isco, Inc.
4700 Superior St.
Lincoln, NE 68504
Phone: 402-464-0231 Fax: 402-464-4543
CEO: Robert W. Allington
CFO: Philip M. Wittig
1991 Sales: $37 million Employees: 504
Symbol: ISKO Exchange: NASDAQ
Industry: Instruments - scientific

Isis Pharmaceuticals, Inc.
2280 Faraday Ave.
Carlsbad, CA 92008
Phone: 619-931-9200 Fax: 619-931-9639
CEO: Stanley T. Crooke
CFO: Yasunori Kaneko
1991 Sales: $6.3 million Employees: 105
Symbol: ISIP Exchange: NASDAQ
Industry: Drugs

Island Lincoln-Mercury
1850 E. Merritt Island Causeway
Merritt Island, FL 32952
Phone: 407-452-9220 Fax: 407-453-3498
CEO: R. Bruce Deardoff
CFO: Phyllis Walker
1990 Sales: $732 million Employees: 52
Ownership: Privately held
Industry: Retail - auto dealerships

Isomedix Inc.
11 Apollo Dr.
Whippany, NJ 07981
Phone: 201-887-4700 Fax: 201-887-1476
CEO: John Masefield
CFO: Thomas J. DeAngelo
1991 Sales: $29 million Employees: 210
Symbol: ISMX Exchange: NASDAQ
Industry: Medical & dental supplies

Itel Corp.
Two N. Riverside Plaza, 19th Fl.
Chicago, IL 60606
Phone: 312-902-1515 Fax: 312-902-1573
CEO: Samuel Zell
CFO: Gary M. Hill
1992 Sales: $1,682 million Employees: 5,300
Symbol: ITL Exchange: NYSE
Industry: Diversified operations - marine construction, rail operations

Item Products
6703 Theall Rd.
Houston, TX 77066
Phone: 713-893-0100 Fax: 713-893-4836
CEO: Paul Schnizler
CFO: Paul Schnizler
1991 Sales: $3.8 million Employees: 31
Ownership: Privately held
Industry: Building products - modular building systems

Ithaca Bancorp, Inc.
118 N. Tioga St.
Ithaca, NY 14850
Phone: 607-273-7111 Fax: —
CEO: Arthur M. Pivirotto, Jr.
CFO: Edward S. Elles, Jr.
1991 Sales: $49 million Employees: 227
Symbol: ITHB Exchange: NASDAQ
Industry: Financial - savings and loans

Ithaca Software
1301 Marina Village Pkwy., Ste. 300
Alameda, CA 94501
Phone: 510-523-5900 Fax: 510-523-2880
CEO: Stephen Mendel
CFO: Shelly Cruze
1991 Sales: $2.8 million Employees: 34
Ownership: Privately held
Industry: Computers - portable 3-D graphics software

Ito-Yokado Co.
One Union Sq., 600 University St., Ste. 2829
Seattle, WA 98101
Phone: 206-624-6682 Fax: 206-624-6778
CEO: Akinari Uehira
CFO: —
1992 Sales: $22,266 million Employees: 32,076
Parent: Ito-Yokado Co., Ltd.
Industry: Retail - superstores, convenience stores & restaurants

indicates company is in *Hoover's Handbook of American Business.*

indicates company is in *Hoover's Handbook of World Business;* sales and employee numbers are for parent company.

ITOCHU International Inc.
335 Madison Ave.
New York, NY 10017
Phone: 212-818-8000 Fax: 212-818-8361
CEO: Jay W. Chai
CFO: —
1992 Sales: $164,884 million Employees: 7,149
Parent: ITOCHU Corporation
Industry: Diversified operations - machinery & construction, metals, energy & chemicals

ITT Corp.
1330 Avenue of the Americas
New York, NY 10019
Phone: 212-258-1000 Fax: 212-258-1037
CEO: Rand V. Araskog
CFO: M. Cabell Woodward, Jr.
1992 Sales: $21,645 million Employees: 110,000
Symbol: ITT Exchange: NYSE
Industry: Diversified operations - insurance, automotive components

IVAX Corp.
8800 NW 36th St. Ext.
Miami, FL 33178
Phone: 305-590-2200 Fax: 305-590-2252
CEO: Phillip Frost
CFO: Frederick E. Baxter
1991 Sales: $182 million Employees: 1,471
Symbol: IVX Exchange: AMEX
Industry: Medical products - pharmaceuticals & test kits; specialty chemicals

IVT Limited
315 Walt Whitman Rd.
Huntington Station, NY 11746
Phone: 516-385-8811 Fax: 516-385-8815
CEO: Leo Wasserman
CFO: Leo Wasserman
1991 Sales: $2.7 million Employees: 4
Ownership: Privately held
Industry: Business services - consulting & financial research services

IWC Resources Corp.
1220 Waterway Blvd.
Indianapolis, IN 46206
Phone: 317-639-1501 Fax: —
CEO: James T. Morris
CFO: Michael G. Hinkle
1991 Sales: $60 million Employees: 392
Symbol: IWCR Exchange: NASDAQ
Industry: Utility - water supply

J and M Laboratories
23 J and M Overlook
Dawsonville, GA 30534
Phone: 706-216-1520 Fax: 706-216-1517
CEO: Martin Allen
CFO: John T. Fetcko
1991 Sales: $3 million Employees: 50
Ownership: Privately held
Industry: Machinery - general industrial

J.B. Dollar-Stretcher Magazine
3105 Farnham Rd.
Richfield, OH 44286
Phone: 216-659-3590 Fax: 216-659-6741
CEO: Robert Minchak
CFO: Robert Minchak
1991 Sales: $1.6 million Employees: 7
Ownership: Privately held
Industry: Publishing - advertising coupon magazine

J.B. Hunt Transport Services, Inc.
PO Box 130
Lowell, AR 72745
Phone: 501-820-0000 Fax: 501-820-8395Attn: Mrs. Hunt
CEO: Kirk Thompson
CFO: Jerry W. Walton
1992 Sales: $912 million Employees: 9,445
Symbol: JBHT Exchange: NASDAQ
Industry: Transportation - truck

J. Baker, Inc.
65 Sprague St.
Readville, MA 02137
Phone: 617-364-3000 Fax: 617-361-8694
CEO: Jerry M. Socol
CFO: Alan I. Weinstein
1991 Sales: $494 million Employees: 6,080
Symbol: JBAK Exchange: NASDAQ
Industry: Retail - apparel & shoes

J. C. Penney Co., Inc.
14841 N. Dallas Pkwy.
Dallas, TX 75240
Phone: 214-591-1000 Fax: 214-591-1315
CEO: William R. Howell
CFO: Robert E. Northam
1992 Sales: $18,383 million Employees: 185,000
Symbol: JCP Exchange: NYSE
Industry: Retail - major department stores, catalog stores & drug stores

J & J Snack Foods Corp.
6000 Central Hwy.
Pennsauken, NJ 08109
Phone: 609-665-9533 Fax: 609-665-6359
CEO: Gerald B. Shreiber
CFO: Arnold J. Goldstein
1991 Sales: $110 million Employees: 1,000
Symbol: JJSF Exchange: NASDAQ
Industry: Food - snack foods & baked goods; beverages

J.L. Honigberg & Associates
310 N. Peoria St.
Chicago, IL 60607
Phone: 312-243-6633 Fax: 312-243-6611
CEO: Janice Honigberg
CFO: Janice Honigberg
1991 Sales: $6.5 million Employees: 14
Ownership: Privately held
Industry: Food - specialty fruits & vegetables importing

J. M. Huber Corporation
333 Thornall St.
Edison, NJ 08818
Phone: 908-549-8600 Fax: 908-549-2239
CEO: George Schenk
CFO: James Ryan
1992 Sales: $1,100 million Employees: 6,000
Ownership: Privately held
Industry: Diversified operations - natural resources, plastics, electronics, ink

J.M. Peters Co., Inc.
3501 Jamboree Rd., Ste. 200
Newport Beach, CA 92660
Phone: 714-854-2500 Fax: 714-854-0514
CEO: Hadi Makarechian
CFO: Gregory R. Petersen
1992 Sales: $185 million Employees: 75
Symbol: JMP Exchange: AMEX
Industry: Building - residential & commercial

J. M. Smucker Co.
Strawberry Lane
Orrville, OH 44667
Phone: 216-682-3000 Fax: 216-684-3370
CEO: Paul H. Smucker
CFO: Richard K. Smucker
1992 Sales: $484 million Employees: 1,900
Symbol: SJMA Exchange: NYSE
Industry: Food - confectionery

J. P. Morgan & Co. Inc.
60 Wall St.
New York, NY 10260
Phone: 212-483-2323 Fax: 212-235-4945
CEO: Dennis Weatherstone
CFO: James T. Flynn
1992 Sales: $10,231 million Employees: 13,323
Symbol: JPM Exchange: NYSE
Industry: Banks - money center

J. W. Mays, Inc.
9 Bond St.
Brooklyn, NY 11201
Phone: 718-624-7400 Fax: —
CEO: Max L. Shulman
CFO: Alex Slobodin
1991 Sales: $8.2 million Employees: 40
Symbol: MAYS Exchange: NASDAQ
Industry: Retail - regional department stores

Jack Eckerd Corporation
8333 Bryan Dairy Rd.
Largo, FL 34647
Phone: 813-397-7461 Fax: 813-398-8369
CEO: Stewart Turley
CFO: John W. Boyle
1992 Sales: $3,657 million Employees: 39,800
Ownership: Privately held
Industry: Retail - drug stores, optical & photo stores

Jack Henry & Associates, Inc.
West Hwy. 60
Monett, MO 65708
Phone: 417-235-6652 Fax: 417-235-8406
CEO: Jerry D. Hall
CFO: Terry W. Thompson
1992 Sales: $24 million Employees: 121
Symbol: JKHY Exchange: NASDAQ
Industry: Computers - software

Jackpot Enterprises, Inc.
2900 S. Highland Dr.
Las Vegas, NV 89109
Phone: 702-369-3424 Fax: 702-369-8733
CEO: Neil Rosenstein
CFO: Frederick Sandvick
1991 Sales: $55 million Employees: 700
Symbol: J Exchange: NYSE
Industry: Gaming machines & casinos

Jackson Hewitt Tax Service
2217 Commerce Pkwy.
Virginia Beach, VA 23454
Phone: 804-463-3300 Fax: 804-463-8612
CEO: John Hewitt
CFO: Chris Drake
1991 Sales: $12 million Employees: 130
Ownership: Privately held
Industry: Business services - income tax preparation franchiser

Jaclyn, Inc.
635 59th St.
West New York, NJ 07093
Phone: 201-868-9400 Fax: 201-854-7202
CEO: Robert Chestnov
CFO: Murray Richman
1991 Sales: $55 million Employees: 470
Symbol: JLN Exchange: AMEX
Industry: Shoes & related apparel

Jaco Electronics, Inc.
145 Oser Ave.
Hauppauge, NY 11788
Phone: 516-273-5500 Fax: 516-273-5528
CEO: Joel H. Girsky
CFO: Jeffrey D. Gash
1992 Sales: $77 million Employees: 228
Symbol: JACO Exchange: NASDAQ
Industry: Electronics - parts distribution

Jacobs Engineering Group Inc.
251 S. Lake Ave.
Pasadena, CA 91101
Phone: 818-449-2171 Fax: 818-578-6893
CEO: Joseph J. Jacobs
CFO: John W. Prosser, Jr.
1992 Sales: $1,138 million Employees: 10,750
Symbol: JEC Exchange: NYSE
Industry: Construction - heavy

A indicates company is in *Hoover's Handbook of American Business.*

W indicates company is in *Hoover's Handbook of World Business*; sales and employee numbers are for parent company.

Jacobson Stores Inc.
3333 Sargent Rd.
Jackson, MI 49201
Phone: 517-764-6400 Fax: 517-764-6427
CEO: J. R. Fowler
CFO: Paul W. Gilbert
1991 Sales: $402 million Employees: 6,600
Symbol: JCBS Exchange: NASDAQ
Industry: Retail - regional department stores

James River Corporation
120 Tredegar St.
Richmond, VA 23219
Phone: 804-644-5411 Fax: 804-649-4428
CEO: Robert C. Williams
CFO: Stephen E. Hare
1992 Sales: $4,728 million Employees: 39,000
Symbol: JR Exchange: NYSE
Industry: Paper & paper products & consumer products

Jamesway Corp.
40 Hartz Way
Secaucus, NJ 07096
Phone: 201-330-6000 Fax: 201-330-6206
CEO: Herbert Fisher
CFO: Kevin Regan
1992 Sales: $862 million Employees: 7,900
Symbol: JMY Exchange: NYSE
Industry: Retail - discount & variety

Jan Bell Marketing, Inc.
13801 NW 14th St.
Sunrise, FL 33323
Phone: 305-846-8000 Fax: 305-846-2887
CEO: Alan H. Lipton
CFO: Rosemary B. Trudeau
1991 Sales: $224 million Employees: 625
Symbol: JBM Exchange: AMEX
Industry: Precious metals & jewelry

Japan Airlines Company, Ltd.
655 Fifth Ave.
New York, NY 10022
Phone: 212-310-1221 Fax: 212-310-1230
CEO: Susumu Ashino
CFO: —
1992 Sales: $11,048 million Employees: 21,451
Parent: Japan Airlines Company, Ltd.
Industry: Transportation - airline

Jason Inc.
411 E. Wisconsin Ave.
Milwaukee, WI 53202
Phone: 414-277-9300 Fax: 414-277-9445
CEO: Vincent L. Martin
CFO: Mark Train
1991 Sales: $161 million Employees: 1,698
Symbol: JASN Exchange: NASDAQ
Industry: Automotive & trucking - original equipment

Jay Jacobs, Inc.
1530 Fifth Ave.
Seattle, WA 98101
Phone: 206-622-5400 Fax: 206-621-9830
CEO: J. Jay Jacobs
CFO: Craig Bohman
1992 Sales: $146 million Employees: 1,990
Symbol: JAYJ Exchange: NASDAQ
Industry: Retail - apparel & shoes

JB's Restaurants, Inc.
1010 West 2610 South
Salt Lake City, UT 84119
Phone: 801-974-4300 Fax: 801-974-4395
CEO: Fred P. Gonzales
CFO: David E. Pertl
1991 Sales: $127 million Employees: 5,800
Symbol: JBBB Exchange: NASDAQ
Industry: Retail - food & restaurants

Jean Philippe Fragrances, Inc.
551 Fifth Ave., Ste. 1500
New York, NY 10176
Phone: 212-983-2640 Fax: 212-983-4197
CEO: Jean Madar
CFO: Philippe Benacin
1991 Sales: $26 million Employees: 55
Symbol: JEAN Exchange: NASDAQ
Industry: Cosmetics & toiletries

Jefferies Group, Inc.
55 W. Monroe St., Ste. 4000
Chicago, IL 60603
Phone: 312-750-4400 Fax: 312-750-4790
CEO: Frank E. Baxter
CFO: Alan D. Browning
1991 Sales: $196 million Employees: 467
Symbol: JEFG Exchange: NASDAQ
Industry: Financial - investment bankers

Jefferson Bank
250 S. 18th St.
Philadelphia, PA
Phone: 215-564-5040 Fax: —
CEO: Betsy Z. Cohen
CFO: Paul Frenkiel
1992 Sales: — Employees: —
Symbol: JFFN Exchange: NASDAQ
Industry: Banks - Northeast

Jefferson Bankshares, Inc.
123 E. Main St.
Charlottesville, VA 22901
Phone: 804-972-1100 Fax: —
CEO: Hovey S. Dabney
CFO: Walter A. Pace, Jr.
1991 Sales: $149 million Employees: 1,000
Symbol: JBNK Exchange: NASDAQ
Industry: Banks - Southeast

Jefferson-Pilot Corp.
100 N. Greene St.
Greensboro, NC 27401
Phone: 919-691-3000 Fax: 919-691-3938
CEO: W. Roger Soles
CFO: Thomas Fee
1992 Sales: $1,202 million Employees: —
Symbol: JP Exchange: NYSE
Industry: Insurance - life

Jelyn Co., Inc./Old Glory
375 Commerce Dr., Ste. B
Ft. Washington, PA 19034
Phone: 215-540-0324 Fax: 215-540-0263
CEO: Jeff Soowal
CFO: Jeff Crago
1991 Sales: $8.8 million Employees: 15
Ownership: Privately held
Industry: Textiles - sweaters

Jennifer Convertibles, Inc.
331 Route 4 West
Paramus, NJ 07652
Phone: 201-343-1610 Fax: —
CEO: Harley J. Greenfield
CFO: Isabelle Silverman
1991 Sales: $26 million Employees: 78
Symbol: JENN Exchange: NASDAQ
Industry: Retail - sofas & sofabeds

Jenny Craig, Inc.
445 Marine View Ave., Ste. 300
Del Mar, CA 92014
Phone: 619-259-7000 Fax: 619-259-2812
CEO: Sid Craig
CFO: W. James Mallen
1992 Sales: $461 million Employees: 5,370
Symbol: JC Exchange: NYSE
Industry: Retail - weight control

Jetronic Industries, Inc.
4200 Mitchell St.
Philadelphia, PA 19128
Phone: 215-482-7660 Fax: 215-482-3323
CEO: Daniel R. Kursman
CFO: Leonard W. Pietrzak
1990 Sales: $42 million Employees: 294
Symbol: JET Exchange: AMEX
Industry: Diversified operations - energy conversion products, furniture & appliances, electronic equipment

Jewelmasters, Inc.
777 S. Flagler Dr.
West Palm Beach, FL 33401
Phone: 407-655-7260 Fax: 407-659-5976
CEO: Josef J. Barr
CFO: David Natan
1991 Sales: $32 million Employees: 350
Symbol: JEM Exchange: AMEX
Industry: Retail - jewelry stores

JG Industries, Inc.
919 N. Michigan Ave., Ste. 540
Chicago, IL 60611
Phone: 312-787-0022 Fax: 312-421-4565
CEO: William Hellman
CFO: Thomas Pabst
1991 Sales: $207 million Employees: 2,061
Symbol: JGIN Exchange: NASDAQ
Industry: Retail - regional department stores

JHM Mortgage Securities L.P.
8300 Greensboro Dr., Ste. 900
McLean, VA 22102
Phone: 703-883-2900 Fax: —
CEO: Steven P. Gavula
CFO: Arthur F. Trudel
1992 Sales: — Employees: —
Symbol: JHM Exchange: NYSE
Industry: Financial - mortgages & related services

Jim Walter Corp.
4010 Boy Scout Blvd., 1 Metro Ctr.
Tampa, FL 33607
Phone: 813-873-4194 Fax: 813-873-4430
CEO: Dennis M. Ross
CFO: Blair Kreiver
1991 Sales: $543 million Employees: 3,000
Ownership: Privately held
Industry: Building products - retail & wholesale

Jimbo's Jumbos, Inc.
185 Peanut Dr.
Edenton, NC 27932
Phone: 919-482-2193 Fax: 919-482-7857
CEO: J. Tilmon Keel, Jr.
CFO: Charles F. Schwartz
1991 Sales: $70 million Employees: 169
Symbol: PNUT Exchange: NASDAQ
Industry: Food - peanuts

Jitney Jungle Stores of America Inc.
453 N. Mill St.
Jackson, MS 39202
Phone: 601-948-0361 Fax: 601-352-0483
CEO: W. H. Holman, Jr.
CFO: Rodger P. Friou
1991 Sales: $1,046 million Employees: 9,000
Ownership: Privately held
Industry: Retail - supermarkets

JLG Industries, Inc.
JLG Dr.
McConnellsburg, PA 17233
Phone: 717-485-5161 Fax: 717-485-6417
CEO: L. David Black
CFO: Charles H. Diller, Jr.
1991 Sales: $94 million Employees: 1,182
Symbol: JLGI Exchange: NASDAQ
Industry: Machinery - construction & mining

JM Family Enterprises
100 Northwest 12th Ave.
Deerfield Beach, FL 33442
Phone: 305-429-2000 Fax: 305-429-2300
CEO: Patricia Moran
CFO: Casey L. Gunnell
1992 Sales: $2,400 million Employees: 2,300
Ownership: Privately held
Industry: Retail - auto dealership

JMB Realty Corp.
900 N. Michigan Ave.
Chicago, IL 60611
Phone: 312-440-4800 Fax: 312-915-2310
CEO: Neil Bluhm
CFO: Howard Kogen
1991 Sales: $500 million Employees: 17,000
Ownership: Privately held
Industry: Real estate operations

JMR Electronics
19320 Londelius St.
Northridge, CA 91324
Phone: 818-993-4801 Fax: 818-993-9173
CEO: Josef Rabinovitz
CFO: Mirit Rabinovitz
1992 Sales: $18 million Employees: 220
Ownership: Privately held
Industry: Computers - peripheral equipment

Joe Koch Construction
352 Wyndclift Place
Youngstown, OH 44515
Phone: 216-793-2464 Fax: 216-793-6371
CEO: Joe Koch
CFO: Joe Koch
1991 Sales: $5.5 million Employees: 21
Ownership: Privately held
Industry: Construction - single-family homes

John Adams Life Corp.
11845 W. Olympic Blvd.
Los Angeles, CA 90064
Phone: 213-444-5252 Fax: —
CEO: Benjamin A. DeMotto
CFO: Peter Hagopian
1991 Sales: $3.1 million Employees: 14
Symbol: JALC Exchange: NASDAQ
Industry: Insurance - life

John Alden Financial Corp.
7300 Corporate Center Dr.
Miami, FL 33126
Phone: 305-470-3100 Fax: 305-470-3009
CEO: Glendon E. Johnson
CFO: Syed A. Ali
1991 Sales: $1,339 million Employees: 2,540
Ownership: Privately held
Industry: Insurance - life

John B. Sanfilippo & Son, Inc.
2299 Busse Rd.
Elk Grove Village, IL 60007
Phone: 708-593-2300 Fax: 708-593-3085
CEO: Jasper B. Sanfilippo
CFO: Larry D. Ray
1991 Sales: $161 million Employees: 810
Symbol: JBSS Exchange: NASDAQ
Industry: Food - wholesale

John Fluke Mfg. Co., Inc.
6920 Seaway Blvd.
Everett, WA 98203
Phone: 206-347-6100 Fax: 206-356-5116
CEO: George M. Winn
CFO: John R. Smith
1991 Sales: $240 million Employees: 2,214
Symbol: FKM Exchange: AMEX
Industry: Electronics - measuring instruments

John H. Harland Co.
2939 Miller Rd.
Decatur, GA 30035
Phone: 404-981-9460 Fax: 404-593-5200
CEO: Robert R. Woodson
CFO: William M. Dollar
1991 Sales: $379 million Employees: 5,600
Symbol: JH Exchange: NYSE
Industry: Paper - business forms

John Hancock Mutual Life Insurance Co.
PO Box 111
Boston, MA 02117
Phone: 617-572-6000 Fax: 617-572-1899
CEO: Stephen L. Brown
CFO: Thomas E. Moloney
1991 Sales: $10,072 million Employees: 16,500
Ownership: Privately held
Industry: Insurance - life

John Nuveen Co.
333 W. Wacker Dr.
Chicago, IL 60606
Phone: 312-917-7700 Fax: 312-917-8034
CEO: Richard J. Franke
CFO: H. William Stabenow
1991 Sales: $180 million Employees: 518
Symbol: JHC Exchange: NYSE
Industry: Financial - investment management

John Swire & Sons, Inc.
PO Box 140
Milford, DE 19963
Phone: 302-422-7536 Fax: 302-422-6311
CEO: Tim Bridgman
CFO: —
1991 Sales: $4,321 million Employees: 36,300
Parent: Swire Pacific Ltd.
Industry: Transportation - airline

John Wiley & Sons, Inc.
605 Third Ave.
New York, NY 10158
Phone: 212-850-6000 Fax: 212-850-6088
CEO: Charles R. Ellis
CFO: Robert D. Wilder
1992 Sales: $248 million Employees: 1,580
Symbol: WILLA Exchange: NASDAQ
Industry: Publishing - books

Johnson & Co. Wilderness Products, Inc.
125 Broad St.
New York, NY 10004
Phone: 212-574-7000 Fax: 212-574-7676
CEO: Kenneth Johnson
CFO: Kenneth Johnson
1991 Sales: $1 million Employees: 8
Ownership: Privately held
Industry: Wilderness products, leathercare, cold-weather clothing

Johnson Controls, Inc.
5757 N. Green Bay Ave.
Milwaukee, WI 53201
Phone: 414-228-1200 Fax: 414-228-2302
CEO: James H. Keyes
CFO: Stephen A. Roell
1992 Sales: $5,452 million Employees: 42,700
Symbol: JCI Exchange: NYSE
Industry: Diversified operations - controls, automotive products, plastics & batteries

Johnson & Higgins
125 Broad St.
New York, NY 10004
Phone: 212-574-7000 Fax: 212-574-7676
CEO: David A. Olsen
CFO: Joseph D. Roxe
1991 Sales: $933 million Employees: 8,200
Ownership: Privately held
Industry: Business services - risk management consulting, insurance brokerage

Johnson & Johnson
One Johnson & Johnson Plaza
New Brunswick, NJ 08933
Phone: 908-524-0400 Fax: 908-214-0332
CEO: Ralph S. Larsen
CFO: Clark H. Johnson
1992 Sales: $13,753 million Employees: 82,700
Symbol: JNJ Exchange: NYSE
Industry: Medical & dental supplies - consumer products, pharmaceuticals

Johnson Products Co.
8522 S. Lafayette Ave.
Chicago, IL 60620
Phone: 312-483-4100 Fax: 312-962-5741
CEO: Eric G. Johnson
CFO: Thomas P. Polke
1991 Sales: $38 million Employees: 224
Symbol: JPC Exchange: AMEX
Industry: Cosmetics & toiletries

Johnson Publishing Company, Inc.
820 S. Michigan Ave.
Chicago, IL 60605
Phone: 312-322-9200 Fax: 312-322-0918
CEO: John H. Johnson
CFO: Eunice W. Johnson
1991 Sales: $261 million Employees: 2,710
Ownership: Privately held
Industry: Publishing - periodicals; radio broadcasting

Johnson Worldwide Associates, Inc.
222 Main St.
Racine, WI 53403
Phone: 414-631-2100 Fax: 414-631-4426
CEO: Terence S. Malone
CFO: John S. Cahill
1991 Sales: $311 million Employees: 2,043
Symbol: JWAIA Exchange: NASDAQ
Industry: Leisure & recreational products - fishing, camping & marine activities products

Johnston Coca-Cola Bottling Group
600 Krystal Bldg., Ste. 600
Chattanooga, TN 37402
Phone: 615-756-1202 Fax: 615-756-5661
CEO: Summerfield K. Johnston, Jr.
CFO: Philip Sanford
1990 Sales: $1,133 million Employees: 5,000
Ownership: Privately held
Industry: Beverages - soft drinks

Johnston Industries, Inc.
111 W. 40th St., Ste. 2106
New York, NY 10018
Phone: 212-768-3760 Fax: 212-768-3764
CEO: David L. Chandler
CFO: Charles E. Wieser
1992 Sales: $138 million Employees: 1,395
Symbol: JII Exchange: NYSE
Industry: Textiles - mill products

Johnstown Savings Bank, F.S.B.
Market at Main St.
Johnstown, PA 15901
Phone: 814-535-8900 Fax: —
CEO: Patrick J. Coyne
CFO: Walter F. Rusnak
1992 Sales: — Employees: —
Symbol: JSBK Exchange: NASDAQ
Industry: Financial - savings and loans

Jones Apparel Group, Inc.
250 Rittenhouse Circle
Bristol, PA 19007
Phone: 215-785-4000 Fax: 215-785-1795
CEO: Sidney Kimmel
CFO: Wesley R. Card
1991 Sales: $334 million Employees: 850
Symbol: JNY Exchange: NYSE
Industry: Textiles - apparel

indicates company is in *Hoover's Handbook of American Business.*

indicates company is in *Hoover's Handbook of World Business;* sales and employee numbers are for parent company.

Jones Intercable, Inc.
9697 E. Mineral Ave.
Englewood, CO 80112
Phone: 303-792-3111 Fax: 303-790-0533
CEO: Glenn R. Jones
CFO: Kevin P. Coyle
1992 Sales: $131 million Employees: 2,750
Symbol: JOIN Exchange: NASDAQ
Industry: Cable TV

Jones Intercable Investors, L.P.
9697 E. Mineral Ave.
Englewood, CO 80112
Phone: 303-792-3111 Fax: —
CEO: Glenn R. Jones
CFO: Kevin P. Coyle
1991 Sales: $38 million Employees: —
Symbol: JTV Exchange: AMEX
Industry: Cable TV

Jones Medical Industries, Inc.
11604 Lilburn Park Rd.
St. Louis, MO 63146
Phone: 314-432-7557 Fax: 314-432-3785
CEO: Dennis M. Jones
CFO: Judith A. Jones
1991 Sales: $21 million Employees: 145
Symbol: JMED Exchange: NASDAQ
Industry: Drugs

Jones Plumbing Systems, Inc.
6247 Amber Hills Rd.
Birmingham, AL 35210
Phone: 205-956-5511 Fax: —
CEO: Kenneth R. Wells
CFO: Clifford N. Mabie III
1991 Sales: $38 million Employees: 369
Symbol: JPS Exchange: AMEX
Industry: Building products - plumbing & related products

Jordache Enterprises Inc.
226 W. 37th St.
New York, NY 10018
Phone: 212-643-8400 Fax: 212-629-9223
CEO: J. Nakash
CFO: Stephen Tuccillo
1991 Sales: $610 million Employees: 6,250
Ownership: Privately held
Industry: Apparel

Jordan Co.
315 Park Ave. South, 20th Fl.
New York, NY 10010
Phone: 212-460-1915 Fax: 212-477-2461
CEO: John W. Jordan II
CFO: Paul Rodzevik
1991 Sales: $1,500 million Employees: 9,900
Ownership: Privately held
Industry: Diversified operations

Jordan Motors
609 E. Jefferson Blvd.
Mishawaka, IN 46545
Phone: 219-259-1981 Fax: 219-255-0984
CEO: Jordan Kapson
CFO: George Merryman
1992 Sales: $1,240 million Employees: 125
Ownership: Privately held
Industry: Retail - auto dealerships

Joseph E. Seagram & Sons, Inc.
375 Park Ave.
New York, NY 10152
Phone: 212-572-7000 Fax: 212-572-7082
CEO: Edgar Bronfman, Jr.
CFO: —
1991 Sales: 5,278 Employees: 16,800
Parent: The Seagram Company Ltd.
Industry: Beverages - spirits, juices & mixers

Joslyn Corp.
30 S. Wacker Dr., Ste. 2706
Chicago, IL 60606
Phone: 312-454-2900 Fax: 312-454-2930
CEO: Donald B. Hamister
CFO: Lawrence G. Wolski
1991 Sales: $204 million Employees: 1,900
Symbol: JOSL Exchange: NASDAQ
Industry: Electrical products - electrical hardware, protective equipment

Jostens, Inc.
5501 Norman Center Dr.
Minneapolis, MN 55437
Phone: 612-830-3300 Fax: 612-830-0818
CEO: H. William Lurton
CFO: Gerald A. Haugen
1992 Sales: $878 million Employees: 8,000
Symbol: JOS Exchange: NYSE
Industry: Precious metals & jewelry

Joule Inc.
1245 U.S. Route 1 South
Edison, NJ 08837
Phone: 908-494-6500 Fax: —
CEO: Emanuel N. Logothetis
CFO: Bernard G. Clarkin
1991 Sales: $27 million Employees: 770
Symbol: JOL Exchange: AMEX
Industry: Business services - temporary office personnel

Journal Communications
333 W. State St.
Milwaukee, WI 53201
Phone: 414-224-2000 Fax: 414-224-2599
CEO: Robert Kahlor
CFO: Peter P. Jarzembinski
1991 Sales: $466 million Employees: 4,800
Ownership: Privately held
Industry: Publishing - newspapers; broadcasting, printing & telecommunications

Joy Technologies Inc.
301 Grant St.
Pittsburgh, PA 15219
Phone: 412-562-4500 Fax: 412-562-4548
CEO: Marc F. Wray
CFO: James O. Grimshaw
1992 Sales: $609 million Employees: 4,200
Symbol: JOY Exchange: NYSE
Industry: Machinery - general industrial

JP Foodservice
7250 Parkway Dr., Ste. 300
Hanover, MD 21076
Phone: 410-712-6150 Fax: 410-712-4591
CEO: James Miller
CFO: Lew Hay
1991 Sales: $1,015 million Employees: 2,300
Ownership: Privately held
Industry: Food - wholesale

JPS Textile Group Inc.
555 N. Pleasantburg Dr., Ste. 202
Greenville, SC 29607
Phone: 803-271-9919 Fax: 803-271-9939
CEO: Steven Friedman
CFO: David Taylor
1991 Sales: $761 million Employees: 8,000
Ownership: Privately held
Industry: Textiles - carpet, industrial fabrics, apparel, elastics

JR Simplot Co.
999 Main St.
Boise, ID 83702
Phone: 208-336-2110 Fax: 208-389-7515
CEO: Gordon Smith
CFO: L. E. Costello
1991 Sales: $1,600 million Employees: 9,000
Ownership: Privately held
Industry: Diversified operations - food processing, fertilizer & livestock

JRL Systems Inc.
8305 Hwy 71 West
Austin, TX 78735
Phone: 512-288-6750 Fax: 512-288-7676
CEO: Fred Klingensmith
CFO: Jean Richards
1991 Sales: $2.9 million Employees: 18
Ownership: Privately held
Industry: Computers - peripheral equipment

JSB Financial, Inc.
303 Merrick Rd.
Lynbrook, NY 11563
Phone: 516-887-7000 Fax: 516-599-8061
CEO: Park T. Adikes
CFO: Edward P. Henson
1991 Sales: $140 million Employees: 462
Symbol: JSBF Exchange: NASDAQ
Industry: Financial - savings and loans

JTS Enterprises Inc.
4600 Post Oak Pl. Dr.
Houston, TX 77027
Phone: 713-621-6740 Fax: 713-621-2454
CEO: Forrest Henson, Jr.
CFO: Forrest Henson, Jr.
1991 Sales: $19 million Employees: 3
Ownership: Privately held
Industry: Diversified operations - chemical trading & consulting services

Juno Lighting, Inc.
2001 S. Mt. Prospect Rd.
Des Plaines, IL 60018
Phone: 708-827-9880 Fax: 708-827-2925
CEO: Robert S. Fremont
CFO: George J. Bilek
1991 Sales: $80 million Employees: 700
Symbol: JUNO Exchange: NASDAQ
Industry: Building products - lighting fixtures

Jupiter Industries
919 North Michigan Ave.
Chicago, IL 60611
Phone: 312-642-6000 Fax: 312-642-2316
CEO: Edward Ross
CFO: George Murphy
1991 Sales: $501 million Employees: 7,000
Ownership: Privately held
Industry: Diversified operations - real estate, transport services, natural gas & insurance

Jupiter National, Inc.
5454 Wisconsin Ave.
Chevy Chase, MD 20815
Phone: 301-656-0626 Fax: 301-656-4053
CEO: David L. Chandler
CFO: Kurt R. Harrington
1992 Sales: — Employees: —
Symbol: JPI Exchange: AMEX
Industry: Financial - SBIC & commercial

Justin Industries, Inc.
2821 W. 7th St.
Ft. Worth, TX 76107
Phone: 817-336-5125 Fax: 817-390-2477
CEO: John Justin
CFO: Richard J. Savitz
1991 Sales: $368 million Employees: 4,585
Symbol: JSTN Exchange: NASDAQ
Industry: Shoes & related apparel

JWP Inc.
6 International Dr.
Ryebrook, NY 10557
Phone: 914-935-4000 Fax: 914-935-4179
CEO: Andrew T. Dwyer
CFO: Edward F. Kosnik
1991 Sales: $3,594 million Employees: 22,400
Symbol: JWP Exchange: NYSE
Industry: Diversified operations - facility systems, information systems, water supply

indicates company is in *Hoover's Handbook of American Business.*

indicates company is in *Hoover's Handbook of World Business;* sales and employee numbers are for parent company.

K N Energy, Inc.
12055 W. 2nd Place
Lakewood, CO 80215
Phone: 303-989-1740 Fax: —
CEO: Charles W. Battey
CFO: E. Wayne Lundhagen
1991 Sales: $395 million Employees: 1,600
Symbol: KNE Exchange: NYSE
Industry: Utility - gas distribution

K&B
K&B Plaza, Lee Circle
New Orleans, LA 70130
Phone: 504-586-1234 Fax: 504-585-4482
CEO: Sydney J. Besthoff III
CFO: Ronald Dyer
1991 Sales: $490 million Employees: 4,200
Ownership: Privately held
Industry: Retail - drug stores

K-III Communications
745 5th Ave.
New York, NY 10151
Phone: 212-745-0100 Fax: 212-745-0199
CEO: William F. Reilly
CFO: Charles G. McCurdy
1991 Sales: $795 million Employees: 3,473
Ownership: Privately held
Industry: Publishing - periodicals; information services

K-Swiss, Inc.
12300 Montague St.
Pacoima, CA 91331
Phone: 818-897-3433 Fax: —
CEO: Steven Nichols
CFO: George Powlick
1991 Sales: $119 million Employees: 281
Symbol: KSWS Exchange: NASDAQ
Industry: Shoes & related apparel

K-Tron International, Inc.
Routes 55 and 553
Pitman, NJ 08071
Phone: 609-589-0500 Fax: 609-582-8113
CEO: Leo C. Beebe
CFO: Ronald G. Larson
1991 Sales: $80 million Employees: 573
Symbol: KTII Exchange: NASDAQ
Industry: Instruments - control

K-VA-T Food Stores
329 North Main St.
Grundy, VA 24614
Phone: 703-935-4587 Fax: 703-935-4587
CEO: Jack Smith
CFO: Robert Neeley
1991 Sales: $492 million Employees: 4,600
Ownership: Privately held
Industry: Retail - supermarkets

Kahler Hotel
20 SW 2nd Ave.
Rochester, MN 55902
Phone: 507-282-2581 Fax: 507-285-2772
CEO: Harold W. Milner
CFO: Steven R. Stenhaug
1991 Sales: $64 million Employees: 2,450
Symbol: KHLR Exchange: NASDAQ
Industry: Hotels & motels

Kaiser Aluminum Corp.
5847 San Felipe, Ste. 2600
Houston, TX 77057
Phone: 713-267-3777 Fax: 713-267-3710
CEO: John M. Seidl
CFO: John T. La Duc
1992 Sales: $1,909 million Employees: 10,270
Symbol: KLU Exchange: NYSE
Industry: Metals - nonferrous

Kaiser Steel Resources, Inc.
8300 Utica Ave., Ste. 301
Rancho Cucamonga, CA 91730
Phone: 909-944-4155 Fax: 909-994-4158
CEO: Richard E. Stoddard
CFO: Stewart W. Dillingham III
1991 Sales: $7.5 million Employees: 33
Symbol: KSRI Exchange: NASDAQ
Industry: Leasing & rental

Kaman Corp.
Blue Hills Ave.
Bloomfield, CT 06002
Phone: 203-243-8311 Fax: 203-243-6365
CEO: Charles H. Kaman
CFO: Harvey S. Levenson
1992 Sales: $785 million Employees: 5,544
Symbol: KAMNA Exchange: NASDAQ
Industry: Aerospace - aircraft equipment

Kaneb Pipe Line Partners, L.P.
2400 Lakeside Blvd.
Richardson, TX 75082
Phone: 214-699-4000 Fax: —
CEO: Murray R. Biles
CFO: Howard C. Wadsworth
1991 Sales: $39 million Employees: —
Symbol: KPP Exchange: NYSE
Industry: Oil & gas - production & pipeline

Kaneb Services, Inc.
2400 Lakeside Blvd., Ste. 600
Richardson, TX 75082
Phone: 214-699-4000 Fax: 214-699-4025
CEO: John R. Barnes
CFO: Howard C. Wadsworth
1991 Sales: $135 million Employees: 1,722
Symbol: KAB Exchange: NYSE
Industry: Oil & gas - production & pipeline

Kansas City Power & Light Co.
1330 Baltimore Ave.
Kansas City, MO 64105
Phone: 816-556-2200 Fax: 816-556-2446
CEO: A. Drue Jennings
CFO: Bernard J. Beaudoin
1991 Sales: $825 million Employees: 3,282
Symbol: KLT Exchange: NYSE
Industry: Utility - electric power

Kansas City Southern Industries, Inc.
114 W. 11th St.
Kansas City, MO 64105
Phone: 816-556-0303 Fax: 816-556-0297
CEO: Landon H. Rowland
CFO: Donald L. Graf
1992 Sales: $741 million Employees: 5,329
Symbol: KSU Exchange: NYSE
Industry: Transportation - rail

Kash n' Karry Food Stores Inc.
6422 Harney Rd.
Tampa, FL 33610
Phone: 813-621-0200 Fax: 813-621-0293
CEO: Ronald J. Floto
CFO: Ray Springer
1991 Sales: $1,071 million Employees: 4,500
Ownership: Privately held
Industry: Retail - supermarkets

Kasler Corp.
27400 E. Fifth St.
Highland, CA 92346
Phone: 909-884-4811 Fax: 909-862-8433
CEO: E. Robert Ferguson
CFO: W. John Cash
1991 Sales: $195 million Employees: 569
Symbol: KAS Exchange: NYSE
Industry: Construction - heavy

Katy Industries, Inc.
853 Dundee Ave.
Elgin, IL 60120
Phone: 708-697-8900 Fax: 312-379-1130
CEO: Jacob Saliba
CFO: William H. Murphy
1991 Sales: $182 million Employees: 2,078
Symbol: KT Exchange: NYSE
Industry: Diversified operations - industrial machinery, industrial components

Kaufman and Broad Home Corp.
10877 Wilshire Blvd., 12th Fl.
Los Angeles, CA 90024
Phone: 213-443-8000 Fax: 213-443-8089
CEO: Bruce E. Karatz
CFO: R. Chad Dreier
1992 Sales: $1,094 million Employees: 820
Symbol: KBH Exchange: NYSE
Industry: Building - residential & commercial

Kaydon Corp.
19329 U.S. 19 North, Ste. 101
Clearwater, FL 34624
Phone: 813-531-1101 Fax: 813-530-9247
CEO: Lawrence J. Cawley
CFO: Lawrence J. Cawley
1991 Sales: $161 million Employees: 1,441
Symbol: KDON Exchange: NASDAQ
Industry: Metal processing & fabrication

KCS Group Inc.
379 Thornall St.
Edison, NJ 08837
Phone: 908-632-1770 Fax: 908-603-8960
CEO: James W. Christmas
CFO: Henry A. Jurand
1991 Sales: $99 million Employees: 69
Symbol: KCSE Exchange: NASDAQ
Industry: Oil & gas - production & pipeline

Keane, Inc.
Ten City Square
Boston, MA 02129
Phone: 617-241-9200 Fax: 617-241-9507
CEO: John F. Keane
CFO: Wallace A. Cataldo
1991 Sales: $96 million Employees: 1,386
Symbol: KEA Exchange: AMEX
Industry: Computers - services

Keene Corp.
200 Park Ave.
New York, NY 10166
Phone: 212-557-1900 Fax: 212-972-3959
CEO: Glenn W. Bailey
CFO: Timothy E. Coyne
1991 Sales: $9.6 million Employees: 89
Symbol: KEEN Exchange: NASDAQ
Industry: Aerospace - materials

Keithley Instruments, Inc.
28775 Aurora Rd.
Solon, OH 44139
Phone: 216-248-0400 Fax: 216-248-6168
CEO: Thomas G. Brick
CFO: Ronald M. Rebner
1991 Sales: $100 million Employees: 716
Symbol: KEI Exchange: AMEX
Industry: Instruments - scientific

Kelley Oil Corp.
601 Jefferson St., Ste. 1100
Houston, TX 77002
Phone: 713-652-5200 Fax: —
CEO: David L. Kelley
CFO: W. Matt Ralls
1991 Sales: $56 million Employees: 123
Symbol: KOIL Exchange: NASDAQ
Industry: Oil & gas - US exploration & production

indicates company is in *Hoover's Handbook of American Business.*
indicates company is in *Hoover's Handbook of World Business;* sales and employee numbers are for parent company.

Kelley Oil & Gas Partners, Ltd.
601 Jefferson St., Ste. 1100
Houston, TX 77002
Phone: 713-652-5200 Fax: —
CEO: David L. Kelley
CFO: W. Matt Ralls
1991 Sales: $34 million Employees: —
Symbol: KLY Exchange: AMEX
Industry: Oil & gas - US exploration & production

Kellogg Co.
One Kellogg Square
Battle Creek, MI 49016
Phone: 616-961-2000 Fax: 616-961-2871
CEO: Arnold G. Langbo
CFO: Charles W. Elliott
1992 Sales: $6,191 million Employees: 17,017
Symbol: K Exchange: NYSE
Industry: Food - cereals, baked goods, beverages

Kellwood Co.
600 Kellwood Pkwy.
St. Louis, MO 63017
Phone: 314-576-3100 Fax: 314-576-3180
CEO: William J. McKenna
CFO: James C. Jacobsen
1992 Sales: $988 million Employees: 15,750
Symbol: KWD Exchange: NYSE
Industry: Textiles - apparel

Kelly Services, Inc.
999 W. Big Beaver Rd.
Troy, MI 48084
Phone: 313-362-4444 Fax: 313-362-2258
CEO: Terence E. Adderley
CFO: Robert F. Stoner
1992 Sales: $1,723 million Employees: 553,900
Symbol: KELYA Exchange: NASDAQ
Industry: Business services - temporary personnel services

Kemper Corp.
One Kemper Dr.
Long Grove, IL 60049
Phone: 708-540-2000 Fax: 708-540-2494
CEO: David B. Mathis
CFO: John H. Fitzpatrick
1992 Sales: $2,201 million Employees: 9,150
Symbol: KEM Exchange: NYSE
Industry: Insurance - multiline; reinsurance, asset management, securities brokerage

Kenan Transport Co.
143 W. Franklin St., University Square West
Chapel Hill, NC 27515
Phone: 919-967-8221 Fax: 919-929-5295
CEO: Frank H. Kenan
CFO: William L. Boone
1991 Sales: $49 million Employees: 700
Symbol: KTCO Exchange: NASDAQ
Industry: Transportation - truck

Kendall Co.
15 Hampshire St.
Mansfield, MA 02048
Phone: 508-261-8000 Fax: 508-261-8102
CEO: Richard A. Gilleland
CFO: G. Khan
1991 Sales: $720 million Employees: 9,000
Ownership: Privately held
Industry: Medical products - healthcare products

Kendall Square Research Corp.
170 Tracer Lane
Waltham, MA 02154
Phone: 617-895-9400 Fax: —
CEO: Henry Burkhardt III
CFO: Karl G. Wassman III
1991 Sales: $0.9 million Employees: 152
Symbol: KSRC Exchange: NASDAQ
Industry: Computers - software

Kendall-Jackson Winery
4825 Old Redwood Hwy.
Santa Rosa, CA 95403
Phone: 707-544-4000 Fax: 707-544-4013
CEO: Mike Haarstad
CFO: Pete Scott
1992 Sales: — Employees: —
Ownership: Privately held
Industry: Beverages - wine

Kenley Corp
5125 Enterprise Dr.
Mason, OH 45040
Phone: 513-459-9000 Fax: 513-459-1955
CEO: Joe Beck
CFO: Ellen Hewitt
1991 Sales: $2.6 million Employees: 6
Ownership: Privately held
Industry: Leisure & recreational products

Kennametal Inc.
Rt. 981 South
Latrobe, PA 15650
Phone: 412-539-5000 Fax: 412-539-4629
CEO: Robert L. McGeehan
CFO: Henry L. Dykema
1992 Sales: $594 million Employees: 4,980
Symbol: KMT Exchange: NYSE
Industry: Machine tools & related products

Kennecott Corporation
PO Box 11248
Salt Lake City, UT 84147
Phone: 801-322-7000 Fax: 801-322-8181
CEO: G.F. Joklik
CFO: —
1991 Sales: $9,135 million Employees: 73,495
Parent: The RTZ Corporation PLC
Industry: Mining - metals and industrial minerals

Kennedy-Wilson, Inc.
2950 31st St.
Santa Monica, CA 90405
Phone: 310-314-8400 Fax: —
CEO: William J. McMorrow
CFO: William M. McKay
1991 Sales: $20 million Employees: 330
Symbol: KWIC Exchange: NASDAQ
Industry: Real estate operations

Kent Electronics Corp.
5600 Bonhomme Rd.
Houston, TX 77036
Phone: 713-780-7770 Fax: 713-978-5890
CEO: Morrie K. Abramson
CFO: Clarence J. Metzger
1992 Sales: $95 million Employees: 612
Symbol: KNT Exchange: NYSE
Industry: Electrical components - wire, cable & electronic connectors & components

Kentucky Central Life Insurance Co.
Kincaid Towers
Lexington, KY 40507
Phone: 606-253-5111 Fax: —
CEO: W. E. Burnett, Jr.
CFO: Wendell L. Gunn
1991 Sales: $301 million Employees: 875
Symbol: KENCA Exchange: NASDAQ
Industry: Insurance - life

Kentucky Medical Insurance Co.
303 N. Hurstbourne Pkwy.
Louisville, KY 40222
Phone: 502-339-5700 Fax: 502-339-5757
CEO: Steven L. Salman
CFO: S. Randolph Scheen, Jr.
1991 Sales: $20 million Employees: 48
Symbol: KYMDA Exchange: NASDAQ
Industry: Insurance - accident & health

Kenwin Shops, Inc.
4747 Granite Dr.
Tucker, GA 30084
Phone: 404-938-0451 Fax: —
CEO: Robert Schwartz
CFO: Kenneth Silberstein
1991 Sales: $30 million Employees: 465
Symbol: KWN Exchange: AMEX
Industry: Retail - apparel & shoes

Keptel Inco
56 Park Rd.
Tinton Falls, NJ 07724
Phone: 908-389-8800 Fax: 908-389-4595
CEO: Richard K. Laird
CFO: Mark J. Scagliuso
1991 Sales: $48 million Employees: 176
Symbol: KPTL Exchange: NASDAQ
Industry: Telecommunications equipment

Kerr Group, Inc.
1840 Century Park East, Ste. 500
Los Angeles, CA 90067
Phone: 310-556-2200 Fax: 310-201-5943
CEO: Roger W. Norian
CFO: D. Gordon Strickland
1991 Sales: $145 million Employees: 1,200
Symbol: KGM Exchange: NYSE
Industry: Glass products

Kerr-McGee Ctr.
123 Robert S. Kerr Ave., Kerr-McGee Ctr.
Oklahoma City, OK 73102
Phone: 405-270-1313 Fax: 405-270-3132
CEO: Frank A. McPherson
CFO: John C. Linehan
1992 Sales: $3,382 million Employees: 6,072
Symbol: KMG Exchange: NYSE
Industry: Oil & gas - US integrated

Ketema Aerospace & Electronics
2233 State Rd.
Bensalem, PA 19020
Phone: 215-639-2255 Fax: 215-639-1533
CEO: Hugh H. Williamson III
CFO: Otto W. Richards
1992 Sales: $168 million Employees: 1,600
Symbol: KTM Exchange: AMEX
Industry: Machinery - general industrial

Kevlin Corp.
5 Cornell Place
Wilmington, MA 01887
Phone: 508-657-3900 Fax: 508-658-5170
CEO: Arthur C. Williams
CFO: Arthur C. Williams
1992 Sales: $11 million Employees: 93
Symbol: KVLM Exchange: NASDAQ
Industry: Telecommunications equipment

Kewaunee Scientific Corp.
1144 Wilmette Ave.
Wilmette, IL 60091
Phone: 708-251-7100 Fax: —
CEO: Eli Manchester, Jr.
CFO: James J. Habschmidt
1992 Sales: $75 million Employees: 747
Symbol: KEQU Exchange: NASDAQ
Industry: Furniture

Key Centurion Bancshares, Inc.
PO Box 1113
Charleston, WV 25324
Phone: 304-526-4336 Fax: 304-526-4318
CEO: A. Michael Perry
CFO: Edsel R. Burns
1991 Sales: $276 million Employees: 1,600
Symbol: KEYC Exchange: NASDAQ
Industry: Banks - Southeast

Key Construction
741 W. 2nd St.
Wichita, KS 67203
Phone: 316-263-3515 Fax: 316-263-1161
CEO: Ken Wells
CFO: May Porter
1991 Sales: $12 million Employees: 50
Ownership: Privately held
Industry: Construction - general contracting

Key Production Co.
1700 Lincoln St., Ste. 1900
Denver, CO 80203
Phone: 303-837-5000 Fax: —
CEO: Raymond Plank
CFO: Wayne W. Murdy
1991 Sales: $23 million Employees: —
Symbol: KPCI Exchange: NASDAQ
Industry: Oil & gas - US exploration & production

Key Tronic Corp.
N. 4424 Sullivan Rd.
Spokane, WA 99216
Phone: 509-928-8000 Fax: 509-927-5248
CEO: Wendell J. Satre
CFO: Steven P. Benner
1991 Sales: $141 million Employees: 2,241
Symbol: KTCC Exchange: NASDAQ
Industry: Computers - keyboards & input devices

KeyCorp, Inc.
One KeyCorp Plaza, 30 S. Pearl St.
Albany, NY 12207
Phone: 518-486-8000 Fax: 518-486-8221
CEO: Victor J. Riley, Jr.
CFO: William H. Dougherty
1992 Sales: $2,239 million Employees: 13,000
Symbol: KEY Exchange: NYSE
Industry: Banks - Northeast

Keypoint Technology
21087 Commerce Point Dr.
Walnut, CA 91789
Phone: 714-468-5555 Fax: 714-468-5561
CEO: Iris So
CFO: Iris So
1991 Sales: $60 million Employees: 54
Ownership: Privately held
Industry: Computers - peripheral equipment

Keystone Consolidated Industries, Inc.
5430 LBJ Fwy., Ste. 1440
Dallas, TX 75240
Phone: 214-458-0028 Fax: 214-458-8108
CEO: Glenn R. Simmons
CFO: Harold M. Curdy
1991 Sales: $302 million Employees: 2,000
Symbol: KES Exchange: NYSE
Industry: Wire & cable products

Keystone Financial, Inc.
The 225 Market Bldg.
Harrisburg, PA 17105
Phone: 717-233-1555 Fax: —
CEO: Carl L. Campbell
CFO: Mark L. Pulaski
1991 Sales: $267 million Employees: 1,666
Symbol: KSTN Exchange: NASDAQ
Industry: Banks - Northeast

Keystone Heritage Group, Inc.
555 Willow St.
Lebanon, PA 17042
Phone: 717-274-6800 Fax: —
CEO: Albert B. Murry
CFO: Kurt A. Phillips
1991 Sales: $53 million Employees: 302
Symbol: KHGI Exchange: NASDAQ
Industry: Banks - Northeast

Keystone International, Inc.
9600 West Gulf Bank Dr.
Houston, TX 77040
Phone: 713-466-1176 Fax: 713-937-5406
CEO: Raymond A. LeBlanc
CFO: Mark E. Baldwin
1991 Sales: $520 million Employees: 4,100
Symbol: KII Exchange: NYSE
Industry: Instruments - control

Killearn Properties, Inc.
7118 Beech Ridge Trail
Tallahassee, FL 32312
Phone: 904-893-2111 Fax: 904-893-3730
CEO: J. T. Williams, Jr.
CFO: Juanice M. Hagan
1992 Sales: $18 million Employees: 235
Symbol: KPI Exchange: AMEX
Industry: Real estate development

Kimball International, Inc.
1600 Royal St.
Jasper, IN 47549
Phone: 812-482-1600 Fax: 812-482-8012
CEO: Thomas L. Habig
CFO: James C. Thyen
1992 Sales: $678 million Employees: 7,641
Symbol: KBALB Exchange: NASDAQ
Industry: Furniture

Kimberly-Clark Corp.
545 E. John W. Carpenter Fwy., Ste. 1300
Irving, TX 75062
Phone: 214-830-1200 Fax: 214-830-1289
CEO: Wayne R. Sanders
CFO: Brendan M. O'Neill
1992 Sales: $7,091 million Employees: 41,286
Symbol: KMB Exchange: NYSE
Industry: Paper & paper products - tissue, diapers, towels, napkins

Kimco Development Corp.
1044 Northern Blvd.
Roslyn, NY 11576
Phone: 516-484-5858 Fax: 516-484-5637
CEO: David M. Samber
CFO: Louis J. Petra
1992 Sales: — Employees: 120
Symbol: KIM Exchange: NYSE
Industry: Real estate operations

Kimmins Environmental Service Corp.
1501 E 2nd Ave.
Tampa, FL 33605
Phone: 813-248-3878 Fax: 813-247-0180
CEO: Francis M. Williams
CFO: John R. Hindman
1991 Sales: $101 million Employees: 720
Symbol: KVN Exchange: NYSE
Industry: Asbestos abatement, solid waste management, environmental contracting services

Kinark Corp.
7060 S. Yale Ave., Ste. 603
Tulsa, OK 74136
Phone: 918-494-0964 Fax: 918-494-3999
CEO: Paul R. Chastain
CFO: J. Bruce Lancaster
1991 Sales: $34 million Employees: 359
Symbol: KIN Exchange: AMEX
Industry: Chemicals - specialty

Kinder-Care Learning Centers, Inc.
2400 Presidents Dr.
Montgomery, AL 36116
Phone: 205-277-5090 Fax: 205-271-1717
CEO: Tull N. Gearreald, Jr.
CFO: Tull N. Gearreald, Jr.
1991 Sales: $411 million Employees: 20,500
Symbol: KINDC Exchange: NASDAQ
Industry: Schools - daycare

Kinetic Concepts, Inc.
3440 E. Houston St.
San Antonio, TX 78219
Phone: 210-225-4092 Fax: 210-554-1727
CEO: James R. Leininger
CFO: Howard W. Deichen
1991 Sales: $249 million Employees: 2,200
Symbol: KNCI Exchange: NASDAQ
Industry: Medical products - therapeutic beds

King Kullen Grocery Co., Inc.
1194 Prospect Ave.
Westbury, NY 11590
Phone: 516-333-7100 Fax: 516-333-7929
CEO: John B. Cullen
CFO: J. Donald Kennedy
1991 Sales: $720 million Employees: 5,000
Ownership: Privately held
Industry: Retail - supermarkets

King Ranch, Inc.
Two Greenspoint Plaza, 16825 Northchase, Ste. 1450
Houston, TX 77060
Phone: 713-872-5566 Fax: 713-872-7209
CEO: Roger L. Jarvis
CFO: Mark Kent
1992 Sales: — Employees: 700
Ownership: Privately held
Industry: Agricultural operations

King World Productions, Inc.
830 Morris Tnpk.
Short Hills, NJ 07078
Phone: 201-376-1313 Fax: 201-376-7674
CEO: Michael King
CFO: Jeffrey E. Epstein
1992 Sales: $474 million Employees: 474
Symbol: KWP Exchange: NYSE
Industry: Broadcasting - first-run syndicated programs, TV station, advertising

Kings Road Entertainment, Inc.
1901 Avenue of the Stars, Ste. 605
Los Angeles, CA 90067
Phone: 213-552-0057 Fax: 213-277-4468
CEO: Stephen J. Friedman
CFO: Suzanne Jealous
1992 Sales: $20 million Employees: 10
Symbol: KREN Exchange: NASDAQ
Industry: Motion pictures & services

Kingston Technology Corp.
17600 Newhope St.
Fountain Valley, CA 92708
Phone: 714-435-2600 Fax: 714-434-2699
CEO: John Tu
CFO: Albert Kong
1992 Sales: $251 million Employees: 183
Ownership: Privately held
Industry: Computers - peripheral equipment

Kinnard Investments, Inc.
110 S. 7th St., Ste. 1700
Minneapolis, MN 55402
Phone: 612-370-2700 Fax: 612-370-2725
CEO: Robert R. Martin
CFO: Gerald M. Gifford
1991 Sales: $43 million Employees: 389
Symbol: KINN Exchange: NASDAQ
Industry: Financial - business services

Kirby Corp.
1775 St. James Place, Ste. 300
Houston, TX 77056
Phone: 713-629-9370 Fax: 713-964-2200
CEO: George A. Peterkin, Jr.
CFO: Brian K. Harrington
1991 Sales: $187 million Employees: 1,450
Symbol: KEX Exchange: AMEX
Industry: Diversified operations - petrochemical transport, diesel repair, insurance

indicates company is in *Hoover's Handbook of American Business.*

indicates company is in *Hoover's Handbook of World Business;* sales and employee numbers are for parent company.

Kirin USA, Inc.
600 3rd Ave., 21st Fl.
New York, NY 10016
Phone: 212-687-1865 Fax: 212-286-8065
CEO: Kazuyasu Kato
CFO: —
1991 Sales: $6,576 million Employees: 7,856
Parent: Kirin Brewery Company, Ltd.
Industry: Beverages - beer

Kirschner Medical Corp.
9690 Deereco Rd., Ste. 600
Timonium, MD 21093
Phone: 410-560-3333 Fax: 410-560-3376
CEO: Bruce J. Hegstad
CFO: John A. Kravitz
1991 Sales: $71 million Employees: 519
Symbol: KMDC Exchange: NASDAQ
Industry: Medical instruments - orthopedics

KIT Manufacturing Co.
530 E. Wardlow Rd.
Long Beach, CA 90807
Phone: 310-595-7451 Fax: 310-426-8463
CEO: Dan Pocapalia
CFO: Dale J. Gonzalez
1991 Sales: $57 million Employees: 726
Symbol: KIT Exchange: AMEX
Industry: Building - mobile homes & RVs

KLA Instruments Corp.
160 Rio Robles
San Jose, CA 95134
Phone: 408-434-4200 Fax: 408-434-4266
CEO: Kenneth Levy
CFO: Robert J. Boehlke
1992 Sales: $156 million Employees: —
Symbol: KLAC Exchange: NASDAQ
Industry: Optical character recognition

Kleer-Vu Industries, Inc.
14202 Woodforest Blvd.
Houston, TX 77015
Phone: 713-654-7777 Fax: —
CEO: Daniel Dror
CFO: Barry E. Reifler
1991 Sales: $20 million Employees: 246
Symbol: KVU Exchange: AMEX
Industry: Rubber & plastic products

Kleinert's, Inc.
120 W. Germantown Pike, Ste. 100
Plymouth Meeting, PA 19462
Phone: 215-828-7261 Fax: 215-828-4589
CEO: Jack Brier
CFO: Jack Brier
1991 Sales: $62 million Employees: 1,100
Symbol: KLRT Exchange: NASDAQ
Industry: Apparel

KLLM Transport Services, Inc.
3475 Lakeland Dr.
Jackson, MS 39208
Phone: 601-939-2545 Fax: 601-936-7151
CEO: William J. Liles, Jr.
CFO: J. Kirby Lane
1991 Sales: $130 million Employees: 1,682
Symbol: KLLM Exchange: NASDAQ
Industry: Transportation - truck

KLM Royal Dutch Airlines
565 Taxter Rd.
Elmsford, NY 10523
Phone: 914-784-2000 Fax: 914-784-2103
CEO: Toon Woltman
CFO: —
1992 Sales: $4,267 million Employees: 29,075
Parent: KLM Royal Dutch Airlines
Industry: Transportation - airline

Kmart Corp.
3100 W. Big Beaver Rd.
Troy, MI 48084
Phone: 313-643-1000 Fax: 313-643-5249
CEO: Joseph E. Antonini
CFO: Thomas F. Murasky
1992 Sales: $37,200 million Employees: 349,000
Symbol: KM Exchange: NYSE
Industry: Retail - major department stores, book stores; home improvement stores

KMC Enterprises, Inc.
1798 Technology Dr.
San Jose, CA 95110
Phone: 408-453-1800 Fax: —
CEO: Kenneth W. Keegan
CFO: Robert G. Sharpe
1991 Sales: $55 million Employees: 867
Symbol: KMCI Exchange: NASDAQ
Industry: Retail - food & restaurants

KMS Fusion Inc.
700 KMS Place
Ann Arbor, MI 48106
Phone: 313-769-8500 Fax: 313-769-1765
CEO: Patrick B. Long
CFO: Neil W. Hennessey
1991 Sales: $17 million Employees: 50
Symbol: KMSI Exchange: NASDAQ
Industry: Engineering - R&D services

Knape & Vogt Manufacturing Co.
2700 Oak Industrial Dr. NE
Grand Rapids, MI 49505
Phone: 616-459-3311 Fax: 616-459-3290
CEO: Raymond E. Knape
CFO: Richard C. Simkins
1992 Sales: $125 million Employees: 1,083
Symbol: KNAP Exchange: NASDAQ
Industry: Furniture

Knight-Ridder, Inc.
One Herald Plaza, 6th Fl.
Miami, FL 33132
Phone: 305-376-3800 Fax: 305-376-3828
CEO: James K. Batten
CFO: Robert F. Singleton
1992 Sales: $2,330 million Employees: 20,000
Symbol: KRI Exchange: NYSE
Industry: Publishing - newspapers; electronic publishing, financial information database

Knogo Corp.
350 Wireless Blvd.
Hauppauge, NY 11788
Phone: 516-232-2100 Fax: 516-232-2124
CEO: Arthur J. Minasy
CFO: Robert T. Abbott
1992 Sales: $81 million Employees: 789
Symbol: KNO Exchange: NYSE
Industry: Protection - safety equipment & services

Knowledge Products Company, Inc.
102 Fountain Brook Circle
Cary, NC 27511
Phone: 919-481-1020 Fax: 919-481-0469
CEO: Bruce Speicher
CFO: Kevin Fox
1992 Sales: $2 million Employees: 25
Ownership: Privately held
Industry: Business services - employee involvement consulting

KnowledgeWare, Inc.
3340 Peachtree Rd. NE
Atlanta, GA 30326
Phone: 404-231-8575 Fax: 404-364-0883
CEO: Francis A. Tarkenton
CFO: Richard M. Haddrill
1992 Sales: $115 million Employees: 840
Symbol: KNOW Exchange: NASDAQ
Industry: Computers - engineering software

Koch Industries, Inc.
4111 E. 37th St. North
Wichita, KS 67220
Phone: 316-832-5500 Fax: 316-832-5739
CEO: Charles Koch
CFO: F. Lynn Markel
1991 Sales: $19,914 million Employees: 12,000
Ownership: Privately held
Industry: Oil & gas - US integrated, chemicals, minerals & agriculture

Koch International Inc.
177 Cantiague Rock Rd.
Westbury, NY 11590
Phone: 516-938-8047 Fax: 516-938-8055
CEO: Michael Koch
CFO: Michael Rosenberg
1991 Sales: $14 million Employees: 60
Ownership: Privately held
Industry: Prerecorded music

Kofax Image Products
3 Jenner St.
Irvine, CA 92718
Phone: 714-727-1733 Fax: 714-727-3144
CEO: David Silver
CFO: Ron Fikert
1991 Sales: $10.3 million Employees: 96
Ownership: Privately held
Industry: Computers - image processing software & hardware

Koger Properties, Inc.
3986 Boulevard Center Dr.
Jacksonville, FL 32207
Phone: 904-396-4811 Fax: 904-398-3646
CEO: Jack H. Chambers
CFO: John W. Brent
1992 Sales: $72 million Employees: 245
Symbol: KOG Exchange: NYSE
Industry: Real estate development

Kohl's Corp.
N. 54 W. 13600 Woodale Dr.
Menomenee Falls, WI 53051
Phone: 414-783-5800 Fax: 414-783-6501
CEO: William Kellogg
CFO: Jules Allen
1991 Sales: $863 million Employees: 12,900
Symbol: KSS Exchange: NYSE
Industry: Retail - supermarkets

Kohlberg Kravis Roberts & Co.
9 W. 57th St., Ste. 4200
New York, NY 10019
Phone: 212-750-8300 Fax: 212-593-2430
CEO: Henry R. Kravis
CFO: George R. Roberts
1992 Sales: — Employees: —
Ownership: Privately held
Industry: Financial - business services

Kohler Company
444 Highland Dr.
Kohler, WI 53044
Phone: 414-457-4441 Fax: 414-457-1271
CEO: Herbert V. Kohler, Jr.
CFO: Richard A. Wells
1991 Sales: $1,340 million Employees: 13,778
Ownership: Privately held
Industry: Building products - plumbing products, generators & engines, fine furniture

Koll Co.
4343 Von Karman Ave.
Newport Beach, CA 92660
Phone: 714-833-3030 Fax: 714-833-3755
CEO: Donald M. Koll
CFO: James Summerford
1990 Sales: $482 million Employees: 1,100
Ownership: Privately held
Industry: Real estate development

indicates company is in *Hoover's Handbook of American Business.*

indicates company is in *Hoover's Handbook of World Business;* sales and employee numbers are for parent company.

Koll Management Services, Inc.
4343 Von Karman Ave.
Newport Beach, CA 92660
Phone: 714-833-3030 Fax: 714-833-2834
CEO: Ray Wirta
CFO: Lawrence W. Kellner
1992 Sales: $29 million Employees: 623
Symbol: KOLL Exchange: NASDAQ
Industry: Real estate operations

Kollmorgen Corp.
1601 Trapelo Rd., Reservoir Place
Waltham, MA 02154
Phone: 617-890-5655 Fax: 203-658-6947
CEO: Gideon Argov
CFO: Robert J. Cobuzzi
1991 Sales: $200 million Employees: 2,000
Symbol: KOL Exchange: NYSE
Industry: Electrical products - electronic interconnections, motors & controls

Komag, Inc.
275 S. Hillview Dr.
Milpitas, CA 95035
Phone: 408-946-2300 Fax: 408-946-1126
CEO: Stephen C. Johnson
CFO: William L. Potts
1991 Sales: $279 million Employees: 2,637
Symbol: KMAG Exchange: NASDAQ
Industry: Computers - disk drive film

Koor USA Inc.
1270 Avenue of the Americas, Ste. 2307
New York, NY 10020
Phone: 212-765-5050 Fax: 212-765-3375
CEO: Dov Roschman
CFO: —
1991 Sales: $2,402 million Employees: 16,000
Parent: Koor Industries, Ltd.
Industry: Diversified operations - construction, agrochemicals, food & electronics

Kopin Corp.
695 Myles Standish Blvd.
Taunton, MA 02780
Phone: 508-824-6696 Fax: —
CEO: John C. C. Fan
CFO: Paul J. Mitchell
1991 Sales: $6.1 million Employees: 56
Symbol: KOPN Exchange: NASDAQ
Industry: Electrical components

Koss Corp.
4129 N. Port Washington Ave.
Milwaukee, WI 53212
Phone: 414-964-5000 Fax: 414-964-8615
CEO: John C. Koss
CFO: Michael J. Koss
1992 Sales: $26 million Employees: 137
Symbol: KOSS Exchange: NASDAQ
Industry: Audio & video home products

KPMG Peat Marwick
767 Fifth Ave.
New York, NY 10153
Phone: 212-909-5000 Fax: 212-909-5299
CEO: Jon C. Madonna
CFO: —
1991 Sales: $6,011 million Employees: 75,000
Ownership: Privately held
Industry: Business services - accounting & consulting

Kreisler Manufacturing Corp.
5960 Central Ave., Ste. H
St. Petersburg, FL 33707
Phone: 813-347-1144 Fax: —
CEO: Edward L. Stern
CFO: Edward L. Stern
1992 Sales: $6 million Employees: 68
Symbol: KRSL Exchange: NASDAQ
Industry: Aerospace - aircraft equipment

Kroger Co., The
1014 Vine St.
Cincinnati, OH 45202
Phone: 513-762-4000 Fax: 513-762-4454
CEO: Joseph A. Pichler
CFO: William J. Sinkula
1992 Sales: $22,145 million Employees: 170,000
Symbol: KR Exchange: NYSE
Industry: Retail - supermarkets & convenience stores

Krug International Corp.
6 Gem Plaza, Ste. 500
Dayton, OH 45402
Phone: 513-224-9066 Fax: 513-224-3654
CEO: Maurice F. Krug
CFO: Thomas W. Kemp
1992 Sales: $99 million Employees: 945
Symbol: KRUG Exchange: NASDAQ
Industry: Diversified operations - housewares, aerospace, leisure marine equipment

Krystal Co.
One Union Square
Chattanooga, TN 37402
Phone: 615-756-5100 Fax: 615-757-1590
CEO: Carl D. Long
CFO: Camden B. Scearce
1991 Sales: $210 million Employees: 8,370
Symbol: KRYS Exchange: NASDAQ
Industry: Retail - food & restaurants

KU Energy Corp.
One Quality St.
Lexington, KY 40507
Phone: 606-255-2100 Fax: —
CEO: John T. Newton
CFO: Michael R. Whitley
1991 Sales: $588 million Employees: 2,093
Symbol: KU Exchange: NYSE
Industry: Utility - electric power

Kuhlman Corp.
2343 Alexandria Dr., Ste. 200
Lexington, KY 40504
Phone: 606-224-4300 Fax: 606-223-1207
CEO: Donald O. Dulude
CFO: Richard W. Spicka
1991 Sales: $126 million Employees: 889
Symbol: KUH Exchange: NYSE
Industry: Electrical products - transformers

Kulicke and Soffa Industries, Inc.
2101 Blair Mill Rd.
Willow Grove, PA 19090
Phone: 215-784-6000 Fax: 215-659-7588
CEO: C. Scott Kulicke
CFO: Clifford G. Sprague
1991 Sales: $100 million Employees: 1,013
Symbol: KLIC Exchange: NASDAQ
Industry: Electrical components - semiconductors

Kushner-Locke Co.
11601 Wilshire Blvd., 21st Fl.
Los Angeles, CA 90025
Phone: 213-445-1111 Fax: 213-445-1191
CEO: Donald Kushner
CFO: Ann Evans
1991 Sales: $28 million Employees: 32
Symbol: KLOC Exchange: NASDAQ
Industry: TV series, mini-series production & animated programming

KV Pharmaceutical Co.
2503 S. Hanley Rd.
St. Louis, MO 63144
Phone: 314-645-6600 Fax: 314-645-6732
CEO: Marc S. Hermelin
CFO: Gerald R. Mitchell
1992 Sales: $41 million Employees: 357
Symbol: KV Exchange: AMEX
Industry: Drugs

Kyocera International, Inc.
8611 Balboa Ave.
San Diego, CA 92123
Phone: 619-576-2600 Fax: 619-492-1456
CEO: Rodney Lanthorne
CFO: —
1992 Sales: $3,401 million Employees: 14,473
Parent: Kyocera Corporation
Industry: Ceramics & ceramic products

Kysor Industrial Corp.
One Madison Ave.
Cadillac, MI 49601
Phone: 616-779-2200 Fax: 616-775-2661
CEO: George R. Kempton
CFO: Terry M. Murphy
1991 Sales: $224 million Employees: 1,809
Symbol: KZ Exchange: NYSE
Industry: Automotive & trucking - original equipment

L.A. Gear, Inc.
4221 Redwood Ave.
Los Angeles, CA 90066
Phone: 310-822-1995 Fax: 310-822-0843
CEO: Stanley P. Gold
CFO: William L. Benford
1991 Sales: $618 million Employees: 900
Symbol: LA Exchange: NYSE
Industry: Shoes - athletic, casual, fashion & children's

L. B. Foster Co.
415 Holiday Dr.
Pittsburgh, PA 15220
Phone: 412-928-3417 Fax: 412-928-7891
CEO: Lee B. Foster II
CFO: Roger F. Nejes
1991 Sales: $221 million Employees: 524
Symbol: FSTRA Exchange: NASDAQ
Industry: Steel - pipes & tubes

L. E. Myers Co. Group
2550 W. Golf Rd., Ste. 200
Rolling Meadows, IL 60008
Phone: 708-290-1891 Fax: 708-290-1892
CEO: Charles M. Brennan III
CFO: Elliott C. Robbins
1991 Sales: $93 million Employees: 1,199
Symbol: MYR Exchange: NYSE
Industry: Construction - heavy

L.L. Bean Inc.
Casco St.
Freeport, ME 04033
Phone: 207-865-4761 Fax: 207-865-6738
CEO: Leon A. Gorman
CFO: Norman A. Poole
1992 Sales: $700 million Employees: 3,600
Ownership: Privately held
Industry: Retail - mail-order outdoor sporting specialties & clothing

L. Luria & Son, Inc.
5770 Miami Lakes Dr.
Miami, FL 33014
Phone: 305-557-9000 Fax: 305-557-6133
CEO: Leonard Luria
CFO: Wallace D. Ruiz
1991 Sales: $208 million Employees: 2,262
Symbol: LUR Exchange: AMEX
Industry: Retail - catalog showrooms

L. S. Starrett Co.
121 Crescent St.
Athol, MA 01331
Phone: 508-249-3551 Fax: 508-249-8495
CEO: Douglas R. Starrett
CFO: Roger U. Wellington, Jr.
1992 Sales: $180 million Employees: 2,553
Symbol: SCX Exchange: NYSE
Industry: Tools - hand held

indicates company is in *Hoover's Handbook of American Business.*

indicates company is in *Hoover's Handbook of World Business;* sales and employee numbers are for parent company.

La Petite Academy, Inc.
1100 Main St., Ste. 1050
Kansas City, MO 64105
Phone: 816-474-4750 Fax: 816-471-0398
CEO: Robert F. Brozman
CFO: Nora K. Gosney
1991 Sales: $219 million Employees: 11,500
Symbol: LPAI Exchange: NASDAQ
Industry: Schools - childcare & preschools

La Quinta Motor Inns, Inc.
10010 San Pedro Ave.
San Antonio, TX 78216
Phone: 210-366-6000 Fax: 210-366-6109
CEO: Sam Barshop
CFO: Walter J. Biegler
1991 Sales: $242 million Employees: 5,900
Symbol: LQM Exchange: NYSE
Industry: Hotels & motels

La Quinta Motor Inns L.P.
10010 San Pedro Ave.
San Antonio, TX 78216
Phone: 210-366-6030 Fax: —
CEO: Sam Barshop
CFO: Francis P. Bissaillon
1991 Sales: $42 million Employees: —
Symbol: LQP Exchange: NYSE
Industry: Hotels & motels

La-Z-Boy Chair Co.
1284 N. Telegraph Rd.
Monroe, MI 48161
Phone: 313-241-4414 Fax: 313-241-4422
CEO: Charles T. Knabusch
CFO: Frederick H. Jackson
1992 Sales: $640 million Employees: 8,153
Symbol: LZB Exchange: NYSE
Industry: Furniture

LaBarge Electronics, Inc.
707 N. Second St.
St. Louis, MO 63102
Phone: 314-231-5960 Fax: 314-982-9437
CEO: Craig E. LaBarge
CFO: William J. Maender
1992 Sales: $78 million Employees: 1,140
Symbol: LB Exchange: AMEX
Industry: Electronics - military

Labatt's USA
23 Old King's Hwy. South
Darien, CT 06820
Phone: 203-656-1876 Fax: 203-656-0838
CEO: Richard R. Fogarty
CFO: —
1991 Sales: $3,308 million Employees: 11,100
Parent: John Labatt Ltd.
Industry: Beverages - beer; dairy products, entertainment

Label Technology, Inc.
450 Grogan Ave.
Merced, CA 95340
Phone: 209-384-2113 Fax: 209-384-0322
CEO: John Bankson
CFO: John Bankson
1991 Sales: $3.3 million Employees: 30
Ownership: Privately held
Industry: Paper - labels

Laclede Gas Co.
720 Olive St.
St. Louis, MO 63101
Phone: 314-342-0500 Fax: 314-421-1979
CEO: Lee M. Liberman
CFO: Glenn F. Smith
1991 Sales: $438 million Employees: 2,096
Symbol: LG Exchange: NYSE
Industry: Utility - gas distribution

Laclede Steel Co.
One Metropolitan Square
St. Louis, MO 63102
Phone: 314-425-1400 Fax: 314-425-1561
CEO: John B. McKinney
CFO: Michael H. Lane
1991 Sales: $261 million Employees: 1,800
Symbol: LCLD Exchange: NASDAQ
Industry: Steel - specialty alloys

Ladd Furniture, Inc.
One Plaza Center, Box HP-3
High Point, NC 27261
Phone: 919-889-0333 Fax: 919-889-5839
CEO: Richard R. Allen
CFO: Fred L. Schuermann, Jr.
1991 Sales: $429 million Employees: 6,340
Symbol: LADF Exchange: NASDAQ
Industry: Furniture

Lafarge Corp.
11130 Sunrise Valley Dr., Ste. 300
Reston, VA 22091
Phone: 703-264-3600 Fax: 703-264-0634
CEO: Robert W. Murdoch
CFO: Jean-Pierre Cloiseau
1992 Sales: $1,511 million Employees: 8,300
Symbol: LAF Exchange: NYSE
Industry: Construction - cement & concrete

Lafayette American Bancorp, Inc.
2321 Whitney Ave.
Hamden, CT 06518
Phone: 203-287-3545 Fax: —
CEO: Donald P. Calcagnini
CFO: Thomas A. Sebastian
1991 Sales: $79 million Employees: 371
Symbol: LABK Exchange: NASDAQ
Industry: Banks - Northeast

Lai, Venuti & Lai
2880 Lakeside Dr. , Ste. 116
Santa Clara, CA 95054
Phone: 408-982-0445 Fax: 408-982-0560
CEO: Stephen Venuti
CFO: Stephen Venuti
1991 Sales: $2.5 million Employees: 17
Ownership: Privately held
Industry: Advertising

Lake Shore Bancorp., Inc.
605 N. Michigan Ave.
Chicago, IL 60611
Phone: 312-787-1900 Fax: —
CEO: James W. Aldrich
CFO: Sharon Smith Peterson
1991 Sales: $99 million Employees: 436
Symbol: LSNB Exchange: NASDAQ
Industry: Banks - Midwest

Lakehead Pipeline Co., Inc.
119 N. 25th St. East
Superior, WI 54880
Phone: 715-394-1400 Fax: 715-394-1564
CEO: B. F. MacNeill
CFO: D. P. Truswell
1991 Sales: $202 million Employees: —
Symbol: LHP Exchange: NYSE
Industry: Oil & gas - production & pipeline

Lakeland First Financial Group, Inc.
250 Route 10
Succasunna, NJ 07876
Phone: 201-584-6666 Fax: —
CEO: Henry A. Becker
CFO: Harry L. Still, Jr.
1991 Sales: $30 million Employees: 97
Symbol: LLSL Exchange: NASDAQ
Industry: Financial - savings and loans

Lakeland Industries, Inc.
1 Comac Loop
Ronkonkoma, NY 11779
Phone: 516-981-9700 Fax: 516-981-9751
CEO: Raymond J. Smith
CFO: James M. McCormick
1991 Sales: $26 million Employees: 175
Symbol: LAKE Exchange: NASDAQ
Industry: Textiles - apparel

Lam Research Corp.
4650 Cushing Rd.
Fremont, CA 94538
Phone: 510-659-0200 Fax: 510-659-1560
CEO: Roger D. Emerick
CFO: Henk J. Evenhuis
1992 Sales: $171 million Employees: 976
Symbol: LRCX Exchange: NASDAQ
Industry: Electrical components - semiconductors

Lamson & Sessions Co.
25701 Science Park Dr.
Beachwood, OH 44122
Phone: 216-464-3400 Fax: 216-464-1455
CEO: John B. Schulze
CFO: James J. Abel
1991 Sales: $291 million Employees: 1,696
Symbol: LMS Exchange: NYSE
Industry: Rubber & plastic products

Lancaster Colony Corp.
37 W. Broad St., 5th Fl.
Columbus, OH 43215
Phone: 614-224-7141 Fax: 614-469-8219
CEO: John B. Gerlach
CFO: John B. Gerlach
1992 Sales: $600 million Employees: 4,700
Symbol: LANC Exchange: NASDAQ
Industry: Diversified operations - specialty foods, automotive products, glassware & candles

Lance, Inc.
8600 S. Blvd.
Charlotte, NC 28273
Phone: 704-554-1421 Fax: 704-554-5586
CEO: J. William Disher
CFO: Earl D. Leake
1991 Sales: $450 million Employees: 5,916
Symbol: LNCE Exchange: NASDAQ
Industry: Food - snack foods

Lancer Corp.
235 W. Turbo Dr.
San Antonio, TX 78216
Phone: 210-344-3071 Fax: 210-344-8174
CEO: George F. Schroeder
CFO: Dennis D. Stout
1991 Sales: $36 million Employees: 539
Symbol: LAN Exchange: AMEX
Industry: Machinery - material handling

Landauer, Inc.
2 Science Rd.
Glenwood, IL 60425
Phone: 708-755-7000 Fax: 708-755-7016
CEO: Thomas M. Fulton
CFO: James M. O'Connell
1991 Sales: $27 million Employees: 260
Symbol: LDR Exchange: AMEX
Industry: Engineering - R&D services

Landex Construction Corp.
3944 Murphy Canyon Rd. #C207
San Diego, CA 92123
Phone: 619-278-9885 Fax: 619-278-9204
CEO: Louis Ramzi
CFO: Louis Ramzi
1991 Sales: $7 million Employees: 21
Ownership: Privately held
Industry: Construction - commercial & light industrial

indicates company is in *Hoover's Handbook of American Business.*

indicates company is in *Hoover's Handbook of World Business;* sales and employee numbers are for parent company.

Landmark Graphics Corp.
15150 Memorial Dr.
Houston, TX 77079
Phone: 713-560-1000 Fax: 713-560-1410
CEO: C. Eugene Ennis
CFO: Hardie W. Morgan
1992 Sales: $82 million Employees: 542
Symbol: LMRK Exchange: NASDAQ
Industry: Computers - geoscientific exploration software

Lands' End, Inc.
1 Lands' End Lane
Dodgeville, WI 53595
Phone: 608-935-9341 Fax: 608-935-4260
CEO: William T. End
CFO: Stephen A. Orum
1992 Sales: $724 million Employees: 6,500
Symbol: LE Exchange: NYSE
Industry: Retail - mail order & direct

Lanoga
17946 NE 65th St.
Redmond, WA 98073
Phone: 206-883-4125 Fax: 206-882-2959
CEO: Daryl D. Nagel
CFO: William P. Brakken
1992 Sales: $557 million Employees: 2,900
Ownership: Privately held
Industry: Building products

Larizza Industries, Inc.
201 W. Big Beaver Rd., Ste. 1040
Troy, MI 48084
Phone: 313-689-5800 Fax: 313-524-4996
CEO: Ronald T. Larizza
CFO: Terence C. Seikel
1991 Sales: $86 million Employees: 1,199
Symbol: LII Exchange: AMEX
Industry: Automotive & trucking - original equipment

Laser Precision Corp.
109 N. Genesse St.
Utica, NY 13502
Phone: 315-797-4449 Fax: 315-798-4038
CEO: C. Fredrick Sehnert
CFO: Gregory A. Miner
1991 Sales: $26 million Employees: 177
Symbol: LASR Exchange: NASDAQ
Industry: Electronics - measuring instruments

Laser-Pacific Media Corp.
809 N. Cahuenga Blvd.
Hollywood, CA 90038
Phone: 213-462-6266 Fax: —
CEO: Robert E. Seidenglanz
CFO: Ralph E. Walters
1991 Sales: $36 million Employees: 261
Symbol: LPAC Exchange: NASDAQ
Industry: Motion pictures & services

LaserMaster Technologies, Inc.
7156 Shady Oak Rd.
Eden Prairie, MN 55344
Phone: 612-944-9457 Fax: —
CEO: Melvin L. Master
CFO: Timothy N. Thurn
1992 Sales: $60 million Employees: 392
Symbol: LMTS Exchange: NASDAQ
Industry: Computers - laser printers & display systems

Laserscope
3052 Orchard Dr.
San Jose, CA 95134
Phone: 408-943-0636 Fax: 408-943-1462
CEO: Rodney Perkins
CFO: Alfred G. Merriweather
1991 Sales: $42 million Employees: 259
Symbol: LSCP Exchange: NASDAQ
Industry: Lasers - systems & components

Lattice Semiconductor Corp.
5555 NE Moore Court
Hillsboro, OR 97124
Phone: 503-681-0118 Fax: 503-681-0347
CEO: Cyrus Y. Tsui
CFO: John Johannessen
1992 Sales: $71 million Employees: 263
Symbol: LSCC Exchange: NASDAQ
Industry: Electrical components - semiconductors

Laurentian Capital Corp.
640 Lee Rd., Ste. 303
Wayne, PA 19087
Phone: 215-889-7400 Fax: 215-889-7406
CEO: Robert T. Rakich
CFO: Bernhard M. Koch
1991 Sales: $131 million Employees: —
Symbol: LQ Exchange: AMEX
Industry: Insurance - life

Lawrence Insurance Group, Inc.
500 Fifth Ave., Ste. 3520
New York, NY 10110
Phone: 212-674-8753 Fax: 518-783-8009
CEO: Lawrence A. Shore
CFO: Floyd N. Adams
1991 Sales: $134 million Employees: 254
Symbol: LWR Exchange: AMEX
Industry: Insurance - property & casualty

Lawrence Savings Bank
30 Massachusetts Ave.
North Andover, MA 01845
Phone: 508-687-1131 Fax: 508-681-0813
CEO: Paul A. Miller
CFO: Timothy L. Felter
1992 Sales: — Employees: —
Symbol: LSBX Exchange: NASDAQ
Industry: Banks - Northeast

Lawson Products, Inc.
1666 E. Touhy Ave.
Des Plaines, IL 60018
Phone: 708-827-9666 Fax: 708-827-8277
CEO: Bernard Kalish
CFO: Jerome Shaffer
1991 Sales: $182 million Employees: 779
Symbol: LAWS Exchange: NASDAQ
Industry: Metal products - distribution

Lawter International, Inc.
990 Skokie Blvd.
Northbrook, IL 60062
Phone: 708-498-4700 Fax: 708-498-0066
CEO: Daniel J. Terra
CFO: William S. Russell
1991 Sales: $153 million Employees: 498
Symbol: LAW Exchange: NYSE
Industry: Chemicals - specialty

Lawyers Title Insurance Corp.
6630 W. Broad St.
Richmond, VA 23230
Phone: 804-281-6700 Fax: 804-282-5453
CEO: Charles H. Foster, Jr.
CFO: John R. Blanchard
1991 Sales: $387 million Employees: 2,952
Symbol: LTCO Exchange: NASDAQ
Industry: Business services

Layne, Inc.
1900 Shawnee Mission Pkwy.
Mission Woods, KS 66205
Phone: 913-362-0510 Fax: 913-362-0170
CEO: Robert C. Dymond
CFO: Frank R. Clark
1992 Sales: $167 million Employees: 1,408
Symbol: LAYN Exchange: NASDAQ
Industry: Water well drilling, well & pump repair & maintenance

Lazare Kaplan International Inc.
529 Fifth Ave.
New York, NY 10017
Phone: 212-972-9700 Fax: 212-972-8561
CEO: Maurice Tempelsman
CFO: Sheldon L. Ginsberg
1992 Sales: $152 million Employees: 303
Symbol: LKI Exchange: AMEX
Industry: Precious metals & jewelry

LBS Capital Management
129 6th Ave. North
Safety Harbor, FL 34695
Phone: 813-726-5656 Fax: 813-726-2517
CEO: Walter J. Loick
CFO: James A. Ackles
1992 Sales: $3 million Employees: 15
Ownership: Privately held
Industry: Business services - investment advice & money management services

LCS Industries, Inc.
120 Brighton Rd.
Clifton, NJ 07012
Phone: 201-778-5588 Fax: 201-778-6001
CEO: Arnold J. Scheine
CFO: Donald L. Flamm
1991 Sales: $42 million Employees: 635
Symbol: LCSI Exchange: NASDAQ
Industry: Retail - mail order & direct

LDB Corp.
444 Sidney Baker South
Kerrville, TX 78028
Phone: 210-257-2000 Fax: 210-257-2003
CEO: L. D. Brinkman
CFO: Joel C. Longtin
1991 Sales: $61 million Employees: 2,303
Symbol: LDBC Exchange: NASDAQ
Industry: Retail - food & restaurants

LDDS Communications, Inc.
4780 I-55 North, Ste. 500
Jackson, MS 39211
Phone: 601-364-7000 Fax: 601-364-7103
CEO: Bernard J. Ebbers
CFO: Charles T. Cannada
1991 Sales: $263 million Employees: 901
Symbol: LDDSA Exchange: NASDAQ
Industry: Telecommunications services - long distance

LDI Corp.
1375 E. Ninth St.
Cleveland, OH 44114
Phone: 216-687-0100 Fax: —
CEO: Robert S. Kendall
CFO: Jerry E. Kish
1991 Sales: $361 million Employees: 674
Symbol: LDIC Exchange: NASDAQ
Industry: Computers - services

Le Studio Canal+
9454 Wilshire Blvd., Ste. 903
Beverly Hills, CA 90212
Phone: 310-247-0994 Fax: 310-247-0998
CEO: Gilbert Dumontet
CFO: —
1991 Sales: $1,351 million Employees: 1,550
Parent: Canal+
Industry: Cable TV

Lear Seating Corp.
21557 Telegraph Rd.
Southfield, MI 48034
Phone: 313-746-1500 Fax: 313-746-1722
CEO: Kenneth Way
CFO: James Vandenberghe
1991 Sales: $1,423 million Employees: 14,500
Ownership: Privately held
Industry: Automotive & trucking - original equipment; automobile seats

indicates company is in *Hoover's Handbook of American Business.*

indicates company is in *Hoover's Handbook of World Business;* sales and employee numbers are for parent company.

Lear Siegler Inc.
220 S. Orange Ave.
Livingston, NJ 07039
Phone: 201-535-9522 Fax: 201-535-9837
CEO: William J. Turner
CFO: John A. Gockeler
1991 Sales: $447 million Employees: 3,740
Ownership: Privately held
Industry: Machinery - general industrial & material handling systems

LeaRonal, Inc.
272 Buffalo Ave.
Freeport, NY 11520
Phone: 516-868-8800 Fax: 516-868-8824
CEO: Ronald Ostrow
CFO: David Rosenthal
1992 Sales: $129 million Employees: 500
Symbol: LRI Exchange: NYSE
Industry: Chemicals - specialty

Leaseway Transportation Corp.
3700 Park East Dr.
Cleveland, OH 44122
Phone: 216-765-5500 Fax: 216-765-5077
CEO: Richard A. Damsel
CFO: Charles B. Carden
1991 Sales: $780 million Employees: 10,500
Ownership: Privately held
Industry: Transportation - truck & related services

Leasing Solutions Inc.
10 Almaden Blvd., Ste. 500
San Jose, CA 95113
Phone: 408-995-6565 Fax: 408-995-0696
CEO: Hal Krauter
CFO: Ed Phillippe
1991 Sales: $23 million Employees: 48
Ownership: Privately held
Industry: Computers - leasing services

Lechmere Inc.
275 Wildwood St.
Woburn, MA 01801
Phone: 617-935-8320 Fax: 617-935-2980
CEO: J. Kent Flummerfelt
CFO: Robert Trabucco
1991 Sales: $672 million Employees: 4,500
Ownership: Privately held
Industry: Retail - discount electronics, appliances & houseware

Lechters, Inc.
1 Cape May St.
Harrison, NJ 07029
Phone: 201-481-1100 Fax: 201-481-5493
CEO: Donald Jonas
CFO: Philip J. Reilly
1991 Sales: $234 million Employees: 1,898
Symbol: LECH Exchange: NASDAQ
Industry: Retail - discount & variety

LecTec Corp.
10701 Red Circle Dr.
Minnetonka, MN 55343
Phone: 612-933-2291 Fax: 612-933-4808
CEO: George B. Ingebrand
CFO: Bruce E. LaCoe
1992 Sales: $8.1 million Employees: 48
Symbol: LECT Exchange: NASDAQ
Industry: Medical products - diagnostic & monitoring electrodes, medical tapes

Lee Enterprises, Inc.
215 N. Main St.
Davenport, IA 52801
Phone: 319-383-2100 Fax: 319-323-9609
CEO: Richard D. Gottlieb
CFO: Michael J. Riley
1991 Sales: $340 million Employees: 5,000
Symbol: LEE Exchange: NYSE
Industry: Publishing - newspapers

Lee Pharmaceuticals
1444 Santa Anita Ave.
South El Monte, CA 91733
Phone: 818-442-3141 Fax: 818-575-8607
CEO: Henry L. Lee, Jr.
CFO: Michael L. Agresti
1991 Sales: $13 million Employees: 107
Symbol: LPH Exchange: AMEX
Industry: Cosmetics & toiletries

Lefrak Organization
97-77 Queens Blvd.
Rego Park, NY 11374
Phone: 718-459-9021 Fax: 718-897-0688
CEO: Arthur Klein
CFO: Gerald Weinstein
1991 Sales: $3,100 million Employees: 18,000
Ownership: Privately held
Industry: Real estate development & management; entertainment; oil & gas exploration

LEGENT Corp.
2 Allegheny Dr.
Pittsburgh, PA 15212
Phone: 412-323-2600 Fax: 412-323-2038
CEO: Joe M. Henson
CFO: Franchon M. Smithson
1991 Sales: $203 million Employees: 1,138
Symbol: LGNT Exchange: NASDAQ
Industry: Computers - productivity enhancement software

Legg Mason, Inc.
111 S. Calvert St.
Baltimore, MD 21202
Phone: 410-539-3400 Fax: 410-539-4096
CEO: Raymond A. Mason
CFO: F. Barry Bilson
1992 Sales: $292 million Employees: 2,253
Symbol: LM Exchange: NYSE
Industry: Financial - investment bankers

Leggett & Platt, Inc.
1 Leggett Rd.
Carthage, MO 64836
Phone: 417-358-8131 Fax: 417-358-8449
CEO: Harry M. Cornell, Jr.
CFO: Michael A. Glauber
1992 Sales: $1,171 million Employees: 10,400
Symbol: LEG Exchange: NYSE
Industry: Furniture

Leisure Concepts, Inc.
1414 Avenue of the Americas
New York, NY 10019
Phone: 212-758-7666 Fax: —
CEO: Alfred R. Kahn
CFO: Joseph P. Garrity
1991 Sales: $7 million Employees: 22
Symbol: LCIC Exchange: NASDAQ
Industry: Business services - manufacturing consulting, juvenile product development

Lennar Corp.
700 NW 107th Ave.
Miami, FL 33172
Phone: 305-559-4000 Fax: 305-226-4158
CEO: Leonard Miller
CFO: Allan J. Pekor
1991 Sales: $323 million Employees: 1,017
Symbol: LEN Exchange: NYSE
Industry: Building - residential & commercial

Lennox International Inc.
PO Box 799900
Dallas, TX 75379
Phone: 214-497-5000 Fax: 214-497-5299
CEO: John W. Norris, Jr.
CFO: Clyde Wyant
1991 Sales: $1,047 million Employees: 8,000
Ownership: Privately held
Industry: Building products - a/c & heating

Leo Burnett Co. Inc.
35 W. Wacker Dr., 21st. Fl.
Chicago, IL 60601
Phone: 312-220-5959 Fax: 312-220-3299
CEO: Richard B. Fizdale
CFO: J. C. Kraft
1991 Sales: $584 million Employees: 6,440
Ownership: Privately held
Industry: Advertising

Leopardo Construction Inc.
115 N. Brandon Dr.
Glendale Heights, IL 60139
Phone: 708-894-7200 Fax: 708-894-6678
CEO: James Leopardo
CFO: John D. Ward, Jr.
1992 Sales: $60 million Employees: 105
Ownership: Privately held
Industry: Construction - general contracting & consulting services

LESCO, Inc.
20005 Lake Rd.
Rocky River, OH 44116
Phone: 216-333-9250 Fax: 216-333-6832
CEO: James I. FitzGibbon
CFO: Kennth W. Didion
1991 Sales: $131 million Employees: 604
Symbol: LSCO Exchange: NASDAQ
Industry: Building - maintenance & services

Leslie Fay Companies, Inc.
1400 Broadway, 16th Fl.
New York, NY 10018
Phone: 212-221-4000 Fax: 212-221-4146
CEO: John J. Pomerantz
CFO: Paul F. Polishan
1991 Sales: $837 million Employees: 4,600
Symbol: LES Exchange: NYSE
Industry: Textiles - apparel

Leslie's Poolmart
20222 Plummer St.
Chatsworth, CA 91311
Phone: 818-993-4212 Fax: 818-349-1059
CEO: Brian P. McDermott
CFO: Hugh O. Pierce
1991 Sales: $83 million Employees: 427
Symbol: LESL Exchange: NASDAQ
Industry: Retail - pool supplies & equipment, accessories

Leucadia National Corp.
315 Park Ave. South, 20th Fl.
New York, NY 10010
Phone: 212-460-1900 Fax: 212-598-4869
CEO: Joseph S. Steinberg
CFO: Norman P. Kiken
1991 Sales: $1,096 million Employees: 5,332
Symbol: LUK Exchange: NYSE
Industry: Diversified operations - insurance, manufacturing, real estate development

Levi Strauss Associates Inc.
1155 Battery St.
San Francisco, CA 94111
Phone: 415-544-6000 Fax: 415-544-3939
CEO: Robert D. Haas
CFO: George B. James
1991 Sales: $4,903 million Employees: 32,100
Ownership: Privately held
Industry: Textiles - apparel

Levitz Furniture
6111 Broken Sound Pkwy. NW
Boca Raton, FL 33487
Phone: 407-994-6006 Fax: 407-998-5615
CEO: Robert M. Elliott
CFO: Patrick J. Nolan
1991 Sales: $893 million Employees: 6,100
Ownership: Privately held
Industry: Retail - home furnishings

indicates company is in *Hoover's Handbook of American Business.*

indicates company is in *Hoover's Handbook of World Business;* sales and employee numbers are for parent company.

Lewis Galoob Toys, Inc.
500 Forbes Blvd.
South San Francisco, CA 94080
Phone: 415-952-1678 Fax: 415-583-4996
CEO: Mark Goldman
CFO: David Yankey
1991 Sales: $151 million Employees: 263
Symbol: GAL Exchange: NYSE
Industry: Toys - games & hobby products

Lewis Homes Management
1156 N. Mountain Ave.
Upland, CA 91786
Phone: 909-985-0971 Fax: 909-949-6700
CEO: John M. Goodman
CFO: Jim Price
1991 Sales: $507 million Employees: 793
Ownership: Privately held
Industry: Real estate development & residential construction

Lexicon Corp.
2400 E. Commercial Blvd.
Ft. Lauderdale, FL 33308
Phone: 305-772-7221 Fax: 305-772-6110
CEO: Michael Levy
CFO: Steven W. Lowe
1991 Sales: $8.6 million Employees: 96
Symbol: LEXI Exchange: NASDAQ
Industry: Electronics - military

Lexington Savings Bank
1776 Massachusetts Ave.
Lexington, MA 02173
Phone: 617-862-1775 Fax: —
CEO: William G. Gothorpe
CFO: Douglas R. Keyes
1992 Sales: — Employees: —
Symbol: LEXB Exchange: NASDAQ
Industry: Financial - savings and loans

Lexmark International Inc.
55 Railroad Ave.
Greenwich, CT 06836
Phone: 203-629-6700 Fax: 203-629-6725
CEO: Marvin L. Mann
CFO: Achim Knust
1991 Sales: $2,000 million Employees: 4,000
Ownership: Privately held
Industry: Computers - printers & keyboards

LG&E Energy Corp.
220 Main St.
Louisville, KY 40232
Phone: 502-627-2000 Fax: 502-627-2023
CEO: Roger W. Hale
CFO: Charles A. Markel III
1991 Sales: $715 million Employees: 4,328
Symbol: LGE Exchange: NYSE
Industry: Utility - electric power

Liberty Bancorp, Inc.
5700 N. Lincoln Ave.
Chicago, IL 60659
Phone: 312-334-1200 Fax: 405-231-6002
CEO: Edward J. Burns
CFO: Joseph W. Stachnik
1991 Sales: $41 million Employees: 144
Symbol: LBCI Exchange: NASDAQ
Industry: Financial - savings and loans

Liberty Bancorp, Inc.
100 N. Broadway
Oklahoma City, OK 73102
Phone: 405-231-6000 Fax: —
CEO: Charles E. Nelson
CFO: Mischa Gorkuscha
1991 Sales: $188 million Employees: 1,252
Symbol: LBNA Exchange: NASDAQ
Industry: Banks - Southwest

Liberty Corp.
2000 Wade Hampton Blvd.
Greenville, SC 29602
Phone: 803-268-8111 Fax: 803-292-4411
CEO: W. Hayne Hipp
CFO: Barry L. Edwards
1991 Sales: $364 million Employees: —
Symbol: LC Exchange: NYSE
Industry: Insurance - life

Liberty Homes, Inc.
1101 Eisenhower Dr. North
Goshen, IN 46526
Phone: 219-533-0431 Fax: 219-533-0438
CEO: Edward J. Hussey
CFO: Michael F. Hussey
1991 Sales: $52 million Employees: 540
Symbol: LIBHA Exchange: NASDAQ
Industry: Building - mobile homes & RVs

Liberty Media Corp.
2232 Dell Range Blvd., Ste. 305
Cheyenne, WY 82009
Phone: 307-637-8253 Fax: 307-637-8448
CEO: Peter R. Barton
CFO: Robert R. Bennet
1991 Sales: $107 million Employees: 439
Symbol: LBTYA Exchange: NASDAQ
Industry: Cable TV programming

Liberty National Bancorp, Inc.
416 W. Jefferson St.
Louisville, KY 40202
Phone: 502-566-2000 Fax: 502-566-3956
CEO: Joseph W. Phelps
CFO: Carl E. Weigel
1991 Sales: $396 million Employees: 2,127
Symbol: LNBC Exchange: NASDAQ
Industry: Banks - Southeast

Lida, Inc.
2222 S. Blvd.
Charlotte, NC 28203
Phone: 704-376-5609 Fax: 704-332-2434
CEO: Isaac Kier
CFO: Nelson Kier
1991 Sales: $108 million Employees: 641
Symbol: LIDA Exchange: NASDAQ
Industry: Textiles - mill products

Life Technologies, Inc.
8717 Grovemont Circle
Gaithersburg, MD 20877
Phone: 301-840-8000 Fax: 301-921-2149
CEO: J. Stark Thompson
CFO: Joseph C. Stokes, Jr.
1991 Sales: $171 million Employees: 1,285
Symbol: LTEK Exchange: NASDAQ
Industry: Biomedical & genetic products

Life USA Holding, Inc.
300 S. Hwy. 169
Minneapolis, MN 55426
Phone: 612-546-7386 Fax: 612-525-6000
CEO: Robert W. MacDonald
CFO: Joseph W. Carlson
1991 Sales: $114 million Employees: 273
Symbol: LUSA Exchange: NASDAQ
Industry: Insurance - life

LifeCore Biomedical, Inc.
3515 Lyman Blvd.
Chaska, MN 55318
Phone: 612-368-4300 Fax: 612-368-3411
CEO: James W. Bracke
CFO: John C. Heinmiller
1992 Sales: $4.5 million Employees: 106
Symbol: LCBM Exchange: NASDAQ
Industry: Biomedical & genetic products

Lifeline Systems, Inc.
One Arsenal Marketplace Mall
Watertown, MA 02172
Phone: 617-923-4141 Fax: 617-923-1384
CEO: Arthur R. Phipps
CFO: Kathleen A. Barry
1991 Sales: $38 million Employees: 270
Symbol: LIFE Exchange: NASDAQ
Industry: Healthcare - outpatient & home

LifeQuest Medical, Inc.
9601 McAllister Fwy.
San Antonio, TX 78216
Phone: 210-366-2100 Fax: 210-349-0500
CEO: Herbert H. Spoon
CFO: Herbert H. Spoon
1992 Sales: — Employees: 6
Symbol: LQMD Exchange: NASDAQ
Industry: Medical products

Lifetime Corp.
75 State St.
Boston, MA 02109
Phone: 617-330-5080 Fax: 617-330-7995
CEO: Anthony H. Reeves
CFO: Barry P. Coombes
1992 Sales: $886 million Employees: 63,425
Symbol: LFT Exchange: NYSE
Industry: Healthcare - outpatient & home

Lifetime Hoan Corp.
820 Third Ave.
Brooklyn, NY 11232
Phone: 718-499-9500 Fax: 718-499-9560
CEO: Milton L. Cohen
CFO: Fred Spivak
1991 Sales: $55 million Employees: 275
Symbol: LCUT Exchange: NASDAQ
Industry: Housewares

Lifetime Products Inc.
Freeport Center
Clearfield, UT 84016
Phone: 801-776-1532 Fax: 801-776-4397
CEO: Barry Mower
CFO: Brent Allen
1992 Sales: $40 million Employees: 322
Ownership: Privately held
Industry: Leisure & recreational products - basketball equipment

Lifetime Products, Inc.
5000 Quorum Dr., Ste. 660
Dallas, TX 75240
Phone: 214-980-2886 Fax: 214-980-0790
CEO: Jennifer P. Runyeon
CFO: Gary J. Martin
1991 Sales: $45 million Employees: 188
Symbol: LPI Exchange: AMEX
Industry: Automotive & trucking - replacement parts

Lillian Vernon Corp.
510 S. Fulton Ave.
Mt. Vernon, NY 10550
Phone: 914-699-4131 Fax: 914-699-7698
CEO: Lillian Vernon
CFO: Edward L. Larsen
1992 Sales: $162 million Employees: 1,940
Symbol: LVC Exchange: AMEX
Industry: Retail - mail order & direct

Lilly Industries, Inc.
546 Abbott St.
Indianapolis, IN 46225
Phone: 317-634-8512 Fax: 317-687-6741
CEO: Douglas J. Huemme
CFO: Roman J. Klusas
1991 Sales: $213 million Employees: 1,140
Symbol: LICIA Exchange: NASDAQ
Industry: Chemicals - specialty

Limited, Inc., The
Two Limited Pkwy.
Columbus, OH 43230
Phone: 614-479-7000 Fax: 614-479-7080
CEO: Leslie H. Wexner
CFO: Kenneth B. Gilman
1992 Sales: $6,573 million Employees: 83,800
Symbol: LTD Exchange: NYSE
Industry: Retail - apparel & shoes, bath products

LIN Broadcasting Corp.
5295 Carillon Point
Kirkland, WA 98033
Phone: 206-828-1902 Fax: 206-828-1900
CEO: Craig O. McCaw
CFO: Donald Guthrie
1991 Sales: $468 million Employees: 1,141
Symbol: LINB Exchange: NASDAQ
Industry: Broadcasting - radio & TV

Lincare Holdings, Inc.
19337 US 19 North, Ste. 500
Clearwater, FL 34624
Phone: 813-530-7700 Fax: —
CEO: James T. Kelly
CFO: James M. Emanuel
1991 Sales: $89 million Employees: 1,000
Symbol: LNCR Exchange: NASDAQ
Industry: Medical services

Lincoln Financial Corp.
116 E. Berry St.
Ft. Wayne, IN 46802
Phone: 219-461-6000 Fax: 219-461-6492
CEO: Douglas E. Ebert
CFO: Robert K. Chapman
1991 Sales: $234 million Employees: 1,310
Symbol: LFIN Exchange: NASDAQ
Industry: Banks - Midwest

Lincoln Foodservice Products, Inc.
1111 N. Hadley Rd.
Ft. Wayne, IN 46804
Phone: 219-432-9511 Fax: 219-436-0735
CEO: William A. Thomas
CFO: David O. Cole
1991 Sales: $44 million Employees: 333
Symbol: LINN Exchange: NASDAQ
Industry: Machinery - general industrial

Lincoln Logs Ltd.
Riverside Dr.
Chestertown, NY 12817
Phone: 518-494-4777 Fax: 518-494-7495
CEO: Richard Considine
CFO: William J. Thyne
1991 Sales: $7 million Employees: 46
Symbol: LLOG Exchange: NASDAQ
Industry: Toys - games & hobby products

Lincoln National Corp.
1300 S. Clinton St.
Ft. Wayne, IN 46802
Phone: 219-455-2000 Fax: 219-455-2733
CEO: Ian M. Rolland
CFO: Richard S. Robertson
1992 Sales: $8,034 million Employees: —
Symbol: LNC Exchange: NYSE
Industry: Insurance - property & casualty

Lincoln Property Co.
500 N. Akard, Ste. 3300
Dallas, TX 75201
Phone: 214-740-3300 Fax: 214-740-3313
CEO: A. Mack Pogue
CFO: Mark Wallis
1992 Sales: $1,173 million Employees: 4,059
Ownership: Privately held
Industry: Real estate development & management

Lincoln Savings Bank
102 Broadway Ave.
Carnegie, PA 15106
Phone: 412-276-4860 Fax: —
CEO: David B. Hartman
CFO: Gary T. Jenkins
1992 Sales: — Employees: —
Symbol: LNSB Exchange: NASDAQ
Industry: Financial - savings and loans

Lincoln Telecommunications Co.
1440 M St.
Lincoln, NE 68508
Phone: 402-476-4321 Fax: 402-475-9195
CEO: James E. Geist
CFO: Michael J. Tavlin
1991 Sales: $176 million Employees: 1,597
Symbol: LTEC Exchange: NASDAQ
Industry: Utility - telephone

Lindal Cedar Homes, Inc.
4300 S. 104th Place
Seattle, WA 98178
Phone: 206-725-0900 Fax: 206-725-1615
CEO: Robert W. Lindal
CFO: John F. Dacy
1991 Sales: $37 million Employees: 195
Symbol: LNDL Exchange: NASDAQ
Industry: Building - residential & commercial

Lindberg Corp.
6133 N. River Rd., Ste. 700
Rosemont, IL 60018
Phone: 708-823-2021 Fax: 708-823-0795
CEO: Leo G. Thompson
CFO: Stephen S. Penley
1991 Sales: $74 million Employees: 803
Symbol: LIND Exchange: NASDAQ
Industry: Metal processing & fabrication

Lindsay Manufacturing Co., Inc.
E. Hwy. 91
Lindsay, NE 68644
Phone: 402-428-2131 Fax: 402-428-2795
CEO: Gary D. Parker
CFO: Bruce C. Karsk
1991 Sales: $99 million Employees: 511
Symbol: LINZ Exchange: NASDAQ
Industry: Machinery - farm

Linear Technology Corp.
1630 McCarthy Blvd.
Milpitas, CA 95035
Phone: 408-432-1900 Fax: 408-434-0507
CEO: Robert H. Swanson, Jr.
CFO: Paul Coghlan
1992 Sales: $119 million Employees: 802
Symbol: LLTC Exchange: NASDAQ
Industry: Electrical components - semiconductors

Lionel Corp.
220 Mill Rd.
Edison, NJ 08817
Phone: 908-572-0054 Fax: 215-969-0522
CEO: Michael J. Vastola
CFO: Michael J. Vastola
1991 Sales: $309 million Employees: 2,500
Symbol: LIO Exchange: AMEX
Industry: Retail - discount & variety

Liposome Co., Inc.
One Research Way
Princeton, NJ 08540
Phone: 609-452-7060 Fax: 609-452-1890
CEO: Charles A. Baker
CFO: Anne M. Van Lent
1991 Sales: $6.3 million Employees: 80
Symbol: LIPO Exchange: NASDAQ
Industry: Biomedical & genetic products

Liposome Technology, Inc.
1050 Hamilton Court
Menlo Park, CA 94025
Phone: 415-323-9011 Fax: 415-323-9106
CEO: Nicolaos V. Arvanitidis
CFO: Donald J. Stewart
1991 Sales: $0.3 million Employees: 72
Symbol: LTIZ Exchange: NASDAQ
Industry: Drugs

Liqui-Box Corp.
6950 Worthington-Galena Rd.
Worthington, OH 43085
Phone: 614-888-9280 Fax: 614-888-0982
CEO: Samuel B. Davis
CFO: Samuel B. Davis
1991 Sales: $108 million Employees: 738
Symbol: LIQB Exchange: NASDAQ
Industry: Containers - paper & plastic

Litchfield Financial Corp.
25 Main St.
Williamstown, MA 01267
Phone: 413-458-2551 Fax: —
CEO: Donald R. Dion, Jr.
CFO: Heather A. Sica
1990 Sales: $2.6 million Employees: 21
Symbol: LTCH Exchange: NASDAQ
Industry: Financial - consumer loans

Litle & Co.
54 Stiles Rd
Salem, NH 03079
Phone: 603-893-9333 Fax: 603-894-5357
CEO: Tim Litle
CFO: Michael Duffy
1991 Sales: $46 million Employees: 101
Ownership: Privately held
Industry: Financial - credit card processing

Little Caesar Enterprises Inc.
2211 Woodward Ave.
Detroit, MI 48201
Phone: 313-983-6000 Fax: 313-983-6494
CEO: Michael Ilitch
CFO: Marian Ilitch
1992 Sales: $2,050 million Employees: 90,000
Ownership: Privately held
Industry: Retail - food & restaurants, pizza restaurants, sports arenas, pro sports

Littlefield, Adams & Co.
1302 Rockland Ave. NW
Roanoke, VA 24012
Phone: 703-366-2451 Fax: —
CEO: J. William Stephens
CFO: Michael A. Fleshman
1991 Sales: $5.2 million Employees: 60
Symbol: LFA Exchange: AMEX
Industry: Textiles - apparel

Litton Industries, Inc.
360 N. Crescent Dr.
Beverly Hills, CA 90210
Phone: 310-859-5000 Fax: 310-859-5940
CEO: Orion L. Hoch
CFO: Joseph T. Casey
1992 Sales: $5,699 million Employees: 52,300
Symbol: LIT Exchange: NYSE
Industry: Diversified operations - defense contracting, seismic exploration

Liuski International, Inc.
10 Hub Dr.
Melville, NY 11747
Phone: 516-454-8220 Fax: 516-454-8266
CEO: Morries Liu
CFO: Edward J. Feinberg
1991 Sales: $137 million Employees: 360
Symbol: LSKI Exchange: NASDAQ
Industry: Computers - peripheral equipment

indicates company is in *Hoover's Handbook of American Business.*

indicates company is in *Hoover's Handbook of World Business;* sales and employee numbers are for parent company.

LIVE Entertainment Inc.
15400 Sherman Way, Ste. 500
Van Nuys, CA 94106
Phone: 818-988-5060 Fax: —
CEO: Wayne H. Patterson
CFO: Roger R. Smith
1991 Sales: $361 million Employees: 1,472
Symbol: LVE Exchange: NYSE
Industry: Leisure & recreational products - music & video recordings

Living Centers of America, Inc.
15415 Katy Fwy., Ste. 800
Houston, TX 77094
Phone: 713-578-4600 Fax: 713-578-4735
CEO: Edward L. Kuntz
CFO: Leroy D. Williams
1991 Sales: $397 million Employees: 15,200
Symbol: LCA Exchange: NYSE
Industry: Healthcare - outpatient & home

Liz Claiborne, Inc.
1441 Broadway
New York, NY 10018
Phone: 212-354-4900 Fax: 212-719-9049
CEO: Jerome A. Chazen
CFO: Samuel M. Miller
1992 Sales: $2,194 million Employees: 7,000
Symbol: LIZ Exchange: NYSE
Industry: Textiles - women's and men's apparel; cosmetics

Lloyd's New York
1 World Trade Center
New York, NY 10048
Phone: 212-269-6700 Fax: 212-269-6758
CEO: Winslow Stillwell
CFO: —
1992 Sales: — Employees: 2,136
Parent: Lloyd's of London
Industry: Insurance - multiline & misc

Loan America Financial Corp.
8100 Oak Lane
Miami Lakes, FL 33016
Phone: 305-557-9282 Fax: —
CEO: Charles B. Stuzin
CFO: M. Frances Vega
1991 Sales: $37 million Employees: 327
Symbol: LAFCB Exchange: NASDAQ
Industry: Financial - mortgages & related services

Loan Pricing Corp.
135 W. 50th St., 13th Fl.
New York, NY 10020
Phone: 212-489-5455 Fax: 212-765-4983
CEO: Christopher Snyder
CFO: Michael Sepesi
1991 Sales: $3.7 million Employees: 41
Ownership: Privately held
Industry: Business services - database services to financial institutions

Lockheed Corp.
4500 Park Granada Blvd.
Calabasas, CA 91399
Phone: 818-876-2000 Fax: 818-876-2329
CEO: David M. Tellep
CFO: Vincent N. Marafino
1992 Sales: $10,100 million Employees: 72,300
Symbol: LK Exchange: NYSE
Industry: Aerospace - missiles & space systems, aeronautical systems & technology services

Loctite Corp.
10 Columbus Blvd., Hartford Square North
Hartford, CT 06106
Phone: 203-520-5000 Fax: 203-520-5073
CEO: Kenneth W. Butterworth
CFO: Robert L. Aller
1991 Sales: $561 million Employees: 3,587
Symbol: LOC Exchange: NYSE
Industry: Paints & allied products

Loews Corp.
667 Madison Ave.
New York, NY 10021
Phone: 212-545-2000 Fax: 212-545-2498
CEO: Laurence A. Tisch
CFO: Roy E. Posner
1992 Sales: $13,692 million Employees: 26,800
Symbol: LTR Exchange: NYSE
Industry: Diversified operations - insurance, tobacco, hotels

Loflin Environmental Services
2020 Montrose, Ste. 100
Houston, TX 77006
Phone: 713-521-3300 Fax: 713-523-0829
CEO: Joe Loflin
CFO: Beth Waguespack
1991 Sales: $1.8 million Employees: 14
Ownership: Privately held
Industry: Business services - industrial hygiene consulting services

Logic Devices Inc.
2 Larson Dr.
Danbury, CT 06810
Phone: 203-797-0800 Fax: 203-797-1086
CEO: William J. Volz
CFO: Todd J. Ashford
1991 Sales: $19 million Employees: 87
Symbol: LOGC Exchange: NASDAQ
Industry: Electrical components - integrated circuits

Logicon, Inc.
3701 Skypark Dr.
Torrance, CA 90505
Phone: 310-373-0220 Fax: Call co. operator
CEO: John R. Woodhull
CFO: Ralph L. Webster
1992 Sales: $298 million Employees: 3,500
Symbol: LGN Exchange: NYSE
Industry: Electronics - military

Logos Systems Inc.
8303 Southwest Fwy. #500
Houston, TX 77074
Phone: 713-777-8229 Fax: 713-777-9512
CEO: Robert S. Butnem
CFO: —
1991 Sales: $0.9 million Employees: 10
Ownership: Privately held
Industry: Computers - healthcare software & services

Lomas Financial Corp.
2001 Bryan Tower, 36th Fl.
Dallas, TX 75201
Phone: 214-746-7111 Fax: 214-746-7119
CEO: Jess Hay
CFO: Gene H. Bishop
1992 Sales: $282 million Employees: 2,163
Symbol: LFC Exchange: NYSE
Industry: Financial - investment management

Lone Star Industries, Inc.
300 First Stamford Place
Stamford, CT 06902
Phone: 203-969-8600 Fax: 203-969-8546
CEO: David W. Wallace
CFO: Joseph F. Smorada
1991 Sales: $239 million Employees: 1,700
Symbol: LCE Exchange: NYSE
Industry: Construction - cement & concrete

Lone Star Steakhouse & Saloon, Inc.
224 E. Douglas, Ste. 700
Wichita, KS 67202
Phone: 316-264-8899 Fax: —
CEO: Jamie B. Coulter
CFO: John D. White
1991 Sales: $11 million Employees: 560
Symbol: STAR Exchange: NASDAQ
Industry: Retail - food & restaurants

Lone Star Technologies, Inc.
2200 W. Mockingbird Lane
Dallas, TX 75235
Phone: 214-352-3981 Fax: 214-353-6409
CEO: John P. Harbin
CFO: W. Preston Holsinger
1991 Sales: $487 million Employees: 1,841
Symbol: LSST Exchange: NASDAQ
Industry: Steel - production

Long Island Lighting Co.
175 E. Old Country Rd.
Hicksville, NY 11801
Phone: 516-933-4590 Fax: 516-935-1729
CEO: William J. Catacosinos
CFO: George J. Sideris
1992 Sales: $2,622 million Employees: 6,605
Symbol: LIL Exchange: NYSE
Industry: Utility - electric power

Long John Silver's Inc.
101 Jerrico Dr.
Lexington, KY 40509
Phone: 606-263-6000 Fax: 606-263-6145
CEO: Clinton A. Clark
CFO: Gerald Deitchle
1991 Sales: $830 million Employees: 18,000
Ownership: Privately held
Industry: Retail - food & restaurants

Longhorn Steaks, Inc.
8215 Roswell Rd.
Atlanta, GA 30350
Phone: 404-399-9595 Fax: —
CEO: George W. McKerrow, Sr.
CFO: Ronald W. San Martin
1991 Sales: $39 million Employees: 915
Symbol: LOHO Exchange: NASDAQ
Industry: Retail - food & restaurants

Longs Drug Stores Inc.
141 N. Civic Dr.
Walnut Creek, CA 94596
Phone: 510-937-1170 Fax: 510-210-6886
CEO: Robert M. Long
CFO: W. G. Combs
1992 Sales: $2,457 million Employees: 15,000
Symbol: LDG Exchange: NYSE
Industry: Retail - drug stores

Longview Fibre Co.
Fibre Way
Longview, WA 98632
Phone: 206-425-1550 Fax: 206-425-3116
CEO: Richard P. Wollenberg
CFO: Lisa J. Holbrook
1992 Sales: $691 million Employees: 3,400
Symbol: LFB Exchange: NYSE
Industry: Paper & paper products

Loop Restaurant, The
One San Jose Place, Ste. 3
Jacksonville, FL 32257
Phone: 904-268-2609 Fax: 904-268-5809
CEO: Mike Schneider
CFO: Stephen Joost
1991 Sales: $4.8 million Employees: 200
Ownership: Privately held
Industry: Retail - food & restaurants

Loral Corp.
600 Third Ave.
New York, NY 10016
Phone: 212-697-1105 Fax: 212-661-8988
CEO: Bernard L. Schwartz
CFO: Michael P. DeBlasio
1992 Sales: $3,155 million Employees: 22,000
Symbol: LOR Exchange: NYSE
Industry: Electronics - military

indicates company is in *Hoover's Handbook of American Business.*

indicates company is in *Hoover's Handbook of World Business;* sales and employee numbers are for parent company.

Lori Corp.
500 Central Ave.
Northfield, IL 60093
Phone: 708-441-7300 Fax: 708-441-6959
CEO: John J. Harvey
CFO: James D. Doering
1991 Sales: $107 million Employees: 2,000
Symbol: LRC Exchange: AMEX
Industry: Precious metals & jewelry

Lotus Development Corp.
55 Cambridge Pkwy.
Cambridge, MA 02142
Phone: 617-577-8500 Fax: 617-693-1299
CEO: Jim P. Manzi
CFO: Edwin J. Gillis
1992 Sales: $900 million Employees: 4,300
Symbol: LOTS Exchange: NASDAQ
Industry: Computers - spreadsheet, graphics, & word processing software

Louisiana Land and Exploration Co.
909 Poydras St., Ste. 3600
New Orleans, LA 70112
Phone: 504-566-6500 Fax: 504-566-6874
CEO: H. Leighton Steward
CFO: Richard A. Bachmann
1992 Sales: $787 million Employees: 785
Symbol: LLX Exchange: NYSE
Industry: Oil & gas - US integrated

Louisiana Power & Light Co.
317 Baronne St.
New Orleans, LA 70112
Phone: 504-595-3100 Fax: Call co. operator
CEO: Jerry L. Maulden
CFO: Gerald D. McInvale
1991 Sales: $1.5 million Employees: 2,025
Symbol: LPLAp Exchange: NYSE
Industry: Utility - electric power

Louisiana-Pacific Corp.
111 SW Fifth Ave.
Portland, OR 97204
Phone: 503-221-0800 Fax: Call co. operator
CEO: Harry A. Merlo
CFO: John C. Hart
1992 Sales: $2,185 million Employees: 12,500
Symbol: LPX Exchange: NYSE
Industry: Building products - wood

Lowe's Companies, Inc.
Hwy. 268 East
North Wilkesboro, NC 28656
Phone: 919-651-4000 Fax: 919-651-4766
CEO: Leonard G. Herring
CFO: Harry B. Underwood II
1992 Sales: $3,646 million Employees: 18,368
Symbol: LOW Exchange: NYSE
Industry: Building products - retail & wholesale

Lowrance Electronics, Inc.
12000 E. Skelly Dr.
Tulsa, OK 74128
Phone: 918-437-6881 Fax: 918-438-6149
CEO: Darrell J. Lowrance
CFO: Graham A. Wilson
1991 Sales: $54 million Employees: 467
Symbol: LEIX Exchange: NASDAQ
Industry: Leisure & recreational products - sonars for boating

Loyola Capital Corp.
1300 N. Charles St.
Baltimore, MD 21201
Phone: 410-332-7000 Fax: —
CEO: Joseph W. Mosmiller
CFO: James V. McAveney
1991 Sales: $205 million Employees: 732
Symbol: LOYC Exchange: NASDAQ
Industry: Financial - savings and loans

LSB Bancshares, Inc.
One LSB Plaza
Lexington, NC 27293
Phone: 704-246-6500 Fax: —
CEO: Robert F. Lowe
CFO: Monty J. Oliver
1990 Sales: $30 million Employees: 225
Symbol: LXBK Exchange: NASDAQ
Industry: Banks - Southeast

LSB Industries, Inc.
16 S. Pennsylvania Ave.
Oklahoma City, OK 73107
Phone: 405-235-4546 Fax: 405-235-5067
CEO: Jack E. Golsen
CFO: Tony M. Shelby
1991 Sales: $234 million Employees: 1,344
Symbol: LSB Exchange: AMEX
Industry: Diversified operations - chemicals, environmental controls, financial services

LSI Industries Inc.
10000 Alliance Rd.
Cincinnati, OH 45242
Phone: 513-793-3200 Fax: 513-984-1335
CEO: Robert J. Ready
CFO: James S. Cox
1992 Sales: $69 million Employees: 590
Symbol: LYTS Exchange: NASDAQ
Industry: Building products - lighting fixtures

LSI Logic Corp.
1551 McCarthy Blvd.
Milpitas, CA 95035
Phone: 408-433-8000 Fax: 408-434-6457
CEO: Wilfred J. Corrigan
CFO: Patrick S. Jones
1992 Sales: $618 million Employees: 4,204
Symbol: LSI Exchange: NYSE
Industry: Electrical components - semiconductors

LTV Corp., The
2001 Ross Ave., 42nd Fl.
Dallas, TX 75201
Phone: 214-979-7711 Fax: 214-979-7946
CEO: David H. Hoag
CFO: James F. Powers
1992 Sales: $3,826 million Employees: 34,600
Trading Status: Suspended
Industry: Steel - production, oil & gas drilling equipment

LTX Corp.
LTX Park at University Ave.
Westwood, MA 02090
Phone: 617-329-7550 Fax: Call co. operator
CEO: Graham C.C. Miller
CFO: John J. Arcari
1991 Sales: $200 million Employees: 1,144
Symbol: LTXX Exchange: NASDAQ
Industry: Electronics - measuring instruments

Lubrizol Corp.
29400 Lakeland Blvd.
Wickliffe, OH 44092
Phone: 216-943-4200 Fax: 216-943-5337
CEO: L. E. Coleman
CFO: Ray A. Andreas
1992 Sales: $1,552 million Employees: 5,299
Symbol: LZ Exchange: NYSE
Industry: Oil refining & marketing

Luby's Cafeterias, Inc.
2211 Northeast Loop 410
San Antonio, TX 78217
Phone: 210-654-9000 Fax: 210-654-3211
CEO: Ralph Erben
CFO: John E. Curtis, Jr.
1991 Sales: $328 million Employees: 9,000
Symbol: LUB Exchange: NYSE
Industry: Retail - food & restaurants

Lucky-Goldstar International (America)
1000 Sylvan Ave.
Englewood Cliffs, NJ 07632
Phone: 201-816-2300 Fax: 201-816-0636
CEO: Y.K. Jin
CFO: —
1991 Sales: $2,422 million Employees: 18,000
Parent: Lucky-Goldstar International
Industry: Diversified operations - electronics, petrochemicals, chemicals & foodstuffs

Lufkin Industries, Inc.
407 Kilen St.
Lufkin, TX 75901
Phone: 409-634-2211 Fax: 409-637-5474
CEO: F. B. Stevenson
CFO: C. J. Haley, Jr.
1991 Sales: $194 million Employees: 2,400
Symbol: LUFK Exchange: NASDAQ
Industry: Oil field machinery & equipment

Lufthansa German Airlines
750 Lexington Ave.
New York, NY 10022
Phone: 212-745-0700 Fax: 212-745-0795
CEO: Frederick Reid
CFO: —
1991 Sales: $10,592 million Employees: 61,791
Parent: Deutsche Lufthansa AG
Industry: Transportation - airline

Lukens Inc.
50 S. First Ave.
Coatesville, PA 19320
Phone: 215-383-2000 Fax: 215-383-2436
CEO: R. William Van Sant
CFO: John R. Bartholdson
1992 Sales: $881 million Employees: 3,884
Symbol: LUC Exchange: NYSE
Industry: Steel - specialty alloys

Lumex, Inc.
100 Spence St.
Bay Shore, NY 11706
Phone: 516-273-2200 Fax: 516-273-2408
CEO: Lawrence N. Cohen
CFO: Robert McNally
1991 Sales: $100 million Employees: 1,085
Symbol: LUM Exchange: AMEX
Industry: Medical & dental supplies

Lunar Corp.
313 W. Beltline Hwy.
Madison, WI 53713
Phone: 608-274-2663 Fax: 608-274-5374
CEO: Richard B. Mazess
CFO: Robert A. Beckman
1992 Sales: $24 million Employees: 95
Symbol: LUNR Exchange: NASDAQ
Industry: Medical products - bone disease treatment products

Lund International Holdings, Inc.
9055 Evergreen Blvd. NW
Coon Rapids, MN 55433
Phone: 612-780-2520 Fax: —
CEO: James K. Pfleider
CFO: John T. Kubinski
1992 Sales: $17 million Employees: —
Symbol: LUND Exchange: NASDAQ
Industry: Automotive & trucking - replacement parts

LVI Group Inc.
470 Park Ave. South
New York, NY 10016
Phone: 212-951-3660 Fax: 212-481-9136
CEO: Salvatore J. Zizza
CFO: R. Gene Kemp, Jr.
1991 Sales: $42 million Employees: 471
Symbol: LVI Exchange: NYSE
Industry: Diversified operations - construction management, asbestos abatement

A indicates company is in *Hoover's Handbook of American Business*.

W indicates company is in *Hoover's Handbook of World Business*; sales and employee numbers are for parent company.

LVMH U.S. Corporation
2 Park Ave., Ste. 1830
New York, NY 10016
Phone: 212-340-7480 Fax: 212-340-7620
CEO: Evan G. Galbraith
CFO: —
1991 Sales: $4,242 million Employees: 14,650
Parent: LVMH Moet Henessy Louis Vuitton
Industry: Beverages - spirits & wines; leather goods, perfume

LXE
303 Research Dr.
Norcross, GA 30092
Phone: 404-447-4224 Fax: —
CEO: John E. Pippin
CFO: Don T. Scartz
1991 Sales: $39 million Employees: 330
Symbol: LXEI Exchange: NASDAQ
Industry: Telecommunications equipment

Lydall, Inc.
One Colonial Rd.
Manchester, CT 06040
Phone: 203-646-1233 Fax: 203-646-4917
CEO: Leonard R. Jaskol
CFO: John E. Hanley
1991 Sales: $136 million Employees: 947
Symbol: LDL Exchange: NYSE
Industry: Paper & paper products

Lykes Bros. Inc.
111 E. Madison St., 18th Fl.
Tampa, FL 33602
Phone: 813-223-3981 Fax: 813-273-5493
CEO: Thompson L. Rankin
CFO: A. Thayer
1991 Sales: $850 million Employees: 3,000
Ownership: Privately held
Industry: Diversified operations - food processing and insurance

Lynch Corp.
8 Sound Shore Dr., Ste. 290
Greenwich, CT 06830
Phone: 203-629-3333 Fax: 203-629-3718
CEO: Mario J. Gabelli
CFO: Robert E. Dolan
1991 Sales: $97 million Employees: 534
Symbol: LGL Exchange: AMEX
Industry: Diversified operations - telecommunications, transportation, investments

Lyondell Petrochemical Co.
1221 McKinney Ave., Ste. 1600
Houston, TX 77010
Phone: 713-652-7200 Fax: 713-652-7430
CEO: Bob G. Gower
CFO: Russell S. Young
1992 Sales: $4,805 million Employees: 2,270
Symbol: LYO Exchange: NYSE
Industry: Chemicals - plastics

M. A. Hanna Co.
1301 E. Ninth St., Ste. 3600
Cleveland, OH 44114
Phone: 216-589-4000 Fax: 216-589-4109
CEO: Martin D. Walker
CFO: Ronald G. Fountain
1992 Sales: $1,330 million Employees: 5,800
Symbol: MAH Exchange: NYSE
Industry: Diversified operations - formulated polymers, roofing materials

M.D.C. Holdings, Inc.
3600 S. Yosemite St., Ste. 900
Denver, CO 80237
Phone: 303-773-1100 Fax: —
CEO: Larry A. Mizel
CFO: Paris G. Reece III
1991 Sales: $422 million Employees: 630
Symbol: MDC Exchange: NYSE
Industry: Financial - investment management

M.D. Enterprises of Connecticut
6 Divine St.
New Haven, CT 06473
Phone: 203-776-5759 Fax: 203-230-0045
CEO: Douglas Hayward
CFO: Alex Sommers
1991 Sales: $81 million Employees: 185
Ownership: Privately held
Industry: Health maintenance organization

M. I. C. Industries, Inc.
11911 Freedom Dr. #1000
Reston, VA 22090
Phone: 703-734-2844 Fax: 703-318-9321
CEO: Michael Ansari
CFO: Eileen O. Penland
1991 Sales: $21 million Employees: 98
Ownership: Privately held
Industry: Industrial automation - automatic building machines

M.S. Carriers, Inc.
3171 Directors Row
Memphis, TN 38116
Phone: 901-332-2500 Fax: 901-344-4599
CEO: Michael S. Starnes
CFO: M. J. Barrow
1991 Sales: $153 million Employees: 1,897
Symbol: MSCA Exchange: NASDAQ
Industry: Transportation - truck

M-Wave, Inc.
216 Evergreen St.
Bensenville, IL 60106
Phone: 708-860-9542 Fax: —
CEO: Joel S. Dryer
CFO: David J. Wisher
1991 Sales: $14 million Employees: 112
Symbol: MWAV Exchange: NASDAQ
Industry: Electrical components

M/A-COM, Inc.
401 Edgewater Place, Ste. 560
Wakefield, MA 01880
Phone: 617-272-3000 Fax: 617-224-5655
CEO: Thomas A. Vanderslice
CFO: Denis N. Maiorani
1991 Sales: $382 million Employees: 4,648
Symbol: MAI Exchange: NYSE
Industry: Electronics - military

M/A/R/C Group, The
7850 N. Belt Line Rd.
Irving, TX 75063
Phone: 214-506-3400 Fax: —
CEO: Cecil B. Phillips
CFO: Harold R. Curtis
1991 Sales: $71 million Employees: 1,382
Symbol: MARC Exchange: NASDAQ
Industry: Business services

Ma Laboratories
1972 Concourse Dr.
San Jose, CA 95131
Phone: 408-954-8188 Fax: 408-954-0944
CEO: Abraham Ma
CFO: Abraham Ma
1992 Sales: $155 million Employees: 80
Ownership: Privately held
Industry: Computers - memory module, CPUs & hard disk drives

MA Mortenson Co. Inc.
PO Box 710
Minneapolis, MN 55440
Phone: 612-522-2100 Fax: 612-520-3430
CEO: M. A. Mortenson, Jr.
CFO: Peter Conzemius
1991 Sales: $802 million Employees: 1,700
Ownership: Privately held
Industry: Construction - general contracting, design, construction management

Mac Frugal's Bargains - Close-outs, Inc.
2430 E. Del Amo Blvd.
Dominguez, CA 90220
Phone: 310-537-9220 Fax: 310-632-4477
CEO: Leonard S. Williams
CFO: Philip L. Carter
1991 Sales: $543 million Employees: 5,700
Symbol: MFI Exchange: NYSE
Industry: Retail - discount & variety

MacAndrews & Forbes Holdings Inc.
36 E. 63rd St.
New York, NY 10021
Phone: 212-688-9000 Fax: 212-572-5022
CEO: Ronald O. Perelman
CFO: Irwin Engelman
1991 Sales: $3,496 million Employees: 25,700
Ownership: Privately held
Industry: Diversified operations - cosmetics, banking, financial services & publishing

MacDermid, Inc.
245 Freight St.
Waterbury, CT 06702
Phone: 203-575-5700 Fax: 203-575-5630
CEO: Daniel H. Leever
CFO: Charles D. Rice
1992 Sales: $145 million Employees: 798
Symbol: MACD Exchange: NASDAQ
Industry: Chemicals - specialty

Machine Technology, Inc.
25 Eastmans Rd.
Parsippany, NJ 07054
Phone: 201-386-0600 Fax: 201-386-0375
CEO: Gary Hillman
CFO: Sanford R. Gildenberg
1991 Sales: $31 million Employees: 183
Symbol: MTEC Exchange: NASDAQ
Industry: Electrical components - semiconductors

Mack Trucks, Inc.
2100 Mack Blvd.
Allentown, PA 18105
Phone: 215-439-3011 Fax: 215-439-3308
CEO: Elios Pascual
CFO: —
1991 Sales: $32,041 million Employees: 147,185
Parent: Renault
Industry: Automotive manufacturing

Macmillan, Inc.
55 Railroad Ave.
Greenwich, CT 08630
Phone: 203-862-7500 Fax: 203-862-7712
CEO: Mark Homan
CFO: Susan Aldridge
1992 Sales: — Employees: —
Parent: Maxwell Communication Corp. PLC
Industry: Publishing - books

MacNeal-Schwendler Corp.
815 Colorado Blvd.
Los Angeles, CA 90041
Phone: 213-258-9111 Fax: 213-259-3838
CEO: Richard H. MacNeal
CFO: Louis A. Greco
1991 Sales: $56 million Employees: 280
Symbol: MNS Exchange: AMEX
Industry: Computers - engineering software

MacTemps, Inc.
54 Church St., Harvard Square
Cambridge, MA 02138
Phone: 617-868-6800 Fax: 617-868-6820
CEO: John Scuang
CFO: Steve Kapner
1991 Sales: $13 million Employees: 72
Ownership: Privately held
Industry: Business services - Macintosh & Windows temporary personnel

 indicates company is in *Hoover's Handbook of American Business.*

indicates company is in *Hoover's Handbook of World Business;* sales and employee numbers are for parent company.

Madison Gas and Electric Co.
133 S. Blair St.
Madison, WI 53701
Phone: 608-252-7000 Fax: 608-252-7098
CEO: Frank C. Vondrasek
CFO: Joseph T. Krzos
1991 Sales: $232 million Employees: 758
Symbol: MDSN Exchange: NASDAQ
Industry: Utility - electric power

MAF Bancorp, Inc.
55th St. & Holmes Ave.
Clarendon Hills, IL 60514
Phone: 708-325-7300 Fax: 708-325-1193
CEO: Allen M. Koranda
CFO: Jerry A. Weberling
1991 Sales: $144 million Employees: 460
Symbol: MAFB Exchange: NASDAQ
Industry: Banks - Midwest

Magainin Pharmaceuticals Inc.
5110 Campus Dr.
Plymouth Meeting, PA 19462
Phone: 215-941-4020 Fax: 215-941-5399
CEO: Jay Moorin
CFO: Scott Horvitz
1992 Sales: $0.4 million Employees: —
Symbol: MAGN Exchange: NASDAQ
Industry: Drugs

Magma Copper Co.
7400 N. Oracle Rd., Ste. 200
Tucson, AZ 85704
Phone: 602-575-5600 Fax: Call co. operator
CEO: J. Burgess Winter
CFO: Douglas J. Purdom
1992 Sales: $820 million Employees: 4,487
Symbol: MCU Exchange: NYSE
Industry: Metals - nonferrous

Magma Power Co.
11770 Bernardo Plaza Court, Ste. 366
San Diego, CA 92128
Phone: 619-622-7800 Fax: 619-487-9416
CEO: Paul M. Pankrantz
CFO: Wallace C. Dieckmann
1991 Sales: $84 million Employees: 241
Symbol: MGMA Exchange: NASDAQ
Industry: Energy - alternative sources

Magna Bancorp, Inc.
100 W. Front St.
Hattiesburg, MS 39402
Phone: 601-545-4722 Fax: 601-583-7132
CEO: Robert S. Duncan
CFO: Lou Ann Poynter
1991 Sales: $101 million Employees: 879
Symbol: MGNL Exchange: NASDAQ
Industry: Financial - savings and loans

Magna Group, Inc.
19 Public Sq.
Belleville, IL 62220
Phone: 618-234-0020 Fax: 618-236-9236
CEO: William S. Badgley
CFO: George R. Klann
1991 Sales: $220 million Employees: 2,455
Symbol: MAGI Exchange: NASDAQ
Industry: Banks - Midwest

Magnet, Inc.
7 Chamber Dr.
Washington, MO 63090
Phone: 314-239-5661 Fax: 314-239-4490
CEO: Joseph M. Patane
CFO: Walter W. Luther, Jr.
1991 Sales: $13 million Employees: 192
Ownership: Privately held
Industry: Advertising refrigerator magnets

MagneTek, Inc.
11150 Santa Monica Blvd., 15th Fl.
Los Angeles, CA 90025
Phone: 310-473-6681 Fax: 310-477-9105
CEO: Frank Perna, Jr.
CFO: David P. Reiland
1992 Sales: $1,360 million Employees: 15,500
Symbol: MAG Exchange: NYSE
Industry: Electrical products - motors, uninterruptible power supplies, wire, etc.

MAI Systems Corp.
14192 Franklin Ave.
Tustin, CA 92680
Phone: 714-731-5100 Fax: 714-730-3185
CEO: Bennett S. LeBow
CFO: Michael L. Veuve
1991 Sales: $336 million Employees: 2,642
Symbol: MCO Exchange: NYSE
Industry: Computers - mini & micro

Maier Group
235 E. 95th St., Ste. 1-J
New York, NY 10128
Phone: 212-534-4100 Fax: 212-410-2145
CEO: Howard Maier
CFO: Tom Morton
1991 Sales: $6 million Employees: 25
Ownership: Privately held
Industry: Video home & fitness products

Mail Boxes Etc.
6060 Cornerstone Court West
San Diego, CA 92121
Phone: 619-455-8800 Fax: 619-452-9937
CEO: Anthony W. DeSio
CFO: Gary S. Grahn
1992 Sales: $36 million Employees: 130
Symbol: MAIL Exchange: NASDAQ
Industry: Business services - postal operations & communications

Main Street Muffins Inc.
198 Wooster Ave.
Akron, OH 44307
Phone: 216-762-0000 Fax: 216-762-0329
CEO: Steven Marks
CFO: Steven Marks
1992 Sales: $3 million Employees: 25
Ownership: Privately held
Industry: Food - frozen bakery products

Maine Public Service Co.
209 State St.
Presque Isle, ME 04769
Phone: 207-768-5811 Fax: Ext. 118
CEO: G. Melvin Hovey
CFO: Paul R. Cariani
1991 Sales: $58 million Employees: 203
Symbol: MAP Exchange: AMEX
Industry: Utility - electric power

Major Realty Corp.
5728 Major Blvd., Ste. 700
Orlando, FL 32819
Phone: 407-351-1111 Fax: 407-345-0439
CEO: Randon A. Samelson
CFO: Richard A. Petterson
1991 Sales: $1.5 million Employees: —
Symbol: MAJR Exchange: NASDAQ
Industry: Real estate development

Mallon Resources Corp.
1099 18th St., Ste. 2750
Denver, CO 80202
Phone: 303-293-2333 Fax: 303-293-3601
CEO: George O. Mallon, Jr.
CFO: David L. Heppe
1991 Sales: $1.5 million Employees: 31
Symbol: MLRC Exchange: NASDAQ
Industry: Oil & gas - US exploration & production

Manatron, Inc.
2970 S. 9th St.
Kalamazoo, MI 49009
Phone: 616-375-5300 Fax: 616-375-9826
CEO: Allen F. Peat
CFO: Paul R. Sylvester
1992 Sales: $10.1 million Employees: 144
Symbol: MANA Exchange: NASDAQ
Industry: Computers - software

Manitowoc Co., Inc.
500 S. 16th St.
Manitowoc, WI 54220
Phone: 414-684-6621 Fax: 414-683-6277
CEO: Fred M. Butler
CFO: Robert R. Friedl
1992 Sales: $246 million Employees: 1,800
Symbol: MANT Exchange: NASDAQ
Industry: Diversified operations - crane construction, food service, ship repair

Mannesmann Capital Corporation
450 Park Ave.
New York, NY 10022
Phone: 212-702-9439 Fax: 212-826-0074
CEO: Peter Prinz Wittgenstein
CFO: —
1991 Sales: $15,997 million Employees: 125,188
Parent: Mannesmann AG
Industry: Diversified operations - plant & machinery construction, trading, automotive technology

Manor Care, Inc.
10750 Columbia Pike
Silver Spring, MD 20901
Phone: 301-681-9400 Fax: Call co. operator
CEO: Stewart Bainum, Jr.
CFO: James A. MacCutcheon
1992 Sales: $964 million Employees: 23,100
Symbol: MNR Exchange: NYSE
Industry: Nursing homes

Manville Corp.
717 17th St.
Denver, CO 80202
Phone: 303-978-2000 Fax: 303-978-2363
CEO: W. Thomas Stephens
CFO: Robert E. Cole
1992 Sales: $2,224 million Employees: 16,000
Symbol: MVL Exchange: NYSE
Industry: Building products, paperboard & packaging products, engineered products

MAPCO Petroleum Inc.
1800 S. Baltimore Ave.
Tulsa, OK 74119
Phone: 918-581-1800 Fax: 918-599-3634
CEO: James E. Barnes
CFO: Frank S. Dickerson III
1992 Sales: $2,787 million Employees: 6,057
Symbol: MDA Exchange: NYSE
Industry: Oil & gas - production & pipeline

MapInfo Corporation
200 Broadway
Troy, NY 12180
Phone: 518-274-8673 Fax: 518-274-6066
CEO: Michael Marvin
CFO: Jessica Dembo
1991 Sales: $7 million Employees: 80
Ownership: Privately held
Industry: Computers - software

MAR Oil & Gas Corp.
1208 Galisteo Pkwy.
Santa Fe, NM 87501
Phone: 505-988-2012 Fax: 505-982-6398
CEO: Leon Romero
CFO: Leon Romero
1991 Sales: $2.4 million Employees: 4
Ownership: Privately held
Industry: Oil & natural gas refining & marketing

indicates company is in *Hoover's Handbook of American Business.*

indicates company is in *Hoover's Handbook of World Business;* sales and employee numbers are for parent company.

Marathon Systems
#4 Embarcadero Center 780
San Francisco, CA 94111
Phone: 415-362-0500 Fax: 415-362-5528
CEO: Fred Greifenstein
CFO: John Scemion
1991 Sales: $4.7 million Employees: 47
Ownership: Privately held
Industry: Computers - business systems software

Marble Financial Corp.
47 Merchants Row
Rutland, VT 05701
Phone: 802-775-0025 Fax: —
CEO: William B. Wright
CFO: George B. Williams
1991 Sales: $37 million Employees: 153
Symbol: MRBL Exchange: NASDAQ
Industry: Financial - savings and loans

Marcade Group Inc.
805 Third Ave., 26th Fl.
New York, NY 10022
Phone: 212-935-8484 Fax: 212-935-9216
CEO: Charles S. Ramat
CFO: Kenneth F. Korb
1991 Sales: $237 million Employees: 2,500
Symbol: MAR Exchange: NYSE
Industry: Textiles - apparel

Marcam Corp.
95 Wells Ave.
Newton, MA 02159
Phone: 617-965-0220 Fax: —
CEO: Paul Margolis
CFO: David Cairns
1991 Sales: $56 million Employees: 470
Symbol: MCAM Exchange: NASDAQ
Industry: Computers - application software & services for process manufacturers

Marcus Corp.
212 W. Wisconsin Ave., 7th Fl.
Milwaukee, WI 53203
Phone: 414-272-6020 Fax: 414-272-0669
CEO: Stephen H. Marcus
CFO: Kenneth A. MacKenzie
1992 Sales: $194 million Employees: 7,500
Symbol: MRCS Exchange: NASDAQ
Industry: Hotels & motels

Margaretten & Co. Inc.
205 Smith St.
Perth Amboy, NJ 08861
Phone: 908-324-4000 Fax: 908-324-8416
CEO: F. M. Beck
CFO: B. M. Schnelwar
1991 Sales: $169 million Employees: 1,270
Symbol: MRG Exchange: NYSE
Industry: Financial - mortgages & related services

Marietta Corp.
37 Huntington St.
Cortland, NY 13045
Phone: 607-753-6746 Fax: 607-753-7456
CEO: John S. Nadolski
CFO: William T. Nanovsky
1991 Sales: $58 million Employees: —
Symbol: MRTA Exchange: NASDAQ
Industry: Cosmetics & toiletries

MariFarms, Inc.
10 Woodbridge Center Dr.
Woodbridge, NJ 07095
Phone: 908-750-1122 Fax: —
CEO: C. F. Woodhouse
CFO: Audrey M. Vasey
1991 Sales: $70 million Employees: 1,365
Symbol: MRF Exchange: AMEX
Industry: Food - shrimp & tuna

Marine Drilling Companies, Inc.
14141 Southwest Fwy.
Sugar Land, TX 77478
Phone: 713-491-2002 Fax: 713-242-3826
CEO: William O. Keyes
CFO: William H. Flores
1991 Sales: $67 million Employees: 390
Symbol: MDCO Exchange: NASDAQ
Industry: Oil & gas - field services

Marion Merrell Dow Inc.
9300 Ward Pkwy.
Kansas City, MO 64114
Phone: 816-966-5000 Fax: 816-966-4001
CEO: Fred W. Lyons, Jr.
CFO: Edward W. Mehrer
1992 Sales: $3,320 million Employees: 9,170
Symbol: MKC Exchange: NYSE
Industry: Drugs

Maritime Services Corp
3457 Guignard Dr.
Hood River, OR 97031
Phone: 503-386-1010 Fax: 503-386-2269
CEO: George Selfridge
CFO: Dianna Boyer
1992 Sales: $6.5 million Employees: 50
Ownership: Privately held
Industry: Ship building

Maritrans Partners L.P.
300 Delaware Ave., Ste. 1130
Wilmington, DE 19801
Phone: 302-656-7242 Fax: 302-864-1213
CEO: Stephen A. Van Dyck
CFO: Gary L. Schaefer
1991 Sales: $147 million Employees: 792
Symbol: TUG Exchange: NYSE
Industry: Transportation - shipping

Maritz Communication
1375 N. Highway Dr.
Fenton, MO 63099
Phone: 314-827-4000 Fax: 314-827-1739
CEO: William E. Maritz
CFO: D. L. Fleisher
1991 Sales: $552 million Employees: 5,500
Ownership: Privately held
Industry: Business services - market research

Mark Controls Corp.
5202 Old Orchard Rd.
Skokie, IL 60077
Phone: 708-470-8585 Fax: 708-470-9774
CEO: William E. Bendix
CFO: J. Emmett Hammond
1991 Sales: $93 million Employees: 590
Symbol: MRCC Exchange: NASDAQ
Industry: Instruments - control

Mark IV Industries, Inc.
501 John James Audubon Pkwy.
Amherst, NY 14228
Phone: 716-689-4072 Fax: 716-689-6098
CEO: Sal H. Alfiero
CFO: William P. Montague
1992 Sales: $1,203 million Employees: 11,900
Symbol: IV Exchange: NYSE
Industry: Diversified operations - transportation & process control equipment

Mark Twain Bancshares, Inc.
8820 Ladue Rd.
St. Louis, MO 63124
Phone: 314-727-1000 Fax: 314-746-2609
CEO: John P. Dubinsky
CFO: Keith Miller
1991 Sales: $223 million Employees: —
Symbol: MTWN Exchange: NASDAQ
Industry: Banks - Midwest

Markel Corp.
School Lane
Norristown, PA 19404
Phone: 215-272-8960 Fax: 215-270-3138
CEO: Alan I. Kirshner
CFO: Darrell D. Martin
1991 Sales: $223 million Employees: 853
Symbol: MAKL Exchange: NASDAQ
Industry: Insurance - property & casualty

Market Facts, Inc.
3040 W. Salt Creek Lane
Arlington Heights, IL 60005
Phone: 708-590-7000 Fax: 312-280-8756
CEO: Verne B. Churchill
CFO: Timothy J. Sullivan
1991 Sales: $41 million Employees: 976
Symbol: MFAC Exchange: NASDAQ
Industry: Business services - market research

Marketing Profiles, Inc.
2301 Lucien Way, Ste. 260
Maitland, FL 32751
Phone: 407-660-9009 Fax: 407-660-0064
CEO: John Dean
CFO: Brad Mathewson
1991 Sales: $8.4 million Employees: 53
Ownership: Privately held
Industry: Computers - database software

Marks and Spencer US Holdings Inc.
3046 Madison Ave.
New York, NY 10017
Phone: 212-697-3886 Fax: 212-697-3857
CEO: Paul Smith
CFO: —
1992 Sales: $10,833 million Employees: 67,894
Parent: Marks and Spencer PLC
Industry: Retail - major department stores

Marley Co.
1900 Shawnee Mission Pkwy.
Mission Woods, KS 66205
Phone: 913-362-5440 Fax: 913-432-1451
CEO: Robert J. Dineen
CFO: Errol P. Mitlyng
1992 Sales: $440 million Employees: 2,700
Ownership: Privately held
Industry: Building products - a/c & heating; cooling towers, boilers, pumps, heating equipment

Marlton Technologies, Inc.
111 Presidential Blvd.
Bala Cynwyd, PA 19004
Phone: 215-664-6900 Fax: —
CEO: Robert B. Ginsburg
CFO: Edmond D. Costantini, Jr.
1991 Sales: $12 million Employees: 125
Symbol: MTY Exchange: AMEX
Industry: Business services - trade show exhibit design & on-line information services

Marmon Group, Inc.
225 W. Washington St., Ste. 1900
Chicago, IL 60606
Phone: 312-372-9500 Fax: 312-845-5305
CEO: Robert A. Pritzker
CFO: Dennis Brown
1991 Sales: $3,869 million Employees: 27,050
Ownership: Privately held
Industry: Diversified operations - industrial materials, automobile & medical products

Marquest Medical Products, Inc.
11039 Lansing Circle
Englewood, CO 80112
Phone: 303-790-4835 Fax: 303-799-0210
CEO: Robert J. McKinnon
CFO: Alexander McKinnon
1992 Sales: $30 million Employees: 440
Symbol: MMPI Exchange: NASDAQ
Industry: Medical products - cardiopulmonary & anesthesiology support products

indicates company is in *Hoover's Handbook of American Business.*

indicates company is in *Hoover's Handbook of World Business;* sales and employee numbers are for parent company.

Marquette Electronics, Inc.
8200 W. Tower Ave.
Milwaukee, WI 53223
Phone: 414-355-5000 Fax: 414-355-3790
CEO: Michael J. Cudahy
CFO: Mary M. Kabacinski
1992 Sales: $233 million Employees: 1,384
Symbol: MARQA Exchange: NASDAQ
Industry: Medical products - critical care monitors

Marriott Corp.
10400 Fernwood Rd.
Bethesda, MD 20817
Phone: 301-380-9000 Fax: 301-897-9014
CEO: J. Willard Marriott, Jr.
CFO: Stephen F. Bollenbach
1992 Sales: $8,722 million Employees: 202,000
Symbol: MHS Exchange: NYSE
Industry: Hotels & motels, retirement communities, food & services management

Mars, Inc.
6885 Elm St.
McLean, VA 22101
Phone: 703-821-4900 Fax: 703-448-9678
CEO: Forrest E. Mars, Jr.
CFO: V. J. Spitaleri
1991 Sales: $11,000 million Employees: 28,000
Ownership: Privately held
Industry: Food - confectionery, pet food & rice

Marsam Pharmaceuticals Inc.
Bldg. 31, Olney Ave.
Cherry Hill, NJ 08034
Phone: 609-424-5600 Fax: 609-751-8784
CEO: Marvin Samson
CFO: Judith U. Arnoff
1991 Sales: $16 million Employees: 82
Symbol: MSAM Exchange: NASDAQ
Industry: Drugs

Marsh & McLennan Companies, Inc.
1166 Avenue of the Americas
New York, NY 10036
Phone: 212-345-5000 Fax: 212-345-4838
CEO: A. J. C. Smith
CFO: Frank J. Borelli
1992 Sales: $2,937 million Employees: 23,400
Symbol: MMC Exchange: NYSE
Industry: Insurance - brokerage, consulting, investment management

Marsh Supermarkets, Inc.
9800 Crosspoint Blvd.
Indianapolis, IN 46256
Phone: 317-594-2100 Fax: 317-594-2704
CEO: Don E. Marsh
CFO: John S. Hayford
1992 Sales: $1,151 million Employees: 10,500
Symbol: MARSB Exchange: NASDAQ
Industry: Retail - supermarkets

Marshall & Ilsley Corp.
770 N. Water St.
Milwaukee, WI 53202
Phone: 414-765-7801 Fax: 414-765-7899
CEO: J. A. Puelicher
CFO: W. A. Diaz
1991 Sales: $835 million Employees: 6,137
Symbol: MRIS Exchange: NASDAQ
Industry: Banks - Midwest

Marshall Industries
9320 Telstar Ave.
El Monte, CA 91731
Phone: 818-307-6000 Fax: 818-307-6348
CEO: Gordon S. Marshall
CFO: Henry W. Chin
1992 Sales: $575 million Employees: 1,600
Symbol: MI Exchange: NYSE
Industry: Electronics - parts distribution

Martech USA, Inc.
300 E. 54th Ave.
Anchorage, AK 99518
Phone: 907-561-1970 Fax: 907-563-0830
CEO: Benjamin C. Tisdale III
CFO: Mark T. Glore
1991 Sales: $40 million Employees: 291
Symbol: MUS Exchange: NYSE
Industry: Oil & gas exploration environmental services

Marten Transport, Ltd.
129 Marten St.
Mondovi, WI 54755
Phone: 715-926-4216 Fax: 715-926-4530
CEO: Roger R. Marten
CFO: Darrell D. Rubel
1991 Sales: $88 million Employees: 928
Symbol: MRTN Exchange: NASDAQ
Industry: Transportation - truck

Martin Lawrence Limited Editions, Inc.
16250 Stagg St.
Van Nuys, CA 91406
Phone: 818-988-0630 Fax: 818-785-4330
CEO: Martin S. Blinder
CFO: Allen A. Baron
1991 Sales: $24 million Employees: 225
Symbol: MLE Exchange: NYSE
Industry: Retail - artwork

Martin Marietta Corp.
6801 Rockledge Dr.
Bethesda, MD 20817
Phone: 301-897-6000 Fax: 301-897-6704
CEO: Norman R. Augustine
CFO: Marcus C. Bennett
1992 Sales: $5,943 million Employees: 60,500
Symbol: ML Exchange: NYSE
Industry: Diversified operations - astronautics; electronics & missiles; materials

Marubeni America Corp.
200 Park Ave.
New York, NY 10166
Phone: 212-599-3700 Fax: 212-953-0388
CEO: Ryuhei Nakamura
CFO: —
1992 Sales: $149,847 million Employees: 9,949
Parent: Marubeni Corporation
Industry: Diversified operations - machinery, metals, energy & chemicals

Marvel Entertainment Group, Inc.
387 Park Ave. South
New York, NY 10016
Phone: 212-696-0808 Fax: 212-576-8598
CEO: William C. Bevins, Jr.
CFO: Robert J. Riscica
1991 Sales: $115 million Employees: 278
Symbol: MRV Exchange: NYSE
Industry: Publishing - comic books; sports picture cards

Mary Kay Cosmetics Inc.
8787 Stemmons Fwy.
Dallas, TX 75247
Phone: 214-630-8787 Fax: 214-905-5699
CEO: Richard R. Rogers
CFO: John P. Rochon
1991 Sales: $520 million Employees: 1,900
Ownership: Privately held
Industry: Cosmetics

Maryland Federal Bancorp, Inc.
3505 Hamilton St.
Hyattsville, MD 20782
Phone: 301-779-1200 Fax: —
CEO: Robert H. Halleck
CFO: Teresa A. Gray
1992 Sales: $72 million Employees: 198
Symbol: MFSL Exchange: NASDAQ
Industry: Banks - Northeast

Masco Corp.
21001 Van Born Rd.
Taylor, MI 48180
Phone: 313-274-7400 Fax: 313-374-6787
CEO: Richard A. Manoogian
CFO: Richard G. Mosteller
1992 Sales: $3,525 million Employees: 40,000
Symbol: MAS Exchange: NYSE
Industry: Building products - plumbing, cabinets, hardware; home furnishings

Masco Industries, Inc.
21001 Van Born Rd.
Taylor, MI 48180
Phone: 313-274-7400 Fax: 313-374-6315
CEO: Richard A. Manoogian
CFO: James J. Sigouin
1992 Sales: $1,657 million Employees: 12,800
Symbol: MASX Exchange: NASDAQ
Industry: Diversified operations - automotive design, transportation-related components

Massachusetts Mutual Life Insurance Co.
1295 State St.
Springfield, MA 01111
Phone: 413-788-8411 Fax: 413-744-6003
CEO: Thomas B. Wheeler
CFO: Gary E. Wendlandt
1991 Sales: $6,738 million Employees: 10,463
Ownership: Privately held
Industry: Insurance - life

MASSBANK Corp.
123 Haven St.
Reading, MA 01867
Phone: 617-662-0100 Fax: 617-942-1022
CEO: John H. Wood
CFO: Gerard H. Brandi
1991 Sales: $10.4 million Employees: 124
Symbol: MASB Exchange: NASDAQ
Industry: Banks - Northeast

Masstor Systems Corp.
5200 Great America Pkwy.
Santa Clara, CA 95052
Phone: 408-988-1008 Fax: 408-737-0676
CEO: David R. Addison
CFO: Charles B. Griffis, Jr.
1991 Sales: $46 million Employees: 189
Symbol: MSCO Exchange: NASDAQ
Industry: Computers - mainframe storage equipment

Mastech Systems Corp.
2090 Greentree Rd., 1st Fl.
Pittsburgh, PA 15220
Phone: 412-279-6400 Fax: 412-279-6870
CEO: Sunil Wadhwani
CFO: Sunil Wadhwani
1991 Sales: $14 million Employees: 450
Ownership: Privately held
Industry: Computers - systems integration services & custom programming

Mastersoft
6991 E. Camelback Rd. #A-320
Scottsdale, AZ 85251
Phone: 602-970-0800 Fax: 602-970-0706
CEO: Kent Mueller
CFO: Sally Lauden
1991 Sales: $2 million Employees: 19
Ownership: Privately held
Industry: Computers - software

Matec Corp.
75 South St.
Hopkinton, MA 01748
Phone: 508-435-9039 Fax: 508-435-5289
CEO: Robert Gill
CFO: Michael J. Kroll
1991 Sales: $24 million Employees: 328
Symbol: MXC Exchange: AMEX
Industry: Diversified operations - high technology

 indicates company is in *Hoover's Handbook of American Business.*

indicates company is in *Hoover's Handbook of World Business;* sales and employee numbers are for parent company.

Material Sciences Corp.
2300 E. Pratt Blvd.
Elk Grove Village, IL 60007
Phone: 708-439-8270 Fax: 708-806-2134
CEO: G. Robert Evans
CFO: William H. Vrba
1992 Sales: $143 million Employees: 639
Symbol: MSC Exchange: AMEX
Industry: Steel - specialty alloys

Matlack, Inc.
2200 Concord Pike
Wilmington, DE 19803
Phone: 302-426-2700 Fax: 302-426-3298
CEO: Gerard J. Trippitelli
CFO: Patrick J. Bagley
1991 Sales: $199 million Employees: 1,155
Symbol: MLK Exchange: AMEX
Industry: Transportation - truck

Matrix Pharmaceutical, Inc.
1430 O'Brien Dr., Ste. H
Menlo Park, CA 94025
Phone: 415-326-6100 Fax: 415-326-1407
CEO: Craig R. McMullen
CFO: Ronald W. Edinger
1992 Sales: — Employees: —
Symbol: MATX Exchange: NASDAQ
Industry: Biomedical & genetic products

Matrix Service Co.
10701 E. Ute St.
Tulsa, OK 74116
Phone: 918-838-8822 Fax: 918-838-8810
CEO: Doyl D. West
CFO: C. William Lee
1992 Sales: $123 million Employees: 142
Symbol: MTRX Exchange: NASDAQ
Industry: Oil & gas - field services

Matsushita Electric Corp. of America
One Panasonic Way
Secaucus, NJ 07094
Phone: 201-348-7000 Fax: 201-348-8378
CEO: Akiya Imura
CFO: —
1992 Sales: $56,015 million Employees: 242,246
Parent: Matsushita Electric
Industry: Video, communication & industrial equipment, appliances

Mattel, Inc.
333 Continental Blvd.
El Segundo, CA 90245
Phone: 310-524-2000 Fax: 310-524-3861
CEO: John W. Amerman
CFO: James A. Eskridge
1992 Sales: $1,848 million Employees: 12,500
Symbol: MAT Exchange: NYSE
Industry: Toys - dolls, games, action & activity toys

Mattern Construction Inc.
148 Route 2
Preston, CT 06365
Phone: 203-887-1998 Fax: 203-886-8091
CEO: George Mattern
CFO: George Mattern
1991 Sales: $2.9 million Employees: 9
Ownership: Privately held
Industry: Construction - general contracting services

Matthews Studio Equipment Group
2405 Empire Ave.
Burbank, CA 91504
Phone: 818-843-6715 Fax: —
CEO: Carlos De Mattos
CFO: Allan Klein
1991 Sales: $23 million Employees: 168
Symbol: MATT Exchange: NASDAQ
Industry: Motion pictures & services

Mauna Loa Macadamia Partners, L.P.
827 Fort St.
Honolulu, HI 96813
Phone: 808-544-6112 Fax: 808-544-6182
CEO: J. W. A. Buyers
CFO: E. Dunford
1991 Sales: $12 million Employees: —
Symbol: NUT Exchange: NYSE
Industry: Agricultural operations

Maverick Tube Corp.
400 Chesterfield Center
Chesterfield, MO 63017
Phone: 314-537-1314 Fax: 314-537-1363
CEO: Gregg M. Eisenberg
CFO: Dan P. Boxdorfer
1991 Sales: $126 million Employees: 448
Symbol: MAV Exchange: AMEX
Industry: Oil field machinery & equipment

Max & Erma's Restaurants, Inc.
4849 Evanswood Dr.
Columbus, OH 43229
Phone: 614-431-5800 Fax: —
CEO: Todd B. Barnum
CFO: William C. Niegsch, Jr.
1991 Sales: $36 million Employees: 1,491
Symbol: MAXE Exchange: NASDAQ
Industry: Retail - food & restaurants

Maxco, Inc.
1118 Centennial Way
Lansing, MI 48908
Phone: 517-321-3130 Fax: 517-321-1022
CEO: Max A. Coon
CFO: Vincent Shunsky
1992 Sales: $92 million Employees: 600
Symbol: MAXC Exchange: NASDAQ
Industry: Machinery - construction & mining

Maxicare Health Plans, Inc.
1149 S. Hill St.
Los Angeles, CA 90015
Phone: 213-765-2000 Fax: 310-642-5995
CEO: Peter J. Ratican
CFO: Eugene L. Froelich
1991 Sales: $393 million Employees: 462
Symbol: MAXI Exchange: NASDAQ
Industry: Health maintenance organization

Maxim Integrated Products, Inc.
120 San Gabriel Dr.
Sunnyvale, CA 94086
Phone: 408-737-7600 Fax: 408-737-7194
CEO: John F. Gifford
CFO: John H. Trollman
1992 Sales: $87 million Employees: 646
Symbol: MXIM Exchange: NASDAQ
Industry: Electrical components - integrated circuits

Maximum Strategy, Inc.
2185 Old Oakland Rd.
San Jose, CA 95131
Phone: 408-456-8880 Fax: 408-456-8887
CEO: Del Masters
CFO: Bobbi Day
1992 Sales: $11 million Employees: 28
Ownership: Privately held
Industry: Computers - storage systems

Maxtor Corp.
211 River Oaks Pkwy.
San Jose, CA 95134
Phone: 408-432-1700 Fax: 408-432-4510
CEO: Laurence R. Hootnick
CFO: Walter D. Amaral
1992 Sales: $1,389 million Employees: 8,822
Symbol: MXTR Exchange: NASDAQ
Industry: Computers - disk drives

Maxum Health Corp.
14850 Quorum Dr., Ste. 400
Dallas, TX 75240
Phone: 214-716-6200 Fax: —
CEO: William L. MacKnight
CFO: Glenn P. Cato
1991 Sales: $35 million Employees: 346
Symbol: MXH Exchange: NASDAQ
Industry: Medical services - diagnostic imaging services

Maxus Energy Corp.
717 N. Harwood St.
Dallas, TX 75201
Phone: 214-953-2000 Fax: 214-953-2901
CEO: Charles L. Blackburn
CFO: Michael J. Barron
1992 Sales: $718 million Employees: 1,926
Symbol: MXS Exchange: NYSE
Industry: Oil & gas - international specialty

Maxwell Laboratories, Inc.
8888 Balboa Ave.
San Diego, CA 92123
Phone: 619-279-5100 Fax: 619-277-6754
CEO: Alan C. Kolb
CFO: Sean M. Maloy
1991 Sales: $86 million Employees: 800
Symbol: MXWL Exchange: NASDAQ
Industry: Electronics - military

MAXXAM Inc.
5847 San Felipe, Ste. 2600
Houston, TX 77057
Phone: 713-975-7600 Fax: 713-267-3701
CEO: Charles E. Hurwitz
CFO: John T. La Duc
1992 Sales: $2,203 million Employees: 12,260
Symbol: MXM Exchange: AMEX
Industry: Diversified operations - forest products, real estate development & aluminum

May Department Stores Co., The
611 Olive St.
St. Louis, MO 63101
Phone: 314-342-6300 Fax: 314-342-6584
CEO: David C. Farrell
CFO: Jerome T. Loeb
1992 Sales: $10,907 million Employees: 115,000
Symbol: MA Exchange: NYSE
Industry: Retail - major department stores & shoe stores

Mayfair Supermarkets Inc.
681 Newark Ave.
Elizabeth, NJ 07208
Phone: 908-352-6400 Fax: 908-352-0103
CEO: Stanley P. Kaufelt
CFO: Frank Curci
1991 Sales: $600 million Employees: 4,500
Ownership: Privately held
Industry: Retail - supermarkets

Mayflower Co-operative Bank
30 S. Main St.
Middleboro, MA 02346
Phone: 508-947-4343 Fax: —
CEO: William C. MacLeod
CFO: William C. MacLeod
1992 Sales: — Employees: —
Symbol: MFLR Exchange: NASDAQ
Industry: Banks - Northeast

Mayflower Group
9998 N. Michigan Rd.
Carmel, IN 46032
Phone: 317-875-1469 Fax: 317-875-2214
CEO: Michael L. Smith
CFO: Patrick F. Carr
1991 Sales: $627 million Employees: 2,800
Ownership: Privately held
Industry: Transportation - truck-moving services & bus transportation

indicates company is in *Hoover's Handbook of American Business.*

indicates company is in *Hoover's Handbook of World Business;* sales and employee numbers are for parent company.

Maynard Oil Co.
8080 N. Central Expressway, Ste. 660
Dallas, TX 75206
Phone: 214-891-8880 Fax: 214-891-8827
CEO: James G. Maynard
CFO: Kenneth W. Hatcher
1991 Sales: $26 million Employees: 113
Symbol: MOIL Exchange: NASDAQ
Industry: Oil & gas - US exploration & production

Mayo Foundation
Mayo Clinic
Rochester, MN 55905
Phone: 507-284-2511 Fax: 507-284-8713
CEO: Robert Waller
CFO: John Herrell
1992 Sales: — Employees: 18,775
Ownership: Privately held
Industry: Hospitals

Maytag Corp.
403 W. Fourth St. North
Newton, IA 50208
Phone: 515-792-8000 Fax: 515-791-8395
CEO: Leonard A. Hadley
CFO: Jerry A. Schiller
1992 Sales: $3,041 million Employees: 22,533
Symbol: MYG Exchange: NYSE
Industry: Appliances - household; drink vending machines

MBIA Corp.
113 King St.
Armonk, NY 10504
Phone: 914-273-4545 Fax: 914-765-3163
CEO: David H. Elliott
CFO: Arthur M. Warren
1991 Sales: $269 million Employees: —
Symbol: MBI Exchange: NYSE
Industry: Insurance - multiline & misc.

MBM
PO Box 2856
Rocky Mount, NC 27802
Phone: 919-985-7200 Fax: 919-446-3818
CEO: Jerry L. Wordsworth
CFO: Ernest Avert
1991 Sales: $900 million Employees: 1,050
Ownership: Privately held
Industry: Food - wholesale

MBNA
400 Christiana Rd.
Newark, DE 19713
Phone: 302-453-9930 Fax: 302-456-8150
CEO: Alfred Lerner
CFO: M. Scot Kaufman
1991 Sales: $1,134 million Employees: 4,969
Symbol: KRB Exchange: NYSE
Industry: Financial - business services

MBS Communications
286 Maple Ave.
Cheshire, CT 06410
Phone: 203-271-3988 Fax: 203-271-2544
CEO: Robert Roscoe
CFO: Robert Roscoe
1991 Sales: $1.2 million Employees: 33
Ownership: Privately held
Industry: Business services - telephone answering services

MC Strategies
4751 Best Rd., #120
Atlanta, GA 30337
Phone: 404-669-9400 Fax: 404-669-9339
CEO: Don Galimore
CFO: Don Galimore
1991 Sales: $4 million Employees: 110
Ownership: Privately held
Industry: Business services - consulting for healthcare organizations

McArthur/Glen Group
8400 Westpark Dr., 5th Fl.
McLean, VA 22102
Phone: 703-556-6444 Fax: 703-556-9151
CEO: Cheryl McArthur
CFO: Lee Campbell
1991 Sales: $24 million Employees: 124
Ownership: Privately held
Industry: Real estate development

McCarthy Co.
1341 N. Rock Hill Rd.
St. Louis, MO 63124
Phone: 314-968-3300 Fax: 314-968-0032
CEO: Michael M. McCarthy
CFO: George Scherer
1991 Sales: $565 million Employees: 450
Ownership: Privately held
Industry: Construction - general contracting, construction management

McCaw Cellular Communications, Inc.
5400 Carillon Point
Kirkland, WA 98033
Phone: 206-827-4500 Fax: 206-828-8616
CEO: Craig O. McCaw
CFO: Peter L. S. Currie
1992 Sales: $1,743 million Employees: 6,373
Symbol: MCAWA Exchange: NASDAQ
Industry: Telecommunications services - cellular telephone services, radio paging

McClain Industries, Inc.
6200 Elmridge Rd.
Sterling Heights, MI 48310
Phone: 313-264-3611 Fax: 313-264-2229
CEO: Kenneth D. McClain
CFO: Carl Jaworski
1991 Sales: $28 million Employees: 190
Symbol: MCCL Exchange: NASDAQ
Industry: Transportation - equipment & leasing

McClatchy Newspapers, Inc.
2100 "Q" St.
Sacramento, CA 95816
Phone: 916-321-1000 Fax: 916-321-1996
CEO: Erwin Potts
CFO: James P. Smith
1991 Sales: $427 million Employees: 6,433
Symbol: MNI Exchange: NYSE
Industry: Publishing - newspapers

McCool's Carpet Outlet
329 S. OO EW
Kokomo, IN 46902
Phone: 317-453-3039 Fax: 317-453-6096
CEO: Virgil McCool
CFO: Virgil McCool
1991 Sales: $2 million Employees: 7
Ownership: Privately held
Industry: Building products - flooring

McCormick & Co., Inc.
18 Loveton Creek
Sparks, MD 21152
Phone: 410-771-7301 Fax: 410-771-7462
CEO: Charles P. McCormick, Jr.
CFO: James A. Hooker
1992 Sales: $1,471 million Employees: 7,700
Symbol: MCCRK Exchange: NASDAQ
Industry: Food - seasonings & flavorings; plastic packaging

McDermott International, Inc.
1010 Common St.
New Orleans, LA 70112
Phone: 504-587-5400 Fax: 504-587-6433
CEO: Robert E. Howson
CFO: Brock A. Hattox
1992 Sales: $3,200 million Employees: 29,500
Symbol: MDR Exchange: NYSE
Industry: Machinery - electric utility

McDonald & Company Securities, Inc.
800 Superior Ave., Ste. 2100
Cleveland, OH 44114
Phone: 216-443-2300 Fax: 216-443-2699
CEO: Thomas M. O'Donnell
CFO: Gordon A. Price
1992 Sales: $128 million Employees: 840
Symbol: MDD Exchange: NYSE
Industry: Financial - investment bankers

McDonald's Corp.
McDonald's Plaza
Oak Brook, IL 60521
Phone: 708-575-3000 Fax: 708-575-5211
CEO: Michael R. Quinlan
CFO: Jack M. Greenberg
1992 Sales: $7,133 million Employees: 168,000
Symbol: MCD Exchange: NYSE
Industry: Retail - food & restaurants

McDonnell Douglas Corp.
McDonnell Blvd. & Airport Rd.
St. Louis, MO 63134
Phone: 314-232-0232 Fax: 314-777-1739
CEO: John F. McDonnell
CFO: Herbert J. Lanese
1992 Sales: $17,373 million Employees: 109,123
Symbol: MD Exchange: NYSE
Industry: Aerospace - aircraft equipment, defense electronics, financial services

McFarland Energy, Inc.
10425 S. Painter Ave.
Santa Fe Springs, CA 90670
Phone: 310-944-0181 Fax: 310-946-4608
CEO: J. C. McFarland
CFO: Robert E. Ransom
1991 Sales: $16 million Employees: 70
Symbol: MCFE Exchange: NASDAQ
Industry: Oil & gas - US exploration & production

McGinnis Farms, Inc.
5610 McGinnis Ferry Rd.
Alpharetta, GA 30202
Phone: 404-442-8881 Fax: 404-442-3214
CEO: Stan Walker
CFO: Victor Logan
1991 Sales: $7.1 million Employees: 44
Ownership: Privately held
Industry: Nursery stock, landscaping supplies & irrigation products

McGrath RentCorp
2500 Grant Ave.
San Lorenzo, CA 94580
Phone: 415-276-2626 Fax: 415-276-3905
CEO: Robert P. McGrath
CFO: Robert P. McGrath
1991 Sales: $56 million Employees: 150
Symbol: MGRC Exchange: NASDAQ
Industry: Leasing

McGraw-Hill, Inc.
1221 Avenue of the Americas
New York, NY 10020
Phone: 212-512-2000 Fax: 212-512-4871
CEO: Joseph L. Dionne
CFO: Robert J. Bahash
1992 Sales: $2,051 million Employees: 13,539
Symbol: MHP Exchange: NYSE
Industry: Publishing - books & electronic, financial services, broadcasting

MCI Communications Corp.
1801 Pennsylvania Ave. NW
Washington, DC 20006
Phone: 202-872-1600 Fax: 202-887-3140
CEO: Bert C. Roberts, Jr.
CFO: Douglas L. Maine
1992 Sales: $10,562 million Employees: 27,857
Symbol: MCIC Exchange: NASDAQ
Industry: Telecommunications services - long distance & messaging services

 indicates company is in *Hoover's Handbook of American Business.*

indicates company is in *Hoover's Handbook of World Business;* sales and employee numbers are for parent company.

McJunkin Corp.
835 Hillcrest Dr. East
Charleston, WV 25311
Phone: 304-348-5211 Fax: 304-348-4922
CEO: H. B. Wehrle III
CFO: M. H. Wehrle
1991 Sales: $517 million Employees: 1,245
Ownership: Privately held
Industry: Electrical products - piping & electrical equipment; oil & gas field equipment

McKee Foods
PO Box 750
Collegedale, TN 37315
Phone: 615-238-7111 Fax: 615-238-7170
CEO: Ellsworth McKee
CFO: Barry Patterson
1991 Sales: $525 million Employees: 4,200
Ownership: Privately held
Industry: Food - snacks

McKesson Corp.
McKesson Plaza, One Post St.
San Francisco, CA 94104
Phone: 415-983-8300 Fax: 415-983-7160
CEO: Alan J. Seelenfreund
CFO: Garret A. Scholz
1992 Sales: $11,493 million Employees: 14,150
Symbol: MCK Exchange: NYSE
Industry: Drugs & sundries - wholesale, service merchandising, water

McKinsey & Company, Inc.
55 E. 52nd St.
New York, NY 10022
Phone: 212-446-7000 Fax: 212-446-8575
CEO: Frederick W. Gluck
CFO: James Rogers
1991 Sales: $1,050 million Employees: 4,500
Ownership: Privately held
Industry: Business services - management consulting

MCN Corp.
500 Griswold St.
Detroit, MI 48226
Phone: 313-965-2430 Fax: 313-256-5871
CEO: Alfred R. Glancy III
CFO: William K. McCrackin
1992 Sales: $1,438 million Employees: 3,882
Symbol: MCN Exchange: NYSE
Industry: Utility - gas distribution

McNerney Heintz Inc.
509 W. Old Northwest Hwy.
Barrington, IL 60010
Phone: 708-381-0424 Fax: 708-381-0453
CEO: Duane Heintz
CFO: Charles Page
1991 Sales: $9.4 million Employees: 171
Ownership: Privately held
Industry: Business services - administrative management services for medical organizations

McRae Industries, Inc.
Hwy. 109 North
Mt. Gilead, NC 27306
Phone: 919-439-6147 Fax: 919-439-9596
CEO: Branson J. McRae
CFO: Harold W. Smith
1991 Sales: $37 million Employees: 473
Symbol: MRI.A Exchange: AMEX
Industry: Shoes & related apparel

MDM Engineering Corp.
635 Camino de los Mares, Ste. 100
San Clemente, CA 92673
Phone: 714-240-0153 Fax: 714-496-7793
CEO: Michael Flower
CFO: Cynthia Browder
1991 Sales: $10.1 million Employees: 125
Ownership: Privately held
Industry: Engineering & technical services

MDT Corp.
2300 205th St.
Torrance, CA 90501
Phone: 310-618-9269 Fax: 310-618-9105
CEO: J. Miles Branagan
CFO: Thomas M. Hein
1992 Sales: $119 million Employees: 1,128
Symbol: MDTC Exchange: NASDAQ
Industry: Medical & dental supplies

MDU Resources Group, Inc.
400 N. Fourth St.
Bismarck, ND 58501
Phone: 701-222-7900 Fax: 701-222-7606
CEO: John A. Schuchart
CFO: Harold J. Mellen, Jr.
1991 Sales: $367 million Employees: 1,759
Symbol: MDU Exchange: NYSE
Industry: Utility - electric power

Mead Corp., The
Courthouse Plaza NE, 10 W. 2nd St.
Dayton, OH 45463
Phone: 513-495-6323 Fax: 513-461-2424
CEO: Steven C. Mason
CFO: William A. Enouen
1992 Sales: $4,703 million Employees: 21,600
Symbol: MEA Exchange: NYSE
Industry: Paper & paper products - packaging, school & office products, & on-line information network

Meadowbrook Rehabilitation Group, Inc.
2200 Powell St., Ste. 800
Emeryville, GA 94608
Phone: 510-420-0900 Fax: 510-547-4323
CEO: Harvey Wm. Glasser
CFO: Thomas F. Still
1992 Sales: $34 million Employees: 530
Symbol: MBRK Exchange: NASDAQ
Industry: Healthcare - outpatient & home

Measurex Corp.
One Results Way
Cupertino, CA 95014
Phone: 408-255-1500 Fax: 408-864-7570
CEO: David A. Bossen
CFO: Robert McAdams, Jr.
1991 Sales: $254 million Employees: 2,530
Symbol: MX Exchange: NYSE
Industry: Instruments - control

MECA Software, Inc.
55 Walls Dr.
Fairfield, CT 06430
Phone: 203-256-5000 Fax: 203-255-6300
CEO: Daniel Schley
CFO: Paul Harrison
1992 Sales: $21 million Employees: 174
Symbol: MECA Exchange: NASDAQ
Industry: Computers - personal productivity software

Mechanical Technology Inc.
968 Albany-Shaker Rd.
Latham, NY 12110
Phone: 518-785-2211 Fax: 518-785-2420
CEO: Harry Apkarian
CFO: Harry Apkarian
1991 Sales: $65 million Employees: 567
Symbol: MTIX Exchange: NASDAQ
Industry: Electronics - military

Medalist Industries, Inc.
10850 W. Park Place, Ste. 150
Milwaukee, WI 53224
Phone: 414-359-3000 Fax: 414-359-3005
CEO: Edward D. Hopkins
CFO: James L. Sievert
1991 Sales: $55 million Employees: 479
Symbol: MDIN Exchange: NASDAQ
Industry: Diversified operations - sporting apparel, fasteners, machine tools

Medaphis Corp.
2700 Cumberland Pkwy., Ste. 300
Atlanta, GA 30339
Phone: 404-319-3300 Fax: 404-957-0670
CEO: Randolph G. Brown
CFO: Timothy J. Kilgallon
1991 Sales: $56 million Employees: 2,039
Symbol: MEDA Exchange: NASDAQ
Industry: Business services - accounts receivable management services

Medar, Inc.
38700 Grand River Ave.
Farmington Hills, MI 48335
Phone: 313-477-3900 Fax: 313-477-8897
CEO: Charles J. Drake
CFO: Gerald R. Smith
1991 Sales: $17 million Employees: 149
Symbol: MDXR Exchange: NASDAQ
Industry: Industrial automation & robotics

Medarex, Inc.
22 Chambers St.
Princeton, NJ 08542
Phone: 609-921-7121 Fax: 609-921-7450
CEO: Donald L. Drakeman
CFO: Michael A. Appelbaum
1991 Sales: $1.7 million Employees: 23
Symbol: MEDX Exchange: NASDAQ
Industry: Drugs

MedChem Products, Inc.
232 W. Cummings Park
Woburn, MA 01801
Phone: 617-938-9328 Fax: 617-938-0657
CEO: David A. Swann
CFO: Sean F. Moran
1991 Sales: $18 million Employees: —
Symbol: MCH Exchange: AMEX
Industry: Medical products - hemostats & surgical devices

Medco Containment Services, Inc.
100 Summit Ave.
Montvale, NJ 07645
Phone: 201-358-5400 Fax: 201-703-7617
CEO: Richard Braddock
CFO: James V. Manning
1992 Sales: $2,131 million Employees: 6,750
Symbol: MCCS Exchange: NASDAQ
Industry: Medical services - mail order drug distribution

Medco Research, Inc.
8733 Beverly Blvd., Ste. 404
Los Angeles, CA 90048
Phone: 213-854-1954 Fax: 213-659-2105
CEO: Archie W. Prestayko
CFO: Donald B. Siegel
1991 Sales: $2.9 million Employees: 9
Symbol: MRE Exchange: AMEX
Industry: Medical services - cardiovascular drug research

Medex, Inc.
3637 Lacon Rd.
Hilliard, OH 43026
Phone: 614-876-2413 Fax: 614-876-7796
CEO: Craig Waldbillig
CFO: Robert F. Durbin
1992 Sales: $87 million Employees: 1,200
Symbol: MDEX Exchange: NASDAQ
Industry: Medical & dental supplies

Media General, Inc.
333 E. Grace St.
Richmond, VA 23219
Phone: 804-649-6000 Fax: 804-649-6898
CEO: J. Stewart Bryan III
CFO: Marshall N. Morton
1991 Sales: $586 million Employees: 7,500
Symbol: MEGA Exchange: AMEX
Industry: Publishing - newspapers & business information

MediaNews Group
4888 Loop Central Dr., Ste. 525
Houston, TX 77081
Phone: 713-295-3800 Fax: 713-295-3893
CEO: W. Dean Singleton
CFO: E. Michael Fluker
1992 Sales: $450 million Employees: 9,000
Ownership: Privately held
Industry: Publishing - newspaper

Medical Action Industries Inc.
1934 New Hwy.
Farmingdale, NY 11735
Phone: 516-249-7535 Fax: 516-249-7541
CEO: Joseph R. Meringola
CFO: Paul V. Rossi
1992 Sales: $27 million Employees: 133
Symbol: MDCI Exchange: NASDAQ
Industry: Medical products - surgical-related products

Medical Devices, Inc.
833 Third St. SW
St. Paul, MN 55112
Phone: 612-631-0590 Fax: 612-631-8476
CEO: Robert C. Wingrove
CFO: Jeffrey P. Shields
1992 Sales: $4.4 million Employees: 47
Symbol: MDEV Exchange: NASDAQ
Industry: Medical products - rehabilitation & pain relief products

Medical Diagnostics, Inc.
6 New England Executive Park
Burlington, MA 01803
Phone: 617-270-9560 Fax: 617-270-9940
CEO: John A. Lynch
CFO: Thomas V. Hennessey, Jr.
1991 Sales: $16 million Employees: —
Symbol: MDIX Exchange: NASDAQ
Industry: Medical services - magnetic resonance imaging services

Medical Equipment Repair Services
2140 Bispham Rd.
Sarasota, FL 34231
Phone: 813-921-2584 Fax: 813-924-6158
CEO: Will Howe
CFO: Will Howe
1992 Sales: $1.5 million Employees: 19
Ownership: Privately held
Industry: Medical products - respiratory equipment sales & service

Medical Graphics Corp.
350 Oak Grove Pkwy.
St. Paul, MN 55127
Phone: 612-484-4874 Fax: —
CEO: Catherine A. Anderson
CFO: Brian P. King
1991 Sales: $15 million Employees: 124
Symbol: MGCC Exchange: NASDAQ
Industry: Medical products - heart & lung disease testing & treatment systems

Medical Imaging Centers of America, Inc.
9444 Farnham St., Ste. 100
San Diego, CA 92123
Phone: 619-560-0110 Fax: 619-560-0046
CEO: Antone J. Lazos
CFO: Michael L. Jeub
1991 Sales: $88 million Employees: 472
Symbol: MIKA Exchange: NASDAQ
Industry: Healthcare - outpatient & home

Medical Marketing Group, Inc.
2960 Post Rd.
Southport, CT 06490
Phone: 203-254-1388 Fax: 203-259-9582
CEO: Per G. H. Lofberg
CFO: James V. Manning
1992 Sales: $26 million Employees: 275
Symbol: MMGI Exchange: NASDAQ
Industry: Business services - information products & marketing programs; prescription data licensing

Medical Sterilization, Inc.
225 Underhill Blvd.
Syosset, NY 11791
Phone: 516-496-8822 Fax: —
CEO: Kennard H. Morganstern
CFO: John M. Sharpe, Jr.
1991 Sales: $7.4 million Employees: 89
Symbol: MSTI Exchange: NASDAQ
Industry: Medical services - instrument sterilization

Medical Technology Systems, Inc.
12920 Automobile Blvd.
Clearwater, FL 34622
Phone: 813-576-6311 Fax: —
CEO: Harold B. Siegel
CFO: Gerald Courture
1992 Sales: $7.5 million Employees: 108
Symbol: MSYS Exchange: NASDAQ
Industry: Medical products - punch-card medication dispensing systems

MediCenter, Inc.
13 NW 44th St.
Lawton, OK 73505
Phone: 405-357-3686 Fax: 405-357-5622
CEO: Cheryn Williams
CFO: Holly Conway
1991 Sales: $13 million Employees: 92
Ownership: Privately held
Industry: Medical services - company-sponsored medical centers & pharmacies

Medicine Shoppe International, Inc.
1100 N. Lindbergh Blvd.
St. Louis, MO 63132
Phone: 314-993-6000 Fax: 314-569-9780
CEO: David A. Abrahamson
CFO: Donald C. Schreiber
1991 Sales: $37 million Employees: 193
Symbol: MSII Exchange: NASDAQ
Industry: Retail - drug stores

Medicis Pharmaceutical Corp.
100 E. 42nd St., 15th Fl.
New York, NY 10017
Phone: 212-599-2000 Fax: —
CEO: Jonah Shacknai
CFO: Stuart Diamond
1991 Sales: $3.3 million Employees: 35
Symbol: MDRXA Exchange: NASDAQ
Industry: Drugs

Medicore, Inc.
2201 W. 76th St.
Hialeah, FL 33016
Phone: 305-558-4000 Fax: 305-557-1163
CEO: Thomas K. Langbein
CFO: Dennis W. Healey
1991 Sales: $18 million Employees: 338
Symbol: MDK Exchange: AMEX
Industry: Diversified operations - kidney dialysis; electronic & mechanical components

Medicus Systems Corp.
One Rotary Center, Ste. 400
Evanston, IL 60201
Phone: 708-570-7500 Fax: 708-570-7518
CEO: Richard C. Jelinek
CFO: Deborah R. Suckow
1992 Sales: $22 million Employees: 195
Symbol: MECS Exchange: NASDAQ
Industry: Computers - decision-support software

MedImmune, Inc.
35 W. Watkins Mill Rd.
Gaithersburg, MD 20878
Phone: 301-417-0770 Fax: —
CEO: Wayne T. Hockmeyer
CFO: David LeBuhn
1991 Sales: $14 million Employees: 60
Symbol: MEDI Exchange: NASDAQ
Industry: Medical products - therapeutics & vaccines

Mediplex Group, Inc.
15 Walnut St.
Wellesley, MA 02181
Phone: 617-446-6900 Fax: 617-446-6908
CEO: Abraham D. Gosman
CFO: Frederick R. Leathers
1991 Sales: $237 million Employees: 5,450
Symbol: MPX Exchange: NYSE
Industry: Health maintenance organization

MEDIQ Inc.
One MEDIQ Plaza
Pennsauken, NJ 08110
Phone: 609-665-9300 Fax: 609-665-2391
CEO: Bernard J. Korman
CFO: Michael F. Sandler
1991 Sales: $298 million Employees: —
Symbol: MED Exchange: AMEX
Industry: Medical & dental supplies

MediSense
266 2nd Ave.
Waltham, MA 02154
Phone: 617-492-2373 Fax: 617-890-1711
CEO: Rob Coleman
CFO: Jerry Bojas
1991 Sales: $90 million Employees: 786
Ownership: Privately held
Industry: Medical products - equipment

MediServe Information Systems, Inc.
1615 W. University #138
Tempe, AZ 85281
Phone: 602-966-6800 Fax: 602-966-6735
CEO: Randy Scheib
CFO: Trey Cowley
1991 Sales: $2.7 million Employees: 20
Ownership: Privately held
Industry: Computers - software services

Medisys, Inc.
4550 W. 77th St.
Edina, MN 55435
Phone: 612-835-8300 Fax: —
CEO: William J. Brummond
CFO: David J. Byrd
1991 Sales: $9.1 million Employees: 119
Symbol: MEDS Exchange: NASDAQ
Industry: Healthcare - outpatient & home

MedQuist, Inc.
20 E. Clementon Rd.
Gibbsboro, NJ 08026
Phone: 609-782-0300 Fax: —
CEO: Richard J. Censits
CFO: Michael J. Handline
1991 Sales: $23 million Employees: 425
Symbol: MEDQ Exchange: NASDAQ
Industry: Transportation - services

Medrad, Inc.
271 Kappa Dr.
Pittsburgh, PA 15238
Phone: 412-967-9700 Fax: 412-967-9028
CEO: Thomas H. Witmer
CFO: Michael T. Howard
1992 Sales: $58 million Employees: 638
Symbol: MEDR Exchange: NASDAQ
Industry: Medical products - vascular injection systems

MEDSTAT Systems, Inc.
777 E. Eisenhower Pkwy., Ste. 500
Ann Arbor, MI 48108
Phone: 313-996-1180 Fax: 313-996-3740
CEO: Ernest G. Ludy
CFO: Jennifer S. Ponski
1991 Sales: $18 million Employees: 194
Symbol: MDST Exchange: NASDAQ
Industry: Business services - medical benefits analysis computer system & software

Medtronic, Inc.
7000 Central Ave. NE
Minneapolis, MN 55432
Phone: 612-574-4000 Fax: 612-574-4879
CEO: William W. George
CFO: Robert L. Ryan
1992 Sales: $1,295 million Employees: 9,392
Symbol: MDT Exchange: NYSE
Industry: Medical instruments - pacemakers & related cardiovascular products

Medusa Corp.
3008 Monticello Blvd.
Cleveland, OH 44118
Phone: 216-371-4000 Fax: 216-371-2912
CEO: Robert S. Evans
CFO: Brian P. Bammel
1991 Sales: $173 million Employees: 960
Symbol: MSA Exchange: NYSE
Industry: Construction - cement & concrete

Mega-Sys
432 S. Emerson Ave.
Greenwood, IN 46143
Phone: 317-888-7369 Fax: 317-888-0178
CEO: Rob Richardson
CFO: David Yeley
1991 Sales: $7.7 million Employees: 13
Ownership: Privately held
Industry: Transportation - services

Megacards, Inc.
1807 Park 270 Dr., Ste. 318
St. Louis, MO 63146
Phone: 314-576-3555 Fax: 314-576-1469
CEO: Stephan R. Juskewycz
CFO: E. Michael Krebs
1991 Sales: $18 million Employees: 201
Symbol: MEGX Exchange: NASDAQ
Industry: Leisure & recreational products - sports picture cards

Megafoods Stores Inc.
1455 S. Stapley Dr.
Mesa, AZ 85204
Phone: 602-926-1087 Fax: 602-926-1237
CEO: Dean G. Miller
CFO: Jack J. Walker
1991 Sales: $245 million Employees: 1,412
Symbol: MEGF Exchange: NASDAQ
Industry: Retail - supermarkets

Megasource, Inc.
2600 S. Telegraph, Ste. 200
Bloomfield Hills, MI 48302
Phone: 313-332-9400 Fax: 313-338-6342
CEO: David Carney
CFO: Terry McBride
1991 Sales: $7.2 million Employees: 76
Ownership: Privately held
Industry: Medical services - health care consulting services & software

MEI Diversified Inc.
90 S. Sixth St., Ste. 800
Minneapolis, MN 55402
Phone: 612-339-8853 Fax: 612-339-8868
CEO: Donald E. Benson
CFO: James A. Cesario
1991 Sales: $448 million Employees: 16,487
Symbol: MEI Exchange: NYSE
Industry: Diversified operations - snack foods, beauty salons, medical products

Meijer Inc.
2929 Walker Ave. NW
Grand Rapids, MI 49504
Phone: 616-453-6711 Fax: 616-453-6067
CEO: Doug Meijer
CFO: Fred L. Kistler
1991 Sales: $5,390 million Employees: 35,200
Ownership: Privately held
Industry: Retail - supermarkets, discount & retail stores

Melaleuca Inc.
3910 Yellowstone Hwy.
Idaho Falls, ID 83402
Phone: 208-522-0700 Fax: 208-528-2090
CEO: Frank Vandersloot
CFO: Gill Fuller
1992 Sales: $200 million Employees: 950
Ownership: Privately held
Industry: Nutritional, medicinal, personal care & household cleaning products

Melamine Chemicals, Inc.
Hwy. 18 West
Donaldsonville, LA 70346
Phone: 504-473-3121 Fax: 504-473-0550
CEO: Frederic R. Huber
CFO: Wayne D. DeLeo
1992 Sales: $36 million Employees: 89
Symbol: MTWO Exchange: NASDAQ
Industry: Chemicals - specialty

Mellon Bank Corp.
500 Grant St., One Mellon Bank Center
Pittsburgh, PA 15258
Phone: 412-234-5000 Fax: 412-234-6265
CEO: Frank V. Cahouet
CFO: Steven G. Elliott
1992 Sales: $2,972 million Employees: 16,900
Symbol: MEL Exchange: NYSE
Industry: Banks - Northeast; retail & wholesale & middle market banking & service products

Melville Corp.
One Theall Rd.
Rye, NY 10580
Phone: 914-925-4000 Fax: 914-925-4026
CEO: Stanley P. Goldstein
CFO: Robert D. Huth
1992 Sales: $10,433 million Employees: 110,148
Symbol: MES Exchange: NYSE
Industry: Retail - apparel & shoes, drugs, health & beauty aids, toys

Melvin Simon & Associates Inc.
115 W. Washington St.
Indianapolis, IN 46204
Phone: 317-636-1600 — Fax: 317-685-7222
CEO: Melvin Simon
CFO: David Simon
1991 Sales: $625 million — Employees: 3,500
Ownership: Privately held
Industry: Real estate development & management

MEM Co., Inc.
231 Union St.
Northvale, NJ 07647
Phone: 201-767-0100 — Fax: 201-767-0698
CEO: Gay A. Mayer
CFO: Michael G. Kazimir, Jr.
1991 Sales: $58 million — Employees: 438
Symbol: MEM — Exchange: AMEX
Industry: Cosmetics & toiletries

Men's Wearhouse, Inc.
5803 Glenmont Dr.
Houston, TX 77081
Phone: 800-777-8580 — Fax: 713-664-1957
CEO: George Zimmer
CFO: David H. Edwab
1992 Sales: $170 million — Employees: 1,080
Symbol: SUIT — Exchange: NASDAQ
Industry: Retail - apparel & shoes

Menasha Corp.
1645 Bergstrom Rd.
Neenah, WI 54956
Phone: 414-751-1000 — Fax: 414-751-1236
CEO: D. C. Shepard
CFO: William Griffith
1992 Sales: $623 million — Employees: 4,200
Ownership: Privately held
Industry: Diversified operations - packaging, plastics, forest products & printing

Mendez Excavation
10955 W. Polk Dr.
Breckenridge, CO 80127
Phone: 303-453-7827 — Fax: 303-453-4765
CEO: Dan Mendez
CFO: Dan Mendez
1991 Sales: $2.9 million — Employees: 35
Ownership: Privately held
Industry: Construction - general contracting services

Menley & James, Inc.
100 Tournament Dr.
Horsham, PA 19044
Phone: 215-441-6500 — Fax: —
CEO: Lawrence D. White
CFO: William W. Yeager
1991 Sales: $28 million — Employees: 37
Symbol: MENJ — Exchange: NASDAQ
Industry: Cosmetics & toiletries

Mentor Corp.
600 Pine Ave.
Goleta, CA 93117
Phone: 805-967-3451 — Fax: 805-967-3013
CEO: Christopher Conway
CFO: Gary E. Mistlin
1992 Sales: $89 million — Employees: 827
Symbol: MNTR — Exchange: NASDAQ
Industry: Medical & dental supplies

Mentor Graphics Corp.
8005 SW Boeckman Rd.
Wilsonville, OR 97070
Phone: 503-685-7000 — Fax: 503-685-1204
CEO: Thomas H. Bruggere
CFO: Brian C. Henry
1991 Sales: $400 million — Employees: 2,438
Symbol: MENT — Exchange: NASDAQ
Industry: Computers - graphics hardware

Mercantile Bancorporation Inc.
721 Locust St.
St. Louis, MO 63101
Phone: 314-425-2525 — Fax: 314-425-1286
CEO: Thomas H. Jacobsen
CFO: Ralph W. Babb, Jr.
1991 Sales: $776 million — Employees: 4,417
Symbol: MTRC — Exchange: NASDAQ
Industry: Banks - Midwest

Mercantile Bankshares Corp.
2 Hopkins Plaza
Baltimore, MD 21201
Phone: 410-237-5900 — Fax: 410-237-5854
CEO: H. Furlong Baldwin
CFO: Charles C. McGuire, Jr.
1991 Sales: $512 million — Employees: 2,726
Symbol: MRBK — Exchange: NASDAQ
Industry: Banks - Southeast

Mercantile Stores Co., Inc.
9450 Seward Rd.
Fairfield, OH 45014
Phone: 513-860-8000 — Fax: 513-860-8689
CEO: David L. Nichols
CFO: James M. McVicker
1992 Sales: $2,633 million — Employees: 28,850
Symbol: MST — Exchange: NYSE
Industry: Retail - regional department stores

Mercedes-Benz of North America, Inc.
One Mercedes Dr.
Montvale, NJ 07645
Phone: 201-573-0600 — Fax: 201-573-6780
CEO: Michael N. Bassermann
CFO: —
1991 Sales: $62,507 million — Employees: 379,252
Parent: Daimler-Benz AG
Industry: Automotive manufacturing

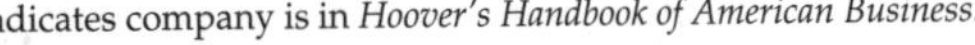
indicates company is in *Hoover's Handbook of American Business.*
indicates company is in *Hoover's Handbook of World Business;* sales and employee numbers are for parent company.

Merchants Bancshares, Inc.
123 Church St.
Burlington, VT 05401
Phone: 802-658-3400 Fax: —
CEO: Dudley H. Davis
CFO: Edward W. Haase
1991 Sales: $67 million Employees: 371
Symbol: MBVT Exchange: NASDAQ
Industry: Banks - Northeast

Merchants Bank of New York
434 Broadway
New York, NY 10013
Phone: 212-669-6600 Fax: —
CEO: James G. Lawrence
CFO: William J. Cardew
1992 Sales: — Employees: —
Symbol: MBNY Exchange: NASDAQ
Industry: Banks - Northeast

Merchants Capital Corp.
125 Tremont St.
Boston, MA 02108
Phone: 617-484-2800 Fax: —
CEO: John R. Lakian
CFO: Joseph A. Anoli
1991 Sales: $18 million Employees: 119
Symbol: MCBKA Exchange: NASDAQ
Industry: Financial - investment management

Merchants Group, Inc.
250 Main St.
Buffalo, NY 14202
Phone: 716-849-3101 Fax: 716-849-3200
CEO: James F. Marino
CFO: Robert M. Zak
1991 Sales: $102 million Employees: —
Symbol: MGP Exchange: AMEX
Industry: Insurance - property & casualty

Merck & Co., Inc.
126 E. Lincoln Ave.
Rahway, NJ 07065
Phone: 908-594-4000 Fax: 908-594-4662
CEO: P. Roy Vagelos
CFO: Judy C. Lewent
1992 Sales: $9,663 million Employees: 37,700
Symbol: MRK Exchange: NYSE
Industry: Drugs - cardiovasculars, antibiotics, anti-ulcerants

Mercury Finance Co.
40 Skokie Blvd., Ste. 200
Northbrook, IL 60062
Phone: 708-564-3720 Fax: 708-564-3758
CEO: John N. Brincat
CFO: Charley A. Pond
1991 Sales: $116 million Employees: 650
Symbol: MFN Exchange: NYSE
Industry: Financial - business services

Mercury General Corp.
4484 Wilshire Blvd.
Los Angeles, CA 90010
Phone: 213-937-1060 Fax: 213-857-7116
CEO: George Joseph
CFO: Keith L. Parker
1991 Sales: $529 million Employees: 1,110
Symbol: MRCY Exchange: NASDAQ
Industry: Insurance - property & casualty

Meredith Corp.
1716 Locust St.
Des Moines, IA 50309
Phone: 515-284-3000 Fax: 512-284-2700
CEO: Jack D. Rehm
CFO: Larry D. Hartsook
1992 Sales: $735 million Employees: 2,025
Symbol: MDP Exchange: NYSE
Industry: Publishing - periodicals

Meridian Bancorp, Inc.
35 N. Sixth St.
Reading, PA 19601
Phone: 215-655-2000 Fax: 215-320-2452
CEO: Samuel A. McCullough
CFO: David E. Sparks
1992 Sales: $1,082 million Employees: 5,360
Symbol: MRDN Exchange: NASDAQ
Industry: Banks - Northeast

Meridian Diagnostics, Inc.
3471 River Hills Dr.
Cincinnati, OH 45244
Phone: 513-271-3700 Fax: 513-271-3762
CEO: William J. Motto
CFO: Frank J. Seurkamp
1991 Sales: $11 million Employees: 99
Symbol: KITS Exchange: NASDAQ
Industry: Medical products - immunodiagnostic test kits

Meridian Insurance Group, Inc.
2955 N. Meridian St.
Indianapolis, IN 46208
Phone: 317-927-8100 Fax: 317-925-5902
CEO: Norma J. Oman
CFO: William E. Denny
1991 Sales: $119 million Employees: —
Symbol: MIGI Exchange: NASDAQ
Industry: Insurance - property & casualty

Meris Laboratories, Inc.
2890 Zanker Rd.
San Jose, CA 95134
Phone: 408-434-9200 Fax: —
CEO: Chris C. Riedel
CFO: John J. DiPietro
1991 Sales: $20 million Employees: 303
Symbol: MERS Exchange: NASDAQ
Industry: Medical services - laboratory & patient service centers

Merisel, Inc.
200 Continental Blvd.
El Segundo, CA 90245
Phone: 310-615-3080 Fax: 310-615-1238
CEO: Michael D. Pickett
CFO: James L. Brill
1992 Sales: $2,239 million Employees: 1,450
Symbol: MSEL Exchange: NASDAQ
Industry: Computers - retail & wholesale

Merit Medical Systems, Inc.
79 West 4500 South, Ste. 9
Salt Lake City, UT 84107
Phone: 801-263-9300 Fax: 801-268-4201
CEO: Fred P. Lampropoulos
CFO: Kent W. Stanger
1991 Sales: $10.5 million Employees: 171
Symbol: MMSI Exchange: NASDAQ
Industry: Medical products - disposable proprietary products for cardiology & radiology

Merrill Corp.
One Merrill Circle
St. Paul, MN 55108
Phone: 612-646-4501 Fax: 800-647-2424
CEO: John W. Castro
CFO: John B. McCain
1992 Sales: $125 million Employees: 831
Symbol: MRLL Exchange: NASDAQ
Industry: Printing - commercial

Merrill Lynch & Co., Inc.
250 Vesey St., 18th Fl.
New York, NY 10281
Phone: 212-449-1000 Fax: 212-236-4384
CEO: William A. Schreyer
CFO: Herbert M. Allison, Jr.
1992 Sales: $13,428 million Employees: 38,300
Symbol: MER Exchange: NYSE
Industry: Financial - business services; securities brokerage, asset management, insurance

Merrimac Industries, Inc.
41 Fairfield Place
West Caldwell, NJ 07006
Phone: 201-575-1300 Fax: 201-575-0531
CEO: Paul Terranova
CFO: Paul Terranova
1991 Sales: $13 million Employees: 138
Symbol: MRM Exchange: AMEX
Industry: Electronics - military

Merry-Go-Round Enterprises, Inc.
3300 Fashion Way
Joppa, MD 21085
Phone: 410-538-1000 Fax: 410-538-1001
CEO: Michael D. Sullivan
CFO: Isaac Kaufman
1992 Sales: $833 million Employees: 11,688
Symbol: MGR Exchange: NYSE
Industry: Retail - apparel & shoes

Mesa Airlines, Inc.
2325 E. 30th St.
Farmington, NM 87401
Phone: 505-327-0271 Fax: 505-326-4485
CEO: Larry L. Risley
CFO: Blaine M. Jones
1992 Sales: $317 million Employees: 2,540
Symbol: MESA Exchange: NASDAQ
Industry: Transportation - airline

Mesa Inc.
2001 Ross Ave.
Dallas, TX 75201
Phone: 214-969-2200 Fax: —
CEO: T. Boone Pickens
CFO: W. Mark Womble
1991 Sales: $250 million Employees: 351
Symbol: MXP Exchange: NYSE
Industry: Oil & gas - US exploration & production

Mestek, Inc.
260 N. Elm St.
Westfield, MA 01085
Phone: 413-568-9571 Fax: 413-568-2969
CEO: John E. Reed
CFO: Stephen M. Shea
1991 Sales: $221 million Employees: 2,600
Symbol: MCC Exchange: NYSE
Industry: Building products - a/c & heating

Met-Coil Systems Corp.
5486 Sixth St. SW
Cedar Rapids, IA 52404
Phone: 319-363-6566 Fax: 319-362-0225
CEO: Raymond H. Blakeman
CFO: Michael E. Canfield
1992 Sales: $47 million Employees: 419
Symbol: METS Exchange: NASDAQ
Industry: Metal products - fabrication

Met-Pro Corp.
160 Cassell Rd.
Harleysville, PA 19438
Phone: 215-723-6751 Fax: 215-723-6758
CEO: Edwin A. Wilcox
CFO: William F. Moffit
1991 Sales: $40 million Employees: —
Symbol: MPR Exchange: AMEX
Industry: Filtration equipment, air & water purification systems

Metalize Texas Inc.
PO Box 520
Bastrop, TX 78602
Phone: 512-321-4477 Fax: 512-321-4437
CEO: Jone Rodgers
CFO: Russell Jenkins
1991 Sales: $0.9 million Employees: 25
Ownership: Privately held
Industry: Metal processing - electrochemical metalizing

indicates company is in *Hoover's Handbook of American Business.*

indicates company is in *Hoover's Handbook of World Business;* sales and employee numbers are for parent company.

Metallurg, Inc.
25 E. 39th St.
New York, NY 10016
Phone: 212-686-4010 Fax: 212-697-2874
CEO: Michael A. Standen
CFO: George J. Udcoff
1991 Sales: $650 million Employees: 2,800
Ownership: Privately held
Industry: Metal products - fabrication, alloys

Methode Electronics, Inc.
7444 W. Wilson Ave.
Chicago, IL 60656
Phone: 708-867-9600 Fax: 708-867-9130
CEO: William J. McGinley
CFO: Kevin J. Hayes
1992 Sales: $148 million Employees: 1,930
Symbol: METHA Exchange: NASDAQ
Industry: Electrical connectors

Metrica, Inc.
8301 Broadway, Ste. 215
San Antonio, TX 78209
Phone: 210-822-6600 Fax: 210-821-6301
CEO: Nancy Dunson
CFO: Nancy Dunson
1991 Sales: $8.2 million Employees: 145
Ownership: Privately held
Industry: Computers - data-processing systems integration & research services

Metricom, Inc.
980 University Ave.
Los Gatos, CA 95030
Phone: 408-399-8200 Fax: —
CEO: Robert P. Dilworth
CFO: William D. Swain
1991 Sales: $10.7 million Employees: 78
Symbol: MCOM Exchange: NASDAQ
Industry: Telecommunications equipment

Metro Bancshares Inc.
100 Jericho Quadrangle
Jericho, NY 11753
Phone: 516-933-8000 Fax: 516-935-3242
CEO: David G. Herold
CFO: Stephen G. Wilson
1991 Sales: $75 million Employees: 295
Symbol: MTO Exchange: AMEX
Industry: Banks - Northeast

Metro-Tel Corp.
500 N. Broadway, Ste. 240
Jericho, NY 11753
Phone: 516-937-3420 Fax: 516-937-3426
CEO: Venerando J. Indelicato
CFO: Venerando J. Indelicato
1992 Sales: $4.4 million Employees: 31
Symbol: MTRO Exchange: NASDAQ
Industry: Telecommunications equipment

Metrobank
10900 Wilshire Blvd.
Los Angeles, CA 90024
Phone: 310-824-5700 Fax: 310-824-1771
CEO: David L. Buell
CFO: David P. Malone
1991 Sales: $70 million Employees: —
Symbol: MBN Exchange: AMEX
Industry: Banks - West

Metrographics Printing & Computer Svcs.
10 Madison Rd.
Fairfield, NJ 07003
Phone: 201-882-6500 Fax: 201-882-5663
CEO: Andrew Duke
CFO: Jeff Bernstein
1991 Sales: $2 million Employees: 12
Ownership: Privately held
Industry: Business services - printing & computer services

Metromedia Company
One Meadowlands Plaza
East Rutherford, NJ 07073
Phone: 201-804-6400 Fax: 201-804-6540
CEO: John W. Kluge
CFO: Stuart Subotnick
1991 Sales: $2,220 million Employees: 49,000
Ownership: Privately held
Industry: Retail - food & restaurants, entertainment & telecommunications industries

Metropolitan Federal Savings and Loan Assoc.
1520 4th Ave.
Seattle, WA 98101
Phone: 206-625-1818 Fax: —
CEO: Patrick F. Patrick
CFO: Ann R. Christensen
1992 Sales: — Employees: —
Symbol: MSEA Exchange: NASDAQ
Industry: Financial - savings and loans

Metropolitan Financial Corp.
6800 France Ave. South
Minneapolis, MN 55435
Phone: 612-928-5000 Fax: 612-928-5099
CEO: Norman M. Jones
CFO: David J. Melroe
1991 Sales: $496 million Employees: 1,790
Symbol: MFC Exchange: NYSE
Industry: Financial - savings and loans

Metropolitan Life Insurance Co.
One Madison Ave.
New York, NY 10010
Phone: 212-578-2211 Fax: 212-685-1224
CEO: Robert G. Schwartz
CFO: Philip Briggs
1991 Sales: $28,488 million Employees: 58,000
Ownership: Privately held
Industry: Insurance - life

Metters Industries Inc.
8200 Greensboro Dr. #500
McLean, VA 22102
Phone: 703-821-3300 Fax: 703-821-3996
CEO: Samuel Metters
CFO: Eugene Lynch
1991 Sales: $29 million Employees: 350
Ownership: Privately held
Industry: Engineering services

MGI PHARMA, Inc.
9900 Bren Rd. East, Ste. 300E
Minneapolis, MN 55343
Phone: 612-935-7335 Fax: 612-935-0468
CEO: Kenneth F. Tempero
CFO: James V. Adam
1991 Sales: $6.1 million Employees: 48
Symbol: MOGN Exchange: NASDAQ
Industry: Drugs

MGIC Investment Corp.
250 E. Kilbourn Ave.
Milwaukee, WI 53202
Phone: 414-347-6480 Fax: 414-347-6696
CEO: William H. Lacy
CFO: J. Michael Lauer
1991 Sales: $294 million Employees: 1,892
Symbol: MTG Exchange: NYSE
Industry: Financial - mortgages & related services

MGM Grand, Inc.
9333 Wilshire Blvd., Ste. 302
Beverly Hills, CA 90210
Phone: 213-271-3793 Fax: 213-271-2961
CEO: Robert R. Maxey
CFO: Joseph T. Murphy
1991 Sales: $147 million Employees: 364
Symbol: MGG Exchange: NYSE
Industry: Hotels & motels

MHI Group, Inc.
2032-D Thomasville Rd.
Tallahassee, FL 32312
Phone: 904-385-8883 Fax: —
CEO: Fred O. Drake, Jr.
CFO: Glynda Jane Harris
1992 Sales: $16 million Employees: 135
Symbol: MH Exchange: NYSE
Industry: Funeral services & related

Miami Subs Corp.
6300 NW 31st Ave.
Ft. Lauderdale, FL 33309
Phone: 305-973-0000 Fax: —
CEO: C. R. Petty
CFO: C. Barnett
1992 Sales: $8.7 million Employees: 355
Symbol: SUBS Exchange: NASDAQ
Industry: Retail - food & restaurants

Michael Anthony Jewelers, Inc.
115 S. MacQuesten Pkwy.
Mt. Vernon, NY 10550
Phone: 914-699-0000 Fax: 914-664-4884
CEO: Michael Paolercio
CFO: Allan Corn
1992 Sales: $113 million Employees: 446
Symbol: MAJ Exchange: AMEX
Industry: Precious metals & jewelry

Michael Baker Corp.
4301 Dutch Ridge Rd.
Beaver, PA 15009
Phone: 412-495-7711 Fax: 412-269-2534
CEO: William G. Thomas
CFO: Donald J. Nelson
1991 Sales: $203 million Employees: 2,603
Symbol: BKR Exchange: AMEX
Industry: Engineering - R&D services

Michael Foods, Inc.
5353 Wayzata Blvd.
Minneapolis, MN 55416
Phone: 612-546-1500 Fax: 612-546-3711
CEO: Richard G. Olson
CFO: John D. Reedy
1991 Sales: $455 million Employees: 2,730
Symbol: MIKL Exchange: NASDAQ
Industry: Food - eggs, dairy & potato products

Michaels Stores, Inc.
5931 Campus Circle Dr.
Irving, TX 75063
Phone: 214-580-8242 Fax: 214-714-7155
CEO: Sam Wyly
CFO: R. Don Morris
1991 Sales: $411 million Employees: 5,490
Symbol: MIKE Exchange: NASDAQ
Industry: Retail - framing materials & arts & crafts

Michelin Tire Corp.
PO Box 19001
Greenville, SC 29602
Phone: 803-458-5000 Fax: 803-458-6359
CEO: Carlos Ghosu
CFO: —
1991 Sales: $13,060 million Employees: 135,610
Parent: Michelin
Industry: Rubber tires

Michigan Financial Corp.
101 W. Washington St.
Marquette, MI 49855
Phone: 906-228-6940 Fax: —
CEO: Howard L. Cohodas
CFO: Kenneth F. Beck
1991 Sales: $30 million Employees: 600
Symbol: MFCB Exchange: NASDAQ
Industry: Banks - Midwest

indicates company is in *Hoover's Handbook of American Business.*

indicates company is in *Hoover's Handbook of World Business;* sales and employee numbers are for parent company.

Michigan National Corp.
2777 Inkster Rd.
Farmington Hills, MI 48334
Phone: 313-473-3000 Fax: —
CEO: Robert J. Mylod
CFO: Eric D. Booth
1992 Sales: $1,004 million Employees: 5,700
Symbol: MNCO Exchange: NASDAQ
Industry: Banks - Midwest

Mickelberry Corp.
405 Park Ave., 10th Fl.
New York, NY 10022
Phone: 212-832-0303 Fax: 212-832-0554
CEO: James C. Marlas
CFO: George Kane
1991 Sales: $106 million Employees: 706
Symbol: MBC Exchange: NYSE
Industry: Advertising, promotions & printing

Micro Bio-Medics, Inc.
846 Pelham Pkwy.
Pelham Manor, NY 10803
Phone: 914-699-1700 Fax: 914-699-1759
CEO: Bruce J. Haber
CFO: Bruce J. Haber
1991 Sales: $51 million Employees: 172
Symbol: MBMI Exchange: NASDAQ
Industry: Medical & dental supplies

Micro Healthsystems, Inc.
414 Eagle Rock Ave.
West Orange, NJ 07052
Phone: 201-731-9252 Fax: —
CEO: S. M. Caravetta
CFO: Walter R. Cruickshank
1992 Sales: $19 million Employees: 160
Symbol: MCHS Exchange: NASDAQ
Industry: Computers - turnkey software management systems

Micro Information Services
10206 N. Port Washington Rd.
Mequon, WI 53092
Phone: 414-241-9410 Fax: 414-241-9528
CEO: Fred Pike
CFO: Fred Pike
1991 Sales: $3.4 million Employees: 25
Ownership: Privately held
Industry: Computers - networking services

Micro-Frame Technologies Inc.
2151 E. D St. 201C
Ontario, CA 91764
Phone: 909-983-2711 Fax: 909-984-5382
CEO: John O'Neil
CFO: John O'Neil
1991 Sales: $9 million Employees: 86
Ownership: Privately held
Industry: Computers - cost-management software

MicroAge Computer Centers, Inc.
2308 S. 55th St.
Tempe, AZ 85282
Phone: 602-968-3168 Fax: 602-966-7339
CEO: Jeffrey D. McKeever
CFO: John H. Andrews
1992 Sales: $1,099 million Employees: 629
Symbol: MICA Exchange: NASDAQ
Industry: Retail - computer hardware & software

Microcom, Inc.
500 River Ridge Dr.
Norwood, MA 02062
Phone: 617-551-1000 Fax: 617-551-1006
CEO: James M. Dow
CFO: Peter J. Minihane
1992 Sales: $74 million Employees: 405
Symbol: MNPI Exchange: NASDAQ
Industry: Telecommunications equipment

Microdyne Corp.
491 Oak Rd.
Ocala, FL 32672
Phone: 904-687-4633 Fax: 904-687-3392
CEO: Donald L. Feller
CFO: Robert K. Michaels
1991 Sales: $56 million Employees: 544
Symbol: MCDY Exchange: NASDAQ
Industry: Telecommunications equipment

Microlog Corp.
20270 Goldenrod Lane
Germantown, MD 20876
Phone: 301-428-3227 Fax: 301-972-6208
CEO: Joe J. Lynn
CFO: William J. Lallas
1991 Sales: $20 million Employees: 290
Symbol: MLOG Exchange: NASDAQ
Industry: Telecommunications equipment

Micron Technology, Inc.
2805 E. Columbia Rd.
Boise, ID 83706
Phone: 208-368-4000 Fax: 208-343-2536
CEO: Joseph L. Parkinson
CFO: Reid N. Langrill
1992 Sales: $506 million Employees: 4,100
Symbol: MU Exchange: NYSE
Industry: Electrical components - semiconductors

Micronics Computers, Inc.
232 E. Warren Ave.
Fremont, CA 94539
Phone: 510-651-2300 Fax: 510-651-5666
CEO: Frank W. Lin
CFO: Steven R. Wade
1991 Sales: $134 million Employees: 254
Symbol: MCRN Exchange: NASDAQ
Industry: Computers - system boards

Micropolis Corp.
21211 Nordhoff St.
Chatsworth, CA 91311
Phone: 818-709-3300 Fax: 818-709-3396
CEO: Stuart P. Mabon
CFO: Dale J. Bartos
1991 Sales: $351 million Employees: 2,780
Symbol: MLIS Exchange: NASDAQ
Industry: Computers - Winchester disk drives

MicroProse Software, Inc.
180 Lakefront Dr.
Hunt Valley, MD 21030
Phone: 410-771-1151 Fax: 410-771-1174
CEO: John W. Stealey, Sr.
CFO: James W. Thomas
1992 Sales: $41 million Employees: 272
Symbol: MPRS Exchange: NASDAQ
Industry: Computers - entertainment software

MICROS Systems, Inc.
12000 Baltimore Ave.
Beltsville, MD 20705
Phone: 301-490-2000 Fax: 301-490-6699
CEO: Reay Sterling, Jr.
CFO: Ronald J. Kolson
1992 Sales: $44 million Employees: 329
Symbol: MCRS Exchange: NASDAQ
Industry: Office automation

Microsemi Corp.
2830 S. Fairview St.
Santa Ana, CA 92704
Phone: 714-979-8220 Fax: 714-557-5989
CEO: Philip Frey, Jr.
CFO: David R. Sonksen
1991 Sales: $83 million Employees: 1,961
Symbol: MSCC Exchange: NASDAQ
Industry: Electrical components - semiconductors

Microserv
11321 NE 120th St.
Kirkland, WA 98034
Phone: 206-820-5605 Fax: 206-820-5665
CEO: Gary Zukowski
CFO: Martin Rae
1991 Sales: $5.5 million Employees: 98
Ownership: Privately held
Industry: Engineering services

Microsoft Corp.
One Microsoft Way
Redmond, WA 98052
Phone: 206-882-8080 Fax: 206-883-8101
CEO: William H. Gates III
CFO: Francis J. Gaudette
1992 Sales: $3,252 million Employees: 11,542
Symbol: MSFT Exchange: NASDAQ
Industry: Computers - systems, operating environment & application software

Microtest, Inc.
4747 N. 22nd St.
Phoenix, AZ 85016
Phone: 602-957-6400 Fax: 602-957-6414
CEO: David Bolles
CFO: Carl Strain
1991 Sales: $17 million Employees: 150
Ownership: Privately held
Industry: Computers - network diagnostic tools & enhancement software

MicroTouch Systems, Inc.
55 Jonspin Rd.
Wilmington, MA 01887
Phone: 508-694-9900 Fax: —
CEO: James D. Logan
CFO: Geoffrey P. Clear
1991 Sales: $19 million Employees: 202
Symbol: MTSI Exchange: NASDAQ
Industry: Computers - peripheral equipment

Microwave Laboratories, Inc.
8917 Glenwood Ave.
Raleigh, NC 27612
Phone: 919-781-4260 Fax: —
CEO: Carl A. Everleigh, Jr.
CFO: Gary L. Allen
1991 Sales: $14 million Employees: 112
Symbol: MWAV Exchange: NASDAQ
Industry: Electronics - military

Mid Atlantic Medical Services Inc.
4 Taft Court
Rockville, MD 20850
Phone: 301-294-5140 Fax: 301-762-1430
CEO: George T. Jochum
CFO: John L. Child
1991 Sales: $398 million Employees: 573
Symbol: MAMS Exchange: NASDAQ
Industry: Healthcare - outpatient & home

Mid Maine Savings Bank, F.S.B.
Great Falls Plaza
Auburn, ME 04210
Phone: 207-784-3581 Fax: —
CEO: Ralph L. Hodgkins, Jr.
CFO: Allen R. Stasulis
1991 Sales: $20 million Employees: 103
Symbol: MMS Exchange: AMEX
Industry: Financial - savings and loans

Mid-Am, Inc.
222 S. Main St.
Bowling Green, OH 43402
Phone: 419-352-5271 Fax: 419-352-2305
CEO: Edward J. Reiter
CFO: Dennis L. Nemec
1991 Sales: $119 million Employees: 761
Symbol: MIAM Exchange: NASDAQ
Industry: Banks - Midwest

 indicates company is in *Hoover's Handbook of American Business.*

indicates company is in *Hoover's Handbook of World Business;* sales and employee numbers are for parent company.

Mid-America Bancorp
500 W. Broadway
Louisville, KY 40202
Phone: 502-589-3351 Fax: 502-562-5468
CEO: Bertram W. Klein
CFO: Bertram W. Klein
1991 Sales: $89 million Employees: 577
Symbol: MAB Exchange: AMEX
Industry: Banks - Southeast

Mid-American Waste Systems, Inc.
1006 Walnut St.
Canal Winchester, OH 43110
Phone: 614-833-9155 Fax: 614-833-9173
CEO: Christopher L. White
CFO: Dennis P. Wilburn
1991 Sales: $119 million Employees: 1,169
Symbol: MAW Exchange: NYSE
Industry: Pollution control equipment & services - solid waste disposal

Mid-Atlantic Cars
10287 Lee Hwy.
Fairfax, VA 22030
Phone: 703-352-5555 Fax: 703-352-5591
CEO: William E. Schuiling
CFO: Charles Stringfellow
1991 Sales: $1,300 million Employees: 3,000
Ownership: Privately held
Industry: Retail - auto dealerships

Mid-South Insurance Co.
4317 Ramsey St.
Fayetteville, NC 28311
Phone: 919-822-1020 Fax: —
CEO: Walter B. Clark
CFO: Walter B. Clark
1991 Sales: $55 million Employees: 98
Symbol: MIDS Exchange: NASDAQ
Industry: Insurance - accident & health

Mid-State Federal Savings Bank
3300 SW 34th Ave., Ste. 101
Ocala, FL 32674
Phone: 904-854-0177 Fax: —
CEO: Charles E. Harris
CFO: James L. Goehler
1992 Sales: — Employees: —
Symbol: MSSB Exchange: NASDAQ
Industry: Financial - savings and loans

MidConn Bank
346 Main St.
Kensington, CT 06037
Phone: 203-828-0301 Fax: —
CEO: Richard J. Toman
CFO: Robert W. Anderson
1992 Sales: — Employees: —
Symbol: MIDC Exchange: NASDAQ
Industry: Banks - Northeast

Middleby Corp.
10255 W. Higgins Rd.
Rosemont, IL 60018
Phone: 708-299-2940 Fax: 708-299-7651
CEO: David P. Riley
CFO: James F. Ott
1991 Sales: $103 million Employees: 909
Symbol: MBY Exchange: AMEX
Industry: Machinery - general industrial

Middlesex Water Co.
1500 Ronson Rd.
Iselin, NJ 08830
Phone: 908-634-1500 Fax: 908-750-5981
CEO: J. Richard Tompkins
CFO: Ernest C. Gere
1991 Sales: $30 million Employees: 135
Symbol: MSEX Exchange: NASDAQ
Industry: Utility - water supply

Midland Co.
537 E. Pete Rose Way
Cincinnati, OH 45202
Phone: 513-721-3777 Fax: 513-721-5284
CEO: J. P. Hayden, Jr.
CFO: John I. Von Lehman
1991 Sales: $203 million Employees: 825
Symbol: MLA Exchange: AMEX
Industry: Diversified operations - insurance, river transportation; financial services

Midlantic Corp.
Metro Park Plaza, 499 Thornhill St.
Edison, NJ 08818
Phone: 908-321-8000 Fax: 908-321-2271
CEO: Gary J. Scheuring
CFO: Donald W. Ebbert, Jr.
1992 Sales: $1,353 million Employees: 9,561
Symbol: MIDL Exchange: NASDAQ
Industry: Banks - Northeast

MidSouth Corp.
111 E. Capitol St.
Jackson, MS 39201
Phone: 601-353-7508 Fax: 601-354-5737
CEO: Mark M. Levin
CFO: John A. Scotto
1991 Sales: $92 million Employees: 587
Symbol: MSRR Exchange: NASDAQ
Industry: Transportation - rail

Midwesco Filter Resources, Inc.
400 Battaile Dr.
Winchester, VA 22601
Phone: 703-667-8500 Fax: 703-667-9074
CEO: David Unger
CFO: Michael D. Bennett
1991 Sales: $22 million Employees: 179
Symbol: MFRI Exchange: NASDAQ
Industry: Filtration products

Midwest Communications Corp.
4 Tesseneer Dr.
Highland Heights, KY 41076
Phone: 606-781-2200 Fax: 606-781-3988
CEO: Leonard L. Brown
CFO: Dennis H. Eaton
1991 Sales: $10.7 million Employees: 78
Symbol: MCOM Exchange: NASDAQ
Industry: Video equipment

Midwest Grain Products, Inc.
1300 Main St.
Atchison, KS 66002
Phone: 913-367-1480 Fax: 913-367-0192
CEO: Laidacker M. Seaberg
CFO: Robert G. Booe
1992 Sales: $174 million Employees: 536
Symbol: MWGP Exchange: NASDAQ
Industry: Food - flour & grain

Midwest Resources Inc.
666 Grand Ave.
Des Moines, IA 50306
Phone: 515-242-4300 Fax: 515-281-2981
CEO: Russell E. Christiansen
CFO: Gary J. Harward
1992 Sales: $1,033 million Employees: 3,100
Symbol: MWR Exchange: NYSE
Industry: Utility - electric power

Miles Inc.
One Mellon Center, 500 Grant St.
Pittsburgh, PA 15219
Phone: 412-394-5500 Fax: 412-394-5578
CEO: Helge H. Wehmeier
CFO: —
1991 Sales: $27,895 million Employees: 164,200
Parent: Bayer AG
Industry: Chemicals - diversified

Milestone Properties, Inc.
5200 Town Center Circle
Boca Raton, FL 33486
Phone: 407-394-9533 Fax: 407-393-8095
CEO: Leonard S. Mandor
CFO: Robert A. Mandor
1991 Sales: $7.7 million Employees: 14
Symbol: MPI Exchange: NYSE
Industry: Real estate development

Miller Building Systems, Inc.
58120 County Rd. 3 South
Elkhart, IN 46517
Phone: 219-295-1214 Fax: 219-295-2232
CEO: John M. Davis
CFO: Thomas M. Martini
1992 Sales: $41 million Employees: 380
Symbol: MTIK Exchange: NASDAQ
Industry: Building - residential & commercial

Millfeld Trading, Inc.
150 Woodbury Rd.
Woodbury, NY 11797
Phone: 516-367-3711 Fax: 516-367-3973
CEO: Barry Feldstein
CFO: Michael P. Callahan
1991 Sales: $4.4 million Employees: 33
Symbol: SHOEC Exchange: NASDAQ
Industry: Shoes & related apparel

Millicom Inc.
153 E. 53rd St., Ste. 5500
New York, NY 10022
Phone: 212-355-3440 Fax: 212-751-2114
CEO: J. Shelby Bryan
CFO: David J. Frear
1991 Sales: $56 million Employees: 1,469
Symbol: MILL Exchange: NASDAQ
Industry: Telecommunications services

Milliken & Co., Inc.
920 Milliken Rd.
Spartanburg, SC 29303
Phone: 803-573-2020 Fax: 803-573-2100
CEO: Roger Milliken
CFO: Minot K. Milliken
1991 Sales: $2,498 million Employees: 14,000
Ownership: Privately held
Industry: Textiles - mill products

Millipore Corp.
80 Ashby Rd.
Bedford, MA 01730
Phone: 617-275-9200 Fax: 617-275-5550
CEO: John A. Gilmartin
CFO: Douglas A. Berthiaume
1992 Sales: $777 million Employees: 5,755
Symbol: MIL Exchange: NYSE
Industry: Filtration products

Miltope Group Inc.
1770 Walt Whitman Rd.
Melville, NY 11747
Phone: 516-420-0200 Fax: 516-756-7606
CEO: Michael H. Alexander
CFO: Bruce M. Crowell
1991 Sales: $103 million Employees: 600
Symbol: MILT Exchange: NASDAQ
Industry: Computers - mini & micro

Milwaukee Insurance Group, Inc.
803 W. Michigan St.
Milwaukee, WI 53233
Phone: 414-271-0525 Fax: —
CEO: Robert W. Doucette
CFO: John A. Weitzel
1991 Sales: $76 million Employees: 721
Symbol: MILW Exchange: NASDAQ
Industry: Insurance - property & casualty

indicates company is in *Hoover's Handbook of American Business.*

indicates company is in *Hoover's Handbook of World Business;* sales and employee numbers are for parent company.

Mine Safety Appliances Co.
121 Gamma Dr.
Pittsburgh, PA 15238
Phone: 412-967-3000 Fax: 412-967-3326
CEO: John T. Ryan III
CFO: James E. Herald
1991 Sales: $501 million Employees: 5,600
Symbol: MNES Exchange: NASDAQ
Industry: Respiratory, eye, ear & face protective equipment, mining safety equipment

Miners National Bancorp, Inc.
120 S. Centre St.
Pottsville, PA 17901
Phone: 717-622-2320 Fax: —
CEO: Allen E. Kiefer
CFO: Guy H. Boyer
1991 Sales: $18 million Employees: 130
Symbol: MNBC Exchange: NASDAQ
Industry: Banks - Northeast

Minnesota Mining and Manufacturing Co.
3M Center
St. Paul, MN 55144
Phone: 612-733-1110 Fax: 612-736-8261
CEO: Livio D. DeSimone
CFO: Giulio Agostini
1992 Sales: $13,883 million Employees: 88,477
Symbol: MMM Exchange: NYSE
Industry: Diversified operations - information & imaging equipment, consumer products

Minnesota Power & Light Co.
30 W. Superior St.
Duluth, MN 55802
Phone: 218-722-2641 Fax: 218-723-3996
CEO: Arend J. Sandbulte
CFO: Robert D. Edwards
1991 Sales: $484 million Employees: 2,719
Symbol: MPL Exchange: NYSE
Industry: Utility - electric power

Minntech Corp.
14905 28th Ave. North
Minneapolis, MN 55447
Phone: 612-553-3300 Fax: 612-553-3371
CEO: Louis C. Cosentino
CFO: Robert M. Rosner
1992 Sales: $35 million Employees: 262
Symbol: MNTX Exchange: NASDAQ
Industry: Medical products

Minolta Corporation (U.S.A.)
101 Williams Dr.
Ramsey, NJ 07446
Phone: 201-825-4000 Fax: 201-423-0590
CEO: Sadahei Kusomoto
CFO: —
1992 Sales: $2,849 million Employees: 6,741
Parent: Minolta Camera Co., Ltd.
Industry: Photographic equipment & supplies, copiers

Minorco (U.S.A.) Inc.
5251 DTC Pkwy., Ste. 700
Englewood, CO 80111
Phone: 303-889-0700 Fax: 303-889-0707
CEO: Gerard E. Munera
CFO: —
1992 Sales: $613 million Employees: —
Parent: Anglo American Corporation
Industry: Gold mining & processing

MinVen Gold Corp.
7596 W. Jewell Ave., Ste. 303
Lakewood, CO 80232
Phone: 303-980-5615 Fax: 303-980-5302
CEO: Alan R. Bell
CFO: Robert R. Gilmore
1991 Sales: $32 million Employees: 208
Symbol: MVG Exchange: AMEX
Industry: Gold mining & processing

Minyard Food Stores Inc.
777 Freeport Pkwy.
Coppell, TX 75019
Phone: 214-393-8700 Fax: 214-462-9407
CEO: Liz Minyard
CFO: John Bennett
1991 Sales: $730 million Employees: 6,100
Ownership: Privately held
Industry: Retail - supermarkets

Mirage Resorts, Inc.
3400 Las Vegas Blvd. South
Las Vegas, NV 89109
Phone: 702-791-5627 Fax: 702-792-7646
CEO: Stephen A. Wynn
CFO: Daniel R. Lee
1991 Sales: $823 million Employees: 11,400
Symbol: MIR Exchange: NYSE
Industry: Leisure & recreational services - casinos

Mission West Properties
6815 Flanders Dr., Ste. 150
San Diego, CA 92121
Phone: 619-450-3135 Fax: 619-450-1618
CEO: G. Joseph LaBreche
CFO: J. Gregory Kasun
1991 Sales: $6.1 million Employees: 17
Symbol: MSW Exchange: AMEX
Industry: Real estate operations

Mitchell Energy & Development Corp.
2001 Timberloch Place
The Woodlands, TX 77380
Phone: 713-377-5500 Fax: 713-377-6910
CEO: George P. Mitchell
CFO: Philip S. Smith
1992 Sales: $908 million Employees: 2,900
Symbol: MND Exchange: NYSE
Industry: Oil & gas - US exploration & production

Mitek Surgical Products, Inc.
57 Providence Hwy.
Norwood, MA 02062
Phone: 617-551-8500 Fax: 617-551-8501
CEO: Kenneth W. Anstey
CFO: Henry Barber
1991 Sales: $8.4 million Employees: 40
Symbol: MYTK Exchange: NASDAQ
Industry: Medical products - surgical implants

Mitsubishi International Corp.
520 Madison Ave.
New York, NY 10022
Phone: 212-605-2000 Fax: 212-605-2597
CEO: Tetsuo Kamimura
CFO: —
1992 Sales: $144,973 million Employees: 13,602
Parent: Mitsubishi Group
Industry: Diversified operations - metals, machinery, information systems & chemicals

Mitsui & Co. (U.S.A.), Inc.
200 Park Ave.
New York, NY 10166
Phone: 212-878-4000 Fax: 212-878-4800
CEO: Junichi Amano
CFO: —
1992 Sales: $134,089 million Employees: 11,773
Parent: Mitsui Group
Industry: Diversified operations - machinery, nonferrous metals, energy & food

MLX Corp.
4781 Lewis Rd.
Stone Mountain, GA 30083
Phone: 404-939-5910 Fax: —
CEO: Brian R. Esher
CFO: Tom Waggoner
1991 Sales: $51 million Employees: 485
Symbol: MLXX Exchange: NASDAQ
Industry: Metal products - fabrication

MMI Medical, Inc.
11155 Jersey Blvd., Unit D
Rancho Cucamonga, CA 91730
Phone: 909-466-9884 Fax: 909-466-8303
CEO: Alan D. Margulis
CFO: Christopher Purcell
1992 Sales: $45 million Employees: 270
Symbol: MMIM Exchange: NASDAQ
Industry: Medical services - diagnostic imaging services

MMI of Mississippi, Inc.
232 Georgetown
Crystal Springs, MS 39059
Phone: 601-892-1105 Fax: 601-892-1150
CEO: William Reeves
CFO: William Reeves
1992 Sales: $3.3 million Employees: 14
Ownership: Privately held
Industry: Medical products - health care furniture & laboratories

MNC Financial, Inc.
100 S. Charles St.
Baltimore, MD 21201
Phone: 410-605-5000 Fax: 410-837-6132
CEO: Alfred Lerner
CFO: Peter L. Gartman
1992 Sales: $1,533 million Employees: 7,820
Symbol: MNC Exchange: NYSE
Industry: Banks - Southeast

MNX Inc.
5310 St. Joseph Ave.
St. Joseph, MO 64505
Phone: 816-233-3158 Fax: 816-387-4201
CEO: J. Michael Head
CFO: Janet K. Pullen
1991 Sales: $289 million Employees: 1,695
Symbol: MNXI Exchange: NASDAQ
Industry: Transportation - truck

Mobil Corp.
3225 Gallows Rd.
Fairfax, VA 22037
Phone: 703-846-3000 Fax: 703-846-4669
CEO: Allen E. Murray
CFO: Robert G. Weeks
1992 Sales: $57,217 million Employees: 67,500
Symbol: MOB Exchange: NYSE
Industry: Oil & gas - international integrated; packaging films, fabricated plastics

Mobile Gas Service Corp.
2828 Dauphin St.
Mobile, AL 36606
Phone: 205-476-2720 Fax: 205-471-2588
CEO: Walter L. Hovell
CFO: Charles P. Huffman
1991 Sales: $45 million Employees: 244
Symbol: MBLE Exchange: NASDAQ
Industry: Utility - gas distribution

Mobile Telecommunications Technologies Corp.
200 S. Lamar
Jackson, MS 39201
Phone: 601-944-1300 Fax: 601-944-7158
CEO: John N. Palmer
CFO: J. Robert Fugate
1991 Sales: $90 million Employees: 1,335
Symbol: MTEL Exchange: NASDAQ
Industry: Telecommunications services

Mobley Environmental Services, Inc.
3800 Stone Rd.
Kilgore, TX 75662
Phone: 903-984-0270 Fax: 903-983-1227
CEO: John A. Mobley
CFO: Steven M. Mobley
1991 Sales: $37 million Employees: 320
Symbol: MBLYA Exchange: NASDAQ
Industry: Pollution control equipment & services - waste disposal & oil field services

indicates company is in *Hoover's Handbook of American Business*.

indicates company is in *Hoover's Handbook of World Business*; sales and employee numbers are for parent company.

Modern Controls, Inc.
7500 Boone Ave. North
Minneapolis, MN 55428
Phone: 612-493-6370 Fax: 612-493-6358
CEO: William N. Mayer
CFO: Ronald A. Meyer
1991 Sales: $14 million Employees: 72
Symbol: MOCO Exchange: NASDAQ
Industry: Instruments - control

Modern Technologies Corp
4032 Linden Ave.
Dayton, OH 45432
Phone: 513-252-9199 Fax: 513--2583863
CEO: Rajesh Soin
CFO: Richard Schott
1992 Sales: $40 million Employees: 570
Ownership: Privately held
Industry: Engineering services, vehicle manufacture & environmental engineering

Modine Manufacturing Co.
1500 DeKoven Ave.
Racine, WI 53403
Phone: 414-636-1200 Fax: 414-636-1424
CEO: Richard T. Savage
CFO: Alan D. Reid
1992 Sales: $527 million Employees: 5,222
Symbol: MODI Exchange: NASDAQ
Industry: Automotive & trucking - original equipment

Modtech, Inc.
2830 Barrett Ave.
Perris, CA 92372
Phone: 714-943-4014 Fax: 909-940-0427
CEO: Evan M. Gruber
CFO: Evan M. Gruber
1991 Sales: $36 million Employees: 275
Symbol: MODT Exchange: NASDAQ
Industry: Building - residential & commercial

Mohawk Carpet Corp.
1755 Exchange NW
Atlanta, GA 30339
Phone: 404-951-6000 Fax: 404-951-6152
CEO: David L. Kolb
CFO: John D. Swift
1991 Sales: $279 million Employees: 2,100
Symbol: MOHK Exchange: NASDAQ
Industry: Textiles - home furnishings

Molecular Biosystems, Inc.
10030 Barnes Canyon Rd.
San Diego, CA 92121
Phone: 619-452-0681 Fax: 619-452-6187
CEO: Kenneth J. Widder
CFO: Joyce L. Comeaux
1992 Sales: $10.7 million Employees: 169
Symbol: MB Exchange: NYSE
Industry: Biomedical & genetic products

Molex Inc.
2222 Wellington Court
Lisle, IL 60532
Phone: 708-969-4550 Fax: 708-969-1352
CEO: Frederick A. Krehbiel
CFO: John C. Psaltis
1992 Sales: $818 million Employees: 7,483
Symbol: MOLX Exchange: NASDAQ
Industry: Electrical connectors

Momentum Distribution Inc.
500 108th Ave. NE, Ste. 1900
Bellevue, WA 98004
Phone: 206-646-6550 Fax: 206-646-6574
CEO: Richard E. Engebrecht
CFO: Patsy R. Turnipseed
1991 Sales: $165 million Employees: 459
Symbol: MMDI Exchange: NASDAQ
Industry: Photographic equipment & supplies

Monarch Avalon Inc.
4517 Harford Rd.
Baltimore, MD 21214
Phone: 410-254-9200 Fax: —
CEO: A. Eric Dott
CFO: Frank E. Fontanazza
1992 Sales: $6.9 million Employees: 119
Symbol: MAHI Exchange: NASDAQ
Industry: Toys - games & hobby products

Monarch Machine Tool Co.
615 Oak Ave.
Sidney, OH 45365
Phone: 513-492-4111 Fax: 513-492-7958
CEO: Robert J. Siewert
CFO: Robert B. Riethman
1991 Sales: $106 million Employees: 827
Symbol: MMO Exchange: NYSE
Industry: Machine tools & related products

Money Store Inc., The
2840 Morris Ave.
Union, NJ 07083
Phone: 908-686-2000 Fax: 908-686-6907
CEO: Marc Turtletaub
CFO: Morton Dear
1991 Sales: $140 million Employees: 900
Symbol: MONE Exchange: AMEX
Industry: Financial - consumer loans

Monongahela Power Co.
1310 Fairmont Ave.
Fairmont, WV 26554
Phone: 304-366-3000 Fax: 304-367-3327
CEO: Klaus Bergman
CFO: Charles S. Mullett
1991 Sales: $625 million Employees: 1,957
Symbol: MPNpA Exchange: AMEX
Industry: Utility - electric power

Monro Muffler Brake, Inc.
2340 Brighton-Henrietta TL Rd.
Rochester, NY 14623
Phone: 716-427-2280 Fax: 716-427-2295
CEO: Jack M. Gallagher
CFO: Jarret J. Lobb
1992 Sales: $70 million Employees: 886
Symbol: MNRO Exchange: NASDAQ
Industry: Retail - auto parts

Monsanto Co.
800 N. Lindbergh Blvd.
St. Louis, MO 63167
Phone: 314-694-1000 Fax: 314-694-7625
CEO: Richard J. Mahoney
CFO: Francis A. Stroble
1992 Sales: $7,763 million Employees: 39,281
Symbol: MTC Exchange: NYSE
Industry: Chemicals - fat substitute, herbicides, industrial, pharmaceuticals

Montana Power Co.
40 E. Broadway
Butte, MT 59701
Phone: 406-723-5421 Fax: 406-496-5099
CEO: Daniel T. Berube
CFO: Jerrold P. Pederson
1991 Sales: $498 million Employees: 2,398
Symbol: MTP Exchange: NYSE
Industry: Utility - electric power

Montclair Bancorp, Inc.
560 Valley Rd.
Upper Montclair, NJ 07043
Phone: 201-744-3500 Fax: —
CEO: Bernard J. Martin
CFO: Louis J. Beierle
1991 Sales: $54 million Employees: 151
Symbol: MSBI Exchange: NASDAQ
Industry: Banks - Northeast

Monterey Homes
6263 N. Scottsdale Rd.
Scottsdale, AZ
Phone: 602-998-8700 Fax: 602-998-8700
CEO: Bill Cleverly
CFO: David Walls
1991 Sales: $21 million Employees: 30
Ownership: Privately held
Industry: Construction - luxury communities

Montgomery Development Corporation
219 South West St., Ste. 300
Syracuse, NY 13202
Phone: 315-474-4418 Fax: 315-471-7098
CEO: Christine M. Edwards
CFO: Christine M. Edwards
1991 Sales: $6.3 million Employees: 25
Ownership: Privately held
Industry: Construction - general commercial

Montgomery Ward Holding Corp.
One Montgomery Ward Plaza
Chicago, IL 60671
Phone: 312-467-2000 Fax: 312-467-2043
CEO: Bernard F. Brennan
CFO: John Workman
1991 Sales: $5,655 million Employees: 62,400
Ownership: Privately held
Industry: Retail - major department stores

Moog Inc.
Seneca St. & Jamison Rd.
East Aurora, NY 14052
Phone: 716-652-2000 Fax: 716-652-0633
CEO: Robert T. Brady
CFO: Robert R. Banta
1991 Sales: $321 million Employees: 3,309
Symbol: MOGA Exchange: AMEX
Industry: Aerospace - aircraft equipment

Moorco International, Inc.
2700 Post Oak Blvd., Ste. 5701
Houston, TX 77056
Phone: 713-993-0999 Fax: 713-993-7488
CEO: George A. Ciotti
CFO: David W. Pfleghar
1992 Sales: $207 million Employees: 1,472
Symbol: MRC Exchange: NYSE
Industry: Instruments - control

Moore Business Forms & Systems, Inc.
275 Field Dr.
Lake Forest, IL 60045
Phone: 708-615-6000 Fax: 708-205-0648
CEO: John R. Anderluh
CFO: —
1991 Sales: $2,492 million Employees: 23,556
Parent: Moore Corporation Ltd.
Industry: Paper - business forms

Moore Medical Corp.
389 John Downey Dr.
New Britain, CT 06051
Phone: 203-826-3600 Fax: 203-223-2382
CEO: Mark E. Karp
CFO: John A. Murray
1991 Sales: $311 million Employees: 400
Symbol: MMD Exchange: AMEX
Industry: Drugs & sundries - wholesale

Moore Products Co.
Sumneytown Pike
Spring House, PA 19477
Phone: 215-646-7400 Fax: 215-283-6358
CEO: William B. Moore
CFO: E. J. Curry
1991 Sales: $97 million Employees: 1,289
Symbol: MORP Exchange: NASDAQ
Industry: Instruments - control

indicates company is in *Hoover's Handbook of American Business.*

indicates company is in *Hoover's Handbook of World Business;* sales and employee numbers are for parent company.

Moore-Handley, Inc.
US Hwy. 31 South
Pelham, AL 35124
Phone: 205-663-8011 Fax: 205-663-8229
CEO: Pierce E. Marks, Jr.
CFO: L. Ward Edwards
1991 Sales: $124 million Employees: 435
Symbol: MHCO Exchange: NASDAQ
Industry: Building products - retail & wholesale

Moorman Manufacturing Co.
1000 N. 30th St.
Quincy, IL 62301
Phone: 217-222-7100 Fax: 217-222-4069
CEO: T. L. Shade
CFO: Richard Jackson
1991 Sales: $809 million Employees: 3,000
Ownership: Privately held
Industry: Veterinary products & services - livestock feed & equipment

Morgan Keegan, Inc.
Fifty N. Front St.
Memphis, TN 38103
Phone: 901-524-4100 Fax: 901-524-4158
CEO: Allen B. Morgan, Jr.
CFO: Joseph C. Weller
1991 Sales: $116 million Employees: 878
Symbol: MOR Exchange: NYSE
Industry: Financial - investment bankers

Morgan Products Ltd.
601 Oregon St.
Oshkosh, WI 54901
Phone: 414-235-7170 Fax: 414-235-5773
CEO: Arthur L. Knight, Jr.
CFO: Douglas H. MacMillan
1991 Sales: $353 million Employees: 1,787
Symbol: MGN Exchange: NYSE
Industry: Building products - doors & trim

Morgan Stanley Group Inc.
1251 Avenue of the Americas
New York, NY 10020
Phone: 212-703-4000 Fax: 212-703-6503
CEO: Richard B. Fisher
CFO: Allen W. Zern
1991 Sales: $6,785 million Employees: 7,053
Symbol: MS Exchange: NYSE
Industry: Financial - investment bankers; merchant banking, stock brokerage

Morgan's Foods, Inc.
6690 Beta Dr., Ste. 300
Cleveland, OH 44143
Phone: 216-461-6200 Fax: 216-461-5439
CEO: Leonard Stein-Sapir
CFO: Richard C. Adamany
1992 Sales: $45 million Employees: 1,142
Symbol: MR Exchange: AMEX
Industry: Retail - food & restaurants

MorningStar Group, Inc.
5956 Sherry Lane, Ste. 1100
Dallas, TX 75225
Phone: 214-360-4700 Fax: 214-360-9100
CEO: James A. Bach
CFO: Tracy L. Noll
1991 Sales: $480 million Employees: 1,826
Symbol: MSTR Exchange: NASDAQ
Industry: Food - dairy products

Morrison, Inc.
4721 Morrison Dr.
Mobile, AL 36609
Phone: 205-344-3000 Fax: 205-344-3066
CEO: Samuel E. Beall III
CFO: Robert G. Crankovic
1992 Sales: $1,067 million Employees: 34,000
Symbol: MORR Exchange: NASDAQ
Industry: Retail - food & restaurants

Morrison Knudsen Corp.
720 Park Blvd.
Boise, ID 83729
Phone: 208-386-5000 Fax: 208-386-7186
CEO: William J. Agee
CFO: Edmund J. Gorman
1992 Sales: $2,285 million Employees: 12,700
Symbol: MRN Exchange: NYSE
Industry: Construction - heavy

Morse Diesel International Inc.
1515 Broadway, 41st Fl.
New York, NY 10036
Phone: 212-730-4000 Fax: 212-704-4143
CEO: Donald H. Piser
CFO: Norman G. Fornella
1991 Sales: $640 million Employees: 525
Ownership: Privately held
Industry: Construction & consulting

Morse Operations
1240 N. Federal Hwy.
Ft. Lauderdale, FL 33304
Phone: 305-568-0770 Fax: 305-568-5190
CEO: Edward J. Morse
CFO: Donald MacInnes
1991 Sales: $1,803 million Employees: 1,338
Ownership: Privately held
Industry: Retail dealership

Morse Shoe Inc.
555 Turnpike St.
Canton, MA 02021
Phone: 617-828-9300 Fax: 617-821-6265
CEO: Malcolm L. Sherman
CFO: Thomas J. Galligan III
1991 Sales: $529 million Employees: 4,000
Ownership: Privately held
Industry: Shoes & related apparel

Morton International, Inc.
100 N. Riverside Plaza
Chicago, IL 60606
Phone: 312-807-2000 Fax: 312-807-2241
CEO: Charles S. Locke
CFO: John R. Bowen
1992 Sales: $2,144 million Employees: 10,700
Symbol: MII Exchange: NYSE
Industry: Chemicals - specialty; salt, automobile airbags

MOSCOM Corp.
3750 Monroe Ave.
Pittsford, NY 14534
Phone: 716-381-6000 Fax: —
CEO: Albert J. Montevecchio
CFO: Paul A. Lipari
1991 Sales: $16 million Employees: 157
Symbol: MSCM Exchange: NASDAQ
Industry: Telecommunications equipment

Mosinee Paper Corp.
1244 Kronenwetter Dr.
Mosinee, WI 54455
Phone: 715-693-4470 Fax: 715-693-4803
CEO: Richard L. Radt
CFO: Gary P. Peterson
1991 Sales: $197 million Employees: 1,246
Symbol: MOSI Exchange: NASDAQ
Industry: Paper & paper products

Moto Photo, Inc.
4444 Lake Center Dr.
Dayton, OH 45426
Phone: 513-854-6686 Fax: 513-854-0140
CEO: Michael F. Adler
CFO: David A. Mason
1991 Sales: $36 million Employees: 544
Symbol: MOTO Exchange: NASDAQ
Industry: Retail - photo processing services & merchandise

Motor Club of America
484 Central Ave.
Newark, NJ 07107
Phone: 201-733-1234 Fax: —
CEO: Archer McWhorter
CFO: Robert E. Dennis
1991 Sales: $79 million Employees: 325
Symbol: MOTR Exchange: NASDAQ
Industry: Insurance - property & casualty

Motorola, Inc.
1303 E. Algonquin Rd.
Schaumburg, IL 60196
Phone: 708-576-5000 Fax: 708-576-8003
CEO: George M.C. Fisher
CFO: Carl F. Koenemann
1992 Sales: $13,303 million Employees: 102,000
Symbol: MOT Exchange: NYSE
Industry: Electrical products - cellular telephones, semiconductors, computers & peripherals

Motts Holdings, Inc.
59 Leggett St.
East Hartford, CT 06108
Phone: 203-289-3301 Fax: —
CEO: Barry P. Baskind
CFO: Stanley M. Baskind
1991 Sales: $3 million Employees: 25
Symbol: MSM Exchange: AMEX
Industry: Retail - supermarkets

Mountain Medical Equipment, Inc.
10488 W. Centennial Rd.
Littleton, CO 80127
Phone: 303-973-1200 Fax: 303-972-3897
CEO: Paul J. Jerde
CFO: Joan F. Lowe
1992 Sales: $19 million Employees: 188
Symbol: MTN Exchange: AMEX
Industry: Medical products - oxygen concentrators, medication nebulizers

Mountain West Savings Bank, F.S.B.
401 Front Ave.
Coeur d'Alene, ID 83814
Phone: 208-667-2566 Fax: 208-667-8420
CEO: Jon W. Hippler
CFO: Ronn C. Rich
1992 Sales: — Employees: —
Symbol: MWSB Exchange: NASDAQ
Industry: Financial - savings and loans

Mountaineer Bankshares of W. Va., Inc.
148 S. Queen St.
Martinsburg, WV 25401
Phone: 304-263-0861 Fax: —
CEO: Lacy I. Rice, Jr.
CFO: Brent D. Robinson
1991 Sales: $24 million Employees: 363
Symbol: MTNR Exchange: NASDAQ
Industry: Banks - Southeast

Moyer Packing Co.
PO Box 395
Souderton, PA 18964
Phone: 215-723-5555 Fax: 215-723-1018
CEO: Curtis F. Moyer
CFO: Bill Morral
1991 Sales: $465 million Employees: 1,200
Ownership: Privately held
Industry: Food - meatpacking

Mr. Bulky Treats & Gifts
755 W. Big Beaver Rd., #1600
Troy, MI 48084
Phone: 313-244-9000 Fax: 313-244-9365
CEO: Sid Rubin
CFO: Tim Cavalli
1992 Sales: $100 million Employees: 690
Ownership: Privately held
Industry: Retail - candy, nuts & gifts

indicates company is in *Hoover's Handbook of American Business.*

indicates company is in *Hoover's Handbook of World Business;* sales and employee numbers are for parent company.

Mr. Coffee, Inc.
24700 Niles Rd.
Bedford Heights, OH 44146
Phone: 216-464-4000 Fax: 216-464-5629
CEO: P. C. McC. Howell
CFO: Thomas P. Evans
1991 Sales: $159 million Employees: 537
Symbol: JAVA Exchange: NASDAQ
Industry: Appliances - household

MRI Manufacturing & Research, Inc.
2045 N. Forbes Blvd.
Tucson, AZ 85745
Phone: 602-882-7794 Fax: 602-882-6849
CEO: Robert Kelliher
CFO: Robert Kelliher
1991 Sales: $3 million Employees: 84
Ownership: Privately held
Industry: Medical instruments - silicone catheters

MTD Products Inc.
5965 Grafton Rd.
Valley City, OH 44280
Phone: 216-225-2600 Fax: 216-225-0896
CEO: Curtis E. Moll
CFO: David R. Campbell
1991 Sales: $485 million Employees: 4,250
Ownership: Privately held
Industry: Machinery - outdoor power equipment

MTS Inc.
2500 Del Monte St., Bldg. C
West Sacramento, CA 95691
Phone: 916-373-2500 Fax: 916-373-2535
CEO: Russ Solomon
CFO: Dee Searson
1992 Sales: $650 million Employees: 5,800
Ownership: Privately held
Industry: Retail - records, books & videos

MTS Systems Corp.
14000 Technology Dr.
Eden Prairie, MN 55344
Phone: 612-937-4000 Fax: 612-937-4515
CEO: Donald M. Sullivan
CFO: Marshall L. Carpenter
1991 Sales: $158 million Employees: 1,372
Symbol: MTSC Exchange: NASDAQ
Industry: Electronics - measuring instruments

Mueller Industries, Inc.
555 N. Woodlawn St., Ste. 102
Wichita, KS 67208
Phone: 316-682-6300 Fax: 316-682-9650
CEO: Harvey L. Karp
CFO: Earl W. Bunkers
1991 Sales: $441 million Employees: 2,400
Symbol: MLI Exchange: NYSE
Industry: Steel - production

Multi-Color Corp.
4575 Eastern Ave.
Cincinnati, OH 45226
Phone: 513-321-5381 Fax: 513-321-6138
CEO: John C. Court
CFO: John D. Littlehale
1992 Sales: $65 million Employees: 453
Symbol: LABL Exchange: NASDAQ
Industry: Printing - commercial

Multibank Financial Corp.
100 Rustcraft Rd.
Dedham, MA 02026
Phone: 617-461-1820 Fax: 617-461-5514
CEO: David B. Lynch
CFO: Peter F. Russo
1991 Sales: $275 million Employees: 1,442
Symbol: MLTF Exchange: NASDAQ
Industry: Banks - Northeast

Multimedia, Inc.
305 S. Main St.
Greenville, SC 29601
Phone: 803-298-4373 Fax: 803-298-4271
CEO: Walter E. Bartlett
CFO: Robert E. Hamby, Jr.
1992 Sales: $577 million Employees: 3,100
Symbol: MMEDC Exchange: NASDAQ
Industry: Broadcasting - radio & TV

Munsingwear, Inc.
8000 W. 78th St.
Minneapolis, MN 55439
Phone: 612-943-5000 Fax: 612-943-5019
CEO: Charles J. Campbell
CFO: James S. Bury
1991 Sales: $37 million Employees: 340
Symbol: MUN Exchange: NYSE
Industry: Textiles - apparel

Murphy Oil USA
200 Peach St.
El Dorado, AR 71730
Phone: 501-862-6411 Fax: 501-862-9057
CEO: Jack W. McNutt
CFO: George E. Breazeal
1992 Sales: $1,685 million Employees: 3,991
Symbol: MUR Exchange: NYSE
Industry: Oil & gas - international specialty

Music Tech of Minneapolis
304 N. Washington
Minneapolis, MN 55401
Phone: 612-338-0175 Fax: 612-338-0804
CEO: Jack McNally
CFO: Jack McNally
1992 Sales: $1.9 million Employees: 50
Ownership: Privately held
Industry: Schools - private music school specializing in popular music

Musicland Group Inc.
7500 Excelsior Blvd.
Minneapolis, MN 55426
Phone: 612-932-7700 Fax: 612-932-7410
CEO: J. W. Eugster
CFO: Keith A. Benson
1992 Sales: $1,021 million Employees: 18,600
Symbol: MLG Exchange: NYSE
Industry: Retail - prerecorded music & video

Mustang Engineering Inc.
16001 Park Ten Place #500
Houston, TX 77084
Phone: 713-578-0070 Fax: 713-578-1304
CEO: Paul Redmon
CFO: Felix W. Covington
1991 Sales: $30 million Employees: 275
Ownership: Privately held
Industry: Oil & gas - field services

Mutual Assurance, Inc.
100 Brookwood Place, Ste. 500
Birmingham, AL 35209
Phone: 205-877-4400 Fax: —
CEO: A. Derrill Crowe
CFO: James J. Morello
1991 Sales: $76 million Employees: 135
Symbol: MAIC Exchange: NASDAQ
Industry: Insurance - multiline & misc.

Mutual of Omaha Interest Shares, Inc.
10235 Regency Circle
Omaha, NE 68114
Phone: 402-397-8555 Fax: —
CEO: John M. Delich
CFO: William J. Bluvas
1992 Sales: — Employees: —
Symbol: MUO Exchange: NYSE
Industry: Financial - investment management

MVM, Inc.
5113 Leesburg Pike #700
Falls Church, VA 22041
Phone: 703-671-9810 Fax: 703-671-9853
CEO: Dario O. Maquez, Jr.
CFO: Bob Schnakenberg
1991 Sales: $24 million Employees: 798
Ownership: Privately held
Industry: Protection - security & investigative services

MWW/Strategic Communications, Inc.
70 Grand Ave.
River Edge, NJ 07661
Phone: 201-342-9500 Fax: 201-342-8807
CEO: Michael Kempner
CFO: Sally Larson-White
1991 Sales: $3.5 million Employees: 40
Ownership: Privately held
Industry: Public relations services

Mycogen Corp.
5451 Oberlin Dr.
San Diego, CA 92121
Phone: 619-453-8030 Fax: 619-453-1053
CEO: Jerry D. Caulder
CFO: James R. Glynn
1991 Sales: $18 million Employees: 279
Symbol: MYCO Exchange: NASDAQ
Industry: Biomedical & genetic products

Myers Industries, Inc.
1293 S. Main St.
Akron, OH 44301
Phone: 216-253-5592 Fax: 216-253-1882
CEO: Stephen E. Myers
CFO: Gregory J. Stodnick
1991 Sales: $196 million Employees: 1,418
Symbol: MYE Exchange: AMEX
Industry: Rubber & plastic products

Mylan Laboratories Inc.
130 Seventh St., Ste. 1030
Pittsburgh, PA 15222
Phone: 412-232-0100 Fax: 412-232-0123
CEO: Roy McKnight
CFO: Roy McKnight
1992 Sales: $132 million Employees: 690
Symbol: MYL Exchange: NYSE
Industry: Drugs - generic

Mylex Corp.
34551 Ardenwood Blvd.
Fremont, CA 94555
Phone: 510-796-6100 Fax: 510-745-7654
CEO: M. Chowdry
CFO: Khaled Ibrahim
1991 Sales: $54 million Employees: 130
Symbol: MYLX Exchange: NASDAQ
Industry: Computers - mini & micro

N.S. Bancorp, Inc.
2300 N. Western Ave.
Chicago, IL 60647
Phone: 312-489-2300 Fax: 312-489-7498
CEO: Henry R. Smogolski
CFO: Steven Skiba
1991 Sales: $129 million Employees: 349
Symbol: NSBI Exchange: NASDAQ
Industry: Financial - savings and loans

N-W Group, Inc.
645 E. Missouri Ave., Ste. 132
Phoenix, AZ 85012
Phone: 602-263-9161 Fax: 602-263-9032
CEO: Clarke H. Bailey
CFO: Vickie M. Sixta
1991 Sales: $73 million Employees: 26
Symbol: NWGI Exchange: NASDAQ
Industry: Real estate operations

NAB Asset Corp.
2401 Fountainview
Houston, TX 77057
Phone: 713-952-6800 Fax: —
CEO: Michael A. Hrebenar
CFO: Michael A. Hrebenar
1991 Sales: $1.8 million Employees: 10
Symbol: NABCV Exchange: NASDAQ
Industry: Banks - Midwest

Nabors Industries, Inc.
515 W. Greens Rd., Ste. 1200
Houston, TX 77067
Phone: 713-874-0035 Fax: 713-872-5205
CEO: Eugene M. Isenberg
CFO: W. John Zygmunt
1992 Sales: $286 million Employees: 2,820
Symbol: NBR Exchange: AMEX
Industry: Oil & gas - field services

NAC Re Corp.
One Greenwich Plaza
Greenwich, CT 06836
Phone: 203-622-5200 Fax: 203-622-1494
CEO: Ronald L. Bornhuetter
CFO: Paul J. Malvasio
1991 Sales: $294 million Employees: 184
Symbol: NREC Exchange: NASDAQ
Industry: Insurance - property & casualty

NACCO Industries, Inc.
5875 Landerbrook Dr., Ste. 300
Mayfield, OH 44124
Phone: 216-449-9600 Fax: 216-449-9581
CEO: Alfred M. Rankin, Jr.
CFO: John R. Cook
1992 Sales: $1,482 million Employees: 9,858
Symbol: NC Exchange: NYSE
Industry: Diversified operations - forklifts, small appliances, coal

Nahama & Weagant Energy Co.
602 H St.
Bakersfield, CA 93304
Phone: 805-323-9075 Fax: —
CEO: Rodney Nahama
CFO: Denis J. Fitzpatrick
1991 Sales: $5.8 million Employees: 20
Symbol: NAWE Exchange: NASDAQ
Industry: Oil & gas - US exploration & production

Nalco Chemical Co.
One Nalco Center
Naperville, IL 60563
Phone: 708-305-1000 Fax: 708-305-2900
CEO: W. H. Clark
CFO: Rodney M. Bloom
1992 Sales: $1,374 million Employees: 6,832
Symbol: NLC Exchange: NYSE
Industry: Chemicals - specialty

NAMIC U.S.A. Corp.
Pruyn's Island
Glens Falls, NY 12801
Phone: 518-798-0067 Fax: 518-798-8096
CEO: Cynthia L. Morris
CFO: David W. Gilmour
1992 Sales: $52 million Employees: 699
Symbol: NUSA Exchange: NASDAQ
Industry: Medical products - cardiovascular disease treatment

Nanometrics Inc.
310 DeGuigne Dr.
Sunnyvale, CA 94086
Phone: 408-746-1600 Fax: 408-720-0196
CEO: Vincent J. Coates
CFO: James A. Smith
1991 Sales: $18 million Employees: 110
Symbol: NANO Exchange: NASDAQ
Industry: Electronics - measuring instruments

Nantucket Industries, Inc.
105 Madison Ave.
New York, NY 10016
Phone: 212-889-5656 Fax: 212-532-3217
CEO: George J. Gold
CFO: Stephen P. Sussman
1992 Sales: $45 million Employees: 376
Symbol: NAN Exchange: AMEX
Industry: Textiles - apparel

Napa Valley Bancorp
Three Financial Plaza, Ste. B
Napa, CA 94558
Phone: 707-257-4900 Fax: 707-255-8452
CEO: Bryan C. Hansen
CFO: Sharon A. Newcomer
1991 Sales: $61 million Employees: 423
Symbol: NVB Exchange: AMEX
Industry: Banks - West

Napco Security Systems, Inc.
333 Bayview Ave.
Amityville, NY 11701
Phone: 516-842-9400 Fax: 516-842-9137
CEO: Richard Soloway
CFO: Kenneth Rosenberg
1992 Sales: $39 million Employees: 1,129
Symbol: NSSC Exchange: NASDAQ
Industry: Protection - security alarms & door security devices

Nash Finch Co.
3381 Gorham Ave.
St. Louis Park, MN 55426
Phone: 612-929-0371 Fax: 612-924-4854
CEO: Harold B. Finch, Jr.
CFO: Robert F. Nash
1992 Sales: $2,521 million Employees: 10,888
Symbol: NAFC Exchange: NASDAQ
Industry: Food - wholesale

Nashua Corp.
44 Franklin St.
Nashua, NH 03060
Phone: 603-880-2323 Fax: 603-880-5671
CEO: Charles E. Clough
CFO: William Luke
1991 Sales: $526 million Employees: 3,869
Symbol: NSH Exchange: NYSE
Industry: Diversified operations - coated paper & computer products, photo-finishing

NaTec Resources, Inc.
1177 West Loop South
Houston, TX 77027
Phone: 713-552-2552 Fax: —
CEO: Socrates S. Christopher
CFO: M. Glenn Hobratschk
1991 Sales: $2.1 million Employees: 42
Symbol: NATC Exchange: NASDAQ
Industry: Chemicals - specialty

National Association of Securities Dealers
1735 K St. NW
Washington, DC 20006
Phone: 202-728-8000 Fax: 202-728-8147
CEO: Joseph R. Hardiman
CFO: James P. O'Donnell
1991 Sales: $216 million Employees: 2,000
Ownership: Privately held
Industry: Stock exchange

National Banc of Commerce Co.
One Commerce Square
Charleston, WV 25301
Phone: 304-348-5000 Fax: —
CEO: Charles R. Smith
CFO: Richeard D. Wolford
1991 Sales: $68 million Employees: 511
Symbol: NBCC Exchange: NASDAQ
Industry: Banks - Southeast

National Bancorp of Alaska, Inc.
310 W. Northern Lights Blvd.
Anchorage, AK 99503
Phone: 907-276-1132 Fax: 907-265-2139
CEO: Edward B. Rasmuson
CFO: Kathleen Knowles
1991 Sales: $94 million Employees: 1,138
Symbol: NBAK Exchange: NASDAQ
Industry: Banks - West

National Beverage Corp.
One N. University Dr.
Plantation, FL 33324
Phone: 305-581-0922 Fax: 305-473-4710
CEO: Nick A. Caporella
CFO: Nick A. Caporella
1992 Sales: $336 million Employees: 1,100
Symbol: POPS Exchange: NASDAQ
Industry: Beverages - soft drinks

National Business Group Inc.
2840 Mt. Wilkinson Pkwy., #200
Atlanta, GA 30339
Phone: 404-319-8300 Fax: 404-319-1416
CEO: Rich Basich
CFO: Jim Hughes
1991 Sales: $8.7 million Employees: 13
Ownership: Privately held
Industry: Computers - connectivity hardware & software

National Capital Management Corp.
50 California St., Ste. 3300
San Francisco, CA 94111
Phone: 415-989-2661 Fax: 415-989-1204
CEO: Herbert J. Jaffe
CFO: Leslie A. Filler
1991 Sales: $2.6 million Employees: —
Symbol: NCMC Exchange: NASDAQ
Industry: Financial - investment management

National City Bancorporation
75 S. Fifth St.
Minneapolis, MN 55402
Phone: 612-340-3183 Fax: 612-340-3181
CEO: David L. Andreas
CFO: Thomas J. Freed
1991 Sales: $58 million Employees: 322
Symbol: NCBM Exchange: NASDAQ
Industry: Banks - Midwest

National City Bancshares, Inc.
227 Main St.
Evansville, IN 47705
Phone: 812-464-9800 Fax: —
CEO: John D. Lippert
CFO: Harold A. Mann
1991 Sales: $43 million Employees: 285
Symbol: NCBE Exchange: NASDAQ
Industry: Banks - Midwest

National City Corp.
1900 E. Ninth St.
Cleveland, OH 44114
Phone: 216-575-2000 Fax: 216-575-3332
CEO: Edward B. Brandon
CFO: Robert G. Siefers
1992 Sales: $2,784 million Employees: 15,721
Symbol: NCC Exchange: NYSE
Industry: Banks - Midwest

National Commerce Bancorporation
One Commerce Square
Memphis, TN 38150
Phone: 901-523-3242 Fax: 901-523-3310
CEO: Bruce E. Campbell, Jr.
CFO: Walter B. Howell, Jr.
1991 Sales: $84 million Employees: 868
Symbol: NCBC Exchange: NASDAQ
Industry: Banks - Southeast

National Community Banks, Inc.
385 Risle Camp Rd.
West Paterson, NJ 07424
Phone: 201-357-7000 Fax: 201-357-7623
CEO: Robert M. Kossick
CFO: Anthony J. Franchina
1991 Sales: $354 million Employees: 1,913
Symbol: NCBR Exchange: NASDAQ
Industry: Banks - Northeast

National Computer Systems, Inc.
11000 Prairie Lakes Dr.
Minneapolis, MN 55344
Phone: 612-829-3000 Fax: 612-829-3167
CEO: Charles W. Oswald
CFO: Charles W. Oswald
1991 Sales: $302 million Employees: 2,650
Symbol: NLCS Exchange: NASDAQ
Industry: Optical character recognition

National Contract Staffing
5650 W. Flamingo Rd., Ste. B
Las Vegas, NV 89103
Phone: 702-364-8100 Fax: 702-367-1117
CEO: Kevin Morley
CFO: Kevin Morley
1991 Sales: $25 million Employees: 20
Ownership: Privately held
Industry: Business services - employee leasing

National Data Corp.
2 National Data Plaza
Atlanta, GA 30329
Phone: 404-728-2000 Fax: 404-728-2551
CEO: O. G. Greene
CFO: O. G. Greene
1992 Sales: $219 million Employees: 2,000
Symbol: NDTA Exchange: NASDAQ
Industry: Computers - data processing services

National Distributing Company Inc.
One National Dr. SW
Atlanta, GA 30336
Phone: 404-696-9440 Fax: 404-691-0364
CEO: Michael C. Carlos
CFO: Andrew C. Carlos
1991 Sales: $470 million Employees: 2,000
Ownership: Privately held
Industry: Beverages - wholesale wine & liquor

National Education Corp.
18400 Von Karman Ave.
Irvine, CA 92715
Phone: 714-474-9400 Fax: 714-474-9494
CEO: Jerome W. Cwiertnia
CFO: Keith K. Ogata
1991 Sales: $385 million Employees: 4,200
Symbol: NEC Exchange: NYSE
Industry: Business services - computer training

National Enterprises, Inc.
Earle Ave. at Wallace St.
Lafayette, IN 47904
Phone: 317-448-2000 Fax: —
CEO: John B. Overzet
CFO: Wilmer R. Files
1992 Sales: — Employees: —
Symbol: NEI Exchange: NYSE
Industry: Building - residential & commercial

National Environmental Group, Inc.
700 Ashland Ave.
Folcroft, PA 19032
Phone: 215-237-0700 Fax: —
CEO: Francis D. John
CFO: Daniel P. Wisniewski
1991 Sales: $24 million Employees: 430
Symbol: NEG Exchange: AMEX
Industry: Oil & gas - field services

National Fuel Gas Co.
30 Rockefeller Plaza, Ste. 4545
New York, NY 10112
Phone: 212-541-7533 Fax: 212-541-7841
CEO: Bernard J. Kennedy
CFO: P. C. Ackerman
1992 Sales: $942 million Employees: 3,494
Symbol: NFG Exchange: NYSE
Industry: Utility - gas distribution

National Gas & Oil Co.
1500 Granville Rd.
Newark, OH 43055
Phone: 614-344-2102 Fax: 614-344-2054
CEO: Richard A. Jacobs
CFO: Lawrence P. Haren
1991 Sales: $31 million Employees: 128
Symbol: NLG Exchange: AMEX
Industry: Utility - gas distribution

National Geographic Society
1600 M St. NW
Washington, DC 20036
Phone: 202-857-7000 Fax: 202-828-6679
CEO: Gilbert M. Grosvenor
CFO: H. Gregory Platts
1991 Sales: $436 million Employees: 2,189
Ownership: Privately held
Industry: Nonprofit educational organization

National Health Laboratories, Inc.
7590 Fay Ave.
La Jolla, CA 92037
Phone: 619-454-3314 Fax: 619-456-0688
CEO: Robert E. Draper
CFO: David C. Flaugh
1992 Sales: $721 million Employees: 7,390
Symbol: NH Exchange: NYSE
Industry: Medical & dental supplies

National HealthCorp L.P.
100 E. Vine St.
Murfreesboro, TN 37130
Phone: 615-890-2020 Fax: 615-890-0123
CEO: W. Andrew Adams
CFO: W. Andrew Adams
1991 Sales: $176 million Employees: 9,769
Symbol: NHC Exchange: AMEX
Industry: Nursing homes

National Home Health Care Corp.
850 Bronx River Rd.
Yonkers, NY 10708
Phone: 914-776-2800 Fax: —
CEO: Frederick H. Fialkow
CFO: Robert P. Heller
1991 Sales: $17 million Employees: 700
Symbol: NHHC Exchange: NASDAQ
Industry: Healthcare - outpatient & home

National Insurance Group
1250 Bayhill Dr., Ste. 100
San Bruno, CA 94066
Phone: 415-872-6772 Fax: —
CEO: Mark A. Speizer
CFO: Howard L. Herman
1991 Sales: $26 million Employees: 162
Symbol: NAIG Exchange: NASDAQ
Industry: Insurance - property & casualty

National Intergroup, Inc.
1220 Seniac Dr.
Carrollton, TX 75006
Phone: 214-446-9090 Fax: 214-446-4499
CEO: Robert L. King
CFO: Dennis J. Letham
1992 Sales: $4,446 million Employees: 3,138
Symbol: NII Exchange: NYSE
Industry: Diversified operations - pharmaceuticals, health & beauty aids, crude oil

National Interrent
7700 France Ave. South
Minneapolis, MN 55435
Phone: 612-830-2121 Fax: 612-830-2921
CEO: Thomas N. Murphy
CFO: Robert McKenna
1991 Sales: $936 million Employees: 8,500
Ownership: Privately held
Industry: Leasing - auto rentals

National Loan Bank
PO Box 2558
Houston, TX 77252
Phone: 713-236-4358 Fax: —
CEO: Harry K. Smith
CFO: Harry K. Smith
1992 Sales: — Employees: —
Symbol: NLBK Exchange: NASDAQ
Industry: Banks - Midwest

National Media Corp.
4360 Main St.
Philadelphia, PA 19127
Phone: 215-482-9800 Fax: 215-482-9805
CEO: John J. Turchi, Jr.
CFO: J. Jeffrey Fox
1992 Sales: $102 million Employees: 236
Symbol: NM Exchange: NYSE
Industry: Retail - mail order & direct

National Medical Enterprises, Inc.
2700 Colorado Ave.
Santa Monica, CA 90404
Phone: 310-315-8000 Fax: 310-315-8329
CEO: Richard K. Eamer
CFO: Taylor R. Jenson
1992 Sales: $3,845 million Employees: 51,906
Symbol: NME Exchange: NYSE
Industry: Hospitals - general & specialty

National Mercantile Bancorp
1840 Century Park East
Los Angeles, CA 90067
Phone: 213-277-2265 Fax: —
CEO: Donald D. Thornburg
CFO: Donald D. Thornburg
1991 Sales: $20 million Employees: 143
Symbol: MBLA Exchange: NASDAQ
Industry: Banks - Midwest

National Patent Development Corp.
9 W. 57th St., Ste. 4170
New York, NY 10019
Phone: 212-230-9500 Fax: 212-230-9545
CEO: Jerome I. Feldman
CFO: Scott N. Greenberg
1991 Sales: $259 million Employees: 2,570
Symbol: NPD Exchange: AMEX
Industry: Medical & dental supplies

National Penn Bancshares, Inc.
Philadelphia & Reading Avenues
Boyertown, PA 19512
Phone: 215-367-6001 Fax: 215-369-6349
CEO: Lawrence T. Jilk, Jr.
CFO: Gary L. Rhoads
1991 Sales: $76 million Employees: 357
Symbol: NPBC Exchange: NASDAQ
Industry: Banks - Northeast

National Pizza Co.
720 W. 20th St.
Pittsburg, KS 66762
Phone: 316-231-3390 Fax: 316-231-1188
CEO: O. Gene Bicknell
CFO: Joseph J. Fitzsimmons
1992 Sales: $299 million Employees: 11,097
Symbol: PIZA Exchange: NASDAQ
Industry: Retail - food & restaurants

 indicates company is in *Hoover's Handbook of American Business.*
indicates company is in *Hoover's Handbook of World Business;* sales and employee numbers are for parent company.

National Presto Industries, Inc.
3925 N. Hastings Way
Eau Claire, WI 54703
Phone: 715-839-2121 Fax: 715-839-2148
CEO: Melvin S. Cohen
CFO: Maryjo Cohen
1991 Sales: $162 million Employees: 607
Symbol: NPK Exchange: NYSE
Industry: Appliances - household

National Properties Corp.
4500 Merle Hay Rd.
Des Moines, IA 50310
Phone: 515-278-1132 Fax: —
CEO: Raymond DiPaglia
CFO: Robert W. Guely
1991 Sales: $2.4 million Employees: 7
Symbol: NAPE Exchange: NASDAQ
Industry: Real estate operations

National RE Holdings Corp.
777 Long Ridge Rd.
Stamford, CT 06904
Phone: 203-329-7700 Fax: 203-329-9027
CEO: W. D. Warren
CFO: P. A. Chesney
1991 Sales: $368 million Employees: —
Symbol: NRE Exchange: NYSE
Industry: Insurance - property & casualty

National Realty, L.P.
10670 N. Central Expressway
Dallas, TX 75231
Phone: 214-692-4800 Fax: 214-890-0752
CEO: William S. Friedman
CFO: William S. Friedman
1991 Sales: $97 million Employees: —
Symbol: NLP Exchange: AMEX
Industry: Real estate operations

National Rehabilitation Centers, Inc.
200 Powell Place, Ste. 210
Brentwood, TN 37027
Phone: 615-377-2937 Fax: —
CEO: William F. Youree
CFO: William F. Youree
1991 Sales: $24 million Employees: 466
Symbol: NRCT Exchange: NASDAQ
Industry: Healthcare - outpatient & home

National Safety Associates
4260 E. Raines Rd.
Memphis, TN 38118
Phone: 901-366-9288 Fax: 901-541-1298
CEO: A. Jay Martin
CFO: L. Frank Swords
1991 Sales: $285 million Employees: 650
Ownership: Privately held
Industry: Filtration products - water & air

National Sanitary Supply Co.
255 E. Fifth St., Ste. 2900
Cincinnati, OH 45202
Phone: 513-762-6500 Fax: 513-762-6644
CEO: Paul C. Voet
CFO: Gary H. Sander
1991 Sales: $268 million Employees: 1,659
Symbol: NSSX Exchange: NASDAQ
Industry: Soap & cleaning preparations

National Savings Bank of Albany
90 State St.
Albany, NY 12207
Phone: 518-472-6800 Fax: —
CEO: George O. Pfaff
CFO: Paul B. Lederman
1991 Sales: $57 million Employees: —
Symbol: NSBA Exchange: NASDAQ
Industry: Financial - savings and loans

National Security Group, Inc.
661 E. Davis St.
Elba, AL 36323
Phone: 205-897-2273 Fax: —
CEO: J. R. Brunson
CFO: M. L. Murdock
1991 Sales: $25 million Employees: 1,200
Symbol: NSEC Exchange: NASDAQ
Industry: Insurance - multiline & misc.

National Semiconductor Corp.
2900 Semiconductor Dr.
Santa Clara, CA 95051
Phone: 408-721-5000 Fax: 408-739-9803
CEO: Gilbert F. Amelio
CFO: Donald McLeod
1992 Sales: $1,858 million Employees: 27,200
Symbol: NSM Exchange: NYSE
Industry: Electrical components - semiconductors

National Service Industries, Inc.
1420 Peachtree St. NE
Atlanta, GA 30309
Phone: 404-853-1000 Fax: 404-853-1015
CEO: Erwin Zaban
CFO: J. Robert Hipps
1992 Sales: $1,667 million Employees: 20,900
Symbol: NSI Exchange: NYSE
Industry: Diversified operations - textile rental, chemicals, lighting equipment

National Tea Co.
6050 N. Lindbergh St.
Hazelwood, MO 63042
Phone: 314-731-5511 Fax: 314-731-1252
CEO: H. A. Seitz
CFO: —
1991 Sales: $9,284 million Employees: 63,700
Parent: George Weston Limited
Industry: Retail - supermarkets

National Technical Systems, Inc.
24007 Ventura Blvd., Ste. 200
Calabasas, CA 91302
Phone: 818-591-0776 Fax: 818-591-0899
CEO: Jack Lin
CFO: Lloyd Blonder
1991 Sales: $41 million Employees: 480
Symbol: NTSC Exchange: NASDAQ
Industry: Engineering - R&D services

National Western Life Insurance Co.
850 E. Anderson Lane
Austin, TX 78752
Phone: 512-836-1010 Fax: 512-835-2729
CEO: Robert L. Moody
CFO: Robert L. Busby III
1991 Sales: $297 million Employees: 233
Symbol: NWLIA Exchange: NASDAQ
Industry: Insurance - life

National Westminster Bancorp
175 Water St.
New York, NY 10038
Phone: 212-602-1000 Fax: 201-547-7179
CEO: John Tugwell
CFO: —
1991 Sales: $1,974 million Employees: 102,400
Parent: National Westminster Bank PLC
Industry: Banks - money center

National-Standard Co.
1618 Terminal Rd.
Niles, MI 49120
Phone: 616-683-8100 Fax: 616-683-6249
CEO: Michael B. Savitske
CFO: William D. Grafer
1991 Sales: $233 million Employees: 1,473
Symbol: NSD Exchange: NYSE
Industry: Wire & cable products

NationsBank Corp.
101 S. Tryon St., 1 NationsBank Plaza
Charlotte, NC 28255
Phone: 704-386-5000 Fax: 704-386-6655
CEO: Hugh L. McColl, Jr.
CFO: James H. Hance, Jr.
1992 Sales: $9,941 million Employees: 57,177
Symbol: NB Exchange: NYSE
Industry: Banks - Southeast

Nationwide Cellular Service, Inc.
20 E. Sunrise Hwy.
Valley Stream, NY 11581
Phone: 516-568-2000 Fax: 516-568-0554
CEO: Stephen Katz
CFO: Jerome Sanders
1991 Sales: $115 million Employees: 368
Symbol: NCEL Exchange: NASDAQ
Industry: Telecommunications services

Nationwide Remittance Centers
7926 Jones Branch Dr. #500
McLean, VA 22102
Phone: 703-827-5090 Fax: 703-790-5181
CEO: Joseph Loughry
CFO: William Doescher
1992 Sales: $15 million Employees: 475
Ownership: Privately held
Industry: Financial - lockbox services

Natural Wonders, Inc.
30031 Ahern St.
Union City, CA 94587
Phone: 510-429-9900 Fax: 510-429-8428
CEO: Robert S. Rubinstein
CFO: John F. Sauerland
1992 Sales: $88 million Employees: 951
Symbol: NATW Exchange: NASDAQ
Industry: Retail - educational & scientific products

Nature Food Centers, Inc.
1 Nature Way
Wilmington, MA 01887
Phone: 508-657-5000 Fax: 508-657-5679
CEO: James F. Leary
CFO: Dora S. Chiu
1991 Sales: $54 million Employees: —
Symbol: NAFD Exchange: NASDAQ
Industry: Vitamins & nutritional products

Nature's Bounty, Inc.
90 Orville Dr.
Bohemia, NY 11716
Phone: 516-567-9500 Fax: 516-563-1623
CEO: Arthur Rudolph
CFO: Arthur Rudolph
1991 Sales: $74 million Employees: 700
Symbol: NBTY Exchange: NASDAQ
Industry: Vitamins & nutritional products

Nature's Recipe Pet Foods
341 Bonnie Circle
Corona, CA 91720
Phone: 909-278-4280 Fax: 909-278-9727
CEO: Jeffery Paul Bennett
CFO: Jeffery Paul Bennett
1991 Sales: $21 million Employees: 40
Ownership: Privately held
Industry: Veterinary products - premium pet foods

Nature's Sunshine Products, Inc.
1655 N. Main St.
Spanish Fork, UT 84660
Phone: 801-342-4300 Fax: 801-342-4308
CEO: Alan D. Kennedy
CFO: Douglas Faggioli
1991 Sales: $73 million Employees: 344
Symbol: NATR Exchange: NASDAQ
Industry: Nutritional & personal care products

A indicates company is in *Hoover's Handbook of American Business.*

W indicates company is in *Hoover's Handbook of World Business;* sales and employee numbers are for parent company.

Navigators Group, Inc.
123 Williams St.
New York, NY 10038
Phone: 212-406-2900 Fax: 212-406-3042
CEO: Terence N. Deeks
CFO: W. Allen Barnett
1991 Sales: $62 million Employees: —
Symbol: NAVG Exchange: NASDAQ
Industry: Insurance - property & casualty

Navistar International Corp.
455 N. Cityfront Plaza Dr.
Chicago, IL 60611
Phone: 312-836-2000 Fax: 312-836-2192
CEO: James C. Cotting
CFO: Robert C. Lannert
1992 Sales: $3,875 million Employees: 13,472
Symbol: NAV Exchange: NYSE
Industry: Trucking - original equipment

Naylor Industries, Inc.
131 N. Richey
Pasadena, TX 77506
Phone: 713-473-9311 Fax: —
CEO: William S. Naylor
CFO: Lawrence D. Keister
1991 Sales: $36 million Employees: 397
Symbol: NALR Exchange: NASDAQ
Industry: Building products

NBB Bancorp, Inc.
174 Union St.
New Bedford, MA 02740
Phone: 508-996-5000 Fax: 508-997-9708
CEO: Robert McCarter
CFO: Irving J. Goss
1991 Sales: $141 million Employees: 411
Symbol: NBB Exchange: NYSE
Industry: Banks - Northeast

NBD Bancorp, Inc.
611 Woodward Ave.
Detroit, MI 48226
Phone: 313-225-1000 Fax: Call co. operator
CEO: Charles T. Fisher III
CFO: Louis Betanzos
1992 Sales: $3,373 million Employees: 13,129
Symbol: NBD Exchange: NYSE
Industry: Banks - Midwest

NBSC Corp.
13 E. Canal St.
Sumter, SC 29150
Phone: 803-775-1211 Fax: —
CEO: Robert V. Royall, Jr.
CFO: William L. Pherigo
1991 Sales: $59 million Employees: 463
Symbol: NSCB Exchange: NASDAQ
Industry: Banks - Southeast

NBT Bancorp, Inc.
52 S. Broad St.
Norwich, NY 13815
Phone: 607-335-6000 Fax: 607-336-7538
CEO: Joseph J. Butare, Jr.
CFO: Joseph J. Butare, Jr.
1991 Sales: $86 million Employees: 638
Symbol: NBTB Exchange: NASDAQ
Industry: Banks - Northeast

NCH Corp.
2727 Chemsearch Blvd.
Irving, TX 75062
Phone: 214-438-0211 Fax: 214-438-0186
CEO: Irvin L. Levy
CFO: Allen Piassick
1992 Sales: $686 million Employees: 10,477
Symbol: NCH Exchange: NYSE
Industry: Soap & cleaning preparations

NEC America, Inc.
8 Old Sod Farm Rd.
Melville, NY 11747
Phone: 516-753-7000 Fax: 516-753-7041
CEO: Hisashi Kaneko
CFO: —
1992 Sales: $28,375 million Employees: 128,320
Parent: NEC Corporation
Industry: Computers, communication systems

Neiman Marcus Group, Inc.
27 Boylston St.
Chestnut Hill, MA 02167
Phone: 617-232-0760 Fax: Ext. 2429
CEO: Robert J. Tarr, Jr.
CFO: John R. Cook
1992 Sales: $1,853 million Employees: 15,700
Symbol: NMG Exchange: NYSE
Industry: Retail - regional department stores

Nellcor Inc.
2549 Whitesell St.
Hayward, CA 94545
Phone: 510-887-5858 Fax: 510-782-0616
CEO: C. Raymond Larkin, Jr.
CFO: Michael P. Downey
1992 Sales: $196 million Employees: 1,512
Symbol: NELL Exchange: NASDAQ
Industry: Medical products - patient monitoring & measurement instruments

NeoRx Corp.
410 W. Harrison St.
Seattle, WA 98119
Phone: 206-281-7001 Fax: 206-284-7112
CEO: Paul G. Abrams
CFO: Robert M. Littauer
1991 Sales: $0.4 million Employees: 63
Symbol: NERX Exchange: NASDAQ
Industry: Biomedical & genetic products

Neozyme Corp.
One Kendall Square
Cambridge, MA 02139
Phone: 617-252-7500 Fax: 617-252-7600
CEO: Elliott D. Hillback
CFO: David J. McLachlan
1992 Sales: — Employees: 4
Symbol: NEOZ Exchange: NASDAQ
Industry: Medical products - cholesterol tests, thyroid cancer diagnosis products

NERCO, Inc.
500 NE Multnomah, Ste. 1500
Portland, OR 97232
Phone: 503-731-6600 Fax: 503-230-9045
CEO: Lawrence E. Heiner
CFO: Richard T. O'Brien
1991 Sales: $901 million Employees: 1,712
Symbol: NER Exchange: NYSE
Industry: Coal

NESB Corp.
63 Eugene O'Neill Dr.
New London, CT 06320
Phone: 203-444-3400 Fax: 203-444-3427
CEO: Robin Honiss
CFO: Seymour M. Smith
1991 Sales: $98 million Employees: 382
Symbol: NESB Exchange: NASDAQ
Industry: Banks - Northeast

Nestlé USA Inc.
800 N. Brand Blvd.
Glendale, CA 91203
Phone: 818-549-6000 Fax: 818-549-5884
CEO: Timm Crull
CFO: —
1991 Sales: $37,122 million Employees: 201,139
Parent: Nestlé SA
Industry: Food - confectionery, cereals; beverages

Netframe Systems, Inc.
1545 Barber Lane
Milpitas, CA 95035
Phone: 408-944-0600 Fax: —
CEO: Enzo Torresi
CFO: Robert P. Verheecke
1991 Sales: $21 million Employees: 118
Symbol: NETF Exchange: NASDAQ
Industry: Computers - network servers

Network Computing Devices, Inc.
350 N. Bernardo Ave.
Mountain View, CA 94043
Phone: 415-694-0650 Fax: 415-961-7711
CEO: William N. Carrico
CFO: Jack A. Bradley
1991 Sales: $61 million Employees: 211
Symbol: NCDI Exchange: NASDAQ
Industry: Computers - x terminal systems

Network Equipment Technologies, Inc.
800 Saginaw Dr.
Redwood City, CA 94063
Phone: 415-366-4400 Fax: 415-366-5675
CEO: Daniel J. Warmenhoven
CFO: Craig M. Gentner
1992 Sales: $181 million Employees: 1,087
Symbol: NWK Exchange: NYSE
Industry: Telecommunications equipment

Network General Corp.
4200 Bohannon Dr.
Menlo Park, CA 94025
Phone: 415-688-2700 Fax: 415-321-0855
CEO: Harry J. Saal
CFO: Roger C. Ferguson
1992 Sales: $64 million Employees: 259
Symbol: NETG Exchange: NASDAQ
Industry: Computers - LAN-analysis software

Network Systems Corp.
7600 Boone Ave. North
Minneapolis, MN 55428
Phone: 612-424-4888 Fax: 612-424-2853
CEO: Lyle D. Altman
CFO: Richard A. Fisher
1991 Sales: $199 million Employees: 1,392
Symbol: NSCO Exchange: NASDAQ
Industry: Computers - data communications equipment

Networks Electronic Corp.
9750 De Soto Ave.
Chatsworth, CA 91311
Phone: 818-341-0440 Fax: 818-718-7133
CEO: Mihai D. Patrichi
CFO: Mihai D. Patrichi
1992 Sales: $6.6 million Employees: 84
Symbol: NWRK Exchange: NASDAQ
Industry: Military equipment

Neumann Homes, Inc.
4450 Milton Ave., Ste. 206
Janesville, WI 53546
Phone: 608-754-4663 Fax: 608-754-4680
CEO: Paul Giusti
CFO: Ken Neumann
1991 Sales: $17 million Employees: 40
Ownership: Privately held
Industry: Building - residential & commercial projects; real estate development

Neutrogena Corp.
5760 W. 96th St.
Los Angeles, CA 90045
Phone: 310-642-1150 Fax: 310-337-5564
CEO: Lloyd E. Cotsen
CFO: Dasha Lewin
1991 Sales: $231 million Employees: 719
Symbol: NGNA Exchange: NASDAQ
Industry: Cosmetics & toiletries

indicates company is in *Hoover's Handbook of American Business.*

indicates company is in *Hoover's Handbook of World Business;* sales and employee numbers are for parent company.

Nevada Power Co.
6226 W. Sahara Ave.
Las Vegas, NV 89102
Phone: 702-367-5000 Fax: 702-367-8803
CEO: Charles A. Lenzie
CFO: Richard G. Hyte
1991 Sales: $546 million Employees: 1,689
Symbol: NVP Exchange: NYSE
Industry: Utility - electric power

New Brunswick Scientific Co., Inc.
44 Talmadge Rd.
Edison, NJ 08817
Phone: 908-287-1200 Fax: 908-287-4222
CEO: Ezra Weisman
CFO: Samuel Eichenbaum
1991 Sales: $33 million Employees: 350
Symbol: NBSC Exchange: NASDAQ
Industry: Instruments - scientific

New England Business Service, Inc.
500 Main St.
Groton, MA 01471
Phone: 508-448-6111 Fax: 508-448-2369
CEO: Bartley H. Calder
CFO: Russell V. Corsini, Jr.
1992 Sales: $232 million Employees: 2,180
Symbol: NEBS Exchange: NASDAQ
Industry: Paper - business forms

New England Electric Co.
25 Research Dr.
Westborough, MA 01582
Phone: 508-366-9011 Fax: Ext. 2698
CEO: John W. Rowe
CFO: Alfred D. Houston
1992 Sales: $2,182 million Employees: 5,616
Symbol: NES Exchange: NYSE
Industry: Utility - electric power

New Hampshire Oak Inc.
Liberty Lane
Hampton, NH 03842
Phone: 603-926-1340 Fax: 603-929-2404
CEO: Michael D. Dingman
CFO: Laurence Brock
1991 Sales: $675 million Employees: 3,500
Ownership: Privately held
Industry: Chemicals & industrial products

New Hampshire Thrift Bancshares, Inc.
The Carriage House
New London, NH 03257
Phone: 603-526-2116 Fax: 603-863-5025
CEO: John J. Kiernan
CFO: Steven R. Theroux
1991 Sales: $20 million Employees: 81
Symbol: NHTB Exchange: NASDAQ
Industry: Financial - savings and loans

New Horizons Savings and Loan Association
1050 Fourth St.
San Rafael, CA 94901
Phone: 415-457-6990 Fax: —
CEO: James W. Barnett
CFO: Georgia A. Athanasiou
1992 Sales: — Employees: —
Symbol: NHSL Exchange: NASDAQ
Industry: Financial - savings and loans

New Image Industries Inc.
21218 Vanowen St.
Canoga Park, CA 91303
Phone: 818-702-0285 Fax: 818-702-8868
CEO: Robert J. Gurevitch
CFO: Dennis J. Smolinski
1991 Sales: $8.3 million Employees: 56
Symbol: NIIS Exchange: NASDAQ
Industry: Computers - graphics

New Jersey Resources Corp.
1415 Wyckoff Rd.
Wall, NJ 07719
Phone: 908-938-1480 Fax: 908-938-2620
CEO: Oliver G. Richard III
CFO: Laurence M. Downes
1991 Sales: $335 million Employees: 809
Symbol: NJR Exchange: NYSE
Industry: Utility - gas distribution

New Jersey Steel Corp.
N. Crossman Rd.
Sayreville, NJ 08872
Phone: 908-721-6600 Fax: 908-721-9687
CEO: Robert J. Pasquarelli
CFO: Paul Roik
1991 Sales: $120 million Employees: 364
Symbol: NJST Exchange: NASDAQ
Industry: Steel - production

New Line Cinema Corp.
575 Eighth Ave., 16th Fl.
New York, NY 10018
Phone: 212-649-4900 Fax: 212-239-9104
CEO: Robert K. Shaye
CFO: Stephen Abramson
1991 Sales: $225 million Employees: 200
Symbol: NLN Exchange: AMEX
Industry: Motion pictures & services - production

New London Inc.
12500 San Pedro, Ste. 500
San Antonio, TX 78216
Phone: 210-494-1179 Fax: 210-494-2318
CEO: Paul N. Kesterton
CFO: Kendal A. Gladys
1992 Sales: $29 million Employees: 325
Symbol: NLON Exchange: NASDAQ
Industry: Oil & gas - field services

New Mexico and Arizona Land Co.
2810 N. 3rd St.
Phoenix, AZ 85004
Phone: 602-266-5455 Fax: —
CEO: Richard E. Leonard
CFO: W. Clarence McComack
1991 Sales: $7.2 million Employees: 19
Symbol: NZ Exchange: AMEX
Industry: Real estate operations

New Valley Corp.
One Lake St.
Upper Saddle River, NJ 07458
Phone: 201-818-5000 Fax: —
CEO: Robert J. Amman
CFO: Donald F. McKee
1991 Sales: $426 million Employees: 1,800
Symbol: NVL Exchange: NYSE
Industry: Telecommunications services

New York Bancorp Inc.
241-02 Northern Blvd.
Douglaston, NY 11363
Phone: 718-631-8100 Fax: —
CEO: Michael A. McManus, Jr.
CFO: Gerald E. Lundgren
1991 Sales: $104 million Employees: 275
Symbol: NYBC Exchange: NASDAQ
Industry: Banks - Northeast

New York Life Insurance Co.
51 Madison Ave.
New York, NY 10010
Phone: 212-576-7000 Fax: 212-576-6794
CEO: Harry G. Hohn
CFO: Bruce J. Davey
1991 Sales: $13,429 million Employees: 18,848
Ownership: Privately held
Industry: Insurance - life

New York State Electric & Gas Corp.
PO Box 287
Ithaca, NY 14850
Phone: 607-347-4142 Fax: 607-347-4034
CEO: James A. Carrigg
CFO: Sherwood J. Rafferty
1992 Sales: $1,692 million Employees: 4,782
Symbol: NGE Exchange: NYSE
Industry: Utility - electric power

New York Stock Exchange, Inc.
11 Wall St.
New York, NY 10005
Phone: 212-656-3000 Fax: 212-269-4830
CEO: William H. Donaldson
CFO: David L. Domijan
1991 Sales: $375 million Employees: —
Ownership: Privately held
Industry: Stock exchange

New York Times Co., The
229 W. 43rd St.
New York, NY 10036
Phone: 212-556-1234 Fax: 212-556-4607
CEO: Arthur Ochs Sulzberger
CFO: David L. Gorham
1992 Sales: $1,774 million Employees: 10,100
Symbol: NYTA Exchange: AMEX
Industry: Publishing - newspapers, magazines, broadcasting, information services

Newark Group
20 Jackson Dr.
Cranford, NJ 07016
Phone: 908-276-4000 Fax: 908-276-2888
CEO: Edward K. Mullen
CFO: William Harper
1991 Sales: $500 million Employees: 2,700
Ownership: Privately held
Industry: Paper & paper products - recycled paperboard & converted products

Newcor, Inc.
3270 W. Big Beaver Rd., Ste. 430
Troy, MI 48084
Phone: 313-643-7730 Fax: 313-643-2714
CEO: Richard A. Smith
CFO: John J. Garber
1991 Sales: $99 million Employees: 465
Symbol: NEWC Exchange: NASDAQ
Industry: Machinery - general industrial

Newell Co.
29 E. Stephenson St.
Freeport, IL 61032
Phone: 815-235-4171 Fax: 815-233-8060
CEO: Daniel C. Ferguson
CFO: William T. Alldredge
1992 Sales: $1,452 million Employees: 10,600
Symbol: NWL Exchange: NYSE
Industry: Diversified operations - hardware, housewares, office & industrial products

Newhall Land and Farming Co.
23823 Valencia Blvd.
Valencia, CA 91355
Phone: 805-255-4000 Fax: 805-255-3960
CEO: Thomas L. Lee
CFO: Robert D. Wilke
1991 Sales: $152 million Employees: 380
Symbol: NHL Exchange: NYSE
Industry: Agricultural operations

NewMil Bancorp, Inc.
19 Main St.
New Milford, CT 06776
Phone: 203-354-4411 Fax: —
CEO: F. Wayne Arnold
CFO: Jordan E. Barrows
1991 Sales: $20 million Employees: 94
Symbol: NMSB Exchange: NASDAQ
Industry: Financial - savings and loans

indicates company is in *Hoover's Handbook of American Business.*

indicates company is in *Hoover's Handbook of World Business;* sales and employee numbers are for parent company.

Newmont Gold Co.
1700 Lincoln St.
Denver, CO 80203
Phone: 303-863-7414 Fax: 303-837-5837
CEO: Gordon R. Parker
CFO: Paul L. Maroni
1991 Sales: $573 million Employees: 2,150
Symbol: NGC Exchange: NYSE
Industry: Gold mining & processing

Newmont Mining Corp.
1700 Lincoln St.
Denver, CO 80203
Phone: 303-863-7414 Fax: 303-837-5837
CEO: Gordon R. Parker
CFO: Paul L. Maroni
1991 Sales: $623 million Employees: 2,550
Symbol: NEM Exchange: NYSE
Industry: Gold mining & processing

Newnan Savings Bank, FSB
19 Jefferson St.
Newnan, GA 30264
Phone: 404-253-5017 Fax: —
CEO: Thomas J. Moat
CFO: Douglas J. Hertha
1992 Sales: — Employees: —
Symbol: NFSL Exchange: NASDAQ
Industry: Financial - savings and loans

Neworld Bancorp, Inc.
55 Summer St.
Boston, MA 02110
Phone: 617-482-2600 Fax: 617-482-2411
CEO: James M. Oates
CFO: Thomas J. Treacy, Jr.
1991 Sales: $114 million Employees: 338
Symbol: NWOR Exchange: NASDAQ
Industry: Banks - Northeast

Newpark Resources, Inc.
2900 Ridgelake Dr.
Metairie, LA 70002
Phone: 504-838-8222 Fax: 504-833-9506
CEO: James D. Cole
CFO: Matthew W. Hardey
1991 Sales: $60 million Employees: 850
Symbol: NPRS Exchange: NASDAQ
Industry: Oil & gas - field services

Newport Corp.
1791 Deere Ave.
Irvine, CA 92714
Phone: 714-963-9811 Fax: 714-963-2015
CEO: Richard E. Schmidt
CFO: Robert C. Hewitt
1991 Sales: $60 million Employees: 495
Symbol: NEWP Exchange: NASDAQ
Industry: Instruments - scientific

Newport Electronics, Inc.
2229 S. Yale St.
Santa Ana, CA 92704
Phone: 714-540-4914 Fax: 714-546-3022
CEO: Milton B. Hollander
CFO: Milton B. Hollander
1991 Sales: $20 million Employees: 172
Symbol: NEWE Exchange: NASDAQ
Industry: Instruments - control

News America Publishing, Inc.
1211 Avenue of the Americas, 3rd Fl.
New York, NY 10036
Phone: 212-852-7000 Fax: 212-852-7145
CEO: Patrick Purcell
CFO: —
1991 Sales: $8,587 million Employees: 30,700
Parent: The News Corporation Limited
Industry: Publishing - newspapers & magazines; film & TV

NeXT Inc.
900 Chesapeake Dr.
Redwood City, CA 94063
Phone: 415-366-0900 Fax: 415-780-3714
CEO: Steven P. Jobs
CFO: Susan Kelly Barnes
1992 Sales: $140 million Employees: 530
Ownership: Privately held
Industry: Computers - operating systems

NFS Financial Corp.
157 Main St.
Nashua, NH 03061
Phone: 603-880-2011 Fax: —
CEO: James H. Adams
CFO: Albert R. Rietheimer
1991 Sales: $46 million Employees: 208
Symbol: NFSF Exchange: NASDAQ
Industry: Banks - Northeast

NHD Stores, Inc.
365 Washington St.
Stoughton, MA 02072
Phone: 617-341-1810 Fax: 617-341-2291
CEO: Sheldon M. Woolf
CFO: Theodore G. Dawe
1991 Sales: $57 million Employees: 615
Symbol: NHDI Exchange: NASDAQ
Industry: Retail - building products

Niagara Mohawk Power Corp.
300 Erie Blvd. West
Syracuse, NY 13202
Phone: 315-474-1511 Fax: 315-428-5101
CEO: William J. Donlon
CFO: John W. Powers
1992 Sales: $3,702 million Employees: 11,837
Symbol: NMK Exchange: NYSE
Industry: Utility - electric power

Nichols Institute
33608 Ortega Hwy.
San Juan Capistrano, CA 92690
Phone: 714-661-8000 Fax: 714-240-4507
CEO: Paul Bellamy
CFO: Paul Bellamy
1991 Sales: $236 million Employees: 3,300
Symbol: LABA Exchange: AMEX
Industry: Medical & dental supplies

Nichols Research Corp.
4040 S. Memorial Pkwy.
Huntsville, AL 35802
Phone: 205-883-1140 Fax: 205-880-0367
CEO: Chris H. Horgen
CFO: Charles F. Lofty
1991 Sales: $91 million Employees: 902
Symbol: NRES Exchange: NASDAQ
Industry: Engineering - R&D services

NICOR Inc.
1700 W. Ferry Rd.
Naperville, IL 60563
Phone: 708-305-9500 Fax: 708-983-4566
CEO: Richard G. Cline
CFO: John J. Lannon
1992 Sales: $1,612 million Employees: 3,600
Symbol: GAS Exchange: NYSE
Industry: Utility - gas distribution

NIKE, Inc.
One Bowerman Dr.
Beaverton, OR 97005
Phone: 503-671-6453 Fax: 503-671-7252
CEO: Philip H. Knight
CFO: Robert S. Falcone
1992 Sales: $3,690 million Employees: 6,500
Symbol: NKE Exchange: NYSE
Industry: Shoes & related apparel - athletic

Nintendo of America Inc.
4820 150th Ave. NE
Redmond, WA 98052
Phone: 206-882-2040 Fax: 206-882-3585
CEO: Minoru Arakawa
CFO: —
1992 Sales: $4,500 million Employees: 825
Parent: Nintendo Co., Ltd.
Industry: Toys - electronic game hardware & software

Nippon Steel U.S.A., Inc.
10 E. 50th St., 29th Fl.
New York, NY 10022
Phone: 212-486-7150 Fax: 212-593-3049
CEO: Aki Zuki
CFO: —
1992 Sales: $25,837 million Employees: 53,290
Parent: Nippon Steel Corporation
Industry: Steel - production; chemicals, engineering & construction

NIPSCO Industries, Inc.
5265 Hohman Ave.
Hammond, IN 46320
Phone: 219-853-5200 Fax: 219-853-5161
CEO: Edmund A. Schroer
CFO: Stephen P. Adik
1992 Sales: $1,582 million Employees: 4,570
Symbol: NI Exchange: NYSE
Industry: Utility - electric power

Nissan Motor Corporation
18501 S. Figueroa St.
Gardena, CA 90248
Phone: 310-532-3111 Fax: 310-719-5656
CEO: Thomas D. Mignanelli
CFO: —
1992 Sales: $51,343 million Employees: 143,916
Parent: Nissan Motor Co., Ltd.
Industry: Automotive manufacturing

NL Industries, Inc.
3000 N. Sam Houston Pkwy. East
Houston, TX 77032
Phone: 713-987-5000 Fax: 713-987-5742
CEO: J. Landis Martin
CFO: Susan E. Alderton
1992 Sales: $894 million Employees: 3,500
Symbol: NL Exchange: NYSE
Industry: Chemicals - specialty

NMR of America, Inc.
355 Madison Ave.
Morristown, NJ 07960
Phone: 201-539-1082 Fax: 201-993-1991
CEO: Joseph G. Dasti
CFO: Bruce A. Phillips
1992 Sales: $15 million Employees: 127
Symbol: NMRR Exchange: NASDAQ
Industry: Medical services - magnetic resonance imaging

Nobel Industries USA, Inc.
595 Skippack Pike, Ste. 300
Blue Bell, PA 19422
Phone: 215-641-9330 Fax: 215-641-9334
CEO: Jan Kihlberg
CFO: —
1991 Sales: $4,462 million Employees: 22,922
Parent: Nobel Industries Sweden AB
Industry: Diversified operations - adhesives & paints, pulp & paper chemicals, lasers

Noble Affiliates, Inc.
110 W. Broadway St.
Ardmore, OK 73401
Phone: 405-223-4110 Fax: 405-221-1210
CEO: Robert Kelley
CFO: William D. Dickson
1991 Sales: $226 million Employees: 420
Symbol: NBL Exchange: NYSE
Industry: Oil & gas - US exploration & production

indicates company is in *Hoover's Handbook of American Business.*
indicates company is in *Hoover's Handbook of World Business;* sales and employee numbers are for parent company.

Noble Drilling Corp.
10370 Richmond Ave., Ste. 400
Houston, TX 77042
Phone: 713-974-3131 Fax: 713-974-3181
CEO: James C. Day
CFO: Byron L. Welliver
1991 Sales: $177 million Employees: 1,847
Symbol: NDCO Exchange: NASDAQ
Industry: Oil & gas - field services

Noble Oil Services Inc.
5617 Clyde Rhyne Dr.
Sanford, NC 27330
Phone: 919-774-8180 Fax: 919-775-7732
CEO: Jim Noble
CFO: Bill Morgan
1991 Sales: $2.6 million Employees: 36
Ownership: Privately held
Industry: Pollution control equipment & services - petroleum waste recycling

Noel Group, Inc.
667 Madison Ave.
New York, NY 10021
Phone: 212-371-1400 Fax: —
CEO: William L. Bennett
CFO: William L. Bennett
1991 Sales: $14 million Employees: —
Symbol: NOEL Exchange: NASDAQ
Industry: Diversified operations - oil & gas, medical technology & mushroom production

Noise Cancellation Technologies, Inc.
1015 W. Nursery Rd.
Linthicum, MD 21090
Phone: 410-636-8700 Fax: —
CEO: John J. McCloy II
CFO: John J. McCloy II
1991 Sales: $5.9 million Employees: 77
Symbol: NCTI Exchange: NASDAQ
Industry: Engineering - R&D services

Nokia Mobile Phones Inc.
PO Box 2930
Largo, FL 34641
Phone: 813-536-5553 Fax: 813-530-7245
CEO: Paul Chellgren
CFO: —
1991 Sales: $3,743 million Employees: 29,167
Parent: Nokia Group
Industry: Telecommunications equipment - mobile phones

Noland Co.
2700 Warwick Blvd.
Newport News, VA 23607
Phone: 804-928-9000 Fax: 804-245-6532
CEO: Lloyd U. Noland III
CFO: Arthur P. Henderson, Jr.
1991 Sales: $384 million Employees: 1,704
Symbol: NOLD Exchange: NASDAQ
Industry: Building products - retail & wholesale

Nomura Securities International, Inc.
2 World Financial Center, Bldg. B
New York, NY 10281
Phone: 212-667-9300 Fax: 212-667-1058
CEO: Max C. Chapman, Jr.
CFO: —
1992 Sales: $5,249 million Employees: 16,800
Parent: The Nomura Securities Co., Ltd.
Industry: Financial - business services; securities brokerage

Nord Resources Corp.
8150 Washington Village Dr.
Dayton, OH 45458
Phone: 513-433-6307 Fax: 513-435-7285
CEO: Edgar F. Cruft
CFO: Terence H. Lang
1991 Sales: $107 million Employees: 2,174
Symbol: NRD Exchange: NYSE
Industry: Metal ores

Nordson Corp.
28601 Clemens Rd.
Westlake, OH 44145
Phone: 216-892-1580 Fax: 216-892-9507
CEO: William P. Madar
CFO: Nicholas D. Pellecchia
1991 Sales: $388 million Employees: 2,827
Symbol: NDSN Exchange: NASDAQ
Industry: Machinery - general industrial

Nordstrom, Inc.
1501 Fifth Ave.
Seattle, WA 98101
Phone: 206-628-2111 Fax: 206-628-1289
CEO: Bruce A. Nordstrom
CFO: John A. Goesling
1992 Sales: $3,331 million Employees: 31,000
Symbol: NOBE Exchange: NASDAQ
Industry: Retail - regional department stores

Norfolk Southern Corp.
Three Commercial Place
Norfolk, VA 23510
Phone: 804-629-2680 Fax: 804-629-2777
CEO: Arnold B. McKinnon
CFO: John R. Turbyfill
1992 Sales: $4,607 million Employees: 31,952
Symbol: NSC Exchange: NYSE
Industry: Transportation - rail & truck, coal

Norrell Corporation
3535 Piedmont Rd. NE
Atlanta, GA 30305
Phone: 404-240-3000 Fax: 404-240-3312
CEO: Guy W. Millner
CFO: Larry Bryan
1991 Sales: $473 million Employees: 2,072
Ownership: Privately held
Industry: Business services - temporary employment services, health care services

Norsk Hydro USA Inc.
800 Third Ave.
New York, NY 10022
Phone: 212-688-6606 Fax: 212-750-1252
CEO: Rolf E. Kogstad
CFO: —
1991 Sales: $10,264 million Employees: 34,957
Parent: Norsk Hydro AS
Industry: Diversified operations - agriculture, light metals & oil & gas

Norstan Communications, Inc.
6900 Wedgwood Rd., Ste. 150
Maple Grove, MN 55369
Phone: 612-420-1100 Fax: 612-420-1178
CEO: Paul Baszucki
CFO: Richard Cohen
1992 Sales: $142 million Employees: 1,524
Symbol: NRRD Exchange: NASDAQ
Industry: Telecommunications equipment

Nortek, Inc.
50 Kennedy Plaza
Providence, RI 02903
Phone: 401-751-1600 Fax: 401-751-4610
CEO: Richard L. Bready
CFO: Richard L. Bready
1992 Sales: $800 million Employees: 7,188
Symbol: NTK Exchange: NYSE
Industry: Diversified operations - building products, electrical material products, industrial products

North American Biologicals, Inc.
16500 NW 15th Ave.
Miami, FL 33169
Phone: 305-625-5303 Fax: 305-625-0925
CEO: Thomas Halasz
CFO: Alfred J. Fernandez
1991 Sales: $68 million Employees: 849
Symbol: NBIO Exchange: NASDAQ
Industry: Biomedical & genetic products

North American Mortgage Co.
3883 Airway Dr.
Santa Rosa, CA 95463
Phone: 707-523-5000 Fax: —
CEO: J. F. Farrell, Jr.
CFO: Robert J. Gallagher
1992 Sales: — Employees: —
Symbol: NAC Exchange: NYSE
Industry: Financial - mortgages & related services

North American National Corp.
PO Box 625
Columbus, OH 43216
Phone: 614-488-4881 Fax: —
CEO: George R. Manser
CFO: Rosemarie Coleman
1992 Sales: $18 million Employees: 55
Symbol: NAMC Exchange: NASDAQ
Industry: Insurance - life

North American Philips Corp.
100 E. 42nd St.
New York, NY 10017
Phone: 212-850-5000 Fax: 212-850-7314
CEO: Stephen C. Tumminello
CFO: —
1991 Sales: $33,274 million Employees: 240,001
Parent: Philips Electronics NV
Industry: Audio & video equipment, lighting, consumer products

North American Processing
741 N. Milwaukee Ave.
Niles, IL 60714
Phone: 708-647-1210 Fax: 708-647-1299
CEO: Robert Lenahan
CFO: Frank Lenahan
1991 Sales: $137 million Employees: 15
Ownership: Privately held
Industry: Food - meat products

North American Recycling Systems, Inc.
14 Wing St.
Ft. Edward, NY 12828
Phone: 518-747-4183 Fax: —
CEO: Robert R. Barber
CFO: Stephen R. Brown
1991 Sales: $6 million Employees: —
Symbol: NAR Exchange: AMEX
Industry: Recycling & solid waste management

North Atlantic Industries, Inc.
60 Plant Ave.
Hauppauge, NY 11788
Phone: 516-582-6500 Fax: 516-582-8652
CEO: Robert A. Carlson
CFO: Richard A. Schneider
1991 Sales: $59 million Employees: 390
Symbol: NATL Exchange: NASDAQ
Industry: Computers - peripheral equipment

North Carolina Natural Gas Corp.
150 Rowan St.
Fayetteville, NC 28301
Phone: 919-483-0315 Fax: 919-483-0336
CEO: Calvin B. Wells
CFO: Cecil C. Dew
1991 Sales: $127 million Employees: 497
Symbol: NCG Exchange: NYSE
Industry: Utility - gas distribution

North Fork Bancorporation, Inc.
9025 Main Rd. (Route 25)
Mattituck, NY 11952
Phone: 516-298-8366 Fax: 516-298-5182
CEO: John Adam Kanas
CFO: Daniel M. Healy
1991 Sales: $173 million Employees: 654
Symbol: NFB Exchange: NYSE
Industry: Banks - Northeast

indicates company is in *Hoover's Handbook of American Business.*

indicates company is in *Hoover's Handbook of World Business;* sales and employee numbers are for parent company.

North Pacific Lumber Co.
1505 SE Gideon St.
Portland, OR 97202
Phone: 503-231-1166 Fax: 503-238-2650
CEO: T. J. Tomjack
CFO: George R. Thurston
1991 Sales: $490 million Employees: 370
Ownership: Privately held
Industry: Diversified operations - forest, agriculture & steel products wholesaling

North Side Savings Bank
170 Tulip Ave.
Floral Park, NY 11001
Phone: 516-488-6900 Fax: —
CEO: Thomas M. O'Brien
CFO: Donald C. Fleming
1992 Sales: — Employees: —
Symbol: NSBK Exchange: NASDAQ
Industry: Financial - savings and loans

North Star Universal, Inc.
5353 Wayzata Blvd., Ste. 610
Minneapolis, MN 55416
Phone: 612-546-7500 Fax: 612-540-9100
CEO: Jeffrey J. Michael
CFO: Peter E. Flynn
1991 Sales: $72 million Employees: 468
Symbol: NSRU Exchange: NASDAQ
Industry: Diversified operations - food processing, computer cable, managed health care

Northbay Financial Corp.
20 Petaluma Blvd. South
Petaluma, CA 94952
Phone: 707-778-3300 Fax: —
CEO: Alfred A. Alys
CFO: Gregory L. Jahn
1991 Sales: $27 million Employees: 108
Symbol: NBF Exchange: AMEX
Industry: Financial - savings and loans

Northeast Bancorp, Inc.
205 Church St.
New Haven, CT 06502
Phone: 203-773-0500 Fax: 203-926-9956
CEO: Frank J. Kugler, Jr.
CFO: George R. Kabureck
1991 Sales: $331 million Employees: 1,710
Symbol: NBIC Exchange: NASDAQ
Industry: Banks - Northeast

Northeast Federal Corp.
50 State House Square
Hartford, CT 06103
Phone: 203-280-1000 Fax: 203-280-1170
CEO: George P. Rutland
CFO: Kirk W. Walters
1992 Sales: $343 million Employees: 1,089
Symbol: NSB Exchange: NYSE
Industry: Financial - savings and loans

Northeast Utilities
174 Brush Hill Ave.
West Springfield, MA 01090
Phone: 413-785-5871 Fax: 413-787-9352
CEO: William B. Ellis
CFO: Robert E. Busch
1992 Sales: $3,258 million Employees: 8,099
Symbol: NU Exchange: NYSE
Industry: Utility - electric power

Northern Indiana Public Service Co.
5265 Hohman Ave.
Hammond, IN 46320
Phone: 219-853-5200 Fax: —
CEO: Edmund A. Schroer
CFO: Jerry M. Springer
1991 Sales: $1.5 million Employees: 4,576
Symbol: NIp Exchange: AMEX
Industry: Utility - gas distribution

Northern States Power Co.
414 Nicollet Mall
Minneapolis, MN 55401
Phone: 612-330-5500 Fax: 612-330-2900
CEO: James J. Howard
CFO: James T. Doudiet
1992 Sales: $2,160 million Employees: 7,926
Symbol: NSP Exchange: NYSE
Industry: Utility - electric power

Northern Telecom Inc.
200 Athens Way
Nashville, TN 37228
Phone: 615-734-4000 Fax: 615-734-5190
CEO: Paul George Stern
CFO: —
1991 Sales: $17,204 million Employees: 124,000
Parent: BCE Inc.
Industry: Utility - telephone; telecommunications services

Northern Trust Corp.
50 S. La Salle St.
Chicago, IL 60675
Phone: 312-630-6000 Fax: 312-630-1512
CEO: David W. Fox
CFO: Perry R. Pero
1992 Sales: $1,231 million Employees: 5,798
Symbol: NTRS Exchange: NASDAQ
Industry: Banks - Midwest

Northland Cranberries, Inc.
800 First Ave. South
Wisconsin Rapids, WI 54494
Phone: 715-424-4444 Fax: —
CEO: John Swendrowski
CFO: John A. Pazurek
1992 Sales: $12 million Employees: 256
Symbol: CBRYA Exchange: NASDAQ
Industry: Agricultural operations

Northrop Corp.
1840 Century Park East
Los Angeles, CA 90067
Phone: 310-553-6262 Fax: 310-553-2076
CEO: Kent Kresa
CFO: Richard B. Waugh, Jr.
1992 Sales: $5,550 million Employees: 36,200
Symbol: NOC Exchange: NYSE
Industry: Aerospace - aircraft equipment & electronic systems

Northstar Computer Forms, Inc.
1226 Linden Ave.
Minneapolis, MN 55403
Phone: 612-338-8601 Fax: 612-339-2332
CEO: Roger T. Bredesen
CFO: Roger T. Bredesen
1991 Sales: $16 million Employees: 200
Symbol: NSCF Exchange: NASDAQ
Industry: Paper - business forms

Northwest Illinois Bancorp, Inc.
50 W. Douglas St.
Freeport, IL 61032
Phone: 815-235-8459 Fax: —
CEO: Dan Heine
CFO: R. William Owen
1991 Sales: $30 million Employees: 187
Symbol: NWIB Exchange: NASDAQ
Industry: Banks - Midwest

Northwest Micro Inc.
9610 SW Sunshine Ct., Ste. 800
Beaverton, OR 97005
Phone: 503-626-2555 Fax: 503-626-2333
CEO: Max K. Chau
CFO: Max K. Chau
1991 Sales: $7.4 million Employees: 19
Ownership: Privately held
Industry: Computers - microcomputer systems integration & component distribution

Northwest Natural Gas Co.
220 NW Second Ave.
Portland, OR 97209
Phone: 503-226-4211 Fax: 503-273-4824
CEO: Robert L. Ridgley
CFO: Bruce R. DeBolt
1991 Sales: $296 million Employees: 1,283
Symbol: NWNG Exchange: NASDAQ
Industry: Utility - gas distribution

Northwest Pine Products Inc.
53 NW Irving
Bend, OR 97709
Phone: 503-382-2274 Fax: 503-389-5885
CEO: Tom Hicks
CFO: Tom Hicks
1991 Sales: $13 million Employees: 34
Ownership: Privately held
Industry: Wood chips for pulp & paper industry

Northwest Teleproductions, Inc.
4455 W. 77th St.
Minneapolis, MN 55435
Phone: 612-835-4455 Fax: 612-835-0971
CEO: Robert C. Mitchell
CFO: James N. Steffen
1992 Sales: $14 million Employees: 122
Symbol: NWTL Exchange: NASDAQ
Industry: Motion pictures & services

Northwestern Mutual Life Insurance Co.
720 E. Wisconsin Ave.
Milwaukee, WI 53202
Phone: 414-271-1444 Fax: 414-299-7022
CEO: Donald J. Schuenke
CFO: Walt J. Wojcik
1991 Sales: $7,694 million Employees: 3,100
Ownership: Privately held
Industry: Insurance - life

Northwestern Public Service Co.
33 Third St. SE
Huron, SD 57350
Phone: 605-352-8411 Fax: 605-353-8286
CEO: Robert A. Wilkens
CFO: Richard R. Hylland
1991 Sales: $123 million Employees: 457
Symbol: NPS Exchange: NYSE
Industry: Utility - electric power

Northwestern Steel & Wire
121 Wallace St.
Sterling, IL 61081
Phone: 815-625-2500 Fax: 815-625-0440
CEO: Robert N. Gurnitz
CFO: Edward Maris
1991 Sales: $470 million Employees: 2,700
Ownership: Privately held
Industry: Wire & cable products - steel, rod & wire products

Norwest Corp.
Sixth & Marquette Streets
Minneapolis, MN 55479
Phone: 612-667-1234 Fax: —
CEO: Lloyd P. Johnson
CFO: John T. Thornton
1992 Sales: $4,628 million Employees: 25,500
Symbol: NOB Exchange: NYSE
Industry: Banks - Midwest

Norwich Financial Corp.
4 Broadway
Norwich, CT 06360
Phone: 203-889-2621 Fax: —
CEO: Daniel R. Dennis, Jr.
CFO: Michael J. Hartl
1991 Sales: $53 million Employees: 210
Symbol: NSSB Exchange: NASDAQ
Industry: Financial - savings and loans

indicates company is in *Hoover's Handbook of American Business.*

indicates company is in *Hoover's Handbook of World Business;* sales and employee numbers are for parent company.

NovaCare, Inc.
2570 Boulevard of the Generals
Valley Forge, PA 19482
Phone: 215-631-9300 Fax: 215-631-0808
CEO: John H. Foster
CFO: Timothy E. Foster
1992 Sales: $385 million Employees: 5,650
Symbol: NOV Exchange: NYSE
Industry: Healthcare - outpatient & home

Novametrix Medical Systems Inc.
1 Barnes Industrial Park Rd.
Wallingford, CT 06492
Phone: 203-265-7701 Fax: 203-284-0753
CEO: Louis P. Pelligrino
CFO: James E. Lordi
1992 Sales: $21 million Employees: 154
Symbol: NMTX Exchange: NASDAQ
Industry: Medical instruments

Novell, Inc.
122 East 1700 South
Provo, UT 84606
Phone: 801-429-7000 Fax: 801-429-5775
CEO: Raymond J. Noorda
CFO: James R. Tolonen
1992 Sales: $933 million Employees: 2,843
Symbol: NOVL Exchange: NASDAQ
Industry: Computers - network software

Novellus Systems, Inc.
81 Vista Montana
San Jose, CA 95134
Phone: 408-943-9700 Fax: 408-943-0202
CEO: Robert F. Graham
CFO: Gary Harmon
1991 Sales: $80 million Employees: 265
Symbol: NVLS Exchange: NASDAQ
Industry: Electrical components - semiconductors

Noven Pharmaceuticals, Inc.
1330 SW 128th St.
Miami, FL 33186
Phone: 305-253-5099 Fax: —
CEO: Steven Sablotsky
CFO: Sheldon H. Becher
1991 Sales: $0.1 million Employees: 23
Symbol: NOVN Exchange: NASDAQ
Industry: Drugs

Novo Nordisk of North America, Inc.
405 Lexington Ave., Ste. 6200
New York, NY 10017
Phone: 212-867-0131 Fax: 212-867-0299
CEO: Harry H. Penner
CFO: —
1991 Sales: $1,632 million Employees: 9,627
Parent: Novo Nordisk A/S
Industry: Biomedical & genetic products

NS Group, Inc.
Ninth & Lowell Streets
Newport, KY 41072
Phone: 606-292-6809 Fax: 606-292-0593
CEO: Clifford R. Borland
CFO: John R. Parker
1991 Sales: $212 million Employees: 1,823
Symbol: NSS Exchange: NYSE
Industry: Steel - pipes & tubes

NSC Corp.
4300 W. Lake St.
Chicago, IL 60624
Phone: 312-379-9190 Fax: 312-379-9199
CEO: Anthony Mesiti
CFO: Gene J. Ostrow
1991 Sales: $38 million Employees: 918
Symbol: NSCC Exchange: NASDAQ
Industry: Pollution control equipment & services

NTT America, Inc.
101 Park Ave., 40th & 41st Floors
New York, NY 10178
Phone: 212-661-0810 Fax: 212-661-1078
CEO: Koichiro Hayashi
CFO: —
1992 Sales: $51,184 million Employees: 257,663
Parent: Nippon Telegraph and Telephone Corp.
Industry: Telecommunications services

Nu Horizons Electronic Corp.
6000 New Horizons Blvd.
Amityville, NY 11701
Phone: 516-226-6000 Fax: 516-226-6140
CEO: Irving Lubman
CFO: Paul Durando
1992 Sales: $42 million Employees: 140
Symbol: NUH Exchange: AMEX
Industry: Electronics - parts distribution

Nu-West Industries, Inc.
8400 E. Prentice Ave., Ste. 1320
Englewood, CO 80111
Phone: 303-721-1396 Fax: 303-721-1402
CEO: Craig D. Harlen
CFO: Mark R. Sanders
1992 Sales: $98 million Employees: 239
Symbol: FERT Exchange: NASDAQ
Industry: Fertilizers

Nuclear Metals, Inc.
2229 Main St.
Concord, MA 01742
Phone: 508-369-5410 Fax: 508-263-8884
CEO: Wilson B. Tuffin
CFO: Daral D. Ferguson
1991 Sales: $48 million Employees: 456
Symbol: NUCM Exchange: NASDAQ
Industry: Metal processing & fabrication

Nuclear Support Services, Inc.
W. Market St.
Campbelltown, PA 17010
Phone: 717-838-8125 Fax: 717-838-8400
CEO: Joe C. Quick
CFO: C. David Williams
1991 Sales: $71 million Employees: 1,246
Symbol: NSSI Exchange: NASDAQ
Industry: Engineering - R&D services

Nucor Corp.
2100 Rexford Rd.
Charlotte, NC 28211
Phone: 704-366-7000 Fax: 704-362-4208
CEO: F. Kenneth Iverson
CFO: Samuel Siegel
1992 Sales: $1,619 million Employees: 5,600
Symbol: NUE Exchange: NYSE
Industry: Steel - production

Nucorp, Inc.
Two N. Riverside Plaza
Chicago, IL 60606
Phone: 312-454-0100 Fax: 312-454-9190
CEO: Donald W. Phillips
CFO: Arthur A. Greenberg
1991 Sales: $35 million Employees: 52
Symbol: NUCO Exchange: NASDAQ
Industry: Oil & gas - US exploration & production

Nuevo Energy Co.
1221 Lamar, Ste. 1600
Houston, TX 77010
Phone: 713-652-0706 Fax: —
CEO: James P. Bryan
CFO: John J. Lendrum III
1991 Sales: $36 million Employees: 16
Symbol: NEV Exchange: NYSE
Industry: Oil & gas - US exploration & production

NUI Corp.
550 Route 202-206
Bedminster, NJ 07921
Phone: 908-685-3900 Fax: 908-781-0718
CEO: John Kean, Sr.
CFO: John Kean, Jr.
1991 Sales: $291 million Employees: 959
Symbol: NUI Exchange: NYSE
Industry: Utility - gas distribution

Nutech Laundry & Textiles Inc.
5214 Monroe Pl.
Hyattsville, MD 20781
Phone: 301-985-6500 Fax: 301-277-7496
CEO: Jack Robinson
CFO: Jack Robinson
1991 Sales: $3.9 million Employees: 130
Ownership: Privately held
Industry: Linen supply - laundry plant services & hotel laundry systems

Nutmeg Industries, Inc.
4408 W. Linebaugh Ave.
Tampa, FL 33624
Phone: 813-963-6153 Fax: 813-968-6312
CEO: Richard E. Jacobsen
CFO: George N. Derhofer
1991 Sales: $122 million Employees: 1,560
Symbol: NTM Exchange: NYSE
Industry: Textiles - apparel

NutraMax Products, Inc.
9 Blackburn Dr.
Gloucester, MA 01930
Phone: 508-283-1800 Fax: 508-283-4067
CEO: Donald E. Lepone
CFO: Michael F. Sandler
1991 Sales: $20 million Employees: 150
Symbol: NMPC Exchange: NASDAQ
Industry: Cosmetics & toiletries

NuVision Optical
2284 S. Ballenger Hwy.
Flint, MI 48503
Phone: 313-767-0900 Fax: 313-767-6390
CEO: Eli Shapiro
CFO: Stephen L. Hirsch
1991 Sales: $48 million Employees: 850
Symbol: NUVI Exchange: NASDAQ
Industry: Retail - optical offices

nVIEW Corp.
11835 Canon Blvd.
Newport News, VA 23606
Phone: 804-873-1354 Fax: 804-873-2153
CEO: James H. Vogeley
CFO: William M. Donaldson
1991 Sales: $17 million Employees: 47
Symbol: NVUE Exchange: NASDAQ
Industry: Video equipment

NVR L.P.
7601 Lewinsville Rd., Ste. 300
McLean, VA 22102
Phone: 703-761-2000 Fax: 703-761-2030
CEO: Dwight C. Schar
CFO: Paul C. Saville
1992 Sales: — Employees: —
Symbol: NVR Exchange: AMEX
Industry: Building - residential & commercial

NWA Inc.
5101 Northwest Dr.
St. Paul, MN 55111
Phone: 612-726-2111 Fax: 612-726-3942
CEO: John H. Dasburg
CFO: Joseph Francht
1992 Sales: $8,500 million Employees: 45,000
Ownership: Privately held
Industry: Transportation - airline

indicates company is in *Hoover's Handbook of American Business.*

indicates company is in *Hoover's Handbook of World Business;* sales and employee numbers are for parent company.

NWNL Companies, Inc.
20 Washington Ave. South
Minneapolis, MN 55401
Phone: 612-372-5432 Fax: 612-342-3966
CEO: John G. Turner
CFO: John H. Flittie
1992 Sales: $1,378 million Employees: —
Symbol: NWN Exchange: NYSE
Industry: Insurance - life

NYCAL Corp.
3050 K St., NW, Ste. 310
Washington, DC 20007
Phone: 202-944-4424 Fax: 202-944-4426
CEO: Graham F. Lacey
CFO: William C. Horn
1992 Sales: $4.7 million Employees: 91
Symbol: NYCL Exchange: NASDAQ
Industry: Diversified operations - mineral claim exploration, insurance brokerage, financial services

NYCOR, Inc.
287 Childs Rd.
Basking Ridge, NJ 07920
Phone: 908-953-8200 Fax: 908-953-0100
CEO: Salvatore Giordano, Jr.
CFO: Robert E. Logan, Jr.
1991 Sales: $6.4 million Employees: —
Symbol: NYCO Exchange: NASDAQ
Industry: Investors

NYMAGIC, INC.
330 Madison Ave.
New York, NY 10017
Phone: 212-551-0600 Fax: 212-986-1310
CEO: Mark W. Blackman
CFO: Thomas J. Iacopelli
1991 Sales: $98 million Employees: 136
Symbol: NYM Exchange: NYSE
Industry: Insurance - property & casualty

NYNEX Corp.
335 Madison Ave.
New York, NY 10017
Phone: 212-370-7400 Fax: 212-682-1324
CEO: William C. Ferguson
CFO: Robert J. Eckenrode
1992 Sales: $13,155 million Employees: 83,900
Symbol: NYN Exchange: NYSE
Industry: Utility - telephone; publishing

O.I. Corp.
151 Graham Rd.
College Station, TX 77841
Phone: 409-690-1711 Fax: 409-690-0440
CEO: William W. Botts
CFO: William W. Botts
1991 Sales: $18 million Employees: 131
Symbol: OICO Exchange: NASDAQ
Industry: Instruments - scientific

O'Brien Energy Systems, Inc.
225 S. Eighth St.
Philadelphia, PA 19106
Phone: 215-627-5500 Fax: 215-922-5227
CEO: Frank L. O'Brien III
CFO: Joel D. Cooperman
1992 Sales: $100 million Employees: 195
Symbol: OBS Exchange: AMEX
Industry: Energy - alternative sources

O'Charley's Inc.
25 Century Blvd. South, Ste. 102
Nashville, TN 37214
Phone: 615-256-8500 Fax: 615-256-8443
CEO: David K. Wachtel
CFO: Gregory L. Burns
1991 Sales: $58 million Employees: 2,800
Symbol: CHUX Exchange: NASDAQ
Industry: Retail - food & restaurants

O'Sullivan Corp.
1944 Valley Ave.
Winchester, VA 22601
Phone: 703-667-6666 Fax: 703-722-2695
CEO: Arthur H. Bryant II
CFO: C. Bryant Nickerson
1991 Sales: $196 million Employees: 1,900
Symbol: OSL Exchange: AMEX
Industry: Rubber & plastic products

Oak Hill Sportswear Corp.
1411 Broadway, 34th Fl.
New York, NY 10018
Phone: 212-789-8900 Fax: 212-944-2065
CEO: Arthur L. Asch
CFO: Martin Jacobson
1991 Sales: $91 million Employees: 803
Symbol: OHSC Exchange: NASDAQ
Industry: Textiles - apparel

Oak Industries Inc.
1000 Winter St.
Waltham, MA 02154
Phone: 617-890-0400 Fax: 617-890-8585
CEO: William S. Antle III
CFO: William C. Weaver
1991 Sales: $124 million Employees: 1,620
Symbol: OAK Exchange: NYSE
Industry: Electrical products - controls & components, quartz crystals

Oakville Forest Products
208 Park St.
Oakville, WA 98568
Phone: 206-273-5575 Fax: 206-273-5576
CEO: Dan Basler
CFO: Dan Basler
1991 Sales: $6.9 million Employees: 17
Ownership: Privately held
Industry: Building & paper products - wood chips for paper industry & lumber; drying equipment

Oakwood Homes Corp.
2225 S. Holden Rd.
Greensboro, NC 27407
Phone: 919-855-2400 Fax: 919-852-1537
CEO: Nicholas J. St. George
CFO: C. Michael Kilbourne
1991 Sales: $160 million Employees: 1,290
Symbol: OH Exchange: NYSE
Industry: Building - mobile homes & RVs

Occidental Petroleum Corp.
10889 Wilshire Blvd.
Los Angeles, CA 90024
Phone: 310-208-8800 Fax: 310-824-2372
CEO: Ray R. Irani
CFO: Anthony R. Leach
1992 Sales: $8,494 million Employees: 24,700
Symbol: OXY Exchange: NYSE
Industry: Oil & gas - US integrated; chemicals & pipelines

Oceaneering International, Inc.
16001 Park Ten Place, Ste. 600
Houston, TX 77084
Phone: 713-578-8868 Fax: 713-578-5243
CEO: John R. Huff
CFO: Thomas R. Hix
1992 Sales: $168 million Employees: 1,200
Symbol: OII Exchange: NYSE
Industry: Oil & gas - field services

OCS Group Inc.
1170 Pittsford Victor Rd. #260
Pittsford, NY 14534
Phone: 716-586-7530 Fax: 716-381-8518
CEO: Cindy Stewart
CFO: Cindy Stewart
1991 Sales: $5.7 million Employees: 119
Ownership: Privately held
Industry: Diversified operations - information management, engineering & technical writing services

Octel Communications Corp.
890 Tasman Dr.
Milpitas, CA 95035
Phone: 408-321-2000 Fax: 408-321-9801
CEO: Douglas C. Chance
CFO: Gary A. Wetsel
1992 Sales: $189 million Employees: 1,292
Symbol: OCTL Exchange: NASDAQ
Industry: Telecommunications equipment

Odds-N-End's, Inc.
20 Churchill St.
Buffalo, NY 14207
Phone: 716-874-9004 Fax: —
CEO: John H. Clark
CFO: John H. Clark
1991 Sales: $16 million Employees: —
Symbol: ODDE Exchange: NASDAQ
Industry: Retail - discount & variety

Odetics, Inc.
1515 S. Manchester Ave.
Anaheim, CA 92802
Phone: 714-774-5000 Fax: 714-535-8532
CEO: Joel Slutzky
CFO: Eugene T. Juengel
1992 Sales: $70 million Employees: 586
Symbol: O.A Exchange: AMEX
Industry: Electronics - measuring instruments

OEA, Inc.
34501 E. Quincy Ave.
Denver, CO 80250
Phone: 303-693-1248 Fax: 303-699-6991
CEO: Ahmed D. Kafadar
CFO: John E. Banko
1991 Sales: $84 million Employees: 775
Symbol: OEA Exchange: NYSE
Industry: Electronics - military

OESI Power Corp.
610 E. Glendale Ave.
Sparks, NV 89431
Phone: 702-355-5666 Fax: 702-355-5656
CEO: James W. Porter, Jr.
CFO: Robert C. Anderson, Jr.
1991 Sales: $26 million Employees: 131
Symbol: OESI Exchange: NASDAQ
Industry: Energy - alternative sources

Office Depot, Inc.
2200 Old Germantown Rd.
Delray Beach, FL 33445
Phone: 407-278-4800 Fax: 407-265-4003
CEO: David I. Fuente
CFO: Barry J. Goldstein
1992 Sales: $1,733 million Employees: 9,000
Symbol: ODP Exchange: NYSE
Industry: Retail - office equipment & supplies

Offshore Logistics, Inc.
224 Rue de Jean
Lafayette, LA 70505
Phone: 318-233-1221 Fax: 318-235-6678
CEO: James B. Clement
CFO: George M. Small
1992 Sales: $82 million Employees: 533
Symbol: OLOG Exchange: NASDAQ
Industry: Oil & gas - field services

Offshore Pipelines, Inc.
5718 Westheimer
Houston, TX 77057
Phone: 713-952-1000 Fax: 713-268-6891
CEO: Franklin C. Wade
CFO: Howard D. Loyd III
1991 Sales: $214 million Employees: 1,965
Symbol: OFP Exchange: NYSE
Industry: Oil & gas - field services

A indicates company is in *Hoover's Handbook of American Business.*

W indicates company is in *Hoover's Handbook of World Business*; sales and employee numbers are for parent company.

Ogden Corp.
Two Pennsylvania Plaza, 26th Fl.
New York, NY 10121
Phone: 212-868-6100 Fax: 212-868-4578
CEO: R. Richard Ablon
CFO: Philip G. Husby
1992 Sales: $1,769 million Employees: 42,000
Symbol: OG Exchange: NYSE
Industry: Diversified operations - housekeeping, entertainment promotion

Ogden Projects, Inc.
40 Lane Rd.
Fairfield, NJ 07007
Phone: 201-882-9000 Fax: 201-882-4167
CEO: David L. Sokol
CFO: Martin N. Hausman
1991 Sales: $364 million Employees: 305
Symbol: OPI Exchange: NYSE
Industry: Energy - alternative sources

Oglebay Norton Co.
1100 Superior Ave. East
Cleveland, OH 44114
Phone: 216-861-3300 Fax: 216-861-2863
CEO: Renold D. Thompson
CFO: Richard J. Kessler
1991 Sales: $173 million Employees: 1,889
Symbol: OGLE Exchange: NASDAQ
Industry: Diversified operations - transportation & transport facilities, iron ore

Ohio Art Co.
One Toy St.
Bryan, OH 43506
Phone: 419-636-3141 Fax: 419-636-7614
CEO: William C. Killgallon
CFO: W. H. Martens
1991 Sales: $50 million Employees: 405
Symbol: OAR Exchange: AMEX
Industry: Toys - games & hobby products

Ohio Bancorp
801 Dollar Bank Bldg.
Youngstown, OH 44503
Phone: 216-744-2093 Fax: 216-743-1572
CEO: T. R. Hollern
CFO: William G. Weber
1991 Sales: $159 million Employees: 1,078
Symbol: OHBC Exchange: NASDAQ
Industry: Banks - Midwest

Ohio Casualty Group of Insurance Cos.
136 N. Third St.
Hamilton, OH 45025
Phone: 513-867-3000 Fax: 513-867-3215
CEO: Joseph L. Marcum
CFO: Joseph L. Marcum
1992 Sales: $1,812 million Employees: 5,100
Symbol: OCAS Exchange: NASDAQ
Industry: Insurance - property & casualty

Ohio Edison Co.
76 S. Main St.
Akron, OH 44308
Phone: 216-384-5100 Fax: 216-384-5791
CEO: Justin T. Rogers, Jr.
CFO: H. Peter Burg
1992 Sales: $2,332 million Employees: 6,567
Symbol: OEC Exchange: NYSE
Industry: Utility - electric power

Ohio Power Co.
301 Cleveland Ave. SW
Canton, OH 44702
Phone: 216-456-8173 Fax: 216-438-7340
CEO: R. E. Disbrow
CFO: Gerald P. Maloney
1991 Sales: $1.7 million Employees: 7,044
Symbol: OPWp Exchange: NYSE
Industry: Utility - electric power

OHM Corp. Environmental Treatment Technologies
16406 U.S. Route 224 East
Findlay, OH 45840
Phone: 419-423-3526 Fax: 419-424-4990
CEO: James L. Kirk
CFO: Samuel H. Iapalucci
1991 Sales: $176 million Employees: 2,423
Symbol: OHM Exchange: NYSE
Industry: Pollution control equipment & services - asbestos abatement

Oil-Dri Corporation of America
520 N. Michigan Ave.
Chicago, IL 60611
Phone: 312-321-1515 Fax: 312-321-1271
CEO: Richard M. Jaffee
CFO: Richard Pietrowski
1991 Sales: $102 million Employees: 660
Symbol: OILC Exchange: NASDAQ
Industry: Chemicals - specialty

Oilgear Co.
2300 S. 51st St.
Milwaukee, WI 53219
Phone: 414-327-1700 Fax: 414-327-0532
CEO: Otto F. Klieve
CFO: David A. Zuege
1991 Sales: $66 million Employees: 848
Symbol: OLGR Exchange: NASDAQ
Industry: Machinery - general industrial

Oki America, Inc.
Three University Plaza
Hackensack, NJ 07601
Phone: 201-646-0011 Fax: 201-646-9229
CEO: Bernard Herman
CFO: —
1992 Sales: $5,450 million Employees: 21,593
Parent: Oki Electric Industry Co., Ltd.
Industry: Computers - mini & micro, peripherals; telecommunications

Oklahoma Gas and Electric Co.
321 N. Harvey Ave.
Oklahoma City, OK 73101
Phone: 405-272-3000 Fax: 405-272-3290
CEO: James G. Harlow, Jr.
CFO: Al M. Strecker
1992 Sales: $1,315 million Employees: 3,796
Symbol: OGE Exchange: NYSE
Industry: Utility - electric power

Old Dominion Freight Line, Inc.
1730 Westchester Dr.
High Point, NC 27262
Phone: 919-889-5000 Fax: 919-883-8864
CEO: Earl E. Congdon
CFO: J. Wes Frye
1991 Sales: $156 million Employees: 2,303
Symbol: ODFL Exchange: NASDAQ
Industry: Transportation - shipping

Old Kent Financial Corp.
One Vandenberg Center
Grand Rapids, MI 49503
Phone: 616-771-5000 Fax: 617-771-1119
CEO: John C. Canepa
CFO: Richard W. Wroten
1991 Sales: $862 million Employees: 4,610
Symbol: OKEN Exchange: NASDAQ
Industry: Banks - Midwest

Old National Bancorp
420 Main St.
Evansville, IN 47708
Phone: 812-464-1434 Fax: 812-464-1567
CEO: Dan W. Mitchell
CFO: Steve H. Parker
1991 Sales: $239 million Employees: 1,309
Symbol: OLDB Exchange: NASDAQ
Industry: Banks - Midwest

Old Republic International Corp.
307 N. Michigan Ave.
Chicago, IL 60601
Phone: 312-346-8100 Fax: 312-726-0309
CEO: A. C. Zucaro
CFO: Paul D. Adams
1991 Sales: $1,374 million Employees: —
Symbol: ORI Exchange: NYSE
Industry: Insurance - property & casualty

Old Stone Corp.
150 S. Main St.
Providence, RI 02903
Phone: 401-738-5000 Fax: —
CEO: James V. Rosati
CFO: Edward J. Braks
1991 Sales: $53 million Employees: 962
Symbol: OSTN Exchange: NASDAQ
Industry: Banks - Northeast

Olin Corp.
120 Long Ridge Rd.
Stamford, CT 06902
Phone: 203-356-2000 Fax: 203-356-3595
CEO: John W. Johnstone, Jr.
CFO: James A. Riggs
1992 Sales: $2,376 million Employees: 14,400
Symbol: OLN Exchange: NYSE
Industry: Diversified operations - chemicals, defense & ammunition, metals

Olivetti USA, Inc.
765 US Hwy. 202
Somerville, NJ 00807
Phone: 908-526-8200 Fax: 908-526-8405
CEO: Leon Harris
CFO: —
1991 Sales: $7,497 million Employees: 46,484
Parent: Ing. C. Olivetti & C., SpA
Industry: Computers - PCs, software, minicomputers & peripheral equipment

Olsten Corp.
One Merrick Ave.
Westbury, NY 11590
Phone: 516-832-8200 Fax: 516-832-8019
CEO: Frank N. Liguori
CFO: Robert J. Vitamante
1992 Sales: $987 million Employees: 281,800
Symbol: OLS Exchange: AMEX
Industry: Business services - temporary personnel

Olympus Capital Corp.
115 S. Main St.
Salt Lake City, UT 84111
Phone: 801-363-8111 Fax: —
CEO: A. Blaine Huntsman
CFO: K. John Jones
1991 Sales: $40 million Employees: 131
Symbol: OLCC Exchange: NASDAQ
Industry: Financial - savings and loans

Omega Financial Corp.
366 Walker Dr.
State College, PA 16801
Phone: 814-231-7680 Fax: —
CEO: David B. Lee
CFO: Daniel L. Warfel
1991 Sales: $21 million Employees: 326
Symbol: OMEF Exchange: NASDAQ
Industry: Banks - Northeast

OMI Bulk Management Co.
90 Park Ave.
New York, NY 10016
Phone: 212-986-1960 Fax: 212-297-2100
CEO: Jack Goldstein
CFO: Jack Goldstein
1991 Sales: $284 million Employees: 757
Symbol: OMM Exchange: NYSE
Industry: Transportation - shipping

Omnicare, Inc.
255 E. Fifth St., Chemed Ctr., Ste. 2800
Cincinnati, OH 45202
Phone: 513-762-6666 Fax: 513-762-6678
CEO: Edward L. Hutton
CFO: Judi K. O'Steen
1991 Sales: $116 million Employees: 1,103
Symbol: OCR Exchange: NYSE
Industry: Medical & dental supplies

Omnicom Group Inc.
437 Madison Ave., 9th Fl.
New York, NY 10022
Phone: 212-415-3600 Fax: 212-415-3530
CEO: Bruce Crawford
CFO: Fred J. Meyer
1992 Sales: $1,385 million Employees: 12,300
Symbol: OMC Exchange: NYSE
Industry: Advertising

On The Border Cafes, Inc.
7800 N. Stemmons Fwy.
Dallas, TX 75247
Phone: 214-905-7500 Fax: 214-905-7505
CEO: Stephen F. Fenstermacher
CFO: Raymond E. Yoakum
1991 Sales: $21 million Employees: 730
Symbol: OTBC Exchange: NASDAQ
Industry: Retail - food & restaurants

ONBANCorp, Inc.
101 S. Salina St.
Syracuse, NY 13202
Phone: 315-424-4400 Fax: 315-442-1877
CEO: Robert J. Bennett
CFO: Robert J. Berger
1991 Sales: $184 million Employees: 530
Symbol: ONBK Exchange: NASDAQ
Industry: Banks - Northeast

Oncogene Science, Inc.
106 Charles Lindbergh Blvd.
Uniondale, NY 11553
Phone: 516-222-0023 Fax: 516-222-0114
CEO: Gary E. Frashier
CFO: Robert L. Van Nostrand
1991 Sales: $7.8 million Employees: 95
Symbol: ONCS Exchange: NASDAQ
Industry: Biomedical & genetic products

ONCOR, Inc.
209 Perry Pkwy.
Gaithersburg, MD 20877
Phone: 301-963-3500 Fax: 301-926-6129
CEO: Stephen Turner
CFO: Rodney E. Dausch
1991 Sales: $4.5 million Employees: 83
Symbol: ONCR Exchange: NASDAQ
Industry: Biomedical & genetic products

One Price Clothing Stores, Inc.
Hwy. 290, Commerce Park
Duncan, SC 29334
Phone: 803-439-6666 Fax: 803-439-9584
CEO: Henry D. Jacobs, Jr.
CFO: Gregory R. Moxley
1991 Sales: $130 million Employees: 2,829
Symbol: ONPR Exchange: NASDAQ
Industry: Retail - apparel & shoes

One Valley Bancorp of West Virginia, Inc.
PO Box 1793
Charleston, WV 25326
Phone: 304-348-7000 Fax: —
CEO: J. Holmes Morrison
CFO: Laurance G. Jones
1991 Sales: $207 million Employees: 1,500
Symbol: OVWV Exchange: NASDAQ
Industry: Banks - Southeast

Oneida Ltd.
Kenwood Ave.
Oneida, NY 13421
Phone: 315-361-3000 Fax: 315-829-3950
CEO: William D. Matthews
CFO: Edward W. Thoma
1991 Sales: $447 million Employees: 5,252
Symbol: OCQ Exchange: NYSE
Industry: Housewares, tableware & china; industrial wire

Oneita Industries, Inc.
Hwy. 41, Conifer St.
Andrews, SC 29510
Phone: 803-264-5225 Fax: 803-264-4262
CEO: Harvey R. Blau
CFO: Dougles E. Pease
1991 Sales: $151 million Employees: 3,200
Symbol: ONA Exchange: AMEX
Industry: Textiles - apparel

Oneok Inc.
100 W. Fifth St.
Tulsa, OK 74103
Phone: 918-588-7000 Fax: 918-588-7273
CEO: J. D. Scott
CFO: J. D. Neal
1991 Sales: $690 million Employees: 2,273
Symbol: OKE Exchange: NYSE
Industry: Utility - gas distribution

Oppenheimer & Co., Inc.
World Financial Center, Oppenheimer Tower
New York, NY 10281
Phone: 212-667-7000 Fax: 212-667-5988
CEO: Joseph M. La Motta
CFO: Sheldon M. Siegel
1992 Sales: $3.2 million Employees: —
Symbol: OCC Exchange: NYSE
Industry: Financial - investment management

Opta Food Ingredients, Inc.
64 Sidney St.
Cambridge, MA 02139
Phone: 617-252-0005 Fax: —
CEO: Mark B. Skaletsky
CFO: Mark B. Skaletsky
1991 Sales: $0.4 million Employees: 18
Symbol: OPTS Exchange: NASDAQ
Industry: Food - new food ingredients

Optek Technology, Inc.
1215 W. Crosby Rd.
Carrollton, TX 75006
Phone: 214-323-2200 Fax: 214-323-2392
CEO: Thomas R. Filesi
CFO: James M. Barry
1991 Sales: $52 million Employees: 1,847
Symbol: OPTX Exchange: NASDAQ
Industry: Electrical components - optoelectronic components; semiconductor products

Optical Coating Laboratory, Inc.
2789 Northpoint Pkwy.
Santa Rosa, CA 95407
Phone: 707-545-6440 Fax: 707-525-7410
CEO: Herbert M. Dwight, Jr.
CFO: Gilbert L. Whissen
1991 Sales: $104 million Employees: 1,039
Symbol: OCLI Exchange: NASDAQ
Industry: Instruments - scientific

Optical Data Systems, Inc.
1101 E. Arapaho Rd.
Richardson, TX 75081
Phone: 214-234-6400 Fax: 214-234-1467
CEO: G. Ward Paxton
CFO: G. Ward Paxton
1991 Sales: $37 million Employees: 176
Symbol: ODSI Exchange: NASDAQ
Industry: Telecommunications equipment

Optical Radiation Corp.
1300 Optical Dr.
Azusa, CA 91702
Phone: 818-969-3344 Fax: 818-969-3681
CEO: Richard D. Wood
CFO: Gary N. Patten
1991 Sales: $146 million Employees: 1,570
Symbol: ORCO Exchange: NASDAQ
Industry: Medical & dental supplies

Optimation Technology
50 High Tech Dr.
Rush, NY 14543
Phone: 716-359-0700 Fax: 716-359-0701
CEO: Bill Pollock
CFO: Tim Lasch
1992 Sales: $2.6 million Employees: 30
Ownership: Privately held
Industry: Engineering - industrial systems integration services

Option Care, Inc.
100 Corporate North, Ste. 212
Bannockburn, IL 60015
Phone: 708-615-1690 Fax: 708-615-1794
CEO: Sheldon D. Asher
CFO: Robert J. Sullivan
1991 Sales: $24 million Employees: 129
Symbol: OPTN Exchange: NASDAQ
Industry: Healthcare - outpatient & home

Option Technologies
1275 Knollwood
Mendota Heights, MN 55118
Phone: 612-450-1700 Fax: 612-450-9413
CEO: William A. Flexner
CFO: Kimbal L. Wheatley
1991 Sales: $1 million Employees: 7
Ownership: Privately held
Industry: Computers - brainstorming, voting & decision-making enhancement software

Opto Mechanik, Inc.
425 North Dr.
Melbourne, FL 32935
Phone: 407-254-1212 Fax: 407-254-4497
CEO: Ottmar Dippold
CFO: Ronald K. Urich
1991 Sales: $32 million Employees: 233
Symbol: OPTO Exchange: NASDAQ
Industry: Electronics - military

Oracle Systems Corp.
500 Oracle Pkwy.
Redwood City, CA 94065
Phone: 415-506-7000 Fax: 415-506-7150
CEO: Lawrence J. Ellison
CFO: Jeffrey L. Kenley
1992 Sales: $1,310 million Employees: 8,160
Symbol: ORCL Exchange: NASDAQ
Industry: Computers - database management systems & software

Orange Co. of Florida, Inc.
2022 U.S. Hwy. 17 South
Bartow, FL 33830
Phone: 813-533-0551 Fax: 813-533-6357
CEO: Robert A. Peiser
CFO: Dale A. Bruwelheide
1991 Sales: $80 million Employees: 829
Symbol: OJ Exchange: NYSE
Industry: Agricultural operations

Orange & Rockland Utilities, Inc.
One Blue Hill Plaza
Pearl River, NY 10965
Phone: 914-352-6000 Fax: 914-577-2730
CEO: James F. Smith
CFO: Patrick J. Chambers, Jr.
1991 Sales: $732 million Employees: 1,750
Symbol: ORU Exchange: NYSE
Industry: Utility - electric power

AHH indicates company is in *Hoover's Handbook of American Business.*

WHH indicates company is in *Hoover's Handbook of World Business;* sales and employee numbers are for parent company.

Orbit Instrument Corp.
80 Cabot Court
Hauppauge, NY 11788
Phone: 516-435-8300 Fax: 516-435-8458
CEO: Max Reissman
CFO: Mitchell Binder
1991 Sales: $48 million Employees: 1,205
Symbol: ORBT Exchange: NASDAQ
Industry: Electronics - military

Orbital Sciences Corp.
12500 Fair Lakes Circle, Ste. 350
Fairfax, VA 22033
Phone: 703-631-3600 Fax: 703-631-3610
CEO: David W. Thompson
CFO: Carlton B. Crenshaw
1991 Sales: $135 million Employees: 869
Symbol: ORBI Exchange: NASDAQ
Industry: Aerospace - aircraft & space launch equipment

Oregon Metallurgical Corp.
530 W. 34th Ave. SW
Albany, OR 97321
Phone: 503-926-4281 Fax: 503-967-8669
CEO: Frank Caputo
CFO: Frederick G. Gent
1991 Sales: $54 million Employees: 354
Symbol: OREM Exchange: NASDAQ
Industry: Steel - specialty alloys

Oregon Steel Mills, Inc.
14400 N. Rivergate Blvd.
Portland, OR 97203
Phone: 503-286-9651 Fax: 503-240-5291
CEO: Thomas B. Boklund
CFO: V. Neil Fulton
1991 Sales: $489 million Employees: 1,270
Symbol: OS Exchange: NYSE
Industry: Steel - specialty alloys

Oreman Sales Inc.
2725 Lexington Ave.
Kenner, LA 70062
Phone: 504-468-2001 Fax: 504-479-5765
CEO: Gary Oreman
CFO: Richard Lindholm
1991 Sales: $62 million Employees: 72
Ownership: Privately held
Industry: Computers - wholesale computers & accessories

Organogenesis Inc.
83 Rogers St.
Cambridge, MA 02142
Phone: 617-577-1717 Fax: —
CEO: Herbert M. Stein
CFO: Michael T. Pieniazek
1991 Sales: $3.8 million Employees: 90
Symbol: ORG Exchange: AMEX
Industry: Medical services - living-organ equivalent fabrication

Orient-Express Hotels Inc.
1155 Avenue of the Americas
New York, NY 10036
Phone: 212-302-5055 Fax: 212-302-5073
CEO: James B. Sherwood
CFO: Daniel J. O'Sullivan
1991 Sales: $50 million Employees: 500
Symbol: OEH Exchange: NYSE
Industry: Diversified operations - hotels, tourist trains & cruise ships

Oriole Homes Corp.
1151 NW 24th St.
Pompano Beach, FL 33064
Phone: 407-747-0244 Fax: 305-977-3589
CEO: Richard D. Levy
CFO: A. Nunez
1991 Sales: $79 million Employees: 237
Symbol: OHCB Exchange: AMEX
Industry: Building - residential & commercial

Orion Capital Corp.
30 Rockefeller Plaza, Rm. 2820
New York, NY 10112
Phone: 212-332-8080 Fax: 212-581-7261
CEO: Alan R. Gruber
CFO: Vincent T. Papa
1991 Sales: $838 million Employees: —
Symbol: OC Exchange: NYSE
Industry: Insurance - property & casualty

Orion Pictures Corp.
1325 Sixth Ave.
New York, NY 10019
Phone: 212-956-3800 Fax: 212-956-7449
CEO: Eric Pleskow
CFO: Lawrence Bernstein
1992 Sales: $491 million Employees: 420
Symbol: OPC Exchange: NYSE
Industry: Motion pictures & services - production

Ormet Corp.
State Route Seven
Hannibal, OH 43931
Phone: 614-483-1381 Fax: 614-483-2622
CEO: R. Emmett Boyle
CFO: John F. Kelly
1991 Sales: $550 million Employees: 2,100
Ownership: Privately held
Industry: Metals - aluminum

OrNda Healthcorp
3401 W. End Ave., Ste. 700
Nashville, TN 37203
Phone: 615-383-8599 Fax: 615-783-1270
CEO: Charles N. Martin
CFO: Keith Pitts
1991 Sales: $454 million Employees: 5,300
Symbol: ORND Exchange: NASDAQ
Industry: Hospitals

Orthomet, Inc.
6301 Cecilia Circle
Bloomington, MN 55435
Phone: 612-944-6112 Fax: 612-944-1389
CEO: Richard D. Nikolaev
CFO: James C. Hawley
1992 Sales: $16 million Employees: 128
Symbol: OMET Exchange: NASDAQ
Industry: Medical products - orthopedic products

Oryx Energy Co.
13155 Noel Rd.
Dallas, TX 75240
Phone: 214-715-4000 Fax: 214-715-3798
CEO: Robert P. Hauptfuhrer
CFO: Edward W. Moneypenny
1992 Sales: $1,392 million Employees: 2,500
Symbol: ORX Exchange: NYSE
Industry: Oil & gas - US exploration & production

Osborn Communications Corp.
405 Lexington Ave., 54th Fl.
New York, NY 10174
Phone: 212-697-2280 Fax: 212-697-2249
CEO: Frank D. Osborn
CFO: Barry M. Wolper
1991 Sales: $25 million Employees: 275
Symbol: OSBN Exchange: NASDAQ
Industry: Broadcasting - radio & TV

Oshkosh B'Gosh, Inc.
112 Otter Ave.
Oshkosh, WI 54901
Phone: 414-231-8800 Fax: 414-231-8621
CEO: Douglas W. Hyde
CFO: William P. Jacobsen
1991 Sales: $365 million Employees: 8,000
Symbol: GOSHA Exchange: NASDAQ
Industry: Textiles - apparel

Oshkosh Truck Corp.
2307 Oregon St.
Oshkosh, WI 54901
Phone: 414-235-9150 Fax: 414-233-9540
CEO: R. Eugene Goodson
CFO: Fred S. Schulte
1991 Sales: $420 million Employees: 2,400
Symbol: OTRKB Exchange: NASDAQ
Industry: Automotive & trucking - original equipment

Oshman's Sporting Goods, Inc.
2302 Maxwell Lane
Houston, TX 77023
Phone: 713-928-3171 Fax: 713-921-6545
CEO: Alvin N. Lubetkin
CFO: Edward R. Carlin
1991 Sales: $298 million Employees: 3,700
Symbol: OSHM Exchange: NASDAQ
Industry: Retail - sporting goods

Osicom Technologies, Inc.
198 Green Pond Rd.
Rockaway, NJ 07866
Phone: 201-586-2550 Fax: 201-586-9740
CEO: Parvinder S. Chadha
CFO: Sharon Gill Chadha
1990 Sales: $46 million Employees: 105
Symbol: OSICE Exchange: NASDAQ
Industry: Computers - mini & micro

Osmonics, Inc.
5951 Clearwater Dr.
Minnetonka, MN 55343
Phone: 612-933-2277 Fax: 612-933-0141
CEO: D. Dean Spatz
CFO: L. Lee Runzheimer
1991 Sales: $47 million Employees: 559
Symbol: OSMO Exchange: NASDAQ
Industry: Pollution control equipment & services - fluid handling & processing

Osteotech, Inc.
1151 Shrewsbury Ave.
Shrewsbury, NJ 07702
Phone: 908-542-2800 Fax: —
CEO: Patrick A. McBrayer
CFO: Michael J. Jeffries
1991 Sales: $9.7 million Employees: 98
Symbol: OSTE Exchange: NASDAQ
Industry: Medical services - bone, ligament & tendon processing

Otter Tail Power Co.
215 S. Cascade St.
Fergus Falls, MN 56537
Phone: 218-739-8200 Fax: 218-739-8218
CEO: John MacFarlane
CFO: Dennis R. Emmen
1991 Sales: $180 million Employees: 853
Symbol: OTTR Exchange: NASDAQ
Industry: Utility - electric power

Outback Steakhouse, Inc.
550 N. Reo St., Ste. 204
Tampa, FL 33609
Phone: 813-282-1225 Fax: 813-282-1209
CEO: Chris T. Sullivan
CFO: Robert S. Merritt
1992 Sales: $124 million Employees: 1,681
Symbol: OSSI Exchange: NASDAQ
Industry: Retail - food & restaurants

Outboard Marine Corp.
100 Sea Horse Dr.
Waukegan, IL 60085
Phone: 708-689-6200 Fax: 708-689-5555
CEO: James C. Chapman
CFO: Michael T. Cantwell
1992 Sales: $1,050 million Employees: 8,100
Symbol: OM Exchange: NYSE
Industry: Leisure & recreational products - powerboats, marine motors

 indicates company is in *Hoover's Handbook of American Business.*

indicates company is in *Hoover's Handbook of World Business;* sales and employee numbers are for parent company.

Outlet Communications, Inc.
111 Dorrance St.
Providence, RI 02903
Phone: 401-455-9200 Fax: 401-455-9216
CEO: James Babb
CFO: Felix W. Oziemblewski
1991 Sales: $39 million Employees: 280
Symbol: OCOAC Exchange: NASDAQ
Industry: Broadcasting - radio & TV

Outlook Graphics Corp.
1180 American Dr.
Neenah, WI 54956
Phone: 414-722-2333 Fax: 414-727-4787
CEO: David L. Edrmann
CFO: Jeffrey P. Stilp
1992 Sales: $64 million Employees: 1,271
Symbol: OUTL Exchange: NASDAQ
Industry: Business services - printing, converting & packaging

Overseas Shipholding Group, Inc.
1114 Avenue of the Americas
New York, NY 10036
Phone: 212-869-1222 Fax: 212-536-3776
CEO: Morton P. Hyman
CFO: Michael A. Recanati
1991 Sales: $411 million Employees: 2,275
Symbol: OSG Exchange: NYSE
Industry: Transportation - shipping

Owens & Minor, Inc.
4800 Cox Rd.
Glen Allen, VA 23060
Phone: 804-747-9794 Fax: 804-270-7281
CEO: G. Gilmer Minor III
CFO: Glenn J. Dozier
1992 Sales: $1,177 million Employees: 1,650
Symbol: OMI Exchange: NYSE
Industry: Drugs & sundries - wholesale

Owens-Corning Fiberglas Corp.
Fiberglas Tower
Toledo, OH 43659
Phone: 419-248-8000 Fax: 419-248-5337
CEO: Glen H. Hiner
CFO: Paul V. Daverio
1992 Sales: $2,878 million Employees: 16,000
Symbol: OCF Exchange: NYSE
Industry: Building products - insulation, roofing; industrial materials; resins, textile yarns

Owens-Illinois, Inc.
One Seagate
Toledo, OH 43666
Phone: 419-247-5000 Fax: 419-247-2839
CEO: Joseph H. Lemieux
CFO: Lee A. Wesselman
1992 Sales: $3,672 million Employees: 34,300
Symbol: OI Exchange: NYSE
Industry: Glass products - containers & specialized; plastics & closures

Oxbow Corp.
1601 Forum Place
West Palm Beach, FL 33401
Phone: 407-697-4300 Fax: 407-640-8740
CEO: William Koch
CFO: Zachary Shipley
1991 Sales: $1,300 million Employees: 300
Ownership: Privately held
Industry: Diversified operations - energy, fossil fuel & real estate

Oxford Energy Co.
330 Town Center Dr., Fairlane Plaza South, Ste. 900
Dearborn, MI 48126
Phone: 313-436-9595 Fax: 707-575-9852
CEO: Robert J. Cushman
CFO: Robert J. Cushman
1991 Sales: $33 million Employees: 285
Symbol: OEN Exchange: AMEX
Industry: Energy - alternative sources

Oxford Health Plans, Inc.
320 Post Rd.
Darien, CT 06820
Phone: 203-656-1442 Fax: 203-656-0747
CEO: Stephen F. Wiggins
CFO: Andrew B. Cassidy
1991 Sales: $95 million Employees: 239
Symbol: OXHP Exchange: NASDAQ
Industry: Health maintenance organization

Oxford Industries, Inc.
222 Piedmont Ave. NE
Atlanta, GA 30308
Phone: 404-659-2424 Fax: 404-525-3650
CEO: J. Hicks Lanier
CFO: R. William Lee, Jr.
1992 Sales: $560 million Employees: 9,857
Symbol: OXM Exchange: NYSE
Industry: Textiles - apparel

P & F Industries, Inc.
300 Smith St.
Farmingdale, NY 11735
Phone: 516-694-1800 Fax: 516-694-1836
CEO: Sidney Horowitz
CFO: Leon D. Feldman
1991 Sales: $54 million Employees: 444
Symbol: PFINA Exchange: NASDAQ
Industry: Metal products - fabrication

P. H. Glatfelter Co.
228 S. Main St.
Spring Grove, PA 17362
Phone: 717-225-4711 Fax: 717-225-6834
CEO: T. C. Norris
CFO: M. A. Johnson II
1991 Sales: $568 million Employees: 3,393
Symbol: GLT Exchange: AMEX
Industry: Paper & paper products

Pac Rim Holding Corp.
6200 Canoga Ave.
Woodland Hills, CA 91367
Phone: 818-226-6200 Fax: 818-595-0099
CEO: Stanley Braun
CFO: Paul W. Souza
1991 Sales: $106 million Employees: 240
Symbol: PRIM Exchange: NASDAQ
Industry: Insurance - accident & health

PACCAR Inc.
777 106th Ave. NE
Bellevue, WA 98004
Phone: 206-455-7400 Fax: 206-453-4900
CEO: Charles M. Pigott
CFO: William E. Boisvert
1992 Sales: $2,735 million Employees: 10,163
Symbol: PCAR Exchange: NASDAQ
Industry: Trucking - original equipment, auto supply

Pacific Bancorporation
5100 N. Sixth St., Ste. 103
Fresno, CA 93710
Phone: 209-221-7381 Fax: —
CEO: Harry L. Wheeler
CFO: Richard B. Shupe
1991 Sales: $22 million Employees: 220
Symbol: PABC Exchange: NASDAQ
Industry: Banks - West

Pacific Bank, N.A.
351 California St.
San Francisco, CA 94104
Phone: 415-576-2700 Fax: 415-362-4549
CEO: Norman C. Eckersley
CFO: Roger R. Peters
1992 Sales: — Employees: —
Symbol: PBSF Exchange: NASDAQ
Industry: Banks - West

Pacific Enterprises
633 W. Fifth St.
Los Angeles, CA 90071
Phone: 213-895-5000 Fax: 213-629-1225
CEO: Willis B. Wood, Jr.
CFO: Lloyd A. Levitin
1992 Sales: $2,912 million Employees: 41,000
Symbol: PET Exchange: NYSE
Industry: Utility - gas distribution

Pacific Gas and Electric Co.
77 Beale St.
San Francisco, CA 94106
Phone: 415-973-7000 Fax: 415-543-7813
CEO: Richard A. Clarke
CFO: Gordon R. Smith
1992 Sales: $10,296 million Employees: 26,747
Symbol: PCG Exchange: NYSE
Industry: Utility - electric power & gas power

Pacific Holding Co.
10900 Wilshire Blvd., 16th Fl.
Los Angeles, CA 90024
Phone: 310-208-6055 Fax: 310-824-2159
CEO: David H. Murdock
CFO: Jeff Henley
1991 Sales: $968 million Employees: 5,000
Ownership: Privately held
Industry: Diversified operations - real estate & building materials

Pacific International Services Corp.
1600 Kapiolani Blvd., Ste. 825
Honolulu, HI 96814
Phone: 808-926-4242 Fax: 808-926-4255
CEO: Alan M. Robin
CFO: Lawrence Trachtenberg
1991 Sales: $68 million Employees: 449
Symbol: PISC Exchange: NASDAQ
Industry: Transportation - equipment & leasing

Pacific Nuclear Systems, Inc.
1010 S. 336th St., Ste. 220
Federal Way, WA 98003
Phone: 206-874-2235 Fax: 206-874-2401
CEO: Michael J. Scholtens
CFO: Phillip L. Jordan
1991 Sales: $66 million Employees: 475
Symbol: PACN Exchange: NASDAQ
Industry: Pollution control equipment & services - radioactive waste management

Pacific Physician Services, Inc.
1826 Orange Tree Lane
Redlands, CA 92374
Phone: 714-825-4401 Fax: 714-798-9640
CEO: Gary L. Grove
CFO: Ronald D. Lossett
1991 Sales: $74 million Employees: 775
Symbol: PPSI Exchange: NASDAQ
Industry: Health maintenance organization

Pacific Scientific Co.
620 Newport Center Dr., Ste. 700
Newport Beach, CA 92660
Phone: 714-720-1714 Fax: 714-720-1083
CEO: Edgar S. Brower
CFO: Richard V. Plat
1991 Sales: $173 million Employees: 1,382
Symbol: PSX Exchange: NYSE
Industry: Electronics - measuring instruments

Pacific Telecom, Inc.
805 Broadway
Vancouver, WA 98660
Phone: 206-696-0983 Fax: 206-696-6925
CEO: Charles E. Robinson
CFO: James H. Huesgen
1992 Sales: $705 million Employees: 3,050
Symbol: PTCM Exchange: NASDAQ
Industry: Utility - telephone

Pacific Telesis Group
130 Kearny St.
San Francisco, CA 94108
Phone: 415-394-3000 Fax: 415-362-2913
CEO: Sam Ginn
CFO: Lydell L. Christensen
1992 Sales: $9,935 million Employees: 62,236
Symbol: PAC Exchange: NYSE
Industry: Utility - telephone

Pacific Trading Overseas Corporation
1390 Brickell Ave., Ste. 240
Miami, FL 33131
Phone: 305-358-1900 Fax: 305-381-8519
CEO: Jose M. Massuh
CFO: Jose M. Massuh
1991 Sales: $5 million Employees: 4
Ownership: Privately held
Industry: Chemicals, plastics & resins - export

Pacific Western Bancshares, Inc.
333 W. Santa Clara St.
San Jose, CA 95113
Phone: 408-244-1700 Fax: 408-286-5242
CEO: Phillip R. Boyce
CFO: Eugene E. Blakeslee
1991 Sales: $124 million Employees: 626
Symbol: PWB Exchange: AMEX
Industry: Banks - West

PacifiCare Health Systems, Inc.
5995 Plaza Dr.
Cypress, CA 90630
Phone: 714-952-1121 Fax: 714-220-3690
CEO: Terry Hartshorn
CFO: Wayne Lowell
1992 Sales: $1,829 million Employees: 2,186
Symbol: PHSYA Exchange: NASDAQ
Industry: Health maintenance organization

PacifiCorp
700 NE Multnomah, Ste. 1600
Portland, OR 97232
Phone: 503-731-2000 Fax: 503-731-2136
CEO: A. M. Gleason
CFO: Robert F. Lanz
1992 Sales: $3,242 million Employees: 15,722
Symbol: PPW Exchange: NYSE
Industry: Utility - electric power

Packard Bell Electronics
9425 Canoga Ave.
Chatsworth, CA 91311
Phone: 818-886-4600 Fax: 818-733-9521
CEO: Beny Alagem
CFO: Brent Cohen
1991 Sales: $676 million Employees: 959
Ownership: Privately held
Industry: Computers - PCs & peripheral equipment

Paco Pharmaceutical Services, Inc.
1200 Paco Way
Lakewood, NJ 08701
Phone: 908-367-9000 Fax: 908-364-5266
CEO: Russell R. Haines
CFO: Clifford H. Straub, Jr.
1992 Sales: $70 million Employees: 1,284
Symbol: PACO Exchange: NASDAQ
Industry: Medical products - drug packaging

Page America Group, Inc.
125 State St., Ste. 100
Hackensack, NJ 07601
Phone: 201-342-6676 Fax: 201-342-0046
CEO: Steven L. Sinn
CFO: John X. Adiletta
1991 Sales: $25 million Employees: 235
Symbol: PGG Exchange: AMEX
Industry: Telecommunications services

PAGES, Inc.
5720 Avery Rd.
Amlin, OH 43002
Phone: 614-793-8749 Fax: —
CEO: S. Robert Davis
CFO: Richard A. Stimmel
1992 Sales: — Employees: —
Symbol: PAGZ Exchange: NASDAQ
Industry: Building - commercial

Paging Network, Inc.
4965 Preston Park Blvd.
Plano, TX 75093
Phone: 214-985-4100 Fax: 214-985-7076
CEO: George M. Perrin
CFO: Terry L. Scott
1991 Sales: $166 million Employees: 1,675
Symbol: PAGE Exchange: NASDAQ
Industry: Telecommunications services

PAI Corp.
116 Milan Way
Oak Ridge, TN 37830
Phone: 615-483-0666 Fax: 615-481-0003
CEO: Doan Phung
CFO: Bruce Bowland
1991 Sales: $7.5 million Employees: 65
Ownership: Privately held
Industry: Environmental consulting & engineering

Paine Webber Group Inc.
1285 Avenue of the Americas
New York, NY 10019
Phone: 212-713-2000 Fax: 212-713-4889
CEO: Donald B. Marron
CFO: Robert H. Silver
1992 Sales: $3,364 million Employees: 12,900
Symbol: PWJ Exchange: NYSE
Industry: Financial - investment banking, retail sales, asset management, capital markets

PALFED, Inc.
107 Chesterfield St. South
Aiken, SC 29801
Phone: 803-642-1400 Fax: —
CEO: Richard W. Herring
CFO: Darrell R. Rains
1991 Sales: $73 million Employees: 263
Symbol: PALM Exchange: NASDAQ
Industry: Financial - savings and loans

Pall Corp.
2200 Northern Blvd.
East Hills, NY 11546
Phone: 516-484-5400 Fax: 516-671-4066
CEO: Maurice G. Hardy
CFO: Stanley Wernick
1991 Sales: $657 million Employees: 6,400
Symbol: PLL Exchange: NYSE
Industry: Filtration products

Palm Tree Packaging
1126 Ocoee
Apopka, FL 32704
Phone: 407-886-3663 Fax: 407-886-9360
CEO: Joe Persaud
CFO: Joe Persaud
1991 Sales: $2.2 million Employees: 17
Ownership: Privately held
Industry: Containers - floral packaging

PAM Transportation Services, Inc.
Hwy. 68 West
Tontitown, AR 72770
Phone: 501-361-9111 Fax: 501-361-5335
CEO: Robert W. Weaver
CFO: Larry J. Goddard
1991 Sales: $66 million Employees: 902
Symbol: PTSI Exchange: NASDAQ
Industry: Transportation - truck

Pamida Inc.
8800 "F" St.
Omaha, NE 68127
Phone: 402-339-2400 Fax: 402-393-3230
CEO: C. Clayton Burkstrand
CFO: Richard W. Ramm
1991 Sales: $636 million Employees: 6,300
Symbol: PAM Exchange: AMEX
Industry: Retail - discount & variety

Pamrapo Bancorp, Inc.
611 Ave. C
Bayonne, NJ 07002
Phone: 201-339-4600 Fax: —
CEO: William J. Campbell
CFO: Gary J. Thomas
1991 Sales: $36 million Employees: 120
Symbol: PBCI Exchange: NASDAQ
Industry: Banks - Northeast

Pan Atlantic Inc.
4 W. Red Oak Lane
White Plains, NY 10604
Phone: 914-694-4757 Fax: 914-694-4762
CEO: Lionel J. Goetz
CFO: Lionel J. Goetz
1991 Sales: $32 million Employees: 161
Symbol: PATL Exchange: NASDAQ
Industry: Insurance - property & casualty

PANACO, Inc.
1011 W. 103rd St., Ste. 211
Kansas City, MO 64114
Phone: 816-942-6300 Fax: 816-942-6305
CEO: H. James Maxwell
CFO: H. James Maxwell
1992 Sales: — Employees: —
Symbol: PANA Exchange: NASDAQ
Industry: Oil & gas - US exploration & production

Panatech Research and Development Corp.
6565 American Pkwy. NE, Ste. 850
Albuquerque, NM 87110
Phone: 505-880-1717 Fax: 505-880-3158
CEO: Arthur J. Rosenberg
CFO: Arthur J. Rosenberg
1992 Sales: $4.6 million Employees: 38
Symbol: PNTC Exchange: NASDAQ
Industry: Telecommunications equipment

Pancho's Mexican Buffet, Inc.
3500 Noble Ave.
Ft. Worth, TX 76111
Phone: 817-831-0081 Fax: 817-838-1480
CEO: Hollis Taylor
CFO: David Oden
1991 Sales: $74 million Employees: 3,207
Symbol: PAMX Exchange: NASDAQ
Industry: Retail - food & restaurants

Panhandle Eastern Corp.
5400 Westheimer Ct.
Houston, TX 77056
Phone: 713-627-5400 Fax: 713-627-4145
CEO: Dennis R. Hendrix
CFO: James B. Hipple
1992 Sales: $2,342 million Employees: 5,300
Symbol: PEL Exchange: NYSE
Industry: Oil & gas - production & pipeline

Panoramic
4321 Goshen Rd.
Ft. Wayne, IN 46818
Phone: 219-489-2291 Fax: 219-489-5683
CEO: Eric Stetzel
CFO: Neil Miller
1991 Sales: $8 million Employees: 20
Ownership: Privately held
Industry: Medical instruments - X-ray equipment

indicates company is in *Hoover's Handbook of American Business.*

indicates company is in *Hoover's Handbook of World Business;* sales and employee numbers are for parent company.

Papa John's International
11492 Bluegrass Pkwy., Ste. 175
Louisville, KY 40299
Phone: 502-266-5200 Fax: 502-266-2925
CEO: John Schnatter
CFO: Drew Milby
1991 Sales: $19 million Employees: 220
Ownership: Privately held
Industry: Food - take-out pizza

PAR Technology Corp.
220 Seneca Tnpk.
New Hartford, NY 13413
Phone: 315-738-0600 Fax: 315-738-0562
CEO: John W. Sammon, Jr.
CFO: A. Kenneth Patterson
1991 Sales: $79 million Employees: 874
Symbol: PTC Exchange: NYSE
Industry: Computers - software services, transaction-processing systems

Paragon Group
7557 Rambler Rd., Ste. 1200
Dallas, TX 75231
Phone: 214-891-2000 Fax: 214-891-2019
CEO: W. R. Cooper
CFO: Jerry Bonner
1992 Sales: $550 million Employees: 1,646
Ownership: Privately held
Industry: Real estate development & management

Parametric Technology Corp.
128 Technology Dr.
Waltham, MA 02154
Phone: 617-894-7111 Fax: 617-891-1069
CEO: Steven Walske
CFO: Samuel Geisberg
1992 Sales: $87 million Employees: 525
Symbol: PMTC Exchange: NASDAQ
Industry: Computers - software

Paramount Communications Inc.
15 Columbus Circle
New York, NY 10023
Phone: 212-373-8000 Fax: 212-373-8228
CEO: Martin S. Davis
CFO: Ronald L. Nelson
1992 Sales: $4,265 million Employees: 12,200
Symbol: PCI Exchange: NYSE
Industry: Motion pictures & services - production; publishing, broadcasting

Parexel International Corp.
195 West St.
Waltham, MA 02154
Phone: 617-487-9900 Fax: 617-487-0525
CEO: Josef von Rickenbach
CFO: William T. Sobo
1991 Sales: $26 million Employees: 700
Ownership: Privately held
Industry: Drugs & biotechnology products - clinical trials management

Paris Business Forms, Inc.
122 Kissel Rd.
Burlington, NJ 08016
Phone: 609-387-7300 Fax: 609-387-7308
CEO: Dominic P. Toscani, Sr.
CFO: James W. Thompson
1991 Sales: $60 million Employees: 280
Symbol: PBFI Exchange: NASDAQ
Industry: Paper - business forms

Park Communications, Inc.
Terrace Hill
Ithaca, NY 14850
Phone: 607-272-9020 Fax: 607-272-6057
CEO: Roy H. Park
CFO: Wright M. Thomas
1991 Sales: $149 million Employees: 2,370
Symbol: PARC Exchange: NASDAQ
Industry: Broadcasting - radio & TV

Park Electrochemical Corp.
5 Dakota Dr.
Lake Success, NY 11042
Phone: 516-354-4100 Fax: 516-354-4128
CEO: Jerry Shore
CFO: Allen Levine
1992 Sales: $166 million Employees: 1,390
Symbol: PKE Exchange: NYSE
Industry: Electrical components - circuit board materials

Park National Corp.
50 N. Third St.
Newark, OH 43055
Phone: 614-349-8451 Fax: 614-349-3787
CEO: John W. Alford
CFO: John W. Alford
1991 Sales: $115 million Employees: 617
Symbol: PARK Exchange: NASDAQ
Industry: Financial - savings and loans

Park-Ohio Industries, Inc.
20600 Chagrin Blvd., Tower East, Ste. 600
Shaker Heights, OH 44122
Phone: 216-991-9700 Fax: 216-991-9319
CEO: Stanley V. Intihar
CFO: Joseph P. Rattigan
1991 Sales: $116 million Employees: 1,160
Symbol: PKOH Exchange: NASDAQ
Industry: Metal products - fabrication

Parker Drilling Co.
Eight E. Third St.
Tulsa, OK 74103
Phone: 918-585-8221 Fax: 918-585-1058
CEO: Robert L. Parker, Jr.
CFO: James J. Davis
1991 Sales: $113 million Employees: 1,695
Symbol: PKD Exchange: NYSE
Industry: Oil & gas - field services

Parker Hannifin Corp.
17325 Euclid Ave.
Cleveland, OH 44112
Phone: 216-531-3000 Fax: 216-531-6525
CEO: Paul G. Schloemer
CFO: Michael J. Hiemstra
1992 Sales: $2,428 million Employees: 26,669
Symbol: PH Exchange: NYSE
Industry: Instruments - control

Parker & Parsley Development Partners, L.P.
600 W. Illinois, Ste. 103
Midland, TX 79701
Phone: 915-683-4768 Fax: 915-686-4063
CEO: Scott D. Sheffield
CFO: A. Frank Kubica
1991 Sales: $143 million Employees: 641
Symbol: PDP Exchange: AMEX
Industry: Oil & gas - US exploration & production

Parkvale Financial Corp.
4220 William Penn Hwy.
Monroeville, PA 15146
Phone: 412-373-7200 Fax: —
CEO: Robert J. McCarthy, Jr.
CFO: Timothy G. Rubritz
1991 Sales: $71 million Employees: 240
Symbol: PVSA Exchange: NASDAQ
Industry: Financial - savings and loans

Parlex Corp.
145 Milk St.
Methuen, MA 01844
Phone: 508-685-4341 Fax: 508-685-8809
CEO: Herbert W. Pollack
CFO: Steven M. Millstein
1992 Sales: $29 million Employees: 385
Symbol: PRLX Exchange: NASDAQ
Industry: Electrical connectors

Parsons Corporation, The
100 W. Walnut St.
Pasadena, CA 91124
Phone: 818-440-2000 Fax: 818-440-2630
CEO: Leonard J. Pieroni
CFO: Curtis A. Bower
1991 Sales: $1,303 million Employees: 10,000
Ownership: Privately held
Industry: Construction - engineering & design

Parsons Technology
One Parsons Dr.
Hiawatha, IA 52233
Phone: 319-395-9626 Fax: 319-395-0217
CEO: Bob Parsons
CFO: Scott Porter
1991 Sales: $28 million Employees: 235
Ownership: Privately held
Industry: Computers - financial & tax preparation software

Parsons & Whittemore Inc.
Four International Dr.
Ryebrook, NY 10573
Phone: 914-937-9009 Fax: 914-937-2259
CEO: George F. Landegger
CFO: S. J. Napolitano
1991 Sales: $710 million Employees: 2,500
Ownership: Privately held
Industry: Diversified operations - pulp & paper, industrial machinery

Partnership Group, The
840 W. Main St.
Lansdale, PA 19446
Phone: 215-362-5070 Fax: 215-362-5918
CEO: Tyler Phillips
CFO: Michael Graham
1991 Sales: $7.4 million Employees: 100
Ownership: Privately held
Industry: Business services - child care, elder care & referral services

Patlex Corp.
250 Cotorro Court, Ste. A
Las Cruces, NM 88005
Phone: 505-524-4050 Fax: 505-523-8081
CEO: Frank Borman
CFO: Richard Laitinen
1991 Sales: $7 million Employees: 6
Symbol: PTLX Exchange: NASDAQ
Industry: Financial - business services

Patrick Industries, Inc.
1800 S. 14th St.
Elkhart, IN 46515
Phone: 219-294-7511 Fax: 219-522-5213
CEO: Mervin D. Lung
CFO: Keith V. Kankel
1991 Sales: $143 million Employees: 813
Symbol: PATK Exchange: NASDAQ
Industry: Building products - retail & wholesale

Patrick Petroleum Co.
301 W. Michigan Ave.
Jackson, MI 49201
Phone: 517-787-6633 Fax: 517-787-6630
CEO: Ueal E. Patrick
CFO: Russell C. Youngdahl, Jr.
1991 Sales: $10.6 million Employees: 40
Symbol: PPC Exchange: NYSE
Industry: Oil & gas - US exploration & production

Patten Corp.
5295 Town Center Rd., Ste. 400
Boca Raton, FL 33486
Phone: 407-391-6336 Fax: 407-391-6337
CEO: Harry S. Patten
CFO: Alan L. Murray
1992 Sales: $62 million Employees: 218
Symbol: PAT Exchange: NYSE
Industry: Real estate development

indicates company is in *Hoover's Handbook of American Business.*

indicates company is in *Hoover's Handbook of World Business*; sales and employee numbers are for parent company.

Paul Mueller Co.
1600 W. Phelps
Springfield, MO 65802
Phone: 417-831-3000 Fax: 417-831-3528
CEO: Daniel C. Manna
CFO: Donald E. Golik
1991 Sales: $75 million Employees: 810
Symbol: MUEL Exchange: NASDAQ
Industry: Machinery - farm

PAXAR Corp.
275 N. Middletown Rd.
Pearl River, NY 10965
Phone: 914-735-9200 Fax: 914-735-9037
CEO: Arthur Hershaft
CFO: Bruce E. Hagen
1991 Sales: $89 million Employees: 969
Symbol: PXR Exchange: NYSE
Industry: Machinery - general industrial

Pay-Fone Systems, Inc.
8100 Balboa Blvd.
Van Nuys, CA 91406
Phone: 818-997-0808 Fax: 818-787-1850
CEO: Guy Lundberg
CFO: Mark Leekley
1991 Sales: $5.2 million Employees: 96
Symbol: PYF Exchange: AMEX
Industry: Business services - automated payroll services

Paychex, Inc.
911 Panorama Trail South
Rochester, NY 14625
Phone: 716-385-6666 Fax: 716-385-4299
CEO: B. Thomas Golisano
CFO: G. Thomas Clark
1992 Sales: $161 million Employees: 2,500
Symbol: PAYX Exchange: NASDAQ
Industry: Business services - payroll processing

Payco American Corp.
180 N. Executive Dr.
Brookfield, WI 53005
Phone: 414-784-9035 Fax: 414-784-9789
CEO: Neal R. Sparby
CFO: James R. Bohmann
1991 Sales: $112 million Employees: 2,551
Symbol: PAYC Exchange: NASDAQ
Industry: Financial - business services

Payless Cashways Inc.
2300 Main St.
Kansas City, MO 64141
Phone: 816-234-6000 Fax: 816-234-6142
CEO: David Stanley
CFO: Stephen A. Lightstone
1992 Sales: $2,496 million Employees: 11,700
Ownership: Privately held
Industry: Retail - building products; home improvement centers

Payroll 1
333 West Seventh St.
Royal Oak, MI 48067
Phone: 313-548-7020 Fax: 313-548-3879
CEO: Donald Dawson
CFO: Peter Hanley
1992 Sales: $5 million Employees: 110
Ownership: Privately held
Industry: Business services - payrolls & payroll taxes

Payroll 1 MidAtlantic
2000 Corporate Ridge, Ste. 570
McLean, VA 22102
Phone: 703-356-9500 Fax: 703-827-5465
CEO: Tom Tracy
CFO: Connie Puchrik
1991 Sales: $2.5 million Employees: 52
Ownership: Privately held
Industry: Business services - payrolls & payroll taxes

PBR Consulting Group
1500 Market St., Ste. 2300
Philadelphia, PA 19102
Phone: 215-854-0778 Fax: 215-854-0079
CEO: Randy Pritzken
CFO: Scott Baron
1992 Sales: $6 million Employees: 70
Ownership: Privately held
Industry: Computers - system consulting services

PCA International, Inc.
815 Matthews-Mint Hill Rd.
Matthews, NC 28105
Phone: 704-847-8011 Fax: Ext. 2686
CEO: John Grosso
CFO: Bruce A. Fisher
1991 Sales: $147 million Employees: 3,000
Symbol: PCAI Exchange: NASDAQ
Industry: Retail - portrait photographs

PCI Services, Inc.
K St. and Erie Ave.
Philadelphia, PA 19803
Phone: 215-537-8100 Fax: 215-743-4818
CEO: Richard S. Sauter
CFO: Michael F. Sandler
1991 Sales: $68 million Employees: 876
Symbol: PCIS Exchange: NASDAQ
Industry: Containers - paper & plastic

PDA Engineering
2975 Red Hill Ave.
Costa Mesa, CA 92626
Phone: 714-540-8900 Fax: 714-545-9434
CEO: Louis A. Delmonico
CFO: James W. Kerrigan
1992 Sales: $38 million Employees: 248
Symbol: PDAS Exchange: NASDAQ
Industry: Computers - engineering software

PDK Labs, Inc.
145 Ricefield Lane
Hauppauge, NY 11779
Phone: 516-273-2630 Fax: —
CEO: Michael B. Krasnoff
CFO: Michael B. Krasnoff
1991 Sales: $8.5 million Employees: 59
Symbol: PDKL Exchange: NASDAQ
Industry: Vitamins & nutritional products - nonprescription pharmaceuticals

Peak Technologies Group, Inc.
600 Madison Ave.
New York, NY 10022
Phone: 212-832-2833 Fax: 212-832-3151
CEO: Nicholas R. Toms
CFO: Donald W. Rowley
1991 Sales: $44 million Employees: 270
Symbol: PEAK Exchange: NASDAQ
Industry: Machinery - bar code printing

Pearson, Inc.
One Rockefeller Plaza
New York, NY 10020
Phone: 212-713-1919 Fax: 212-247-4616
CEO: David Veit
CFO: —
1991 Sales: $2,992 million Employees: 28,492
Parent: Pearson PLC
Industry: Publishing - books & periodicals; oil services & fine china

PEC Israel Economic Corp.
511 Fifth Ave.
New York, NY 10017
Phone: 212-687-2400 Fax: —
CEO: Joseph Ciechanover
CFO: Frank J. Klein
1991 Sales: $12 million Employees: —
Symbol: IEC Exchange: AMEX
Industry: Financial - investment management

Peck/Jones Construction Corporation
10866 Wilshire Blvd., 7th Fl.
Los Angeles, CA 90024
Phone: 310-470-1885 Fax: 310-470-3175
CEO: Jerve M. Jones
CFO: Dan Penn
1991 Sales: $515 million Employees: 338
Ownership: Privately held
Industry: Construction - commercial; general contracting & project management

Peer Review Analysis, Inc.
380 Pleasant St.
Malden, MA 02148
Phone: 617-322-6400 Fax: —
CEO: Eric R. Spitzer
CFO: William E. Nixon
1991 Sales: $8.2 million Employees: 81
Symbol: PRAI Exchange: NASDAQ
Industry: Medical services - management & administration

Peerless Mfg. Co.
2819 Walnut Hill Lane
Dallas, TX 75229
Phone: 214-357-6181 Fax: 214-351-0194
CEO: Donald A. Sillers, Jr.
CFO: Donald H. Newman
1992 Sales: $23 million Employees: 170
Symbol: PMFG Exchange: NASDAQ
Industry: Filtration products

Peerless Tube Co.
58 Locust Ave.
Bloomfield, NJ 07003
Phone: 201-743-5100 Fax: 201-743-5954
CEO: Frederic Remington, Jr.
CFO: Thomas J. Lynch, Jr.
1991 Sales: $43 million Employees: 375
Symbol: PLS Exchange: AMEX
Industry: Containers - metal

Pegasus Gold Inc.
9 N. Post St., Ste. 400
Spokane, WA 99201
Phone: 509-624-4653 Fax: 509-838-8317
CEO: John M. Willson
CFO: John L. Azlant
1991 Sales: $156 million Employees: 630
Symbol: PGU Exchange: AMEX
Industry: Gold mining & processing

Pelton & Associates
308 S. Catalina Ave.
Redondo Beach, CA 90277
Phone: 310-376-8061 Fax: 310-376-8064
CEO: Robert Pelton
CFO: Hank Porpor
1991 Sales: $9 million Employees: 22
Ownership: Privately held
Industry: Business services - marketing

Penn Central Corp.
One E. Fourth St.
Cincinnati, OH 45202
Phone: 513-579-6600 Fax: 513-579-0108
CEO: Carl H. Lindner
CFO: David H. Street
1992 Sales: $1,797 million Employees: 12,100
Symbol: PC Exchange: NYSE
Industry: Diversified operations - insurance, communications, wire & cable

Penn Engineering & Manufacturing Co.
5190 Old Easton Hwy.
Danboro, PA 18916
Phone: 215-766-8853 Fax: 215-766-0143
CEO: K. A. Swanstrom
CFO: Mark W. Simon
1991 Sales: $71 million Employees: 806
Symbol: PNN Exchange: AMEX
Industry: Metal products - fasteners

indicates company is in *Hoover's Handbook of American Business.*

indicates company is in *Hoover's Handbook of World Business;* sales and employee numbers are for parent company.

Penn Property & Casualty Inc.
1023 Mumma Rd.
Lemoyne, PA 17043
Phone: 717-761-2919 Fax: 717-761-6159
CEO: Greg Gunn
CFO: Ted Mowery
1991 Sales: $4.2 million Employees: 12
Ownership: Privately held
Industry: Insurance - property & casualty; surety bond brokerage services

Penn Traffic Co.
319 Washington St.
Johnstown, PA 15901
Phone: 814-536-9900 Fax: 814-536-9926
CEO: Claude J. Incaudo
CFO: John M. Kriak
1992 Sales: $2,790 million Employees: 22,186
Symbol: PNF Exchange: AMEX
Industry: Retail - supermarkets

Penn Treaty American Corp.
3440 Lehigh St.
Allentown, PA 18103
Phone: 215-965-2222 Fax: 215-967-4616
CEO: Irving Levit
CFO: Michael F. Grill
1992 Sales: — Employees: —
Symbol: PTAC Exchange: NASDAQ
Industry: Insurance - accident & health

Penn Virginia Corp.
200 S. Broad St., Ste. 800
Philadelphia, PA 19102
Phone: 215-545-6600 Fax: 215-545-6608
CEO: John A. H. Shober
CFO: Robert J. Jaeger
1991 Sales: $49 million Employees: 297
Symbol: PVIR Exchange: NASDAQ
Industry: Computers - graphics

PennFirst Bancorp, Inc.
600 Lawrence Ave.
Ellwood City, PA 16117
Phone: 412-758-5584 Fax: —
CEO: Charlotte A. Zuschlag
CFO: Eugene J. Baur, Jr.
1991 Sales: $21 million Employees: 91
Symbol: PWBC Exchange: NASDAQ
Industry: Financial - savings and loans

Pennsylvania Enterprises, Inc.
39 Public Square
Wilkes-Barre, PA 18711
Phone: 717-829-8600 Fax: 717-829-8652
CEO: Dean T. Casady
CFO: John F. Kell, Jr.
1991 Sales: $183 million Employees: 990
Symbol: PENT Exchange: NASDAQ
Industry: Utility - gas distribution

Pennsylvania Power & Light Co.
Two N. Ninth St.
Allentown, PA 18101
Phone: 215-774-5151 Fax: 215-770-5408
CEO: John T. Kauffman
CFO: Charles E. Russoli
1992 Sales: $2,744 million Employees: 8,139
Symbol: PPL Exchange: NYSE
Industry: Utility - electric power

Pennzoil Co.
700 Milam St.
Houston, TX 77002
Phone: 713-546-4000 Fax: 713-546-7591
CEO: James L. Pate
CFO: David P. Alderson II
1992 Sales: $2,357 million Employees: 11,694
Symbol: PZL Exchange: NYSE
Industry: Oil & gas - US integrated; automotive products

Penobscot Shoe Co.
450 N. Main St.
Old Town, ME 04468
Phone: 207-827-4431 Fax: 207-827-4834
CEO: Irving Kagan
CFO: David L. Keane
1991 Sales: $13 million Employees: 135
Symbol: PSO Exchange: AMEX
Industry: Shoes & related apparel

Penril DataComm Networks, Inc.
1300 Quince Orchard Blvd.
Gaithersburg, MD 20878
Phone: 301-921-8600 Fax: 301-948-5761
CEO: Henry D. Epstein
CFO: Harry O. Christenson
1991 Sales: $53 million Employees: 427
Symbol: PNRL Exchange: NASDAQ
Industry: Telecommunications equipment

Penske Corporation
13400 Outer Dr. West
Detroit, MI 48239
Phone: 313-592-5000 Fax: 313-592-5256
CEO: Roger S. Penske
CFO: Rich Peters
1992 Sales: $2,800 million Employees: 10,100
Ownership: Privately held
Industry: Diversified operations - auto dealerships, truck leasing & rental, diesel engine manufacturing

Pentair, Inc.
1700 W. Hwy. 36, Ste. 700
St. Paul, MN 55113
Phone: 612-636-7920 Fax: 612-636-5508
CEO: D. Eugene Nugent
CFO: J. H. Grunewald
1992 Sales: $1,239 million Employees: 8,400
Symbol: PNTA Exchange: NASDAQ
Industry: Paper & paper products

Pentech International, Inc.
2 Ethel Rd., Ste. 204-B
Edison, NJ 08817
Phone: 908-287-6640 Fax: 908-287-6610
CEO: Norman Melnick
CFO: David Melnick
1991 Sales: $34 million Employees: 55
Symbol: PNTK Exchange: NASDAQ
Industry: Office & art materials

Penwest, Ltd.
777-108th Ave. NE, Ste. 2390
Bellevue, WA 98004
Phone: 206-462-6000 Fax: 206-462-2819
CEO: Tod R. Hamachek
CFO: Jeffrey T. Cook
1991 Sales: $111 million Employees: 384
Symbol: PENW Exchange: NASDAQ
Industry: Chemicals - specialty

People's Bank
850 Main St.
Bridgeport, CT 06604
Phone: 203-579-7171 Fax: —
CEO: David E. A. Carson
CFO: George W. Morriss
1992 Sales: — Employees: —
Symbol: PBCT Exchange: NASDAQ
Industry: Banks - Northeast

People's Savings Bank of Brockton
221 Main St.
Brockton, MA 02403
Phone: 617-588-6600 Fax: —
CEO: Roger A. Kibart
CFO: John M. Dean
1992 Sales: — Employees: —
Symbol: PBKB Exchange: NASDAQ
Industry: Financial - savings and loans

People's Savings Financial Corp.
123 Broad St.
New Britain, CT 06050
Phone: 203-224-7771 Fax: —
CEO: Richard S. Mansfield
CFO: John G. Medvec
1991 Sales: $27 million Employees: 67
Symbol: PBNB Exchange: NASDAQ
Industry: Financial - savings and loans

Peoples Bancorp
212 W. 7th St.
Auburn, IN 46706
Phone: 219-925-2500 Fax: —
CEO: Robert J. Wertenberger
CFO: Robert J. Wertenberger
1991 Sales: $21 million Employees: 77
Symbol: PFDC Exchange: NASDAQ
Industry: Financial - savings and loans

Peoples Bancorp of Worcester, Inc.
120 Front St.
Worcester, MA 01608
Phone: 508-791-3861 Fax: 508-798-3743
CEO: Woodbury C. Titcomb
CFO: Michael S. Shaw
1991 Sales: $86 million Employees: 340
Symbol: PEBW Exchange: NASDAQ
Industry: Banks - Northeast

Peoples Energy Corp.
122 S. Michigan Ave.
Chicago, IL 60603
Phone: 312-431-4000 Fax: 312-431-0112
CEO: Richard E. Terry
CFO: John A. Lawrisuk
1992 Sales: $1,127 million Employees: 3,428
Symbol: PGL Exchange: NYSE
Industry: Utility - gas distribution

Peoples First Corp.
100 S. Fourth St.
Paducah, KY 42001
Phone: 502-444-6371 Fax: —
CEO: Aubrey W. Lippert
CFO: Allan B. Kleet
1991 Sales: $20 million Employees: 295
Symbol: PFKY Exchange: NASDAQ
Industry: Banks - Midwest

Peoples Heritage Financial Group, Inc.
One Portland Square
Portland, ME 04112
Phone: 207-761-8500 Fax: 207-761-8536
CEO: William J. Ryan
CFO: Peter J. Verrill
1991 Sales: $74 million Employees: 1,175
Symbol: PHBK Exchange: NASDAQ
Industry: Financial - savings and loans

Peoples Holding Co.
209 Troy St.
Tupelo, MS 38802
Phone: 601-680-1001 Fax: —
CEO: E. C. Neelly
CFO: E. C. Neelly
1991 Sales: $63 million Employees: 495
Symbol: PHCO Exchange: NASDAQ
Industry: Banks - Southeast

Peoples Telephone Co., Inc.
8041 NW 14th St.
Miami, FL 33126
Phone: 305-593-9667 Fax: 305-593-0479
CEO: Jeffrey Hanft
CFO: Richard F. Militello
1991 Sales: $56 million Employees: 256
Symbol: PTEL Exchange: NASDAQ
Industry: Telecommunications equipment

Peoples Westchester Savings Bank
Three Skyline Dr.
Hawthorne, NY 10532
Phone: 914-347-3800 Fax: 914-347-7665
CEO: William F. Olson
CFO: James G. Kane
1992 Sales: — Employees: —
Symbol: PWSB Exchange: NASDAQ
Industry: Financial - savings and loans

Pep Boys - Manny, Moe & Jack, The
3111 W. Allegheny Ave.
Philadelphia, PA 19132
Phone: 215-229-9000 Fax: 215-226-2323
CEO: Mitchell G. Leibovitz
CFO: Michael J. Holden
1992 Sales: $1,127 million Employees: 11,965
Symbol: PBY Exchange: NYSE
Industry: Retail - auto parts

Pepper Cos. Inc.
643 N. Orleans St.
Chicago, IL 60610
Phone: 312-266-4703 Fax: 312-266-2792
CEO: Richard S. Pepper
CFO: Thomas M. O'Leary
1992 Sales: $420 million Employees: 800
Ownership: Privately held
Industry: Construction - general contracting

PepsiCo, Inc.
700 Anderson Hill Rd.
Purchase, NY 10577
Phone: 914-253-2000 Fax: 914-253-2070
CEO: D. Wayne Calloway
CFO: Robert G. Dettmer
1992 Sales: $21,970 million Employees: 338,000
Symbol: PEP Exchange: NYSE
Industry: Beverages - soft drinks, snack foods, restaurants

Perception Technology Corp.
40 Shawmut Rd.
Canton, MA 02021
Phone: 617-821-0320 Fax: 617-828-7886
CEO: Leon A. Ferber
CFO: Paul R. Yecies
1991 Sales: $17 million Employees: 109
Symbol: PCEP Exchange: NASDAQ
Industry: Telecommunications equipment

Perceptronics, Inc.
21135 Erwin St.
Woodland Hills, CA 91367
Phone: 818-884-7470 Fax: 818-348-0540
CEO: Gershon Weltman
CFO: David P. Nelson
1992 Sales: $25 million Employees: 118
Symbol: PERC Exchange: NASDAQ
Industry: Electronics - military

Perdue Farms Inc.
Rt. 346
Salisbury, MD 21801
Phone: 410-543-3000 Fax: 410-543-3292
CEO: James Perdue
CFO: George Reiswig
1991 Sales: $1,239 million Employees: 13,300
Ownership: Privately held
Industry: Food - poultry processing

Perfumania, Inc.
7875 NW 64th St.
Miami, FL 33166
Phone: 305-591-8317 Fax: 305-592-5774
CEO: Ilia Lekach
CFO: Ron A. Friedman
1991 Sales: $86 million Employees: 482
Symbol: PRFM Exchange: NASDAQ
Industry: Cosmetics & toiletries

Perini Corp.
73 Mt. Wayte Ave.
Framingham, MA 01701
Phone: 508-875-6171 Fax: 508-820-2530
CEO: David B. Perini
CFO: James M. Markert
1992 Sales: $1,071 million Employees: 5,100
Symbol: PCR Exchange: AMEX
Industry: Construction - heavy

Peripheral Land, Inc.
47421 Bayside Pkwy.
Fremont, CA 94538
Phone: 510-657-2211 Fax: 510-683-9713
CEO: Leo Berenguel
CFO: Bruce Linpon
1991 Sales: $25 million Employees: 106
Ownership: Privately held
Industry: Computers - mass storage products

Perkin-Elmer Corp.
761 Main Ave.
Norwalk, CT 06859
Phone: 203-762-1000 Fax: 203-762-6000
CEO: Gaynor N. Kelley
CFO: F. Gordon Bitter
1992 Sales: $946 million Employees: 6,085
Symbol: PKN Exchange: NYSE
Industry: Instruments - scientific

Perkins Family Restaurants, L.P.
6075 Poplar Ave., Ste. 800
Memphis, TN 38119
Phone: 901-766-6400 Fax: 901-766-6482
CEO: Donald N. Smith
CFO: Michael P. Donahoe
1991 Sales: $180 million Employees: 6,800
Symbol: PFR Exchange: NYSE
Industry: Retail - food & restaurants

Perrier Group, The
777 W. Putnam Ave.
Greenwich, CT 06830
Phone: 203-531-4100 Fax: 203-863-0297
CEO: Ron Davis
CFO: —
1991 Sales: $2,546 million Employees: 15,261
Parent: Source Perrier, SA
Industry: Beverages - bottled water

Perrigo Co.
117 Water St.
Allegan, MI 49010
Phone: 616-673-8451 Fax: 616-673-7534
CEO: Michael J. Jandernoa
CFO: M. James Gunberg
1992 Sales: $410 million Employees: 3,171
Symbol: PRGO Exchange: NASDAQ
Industry: Cosmetics & toiletries

Perry Drug Stores, Inc.
5400 Perry Dr.
Pontiac, MI 48343
Phone: 313-334-1300 Fax: 313-674-7849
CEO: Jack A. Robinson
CFO: Jerry E. Stone
1992 Sales: $674 million Employees: 5,000
Symbol: PDS Exchange: NYSE
Industry: Retail - drug stores

Perry H. Koplik & Sons Inc.
505 Park Ave.
New York, NY 10022
Phone: 212-752-2288 Fax: 212-838-8790
CEO: Michael R. Koplik
CFO: Edward Stein
1990 Sales: $481 million Employees: 67
Ownership: Privately held
Industry: Paper & paper products - forest products

PerSeptive Biosystems, Inc.
38 Sidney St.
Cambridge, MA 02139
Phone: 617-621-1787 Fax: —
CEO: Noubar B. Aleyan
CFO: Robert A. Fein
1991 Sales: $0.9 million Employees: —
Symbol: PBIO Exchange: NASDAQ
Industry: Medical products - diagnostics

Personnel Management, Inc.
16 Public Square, Ste. A
Shelbyville, IN 46176
Phone: 317-392-7400 Fax: 317-392-7401
CEO: Don Taylor
CFO: Jim Burnette
1991 Sales: $9.5 million Employees: 45
Ownership: Privately held
Industry: Business services - temporary personnel

PET Inc.
400 S. Fourth St.
St. Louis, MO 63102
Phone: 314-621-5400 Fax: 314-622-6525
CEO: Miles L. Marsh
CFO: John C. Elbin
1992 Sales: $1,769 million Employees: 7,465
Symbol: PT Exchange: NYSE
Industry: Food - canned & baked goods, pasta, evaporated milk

Pet Ventures Inc.
200 N. Glebe Rd. #809
Arlington, VA 22203
Phone: 703-276-7746 Fax: 703-276-8416
CEO: Mike Molony
CFO: Mary-Clare Molony
1991 Sales: $5.8 million Employees: 70
Ownership: Privately held
Industry: Veterinary products & services - pet food & supplies

Peter J. Schmitt Co. Inc.
355 Harlem Rd.
West Seneca, NY 14224
Phone: 716-825-1111 Fax: 716-821-1645
CEO: D. Clark Ogle
CFO: Mark Flint
1991 Sales: $500 million Employees: 700
Ownership: Privately held
Industry: Food - wholesale

Peter Kiewit Sons', Inc.
1000 Kiewit Plaza
Omaha, NE 68131
Phone: 402-342-2052 Fax: 402-271-2829
CEO: Walter Scott, Jr.
CFO: Robert E. Julian
1991 Sales: $2,086 million Employees: 8,000
Ownership: Privately held
Industry: Construction - heavy; coal mining & telecommunications

Petrie Stores Corp.
70 Enterprise Ave. North
Secaucus, NJ 07094
Phone: 201-866-3600 Fax: 201-866-5483
CEO: Milton Petrie
CFO: Peter A. Left
1992 Sales: $1,398 million Employees: 17,000
Symbol: PST Exchange: NYSE
Industry: Retail - apparel & shoes

Petrobrás
1330 Avenue of the Americas, 16th Fl.
New York, NY 10019
Phone: 212-974-0777 Fax: 212-974-1169
CEO: Gerson N. Braune
CFO: —
1991 Sales: $16,996 million Employees: 53,857
Parent: Petróleo Brasileiro S.A.
Industry: Oil & gas - international integrated

indicates company is in *Hoover's Handbook of American Business.*

indicates company is in *Hoover's Handbook of World Business;* sales and employee numbers are for parent company.

Petróleos de Venezuela (USA) Corp.
750 Lexington Ave., 59th St., 10th/21st Fl.
New York, NY 10022
Phone: 212-339-7770 Fax: 212-339-7725
CEO: Eglé Iturbe de Blanco
CFO: —
1991 Sales: $20,591 million Employees: 54,850
Parent: Petróleos de Venezuela, SA
Industry: Oil & gas - international integrated

Petróleos Mexicanos
3600 S. Gessner, Ste. 100
Houston, TX 77063
Phone: 713-978-7974 Fax: 713-978-5997
CEO: Ramon Guerrero
CFO: —
1991 Sales: $19,165 million Employees: 166,896
Parent: Petróleos Mexicanos
Industry: Oil & gas - international integrated

Petroleum Development Corp.
103 E. Main St.
Bridgeport, WV 26330
Phone: 304-842-6256 Fax: Ext. 30
CEO: James N. Ryan
CFO: Dale G. Rettinger
1991 Sales: $17 million Employees: 74
Symbol: PETD Exchange: NASDAQ
Industry: Oil & gas - US exploration & production

Petroleum Heat and Power Co., Inc.
Davenport St.
Stamford, CT 06902
Phone: 203-323-2121 Fax: 203-323-5156
CEO: Malvin P. Sevin
CFO: Irik P. Sevin
1991 Sales: $523 million Employees: 2,081
Symbol: PHP Exchange: AMEX
Industry: Oil refining & marketing

Petroleum & Resources Corp.
Seven St. Paul St., Ste. 1140
Baltimore, MD 21202
Phone: 410-752-5900 Fax: —
CEO: Douglas G. Ober
CFO: Simeon F. Wooten III
1992 Sales: — Employees: —
Symbol: PEO Exchange: NYSE
Industry: Financial - investment management

Petrolite Corp.
100 N. Broadway, Ste. 1900
St. Louis, MO 63102
Phone: 314-241-8370 Fax: 314-241-1833
CEO: Ellis L. Brown
CFO: Herbert F. Eggerding, Jr.
1991 Sales: $324 million Employees: 1,925
Symbol: PLIT Exchange: NASDAQ
Industry: Oil & gas - field services

Petrominerals Corp.
2472 Chambers Rd., Ste. 230
Tustin, CA 92680
Phone: 714-730-5400 Fax: —
CEO: Larry S. Dodson
CFO: Kenneth M. Padula
1991 Sales: $8.7 million Employees: 103
Symbol: PTRO Exchange: NASDAQ
Industry: Oil & gas - field services

Pettibone Corp.
425 Naperville Rd., Ste. 200
Lisle, IL 60532
Phone: 708-955-2238 Fax: 708-955-2230
CEO: Larry C. Klumpp
CFO: Larry W. Gies
1992 Sales: $113 million Employees: 799
Symbol: PETT Exchange: NASDAQ
Industry: Machinery - construction & mining

Peugeot Motors of America, Inc.
One Peugeot Plaza
Lyndhurst, NJ 07071
Phone: 201-935-8400 Fax: 201-935-6425
CEO: Serge Banzet
CFO: —
1991 Sales: $30,921 million Employees: 156,800
Parent: PSA Peugeot Citroën
Industry: Automotive manufacturing

Pfizer Inc.
235 E. 42nd St.
New York, NY 10017
Phone: 212-573-2323 Fax: 212-573-7851
CEO: William C. Steere, Jr.
CFO: Henry A. McKinnell
1992 Sales: $7,230 million Employees: 44,100
Symbol: PFE Exchange: NYSE
Industry: Drugs, specialty chemicals & minerals, consumer products

Phar-Mor
20 Federal Plaza West
Youngstown, OH 44501
Phone: 216-746-6641 Fax: 216-740-2915
CEO: Antonio Alvarez
CFO: Daniel O'Leary
1991 Sales: $3,144 million Employees: 20,000
Ownership: Privately held
Industry: Retail - discount drug & variety stores

Pharmaceutical Data Services, Inc.
9501 E. Shea Blvd.
Scottsdale, AZ 85260
Phone: 602-391-4731 Fax: 602-391-4298
CEO: Dennis M.J. Turner
CFO: Roger L. Mansbridge
1991 Sales: $60 million Employees: 426
Symbol: PMRX Exchange: NASDAQ
Industry: Drugs

Pharmaceutical Resources, Inc.
One Ram Ridge Rd.
Spring Valley, NY 10977
Phone: 914-425-7100 Fax: 914-425-7907
CEO: Kenneth I. Sawyer
CFO: Richard J. Nadler
1991 Sales: $34 million Employees: 325
Symbol: PRX Exchange: NYSE
Industry: Drugs - generic

Pharmacy Management Services, Inc.
3611 Queen Palm Dr.
Tampa, FL 33619
Phone: 813-626-7788 Fax: 813-622-7822
CEO: Cecil S. Harrell
CFO: David L. Redmond
1991 Sales: $82 million Employees: 1,050
Symbol: PMSV Exchange: NASDAQ
Industry: Medical services

PharmChem Laboratories, Inc.
1505-A O'Brien Dr.
Menlo Park, CA 94025
Phone: 415-328-6200 Fax: —
CEO: Jay Whitney
CFO: Lloyd Leanse
1991 Sales: $24 million Employees: 250
Symbol: PCHM Exchange: NASDAQ
Industry: Medical services - drug testing

Phelps Dodge Corp.
2600 N. Central Ave.
Phoenix, AZ 85004
Phone: 602-234-8100 Fax: 602-234-8337
CEO: Douglas C. Yearley
CFO: Thomas M. St. Clair
1992 Sales: $2,579 million Employees: 13,931
Symbol: PD Exchange: NYSE
Industry: Metals - nonferrous; copper

PHH Corp.
11333 McCormick Rd.
Hunt Valley, MD 21031
Phone: 410-771-3600 Fax: 410-771-1123
CEO: Robert D. Kunisch
CFO: Roy A. Meierhenry
1992 Sales: $1,987 million Employees: 4,834
Symbol: PHH Exchange: NYSE
Industry: Leasing

Philadelphia Electric Co.
2301 Market St.
Philadelphia, PA 19101
Phone: 215-841-4000 Fax: 215-841-6830
CEO: Joseph F. Paquette, Jr.
CFO: W. L. Bardeen
1992 Sales: $3,963 million Employees: 9,933
Symbol: PE Exchange: NYSE
Industry: Utility - electric power

Philadelphia Suburban Corp.
762 W. Lancaster Ave.
Bryn Mawr, PA 19010
Phone: 215-527-8000 Fax: 215-645-1055
CEO: John W. Boyer, Jr.
CFO: Michael P. Graham
1991 Sales: $89 million Employees: 526
Symbol: PSC Exchange: NYSE
Industry: Utility - water supply

Philip Morris Companies Inc.
120 Park Ave.
New York, NY 10017
Phone: 212-880-5000 Fax: 212-878-2167
CEO: Michael A. Miles
CFO: Hans G. Storr
1992 Sales: $50,095 million Employees: 166,000
Symbol: MO Exchange: NYSE
Industry: Tobacco, food & beer

Phillips Petroleum Co.
4th & Keeler Streets
Bartlesville, OK 74004
Phone: 918-661-6600 Fax: 918-661-7636
CEO: C. J. Silas
CFO: James J. Mulva
1992 Sales: $11,933 million Employees: 22,682
Symbol: P Exchange: NYSE
Industry: Oil & gas - US integrated

Phillips-Van Heusen Corp.
1290 Avenue of the Americas
New York, NY 10104
Phone: 212-541-5200 Fax: 212-247-5309
CEO: Lawrence S. Phillips
CFO: Irwin W. Winter
1992 Sales: $1,002 million Employees: 9,600
Symbol: PVH Exchange: NYSE
Industry: Textiles - apparel

PHLCorp, Inc.
315 Park Ave. South
New York, NY 10010
Phone: 212-598-3200 Fax: 212-598-4869
CEO: Ian M. Cumming
CFO: Norman P. Kiken
1991 Sales: $369 million Employees: 1,273
Symbol: PHX Exchange: NYSE
Industry: Diversified operations - insurance, motivation services, trading stamps

PHM Corp.
33 Bloomfield Hills Pkwy., Ste. 200
Bloomfield Hills, MI 48304
Phone: 313-647-2750 Fax: 313-433-4598
CEO: William J. Pulte
CFO: William J. Crombie
1992 Sales: $1,370 million Employees: 1,976
Symbol: PHM Exchange: NYSE
Industry: Building - residential & commercial

Phoenix Control Corp.
55 Chapel St.
Newton, MA 02158
Phone: 617-964-6670 Fax: 617-965-4503
CEO: Art Doland
CFO: Art Doland
1991 Sales: $7.7 million Employees: 74
Ownership: Privately held
Industry: Instruments - laboratory airflow control systems

Phoenix Reinsurance Co.
80 Maiden Lane
New York, NY 10038
Phone: 212-269-7640 Fax: 212-809-9028
CEO: Gerald L. Radke
CFO: Jeffrey D. Cropsey
1991 Sales: $49 million Employees: —
Symbol: PXRE Exchange: NASDAQ
Industry: Insurance - property & casualty

Phoenix Resource Cos., Inc.
6525 N. Meridian Ave., Ste. 102
Oklahoma City, OK 73116
Phone: 405-728-5100 Fax: 405-728-5259
CEO: George D. Lawrence, Jr.
CFO: George D. Lawrence, Jr.
1991 Sales: $15 million Employees: 21
Symbol: PHN Exchange: AMEX
Industry: Oil & gas - international specialty

Phoenix Technologies Ltd.
846 University Ave.
Norwood, MA 02062
Phone: 617-551-4000 Fax: 617-551-3750
CEO: Ronald D. Fisher
CFO: Robert R. Langer
1991 Sales: $52 million Employees: 309
Symbol: PTEC Exchange: NASDAQ
Industry: Computers - bios software

Photo Control Corp.
4800 Quebec Ave. North
Minneapolis, MN 55428
Phone: 612-537-3601 Fax: 612-537-2852
CEO: Leslie A. Willig
CFO: Curtis R. Jackels
1991 Sales: $12 million Employees: 129
Symbol: PHOC Exchange: NASDAQ
Industry: Photographic equipment & supplies

Photronic Labs Inc.
15 Secor Rd.
Brookfield, CT 06804
Phone: 203-775-9000 Fax: 203-775-5944
CEO: Constantine Macricostas
CFO: Michael J. Yomazzo
1991 Sales: $42 million Employees: 350
Symbol: PLAB Exchange: NASDAQ
Industry: Electrical components - photomasks (photographic glass plates)

PHP Healthcare
4900 Seminary Rd., 12th Fl.
Alexandria, VA 22308
Phone: 703-998-7808 Fax: 709-998-5040
CEO: Charles H. Robbins
CFO: Anthony M. Picini
1992 Sales: $118 million Employees: 2,745
Symbol: PPH Exchange: NYSE
Industry: Healthcare - outpatient & home

PhyCor, Inc.
30 Burton Hills Blvd.
Nashville, TN 37215
Phone: 615-665-9066 Fax: 615-665-9088
CEO: Joseph C. Hutts
CFO: Joseph C. Hutts
1991 Sales: $90 million Employees: 1,700
Symbol: PHYC Exchange: NASDAQ
Industry: Hospitals

Physician Computer Network, Inc.
100 Metro Park South
Laurence Harbor, NJ 08878
Phone: 908-290-7711 Fax: —
CEO: Jerry Brager
CFO: Vincent M. Achilarre
1991 Sales: $2.1 million Employees: 86
Symbol: PCNI Exchange: NASDAQ
Industry: Medical services - computer network for physicians & health care organizations

Physicians Insurance Co. of Ohio
13515 Yarmouth Dr. NW
Pickerington, OH 43147
Phone: 614-864-7100 Fax: —
CEO: Robert L. Dion
CFO: William Henderly
1992 Sales: — Employees: —
Symbol: PICOA Exchange: NASDAQ
Industry: Real estate operations - rural property

Piccadilly Cafeterias, Inc.
3232 Sherwood Forest Blvd.
Baton Rouge, LA 70816
Phone: 504-293-9440 Fax: 504-296-8370
CEO: James W. Bennett
CFO: Ronald A. LaBorde
1992 Sales: $295 million Employees: 8,737
Symbol: PICC Exchange: NASDAQ
Industry: Retail - food & restaurants

Pico Products, Inc.
1001 Zine St.
Liverpool, NY 13008
Phone: 315-451-7700 Fax: 315-451-7904
CEO: Everett T. Keech
CFO: Peter J. Moerbeek
1991 Sales: $18 million Employees: 210
Symbol: PPI Exchange: AMEX
Industry: Telecommunications equipment

PictureTel Corp.
222 Rosewood Dr.
Danvers, MA 01923
Phone: 508-762-5000 Fax: 508-762-5245
CEO: Norman Gaut
CFO: Les B. Strauss
1991 Sales: $78 million Employees: 449
Symbol: PCTL Exchange: NASDAQ
Industry: Telecommunications services

Piedmont BankGroup Inc.
200 E. Church St.
Martinsville, VA 24115
Phone: 703-632-2971 Fax: —
CEO: Irving M. Groves, Jr.
CFO: R. Bruce Valley
1991 Sales: $70 million Employees: 465
Symbol: PBGI Exchange: NASDAQ
Industry: Banks - Southeast

Piedmont Group
3871 Piedmont Ave.
Oakland, CA 94611
Phone: 510-428-2698 Fax: 510-428-9132
CEO: Ann Kraynak
CFO: Ann Kraynak
1991 Sales: $2 million Employees: 25
Ownership: Privately held
Industry: Business services - photocopying & desktop publishing services

Piedmont Management Co. Inc.
80 Maiden Lane
New York, NY 10038
Phone: 212-363-4650 Fax: 212-363-4658
CEO: Robert M. DeMichele
CFO: Peter J. Palenzona
1991 Sales: $105 million Employees: 170
Symbol: PMAN Exchange: NASDAQ
Industry: Insurance - property & casualty

Piedmont Natural Gas Co., Inc.
1915 Rexford Rd.
Charlotte, NC 28211
Phone: 704-364-3120 Fax: 704-365-3849
CEO: John H. Maxheim
CFO: Everette C. Hinson
1991 Sales: $412 million Employees: 1,893
Symbol: PNY Exchange: NYSE
Industry: Utility - gas distribution

Pier 1 Imports, Inc.
301 Commerce St., Ste. 600
Ft. Worth, TX 76102
Phone: 817-878-8000 Fax: 817-878-7883
CEO: Clark A. Johnson
CFO: Robert G. Herndon
1992 Sales: $587 million Employees: 7,787
Symbol: PIR Exchange: NYSE
Industry: Retail - imported apparel & home furnishings

Pilgrim Regional Bank Shares Inc.
10100 Santa Monica Blvd.
Los Angeles, CA 90067
Phone: 800-331-1080 Fax: —
CEO: Palomba Weingarten
CFO: Palomba Weingarten
1992 Sales: — Employees: —
Symbol: PBS Exchange: NYSE
Industry: Financial - investment management

Pilgrim's Pride Corp.
110 S. Texas St.
Pittsburg, TX 75686
Phone: 903-856-7901 Fax: 903-856-7505
CEO: Lonnie A. Pilgrim
CFO: Clifford E. Butler
1992 Sales: $842 million Employees: 10,341
Symbol: CHX Exchange: NYSE
Industry: Food - meat products

Pinkerton's Security & Investigation Services
6727 Odessa Ave.
Van Nuys, CA 91406
Phone: 818-373-8000 Fax: 818-902-9512
CEO: Thomas W. Wathen
CFO: Daniel C. Weaver
1992 Sales: $704 million Employees: 45,000
Symbol: PKTN Exchange: NASDAQ
Industry: Protection - security & investigative services

Pinnacle West Capital Corp.
400 E. Van Buren, Ste. 700
Phoenix, AZ 85004
Phone: 602-379-2500 Fax: 602-379-2640
CEO: Richard Snell
CFO: Henry B. Sargent
1992 Sales: $1,690 million Employees: 7,800
Symbol: PNW Exchange: NYSE
Industry: Utility - electric power

Pioneer Bancorp, Inc.
325 Nash St.
Rocky Mount, NC 27804
Phone: 919-446-0611 Fax: —
CEO: Theo H. Pitt, Jr.
CFO: William L. Wall
1991 Sales: $56 million Employees: 255
Symbol: PSBN Exchange: NASDAQ
Industry: Banks - Southeast

Pioneer Electronics (USA), Inc.
2265 E. 220th St.
Long Beach, CA 90810
Phone: 213-746-6337 Fax: 310-952-2402
CEO: Shoichi Yamada
CFO: —
1992 Sales: $4,609 million Employees: 16,574
Parent: Pioneer Electronic Corporation
Industry: Audio & video products

 indicates company is in *Hoover's Handbook of American Business.*

 indicates company is in *Hoover's Handbook of World Business*; sales and employee numbers are for parent company.

Pioneer Fed BanCorp, Inc.
900 Fort St. Mall
Honolulu, HI 96813
Phone: 808-522-6690 Fax: —
CEO: Lily K. Yao
CFO: Albert M. Yamada
1991 Sales: $61 million Employees: 272
Symbol: PFBC Exchange: NASDAQ
Industry: Financial - savings and loans

Pioneer Financial Corp.
5601 Ironbridge Pkwy.
Chester, VA 23831
Phone: 804-748-9733 Fax: —
CEO: George R. Whittemore
CFO: John F. B. Jurgens III
1991 Sales: $55 million Employees: 150
Symbol: PION Exchange: NASDAQ
Industry: Financial - savings and loans

Pioneer Financial Services Co.
304 N. Main St.
Rockford, IL 61101
Phone: 815-987-5000 Fax: 815-987-9853
CEO: Peter W. Nauert
CFO: Gregory W. Peternell
1991 Sales: $708 million Employees: —
Symbol: PFS Exchange: NYSE
Industry: Insurance - accident & health

Pioneer Group, Inc.
60 State St.
Boston, MA 02109
Phone: 617-742-7825 Fax: 617-227-9826
CEO: John F. Cogan, Jr.
CFO: William H. Keough
1991 Sales: $81 million Employees: —
Symbol: PIOG Exchange: NASDAQ
Industry: Financial - investment management

Pioneer Hi-Bred International, Inc.
400 Locust, Ste. 700
Des Moines, IA 50309
Phone: 515-245-3500 Fax: 512-245-3650
CEO: Thomas N. Urban
CFO: Jerry L. Chicoine
1991 Sales: $1,125 million Employees: 4,768
Symbol: PHYB Exchange: NASDAQ
Industry: Agricultural operations

Pioneer Software, Inc.
5540 Centerview Dr., #324
Raleigh, NC 27606
Phone: 919-859-2220 Fax: 919-859-9334
CEO: Richard Holcomb
CFO: Lee N. Palles
1992 Sales: $7.5 million Employees: 92
Ownership: Privately held
Industry: Computers - software

Pioneer-Standard Electronics, Inc.
4800 E. 131st St.
Cleveland, OH 44105
Phone: 216-587-3600 Fax: 216-587-3906
CEO: Preston B. Heller, Jr.
CFO: John V. Goodger
1992 Sales: $362 million Employees: 905
Symbol: PIOS Exchange: NASDAQ
Industry: Electronics - parts distribution

Piper Jaffray Inc.
222 S. Ninth St.
Minneapolis, MN 55402
Phone: 612-342-6000 Fax: 612-342-6996
CEO: Addison L. Piper
CFO: Charles N. Hayssen
1991 Sales: $294 million Employees: 1,928
Symbol: PJC Exchange: NYSE
Industry: Financial - investment bankers

Pirelli Armstrong Tire Corporation
500 Sargent Dr.
New Haven, CT 06536
Phone: 203-784-2200 Fax: 203-784-2579
CEO: Giuseppe Morchio
CFO: —
1991 Sales: $8,732 million Employees: 64,854
Parent: Pirella SpA
Industry: Tires & cables

Pitney Bowes Inc.
1 Elmcroft
Stamford, CT 06926
Phone: 203-356-5000 Fax: 203-351-6303
CEO: George B. Harvey
CFO: Carmine F. Adimando
1992 Sales: $3,434 million Employees: 29,421
Symbol: PBI Exchange: NYSE
Industry: Office equipment & supplies - mailing & copier systems, facsimile machines

Pitt-Des Moines, Inc.
3400 Grand Ave.
Pittsburgh, PA 15225
Phone: 412-331-3000 Fax: Call co. operator
CEO: W. W. McKee
CFO: R. A. Byers
1991 Sales: $392 million Employees: 2,285
Symbol: PDM Exchange: AMEX
Industry: Construction - heavy

Pittston Co.
100 First Stamford Place
Stamford, CT 06912
Phone: 203-978-5200 Fax: 203-978-5210
CEO: Joseph C. Farrell
CFO: David L. Marshall
1992 Sales: $2,073 million Employees: 20,100
Symbol: PCO Exchange: NYSE
Industry: Coal

Pittway Corp.
200 S. Wacker Dr., Ste. 700
Chicago, IL 60606
Phone: 312-831-1070 Fax: 312-831-0808
CEO: King Harris
CFO: Paul R. Gauvreau
1991 Sales: $982 million Employees: 8,300
Symbol: PRY Exchange: AMEX
Industry: Diversified operations - burglar & fire alarms, publishing, real estate

Placid Oil Co.
3800 Thanksgiving Tower
Dallas, TX 75201
Phone: 214-880-1000 Fax: 214-880-1185
CEO: Jerry R. Wright
CFO: Walter V. Fraker
1991 Sales: $500 million Employees: 591
Ownership: Privately held
Industry: Oil & gas - US exploration & production

Plains Petroleum Co.
12596 W. Bayaud Ave., Ste. 400
Lakewood, CO 80228
Phone: 303-969-9325 Fax: 303-969-3157
CEO: James A. Miller
CFO: Darrel Reed
1991 Sales: $59 million Employees: 98
Symbol: PLP Exchange: NYSE
Industry: Oil & gas - US exploration & production

Plains Resources Inc.
1600 Smith St., Ste. 1500
Houston, TX 77002
Phone: 713-654-1414 Fax: 713-654-1523
CEO: Greg L. Armstrong
CFO: Greg L. Armstrong
1991 Sales: $79 million Employees: 100
Symbol: PLX Exchange: AMEX
Industry: Oil & gas - US exploration & production

Plasti-Line, Inc.
623 E. Emory Rd.
Powell, TN 37849
Phone: 615-938-1511 Fax: 615-947-8431
CEO: James R. Martin
CFO: Teresa W. Ayers
1991 Sales: $72 million Employees: 719
Symbol: SIGN Exchange: NASDAQ
Industry: Advertising

Plastronics Plus
2735 Main
E. Troy, WI 53120
Phone: 414-642-6500 Fax: 414-642-6507
CEO: Chris Hubertz
CFO: Chris Hubertz
1991 Sales: $5 million Employees: 80
Ownership: Privately held
Industry: Rubber & plastic products - custom plastic injection molding

PLATINUM technology, inc.
555 Waters Edge Dr., Ste. 200
Lombard, IL 60148
Phone: 708-620-5000 Fax: 708-691-0710
CEO: Andrew J. Filipowski
CFO: Michael P. Cullinane
1991 Sales: $29 million Employees: 163
Symbol: PLAT Exchange: NASDAQ
Industry: Computers - system software

Playboy Enterprises, Inc.
680 N. Lake Shore Dr.
Chicago, IL 60611
Phone: 312-751-8000 Fax: 312-751-2818
CEO: Christie Hefner
CFO: David I. Chemerow
1992 Sales: $194 million Employees: 637
Symbol: PLAA Exchange: NYSE
Industry: Publishing - periodicals

PLC Systems, Inc.
113 Cedar St., Ste. S-2
Milford, MA 01737
Phone: 508-478-5991 Fax: —
CEO: Robert I. Rudko
CFO: Patricia L. Murphy
1992 Sales: — Employees: 34
Symbol: PLC Exchange: AMEX
Industry: Lasers - systems & components

Pleasant Co.
8400 Fairway Pl.
Middleton, WI 53562
Phone: 608-836-4848 Fax: 608-836-1999
CEO: Pleasant Rowland
CFO: Pleasant Rowland
1991 Sales: $64 million Employees: 280
Ownership: Privately held
Industry: Children's products

Plenum Publishing Corp.
233 Spring St.
New York, NY 10013
Phone: 212-620-8000 Fax: 212-463-0742
CEO: Martin E. Tash
CFO: Ghanshyam A. Patel
1991 Sales: $53 million Employees: 320
Symbol: PLEN Exchange: NASDAQ
Industry: Publishing - books

Plexus Corp.
55 Jewelers Park Dr.
Neenah, WI 54956
Phone: 414-722-3451 Fax: 414-722-3220
CEO: Peter Strandwitz
CFO: Thomas N. Turriff
1991 Sales: $120 million Employees: 1,450
Symbol: PLXS Exchange: NASDAQ
Industry: Electrical products & related test equipment

PLM International, Inc.
One Market Plaza, Ste. 900
San Francisco, CA 94111
Phone: 415-989-1860 Fax: 415-882-0860
CEO: Robert N. Tidball
CFO: David P. Jones
1991 Sales: $67 million Employees: 241
Symbol: PLM Exchange: AMEX
Industry: Leasing

Plum Creek Timber Co., L.P.
999 Third Ave., Ste. 2300
Seattle, WA 98104
Phone: 206-467-3600 Fax: 206-467-3795
CEO: David D. Leland
CFO: Rick R. Holley
1991 Sales: $390 million Employees: 1,750
Symbol: PCL Exchange: NYSE
Industry: Building products - wood

Ply Gem Industries, Inc.
777 Third Ave., 30th Fl.
New York, NY 10017
Phone: 212-832-1550 Fax: 212-888-0472
CEO: Jeffrey S. Silverman
CFO: Stanford Zeisel
1991 Sales: $562 million Employees: 3,400
Symbol: PGI Exchange: AMEX
Industry: Building products - wood

Plymouth Rubber Co., Inc.
104 Revere St.
Canton, MA 02021
Phone: 617-828-0220 Fax: 617-828-6041
CEO: Maurice J. Hamilburg
CFO: Duane E. Wheeler
1991 Sales: $40 million Employees: 325
Symbol: PLRB Exchange: AMEX
Industry: Rubber & plastic products

PMC Inc.
12243 Branford St.
Sun Valley, CA 91352
Phone: 818-896-1101 Fax: 818-897-4087
CEO: Philip Kamins
CFO: Lori M. Johnson
1991 Sales: $957 million Employees: 3,500
Ownership: Privately held
Industry: Chemicals - plastic, specialty & foam

PNC Bank Corp
Fifth Ave. and Wood St., 30th Fl.
Pittsburgh, PA 15222
Phone: 412-762-2000 Fax: 412-762-6238
CEO: Thomas H. O'Brien
CFO: Walter E. Gregg, Jr.
1992 Sales: $4,106 million Employees: 16,900
Symbol: PNC Exchange: NYSE
Industry: Banks - Northeast

Poe & Associates, Inc.
702 N. Franklin St.
Tampa, FL 33602
Phone: 813-222-4100 Fax: 813-223-5874
CEO: William F. Poe
CFO: Robert P. Cuthbert
1991 Sales: $49 million Employees: 600
Symbol: POEA Exchange: NASDAQ
Industry: Insurance - brokerage

Pogo Producing Co.
5 Greenway Plaza, Ste. 2700
Houston, TX 77046
Phone: 713-297-5000 Fax: 713-297-5100
CEO: Paul B. Van Wagenen
CFO: D. Stephen Slack
1991 Sales: $121 million Employees: 98
Symbol: PPP Exchange: NYSE
Industry: Oil & gas - US exploration & production

Polaris Industries Partners L.P.
2424 S. 130th Circle
Omaha, NE 68144
Phone: 800-255-1345 Fax: 402-330-8688
CEO: W. Hall Wendel, Jr.
CFO: Michael Malone
1991 Sales: $298 million Employees: 1,100
Symbol: SNO Exchange: AMEX
Industry: Automotive manufacturing - snowmobiles & all-terrain vehicles

Polaroid Corp.
549 Technology Square
Cambridge, MA 02139
Phone: 617-577-2000 Fax: 617-577-5618
CEO: I. MacAllister Booth
CFO: William J. O'Neill, Jr.
1992 Sales: $2,152 million Employees: 12,003
Symbol: PRD Exchange: NYSE
Industry: Photographic equipment & supplies - cameras & film, medical imaging systems

Policy Management Systems Corp.
PO Box 10
Columbia, SC 29202
Phone: 803-735-4000 Fax: 803-735-5544
CEO: G. Larry Wilson
CFO: Robert L. Gresham
1991 Sales: $415 million Employees: 4,403
Symbol: PMS Exchange: NYSE
Industry: Computers - insurance industry software & services

Polifly Financial Corp.
730 River Rd.
New Milford, NJ 07646
Phone: 201-261-6900 Fax: —
CEO: Joseph S. Paparatto
CFO: Peter M. Levine
1991 Sales: $50 million Employees: 139
Symbol: PFLY Exchange: NASDAQ
Industry: Financial - savings and loans

Polk Audio, Inc.
5601 Metro Dr.
Baltimore, MD 21215
Phone: 410-358-3600 Fax: 410-764-5266
CEO: George M. Klopfer
CFO: Gary B. Davis
1992 Sales: $28 million Employees: 157
Symbol: POLK Exchange: NASDAQ
Industry: Audio & video home products

Polo Ralph Lauren Corp.
650 Madison Ave.
New York, NY 10022
Phone: 212-318-7000 Fax: 212-888-5780
CEO: Ralph Lauren
CFO: Michael J. Newman
1991 Sales: $1,700 million Employees: 3,000
Ownership: Privately held
Industry: Apparel, home furnishings & accessories

PolyMedica Industries, Inc.
2 Constitution Way
Woburn, MA 01801
Phone: 617-933-2020 Fax: —
CEO: Steven J. Lee
CFO: Eric G. Walters
1992 Sales: $2.8 million Employees: 38
Symbol: POLY Exchange: NASDAQ
Industry: Medical products

Polyphase Corp.
175 Commerce Dr.
Ft. Washington, PA 19034
Phone: 215-643-6950 Fax: 215-643-5237
CEO: P. Stevens
CFO: K. A. Harper
1991 Sales: $7.6 million Employees: 145
Symbol: PLY Exchange: AMEX
Industry: Electrical products - transformers & communications filters

Pomeroy Computer Resources, Inc.
1840 Airport Exchange Blvd., Ste. 240
Erlanger, KY 45246
Phone: 606-282-7111 Fax: 606-283-8281
CEO: David B. Pomeroy
CFO: Edwin S. Weinstein
1991 Sales: $54 million Employees: 222
Symbol: PMRY Exchange: NASDAQ
Industry: Computers - retail & wholesale

Pool Energy Services Co.
10375 Richmond Ave.
Houston, TX 77042
Phone: 713-954-3000 Fax: 713-954-3319
CEO: James T. Jongebloed
CFO: Ernest J. Spillard
1991 Sales: $225 million Employees: 3,916
Symbol: PESC Exchange: NASDAQ
Industry: Oil & gas - field services

Pope Resources
PO Box 1780
Poulsbo, WA 98370
Phone: 206-697-6626 Fax: —
CEO: George H. Folquet
CFO: Thomas M. Ringo
1991 Sales: $27 million Employees: 68
Symbol: POPEZ Exchange: NASDAQ
Industry: Agricultural operations

Pope & Talbot, Inc.
1500 SW First Ave.
Portland, OR 97201
Phone: 503-228-9161 Fax: 503-220-2755
CEO: Peter T. Pope
CFO: Carlos M. Lamadrid
1991 Sales: $502 million Employees: 3,000
Symbol: POP Exchange: NYSE
Industry: Paper & paper products

Porta Systems Corp.
575 Underhill Blvd.
Syosset, NY 11791
Phone: 516-364-9300 Fax: 516-682-4655
CEO: Vincent F. Santulli
CFO: Michael A. Tancredi
1991 Sales: $95 million Employees: 966
Symbol: PSI Exchange: AMEX
Industry: Telecommunications equipment

Portage Industries Corp.
1325 Adams St.
Portage, WI 53901
Phone: 608-742-7123 Fax: 608-742-5707
CEO: John A. Becker
CFO: Bertren D. Figi
1991 Sales: $24 million Employees: —
Symbol: PTG Exchange: AMEX
Industry: Rubber & plastic products

Portec, Inc.
300 Windsor Dr.
Oak Brook, IL 60521
Phone: 708-573-4600 Fax: 708-573-4604
CEO: Michael T. Yonker
CFO: Nancy A. Dedert
1991 Sales: $65 million Employees: 499
Symbol: POR Exchange: NYSE
Industry: Diversified operations - construction & railroad equipment, materials handling

Portland General Corp.
101 SW Salmon St., Ste. 1000
Portland, OR 97204
Phone: 503-464-8000 Fax: 503-464-2233
CEO: Ken L. Harrison
CFO: C. D. Hobbs
1991 Sales: $890 million Employees: 3,256
Symbol: PGN Exchange: NYSE
Industry: Utility - electric power

Portsmouth Bank Shares, Inc.
PO Box 6700
Portsmouth, NH 03802
Phone: 603-436-6630 Fax: —
CEO: Robert W. Simpson
CFO: Robert W. Simpson
1991 Sales: $23 million Employees: 59
Symbol: POBS Exchange: NASDAQ
Industry: Banks - Northeast

Posi-Clean Corp.
3301 Chapline St.
Wheeling, WV 26003
Phone: 304-233-6282 Fax: 304-233-4319
CEO: William H. Blair
CFO: Craig Deemer
1991 Sales: $2 million Employees: 28
Ownership: Privately held
Industry: Industrial processing - engine oil coolers & heat exchangers

Possis Corp.
750 Pennsylvania Ave. South
Minneapolis, MN 55426
Phone: 612-545-1471 Fax: 612-545-5670
CEO: Zinon C. Possis
CFO: Thomas E. Bower
1991 Sales: $8.3 million Employees: 125
Symbol: POSS Exchange: NASDAQ
Industry: Diversified operations - medical products, waterjet equipment

Potamkin Manhattan Leasing Corp.
787 Eleventh Ave.
New York, NY 10019
Phone: 212-603-7231 Fax: 212-603-7034
CEO: Victor Potamkin
CFO: Lou Turco
1991 Sales: $789 million Employees: 2,000
Ownership: Privately held
Industry: Retail - auto dealership, communications

Potlatch Corp.
One Maritime Plaza, Ste. 2400
San Francisco, CA 94111
Phone: 415-576-8800 Fax: 415-576-8840
CEO: Richard B. Madden
CFO: George E. Pfautsch
1992 Sales: $1,327 million Employees: 7,400
Symbol: PCH Exchange: NYSE
Industry: Paper & paper products

Potomac Electric Power Co.
1900 Pennsylvania Ave. NW
Washington, DC 20068
Phone: 202-872-2000 Fax: 202-872-2216
CEO: Edward F. Mitchell
CFO: H. Lowell Davis
1992 Sales: $1,602 million Employees: 5,157
Symbol: POM Exchange: NYSE
Industry: Utility - electric power

Poughkeepsie Savings Bank, FSB
249 Main Mall
Poughkeepsie, NY 12601
Phone: 914-431-6200 Fax: —
CEO: Joseph B. Tockarshewsky
CFO: Stephen R. Brown
1992 Sales: — Employees: —
Symbol: PKPS Exchange: NASDAQ
Industry: Financial - savings and loans

Powell Industries, Inc.
8550 Mosley Rd.
Houston, TX 77075
Phone: 713-944-6900 Fax: 713-947-4453
CEO: Thomas W. Powell
CFO: J. F. Ahart
1991 Sales: $147 million Employees: 808
Symbol: POWL Exchange: NASDAQ
Industry: Machinery - electrical

Powerfood Inc.
1442 A Walnut St.
Berkeley, CA 94709
Phone: 510-843-1330 Fax: 510-843-1446
CEO: Brian Maxwell
CFO: Jennifer Maxwell
1991 Sales: $10 million Employees: 56
Ownership: Privately held
Industry: Food - sports energy bar

PPG Industries, Inc.
One PPG Place
Pittsburgh, PA 15272
Phone: 412-434-3131 Fax: 412-434-2448
CEO: Vincent A. Sarni
CFO: Raymond W. LeBoeuf
1992 Sales: $5,814 million Employees: 33,700
Symbol: PPG Exchange: NYSE
Industry: Chemicals - diversified, glass, coatings & resins, biomedical products

PPOM
28588 Northwestern Hwy. #380
Southfield, MI 48034
Phone: 313-357-7766 Fax: 313-357-3169
CEO: Richard Rogel
CFO: Naomi Ashel
1991 Sales: $12 million Employees: 115
Ownership: Privately held
Industry: Medical services - preferred provider programs

Pratt Hotel Corp.
13455 Noel Rd., LB 48
Dallas, TX 75240
Phone: 214-386-9777 Fax: 214-386-7411
CEO: Jack E. Pratt
CFO: Albert J. Cohen
1991 Sales: $268 million Employees: 3,100
Symbol: PHC Exchange: AMEX
Industry: Hotels & motels

Pratt & Lambert, Inc.
75 Tonawanda St.
Buffalo, NY 14207
Phone: 716-873-6000 Fax: 716-877-9646
CEO: Joseph J. Castiglia
CFO: James R. Boldt
1991 Sales: $239 million Employees: 1,578
Symbol: PM Exchange: AMEX
Industry: Paints & allied products

Praxair, Inc.
39 Old Ridgebury Rd.
Danbury, CT 06817
Phone: 203-794-2000 Fax: Call co. operator
CEO: H. W. Lichtenberger
CFO: J. A. Clerico
1992 Sales: $2,604 million Employees: 19,992
Symbol: PX Exchange: NYSE
Industry: Industrial gases

Pre-Paid Legal Services, Inc.
321 E. Main St.
Ada, OK 74820
Phone: 405-436-1234 Fax: 405-436-7409
CEO: Harland C. Stonecipher
CFO: Harland C. Stonecipher
1991 Sales: $21 million Employees: 90
Symbol: PPD Exchange: AMEX
Industry: Business services - legal service contracts

Precision Aerotech, Inc.
7777 Fay Ave., Ste. 120
La Jolla, CA 92037
Phone: 619-456-2992 Fax: 619-456-3809
CEO: Richard W. Detweiler
CFO: Steven R. Greene
1992 Sales: $51 million Employees: 467
Symbol: PAR Exchange: AMEX
Industry: Machine tools & related products

Precision Castparts Corp.
4600 S.E. Harney Dr.
Portland, OR 97206
Phone: 503-777-3881 Fax: 503-777-7632
CEO: William C. McCormick
CFO: William D. Larsson
1992 Sales: $583 million Employees: 6,372
Symbol: PCP Exchange: NYSE
Industry: Aerospace - aircraft equipment

Precision Standard, Inc.
1943 50th St.
Birmingham, AL 35212
Phone: 205-591-3009 Fax: 205-595-6631
CEO: Matthew L. Gold
CFO: Walter M. Moede
1991 Sales: $137 million Employees: 2,224
Symbol: PCSNC Exchange: NASDAQ
Industry: Aerospace - aircraft equipment

Preferred Health Care Ltd.
15 River Rd., Ste. 300
Wilton, CT 06897
Phone: 203-762-0993 Fax: 203-834-9587
CEO: David J. McDonnell
CFO: James T. Buonincontri
1991 Sales: $40 million Employees: 598
Symbol: PY Exchange: AMEX
Industry: Business services - healthcare administration & advisory services

Premark International, Inc.
1717 Deerfield Rd.
Deerfield, IL 60015
Phone: 708-405-6000 Fax: 708-405-6013
CEO: Warren L. Batts
CFO: Lawrence B. Skatoff
1992 Sales: $2,946 million Employees: 24,000
Symbol: PMI Exchange: NYSE
Industry: Diversified operations - plastic containers, food equipment, consumer & decorative products

Premier Anesthesia, Inc.
2300 Peachford Rd.
Atlanta, GA 30338
Phone: 404-458-4842 Fax: —
CEO: R. D. Ballard
CFO: Linda S. Hammock
1991 Sales: $40 million Employees: 103
Symbol: PRAN Exchange: NASDAQ
Industry: Medical services

Premier Bancorp, Inc.
451 Florida St.
Baton Rouge, LA 70801
Phone: 504-389-4011 Fax: 504-334-7213
CEO: G. Lee Griffin
CFO: R. Neil Williams
1991 Sales: $376 million Employees: 2,731
Symbol: PRBC Exchange: NASDAQ
Industry: Banks - Southeast

Premier Bankshares Corp.
201 W. Main St.
Tazewell, VA 24651
Phone: 703-988-7145 Fax: 216-391-8327
CEO: Jack P. Chambers
CFO: Jack P. Chambers
1991 Sales: $42 million Employees: 239
Symbol: PBKC Exchange: NASDAQ
Industry: Banks - Midwest

Premier Financial Services, Inc.
27 W. Main St.
Freeport, IL 60132
Phone: 815-233-3671 Fax: —
CEO: Richard L. Geach
CFO: David L. Murray
1991 Sales: $31 million Employees: 251
Symbol: PREM Exchange: NASDAQ
Industry: Banks - Midwest

indicates company is in *Hoover's Handbook of American Business*

indicates company is in *Hoover's Handbook of World Business*; sales and employee numbers are for parent company.

Premier Industrial Corp.
4500 Euclid Ave.
Cleveland, OH 44103
Phone: 216-391-8300 Fax: 216-391-8327
CEO: Morton L. Mandel
CFO: Philip S. Sims
1992 Sales: $663 million Employees: 4,400
Symbol: PRE Exchange: NYSE
Industry: Electronics - parts distribution

Premiere Merchandising, Inc.
811 W. Arbor Vitae
Inglewood, CA 90301
Phone: 310-410-4010 Fax: 310-410-2916
CEO: Brian Shniderson
CFO: Greg M. Klein
1992 Sales: $7.9 million Employees: 12
Ownership: Privately held
Industry: Business services - promotional & marketing

Premiere Radio Networks, Inc.
6255 Sunset Blvd., Ste. 2203
Hollywood, CA 90028
Phone: 213-467-2346 Fax: —
CEO: Stephen C. Lehman
CFO: Robert W. Crawford
1991 Sales: $9.6 million Employees: 42
Symbol: PRNI Exchange: NASDAQ
Industry: Leisure & recreational products

Presidential Life Corp.
69 Lydecker St.
Nyack, NY 10960
Phone: 914-358-2300 Fax: 914-332-4573
CEO: Herbert Kurz
CFO: Charles Fausel
1991 Sales: $201 million Employees: —
Symbol: PLFE Exchange: NASDAQ
Industry: Insurance - life

Presidio Corporation, The
5100-J Philadelphia Way
Lanham, MD 20706
Phone: 301-459-2200 Fax: 301-459-2201
CEO: Babielyn Hernandez Trabbic
CFO: Babielyn Hernandez Trabbic
1991 Sales: $4.1 million Employees: 15
Ownership: Privately held
Industry: Computers - computer systems, integration, products & services

Presidio Oil Co.
3131 Turtle Creek Blvd., Ste. 400
Dallas, TX 75219
Phone: 214-528-5898 Fax: 214-528-2160
CEO: George P. Giard, Jr.
CFO: Lon McCain
1991 Sales: $144 million Employees: 237
Symbol: PRSA Exchange: AMEX
Industry: Oil & gas - US exploration & production

Presley Companies
19 Corporate Plaza Dr.
Newport Beach, CA 92660
Phone: 714-640-6400 Fax: 714-640-1643
CEO: Wade H. Cable
CFO: David M. Siegel
1991 Sales: $173 million Employees: 429
Symbol: PDC Exchange: NYSE
Industry: Building - residential & commercial

Preston Corp.
151 Easton Blvd.
Preston, MD 21655
Phone: 410-673-7151 Fax: 410-673-2644
CEO: William B. Potter
CFO: J. Sean Callahan
1991 Sales: $565 million Employees: 8,895
Symbol: PTRK Exchange: NASDAQ
Industry: Transportation - truck

Price Co., The
4649 Morena Blvd.
San Diego, CA 92117
Phone: 619-581-4600 Fax: 619-581-4773
CEO: Robert E. Price
CFO: Robert Hunt
1992 Sales: $7,642 million Employees: 19,142
Symbol: PCLB Exchange: NASDAQ
Industry: Retail - discount clubs

Price Communications Corp.
45 Rockefeller Plaza, Ste. 3201
New York, NY 10020
Phone: 212-757-5600 Fax: 212-397-3755
CEO: Robert Price
CFO: Kim I. Pressman
1991 Sales: $48 million Employees: 430
Symbol: PR Exchange: AMEX
Industry: Broadcasting - radio & TV

Price Stern Sloan, Inc.
360 N. La Cienega Blvd.
Los Angeles, CA 90048
Phone: 213-657-6100 Fax: 213-855-8993
CEO: L. Lawrence Sloan
CFO: Dan P. Reavis
1991 Sales: $37 million Employees: 164
Symbol: PSSP Exchange: NASDAQ
Industry: Publishing - books

Price Waterhouse
1251 Sixth Ave.
New York, NY 10020
Phone: 212-819-5000 Fax: 212-790-6620
CEO: Shaun F. O'Malley
CFO: Thomas H. Chamberlain
1992 Sales: $3,800 million Employees: 49,000
Ownership: Privately held
Industry: Business services - accounting & consulting

Pricor Inc.
805 S. Church St.
Murfreesboro, TN 37130
Phone: 615-896-3100 Fax: 615-896-5068
CEO: Hubert L. McCullough
CFO: William J. Ballard
1992 Sales: $30 million Employees: 894
Symbol: PRCO Exchange: NASDAQ
Industry: Protection - safety equipment & services

Pride Companies, L.P.
500 Chestnut, Ste. 1300
Abilene, TX 79602
Phone: 915-674-8000 Fax: —
CEO: R. J. Schumacher
CFO: Brad Stephens
1992 Sales: — Employees: —
Symbol: PRF Exchange: NYSE
Industry: Oil & gas - production & pipeline

Pride Petroleum Services, Inc.
3040 Post Oak Blvd., Ste. 1500
Houston, TX 77056
Phone: 713-871-8567 Fax: 713-871-1836
CEO: Ray H. Tolson
CFO: Eugene C. Fowler
1991 Sales: $112 million Employees: 1,950
Symbol: PRDE Exchange: NASDAQ
Industry: Oil & gas - field services

Prima Energy Corp.
1801 Broadway, Ste. 500
Denver, CO 80202
Phone: 303-297-2100 Fax: —
CEO: Richard H. Lewis
CFO: Richard H. Lewis
1992 Sales: $10.1 million Employees: 51
Symbol: PENG Exchange: NASDAQ
Industry: Oil & gas - US exploration & production

Primark Corp.
8251 Greensboro Dr., Ste. 700
McLean, VA 22102
Phone: 703-790-7600 Fax: 703-790-7677
CEO: Joseph E. Kasputys
CFO: Steven H. Curran
1991 Sales: $153 million Employees: 2,950
Symbol: PMK Exchange: NYSE
Industry: Diversified operations - leasing services, ground transport, mortgage banking

Prime Bancorp, Inc.
6425 Rising Sun Ave.
Philadelphia, PA 19111
Phone: 215-742-5300 Fax: —
CEO: Erwin T. Straw
CFO: Thomas P. Kirwin
1991 Sales: $18 million Employees: 120
Symbol: PSAB Exchange: NASDAQ
Industry: Banks - Northeast

Prime Bancshares, Inc.
101 W. Ponce de Leon Ave.
Decatur, GA 30030
Phone: 404-377-0211 Fax: 404-373-8750
CEO: Darrell D. Pittard
CFO: Dale E. Johnson
1991 Sales: $64 million Employees: —
Symbol: PMB Exchange: AMEX
Industry: Banks - Southeast

Prime Hospitality Corp.
700 Route 46 East
Fairfield, NJ 07004
Phone: 201-882-1010 Fax: 201-808-7733
CEO: John Elwood
CFO: Michael J. Clarke
1992 Sales: — Employees: —
Symbol: PDQ Exchange: NYSE
Industry: Hotels & motels

Prime Medical Services, Inc.
1301 S. Capital of Texas Hwy., Ste. A300
Austin, TX 78746
Phone: 512-328-2892 Fax: 512-328-8510
CEO: Jackie C. Majors
CFO: Cheryl L. McLeod
1991 Sales: $13 million Employees: 168
Symbol: PMSI Exchange: NASDAQ
Industry: Business services - rehabilitation center management

Primerica Corp.
65 E. 55th St.
New York, NY 10022
Phone: 212-891-8900 Fax: 212-891-8910
CEO: Sanford I. Weill
CFO: James Dimon
1992 Sales: $5,096 million Employees: 16,500
Symbol: PA Exchange: NYSE
Industry: Financial - insurance & brokerage services

Princeton Diagnostic Laboratories of America
100 Corporate Court
South Plainfield, NJ 07080
Phone: 908-769-8500 Fax: 908-769-2444
CEO: Carlton E. Turner
CFO: Frank M. Thiry
1991 Sales: $6.8 million Employees: 70
Symbol: PDA Exchange: AMEX
Industry: Medical services - psychiatric testing

Princeton National Bancorp, Inc.
606 S. Main St.
Princeton, IL 61356
Phone: 815-875-4444 Fax: —
CEO: D. E. Van Ordstrand
CFO: Dennis B. Guthrie
1991 Sales: $24 million Employees: 184
Symbol: PNBC Exchange: NASDAQ
Industry: Banks - Midwest

indicates company is in *Hoover's Handbook of American Business*

indicates company is in *Hoover's Handbook of World Business*; sales and employee numbers are for parent company.

Printronix, Inc.
17500 Cartwright Rd.
Irvine, CA 92713
Phone: 714-863-1900 Fax: 714-660-8682
CEO: Robert A. Kleist
CFO: George L. Harwood
1992 Sales: $89 million Employees: 920
Symbol: PTNX Exchange: NASDAQ
Industry: Computers - printers

Prism Entertainment Corp.
1888 Century Park East, Ste. 350
Los Angeles, CA 90067
Phone: 213-277-3270 Fax: 213-203-8036
CEO: Barry Collier
CFO: Earl Rosenstein
1991 Sales: $10.6 million Employees: 24
Symbol: PRZ Exchange: AMEX
Industry: Motion pictures & services

Procter & Gamble Co., The
One Procter & Gamble Plaza
Cincinnati, OH 45202
Phone: 513-983-1100 Fax: 513-562-4500
CEO: Edwin L. Artzt
CFO: Erik G. Nelson
1992 Sales: $30,368 million Employees: 106,000
Symbol: PG Exchange: NYSE
Industry: Soap & cleaning preparations, personal care products, food & beverages

ProCyte Corp.
12040 115th Ave. NE
Kirkland, WA 98034
Phone: 206-820-4548 Fax: 206-820-4111
CEO: Joseph Ashley
CFO: Joseph Ashley
1991 Sales: $0.1 million Employees: 38
Symbol: PRCY Exchange: NASDAQ
Industry: Drugs

Production Operators Corp.
11302 Tanner Rd.
Houston, TX 77041
Phone: 713-466-0980 Fax: 713-896-2528
CEO: Carl W. Knobloch, Jr.
CFO: Ralph E. Wilgus
1991 Sales: $66 million Employees: 388
Symbol: PROP Exchange: NASDAQ
Industry: Oil & gas - field services

Professional Bancorp, Inc.
606 Broadway
Santa Monica, CA 90401
Phone: 310-458-1521 Fax: —
CEO: J. W. Kovner
CFO: D. S. Rader
1991 Sales: $17 million Employees: 85
Symbol: MDB Exchange: AMEX
Industry: Banks - West

Proffitt's, Inc.
115 N. Calderwood St.
Alcoa, TN 37701
Phone: 615-983-7000 Fax: 615-982-0690
CEO: R. Brad Martin
CFO: Julia A. Bentley
1991 Sales: $109 million Employees: 1,425
Symbol: PRFT Exchange: NASDAQ
Industry: Retail - regional department stores

Progress Financial Corp.
600 W. Germantown Pike
Plymouth Meeting, PA 19462
Phone: 215-825-8800 Fax: —
CEO: W. Kirk Wycoff
CFO: Gerald P. Plush
1991 Sales: $29 million Employees: 111
Symbol: PFNC Exchange: NASDAQ
Industry: Financial - savings and loans

Progress Software Corp.
5 Oak Park Dr.
Bedford, MA 01730
Phone: 617-275-4500 Fax: 617-275-4595
CEO: Joseph W. Alsop
CFO: Joni M. Mace
1991 Sales: $58 million Employees: 452
Symbol: PRGS Exchange: NASDAQ
Industry: Computers - database management software

Progressive Bank, Inc.
Akindale Rd.
Pawling, NY 12564
Phone: 914-855-1333 Fax: —
CEO: Peter Van Kleeck
CFO: Robert J. Soraci
1991 Sales: $58 million Employees: 241
Symbol: PSBK Exchange: NASDAQ
Industry: Financial - savings and loans

Progressive Corp.
6000 Parkland Blvd.
Mayfield Heights, OH 44124
Phone: 216-464-8000 Fax: 216-446-7097
CEO: Peter B. Lewis
CFO: Daniel R. Lewis
1992 Sales: $1,739 million Employees: —
Symbol: PGR Exchange: NYSE
Industry: Insurance - property & casualty

ProGroup, Inc.
6201 Mountain View Rd.
Ooltewah, TN 37363
Phone: 615-238-5890 Fax: 615-238-9831
CEO: Richard E. Wenz
CFO: Mark D. Renfree
1991 Sales: $33 million Employees: 646
Symbol: PRGR Exchange: NASDAQ
Industry: Leisure & recreational products - golf equipment & apparel

Proler International Corp.
7501 Wallisville Rd.
Houston, TX 77020
Phone: 713-675-2281 Fax: 713-675-5968
CEO: Herman Proler
CFO: David A. Juengel
1991 Sales: $111 million Employees: 328
Symbol: PS Exchange: NYSE
Industry: Metal processing & fabrication

Promus Companies Inc., The
1023 Cherry Rd.
Memphis, TN 38117
Phone: 901-762-8600 Fax: 901-762-8637
CEO: Michael D. Rose
CFO: Charles A. Ledsinger, Jr.
1992 Sales: $1,113 million Employees: 23,000
Symbol: PRI Exchange: NYSE
Industry: Hotels & motels, casinos

ProNet Inc.
600 Data Dr., Ste. 100
Plano, TX 75075
Phone: 214-964-9500 Fax: 214-964-9570
CEO: Jackie R. Kimzey
CFO: Jan E. Clinger
1991 Sales: $18 million Employees: 170
Symbol: PNET Exchange: NASDAQ
Industry: Telecommunications equipment

ProServe Corp.
730 17th St. #817
Denver, CO 80202
Phone: 303-571-0900 Fax: 303-571-1144
CEO: Joseph Aragon
CFO: Larry Hanson
1991 Sales: $8.3 million Employees: 325
Ownership: Privately held
Industry: Food - institutional food services programs

Prospect Group, Inc.
667 Madison Ave.
New York, NY 10021
Phone: 212-758-8500 Fax: 212-593-6127
CEO: Gilbert H. Lamphere
CFO: Todd K. West
1992 Sales: — Employees: 10
Symbol: PROSZ Exchange: NASDAQ
Industry: Diversified operations - insurance, mushrooms, venture capital

Prospect Motors Inc.
645 Hwy. 49 & 88 North
Jackson, CA 95642
Phone: 209-223-1740 Fax: 209-223-0395
CEO: William Halvorson
CFO: Ron Caruso
1992 Sales: $1,221 million Employees: 90
Ownership: Privately held
Industry: Retail - auto dealership

Protective Life Corp.
2801 Hwy. 280 South
Birmingham, AL 35223
Phone: 205-879-9230 Fax: 205-868-3270
CEO: William J. Rushton III
CFO: Dennis R. Glass
1992 Sales: $626 million Employees: —
Symbol: PROT Exchange: NASDAQ
Industry: Insurance - life

Protein Design Labs, Inc.
2375 Garcia Ave.
Mountain View, CA 94043
Phone: 415-903-3700 Fax: 415-903-3730
CEO: Laurence Jay Korn
CFO: Harold J. Voelkek
1991 Sales: $4.4 million Employees: 44
Symbol: PDLI Exchange: NASDAQ
Industry: Biomedical & genetic products

Proteon, Inc.
9 Technology Dr.
Westborough, MA 01581
Phone: 508-898-2800 Fax: 508-366-8901
CEO: Patrick Courtin
CFO: Elliot F. Honan
1991 Sales: $95 million Employees: 464
Symbol: PTON Exchange: NASDAQ
Industry: Telecommunications equipment

Proteus Corp.
10010 Indian School Rd. NE
Albuquerque, NM 87112
Phone: 505-275-3013 Fax: 505-292-6406
CEO: Roy Martinez
CFO: Jimmy Abalos
1991 Sales: $4.9 million Employees: 79
Ownership: Privately held
Industry: Computers - systems integration products

Protocol Systems, Inc.
8500 SW Creekside Place
Beaverton, OR 97005
Phone: 503-526-8500 Fax: —
CEO: James B. Moon
CFO: Craig M. Swanson
1991 Sales: $23 million Employees: 160
Symbol: PCOL Exchange: NASDAQ
Industry: Medical instruments

Provena Foods Inc.
5010 Eucalyptus Ave.
Chino, CA 91710
Phone: 909-627-1082 Fax: —
CEO: James H. Bolton
CFO: Thomas J. Mulroney
1991 Sales: $30 million Employees: 132
Symbol: PZA Exchange: AMEX
Industry: Food - meat products

indicates company is in *Hoover's Handbook of American Business*
indicates company is in *Hoover's Handbook of World Business*; sales and employee numbers are for parent company.

Providence Energy Corp.
100 Weybosset St.
Providence, RI 02903
Phone: 401-272-5040 Fax: 401-751-0698
CEO: James H. Dodge
CFO: Robert W. Owens
1991 Sales: $169 million Employees: 711
Symbol: PVY Exchange: AMEX
Industry: Utility - gas distribution

Providence & Worcester Railroad Co.
75 Hammond St.
Worcester, MA 01610
Phone: 508-755-4000 Fax: 508-795-0748
CEO: Robert H. Eder
CFO: Robert J. Easton
1991 Sales: $16 million Employees: 130
Symbol: PWRR Exchange: NASDAQ
Industry: Transportation - rail

Provident Bancorp, Inc.
One E. Fourth St.
Cincinnati, OH 45202
Phone: 513-579-2000 Fax: 513-763-4270
CEO: Allen L. Davis
CFO: Jerry L. Grace
1991 Sales: $122 million Employees: 1,400
Symbol: PRBK Exchange: NASDAQ
Industry: Banks - Midwest

Provident Bankshares Corp.
114 E. Lexington St.
Baltimore, MD 21202
Phone: 410-281-7000 Fax: 410-281-7334
CEO: Carl W. Stearn
CFO: Harold H. Johnson III
1991 Sales: $139 million Employees: 690
Symbol: PBKS Exchange: NASDAQ
Industry: Banks - Southeast

Provident Life and Accident Ins. Co. of America
One Fountain Square
Chattanooga, TN 37402
Phone: 615-755-1011 Fax: 615-755-7013
CEO: Winston W. Walker
CFO: Thomas C. Hardy
1992 Sales: $2,867 million Employees: —
Symbol: PVB Exchange: NYSE
Industry: Insurance - accident & health

Providential Corp.
Three Embarcadero Center
San Francisco, CA 94111
Phone: 415-956-2700 Fax: —
CEO: William J. Texido
CFO: Feroze A. Waheed
1991 Sales: $4.3 million Employees: —
Symbol: PHIP Exchange: NASDAQ
Industry: Financial - mortgages & related services

Prudential Insurance Co. of America, The
751 Broad St.
Newark, NJ 07102
Phone: 201-802-6000 Fax: 201-802-6092
CEO: Robert C. Winters
CFO: Eugene M. O'Hara
1991 Sales: $50,958 million Employees: 103,284
Ownership: Privately held
Industry: Insurance - health & life

PS Group, Inc.
4370 La Jolla Village Dr., Ste. 1050
San Diego, CA 92122
Phone: 619-546-5001 Fax: 619-546-5017
CEO: George M. Shortley
CFO: Lawrence A. Guske
1991 Sales: $278 million Employees: 2,513
Symbol: PSG Exchange: NYSE
Industry: Leasing

PSI Resources, Inc.
1000 E. Main St.
Plainfield, IN 46168
Phone: 317-839-9611 Fax: 317-838-1484
CEO: James E. Rogers, Jr.
CFO: J. Wayne Leonard
1991 Sales: $1,122 million Employees: 4,162
Symbol: PIN Exchange: NYSE
Industry: Utility - electric power

PSICOR, Inc.
16818 Via del Campo Court
San Diego, CA 92127
Phone: 619-485-5599 Fax: 619-485-0612
CEO: Michael W. Dunaway
CFO: George R. Pache
1991 Sales: $67 million Employees: 476
Symbol: PCOR Exchange: NASDAQ
Industry: Medical services - personnel & equipment supply

Pubco Corp.
3830 Kelley Ave.
Cleveland, OH 44114
Phone: 216-881-5300 Fax: 216-881-8380
CEO: Robert H. Kanner
CFO: Robert H. Kanner
1991 Sales: $125 million Employees: 2,150
Symbol: PUBO Exchange: NASDAQ
Industry: Diversified operations - outerwear, sales, apparel manufacturing

Public Service Co. of Colorado
1225 17th. St.
Denver, CO 80202
Phone: 303-571-7511 Fax: 303-571-7940
CEO: Delwin D. Hock
CFO: Richard C. Kelly
1992 Sales: $1,862 million Employees: 6,719
Symbol: PSR Exchange: NYSE
Industry: Utility - electric power

Public Service Co. of New Mexico
414 Silver Ave.
Albuquerque, NM 87102
Phone: 505-848-2700 Fax: 505-848-2359
CEO: John T. Ackerman
CFO: Max H. Maerki
1991 Sales: $857 million Employees: 3,196
Symbol: PNM Exchange: NYSE
Industry: Utility - electric power

Public Service Co. of North Carolina, Inc.
400 Cox Rd.
Gastonia, NC 28054
Phone: 704-864-6731 Fax: 704-861-8966
CEO: Charles E. Zeigler, Jr.
CFO: Charles E. Zeigler, Jr.
1991 Sales: $193 million Employees: 1,186
Symbol: PSNC Exchange: NASDAQ
Industry: Utility - gas distribution

Public Service Enterprise Group Inc.
80 Park Plaza
Newark, NJ 07102
Phone: 201-430-7000 Fax: 201-430-5983
CEO: E. James Ferland
CFO: Robert C. Murray
1992 Sales: $5,357 million Employees: 13,253
Symbol: PEG Exchange: NYSE
Industry: Utility - electric power & gas power

Publicker Industries Inc.
1445 E. Putnam Ave.
Old Greenwich, CT 06870
Phone: 203-637-4500 Fax: —
CEO: David L. Herman
CFO: James J. Weis
1991 Sales: $94 million Employees: 950
Symbol: PUL Exchange: NYSE
Industry: Chemicals - specialty

Publishers Equipment Corp.
16660 Dallas Pkwy., Ste. 1100
Dallas, TX 75248
Phone: 214-931-2312 Fax: 214-931-2399
CEO: Evans Kostas
CFO: Roger R. Baier
1991 Sales: $19 million Employees: 177
Symbol: PECN Exchange: NASDAQ
Industry: Machinery - printing

Publishers Group West
4065 Hollis
Emeryville, CA 94608
Phone: 510-658-3453 Fax: 510-658-1834
CEO: Charles Winton
CFO: Randall Fleming
1992 Sales: $70 million Employees: 163
Ownership: Privately held
Industry: Wholesale distribution - books

Publix Super Markets, Inc.
1936 George Jenkins Blvd.
Lakeland, FL 33802
Phone: 813-688-1188 Fax: 813-680-5257
CEO: Howard M. Jenkins
CFO: William H. Vass
1991 Sales: $6,140 million Employees: 68,606
Ownership: Privately held
Industry: Retail - supermarkets

Pueblo International, Inc.
1300 NW 22nd St.
Pompano Beach, FL 33069
Phone: 305-977-2500 Fax: 305-973-8889
CEO: David W. Morrow
CFO: Jeffrey P. Freimark
1991 Sales: $1,132 million Employees: 11,000
Ownership: Privately held
Industry: Retail - supermarkets

Puget Sound Bancorp
1119 Pacific Ave.
Tacoma, WA 98402
Phone: 206-593-3600 Fax: 206-597-4949
CEO: W. W. Philip
CFO: Don G. Vandenheuvel
1991 Sales: $500 million Employees: 2,781
Symbol: PSNB Exchange: NASDAQ
Industry: Banks - West

Puget Sound Power & Light Co.
10608 NE 4th St.
Bellevue, WA 98004
Phone: 206-454-6363 Fax: 206-462-3307
CEO: John W. Ellis
CFO: William S. Weaver
1992 Sales: $1,025 million Employees: 2,688
Symbol: PSD Exchange: NYSE
Industry: Utility - electric power

Pulaski Furniture Corp.
One Pulaski Sq.
Pulaski, VA 24301
Phone: 703-980-7330 Fax: 703-980-0617
CEO: Bernard C. Wampler
CFO: Jason A. Gibbs
1991 Sales: $121 million Employees: 2,100
Symbol: PLFC Exchange: NASDAQ
Industry: Furniture

Pulitzer Publishing Co.
900 N. Tucker Blvd.
St. Louis, MO 63101
Phone: 314-622-7000 Fax: 314-622-7093
CEO: Michael E. Pulitzer
CFO: Ronald H. Ridgway
1991 Sales: $393 million Employees: 2,900
Symbol: PLTZ Exchange: NASDAQ
Industry: Broadcasting - radio & TV

indicates company is in *Hoover's Handbook of American Business*

indicates company is in *Hoover's Handbook of World Business*; sales and employee numbers are for parent company.

Pullman Co.
220 S. Orange Ave.
Livingston, NJ 07039
Phone: 201-535-9522 Fax: 201-535--9837
CEO: William Turner
CFO: Vince Toscano
1990 Sales: $500 million Employees: 6,200
Ownership: Privately held
Industry: Transportation - equipment & auto parts

Pulse Bancorp, Inc.
6 Jackson St.
South River, NJ 08882
Phone: 908-257-2400 Fax: —
CEO: Benjamin S. Konopacki
CFO: George T. Hornyak, Jr.
1991 Sales: $31 million Employees: 60
Symbol: PULS Exchange: NASDAQ
Industry: Financial - savings and loans

Pulse Engineering, Inc.
12220 World Trade Ctr.
San Diego, CA 92128
Phone: 619-674-8100 Fax: 619-674-8263
CEO: David R. Flowers
CFO: Dale W. Hornback
1992 Sales: $62 million Employees: 1,518
Symbol: PLSE Exchange: NASDAQ
Industry: Electrical components - data processing & telecommunications components

Pure Tech International, Inc.
100 Franklin Square Dr.
Somerset, NJ 08873
Phone: 908-271-1355 Fax: —
CEO: David Katz
CFO: David Katz
1992 Sales: $15 million Employees: 370
Symbol: PURT Exchange: NASDAQ
Industry: Pollution control equipment & services - plastic recycling

Purepac, Inc.
200 Elmora Ave.
Elizabeth, NJ 07207
Phone: 908-527-9100 Fax: 908-527-0649
CEO: Michael R.D. Ashton
CFO: Russell J. Reardon
1992 Sales: $64 million Employees: 291
Symbol: MBIO Exchange: NASDAQ
Industry: Drugs - generic

Puritan-Bennett Corp.
9401 Indian Creek Pkwy.
Overland Park, KS 66210
Phone: 913-661-0444 Fax: 913-661-0234
CEO: Burton A. Dole Jr.
CFO: Lee A. Robbins
1991 Sales: $256 million Employees: 2,418
Symbol: PBEN Exchange: NASDAQ
Industry: Medical instruments

Purity Supreme Inc.
101 Billerica Ave.
North Billerica, MA 01862
Phone: 508-663-0750 Fax: 508-671-1511
CEO: Peter J. Sodini
CFO: Bill Flyg
1991 Sales: $1,142 million Employees: 6,100
Ownership: Privately held
Industry: Retail - supermarkets

Pyramid Technology Corp.
1295 Charleston Rd.
Mountain View, CA 94039
Phone: 415-965-7200 Fax: 415-335-8208
CEO: Richard H. Lussier
CFO: Kent L. Robertson
1991 Sales: $227 million Employees: 1,193
Symbol: PYRD Exchange: NASDAQ
Industry: Computers - mini & micro

Pyxis Corp.
11425 Sorrento Valley Rd.
San Diego, CA 92121
Phone: 619-792-0966 Fax: —
CEO: Ronald R. Taylor
CFO: Gerald E. Forth
1991 Sales: $13 million Employees: 115
Symbol: PYXS Exchange: NASDAQ
Industry: Medical services - medication & supply management & control

Q-Med, Inc.
67 Walnut Ave., Ste. 403
Clark, NJ 07066
Phone: 908-381-6680 Fax: 908-815-9530
CEO: Michael W. Cox
CFO: Michael W. Cox
1991 Sales: $7.7 million Employees: 91
Symbol: QEKG Exchange: NASDAQ
Industry: Medical products

Qantas Airways
360 Post St.
San Francisco, CA 94108
Phone: 415-445-1400 Fax: 415-981-1152
CEO: Richard Porter
CFO: —
1991 Sales: $2,925 million Employees: 20,430
Parent: Qantas Airways Ltd.
Industry: Transportation - airline

QMS, Inc.
One Magnum Pass
Mobile, AL 36618
Phone: 205-633-4300 Fax: 205-633-0013
CEO: James L. Busby
CFO: Charles D. Daley
1991 Sales: $304 million Employees: 1,538
Symbol: AQM Exchange: NYSE
Industry: Computers - intelligent print controllers

Quad/Graphics
W224 N3322 DuPlainville Rd.
Pewaukee, WI 53072
Phone: 414-246-9200 Fax: 414-691-5608
CEO: Harry V. Quadracci
CFO: John Fowler
1991 Sales: $509 million Employees: 5,365
Ownership: Privately held
Industry: Printing - commercial

Quadrex Corp.
1940 NW 67th Place
Gainesville, FL 32606
Phone: 904-373-6066 Fax: 904-373-0040
CEO: William P. Derrickson
CFO: Russell J. Hammer
1991 Sales: $43 million Employees: 401
Symbol: QUAD Exchange: NASDAQ
Industry: Engineering - R&D services

Quaker Chemical Corp.
E. Elm and Lee Streets
Conshohocken, PA 19428
Phone: 215-832-4000 Fax: 215-832-4495
CEO: Peter A. Benoliel
CFO: William G. Hamilton
1991 Sales: $191 million Employees: 1,027
Symbol: QCHM Exchange: NASDAQ
Industry: Chemicals - specialty

Quaker Oats Co., The
Quaker Tower
Chicago, IL 60604
Phone: 312-222-7111 Fax: 312-222-2734
CEO: William D. Smithburg
CFO: Terry G. Westbrook
1992 Sales: $5,705 million Employees: 21,100
Symbol: OAT Exchange: NYSE
Industry: Food - cereals, pet food, beverages

Quaker State Corp.
225 Elm St.
Oil City, PA 16301
Phone: 814-676-7676 Fax: 814-676-7030
CEO: Jack W. Corn
CFO: R. Scott Keefer
1992 Sales: $724 million Employees: 4,969
Symbol: KSF Exchange: NYSE
Industry: Oil refining & marketing

Qual-Med, Inc.
720 N. Main St., Ste. 320
Pueblo, CO 81144
Phone: 719-542-0500 Fax: 719-542-4921
CEO: Malik M. Hasan
CFO: E. Keith Hovland
1991 Sales: $283 million Employees: 511
Symbol: QLMD Exchange: NASDAQ
Industry: Healthcare - outpatient & home

QUALCOMM Inc.
10555 Sorrento Valley Rd.
San Diego, CA 92121
Phone: 619-587-1121 Fax: 619-452-9096
CEO: Irwin M. Jacobs
CFO: Adelia A. Coffman
1991 Sales: $90 million Employees: 619
Symbol: QCOM Exchange: NASDAQ
Industry: Telecommunications equipment

Quality Food Centers, Inc.
10116 NE 8th St.
Bellevue, WA 98004
Phone: 206-455-3761 Fax: 206-462-2159
CEO: Stuart M. Sloan
CFO: Marc W. Evanger
1991 Sales: $395 million Employees: 2,400
Symbol: QFCI Exchange: NASDAQ
Industry: Retail - supermarkets

Quality King Distributors Inc.
2060 Ninth Ave.
Ronkonkoma, NY 11779
Phone: 516-737-5555 Fax: 516-737-3309
CEO: Dennis Barkey
CFO: Dennis Barkey
1991 Sales: $760 million Employees: 500
Ownership: Privately held
Industry: Drugs & sundries - wholesale

Quanex Corp.
1900 W. Loop South, Ste. 1500
Houston, TX 77027
Phone: 713-961-4600 Fax: 713-877-5333
CEO: Robert C. Snyder
CFO: Wayne M. Rose
1991 Sales: $589 million Employees: 2,603
Symbol: NX Exchange: NYSE
Industry: Steel - pipes & tubes

Quantum Chemical Corp.
99 Park Ave.
New York, NY 10016
Phone: 212-949-5000 Fax: 212-551-0307
CEO: John Hoyt Stookey
CFO: David W. Lodge
1992 Sales: $2,367 million Employees: 8,850
Symbol: CUE Exchange: NYSE
Industry: Chemicals - plastics

Quantum Corp.
1820 McCarthy Blvd.
Milpitas, CA 95035
Phone: 408-432-1100 Fax: 408-434-0420
CEO: William J. Miller
CFO: Joseph T. Rodgers
1992 Sales: $1,536 million Employees: 782
Symbol: QNTM Exchange: NASDAQ
Industry: Computers - rigid disk drives

indicates company is in *Hoover's Handbook of American Business*

indicates company is in *Hoover's Handbook of World Business*; sales and employee numbers are for parent company.

Quantum Health Resources, Inc.
790 The City Drive South
Orange, CA 92668
Phone: 714-750-1610 Fax: 714-750-3235
CEO: Douglas H. Stickney
CFO: Wm. James Nicol
1991 Sales: $77 million Employees: 403
Symbol: QHRI Exchange: NASDAQ
Industry: Medical services - therapy & support services

Quantum Restaurant Group, Inc.
97 Powerhouse Rd., Ste. 101
Roslyn Heights, NY 11577
Phone: 516-484-0777 Fax: 516-484-0715
CEO: Allen J. Bernstein
CFO: Thomas J. Baldwin
1991 Sales: $78 million Employees: 2,003
Symbol: QRST Exchange: NASDAQ
Industry: Retail - food & restaurants

Quarex Industries, Inc.
47-05 Metropolitan Ave.
Flushing, NY 11385
Phone: 718-821-0011 Fax: 718-381-8943
CEO: Frank Castellana
CFO: Jules L. Verner
1991 Sales: $215 million Employees: 695
Symbol: QRXI Exchange: NASDAQ
Industry: Food - wholesale

Quarterdeck Office Systems, Inc.
1901 Main St.
Santa Monica, CA 90405
Phone: 310-392-9851 Fax: 310-314-3219
CEO: Therese E. Myers
CFO: Ronald B. Hammond
1992 Sales: $44 million Employees: 302
Symbol: QDEK Exchange: NASDAQ
Industry: Computers - multi-tasking, windowing & memory management software

Quest Medical, Inc.
4103 Billy Mitchell Dr.
Dallas, TX 75244
Phone: 214-387-2740 Fax: 214-387-0501
CEO: Thomas C. Thompson
CFO: F. Robert Merrill III
1991 Sales: $10.7 million Employees: 138
Symbol: QMED Exchange: NASDAQ
Industry: Medical products - surgical refracting tapes, IV systems

Questar Corp.
180 East 100 South
Salt Lake City, UT 84111
Phone: 801-534-5000 Fax: 801-534-5166
CEO: R. D. Cash
CFO: William F. Edwards
1991 Sales: $632 million Employees: 2,610
Symbol: STR Exchange: NYSE
Industry: Utility - gas distribution

QuestTech, Inc.
7600-A Leesburg Pike
Falls Church, VA 22043
Phone: 703-760-1000 Fax: 703-760-1062
CEO: Vincent L. Salvatori
CFO: Joseph P. O'Connell, Jr.
1991 Sales: $39 million Employees: 435
Symbol: QTEC Exchange: NASDAQ
Industry: Engineering - R&D services

Quick & Reilly Group, Inc.
230 S. County Rd.
Palm Beach, FL 33480
Phone: 407-655-8000 Fax: 407-655-9010
CEO: Leslie C. Quick, Jr.
CFO: Leslie C. Quick, Jr.
1992 Sales: $154 million Employees: 717
Symbol: BQR Exchange: NYSE
Industry: Financial - investment bankers

Quidel Corp.
10165 McKellar Court
San Diego, CA 92121
Phone: 619-552-1100 Fax: 619-453-4338
CEO: Scott L. Glenn
CFO: Steven C. Burke
1992 Sales: $27 million Employees: 258
Symbol: QDEL Exchange: NASDAQ
Industry: Medical products - diagnostics

Quiksilver, Inc.
1740 Monrovia Ave.
Costa Mesa, CA 92627
Phone: 714-645-1395 Fax: 714-645-0313
CEO: Robert B. McKnight, Jr.
CFO: Randall L. Herrel
1991 Sales: $97 million Employees: 402
Symbol: QUIK Exchange: NASDAQ
Industry: Textiles - apparel; shirts & shorts

QuikTrip
901 N. Mingo Rd.
Tulsa, OK 74116
Phone: 918-836-8551 Fax: 918-834-4117
CEO: Chester Cadieux
CFO: Terry Carter
1991 Sales: $673 million Employees: 1,892
Ownership: Privately held
Industry: Gasoline convenience stores

Quincy Savings Bank
1200 Hancock St.
Quincy, MA 02169
Phone: 617-471-3500 Fax: —
CEO: Charles R. Simpson, Jr.
CFO: John A. Fanciullo
1992 Sales: — Employees: —
Symbol: QUIN Exchange: NASDAQ
Industry: Banks - Northeast

Quintiles Transnational
PO Box 13979
Research Triangle Park, NC 27709
Phone: 919-941-2888 Fax: 919-941-9113
CEO: Dennis Gillings
CFO: Rachel Selisker
1992 Sales: $60 million Employees: 650
Ownership: Privately held
Industry: Medical services - pharmaceutical product development & registration

Quipp, Inc.
4800 NW 157th St.
Hialeah, FL 33014
Phone: 305-623-8700 Fax: —
CEO: James E. Pruitt
CFO: Louis D. Kipp
1991 Sales: $13 million Employees: 119
Symbol: QUIP Exchange: NASDAQ
Industry: Machinery - material handling

Quixote Corp.
One E. Wacker Dr., 30th Fl.
Chicago, IL 60601
Phone: 312-467-6755 Fax: 312-467-1356
CEO: Philip E. Rollhaus
CFO: Myron R. Shain
1992 Sales: $129 million Employees: 986
Symbol: QUIX Exchange: NASDAQ
Industry: Diversified operations - highway safety devices, stenographic equipment, compact discs

Qume Corp.
500 Yosemite Dr.
Milpitas, CA 95035
Phone: 408-952-4000 Fax: 408-942-4062
CEO: David S. Lee
CFO: Stephen R. Bowling
1992 Sales: $230 million Employees: 722
Symbol: QUME Exchange: NASDAQ
Industry: Computers - disk drives, printers & terminals

QVC Network, Inc.
1365 Enterprise Dr.
West Chester, PA 19380
Phone: 215-430-1000 Fax: 215-430-1051
CEO: Barry Diller
CFO: William F. Costello
1992 Sales: $1,010 million Employees: 4,485
Symbol: QVCN Exchange: NASDAQ
Industry: Retail - mail order & direct cable television shopping

R. B. Pamplin Corporation
900 SW Fifth Ave., Ste. 1800
Portland, OR 97204
Phone: 503-248-1133 Fax: 503-248-1175
CEO: Robert B. Pamplin
CFO: Robert B. Pamplin, Jr.
1991 Sales: $573 million Employees: 5,200
Ownership: Privately held
Industry: Diversified operations - textiles, concrete & asphalt

R. G. Barry Corp.
13405 Yarmouth Dr. NW
Pickerington, OH 43147
Phone: 614-864-6400 Fax: 614-866-9787
CEO: Gordon Zacks
CFO: Richard L. Burrell
1991 Sales: $103 million Employees: 2,500
Symbol: RGB Exchange: AMEX
Industry: Shoes & related apparel

R. H. Macy & Co., Inc.
151 W. 34th St.
New York, NY 10001
Phone: 212-695-4400 Fax: 212-629-6814
CEO: Myron Ullman III
CFO: Diane P. Baker
1992 Sales: $6,330 million Employees: 60,000
Ownership: Privately held
Industry: Retail - major department stores

R.O.W. Sciences, Inc.
1700 Research Blvd., Ste. 400
Rockville, MD 20850
Phone: 301-294-5400 Fax: 301-294-5401
CEO: Ralph O. Williams
CFO: John Smith
1992 Sales: $25 million Employees: 380
Ownership: Privately held
Industry: Biomedical and health services research & information systems

R.P. Scherer Corp.
2075 W. Big Beaver Rd.
Troy, MI 48084
Phone: 313-649-0900 Fax: 313-649-2079
CEO: John P. Cashman
CFO: Robert J. Lollini
1992 Sales: $338 million Employees: 2,485
Symbol: SHR Exchange: NYSE
Industry: Medical products - drug delivery systems

R.R. Donnelley & Sons Co.
2223 S. Martin Luther King Dr.
Chicago, IL 60616
Phone: 312-326-8000 Fax: 312-326-8543
CEO: John R. Walter
CFO: Frank R. Jarc
1992 Sales: $4,193 million Employees: 30,000
Symbol: DNY Exchange: NYSE
Industry: Printing - commercial

R&B, Inc.
3400 E. Walnut St.
Colmar, PA 18915
Phone: 215-997-1800 Fax: —
CEO: Richard Berman
CFO: Robert Gollon
1991 Sales: $41 million Employees: 391
Symbol: RBIN Exchange: NASDAQ
Industry: Automotive & trucking - replacement parts

indicates company is in *Hoover's Handbook of American Business*

indicates company is in *Hoover's Handbook of World Business*; sales and employee numbers are for parent company.

R&M Business Systems Inc.
1683 Elmhurst Rd.
Elk Grove Village, IL 60007
Phone: 708-228-8600 Fax: 708-228-8620
CEO: Joe Phillips
CFO: Michael Ryan
1991 Sales: $3.5 million Employees: 38
Ownership: Privately held
Industry: Office equipment & supplies

Rabco Health Services
444 Madison Ave., Ste. 601
New York, NY 10022
Phone: 212-688-4500 Fax: 212-888-5025
CEO: Richard A. Bernstein
CFO: Stuart Turner
1991 Sales: $1,386 million Employees: 2,600
Ownership: Privately held
Industry: Medical products - medical & surgical equipment, pharmaceuticals

Racetrac Petroleum Inc.
300 Technology Ct.
Smyrna, GA 30082
Phone: 404-431-7600 Fax: 404-431-7612
CEO: Carl Bolch, Jr.
CFO: Robert Dumbacher
1991 Sales: $746 million Employees: 2,100
Ownership: Privately held
Industry: Oil refining & marketing, convenience stores

Radiation Care, Inc.
1155 Hammond Dr., Bldg. A
Atlanta, GA 30328
Phone: 404-399-0663 Fax: —
CEO: Thomas E. Haire
CFO: Christi K. Haire
1992 Sales: $6.8 million Employees: —
Symbol: RDCR Exchange: NASDAQ
Industry: Medical services - radiation therapy centers

Radiation Systems, Inc.
1501 Moran Rd.
Sterling, VA 22170
Phone: 703-450-5680 Fax: 703-450-4706
CEO: Richard E. Thomas
CFO: Mark D. Funston
1992 Sales: $127 million Employees: 893
Symbol: RADS Exchange: NASDAQ
Industry: Telecommunications equipment - antenna products

Radius, Inc.
1710 Fortune Dr.
San Jose, CA 95131
Phone: 408-434-1010 Fax: 408-434-0770
CEO: Michael D. Boich
CFO: Richard A. Heddleson
1991 Sales: $119 million Employees: 347
Symbol: RDUS Exchange: NASDAQ
Industry: Computers - computer monitors

Rag Shop, The
111 Wagaraw Rd.
Hawthorne, NJ 07506
Phone: 201-423-1303 Fax: 201-427-6568
CEO: Stanley Berenzweig
CFO: Steven Barnett
1991 Sales: $58 million Employees: 1,000
Symbol: RAGS Exchange: NASDAQ
Industry: Retail - fabric & craft merchandise

Railroad Savings & Loan Assn.
110 S. Main St.
Wichita, KS 67202
Phone: 316-269-0300 Fax: 316-269-0378
CEO: Robert D. Taylor
CFO: Donald J. Voth
1991 Sales: $46 million Employees: 180
Symbol: RF Exchange: AMEX
Industry: Banks - Midwest

Railroadmen's Federal Savings and Loan Assoc.
21 Virginia Ave.
Indianapolis, IN 46204
Phone: 317-637-0400 Fax: —
CEO: James R. Kocher
CFO: John J. Dee
1992 Sales: — Employees: —
Symbol: RRMN Exchange: NASDAQ
Industry: Financial - savings and loans

Rainbow Technologies, Inc.
9292 Jeronimo Rd.
Irvine, CA 92718
Phone: 714-454-2100 Fax: 714-454-8557
CEO: Walter W. Straub
CFO: Walter W. Straub
1991 Sales: $19 million Employees: 93
Symbol: RNBO Exchange: NASDAQ
Industry: Computers - computer-related security products

Raley's Inc.
500 W. Capitol Ave.
West Sacramento, CA 95605
Phone: 916-373-3333 Fax: 916-444-3733
CEO: Charles L. Collings
CFO: Keith F. Tronson
1992 Sales: $1,800 million Employees: 11,000
Ownership: Privately held
Industry: Retail - supermarkets & drug stores

Rally's, Inc.
10002 Shelbyville Rd., Ste. 150
Louisville, KY 40223
Phone: 502-245-8900 Fax: 502-245-7407
CEO: Burt Sugarman
CFO: Donald C. Moore
1992 Sales: $121 million Employees: 4,500
Symbol: RLLY Exchange: NASDAQ
Industry: Retail - food & restaurants

Ralston Purina Co.
Checkerboard Square
St. Louis, MO 63164
Phone: 314-982-1000 Fax: 314-982-1211
CEO: William P. Stiritz
CFO: James R. Elser
1992 Sales: $7,901 million Employees: 57,996
Symbol: RAL Exchange: NYSE
Industry: Food - pet food, cereals, batteries

Ramapo Financial Corp.
64 Mountain View Blvd.
Wayne, NJ 07470
Phone: 201-696-6100 Fax: —
CEO: Robert R. Peacock
CFO: Walter A. Wojcik, Jr.
1991 Sales: $32 million Employees: 276
Symbol: RMPO Exchange: NASDAQ
Industry: Banks - Northeast

Ramerica International, Inc.
350 5th Ave., Ste. 4721
New York, NY 10118
Phone: 212-971-9100 Fax: 212-736-4958
CEO: Davut Okutcu
CFO: —
1991 Sales: $9,905 million Employees: 39,169
Parent: Koç Holding AS
Industry: Diversified operations - automobiles, appliances, gas

Ramsay Health Care, Inc.
639 Loyola Ave., One Poydras Plaza, Ste. 1400
New Orleans, LA 70113
Phone: 504-525-2505 Fax: 504-585-0505
CEO: Ralph J. Watts
CFO: Bruce R. Soden
1992 Sales: $137 million Employees: 2,323
Symbol: RHCI Exchange: NASDAQ
Industry: Hospitals

Randall's Food Markets, Inc.
3663 Briarpark
Houston, TX 77042
Phone: 713-268-3500 Fax: 713-268-3601
CEO: Robert R. Onstead
CFO: Bob Gowens
1992 Sales: $2,000 million Employees: 8,500
Ownership: Privately held
Industry: Retail - supermarkets

Random Access, Inc.
8000 E. Iliff
Denver, CO 80231
Phone: 303-745-9600 Fax: 303-745-0242
CEO: Bruce A. Milliken
CFO: John Gierscher
1992 Sales: $75 million Employees: 203
Symbol: RNDM Exchange: NASDAQ
Industry: Computers - services

Rank America Inc.
5 Concourse Pkwy., Ste. 2400
Atlanta, GA 30328
Phone: 404-392-9029 Fax: 404-392-0585
CEO: John Watson
CFO: —
1991 Sales: $3,953 million Employees: 42,993
Parent: The Rank Organisation PLC
Industry: Film & TV, holidays & hotels, recreation

Raritan Bancorp Inc.
9 W. Somerset St.
Raritan, NJ 08869
Phone: 908-725-0080 Fax: —
CEO: Arlyn D. Rus
CFO: Thomas F. Tansey
1991 Sales: $21 million Employees: 74
Symbol: RARB Exchange: NASDAQ
Industry: Banks - Northeast

RasterOps
2500 Walsh Ave.
Santa Clara, CA 95051
Phone: 408-562-4200 Fax: 408-562-4065
CEO: Kieth E. Sorenson
CFO: Ken J. McEwan
1992 Sales: $89 million Employees: 205
Symbol: ROPS Exchange: NASDAQ
Industry: Computers - photo-realistic imaging systems

Rauch Industries, Inc.
6048 S. York Rd.
Gastonia, NC 28053
Phone: 704-867-5333 Fax: 704-864-2081
CEO: Marshall A. Rauch
CFO: Donald G. Walser
1991 Sales: $38 million Employees: 582
Symbol: RCHI Exchange: NASDAQ
Industry: Glass products

Raven Industries, Inc.
205 E. 6th. St.
Sioux Falls, SD 57102
Phone: 605-336-2750 Fax: 605-335-0268
CEO: David A. Christensen
CFO: Arnold J. Thue
1991 Sales: $101 million Employees: 1,252
Symbol: RAVN Exchange: NASDAQ
Industry: Diversified operations - plastics, electronics, sewn products

Ravenswood Aluminum Corporation
Willow Grove Rd.
Ravenswood, WV 26164
Phone: 304-273-6000 Fax: 304-273-6241 ext.6846
CEO: Craig A. Davis
CFO: Steven Schneider
1991 Sales: $500 million Employees: 2,012
Ownership: Privately held
Industry: Metals - aluminum

A indicates company is in *Hoover's Handbook of American Business*
W indicates company is in *Hoover's Handbook of World Business;* sales and employee numbers are for parent company.

Raychem Corp.
300 Constitution Dr.
Menlo Park, CA 94025
Phone: 415-361-3333 Fax: 415-361-2108
CEO: Robert J. Saldich
CFO: Michael T. Everett
1992 Sales: $1,362 million Employees: 11,187
Symbol: RYC Exchange: NYSE
Industry: Electrical products - insulation products, telephone & cable accessories

Raymond Corp.
20 South Canal St.
Greene, NY 13778
Phone: 607-656-2311 Fax: 607-656-9005
CEO: Ross K. Colquhoun
CFO: William B. Lynn
1991 Sales: $139 million Employees: 1,137
Symbol: RAYM Exchange: NASDAQ
Industry: Machinery - material handling

Raymond James Financial, Inc.
880 Carillon Pkwy.
St. Petersburg, FL 33716
Phone: 813-573-3800 Fax: 813-573-8244
CEO: Thomas A. James
CFO: Jeffrey P. Julian
1992 Sales: $361 million Employees: 1,637
Symbol: RJF Exchange: NYSE
Industry: Financial - stock brokerage

Rayonier Timberlands, L.P.
1177 Summer St.
Stamford, CT 06904
Phone: 203-348-7000 Fax: 203-964-4528
CEO: Ronald M. Gross
CFO: Gerald J. Pollack
1991 Sales: $103 million Employees: —
Symbol: LOG Exchange: NYSE
Industry: Building products - wood

Raytech Corp.
One Corporate Dr., Ste. 512
Shelton, CT 06484
Phone: 203-925-8000 Fax: 203-925-8088
CEO: Craig R. Smith
CFO: Albert A. Canosa
1991 Sales: $103 million Employees: 962
Symbol: RAY Exchange: NYSE
Industry: Automotive & trucking - original equipment

Raytheon Co.
141 Spring St.
Lexington, MA 02173
Phone: 617-862-6600 Fax: 617-860-2172
CEO: Dennis J. Picard
CFO: Sheldon Rutstein
1992 Sales: $9,058 million Employees: 71,600
Symbol: RTN Exchange: NYSE
Industry: Diversified operations - electronics, energy & environmental products, aircraft products

RB&W Corp.
5970 Heisley Rd.
Mentor, OH 44060
Phone: 216-357-1200 Fax: 216-639-1944
CEO: John J. Lohrman
CFO: Ronald C. Drabik
1991 Sales: $164 million Employees: 1,137
Symbol: RBW Exchange: AMEX
Industry: Metal products - fabrication

Re Capital Corp.
Six Stamford Forum
Stamford, CT 06904
Phone: 203-977-6100 Fax: 203-325-8968
CEO: James E. Roberts
CFO: R. Richard Mueller
1991 Sales: $151 million Employees: 40
Symbol: RCC Exchange: AMEX
Industry: Insurance - property & casualty

Read-Rite Corp.
345 Los Coches St.
Milpitas, CA 95035
Phone: 408-262-6700 Fax: 408-956-3205
CEO: Cyril J. Yansouni
CFO: Lori Holland
1992 Sales: $389 million Employees: 7,522
Symbol: RDRT Exchange: NASDAQ
Industry: Computers - magnetic recording heads

Reader's Digest Association, Inc., The
One Readers Digest Rd.
Pleasantville, NY 10570
Phone: 914-238-1000 Fax: 914-238-4559
CEO: George V. Grune
CFO: Anthony W. Ruggiero
1992 Sales: $2,811 million Employees: 7,400
Symbol: RDA Exchange: NYSE
Industry: Publishing - periodicals, books, records & videos

ReadiCare, Inc.
2600 Michelson Dr., Ste. 1130
Irvine, CA 92715
Phone: 714-476-8743 Fax: —
CEO: Dennis G. Danko
CFO: James A. Ripp
1992 Sales: $36 million Employees: 790
Symbol: RDI Exchange: AMEX
Industry: Healthcare - outpatient & home

Reading & Bates Corp.
901 Threadneedle, Ste. 200
Houston, TX 77079
Phone: 713-496-5000 Fax: 713-496-2298
CEO: Paul B. Loyd, Jr.
CFO: Tim W. Nagle
1991 Sales: $127 million Employees: 1,500
Symbol: RB Exchange: NYSE
Industry: Oil & gas - offshore drilling

Reading Co.
121 S. Broad St., 20th Fl.
Philadelphia, PA 19107
Phone: 215-735-8300 Fax: 215-735-1271
CEO: Edward L. Kane
CFO: James A. Wunderle
1991 Sales: $6 million Employees: 13
Symbol: RDGCA Exchange: NASDAQ
Industry: Real estate operations

Receptech Corp.
51 University St.
Seattle, WA 98101
Phone: 206-587-0430 Fax: —
CEO: Alan D. Frazier
CFO: James A. Johnson
1992 Sales: — Employees: —
Symbol: RECP Exchange: NASDAQ
Industry: Medical products - autoimmune disease treatment products

Recognition Equipment Inc.
2701 E. Grauwyler Rd.
Irving, TX 75061
Phone: 214-579-6000 Fax: 214-579-6830
CEO: Robert A. Vanourek
CFO: Robert M. Swartz
1991 Sales: $155 million Employees: 1,368
Symbol: REC Exchange: NYSE
Industry: Optical character recognition

Recom Technologies Inc.
1245 S. Winchester Blvd., Ste. 201
San Jose, CA 95128
Phone: 408-261-7688 Fax: 408-261-7699
CEO: G. K. Lee
CFO: Donald St. Louis
1991 Sales: $9.2 million Employees: 209
Ownership: Privately held
Industry: Computers - engineering & technical support systems

Recoton Corp.
46-23 Crane St.
Long Island City, NY 11101
Phone: 718-392-6442 Fax: 718-784-1080
CEO: Robert L. Borchardt
CFO: Joseph H. Massot
1991 Sales: $58 million Employees: 443
Symbol: RCOT Exchange: NASDAQ
Industry: Audio & video home products

Red Apple Group
823 Eleventh Ave.
New York, NY 10019
Phone: 212-956-5803 Fax: 212-262-4979
CEO: John Andreas Catsimatidis
CFO: Stuart Spivak
1991 Sales: $2,350 million Employees: 9,500
Ownership: Privately held
Industry: Diversified operations - supermarkets & convenience stores, oil, real estate

Red Eagle Resources Corp.
1601 Northwest Expwy., Ste. 1700
Oklahoma City, OK 73118
Phone: 405-843-8066 Fax: 405-842-5473
CEO: Harry C. Johnson
CFO: Allen R. Clark
1991 Sales: $30 million Employees: 384
Symbol: REDX Exchange: NASDAQ
Industry: Oil & gas - US exploration & production

Red Lion Hotels & Inns
4001 Main St.
Vancouver, WA 98663
Phone: 206-696-0001 Fax: 206-696-4964
CEO: David J. Johnson
CFO: H. Raymond Bingham
1991 Sales: $97 million Employees: 11,000
Symbol: RED Exchange: AMEX
Industry: Hotels & motels

Red Rose Collection, Inc.
42 Adrian Court
Burlingame, CA 94010
Phone: 415-692-4500 Fax: 415-692-1750
CEO: Rinaldo Brutoco
CFO: Ray Afshordi
1992 Sales: $10.2 million Employees: 80
Ownership: Privately held
Industry: Retail - mail order; publishing & wholesale

Redwood Empire Bancorp
111 Santa Rosa Ave.
Santa Rosa, CA 95404
Phone: 707-573-4800 Fax: —
CEO: Patrick W. Kilkenny
CFO: Dennis E. Kelley
1991 Sales: $29 million Employees: 186
Symbol: REB Exchange: AMEX
Industry: Banks - West

Reebok International Ltd.
100 Technology Center Dr.
Stoughton, MA 02072
Phone: 617-341-5000 Fax: 617-341-5087
CEO: Paul B. Fireman
CFO: Paul R. Duncan
1992 Sales: $3,023 million Employees: 4,220
Symbol: RBK Exchange: NYSE
Industry: Shoes & related apparel - athletic

Reed Publishing (USA) Inc.
275 Washington St.
Newton, MA 02158
Phone: 617-964-3030 Fax: 617-558-4667
CEO: Robert L. Krakoff
CFO: —
1992 Sales: $3,050 million Employees: 18,300
Parent: Reed International PLC
Industry: Publishing - consumer & business publications, books

 indicates company is in *Hoover's Handbook of American Business*

indicates company is in *Hoover's Handbook of World Business*; sales and employee numbers are for parent company.

Reeds Jewelers, Inc.
2525 S. Seventeenth St.
Wilmington, NC 28401
Phone: 919-350-3100 Fax: 919-350-3277
CEO: Alan M. Zimmer
CFO: James R. Rouse
1992 Sales: $58 million Employees: 709
Symbol: REED Exchange: NASDAQ
Industry: Retail - jewelry stores

Refac Technology Development Corp.
100 E. 42nd St.
New York, NY 10017
Phone: 212-687-4741 Fax: 212-949-8716
CEO: Eugene M. Lang
CFO: Karl H. Lohse
1991 Sales: $14 million Employees: 14
Symbol: REFC Exchange: NASDAQ
Industry: Business services - license & joint venture administration

Reference Press, Inc., The
6448 Hwy. 290 East, Ste. E-104
Austin, TX 78723
Phone: 512-454-7778 Fax: 512-454-9401
CEO: Patrick J. Spain
CFO: Alan Chai
1992 Sales: $1 million Employees: 9
Ownership: Privately held
Industry: Publishing - business reference books & software

Reflectone, Inc.
4908 Tampa West Blvd.
Tampa, FL 33634
Phone: 813-885-7481 Fax: 813-888-6871
CEO: Richard G. Snyder
CFO: Richard W. Welshhans
1991 Sales: $51 million Employees: 556
Symbol: RFTN Exchange: NASDAQ
Industry: Electronics - military

Regal Communications Corp.
1035 Camphill Rd.
Ft. Washington, PA 19034
Phone: 215-540-1190 Fax: —
CEO: Arthur L. Toll
CFO: Bruce B. Edmondson
1991 Sales: $18 million Employees: 274
Symbol: RCOM Exchange: NASDAQ
Industry: Telecommunications services - audiotex services

Regal International, Inc.
256 N. Belt East, Ste. 252
Houston, TX 77060
Phone: 713-445-7700 Fax: 713-445-5006
CEO: Ruben V. Aragon
CFO: Charles T. Worsham
1991 Sales: $10.1 million Employees: 150
Symbol: RGL Exchange: NYSE
Industry: Oil field machinery & equipment

Regal-Beloit Corp.
200 State St.
Beloit, WI 53511
Phone: 608-365-2563 Fax: 608-365-2182
CEO: James L. Packard
CFO: Robert C. Burress
1991 Sales: $152 million Employees: 2,200
Symbol: RBC Exchange: AMEX
Industry: Tools - hand held

Regency Coffee
One 19th Ave. South
Minneapolis, MN 55454
Phone: 612-333-3045 Fax: 612-333-7090
CEO: Ron Burton
CFO: Ron Burton
1992 Sales: $3.3 million Employees: 75
Ownership: Privately held
Industry: Retail - gourmet coffee

Regency Cruises Inc.
260 Madison Ave.
New York, NY 10016
Phone: 212-972-4499 Fax: 212-687-2290
CEO: William Schanz
CFO: William Schanz
1991 Sales: $134 million Employees: 586
Symbol: SHIP Exchange: NASDAQ
Industry: Leisure & recreational services - cruises

Regency Equities Corp.
11400 W. Olympic Blvd.
Los Angeles, CA 90064
Phone: 310-575-1500 Fax: —
CEO: Robert N. Goodman
CFO: Morris Engel
1991 Sales: $1.2 million Employees: 2
Symbol: RGEQ Exchange: NASDAQ
Industry: Real estate operations

Regency Health Services, Inc.
3636 Birch St., Ste. 195
Newport Beach, CA 92660
Phone: 714-851-9512 Fax: —
CEO: Cecil R. Mays
CFO: Carol Mays
1991 Sales: $57 million Employees: —
Symbol: RHS Exchange: AMEX
Industry: Medical services - nursing care

Regeneron Pharmaceuticals, Inc.
777 Old Saw Mill River Rd.
Tarrytown, NY 10591
Phone: 914-347-7000 Fax: 914-347-2113
CEO: Leonard Schleifer
CFO: Frederic D. Price
1991 Sales: $7.3 million Employees: 169
Symbol: REGN Exchange: NASDAQ
Industry: Biomedical & genetic products

Regional Bancorp, Inc.
29 High St.
Medford, MA 02155
Phone: 617-395-7700 Fax: —
CEO: Thomas F. O'Connor
CFO: Leonard V. Siuda
1991 Sales: $49 million Employees: 173
Symbol: REGB Exchange: NASDAQ
Industry: Banks - Northeast

Regis Corp.
5000 Normandale Rd.
Minneapolis, MN 55436
Phone: 612-929-6776 Fax: 612-925-5357
CEO: Myron Kunin
CFO: Frank E. Evangelist
1992 Sales: $306 million Employees: 14,000
Symbol: RGIS Exchange: NASDAQ
Industry: Retail - hair salons

Registry, Inc.
42 Washington St.
Wellesley, MA 02181
Phone: 617-237-9119 Fax: 617-235-5580
CEO: G. Drew Conway
CFO: Robert E. Foley
1991 Sales: $17 million Employees: 54
Ownership: Privately held
Industry: Business services - computer personnel services

RehabCare Corp.
112 S. Hanley Rd.
St. Louis, MO 63105
Phone: 314-863-7422 Fax: 314-863-0769
CEO: James M. Usdan
CFO: Alan C. Henderson
1992 Sales: $44 million Employees: 753
Symbol: RHBC Exchange: NASDAQ
Industry: Healthcare - outpatient & home

Reich & Tang L.P.
100 Park Ave., Ste. 2800
New York, NY 10017
Phone: 212-370-1110 Fax: 212-370-1265
CEO: Oscar L. Tang
CFO: Oscar L. Tang
1991 Sales: $54 million Employees: 124
Symbol: RTP Exchange: NYSE
Industry: Financial - investment management

Reliability Inc.
16400 Park Row
Houston, TX 77084
Phone: 713-492-0550 Fax: 713-492-0615
CEO: Everett Hanlon
CFO: Max T. Langley
1991 Sales: $30 million Employees: 533
Symbol: REAL Exchange: NASDAQ
Industry: Electronics - measuring instruments

Reliance Electric Co.
6065 Parkland Blvd.
Cleveland, OH 44124
Phone: 216-266-5800 Fax: 216-266-7666
CEO: John C. Morley
CFO: Keith C. Moore, Jr.
1992 Sales: $1,553 million Employees: 14,118
Symbol: REE Exchange: NYSE
Industry: Electrical products - industrial & telecommunications products

Reliance Group Holdings, Inc.
55 E. 52nd St.
New York, NY 10055
Phone: 212-909-1100 Fax: 212-909-1864
CEO: Saul P. Steinberg
CFO: Lowell C. Freiberg
1991 Sales: $3,392 million Employees: —
Symbol: REL Exchange: NYSE
Industry: Insurance - multiline & misc.

ReLife, Inc.
813 Shades Creek Pkwy., Ste. 300
Birmingham, AL 35209
Phone: 205-870-8099 Fax: 205-870-8128
CEO: Michael E. Stephens
CFO: Thomas W. Marshall
1992 Sales: $57 million Employees: 1,664
Symbol: RELF Exchange: NASDAQ
Industry: Healthcare - outpatient & home

Remote Control International
5928 Pascal Court, #150
Carlsbad, CA 92008
Phone: 619-431-4000 Fax: 619-431-4006
CEO: Michael McCafferty
CFO: Frank Ryason
1992 Sales: $5.1 million Employees: 62
Ownership: Privately held
Industry: Computers - software publishing services

REN Corporation - USA
6820 Charlotte Pike
Nashville, TN 37209
Phone: 615-353-4200 Fax: 615-353-1635
CEO: Jerome S. Tannenbaum
CFO: Bradley S. Wear
1992 Sales: $81 million Employees: 832
Symbol: RENL Exchange: NASDAQ
Industry: Healthcare - outpatient & home

Rentrak Corp.
7227 NE 55th Ave.
Portland, OR 97218
Phone: 503-284-7581 Fax: 503-288-1563
CEO: Ron Berger
CFO: Karl D. Wetzel
1992 Sales: $47 million Employees: 157
Symbol: RENT Exchange: NASDAQ
Industry: Leisure & recreational services - prerecorded videotapes

 indicates company is in *Hoover's Handbook of American Business*

indicates company is in *Hoover's Handbook of World Business*; sales and employee numbers are for parent company.

Repligen Corp.
One Kendall Square
Cambridge, MA 02139
Phone: 617-225-6000 Fax: 617-494-1786
CEO: Sandford D. Smith
CFO: Ramesh L. Ratan
1992 Sales: $8.7 million Employees: 191
Symbol: RGEN Exchange: NASDAQ
Industry: Biomedical & genetic products

Repossession Auction, Inc.
11401 NW Seventh Ave.
Miami, FL 33168
Phone: 305-756-1000 Fax: —
CEO: Lloyd Lyons
CFO: Lloyd Lyons
1991 Sales: $9.8 million Employees: 13
Symbol: REPO Exchange: NASDAQ
Industry: Retail - used vehicles

Repsol Oil, USA
405 Lexington Ave.
New York, NY 10174
Phone: 212-953-9662 Fax: 212-986-0211
CEO: Everardo Santamarina
CFO: —
1991 Sales: $17,507 million Employees: 20,848
Parent: Repsol, SA
Industry: Oil & gas - international integrated

Republic Automotive Parts, Inc.
500 Wilson Pike Circle, Ste. 115
Brentwood, TN 37027
Phone: 615-373-2050 Fax: 615-373-1629
CEO: Keith M. Thompson
CFO: Donald B. Hauk
1991 Sales: $80 million Employees: 691
Symbol: RAUT Exchange: NASDAQ
Industry: Automotive & trucking - replacement parts

Republic Bancorp Inc.
1070 E. Main St.
Owosso, MI 48867
Phone: 517-725-7337 Fax: —
CEO: Jerry D. Campbell
CFO: Dana M. Cluckey
1991 Sales: $54 million Employees: 370
Symbol: RBNC Exchange: NASDAQ
Industry: Banks - Midwest

Republic Bank
23133 Hawthorne Blvd.
Torrance, CA 90505
Phone: 310-378-8483 Fax: —
CEO: William B. Oberholzer
CFO: Carl C. Maier
1992 Sales: — Employees: —
Symbol: ARBC Exchange: NASDAQ
Industry: Banks - West

Republic Capital Group, Inc.
500 W. Brown Deer Rd.
Milwaukee, WI 53217
Phone: 414-352-3500 Fax: 414-351-8680
CEO: Frank J. Banholzer
CFO: Mark A. Roble
1991 Sales: $93 million Employees: 544
Symbol: RSLA Exchange: NASDAQ
Industry: Financial - savings and loans

Republic Engineered Steels
410 Oberlin Rd. SW
Massillon, OH 44647
Phone: 800-331-9420 Fax: 216-837-6083
CEO: Russell W. Maier
CFO: James B. Riley
1991 Sales: $650 million Employees: 4,725
Ownership: Privately held
Industry: Steel production

Republic Gypsum Co.
3625 Miller Park Dr.
Garland, TX 75042
Phone: 214-272-0441 Fax: 214-272-7289
CEO: Phil Simpson
CFO: Stephen L. Gagnon
1992 Sales: $42 million Employees: —
Symbol: RGC Exchange: NYSE
Industry: Building products - gypsum paperboard & wallboard

Republic New York Corp.
452 Fifth Ave.
New York, NY 10018
Phone: 212-525-6225 Fax: —
CEO: Walter H. Weiner
CFO: John D. Kaberle, Jr.
1992 Sales: $2,341 million Employees: 4,600
Symbol: RNB Exchange: NYSE
Industry: Banks - Northeast

Republic Pictures Corp.
12636 Beatrice St.
Los Angeles, CA 90066
Phone: 310-306-4040 Fax: 310-301-0142
CEO: Russell Goldsmith
CFO: David M. Kirchheimer
1991 Sales: $82 million Employees: 133
Symbol: RPICA Exchange: NASDAQ
Industry: Motion pictures & services

Republic Savings Financial Corp.
3970 RCA Blvd., Ste. 7000
Palm Beach Gardens, FL 33410
Phone: 407-775-2100 Fax: —
CEO: R. E. Schupp
CFO: Richard J. Haskins
1992 Sales: $15 million Employees: 86
Symbol: RSFC Exchange: NASDAQ
Industry: Financial - savings and loans

Research, Inc.
6425 Flying Cloud Dr.
Eden Prairie, MN 55344
Phone: 612-941-3300 Fax: 612-941-3628
CEO: Fred Tucker Renshaw
CFO: Claude C. Johnson
1991 Sales: $13 million Employees: 141
Symbol: RESR Exchange: NASDAQ
Industry: Electrical components - control systems

Research Industries Corp.
6864 South 300 West
Midvale, UT 84047
Phone: 801-562-0200 Fax: 801-972-8393
CEO: Gary L. Crocker
CFO: F. Lynn Michelsen
1991 Sales: $12 million Employees: 125
Symbol: REIC Exchange: NASDAQ
Industry: Medical products - pharmaceuticals & disposable cardiovascular products

Research Information Systems
2355 Camina Vida Roble
Carlsbad, CA 92009
Phone: 619-438-5526 Fax: 619-438-5573
CEO: Earl Beutler
CFO: Colleen Baer
1991 Sales: $3.9 million Employees: 45
Ownership: Privately held
Industry: Computers - software & information services

Reserve Industries Corp.
20 First Plaza NW, Ste. 308
Albuquerque, NM 87102
Phone: 505-247-2384 Fax: 505-247-2379
CEO: James J. Melfi, Jr.
CFO: William J. Melfi
1991 Sales: $7.2 million Employees: 87
Symbol: ROIL Exchange: NASDAQ
Industry: Metals - nonferrous

Resorts International Casino Hotel
North Carolina Ave. & Boardwalk
Atlantic City, NJ 08404
Phone: 609-344-6000 Fax: 609-340-6284
CEO: David P. Hanlon
CFO: Matthew B. Kearney
1991 Sales: $418 million Employees: 7,100
Symbol: RT Exchange: AMEX
Industry: Leisure & recreational services - casinos

Resource America, Inc.
1609 Walnut St.
Philadelphia, PA 19103
Phone: 215-557-8454 Fax: —
CEO: Edward F. Cohen
CFO: Nancy J. McGurk
1991 Sales: $8.1 million Employees: 45
Symbol: REXI Exchange: NASDAQ
Industry: Oil & gas - production & pipeline

Resource Recycling Technologies, Inc.
300 Plaza Dr.
Binghamton, NY 13903
Phone: 607-729-9331 Fax: 607-797-7103
CEO: Burton I. Koffman
CFO: Thomas F. Recny
1991 Sales: $46 million Employees: 350
Symbol: RRT Exchange: AMEX
Industry: Pollution control equipment & services - recyclable materials marketing

Respironics, Inc.
1001 Murry Ridge Dr.
Monroeville, PA 15668
Phone: 412-733-0200 Fax: 412-733-0299
CEO: Gerald E. McGinnis
CFO: Dennis S. Meteny
1992 Sales: $49 million Employees: 961
Symbol: RESP Exchange: NASDAQ
Industry: Medical products - respiratory products

Response Technologies, Inc.
1775 Moriah Woods Blvd.
Memphis, TN 38117
Phone: 901-683-0212 Fax: 901-683-0313
CEO: William H. West
CFO: Daryl P. Johnson
1991 Sales: $8.9 million Employees: 115
Symbol: RTK Exchange: AMEX
Industry: Medical services - outpatient cancer centers

Restaurant Enterprises Group
One Park Plaza Jamboree Ctr., Ste. 900
Irvine, CA 92714
Phone: 714-852-5700 Fax: 714-724-9914
CEO: Norman N. Habermann
CFO: Mike Casey
1991 Sales: $978 million Employees: 19,980
Ownership: Privately held
Industry: Retail - food & restaurants

Restek Corp.
110 Benner Circle
Bellefonte, PA 16823
Phone: 814-353-1300 Fax: 814-353-1309
CEO: Paul Silvis
CFO: Anthony Cepullio
1991 Sales: $6.4 million Employees: 69
Ownership: Privately held
Industry: Gas chromatography columns & accessories

Restor Industries, Inc.
333 Enterprise St.
Ocoee, FL 34761
Phone: 407-877-0908 Fax: —
CEO: Richard H. Williams
CFO: Mark A. Gergel
1991 Sales: $20 million Employees: 228
Symbol: REST Exchange: NASDAQ
Industry: Industrial maintenance - electrical repair

Resurgens Communications Group, Inc.
945 E. Paces Ferry Rd., Ste. 2210
Atlanta, GA 30326
Phone: 404-261-6190 Fax: 404-233-2280
CEO: John D. Phillips
CFO: H. Hobart Corwin
1991 Sales: $25 million Employees: 313
Symbol: RCG Exchange: AMEX
Industry: Telecommunications services - long distance

Retailing Corporation of America
PO Box 339
Wheelersburg, OH 53202
Phone: 614-574-2583 Fax: 614-574-2113
CEO: Dean T. Johnson
CFO: Dean T. Johnson
1991 Sales: $96 million Employees: 248
Symbol: RCOA Exchange: NASDAQ
Industry: Retail - discount & variety

Retix Inc.
2401 Colorado Ave.
Santa Monica, CA 90404
Phone: 310-828-3400 Fax: 310-828-2255
CEO: Stephen W. Frankel
CFO: Ronald W. Rudolph
1991 Sales: $60 million Employees: 423
Symbol: RETX Exchange: NASDAQ
Industry: Computers - networking software

Reunion Time
766 Shrewsbury Ave.
Tinton Falls, NJ 07724
Phone: 908-758-0222 Fax: 908-758-9567
CEO: David Siore
CFO: Nancy Carney
1991 Sales: $2.5 million Employees: 11
Ownership: Privately held
Industry: Business services - class reunion planning

Reuters America Inc.
1700 Broadway
New York, NY 10019
Phone: 212-603-3300 Fax: 212-912-7394
CEO: Brian Michael Douglas Vaughan
CFO: —
1991 Sales: $2,737 million Employees: 10,335
Parent: Reuters Holdings PLC
Industry: Computers - on-line information services

Revco D.S., Inc.
1925 Enterprise Pkwy.
Twinsburg, OH 44087
Phone: 216-425-9811 Fax: Call co. operator
CEO: Boake A. Sells
CFO: Gregory K. Raven
1992 Sales: $2,142 million Employees: 16,000
Symbol: RXR Exchange: NYSE
Industry: Retail - drug stores

Revell Monogram
363 N. 3rd Ave.
Des Plaines, IL 60016
Phone: 708-390-8910 Fax: 708-390-7377
CEO: Timothy Cawley
CFO: Theodore J. Eischeid
1991 Sales: $106 million Employees: 766
Symbol: RVL Exchange: AMEX
Industry: Toys - hobby products

Rexene Corp.
5005 LBJ Fwy.
Dallas, TX 75244
Phone: 915-333-7200 Fax: 915-333-8238
CEO: Andrew J. Smith
CFO: Kevin W. McAleer
1991 Sales: $450 million Employees: 1,283
Symbol: RXN Exchange: NYSE
Industry: Chemicals - diversified

Rexhall Industries, Inc.
25655 Springbrook Ave.
Saugus, CA 91350
Phone: 805-253-1295 Fax: 805-253-2422
CEO: William J. Rex
CFO: William J. Rex
1991 Sales: $26 million Employees: 96
Symbol: REXL Exchange: NASDAQ
Industry: Building - mobile homes & RVs

Rexnord Corp.
4701 W. Greenfield Ave.
Milwaukee, WI 53214
Phone: 414-643-3000 Fax: 414-797-5543
CEO: James R. Swenson
CFO: Thomas J. Jansen
1991 Sales: $552 million Employees: 5,335
Symbol: REX Exchange: NYSE
Industry: Machinery - general industrial

Rexon Inc.
1334 Parkview Ave., Ste. 200
Manhattan Beach, CA 90266
Phone: 310-545-4441 Fax: 310-546-2822
CEO: Michael O. Preletz
CFO: Irvin R. Reuling
1991 Sales: $183 million Employees: 808
Symbol: REXN Exchange: NASDAQ
Industry: Computers - tape drives & related equipment

Rexworks Inc.
445 W. Oklahoma Ave.
Milwaukee, WI 53207
Phone: 414-747-7200 Fax: 414-747-7345
CEO: M. C. Hadjinian
CFO: E. R. Sisolak
1991 Sales: $33 million Employees: 243
Symbol: REXW Exchange: NASDAQ
Industry: Machinery - construction & mining

Reynolds and Reynolds Co.
115 S. Ludlow St.
Dayton, OH 45402
Phone: 513-443-2000 Fax: 513-449-4416
CEO: David R. Holmes
CFO: Dale L. Medford
1992 Sales: $657 million Employees: 4,826
Symbol: REY Exchange: NYSE
Industry: Paper - business forms

Reynolds Metals Co.
6601 W. Broad St.
Richmond, VA 23230
Phone: 804-281-2000 Fax: 804-281-4160
CEO: Richard G. Holder
CFO: Henry S. Savedge, Jr.
1992 Sales: $5,593 million Employees: 30,900
Symbol: RLM Exchange: NYSE
Industry: Metals - nonferrous

Rheometrics, Inc.
One Possumtown Rd.
Piscataway, NJ 08854
Phone: 908-560-8550 Fax: 908-560-7451
CEO: Joseph M. Starita
CFO: Neil J. Abitabilo
1991 Sales: $26 million Employees: 223
Symbol: RHEM Exchange: NASDAQ
Industry: Instruments - control

Rhône-Poulenc Inc.
CN 5266
Princeton, NJ 08543
Phone: 908-297-0100 Fax: 908-297-1597
CEO: Peter J. Neff
CFO: —
1992 Sales: $7,230 million Employees: 89,051
Parent: Rhône-Poulenc SA
Industry: Chemicals - diversified

Rhône-Poulenc Rorer Inc.
500 Arcola Rd.
Collegeville, PA 19426
Phone: 215-628-6000 Fax: 215-283-4915
CEO: Robert E. Cawthorn
CFO: Patrick Langlois
1992 Sales: $4,096 million Employees: 22,500
Symbol: RPR Exchange: NYSE
Industry: Drugs

Ribbon Outlet Inc.
3434 U.S. Hwy. 22 West
Somerville, NJ 08876
Phone: 908-707-9800 Fax: 908-707-1040
CEO: Gregory Link
CFO: Kevin R. Wood
1991 Sales: $14 million Employees: 450
Ownership: Privately held
Industry: Retail - ribbon, lace & trim

RIBI ImmunoChem Research, Inc.
PO Box 1409
Hamilton, MT 59840
Phone: 406-363-6214 Fax: 406-363-6129
CEO: Robert E. Ivy
CFO: Vern D. Child
1991 Sales: $0.9 million Employees: 60
Symbol: RIBI Exchange: NASDAQ
Industry: Biomedical & genetic products

Rich Products Corp.
1150 Niagara St.
Buffalo, NY 14213
Phone: 716-878-8000 Fax: 716-878-8266
CEO: Robert E. Rich, Jr.
CFO: Charles Trego
1991 Sales: $890 million Employees: 7,000
Ownership: Privately held
Industry: Diversified operations - frozen foods, pro sports, broadcasting

Richardson Electronics, Ltd.
40 W. 267 Keslinger Rd.
Lafox, IL 60147
Phone: 708-208-2200 Fax: 708-208-2550
CEO: Edward J. Richardson
CFO: Leonard R. Prange
1992 Sales: $159 million Employees: 655
Symbol: RELL Exchange: NASDAQ
Industry: Electronics - parts distribution

Richfood Holdings, Inc.
2000 Richfood Rd.
Mechanicsville, VA 23111
Phone: 804-746-6000 Fax: 804-746-6144
CEO: Donald D. Bennett
CFO: John E. Stokely
1992 Sales: $1,072 million Employees: 1,347
Symbol: RCHF Exchange: NASDAQ
Industry: Food - wholesale

Richton International Corp.
1345 Avenue of the Americas, 36th Fl.
New York, NY 10105
Phone: 212-765-6480 Fax: 212-397-9219
CEO: Fred R. Sullivan
CFO: Cornelius F. Griffin
1992 Sales: $17 million Employees: 200
Symbol: RHT Exchange: AMEX
Industry: Precious metals & jewelry

Riddell Sports, Inc.
810 Seventh Ave.
New York, NY 10019
Phone: 212-586-6800 Fax: —
CEO: Robert Nederlander
CFO: Lawrence F. Simon
1991 Sales: $36 million Employees: 613
Symbol: RIDL Exchange: NASDAQ
Industry: Leisure & recreational products - football helmets

indicates company is in *Hoover's Handbook of American Business*

indicates company is in *Hoover's Handbook of World Business*; sales and employee numbers are for parent company.

Riedel Environmental Technologies, Inc.
4611 N. Channel Ave.
Portland, OR 97217
Phone: 503-286-4656 Fax: 503-283-2602
CEO: Arthur A. Riedel
CFO: Joseph R. McGuinn
1991 Sales: $80 million Employees: 832
Symbol: RIE Exchange: AMEX
Industry: Pollution control equipment & services - hazardous waste management

Riggs National Corp.
800 17th St. NW
Washington, DC 20006
Phone: 202-835-6000 Fax: 202-835-4009
CEO: Joe L. Allbritton
CFO: Joe L. Allbritton
1991 Sales: $582 million Employees: 2,187
Symbol: RIGS Exchange: NASDAQ
Industry: Banks - Southeast

Right Management Consultants, Inc.
1818 Market St., 14th Fl.
Philadelphia, PA 19103
Phone: 215-988-1588 Fax: 215-988-9112
CEO: Stanley R. Tilton
CFO: G. Lee Bohs
1991 Sales: $48 million Employees: 377
Symbol: RMCI Exchange: NASDAQ
Industry: Business services - consulting

Right Start, Inc., The
5334 Sterling Center Dr.
Westlake Village, CA 91361
Phone: 818-707-7100 Fax: 818-707-7132
CEO: Lenny M. Targon
CFO: Lenny M. Targon
1992 Sales: $27 million Employees: 120
Symbol: RTST Exchange: NASDAQ
Industry: Retail - mail order & direct

Riklis Family Corporation
667 Madison Ave., 12th Fl.
New York, NY 10022
Phone: 212-735-9500 Fax: 212-735-9450
CEO: Meshulam Riklis
CFO: Paul Weiner
1991 Sales: $1,520 million Employees: 23,300
Ownership: Privately held
Industry: Retail - discount & variety stores

Ringer Corp.
9959 Valley View Rd.
Eden Prairie, MN 55344
Phone: 612-941-4180 Fax: 612-941-5036
CEO: Udo E. Schulz
CFO: Mark S. Robinow
1991 Sales: $21 million Employees: 71
Symbol: RING Exchange: NASDAQ
Industry: Chemicals - specialty

Rio Grande Industries, Inc.
Southern Pacific Bldg., One Market Plaza
San Francisco, CA 94105
Phone: 415-541-1000 Fax: 415-541-1256
CEO: Philip F. Anschutz
CFO: L. C. Yarberry
1991 Sales: $2,780 million Employees: 23,396
Ownership: Privately held
Industry: Transportation - rail

Rio Hotel and Casino, Inc.
3700 W. Flamingo Rd.
Las Vegas, NV 89103
Phone: 702-252-7733 Fax: —
CEO: Anthony A. Marnell II
CFO: James A. Barrett, Jr.
1991 Sales: $66 million Employees: 1,282
Symbol: RIOH Exchange: NASDAQ
Industry: Leisure & recreational services - hotels & casinos

Riser Foods, Inc.
5300 Richmond Rd.
Bedford Heights, OH 44146
Phone: 216-292-7000 Fax: 216-591-2640
CEO: Anthony C. Rego
CFO: Ronald W. Ocasek
1992 Sales: $1,040 million Employees: 5,800
Symbol: RSR Exchange: AMEX
Industry: Retail - supermarkets

Rite Aid Corp.
431 Railroad Ave.
Shiremanstown, PA 17011
Phone: 717-761-2633 Fax: 717-975-5871
CEO: Alex Grass
CFO: Frank M. Bergonzi
1992 Sales: $3,987 million Employees: 30,490
Symbol: RAD Exchange: NYSE
Industry: Retail - discount drug stores

Rival Co.
800 E. 101st Terrace
Kansas City, MO 64131
Phone: 816-943-4100 Fax: 816-943-4123
CEO: Thomas K. Manning
CFO: Stanley D. Briggs
1992 Sales: $164 million Employees: 2,000
Symbol: RIVL Exchange: NASDAQ
Industry: Appliances - household

River Forest Bancorp, Inc.
3959 N. Lincoln Ave.
Chicago, IL 60613
Phone: 312-989-5100 Fax: —
CEO: Joseph C. Glickman
CFO: Alan J. Lorr
1991 Sales: $54 million Employees: 540
Symbol: RFBC Exchange: NASDAQ
Industry: Banks - Midwest

Riverside Group, Inc.
10 W. Adams St.
Jacksonville, FL 32202
Phone: 904-359-3076 Fax: 904-359-3092
CEO: J. Steven Wilson
CFO: Suzanne T. Gilstrap
1991 Sales: $128 million Employees: 217
Symbol: RSGI Exchange: NASDAQ
Industry: Insurance - multiline & misc.

Riverside National Bank
3484 Central Ave.
Riverside, CA 92506
Phone: 714-686-9075 Fax: —
CEO: Michael C. Billings
CFO: J. Richard Swartz
1992 Sales: — Employees: —
Symbol: RNRC Exchange: NASDAQ
Industry: Banks - West

Riverwood International Corp.
3350 Cumberland Circle
Atlanta, GA 30339
Phone: 404-916-7900 Fax: —
CEO: Thomas H. Johnson
CFO: Frank R. McCauley
1992 Sales: $1.1 million Employees: 8,000
Symbol: RVW Exchange: NYSE
Industry: Building products - wood

RJR Nabisco, Inc.
1301 Avenue of the Americas
New York, NY 10019
Phone: 212-258-5600 Fax: 212-969-9173
CEO: Louis V. Gerstner, Jr.
CFO: Karl M. von der Heyden
1992 Sales: $15,734 million Employees: 56,000
Symbol: RN Exchange: NYSE
Industry: Tobacco & food

RLI Insurance Co.
9025 N. Lindberg Dr.
Peoria, IL 61615
Phone: 309-692-1000 Fax: 309-692-1068
CEO: Gerald D. Stephens
CFO: Jonathan E. Michael
1991 Sales: $102 million Employees: —
Symbol: RLI Exchange: NYSE
Industry: Insurance - accident & health

RMI Titanium Co.
1000 Warren Ave.
Niles, OH 44446
Phone: 216-652-7633 Fax: 216-544-7796
CEO: L. Frederick Gieg, Jr.
CFO: Timothy G. Rupert
1991 Sales: $166 million Employees: 1,556
Symbol: RTI Exchange: NYSE
Industry: Metals - nonferrous

Roadshow International, Inc.
8300 Greensboro Dr., Ste. 400
McLean, VA 22102
Phone: 703-790-8300 Fax: 703-790-8333
CEO: Donald J. Soults
CFO: Steward Curly
1992 Sales: $8 million Employees: 100
Ownership: Privately held
Industry: Computers - vehicle routing & scheduling system

Roadway Services, Inc.
1077 Gorge Blvd.
Akron, OH 44310
Phone: 216-384-8184 Fax: 216-258-6042
CEO: Joseph M. Clapp
CFO: D. A. Wilson
1992 Sales: $3,578 million Employees: 37,900
Symbol: ROAD Exchange: NASDAQ
Industry: Transportation - truck

Roanoke Electric Steel Corp.
102 Westside Blvd. NW, Ste. 650
Roanoke, VA 24017
Phone: 703-342-1831 Fax: 703-342-9437
CEO: Donald G. Smith
CFO: Donald G. Smith
1991 Sales: $127 million Employees: 966
Symbol: RESC Exchange: NASDAQ
Industry: Steel - production

Robbins & Myers, Inc.
1400 Kettering Tower
Dayton, OH 45423
Phone: 513-222-2610 Fax: 513-225-3314
CEO: Daniel W. Duval
CFO: George M. Walker
1991 Sales: $79 million Employees: 593
Symbol: ROBN Exchange: NASDAQ
Industry: Machinery - electrical

Robec, Inc.
425 Privet Rd.
Horsham, PA 19044
Phone: 215-675-9300 Fax: 215-672-5945
CEO: Robert H. Beckett
CFO: Mark Dorfman
1991 Sales: $201 million Employees: 400
Symbol: ROBC Exchange: NASDAQ
Industry: Computers - retail & wholesale

Robert Bosch Corp.
2800 S. 25th Ave.
Broadview, IL 60153
Phone: 708-865-5200 Fax: 708-865-5203
CEO: Friedrich W. Schiefer
CFO: —
1991 Sales: $22,106 million Employees: 181,000
Parent: Robert Bosch GMBH
Industry: Automotive & trucking - electronic equipment; communications technology

indicates company is in *Hoover's Handbook of American Business*

indicates company is in *Hoover's Handbook of World Business;* sales and employee numbers are for parent company.

Robert Half International Inc.
2884 Sand Hill Rd.
Menlo Park, CA 94025
Phone: 415-854-9700 Fax: 415-854-9735
CEO: Harold M. Messmer, Jr.
CFO: M. Keith Waddell
1991 Sales: $210 million Employees: 40,850
Symbol: RHI Exchange: NYSE
Industry: Business services - personnel services

Roberts Pharmaceutical Corp.
6 Industrial Way West
Eatontown, NJ 07724
Phone: 908-389-1182 Fax: 908-389-1014
CEO: Robert A. Vukovich
CFO: Anthony P. Maris
1991 Sales: $14 million Employees: 174
Symbol: RPCX Exchange: NASDAQ
Industry: Drugs

Robertson-Ceco Corp.
Two Gateway Center
Pittsburgh, PA 15222
Phone: 412-281-3200 Fax: 412-338-6425
CEO: Richard Broyd
CFO: Camillo J. DiFrancesco
1991 Sales: $652 million Employees: 4,288
Symbol: RHH Exchange: NYSE
Industry: Diversified operations - building products, metal buildings, door products

Robins Engineering & Constructors
7730 E. Belleview Ave., Ste. 404
Englewood, CO 80111
Phone: 303-770-0808 Fax: 303-770-8233
CEO: Manfred Koppers
CFO: —
1992 Sales: — Employees: —
Parent: Fried. Krupp AG Hoesch-Krupp
Industry: Steel, mechanical engineering & plantmaking

Robinson Nugent, Inc.
800 E. Eighth St.
New Albany, IN 47151
Phone: 812-945-0211 Fax: 812-945-0804
CEO: Larry W. Burke
CFO: Clifford G. Boggs
1992 Sales: $51 million Employees: 470
Symbol: RNIC Exchange: NASDAQ
Industry: Electrical connectors

Rochester Community Savings Bank
40 Franklin St.
Rochester, NY 14604
Phone: 716-258-3000 Fax: —
CEO: Leonard S. Simon
CFO: Edward J. Pettinella
1992 Sales: — Employees: —
Symbol: RCSB Exchange: NASDAQ
Industry: Financial - savings and loans

Rochester Gas and Electric Corp.
89 East Ave.
Rochester, NY 14649
Phone: 716-546-2700 Fax: 716-724-8668
CEO: Roger W. Kober
CFO: Robert C. Henderson
1991 Sales: $853 million Employees: 2,770
Symbol: RGS Exchange: NYSE
Industry: Utility - electric power

Rochester Telephone Corp.
180 S. Clinton Ave.
Rochester, NY 14646
Phone: 716-955-9800 Fax: 716-777-7029
CEO: Alan C. Hasselwander
CFO: Frederick R. Pestorius
1992 Sales: $804 million Employees: 4,559
Symbol: RTC Exchange: NYSE
Industry: Utility - telephone

Rock Financial Corp.
350 Rock Ave.
North Plainfield, NJ 07061
Phone: 908-561-4600 Fax: 908-753-1276
CEO: Arthur Zemel
CFO: Edward R. Wright
1991 Sales: $16 million Employees: 77
Symbol: RFIN Exchange: NASDAQ
Industry: Banks - Northeast

Rock-Tenn Co.
504 Thrasher St.
Norcross, GA 30071
Phone: 404-448-2193 Fax: 404-263-4483
CEO: Bradley Currey, Jr.
CFO: David Nicholson
1992 Sales: $655 million Employees: 5,054
Ownership: Privately held
Industry: Paper & paper products - recycled paperboard & packaging products

Rockwell International Corp.
2201 Seal Beach Blvd.
Seal Beach, CA 90740
Phone: 310-797-3311 Fax: 310-797-5690
CEO: Donald R. Beall
CFO: William M. Barnes
1992 Sales: $10,838 million Employees: 87,004
Symbol: ROK Exchange: NYSE
Industry: Aerospace - aircraft equipment; electronics, automotive & graphics

Rocky Mount Undergarment Co., Inc.
1536 Boone St.
Rocky Mount, NC 27803
Phone: 919-446-6161 Fax: 919-442-4412
CEO: David Greenberg
CFO: Charles Kralick
1991 Sales: $19 million Employees: 560
Symbol: RMUC Exchange: NASDAQ
Industry: Textiles - apparel

Rocky Mountain Helicopters, Inc.
800 South 3110 West
Provo, UT 84601
Phone: 801-375-1124 Fax: 801-375-6712
CEO: James B. Burr
CFO: David R. Anderson
1992 Sales: $83 million Employees: 880
Symbol: RMHI Exchange: NASDAQ
Industry: Transportation - services

Rodman & Renshaw Inc.
120 S. LaSalle St., 10th Fl.
Chicago, IL 60603
Phone: 312-977-7800 Fax: 312-732-0298
CEO: Kurt B. Karmin
CFO: Peter J. Schild
1992 Sales: $84 million Employees: 535
Symbol: RR Exchange: NYSE
Industry: Financial - investment management

Roelynn Business Products
1 Bethany Rd., Ste. 1
Hazlet, NJ 07730
Phone: 908-739-8780 Fax: 908-739-8783
CEO: Vincent J. Praino
CFO: Vincent J. Praino
1991 Sales: $1 million Employees: 6
Ownership: Privately held
Industry: Printing - commercial, farm & business

Rogers Corp.
One Technology Dr.
Rogers, CT 06263
Phone: 203-774-9605 Fax: 203-774-9630
CEO: Norman L. Greenman
CFO: Stuart J. Safft
1991 Sales: $182 million Employees: 2,989
Symbol: ROG Exchange: AMEX
Industry: Electrical components - interconnection products, polymers

Rohm and Haas Co.
Independence Mall West
Philadelphia, PA 19105
Phone: 215-592-3000 Fax: 215-592-3377
CEO: J. Lawrence Wilson
CFO: Fred W. Shaffer
1992 Sales: $3,063 million Employees: 12,872
Symbol: ROH Exchange: NYSE
Industry: Chemicals - diversified

Rohr Inc.
Foot of H St.
Chula Vista, CA 91910
Phone: 619-691-4111 Fax: 619-691-3030
CEO: Robert H. Goldsmith
CFO: David J. Ruggles
1992 Sales: $1,239 million Employees: 11,500
Symbol: RHR Exchange: NYSE
Industry: Aerospace - aircraft equipment

Rollins Environmental Services, Inc.
2200 Concord Pike
Wilmington, DE 19803
Phone: 302-426-2700 Fax: 302-479-3339
CEO: John W. Rollins
CFO: Harold D. Castle
1991 Sales: $221 million Employees: —
Symbol: REN Exchange: NYSE
Industry: Pollution control equipment & services - concentrated industrial waste management

Rollins, Inc.
2170 Piedmont Rd. NE
Atlanta, GA 30324
Phone: 404-888-2000 Fax: Call co. operator
CEO: R. Randall Rollins
CFO: Gene L. Smith
1991 Sales: $476 million Employees: 7,910
Symbol: ROL Exchange: NYSE
Industry: Building - maintenance & services

Rollins Leasing Corp.
2200 Concord Pike
Wilmington, DE 19803
Phone: 302-426-2700 Fax: 302-426-3013
CEO: John W. Rollins
CFO: Patrick J. Bagley
1991 Sales: $342 million Employees: 2,553
Symbol: RLC Exchange: NYSE
Industry: Leasing

Rolls-Royce Inc.
11911 Freedom Dr.
Reston, VA 22090
Phone: 703-834-1700 Fax: 703-625-0634
CEO: J. W. Sandford
CFO: —
1991 Sales: $6,573 million Employees: 57,100
Parent: Rolls-Royce PLC
Industry: Aerospace - aircraft equipment; industrial power

Roosevelt Financial Group, Inc.
900 Roosevelt Pkwy.
Chesterfield, MO 63017
Phone: 314-532-6200 Fax: 314-532-6641
CEO: Stanley J. Bradshaw
CFO: Loyd W. Garrison
1991 Sales: $194 million Employees: 403
Symbol: RFED Exchange: NASDAQ
Industry: Financial - savings and loans

Ropak Corp.
660 S. State College Blvd.
Fullerton, CA 92631
Phone: 714-870-9757 Fax: 714-447-3871
CEO: William H. Roper
CFO: Ronald W. Cameron
1991 Sales: $94 million Employees: 643
Symbol: ROPK Exchange: NASDAQ
Industry: Containers - paper & plastic

indicates company is in *Hoover's Handbook of American Business*

indicates company is in *Hoover's Handbook of World Business;* sales and employee numbers are for parent company.

Roper Pump Co.
Old Maysville Rd.
Commerce, GA 30529
Phone: 706-335-5551 Fax: 706-335-5505
CEO: Derrick N. Key
CFO: Zane E. Metcalf
1991 Sales: $75 million Employees: 618
Symbol: ROPR Exchange: NASDAQ
Industry: Instruments - control

Rose's Stores, Inc.
218 S. Garnett St.
Henderson, NC 27536
Phone: 919-430-2600 Fax: 919-430-2401
CEO: George L. Jones
CFO: R. Edward Anderson
1992 Sales: $1,330 million Employees: 18,000
Symbol: RSTOB Exchange: NASDAQ
Industry: Retail - discount & variety

Roseburg Forest Products Co.
PO Box 1088
Roseburg, OR 97470
Phone: 503-679-3311 Fax: 503-679-9683
CEO: William A. Whelan
CFO: Ron Parker
1991 Sales: $712 million Employees: 3,900
Ownership: Privately held
Industry: Forest products

Rosenthal Cos.
1550 Wilson Blvd., Ste. 700
Arlington, VA 22209
Phone: 703-522-2300 Fax: 703-527-7392
CEO: Robert M. Rosenthal
CFO: Donald B. Bavely
1991 Sales: $581 million Employees: 1,250
Ownership: Privately held
Industry: Retail - auto dealerships

Ross Cosmetics Distribution Centers, Inc.
111 Commerce Court
Duncan, SC 29334
Phone: 803-439-7854 Fax: 803-439-4848
CEO: Viren Sheth
CFO: T. Legrand Crapps
1991 Sales: $31 million Employees: 110
Symbol: RCDC Exchange: NASDAQ
Industry: Cosmetics & toiletries

Ross Stores, Inc.
8333 Central Ave.
Newark, CA 94560
Phone: 510-505-4400 Fax: 510-505-4181
CEO: Norman A. Ferber
CFO: Earl T. Benson
1992 Sales: $1,003 million Employees: 7,397
Symbol: ROST Exchange: NASDAQ
Industry: Retail - apparel & shoes

Ross Systems, Inc.
555 Twin Dolphin Dr.
Redwood City, CA 94065
Phone: 415-593-2500 Fax: 415-592-9364
CEO: Dennis V. Vohs
CFO: Rick L. Smith
1992 Sales: $76 million Employees: 585
Symbol: ROSS Exchange: NASDAQ
Industry: Computers - software

RoTech Medical Corp.
4506 L. B. McLeod Rd., Ste. F
Orlando, FL 32811
Phone: 407-841-2115 Fax: 407-841-9318
CEO: William P. Kennedy
CFO: Stephen P. Griggs
1991 Sales: $24 million Employees: —
Symbol: ROTC Exchange: NASDAQ
Industry: Medical products - respiratory & convalescent therapy equipment

Roto-Rooter Services Co.
255 E. Fifth St., Chemed Ctr., Ste. 2500
Cincinnati, OH 45202
Phone: 513-762-6690 Fax: 513-762-6590
CEO: William R. Griffin
CFO: Brian A. Brumm
1991 Sales: $85 million Employees: 1,589
Symbol: ROTO Exchange: NASDAQ
Industry: Building - maintenance & services

Rouse Co.
10275 Little Patuxent Pkwy.
Columbia, MD 21044
Phone: 410-992-6000 Fax: 410-992-6363
CEO: Mathias J. DeVito
CFO: Anthony W. Deering
1992 Sales: $597 million Employees: 5,488
Symbol: ROUS Exchange: NASDAQ
Industry: Real estate operations

Roux Associates
775 Park Ave., Ste. 255
Huntington, NY 11743
Phone: 516-673-7200 Fax: 516-673-7216
CEO: Amy Potter
CFO: Amy Potter
1991 Sales: $12 million Employees: 108
Ownership: Privately held
Industry: Environmental consulting

Rowan Companies, Inc.
2800 Post Oak Blvd., Transco Bldg., Ste. 5450
Houston, TX 77056
Phone: 713-621-7800 Fax: 713-960-7560
CEO: C. R. Palmer
CFO: E. E. Thiele
1991 Sales: $272 million Employees: 2,573
Symbol: RDC Exchange: NYSE
Industry: Oil & gas - offshore drilling

Rowe Furniture Corp.
239 Rowan St.
Salem, VA 24153
Phone: 703-389-8671 Fax: 703-389-8217
CEO: Gerald M. Birnbach
CFO: Arthur H. Dunkin
1991 Sales: $64 million Employees: 900
Symbol: ROW Exchange: AMEX
Industry: Furniture

Roy F. Weston, Inc.
1 Weston Way
West Chester, PA 19380
Phone: 215-692-3030 Fax: 215-430-3124
CEO: William J. Marrazzo
CFO: John W. Poling
1991 Sales: $211 million Employees: 3,000
Symbol: WSTNA Exchange: NASDAQ
Industry: Pollution control equipment & services - environmental consulting

Royal Appliance Mfg. Co.
650 Alpha Dr.
Highland Heights, OH 44143
Phone: 216-449-6150 Fax: 216-449-7806
CEO: John A. Balch
CFO: Richard R. Goebel
1991 Sales: $273 million Employees: 719
Symbol: RAM Exchange: NYSE
Industry: Appliances - vacuum cleaners

Royal Bank of Canada
Financial Square, 23rd Fl.
New York, NY 10005
Phone: 212-428-6200 Fax: 212-968-1293
CEO: David Robertson
CFO: —
199 Sales: $12,029 million Employees: 57,596
Parent: Royal Bank of Canada
Industry: Banks - money center

Royal Bank of Pennsylvania
732 Montgomery Ave.
Narberth, PA 19072
Phone: 215-668-4700 Fax: —
CEO: Daniel M. Tabas
CFO: Eileen M. Knott
1992 Sales: — Employees: —
Symbol: RBPAA Exchange: NASDAQ
Industry: Banks - Northeast

Royal Gold, Inc.
1660 Wynkoop St., Ste. 1000
Denver, CO 80202
Phone: 303-573-1660 Fax: 303-595-9385
CEO: Stanley Dempsey
CFO: Thomas A. Loucks
1991 Sales: $0.9 million Employees: 7
Symbol: RGLD Exchange: NASDAQ
Industry: Gold mining & processing

Royal Palm Beach Colony, L.P.
2501 South Ocean Dr.
Hollywood, FL 33169
Phone: 305-927-3080 Fax: 305-927-3081
CEO: Martin J. Katz
CFO: Jose E. Fuente
1991 Sales: $3.6 million Employees: 2
Symbol: RPB Exchange: AMEX
Industry: Real estate operations

RPC Energy Services, Inc.
2170 Piedmont Rd. NE
Atlanta, GA 30324
Phone: 404-888-2950 Fax: 404-888-2722
CEO: R. Randall Rollins
CFO: Debra G. Herron
1991 Sales: $97 million Employees: 978
Symbol: RES Exchange: NYSE
Industry: Oil & gas - field services

RPM, Inc.
2628 Pearl Rd.
Medina, OH 44256
Phone: 216-225-3192 Fax: 216-225-8743
CEO: Thomas C. Sullivan
CFO: Richard E. Klar
1992 Sales: $552 million Employees: 3,100
Symbol: RPOW Exchange: NASDAQ
Industry: Paints & allied products

RS Financial Corp.
219 Fayetteville St. Mall
Raleigh, NC 27601
Phone: 919-833-7511 Fax: —
CEO: Stanley E. Wright
CFO: Rex D. Williams
1991 Sales: $74 million Employees: 272
Symbol: RFBK Exchange: NASDAQ
Industry: Financial - savings and loans

Rubbermaid Inc.
1147 Akron Rd.
Wooster, OH 44691
Phone: 216-264-6464 Fax: 216-287-2739
CEO: Walter W. Williams
CFO: Joseph G. Meehan
1992 Sales: $1,805 million Employees: 9,754
Symbol: RBD Exchange: NYSE
Industry: Rubber & plastic products - consumer & industrial

Ruddick Corp.
Two First Union Center, Ste. 2000
Charlotte, NC 28282
Phone: 704-372-5404 Fax: 704-372-6409
CEO: Alan T. Dickson
CFO: Richard N. Brigden
1992 Sales: $1,603 million Employees: 13,500
Symbol: RDK Exchange: NYSE
Industry: Retail - supermarkets

indicates company is in *Hoover's Handbook of American Business*

indicates company is in *Hoover's Handbook of World Business;* sales and employee numbers are for parent company.

Rugby-Darby Group Companies Inc.
100 Banks Ave.
Rockville Centre, NY 11570
Phone: 516-536-3636 Fax: 516-536-8570
CEO: Michael Ashkin
CFO: —
1991 Sales: $575 million Employees: 2,300
Ownership: Privately held
Industry: Retail - mail-order vitamins

Rule Industries, Inc.
70 Blanchard Rd.
Burlington, MA 01803
Phone: 617-272-7400 Fax: 617-272-0920
CEO: William N. Anastos
CFO: John A. Geishecker, Jr.
1991 Sales: $52 million Employees: 493
Symbol: RULE Exchange: NASDAQ
Industry: Diversified operations - hardware & marine products, patent licensing

Russ & Berrie Co., Inc.
111 Bauer Dr.
Oakland, NJ 07436
Phone: 201-337-9000 Fax: 201-337-9634
CEO: Russell Berrie
CFO: Paul Cargotch
1991 Sales: $268 million Employees: 2,333
Symbol: RUS Exchange: NYSE
Industry: Drugs & sundries - wholesale

Russell Corp.
PO Box 272
Alexander City, AL 35010
Phone: 205-329-4000 Fax: 205-329-4474
CEO: Eugene C. Gwaltney
CFO: James D. Nabors
1992 Sales: $899 million Employees: 14,976
Symbol: RML Exchange: NYSE
Industry: Textiles - apparel

Ryan, Beck & Co., Inc.
80 Main St.
West Orange, NJ 07052
Phone: 201-325-3000 Fax: 201-325-7962
CEO: Fenwick H. Garvey
CFO: John S. Baran
1991 Sales: $14 million Employees: 133
Symbol: RBCO Exchange: NASDAQ
Industry: Financial - investment bankers

Ryan's Family Steak Houses, Inc.
405 Lancaster Ave.
Greer, SC 29650
Phone: 803-879-1000 Fax: 803-877-0974
CEO: Charles D. Way
CFO: Fred T. Grant, Jr.
1991 Sales: $299 million Employees: 12,000
Symbol: RYAN Exchange: NASDAQ
Industry: Retail - food & restaurants

Ryder System, Inc.
3600 NW 82nd Ave.
Miami, FL 33166
Phone: 305-593-3726 Fax: 305-593-3336
CEO: M. Anthony Burns
CFO: Edwin A. Huston
1992 Sales: $5,192 million Employees: 40,196
Symbol: R Exchange: NYSE
Industry: Leasing - transportation

Ryland Group, Inc.
10221 Wincopin Circle
Columbia, MD 21044
Phone: 410-730-7222 Fax: 410-730-6090
CEO: Roger W. Schipke
CFO: Alan P. Hoblitzell, Jr.
1992 Sales: $1,442 million Employees: 2,452
Symbol: RYL Exchange: NYSE
Industry: Building - residential & commercial

Rymer Foods, Inc.
4600 S. Packers Ave., Ste. 400
Chicago, IL 60609
Phone: 312-927-7777 Fax: 312-927-7278
CEO: Barry Rymer
CFO: Edward M. Hebert
1991 Sales: $255 million Employees: 1,160
Symbol: RYR Exchange: NYSE
Industry: Food - meat

S. C. Johnson & Son, Inc.
1525 Howe St.
Racine, WI 53403
Phone: 414-631-2000 Fax: 414-631-2133
CEO: William D. George, Jr.
CFO: Neal R. Nottleson
1992 Sales: $3,600 million Employees: 13,400
Ownership: Privately held
Industry: Chemicals - specialty & home care products

S. Cohen & Associates
1355 Beverly Rd.
McLean, VA 22101
Phone: 703-893-6600 Fax: 703-821-8236
CEO: Sanford Cohen
CFO: Sanford Cohen
1991 Sales: $10 million Employees: 45
Ownership: Privately held
Industry: Environmental & energy consulting services

S.E. Rykoff & Co.
761 Terminal St.
Los Angeles, CA 90021
Phone: 213-622-4131 Fax: 213-486-9161
CEO: Roger W. Coleman
CFO: R. Keith McCann
1992 Sales: $1,533 million Employees: 5,730
Symbol: RYK Exchange: NYSE
Industry: Food - wholesale

S & T Bancorp, Inc.
800 Philadelphia St.
Indiana, PA 15701
Phone: 412-349-2900 Fax: —
CEO: Robert D. Duggan
CFO: Delbert M. Baker
1991 Sales: $38 million Employees: 516
Symbol: STBA Exchange: NASDAQ
Industry: Banks - Northeast

S&K Famous Brands, Inc.
11100 W. Broad St.
Glen Allen, VA 23060
Phone: 804-346-2500 Fax: 804-346-2627
CEO: Stuart C. Siegel
CFO: Robert E. Knowles
1991 Sales: $75 million Employees: 1,100
Symbol: SKFB Exchange: NASDAQ
Industry: Retail - apparel & shoes

S&P Co.
100 Shoreline Hwy., Bldg. B, Ste. 39
Mill Valley, CA 94941
Phone: 415-332-0550 Fax: 415-332-0567
CEO: Lutz Isslieb
CFO: John Schless
1991 Sales: $566 million Employees: 2,800
Ownership: Privately held
Industry: Beverages - beer & real estate

S&W Foundation
1030 E. Beltline
Richardson, TX 75081
Phone: 214-235-3267 Fax: 214-437-2286
CEO: Tom Witherspoon
CFO: Tom Witherspoon
1991 Sales: $2 million Employees: 45
Ownership: Privately held
Industry: Construction - foundation, drainage & structural repair services

S-K-I Ltd.
c/o Killington Ltd.
Killington, VT 05751
Phone: 802-422-3333 Fax: 802-422-4391
CEO: Preston L. Smith
CFO: Martel D. Wilson, Jr.
1991 Sales: $83 million Employees: 2,836
Symbol: SKII Exchange: NASDAQ
Industry: Leisure & recreational services - ski resorts

W **Saab Cars USA, Inc.**
4405A Saab Dr.
Norcross, GA 30091
Phone: 404-279-0100 Fax: 404-279-6499
CEO: William Kelly
CFO: —
1991 Sales: $5,289 million Employees: 29,329
Parent: Saab-Scania AB
Industry: Automotive manufacturing; aircraft manufacuring

W **Saatchi & Saatchi Advertising Worldwide**
375 Hudson St.
New York, NY 10014
Phone: 212-463-2000 Fax: 212-463-9855
CEO: Ed Wax
CFO: —
1991 Sales: $1,380 million Employees: 12,400
Parent: Saatchi & Saatchi Company PLC
Industry: Advertising

SafeCard Services, Inc.
6400 NW 6th Way
Ft. Lauderdale, FL 33309
Phone: 305-776-2500 Fax: 305-776-2588
CEO: W. W. Stalcup, Jr.
CFO: Gerald R. Cahill
1991 Sales: $141 million Employees: 378
Symbol: SSI Exchange: NYSE
Industry: Financial - business services

SAFECO Corp.
4333 Brooklyn Ave. NE, SAFECO Plaza
Seattle, WA 98185
Phone: 206-545-5000 Fax: 206-545-5995
CEO: Roger H. Eigsti
CFO: Boh A. Dickey
1992 Sales: $3,481 million Employees: —
Symbol: SAFC Exchange: NASDAQ
Industry: Insurance - property & casualty

Safeguard Health Enterprises, Inc.
505 N. Euclid St., Ste. 200
Anaheim, CA 92801
Phone: 714-778-1284 Fax: 714-758-4338
CEO: Alvin M. Baileys
CFO: Ronald I. Brendzel
1991 Sales: $61 million Employees: 324
Symbol: SFGD Exchange: NASDAQ
Industry: Medical services - dental care programs

Safeguard Scientifics, Inc.
435 Devon Park Dr.
Wayne, PA 19087
Phone: 215-293-0600 Fax: 215-293-0601
CEO: Warren V. Musser
CFO: Gerald M. Wilk
1992 Sales: $845 million Employees: 2,150
Symbol: SFE Exchange: NYSE
Industry: Investors - technology companies

Safesite Records Management Corp.
96 High St.
North Billerica, MA 01862
Phone: 508-663-7100 Fax: 508-670-5406
CEO: Jim Wayman
CFO: Thomas J. Reilly, Jr.
1992 Sales: $9 million Employees: 190
Ownership: Privately held
Industry: Business services - business records storage

Safety-Kleen Corp.
777 Big Timber Rd.
Elgin, IL 60123
Phone: 708-697-8460 Fax: 708-697-4295
CEO: Donald W. Brinckman
CFO: Robert W. Willmschen, Jr.
1992 Sales: $795 million Employees: 6,500
Symbol: SK Exchange: NYSE
Industry: Pollution control equipment & services - contaminated fluid recycling

SafetyTek Corp.
49050 Milmont Dr.
Fremont, CA 94538
Phone: 510-226-9600 Fax: 415-444-5135
CEO: James Hawkins
CFO: Jack Glenn
1992 Sales: $14 million Employees: 127
Symbol: SAFE Exchange: NASDAQ
Industry: Instruments - control

Safeway Inc.
4th and Jackson Streets
Oakland, CA 94660
Phone: 415-891-3000 Fax: 415-444-5135
CEO: Steve Burd
CFO: Michael M. Pharr
1992 Sales: $15,152 million Employees: 110,100
Symbol: SWY Exchange: NYSE
Industry: Retail - supermarkets

Sahara Construction
505 S. Main
Bountiful, UT 84010
Phone: 801-298-7724 Fax: 801-298-2791
CEO: Tom Mabey
CFO: Tom Mabey
1991 Sales: $15 million Employees: 27
Ownership: Privately held
Industry: Construction - buildings, industrial, institutions & construction management

Sahara Hotel
2535 Las Vegas Blvd. South
Las Vegas, NV 89109
Phone: 702-737-2111 Fax: 702-791-2027
CEO: Paul W. Lowden
CFO: Ronald J. Radcliffe
1991 Sales: $183 million Employees: 4,328
Symbol: SHRE Exchange: NASDAQ
Industry: Leisure & recreational services - casinos & hotels

Salant Corp.
1114 Avenue of the Americas, 17th Fl.
New York, NY 10036
Phone: 212-221-7500 Fax: 212-302-2431
CEO: Nicholas P. DiPaolo
CFO: Richard P. Randall
1991 Sales: $398 million Employees: 4,700
Symbol: SLT Exchange: NYSE
Industry: Textiles - apparel

Salem Corp.
PO Box 2222
Pittsburgh, PA 15230
Phone: 412-923-2200 Fax: 412-923-1265
CEO: Victor Posner
CFO: Jack Coppersmith
1991 Sales: $127 million Employees: 885
Symbol: SBS Exchange: AMEX
Industry: Machinery - construction & mining

Salem Sportswear Corp.
One Delaware Dr.
Salem, NH 03079
Phone: 603-886-1285 Fax: 603-886-1317
CEO: Kyle W. Nagel
CFO: John G. Demeritt
1991 Sales: $68 million Employees: —
Symbol: SALM Exchange: NASDAQ
Industry: Apparel

SalePoint
6197 Cornerstone Ct. East, Ste. 103
San Diego, CA 92121
Phone: 619-546-9400 Fax: 619-546-0725
CEO: Larry Haworth
CFO: Adele Warner
1991 Sales: $8 million Employees: 30
Ownership: Privately held
Industry: Computers - IBM products

SalesTalk, Inc.
1161-B San Antonio Rd.
Mountain View, CA 94043
Phone: 415-964-2000 Fax: 415-964-2193
CEO: Jeff Wise
CFO: Greg Redican
1991 Sales: $7.4 million Employees: 40
Ownership: Privately held
Industry: Business services - product demonstrators for manufacturers

Salick Health Care, Inc.
407 N. Maple Dr.
Beverly Hills, CA 90210
Phone: 310-276-0732 Fax: —
CEO: Bernard Salick
CFO: Leslie F. Bell
1991 Sales: $74 million Employees: 840
Symbol: SHCI Exchange: NASDAQ
Industry: Healthcare - outpatient & home

Salomon Inc.
7 World Trade Center
New York, NY 10048
Phone: 212-783-7000 Fax: 212-783-2110
CEO: Robert E. Denham
CFO: Donald S. Howard
1992 Sales: $8,196 million Employees: 8,972
Symbol: SB Exchange: NYSE
Industry: Financial - investment bankers & securities trading, oil refining & marketing

Saloom Furniture Co. Inc.
256 Murdock Ave.
Winchendon, MA 01475
Phone: 508-297-1901 Fax: 508-297-4944
CEO: Peter Saloom
CFO: Linda Saloom
1991 Sales: $5.7 million Employees: 65
Ownership: Privately held
Industry: Furniture - tables & chairs

Salton/Maxim Housewares, Inc.
550 Business Center Dr.
Mt. Prospect, IL 60056
Phone: 708-803-4600 Fax: 708-803-1186
CEO: Leonhard Dreimann
CFO: William B. Rue
1992 Sales: $49 million Employees: 71
Symbol: SALT Exchange: NASDAQ
Industry: Appliances - household

Sam & Libby, Inc.
1123 Industrial Rd., Ste. C
San Carlos, CA 94070
Phone: 415-598-9211 Fax: 415-592-6846
CEO: Samuel L. Edelman
CFO: Robert W. Schultz
1991 Sales: $85 million Employees: 209
Symbol: SAML Exchange: NASDAQ
Industry: Shoes & related apparel

Sammons Enterprises
300 Crescent Court, Ste. 700
Dallas, TX 75201
Phone: 214-855-2800 Fax: 214-855-2899
CEO: Robert W. Korba
CFO: Joe Ethridge
1991 Sales: $1,326 million Employees: 4,400
Ownership: Privately held
Industry: Diversified operations - insurance, cable TV, industrial equipment

Samson Energy Co. L.P.
Two W. Second St.
Tulsa, OK 74103
Phone: 918-583-1791 Fax: 918-583-9096
CEO: Charles Schusterman
CFO: C. Philip Tholen
1991 Sales: $26 million Employees: —
Symbol: SAM Exchange: AMEX
Industry: Oil & gas - US exploration & production

Samsung America, Inc.
105 Challenger Rd.
Ridgefield Park, NJ 07660
Phone: 201-229-5000 Fax: 201-229-5080
CEO: Bangun Chung
CFO: —
1991 Sales: $13,437 million Employees: 5,032
Parent: Samsung Group
Industry: Diversified operations - financial & information services, electronics & engineering

Samuel Goldwyn Co.
10203 Santa Monica Blvd.
Los Angeles, CA 90067
Phone: 310-552-2255 Fax: 310-284-8493
CEO: Samuel Goldwyn, Jr.
CFO: Hans W. Turner
1991 Sales: $42 million Employees: 890
Symbol: SG Exchange: AMEX
Industry: Motion pictures & services - production & distribution

San Diego Gas & Electric Co.
101 Ash St.
San Diego, CA 92101
Phone: 619-696-2000 Fax: 619-231-0169
CEO: Thomas A. Page
CFO: R. Lee Haney
1992 Sales: $1,871 million Employees: 5,064
Symbol: SDO Exchange: NYSE
Industry: Utility - electric power

San Miguel (U.S.A.) Inc.
1400 Fashion Island Blvd., Ste. 111
San Mateo, CA 94404
Phone: 415-345-1330 Fax: 415-341-1519
CEO: Vincent Tarroja
CFO: —
1991 Sales: $2,039 million Employees: 36,060
Parent: San Miguel Corporation
Industry: Beverages - beer

Sanborn, Inc.
25 Commercial Dr.
Wrentham, MA 02093
Phone: 508-384-3181 Fax: 508-384-5346
CEO: George W. Sanborn
CFO: Brian M. Adley
1991 Sales: $12 million Employees: 188
Symbol: SBRN Exchange: NASDAQ
Industry: Instruments - scientific; high-technology separation devices

Sanderson Farms, Inc.
225 N. 13th Ave.
Laurel, MS 39441
Phone: 601-649-4030 Fax: 601-426-1461
CEO: Joe Frank Sanderson, Jr.
CFO: Wyatt J. Davis, Jr.
1991 Sales: $186 million Employees: 2,404
Symbol: SAFM Exchange: NASDAQ
Industry: Food - meat products

Sandestin Resorts, Inc.
5500 Hwy. 98 East
Destin, FL 32541
Phone: 904-837-2121 Fax: 904-267-8222
CEO: JimDato' Rester
CFO: —
1991 Sales: $2,050 million Employees: 30,000
Parent: Sime Darby Berhad
Industry: Diversified operations - plantations, property development, insurance & trading

Sandoz Corp.
608 Fifth Ave.
New York, NY 10020
Phone: 212-307-1122 Fax: 212-246-0185
CEO: Daniel Wagniere
CFO: —
1991 Sales: $9,885 million Employees: 53,400
Parent: Sandoz Ltd.
Industry: Drugs, chemicals, nutritional products

Sands Regent, The
345 N. Arlington Ave.
Reno, NV 89501
Phone: 702-348-2200 Fax: 702-348-2226
CEO: Pete Cladianos, Jr.
CFO: David R. Wood
1992 Sales: $41 million Employees: 996
Symbol: SNDS Exchange: NASDAQ
Industry: Leisure & recreational services - casinos & liquor stores

Sandwich Chef, Inc.
3514 Lorna Ridge Dr.
Birmingham, AL 35216
Phone: 205-822-3960 Fax: 205-822-5241
CEO: Alan V. Kaufman
CFO: J. Ronald Cooper
1992 Sales: $43 million Employees: 935
Symbol: SHEF Exchange: NASDAQ
Industry: Retail - food & restaurants

Sandwich Co-operative Bank
100 Old Kings Hwy.
Sandwich, MA 02563
Phone: 508-888-0026 Fax: —
CEO: Frederic D. Legate
CFO: George L. Larson
1992 Sales: — Employees: —
Symbol: SWCB Exchange: NASDAQ
Industry: Banks - Northeast

Sandy Corp.
1500 W. Big Beaver Rd.
Troy, MI 48084
Phone: 313-649-0800 Fax: 313-649-3614
CEO: William H. Sandy
CFO: Peter E. Steffes
1991 Sales: $35 million Employees: 130
Symbol: SDY Exchange: AMEX
Industry: Business services - training & communication programs

Sanifill, Inc.
1225 N. Loop West, Ste. 550
Houston, TX 77008
Phone: 713-865-9800 Fax: —
CEO: Lorne D. Bain
CFO: J. Chris Brewster
1991 Sales: $65 million Employees: 410
Symbol: FIL Exchange: NYSE
Industry: Pollution control equipment & services - solid waste disposal

Sanmark-Stardust Inc.
136 Madison Ave.
New York, NY 10016
Phone: 212-679-7260 Fax: 212-213-1873
CEO: Mark M. David
CFO: Saul Pomerantz
1991 Sales: $121 million Employees: 2,500
Symbol: SMK Exchange: AMEX
Industry: Textiles - apparel

Santa Cruz Operations, Inc.
PO Box 1900
Santa Cruz, CA 95061
Phone: 408-425-7222 Fax: 408-427-5448
CEO: Larry Michels
CFO: David Zacharias
1991 Sales: $135 million Employees: 1,300
Ownership: Privately held
Industry: Computers - software

Santa Fe Energy Partners, L.P.
1616 S. Voss Rd., Ste. 1000
Houston, TX 77057
Phone: 713-783-2401 Fax: 713-268-5341
CEO: James L. Payne
CFO: Lawrence J. Nilles
1991 Sales: $127 million Employees: —
Symbol: SFP Exchange: NYSE
Industry: Oil & gas - US exploration & production

Santa Fe Energy Resources, Inc.
1616 S. Voss, Ste. 1000
Houston, TX 77057
Phone: 713-783-2401 Fax: 713-268-4542
CEO: James L. Payne
CFO: Richard B. Bonneville
1991 Sales: $380 million Employees: 724
Symbol: SFR Exchange: NYSE
Industry: Oil & gas - US exploration & production

Santa Fe Pacific Corp.
1700 E. Golf Rd.
Schaumburg, IL 60173
Phone: 708-995-6000 Fax: 708-995-6219
CEO: Robert D. Krebs
CFO: Denis E. Springer
1992 Sales: $2,496 million Employees: 15,650
Symbol: SFX Exchange: NYSE
Industry: Transportation - rail; minerals

Santa Fe Pacific Pipeline Partners, L.P.
888 S. Figueroa St.
Los Angeles, CA 90017
Phone: 213-614-1095 Fax: 213-486-7940
CEO: Irvin Toole, Jr.
CFO: Robert L. Edwards
1991 Sales: $193 million Employees: —
Symbol: SFL Exchange: NYSE
Industry: Oil & gas - production & pipeline

Santa Monica Bank
1251 Fourth St.
Santa Monica, CA 90401
Phone: 310-394-9611 Fax: 310-394-8444
CEO: Joe L. Walling
CFO: Dario Quiroga
1991 Sales: $86 million Employees: 381
Symbol: SMO Exchange: AMEX
Industry: Banks - West

Sanyo North America Corp.
666 Fifth Ave.
New York, NY 10103
Phone: 212-315-3232 Fax: 212-315-3263
CEO: Motoharu Iue
CFO: —
1991 Sales: $12,697 million Employees: 56,079
Parent: Sanyo Electric Co., Ltd.
Industry: Audio & video equipment, information systems, appliances

Sara Lee Corp.
Three First National Plaza
Chicago, IL 60602
Phone: 312-726-2600 Fax: 312-726-3712
CEO: John H. Bryan
CFO: Michael E. Murphy
1992 Sales: $13,965 million Employees: 128,000
Symbol: SLE Exchange: NYSE
Industry: Diversified operations - foods & coffee, hosiery, shoecare & leather goods

Satellite Technology Management, Inc.
3530 Hyland Ave.
Costa Mesa, CA 92626
Phone: 714-557-2400 Fax: —
CEO: Emil Youssefzadeh
CFO: Wayne L. Blair
1991 Sales: $12 million Employees: 64
Symbol: STMI Exchange: NASDAQ
Industry: Telecommunications equipment

Saturn Electronics & Engineering
2119 Austin Dr.
Rochester Hills, MI 48309
Phone: 313-852-2120 Fax: 313-852-8340
CEO: Wally Tsuha
CFO: Sherman Crue
1991 Sales: $15 million Employees: 325
Ownership: Privately held
Industry: Engineering - electronic & electromechanical

Savannah Foods & Industries, Inc.
2 E. Bryan St., First Union Bldg., 8th Fl.
Savannah, GA 31401
Phone: 912-234-1261 Fax: 912-238-0252
CEO: William W. Sprague, Jr.
CFO: William R. Steinhauer
1991 Sales: $1,200 million Employees: 2,019
Symbol: SFI Exchange: NYSE
Industry: Food - sugar & refining

Save Mart Supermarkets Inc.
1800 Standiford Ave.
Modesto, CA 95350
Phone: 209-577-1600 Fax: 209-526-4396
CEO: Robert Piccinini
CFO: Robert Piccinini
1991 Sales: $1,200 million Employees: 7,000
Ownership: Privately held
Industry: Retail - supermarkets

Sayett Group, Inc.
17 Tobey Village Office Park
Pittsford, NY 14534
Phone: 716-264-9250 Fax: —
CEO: Raymond L. Bauch
CFO: Jeffrey B. Spear
1991 Sales: $8 million Employees: —
Symbol: SAYT Exchange: NASDAQ
Industry: Protection - safety equipment & services

Sbarro, Inc.
763 Larkfield Rd.
Commack, NY 11725
Phone: 516-864-0200 Fax: 516-462-9058
CEO: Mario Sbarro
CFO: Robert S. Koebele
1991 Sales: $208 million Employees: 7,200
Symbol: SBA Exchange: AMEX
Industry: Retail - food & restaurants

SBE, Inc.
4550 North Canyon Rd.
San Ramon, CA 94583
Phone: 510-355-2000 Fax: 510-355-2020
CEO: William Heye
CFO: Timothy Repp
1991 Sales: $128 million Employees: 146
Symbol: SBEI Exchange: NASDAQ
Industry: Computers - microcomputer design and manufacture

SBM Industries, Inc.
3833 Swanson Court
Gurnee, IL 60031
Phone: 708-249-8000 Fax: 708-249-8110
CEO: Peter Nisselson
CFO: Seymour Mogal
1991 Sales: $0.4 million Employees: 3
Symbol: SBM Exchange: AMEX
Industry: Office equipment & supplies

SC Bancorp
9040 E. Telegraph Rd.
Downey, CA 90240
Phone: 310-923-9811 Fax: —
CEO: Larry D. Hartwig
CFO: Norman A. Morales
1991 Sales: $45 million Employees: 252
Symbol: SCK Exchange: AMEX
Industry: Banks - West

Scan-Optics, Inc.
22 Prestige Park Circle
East Hartford, CT 06108
Phone: 203-289-6001 Fax: 203-289-9034
CEO: Richard I. Tanaka
CFO: Carolyn M. Skahill
1991 Sales: $42 million Employees: 407
Symbol: SOCR Exchange: NASDAQ
Industry: Computers - data entry & remittance processing systems

SCANA Corp.
1426 Main St.
Columbia, SC 29201
Phone: 803-748-3000 Fax: 803-733-2435
CEO: Lawrence M. Gressette, Jr.
CFO: William B. Timmerman
1992 Sales: $1,138 million Employees: 4,672
Symbol: SCG Exchange: NYSE
Industry: Utility - electric power

Scandinavian Airlines System of North America, Inc.
9 Polito Ave.
Lyndhurst, NJ 07071
Phone: 201-896-3600 Fax: 201-896-3725
CEO: Owe Lowenborg
CFO: —
1991 Sales: $5,828 million Employees: 38,940
Parent: Scandinavian Airlines System
Industry: Transportation - airline

Scanforms, Inc.
181 Rittenhouse Circle
Bristol, PA 19007
Phone: 215-785-0101 Fax: 215-785-6451
CEO: J. Roy Morris
CFO: J. Roy Morris
1991 Sales: $19 million Employees: 146
Symbol: SCFM Exchange: NASDAQ
Industry: Paper - business forms

SCEcorp
2244 Walnut Grove Ave.
Rosemead, CA 91770
Phone: 818-302-2222 Fax: 818-302-4815
CEO: John E. Bryson
CFO: Alan J. Fohrer
1992 Sales: $7,969 million Employees: 17,511
Symbol: SCE Exchange: NYSE
Industry: Utility - electric power

Schal Associates
200 W. Hubbard St.
Chicago, IL 60610
Phone: 312-245-1000 Fax: 312-245-1379
CEO: Richard C. Halpern
CFO: Ronald Garsha
1990 Sales: $820 million Employees: 260
Ownership: Privately held
Industry: Construction - residential construction & consulting

Schering-Plough Corp.
One Giralda Farms
Madison, NJ 07940
Phone: 201-822-7000 Fax: 201-822-7447
CEO: Robert P. Luciano
CFO: Harold R. Hiser, Jr.
1992 Sales: $4,056 million Employees: 20,200
Symbol: SGP Exchange: NYSE
Industry: Drugs & consumer healthcare products

Schlumberger NV
277 Park Ave.
New York, NY 10172
Phone: 212-350-9400 Fax: 212-350-9564
CEO: D. Euan Baird
CFO: Arthur Lindenauer
1992 Sales: $6,332 million Employees: 53,000
Symbol: SLB Exchange: NYSE
Industry: Oil & gas - field services; measurement systems

Schnaubelt Shorts
1128 4th Ave.
Coraopolis, PA 15108
Phone: 412-262-0993 Fax: 412-262-9016
CEO: Cathy Rodgers
CFO: Paul Rodgers
1991 Sales: $1.4 million Employees: 47
Ownership: Privately held
Industry: Apparel - designer bicycle apparel

Schneider National Inc.
3101 S. Packerland Dr.
Green Bay, WI 54304
Phone: 414-592-5100 Fax: 414-592-3565
CEO: Donald J. Schneider
CFO: Marc L. Schneider
1992 Sales: $1,000 million Employees: 12,500
Ownership: Privately held
Industry: Transportation - trucks

Schnuck Markets Inc.
11420 Lackland Rd.
St. Louis, MO 63146
Phone: 314-994-4400 Fax: 314-344-9739
CEO: Craig D. Schnuck
CFO: Todd Schnuck
1991 Sales: $1,100 million Employees: 6,300
Ownership: Privately held
Industry: Retail - supermarkets

Scholastic Corporation
730 Broadway, 9th Fl.
New York, NY 10003
Phone: 212-505-3000 Fax: 212-505-3377
CEO: Richard Robinson
CFO: Frederic J. Bischoff
1992 Sales: $518 million Employees: 2,236
Symbol: SCHL Exchange: NASDAQ
Industry: Publishing - periodicals & books

Schottenstein Stores
1800 Moler Rd.
Columbus, OH 43207
Phone: 614-221-9200 Fax: 614-443-0225
CEO: Jerome Schottenstein
CFO: Thomas Ketteler
1991 Sales: $1,200 million Employees: 15,000
Ownership: Privately held
Industry: Retail - home furnishings & department stores

Schreiber Foods Inc.
425 Pine St.
Green Bay, WI 54301
Phone: 414-437-7601 Fax: 414-437-1617
CEO: Jack Meng
CFO: Emerson Flye
1991 Sales: $1,100 million Employees: 2,300
Ownership: Privately held
Industry: Food - meat products & cheese

Schuler Homes, Inc.
1001 Bishop St., Ste. 1060
Honolulu, HI 96813
Phone: 808-521-5661 Fax: —
CEO: James K. Schuler
CFO: Pamela S. Jones
1991 Sales: $57 million Employees: 16
Symbol: SHLR Exchange: NASDAQ
Industry: Building - residential & commercial

Schult Homes Corp.
221 US 20 West
Middlebury, IN 46540
Phone: 219-825-5881 Fax: Call co. operator
CEO: Walter E. Wells
CFO: John P. Guequierre
1991 Sales: $162 million Employees: 1,446
Symbol: SHC Exchange: AMEX
Industry: Building - residential & commercial

Schultz Sav-O Stores, Inc.
2215 Union Ave.
Sheboygan, WI 53081
Phone: 414-457-4433 Fax: 414-457-6684
CEO: James H. Dickelman
CFO: John H. Dahly
1991 Sales: $480 million Employees: 2,570
Symbol: SAVO Exchange: NASDAQ
Industry: Retail - supermarkets

Schwan's Sales Enterprise Inc.
115 W. College Dr.
Marshall, MN 56258
Phone: 507-532-3274 Fax: 507-537-8145
CEO: Marvin Schwan
CFO: —
1991 Sales: $1,680 million Employees: 872
Ownership: Privately held
Industry: Food - home delivery of frozen food

Schweitzer Engineering Laboratories
NE 2350 Hopkins Court
Pullman, WA 99163
Phone: 509-332-1890 Fax: 509-332-7990
CEO: Suzan Carter
CFO: Nance Hindman
1991 Sales: $16 million Employees: 84
Ownership: Privately held
Industry: Machinery - protective relays for electric utility companies

Schwitzer, Inc.
1020 Milwaukee Rd., Ste. 205
Deerfield, IL 60015
Phone: 708-520-2553 Fax: 708-520-2997
CEO: Gary G. Dillon
CFO: Richard H. Prange
1991 Sales: $111 million Employees: 1,000
Symbol: SCZ Exchange: NYSE
Industry: Automotive & trucking - original equipment

SCI Systems, Inc.
2101 W. Clinton Ave.
Huntsville, AL 35805
Phone: 205-882-4800 Fax: 205-882-4804
CEO: Olin B. King
CFO: Robert DeLaurentis
1992 Sales: $1,386 million Employees: 9,512
Symbol: SCIS Exchange: NASDAQ
Industry: Electrical products - printed circuit boards, aerospace & defense computers

SciClone Pharmaceuticals, Inc.
901 Mariner's Island Blvd.
San Mateo, CA 94404
Phone: 415-358-3456 Fax: 415-358-3469
CEO: Thomas E. Moore
CFO: Nelson N. Schneider
1991 Sales: $0.3 million Employees: 10
Symbol: SCLN Exchange: NASDAQ
Industry: Drugs

Science Applications International Corp.
10260 Campus Point Dr.
San Diego, CA 92121
Phone: 619-546-6000 Fax: 619-546-6777
CEO: J. R. Beyster
CFO: W. A. Roper
1992 Sales: $1,500 million Employees: 15,000
Ownership: Privately held
Industry: Engineering - R&D services, systems integration

Science Dynamics Corp.
1919 Springdale Rd.
Cherry Hill, NJ 08003
Phone: 609-424-0068 Fax: —
CEO: Lyndon A. Keele
CFO: Lyndon A. Keele
1991 Sales: $6.9 million Employees: 79
Symbol: SIDY Exchange: NASDAQ
Industry: Telecommunications equipment

Science Management Corp.
PO Box 0600
Basking Ridge, NJ 07920
Phone: 908-647-7000 Fax: 908-647-1446
CEO: James A. Skidmore, Jr.
CFO: Edward J. Hughes
1991 Sales: $46 million Employees: 378
Symbol: SMG Exchange: AMEX
Industry: Business services - management & technological services

SCIENTECH, Inc.
1690 International Way
Idaho Falls, ID 83402
Phone: 208-523-2077 Fax: 208-529-4721
CEO: Larry Ybarrondo
CFO: Scott Robuck
1991 Sales: $21 million Employees: 270
Ownership: Privately held
Industry: Nuclear safety, environmental, security services & systems engineering

Scientific Software-Intercomp, Inc.
1801 California St., Ste. 295
Denver, CO 80202
Phone: 303-292-1111 Fax: 303-295-2235
CEO: E. Allen Breitenbach
CFO: Edward S. Wittman
1991 Sales: $25 million Employees: 229
Symbol: SSFT Exchange: NASDAQ
Industry: Diversified operations - software licenses, engineering consulting services

Scientific Technologies Inc.
31069 Genstar Rd.
Hayward, CA 94544
Phone: 415-471-9717 Fax: 415-471-9752
CEO: Anthony R. Lazzara
CFO: Joseph J. Lazzara
1991 Sales: $10.6 million Employees: 109
Symbol: STIZ Exchange: NASDAQ
Industry: Instruments - control

Scientific-Atlanta, Inc.
One Technology Pkwy. South
Atlanta, GA 30092
Phone: 404-903-5000 Fax: 404-441-4617
CEO: William E. Johnson
CFO: Julian W. Eidson
1992 Sales: $677 million Employees: 3,200
Symbol: SFA Exchange: NYSE
Industry: Telecommunications equipment

SciGenics, Inc.
87 Cambridge Park Dr.
Cambridge, MA 02140
Phone: 617-876-1170 Fax: 617-876-1504
CEO: Gabriel Schmergel
CFO: Joseph Grimm
1991 Sales: $0.9 million Employees: 4
Symbol: SCGN Exchange: NASDAQ
Industry: Medical products - protein based pharmaceuticals

SCIMED Life Systems, Inc.
6655 Wedgwood Rd.
Maple Grove, MN 55369
Phone: 612-420-0700 Fax: 612-420-0717
CEO: Dale A. Spencer
CFO: Craig R. Dvorak
1992 Sales: $184 million Employees: 1,240
Symbol: SMLS Exchange: NASDAQ
Industry: Medical instruments

Scios Nova, Inc.
2450 Bayshore Pkwy.
Mountain View, CA 94043
Phone: 415-966-1550 Fax: 415-968-2438
CEO: Richard L. Casey
CFO: W. Virginia Walker
1991 Sales: $7.4 million Employees: 167
Symbol: SCIO Exchange: NASDAQ
Industry: Biomedical & genetic products

Scope Industries
233 Wilshire Blvd., Ste. 790
Santa Monica, CA 90401
Phone: 310-458-1574 Fax: 310-451-5371
CEO: Meyer Luskin
CFO: John J. Crowley
1992 Sales: $21 million Employees: —
Symbol: SCP Exchange: AMEX
Industry: Agricultural operations

SCOR Reinsurance U.S. Corp.
110 William St.
New York, NY 10038
Phone: 212-513-1777 Fax: 212-406-9296
CEO: Patrick Peugeot
CFO: William K. Lowry, Jr.
1991 Sales: $222 million Employees: —
Symbol: SUR Exchange: NYSE
Industry: Insurance - property & casualty

Score Board, Inc., The
1951 Old Cuthbert Rd.
Cherry Hill, NJ 08034
Phone: 609-354-9000 Fax: 609-795-1942
CEO: Paul Goldin
CFO: Rick Wasserman
1991 Sales: $59 million Employees: 152
Symbol: BSBL Exchange: NASDAQ
Industry: Leisure & recreational services - sports picture cards

Scotsman Industries, Inc.
775 Corporate Woods Pkwy.
Vernon Hills, IL 60061
Phone: 708-215-4500 Fax: 708-913-9844
CEO: Richard C. Osborne
CFO: Donald D. Holmes
1991 Sales: $164 million Employees: 1,075
Symbol: SCT Exchange: NYSE
Industry: Building products - a/c & heating

Scott Paper Co.
Scott Plaza
Philadelphia, PA 19113
Phone: 215-522-5000 Fax: 215-522-5129
CEO: Philip E. Lippincott
CFO: Basil L. Anderson
1992 Sales: $4,886 million Employees: 29,100
Symbol: SPP Exchange: NYSE
Industry: Paper & paper products - personal & printing & publishing paper

Scott & Stringfellow Financial, Inc.
909 E. Main St.
Richmond, VA 23219
Phone: 804-643-1811 Fax: —
CEO: William P. Schubmehl
CFO: Jeffrey D. Levin
1992 Sales: $46 million Employees: 387
Symbol: SCOT Exchange: NASDAQ
Industry: Financial - investment management

Scottish Heritable, Inc.
501 S. Wilhite St.
Cleburne, TX 76031
Phone: 817-645-9111 Fax: —
CEO: Neville C. Platt
CFO: Avelino Martinez
1991 Sales: $40 million Employees: 399
Symbol: SHER Exchange: NASDAQ
Industry: Construction - cement & concrete

Scotts Co.
14111 Scottslawn Rd.
Marysville, OH 43041
Phone: 513-644-0011 Fax: —
CEO: Tadd C. Seitz
CFO: Paul D. Yeager
1991 Sales: $388 million Employees: 1,731
Symbol: SCTT Exchange: NASDAQ
Industry: Chemicals - specialty

Scoular Company, The
2027 Dodge St.
Omaha, NE 68102
Phone: 402-342-3500 Fax: 402-342-5568
CEO: Marshall E. Faith
CFO: Timothy J. Regan
1991 Sales: $1,286 million Employees: 250
Ownership: Privately held
Industry: Food - grain trading & storing

Scripps Howard Broadcasting Div.
Central Trust Tower, Ste. 1100
Cincinnati, OH 45202
Phone: 513-977-3000 Fax: 513-621-6541
CEO: Richard J. Janssen
CFO: Daniel J. Castellini
1991 Sales: $348 million Employees: 2,000
Symbol: SCRP Exchange: NASDAQ
Industry: Broadcasting - radio & TV

SCS/Compute, Inc.
12444 Powerscourt Dr., Ste. 400
St. Louis, MO 63131
Phone: 314-966-1040 Fax: 314-966-5915
CEO: Robert W. Nolan
CFO: Charles G. Wilson
1991 Sales: $37 million Employees: 942
Symbol: SCOM Exchange: NASDAQ
Industry: Computers - tax & accounting software

SDNB Financial Corp.
1420 Kettner Blvd.
San Diego, CA 92101
Phone: 619-233-1234 Fax: —
CEO: Murray L. Galinson
CFO: Howard W. Brotman
1991 Sales: $15 million Employees: 101
Symbol: SDNB Exchange: NASDAQ
Industry: Banks - West

Seaboard Bancorp, Inc.
501 S. Independence Blvd.
Virginia Beach, VA 23450
Phone: 804-490-3181 Fax: —
CEO: Clarence W. Keel
CFO: Willis E. Watson
1991 Sales: $10 million Employees: 42
Symbol: SEAB Exchange: NASDAQ
Industry: Financial - savings and loans

Seaboard Corp.
200 Boylston St.
Chestnut Hill, MA 02167
Phone: 617-332-8492 Fax: 617-244-5463
CEO: H. H. Bresky
CFO: Joe E. Rodrigues
1991 Sales: $876 million Employees: 10,970
Symbol: SEB Exchange: AMEX
Industry: Food - meat products

Seacoast Banking Corporation of Florida
U.S. 1 and Colorado Ave.
Stuart, FL 34995
Phone: 305-287-4000 Fax: —
CEO: Dennis S. Hudson, Jr.
CFO: Dennis S. Hudson III
1991 Sales: $29 million Employees: 373
Symbol: SBCFA Exchange: NASDAQ
Industry: Banks - Southeast

Seafield Capital Corp.
2600 Grand Ave., Ste. 500
Kansas City, MO 64108
Phone: 816-842-7000 Fax: 816-842-2101
CEO: W. Thomas Grant II
CFO: James R. Seward
1991 Sales: $104 million Employees: —
Symbol: SFLD Exchange: NASDAQ
Industry: Insurance - life

indicates company is in *Hoover's Handbook of American Business*

indicates company is in *Hoover's Handbook of World Business;* sales and employee numbers are for parent company.

Seagate Technology, Inc.
920 Disc Dr.
Scotts Valley, CA 95066
Phone: 408-438-6550 Fax: 408-438-6172
CEO: Alan F. Shugart
CFO: Donald L. Waite
1992 Sales: $3,079 million Employees: 43,000
Symbol: SGAT Exchange: NASDAQ
Industry: Computers - disk drives

Seagull Energy Corp.
1001 Fannin St., Ste. 1700
Houston, TX 77002
Phone: 713-951-4700 Fax: 713-951-4819
CEO: Barry J. Galt
CFO: Robert W. Shower
1991 Sales: $248 million Employees: 507
Symbol: SGO Exchange: NYSE
Industry: Oil & gas - production & pipeline

Sealed Air Corp.
One Park 80 Plaza East
Saddle Brook, NJ 07662
Phone: 201-791-7600 Fax: 201-368-2674
CEO: T. J. Dermot Dunphy
CFO: William V. Hickey
1991 Sales: $435 million Employees: 2,770
Symbol: SEE Exchange: NYSE
Industry: Containers - paper & plastic

Sealright Co., Inc.
7101 College Blvd., Ste. 1400
Overland Park, KS 66210
Phone: 913-344-9000 Fax: 913-344-9005
CEO: Marvin W. Ozley
CFO: John L. Wempe
1991 Sales: $258 million Employees: 1,793
Symbol: SRCO Exchange: NASDAQ
Industry: Containers - paper & plastic

Sealy, Inc.
1228 Euclid Ave., 10th Fl.
Cleveland, OH 44115
Phone: 216-522-1310 Fax: 216-522-0602
CEO: Lyman Beggs
CFO: Thomas L. Smudz
1991 Sales: $624 million Employees: 4,500
Ownership: Privately held
Industry: Furniture - mattresses, waterbeds, sofa beds

Sears, Roebuck and Co.
Sears Tower, 233 S. Wacker Dr.
Chicago, IL 60684
Phone: 312-875-2500 Fax: 312-875-8351
CEO: Edward A. Brennan
CFO: Edward M. Liddy
1992 Sales: $52,345 million Employees: 450,000
Symbol: S Exchange: NYSE
Industry: Diversified operations - retail sales, insurance, financial services

Seattle FilmWorks, Inc.
1260 16th Ave. West
Seattle, WA 98119
Phone: 206-281-1390 Fax: 206-284-5357
CEO: Gary R. Christophersen
CFO: James H. Smith
1991 Sales: $37 million Employees: 290
Symbol: FOTO Exchange: NASDAQ
Industry: Retail - mail order & direct; photo processing

Seaway Food Town, Inc.
1020 Ford St.
Maumee, OH 43537
Phone: 419-893-9401 Fax: 419-891-4214
CEO: Wallace D. Iott
CFO: Waldo E. Yeager
1991 Sales: $571 million Employees: 4,762
Symbol: SEWY Exchange: NASDAQ
Industry: Retail - supermarkets

Secom General Corp.
46035 Grand River
Novi, MI 48376
Phone: 313-349-8970 Fax: 313-349-7566
CEO: Roy A. McKnight
CFO: David J. Marczak
1991 Sales: $17 million Employees: 409
Symbol: SECM Exchange: NASDAQ
Industry: Machine tools & related products

Second National Bancorp
2045 West St. at Route 2
Annapolis, MD 21401
Phone: 410-266-9200 Fax: —
CEO: Henry A. Berliner, Jr.
CFO: Henry A. Berliner, Jr.
1991 Sales: $165 million Employees: 485
Symbol: SNLB Exchange: NASDAQ
Industry: Financial - savings and loans

Secor Bank, Federal Savings Bank
201 Office Park Dr.
Birmingham, AL 35223
Phone: 205-877-0200 Fax: —
CEO: William L. Watson III
CFO: F. Eugene Woodham
1992 Sales: — Employees: —
Symbol: SECR Exchange: NASDAQ
Industry: Banks - Southeast

Securities Service Network
222 S. Peters Rd.
Knoxville, TN 37923
Phone: 615-690-5400 Fax: 615-691-5243
CEO: Steven Coffey
CFO: Steven Coffey
1991 Sales: $4.6 million Employees: 73
Ownership: Privately held
Industry: Business services - investment brokerage services

Security Capital Bancorp
215-217 S. Main St.
Salisbury, NC 28144
Phone: 704-633-7800 Fax: —
CEO: David B. Jordan
CFO: Pressley Ridgill
1992 Sales: — Employees: —
Symbol: SCBC Exchange: NASDAQ
Industry: Banks - Southeast

Security Federal Savings and Loan
1413 Golden Gate Blvd.
Mayfield Heights, OH 44124
Phone: 216-449-3700 Fax: —
CEO: Charles F. Valentine
CFO: Kenneth M. Haffey
1992 Sales: — Employees: —
Symbol: SFSL Exchange: NASDAQ
Industry: Financial - savings and loans

Security Federal Savings Bank
219 N. 26th St.
Billings, MT 59101
Phone: 406-259-4571 Fax: —
CEO: David W. Jorgenson
CFO: Jerry H. Jones
1992 Sales: — Employees: —
Symbol: SFBM Exchange: NASDAQ
Industry: Financial - savings and loans

Security Financial Holding Co.
505 S. Duke St.
Durham, NC 27701
Phone: 919-687-7200 Fax: —
CEO: Larry D. Brock
CFO: Robert F. Stockwell
1991 Sales: $30 million Employees: 93
Symbol: SECF Exchange: NASDAQ
Industry: Financial - savings and loans

Security Investments Group, Inc.
818 Landis Ave.
Vineland, NJ 08360
Phone: 609-691-2400 Fax: —
CEO: Ronald A. Seagraves
CFO: Ernest T. Szeker, Jr.
1991 Sales: $111 million Employees: 584
Symbol: SSLN Exchange: NASDAQ
Industry: Financial - savings and loans

Security National Financial Corp.
5300 South 360 West, Ste. 310
Salt Lake City, UT 84123
Phone: 801-264-1060 Fax: —
CEO: George R. Quist
CFO: William L. Sargent
1991 Sales: $22 million Employees: —
Symbol: SNFCA Exchange: NASDAQ
Industry: Insurance - multiline & misc.

Security Tag Systems, Inc.
1615 118th Ave. North
St. Petersburg, FL 33716
Phone: 813-576-6399 Fax: 813-579-4438
CEO: Carter W. Clarke, Jr.
CFO: William J. Bufe
1992 Sales: $20 million Employees: 147
Symbol: STAG Exchange: NASDAQ
Industry: Electrical products - electronic surveillance systems

SEEQ Technology, Inc.
1849 Fortune Dr.
San Jose, CA 95131
Phone: 408-432-7400 Fax: 408-432-9549
CEO: J. Daniel McCranie
CFO: Ralph J. Harms
1991 Sales: $49 million Employees: 332
Symbol: SEEQ Exchange: NASDAQ
Industry: Electrical components - semiconductors

SEI Corp.
680 E. Swedesford Rd.
Wayne, PA 19087
Phone: 215-254-1000 Fax: 215-964-8427
CEO: Alfred P. West, Jr.
CFO: Carmen V. Romeo
1991 Sales: $188 million Employees: 1,485
Symbol: SEIC Exchange: NASDAQ
Industry: Computers - information processing & software services

Seiko Corporation of America
1111 MacArthur Blvd.
Mahwah, NJ 07430
Phone: 201-512-3000 Fax: 201-529-1543
CEO: Shigeho Kurashina
CFO: —
1992 Sales: $3,424 million Employees: 1,488
Parent: Seiko Corporation
Industry: Watches, clocks & jewelry, ophthalmic products

Seitel, Inc.
16010 Barker's Point Lane
Houston, TX 77079
Phone: 713-558-1990 Fax: 713-558-2319
CEO: Paul A. Frame
CFO: Debra D. Valice
1991 Sales: $27 million Employees: 31
Symbol: SEI Exchange: NYSE
Industry: Oil & gas - field services

Selas Corporation of America
2034 Limeklin Pike
Dresher, PA 19025
Phone: 215-646-6600 Fax: 215-646-3536
CEO: Stephen F. Ryan
CFO: Robert W. Ross
1991 Sales: $40 million Employees: 250
Symbol: SLS Exchange: AMEX
Industry: Diversified operations - heat processing products & tire holders

indicates company is in *Hoover's Handbook of American Business*

indicates company is in *Hoover's Handbook of World Business*; sales and employee numbers are for parent company.

Select Ticketing Systems, Inc.
327 W. Fayette St.
Syracuse, NY 13202
Phone: 315-479-6663 Fax: 315-471-2715
CEO: Karen Goetz
CFO: Steven Dippolito
1991 Sales: $8 million Employees: 69
Ownership: Privately held
Industry: Computerized box-office & outlet ticketing systems

Selective Insurance Group, Inc.
40 Wantage Ave.
Branchville, NJ 07890
Phone: 201-948-3000 Fax: 201-948-5721
CEO: Frederick H. Jarvis
CFO: Dominic J. Addesso
1992 Sales: $616 million Employees: —
Symbol: SIGI Exchange: NASDAQ
Industry: Insurance - property & casualty

Selfix, Inc.
4501 W. 47th St.
Chicago, IL 60632
Phone: 312-890-1010 Fax: 312-890-0523
CEO: Meyer J. Ragir
CFO: Joseph R. Giglio
1991 Sales: $37 million Employees: 318
Symbol: SLFX Exchange: NASDAQ
Industry: Housewares

Semiconductor Packaging Materials Co.
431 Fayette Ave.
Mamaroneck, NY 10543
Phone: 914-698-5353 Fax: —
CEO: G. D. Raker
CFO: J. McCarron
1991 Sales: $6.8 million Employees: 53
Symbol: SEM Exchange: AMEX
Industry: Wire & cable products

Semtech Corp.
652 Mitchell Rd.
Newbury Park, CA 91320
Phone: 805-498-2111 Fax: 805-498-3804
CEO: John D. Poe
CFO: Steven M. Otterbeck
1991 Sales: $27 million Employees: 315
Symbol: SMH Exchange: AMEX
Industry: Electrical components - silicon rectifiers & capacitors

Seneca Foods Corp.
1162 Pittsford-Victor Rd.
Pittsford, NY 14534
Phone: 716-385-9500 Fax: 716-385-4249
CEO: Frederick W. Leick
CFO: Kraig H. Kayser
1991 Sales: $321 million Employees: 2,964
Symbol: SENE Exchange: NASDAQ
Industry: Food - canned

Sensormatic Electronics Corp.
500 NW 12th Ave.
Deerfield Beach, FL 33442
Phone: 305-427-9700 Fax: 305-427-0408
CEO: Ronald G. Assaf
CFO: Michael E. Pardue
1992 Sales: $310 million Employees: 2,899
Symbol: SRM Exchange: NYSE
Industry: Protection - safety equipment & services

Sentinel Systems Inc.
2713 Magruder Blvd., Ste. I
Hampton, VA 23666
Phone: 804-766-0200 Fax: 804-766-2781
CEO: George Young
CFO: Catherine Young
1991 Sales: $4.6 million Employees: 19
Ownership: Privately held
Industry: Protection - home security products

Sepracor Inc.
33 Locke Dr.
Marlborough, MA 01752
Phone: 508-481-6700 Fax: 508-481-7683
CEO: Timothy J. Barberich
CFO: Victor H. Woolley
1991 Sales: $13 million Employees: 171
Symbol: SEPR Exchange: NASDAQ
Industry: Drugs

Sequa Corp.
200 Park Ave.
New York, NY 10166
Phone: 212-986-5500 Fax: 212-370-1969
CEO: Norman E. Alexander
CFO: Gerald S. Gutterman
1991 Sales: $1,879 million Employees: 15,750
Symbol: SQAA Exchange: NYSE
Industry: Chemicals - specialty

Sequent Computer Systems, Inc.
15450 SW Koll Pkwy.
Beaverton, OR 97006
Phone: 503-626-5700 Fax: 503-578-9890
CEO: Karl C. Powell, Jr.
CFO: Robert S. Gregg
1991 Sales: $213 million Employees: 1,364
Symbol: SQNT Exchange: NASDAQ
Industry: Computers - mainframe

Sequoia Systems, Inc.
400 Nickerson Rd.
Marlborough, MA 01752
Phone: 508-480-0800 Fax: 508-490-0184
CEO: Cornelius P. McMullan
CFO: Richard B. Goldman
1991 Sales: $63 million Employees: 345
Symbol: SEQS Exchange: NASDAQ
Industry: Computers - mini & micro

Seragen, Inc.
97 South St.
Hopkinton, MA 01748
Phone: 508-435-2331 Fax: 508-435-9805
CEO: Richard C. Svrluga
CFO: John J. Curry
1992 Sales: — Employees: 126
Symbol: SRGN Exchange: NASDAQ
Industry: Medical products

Serv-Tech, Inc.
5200 Cedar Crest Blvd.
Houston, TX 77087
Phone: 713-644-9974 Fax: 713-644-0731
CEO: Richard W. Krajicek
CFO: John M. Slack
1991 Sales: $88 million Employees: 1,041
Symbol: STEC Exchange: NASDAQ
Industry: Oil & gas - field services

Service America Corp.
88 Gatehouse Rd.
Stamford, CT 06904
Phone: 203-964-5000 Fax: 203-964-5018
CEO: Steven Leipsner
CFO: Bernard H. Bard
1991 Sales: $893 million Employees: 19,000
Ownership: Privately held
Industry: Food - service & vending

Service Corporation International
1929 Allen Pkwy.
Houston, TX 77019
Phone: 713-522-5141 Fax: 713-525-5586
CEO: Robert L. Waltrip
CFO: Samuel W. Rizzo
1992 Sales: $773 million Employees: 11,577
Symbol: SRV Exchange: NYSE
Industry: Funeral services & related

Service Fracturing Co.
Hwy. 152 West
Pampa, TX 79066
Phone: 806-665-7221 Fax: 806-665-2366
CEO: Jerry H. Guinn
CFO: Danny Seabourn
1992 Sales: $17 million Employees: 175
Symbol: SERF Exchange: NASDAQ
Industry: Oil & gas - field services

Service Merchandise Co., Inc.
7100 Service Merchandise Dr.
Brentwood, TN 37027
Phone: 615-660-6000 Fax: 615-660-7912
CEO: Raymond Zimmerman
CFO: S. P. Braud III
1992 Sales: $3,713 million Employees: 22,400
Symbol: SME Exchange: NYSE
Industry: Retail - catalog showrooms

ServiceMaster L.P.
One ServiceMaster Way
Downers Grove, IL 60515
Phone: 708-964-1300 Fax: 708-719-6878
CEO: C. William Pollard
CFO: Robert F. Keith
1991 Sales: $2,110 million Employees: 21,100
Symbol: SVM Exchange: NYSE
Industry: Building - maintenance & services

Services Group of America
4025 Delridge Way SW, Ste. 500
Seattle, WA 98106
Phone: 206-933-5225 Fax: 206-933-5247
CEO: Thomas J. Stewart
CFO: Dennis Specht
1991 Sales: $1,272 million Employees: 3,000
Ownership: Privately held
Industry: Diversified operations - food distribution, insurance & real estate

Servico, Inc.
1601 Belvedere Rd.
West Palm Beach, FL 33406
Phone: 407-689-9970 Fax: 407-689-8946
CEO: David E. Hawthorne
CFO: David E. Hawthorne
1991 Sales: $135 million Employees: 3,351
Symbol: SER Exchange: AMEX
Industry: Hotels & motels

Servotronics, Inc.
3901 Union Rd.
Buffalo, NY 14225
Phone: 716-633-5990 Fax: 716-633-8286
CEO: Nicholas D. Trbovich
CFO: Nicholas D. Trbovich
1991 Sales: $16 million Employees: 245
Symbol: SVT Exchange: AMEX
Industry: Diversified operations - advanced technology & cutlery products

Seven Oaks International, Inc.
700 Colonial Rd., Ste. 100
Memphis, TN 38117
Phone: 901-683-7055 Fax: 901-684-6968
CEO: Frank J. Donato
CFO: Tommy R. Thompson
1992 Sales: $7.9 million Employees: 950
Symbol: QPON Exchange: NASDAQ
Industry: Business services - coupon processing

Sevenson Environmental Services Inc.
2749 Lockport Rd.
Niagara Falls, NY 14302
Phone: 716-284-0431 Fax: 716-284-7645
CEO: Arthur Elia
CFO: William J. McDermott
1991 Sales: $48 million Employees: 362
Symbol: SEVN Exchange: NASDAQ
Industry: Pollution control equipment & services - construction site remediation

indicates company is in *Hoover's Handbook of American Business*

indicates company is in *Hoover's Handbook of World Business*; sales and employee numbers are for parent company.

SFFed Corp.
88 Kearny St.
San Francisco, CA 94108
Phone: 415-955-5800 Fax: 415-391-1431
CEO: Roger L. Gordon
CFO: Paul Weinberg
1991 Sales: $328 million Employees: 774
Symbol: SFFD Exchange: NASDAQ
Industry: Financial - savings and loans

SFM Corp.
870 Seventh Ave.
New York, NY 10019
Phone: 212-757-1717 Fax: —
CEO: David A. Segal
CFO: Attila G. Libertiny
1991 Sales: $21 million Employees: 140
Symbol: SFM Exchange: AMEX
Industry: Machinery - electrical

SGI International
1200 Prospect St., Ste. 325
La Jolla, CA 92037
Phone: 619-551-1090 Fax: 619-551-0247
CEO: William M. Owens
CFO: William M. Owens
1991 Sales: $1.1 million Employees: 15
Symbol: SGII Exchange: NASDAQ
Industry: Engineering - R&D services, coal refining technologies

Shapell Industries Inc.
8383 Wilshire Blvd., Ste. 700
Beverly Hills, CA 90211
Phone: 213-655-7330 Fax: 213-655-8135
CEO: Nathan Shapell
CFO: Thomas Zieger
1991 Sales: $575 million Employees: 350
Ownership: Privately held
Industry: Construction & land development

Shared Medical Systems Corp.
51 Valley Stream Pkwy.
Malvern, PA 19355
Phone: 215-296-6300 Fax: 215-251-3124
CEO: R. James Macaleer
CFO: Terrence W. Kyle
1991 Sales: $438 million Employees: 4,093
Symbol: SMED Exchange: NASDAQ
Industry: Computers - services

Sharp Electronics Corporation
Sharp Plaza
Mahwah, NJ 07430
Phone: 201-529-8200 Fax: 201-529-8413
CEO: Sueyiki Hirooka
CFO: —
1992 Sales: $12,144 million Employees: 41,029
Parent: Sharp Corporation
Industry: Audio & video products, information systems & electronic components

Sharper Image Corp.
650 Davis St.
San Francisco, CA 94111
Phone: 415-445-6000 Fax: 415-781-5251
CEO: Richard Thalheimer
CFO: Robert A. Stoffregen
1991 Sales: $142 million Employees: 900
Symbol: SHRP Exchange: NASDAQ
Industry: Retail - mail order & direct

Shaw Industries, Inc.
616 E. Walnut Ave.
Dalton, GA 30721
Phone: 706-278-3812 Fax: 706-275-1040
CEO: Robert E. Shaw
CFO: William C. Lusk, Jr.
1992 Sales: $2,036 million Employees: 19,100
Symbol: SHX Exchange: NYSE
Industry: Textiles - home furnishings

Shaw's Supermarkets, Inc.
140 Laurel St.
East Bridgewater, MA 02333
Phone: 508-378-7211 Fax: 508-378-3916
CEO: D. B. Jenkins
CFO: —
1992 Sales: $16,242 million Employees: 112,784
Parent: J Sainsbury PLC
Industry: Retail - food & beverages, personal care; livestock, superstores

Shawmut National Corp.
777 Main St.
Hartford, CT 06115
Phone: 203-728-2000 Fax: 203-728-4700
CEO: Joel B. Alvord
CFO: Joel B. Alvord
1992 Sales: $2,024 million Employees: 10,792
Symbol: SNC Exchange: NYSE
Industry: Banks - Northeast

Sheffield Industries, Inc.
1190 N.W. 159th Dr.
Miami, FL 33169
Phone: 305-624-8493 Fax: 305-623-1376
CEO: Mitchell A. Hammer
CFO: Michael Mandelblatt
1991 Sales: $29 million Employees: —
Symbol: HOSEE Exchange: NASDAQ
Industry: Apparel

Shelby Williams Industries, Inc.
5303 E. Tennessee Blvd.
Morristown, TN 37813
Phone: 615-586-7000 Fax: 615-586-2260
CEO: Paul N. Steinfeld
CFO: Sam Ferrell
1991 Sales: $140 million Employees: 1,602
Symbol: SY Exchange: NYSE
Industry: Furniture

Sheldahl, Inc.
Hwy. 3 North
Northfield, MN 55057
Phone: 507-663-8000 Fax: 507-663-8365
CEO: James E. Donaghy
CFO: John V. McManus
1991 Sales: $87 million Employees: 1,162
Symbol: SHEL Exchange: NASDAQ
Industry: Electrical components - flexible circuitry, graphic display systems

Shell Oil Co.
One Shell Plaza
Houston, TX 77252
Phone: 713-241-6161 Fax: 713-241-6781
CEO: Frank H. Richardson
CFO: —
1991 Sales: $102,697 million Employees: 133,000
Parent: Royal Dutch/Shell Group
Industry: Oil & gas - international integrated

Shelter Components Corp.
27217 C.R. 6
Elkhart, IN 46514
Phone: 219-262-4541 Fax: 219-262-3936
CEO: Richard E. Summers
CFO: Mark C. Neilson
1991 Sales: $143 million Employees: 523
Symbol: SST Exchange: AMEX
Industry: Building - mobile homes & RVs

Shelton Bancorp, Inc.
427 Howe Ave.
Shelton, CT 06484
Phone: 203-924-4801 Fax: —
CEO: Kenneth E. Schaible
CFO: William C. Nimons
1991 Sales: $5.5 million Employees: 55
Symbol: SSBC Exchange: NASDAQ
Industry: Banks - Northeast

Shepard-Patterson & Associates
15 E. Ridge Pike, Ste. 220
Conshohocken, PA 19428
Phone: 215-941-9010 Fax: 215-941-9022
CEO: Sam Patterson
CFO: Greg Shepard
1991 Sales: $1.4 million Employees: 32
Ownership: Privately held
Industry: Computers - services

Sherikon Inc.
14585 Avion Pkwy. #2500
Chantilly, VA 22021
Phone: 703-803-7000 Fax: 703-803-3730
CEO: Edward R. Fernandez
CFO: Michael Newton
1991 Sales: $14 million Employees: 193
Ownership: Privately held
Industry: Engineering services

Sherwin-Williams Co., The
101 Prospect Ave. NW
Cleveland, OH 44115
Phone: 216-566-2000 Fax: 216-566-3310
CEO: John G. Breen
CFO: Larry J. Pitorak
1992 Sales: $2,748 million Employees: 16,682
Symbol: SHW Exchange: NYSE
Industry: Paints & allied products

Sherwood Group, Inc.
One Exchange Plaza
New York, NY 10006
Phone: 212-482-4000 Fax: —
CEO: Fredric W. Rittereiser
CFO: Phillip Siegel
1992 Sales: $44 million Employees: 141
Symbol: SHD Exchange: AMEX
Industry: Financial - business services

Shields Health Care
265 Westgate Dr.
Brockton, MA 02401
Phone: 508-559-7616 Fax: 508-584-9824
CEO: Thomas F. Shields
CFO: Mark Attarian
1991 Sales: $28 million Employees: 120
Ownership: Privately held
Industry: Medical services - medical diagnostic imaging

Shiseido America Inc.
900 3rd Ave.
New York, NY 10022
Phone: 212-752-2644 Fax: 212-688-0109
CEO: Sadao Abe
CFO: —
1992 Sales: — Employees: 3,605
Parent: Shiseido Co., Ltd.
Industry: Cosmetics & toiletries

Shiva Corporation
Northwest Park, 63 Third Ave.
Burlington, MA 01803
Phone: 617-270-8300 Fax: 617-270-8599
CEO: Dan Schwinn
CFO: Paul Chesterman
1991 Sales: $28 million Employees: 130
Ownership: Privately held
Industry: Computers - remote networking products

ShoLodge, Inc.
217 W. Main St.
Gallatin, TN 37066
Phone: 615-452-7200 Fax: —
CEO: Leon Moore
CFO: Bob Marlowe
1991 Sales: $35 million Employees: 890
Symbol: LODG Exchange: NASDAQ
Industry: Hotels & motels

Shoney's, Inc.
1727 Elm Hill Pike
Nashville, TN 37210
Phone: 615-391-5201 Fax: 615-391-9498
CEO: Taylor H. Henry, Jr.
CFO: W. Craig Barber
1992 Sales: $1,062 million Employees: 28,800
Symbol: SHN Exchange: NYSE
Industry: Retail - food & restaurants

Shopco Laurel Center, L.P.
388 Greenwich St., 28th Fl.
New York, NY 10013
Phone: 212-464-2465 Fax: —
CEO: Paul L. Abbott
CFO: Robert J. Hellman
1991 Sales: $9 million Employees: —
Symbol: LSC Exchange: AMEX
Industry: Real estate operations

ShopKo Stores, Inc.
700 Pilgrim Way
Green Bay, WI 54304
Phone: 414-497-2211 Fax: 414-496-4133
CEO: Dale P. Kramer
CFO: Lawrence J. Clark
1992 Sales: $1,709 million Employees: 17,400
Symbol: SKO Exchange: NYSE
Industry: Retail - regional department stores

Shopsmith, Inc.
3931 Image Dr.
Dayton, OH 45414
Phone: 513-898-6070 Fax: Call co. operator
CEO: John R. Folkerth
CFO: William C. Becker
1992 Sales: $53 million Employees: 460
Symbol: SHOP Exchange: NASDAQ
Industry: Retail - mail order & direct

Shoreline Financial Corp.
823 Riverview Dr.
Benton Harbor, MI 49022
Phone: 616-927-2251 Fax: —
CEO: James F. Murphy
CFO: Wayne R. Koebel
1991 Sales: $44 million Employees: 290
Symbol: SLFC Exchange: NASDAQ
Industry: Banks - Midwest

Shorewood Packaging Corp.
55 Engineers Lane
Farmingdale, NY 11735
Phone: 516-694-2900 Fax: 516-752-9369
CEO: Paul B. Shore
CFO: Murray B. Frischer
1992 Sales: $160 million Employees: 1,090
Symbol: SHOR Exchange: NASDAQ
Industry: Paper & paper products

ShowBiz Pizza Time, Inc.
4441 W. Airport Fwy.
Irving, TX 75015
Phone: 214-258-8507 Fax: 214-258-8545
CEO: Richard M. Frank
CFO: Michael H. Magusiak
1991 Sales: $208 million Employees: 9,475
Symbol: SHBZ Exchange: NASDAQ
Industry: Retail - food & restaurants

Showboat, Inc.
2800 Fremont St.
Las Vegas, NV 89104
Phone: 702-385-9141 Fax: 702-385-9163
CEO: J. K. Houssels
CFO: Leann Schneider
1991 Sales: $331 million Employees: 4,950
Symbol: SBO Exchange: NYSE
Industry: Leisure & recreational services - casinos, hotels & bowling centers

Showscan Corp.
1801 Century Park East
Los Angeles, CA 90067
Phone: 213-553-2364 Fax: —
CEO: Roy H. Aaron
CFO: James A. Sorenson
1992 Sales: $10.2 million Employees: 51
Symbol: SHOW Exchange: NASDAQ
Industry: Motion pictures & services

SI Handling Systems, Inc.
Kesslersville Rd.
Easton, PA 18044
Phone: 215-252-7321 Fax: —
CEO: Leonard S. Yurkovic
CFO: Leonard S. Yurkovic
1992 Sales: $21 million Employees: 156
Symbol: SIHS Exchange: NASDAQ
Industry: Machinery - material handling

Siciliano Inc.
154 W. Lake Dr.
Springfield, IL 62703
Phone: 217-585-1200 Fax: 217-585-1211
CEO: Patricia J. Siciliano
CFO: Patricia J. Siciliano
1991 Sales: $7.6 million Employees: 50
Ownership: Privately held
Industry: Construction - commercial & industrial; restoration, (sitework, utilities) demolition

Siemens Corp.
1301 Avenue of the Americas
New York, NY 10019
Phone: 212-258-4000 Fax: 212-258-4370
CEO: Albert Hoser
CFO: —
1991 Sales: $48,032 million Employees: 402,000
Parent: Siemens AG
Industry: Diversified operations - electronics, communications systems

Sierra Health Services, Inc.
333 N. Rancho Dr., Ste. 900
Las Vegas, NV 89106
Phone: 702-646-8100 Fax: 702-646-0144
CEO: Anthony M. Marlon
CFO: Robert A. Mayer
1991 Sales: $209 million Employees: 1,281
Symbol: SIE Exchange: AMEX
Industry: Health maintenance organization

Sierra On-Line, Inc.
40033 Sierra Way
Oakhurst, CA 93644
Phone: 209-683-4468 Fax: 209-683-3633
CEO: Kenneth A. Williams
CFO: Bruce E. Grant
1992 Sales: $42 million Employees: 527
Symbol: SIER Exchange: NASDAQ
Industry: Computers - entertainment software

Sierra Pacific Industries
PO Box 496028
Redding,, CA 96049
Phone: 916-365-3721 Fax: 916-275-4811
CEO: Red Emmerson
CFO: Mark Emmerson
1991 Sales: $507 million Employees: 2,500
Ownership: Privately held
Industry: Building products - wholesale lumber

Sierra Pacific Resources
6100 Neil Rd., 5th Fl.
Reno, NV 89511
Phone: 702-689-3600 Fax: 702-689-3815
CEO: Austin W. Stedham
CFO: John E. Taulbee
1991 Sales: $469 million Employees: 1,818
Symbol: SRP Exchange: NYSE
Industry: Utility - electric power

Sierra Semiconductor Corp.
2075 N. Capitol Ave.
San Jose, CA 95132
Phone: 408-263-9300 Fax: 408-263-3337
CEO: James V. Diller
CFO: C. Stephen Cordial
1991 Sales: $86 million Employees: 328
Symbol: SERA Exchange: NASDAQ
Industry: Electrical components - semiconductors

Sierra Tahoe Bancorp
10059 Palisades Dr.
Truckee, CA 95734
Phone: 916-582-3000 Fax: —
CEO: Jerrold T. Henley
CFO: David C. Broadley
1991 Sales: $33 million Employees: 188
Symbol: STBS Exchange: NASDAQ
Industry: Banks - West

Sierra Tucson Companies, Inc.
16500 N. Lago del Oro Pkwy.
Tucson, AZ 85737
Phone: 602-624-4000 Fax: Call co. operator
CEO: William T. O'Donnell, Jr.
CFO: John H. Schmitz
1991 Sales: $44 million Employees: 532
Symbol: STSN Exchange: NASDAQ
Industry: Healthcare - outpatient & home

SIFCO Industries, Inc.
970 E. 64th St.
Cleveland, OH 44103
Phone: 216-881-8600 Fax: 216-881-1828
CEO: Jeffrey P. Gotschall
CFO: Richard A. Demetter
1991 Sales: $65 million Employees: 577
Symbol: SIF Exchange: AMEX
Industry: Metal processing & fabrication

Sigma Designs, Inc.
47900 Bayside Pkwy.
Fremont, CA 94538
Phone: 510-770-0100 Fax: 510-770-0110
CEO: Thinh Q. Tran
CFO: Q. Binh Trinh
1991 Sales: $28 million Employees: 197
Symbol: SIGM Exchange: NASDAQ
Industry: Computers - graphics & display products

Sigma-Aldrich Corp.
3050 Spruce St.
St. Louis, MO 63103
Phone: 314-771-5765 Fax: 1-800-325-5052
CEO: Carl T. Cori
CFO: Peter A. Gleich
1991 Sales: $589 million Employees: 4,192
Symbol: SIAL Exchange: NASDAQ
Industry: Chemicals - specialty

Signal Apparel Co., Inc.
200 Manufacturers Rd.
Chattanooga, TN 37405
Phone: 615-756-8146 Fax: 615-755-6662
CEO: Roger Holland
CFO: Donald R. Sherman
1991 Sales: $90 million Employees: 2,500
Symbol: SIA Exchange: NYSE
Industry: Textiles - apparel

Signet Banking Corp.
7 N. Eighth St.
Richmond, VA 23219
Phone: 804-747-2000 Fax: 804-771-7599
CEO: Robert M. Freeman
CFO: Wallace B. Millner III
1992 Sales: $1,041 million Employees: 5,732
Symbol: SBK Exchange: NYSE
Industry: Banks - Southeast

Silgan Corp.
Four Landmark Square, Ste. 301
Stamford, CT 06901
Phone: 203-975-7110 Fax: 203-975-7902
CEO: D. Greg Horrigan
CFO: Harley Rankin, Jr.
1991 Sales: $678 million Employees: 3,560
Ownership: Privately held
Industry: Containers - plastic, steel & aluminum

Silicon General, Inc.
85 W. Tasman Dr.
San Jose, CA 95134
Phone: 408-433-1900 Fax: 408-428-7895
CEO: William D. Rasdal
CFO: J. Scott Kamsler
1992 Sales: $69 million Employees: 523
Symbol: SILN Exchange: NASDAQ
Industry: Computers - graphics

Silicon Graphics, Inc.
2011 N. Shoreline Blvd.
Mountain View, CA 94039
Phone: 415-960-1980 Fax: 415-960-1737
CEO: Edward R. McCracken
CFO: Stanley J. Meresman
1992 Sales: $949 million Employees: 2,568
Symbol: SGI Exchange: NYSE
Industry: Computers - graphics hardware & software

Silicon Valley Bancshares
3000 Lakeside Dr.
Santa Clara, CA 95054
Phone: 408-435-0766 Fax: —
CEO: Roger V. Smith
CFO: Thomas J. O'Connor
1991 Sales: $76 million Employees: 181
Symbol: SIVB Exchange: NASDAQ
Industry: Banks - West

Silicon Valley Group, Inc.
541 E. Trimble Rd.
San Jose, CA 95131
Phone: 408-432-9300 Fax: 408-432-8629
CEO: Papken S. Der Torossian
CFO: Russell G. Weinstock
1991 Sales: $235 million Employees: 1,806
Symbol: SVGI Exchange: NASDAQ
Industry: Electrical components - semiconductors

Siliconix Inc.
2201 Laurelwood Rd.
Santa Clara, CA 95056
Phone: 408-988-8000 Fax: 408-727-5414
CEO: Richard J. Kulle
CFO: Jurgen F. Biehn
1991 Sales: $140 million Employees: 1,247
Symbol: SILI Exchange: NASDAQ
Industry: Electrical components - semiconductors

Simpson Industries, Inc.
32100 Telegraph Rd., Ste. 120
Birmingham, MI 48025
Phone: 313-540-6200 Fax: 313-540-7484
CEO: Robert W. Navarre
CFO: Kenneth E. Berman
1991 Sales: $192 million Employees: 1,471
Symbol: SMPS Exchange: NASDAQ
Industry: Automotive & trucking - original equipment

Simpson Investment Co.
1201 Third Ave., Ste. 4900
Seattle, WA 98101
Phone: 206-224-5000 Fax: 206-224-5060
CEO: William G. Reed, Jr.
CFO: J. Thurston Roach
1991 Sales: $826 million Employees: 8,000
Ownership: Privately held
Industry: Building products - wood; lumber, logging, plywood doors

Simtek Corp.
1465 Kelly Johnson Blvd.
Colorado Springs, CO 80920
Phone: 719-531-9444 Fax: 719-531-9481
CEO: Richard L. Petritz
CFO: William G. Skolout
1991 Sales: $0.7 million Employees: 43
Symbol: SRAMC Exchange: NASDAQ
Industry: Electrical components - semiconductors

Simula, Inc.
10016 S. 51st St.
Phoenix, AZ 85044
Phone: 602-893-7533 Fax: —
CEO: Stanley P. Desjardins
CFO: Donald W. Townsend
1991 Sales: $15 million Employees: 180
Symbol: SIMU Exchange: NASDAQ
Industry: Aerospace - aircraft equipment

Singapore Airlines Ltd.
5670 Wilshire Blvd.
Los Angeles, CA 90036
Phone: 213-934-8833 Fax: 213-934-4482
CEO: Hwang Teng Aun
CFO: —
1992 Sales: $3,346 million Employees: 21,891
Parent: Singapore Airlines Ltd.
Industry: Transportation - airline

Siskon Gold Corp.
350 Crown Point Circle
Grass Valley, CA 95945
Phone: 916-273-4311 Fax: —
CEO: Timothy A. Callaway
CFO: Douglas E. Eacrett
1991 Sales: $1.2 million Employees: —
Symbol: SISK Exchange: NASDAQ
Industry: Gold mining & processing

Sizzler International, Inc.
12655 W. Jefferson Blvd.
Los Angeles, CA 90066
Phone: 310-827-2300 Fax: 310-822-5786
CEO: Richard P. Bermingham
CFO: Christopher Thomas
1992 Sales: $543 million Employees: 17,800
Symbol: SZ Exchange: NYSE
Industry: Retail - food & restaurants

SJNB Financial Corp.
One N. Market St.
San Jose, CA 95113
Phone: 408-947-7562 Fax: —
CEO: James R. Kenny
CFO: Eugene E. Blakeslee
1991 Sales: $5.6 million Employees: 51
Symbol: SJNB Exchange: NASDAQ
Industry: Banks - West

SJW Corp.
374 W. Santa Clara St.
San Jose, CA 95196
Phone: 408-279-7810 Fax: —
CEO: J. W. Weinhardt
CFO: W. R. Roth
1991 Sales: $76 million Employees: 267
Symbol: SJW Exchange: AMEX
Industry: Utility - water supply

Skadden, Arps, Slate, Meagher & Flom
919 Third Ave.
New York, NY 10022
Phone: 212-371-6000 Fax: 212-735-2000
CEO: Peter P. Mullen
CFO: Karl Duchek
1991 Sales: $490 million Employees: 2,900
Ownership: Privately held
Industry: Business services - law firm

Skender Construction Inc.
10101 Roberts Rd.
Palos Hills, IL 60465
Phone: 708-430-8488 Fax: 708-430-8472
CEO: J. Skender
CFO: J. Skender
1991 Sales: $4.3 million Employees: 28
Ownership: Privately held
Industry: Construction management services

Skidmore, Owings & Merrill
220 E. 42nd St.
New York, NY 10017
Phone: 212-309-9500 Fax: 212-309-9750
CEO: David M. Childs
CFO: Dan A. DeCanniere
1991 Sales: $92 million Employees: 804
Ownership: Privately held
Industry: Building - architectural & engineering

Skyline Corp.
2520 By-Pass Rd.
Elkhart, IN 46515
Phone: 219-294-6521 Fax: 219-293-0693
CEO: Arthur J. Decio
CFO: Joseph B. Fanchi
1992 Sales: $339 million Employees: 2,820
Symbol: SKY Exchange: NYSE
Industry: Building - mobile homes & RVs

SkyWest Airlines, Inc.
50 East 100 South, Ste. 201
St. George, UT 84770
Phone: 801-628-2655 Fax: 801-634-2330
CEO: Jerry C. Atkin
CFO: Bradford R. Rich
1992 Sales: $125 million Employees: 1,541
Symbol: SKYW Exchange: NASDAQ
Industry: Transportation - airline

SL Industries, Inc.
8000 Midlantic Dr., Ste. 110
Mt. Laurel, NJ 08054
Phone: 609-727-1500 Fax: 609-727-1683
CEO: Owen Farren
CFO: Ted D. Taubeneck
1992 Sales: $51 million Employees: 663
Symbol: SL Exchange: NYSE
Industry: Electrical products, metal working & plastic products

SLM International, Inc.
200 Fifth Ave.
New York, NY 10010
Phone: 212-675-0070 Fax: 212-206-7098
CEO: David Zunenshire
CFO: Kenneth A. Bloom
1991 Sales: $164 million Employees: 1,050
Symbol: SLMI Exchange: NASDAQ
Industry: Toys - games & hobby products

Small Systems Management Corp.
263 Quigley Blvd., Ste. 12
New Castle, DE 19720
Phone: 302-324-5000 Fax: 302-324-5008
CEO: Marc L. Greenberg
CFO: Geoffrey R. Snelling, Jr.
1991 Sales: $7 million Employees: 15
Ownership: Privately held
Industry: Computers - PC & network installation & services

Small's Oilfield Services Corp.
2008 N. Service Rd. I-20
Big Spring, TX 79721
Phone: 915-267-8885 Fax: —
CEO: Carl W. Small
CFO: Kenneth C. Boothe
1991 Sales: $4.9 million Employees: —
Symbol: FISH Exchange: NASDAQ
Industry: Oil & gas - field services

indicates company is in *Hoover's Handbook of American Business*

indicates company is in *Hoover's Handbook of World Business;* sales and employee numbers are for parent company.

Smart & Final Inc.
524 Chapala St.
Santa Barbara, CA 93101
Phone: 805-564-6700 Fax: 805-564-6729
CEO: Robert J. Emmons
CFO: Martin A. Lynch
1992 Sales: $765 million Employees: 2,329
Symbol: SMF Exchange: NYSE
Industry: Retail - supermarkets

Smith Corona Corp.
65 Locust Ave.
New Canaan, CT 06840
Phone: 203-972-1471 Fax: 203-972-4220
CEO: G. Lee Thompson
CFO: Herbert H. Egli
1992 Sales: $372 million Employees: 3,600
Symbol: SCO Exchange: NYSE
Industry: Office equipment & supplies

Smith International, Inc.
16740 Hardy Rd.
Houston, TX 77032
Phone: 713-443-3370 Fax: 713-443-1591
CEO: Doug Rock
CFO: Dan Steigerwald
1991 Sales: $403 million Employees: 2,600
Symbol: SII Exchange: NYSE
Industry: Oil field machinery & equipment

Smith's Food & Drug Centers, Inc.
1550 S. Redwood Rd.
Salt Lake City, UT 84104
Phone: 801-974-1400 Fax: 801-974-1310
CEO: Jeffrey P. Smith
CFO: Robert D. Bolinder
1992 Sales: $2,650 million Employees: 18,303
Symbol: SFD Exchange: NYSE
Industry: Retail - supermarkets

Smithfield Companies, Inc.
311 County St., Ste. 203
Portsmouth, VA 23704
Phone: 804-399-3100 Fax: 804-399-0916
CEO: Richard S. Fuller
CFO: Mark D. Bedard
1992 Sales: $37 million Employees: 254
Symbol: HAMS Exchange: NASDAQ
Industry: Food - meat products

Smithfield Foods, Inc.
816 Connecticut Ave. NW
Washington, DC 20006
Phone: 202-223-4224 Fax: 202-785-2355
CEO: Joseph W. Luter III
CFO: Aaron D. Trub
1992 Sales: $1,044 million Employees: 5,400
Symbol: SFDS Exchange: NASDAQ
Industry: Food - meat products

SmithKline Beecham Corporation
One Franklin Plaza
Philadelphia, PA 19102
Phone: 215-751-4000 Fax: 215-751-7655
CEO: Jan Leschly
CFO: —
1991 Sales: $8,761 million Employees: 54,000
Parent: SmithKline Beecham PLC
Industry: Drugs & health care products, clinical labs

SMTEK Incorporated
2151 Anchor Ct.
Newbury Park, CA 91320
Phone: 805-376-2595 Fax: 805-376-2686
CEO: Greg Horton
CFO: Stuart Siegel
1991 Sales: $9.2 million Employees: 85
Ownership: Privately held
Industry: Electronics - military, space & medical

Snap-on Tools Corp.
2801 80th St.
Kenosha, WI 53143
Phone: 414-656-5200 Fax: 414-656-5123
CEO: Robert A. Cornog
CFO: Michael F. Montemurro
1992 Sales: $984 million Employees: 6,800
Symbol: SNA Exchange: NYSE
Industry: Tools - hand held & power tools

SNL Securities
410 E. Main St.
Charlottesville, VA 22902
Phone: 804-977-1600 Fax: 804-977-4466
CEO: Reid Nagle
CFO: Reid Nagle
1991 Sales: $2.3 million Employees: 27
Ownership: Privately held
Industry: Publishing - newsletters & databases for financial services industry

Snyder Oil Corp.
2500 First RepublicBank Tower, Ste. 2500
Ft. Worth, TX 76102
Phone: 817-338-4043 Fax: 817-338-4048
CEO: John C. Snyder
CFO: John C. Snyer
1991 Sales: $87 million Employees: 265
Symbol: SNY Exchange: NYSE
Industry: Oil & gas - US exploration & production

SnyderGeneral Corp.
3219 McKinney Ave.
Dallas, TX 75204
Phone: 214-754-0500 Fax: 214-754-0949
CEO: Richard W. Snyder
CFO: James F. Brum
1991 Sales: $800 million Employees: 6,500
Ownership: Privately held
Industry: Air quality control equipment and services

Society Corp.
800 Superior Ave. East, 7th Fl.
Cleveland, OH 44114
Phone: 216-689-3000 Fax: —
CEO: Robert W. Gillespie
CFO: James W. Wert
1992 Sales: $2,405 million Employees: —
Symbol: SCY Exchange: NYSE
Industry: Banks - Midwest

Society for Savings Bancorp, Inc.
31 Pratt St.
Hartford, CT 06103
Phone: 203-727-5000 Fax: —
CEO: Lawrence Connell
CFO: Albert E. Fiacre, Jr.
1991 Sales: $105 million Employees: 1,236
Symbol: SOCS Exchange: NASDAQ
Industry: Financial - savings and loans

SofTech, Inc.
460 Totten Pond Rd.
Waltham, MA 02154
Phone: 617-890-6900 Fax: 617-890-6055
CEO: Norman L. Rasmussen
CFO: Douglas R. Potter
1992 Sales: $52 million Employees: 453
Symbol: SOFT Exchange: NASDAQ
Industry: Computers - custom software

Softub Inc.
21100 Superior St.
Chatsworth, CA 91311
Phone: 818-407-4646 Fax: 818-407-4658
CEO: Tom Thornbury
CFO: Kim Nguyen
1991 Sales: $6.4 million Employees: 105
Ownership: Privately held
Industry: Soft-sided portable spas

Software Etc. Stores, Inc.
7505 Metro Blvd.
Edina, MN 55439
Phone: 612-893-7644 Fax: —
CEO: Daniel A. DeMatteo
CFO: Daniel A. DeMatteo
1991 Sales: $166 million Employees: 2,025
Symbol: SFWR Exchange: NASDAQ
Industry: Retail - software

Software Publishing Corp.
3165 Kifer Rd.
Santa Clara, CA 95056
Phone: 408-986-8000 Fax: 408-450-7916
CEO: Fred M. Gibbons
CFO: Truman Cole
1992 Sales: $156 million Employees: 717
Symbol: SPCO Exchange: NASDAQ
Industry: Computers - word processing, database & graphics software

Software Spectrum, Inc.
2140 Merritt Dr.
Garland, TX 75041
Phone: 214-840-6600 Fax: 214-864-7878
CEO: Judy O. Sims
CFO: Keith R. Coogan
1992 Sales: $159 million Employees: 303
Symbol: SSPE Exchange: NASDAQ
Industry: Computers - software

Software Technical Services Inc.
3020 Holcomb Bridge Rd.
Norcross, GA 30071
Phone: 404-449-8966 Fax: 404-449-5407
CEO: Rita Narasimham
CFO: Pundi Narasimham
1992 Sales: $5.6 million Employees: 17
Ownership: Privately held
Industry: Computers - software consulting services

Software Toolworks, Inc.
60 Leveroni Court
Novato, CA 94949
Phone: 415-883-3000 Fax: 415-883-3303
CEO: Leslie Crane
CFO: Margo G. Hober
1992 Sales: $103 million Employees: 295
Symbol: TWRX Exchange: NASDAQ
Industry: Computers - educational & game software

Solectron Corp.
777 Gibraltar Dr.
Milpitas, CA 95035
Phone: 408-957-8500 Fax: 408-956-6075
CEO: Koichi Nishimura
CFO: Susan Wang
1992 Sales: $407 million Employees: 2,979
Symbol: SLR Exchange: NYSE
Industry: Electrical components - printed circuit boards

Solitron Devices, Inc.
1177 Blue Heron Blvd.
Riviera Beach, FL 33404
Phone: 305-848-4311 Fax: —
CEO: John J. Stayduhar
CFO: John J. Stayduhar
1992 Sales: $23 million Employees: 336
Symbol: SOD Exchange: NYSE
Industry: Electronics - military

Solo Serv Corp.
1610 Cornerway Blvd.
San Antonio, TX 78219
Phone: 210-225-7163 Fax: 210-662-6451
CEO: Robert J. Grimm
CFO: Timothy L. Grady
1991 Sales: $124 million Employees: 1,850
Symbol: SOLO Exchange: NASDAQ
Industry: Retail - discount fragrances, apparel, home furnishings

Somanetics Corp.
1653 E. Maple Rd.
Troy, MI 48083
Phone: 313-689-3050 Fax: —
CEO: Gary D. Lewis
CFO: Raymond W. Gunn
1991 Sales: $0.2 million Employees: 32
Symbol: SMTS Exchange: NASDAQ
Industry: Medical instruments - diagnostics

SoMat Corp.
702 Killarney
Urbana, IL 61801
Phone: 217-328-5359 Fax: 217-328-6576
CEO: Darrell Socie
CFO: Norm Miller
1991 Sales: $1.8 million Employees: 10
Ownership: Privately held
Industry: Computers - data acquisition & analysis

Somatix Therapy Corp.
850 Marina Village Pkwy.
Alameda, CA 94501
Phone: 415-748-3000 Fax: 415-769-8533
CEO: David W. Carter
CFO: Mark N. K. Bagnall
1991 Sales: $2.6 million Employees: 67
Symbol: SOMA Exchange: NASDAQ
Industry: Biomedical & genetic products

Somatogen, Inc.
2545 Central Ave.
Boulder, CO 80301
Phone: 303-440-9988 Fax: 303-444-3013
CEO: Charles H. Scoggin
CFO: Timothy D. Hoogheem
1992 Sales: $3.7 million Employees: 173
Symbol: SMTG Exchange: NASDAQ
Industry: Medical products

Somerset Group, Inc.
135 N. Pennsylvania St.
Indianapolis, IN 46204
Phone: 317-634-1400 Fax: 317-269-1341
CEO: Robert H. McKinney
CFO: Joseph M. Richter
1991 Sales: $15 million Employees: —
Symbol: SOMR Exchange: NASDAQ
Industry: Diversified operations - concrete products, mortgage banking, environmental testing

Somerset Savings Bank
212 Elm St.
Somerville, MA 02144
Phone: 617-625-6000 Fax: —
CEO: Thomas J. Kelly
CFO: Michael F. Tracey
1992 Sales: — Employees: —
Symbol: SOSA Exchange: NASDAQ
Industry: Banks - Northeast

Sonat Inc.
1900 5th Ave. North
Birmingham, AL 35203
Phone: 205-325-3800 Fax: 205-325-7490
CEO: Ronald L. Kuehn, Jr.
CFO: J. Robert Doody
1992 Sales: $1,484 million Employees: 5,300
Symbol: SNT Exchange: NYSE
Industry: Oil & gas - production & pipeline

Sonesta International Hotels Corp.
200 Clarendon St.
Boston, MA 02116
Phone: 617-421-5400 Fax: 617-421-5402
CEO: Roger P. Sonnabend
CFO: Brian T. Owen
1991 Sales: $50 million Employees: 1,444
Symbol: SNSTA Exchange: NASDAQ
Industry: Hotels & motels

Sonetics Corp.
7340 SW Durham Rd.
Portland, OR 97224
Phone: 503-684-7080 Fax: 503-620-2943
CEO: Michael Staeheli
CFO: Allan Schrader
1991 Sales: $3 million Employees: 28
Ownership: Privately held
Industry: Communications equipment for high-noise environments

Sonic Corp.
120 Robert S. Kerr Ave.
Oklahoma City, OK 73102
Phone: 405-232-4334 Fax: 405-272-8290
CEO: C. Stephen Lynn
CFO: J. Clifford Hudson
1992 Sales: $67 million Employees: 105
Symbol: SONC Exchange: NASDAQ
Industry: Retail - food & restaurants

Sonic Solutions
1891 E. Francisco Blvd.
San Rafael, CA 94901
Phone: 415-485-4800 Fax: 415-485-4877
CEO: Robert Doris
CFO: Robert Doris
1991 Sales: $5.8 million Employees: 35
Ownership: Privately held
Industry: Manufactures software & hardware for digital audio systems

Sonny Hill Motors Inc.
1600 E. Prairie View Rd.
Platte City, MO 64079
Phone: 816-431-2144 Fax: 816-431-5040
CEO: Sonny Haughland
CFO: Sonny Haughland
1991 Sales: $140 million Employees: 350
Ownership: Privately held
Industry: Retail - auto dealerships

Sonoco Products Co.
N. Second St.
Hartsville, SC 29550
Phone: 803-383-7000 Fax: 803-383-7731
CEO: Charles W. Coker
CFO: Carl T. Tsang
1992 Sales: $1,838 million Employees: 14,490
Symbol: SONO Exchange: NASDAQ
Industry: Containers - paper & plastic

Sony Corp. of America
Sony Dr.
Park Ridge, NJ 07656
Phone: 201-930-6440 Fax: 201-358-4058
CEO: Ken Iwaki
CFO: —
1992 Sales: $29,439 million Employees: 119,000
Parent: Sony Corporation
Industry: Audio & video products, music & filmed entertainment

Sotheby's Holdings, Inc.
1334 York Ave.
New York, NY 10021
Phone: 212-606-7000 Fax: 212-606-7564
CEO: Michael L. Ainslie
CFO: Russell R. Roth
1991 Sales: $222 million Employees: 1,488
Symbol: BID Exchange: NYSE
Industry: Retail - auctions

Sound Advice, Inc.
1901 Tigertail Blvd.
Dania, FL 33004
Phone: 305-922-4434 Fax: 305-992-1089
CEO: Peter Beshouri
CFO: Roy C. Casey
1991 Sales: $118 million Employees: 557
Symbol: SUNDE Exchange: NASDAQ
Industry: Retail - consumer electronics

Source Capital, Inc.
10301 W. Pico Blvd.
Los Angeles, CA 90064
Phone: 213-277-4900 Fax: —
CEO: George H. Michaelis
CFO: Julio J. de Puzo, Jr.
1992 Sales: — Employees: —
Symbol: SOR Exchange: NYSE
Industry: Financial - investment management

Source Technologies Inc.
588 Griffith Rd.
Charlotte, NC 28217
Phone: 704-522-8500 Fax: 704-522-7533
CEO: Miles Busby
CFO: —
1992 Sales: $10 million Employees: 22
Ownership: Privately held
Industry: Computers - printers

South Carolina Federal Corp.
1500 Hampton St.
Columbia, SC 29201
Phone: 803-254-1500 Fax: —
CEO: John W. Folsom
CFO: George L. McDaniel
1991 Sales: $92 million Employees: 454
Symbol: SCFB Exchange: NASDAQ
Industry: Financial - savings and loans

South Jersey Industries, Inc.
Rt. 54, One S. Jersey Plaza
Folsom, NJ 08037
Phone: 609-561-9000 Fax: 609-561-8225
CEO: William F. Ryan
CFO: Gerald S. Levitt
1991 Sales: $279 million Employees: 1,031
Symbol: SJI Exchange: NYSE
Industry: Utility - gas distribution

Southdown, Inc.
1200 Smith St., Ste. 2400
Houston, TX 77002
Phone: 713-650-6200 Fax: 713-653-6815
CEO: Clarence C. Comer
CFO: James L. Persky
1991 Sales: $505 million Employees: 3,000
Symbol: SDW Exchange: NYSE
Industry: Construction - cement & concrete

Southeastern Michigan Gas Enterprises, Inc.
405 Water St.
Port Huron, MI 48060
Phone: 313-987-2200 Fax: —
CEO: Robert J. Thomson
CFO: Robert F. Caldwell
1991 Sales: $232 million Employees: 576
Symbol: SMGS Exchange: NASDAQ
Industry: Utility - gas distribution

Southern Audio Services
15049 Florida Blvd.
Baton Rouge, LA 70819
Phone: 504-272-7135 Fax: 504-272-9844
CEO: Keith Jordan
CFO: Keith Jordan
1991 Sales: $9 million Employees: 15
Ownership: Privately held
Industry: Automotive & trucking - audio equipment

Southern California Edison Co.
2244 Walnut Grove Ave.
Rosemead, CA 91770
Phone: 818-302-1212 Fax: —
CEO: John E. Bryson
CFO: Alan J. Fohrer
1992 Sales: $8.1 million Employees: 17,110
Symbol: SCEpB Exchange: AMEX
Industry: Utility - electric power

indicates company is in *Hoover's Handbook of American Business.*

indicates company is in *Hoover's Handbook of World Business*; sales and employee numbers are for parent company.

Southern California Water Co.
630 E. Foothill Blvd.
San Dimas, CA 91773
Phone: 909-394-3600 Fax: 909-394-0711
CEO: William V. Caveney
CFO: James B. Gallagher
1991 Sales: $91 million Employees: 422
Symbol: SWTR Exchange: NASDAQ
Industry: Utility - water supply

Southern Co., The
64 Perimeter Center East
Atlanta, GA 30346
Phone: 404-393-0650 Fax: 404-668-3559
CEO: Edward L. Addison
CFO: W. L. Westbrook
1992 Sales: $8,073 million Employees: 30,420
Symbol: SO Exchange: NYSE
Industry: Utility - electric power

Southern Electronics Distribution
4916 N. Royal Atlanta Dr.
Tucker, GA 30084
Phone: 404-491-8962 Fax: 404-938-2814
CEO: G. Diamond
CFO: L. G. Ayers
1992 Sales: $179 million Employees: 224
Symbol: SECX Exchange: NASDAQ
Industry: Wholesale distribution - consumer products

Southern Indiana Gas & Electric Co.
20 NW Fourth St.
Evansville, IN 47741
Phone: 812-424-6411 Fax: 812-464-4554
CEO: Ronald G. Reherman
CFO: Andrew E. Goebel
1991 Sales: $323 million Employees: 975
Symbol: SIG Exchange: NYSE
Industry: Utility - electric power

Southern Mineral Corp.
515 W. Greens Rd., Ste. 775
Houston, TX 77067
Phone: 713-872-7621 Fax: —
CEO: Phinn W. Townsend
CFO: John Misitigh
1991 Sales: $2.2 million Employees: 6
Symbol: SMIN Exchange: NASDAQ
Industry: Oil & gas - US exploration & production

Southern National Corp.
500 N. Chestnut St.
Lumberton, NC 28358
Phone: 919-671-2000 Fax: —
CEO: L. Glenn Orr, Jr.
CFO: John R. Spruill
1991 Sales: $363 million Employees: 2,073
Symbol: SNB Exchange: NYSE
Industry: Banks - Southeast

Southern New England Telecommunications
227 Church St.
New Haven, CT 06506
Phone: 203-771-5200 Fax: 203-772-4855
CEO: Walter H. Monteith, Jr.
CFO: John J. Miller
1992 Sales: $1,614 million Employees: 11,224
Symbol: SNG Exchange: NYSE
Industry: Utility - telephone

Southern Union Exploration Co.
400 W. 15th St., Ste. 615
Austin, TX 78701
Phone: 512-477-5852 Fax: 512-370-3599
CEO: George L. Lindemann
CFO: Ronald J. Endres
1991 Sales: $200 million Employees: 1,046
Symbol: SUG Exchange: AMEX
Industry: Utility - gas distribution

Southington Savings Bank
121 Main St.
Southington, CT 06489
Phone: 203-628-0351 Fax: —
CEO: Robert D. Morton
CFO: Anthony Priore, Jr.
1992 Sales: — Employees: —
Symbol: SSBB Exchange: NASDAQ
Industry: Financial - savings and loans

Southland Corp.
2711 N. Haskell Ave.
Dallas, TX 75204
Phone: 214-828-7011 Fax: 214-828-7848
CEO: C. J. Matthews II
CFO: F. J. Gangi
1992 Sales: $8,010 million Employees: 42,616
Trading Status: Suspended
Industry: Retail - convenience stores

SouthTrust Bank of Alabama
420 N. 20th St.
Birmingham, AL 35203
Phone: 205-254-5000 Fax: 205-254-6688
CEO: Wallace D. Malone, Jr.
CFO: Aubrey D. Barnard
1992 Sales: $965 million Employees: 5,500
Symbol: SOTR Exchange: NASDAQ
Industry: Banks - Southeast

Southwall Technologies Inc.
1029 Corporation Way
Palo Alto, CA 94303
Phone: 415-962-9111 Fax: 415-967-8713
CEO: J. Larry Smart
CFO: Alfred V. Larrenaga
1991 Sales: $18 million Employees: 141
Symbol: SWTX Exchange: NASDAQ
Industry: Chemicals - plastics

Southwest Airlines Co.
2702 Love Field Dr.
Dallas, TX 75235
Phone: 214-904-4000 Fax: 214-904-4200
CEO: Herbert D. Kelleher
CFO: Gary C. Kelly
1992 Sales: $1,685 million Employees: 9,778
Symbol: LUV Exchange: NYSE
Industry: Transportation - airline

Southwest Cafes, Inc.
12200 Stemmons Fwy.
Dallas, TX 75234
Phone: 214-241-5500 Fax: 214-888-8198
CEO: Gilbert Cuellar, Jr.
CFO: Gary W. Coder
1992 Sales: — Employees: 3,450
Symbol: TXMX Exchange: NASDAQ
Industry: Retail - food & restaurants

Southwest Gas Corp.
5241 Spring Mountain Rd.
Las Vegas, NV 89102
Phone: 702-876-7011 Fax: 702-873-3820
CEO: Kenny C. Guinn
CFO: George C. Biehl
1991 Sales: $800 million Employees: 2,892
Symbol: SWX Exchange: NYSE
Industry: Utility - gas distribution

Southwest National Corp.
111 S. Main St.
Greensburg, PA 15601
Phone: 412-834-2310 Fax: —
CEO: David S. Dahlmann
CFO: Donald A. Lawry
1991 Sales: $58 million Employees: 375
Symbol: SWPA Exchange: NASDAQ
Industry: Banks - Northeast

Southwest Royalties Inc.
407 N. Big Spring St.
Midland, TX 79701
Phone: 915-686-9927 Fax: 915-688-0191
CEO: H. H. Wommack III
CFO: Bill Coggin
1991 Sales: $18 million Employees: 75
Ownership: Privately held
Industry: Oil & gas - refining & marketing

Southwest Securities Inc.
1201 Elm St., Ste. 4300
Dallas, TX 75270
Phone: 214-651-1800 Fax: 214-749-0810
CEO: Don A. Buchholz
CFO: Robert A. Buchholz
1992 Sales: $68 million Employees: 376
Symbol: SWST Exchange: NASDAQ
Industry: Financial - investment management

Southwest Water Systems
16340 E. Maplegrove St.
La Puente, CA 91744
Phone: 818-918-1231 Fax: 818-918-5958
CEO: Anton C. Garnier
CFO: R. Joseph Saunders
1991 Sales: $39 million Employees: 369
Symbol: SWWC Exchange: NASDAQ
Industry: Utility - water supply

Southwestern Bell Corp.
One Bell Center
St. Louis, MO 63101
Phone: 314-235-9800 Fax: 314-235-2627
CEO: Edward E. Whitacre, Jr.
CFO: Robert G. Pope
1992 Sales: $10,015 million Employees: 61,230
Symbol: SBC Exchange: NYSE
Industry: Utility - telephone; cellular telephone services, long distance advertising

Southwestern Electric Service Co.
1717 Main St., Ste. 3300
Dallas, TX 75201
Phone: 214-741-3125 Fax: 214-741-5637
CEO: Charles D. Goforth
CFO: Richard C. Hays
1991 Sales: $67 million Employees: 158
Symbol: SWEL Exchange: NASDAQ
Industry: Utility - electric power

Southwestern Energy Co.
1083 Sain St.
Fayetteville, AR 72703
Phone: 501-521-1141 Fax: 501-521-0328
CEO: Charles E. Scharlau
CFO: Stanley D. Green
1991 Sales: $136 million Employees: 618
Symbol: SWN Exchange: NYSE
Industry: Utility - gas distribution

Southwestern Public Service Co.
600 S. Tyler St.
Amarillo, TX 79101
Phone: 806-378-2121 Fax: 806-378-2995
CEO: Bill D. Helton
CFO: Doyle R. Bunch II
1991 Sales: $725 million Employees: 2,026
Symbol: SPS Exchange: NYSE
Industry: Utility - electric power

Southwire Co.
One Southwire Dr.
Carrollton, GA 30119
Phone: 706-832-4242 Fax: 706-832-4929
CEO: Roy Richards, Jr.
CFO: James Richards
1991 Sales: $1,330 million Employees: 5,000
Ownership: Privately held
Industry: Wire & cable products, metal fabricating, rod

indicates company is in *Hoover's Handbook of American Business.*

indicates company is in *Hoover's Handbook of World Business;* sales and employee numbers are for parent company.

Sovereign Bancorp, Inc.
1130 Berkshire Blvd.
Wyomissing, PA 19610
Phone: 215-320-8400 Fax: —
CEO: Jay S. Sidhu
CFO: Karl D. Gerhart
1991 Sales: $132 million Employees: 455
Symbol: SVRN Exchange: NASDAQ
Industry: Financial - savings and loans

SpaceLabs Medical Inc.
15220 NE 40th St.
Redmond, WA 98052
Phone: 206-882-3700 Fax: 206-885-4877
CEO: Carl A. Lombardi
CFO: Patrick J. Walsh
1992 Sales: $225 million Employees: 1,486
Symbol: SLMD Exchange: NASDAQ
Industry: Medical services

Spaghetti Warehouse, Inc.
6120 Aldwick Dr.
Garland, TX 75043
Phone: 214-226-6000 Fax: 214-226-9289
CEO: Robert R. Hawk
CFO: William B. Rea, Jr.
1992 Sales: $56 million Employees: 2,486
Symbol: SWH Exchange: NYSE
Industry: Retail - food & restaurants

Spalding & Evenflo Co. Inc.
PO Box 30101
Tampa, FL 33630
Phone: 813-887-5200 Fax: 813-887-5208
CEO: Donald J. Byrnes
CFO: Paul L. Whiting
1991 Sales: $495 million Employees: 2,750
Ownership: Privately held
Industry: Diversified operations - sporting goods & baby products

Span-America Medical Systems, Inc.
70 Commerce Dr.
Greenville, SC 29615
Phone: 803-288-8877 Fax: 803-288-8692
CEO: Donald C. Spann
CFO: Richard C. Coggins
1991 Sales: $29 million Employees: 214
Symbol: SPAN Exchange: NASDAQ
Industry: Medical products - foam patient positioners & pads

Spartan Motors, Inc.
1000 Reynolds Rd.
Charlotte, MI 48813
Phone: 517-543-6400 Fax: 517-543-7727
CEO: George W. Sztykiel
CFO: Anthony G. Sommer
1991 Sales: $94 million Employees: 372
Symbol: SPAR Exchange: NASDAQ
Industry: Automotive & trucking - original equipment

Spartech Corp.
7777 Bonhomme Ave., Ste. 1001
St. Louis, MO 63105
Phone: 314-721-4242 Fax: 314-721-1447
CEO: Lawrence M. Powers
CFO: David B. Mueller
1991 Sales: $156 million Employees: 590
Symbol: SEH Exchange: AMEX
Industry: Rubber & plastic products

Sparton Corp.
2400 E. Ganson St.
Jackson, MI 49202
Phone: 517-787-8600 Fax: 517-787-8046
CEO: John J. Smith
CFO: Richard L. Langley
1992 Sales: $245 million Employees: —
Symbol: SPA Exchange: NYSE
Industry: Electronics - military

Spear Financial Services, Inc.
505 N. Brand Blvd., 16th Fl.
Glendale, CA 91203
Phone: 818-543-4400 Fax: 818-242-9525
CEO: James K. Mitchell
CFO: Barry J. Laufman
1991 Sales: $30 million Employees: 313
Symbol: SFNS Exchange: NASDAQ
Industry: Financial - business services

Spec's Music, Inc.
1666 NW 82nd Ave.
Miami, FL 33126
Phone: 305-592-7288 Fax: 305-592-0127
CEO: Ann Spector Lieff
CFO: Peter Blei
1991 Sales: $59 million Employees: 692
Symbol: SPEK Exchange: NASDAQ
Industry: Retail - consumer electronics

Spec-Line Laminated Products
2861-G Bankers Industrial Dr.
Doraville, GA 30360
Phone: 404-368-0785 Fax: 404-368-0639
CEO: Carl Polchan
CFO: Vallie Polchan
1991 Sales: $1.5 million Employees: 31
Ownership: Privately held
Industry: Building products - furniture, cabinets, millwork & specialty wood products

Special Devices, Inc.
16830 W. Placerita Canyon Rd.
Newhall, CA 91321
Phone: 805-259-0753 Fax: 805-254-4721
CEO: Thomas F. Treinen
CFO: Robert W. Benson
1991 Sales: $24 million Employees: 319
Symbol: SDII Exchange: NASDAQ
Industry: Electrical components - aerospace pyrotechnics

Specialty Chemical Resources, Inc.
9100 Valley View Rd.
Macedonia, OH 44056
Phone: 216-468-1380 Fax: —
CEO: Edwin M. Roth
CFO: H. Timothy O'Hara
1991 Sales: $44 million Employees: 204
Symbol: CHM Exchange: AMEX
Industry: Chemicals - specialty

Specialty Coatings International
704 E. Franklin ST.
Richmond, VA 23219
Phone: 804-697-3500 Fax: 804-697-3535
CEO: James E. Rogers
CFO: A. William Hamill
1991 Sales: $597 million Employees: 3,702
Ownership: Privately held
Industry: Paper & paper products - specialty

Specialty Retailers
10201 S. Main St.
Houston, TX 77025
Phone: 713-667-5601 Fax: 713-669-2708
CEO: Bernard Fuchs
CFO: Jerry Ivie
1992 Sales: $530 million Employees: 7,500
Ownership: Privately held
Industry: Retail - apparel

SpecTran Corp.
50 Hall Rd.
Sturbridge, MA 01566
Phone: 508-347-2261 Fax: 508-347-2747
CEO: Raymond E. Jaeger
CFO: Bruce A. Cannon
1991 Sales: $16 million Employees: 124
Symbol: SPTR Exchange: NASDAQ
Industry: Fiber optics

Spectranetics Corp.
96 Talamine Court
Colorado Springs, CO 80907
Phone: 719-633-8333 Fax: —
CEO: Robert J. DePasqua
CFO: George H. Rountree
1991 Sales: $6.3 million Employees: 156
Symbol: SPNC Exchange: NASDAQ
Industry: Lasers - systems & components

Spectrum Control, Inc.
2185 W. 8th St.
Erie, PA 16505
Phone: 814-455-0966 Fax: 814-455-2550
CEO: John L. Johnston
CFO: John P. Freeman
1991 Sales: $31 million Employees: 415
Symbol: SPEC Exchange: NASDAQ
Industry: Electrical products - electromagnetic compatability products

Spectrum Information Technologies, Inc.
2710 Stemmons Fwy.
Dallas, TX 75207
Phone: 214-630-9825 Fax: —
CEO: Peter T. Caserta
CFO: Christopher McGowan
1992 Sales: $108 million Employees: 129
Symbol: SPCL Exchange: NASDAQ
Industry: Telecommunications services

Spelling Entertainment Group, Inc.
One E. Fourth St.
Cincinnati, OH 45202
Phone: 513-579-2482 Fax: 513-579-2580
CEO: Carl H. Lindner
CFO: Fred J. Runk
1991 Sales: $123 million Employees: 10
Symbol: SP Exchange: NYSE
Industry: Leisure & recreational products - television programming & feature films

Sphinx Pharmaceuticals Corp.
Two University Place
Durham, NC 27717
Phone: 919-489-0909 Fax: 919-489-9093
CEO: Clayton I. Duncan
CFO: Richard W. Reichow
1992 Sales: $2.4 million Employees: 150
Symbol: SPHX Exchange: NASDAQ
Industry: Drugs

SPI Holding, Inc.
1501 N. Plano Rd.
Richardson, TX 75081
Phone: 214-234-2721 Fax: —
CEO: James H. Boso
CFO: John S. Aylsworth
1991 Sales: $0.2 million Employees: 771
Symbol: SPH Exchange: AMEX
Industry: Cable TV

SPI Pharmaceuticals, Inc.
3300 Hyland Ave.
Costa Mesa, CA 92626
Phone: 714-540-6144 Fax: 714-556-0131
CEO: Milan Panic
CFO: John Phillips
1991 Sales: $364 million Employees: 5,600
Symbol: SPI Exchange: AMEX
Industry: Drugs & sundries - wholesale

Spiegel, Inc.
3500 Lacey Rd.
Downers Grove, IL 60515
Phone: 708-986-8800 Fax: 708-218-7940
CEO: John J. Shea
CFO: Alton M. Withers
1992 Sales: $2,219 million Employees: 12,000
Symbol: SPGLA Exchange: NASDAQ
Industry: Retail - mail order & direct

Spinnaker Software Corp.
201 Broadway
Cambridge, MA 02139
Phone: 617-494-1200 Fax: 617-494-1219
CEO: C. David Seuss
CFO: E. Ronald Goldfuss
1991 Sales: $15 million Employees: 115
Symbol: SPKR Exchange: NASDAQ
Industry: Computers - information management software

Spire Corp.
One Patriots Park
Bedford, MA 01730
Phone: 617-275-6000 Fax: 617-275-7470
CEO: Roger G. Little
CFO: Richard S. Gregorio
1991 Sales: $17 million Employees: 168
Symbol: SPIR Exchange: NASDAQ
Industry: Electrical components - semiconductors

Sport Supply Group, Inc.
1901 Diplomat
Farmers Branch, TX 75234
Phone: 214-484-9484 Fax: —
CEO: Michael J. Blumenfeld
CFO: William R. Estill
1991 Sales: $47 million Employees: 279
Symbol: GYM Exchange: AMEX
Industry: Leisure & recreational products - sports equipment

Sports Heroes, Inc.
550 Kinderkamack Rd.
Oradell, NJ 07649
Phone: 201-262-8020 Fax: —
CEO: Jerome Zuckerman
CFO: Barry M. Levine
1991 Sales: $2.1 million Employees: 3
Symbol: SHRO Exchange: NASDAQ
Industry: Leisure & recreational products

SportsTown, Inc.
680 Engineering Dr.
Norcross, GA 30092
Phone: 404-246-5300 Fax: 404-662-5782
CEO: Thomas K. Haas
CFO: Thomas K. Haas
1991 Sales: $88 million Employees: 628
Symbol: SPTN Exchange: NASDAQ
Industry: Retail - sporting goods

Spray Systems Environmental
1616 S. Edward Dr.
Tempe, AZ 85281
Phone: 602-470-0017 Fax: 602-470-0659
CEO: Chris Boyles
CFO: David Smith
1991 Sales: $8.6 million Employees: 125
Ownership: Privately held
Industry: Environmental services

Spray-Tech Inc.
1086 Florida Central Pkwy.
Longwood, FL 32750
Phone: 407-767-0990 Fax: 407-332-8216
CEO: Ernest Wilding
CFO: Ernest Wilding
1991 Sales: $17 million Employees: 110
Ownership: Privately held
Industry: Building - exterior home improvements

Springs Industries, Inc.
205 N. White St.
Ft. Mill, SC 29715
Phone: 803-547-1500 Fax: 803-547-1636
CEO: Walter Y. Elisha
CFO: Stephen P. Kelbley
1992 Sales: $1,976 million Employees: 21,000
Symbol: SMI Exchange: NYSE
Industry: Textiles - home furnishings, finished fabrics, industrial fabrics

Sprint Corp.
2330 Shawnee Mission Pkwy.
Westwood, KS 66205
Phone: 913-624-3000 Fax: 913-624-3281
CEO: William T. Esrey
CFO: Arthur B. Krause
1992 Sales: $9,230 million Employees: 43,200
Symbol: FON Exchange: NYSE
Industry: Utility - telephone & long distance services

Sprouse-Reitz Stores Inc.
1411 SW Morrison St.
Portland, OR 97205
Phone: 503-224-8220 Fax: 503-796-1087
CEO: Robert A. Sprouse II
CFO: Michael D. Mulholland
1991 Sales: $185 million Employees: 2,244
Symbol: STRS Exchange: NASDAQ
Industry: Retail - discount & variety

SPS Technologies, Inc.
900 Newtown-Yardley Rd.
Newtown, PA 18940
Phone: 215-860-3000 Fax: 215-860-3035
CEO: John R. Selby
CFO: Arthur B. Belden
1991 Sales: $374 million Employees: 4,709
Symbol: ST Exchange: NYSE
Industry: Metal products - fasteners

SPS Transaction Services, Inc.
2500 Lake Cook Rd.
Riverwoods, IL 60015
Phone: 708-405-0900 Fax: —
CEO: Robert L. Wieseneck
CFO: Thomas C. Schneider
1991 Sales: $152 million Employees: 1,860
Symbol: PAY Exchange: NYSE
Industry: Business services

SPX Corp.
700 Terrace Point Dr.
Muskegon, MI 49443
Phone: 616-724-5000 Fax: 616-724-5720
CEO: Dale A. Johnson
CFO: R. Budd Werner
1992 Sales: $801 million Employees: 5,100
Symbol: SPW Exchange: NYSE
Industry: Automotive & trucking - original equipment

Square Industries, Inc.
921 Bergen Ave.
Jersey City, NJ 07306
Phone: 201-798-0090 Fax: 201-798-3179
CEO: Lowell Harwood
CFO: Marvin Fruchtman
1992 Sales: $67 million Employees: 1,136
Symbol: SQAI Exchange: NASDAQ
Industry: Transportation - services

St. Ives Laboratories, Inc.
8944 Mason Ave.
Chatsworth, CA 91311
Phone: 818-709-5500 Fax: 818-341-8569
CEO: Gary H. Worth
CFO: John L. Boyle
1991 Sales: $120 million Employees: 423
Symbol: SWIS Exchange: NASDAQ
Industry: Cosmetics & toiletries

St. Joe Paper Co.
1650 Prudential Dr., Ste. 400
Jacksonville, FL 32207
Phone: 904-396-6600 Fax: 904-396-4042
CEO: Jacob C. Belin
CFO: Edward C. Brownlie
1991 Sales: $582 million Employees: 5,120
Symbol: SJP Exchange: NYSE
Industry: Paper & paper products

St. Joseph Light & Power Co.
520 Francis St.
St. Joseph, MO 64501
Phone: 816-233-8888 Fax: 816-233-7915
CEO: Terry F. Steinbecker
CFO: Larry J. Stoll
1991 Sales: $90 million Employees: 361
Symbol: SAJ Exchange: NYSE
Industry: Utility - electric power

St. Jude Medical, Inc.
One Lillehei Plaza
St. Paul, MN 55117
Phone: 612-483-2000 Fax: 612-482-8318
CEO: Lawrence A. Lehmkuhl
CFO: Stephen L. Wilson
1991 Sales: $210 million Employees: 599
Symbol: STJM Exchange: NASDAQ
Industry: Medical instruments - mechanical heart valves & cardiovascular products

St. Paul Bancorp, Inc.
6700 W. North Ave.
Chicago, IL 60635
Phone: 312-622-5000 Fax: 312-622-2110
CEO: Joseph C. Scully
CFO: Robert N. Parke
1991 Sales: $344 million Employees: 865
Symbol: SPBC Exchange: NASDAQ
Industry: Financial - savings and loans

St. Paul Companies, Inc.
385 Washington St.
St. Paul, MN 55102
Phone: 612-221-7911 Fax: 612-221-8294
CEO: Douglas W. Leatherdale
CFO: Patrick A. Thiele
1992 Sales: $4,499 million Employees: —
Symbol: SPC Exchange: NYSE
Industry: Insurance - property & casualty

St. Supery Vineyards & Winery
8440 St. Helena Hwy.
Rutherford, CA 94573
Phone: 707-963-4507 Fax: 707-963-4526
CEO: Michaela Rodeno
CFO: Donna Brown
1991 Sales: $3.5 million Employees: 60
Ownership: Privately held
Industry: Beverages - wine

Staar Surgical Co.
1911 Walker Ave.
Monrovia, CA 91016
Phone: 818-303-7902 Fax: 818-303-2962
CEO: John R. Wolf
CFO: William C. Huddleston
1991 Sales: $4.3 million Employees: 94
Symbol: STAA Exchange: NASDAQ
Industry: Medical products - surgical lenses, eye surgery implants

Stac Electronics
5993 Avenida Encinas
Carlsbad, CA 92008
Phone: 619-431-7474 Fax: 619-431-0880
CEO: Gary W. Clow
CFO: John R. Witzel
1991 Sales: $8.4 million Employees: 108
Symbol: STAC Exchange: NASDAQ
Industry: Computers - peripheral equipment & software

Staff Builders Inc.
1981 Marcus Ave., Ste. C115
Lake Success, NY 11042
Phone: 516-358-1000 Fax: 516-358-1036
CEO: Stephen Savitsky
CFO: Gordon J. Gerard
1992 Sales: $168 million Employees: 8,000
Symbol: SBLI Exchange: NASDAQ
Industry: Business services - temporary personnel

Staff Leasing Inc
1301 6th Ave. West
Bradenton, FL 34205
Phone: 813-748-4540 Fax: 813-747-1490
CEO: Dion Mullis
CFO: David Varnavore
1991 Sales: $154 million Employees: 11,310
Ownership: Privately held
Industry: Business services - permanent employee leasing

Staff Relief Inc.
10700 Northwest Fwy., Ste. 450
Houston, TX 77092
Phone: 713-680-0343 Fax: 713-956-5463
CEO: Pat Barber
CFO: Dave Reynolds
1991 Sales: $14 million Employees: 600
Ownership: Privately held
Industry: Business services - contract nursing services

Stage II
350 Fifth Ave.
New York, NY 10118
Phone: 212-564-5865 Fax: 212-239-0377
CEO: Jack Clark
CFO: Philip London
1991 Sales: $68 million Employees: 166
Symbol: SA Exchange: AMEX
Industry: Textiles - apparel

Stamina Products Inc.
310-E S. Union
Springfield, MO 65802
Phone: 417-864-6116 Fax: 417-864-8003
CEO: Jeffrey C. Hutchens
CFO: Stanley K. Coggin
1991 Sales: $14 million Employees: 15
Ownership: Privately held
Industry: Home exercise equipment distribution

Standard Brands Paint Co.
4300 W. 190th St.
Torrance, CA 90509
Phone: 310-214-2411 Fax: 310-542-0151
CEO: Stuart D. Buchalter
CFO: Dan Bane
1991 Sales: $253 million Employees: 2,014
Symbol: SBP Exchange: NYSE
Industry: Building products - retail & wholesale

Standard Commercial Corp.
2201 Miller Rd. South
Wilson, NC 27893
Phone: 919-237-1106 Fax: 919-237-1109
CEO: J. Alec G. Murray
CFO: Anthony A.D. Arrowsmith
1992 Sales: $1,200 million Employees: 7,080
Symbol: STW Exchange: NYSE
Industry: Tobacco

Standard Federal Bank
2600 W. Big Beaver Rd.
Troy, MI 48084
Phone: 313-643-9600 Fax: —
CEO: Thomas R. Ricketts
CFO: Joseph E. Krul
1992 Sales: $808 million Employees: 2,400
Symbol: SFB Exchange: NYSE
Industry: Financial - savings and loans

Standard Microsystems Corp.
80 Arkay Dr.
Hauppauge, NY 11788
Phone: 516-435-6000 Fax: 516-273-5550
CEO: Victor F. Trizzino
CFO: Anthony M. D'Agostino
1992 Sales: $133 million Employees: 605
Symbol: SMSC Exchange: NASDAQ
Industry: Computers - circuits

Standard Motor Products, Inc.
37-18 Northern Blvd.
Long Island City, NY 11101
Phone: 718-392-0200 Fax: 718-729-4549
CEO: Bernard Fife
CFO: M. S. Chanko
1991 Sales: $535 million Employees: 3,400
Symbol: SMP Exchange: NYSE
Industry: Automotive & trucking - replacement parts

Standard Pacific, L.P.
1565 W. MacArthur Blvd.
Costa Mesa, CA 92626
Phone: 714-546-1161 Fax: 714-546-6238
CEO: Arthur E. Svendsen
CFO: April J. Morris
1991 Sales: $299 million Employees: 553
Symbol: SPF Exchange: NYSE
Industry: Building - residential & commercial

Standard Products Co.
2130 W. 110th St.
Cleveland, OH 44102
Phone: 216-281-8300 Fax: 216-281-0126
CEO: James S. Reid, Jr.
CFO: Thomas A. Harker
1992 Sales: $686 million Employees: 7,670
Symbol: SPD Exchange: NYSE
Industry: Automotive & trucking - original equipment

Standard Register Co.
600 Albany St.
Dayton, OH 45408
Phone: 513-443-1000 Fax: 513-443-1239
CEO: John K. Darragh
CFO: Craig J. Brown
1992 Sales: $705 million Employees: 5,852
Symbol: SREG Exchange: NASDAQ
Industry: Paper - business forms

Standex International Corp.
6 Manor Pkwy.
Salem, NH 03079
Phone: 603-893-9701 Fax: 603-893-7324
CEO: Thomas L. King
CFO: Lindsay M. Sedwick
1992 Sales: $477 million Employees: —
Symbol: SXI Exchange: NYSE
Industry: Diversified operations - food service equipment, publishing, mail order sales

Stanford Telecommunications, Inc.
2421 Mission College Blvd.
Santa Clara, CA 95054
Phone: 408-748-1010 Fax: 408-980-1066
CEO: James J. Spilker, Jr.
CFO: Gary S. Wolf
1992 Sales: $95 million Employees: 902
Symbol: STII Exchange: NASDAQ
Industry: Electronics - military

Stanhome Inc.
333 Western Ave.
Westfield, MA 01085
Phone: 413-562-3631 Fax: 413-568-2820
CEO: Alejandro D. Vargas
CFO: Allan G. Keirstead
1992 Sales: $744 million Employees: 4,475
Symbol: STH Exchange: NYSE
Industry: Retail - mail order & direct

Stanley Works, The
1000 Stanley Dr.
New Britain, CT 06053
Phone: 203-225-5111 Fax: 203-827-3901
CEO: Richard H. Ayers
CFO: R. Allen Hunter
1992 Sales: $2,218 million Employees: 17,420
Symbol: SWK Exchange: NYSE
Industry: Building products - hand tools, home improvement & industrial products

Staodyn, Inc.
1225 Florida Ave.
Longmont, CO 80501
Phone: 303-772-3631 Fax: 303-651-0266
CEO: W. Bayne Gibson
CFO: Lynda S. Dreiling
1992 Sales: $7.8 million Employees: 62
Symbol: SDYN Exchange: NASDAQ
Industry: Medical products - physical therapy equipment

Staples, Inc.
100 Pennsylvania Ave.
Framingham, MA 01701
Phone: 508-370-8500 Fax: —
CEO: Thomas G. Stemberg
CFO: Robert R. Spellman
1992 Sales: $807 million Employees: 2,086
Symbol: SPLS Exchange: NASDAQ
Industry: Retail - office equipment & supplies

Star Banc Corp.
425 Walnut St.
Cincinnati, OH 45202
Phone: 513-632-4000 Fax: 513-632-5512
CEO: Oliver W. Waddell
CFO: Gust J. Totlis
1991 Sales: $659 million Employees: 3,786
Symbol: STRZ Exchange: NASDAQ
Industry: Banks - Midwest

Star States Corp.
838 Market St.
Wilmington, DE 19899
Phone: 302-792-6000 Fax: —
CEO: Marvin N. Schoenhals
CFO: John D. Waters
1991 Sales: $117 million Employees: 447
Symbol: STSS Exchange: NASDAQ
Industry: Banks - Northeast

Star Technologies, Inc.
515 Shaw Rd.
Sterling, VA 22170
Phone: 703-689-4400 Fax: 703-478-3600
CEO: Robert C. Compton
CFO: Edward J. Larese
1992 Sales: $33 million Employees: 147
Symbol: STRR Exchange: NASDAQ
Industry: Computers - network servers

Starbucks Corp.
2203 Airport Way South
Seattle, WA 98134
Phone: 206-447-1575 Fax: 206-623-8169
CEO: Howard Schultz
CFO: Orin C. Smith
1992 Sales: $93 million Employees: 2,521
Symbol: SBUX Exchange: NASDAQ
Industry: Retail - coffee products & beverages

Starpak, Inc.
100 Garfield St.
Denver, CO 80206
Phone: 303-399-2400 Fax: 303-329-9107
CEO: Michael W. Morgan
CFO: E. Preston Sumner, Jr.
1992 Sales: $20 million Employees: 150
Ownership: Privately held
Industry: Computers - software manufacturing & fulfillment services

Starrett Housing Corp.
909 Third Ave.
New York, NY 10022
Phone: 212-956-7800 Fax: —
CEO: Henry Benach
CFO: Lewis A. Weinfeld
1991 Sales: $103 million Employees: 1,500
Symbol: SHO Exchange: AMEX
Industry: Building - residential & commercial

 indicates company is in *Hoover's Handbook of American Business.*

indicates company is in *Hoover's Handbook of World Business;* sales and employee numbers are for parent company.

State Auto Financial Corp.
518 E. Broad St.
Columbus, OH 43215
Phone: 614-464-5000 Fax: —
CEO: Robert L. Bailey
CFO: Urlin G. Harris, Jr.
1991 Sales: $115 million Employees: 1,200
Symbol: STFC Exchange: NASDAQ
Industry: Insurance - property & casualty

State Farm
One State Farm Plaza
Bloomington, IL 61710
Phone: 309-766-2311 Fax: 309-766-6169
CEO: Edward B. Rust, Jr.
CFO: Roger S. Joslin
1991 Sales: $19,593 million Employees: 58,113
Ownership: Privately held
Industry: Insurance - multiline & miscellaneous

State of the Art, Inc.
56 Technology Dr.
Irvine, CA 92718
Phone: 714-753-1222 Fax: 714-753-1580
CEO: David S. Samuels
CFO: Joseph R. Armstrong
1991 Sales: $19 million Employees: 124
Symbol: SOTA Exchange: NASDAQ
Industry: Computers - accounting software

State Street Boston Corp.
225 Franklin St.
Boston, MA 02110
Phone: 617-786-3000 Fax: 617-654-4173
CEO: Marshall N. Carter
CFO: David A. Spina
1992 Sales: $1,417 million Employees: 8,321
Symbol: STBK Exchange: NASDAQ
Industry: Banks - Northeast

State-O-Maine, Inc.
10 W. 33rd St.
New York, NY 10001
Phone: 212-244-1111 Fax: 212-967-6409
CEO: Harvey Sanders
CFO: Harvey Sanders
1992 Sales: $121 million Employees: 380
Symbol: SOME Exchange: NASDAQ
Industry: Textiles - apparel

Statesman Group, Inc.
1400 Des Moines Bldg.
Des Moines, IA 50309
Phone: 515-284-7500 Fax: —
CEO: D. J. Noble
CFO: J. M. Matovina
1991 Sales: $312 million Employees: 285
Symbol: STTG Exchange: NASDAQ
Industry: Insurance - life

Steel of West Virginia, Inc.
17th St. & 2nd Ave.
Huntington, WV 25703
Phone: 304-696-8200 Fax: 304-529-1479
CEO: Robert L. Bunting, Jr.
CFO: Timothy R. Duke
1991 Sales: $72 million Employees: 432
Symbol: SWVA Exchange: NASDAQ
Industry: Steel - production

Steel Technologies Inc.
15415 Shelbyville Rd.
Louisville, KY 40245
Phone: 502-245-2110 Fax: 502-245-3821
CEO: Merwin J. Ray
CFO: Kenneth R. Bates
1991 Sales: $130 million Employees: 354
Symbol: STTX Exchange: NASDAQ
Industry: Metal processing & fabrication

Steelcase Inc.
PO Box 1967
Grand Rapids, MI 49501
Phone: 616-247-2710 Fax: 616-246-9105
CEO: Jerry K. Myers
CFO: Allwyn Rougier-Chapman
1991 Sales: $2,300 million Employees: 20,500
Ownership: Privately held
Industry: Office equipment - furniture & systems

Stein Mart, Inc.
1200 Gulf Life Dr.
Jacksonville, FL 32207
Phone: 904-346-1501 Fax: —
CEO: Jay Stein
CFO: Jay Stein
1991 Sales: $225 million Employees: 3,500
Symbol: SMRT Exchange: NASDAQ
Industry: Retail - apparel & shoes

Stepan Co.
22 W. Frontage Rd.
Northfield, IL 60093
Phone: 708-446-7500 Fax: 708-501-2443
CEO: F. Quinn Stepan
CFO: William J. Klein
1991 Sales: $414 million Employees: 1,317
Symbol: SCL Exchange: AMEX
Industry: Chemicals - specialty

Stephens, Inc.
111 Center St.
Little Rock, AR 72201
Phone: 501-374-4361 Fax: 501-377-2666
CEO: Warren A. Stephens
CFO: Ray Gash
1991 Sales: $130 million Employees: 450
Ownership: Privately held
Industry: Financial - investment bankers

STERIS Corp.
9450 Pineneedle Dr.
Mentor, OH 44060
Phone: 216-354-2600 Fax: —
CEO: Bill R. Sanford
CFO: Richard R. Goebel
1992 Sales: $13 million Employees: 133
Symbol: STRL Exchange: NASDAQ
Industry: Medical products

Sterling Bancorp
540 Madison Ave.
New York, NY 10022
Phone: 212-826-8000 Fax: 212-826-2413
CEO: Theodore H. Silbert
CFO: Joseph M. Freeman
1991 Sales: $39 million Employees: 186
Symbol: STL Exchange: NYSE
Industry: Banks - Northeast

Sterling Capital Corp.
635 Madison Ave.
New York, NY 10022
Phone: 212-980-3360 Fax: —
CEO: Walter Scheuer
CFO: Richard Kaufman
1992 Sales: — Employees: —
Symbol: SPR Exchange: AMEX
Industry: Financial - investment management

Sterling Chemicals, Inc.
1200 Smith St., Ste. 1900
Houston, TX 77002
Phone: 713-650-3700 Fax: 713-654-9551
CEO: J. Virgil Waggoner
CFO: Douglas W. Metten
1991 Sales: $543 million Employees: 947
Symbol: STX Exchange: NYSE
Industry: Chemicals - diversified

Sterling Electronics Corp.
4201 Southwest Fwy.
Houston, TX 77027
Phone: 713-627-9800 Fax: 713-623-0146
CEO: Michael S. Spolane
CFO: Leon Webb, Jr.
1992 Sales: $118 million Employees: 473
Symbol: SEC Exchange: AMEX
Industry: Electrical components - raw materials & subassemblies

Sterling Environmental Services
4234 Ridge Lea Rd.
Amherst, NY 14226
Phone: 716-834-3558 Fax: 716-834-3599
CEO: Wayne Cameron
CFO: John Rizzo
1991 Sales: $4.1 million Employees: 9
Ownership: Privately held
Industry: Hazardous waste management

Sterling Optical Corp.
255 Route 17 South
Hackensack, NJ 07601
Phone: 201-489-0400 Fax: —
CEO: Robert K. Low
CFO: George Casabona
1991 Sales: $78 million Employees: 930
Symbol: EYE Exchange: NYSE
Industry: Retail - optical stores

Sterling Savings Association
North 120 Wall St.
Spokane, WA 99201
Phone: 509-458-3711 Fax: —
CEO: Harold B. Gilkey
CFO: Daniel G. Byrne
1991 Sales: $68 million Employees: 287
Symbol: STSA Exchange: NASDAQ
Industry: Financial - savings and loans

Sterling Software, Inc.
8080 N. Central Expressway, Ste. 1100
Dallas, TX 75206
Phone: 214-891-8600 Fax: 214-739-0535
CEO: Sterling L. Williams
CFO: George H. Ellis
1992 Sales: $259 million Employees: 2,150
Symbol: SSW Exchange: NYSE
Industry: Computers - software & network services

Stevens Graphics Corp.
5500 Airport Fwy.
Ft. Worth, TX 76117
Phone: 817-831-3911 Fax: 817-838-4344
CEO: Paul I. Stevens
CFO: James A. Cole
1991 Sales: $79 million Employees: 615
Symbol: SVGA Exchange: AMEX
Industry: Machinery - printing

Stewart Enterprises, Inc.
110 Veterans Memorial Blvd.
Metairie, LA 70005
Phone: 504-837-5880 Fax: 504-835-5833
CEO: Lawrence M. Berner
CFO: Ronald H. Patron
1991 Sales: $138 million Employees: 2,300
Symbol: STEI Exchange: NASDAQ
Industry: Funeral services & related

Stewart Information Services Corp.
2200 West Loop South
Houston, TX 77027
Phone: 713-871-1100 Fax: 713-552-9523
CEO: Carloss Morris
CFO: Max Crisp
1991 Sales: $217 million Employees: 2,985
Symbol: SISC Exchange: NASDAQ
Industry: Financial - business services

Stewart & Stevenson Services, Inc.
2707 N. Loop West
Houston, TX 77008
Phone: 713-868-7700 Fax: 713-868-7692
CEO: C. Jim Stewart II
CFO: Robert L. Hargrave
1992 Sales: $776 million Employees: 2,612
Symbol: SSSS Exchange: NASDAQ
Industry: Engines - internal combustion

STI Group, Inc.
4 Stamford Forum
Stamford, CT 06901
Phone: 203-964-8600 Fax: —
CEO: Edward F. Kosnik
CFO: Donald B. Christiansen
1991 Sales: $294 million Employees: 935
Symbol: SPG Exchange: NYSE
Industry: Electrical components

Stifel Nicolaus & Co., Inc.
500 N. Broadway
St. Louis, MO 63102
Phone: 314-342-2000 Fax: 314-342-2051
CEO: George H. Walker III
CFO: Mark D. Knott
1991 Sales: $77 million Employees: 816
Symbol: SF Exchange: NYSE
Industry: Financial - business services

Stokely USA, Inc.
626 E. Wisconsin Ave.
Oconomowoc, WI 53066
Phone: 414-567-9151 Fax: 414-567-0261
CEO: Joseph B. Weix
CFO: Thomas W. Mount
1992 Sales: $280 million Employees: 7,100
Symbol: STKY Exchange: NASDAQ
Industry: Food - canned

Stone Computer & Copier Supply
8753 S. Lewis
Tulsa, OK 74137
Phone: 918-298-2989 Fax: 918-299-9652
CEO: Buddy Stone
CFO: David Brandenburgh
1991 Sales: $2.9 million Employees: 18
Ownership: Privately held
Industry: Computers - computer & copier supplies

Stone Container Corp.
150 N. Michigan Ave.
Chicago, IL 60601
Phone: 312-346-6600 Fax: 312-580-4919
CEO: Roger W. Stone
CFO: Arnold F. Brookstone
1992 Sales: $5,521 million Employees: 31,800
Symbol: STO Exchange: NYSE
Industry: Containers - paper, paperboard & paper packaging, white paper & pulp

Stone & Webster, Inc.
250 W. 34th St.
New York, NY 10119
Phone: 212-290-7500 Fax: 212-290-7507
CEO: William F. Allen, Jr.
CFO: William M. Egan
1991 Sales: $257 million Employees: 8,000
Symbol: SW Exchange: NYSE
Industry: Construction - heavy

Stoneridge Resources
2000 N. Woodward Ave., Ste. 300
Bloomfield Hills, MI 48304
Phone: 313-540-9040 Fax: 313-540-0604
CEO: Kenneth C. Coon
CFO: Timothy J. LaRouere
1991 Sales: $81 million Employees: 181
Symbol: SRE Exchange: NYSE
Industry: Agricultural operations

Stop & Shop Companies, Inc., The
60 Campanelli Park
Braintree, MA 02184
Phone: 617-380-8000 Fax: 617-380-5915
CEO: Lewis G. Schaeneman, Jr.
CFO: Joseph D. McGlinchey
1992 Sales: $3,863 million Employees: 42,000
Symbol: SHP Exchange: NYSE
Industry: Retail - supermarkets

Storage Technology Corp.
2270 S. 88th St.
Louisville, CO 80028
Phone: 303-673-5151 Fax: 303-673-5019
CEO: Ryal R. Poppa
CFO: Gregory A. Tymn
1992 Sales: $1,522 million Employees: 10,100
Symbol: STK Exchange: NYSE
Industry: Computers - storage & retrieval systems

Stratus Computer, Inc.
55 Fairbanks Blvd.
Marlborough, MA 01752
Phone: 508-460-2000 Fax: 508-481-8945
CEO: William E. Foster
CFO: Robert E. Donahue
1992 Sales: $486 million Employees: 2,492
Symbol: SRA Exchange: NYSE
Industry: Computers - mini & micro

Strawbridge & Clothier
8th & Market Streets
Philadelphia, PA 19107
Phone: 215-629-6000 Fax: 215-629-7835
CEO: Francis R. Strawbridge III
CFO: Steven L. Strawbridge
1992 Sales: $973 million Employees: 13,146
Symbol: STRWA Exchange: NASDAQ
Industry: Retail - regional department stores

Stretchco Fabrics
55 Thomas Rd.
Hawthorne, NJ 07506
Phone: 201-423-0556 Fax: 201-423-2077
CEO: Lewis Wolf
CFO: Lewis Wolf
1991 Sales: $10 million Employees: 7
Ownership: Privately held
Industry: Textiles - stretch knit fabrics

Stride Rite Corp.
Five Cambridge Center
Cambridge, MA 02142
Phone: 617-491-8800 Fax: 617-864-1372
CEO: Ervin R. Shames
CFO: John J. Phelan
1991 Sales: $574 million Employees: 3,600
Symbol: SRR Exchange: NYSE
Industry: Shoes & related apparel

Strober Organization, Inc.
550 Hamilton Ave.
Brooklyn, NY 11232
Phone: 718-875-9700 Fax: 718-768-8287
CEO: Gary F. Kulick
CFO: David J. Polishook
1991 Sales: $90 million Employees: 350
Symbol: STRB Exchange: NASDAQ
Industry: Building products - retail & wholesale

Stroh Companies Inc., The
100 River Place
Detroit, MI 48207
Phone: 313-446-2000 Fax: 313-446-2206
CEO: Peter W. Stroh
CFO: Christopher T. Sortwell
1992 Sales: $1,150 million Employees: 3,500
Ownership: Privately held
Industry: Beverages - beer

Structural Dynamics Research Corp.
2000 Eastman Dr.
Milford, OH 45150
Phone: 513-576-2400 Fax: 513-576-2734
CEO: Ronald J. Friedsam
CFO: Ronald H. Hoffman
1991 Sales: $146 million Employees: 1,059
Symbol: SDRC Exchange: NASDAQ
Industry: Computers - engineering software

Struthers Industries, Inc.
1500 34th St.
Gulfport, MS 39501
Phone: 601-864-5410 Fax: 601-864-5555
CEO: John C. Edwards
CFO: John C. Edwards
1991 Sales: $5.5 million Employees: 80
Symbol: SIR Exchange: AMEX
Industry: Aerospace - aircraft equipment

Stryker Corp.
2725 Fairfield Rd.
Kalamazoo, MI 49002
Phone: 616-385-2600 Fax: 616-385-1062
CEO: John W. Brown
CFO: David J. Simpson
1991 Sales: $365 million Employees: 2,448
Symbol: STRY Exchange: NASDAQ
Industry: Medical instruments - surgical products, physical therapy centers, maternity beds

Stuart Entertainment, Inc.
400 E. Mineral Ave.
Littleton, CO 80122
Phone: 303-795-2625 Fax: 303-795-2508
CEO: Leonard A. Stuart
CFO: Richard H. Ellison
1991 Sales: $41 million Employees: 541
Symbol: STUA Exchange: NASDAQ
Industry: Leisure & recreational products - bingo cards, equipment, & supplies

Stuarts Department Stores, Inc.
16 Forge Pkwy.
Franklin, MA 02038
Phone: 508-520-4540 Fax: 508-520-4556
CEO: Marc C. Ostrow
CFO: Antone F. Moreira
1991 Sales: $111 million Employees: 1,072
Symbol: STUSQ Exchange: NASDAQ
Industry: Retail - regional department stores

Student Loan Marketing Association
1050 Thomas Jefferson St. NW
Washington, DC 20007
Phone: 202-333-8000 Fax: 202-337-1976
CEO: Michael Piemonte
CFO: Mitchell A. Johnson
1992 Sales: $2,787 million Employees: 3,423
Symbol: SLM Exchange: NYSE
Industry: Financial - student loans

Sturm, Ruger & Co., Inc.
One Lacey Place
Southport, CT 06490
Phone: 203-259-7843 Fax: 203-254-2195
CEO: William B. Ruger
CFO: John M. Kingsley, Jr.
1991 Sales: $137 million Employees: 1,410
Symbol: RGR Exchange: NYSE
Industry: Leisure & recreational products - guns

STV Group
11 Robinson St.
Pottstown, PA 19464
Phone: 215-326-4600 Fax: 215-326-3833
CEO: Michael Haratunian
CFO: Peter W. Knipe
1991 Sales: $71 million Employees: 879
Symbol: STVI Exchange: NASDAQ
Industry: Engineering - R&D services

indicates company is in *Hoover's Handbook of American Business.*

indicates company is in *Hoover's Handbook of World Business;* sales and employee numbers are for parent company.

Suave Shoe Corp.
14100 NW 60th Ave.
Miami Lakes, FL 33014
Phone: 305-822-7880 Fax: 305-556-8392
CEO: David Egozi
CFO: Pedro Mirones
1991 Sales: $53 million Employees: 1,250
Symbol: SWV Exchange: NYSE
Industry: Shoes & related apparel

Suburban Bancorp, Inc.
50 N. Brockway St.
Palatine, IL 60067
Phone: 708-359-1077 Fax: —
CEO: Gerald F. Fitzgerald, Jr.
CFO: James G. Fitzgerald
1991 Sales: $92 million Employees: 488
Symbol: SUBBA Exchange: NASDAQ
Industry: Banks - Midwest

Suffolk Bancorp
6 W. Second St.
Riverhead, NY 11901
Phone: 516-727-2700 Fax: 516-727-3214
CEO: Edward J. Merz
CFO: Victor F. Bozuhoski, Jr.
1991 Sales: $54 million Employees: 315
Symbol: SUBK Exchange: NASDAQ
Industry: Banks - Northeast

Sulcus Computer Corp.
41 N. Main St.
Greensburg, PA 15601
Phone: 412-836-2000 Fax: —
CEO: Jeffrey S. Rather
CFO: Jeffrey S. Rather
1991 Sales: $18 million Employees: 210
Symbol: SUL Exchange: AMEX
Industry: Computers - software

Sullivan Dental Products, Inc.
10920 W. Lincoln Ave.
West Allis, WI 53227
Phone: 414-321-8881 Fax: 414-321-8865
CEO: Robert J. Sullivan
CFO: Wayne G. Holt
1991 Sales: $75 million Employees: 356
Symbol: SULL Exchange: NASDAQ
Industry: Medical & dental supplies

Sullivan Graphics Inc.
100 Winners Circle
Brentwood, TN 37027
Phone: 615-377-0377 Fax: 615-377-0370
CEO: James T. Sullivan
CFO: Bryan Richardson
1991 Sales: $550 million Employees: 3,800
Ownership: Privately held
Industry: Printing - commercial services

Sumitomo Corp. of America
345 Park Ave., 13th Fl.
New York, NY 10154
Phone: 212-207-0700 Fax: 212-207-0456
CEO: Kenji Miyahara
CFO: —
1992 Sales: $159,496 million Employees: 8,959
Parent: Sumitomo Group
Industry: Diversified operations - metals, machinery & chemicals

Summagraphics Corp.
60 Silvermine Rd.
Seymour, CT 06483
Phone: 203-881-5400 Fax: 203-881-5367
CEO: William J. Lifka
CFO: David G. Osowski
1992 Sales: $74 million Employees: 460
Symbol: SUGR Exchange: NASDAQ
Industry: Computers - digitizing tablets & pen plotters

Summit Bancorp
One Main St.
Chatham, NJ 07928
Phone: 201-701-6200 Fax: 201-701-0464
CEO: Thomas D. Sayles, Jr.
CFO: John R. Feeney
1991 Sales: $351 million Employees: 1,688
Symbol: SUBN Exchange: NASDAQ
Industry: Banks - Northeast

Summit Builders
2601 E. Thomas Rd., Ste. 115
Phoenix, AZ 85106
Phone: 602-840-7700 Fax: 602-840-6897
CEO: Jeff Stone
CFO: Conrad Stone
1991 Sales: $27 million Employees: 49
Ownership: Privately held
Industry: Construction - general contracting

Summit Health Ltd.
2600 W. Magnolia Blvd.
Burbank, CA 91505
Phone: 818-841-8750 Fax: 818-841-4044
CEO: Donald J. Amaral
CFO: Randolph H. Speer
1992 Sales: $452 million Employees: 5,050
Symbol: SUMH Exchange: NASDAQ
Industry: Hospitals

Summit Holding Corp.
129 Main St.
Beckley, WV 25801
Phone: 304-256-7262 Fax: —
CEO: Warren A. Thornhill III
CFO: James W. Word, Jr.
1991 Sales: $8.9 million Employees: 117
Symbol: SUHC Exchange: NASDAQ
Industry: Banks - Southeast

Summit Marketing Group
1425 Jefferson Rd.
Rochester, NY 14623
Phone: 716-272-7360 Fax: 716-272-1421
CEO: Danny Gallant
CFO: Jerry Larrabee
1991 Sales: $4.5 million Employees: 159
Ownership: Privately held
Industry: Publishing - informational dictionaries; markets catalog memberships

Summit Savings Association
400 112th Ave. NE
Bellevue, WA 98004
Phone: 206-451-3585 Fax: —
CEO: James F. Grabicki
CFO: Patricia L. Waldow
1992 Sales: — Employees: —
Symbol: SMMT Exchange: NASDAQ
Industry: Financial - savings and loans

Sun City Industries, Inc.
8600 NW 36th St., Ste. 304
Miami, FL 33166
Phone: 305-730-3333 Fax: 305-592-6288
CEO: Malvin Avchen
CFO: Syed Jafri
1991 Sales: $68 million Employees: 445
Symbol: SNI Exchange: AMEX
Industry: Food - dairy products

Sun Coast Plastics, Inc.
7350 26th Ct. East
Sarasota, FL 34243
Phone: 813-355-7166 Fax: 813-351-2464
CEO: Jon M. Reynolds
CFO: Thomas L. King
1992 Sales: $62 million Employees: 533
Symbol: SUNI Exchange: NASDAQ
Industry: Rubber & plastic products

Sun Coast Resources Inc.
14825 Willis
Houston, TX 77039
Phone: 713-449-7274 Fax: 713-449-7288
CEO: Kathy Prasnicki
CFO: Kathy Prasnicki
1991 Sales: $86 million Employees: 14
Ownership: Privately held
Industry: Wholesale distribution - gasoline & diesel fuel

Sun Company, Inc.
1801 Market St.
Philadelphia, PA 19103
Phone: 215-977-3000 Fax: 215-293-6204
CEO: Robert H. Campbell
CFO: Robert M. Aiken, Jr.
1992 Sales: $10,682 million Employees: 16,963
Symbol: SUN Exchange: NYSE
Industry: Oil refining & marketing

Sun Distributors L.P.
One Logan Square
Philadelphia, PA 19103
Phone: 215-665-3650 Fax: 215-665-3662
CEO: Donald T. Marshall
CFO: Louis J. Cissone
1991 Sales: $574 million Employees: 4,264
Symbol: SDP Exchange: NYSE
Industry: Auto parts - retail & wholesale

Sun Energy Partners, L.P.
13155 Noel Rd.
Dallas, TX 75240
Phone: 214-715-4000 Fax: —
CEO: Robert P. Hauptfuhrer
CFO: Edward W. Moneypenny
1991 Sales: $937 million Employees: —
Symbol: SLP Exchange: NYSE
Industry: Oil & gas - US exploration & production

Sun Microsystems, Inc.
2550 Garcia Ave.
Mountain View, CA 94043
Phone: 415-960-1300 Fax: 415-969-9131
CEO: Scott G. McNealy
CFO: Kevin C. Melia
1992 Sales: $3,832 million Employees: 12,800
Symbol: SUNW Exchange: NASDAQ
Industry: Computers - workstations

Sun Sportswear, Inc.
6520 S. 190th St.
Kent, WA 98032
Phone: 206-251-3565 Fax: —
CEO: Randolph H. Clark
CFO: Kevin C. James
1991 Sales: $72 million Employees: 388
Symbol: SSPW Exchange: NASDAQ
Industry: Apparel

Sun Television & Appliances
1583 Alum Creek Dr.
Columbus, OH 43209
Phone: 614-445-8401 Fax: 614-444-0849
CEO: Macy T. Block
CFO: Robert E. Oyster
1992 Sales: $271 million Employees: 1,670
Symbol: SNTV Exchange: NASDAQ
Industry: Retail - consumer electronics

Sunair Electronics, Inc.
3101 SW Third Ave.
Ft. Lauderdale, FL 33315
Phone: 305-525-1505 Fax: 305-765-1322
CEO: Robert Uricho, Jr.
CFO: Richard H. Hoster
1991 Sales: $4.6 million Employees: 75
Symbol: SNRU Exchange: NASDAQ
Industry: Telecommunications equipment

Sunbeam-Oster Co., Inc.
One Citizen Plaza, 6th Fl.
Providence, RI 02903
Phone: 401-831-8100 Fax: 401-831-0389
CEO: Paul B. Kazarian
CFO: Paul B. Kazarian
1992 Sales: $967 million Employees: 10,000
Symbol: SOC Exchange: NYSE
Industry: Appliances - household

Sunbelt Beverage Corp.
2330 W. Joppa Rd. #330
Lutherville, MD 21093
Phone: 410-832-7740 Fax: 410-832-7730
CEO: Charles Andrews
CFO: Eugene Luciana
1992 Sales: $565 million Employees: 1,400
Ownership: Privately held
Industry: Beverages - wine & spirits

Sunbelt Nursery Group, Inc.
6500 West Fwy., Ste. 600
Ft. Worth, TX 76116
Phone: 817-738-8111 Fax: 817-735-0948
CEO: Donald W. Davis
CFO: Donald W. Davis
1991 Sales: $140 million Employees: 2,000
Symbol: SBN Exchange: AMEX
Industry: Retail - garden centers

Suncoast Savings and Loan Association
4000 Hollywood Blvd.
Hollywood, FL 33021
Phone: 305-981-6400 Fax: —
CEO: Albert J. Finch
CFO: Richard L. Browdy
1992 Sales: — Employees: —
Symbol: SCSL Exchange: NASDAQ
Industry: Financial - savings and loans

Sundowner Offshore Services, Inc.
2707 N. Loop West, Ste. 510
Houston, TX 77008
Phone: 713-868-1294 Fax: 713-868-3827
CEO: Jerry C. Shanklin
CFO: William W. Elting
1991 Sales: $24 million Employees: 340
Symbol: SOSI Exchange: NASDAQ
Industry: Oil & gas - field services

Sundstrand Corp.
4949 Harrison Ave.
Rockford, IL 61108
Phone: 815-226-6000 Fax: 815-226-7488
CEO: Harry C. Stonecipher
CFO: Paul Donovan
1992 Sales: $1,673 million Employees: 12,800
Symbol: SNS Exchange: NYSE
Industry: Aerospace - aircraft equipment

SunGard Data Systems Inc.
1285 Drummers Lane, Ste. 300
Wayne, PA 19087
Phone: 215-341-8700 Fax: 215-341-8739
CEO: James L. Mann
CFO: David D. Gathman
1991 Sales: $284 million Employees: 1,690
Symbol: SNDT Exchange: NASDAQ
Industry: Computers - disaster recovery services

Sunlite, Inc.
1445 Ross Ave.
Dallas, TX 75202
Phone: 214-855-6222 Fax: 214-855-6287
CEO: Graham F. Lacey
CFO: Michael E. Palmer
1991 Sales: $14 million Employees: 120
Symbol: SNLT Exchange: NASDAQ
Industry: Oil & gas - US exploration & production

Sunrise Bancorp
5 SierraGate Plaza
Roseville, CA 95678
Phone: 916-786-7080 Fax: —
CEO: James R. Daley
CFO: James E. Beckwith
1991 Sales: $28 million Employees: 189
Symbol: SRBC Exchange: NASDAQ
Industry: Banks - West

Sunrise Medical Inc.
2355 Crenshaw Blvd., Ste. 150
Torrance, CA 90501
Phone: 310-328-8018 Fax: 310-328-8184
CEO: Richard H. Chandler
CFO: Ted N. Tarbet
1992 Sales: $244 million Employees: 2,238
Symbol: SMD Exchange: NYSE
Industry: Medical & dental supplies

Sunrise Retirement Homes Corp.
9401 Lee Hwy., Ste. 300
Fairfax, VA 22031
Phone: 703-273-7500 Fax: 703-273-7501
CEO: Paul Klaassen
CFO: Kelly Cook
1992 Sales: $24 million Employees: 950
Ownership: Privately held
Industry: Nursing homes - assisted living/senior long-term care

Sunrise Technologies, Inc.
47257 Fremont Blvd.
Fremont, CA 94538
Phone: 510-623-9001 Fax: 510-623-9008
CEO: Arthur Vassilidadis
CFO: Stephen T. Prairie
1991 Sales: $20 million Employees: 73
Symbol: SNRS Exchange: NASDAQ
Industry: Lasers - systems & components

Sunshine JR. Stores, Inc.
Seventeenth St. & June Ave.
Panama City, FL 32402
Phone: 904-769-1661 Fax: 904-769-5499
CEO: Lenard J. Miller
CFO: W. Michael Dreggors
1991 Sales: $218 million Employees: 1,760
Symbol: SJS Exchange: AMEX
Industry: Retail - convenience stores

Sunshine Mining Co.
200 Crescent Court St., Ste. 1350
Dallas, TX 75201
Phone: 214-855-8700 Fax: 214-855-8790
CEO: G. Michael Boswell
CFO: George R. Truitt
1991 Sales: $24 million Employees: 263
Symbol: SSC Exchange: NYSE
Industry: Silver mining & processing

SunTrust Banks, Inc.
25 Park Place NE
Atlanta, GA 30303
Phone: 404-588-7711 Fax: 404-827-6001
CEO: James B. Williams
CFO: John W. Spiegel
1992 Sales: $3,110 million Employees: 19,103
Symbol: STI Exchange: NYSE
Industry: Banks - Southeast

Sunward Technologies, Inc.
5828 Pacific Center Blvd.
San Diego, CA 92121
Phone: 619-587-9140 Fax: 619-587-9614
CEO: Gregorio Reyes
CFO: Ronald J. Scioscia
1992 Sales: $75 million Employees: 2,216
Symbol: SUNT Exchange: NASDAQ
Industry: Computers - magnetic recording heads

Super Food Services, Inc.
3233 Newmark Dr.
Miamisburg, OH 45342
Phone: 513-439-7500 Fax: 513-439-7514
CEO: Jack Twyman
CFO: Robert F. Koogler
1992 Sales: $1,415 million Employees: 2,480
Symbol: SFS Exchange: NYSE
Industry: Food - wholesale

Super Rite Foods Inc.
3900 Industrial Rd.
Harrisburg, PA 17110
Phone: 717-232-6821 Fax: Ext. 4527
CEO: Alex Grass
CFO: William K. Schantzenbach
1992 Sales: $1,244 million Employees: —
Symbol: SUPR Exchange: NASDAQ
Industry: Food - wholesale

Super Valu Stores, Inc.
11840 Valley View Rd.
Eden Prairie, MN 55344
Phone: 612-828-4000 Fax: 612-828-8998
CEO: Michael W. Wright
CFO: Jeffrey C. Girard
1992 Sales: $11,343 million Employees: 24,406
Symbol: SVU Exchange: NYSE
Industry: Food - wholesale

Supercuts, Inc.
555 Northgate Dr.
San Rafael, CA 94903
Phone: 415-472-1170 Fax: 415-492-0982
CEO: Edward E. Faber
CFO: William N. Stirlen
1991 Sales: $32 million Employees: 720
Symbol: CUTS Exchange: NASDAQ
Industry: Retail - hair salons

Superior Industries International, Inc.
7800 Woodley Ave.
Van Nuys, CA 91406
Phone: 818-781-4973 Fax: 818-780-5631
CEO: Louis L. Borick
CFO: R. Jeffrey Ornstein
1991 Sales: $274 million Employees: 3,000
Symbol: SUP Exchange: NYSE
Industry: Automotive & trucking - original equipment

Superior Surgical Manufacturing Co., Inc.
10099 Seminole Blvd.
Seminole, FL 34642
Phone: 813-397-9611 Fax: 813-391-5401
CEO: Gerald M. Benstock
CFO: John W. Johansen
1991 Sales: $118 million Employees: 1,850
Symbol: SGC Exchange: AMEX
Industry: Linen supply & related

Superior TeleTec Inc.
150 Interstate North Pkwy. NW, Ste. 300
Atlanta, GA 30339
Phone: 404-953-8338 Fax: 404-980-2812
CEO: James R. Kanely
CFO: David S. Aldridge
1992 Sales: $132 million Employees: 666
Symbol: STT Exchange: AMEX
Industry: Wire & cable products

SuperMac Technology
485 Potrero Ave.
Sunnyvale, CA 94086
Phone: 408-245-2202 Fax: 408-735-7250
CEO: Michael A. McConnell
CFO: James A. Heisch
1991 Sales: $80 million Employees: 251
Symbol: SMAC Exchange: NASDAQ
Industry: Computers - desktop color graphics systems

indicates company is in *Hoover's Handbook of American Business.*

indicates company is in *Hoover's Handbook of World Business;* sales and employee numbers are for parent company.

Supermarkets General Holdings
301 Blair Rd.
Woodbridge, NJ 07095
Phone: 908-499-3000 Fax: 908-499-3072
CEO: Jack Futterman
CFO: Anthony J. Cuti
1992 Sales: $4,794 million Employees: 31,000
Ownership: Privately held
Industry: Retail - supermarkets, drug stores & home improvement centers

Supertex, Inc.
1225 Bordeaux Dr.
Sunnyvale, CA 94089
Phone: 408-744-0100 Fax: 408-734-5247
CEO: Henry C. Pao
CFO: Henry C. Pao
1992 Sales: $26 million Employees: 238
Symbol: SUPX Exchange: NASDAQ
Industry: Electrical components - semiconductors

Supplemental Health Care Services, Limited
2829 Sheridan Dr.
Tonawanda, NY 14150
Phone: 716-832-8986 Fax: 716-832-3407
CEO: Leo R. Blatz
CFO: Donald P. Ziemann
1991 Sales: $10 million Employees: 1,100
Ownership: Privately held
Industry: Business services - medical staff placement services

Surgical Care Affiliates, Inc.
102 Woodmont Blvd., Ste. 610
Nashville, TN 37205
Phone: 615-385-3541 Fax: 615-385-9939
CEO: Joel C. Gordon
CFO: Tarpley B. Jones
1991 Sales: $170 million Employees: 750
Symbol: SCA Exchange: NYSE
Industry: Healthcare - outpatient & home

Surgical Laser Technologies, Inc.
200 Cresson Blvd.
Oaks, PA 19456
Phone: 215-650-0700 Fax: 215-650-3210
CEO: David S. Joseph
CFO: Joseph F. Sivel
1991 Sales: $29 million Employees: —
Symbol: SLTI Exchange: NASDAQ
Industry: Lasers - systems & components

Surgical Technologies, Inc.
1245 E. Brickyard Rd.
Salt Lake City, UT 84106
Phone: 801-486-8818 Fax: —
CEO: Rex Crosland
CFO: Todd B. Crosland
1992 Sales: $6.7 million Employees: 93
Symbol: SGTI Exchange: NASDAQ
Industry: Medical products

Survival Technology, Inc.
2275 Research Blvd.
Rockville, MD 20850
Phone: 301-926-1800 Fax: 301-926-6186
CEO: James H. Miller
CFO: Jeffrey W. Church
1991 Sales: $47 million Employees: 555
Symbol: STIQ. Exchange: NASDAQ
Industry: Medical products - emergency health treatment

Susquehanna Bancshares, Inc.
26 N. Cedar St.
Lititz, PA 17543
Phone: 717-626-4721 Fax: —
CEO: Robert S. Bolinger
CFO: J. Stanley Mull, Jr.
1991 Sales: $70 million Employees: 1,039
Symbol: SUSQ Exchange: NASDAQ
Industry: Banks - Northeast

Sverdrup Corp.
13723 Riverport Dr.
Maryland Heights, MO 63043
Phone: 314-436-7600 Fax: 314-298-0045
CEO: Brice R. Smith, Jr.
CFO: R. J. Messey
1991 Sales: $600 million Employees: 5,000
Ownership: Privately held
Industry: Diversified operations - engineering, architecture, construction, technical services

Sweet Life Foods Inc.
1120 Harvey Lane
Suffield, CT 06078
Phone: 203-623-1681 Fax: 203-627-5076
CEO: Julian Leavitt
CFO: Gary Kulesza
1991 Sales: $1,050 million Employees: 3,000
Ownership: Privately held
Industry: Food - wholesale

Sweetheart Cups
7575 S. Kostner Ave.
Chicago, IL 60652
Phone: 312-767-3300 Fax: 312-767-9652
CEO: Philip White
CFO: Roger Cregg
1991 Sales: $800 million Employees: 8,000
Ownership: Privately held
Industry: Paper & paper products

SWFTE International Ltd.
Stone Mill Corporate Pk. #150, 724 Yorklyn Rd.
Hockessin, DE 19707
Phone: 302-234-1740 Fax: 302-234-1760
CEO: David Goodman
CFO: Diane Bové
1991 Sales: $2 million Employees: 11
Ownership: Privately held
Industry: Computers - software

Swift Energy Co.
16825 Northchase Dr., Ste. 400
Houston, TX 77060
Phone: 713-874-2700 Fax: 713-874-2726
CEO: A. Earl Swift
CFO: John R. Alden
1991 Sales: $14 million Employees: 171
Symbol: SFY Exchange: NYSE
Industry: Oil & gas - US exploration & production

Swift Transportation Co.
5601 W. Mohave St.
Phoenix, AZ 85043
Phone: 602-269-9700 Fax: 602-272-9917
CEO: Jerry Moyes
CFO: William F. Riley III
1991 Sales: $190 million Employees: 3,000
Symbol: SWFT Exchange: NASDAQ
Industry: Transportation - truck

Swinerton & Walberg Co.
580 California St.
San Francisco, CA 94104
Phone: 415-421-2980 Fax: 415-984-1233
CEO: Milo S. Gates
CFO: James R. Gillette
1990 Sales: $505 million Employees: 1,014
Ownership: Privately held
Industry: Construction - general contracting

Swing-N-Slide Corp.
1212 Barberry Dr.
Janesville, WI 53545
Phone: 608-755-4777 Fax: —
CEO: Thomas R. Baer
CFO: Richard E. Ruegger
1991 Sales: $33 million Employees: 302
Symbol: SNSC Exchange: NASDAQ
Industry: Leisure & recreational products - playground equipment

Sybase, Inc.
6475 Christie Ave.
Emeryville, CA 94608
Phone: 510-596-3500 Fax: 510-658-9441
CEO: Mark B. Hoffman
CFO: Jeanne D. Wohlers
1991 Sales: $159 million Employees: 1,068
Symbol: SYBS Exchange: NASDAQ
Industry: Computers - database management software

Sybron Chemicals, Inc.
Birmingham Rd.
Birmingham, NJ 08011
Phone: 609-893-1100 Fax: 609-894-8641
CEO: Richard M. Klein
CFO: Sidney H. Cohen
1991 Sales: $131 million Employees: 660
Symbol: SYCM Exchange: NASDAQ
Industry: Chemicals - specialty

Sybron Corp.
411 E. Wisconsin Ave., 24th Fl.
Milwaukee, WI 53202
Phone: 414-274-6600 Fax: 414-274-6561
CEO: Kenneth F. Yontz
CFO: Donald G. Rackl
1991 Sales: $350 million Employees: 3,506
Symbol: SYB Exchange: NYSE
Industry: Medical & dental supplies

Sylvan Foods Holdings, Inc.
One Moonlight Dr.
Worthington, PA 16262
Phone: 412-297-3402 Fax: —
CEO: Dennis C. Zensen
CFO: William P. Mooney
1991 Sales: $83 million Employees: 1,930
Symbol: SYLN Exchange: NASDAQ
Industry: Agricultural operations

Sym-Tek Systems, Inc.
17066 Goldentop Rd.
San Diego, CA 92127
Phone: 619-674-6800 Fax: 619-569-8296
CEO: Ray Twigg
CFO: Ray Twigg
1992 Sales: $42 million Employees: 353
Symbol: SYMK Exchange: NASDAQ
Industry: Machinery - material handling

Symantec Corp.
10201 Torre Ave.
Cupertino, CA 95014
Phone: 408-253-9600 Fax: 408-253-4092
CEO: Gordon E. Eubanks, Jr.
CFO: Robert R. B. Dykes
1992 Sales: $217 million Employees: 1,086
Symbol: SYMC Exchange: NASDAQ
Industry: Computers - information management, productivity & development software

Symbion, Inc.
7855 S. River Pkwy., Ste. 211
Tempe, AZ 85284
Phone: 602-831-0472 Fax: —
CEO: Richard W. Alder
CFO: Lane J. Castleton
1990 Sales: $1 million Employees: 15
Symbol: SYMB Exchange: NASDAQ
Industry: Medical products - cardiovascular devices

Symbol Technologies, Inc.
116 Wilbur Place
Bohemia, NY 11716
Phone: 516-563-2400 Fax: 516-563-2831
CEO: Jerome Swartz
CFO: Kenneth M. Schlenker
1991 Sales: $319 million Employees: 2,200
Symbol: SBL Exchange: NYSE
Industry: Optical character recognition

Symbolics, Inc.
8 New England Executive Park East
Burlington, MA 01803
Phone: 617-221-1000 Fax: 617-221-1099
CEO: John S. Wurts
CFO: Ronald R. Benanto
1991 Sales: $44 million Employees: 251
Symbol: SMBX Exchange: NASDAQ
Industry: Computers - artificial intelligence software

Symix Systems
2800 Corporate Exchange Dr., Ste. 400
Columbus, OH 43231
Phone: 614-523-7000 Fax: 614-895-2504
CEO: Lawrence J. Fox
CFO: William E. Tanner
1992 Sales: $27 million Employees: 252
Symbol: SYMX Exchange: NASDAQ
Industry: Computers - accounting & management software

Symmetrix, Inc.
1 Cranberry Hill
Lexington, MA 02173
Phone: 617-862-3200 Fax: 617-674-1300
CEO: George Bennett
CFO: Don Hawley
1991 Sales: $19 million Employees: 115
Ownership: Privately held
Industry: Engineering

Syms Corp.
One Syms Way
Secaucus, NJ 07094
Phone: 201-902-9600 Fax: 201-902-9874
CEO: Sy Syms
CFO: Richard B. Diamond
1991 Sales: $318 million Employees: 1,904
Symbol: SYM Exchange: NYSE
Industry: Retail - apparel & shoes

Synalloy Corp.
2155 W. Croft Cir., Croft Industrial Park
Spartanburg, SC 29304
Phone: 803-585-3605 Fax: 803-596-1501
CEO: James G. Lane, Jr.
CFO: James G. Lane, Jr.
1991 Sales: $90 million Employees: 458
Symbol: SYNC Exchange: NASDAQ
Industry: Steel - pipes & tubes

Synbiotics Corp.
11011 Via Frontera
San Diego, CA 92127
Phone: 619-451-3771 Fax: —
CEO: Edward T. Maggio
CFO: Daniel F. Cain
1992 Sales: $7.2 million Employees: 54
Symbol: SBIO Exchange: NASDAQ
Industry: Biomedical & genetic products

Syncor International Corp.
20001 Prairie St.
Chatsworth, CA 91311
Phone: 818-886-7400 Fax: 818-886-6028
CEO: Gene R. McGrevin
CFO: Michael E. Mikity
1991 Sales: $157 million Employees: 1,762
Symbol: SCOR Exchange: NASDAQ
Industry: Drugs & sundries - wholesale

Synercom Technology, Inc.
2500 City West Blvd., Ste. 1100
Houston, TX 77042
Phone: 713-954-7000 Fax: 713-785-0880
CEO: Robert W. Forsyth
CFO: Robert W. Forsyth
1991 Sales: $15 million Employees: 146
Symbol: SYNR Exchange: NASDAQ
Industry: Computers - database management software

Synergen, Inc.
1885 33rd St.
Boulder, CO 80301
Phone: 303-938-6200 Fax: 303-938-6268
CEO: Jon S. Saxe
CFO: Kenneth J. Collins
1991 Sales: $14 million Employees: 273
Symbol: SYGN Exchange: NASDAQ
Industry: Biomedical & genetic products

Synetic, Inc.
100 Summit Ave.
Montvale, NJ 07645
Phone: 201-358-5300 Fax: 201-358-5772
CEO: Martin J. Wygod
CFO: James V. Manning
1992 Sales: $59 million Employees: 780
Symbol: SNTC Exchange: NASDAQ
Industry: Medical products

Synopsys, Inc.
700 E. Middlefield Rd.
Mountain View, CA 94043
Phone: 415-962-5000 Fax: 415-694-4396
CEO: Harvey C. Jones, Jr.
CFO: A. Brooke Seawell
1992 Sales: $63 million Employees: 412
Symbol: SNPS Exchange: NASDAQ
Industry: Computers - integrated circuit design software

SynOptics Communications, Inc.
4401 Great American Pkwy.
Santa Clara, CA 95052
Phone: 408-988-2400 Fax: 408-988-5525
CEO: Andrew K. Ludwick
CFO: William J. Ruehle
1991 Sales: $248 million Employees: 959
Symbol: SNPX Exchange: NASDAQ
Industry: Computers - local area networks

Synovus Financial Corp.
901 Front Ave., Ste. 301
Columbus, GA 31901
Phone: 706-649-2311 Fax: 706-649-2479
CEO: James H. Blanchard
CFO: Stephen L. Burts, Jr.
1991 Sales: $488 million Employees: 4,085
Symbol: SNV Exchange: NYSE
Industry: Banks - Southeast

Syntellect Inc.
15810 N. 28th Ave.
Phoenix, AZ 85023
Phone: 602-789-2800 Fax: —
CEO: Thomas R. Mayer
CFO: C. Philip Chapman
1991 Sales: $29 million Employees: 189
Symbol: SYNL Exchange: NASDAQ
Industry: Telecommunications equipment

Syntex Corporation
3401 Hillview Ave.
Palo Alto, CA 94304
Phone: 415-855-5050 Fax: 415-855-5103
CEO: Paul E. Freiman
CFO: Richard P. Powers
1992 Sales: $2,069 million Employees: 10,900
Symbol: SYN Exchange: NYSE
Industry: Drugs

Syntro Corp.
9669 Lackman Rd.
Lenaxa, KS 66219
Phone: 913-888-8876 Fax: 913-894-9373
CEO: J. Donald Todd
CFO: Janice E. Katterhenry
1991 Sales: $4 million Employees: 45
Symbol: SYNT Exchange: NASDAQ
Industry: Biomedical & genetic products

SyQuest Technology, Inc.
47071 Bayside Pkwy.
Fremont, CA 94538
Phone: 510-226-4000 Fax: 510-226-4100
CEO: Syed H. Iftiker
CFO: Michael J. Perez
1991 Sales: $115 million Employees: 780
Symbol: SYQT Exchange: NASDAQ
Industry: Computers - removable cartridge disk drives

SYSCO Corp.
1390 Enclave Pkwy.
Houston, TX 77077
Phone: 713-584-1390 Fax: 713-584-1188
CEO: John F. Woodhouse
CFO: E. James Lowrey
1992 Sales: $9,343 million Employees: 22,500
Symbol: SYY Exchange: NYSE
Industry: Food - wholesale

System Connection Inc.
441 E. Bay Blvd.
Provo, UT 84606
Phone: 801-373-9800 Fax: 801-373-9847
CEO: Kirby Cochran
CFO: Jon L. Richards
1992 Sales: $10 million Employees: 75
Ownership: Privately held
Industry: Computers - cable & accessories

System Industries, Inc.
1855 Barber Lane
Milpitas, CA 95035
Phone: 408-432-1212 Fax: 408-943-9368
CEO: Paul W. Emery II
CFO: Robert J. Gannon
1991 Sales: $93 million Employees: 530
Symbol: SYI Exchange: AMEX
Industry: Computers - data enhancement systems

System Resources Corp.
128 Wheeler Rd.
Burlington, MA 01803
Phone: 617-270-9228 Fax: 617-272-2589
CEO: Samir A. Desai
CFO: Donald L. Gelinas
1992 Sales: $18 million Employees: 250
Ownership: Privately held
Industry: Computers - software development, information systems, system integration

System Software Associates, Inc.
500 W. Madison St., Ste. 3200
Chicago, IL 60661
Phone: 312-641-2900 Fax: 312-641-3737
CEO: Larry J. Ford
CFO: David L. Harbert
1991 Sales: $149 million Employees: 781
Symbol: SSAX Exchange: NASDAQ
Industry: Computers - business application software

Systemed, Inc.
140 Columbia
Laguna Hills, CA 92656
Phone: 714-362-1330 Fax: —
CEO: J. Roberts Fosberg
CFO: J. Roberts Fosberg
1991 Sales: $87 million Employees: 363
Symbol: SYSM Exchange: NASDAQ
Industry: Drugs

SyStemix, Inc.
3400 W. Bayshore Rd.
Palo Alto, CA 94303
Phone: 415-856-4901 Fax: 415-856-4919
CEO: Linda D. Sonntag
CFO: Robert G. Beaven
1991 Sales: $1.8 million Employees: 85
Symbol: STMX Exchange: NASDAQ
Industry: Biomedical & genetic products

indicates company is in *Hoover's Handbook of American Business.*

indicates company is in *Hoover's Handbook of World Business;* sales and employee numbers are for parent company.

Systems Center, Inc.
1800 Alexander Bell Dr.
Reston, VA 22091
Phone: 703-264-8000 Fax: 703-264-1308
CEO: Robert E. Cook
CFO: Theodore Kleinman
1991 Sales: $126 million Employees: 939
Symbol: SMX Exchange: NYSE
Industry: Computers - network software

Systems & Computer Technology Corp.
4 Country View Rd.
Malvern, PA 19355
Phone: 215-647-5930 Fax: 215-640-5102
CEO: Michael J. Emmi
CFO: Eric Haskell
1991 Sales: $63 million Employees: 1,050
Symbol: SCTC Exchange: NASDAQ
Industry: Computers - systems integration & information services

Systems & Programming Solutions
9325 N. 107th St.
Milwaukee, WI 53224
Phone: 414-355-5772 Fax: 414-355-7750
CEO: Robert Dumouchel
CFO: Robert Dumouchel
1991 Sales: $1.5 million Employees: 33
Ownership: Privately held
Industry: Computers - consulting services & custom software

T Cell Sciences, Inc.
38 Sidney St.
Cambridge, MA 02139
Phone: 617-621-1400 Fax: 617-621-1420
CEO: James D. Grant
CFO: Geoffrey P. Clear
1992 Sales: $8.9 million Employees: 102
Symbol: TCEL Exchange: NASDAQ
Industry: Biomedical & genetic products

T. Rowe Price Associates, Inc.
100 E. Pratt St.
Baltimore, MD 21202
Phone: 410-547-2000 Fax: 410-385-2026
CEO: George J. Collins
CFO: George A. Roche
1991 Sales: $205 million Employees: 1,400
Symbol: TROW Exchange: NASDAQ
Industry: Financial - investment management

T/SF Communications Corp.
2407 E. Skelly Dr.
Tulsa, OK 74015
Phone: 918-747-2600 Fax: —
CEO: G. Douglas Fox
CFO: J. Gary Mourton
1991 Sales: $94 million Employees: —
Symbol: TCM Exchange: AMEX
Industry: Publishing - periodicals

T^2 Medical, Inc.
1121 Alderman Dr.
Alpharetta, GA 30202
Phone: 404-442-2160 Fax: 404-442-2170
CEO: Thomas E. Haire
CFO: David Hersh
1991 Sales: $142 million Employees: 930
Symbol: TSQ Exchange: NYSE
Industry: Healthcare - outpatient & home

Tab Products Co.
1400 Page Mill Rd.
Palo Alto, CA 94304
Phone: 415-852-2400 Fax: 415-852-2688
CEO: Michael A. Dering
CFO: W. Brandt Brooksby
1992 Sales: $128 million Employees: 1,000
Symbol: TBP Exchange: AMEX
Industry: Office equipment & supplies

Taggart Company
1238 Bleistein
Cody, WY 82414
Phone: 307-527-6204 Fax: 307-527-6802
CEO: Jeffery J. Taggart
CFO: Jeffery J. Taggart
1991 Sales: $16 million Employees: 3
Ownership: Privately held
Industry: Insurance - employee benefits

Takecare Health Plan
2300 Clayton Rd., Ste. 1000
Concord, CA 94524
Phone: 510-246-1300 Fax: —
CEO: Jack R. Anderson
CFO: Dennis L. Gates
1991 Sales: $293 million Employees: 200
Symbol: TKCR Exchange: NASDAQ
Industry: Health maintenance organization

Talley Industries, Inc.
2800 N. 44th St., 9th Fl.
Phoenix, AZ 85008
Phone: 602-957-7711 Fax: 602-852-6972
CEO: William H. Mallender
CFO: Daniel R. Mullen
1991 Sales: $333 million Employees: 3,114
Symbol: TAL Exchange: NYSE
Industry: Diversified operations - architectural & engineering services, avionics

Tambrands Inc.
777 Westchester Ave.
White Plains, NY 10604
Phone: 914-696-6060 Fax: 914-696-6161
CEO: Martin F. C. Emmett
CFO: Raymond F. Wright
1992 Sales: $684 million Employees: 3,800
Symbol: TMB Exchange: NYSE
Industry: Medical & dental supplies

Tampa Bay Vending
7840 Professional Pl.
Tampa, FL 33637
Phone: 813-988-3652 Fax: 813-988-3548
CEO: Brad Bartholomew
CFO: Marie Batholomew
1991 Sales: $2.7 million Employees: 35
Ownership: Privately held
Industry: Retail - vending machines

Tandem Computers Inc.
19333 Vallco Pkwy.
Cupertino, CA 95014
Phone: 408-285-6000 Fax: 408-285-4545
CEO: James G. Treybig
CFO: David J. Rynne
1992 Sales: $2,066 million Employees: 11,167
Symbol: TDM Exchange: NYSE
Industry: Computers - fault-tolerant mini & micro computers

Tandon Corp.
301 Science Dr.
Moorpark, CA 93021
Phone: 805-523-0340 Fax: 805-378-3099
CEO: Sirjang Lal Tandon
CFO: Denis J. Trafecanty
1991 Sales: $461 million Employees: 1,656
Symbol: TCOR Exchange: NASDAQ
Industry: Computers - disk drives & desktop personal computers

Tandy Brands, Inc.
690 E. Lamar Blvd., Ste. 200
Arlington, TX 76011
Phone: 817-548-0090 Fax: 817-548-1144
CEO: J. S. B. Jenkins
CFO: Stanley T. Ninemire
1992 Sales: $36 million Employees: 365
Symbol: TBAC Exchange: NASDAQ
Industry: Leather & related products

Tandy Corp.
1800 One Tandy Center
Ft. Worth, TX 76102
Phone: 817-390-3700 Fax: 817-390-2774
CEO: John V. Roach
CFO: William C. Bousquette
1992 Sales: $4,742 million Employees: 41,000
Symbol: TAN Exchange: NYSE
Industry: Retail - consumer electronics

Tandycrafts, Inc.
1400 Everman Pkwy.
Ft. Worth, TX 76140
Phone: 817-551-9600 Fax: 817-551-5763
CEO: Kenneth L. Gregson
CFO: C. Gary Crow
1992 Sales: $131 million Employees: 2,000
Symbol: TAC Exchange: NYSE
Industry: Diversified operations - retail outlets, leather products, frames, furniture

Tang Industries, Inc.
1965 Pratt Blvd.
Elk Grove Village, IL 60007
Phone: 708-806-7600 Fax: 708-806-7220
CEO: Cyrus Tang
CFO: Michael Tang
1991 Sales: $713 million Employees: 3,222
Ownership: Privately held
Industry: Metal products - fabrication & distribution

Tanknology Environmental, Inc.
5225 Hollister St.
Houston, TX 77040
Phone: 713-690-8265 Fax: 713-690-2255
CEO: Robert L. Waltrip
CFO: Rick Berry
1991 Sales: $32 million Employees: 272
Symbol: TANK Exchange: NASDAQ
Industry: Pollution control equipment & services - storage tank maintenance

Tapistron International, Inc.
735 Broad St., Ste. 212
Chattanooga, TN 37402
Phone: 615-265-1920 Fax: —
CEO: Lanier M. Davenport
CFO: John C. Thomas, Jr.
1992 Sales: — Employees: —
Symbol: TAPI Exchange: NASDAQ
Industry: Machinery - computerized machine for making carpets, rugs, floor coverings

Target Therapeutics, Inc.
47201 Lakeview Blvd.
Fremont, CA 94537
Phone: 510-440-7700 Fax: —
CEO: Richard D. Randall
CFO: A. Larry Tannenbaum
1992 Sales: $19 million Employees: 225
Symbol: TGET Exchange: NASDAQ
Industry: Medical products

Tasty Baking Co. (Tastykake)
2801 W. Hunting Park Ave.
Philadelphia, PA 19129
Phone: 215-221-8500 Fax: 215-223-3288
CEO: Nelson G. Harris
CFO: John M. Pettine
1991 Sales: $288 million Employees: 1,500
Symbol: TBC Exchange: AMEX
Industry: Food - cookies, cakes & snack foods

Tata Incorporated
101 Park Ave.
New York, NY 10178
Phone: 212-557-7979 Fax: 212-557-7987
CEO: F. C. Kohli
CFO: —
1992 Sales: $3,603 million Employees: 251,000
Parent: Tata Group
Industry: Diversified operations - steel, power generation, oil exploration

 indicates company is in *Hoover's Handbook of American Business.*

indicates company is in *Hoover's Handbook of World Business;* sales and employee numbers are for parent company.

Tauber Oil Co.
55 Waugh Dr., Ste. 700
Houston, TX 77007
Phone: 713-869-8700 Fax: 713-869-8069
CEO: O. J. Tauber, Jr.
CFO: Pat O'Neal
1992 Sales: $747 million Employees: 50
Ownership: Privately held
Industry: Oil refining & marketing

Taubman Company, The
200 E. Long Lake Rd.
Bloomfield Hills, MI 48304
Phone: 313-258-6800 Fax: 313-258-7596
CEO: Robert S. Taubman
CFO: Bernard Winograd
1991 Sales: $447 million Employees: 430
Ownership: Privately held
Industry: Real estate development & management

Taylor Medical
2155 I-10 East
Beaumont, TX 77701
Phone: 409-853-7906 Fax: 409-832-1879
CEO: Todd Christopher
CFO: Eugene Humphery
1991 Sales: $81 million Employees: 500
Ownership: Privately held
Industry: Medical products - wholesale

TBC Corp.
4770 Hickory Hill Rd.
Memphis, TN 38141
Phone: 901-363-8030 Fax: —
CEO: Marvin E. Bruce
CFO: Ronald E. McCullough
1991 Sales: $500 million Employees: 240
Symbol: TBCC Exchange: NASDAQ
Industry: Auto parts - retail & wholesale

TCA Cable TV, Inc.
3015 SSE Loop 323
Tyler, TX 75701
Phone: 903-595-3701 Fax: 903-595-1929
CEO: Robert M. Rogers
CFO: Jimmie F. Taylor
1991 Sales: $127 million Employees: 756
Symbol: TCAT Exchange: NASDAQ
Industry: Cable TV

TCBY Enterprises, Inc.
425 W. Capitol Ave., TCBY Tower, Ste. 1100
Little Rock, AR 72201
Phone: 501-688-8229 Fax: 501-688-8246
CEO: Frank D. Hickingbotham
CFO: Gale Law
1991 Sales: $129 million Employees: 1,640
Symbol: TBY Exchange: NYSE
Industry: Retail - food & restaurants

TCF Financial Corp.
801 Marquette Ave.
Minneapolis, MN 55402
Phone: 612-370-7000 Fax: 612-332-1753
CEO: William A. Cooper
CFO: Lynn A. Nagorske
1991 Sales: $437 million Employees: 2,500
Symbol: TCB Exchange: NYSE
Industry: Banks - Midwest

TCI International, Inc.
34175 Ardenwood Blvd.
Fremont, CA 94536
Phone: 510-795-7800 Fax: 510-793-7669
CEO: John W. Ballard
CFO: William L. Gamble
1991 Sales: $57 million Employees: 390
Symbol: TCII Exchange: NASDAQ
Industry: Telecommunications equipment

TCS Enterprises, Inc.
10525 Vista Sorrento Pkwy.
San Diego, CA 92121
Phone: 619-452-8000 Fax: —
CEO: Tom C. Stickel
CFO: Judy Anne Harper
1991 Sales: $12 million Employees: 80
Symbol: TCS Exchange: AMEX
Industry: Financial - mortgages & related services

Teachers Insurance
730 Third Ave.
New York, NY 10017
Phone: 212-490-9000 Fax: 212-916-6231
CEO: Clifton R. Wharton, Jr.
CFO: Thomas W. Jones
1991 Sales: $9,992 million Employees: 3,800
Ownership: Privately held
Industry: Financial - pensions; insurance

Team, Inc.
1019 Hood St.
Alvin, TX 77511
Phone: 713-331-6154 Fax: 713-331-4107
CEO: H. Wesley Hall
CFO: Russell G. Donham
1992 Sales: $73 million Employees: 1,076
Symbol: TMI Exchange: AMEX
Industry: Construction - heavy

Team Spirit
201 Bank of Nebraska Mall
Omaha, NE 68105
Phone: 402-341-2518 Fax: 402-341-0270
CEO: John Dixon
CFO: Dan Dixon
1991 Sales: $13 million Employees: 90
Ownership: Privately held
Industry: Retail - team apparel

Teamsters
25 Louisiana Ave.
Washington, DC 20001
Phone: 202-624-6800 Fax: 202-624-6918
CEO: Ronald Carey
CFO: Tom Sever
1992 Sales: — Employees: —
Ownership: Privately held
Industry: Labor union

Tech Data Corp.
5350 Tech Data Dr.
Clearwater, FL 34620
Phone: 813-539-7429 Fax: 813-538-7050
CEO: Steven A. Raymund
CFO: Jeffery P. Howells
1992 Sales: $895 million Employees: 690
Symbol: TECD Exchange: NASDAQ
Industry: Wholesale distribution - microcomputers, hardware/software

Tech-Sym Corp.
10500 Westoffice Dr., Ste. 200
Houston, TX 77042
Phone: 713-785-7790 Fax: 713-780-3524
CEO: Wendell W. Gamel
CFO: Ray F. Thompson
1991 Sales: $176 million Employees: 1,901
Symbol: TSY Exchange: NYSE
Industry: Electronics - military

Tech/Ops Corp.
One Beacon St.
Boston, MA 02108
Phone: 617-523-2030 Fax: 617-523-0073
CEO: Bernard F. Start
CFO: Paul A. McPartlin
1991 Sales: $18 million Employees: 211
Symbol: TO Exchange: AMEX
Industry: Electrical products - solid state products

Technalysis Corp.
6700 France Ave. South
Minneapolis, MN 55435
Phone: 612-925-5900 Fax: 612-925-6082
CEO: Victor A. Rocchio
CFO: Victor A. Rocchio
1991 Sales: $18 million Employees: 248
Symbol: TECN Exchange: NASDAQ
Industry: Computers - system design and programming services

Techne
614 McKinley Place NE
Minneapolis, MN 55413
Phone: 612-379-8854 Fax: —
CEO: Thomas E. Oland
CFO: Thomas E. Oland
1992 Sales: $22 million Employees: 190
Symbol: TECH Exchange: NASDAQ
Industry: Biomedical & genetic products

Technical Communications Corp.
100 Domino Dr.
Concord, MA 01742
Phone: 508-369-7565 Fax: 508-371-1280
CEO: Arnold M. McCalmont
CFO: Herbert A. Lerner
1991 Sales: $13 million Employees: 50
Symbol: TCCO Exchange: NASDAQ
Industry: Telecommunications equipment

Technical Management Services
4350 N. Fairfax, Ste. 580
Arlington, VA 22203
Phone: 703-516-4440 Fax: 703-516-4368
CEO: Aleta Wilson
CFO: Aleta Wilson
1991 Sales: $6.1 million Employees: 90
Ownership: Privately held
Industry: Computers - systems development consulting services

Technitrol, Inc.
1210 Northbrook Dr., Ste. 385
Trevose, PA 19053
Phone: 215-355-2900 Fax: —
CEO: Roy E. Hock
CFO: Robert J. Citrino
1991 Sales: $81 million Employees: 970
Symbol: TNL Exchange: AMEX
Industry: Electrical products - scales, measuring equipment, electrical contacts

Technology Development Corp.
621 Six Flags Dr.
Arlington, TX 76011
Phone: 817-640-7274 Fax: 817-649-4430
CEO: Thomas M. Cracraft
CFO: Michael R. Buchanan
1990 Sales: $24 million Employees: 152
Symbol: TDCXE Exchange: NASDAQ
Industry: Electronics - measuring instruments

Technology Solutions Co.
205 N. Michigan Ave., Ste. 1500
Chicago, IL 60601
Phone: 312-819-2250 Fax: 312-819-2299
CEO: Albert D. Beedle, Jr.
CFO: Michael E. Mikolajczky
1992 Sales: $68 million Employees: 473
Symbol: TSCC Exchange: NASDAQ
Industry: Computers - consulting services

Technology Works, Inc.
4030 W. Braker Lane
Austin, TX 78759
Phone: 512-794-8533 Fax: 512-794-8520
CEO: Mike Frost
CFO: Mike Fitzpatrick
1991 Sales: $28 million Employees: 100
Ownership: Privately held
Industry: Computers - computer memory add-on products

Tecnol Inc.
7201 Industrial Park Blvd.
Ft. Worth, TX 76180
Phone: 817-581-6424 Fax: 817-581-9354
CEO: Vance M. Hubbard
CFO: Vance M. Hubbard
1991 Sales: $55 million Employees: 572
Symbol: TCNL Exchange: NASDAQ
Industry: Medical products - disposable

Teco Energy Co.
702 N. Franklin St.
Tampa, FL 33602
Phone: 813-228-4111 Fax: 813-228-1219
CEO: Timothy L. Guzzle
CFO: Alan D. Oak
1992 Sales: $1,183 million Employees: 4,640
Symbol: TE Exchange: NYSE
Industry: Utility - electric power

Tecogen Inc.
45 First Ave.
Waltham, MA 02254
Phone: 617-622-1400 Fax: 617-622-1252
CEO: Marshall J. Armstrong
CFO: John N. Hatsopoulos
1991 Sales: $17 million Employees: 124
Symbol: TGN Exchange: AMEX
Industry: Energy - alternative sources

Tecumseh Products Co.
100 E. Patterson St.
Tecumseh, MI 49286
Phone: 517-423-8411 Fax: 517-423-8456
CEO: Todd W. Herrick
CFO: John H. Foss
1992 Sales: $1,259 million Employees: 12,346
Symbol: TECUA Exchange: NASDAQ
Industry: Automotive & trucking - original equipment

Tejas Gas Corp.
1301 McKinney St., Ste. 700
Houston, TX 77010
Phone: 713-658-0509 Fax: 713-658-0278
CEO: Jay A. Precourt
CFO: Maurice D. McNeil
1991 Sales: $454 million Employees: 246
Symbol: TEJS Exchange: NASDAQ
Industry: Oil & gas - production & pipeline

Tejas Power Corp.
14811 St. Mary Lane, Ste. 200
Houston, TX 77079
Phone: 713-584-8200 Fax: 713-584-8212
CEO: Larry W. Bickle
CFO: J. Chris Jones
1991 Sales: $145 million Employees: 77
Symbol: TPC Exchange: AMEX
Industry: Oil & gas - production & pipeline

Tejon Ranch Co.
4436 Lebec Rd.
Lebec, CA 93243
Phone: 805-327-8481 Fax: 805-858-2553
CEO: Jack Hunt
CFO: Allen E. Lyda
1991 Sales: $13 million Employees: 49
Symbol: TRC Exchange: AMEX
Industry: Agricultural operations

Tekelec
26580 Agoura Rd.
Calabasas, CA 91302
Phone: 818-880-5656 Fax: 818-880-6993
CEO: Peter N. Vicars
CFO: Philip J. Alford
1991 Sales: $52 million Employees: 339
Symbol: TKLC Exchange: NASDAQ
Industry: Telecommunications equipment

Teknekron Communications Systems, Inc.
2121 Allston Way
Berkeley, CA 94704
Phone: 510-649-3700 Fax: 510-848-8851
CEO: Roger A. Strauch
CFO: Janelle F. Bradshaw
1991 Sales: $45 million Employees: 203
Symbol: TCSI Exchange: NASDAQ
Industry: Computers - software systems & technologies integration

Tektronix, Inc.
Howard Vollum Industrial Park
Beaverton, OR 97077
Phone: 503-627-7111 Fax: 503-627-5653
CEO: Jerome J. Meyer
CFO: Gary P. Arnold
1992 Sales: $1,344 million Employees: 11,334
Symbol: TEK Exchange: NYSE
Industry: Electronics - measuring instruments

Telamon Corp.
5406 W. 78th St.
Indianapolis, IN 46268
Phone: 317-471-6655 Fax: 317-471-6685
CEO: Albert Chen
CFO: Cyril Lu
1991 Sales: $21 million Employees: 88
Ownership: Privately held
Industry: Telecommunications equipment

Telco Systems, Inc.
63 Nahatan St.
Norwood, MA 02062
Phone: 617-551-0300 Fax: 617-551-0534
CEO: Paul D. Lazay
CFO: John A. Ruggiero
1991 Sales: $103 million Employees: 442
Symbol: TELC Exchange: NASDAQ
Industry: Telecommunications equipment

Tele-Communications, Inc.
5619 DTC Pkwy.
Englewood, CO 80111
Phone: 303-267-5500 Fax: 303-779-1228
CEO: John C. Malone
CFO: Bernard W. Schotters
1991 Sales: $3,827 million Employees: 33,000
Symbol: TCOMA Exchange: NASDAQ
Industry: Cable TV

Tele-Optics, Inc.
1006 W. 15th St.
Riviera Beach, FL 33404
Phone: 305-844-0263 Fax: —
CEO: Harold P. Koenig
CFO: James E. Davis
1990 Sales: $5.6 million Employees: 48
Symbol: TOPT Exchange: NASDAQ
Industry: Electrical products - camera lenses, video cameras & video monitors

Telebit Corp.
1315 Chesapeake Terrace
Sunnyvale, CA 94089
Phone: 408-734-4333 Fax: 408-734-3333
CEO: Paul Baran
CFO: Steven A. Hess
1991 Sales: $44 million Employees: 184
Symbol: TBIT Exchange: NASDAQ
Industry: Telecommunications equipment

TeleCom Corp.
1545 W. Mockingbird Lane, Ste. 7000
Dallas, TX 75235
Phone: 214-638-0638 Fax: 214-638-7043
CEO: Thomas M. Gaubert
CFO: Larry T. Marek
1991 Sales: $52 million Employees: 275
Symbol: TEL Exchange: NYSE
Industry: Building products - a/c & heating

Teledyne, Inc.
1901 Avenue of the Stars
Los Angeles, CA 90067
Phone: 310-277-3311 Fax: 310-551-4365
CEO: William P. Rutledge
CFO: Douglas J. Grant
1992 Sales: $2,888 million Employees: 29,400
Symbol: TDY Exchange: NYSE
Industry: Diversified operations - aviation & electronics, specialty metals

Teleflex Inc.
630 W. Germantown Pike, Ste. 450
Plymouth Meeting, PA 19462
Phone: 215-834-6301 Fax: 215-834-8307
CEO: Lennox K. Black
CFO: Harold L. Zuber, Jr.
1991 Sales: $480 million Employees: 6,160
Symbol: TFX Exchange: AMEX
Industry: Instruments - control

Telefónica - USA, Inc.
535 Madison Ave., 35th Fl.
New York, NY 10022
Phone: 212-221-5991 Fax: 212-759-3084
CEO: Adolpho Suarez
CFO: —
1991 Sales: $11,098 million Employees: 84,344
Parent: Telefónica de España, SA
Industry: Telecommunications services

Telematics International, Inc.
1201 W. Cypress Creek Rd.
Ft. Lauderdale, FL 33309
Phone: 305-772-3070 Fax: 305-351-4404
CEO: William A. Hightower
CFO: Miriam K. Frazer
1991 Sales: $64 million Employees: 358
Symbol: TMAX Exchange: NASDAQ
Industry: Telecommunications equipment

Telephone and Data Systems, Inc.
30 N. LaSalle St., Ste. 4000
Chicago, IL 60602
Phone: 312-630-1900 Fax: 312-630-1908
CEO: LeRoy T. Carlson, Jr.
CFO: Murray L. Swanson
1991 Sales: $354 million Employees: 3,297
Symbol: TDS Exchange: AMEX
Industry: Utility - telephone

Telephone Express
1155 Kelly Johnson Blvd., Ste. 400
Colorado Springs, CO 80920
Phone: 719-592-1200 Fax: 719-592-1201
CEO: J. Street
CFO: K. John
1991 Sales: $18 million Employees: 126
Ownership: Privately held
Industry: Telecommunications services - long distance

TeleVideo Systems, Inc.
550 E. Brokaw Rd.
San Jose, CA 95112
Phone: 408-745-7760 Fax: 408-954-0622
CEO: K. Philip Hwang
CFO: K. Philip Hwang
1991 Sales: $26 million Employees: 136
Symbol: TELV Exchange: NASDAQ
Industry: Computers - video display terminals

Telios Pharmaceuticals, Inc.
4757 Nexus Centre Dr.
San Diego, CA 92121
Phone: 619-622-2600 Fax: 619-535-8269
CEO: Robert J. Erickson
CFO: Robert J. Erickson
1991 Sales: $6.6 million Employees: 124
Symbol: TLIO Exchange: NASDAQ
Industry: Drugs

indicates company is in *Hoover's Handbook of American Business.*

indicates company is in *Hoover's Handbook of World Business;* sales and employee numbers are for parent company.

Tellabs, Inc.
4951 Indiana Ave.
Lisle, IL 60532
Phone: 708-969-8800 Fax: 708-852-7346
CEO: Michael J. Birck
CFO: Peter A. Guglielmi
1991 Sales: $213 million Employees: 2,094
Symbol: TLAB Exchange: NASDAQ
Industry: Telecommunications equipment

Telxon Corp.
3330 W. Market St.
Akron, OH 44333
Phone: 216-867-3700 Fax: 216-869-2220
CEO: Raymond D. Meyo
CFO: Dan R. Wipff
1992 Sales: $215 million Employees: 1,350
Symbol: TLXN Exchange: NASDAQ
Industry: Optical character recognition

Temco Home Health Care Products Inc.
125 South St.
Passaic, NJ 07055
Phone: 201-472-3173 Fax: 201-472-2557
CEO: Marvin D. Kantor
CFO: Sheldon A. Gold
1991 Sales: $20 million Employees: 350
Symbol: TEM Exchange: AMEX
Industry: Medical products, nursing homes, outpatient diagnostic centers

Temple-Inland Inc.
303 S. Temple Dr.
Diboll, TX 75941
Phone: 409-829-5511 Fax: 409-829-1366
CEO: Clifford J. Grum
CFO: Kenneth M. Jastrow II
1992 Sales: $2,713 million Employees: 14,500
Symbol: TIN Exchange: NYSE
Industry: Paper & paper products

Temtex Industries, Inc.
3010 LBJ Fwy., Ste. 605
Dallas, TX 75234
Phone: 214-484-1845 Fax: 214-241-1452
CEO: Edwin R. Buford
CFO: Roger N. Stivers
1991 Sales: $22 million Employees: 351
Symbol: TMTX Exchange: NASDAQ
Industry: Diversified operations

TENERA, L.P.
1995 University Ave., 5th Fl.
Berkeley, CA 94704
Phone: 510-845-5200 Fax: 510-845-8453
CEO: Anthony R. Buhl
CFO: Robert K. Dahl
1991 Sales: $44 million Employees: 361
Symbol: TLP Exchange: AMEX
Industry: Computers - services

Tennant Co.
701 N. Lilac Dr.
Minneapolis, MN 55422
Phone: 612-540-1200 Fax: 612-540-1437
CEO: Roger L. Hale
CFO: Richard A. Snyder
1991 Sales: $199 million Employees: 1,738
Symbol: TANT Exchange: NASDAQ
Industry: Machinery - general industrial

Tenneco, Inc.
Tenneco Bldg., 1010 Milam St.
Houston, TX 77002
Phone: 713-757-2131 Fax: 713-757-1410
CEO: Michael H. Walsh
CFO: Robert T. Blakely
1992 Sales: $13,139 million Employees: 89,000
Symbol: TGT Exchange: NYSE
Industry: Diversified operations - construction & farm equipment, natural gas pipelines

Tennessee Restaurant
One Pierce Place, Ste. 100E
Itasca, IL 60143
Phone: 708-250-0471 Fax: 708-250-0382
CEO: Donald N. Smith
CFO: Mike Donahoe
1991 Sales: $711 million Employees: 9,250
Ownership: Privately held
Industry: Retail - food & restaurants

Tenney Engineering, Inc.
1090 Springfield Rd.
Union, NJ 07083
Phone: 908-686-7870 Fax: 908-686-7971
CEO: Robert S. Schiffman
CFO: Frank E. Colgan
1991 Sales: $17 million Employees: 206
Symbol: TNY Exchange: AMEX
Industry: Pollution control equipment & services - environmental test & vacuum equipment

Teppco Partners, L.P.
2929 Allen Pkwy.
Houston, TX 77019
Phone: 713-759-3636 Fax: —
CEO: Clifford Rackley
CFO: Charles H. Leonard
1991 Sales: $163 million Employees: 550
Symbol: TPP Exchange: NYSE
Industry: Oil & gas - pipeline

Teradyne, Inc.
321 Harrison Ave.
Boston, MA 02118
Phone: 617-482-2700 Fax: 617-422-2910
CEO: Alexander V. D'Arbeloff
CFO: Owen W. Robbins
1991 Sales: $509 million Employees: 4,300
Symbol: TER Exchange: NYSE
Industry: Electronics - measuring instruments

Terex Corp.
201 W. Walnut St.
Green Bay, WI 54303
Phone: 414-435-5322 Fax: 414-432-2596
CEO: Ronald W. Lenz
CFO: Larry L. Skaff
1991 Sales: $784 million Employees: 7,000
Symbol: TEX Exchange: NYSE
Industry: Machinery - construction & mining

Termiflex Corp.
316 Daniel Webster Hwy.
Merrimack, NH 03054
Phone: 603-424-3700 Fax: 603-424-0330
CEO: William E. Fletcher
CFO: Lynn K. Friedel
1992 Sales: $8.4 million Employees: 66
Symbol: TFLX Exchange: NASDAQ
Industry: Electrical products - terminals

Terminal Data Corp.
5898 Condor Dr.
Moorpark, CA 93021
Phone: 805-529-1500 Fax: 805-529-6538
CEO: Jeffrey A. Wilson
CFO: Stephen P. Loomis
1991 Sales: $21 million Employees: 189
Symbol: TERM Exchange: NASDAQ
Industry: Office automation

Terra Industries, Inc.
250 Park Ave.
New York, NY 10177
Phone: 212-503-3100 Fax: 212-503-3178
CEO: Reuben F. Richards
CFO: W. Mark Rosenbury
1991 Sales: $1,033 million Employees: 5,073
Symbol: TRA Exchange: NYSE
Industry: Diversified operations - agricultural chemicals, aggregates, concrete

Terra Vac
PO Box 1591
San Juan, PR 00902
Phone: 809-723-9171 Fax: 809-725-8750
CEO: Jane Malot
CFO: Richard Malot
1991 Sales: $14 million Employees: 32
Ownership: Privately held
Industry: Environmental cleanup services

Tesoro Petroleum Corp.
8700 Tesoro Dr.
San Antonio, TX 78217
Phone: 210-828-8484 Fax: 210-828-8600
CEO: M. Richard Stewart
CFO: James R. Hyslop
1991 Sales: $1,085 million Employees: 2,000
Symbol: TSO Exchange: NYSE
Industry: Oil refining & marketing

Tetra Tech, Inc.
670 N. Rosemead Blvd.
Pasadena, CA 91107
Phone: 818-449-6400 Fax: 818-351-8126
CEO: Li San Hwang
CFO: Robert J. Buscher
1991 Sales: $38 million Employees: 513
Symbol: WATR Exchange: NASDAQ
Industry: Pollution control equipment & services

TETRA Technologies, Inc.
25231 Grogans Mill Rd., Ste. 100
The Woodlands, TX 77380
Phone: 713-367-1983 Fax: 713-364-2240
CEO: Michael L. Jeane
CFO: James R. Hale
1991 Sales: $85 million Employees: 431
Symbol: TTRA Exchange: NASDAQ
Industry: Pollution control equipment & services - environmental engineering & consulting

Teubner & Associates Inc.
623 S. Main
Stillwater, OK 74074
Phone: 405-624-2254 Fax: 405-624-3010
CEO: Russell Teubner
CFO: Brent Phillips
1992 Sales: $3 million Employees: 28
Ownership: Privately held
Industry: Computers - communications software

Texaco Inc.
2000 Westchester Ave.
White Plains, NY 10650
Phone: 914-253-4000 Fax: 914-253-7753
CEO: Alfred C. DeCrane, Jr.
CFO: Allen J. Krowe
1992 Sales: $37,663 million Employees: 40,181
Symbol: TX Exchange: NYSE
Industry: Oil & gas - international integrated

Texas Industries, Inc.
7610 N. Stemmons Fwy.
Dallas, TX 75247
Phone: 214-647-6700 Fax: 214-647-3878
CEO: Robert D. Rogers
CFO: Richard M. Fowler
1992 Sales: $606 million Employees: 2,700
Symbol: TXI Exchange: NYSE
Industry: Diversified operations - steel, concrete, cement

Texas Instruments Inc.
13500 N. Central Expressway
Dallas, TX 75265
Phone: 214-995-2011 Fax: 214-995-3340
CEO: Jerry R. Junkins
CFO: William A. Aylesworth
1992 Sales: $7,440 million Employees: 62,939
Symbol: TXN Exchange: NYSE
Industry: Electrical components - semiconductors

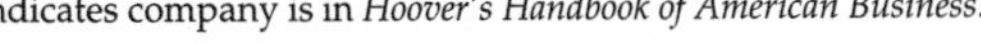
indicates company is in *Hoover's Handbook of American Business.*

indicates company is in *Hoover's Handbook of World Business;* sales and employee numbers are for parent company.

Texas Meridian Resources Ltd.
15995 N. Barkers Landing Rd., Ste. 300
Houston, TX 77079
Phone: 713-558-8080 Fax: 713-558-5595
CEO: Joseph A. Reeves, Jr.
CFO: Joseph A. Reeves, Jr.
1991 Sales: $10.6 million Employees: 11
Symbol: TMR Exchange: AMEX
Industry: Oil & gas - US exploration & production

Texas Utilities Company
2001 Bryan Tower
Dallas, TX 75201
Phone: 214-812-4600 Fax: 214-812-4079
CEO: Jerry S. Farrington
CFO: H. Jarrell Gibbs
1992 Sales: $4,908 million Employees: 15,239
Symbol: TXU Exchange: NYSE
Industry: Utility - electric power

Texfi Industries, Inc.
5400 Glenwood Ave., Ste. 318
Raleigh, NC 27612
Phone: 919-783-4736 Fax: 919-783-4739
CEO: L. Terrell Sovey, Jr.
CFO: Michael A. Miller
1991 Sales: $322 million Employees: 4,022
Symbol: TXF Exchange: NYSE
Industry: Textiles - mill products

Texscan Corp.
10841 Pellicano Dr.
El Paso, TX 79935
Phone: 915-594-3555 Fax: 915-591-6984
CEO: Wm. H. Lambert
CFO: Harold C. Tamburro
1992 Sales: $43 million Employees: 600
Symbol: TSX Exchange: AMEX
Industry: Cable TV

Textron Inc.
40 Westminster St.
Providence, RI 02903
Phone: 401-421-2800 Fax: 401-421-2878
CEO: James F. Hardymon
CFO: Dennis G. Little
1992 Sales: $8,344 million Employees: 52,000
Symbol: TXT Exchange: NYSE
Industry: Diversified operations - commercial products, finance & insurance, helicopters

Thackeray Corp.
20 E. 53rd St., 8th Fl.
New York, NY 10022
Phone: 212-759-3695 Fax: 212-759-4481
CEO: Martin J. Rabinowitz
CFO: Jules Ross
1991 Sales: $12 million Employees: 52
Symbol: THK Exchange: NYSE
Industry: Diversified operations - wire & cable, hardware, real estate management

Theo H. Davies & Co.
Davies Pac. Ctr., 841 Bishop St., Ste. 2300
Honolulu, HI 96802
Phone: 808-531-8531 Fax: 808-521-7352
CEO: David A. Heenan
CFO: —
1991 Sales: $7,190 million Employees: 120,000
Parent: Jardine Matheson Holdings Ltd.
Industry: Diversified operations - real estate, marketing & distribution, insurance

Theragenics Corp.
5325 Oakbrook Pkwy.
Norcross, GA 30093
Phone: 404-381-8338 Fax: 404-381-8447
CEO: John V. Herndon
CFO: Bruce W. Smith
1991 Sales: $2.5 million Employees: 21
Symbol: THRX Exchange: NASDAQ
Industry: Drugs

TheraTech, Inc.
417 Wakara Way, Ste. 100
Salt Lake City, UT 84108
Phone: 801-583-6028 Fax: 801-583-6042
CEO: Dinesh C. Patel
CFO: Steven C. Mayer
1991 Sales: $2.7 million Employees: 64
Symbol: THRT Exchange: NASDAQ
Industry: Medical products

Thermedics Inc.
470 Wildwood St.
Woburn, MA 01801
Phone: 617-938-3786 Fax: 617-933-4476
CEO: John W. Wood Jr.
CFO: John N. Hatsopoulos
1991 Sales: $32 million Employees: 348
Symbol: TMD Exchange: AMEX
Industry: Medical products - medical-grade plastics, drug-delivery systems, wound dressings

Thermo Cardiosystems Inc.
470 Wildwood St.
Woburn, MA 01888
Phone: 617-932-8668 Fax: —
CEO: John W. Wood, Jr.
CFO: John N. Hatsopoulos
1991 Sales: $2 million Employees: 38
Symbol: TCA Exchange: AMEX
Industry: Medical products - cardiac support systems

Thermo Electron Corp.
81 Wyman St.
Waltham, MA 02254
Phone: 617-622-1000 Fax: 617-622-1207
CEO: George N. Hatsopoulos
CFO: John N. Hatsopoulos
1991 Sales: $806 million Employees: 5,965
Symbol: TMO Exchange: NYSE
Industry: Machinery - general industrial

Thermo Electron Technologies Corp.
9550 Distribution Ave.
San Diego, CA 92121
Phone: 619-578-5885 Fax: —
CEO: Firooz Rufeh
CFO: John N. Hatsopoulos
1991 Sales: $17 million Employees: 159
Symbol: TKN Exchange: AMEX
Industry: Engineering - R&D services

Thermo Instrument Systems Inc.
81 Wyman St.
Waltham, MA 02254
Phone: 617-622-1000 Fax: 617-622-1207
CEO: Arvin H. Smith
CFO: John N. Hatsopoulos
1991 Sales: $339 million Employees: 2,585
Symbol: THI Exchange: AMEX
Industry: Instruments - scientific

Thermo Process Systems Inc.
101 First Ave.
Waltham, MA 02254
Phone: 617-622-1000 Fax: —
CEO: Walter J. Bornhorst
CFO: John N. Hatsopoulos
1992 Sales: $47 million Employees: 431
Symbol: TPI Exchange: AMEX
Industry: Machinery - general industrial

Thermwood Corp.
Old Buffaloville Rd.
Dale, IN 47523
Phone: 812-937-4476 Fax: 812-937-2956
CEO: Kenneth J. Susnjara
CFO: Mark D. Brown
1991 Sales: $8.6 million Employees: 81
Symbol: THM Exchange: AMEX
Industry: Machinery - general industrial

Thiokol Corp.
2475 Washington Blvd.
Ogden, UT 84401
Phone: 801-629-2000 Fax: 801-629-2420
CEO: U. Edwin Garrison
CFO: James R. Wilson
1992 Sales: $1,290 million Employees: 11,200
Symbol: TKC Exchange: NYSE
Industry: Aerospace - solid rocket motors, propulsion & missile-launching systems

Thomas & Betts Corp.
1001 Frontier Rd.
Bridgewater, NJ 08807
Phone: 908-685-1600 Fax: 908-707-2145
CEO: T. Kevin Dunnigan
CFO: Ronald P. Babcock
1992 Sales: $1,051 million Employees: 4,700
Symbol: TNB Exchange: NYSE
Industry: Electrical connectors

Thomas Industries Inc.
4360 Brownsboro Rd.
Louisville, KY 40207
Phone: 502-893-4600 Fax: 502-893-4685
CEO: Timothy C. Brown
CFO: Phillip J. Stuecker
1991 Sales: $408 million Employees: 3,530
Symbol: TII Exchange: NYSE
Industry: Building products - lighting fixtures

Thomas Nelson, Inc.
Nelson Place at Elm Hill Pike
Nashville, TN 37214
Phone: 615-889-9000 Fax: 615-391-5225
CEO: Sam Moore
CFO: Phyllis Williams
1992 Sales: $93 million Employees: 600
Symbol: TNEL Exchange: NASDAQ
Industry: Publishing - Bibles & religious books

Thomas-Conrad Corp.
1908-R Kramer Ln.
Austin, TX 78758
Phone: 512-836-1935 Fax: 512-836-2840
CEO: Walt Thirion
CFO: Matt Marnell
1992 Sales: $44 million Employees: 300
Ownership: Privately held
Industry: Computers - local area networks

Thomaston Mills, Inc.
PO Box 311
Thomaston, GA 30286
Phone: 706-647-7131 Fax: 706-647-2742
CEO: Neil H. Hightower
CFO: Rosser R. Raines
1992 Sales: $257 million Employees: 2,451
Symbol: TMSTA Exchange: NASDAQ
Industry: Textiles - mill products

Thomson Advisory Group L.P.
Station Pl.
Stamford, CT 06902
Phone: 203-352-4990 Fax: —
CEO: Donald K. Miller
CFO: Brian J. Girvan
1991 Sales: $42 million Employees: 98
Symbol: TAG Exchange: NYSE
Industry: Financial - investment management

Thomson Corporation, The
245 Park Ave.
New York, NY 10167
Phone: 212-309-8700 Fax: 212-309-8708
CEO: Michael Brown
CFO: —
1991 Sales: $5,589 million Employees: 45,800
Parent: The Bear Stearns Companies Inc.
Industry: Publishing - periodicals & newspapers; travel services

indicates company is in *Hoover's Handbook of American Business.*

indicates company is in *Hoover's Handbook of World Business;* sales and employee numbers are for parent company.

Thomson-CSF, Inc.
2231 Crystal Dr., Ste. 814
Arlington, VA 22202
Phone: 703-486-0780 Fax: 703-486-2646
CEO: Jim D. Bell
CFO: —
1991 Sales: $13,760 million Employees: 105,200
Parent: Thomson SA
Industry: Audio & video equipment, appliances, defense electronics

Thor Energy Resources, Inc.
719 W. Front St.
Tyler, TX 75702
Phone: 214-592-1643 Fax: —
CEO: David M. Fender
CFO: M. Lindsay Sneed
1991 Sales: $4.4 million Employees: 28
Symbol: THR Exchange: AMEX
Industry: Oil & gas - US exploration & production

Thor Industries, Inc.
419 W. Pike St.
Jackson Center, OH 45334
Phone: 513-596-6849 Fax: 513-596-6092
CEO: Wade F.B. Thompson
CFO: Peter B. Orthwein
1991 Sales: $141 million Employees: 1,420
Symbol: THO Exchange: NYSE
Industry: Building - mobile homes & RVs

Thorn Apple Valley, Inc.
18700 W. Ten Mile Rd.
Southfield, MI 48075
Phone: 313-552-0700 Fax: 313-552-0986
CEO: Joel Dorfman
CFO: Louis Glazier
1992 Sales: $715 million Employees: 3,200
Symbol: TAVI Exchange: NASDAQ
Industry: Food - meat products

Thousand Trails, Inc.
12301 NE 10th Place
Bellevue, WA 98005
Phone: 206-455-3155 Fax: 206-455-8596
CEO: George F. Donovan
CFO: Dennis W. Seagraves
1992 Sales: $59 million Employees: 1,197
Symbol: TRLS Exchange: NASDAQ
Industry: Leisure & recreational services - campground operation

THQ, Inc.
5000 N. Parkway Calabasas
Calabasas, CA 91302
Phone: 818-591-1310 Fax: 818-591-1615
CEO: Jack Friedman
CFO: Brian J. Farrell
1991 Sales: $33 million Employees: 23
Symbol: TOYH Exchange: NASDAQ
Industry: Toys - games & hobby products

Three D Departments, Inc.
3200 Bristol St., 8th Fl.
Costa Mesa, CA 92626
Phone: 714-662-0818 Fax: 714-545-8937
CEO: Bernard Abrams
CFO: Frank Kane
1991 Sales: $46 million Employees: 430
Symbol: TDDB Exchange: AMEX
Industry: Retail - bed & bath products

Three Springs Inc.
247-A Chateau Dr.
Huntsville, AL 35802
Phone: 205-880-3339 Fax: 205-880-9569
CEO: Thomas M. Watson
CFO: Thomas M. Watson
1991 Sales: $5 million Employees: 89
Ownership: Privately held
Industry: Health care - residential treatment for troubled adolescents

Thrifty Drug Stores
3424 Wilshire Blvd.
Los Angeles, CA 90010
Phone: 213-251-6000 Fax: 213-386-3079
CEO: William E. Yingling
CFO: Phillip Maslow
1991 Sales: $2,510 million Employees: 14,000
Ownership: Privately held
Industry: Retail - drug & sporting goods stores

Thrifty Oil Co.
10000 Lakewood Blvd.
Downey, CA 90240
Phone: 310-923-9876 Fax: 310-869-9739
CEO: Ted Orden
CFO: Jack Elgin
1991 Sales: $650 million Employees: 1,000
Ownership: Privately held
Industry: Oil refining & marketing, convenience stores

Tidewater Inc.
1440 Canal St.
New Orleans, LA 70112
Phone: 504-568-1010 Fax: 504-566-4582
CEO: John P. Laborde
CFO: Ken C. Tamblyn
1992 Sales: $546 million Employees: 6,500
Symbol: TDW Exchange: NYSE
Industry: Oil & gas - offshore drilling

TIE/communications, Inc.
4 Progress Ave.
Seymour, CT 06483
Phone: 203-888-8000 Fax: 203-888-8231
CEO: Thomas L. Kelly, Jr.
CFO: Anthony T. Guiterman
1991 Sales: $108 million Employees: 1,181
Symbol: TIE Exchange: AMEX
Industry: Telecommunications equipment

Tiffany & Co.
727 Fifth Ave.
New York, NY 10022
Phone: 212-755-8000 Fax: 212-605-4465
CEO: William R. Chaney
CFO: James N. Fernandez
1991 Sales: $493 million Employees: 2,735
Symbol: TIF Exchange: NYSE
Industry: Retail - jewelry stores

Tigera Group, Inc.
950 Third Ave., 21st Fl.
New York, NY 10022
Phone: 212-758-4316 Fax: —
CEO: Richard M. Bliss
CFO: Robert E. Kelly
1991 Sales: $0.5 million Employees: —
Symbol: TYGR Exchange: NASDAQ
Industry: Financial - investment bankers

TII Industries, Inc.
1385 Akron St.
Copiague, NY 11726
Phone: 516-789-5000 Fax: 516-789-5063
CEO: Alfred J. Roach
CFO: Thomas F. Belleau
1992 Sales: $30 million Employees: 992
Symbol: TI Exchange: AMEX
Industry: Electrical products - gas tube overvoltage protectors

Timberland Co.
11 Morrill Dr.
Hampton, NH 03842
Phone: 603-926-1600 Fax: 603-926-9239
CEO: Sidney W. Swartz
CFO: John R. Ranelli
1991 Sales: $226 million Employees: 4,051
Symbol: TBL Exchange: NYSE
Industry: Shoes & related apparel

Timberline Software Corp.
9600 SW Nimbus Dr.
Beaverton, OR 97005
Phone: 503-626-6775 Fax: 503-641-7498
CEO: John Gorman
CFO: Thomas P. Cox
1991 Sales: $13 million Employees: 192
Symbol: TMBS Exchange: NASDAQ
Industry: Computers - information-management software

Time Warner Inc.
75 Rockefeller Plaza
New York, NY 10019
Phone: 212-484-8000 Fax: 212-484-8734
CEO: Gerald M. Levin
CFO: Bert W. Wasserman
1992 Sales: $13,070 million Employees: 41,700
Symbol: TWX Exchange: NYSE
Industry: Publishing - periodicals & books, filmed entertainment, cable systems

Times Mirror Co., The
Times Mirror Square
Los Angeles, CA 90053
Phone: 213-237-3700 Fax: 213-237-3800
CEO: Robert F. Erburu
CFO: Stender E. Sweeney
1992 Sales: $3,702 million Employees: 27,732
Symbol: TMC Exchange: NYSE
Industry: Publishing - newspapers, magazines & books, television & cable

Timken Co.
1835 Dueber Ave. SW
Canton, OH 44706
Phone: 216-438-3000 Fax: 216-438-3452
CEO: W. R. Timken, Jr.
CFO: J. Kevin Ramsey
1992 Sales: $1,642 million Employees: 17,740
Symbol: TKR Exchange: NYSE
Industry: Metal processing & fabrication

Tipperary Corp.
633 17th St., Ste. 1550
Denver, CO 80202
Phone: 303-293-9379 Fax: 303-292-3428
CEO: Carter G. Mathies
CFO: David I. Bradshaw
1991 Sales: $8.3 million Employees: 14
Symbol: TPY Exchange: AMEX
Industry: Oil & gas - US exploration & production

Tishman Realty & Construction Co. Inc.
666 Fifth Ave.
New York, NY 10103
Phone: 212-399-3600 Fax: 212-957-9791
CEO: John Tishman
CFO: Larry Schwarzwalder
1991 Sales: $668 million Employees: 620
Ownership: Privately held
Industry: Real estate operations - construction management

Titan Corp.
3033 Science Park Rd.
San Diego, CA 92121
Phone: 619-552-9500 Fax: 619-552-9645
CEO: Gene W. Ray
CFO: Stephen P. Meyer
1991 Sales: $146 million Employees: 1,350
Symbol: TTN Exchange: NYSE
Industry: Electronics - military

Titan Industrial Corp.
555 Madison Ave., 10th Fl.
New York, NY 10022
Phone: 212-421-6700 Fax: 212-421-6708
CEO: Michael S. Levin
CFO: Michael S. Levin
1991 Sales: $475 million Employees: 400
Ownership: Privately held
Industry: Steel - marketing

indicates company is in *Hoover's Handbook of American Business.*

indicates company is in *Hoover's Handbook of World Business;* sales and employee numbers are for parent company.

TJ International
380 E. ParkCenter Blvd.
Boise, ID 83706
Phone: 208-345-8500 Fax: 208-345-3431
CEO: Walter C. Minnick
CFO: Richard B. Drury
1991 Sales: $283 million Employees: 3,000
Symbol: TJCO Exchange: NASDAQ
Industry: Building products - specialty building products

TJX Companies, Inc.
770 Cochituate Rd.
Framingham, MA 01701
Phone: 508-390-3000 Fax: 508-390-3635
CEO: Bernard Cammarata
CFO: Donald G. Campbell
1992 Sales: $3,063 million Employees: 30,000
Symbol: TJX Exchange: NYSE
Industry: Retail - discount & variety

TL Care Inc.
2415 3rd St. #232
San Francisco, CA 94107
Phone: 415-626-3127 Fax: 415-626-2983
CEO: Tim Leister
CFO: Tim Leister
1991 Sales: $3.4 million Employees: 6
Ownership: Privately held
Industry: Apparel - infant

TLC Beatrice International Holdings, Inc.
9 W. 57th St., 48th Fl.
New York, NY 10019
Phone: 212-756-8900 Fax: 212-888-3093
CEO: Jean S. Fugett, Jr.
CFO: Mark J. Thorne
1991 Sales: $1,542 million Employees: 5,000
Ownership: Privately held
Industry: Food - wholesale & retail distribution, grocery product marketing & manufacturing

TME
8300 Bissonnet St.
Houston, TX 77074
Phone: 713-691-3081 Fax: 713-691-6745
CEO: Larry Luthy
CFO: Gerry Houghton
1991 Sales: $12 million Employees: 171
Ownership: Privately held
Industry: Medical services - outpatient diagnostic imaging centers

TNP Enterprises, Inc.
4100 International Plaza, Tower 2
Ft. Worth, TX 76109
Phone: 817-731-0099 Fax: 817-737-1384
CEO: James M. Tarpley
CFO: D. R. Barnard
1991 Sales: $441 million Employees: 1,104
Symbol: TNP Exchange: NYSE
Industry: Utility - electric power

TNT Freightways Corp.
9700 Higgins Rd., Ste. 570
Rosemont, IL 60018
Phone: 708-696-0200 Fax: 708-696-2080
CEO: John C. Carruth
CFO: Christopher Ellis
1992 Sales: $800 million Employees: 8,912
Symbol: TNTF Exchange: NASDAQ
Industry: Transportation - truck

Toastmaster Inc.
1801 N. Stadium Blvd.
Columbia, MO 65202
Phone: 314-445-8666 Fax: 314-876-0618
CEO: Robert H. Deming
CFO: John E. Thompson
1991 Sales: $153 million Employees: 1,475
Symbol: TM Exchange: NYSE
Industry: Appliances - household

Tocor II, Inc.
244 Great Valley Pkwy.
Malvern, PA 19355
Phone: 215-296-4488 Fax: —
CEO: Hubert J. P. Schoemaker
CFO: Bruce A. Peacock
1990 Sales: — Employees: —
Symbol: TOCRZ Exchange: NASDAQ
Industry: Drugs

Today's Man, Inc.
835 Lancer Dr.
Moorestown, NJ 08057
Phone: 609-235-5656 Fax: 609-235-9323
CEO: David Field
CFO: Zeev Shenkman
1991 Sales: $109 million Employees: 783
Symbol: TMAN Exchange: NASDAQ
Industry: Retail - apparel & shoes

Todd AO Corp.
172 Golden Gate Ave.
San Francisco, CA 94102
Phone: 415-928-3200 Fax: 415-673-3329
CEO: Ronald Zimmerman
CFO: Ronald Zimmerman
1991 Sales: $29 million Employees: 165
Symbol: TODDA Exchange: NASDAQ
Industry: Motion pictures & services

Todd Shipyards Corp.
1102 SW Massachusetts St.
Seattle, WA 98134
Phone: 206-223-1560 Fax: 206-343-9640
CEO: David W. Wallace
CFO: Alfred J. Koontz, Jr.
1992 Sales: $148 million Employees: 800
Symbol: TOD Exchange: NYSE
Industry: Boat building

Todisco Jewelry Co.
30-00 47th Ave.
New York, NY 11001
Phone: 212-997-1963 Fax: 718-784-7366
CEO: Frank Todisco
CFO: Frank Todisco
1991 Sales: $4 million Employees: 100
Ownership: Privately held
Industry: Precious metals & jewelry

Tofutti Brands Inc.
50 Jackson Dr.
Cranford, NJ 07016
Phone: 908-272-2400 Fax: 908-272-9492
CEO: David Mintz
CFO: Steven Kass
1991 Sales: $4.4 million Employees: 7
Symbol: TOF Exchange: AMEX
Industry: Food - non-dairy frozen desserts

Tokheim Corp.
1602 Wabash Ave.
Ft. Wayne, IN 46803
Phone: 219-423-2552 Fax: 219-426-4912
CEO: Douglas K. Pinner
CFO: Jess B. Ford
1991 Sales: $193 million Employees: 2,362
Symbol: TOK Exchange: NYSE
Industry: Oil refining & marketing

Tokio Marine Management, Inc.
101 Park Ave.
New York, NY 10178
Phone: 212-297-6600 Fax: 212-986-6815
CEO: Shinya Yoshikoshi
CFO: —
1992 Sales: $9,062 million Employees: 14,054
Parent: Tokio Marine and Fire
Industry: Insurance - multiline & misc.

Tokos Medical Corp.
1821 E. Dyer Rd., Ste. 200
Santa Ana, CA 92705
Phone: 714-474-1616 Fax: 714-250-1067
CEO: Robert F. Byrnes
CFO: Nicholas A. Mione
1991 Sales: $115 million Employees: 1,300
Symbol: TKOS Exchange: NASDAQ
Industry: Healthcare - outpatient & home

Tokyo Electric Power Co., Inc., The
1901 L St. NW, Ste. 720
Washington, DC 20036
Phone: 202-457-0790 Fax: 202-457-0810
CEO: Konosuke Sugiura
CFO: —
1992 Sales: $36,777 million Employees: 40,081
Parent: The Tokyo Electric Power Co., Inc.
Industry: Utility - electric power

Toledo Edison Co.
300 Madison Ave.
Toledo, OH 43652
Phone: 419-249-5000 Fax: —
CEO: Robert J. Farling
CFO: Edgar H. Maugans
1991 Sales: $887 million Employees: 2,562
Symbol: TED Exchange: NYSE
Industry: Utility - electric power

Toll Brothers, Inc.
3103 Philmont Ave.
Huntingdon Valley, PA 19006
Phone: 215-441-4400 Fax: 215-938-8010
CEO: Robert I. Toll
CFO: Joel H. Rassman
1991 Sales: $182 million Employees: 438
Symbol: TOL Exchange: NYSE
Industry: Building - residential & commercial

Tolland Bank
348 Hartford Tnpk.
Vernon, CT 06066
Phone: 203-875-2500 Fax: 203-875-3856
CEO: Guy Cambria, Jr.
CFO: Joel E. Hyman
1991 Sales: $18 million Employees: 105
Symbol: TBK Exchange: AMEX
Industry: Financial - savings and loans

Tom Brown, Inc.
508 W. Wall St., Ste. 500
Midland, TX 79701
Phone: 915-682-9715 Fax: 915-682-9171
CEO: Donald L. Evans
CFO: Donald L. Evans
1991 Sales: $18 million Employees: 58
Symbol: TMBR Exchange: NASDAQ
Industry: Oil & gas - US exploration & production

Tomlinson Industries
13700 Broadway
Cleveland, OH 44125
Phone: 216-587-3400 Fax: 216-587-0733
CEO: George Blumel
CFO: Donald R. Calkins
1991 Sales: $7 million Employees: —
Symbol: HMNY Exchange: NASDAQ
Industry: Apparel - children's sleepwear & hosiery

Tootsie Roll Industries, Inc.
7401 S. Cicero Ave.
Chicago, IL 60629
Phone: 312-838-3400 Fax: 312-838-3534
CEO: Melvin J. Gordon
CFO: Frederick T. Kushnir
1991 Sales: $208 million Employees: 1,500
Symbol: TR Exchange: NYSE
Industry: Food - confectionery

indicates company is in *Hoover's Handbook of American Business.*

indicates company is in *Hoover's Handbook of World Business;* sales and employee numbers are for parent company.

Topa Equities Ltd.
1800 Avenue of the Stars, Ste. 1400
Los Angeles, CA 90067
Phone: 310-203-9199 Fax: 310-557-1837
CEO: John E. Anderson
CFO: Brenda Seuthe
1991 Sales: $555 million Employees: 1,290
Ownership: Privately held
Industry: Diversified operations - insurance, financial services, beverage distribution

Topps Co., Inc.
254 36th St.
Brooklyn, NY 11232
Phone: 718-768-8900 Fax: 718-965-2638
CEO: Arthur T. Shorin
CFO: John Perillo
1992 Sales: $309 million Employees: 1,400
Symbol: TOPP Exchange: NASDAQ
Industry: Food - confectionery

Torchmark Corp.
2001 Third Ave. South
Birmingham, AL 35233
Phone: 205-325-4200 Fax: 205-325-4198
CEO: Ronald K. Richey
CFO: Ronald K. Richey
1992 Sales: $2,046 million Employees: —
Symbol: TMK Exchange: NYSE
Industry: Insurance - life

Toreador Royalty Corp.
400 N. St. Paul St., Ste. 730
Dallas, TX 75201
Phone: 214-220-2141 Fax: 214-220-3116
CEO: Peter R. Vig
CFO: Peter R. Vig
1991 Sales: $1.2 million Employees: 3
Symbol: TRGL Exchange: NASDAQ
Industry: Oil & gas - US royalty trust

Toro Co.
8111 Lyndale Ave. South
Bloomington, MN 55420
Phone: 612-888-8801 Fax: 612-887-8258
CEO: Kendrick B. Melrose
CFO: Gerald T. Knight
1991 Sales: $712 million Employees: 3,208
Symbol: TTC Exchange: NYSE
Industry: Tools - hand held

Torotel, Inc.
13402 S. 71 Hwy.
Grandview, MO 64030
Phone: 816-761-6314 Fax: 816-763-2278
CEO: Alfred F. Marsh
CFO: Victor K. Brewer, Jr.
1992 Sales: $10.3 million Employees: 230
Symbol: TTL Exchange: AMEX
Industry: Electronics - military

Tosco Corp.
72 Cummings Point Rd.
Stamford, CT 06902
Phone: 203-977-1000 Fax: 203-964-3187
CEO: Thomas D. O'Malley
CFO: Jefferson F. Allen
1992 Sales: $2,155 million Employees: 1,760
Symbol: TOS Exchange: NYSE
Industry: Oil refining & marketing

Toshiba America, Inc.
375 Park Ave., Ste. 1705
New York, NY 10152
Phone: 212-308-2040 Fax: 212-838-1179
CEO: Tadao Taguchi
CFO: —
1992 Sales: $37,779 million Employees: 168,000
Parent: Toshiba Corporation
Industry: Audio & video equipment, electrical apparatus, consumer products

Total Petroleum (North America) Ltd.
999 18th St.
Denver, CO 80202
Phone: 303-291-2000 Fax: 303-291-2113
CEO: Philippe Dunoyer
CFO: —
1991 Sales: $27,610 million Employees: 49,365
Parent: TOTAL
Industry: Oil & gas - international integrated

Total Pharmaceutical Care, Inc.
367 Van Ness Way
Torrance, CA 90501
Phone: 310-212-7501 Fax: 310-212-6272
CEO: Victor M. G. Chaltiel
CFO: Michael A. Piraino
1991 Sales: $31 million Employees: 332
Symbol: TPCA Exchange: NASDAQ
Industry: Medical services - home infusion therapy & support services

Total System Services, Inc.
1200 Sixth Ave.
Columbus, GA 31901
Phone: 706-649-2204 Fax: 706-649-2456
CEO: Richard W. Ussery
CFO: James B. Lipham
1991 Sales: $112 million Employees: 1,264
Symbol: TSS Exchange: NYSE
Industry: Financial - business services

Total-Tel USA Communications, Inc.
140 Little St.
Belleville, NJ 07109
Phone: 201-759-4667 Fax: —
CEO: Manuel Brucker
CFO: Solomon Feldman
1991 Sales: $12 million Employees: 37
Symbol: TELU Exchange: NASDAQ
Industry: Telecommunications services - long-distance

Touchstone Research Laboratory
Millennium Center
Triadelphia, WV 26059
Phone: 304-547-5800 Fax: 304-547-4069
CEO: Elizabeth Kraftician
CFO: William Casto
1991 Sales: $2.3 million Employees: 35
Ownership: Privately held
Industry: Engineering - R&D services, industrial problem-solving

Tova Industries
2902 Blankenbaker Rd.
Louisville, KY 40299
Phone: 502-267-7333 Fax: 502-267-7119
CEO: Zacky Melzer
CFO: Zacky Melzer
1992 Sales: $4 million Employees: 40
Ownership: Privately held
Industry: Food - dehydrated food products

Towers, Perrin Inc.
245 Park Ave., 18th Fl.
New York, NY 10167
Phone: 212-309-3400 Fax: 212-503-0488
CEO: John T. Lynch
CFO: Lawrence N. Margel
1991 Sales: $653 million Employees: 5,000
Ownership: Privately held
Industry: Business services - consulting, reinsurance

Town & Country Corp.
25 Union St.
Chelsea, MA 02150
Phone: 617-884-8500 Fax: 617-889-1473
CEO: C. William Carey
CFO: Francis X. Correra
1992 Sales: $272 million Employees: 2,600
Symbol: TNC Exchange: AMEX
Industry: Precious metals & jewelry

Toyota Motor Sales, U.S.A., Inc.
19001 S. Western Ave.
Torrance, CA 90509
Phone: 310-618-4000 Fax: 310-618-7800
CEO: Shinji Sakai
CFO: —
1991 Sales: $71,414 million Employees: 102,423
Parent: Toyota Motor Corporation
Industry: Automotive manufacturing

Toys "R" Us, Inc.
461 From Rd.
Paramus, NJ 07652
Phone: 201-262-7800 Fax: 201-262-7606
CEO: Charles Lazarus
CFO: Michael Goldstein
1992 Sales: $6,628 million Employees: 78,000
Symbol: TOY Exchange: NYSE
Industry: Retail - toys & children's clothing

TPA of America Inc.
5777 W. Century Blvd.
Los Angeles, CA 90045
Phone: 213-641-1400 Fax: —
CEO: Elliott H. Weir, Jr.
CFO: Elliott H. Weir, Jr.
1991 Sales: $1.4 million Employees: 10
Symbol: TPS Exchange: AMEX
Industry: Medical services - healthcare cost containment services

TPI Enterprises, Inc.
885 Third Ave.
New York, NY 10022
Phone: 212-230-2233 Fax: 212-753-1084
CEO: Stephen R. Cohen
CFO: Joseph P. Gowan
1991 Sales: $263 million Employees: 10,517
Symbol: TPIE Exchange: NASDAQ
Industry: Retail - food & restaurants

Tracer Research Corp.
3855 N. Business Center Dr.
Tucson, AZ 85705
Phone: 602-888-9400 Fax: 602-293-1306
CEO: Shannan Marty
CFO: Shannan Marty
1991 Sales: $8.9 million Employees: 93
Ownership: Privately held
Industry: Contaminant detection in soil, water, tanks & pipelines

Traco Manufacturing Co.
443 South Commerce Rd.
Orem, UT 84058
Phone: 801-225-8040 Fax: 801-226-1509
CEO: John Palica
CFO: Garth Allread
1991 Sales: $2.8 million Employees: 14
Ownership: Privately held
Industry: Machinery - portable shrink wrap machines

Tracor Inc.
6500 Tracor Lane
Austin, TX 78725
Phone: 512-926-2800 Fax: 512-929-2241
CEO: James B. Skaggs
CFO: Robert K. Floyd
1991 Sales: $254 million Employees: 3,600
Symbol: TRAR Exchange: NASDAQ
Industry: Electronics - military & engineering

Trak Auto Corp.
3300 75th Ave.
Landover, MD 20785
Phone: 301-731-1200 Fax: 301-731-1340
CEO: Herbert M. Haft
CFO: Richard J. Koll
1991 Sales: $320 million Employees: 3,700
Symbol: TRKA Exchange: NASDAQ
Industry: Auto parts - retail & wholesale

 indicates company is in *Hoover's Handbook of American Business.*

indicates company is in *Hoover's Handbook of World Business;* sales and employee numbers are for parent company.

Tramex Travel
4505 Spicewood Springs Rd., Ste. 200
Austin, TX 78759
Phone: 512-343-2201 Fax: 512-343-0022
CEO: Juan Portillo
CFO: Juan Portillo
1991 Sales: $15 million Employees: 37
Ownership: Privately held
Industry: Business services - travel agency

Trammell Crow Company
2001 Ross Ave., Ste. 3500
Dallas, TX 75201
Phone: 214-979-5100 Fax: 214-979-6058
CEO: J. McDonald Williams
CFO: Mike Decker
1991 Sales: $1,186 million Employees: 2,700
Ownership: Privately held
Industry: Real estate operations

Trammell Crow Residential
2859 Paces Ferry Rd., Ste. 2100
Atlanta, GA 30339
Phone: 404-433-2000 Fax: 404-431-1055
CEO: J. Ronald Terwilliger
CFO: Marvin Banks
1991 Sales: $895 million Employees: 3,300
Ownership: Privately held
Industry: Real estate development - residential, construction

Trans Financial Bancorp, Inc.
500 E. Main St.
Bowling Green, KY 42101
Phone: 502-781-5000 Fax: 502-843-1016
CEO: Douglas M. Lester
CFO: David A. Blackburn
1992 Sales: — Employees: —
Symbol: TRFI Exchange: NASDAQ
Industry: Banks - Midwest

Trans Leasing International, Inc.
3000 Dundee Rd.
Northbrook, IL 60062
Phone: 708-272-1000 Fax: 708-272-2174
CEO: Richard Grossman
CFO: Susan M. Karich
1992 Sales: $21 million Employees: 103
Symbol: TLII Exchange: NASDAQ
Industry: Leasing

Trans World Airlines, Inc.
100 S. Bedford Rd.
Mt. Kisco, NY 10549
Phone: 914-242-3000 Fax: 914-242-3109
CEO: Carl C. Icahn
CFO: Glenn R. Zander
1991 Sales: $3,651 million Employees: 29,463
Ownership: Privately held
Industry: Transportation - airline

Trans World Music Corp.
38 Corporate Circle
Albany, NY 12203
Phone: 518-452-1242 Fax: 518-452-3547
CEO: Robert J. Higgins
CFO: Jeffrey A. Jones
1991 Sales: $411 million Employees: 4,000
Symbol: TWMC Exchange: NASDAQ
Industry: Retail - prerecorded music & videotapes

Trans-Industries, Inc.
2637 Adams Rd.
Rochester Hills, MI 48309
Phone: 313-852-1990 Fax: 313-852-1211
CEO: Dale S. Coenen
CFO: Kai Kosanke
1991 Sales: $24 million Employees: 259
Symbol: TRNI Exchange: NASDAQ
Industry: Electrical products - electronic sign systems, bus lighting products

Trans-Lux Corp.
110 Richards Ave.
Norwalk, CT 06854
Phone: 203-853-4321 Fax: 203-854-6891
CEO: Victor Liss
CFO: Victor Liss
1991 Sales: $22 million Employees: 308
Symbol: TLX Exchange: AMEX
Industry: Electrical products - signs

Transamerica Corp.
600 Montgomery St.
San Francisco, CA 94111
Phone: 415-983-4000 Fax: 415-983-4234
CEO: Frank C. Herringer
CFO: Robert R. Lindberg
1992 Sales: $4,988 million Employees: 15,000
Symbol: TA Exchange: NYSE
Industry: Insurance - multiline & misc., financial services

Transammonia Inc.
350 Park Ave.
New York, NY 10022
Phone: 212-223-3200 Fax: 212-759-1410
CEO: Ronald P. Stanton
CFO: Edward G. Weiner
1991 Sales: $1,400 million Employees: 190
Ownership: Privately held
Industry: Fertilizers & petroleum products; methanol

Transatlantic Holdings, Inc.
80 Pine St.
New York, NY 10005
Phone: 212-770-2000 Fax: 212-785-7230
CEO: Joseph V. Taranto
CFO: Joseph V. Taranto
1992 Sales: $619 million Employees: —
Symbol: TRH Exchange: NYSE
Industry: Insurance - property & casualty

Transcisco Industries, Inc.
555 California St., Ste. 2420
San Francisco, CA 94104
Phone: 415-477-9700 Fax: —
CEO: Eugene M. Armstrong
CFO: Timothy P. Carlson
1991 Sales: $30 million Employees: 328
Symbol: QTNIB Exchange: AMEX
Industry: Transportation - equipment & leasing

Transco Energy Co.
2800 Post Oak Blvd.
Houston, TX 77056
Phone: 713-439-2000 Fax: 713-439-2440
CEO: John P. DesBarres
CFO: John U. Clarke
1992 Sales: $2,724 million Employees: 5,395
Symbol: E Exchange: NYSE
Industry: Oil & gas - production & pipeline

Transco Exploration Partners, Ltd.
2800 Post Oak Blvd.
Houston, TX 77251
Phone: 713-439-2000 Fax: —
CEO: George S. Slocum
CFO: Jim P. Wise
1992 Sales: — Employees: —
Symbol: EXP Exchange: NYSE
Industry: Oil & gas - US royalty trust

Transcon Inc.
2029 Century Park East, # 3150
Los Angeles, CA 90210
Phone: 310-553-1300 Fax: 310-843-2937
CEO: Orin S. Neiman
CFO: John W. Hollingsworth
1991 Sales: $71 million Employees: 98
Symbol: TCL Exchange: NYSE
Industry: Transportation - truck

Transitional Technology, Inc.
5401 E. La Palma Ave.
Anaheim, CA 92807
Phone: 714-693-1133 Fax: 714-693-0225
CEO: Matthew T. Goldbach
CFO: Hank Lapchak
1991 Sales: $12 million Employees: 46
Ownership: Privately held
Industry: Computers - mass storage devices

Transmation, Inc.
977 Mt. Read Blvd.
Rochester, NY 14606
Phone: 716-254-9000 Fax: 716-254-0273
CEO: William J. Berk
CFO: John A. Misiaszek
1992 Sales: $26 million Employees: 209
Symbol: TRNS Exchange: NASDAQ
Industry: Instruments - control

Transmedia Network, Inc.
11900 Biscayne Blvd.
Miami, FL 33181
Phone: 305-892-3300 Fax: 305-892-3317
CEO: Melvin Chasen
CFO: James M. Callaghan
1991 Sales: $14 million Employees: 21
Symbol: TMNI Exchange: NASDAQ
Industry: Business services - private restaurant credit card

TransNet Corp.
45 Columbia Rd.
Somerville, NJ 08876
Phone: 908-253-0500 Fax: 908-688-7813
CEO: Steven J. Wilk
CFO: John J. Wilk
1992 Sales: $29 million Employees: 81
Symbol: TRNT Exchange: NASDAQ
Industry: Wholesale distribution - computers, hardware & software

Transtech Industries, Inc.
1703 E. 2nd St.
Scotch Plains, NJ 07076
Phone: 908-322-6767 Fax: 908-322-8086
CEO: Robert V. Silva
CFO: Andrew J. Mayer, Jr.
1991 Sales: $7.3 million Employees: 276
Symbol: TRTI Exchange: NASDAQ
Industry: Diversified operations - carbide lime, high-alkali products

Transtechnology Corp.
700 Liberty Ave.
Union, NJ 07083
Phone: 908-964-5666 Fax: 908-688-8518
CEO: Michael J. Berthelot
CFO: Paul Grosher
1992 Sales: $102 million Employees: 903
Symbol: TT Exchange: NYSE
Industry: Electronics - military

Transworld Bancorp
15233 Ventura Blvd.
Sherman Oaks, CA 91403
Phone: 818-783-7501 Fax: —
CEO: David H. Hender
CFO: Howard J. Stanke
1992 Sales: 12.6 million Employees: 223
Symbol: TWBC Exchange: NASDAQ
Industry: Banks - West

Tranzonic Companies
30195 Chagrin Blvd.
Cleveland, OH 44124
Phone: 216-831-5757 Fax: 216-831-5647
CEO: Robert S. Reitman
CFO: Michael J. Gannon
1992 Sales: $111 million Employees: 924
Symbol: TNZ Exchange: AMEX
Industry: Drugs & sundries - wholesale

Travel Store Inc.
11777 San Vicente Blvd.
Los Angeles, CA 90049
Phone: 310-826-3113 Fax: 310-207-3020
CEO: Wido Schaefer
CFO: Osvaldo Ramos
1992 Sales: $34 million Employees: 80
Ownership: Privately held
Industry: Business services - travel management services

Travelers Corp., The
One Tower Square
Hartford, CT 06183
Phone: 203-277-0111 Fax: 203-277-7979
CEO: Edward H. Budd
CFO: Ronald E. Foley, Jr.
1992 Sales: $9,676 million Employees: 32,000
Symbol: TIC Exchange: NYSE
Industry: Insurance - multiline & misc., health care & investment services

Travelpro Luggage-Eiffel Mfg.
501 Fairway Dr.
Deerfield Beach, FL 33441
Phone: 305-426-3281 Fax: 305-426-8686
CEO: Robert Plath
CFO: Robert Plath
1992 Sales: $15 million Employees: 25
Ownership: Privately held
Industry: Wholesale distribution - luggage

TRC Companies, Inc.
5 Waterside Crossing
Windsor, CT 06095
Phone: 203-289-8631 Fax: 203-282-4018
CEO: Vincent A. Rocco
CFO: Harold C. Elston, Jr.
1992 Sales: $56 million Employees: 666
Symbol: TRR Exchange: NYSE
Industry: Pollution control equipment & services - environmental consulting

Treadco, Inc.
1000 S. 21st St.
Ft. Smith, AR 72901
Phone: 501-785-6398 Fax: 501-785-6386
CEO: Robert A. Young III
CFO: Donald L. Neal
1991 Sales: $85 million Employees: 486
Symbol: TRED Exchange: NASDAQ
Industry: Rubber tires

Treasure Chest Advertising Co. Inc.
511 W. Citrus Edge
Glendora, CA 91740
Phone: 818-914-3981 Fax: 818-852-3056
CEO: Sanford G. Scheller
CFO: John F. Whitney
1991 Sales: $540 million Employees: 3,310
Ownership: Privately held
Industry: Printing - commercial

Tredegar Industries, Inc.
1100 Boulders Pkwy.
Richmond, VA 23225
Phone: 804-330-1000 Fax: 804-330-1177
CEO: John D. Gottwald
CFO: Norman A. Scher
1991 Sales: $474 million Employees: 3,500
Symbol: TG Exchange: NYSE
Industry: Diversified operations - plastics, aluminum, coal, oil & gas

Tremont Corp.
1999 Broadway, Ste. 4300
Denver, CO 80202
Phone: 303-296-5600 Fax: —
CEO: J. Landis Martin
CFO: Susan E. Alderton
1991 Sales: $170 million Employees: 1,220
Symbol: TRE Exchange: NYSE
Industry: Metal ores

Trenwick Group Inc.
One Station Place
Stamford, CT 06902
Phone: 203-353-5500 Fax: 203-353-5555
CEO: James F. Billett, Jr.
CFO: Alan L. Hunte
1992 Sales: — Employees: —
Symbol: TREN Exchange: NASDAQ
Industry: Insurance - property & casualty

Tri-Continental Corp.
130 Liberty St.
New York, NY 10006
Phone: 212-488-0200 Fax: —
CEO: William C. Morris
CFO: Edward D. Bedard
1992 Sales: — Employees: —
Symbol: TY Exchange: NYSE
Industry: Financial - investment management

Triad Systems Corp.
3055 Triad Dr.
Livermore, CA 94550
Phone: 510-449-0606 Fax: 510-455-6471
CEO: James R. Porter
CFO: Jerome W. Carlson
1991 Sales: $138 million Employees: 1,356
Symbol: TRSC Exchange: NASDAQ
Industry: Computers - system services

Triangle Corp.
62 Southfield Ave.
Stamford, CT 06902
Phone: 203-327-9050 Fax: 203-359-8014
CEO: H. Arthur Bellows, Jr.
CFO: Don R. Gifford
1991 Sales: $53 million Employees: 910
Symbol: TRG Exchange: AMEX
Industry: Tools - hand held

Tribune Co.
435 N. Michigan Ave.
Chicago, IL 60611
Phone: 312-222-9100 Fax: 312-222-0449
CEO: Charles T. Brumback
CFO: Donald C. Grenesko
1992 Sales: $2,109 million Employees: 12,900
Symbol: TRB Exchange: NYSE
Industry: Publishing - newspapers, radio & TV broadcasting, newsprint operations

TriCare, Inc.
17101 Armstrong Ave., Ste. 200
Irvine, CA 92714
Phone: 714-250-1999 Fax: 714-250-4567
CEO: Stephen F. Bullock
CFO: Nyoka L. Criner
1992 Sales: $47 million Employees: 422
Symbol: TRCR Exchange: NASDAQ
Industry: Healthcare - outpatient & home

Trico Products Corp.
817 Washington St.
Buffalo, NY 14203
Phone: 716-852-5700 Fax: 716-852-0862
CEO: Richard L. Wolf
CFO: Christopher Dunstan
1991 Sales: $229 million Employees: 3,700
Symbol: TRCO Exchange: NASDAQ
Industry: Automotive & trucking - original equipment

Triconex Corp.
15091 Bake Pkwy.
Irvine, CA 92718
Phone: 714-768-3709 Fax: —
CEO: William K. Barkovitz
CFO: Charles W. McBrayer
1991 Sales: $22 million Employees: 96
Symbol: TCNX Exchange: NASDAQ
Industry: Instruments - control

Tridex Corp.
215 Main St.
Westport, CT 06880
Phone: 203-226-1144 Fax: 203-226-8806
CEO: Seth M. Lukash
CFO: George T. Crandall
1992 Sales: $20 million Employees: 193
Symbol: TDX Exchange: AMEX
Industry: Computers - printers, printer mechanisms, data processing terminals

Trigen Energy
1 Water St.
White Plains, NY 10601
Phone: 914-948-9150 Fax: 914-948-9157
CEO: Thomas Casten
CFO: Michael Weiser
1991 Sales: $67 million Employees: 225
Ownership: Privately held
Industry: Energy - cogeneration

Trimark Holdings, Inc.
2901 Ocean Park Blvd.
Santa Monica, CA 90405
Phone: 310-399-8877 Fax: 310-399-4238
CEO: Mark Amin
CFO: James Keegan
1992 Sales: $54 million Employees: 59
Symbol: TMRK Exchange: NASDAQ
Industry: Motion pictures & services

TriMas Corp.
315 E. Eisenhower Pkwy., Ste. 300
Ann Arbor, MI 48108
Phone: 313-747-7025 Fax: —
CEO: Richard A. Manoogian
CFO: Peter C. DeChants
1991 Sales: $339 million Employees: 2,800
Symbol: TMS Exchange: NYSE
Industry: Metal products - fasteners

Trimble Navigation Ltd.
645 N. Mary Ave.
Sunnyvale, CA 94086
Phone: 408-481-8000 Fax: 408-991-6860
CEO: Charles R. Trimble
CFO: William N. Stirlen
1991 Sales: $151 million Employees: 881
Symbol: TRMB Exchange: NASDAQ
Industry: Electronics - measuring instruments

Trimedyne, Inc.
1311 Valencia Ave.
Tustin, CA 92680
Phone: 714-259-1988 Fax: —
CEO: Howard K. Cooper
CFO: D. Joe Atchison
1991 Sales: $8.5 million Employees: 101
Symbol: TMED Exchange: NASDAQ
Industry: Medical instruments

Trinity Industries, Inc.
2525 Stemmons Fwy.
Dallas, TX 75207
Phone: 214-631-4420 Fax: 214-689-0501
CEO: W. Ray Wallace
CFO: K. W. Lewis
1992 Sales: $1,411 million Employees: 10,500
Symbol: TRN Exchange: NYSE
Industry: Transportation - equipment & leasing

TRINOVA Corp.
3000 Strayer Rd.
Maumee, OH 43537
Phone: 419-867-2200 Fax: 419-867-2547
CEO: Darryl F. Allen
CFO: Darryl F. Allen
1992 Sales: $1,696 million Employees: 17,696
Symbol: TNV Exchange: NYSE
Industry: Machinery - general industrial

Trinzic Corp.
138 Technology Dr.
Waltham, MA 02154
Phone: 617-891-6500 Fax: 617-893-8919
CEO: Robert N. Goldman
CFO: Phyllis S. Swersky
1992 Sales: $20 million Employees: 157
Symbol: TRNZ Exchange: NASDAQ
Industry: Computers - software

Trion, Inc.
101 McNeill Rd.
Sanford, NC 27331
Phone: 919-775-2201 Fax: 919-774-8771
CEO: Hugh E. Carr
CFO: William P. Glaser
1991 Sales: $35 million Employees: 383
Symbol: TRON Exchange: NASDAQ
Industry: Machinery - general industrial

TriState Bancorp
7124 Miami Ave.
Cincinnati, OH 45243
Phone: 513-561-4450 Fax: 513-561-4776
CEO: Laird L. Lazelle
CFO: John L. Schinner
1992 Sales: — Employees: —
Symbol: COTG Exchange: NASDAQ
Industry: Financial - savings and loans

Triton Energy Corp.
6688 N. Central Expwy.
Dallas, TX 75206
Phone: 214-691-5200 Fax: 214-987-0571
CEO: William I. Lee
CFO: Robert W. Puetz
1992 Sales: $228 million Employees: —
Symbol: OIL Exchange: NYSE
Industry: Oil & gas - US exploration & production

TRM Copy Centers Corp.
5515 SE Milwaukie Ave.
Portland, OR 97202
Phone: 503-231-0230 Fax: 503-231-3771
CEO: Edwin S. Chan
CFO: Robert A. Bruce
1991 Sales: $17 million Employees: —
Symbol: TRMM Exchange: NASDAQ
Industry: Business services

Trump Organization
725 Fifth Ave.
New York, NY 10022
Phone: 212-832-2000 Fax: 212-935-0141
CEO: Donald J. Trump
CFO: John Burke
1991 Sales: $1,400 million Employees: 17,000
Ownership: Privately held
Industry: Leisure & recreational services - hotels & casinos, real estate, airline

TrustCo Bank Corp NY
320 State St.
Schenectady, NY 12305
Phone: 518-377-3311 Fax: —
CEO: Robert A. McCormick
CFO: William F. Terry
1992 Sales: $104 million Employees: 509
Symbol: TRST Exchange: NASDAQ
Industry: Banks - Northeast

Trustcompany Bancorporation
35 Journal Square
Jersey City, NJ 07306
Phone: 201-420-2500 Fax: —
CEO: Siggi B. Wilzig
CFO: John F. Love
1992 Sales: $157 million Employees: 903
Symbol: TCBC Exchange: NASDAQ
Industry: Banks - Northeast

Trustmark Corp.
248 E. Capitol St.
Jackson, MS 39201
Phone: 601-354-5111 Fax: 601-949-2355
CEO: Frank R. Day
CFO: David R. Carter
1991 Sales: $348 million Employees: 1,955
Symbol: TRMK Exchange: NASDAQ
Industry: Banks - Southeast

TRW Inc.
1900 Richmond Rd.
Cleveland, OH 44124
Phone: 216-291-7000 Fax: 216-291-7629
CEO: Joseph T. Gorman
CFO: Peter S. Hellman
1992 Sales: $8,311 million Employees: 71,262
Symbol: TRW Exchange: NYSE
Industry: Diversified operations - automotive, space & defense, information systems

Tseng Labs, Inc.
6 Terry Dr.
Newtown, PA 18940
Phone: 215-968-0502 Fax: 215-860-7713
CEO: Jack Tseng
CFO: Mark Karsch
1991 Sales: $61 million Employees: 52
Symbol: TSNG Exchange: NASDAQ
Industry: Computers - enhancement packages & integrated circuits

TSI Inc.
500 Cardigan Rd.
Shoreview, MN 55126
Phone: 612-483-0900 Fax: 612-481-1220
CEO: Leroy M. Fingerson
CFO: Lowell D. Nystrom
1992 Sales: $40 million Employees: 347
Symbol: TSII Exchange: NASDAQ
Industry: Instruments - control

TSR, Inc.
400 Oser Ave., Ste. 400
Hauppauge, NY 11788
Phone: 516-231-0333 Fax: 516-435-1428
CEO: Joseph F. Hughes
CFO: John G. Sharkey
1992 Sales: $15 million Employees: 126
Symbol: TSRI Exchange: NASDAQ
Industry: Computers - programming services, database management

Tuboscope Vetco International Corp.
2835 Holmes Rd.
Houston, TX 77051
Phone: 713-799-5100 Fax: 713-799-1460
CEO: Martin R. Reid
CFO: Ronald L. Koons
1991 Sales: $152 million Employees: 2,040
Symbol: TUBO Exchange: NASDAQ
Industry: Oil & gas - field services

Tucker Drilling Co., Inc.
14 E. Beauregard Ave.
San Angelo, TX 76903
Phone: 915-655-6773 Fax: 915-653-4873
CEO: Larry J. Tucker
CFO: Charles B. Middlekauf
1992 Sales: $16 million Employees: 120
Symbol: TUCK Exchange: NASDAQ
Industry: Oil & gas - US exploration & production

Tucson Electric Power Co.
220 W. Sixth St.
Tucson, AZ 85701
Phone: 602-622-6661 Fax: 602-884-3934
CEO: Charles E. Bayless
CFO: Charles E. Bayless
1991 Sales: $589 million Employees: 1,026
Symbol: TEP Exchange: NYSE
Industry: Utility - electric power

Tuesday Morning Corp.
14621 Inwood Rd.
Dallas, TX 75244
Phone: 214-387-3562 Fax: 214-387-2344
CEO: Lloyd L. Ross
CFO: Mark E. Jarvis
1991 Sales: $123 million Employees: 1,725
Symbol: TUES Exchange: NASDAQ
Industry: Retail - discount & variety

Tultex Corp.
22 E. Church St.
Martinsville, VA 24115
Phone: 703-632-2961 Fax: 703-632-8658
CEO: John M. Franck
CFO: Don P. Shook
1992 Sales: $504 million Employees: 6,405
Symbol: TTX Exchange: NYSE
Industry: Textiles - apparel

Turbine Consultants, Inc.
5405 N. 118th Ct.
Milwaukee, WI 53225
Phone: 414-527-3100 Fax: 414-527-1067
CEO: David M. Rasmussen
CFO: David M. Rasmussen
1991 Sales: $5.3 million Employees: 11
Ownership: Privately held
Industry: Business services - electric utility

Turner Broadcasting System, Inc.
One CNN Center, 100 International Blvd.
Atlanta, GA 30303
Phone: 404-827-1700 Fax: 404-827-2437
CEO: R. E. Turner
CFO: Randolph L. Booth
1992 Sales: $1,770 million Employees: 4,370
Symbol: TBS Exchange: AMEX
Industry: Broadcasting - radio & TV, sports teams, real estate

Turner Corp.
375 Hudson St.
New York, NY 10014
Phone: 212-229-6000 Fax: 212-229-6390
CEO: Alfred T. McNeill
CFO: Allen H. Wahlberg
1992 Sales: $2,645 million Employees: 2,806
Symbol: TUR Exchange: AMEX
Industry: Construction - heavy

Tuscarora Plastics, Inc.
800 Fifth Ave.
New Brighton, PA 15066
Phone: 412-843-8200 Fax: 412-847-2140
CEO: John P. O'Leary, Jr.
CFO: Brian C. Mullins
1991 Sales: $84 million Employees: 850
Symbol: TUSC Exchange: NASDAQ
Industry: Chemicals - plastics

TW Holdings, Inc.
203 E. Main St.
Spartanburg, SC 29319
Phone: 803-579-8700 Fax: 803-597-8780
CEO: Jerome J. Richardson
CFO: A. Ray Biggs
1992 Sales: $3,720 million Employees: 112,000
Symbol: TWFS Exchange: NASDAQ
Industry: Retail - food & restaurants

Twin Disc, Inc.
1328 Racine St.
Racine, WI 53403
Phone: 414-634-1981 Fax: 414-634-1989
CEO: Michael E. Batten
CFO: James O. Parrish
1992 Sales: $136 million Employees: 1,221
Symbol: TDI Exchange: NYSE
Industry: Machinery - general industrial

Two Pesos Inc.
10777 Westheimer
Houston, TX 77042
Phone: 713-781-0067 Fax: 713-781-3016
CEO: Ghulam M. Bombaywala
CFO: Maryann F. Antell
1992 Sales: $36 million Employees: 1,162
Symbol: TWP Exchange: AMEX
Industry: Retail - food & restaurants

Tyco Laboratories, Inc.
One Tyco Park
Exeter, NH 03833
Phone: 603-778-9700 Fax: 603-778-7700
CEO: L. Dennis Kozlowski
CFO: Terry L. Hall
1992 Sales: $3,131 million Employees: 23,000
Symbol: TYC Exchange: NYSE
Industry: Diversified operations - fire protection & packing products, electrical components

Tyco Toys, Inc.
6000 Midlantic Dr.
Mt. Laurel, NJ 08054
Phone: 609-234-7400 Fax: 609-722-9343
CEO: Richard E. Grey
CFO: Harry J. Pearce
1992 Sales: $769 million Employees: 1,700
Symbol: TTI Exchange: NYSE
Industry: Toys - games & hobby products

Tycom Limited Partnership
1217 Wakeham Ave.
Santa Ana, CA 92705
Phone: 714-547-5740 Fax: 714-547-8415
CEO: Tim Taylor
CFO: Marty Brogden
1991 Sales: $11 million Employees: 210
Ownership: Privately held
Industry: Machine tools - precision cutting tools

Tyler Corp.
3200 San Jacinto Tower, Ste. 3200
Dallas, TX 75201
Phone: 214-754-7800 Fax: 214-969-9352
CEO: Joseph F. McKinney
CFO: W. Michael Kipphut
1991 Sales: $266 million Employees: 3,445
Symbol: TYL Exchange: NYSE
Industry: Diversified operations - cast iron pipe & fittings, retail auto parts

Tyson Foods, Inc.
2210 W. Oaklawn Dr.
Springdale, AR 72764
Phone: 501-756-4000 Fax: 501-756-4061
CEO: Leland E. Tollett
CFO: Gerald Johnston
1992 Sales: $4,295 million Employees: 47,000
Symbol: TYSNA Exchange: NASDAQ
Industry: Food - meat products

U. S. A. Direct, Inc.
2901 Blackbridge Rd.
York, PA 17402
Phone: 717-852-1000 Fax: 717-852-1030
CEO: Richard Osborne
CFO: Richard Osborne
1991 Sales: $18 million Employees: 331
Ownership: Privately held
Industry: Business services - direct mail

U.S. Alcohol Testing of America, Inc.
10410 Trademark St.
Rancho Cucamonga, CA 91730
Phone: 714-466-8378 Fax: 714-466-0082
CEO: James C. Witham
CFO: Gary S. Wolff
1992 Sales: $0.7 million Employees: —
Symbol: AAA Exchange: AMEX
Industry: Medical instruments - blood-alcohol concentration measuring instruments

U. S. Bancorp
111 S.W. Fifth Ave.
Portland, OR 97204
Phone: 503-275-6111 Fax: 503-275-3452
CEO: Roger L. Breezley
CFO: Paul M. Devore
1992 Sales: $1,935 million Employees: 11,282
Symbol: USBC Exchange: NASDAQ
Industry: Banks - West

U.S. Bioscience, Inc.
920-B Harvest Dr.
Blue Bell, PA 19422
Phone: 215-540-0910 Fax: 215-832-4500
CEO: Philip S. Schein
CFO: Lawrence T. Longacre
1991 Sales: $11 million Employees: 121
Symbol: UBS Exchange: AMEX
Industry: Drugs

U.S. Computer Maintenance Inc.
4 Dubon Ct.
Farmingdale, NY 11735
Phone: 516-753-6080 Fax: 516-753-6105
CEO: Stephen Davies
CFO: James Sutton
1991 Sales: $4.7 million Employees: 50
Ownership: Privately held
Industry: Computers - maintenance services

U.S. Energy Corp.
877 N. 8th St. West
Riverton, WY 82501
Phone: 307-856-9271 Fax: 307-857-3050
CEO: John L. Larsen
CFO: Robert Scott Lorimer
1992 Sales: $5.3 million Employees: 45
Symbol: USEG Exchange: NASDAQ
Industry: Metal ores

U.S. Gold Corp.
55 Madison St., Ste. 280
Denver, CO 80206
Phone: 303-322-8002 Fax: 303-322-7866
CEO: William W. Reid
CFO: William W. Reid
1992 Sales: — Employees: 3
Symbol: USGL Exchange: NASDAQ
Industry: Gold mining & processing

U.S. Healthcare, Inc.
980 Jolly Rd.
Blue Bell, PA 19422
Phone: 215-628-4800 Fax: 215-283-6579
CEO: Leonard Abramson
CFO: Costas C. Nicolaides
1992 Sales: $2,189 million Employees: 2,538
Symbol: USHC Exchange: NASDAQ
Industry: Health maintenance organization

U.S. Home Corp.
1800 W. Loop South, Ste. 1850
Houston, TX 77027
Phone: 713-877-2311 Fax: 713-877-2463
CEO: Robert J. Strudler
CFO: Thomas A. Napoli
1991 Sales: $494 million Employees: 840
Symbol: UH Exchange: NYSE
Industry: Building - residential & commercial

U.S. HomeCare Corp.
141 S. Central Ave.
Hartsdale, NY 10530
Phone: 914-946-9601 Fax: —
CEO: W. Edward Massey
CFO: David N. Slifkin
1991 Sales: $50 million Employees: 3,167
Symbol: USHO Exchange: NASDAQ
Industry: Healthcare - outpatient & home

U.S. Hospitality
325 Plus Park Blvd. #101
Nashville, TN 37217
Phone: 615-367-1208 Fax: 615-367-0719
CEO: Mark Oldham
CFO: Danny Oldham
1991 Sales: $1.4 million Employees: 18
Ownership: Privately held
Industry: Publishing - hotel guest services directories

U.S. Intec, Inc.
1212 Brai Dr.
Port Arthur, TX 77640
Phone: 409-724-7024 Fax: 409-724-2348
CEO: Danny J. Adair
CFO: James B. Poynter
1991 Sales: $66 million Employees: 288
Symbol: USI Exchange: AMEX
Industry: Building products

U.S. Long Distance Corp.
9311 San Pedro Ave., Ste. 300
San Antonio, TX 78216
Phone: 210-525-9009 Fax: 210-342-4030
CEO: Parris H. Holmes, Jr.
CFO: Mark D. Buckner
1991 Sales: $37 million Employees: 368
Symbol: USLD Exchange: NASDAQ
Industry: Telecommunications services

U.S. Paging Corp.
1680 Route 23 North
Wayne, NJ 07470
Phone: 201-305-6000 Fax: —
CEO: Charles F. Schmoyer
CFO: Alan L. Bendes
1991 Sales: $10.8 million Employees: —
Symbol: USPC Exchange: NASDAQ
Industry: Telecommunications services

U.S. Robotics, Inc.
8100 N. McCormick Blvd.
Skokie, IL 60076
Phone: 708-982-5010 Fax: 708-982-5235
CEO: Casey G. Cowell
CFO: John McCartney
1991 Sales: $77 million Employees: 402
Symbol: USRX Exchange: NASDAQ
Industry: Computers - modems

U.S. Structures Inc. (Archadeck)
2112 W. Laburnum Ave. #100
Richmond, VA 23227
Phone: 804-353-6999 Fax: 804-358-1878
CEO: Richard Provost
CFO: Brian Reed
1991 Sales: $11 million Employees: 25
Ownership: Privately held
Industry: Building products - wooden patio decks

U.S. Trust Corp.
114 W. 47th St.
New York, NY 10036
Phone: 212-852-1000 Fax: —
CEO: H. Marshall Schwarz
CFO: Donald M. Roberts
1991 Sales: $405 million Employees: 2,022
Symbol: USTC Exchange: NASDAQ
Industry: Banks - Northeast

U S WEST, Inc.
7800 E. Orchard Rd.
Englewood, CO 80111
Phone: 303-793-6500 Fax: 303-793-6654
CEO: Richard D. McCormick
CFO: James M. Osterhoff
1992 Sales: $10,281 million Employees: 65,829
Symbol: USW Exchange: NYSE
Industry: Utility - telephone, long distance, financial services

U.S. Xpress
1535 New Hope Church Rd.
Tunnel Hill, GA 30755
Phone: 706-673-6592 Fax: 706-673-7350
CEO: Max Fuller
CFO: Nancy Quarles
1991 Sales: $142 million Employees: 2,104
Ownership: Privately held
Industry: Transportation - trucking

UAL Corp.
1200 E. Algonquin Rd.
Elk Grove Village, IL 60007
Phone: 708-952-4000 Fax: 708-952-7680
CEO: Stephen M. Wolf
CFO: John C. Pope
1992 Sales: $12,890 million Employees: 81,242
Symbol: UAL Exchange: NYSE
Industry: Transportation - airline

UBS Holdings Inc.
299 Park Ave.
New York, NY 10171
Phone: 212-715-3000 Fax: 212-715-3285
CEO: Markus Rohrbasser
CFO: —
1991 Sales: $5,733 million Employees: 27,677
Parent: Union Bank of Switzerland
Industry: Banks - money center

UDC-Universal Development L.P.
4820 S. Mill Ave.
Tempe, AZ 85282
Phone: 602-820-4488 Fax: 602-730-3493
CEO: Gary A. Rosenberg
CFO: Robert H. Daskal
1991 Sales: $365 million Employees: 500
Symbol: UDC Exchange: NYSE
Industry: Building - residential & commercial

UF Bancorp, Inc.
501 Main St.
Evansville, IN 47731
Phone: 812-425-7111 Fax: —
CEO: Donald A. Rausch
CFO: Ennis R. Griffith
1992 Sales: — Employees: —
Symbol: UFBI Exchange: NASDAQ
Industry: Banks - Midwest

UGI Corp.
460 N. Gulph Rd.
King of Prussia, PA 19406
Phone: 215-337-1000 Fax: 215-992-3259
CEO: James A. Sutton
CFO: Charles L. Ladner
1991 Sales: $709 million Employees: 3,812
Symbol: UGI Exchange: NYSE
Industry: Utility - gas distribution

UIS Inc.
600 Fifth Ave., 27th Fl.
New York, NY 10020
Phone: 212-581-7660 Fax: 212-581-7517
CEO: Harry Lebensfeld
CFO: Joseph F. Arrigo
1991 Sales: $630 million Employees: 6,700
Ownership: Privately held
Industry: Auto parts - retail

UJB Financial Corp.
301 Carnegie Center
Princeton, NJ 08540
Phone: 609-987-3200 Fax: 609-987-3481
CEO: T. Joseph Semrod
CFO: John R. Haggerty
1992 Sales: $1,130 million Employees: 6,504
Symbol: UJB Exchange: NYSE
Industry: Banks - Northeast

Ultimate Corp.
717 Ridgedale Ave.
East Hanover, NJ 07936
Phone: 201-887-9222 Fax: 201-887-9546
CEO: Michael J. O'Donnell
CFO: John D. Redding
1992 Sales: $142 million Employees: 384
Symbol: ULT Exchange: NYSE
Industry: Computers - software support services

Ultra Bancorp
36 N. Detroit St.
Xenia, OH 45385
Phone: 513-372-6933 Fax: —
CEO: James E. Laughlin
CFO: Steven R. Houser
1991 Sales: $19 million Employees: 79
Symbol: HFOX Exchange: NASDAQ
Industry: Financial - savings and loans

Ultra Pac, Inc.
21925 Industrial Blvd.
Rogers, MN 55374
Phone: 612-428-8340 Fax: 612-428-8344
CEO: Calvin S. Krupa
CFO: Bradley C. Yopp
1991 Sales: $18 million Employees: 125
Symbol: UPAC Exchange: NASDAQ
Industry: Containers - paper & plastic

Ultramar Corp.
120 White Plains Rd.
Tarrytown, NY 10591
Phone: 914-333-2000 Fax: —
CEO: Jean Gaulin
CFO: H. Pete Smith
1992 Sales: $2,596 million Employees: 3,927
Symbol: ULR Exchange: NYSE
Industry: Oil & gas - US exploration & production

UNC Inc.
175 Admiral Cochrane Dr.
Annapolis, MD 21401
Phone: 410-266-7333 Fax: 410-266-5706
CEO: Dan A. Colussy
CFO: Robert L. Pevenstein
1991 Sales: $361 million Employees: 3,852
Symbol: UNC Exchange: NYSE
Industry: Aerospace - aircraft equipment

Uni-Marts, Inc.
477 E. Beaver Ave.
State College, PA 16801
Phone: 814-234-6000 Fax: 814-234-3277
CEO: Henry D. Sahakian
CFO: J. Kirk Gallaher
1991 Sales: $256 million Employees: 2,500
Symbol: UNMAA Exchange: NASDAQ
Industry: Retail - convenience stores

UniCARE Financial Corp.
2201 Dupont Dr., Ste. 600
Irvine, CA 92715
Phone: 714-955-2170 Fax: —
CEO: Russell E. Leatherby
CFO: Ben F. Hernandez
1991 Sales: $126 million Employees: —
Symbol: UFN Exchange: NYSE
Industry: Insurance - accident & health

Unico American Corp.
23251 Mulholland Dr.
Woodland Hills, CA 91364
Phone: 818-591-9800 Fax: 818-591-9822
CEO: Erwin Cheldin
CFO: Lester A. Aaron
1992 Sales: $28 million Employees: 123
Symbol: UNAM Exchange: NASDAQ
Industry: Insurance - multiline & misc.

Unifax
1065 Hwy.315, Ste. 203
Wilkes-Barre, PA 18702
Phone: 717-822-0902 Fax: 717-822-0909
CEO: Frank H. Bevevino
CFO: David McAnally
1991 Sales: $740 million Employees: 2,000
Ownership: Privately held
Industry: Food - wholesale

Unifi, Inc.
7201 W. Friendly Ave.
Greensboro, NC 27410
Phone: 919-294-4410 Fax: 919-316-5422
CEO: William T. Kretzer
CFO: Robert A. Ward
1992 Sales: $1,121 million Employees: —
Symbol: UFI Exchange: NYSE
Industry: Textiles - mill products

UniFirst Corp.
68 Jonspin Rd.
Wilmington, MA 01887
Phone: 508-658-8888 Fax: 508-657-5663
CEO: Ronald D. Croatti
CFO: John B. Bartlett
1991 Sales: $250 million Employees: 4,500
Symbol: UNF Exchange: NYSE
Industry: Linen supply & related

Uniforce Temporary Personnel, Inc.
1335 Jericho Tnpk.
New Hyde Park, NY 11040
Phone: 516-437-3300 Fax: 516-437-3392
CEO: John Fanning
CFO: Harry V. Maccarrone
1991 Sales: $92 million Employees: 51,110
Symbol: UNFR Exchange: NASDAQ
Industry: Financial - business services

Unigene Laboratories, Inc.
110 Little Falls Rd.
Fairfield, NJ 07006
Phone: 201-882-0860 Fax: 201-227-6088
CEO: Warren P. Levy
CFO: Jay Levy
1992 Sales: — Employees: 35
Symbol: UGNE Exchange: NASDAQ
Industry: Biomedical & genetic products

Unilab Corp.
450 Park Ave., Ste. 2603
New York, NY 10022
Phone: 212-832-3130 Fax: 212-832-0599
CEO: Gabriel B. Thomas
CFO: Michael J. Bachich
1991 Sales: $204 million Employees: 2,700
Symbol: ULAB Exchange: NYSE
Industry: Medical services - laboratory testing

Unilever United States, Inc.
390 Park Ave.
New York, NY 10022
Phone: 212-888-1260 Fax: 212-906-4411
CEO: Richard A. Goldstein
CFO: —
1991 Sales: $40,767 million Employees: 298,000
Parent: Unilever
Industry: Food, detergents & personal products

Unimar Co.
120 White Plains Rd.
Tarrytown, NY 10591
Phone: 914-333-2000 Fax: 914-332-0817
CEO: William M. Krips
CFO: William M. Krips
1991 Sales: $208 million Employees: —
Symbol: UMR Exchange: AMEX
Industry: Oil & gas - international integrated

UNIMED, Inc.
2150 E. Lake Cook Rd.
Buffalo Grove, IL 60089
Phone: 708-541-2525 Fax: 708-541-2569
CEO: John J. Kapoor
CFO: David E. Riggs
1991 Sales: $6.3 million Employees: 35
Symbol: UMED Exchange: NASDAQ
Industry: Drugs

Union Bank
350 California St.
San Francisco, CA 94104
Phone: 415-445-0200 Fax: —
CEO: Taisuke Shimizu
CFO: Kanetaka Yoshida
1992 Sales: $1,386 million Employees: 7,283
Symbol: UBNK Exchange: NASDAQ
Industry: Banks - West

Union Camp Corp.
1600 Valley Rd.
Wayne, NJ 07470
Phone: 201-628-2000 Fax: 201-628-2722
CEO: Raymond E. Cartledge
CFO: James M. Reed
1992 Sales: $3,064 million Employees: 20,102
Symbol: UCC Exchange: NYSE
Industry: Paper & paper products

Union Carbide Corp.
39 Old Ridgebury Rd.
Danbury, CT 06817
Phone: 203-794-2000 Fax: 203-794-4336
CEO: Robert D. Kennedy
CFO: John A. Clerico
1992 Sales: $4,872 million Employees: 16,705
Symbol: UK Exchange: NYSE
Industry: Chemicals - diversified

Union Corp.
492 Route 46 East
Fairfield, NJ 07004
Phone: 201-808-2747 Fax: 201-808-5690
CEO: Melvin L. Cooper
CFO: Nicholas P. Gill
1991 Sales: $83 million Employees: 1,040
Symbol: UCO Exchange: NYSE
Industry: Financial - business services

Union Electric Co.
1901 Chouteau Ave.
St. Louis, MO 63103
Phone: 314-621-3222 Fax: 314-554-3268
CEO: William E. Cornelius
CFO: Donald E. Brandt
1992 Sales: $2,015 million Employees: 6,868
Symbol: UEP Exchange: NYSE
Industry: Utility - electric power

Union Holdings
1501 E. 8th St.
Liberal, KS 67905
Phone: 316-624-1851 Fax: 316-626-0685
CEO: Ezra Zilkha
CFO: Norb Schwarz
1991 Sales: $1,200 million Employees: 1,265
Ownership: Privately held
Industry: Food - meat products & food processing

Union Pacific Corp.
Martin Tower, Eighth & Eaton Aves.
Bethlehem, PA 18018
Phone: 215-861-3200 Fax: 215-861-3220
CEO: Drew Lewis
CFO: L. White Matthews III
1992 Sales: $7,294 million Employees: 47,090
Symbol: UNP Exchange: NYSE
Industry: Transportation - rail & trucking, natural resources, waste management

Union Planters Corp.
67 Madison Ave.
Memphis, TN 38103
Phone: 901-523-6000 Fax: 901-523-6409
CEO: Benjamin W. Rawlins, Jr.
CFO: John W. Parker
1991 Sales: $398 million Employees: 2,327
Symbol: UPC Exchange: NYSE
Industry: Banks - Southeast

Union Pointe Construction
2105 W. California Ave.
Salt Lake City, UT 84104
Phone: 801-975-1896 Fax: 801-975-1103
CEO: Douglas K. Anderson
CFO: Richard Mathews
1992 Sales: $13 million Employees: 35
Ownership: Privately held
Industry: Construction - general contracting

Union Texas Petroleum Holdings, Inc.
1330 Post Oak Blvd.
Houston, TX 77056
Phone: 713-623-6544 Fax: 713-968-2771
CEO: A. Clark Johnson
CFO: Larry Kalmbach
1992 Sales: $714 million Employees: 990
Symbol: UTH Exchange: NYSE
Industry: Oil & gas - US exploration & production

UnionFed Financial Corp.
330 E. Lambert Rd.
Brea, CA 92621
Phone: 714-255-8100 Fax: —
CEO: David S. Engelman
CFO: Jeffrey K. Speakes
1992 Sales: $156 million Employees: 361
Symbol: UFF Exchange: NYSE
Industry: Financial - savings and loans

Uniroyal Chemical Co. Inc.
World Headquarters
Middlebury, CT 06749
Phone: 203-573-2000 Fax: 203-573-3077
CEO: Robert J. Mazaika
CFO: Gerry H. Fickensher
1991 Sales: $832 million Employees: 2,800
Ownership: Privately held
Industry: Chemicals - diversified

Unisys Corp.
Township Line & Union Meeting Rds.
Blue Bell, PA 19424
Phone: 215-986-4011 Fax: 215-986-6850
CEO: James A. Unruh
CFO: George T. Robson
1992 Sales: $8,422 million Employees: 60,300
Symbol: UIS Exchange: NYSE
Industry: Computers - mainframe, workstations, software

Unit Corp.
7130 S. Lewis Ave., Ste. 1000
Tulsa, OK 74136
Phone: 918-493-7700 Fax: 918-493-7711
CEO: King P. Kirchner
CFO: Larry D. Pinkston
1991 Sales: $70 million Employees: 208
Symbol: UNT Exchange: NYSE
Industry: Oil & gas - field services

United American Healthcare Corp.
1155 Brewery Pk, Ste. 200
Detroit, MI 48207
Phone: 313-393-0200 Fax: —
CEO: Julius V. Combs
CFO: Jagannathan Vanaharam
1992 Sales: $34 million Employees: 277
Symbol: UAHC Exchange: NASDAQ
Industry: Medical services - healthcare administration & marketing

United Asset Management Corp.
One International Place, 44th Fl.
Boston, MA 02110
Phone: 617-330-8900 Fax: 617-330-1133
CEO: Norton H. Reamer
CFO: William H. Park
1991 Sales: $227 million Employees: 588
Symbol: UAM Exchange: NYSE
Industry: Financial - investment management

United Bankshares, Inc.
500 Virginia St. East
Charleston, WV 25301
Phone: 304-348-8400 Fax: —
CEO: Richard M. Adams
CFO: Steven E. Wilson
1991 Sales: $113 million Employees: 682
Symbol: UBSI Exchange: NASDAQ
Industry: Banks - Southeast

United Capital Corp.
110 E. 59th St., 33rd Fl.
New York, NY 10022
Phone: 212-371-1781 Fax: 212-486-6612
CEO: Attilio F. Petrocelli
CFO: Dennis S. Rosatelli
1991 Sales: $63 million Employees: 425
Symbol: ICU Exchange: AMEX
Industry: Real estate operations

United Carolina Bancshares Corp.
127 W. Webster St.
Whiteville, NC 28472
Phone: 919-642-5131 Fax: 919-642-1265
CEO: E. Rhone Sasser
CFO: Ronald C. Monger
1991 Sales: $265 million Employees: 1,894
Symbol: UCAR Exchange: NASDAQ
Industry: Banks - Southeast

United Cities Gas Co.
5300 Maryland Way
Brentwood, TN 37027
Phone: 615-373-0104 Fax: 615-371-5053
CEO: Gene C. Koonce
CFO: Tom S. Hawkins, Jr.
1991 Sales: $239 million Employees: 1,369
Symbol: UCIT Exchange: NASDAQ
Industry: Utility - gas distribution

United Co.
PO Box 1280
Bristol, VA 24203
Phone: 703-466-3322 Fax: 703-466-5641
CEO: James W. McGlothlin
CFO: Lois Clark
1991 Sales: $610 million Employees: 1,250
Ownership: Privately held
Industry: Diversified operations - coal mining, oil drilling & real estate

United Coasts Corp.
One Corporate Center
Hartford, CT 06103
Phone: 203-560-1670 Fax: —
CEO: Henry W. Nozko, Sr.
CFO: Harold D. Wirth
1991 Sales: $21 million Employees: 350
Symbol: UCOA Exchange: NASDAQ
Industry: Insurance - property & casualty

United Companies Financial Corp.
4041 Essen Lane
Baton Rouge, LA 70821
Phone: 504-924-6007 Fax: —
CEO: J. Terrell Brown
CFO: Dale E. Redman
1991 Sales: $288 million Employees: —
Symbol: UNCF Exchange: NASDAQ
Industry: Insurance - life

United Dominion Industries Inc.
301 S. College St., 1 First Union Center, Ste. 2300
Charlotte, NC 28202
Phone: 704-347-6800 Fax: 704-347-6900
CEO: William R. Holland
CFO: Joseph A. Scopelliti
1991 Sales: $1,350 million Employees: 8,800
Symbol: UDI Exchange: NYSE
Industry: Building - residential & commercial

United Dominion Industries Limited
2300 One First Union Ctr., 301 S. College St.
Charlotte, NC 28202
Phone: 704-347-6800 Fax: 704-347-6940
CEO: William R. Holland
CFO: —
1991 Sales: $8,713 million Employees: 78,200
Parent: Canadian Pacific Ltd.
Industry: Diversified operations - transportation, forest products & telecommunications

United Federal Bancorp, Inc.
1631 S. Atherton St.
State College, PA 16801
Phone: 814-231-1600 Fax: —
CEO: Charles C. Pearson, Jr.
CFO: Donald L. Gross
1991 Sales: $66 million Employees: 264
Symbol: UFBK Exchange: NASDAQ
Industry: Banks - Northeast

United Financial Corp. of South Carolina, Inc.
425 Main St.
Greenwood, SC 29648
Phone: 803-223-8686 Fax: —
CEO: Lynn W. Hodge
CFO: Clifford W. Stumbo
1992 Sales: $52 million Employees: 170
Symbol: UNSA Exchange: NASDAQ
Industry: Financial - savings and loans

United Fire & Casualty Co.
118 Second Ave. SE
Cedar Rapids, IA 52401
Phone: 319-399-5700 Fax: 319-399-5499
CEO: Scott McIntyre, Jr.
CFO: Kent G. Baker
1991 Sales: $185 million Employees: 594
Symbol: UFCS Exchange: NASDAQ
Industry: Insurance - property & casualty

United Foods, Inc.
100 Dawson Ave.
Bells, TN 38006
Phone: 901-422-7600 Fax: 800-634-6171
CEO: James I. Tankersley
CFO: C. W. Gruenewald II
1992 Sales: $154 million Employees: 2,600
Symbol: UFDA Exchange: AMEX
Industry: Food - frozen vegetables & prepared entrees

United Gaming, Inc.
4380 Boulder Hwy.
Las Vegas, NV 89121
Phone: 702-435-4200 Fax: 702-454-0478
CEO: Alfred H. Wilms
CFO: John W. Alderfer
1992 Sales: $94 million Employees: 956
Symbol: UGAM Exchange: NASDAQ
Industry: Leisure & recreational services - casinos & video gaming products

United HealthCare Corp.
9900 Bren Rd. East
Minnetonka, MN 55343
Phone: 612-936-1300 Fax: 612-931-9655
CEO: William W. McGuire
CFO: George B. Borkow
1992 Sales: $1,442 million Employees: 3,200
Symbol: UNH Exchange: NYSE
Industry: Health maintenance organization

United Illuminating Co.
80 Temple St.
New Haven, CT 06506
Phone: 203-787-7200 Fax: 203-777-6037
CEO: Richard J. Grossi
CFO: Robert L. Fiscus
1991 Sales: $673 million Employees: 1,579
Symbol: UIL Exchange: NYSE
Industry: Utility - electric power

United Industrial Corp.
18 E. 48th St.
New York, NY 10017
Phone: 212-752-8787 Fax: 212-838-4629
CEO: Bernard Fein
CFO: Howard M. Bloch
1991 Sales: $258 million Employees: 2,700
Symbol: UIC Exchange: NYSE
Industry: Electronics - military

United Inns, Inc.
5100 Poplar Ave., Ste. 2300
Memphis, TN 38137
Phone: 901-767-2880 Fax: 901-767-4278
CEO: Don William Cockroft
CFO: J. Don Miller
1991 Sales: $106 million Employees: 2,601
Symbol: UI Exchange: NYSE
Industry: Hotels & motels

United Insurance Companies, Inc.
4001 McEwen Dr., Ste. 200
Dallas, TX 75244
Phone: 214-960-8497 Fax: —
CEO: Ronald L. Jensen
CFO: Vernon R. Woelke
1991 Sales: $312 million Employees: 450
Symbol: UICI Exchange: NASDAQ
Industry: Insurance - accident & health

United International Engineering
2201 Buena Vista Dr. SE, Ste. 207
Albuquerque, NM 87106
Phone: 505-242-9200 Fax: 505-242-9096
CEO: David Chou
CFO: David Chou
1992 Sales: $15 million Employees: 226
Ownership: Privately held
Industry: Engineering R&D and engineering services

United Investors Management Co.
2001 Third Ave. South
Birmingham, AL 35233
Phone: 205-325-4200 Fax: 205-325-4157
CEO: R. K. Richey
CFO: Keith A. Tucker
1991 Sales: $311 million Employees: 1,390
Symbol: UTD Exchange: NYSE
Industry: Financial - investment management

United Medical Corp.
56 Haddon Ave.
Haddonfield, NJ 08033
Phone: 609-354-2200 Fax: 609-354-2216
CEO: John Aglialoro
CFO: Arthur W. Hicks, Jr.
1991 Sales: $43 million Employees: 302
Symbol: UM Exchange: AMEX
Industry: Medical services - health & research services & products

United Merchants and Manufacturers, Inc.
980 6th Ave.
New York, NY 10018
Phone: 212-465-3900 Fax: 212-930-7024
CEO: Uzi Ruskin
CFO: Judith A. Nadzick
1991 Sales: $216 million Employees: 3,400
Symbol: UMM Exchange: NYSE
Industry: Textiles - apparel

United Missouri Bancshares, Inc.
1010 Grand Ave.
Kansas City, MO 64106
Phone: 816-860-5600 Fax: 816-421-5411
CEO: R. Crosby Kemper
CFO: William M. Teiwes
1991 Sales: $397 million Employees: 2,925
Symbol: UMSB Exchange: NASDAQ
Industry: Banks - Midwest

United National Bancorp
65 Readington Rd.
Branchburg, NJ 08876
Phone: 908-756-5000 Fax: —
CEO: Kenneth W. Turnbull
CFO: Donald W. Malwitz
1991 Sales: $66 million Employees: 465
Symbol: UNBJ Exchange: NASDAQ
Industry: Banks - Northeast

United New Mexico Financial Corp.
200 Lomas Blvd. NW
Albuquerque, NM 87103
Phone: 505-765-5086 Fax: —
CEO: Gerald J. Ford
CFO: Carl G. Guist
1991 Sales: $122 million Employees: 1,091
Symbol: BNKS Exchange: NASDAQ
Industry: Banks - Southwest

United Parcel Service of America, Inc.
400 Perimeter Center–Terraces North
Atlanta, GA 30346
Phone: 404-913-7123 Fax: 404-913-7123
CEO: Kent Nelson
CFO: Edwin A. Jacoby
1991 Sales: $15,020 million Employees: 256,000
Ownership: Privately held
Industry: Transportation - air & ground package delivery

United Park City Mines Co.
136 S. Main St.
Salt Lake City, UT 84101
Phone: 801-532-4031 Fax: —
CEO: William H. Rothwell
CFO: Edwin L. Osika, Jr.
1991 Sales: $0.6 million Employees: 17
Symbol: UPK Exchange: NYSE
Industry: Real estate operations

United Postal Bancorp, Inc.
10015 Manchester Rd.
St. Louis, MO 63122
Phone: 314-966-2530 Fax: —
CEO: Michael J. Gorman
CFO: Steven M. Rull
1991 Sales: $131 million Employees: 552
Symbol: UPBI Exchange: NASDAQ
Industry: Banks - Midwest

United Retail Group, Inc.
365 W. Passaic St.
Rochelle Park, NJ 07662
Phone: 201-845-0880 Fax: 201-909-2162
CEO: Raphael Benaroyal
CFO: George R. Remeta
1991 Sales: $264 million Employees: 3,172
Symbol: URGI Exchange: NASDAQ
Industry: Retail - apparel & shoes

United Savings Bank, FA
601 First Ave. North
Great Falls, MT 59401
Phone: 406-761-2200 Fax: —
CEO: Bruce K. Weldele
CFO: G. Brent Marvosh
1992 Sales: — Employees: —
Symbol: UBMT Exchange: NASDAQ
Industry: Financial - savings and loans

indicates company is in *Hoover's Handbook of American Business.*

indicates company is in *Hoover's Handbook of World Business;* sales and employee numbers are for parent company.

United Staffing
720 6th Ave.
Troy, NY 12182
Phone: 518-235-5777 Fax: 518-237-3116
CEO: Cherie Fretto
CFO: Cherie Fretto
1991 Sales: $34 million Employees: 42
Ownership: Privately held
Industry: Business services - employee leasing services

United States Antimony Corp.
1250 Prospect Creek Rd.
Thompson Falls, MT 59873
Phone: 406-827-3523 Fax: 406-827-3543
CEO: John C. Lawrence
CFO: Larry E. Ward
1991 Sales: $3.5 million Employees: —
Symbol: USAC Exchange: NASDAQ
Industry: Gold & silver mining

United States Banknote Corp.
345 Hudson St.
New York, NY 10014
Phone: 212-741-8500 Fax: 212-924-0717
CEO: Morris Weissman
CFO: John T. Gorman
1991 Sales: $161 million Employees: 1,220
Symbol: UBK Exchange: AMEX
Industry: Printing - commercial; coupons, securities, etc.

United States Cellular Corp.
8410 W. Bryn Mawr, Ste. 700
Chicago, IL 60631
Phone: 312-399-8900 Fax: 312-399-8936
CEO: H. Donald Nelson
CFO: Kenneth R. Myers
1991 Sales: $100 million Employees: 875
Symbol: USM Exchange: AMEX
Industry: Telecommunications services

United States Shoe Corp., The
One Eastwood Dr.
Cincinnati, OH 45227
Phone: 513-527-7000 Fax: 513-561-2007
CEO: Bannus B. Hudson
CFO: K. Brent Somers
1992 Sales: $2,657 million Employees: 41,000
Symbol: USR Exchange: NYSE
Industry: Retail - apparel & shoes, optical products

United States Surgical Corp.
150 Glover Ave.
Norwalk, CT 06856
Phone: 203-845-1000 Fax: 203-845-4478
CEO: Leon C. Hirsch
CFO: Bruce S. Lustman
1992 Sales: $1,197 million Employees: 7,300
Symbol: USS Exchange: NYSE
Industry: Medical instruments - surgical staplers, sutures & clamps

United Stationers Inc.
2200 E. Golf Rd.
Des Plaines, IL 60016
Phone: 708-699-5000 Fax: 708-699-8046
CEO: Joel D. Spungin
CFO: Allen B. Kravis
1992 Sales: $1,212 million Employees: 2,800
Symbol: USTR Exchange: NASDAQ
Industry: Office equipment & supplies

United Technologies Corp.
United Technologies Bldg., 1 Financial Plaza
Hartford, CT 06101
Phone: 203-728-7000 Fax: 203-728-7979
CEO: Robert F. Daniell
CFO: John A. Rolls
1992 Sales: $22,032 million Employees: 185,100
Symbol: UTX Exchange: NYSE
Industry: Diversified operations - building systems, jet engines, flight systems

United Television, Inc.
8501 Wilshire Blvd., Ste. 340
Beverly Hills, CA 90211
Phone: 310-854-0426 Fax: 310-659-8121
CEO: Herbert J. Siegel
CFO: Garth S. Lindsey
1991 Sales: $113 million Employees: 491
Symbol: UTVI Exchange: NASDAQ
Industry: Broadcasting - radio & TV

United Van Lines Inc.
One United Dr.
Fenton, MO 63026
Phone: 314-326-3100 Fax: 314-326-1106
CEO: Maurice Greenblatt
CFO: Douglas H. Wilton
1992 Sales: $865 million Employees: 950
Ownership: Privately held
Industry: Transportation - truck-moving services

United Water Resources Inc.
200 Old Hook Rd.
Harrington Park, NJ 07640
Phone: 201-784-9434 Fax: 201-767-2892
CEO: Robert A. Gerber
CFO: Donald L. Correll
1991 Sales: $162 million Employees: 752
Symbol: UWR Exchange: NYSE
Industry: Utility - water supply

United Wisconsin Services, Inc.
401 W. Michigan St.
Milwaukee, WI 53201
Phone: 414-226-6900 Fax: 414-226-6229
CEO: Thomas R. Hefty
CFO: C. Edward Mordy
1991 Sales: $322 million Employees: 150
Symbol: UWSI Exchange: NASDAQ
Industry: Insurance - accident & health

United-Guardian, Inc.
230 Marcus Blvd.
Hauppauge, NY 11788
Phone: 516-273-0900 Fax: 516-273-0858
CEO: Alfred R. Globus
CFO: Irma Perlmutter
1991 Sales: $5 million Employees: 47
Symbol: UG Exchange: AMEX
Industry: Drugs

Unitel Video, Inc.
515 W. 57th St.
New York, NY 10019
Phone: 212-265-3600 Fax: 212-765-5801
CEO: Herbert Bass
CFO: Barry Knepper
1991 Sales: $46 million Employees: 256
Symbol: UNV Exchange: AMEX
Industry: Motion pictures & services - studio & mobile production, video editing

UNITIL Corp.
216 Epping Rd.
Exeter, NH 03833
Phone: 603-772-0775 Fax: 603-772-4651
CEO: Peter J. Stulgis
CFO: Gail S. Brown
1991 Sales: $88 million Employees: 208
Symbol: UTL Exchange: AMEX
Industry: Real estate development

Unitog Co.
101 W. 11th St.
Kansas City, MO 64105
Phone: 816-474-7000 Fax: 816-842-1336
CEO: Randolph K. Rolf
CFO: Craig Peterson
1991 Sales: $143 million Employees: 2,645
Symbol: UTOG Exchange: NASDAQ
Industry: Linen supply & related

Unitrin, Inc.
One E. Wacker Dr.
Chicago, IL 60601
Phone: 312-661-4600 Fax: 312-661-4690
CEO: Jerrold V. Jerome
CFO: David F. Bengston
1992 Sales: $1,363 million Employees: —
Symbol: UNIT Exchange: NASDAQ
Industry: Insurance - multiline & misc.

Unitrode Corp.
Five Forbes Rd.
Lexington, MA 02173
Phone: 617-861-6540 Fax: 617-861-6773
CEO: Howard F. Wasserman
CFO: Cosmo S. Trapani
1991 Sales: $108 million Employees: 1,119
Symbol: UTR Exchange: NYSE
Industry: Electrical components - semiconductors

Univar Corp.
6100 Carillon Point
Kirkland, WA 98033
Phone: 206-889-3400 Fax: 206-889-4100
CEO: James W. Bernard
CFO: Gary E. Pruitt
1992 Sales: $1,795 million Employees: 3,268
Symbol: UVX Exchange: NYSE
Industry: Chemicals - diversified

Univax Biologics, Inc.
12280 Wilkins Ave.
Rockville, MD 20852
Phone: 301-770-3099 Fax: 301-770-3097
CEO: Thomas P. Stagnaro
CFO: Cabot R. Caskie
1991 Sales: $1.3 million Employees: 48
Symbol: UNVX Exchange: NASDAQ
Industry: Biomedical & genetic products - vaccines; immunotherapy

Universal Corp.
1501 N. Hamilton St.
Richmond, VA 23230
Phone: 804-359-9311 Fax: 804-254-3584
CEO: Henry H. Harrell
CFO: Hartwell H. Roper
1992 Sales: $3,134 million Employees: 25,000
Symbol: UVV Exchange: NYSE
Industry: Tobacco & agricultural products

Universal Foods Corp.
433 E. Michigan St.
Milwaukee, WI 53202
Phone: 414-271-6755 Fax: 414-347-3785
CEO: Guy A. Osborn
CFO: Geoffrey J. Hibner
1992 Sales: $887 million Employees: 5,924
Symbol: UFC Exchange: NYSE
Industry: Food - frozen potato products, cheeses, dehydrated vegetable products

Universal Health Services, Inc.
367 S. Gulph Rd.
King of Prussia, PA 19406
Phone: 215-768-3300 Fax: 215-768-3336
CEO: Alan B. Miller
CFO: Sidney Miller
1992 Sales: $700 million Employees: 9,950
Symbol: UHS Exchange: NYSE
Industry: Hospitals

Universal Holding Corp.
Two Park Ave.
New York, NY 10016
Phone: 212-779-2448 Fax: 212-689-0136
CEO: Marvin Barasch
CFO: Marvin Barasch
1991 Sales: $9.5 million Employees: 80
Symbol: UHCO Exchange: NASDAQ
Industry: Insurance - life

indicates company is in *Hoover's Handbook of American Business.*

indicates company is in *Hoover's Handbook of World Business;* sales and employee numbers are for parent company.

Universal Hospital Services, Inc.
4220 W. Old Shakopee Rd.
Bloomington, MN 55437
Phone: 612-881-3834 Fax: —
CEO: Thomas A. Minner
CFO: David E. Dovenberg
1991 Sales: $46 million Employees: 292
Symbol: UHOS Exchange: NASDAQ
Industry: Medical products

Universal International, Inc.
5000 Winnetka Ave. North
New Hope, MN 55428
Phone: 612-533-1169 Fax: 612-533-1158
CEO: Mark H. Ravitch
CFO: Mark H. Ravitch
1991 Sales: $62 million Employees: 169
Symbol: UNIV Exchange: NASDAQ
Industry: Wholesale distribution - consumer products

Universal Medical Buildings, L.P.
731 N. Jackson St.
Milwaukee, WI 53202
Phone: 414-278-0100 Fax: 414-278-7285
CEO: Joseph W. Checota
CFO: Joseph W. Checota
1991 Sales: $87 million Employees: 110
Symbol: UMB Exchange: NYSE
Industry: Building - residential & commercial

Universal Security Instruments, Inc.
10324 S. Dolfield Rd.
Owings Mills, MD 21117
Phone: 410-363-3000 Fax: 410-363-2218
CEO: Stephen Knepper
CFO: Harvey Grossblatt
1992 Sales: $26 million Employees: 55
Symbol: USEC Exchange: NASDAQ
Industry: Telecommunications equipment

Universal Seismic Associates, Inc.
12999 Jess Pirtie Blvd.
Sugar Land, TX 77478
Phone: 713-240-3388 Fax: —
CEO: Rick E. Trapp
CFO: Rick E. Trapp
1991 Sales: $3.5 million Employees: —
Symbol: USAC Exchange: NASDAQ
Industry: Oil & gas - field services

Universal Voltronics Corp.
27 Radio Circle Dr.
Mt. Kisco, NY 10549
Phone: 914-241-1300 Fax: —
CEO: Barry Ressler
CFO: John N. Hatsopoulos
1991 Sales: $6.5 million Employees: 68
Symbol: UVL Exchange: AMEX
Industry: Instruments - control

University National Bank & Trust
250 Lytton Ave.
Palo Alto, CA 94301
Phone: 415-327-0210 Fax: —
CEO: Carl J. Schmitt
CFO: Gayle A. Anderson
1992 Sales: — Employees: —
Symbol: UNNB Exchange: NASDAQ
Industry: Banks - West

University Patents, Inc.
1465 Post Rd. East
Westport, CT 06880
Phone: 203-255-6044 Fax: 203-254-1102
CEO: A. Sidney Alpert
CFO: Frank R. McPike, Jr.
1991 Sales: $1.6 million Employees: 21
Symbol: UPT Exchange: AMEX
Industry: Diversified operations - education services, patent & license royalties

Univest Financial Group Inc.
1800 Pkwy. Pl., Ste.1000
Marietta, GA 30067
Phone: 404-429-1994 Fax: 404-429-8409
CEO: Ric Thomlinson
CFO: Michael Boschelti
1991 Sales: $17 million Employees: 104
Ownership: Privately held
Industry: Financial - mortgages & loan portfolios

Uno Restaurant Corp.
100 Charles Park Rd.
West Roxbury, MA 02132
Phone: 617-323-9200 Fax: 617-323-6906
CEO: Aaron D. Spencer
CFO: Robert M. Brown
1992 Sales: $84 million Employees: 3,315
Symbol: UNO Exchange: NYSE
Industry: Retail - food & restaurants

Unocal Corp.
1201 W. Fifth St.
Los Angeles, CA 90017
Phone: 213-977-7600 Fax: 213-977-5185
CEO: Richard J. Stegemeier
CFO: Thomas B. Sleeman
1992 Sales: $9,069 million Employees: 17,248
Symbol: UCL Exchange: NYSE
Industry: Oil & gas - US integrated, chemicals

UNR Industries, Inc.
332 S. Michigan Ave.
Chicago, IL 60604
Phone: 312-341-1234 Fax: 312-341-0349
CEO: William F. Andrews
CFO: Henry Grey
1991 Sales: $354 million Employees: 2,400
Symbol: UNRI Exchange: NASDAQ
Industry: Steel - pipes & tubes

UNSL Financial Corp.
Jefferson at Second, Drawer E
Lebanon, MO 65536
Phone: 417-588-4111 Fax: —
CEO: J. C. Benage
CFO: John W. Donald
1991 Sales: $42 million Employees: 222
Symbol: UNSL Exchange: NASDAQ
Industry: Financial - savings and loans

UNUM Corp.
2211 Congress St.
Portland, ME 04122
Phone: 207-770-2211 Fax: 207-770-6933
CEO: James F. Orr III
CFO: Rodney N. Hook
1992 Sales: $2,641 million Employees: —
Symbol: UNM Exchange: NYSE
Industry: Insurance - multiline & misc.

Upjohn Co., The
7000 Portage Rd.
Kalamazoo, MI 49001
Phone: 616-323-4000 Fax: 616-323-7034
CEO: Theodore Cooper
CFO: Robert C. Salisbury
1992 Sales: $3,669 million Employees: 19,193
Symbol: UPJ Exchange: NYSE
Industry: Drugs, animal health care

Upper Peninsula Energy Corp.
600 Lakeshore Dr.
Houghton, MI 49931
Phone: 906-487-5000 Fax: 906-482-8999
CEO: Elio Argentati
CFO: Burton C. Arola
1991 Sales: $60 million Employees: 593
Symbol: UPEN Exchange: NASDAQ
Industry: Utility - electric power

Urcarco, Inc.
777 Taylor St., Ste. 800
Ft. Worth, TX 76102
Phone: 817-332-7000 Fax: —
CEO: Clifton H. Morris, Jr.
CFO: Daniel E. Berce
1992 Sales: $72 million Employees: 243
Symbol: KAR Exchange: NYSE
Industry: Retail - used cars

URS Corp.
100 California St., Ste. 500
San Francisco, CA 94111
Phone: 415-774-2700 Fax: 415-398-1904
CEO: Martin M. Koffel
CFO: Kent P. Ainsworth
1991 Sales: $123 million Employees: 1,000
Symbol: URS Exchange: NYSE
Industry: Engineering - R&D services

US Facilities Corp.
650 Town Center Dr., Ste. 1600
Costa Mesa, CA 92626
Phone: 714-549-1600 Fax: —
CEO: George Kadonada
CFO: Mark Burke
1991 Sales: $64 million Employees: 145
Symbol: USRE Exchange: NASDAQ
Industry: Insurance - multiline & misc.

US Filter Fluid Systems Corp.
12442 E. Putnam St.
Whittier, CA 90602
Phone: 310-698-9414 Fax: 310-698-1960
CEO: Richard J. Heckmann
CFO: Michael J. Reardon
1992 Sales: $41 million Employees: 602
Symbol: USF Exchange: AMEX
Industry: Filtration products

USA Truck, Inc.
3108 Industrial Park Rd.
Van Buren, AR 72956
Phone: 501-471-2500 Fax: 501-471-2577
CEO: James B. Speed
CFO: Jerry D. Orler
1991 Sales: $52 million Employees: 586
Symbol: USAK Exchange: NASDAQ
Industry: Transportation - truck

USA Waste Services, Inc.
5000 Quorum Dr., Ste. 445
Dallas, TX 75240
Phone: 214-233-4212 Fax: 214-490-9750
CEO: Donald F. Moorehead, Jr.
CFO: Earl E. DeFrates
1991 Sales: $18 million Employees: 406
Symbol: USAS Exchange: NASDAQ
Industry: Pollution control equipment & services - solid waste management

USAir Group, Inc.
2345 Crystal Dr.
Arlington, VA 22227
Phone: 703-418-5306 Fax: 703-418-7312
CEO: Seth E. Schofield
CFO: Frank L. Salizzoni
1992 Sales: $6,686 million Employees: 48,700
Symbol: U Exchange: NYSE
Industry: Transportation - airline

USBANCORP, Inc.
Main & Franklin Streets
Johnstown, PA 15901
Phone: 814-533-5300 Fax: —
CEO: Clifford A. Barton
CFO: Orlando B. Hanselman
1991 Sales: $72 million Employees: 593
Symbol: UBAN Exchange: NASDAQ
Industry: Banks - Northeast

indicates company is in *Hoover's Handbook of American Business.*

indicates company is in *Hoover's Handbook of World Business;* sales and employee numbers are for parent company.

User Technology Associates
4301 N. Fairfax, Ste. 400
Arlington, VA 22203
Phone: 703-522-5132 Fax: 703-522-6457
CEO: Yong K. Kim
CFO: Yong K. Kim
1991 Sales: $12 million Employees: 250
Ownership: Privately held
Industry: Computers - services

USF&G Corp.
100 Light St.
Baltimore, MD 21202
Phone: 301-547-3000 Fax: 301-625-2829
CEO: Norman P. Blake, Jr.
CFO: Edwin G. Pickett
1992 Sales: $3,660 million Employees: —
Symbol: FG Exchange: NYSE
Industry: Insurance - property & casualty & life

USG Corp.
125 S. Franklin St.
Chicago, IL 60606
Phone: 312-606-4000 Fax: 312-606-4093
CEO: Eugene B. Connolly
CFO: J. Bradford James
1992 Sales: $1,777 million Employees: 11,800
Symbol: USG Exchange: NYSE
Industry: Building products - gypsum

USLICO Corp.
4601 Fairfax Dr.
Arlington, VA 22203
Phone: 703-875-3600 Fax: 703-875-3426
CEO: Charles V. Giuffra
CFO: W. Alan Aument
1991 Sales: $393 million Employees: —
Symbol: USC Exchange: NYSE
Industry: Insurance - life

USLIFE Corp.
125 Maiden Lane
New York, NY 10038
Phone: 212-709-6000 Fax: 212-425-8006
CEO: Gordon E. Crosby, Jr.
CFO: Greer F. Henderson
1992 Sales: $1,530 million Employees: —
Symbol: USH Exchange: NYSE
Industry: Insurance - life

USMX, INC.
141 Union Blvd., Ste. 100
Lakewood, CO 80228
Phone: 303-985-4665 Fax: 303-980-1363
CEO: James A. Knox
CFO: Donald E. Nilson
1991 Sales: $17 million Employees: 84
Symbol: USMX Exchange: NASDAQ
Industry: Gold mining & processing

UST Corp.
40 Court St.
Boston, MA 02108
Phone: 617-726-7000 Fax: 617-695-4724
CEO: James V. Sidell
CFO: William C. Brooks
1991 Sales: $261 million Employees: 897
Symbol: USTB Exchange: NASDAQ
Industry: Banks - Northeast

UST Inc.
100 W. Putnam Ave.
Greenwich, CT 06830
Phone: 203-661-1100 Fax: 203-622-3626
CEO: Louis F. Bantle
CFO: John J. Bucchignano
1992 Sales: $1,044 million Employees: 3,569
Symbol: UST Exchange: NYSE
Industry: Tobacco

USX Corp.
600 Grant St.
Pittsburgh, PA 15219
Phone: 412-433-1121 Fax: 412-433-5733
CEO: Charles A. Corry
CFO: Robert M. Hernandez
1992 Sales: $12,782 million Employees: 42,552
Symbol: X & MRO Exchange: NYSE
Industry: Oil & gas - oil & gas & steel production

Utah Medical Products, Inc.
7043 South 300 West
Midvale, UT 84047
Phone: 801-566-1200 Fax: —
CEO: Wm. Dean Wallace
CFO: Evan W. Merrill
1991 Sales: $30 million Employees: 344
Symbol: UTMD Exchange: NASDAQ
Industry: Medical products - respiratory therapy products, pressure monitors

UtiliCorp United Inc.
3000 Commerce Tower, 911 Main, Ste. 3000
Kansas City, MO 64105
Phone: 816-421-6600 Fax: 816-691-3590
CEO: Richard C. Green, Jr.
CFO: Harry L. Winn Jr.
1992 Sales: $1,299 million Employees: 4,197
Symbol: UCU Exchange: NYSE
Industry: Utility - electric power

UTILX Corp.
22404 66th Ave. South
Kent, WA 98032
Phone: 206-395-0200 Fax: 206-395-1040
CEO: John R. Potter
CFO: Charles A. Reilly
1992 Sales: $52 million Employees: 432
Symbol: UTLX Exchange: NASDAQ
Industry: Telecommunications services

V Band Corp.
565 Taxter Rd.
Elmsford, NY 10523
Phone: 914-789-5000 Fax: 914-347-3432
CEO: James J. Boyce
CFO: George J. Rogers
1991 Sales: $24 million Employees: 192
Symbol: VBAN Exchange: NASDAQ
Industry: Telecommunications equipment

V. F. Corp.
1047 N. Park Rd.
Wyomissing, PA 19610
Phone: 215-378-1151 Fax: 215-375-9371
CEO: Lawrence R. Pugh
CFO: Gerard G. Johnson
1992 Sales: $3,824 million Employees: 49,000
Symbol: VFC Exchange: NYSE
Industry: Textiles - apparel

Vader Group Inc.
10 State St.
Moonachie, NJ 07074
Phone: 201-440-2600 Fax: —
CEO: Peter R. Harvey
CFO: Peter R. Harvey
1992 Sales: — Employees: 2
Symbol: VDR Exchange: AMEX
Industry: Retail - artificial flowers

Valassis Communications, Inc.
36111 Schoolcraft Rd.
Livonia, MI 48150
Phone: 313-591-3000 Fax: 313-591-4994
CEO: David A. Brandon
CFO: Robert L. Recchia
1992 Sales: $699 million Employees: 1,174
Symbol: VCI Exchange: NYSE
Industry: Business services

Valence Technology, Inc.
6781 Via Del Ora
San Jose, CA 95119
Phone: 408-365-6125 Fax: —
CEO: Lev M. Dawson
CFO: Christine A. Russell
1992 Sales: $3.8 million Employees: 54
Symbol: VLNC Exchange: NASDAQ
Industry: Engineering - R&D services

Valero Energy Corp.
530 McCullough Ave.
San Antonio, TX 78215
Phone: 210-246-2000 Fax: 210-246-2646
CEO: William E. Greehey
CFO: Edward C. Benninger
1992 Sales: $1,235 million Employees: 1,890
Symbol: VLO Exchange: NYSE
Industry: Oil & gas - production & pipeline

Valero Natural Gas Partners, L.P.
530 McCullough Ave.
San Antonio, TX 78215
Phone: 210-246-2000 Fax: 210-246-2103
CEO: William E. Greehey
CFO: Edward C. Benninger
1991 Sales: $1,144 million Employees: 1,892
Symbol: VLP Exchange: NYSE
Industry: Oil & gas - production & pipeline

Valhi, Inc.
5430 LBJ Fwy., Ste. 1700
Dallas, TX 75240
Phone: 214-233-1700 Fax: 214-385-0586
CEO: Harold C. Simmons
CFO: William C. Timm
1991 Sales: $766 million Employees: 8,050
Symbol: VHI Exchange: NYSE
Industry: Diversified operations - chemicals, refined sugar, forest products

Vallen Corp.
13333 Northwest Fwy.
Houston, TX 77040
Phone: 713-462-8700 Fax: 713-462-5145
CEO: J.M. Wayne Code
CFO: Don B. Hair
1992 Sales: $167 million Employees: 699
Symbol: VALN Exchange: NASDAQ
Industry: Protection - safety equipment & services

Valley Bancorp
100 W. Lawrence St., 2nd Fl.
Appleton, WI 54911
Phone: 414-738-3830 Fax: 414-738-5120
CEO: Peter M. Platten III
CFO: Gary A. Lichtenberg
1991 Sales: $380 million Employees: 2,530
Symbol: VYBN Exchange: NASDAQ
Industry: Banks - Midwest

Valley Forge Corp.
100 Smith Ranch Rd., Ste. 326
San Rafael, CA 94903
Phone: 415-492-1500 Fax: 415-492-0128
CEO: David R. Brining
CFO: Monica J. Burke
1991 Sales: $39 million Employees: 330
Symbol: VF Exchange: AMEX
Industry: Leisure & recreational products - marine products

Valley Industries, Inc.
900 Walnut St.
St. Louis, MO 63102
Phone: 314-231-2160 Fax: Ext. 269
CEO: Lester A. Crancer, Jr.
CFO: Patrick J. Gilligan
1990 Sales: $78 million Employees: 400
Symbol: VI Exchange: NYSE
Industry: Steel - pipes & tubes

indicates company is in *Hoover's Handbook of American Business.*

indicates company is in *Hoover's Handbook of World Business;* sales and employee numbers are for parent company.

Valley National Bancorp
505 Allwood Rd.
Clifton, NJ 07012
Phone: 201-305-8800 Fax: —
CEO: Gerald H. Lipkin
CFO: Gerald H. Lipkin
1991 Sales: $91 million Employees: 924
Symbol: VNBP Exchange: NASDAQ
Industry: Banks - Northeast

Valley National Corp.
241 N. Central Ave.
Phoenix, AZ 85004
Phone: 602-261-2900 Fax: Call co. operator
CEO: Richard J. Lehmann
CFO: Thomas P. Ducharme
1991 Sales: $1,132 million Employees: 7,172
Symbol: VNCP Exchange: NASDAQ
Industry: Banks - Southwest

Valley Resources, Inc.
1595 Mendon Rd.
Cumberland, RI 02864
Phone: 401-333-1595 Fax: 401-333-3527
CEO: Charles H. Goss
CFO: Kenneth W. Hogan
1991 Sales: $60 million Employees: 230
Symbol: VR Exchange: AMEX
Industry: Utility - gas distribution

Valley Systems, Inc.
11580 Lafayette Dr. NW
Canal Fulton, OH 44614
Phone: 216-854-4526 Fax: 216-854-3444
CEO: Eugene R. Valentine
CFO: Nicholas J. Pace
1991 Sales: $18 million Employees: 391
Symbol: VALE Exchange: NASDAQ
Industry: Building - maintenance & services

ValliCorp Holdings, Inc.
4995 E. Clinton Ave.
Fresno, CA 93727
Phone: 209-252-8711 Fax: —
CEO: J. Mike McGown
CFO: David E. Hooston
1991 Sales: $22 million Employees: 274
Symbol: VALY Exchange: NASDAQ
Industry: Banks - West

Valmont Industries, Inc.
W. Hwy. 275
Valley, NE 68064
Phone: 402-359-2201 Fax: 402-359-4025
CEO: William F. Welsh II
CFO: Gary L. Crouch
1991 Sales: $430 million Employees: 4,320
Symbol: VALM Exchange: NASDAQ
Industry: Diversified operations - microcomputer resale, industrial & irrigation products

Valspar Corp.
1101 Third St. South
Minneapolis, MN 55415
Phone: 612-332-7371 Fax: 612-375-7723
CEO: C. Angus Wurtele
CFO: Paul C. Reyelts
1992 Sales: $684 million Employees: 2,530
Symbol: VAL Exchange: AMEX
Industry: Paints & allied products

Value City Department Stores, Inc.
3241 Westerville Rd.
Columbus, OH 43224
Phone: 614-471-4722 Fax: 614-478-2253
CEO: Jay L. Schottenstein
CFO: Robert M. Wysinski
1992 Sales: $752 million Employees: 7,700
Symbol: VCD Exchange: NYSE
Industry: Retail - regional department stores

Value Health, Inc.
22 Waterville Rd.
Avon, CT 06001
Phone: 203-677-4101 Fax: 203-677-1752
CEO: Robert E. Patricelli
CFO: William J. McBride
1991 Sales: $155 million Employees: 533
Symbol: VH Exchange: NYSE
Industry: Health maintenance organization

Value Line, Inc.
711 Third Ave.
New York, NY 10017
Phone: 212-687-3965 Fax: 212-986-3243
CEO: Jean B. Buttner
CFO: Harold T. Read
1992 Sales: $75 million Employees: 343
Symbol: VALU Exchange: NASDAQ
Industry: Financial - investment management & newsletters

Value Merchants, Inc.
710 N. Plankinton Ave., Ste. 900
Milwaukee, WI 53203
Phone: 414-274-2575 Fax: 414-274-2717
CEO: Steven J. Appel
CFO: Ronald E. Skelton
1991 Sales: $235 million Employees: 4,100
Symbol: VMI Exchange: NYSE
Industry: Retail - close-out merchandise & toys

Value-Added Communications, Inc.
1901 S. Meyers Rd., Ste. 530
Oakbrook Terrace, IL 60181
Phone: 708-628-6606 Fax: —
CEO: Dennis R. Casey
CFO: John D. Henry
1991 Sales: $24 million Employees: 82
Symbol: VACI Exchange: NASDAQ
Industry: Telecommunications services

Van Dorn Co.
6000 Lombardo Center, Ste. 300
Cleveland, OH 44131
Phone: 216-447-8777 — Fax: 216-447-8778
CEO: William G. Pryor
CFO: Thomas R. Miklich
1991 Sales: $309 million — Employees: 1,834
Symbol: VDC — Exchange: NYSE
Industry: Containers - metal

Van G. Miller & Assoc.
525 W. 5th St.
Waterloo, IA 50704
Phone: 319-235-7100 — Fax: 319-235-9774
CEO: Vangie Miller
CFO: Tommy Fitzgerald
1991 Sales: $3.1 million — Employees: 13
Ownership: Privately held
Industry: Wholesale distribution - buying group for home medical equipment companies

Van Mar Inc.
122 Tices Ln.
East Brunswick, NJ 08816
Phone: 908-254-5197 — Fax: 908-254-6816
CEO: Marilyn Schulman
CFO: Dan Leff
1991 Sales: $27 million — Employees: 125
Ownership: Privately held
Industry: Apparel - women's intimate

Van Munching & Co. Inc.
1270 Avenue of the Americas, 10th Fl.
New York, NY 10020
Phone: 212-332-8500 — Fax: 212-332-8570
CEO: L. van Munching
CFO: —
1991 Sales: $4,411 million — Employees: 27,502
Parent: Heineken NV
Industry: Beverages - beer

Vanguard Automation, Inc
10900 N. Stallard Pl.
Tucson, AZ 85737
Phone: 602-297-2621 — Fax: 602-544-0535
CEO: Bill Orinski
CFO: Dewey Manzer
1991 Sales: $6.7 million — Employees: 96
Ownership: Privately held
Industry: Industrial automation & robotics - custom automated assembly systems

Vanguard Cellular Systems, Inc.
2002 Pisgah Church Rd., Ste. 300
Greensboro, NC 27408
Phone: 919-282-3690 — Fax: 919-545-2500
CEO: Haynes G. Griffin
CFO: Stephen L. Holcombe
1991 Sales: $69 million — Employees: 600
Symbol: VCELA — Exchange: NASDAQ
Industry: Telecommunications services

Vans, Inc.
2095 N. Batavia St.
Orange, CA 92665
Phone: 714-974-7414 — Fax: —
CEO: Richard P. Leeuwenburg
CFO: Daniel J. Conger
1992 Sales: $91 million — Employees: 2,252
Symbol: VANS — Exchange: NASDAQ
Industry: Shoes & related apparel

Vanzetti Systems, Inc.
111 Island St.
Stoughton, MA 02072
Phone: 617-828-4650 — Fax: 617-341-2084
CEO: John P. Ward
CFO: Ashod S. Dostoomian
1991 Sales: $1.2 million — Employees: 26
Symbol: VANZ — Exchange: NASDAQ
Industry: Electronics - measuring instruments

Varco International, Inc.
743 N. Eckhoff St.
Orange, CA 92668
Phone: 714-978-1900 — Fax: 714-937-5029
CEO: George Boyadjieff
CFO: Richard A. Kertson
1991 Sales: $216 million — Employees: 1,310
Symbol: VRC — Exchange: NYSE
Industry: Oil field machinery & equipment

Vari-Care, Inc.
277 Alexander St., Ste. 800
Rochester, NY 14607
Phone: 716-325-6940 — Fax: 716-325-4086
CEO: Robert H. Hurlbut
CFO: William F. Doud
1991 Sales: $52 million — Employees: 2,307
Symbol: VCRE — Exchange: NASDAQ
Industry: Nursing homes

Varian Associates, Inc.
3100 Hansen Way
Palo Alto, CA 94304
Phone: 415-493-4000 — Fax: 415-493-0307
CEO: J. Tracy O'Rourke
CFO: Robert A. Lemos
1992 Sales: $1,275 million — Employees: 9,300
Symbol: VAR — Exchange: NYSE
Industry: Instruments - scientific

Varitronic Systems, Inc.
300 S. Hwy. 169, Interchange Tower, Ste. 300
Minneapolis, MN 55426
Phone: 612-542-1500 — Fax: 612-541-1503
CEO: Scott F. Drill
CFO: Norbert F. Nicpon
1991 Sales: $39 million — Employees: 217
Symbol: VRSY — Exchange: NASDAQ
Industry: Office equipment & supplies

Varlen Corp.
305 E. Shuman Blvd., Ste. 500
Naperville, IL 60563
Phone: 708-420-0400 Fax: —
CEO: Richard L. Wellek
CFO: Richard A. Nunemaker
1991 Sales: $230 million Employees: 1,880
Symbol: VRLN Exchange: NASDAQ
Industry: Transportation - equipment & leasing

Vector Engineering, Inc.
12438 Loma Rica Dr., Ste. C
Grass Valley, CA 95945
Phone: 916-272-2448 Fax: 916-272-8533
CEO: Mark Smith
CFO: Peter Wolfe
1992 Sales: $2.6 million Employees: 40
Ownership: Privately held
Industry: Solid waste management consulting services

Vencor, Inc.
Brown & Williamson Tower, Ste. 700
Louisville, KY 40202
Phone: 502-569-7300 Fax: 502-569-7499
CEO: W. Bruce Lunsford
CFO: W. Earl Reed III
1991 Sales: $134 million Employees: 2,525
Symbol: VC Exchange: NYSE
Industry: Hospitals

Vendamerica Inc.
104 Field Point Rd.
Greenwich, CT 06830
Phone: 203-629-4676 Fax: 203-629-2273
CEO: Arnold Becker
CFO: —
1991 Sales: $9,649 million Employees: 87,100
Parent: Vendex International NV
Industry: Retail - supermarkets, department stores

Ventritex, Inc.
709 E. Evelyn Ave.
Sunnyvale, CA 94086
Phone: 408-738-4883 Fax: —
CEO: Frank M. Fischer
CFO: Frank E. Wiley
1992 Sales: $9.5 million Employees: 157
Symbol: VNTX Exchange: NASDAQ
Industry: Medical products

Ventura County National Bancorp
500 Esplanade Dr.
Oxnard, CA 93030
Phone: 805-981-2780 Fax: —
CEO: W. E. McAleer
CFO: R. Allen Urban
1991 Sales: $17 million Employees: 221
Symbol: VCNB Exchange: NASDAQ
Industry: Banks - West

Venture Stores, Inc.
2001 E. Terra Lane
O'Fallon, MO 63366
Phone: 314-281-5500 Fax: 314-281-5152
CEO: Julian M. Seeherman
CFO: John F. Burtelow
1992 Sales: $1,665 million Employees: 16,200
Symbol: VEN Exchange: NYSE
Industry: Retail - discount & variety

Venturian Corp.
1600 Second St. South
Hopkins, MN 55343
Phone: 612-931-2500 Fax: 612-931-2402
CEO: Gary B. Rappaport
CFO: Mary F. Jensen
1991 Sales: $25 million Employees: 115
Symbol: VENT Exchange: NASDAQ
Industry: Diversified operations - security, communications, engineering services

Veragon Corp.
1415 West Loop North
Houston, TX 77055
Phone: 713-682-6848 Fax: 713-682-3104
CEO: Terry Tognietti
CFO: Wally Klemp
1991 Sales: $34 million Employees: 110
Ownership: Privately held
Industry: Textiles - diapers

Vercon Construction, Inc.
37 Villa Rd., Ste. 210, B-143
Greenville, SC 29615
Phone: 803-235-5536 Fax: 803-233-6308
CEO: Robert R. Vergnolle
CFO: Robert R. Vergnolle
1991 Sales: $32 million Employees: 55
Ownership: Privately held
Industry: Construction - general contracting services

Verdix Corp.
205 Van Buren St.
Herndon, VA 22070
Phone: 703-318-5800 Fax: 703-318-9304
CEO: Ralph E. Alexander
CFO: Richard H. Diely
1992 Sales: $19 million Employees: 118
Symbol: VRDX Exchange: NASDAQ
Industry: Computers - software development products, trouble-shooting services

VeriFone, Inc.
Three Lagoon Dr., Ste. 400
Redwood City, CA 90465
Phone: 415-591-6500 Fax: 415-598-5504
CEO: Hatim Tyabji
CFO: Thomas W. Hubbs
1991 Sales: $188 million Employees: —
Symbol: VFIC Exchange: NASDAQ
Industry: Telecommunications equipment

Vermont Financial Services Corp.
100 Main St.
Brattleboro, VT 05301
Phone: 802-257-7151 Fax: —
CEO: John D. Hashagen, Jr.
CFO: Richard O. Madden
1991 Sales: $95 million Employees: 623
Symbol: VFSC Exchange: NASDAQ
Industry: Banks - Northeast

Vermont Research Corp.
Precision Park
North Springfield, VT 05150
Phone: 802-886-2256 Fax: 802-886-2682
CEO: Edward D. Winkler, Jr.
CFO: Edward D. Winkler, Jr.
1991 Sales: $3.4 million Employees: 42
Symbol: VRE Exchange: AMEX
Industry: Computers - magnetic & semiconductor memories

Vermont Teddy Bear Co.
2031 Shelburne
Shelburne, VT 05482
Phone: 802-985-3001 Fax: 802-985-8899
CEO: John Sortino
CFO: Spencer Putnam
1992 Sales: $10.4 million Employees: 350
Ownership: Privately held
Industry: Toys - teddy bears

Versa Technologies, Inc.
9301 Washington Ave.
Sturtevant, WI 53177
Phone: 414-886-1174 Fax: 414-886-4614
CEO: James E. Mohrhauser
CFO: Donald W. Peterson
1992 Sales: $49 million Employees: 507
Symbol: VRSA Exchange: NASDAQ
Industry: Rubber & plastic products

Versar, Inc.
6850 Versar Center Dr.
Springfield, VA 22151
Phone: 703-750-3000 Fax: 703-642-6807
CEO: Benjamin M. Rawls
CFO: John J. Rorke
1991 Sales: $58 million Employees: 650
Symbol: VSR Exchange: AMEX
Industry: Pollution control equipment & services - scientific & technical environmental services

Vertex Communications Corp.
2600 N. Longview St.
Kilgore, TX 75662
Phone: 903-984-0555 Fax: 903-984-1826
CEO: J. Rex Vardeman
CFO: James D. Carter
1992 Sales: $49 million Employees: 460
Symbol: VTEX Exchange: NASDAQ
Industry: Telecommunications equipment

Vertex Pharmaceuticals, Inc.
40 Allston St.
Cambridge, MA 02139
Phone: 617-576-3111 Fax: 617-576-2109
CEO: Benno C. Schmidt
CFO: Keith S. Ehrlich
1991 Sales: $3.2 million Employees: 69
Symbol: VRTX Exchange: NASDAQ
Industry: Drugs

Vestar, Inc.
650 Cliffside Dr.
San Dimas, CA 91773
Phone: 909-394-4000 Fax: 909-592-8530
CEO: Roger J. Crossley
CFO: Michael E. Hart
1991 Sales: $15 million Employees: 80
Symbol: VSTR Exchange: NASDAQ
Industry: Drugs

Vestaur Securities, Inc.
Centre Square West, 11th Fl.
Philadelphia, PA 19101
Phone: 215-567-3969 Fax: —
CEO: Stuart T. Saunders, Jr.
CFO: Charles T. Harrison
1992 Sales: — Employees: —
Symbol: VES Exchange: NYSE
Industry: Financial - investment management

Veterinary Centers of America, Inc.
1725 Cloverfield Ave.
Santa Monica, CA 90404
Phone: 310-829-7533 Fax: 310-829-2087
CEO: Robert L. Antin
CFO: Tomas W. Fuller
1991 Sales: $15 million Employees: 257
Symbol: VCAI Exchange: NASDAQ
Industry: Veterinary products & services

Viacom Inc.
1515 Broadway
New York, NY 10036
Phone: 212-258-6000 Fax: 212-258-6597
CEO: Frank J. Biondi, Jr.
CFO: George S. Smith, Jr.
1992 Sales: $1,865 million Employees: 4,900
Symbol: VIA Exchange: NYSE
Industry: Cable TV, radio broadcasting & TV entertainment

Vicon Industries, Inc.
525 Broadhollow Rd.
Melville, NY 11747
Phone: 516-293-2200 Fax: 516-293-2627
CEO: Donald N. Horn
CFO: Henry E. Zorn
1991 Sales: $42 million Employees: 214
Symbol: VII Exchange: AMEX
Industry: Video equipment

Vicor Corp.
23 Frontage Rd.
Andover, MA 01810
Phone: 508-470-2900 Fax: 508-475-6715
CEO: Patrizio Vinciarelli
CFO: Thomas A. St. Germain
1991 Sales: $56 million Employees: 507
Symbol: VICR Exchange: NASDAQ
Industry: Electrical components - modular power converters

VICORP Restaurants, Inc.
400 W. 48th Ave.
Denver, CO 80216
Phone: 303-296-2121 Fax: 303-297-8637
CEO: Charles R. Frederickson
CFO: Dennis L. Kuper
1991 Sales: $422 million Employees: 14,300
Symbol: VRES Exchange: NASDAQ
Industry: Retail - food & restaurants

Victoria Bankshares, Inc.
One O'Connor Plaza
Victoria, TX 77902
Phone: 512-573-9432 Fax: —
CEO: Charles R. Hrdlicka
CFO: Edwin W. Dentler
1991 Sales: $127 million Employees: 831
Symbol: VICT Exchange: NASDAQ
Industry: Banks - Southwest

Victoria Creations, Inc.
30 Jefferson Park Rd.
Warwick, RI 02888
Phone: 401-467-7150 Fax: 401-467-7180
CEO: Paul B. Markovits
CFO: Norman H. Werthwein
1992 Sales: $40 million Employees: 615
Symbol: VITC Exchange: NASDAQ
Industry: Precious metals & jewelry

Video Display Corp.
1868 Tucker Industrial Dr.
Tucker, GA 30084
Phone: 404-938-2080 Fax: 404-493-3903
CEO: Ronald Ordway
CFO: Edward B. Cordell, Jr.
1992 Sales: $54 million Employees: 449
Symbol: VIDE Exchange: NASDAQ
Industry: Video equipment - cathode ray tubes, computer monitors

Video Lottery Technologies, Inc.
2311 South 7th Ave.
Bozeman, MT 59715
Phone: 406-586-4423 Fax: 406-585-6609
CEO: Larry Lipton
CFO: Michael L. Eide
1991 Sales: $32 million Employees: 183
Symbol: VLTS Exchange: NASDAQ
Industry: Leisure & recreational products - video lottery terminals

VideOcart, Inc.
564 W. Randolph St.
Chicago, IL 60606
Phone: 312-466-5000 Fax: —
CEO: Ronald E. Spears
CFO: David E. Riggs
1991 Sales: $3.8 million Employees: 303
Symbol: VCRT Exchange: NASDAQ
Industry: Business services - advertising & promotion

VideoTelecom Corp.
1901 W. Braker Lane
Austin, TX 78758
Phone: 512-834-2700 Fax: —
CEO: F. H. Moeller
CFO: Rodney S. Bond
1991 Sales: $11 million Employees: 101
Symbol: VTEL Exchange: NASDAQ
Industry: Telecommunications equipment

Vie de France Corp.
8201 Greensboro Dr., Ste. 1224
McLean, VA 22102
Phone: 703-442-9205 Fax: 703-790-1158
CEO: Jean-Louis Vilgrain
CFO: Thomas J. Rowe
1992 Sales: $36 million Employees: 1,000
Symbol: VDEF Exchange: NASDAQ
Industry: Food - baked goods

ViewLogic Systems, Inc.
293 Boston Post Rd. West
Marlborough, MA 01752
Phone: 508-480-0881 Fax: 508-480-0882
CEO: Alain J. Hanover
CFO: Ronald R. Benanto
1991 Sales: $42 million Employees: 271
Symbol: VIEW Exchange: NASDAQ
Industry: Computers - engineering software

Vigoro Corp.
225 N. Michigan Ave.
Chicago, IL 60601
Phone: 312-819-2020 Fax: 312-819-2027
CEO: Joseph P. Sullivan
CFO: Jay D. Proops
1992 Sales: $594 million Employees: 1,500
Symbol: VGR Exchange: NYSE
Industry: Chemicals - specialty

Viking Office Products, Inc.
13809 S. Figueroa St.
Los Angeles, CA 90061
Phone: 213-321-4493 Fax: 310-327-2376
CEO: Irwin Helford
CFO: H. B. Richman
1992 Sales: $320 million Employees: 1,067
Symbol: VKNG Exchange: NASDAQ
Industry: Retail - mail order & direct office products

Vikonics, Inc.
210 Meadowland Pkwy.
Secaucus, NJ 07094
Phone: 201-863-6868 Fax: 201-863-0413
CEO: John L. Kaufman
CFO: John L. Strong
1992 Sales: $5 million Employees: 42
Symbol: VKSI Exchange: NASDAQ
Industry: Protection - safety equipment & services

Village Financial Services, Ltd.
One Gateway Plaza
Port Chester, NY 10573
Phone: 914-939-7200 Fax: 914-939-7332
CEO: Edmund C. Grainger, Jr.
CFO: William R. Noble
1991 Sales: $62 million Employees: 139
Symbol: VIFS Exchange: NASDAQ
Industry: Banks - Northeast

Village Supermarket, Inc.
733 Mountain Ave.
Springfield, NJ 07081
Phone: 201-467-2200 Fax: 201-467-6582
CEO: Perry Sumas
CFO: James Sumas
1992 Sales: $721 million Employees: 3,950
Symbol: VLGEA Exchange: NASDAQ
Industry: Retail - supermarkets

Vintage Petroleum, Inc.
One Williams Center, Ste. 4200
Tulsa, OK 74172
Phone: 918-592-0101 Fax: 918-584-7282
CEO: Charles C. Stephenson, Jr.
CFO: William C. Barnes
1991 Sales: $70 million Employees: 190
Symbol: VPI Exchange: NYSE
Industry: Oil & gas - US exploration & production

Viratek, Inc.
3300 Hyland Ave.
Costa Mesa, CA 92626
Phone: 714-545-0100 Fax: 714-556-0131
CEO: Milan Panic
CFO: John E. Giordani
1991 Sales: $4.5 million Employees: 3
Symbol: VIRA Exchange: AMEX
Industry: Drugs

Virco Manufacturing Corp.
15134 S. Vermont Ave.
Gardena, CA 90247
Phone: 310-532-3570 Fax: 310-538-0114
CEO: Robert A. Virtue
CFO: James R. Braam
1991 Sales: $187 million Employees: 2,900
Symbol: VIR Exchange: AMEX
Industry: Furniture

Virgin Atlantic
96 Morton St.
New York, NY 10014
Phone: 212-206-6612 Fax: 212-627-1494
CEO: David Tait
CFO: —
1991 Sales: $1,988 million Employees: 7,450
Parent: Virgin Group PLC
Industry: Diversified operations - airline, retail music & publishing, film

Virginia Beach Federal Financial Corp.
210 25th St.
Virginia Beach, VA 23451
Phone: 804-428-9331 Fax: —
CEO: Timothy F. Miller
CFO: Dennis R. Stewart
1991 Sales: $77 million Employees: 166
Symbol: VABF Exchange: NASDAQ
Industry: Financial - savings and loans

Virginia First Savings, F.S.B.
Franklin and Adams Streets
Petersburg, VA 23804
Phone: 804-733-0333 Fax: —
CEO: William A. Patton
CFO: Stephen R. Kinnier
1992 Sales: — Employees: —
Symbol: VFSB Exchange: NASDAQ
Industry: Financial - savings and loans

ViroGroup, Inc.
428 Pine Island Rd. SW
Cape Coral, FL 33991
Phone: 813-574-1919 Fax: —
CEO: Robert A. Fletcher
CFO: Richard L. Holzinger
1991 Sales: $10.8 million Employees: 118
Symbol: VIRO Exchange: NASDAQ
Industry: Pollution control equipment & services

Virology Testing Services, Inc.
36 Holly Dr.
Newington, CT 06111
Phone: 203-666-5666 Fax: 203-667-3609
CEO: William D. Putt
CFO: William D. Putt
1991 Sales: $7.9 million Employees: 28
Symbol: VTS Exchange: AMEX
Industry: Telecommunications equipment

Vishay Intertechnology, Inc.
63 Lincoln Hwy.
Malvern, PA 19355
Phone: 215-644-1300 Fax: 215-296-0657
CEO: Felix Zandman
CFO: Robert A. Freece
1991 Sales: $442 million Employees: 8,700
Symbol: VSH Exchange: NYSE
Industry: Electronics - measuring instruments

 indicates company is in *Hoover's Handbook of American Business.*

indicates company is in *Hoover's Handbook of World Business;* sales and employee numbers are for parent company.

Vista Resources, Inc.
1201 W. Peachtree St. NW, Ste. 5000
Atlanta, GA 30309
Phone: 404-815-2000 Fax: —
CEO: Samuel W. Norwood III
CFO: Carl J. Simon
1991 Sales: $75 million Employees: 510
Symbol: VS Exchange: NYSE
Industry: Leather & related products

Visual Concepts
35 Griffin Rd. South
Bloomfield, CT 06002
Phone: 203-242-1150 Fax: 203-242-1446
CEO: Steve Shaw
CFO: Steve Shaw
1991 Sales: $0.8 million Employees: 6
Ownership: Privately held
Industry: Business services - corporate video production

VISX, Inc.
1150 Kifer Rd., Ste. 202
Sunnyvale, CA 94086
Phone: 408-732-9880 Fax: —
CEO: Charles R. Munnerlyn
CFO: Alan R. McMillen
1991 Sales: $13 million Employees: 64
Symbol: VSX Exchange: AMEX
Industry: Lasers - systems & components

Vital Signs, Inc.
20 Campus Rd.
Totowa, NJ 07512
Phone: 201-790-1330 Fax: 201-790-3307
CEO: Terence D. Wall
CFO: Anthony J. Dimun
1991 Sales: $47 million Employees: 480
Symbol: VITL Exchange: NASDAQ
Industry: Medical products - anesthesia & respiratory products

Vitalink Pharmacy Services, Inc.
1250 E. Diehl Rd.
Naperville, IL 60563
Phone: 708-505-1320 Fax: —
CEO: Stewart Bainum, Jr.
CFO: S. T. Macomber
1992 Sales: $40 million Employees: 300
Symbol: VTLK Exchange: NASDAQ
Industry: Medical services

Vitesse Semiconductor Corp.
741 Calle Plano
Camarillo, CA 93012
Phone: 805-388-3700 Fax: 805-987-5896
CEO: Louis R. Tomasetta
CFO: Raymond V. Thomas
1991 Sales: $24 million Employees: 252
Symbol: VTSS Exchange: NASDAQ
Industry: Electrical components - semiconductors

Vitronics Corp.
Forbes Rd.
Newmarket, NH 03857
Phone: 603-659-6550 Fax: 603-659-7194
CEO: James J. Mansfield, Jr.
CFO: James J. Mansfield, Jr.
1991 Sales: $14 million Employees: 109
Symbol: VTC Exchange: AMEX
Industry: Machinery - electrical

Vivigen, Inc.
2000 Vivigen Way
Santa Fe, NM 87505
Phone: 505-438-1111 Fax: 505-438-1120
CEO: John H. Pietrie, Jr.
CFO: Annette L. Newton
1991 Sales: $12 million Employees: 145
Symbol: VIV Exchange: AMEX
Industry: Medical services - genetic testing

Vivra Inc.
517 Washington St.
San Francisco, CA 94111
Phone: 415-397-6151 Fax: 415-397-0136
CEO: Robert L. Green
CFO: William H. Malkmus
1991 Sales: $139 million Employees: 1,723
Symbol: V Exchange: NYSE
Industry: Healthcare - outpatient & home

VLSI Technology, Inc.
1109 McKay Dr.
San Jose, CA 95131
Phone: 408-434-3000 Fax: 408-263-2511
CEO: Alfred J. Stein
CFO: Larry R. Carter
1991 Sales: $413 million Employees: 2,315
Symbol: VLSI Exchange: NASDAQ
Industry: Electrical components - semiconductors

VMARK Software, Inc.
30 Speen St.
Natick, MA 01701
Phone: 508-879-3311 Fax: —
CEO: James J. Capeless
CFO: James J. Capeless
1991 Sales: $12 million Employees: 91
Symbol: VMRK Exchange: NASDAQ
Industry: Computers - software

VMX, Inc.
2115 O'Neil Dr.
San Jose, CA 95131
Phone: 408-441-1144 Fax: 408-441-7026
CEO: Patrick S. Howard
CFO: Bruce C. Pollock
1992 Sales: $71 million Employees: 465
Symbol: VMXI Exchange: NASDAQ
Industry: Telecommunications equipment

Volkswagen of America, Inc.
888 W. Big Beaver Rd.
Troy, MI 48007
Phone: 313-362-6000 Fax: 313-362-6047
CEO: William J. Young
CFO: —
1991 Sales: $50,207 million Employees: 267,009
Parent: Volkswagen AG
Industry: Automotive manufacturing

Volt Information Sciences, Inc.
101 Park Ave., 38th Fl.
New York, NY 10178
Phone: 212-309-0200 Fax: 212-309-0317
CEO: William Shaw
CFO: James J. Groberg
1991 Sales: $466 million Employees: 15,200
Symbol: VOLT Exchange: NASDAQ
Industry: Diversified operations - personnel services, telecommunications

Volunteer Capital Corp.
3401 West End Ave.
Nashville, TN 37203
Phone: 615-269-1900 Fax: 615-269-1999
CEO: Lonnie J. Stout II
CFO: R. Gregory Lewis
1991 Sales: $42 million Employees: 1,650
Symbol: VCC Exchange: NYSE
Industry: Retail - food & restaurants

Volvo North America Corporation
535 Madison Ave.
New York, NY 10022
Phone: 212-754-3300 Fax: 212-418-7435
CEO: Albert R. Dowden
CFO: —
1991 Sales: $13,902 million Employees: 63,582
Parent: AB Volvo
Industry: Automobile manufacturing - wholesale

Vons Companies, Inc., The
618 Michillinda Ave.
Arcadia, CA 91007
Phone: 818-821-7000 Fax: 818-821-7933
CEO: Roger E. Stangeland
CFO: Michael F. Henn
1992 Sales: $5,596 million Employees: 32,900
Symbol: VON Exchange: NYSE
Industry: Retail - supermarkets & drug stores

VOPLEX Corp.
1455 Imlay City Rd.
Lapeer, MI 48446
Phone: 313-664-4524 Fax: 313-664-7841
CEO: Joseph W. Bauer
CFO: Walter T. Knollenberg
1990 Sales: $56 million Employees: 764
Symbol: QVOT Exchange: AMEX
Industry: Automotive & trucking - original equipment

Vornado, Inc.
Park 80 West, Plaza II
Saddle Brook, NJ 07662
Phone: 201-587-1000 Fax: 201-587-0600
CEO: Steven Roth
CFO: Joseph Macnow
1991 Sales: $61 million Employees: 50
Symbol: VNO Exchange: NYSE
Industry: Real estate operations

VSB Bancorp, Inc.
15 Ver Valen St.
Closter, NJ 07624
Phone: 201-768-4600 Fax: —
CEO: John A. Ruckstuhl
CFO: Robert W. Collins
1991 Sales: $30 million Employees: 84
Symbol: VSBC Exchange: NASDAQ
Industry: Banks - Northeast

VSE Corp.
2550 Huntington Ave.
Alexandria, VA 22303
Phone: 703-960-4600 Fax: 703-960-2688
CEO: John B. Toomey
CFO: Craig S. Weber
1991 Sales: $68 million Employees: 1,325
Symbol: VSEC Exchange: NASDAQ
Industry: Engineering - R&D services

VT Inc.
8500 Shawnee Mission Pkwy., Ste. 200
Merriam, KS 66202
Phone: 913-432-6400 Fax: 913-789-1039
CEO: Cecil Van Tuyl
CFO: John A. Morford
1992 Sales: $1,088 million Employees: 2,500
Ownership: Privately held
Industry: Retail - auto, aircraft & boat dealerships

VTX Electronics Corp.
61 Executive Blvd.
Farmingdale, NY 11735
Phone: 516-293-9880 Fax: —
CEO: Elliot Levine
CFO: Walter Markowitz
1991 Sales: $47 million Employees: 217
Symbol: VTX Exchange: AMEX
Industry: Wire & cable products

Vulcan International Corp.
Six E. Fourth St.
Cincinnati, OH 45202
Phone: 513-621-2850 Fax: 513-241-8199
CEO: Benjamin Gettler
CFO: Wallace H. Pearson
1991 Sales: $21 million Employees: 391
Symbol: VUL Exchange: AMEX
Industry: Shoes & related apparel

indicates company is in *Hoover's Handbook of American Business.*

indicates company is in *Hoover's Handbook of World Business;* sales and employee numbers are for parent company.

Vulcan Materials Co.
One Metroplex Dr.
Birmingham, AL 35209
Phone: 205-877-3000 Fax: 205-877-3094
CEO: Herbert A. Sklenar
CFO: Peter J. Clemens III
1992 Sales: $1,078 million Employees: 6,404
Symbol: VMC Exchange: NYSE
Industry: Construction - cement & concrete

VWR Corp.
1400 N. Providence Rd.
Media, PA 19063
Phone: 215-891-2770 Fax: 215-565-9058
CEO: Jerrold B. Harris
CFO: Walter S. Sobon
1991 Sales: $441 million Employees: 1,130
Symbol: VWRX Exchange: NASDAQ
Industry: Instruments - scientific

W. H. Brady Co.
727 W. Glendale Ave.
Milwaukee, WI 53201
Phone: 414-332-8100 Fax: 414-332-2887
CEO: Paul G. Gengler
CFO: Donald P. DeLuca
1991 Sales: $211 million Employees: 1,974
Symbol: BRCOA Exchange: NASDAQ
Industry: Office & art materials

W. R. Berkley Corp.
165 Mason St.
Greenwich, CT 06830
Phone: 203-629-2880 Fax: 203-629-3492
CEO: William R. Berkley
CFO: John D. Vollaro
1991 Sales: $541 million Employees: —
Symbol: BKLY Exchange: NASDAQ
Industry: Insurance - property & casualty

W. R. Grace & Co.
One Town Center Rd.
Boca Raton, FL 33486
Phone: 407-362-2000 Fax: 407-362-2193
CEO: J. Peter Grace
CFO: Brian J. Smith
1992 Sales: $5,518 million Employees: 46,560
Symbol: GRA Exchange: NYSE
Industry: Chemicals - diversified, healthcare, specialty businesses

W. W. Grainger, Inc.
5500 W. Howard St.
Skokie, IL 60077
Phone: 708-982-9000 Fax: Ext. 309
CEO: David W. Grainger
CFO: Donald E. Bielinski
1992 Sales: $2,364 million Employees: 8,778
Symbol: GWW Exchange: NYSE
Industry: Machinery - electrical

W. W. Williams Co.
835 W. Goodale Blvd.
Columbus, OH 43212
Phone: 614-228-5000 Fax: 614-228-4490
CEO: David F. Williams
CFO: William S. Williams
1991 Sales: $80 million Employees: 740
Symbol: WWWM Exchange: NASDAQ
Industry: Machinery - general industrial

Waban, Inc.
One Mercer Rd.
Natick, MA 01760
Phone: 508-651-6500 Fax: 508-651-6623
CEO: John F. Levy
CFO: Edward J. Weisberger
1992 Sales: $3,157 million Employees: 15,000
Symbol: WBN Exchange: NYSE
Industry: Retail - home furnishings

Wabash National Corp.
1000 Sagamore Pkwy. South
Lafayette, IN 47905
Phone: 317-448-1591 Fax: 317-447-9405
CEO: Donald J. Ehrlich
CFO: Ronald J. Klimara
1991 Sales: $190 million Employees: 1,124
Symbol: WNC Exchange: NYSE
Industry: Automotive & trucking - original equipment

Wachovia Corp.
301 N. Main St.
Winston-Salem, NC 27101
Phone: 919-770-5000 Fax: 919-770-5959
CEO: John G. Medlin, Jr.
CFO: Anthony L. Furr
1992 Sales: $2,778 million Employees: 17,643
Symbol: WB Exchange: NYSE
Industry: Banks - Southeast

Wackenhut Corp.
1500 San Remo Ave.
Coral Gables, FL 33146
Phone: 305-666-5656 Fax: 305-662-7336
CEO: George R. Wackenhut
CFO: Michael D. DiGregorio
1992 Sales: $630 million Employees: 42,000
Symbol: WAK Exchange: NYSE
Industry: Protection - safety equipment & services

Wahlco Environmental Systems, Inc.
3600 W. Segerstrom Ave.
Santa Ana, CA 92704
Phone: 714-979-7300 Fax: 714-641-9014
CEO: Henry N. Huta
CFO: Charles F. Wilson
1991 Sales: $89 million Employees: 787
Symbol: WAL Exchange: NYSE
Industry: Pollution control equipment & services - process systems

Wainoco Oil Corp.
1200 Smith St., Ste. 1500
Houston, TX 77002
Phone: 713-658-9900 Fax: 713-658-8136
CEO: John B. Ashmun
CFO: Julie H. Edwards
1991 Sales: $122 million Employees: 428
Symbol: WOL Exchange: NYSE
Industry: Oil & gas - US exploration & production

Wainwright Bank & Trust Co.
101 Summer St.
Boston, MA 02110
Phone: 617-542-4451 Fax: —
CEO: Thomas S. Zocco
CFO: Robert L. Chestnut
1992 Sales: — Employees: —
Symbol: WAIN Exchange: NASDAQ
Industry: Banks - Northeast

Wal-Mart Stores, Inc.
702 SW 8th St.
Bentonville, AR 72716
Phone: 501-273-4000 Fax: 501-273-8650
CEO: David D. Glass
CFO: Paul R. Carter
1992 Sales: $52,001 million Employees: 371,000
Symbol: WMT Exchange: NYSE
Industry: Retail - discount & variety

Walbridge, Aldinger Co.
613 Abbott St.
Detroit, MI 48226
Phone: 313-963-8000 Fax: 313-963-8150
CEO: John Rakolta, Jr.
CFO: Keith Penner
1991 Sales: $550 million Employees: 612
Ownership: Privately held
Industry: Construction - general contracting & program management

Walbro Corp.
6242 Garfield St.
Cass City, MI 48726
Phone: 517-872-2131 Fax: 517-872-3090
CEO: Lambert E. Althaver
CFO: Gary L. Vollmar
1991 Sales: $200 million Employees: 2,300
Symbol: WALB Exchange: NASDAQ
Industry: Electrical components - fuel delivery systems, lawn & garden equipment

Walgreen Co.
200 Wilmot Rd.
Deerfield, IL 60015
Phone: 708-940-2500 Fax: 708-940-2804
CEO: Charles R. Walgreen III
CFO: Charles D. Hunter
1992 Sales: $7,681 million Employees: 51,000
Symbol: WAG Exchange: NYSE
Industry: Retail - drug stores

Walker Interactive Systems, Inc.
303 Second St.
San Francisco, CA 94107
Phone: 415-495-8811 Fax: —
CEO: David W. Brownlee
CFO: Joseph G. Girata
1991 Sales: $45 million Employees: 367
Symbol: WALK Exchange: NASDAQ
Industry: Computers - software

Walker Power, Inc.
Mill St.
Warner, NH 03278
Phone: 603-456-3111 Fax: 603-456-2498
CEO: Michael H. Foster
CFO: Dennis M. Deegan
1991 Sales: $10.6 million Employees: 131
Symbol: WPIC Exchange: NASDAQ
Industry: Machinery - general industrial

Walklett Burns, Ltd
5 Great Valley Pkwy.
Malvern, PA 19355
Phone: 215-648-3846 Fax: 215-644-7048
CEO: Thomas Walklett
CFO: Charles Burns
1991 Sales: $2.1 million Employees: 30
Ownership: Privately held
Industry: Computers - systems integration services

Wallace Computer Services, Inc.
4600 Roosevelt Rd.
Hillside, IL 60162
Phone: 708-449-8600 Fax: 708-449-1161
CEO: Theodore Dimitriou
CFO: Michael J. Halloran
1992 Sales: $512 million Employees: 3,386
Symbol: WCS Exchange: NYSE
Industry: Paper - business forms

Walshire Assurance Co.
3350 Whiteford Rd.
York, PA 17402
Phone: 717-757-0000 Fax: —
CEO: Kenneth R. Taylor
CFO: Gary J. Orndorff
1991 Sales: $19 million Employees: 70
Symbol: WALS Exchange: NASDAQ
Industry: Insurance - property & casualty

Walt Disney Co., The
500 S. Buena Vista St.
Burbank, CA 91521
Phone: 818-560-1000 Fax: 818-560-1930
CEO: Michael D. Eisner
CFO: Richard D. Nanula
1992 Sales: $7,979 million Employees: 58,000
Symbol: DIS Exchange: NYSE
Industry: Leisure & recreational products - theme parks & resorts, filmed entertainment

indicates company is in *Hoover's Handbook of American Business.*
indicates company is in *Hoover's Handbook of World Business;* sales and employee numbers are for parent company.

Walter Industries Inc.
1500 N. Dale Mabry Hwy.
Tampa, FL 33607
Phone: 813-871-4811 Fax: 813-871-4430
CEO: G. Robert Durham
CFO: Kenneth J. Matlock
1991 Sales: $1,367 million Employees: 8,100
Ownership: Privately held
Industry: Diversified operations - home building & financing, natural resources & industrial manufacturing

Walton Monroe Mills
PO Box 1046
Monroe, GA 30655
Phone: 404-267-9411 Fax: 404-267-5196
CEO: G. Stephen Felker
CFO: Jack Altherr
1991 Sales: $530 million Employees: 4,200
Ownership: Privately held
Industry: Textiles - mill products

Wang Laboratories, Inc.
One Industrial Ave.
Lowell, MA 01851
Phone: 508-459-5000 Fax: 508-458-8969
CEO: Joseph M. Tucci
CFO: Michael F. Mee
1992 Sales: $1,646 million Employees: 16,792
Symbol: WANB Exchange: AMEX
Industry: Computers - mini & micro

Ward Petroleum Corporation
502 S. Fillmore
Enid, OK 73701
Phone: 405-234-3229 Fax: 405-242-6850
CEO: L.O. Ward
CFO: Richard R. Tozzi
1991 Sales: $147 million Employees: 79
Ownership: Privately held
Industry: Oil & gas - US integrated

Warehouse Club, Inc.
7235 N. Linder Ave.
Skokie, IL 60077
Phone: 708-679-6800 Fax: 708-679-0001
CEO: James V. Walsh
CFO: James V. Walsh
1991 Sales: $250 million Employees: 1,000
Symbol: WCLB Exchange: NASDAQ
Industry: Retail - warehouse store clubs

Warnaco, Inc.
90 Park Ave.
New York, NY 10016
Phone: 212-661-1300 Fax: 212-370-0832
CEO: Linda J. Wachner
CFO: Dariush Ashrafi
1992 Sales: $625 million Employees: 11,500
Symbol: WAC Exchange: NYSE
Industry: Apparel - women's undergarments

Warner Insurance Services, Inc.
17-01 Pollitt Dr.
Fair Lawn, NJ 07410
Phone: 201-794-4800 Fax: —
CEO: Harvey Krieger
CFO: Bradley J. Hughes
1991 Sales: $55 million Employees: 458
Symbol: WCP Exchange: NYSE
Industry: Business services - insurance advisory services

Warner-Lambert Co.
201 Tabor Rd.
Morris Plains, NJ 07950
Phone: 201-540-2000 Fax: 201-540-3761
CEO: Melvin R. Goodes
CFO: Robert J. Dircks
1992 Sales: $5,598 million Employees: 34,000
Symbol: WLA Exchange: NYSE
Industry: Drugs, consumer & healthcare products, confectionery

Warrantech Corp.
300 Atlantic St.
Stamford, CT 06901
Phone: 203-975-1100 Fax: —
CEO: Joel San Antonio
CFO: Joel San Antonio
1992 Sales: $52 million Employees: 150
Symbol: WTEC Exchange: NASDAQ
Industry: Financial - extended warranty services

Warren Bancorp, Inc.
10 Main St.
Peabody, MA 01960
Phone: 508-531-7400 Fax: —
CEO: Stephen F. O'Sullivan
CFO: Paul M. Peduto
1991 Sales: $45 million Employees: 213
Symbol: WRNB Exchange: NASDAQ
Industry: Banks - Northeast

Warren Equities Inc.
10 East 53rd St., 20th Fl.
New York, NY 10022
Phone: 212-751-8100 Fax: 212-758-1798
CEO: Warren Alpert
CFO: John Dziedzic
1991 Sales: $600 million Employees: 1,600
Ownership: Privately held
Industry: Oil refining & marketing, convenience stores, wholesale consumer products

Washington Bancorp, Inc.
101 Washington St.
Hoboken, NJ 07030
Phone: 201-659-0013 Fax: —
CEO: Paul C. Rotondi
CFO: Thomas S. Bingham
1991 Sales: $30 million Employees: 115
Symbol: WBNC Exchange: NASDAQ
Industry: Banks - Northeast

Washington Corporations
PO Box 8182
Missoula, MT 59807
Phone: 406-523-1300 Fax: 406-721-4794
CEO: Dorn Parkinson
CFO: Mike Haight
1991 Sales: $463 million Employees: 3,660
Ownership: Privately held
Industry: Diversified operations - construction, mining & public utilities

Washington Energy Co.
815 Mercer St.
Seattle, WA 98109
Phone: 206-622-6767 Fax: —
CEO: James A. Thorpe
CFO: James P. Torgerson
1991 Sales: $396 million Employees: 1,547
Symbol: WEG Exchange: NASDAQ
Industry: Utility - gas distribution

Washington Federal Savings and Loan Association
425 Pike St.
Seattle, WA 98101
Phone: 206-624-7930 Fax: —
CEO: Elliot K. Knutson
CFO: Guy C. Pinkerton
1991 Sales: $283 million Employees: 414
Symbol: WFSL Exchange: NASDAQ
Industry: Financial - savings and loans

Washington Federal Savings Bank
5101 Wisconsin Ave. NW
Washington, DC 20016
Phone: 202-537-8200 Fax: 206-624-2334
CEO: Carroll E. Amos
CFO: Carroll E. Amos
1990 Sales: $40 million Employees: 198
Symbol: WFSB Exchange: NASDAQ
Industry: Financial - savings and loans

Washington Gas Light Co.
1100 H St. NW
Washington, DC 20080
Phone: 703-750-4440 Fax: 202-624-6277
CEO: Donald J. Heim
CFO: Edmund W. Smallwood
1991 Sales: $698 million Employees: 3,101
Symbol: WGL Exchange: NYSE
Industry: Utility - gas distribution

Washington Mutual Savings Bank
1201 Third Ave.
Seattle, WA 98101
Phone: 206-461-2000 Fax: —
CEO: Kerry K. Killinger
CFO: Willaim A. Longbrake
1991 Sales: $205 million Employees: 2,356
Symbol: WAMU Exchange: NASDAQ
Industry: Financial - savings and loans

Washington National Corp.
1630 Chicago Ave.
Evanston, IL 60201
Phone: 708-570-3208 Fax: 708-570-5566
CEO: Robert W. Patin
CFO: Thomas C. Scott
1991 Sales: $571 million Employees: —
Symbol: WNT Exchange: NYSE
Industry: Insurance - life

Washington Post Co., The
1150 15th St. NW
Washington, DC 20071
Phone: 202-334-6000 Fax: 202-334-4613
CEO: Donald E. Graham
CFO: John B. Morse, Jr.
1992 Sales: $1,451 million Employees: 6,100
Symbol: WPO Exchange: NYSE
Industry: Publishing - newspapers & magazines, TV broadcasting

Washington Savings Bank
Route 301
Waldorf, MD 20603
Phone: 301-843-7200 Fax: —
CEO: Lawrence M. Breneman
CFO: Joseph G. Gross
1991 Sales: $18 million Employees: 80
Symbol: WSBX Exchange: NASDAQ
Industry: Financial - savings and loans

Washington Scientific Industries, Inc.
2605 Wayzata Blvd.
Long Lake, MN 55356
Phone: 612-473-1271 Fax: 612-473-2945
CEO: Clifford W. Dinsmore
CFO: William J. Lucke
1991 Sales: $63 million Employees: 716
Symbol: WSCI Exchange: NASDAQ
Industry: Machine tools & related products

Washington Steel Corp.
90 W. Chestnut St.
Washington, PA 15301
Phone: 412-229-2803 Fax: 412-229-2814
CEO: Thomas C. Graham
CFO: Jerry Felix
1990 Sales: $500 million Employees: 1,200
Ownership: Privately held
Industry: Steel production

Washington Water Power Co.
1411 E. Mission Ave.
Spokane, WA 99202
Phone: 509-489-0500 Fax: 509-482-4184
CEO: Paul A. Redmond
CFO: Jon E. Eliassen
1991 Sales: $567 million Employees: 2,093
Symbol: WWP Exchange: NYSE
Industry: Utility - electric power

indicates company is in *Hoover's Handbook of American Business.*

indicates company is in *Hoover's Handbook of World Business;* sales and employee numbers are for parent company.

Wasser Communication Services
2512 2nd Ave., Ste. 308
Seattle, WA 98121
Phone: 206-441-0707 Fax: 206-441-6628
CEO: Peg Cheirrett
CFO: Peg Cheirrett
1992 Sales: $5 million Employees: 10
Ownership: Privately held
Industry: Business services - technical communications, training & management services

Waste Management, Inc.
3003 Butterfield Rd.
Oak Brook, IL 60521
Phone: 708-572-8800 Fax: 708-572-3094
CEO: Dean L. Buntrock
CFO: James E. Koenig
1992 Sales: $8,661 million Employees: 63,040
Symbol: WMX Exchange: NYSE
Industry: Pollution control equipment & services - waste collection, disposal & recycling

Waste Reduction Systems Inc.
100 Genoa-Red Bluff Rd.
Houston, TX 77034
Phone: 713-922-1000 Fax: 713-922-1474
CEO: Bill Winters
CFO: Jim Goodyear
1991 Sales: $6.6 million Employees: 85
Ownership: Privately held
Industry: Pollution control equipment & services - waste disposal

Waterhouse Securities, Inc.
44 Wall St., 5th Fl.
New York, NY 10005
Phone: 212-344-7500 Fax: 212-809-0274
CEO: Lawrence M. Waterhouse, Jr.
CFO: Kenneth I. Coco
1991 Sales: $31 million Employees: 300
Symbol: WHO Exchange: NYSE
Industry: Financial - business services

Waters Instruments, Inc.
2411 Seventh St. NW
Rochester, MN 55901
Phone: 507-288-7777 Fax: 507-288-7218
CEO: Robert J. Pitel
CFO: Darryl H. Wicklund
1992 Sales: $10.8 million Employees: —
Symbol: WTRS Exchange: NASDAQ
Industry: Diversified operations - farm products, medical systems, electrical products

Watkins-Johnson Co.
3333 Hillview Ave.
Palo Alto, CA 93404
Phone: 415-493-4141 Fax: 415-813-2402
CEO: W. Keith Kennedy, Jr.
CFO: Scott G. Buchanan
1991 Sales: $278 million Employees: 2,620
Symbol: WJ Exchange: NYSE
Industry: Electronics - military

Watsco, Inc.
2665 S. Bayshore Dr., Ste. 901
Coconut Grove, FL 33133
Phone: 305-858-0828 Fax: 305-858-4492
CEO: Albert H. Nahmad
CFO: Ronald P. Newman
1991 Sales: $169 million Employees: 16,719
Symbol: WSOA Exchange: AMEX
Industry: Diversified operations - climate control & personnel services

Watts Industries, Inc.
815 Chestnut St.
North Andover, MA 01845
Phone: 508-688-1811 Fax: 508-794-1848
CEO: Timothy P. Horne
CFO: Kenneth J. McAvoy
1992 Sales: $424 million Employees: 3,000
Symbol: WATTA Exchange: NASDAQ
Industry: Instruments - control

Wausau Paper Mills Co.
One Clark's Island
Wausau, WI 54402
Phone: 715-845-5266 Fax: 715-848-2652
CEO: William L. Goggins
CFO: Thomas B. Pitcher
1991 Sales: $350 million Employees: 1,291
Symbol: WSAU Exchange: NASDAQ
Industry: Paper & paper products

Waverly, Inc.
428 E. Preston St.
Baltimore, MD 21202
Phone: 410-528-4000 Fax: 410-528-8597
CEO: William M. Passano, Jr.
CFO: Samuel G. Macfarlane
1991 Sales: $147 million Employees: 1,168
Symbol: WAVR Exchange: NASDAQ
Industry: Publishing - books

Wawa Inc.
260 W. Baltimore Pike
Wawa, PA 19063
Phone: 215-358-8000 Fax: 215-358-8878
CEO: Richard D. Wood, Jr.
CFO: Thomas J. Payne
1991 Sales: $606 million Employees: 1,899
Ownership: Privately held
Industry: Retail - convenience stores

Waxman Industries, Inc.
24455 Aurora Rd.
Bedford Heights, OH 44146
Phone: 216-439-1830 Fax: 216-439-8494
CEO: Melvin Waxman
CFO: Jerome C. Jacques
1992 Sales: $379 million Employees: 1,698
Symbol: WAX Exchange: NYSE
Industry: Building products - plumbing, electrical & hardware

WB Johnson Properties
3414 Peachtree Rd. NE, Ste. 300
Atlanta, GA 30326
Phone: 404-237-5500 Fax: 404-233-1745
CEO: William B. Johnson
CFO: Richard Stephens
1991 Sales: $540 million Employees: 14,500
Ownership: Privately held
Industry: Hotels & restaurants

WD-40 Co.
1061 Cudahy Place
San Diego, CA 92110
Phone: 619-275-1400 Fax: 619-275-5823
CEO: John S. Barry
CFO: Gerald C. Schleif
1991 Sales: $90 million Employees: 134
Symbol: WDFC Exchange: NASDAQ
Industry: Paints & allied products - lubricant & rust retardant

Wean Inc.
Three Gateway Center, 13th Fl.
Pittsburgh, PA 15222
Phone: 412-456-5300 Fax: 412-456-5309
CEO: R. J. Wean III
CFO: Walter W. Stasik
1991 Sales: $76 million Employees: 456
Symbol: WID Exchange: NYSE
Industry: Machinery - general industrial

Weatherford International Inc.
1360 Post Oak Blvd., Ste. 1000
Houston, TX 77056
Phone: 713-439-9400 Fax: 713-621-0994
CEO: Philip Burguieres
CFO: Norman W. Nolen
1991 Sales: $206 million Employees: 2,063
Symbol: WII Exchange: AMEX
Industry: Oil & gas - field services

Webster Financial Corp.
First Federal Plaza
Waterbury, CT 06720
Phone: 203-753-2921 Fax: —
CEO: James C. Smith
CFO: John V. Brennan
1991 Sales: $72 million Employees: 273
Symbol: WBST Exchange: NASDAQ
Industry: Financial - savings and loans

Wedco Technology, Inc.
Rt. 173
West Portal, NJ 08802
Phone: 908-479-4181 Fax: 908-479-4876
CEO: William E. Willoughby
CFO: Nicholas Ruitenberg
1992 Sales: $30 million Employees: 410
Symbol: WEDC Exchange: NASDAQ
Industry: Machinery - general industrial

Wegener Corp.
11350 Technology Circle
Duluth, GA 30136
Phone: 404-623-0096 Fax: 404-623-0698
CEO: Robert A. Placek
CFO: C. Troy Woodbury, Jr.
1991 Sales: $20 million Employees: 422
Symbol: WGNR Exchange: NASDAQ
Industry: Telecommunications equipment

Wegmans Food Markets Inc.
1500 Brooks Ave.
Rochester, NY 14624
Phone: 716-328-2550 Fax: 716-464-4626
CEO: Robert B. Wegman
CFO: Mark Kindig
1991 Sales: $1,611 million Employees: 6,800
Ownership: Privately held
Industry: Retail - supermarkets

Weirton Steel Corp.
400 Three Springs Dr.
Weirton, WV 26062
Phone: 304-797-2000 Fax: 304-797-2821
CEO: Herbert Elish
CFO: Richard K. Riederer
1992 Sales: $1,079 million Employees: 6,979
Symbol: WS Exchange: NYSE
Industry: Steel - production

Weis Markets, Inc.
1000 S. Second St.
Sunbury, PA 17801
Phone: 717-286-4571 Fax: 717-286-3286
CEO: Sigfried Weis
CFO: Robert F. Weis
1992 Sales: $1,289 million Employees: 14,900
Symbol: WMK Exchange: NYSE
Industry: Retail - supermarkets

Weitek Corp.
1060 E. Arques Ave.
Sunnyvale, CA 94086
Phone: 408-738-8400 Fax: 408-738-1185
CEO: Arthur J. Collmeyer
CFO: Earl E. Fry
1991 Sales: $39 million Employees: 203
Symbol: WWTK Exchange: NASDAQ
Industry: Computers - integrated circuits & software development tools

Wek Enterprises
6910 Aragon Cir.
Buena Park, CA 90620
Phone: 714-522-2008 Fax: 800-832-9935
CEO: Genner Lopez
CFO: Genner Lopez
1991 Sales: $7.4 million Employees: 35
Ownership: Privately held
Industry: Apparel - cotton

 indicates company is in *Hoover's Handbook of American Business.*

indicates company is in *Hoover's Handbook of World Business;* sales and employee numbers are for parent company.

Weldotron Corp.
1532 S. Washington Ave.
Piscataway, NJ 08855
Phone: 908-752-6700 Fax: 908-752-6062
CEO: Martin Siegel
CFO: Roger E. Spreen
1992 Sales: $29 million Employees: 292
Symbol: WLD Exchange: AMEX
Industry: Machinery - material handling

Wellco Enterprises, Inc.
N. Pine St.
Hazelwood, NC 28738
Phone: 704-456-3545 Fax: 704-456-3547
CEO: Rolf Kaufman
CFO: David Lutz
1991 Sales: $24 million Employees: 337
Symbol: WLC Exchange: AMEX
Industry: Military equipment

Wellfleet Communications, Inc.
15 Crosby Dr.
Bedford, MA 01730
Phone: 617-275-2400 Fax: 617-275-5001
CEO: Paul J. Severino
CFO: R. Stephen Cheheyl
1992 Sales: $85 million Employees: 387
Symbol: WFLT Exchange: NASDAQ
Industry: Telecommunications equipment

Wellington Hall, Ltd.
Route 1, US Hwy. 29 & 70
Lexington, NC 27292
Phone: 704-249-4931 Fax: —
CEO: Hoyt M. Hackney, Jr.
CFO: Hoyt M. Hackney, Jr.
1992 Sales: $6.4 million Employees: 420
Symbol: WHAL Exchange: NASDAQ
Industry: Furniture

Wellington Leisure Products, Inc.
1140 Monticello Rd.
Madison, GA 30650
Phone: 706-342-1916 Fax: 706-342-0407
CEO: William R. O'Dell
CFO: Andrew G. Postnieks
1992 Sales: $101 million Employees: 1,290
Symbol: WLPI Exchange: NASDAQ
Industry: Leisure & recreational products

Wellman, Inc.
1040 Broad St., Ste. 302
Shrewsbury, NJ 07702
Phone: 908-542-7300 Fax: 908-542-9344
CEO: Thomas M. Duff
CFO: Clifford J. Christenson
1992 Sales: $828 million Employees: 3,410
Symbol: WLM Exchange: NYSE
Industry: Chemicals - plastics

Wells Fargo & Co.
420 Montgomery St., 2nd Fl.
San Francisco, CA 94163
Phone: 415-477-1000 Fax: 415-362-6958
CEO: Carl E. Reichardt
CFO: Rodney L. Jacobs
1992 Sales: $5,204 million Employees: 21,000
Symbol: WFC Exchange: NYSE
Industry: Banks - West

Wells-Gardner Electronics Corp.
2701 N. Kildare Ave.
Chicago, IL 60639
Phone: 312-252-8220 Fax: 312-252-8072
CEO: Frank J. Myers
CFO: Richard L. Conquest
1991 Sales: $39 million Employees: 286
Symbol: WGA Exchange: AMEX
Industry: Electrical products - video monitors

Wendy's International, Inc.
4288 W. Dublin-Granville Rd.
Dublin, OH 43017
Phone: 614-764-3100 Fax: 614-764-3459
CEO: James W. Near
CFO: John K. Casey
1992 Sales: $1,220 million Employees: 39,000
Symbol: WEN Exchange: NYSE
Industry: Retail - food & restaurants

Werner Enterprises, Inc.
14507 Frontier Rd.
Omaha, NE 68138
Phone: 402-895-6640 Fax: 402-895-1387
CEO: Clarence L. Werner
CFO: Robert E. Synowicki, Jr.
1992 Sales: $323 million Employees: 3,845
Symbol: WERN Exchange: NASDAQ
Industry: Transportation - truck

WesBanco, Inc.
1 Bank Plaza
Wheeling, WV 26003
Phone: 304-234-9000 Fax: —
CEO: Thomas G. Dove
CFO: Thomas G. Dove
1991 Sales: $79 million Employees: 492
Symbol: WSBC Exchange: NASDAQ
Industry: Banks - Southeast

Wesco Financial Corp.
315 E. Colorado Blvd., 3rd Fl.
Pasadena, CA 91101
Phone: 818-449-2345 Fax: 818-449-1455
CEO: Charles T. Munger
CFO: Jeffrey L. Jacobson
1991 Sales: $133 million Employees: 425
Symbol: WSC Exchange: AMEX
Industry: Financial - savings and loans

West Co.
1041 W. Bridge St.
Phoenixville, PA 19460
Phone: 215-935-4500 Fax: 215-935-4600
CEO: William G. Little
CFO: Raymond J. Land
1991 Sales: $330 million Employees: 4,977
Symbol: WST Exchange: NYSE
Industry: Medical & dental supplies

West Coast Bank Idaho
4770 Campus Dr., Ste. 100
Newport Beach, CA 92660
Phone: 714-757-6868 Fax: 714-757-6811
CEO: John B. Joseph
CFO: Frank E. Smith
1991 Sales: $51 million Employees: 290
Symbol: WCBC Exchange: NASDAQ
Industry: Banks - West

West Mass Bankshares, Inc.
45 Federal St.
Greenfield, MA 01301
Phone: 413-774-3713 Fax: —
CEO: Francis L. Lemay
CFO: Kenneth R. Cole
1991 Sales: $20 million Employees: 87
Symbol: WMBS Exchange: NASDAQ
Industry: Banks - Northeast

West Newton Savings Bank
1314 Washington St.
West Newton, MA 02165
Phone: 617-244-2000 Fax: —
CEO: Richard H. Dionne
CFO: Donald Cassidy
1992 Sales: — Employees: —
Symbol: WNSB Exchange: NASDAQ
Industry: Financial - savings and loans

West One Bank Idaho
101 S. Capitol Blvd.
Boise, ID 83702
Phone: 208-383-7000 Fax: —
CEO: Daniel R. Nelson
CFO: Scott M. Hayes
1991 Sales: $520 million Employees: 3,464
Symbol: WEST Exchange: NASDAQ
Industry: Banks - West

West Penn Power Co.
800 Cabin Hill Dr.
Greensburg, PA 15601
Phone: 412-837-3000 Fax: —
CEO: Klaus Bergman
CFO: Kenneth D. Mowl
1991 Sales: $1.1 million Employees: 2,058
Symbol: WSPp Exchange: NYSE
Industry: Utility - electric power

West Point-Pepperell, Inc.
400 W. Tenth St.
West Point, GA 31833
Phone: 706-645-4000 Fax: 706-645-4753
CEO: William Farley
CFO: Stan E. Kees
1991 Sales: $1,203 million Employees: 18,500
Symbol: WPM Exchange: NYSE
Industry: Textiles - mill products

West Publishing Co.
50 W. Kellogg Blvd.
St. Paul, MN 55102
Phone: 612-687-7000 Fax: 612-687-5827
CEO: Dwight D. Opperman
CFO: James G. Lindell
1991 Sales: $500 million Employees: 5,100
Ownership: Privately held
Industry: Publishing - books; law & college textbooks & on-line services

Westamerica Bank
1108 Fifth Ave.
San Rafael, CA 94901
Phone: 415-456-8000 Fax: 415-267-8013
CEO: David L. Payne
CFO: James M. Barnes
1991 Sales: $134 million Employees: 841
Symbol: WAB Exchange: AMEX
Industry: Banks - West

Westbridge Capital Corp.
777 Main St., Ste. 900
Ft. Worth, TX 76102
Phone: 817-878-3300 Fax: 817-878-3480
CEO: Martin E. Kantor
CFO: Michael C. Batte
1991 Sales: $62 million Employees: —
Symbol: WBC Exchange: AMEX
Industry: Insurance - accident & health

Westcorp Financial Services
23 Pasteur Rd.
Irvine, CA 92718
Phone: 714-753-3000 Fax: 714-727-2342
CEO: Ernest S. Rady
CFO: Milton D. Jensen
1991 Sales: $328 million Employees: 930
Symbol: WES Exchange: AMEX
Industry: Financial - savings and loans

Westcott Communications, Inc.
1303 Marsh Lane
Carrollton, TX 75006
Phone: 214-416-4100 Fax: —
CEO: Carl Westcott
CFO: Wayne R. Maynard
1991 Sales: $29 million Employees: 294
Symbol: WCTV Exchange: NASDAQ
Industry: Motion pictures & services

Westerbeke Corp.
Avon Industrial Park
Avon, MA 02322
Phone: 508-588-7700 Fax: 508-559-9323
CEO: John H. Westerbeke, Jr.
CFO: Mark P. Sullivan
1991 Sales: $13 million Employees: 74
Symbol: WTBK Exchange: NASDAQ
Industry: Engines - internal combustion

Western Bank
290 S. Fourth St.
Coos Bay, OR 97420
Phone: 503-269-5171 Fax: 503-269-4285
CEO: Georges C. St. Laurent, Jr.
CFO: Michael L. Sickels
1992 Sales: — Employees: —
Symbol: WSBK Exchange: NASDAQ
Industry: Banks - West

Western Capital Investment Corp.
1675 Broadway, Ste. 1700
Denver, CO 80202
Phone: 303-623-5577 Fax: 303-620-1945
CEO: Robert J. Malone
CFO: Scott A. Crosby
1991 Sales: $216 million Employees: 1,702
Symbol: WECA Exchange: NASDAQ
Industry: Financial - savings and loans

Western Co. of North America
515 Post Oak Blvd.
Houston, TX 77027
Phone: 713-629-2600 Fax: 713-629-2722
CEO: Sheldon R. Erikson
CFO: Sam R. Morrow
1991 Sales: $314 million Employees: 2,606
Symbol: WSN Exchange: NYSE
Industry: Oil & gas - field services

Western Digital Corp.
8105 Irvine Center Dr.
Irvine, CA 92718
Phone: 714-932-5000 Fax: 714-863-1656
CEO: Roger W. Johnson
CFO: George L. Bragg
1992 Sales: $1,138 million Employees: 6,906
Symbol: WDC Exchange: NYSE
Industry: Computers - disk drives & semiconductors

Western Energy Management, Inc.
5777 Madison Ave., Ste. 430
Sacramento, CA 95841
Phone: 916-331-2882 Fax: —
CEO: Jack Wright
CFO: Jack Wright
1991 Sales: $7.5 million Employees: 105
Symbol: WEM Exchange: AMEX
Industry: Engineering - R&D services

Western Fiberglass, Inc.
1555 Copperhill Pkwy.
Santa Rosa, CA 95403
Phone: 707-523-2050 Fax: 707-523-2046
CEO: Michael E. Lewis
CFO: Linda Ebright-Lewis
1991 Sales: $2.1 million Employees: 30
Ownership: Privately held
Industry: Glass products - fiberglass

Western Financial Corp.
10955 Lowell, Ste. 705
Overland Park, KS 66210
Phone: 913-339-9700 Fax: —
CEO: Joe C. Morris
CFO: Stephen M. Carttar
1991 Sales: $74 million Employees: 286
Symbol: WSTF Exchange: NASDAQ
Industry: Financial - mortgages & related services

Western Gas Resources, Inc.
12200 N. Pecos St., Ste. 230
Denver, CO 80234
Phone: 303-452-5603 Fax: 303-452-0186
CEO: Brion G. Wise
CFO: Lonnie R. Brock
1991 Sales: $355 million Employees: 682
Symbol: WGR Exchange: NYSE
Industry: Oil & gas - production & pipeline

Western Micro Technology, Inc.
12900 Saratoga Ave.
Saratoga, CA 95070
Phone: 408-725-1660 Fax: 408-255-6491
CEO: Marshall G. Cox
CFO: Paul A. Araquistain
1991 Sales: $83 million Employees: 202
Symbol: WSTM Exchange: NASDAQ
Industry: Electronics - parts distribution

Western Publishing Co., Inc.
444 Madison Ave.
New York, NY 10022
Phone: 212-688-4500 Fax: 212-888-5025
CEO: Richard A. Bernstein
CFO: Stuart Turner
1992 Sales: $629 million Employees: 3,800
Symbol: WPGI Exchange: NASDAQ
Industry: Publishing - books

Western Resources, Inc.
818 Kansas Ave.
Topeka, KS 66612
Phone: 913-296-6300 Fax: 913-575-6399
CEO: John E. Hayes, Jr.
CFO: Steven L. Kitchen
1992 Sales: $1,556 million Employees: 4,528
Symbol: WR Exchange: NYSE
Industry: Utility - gas distribution

Western Waste Industries
1125 W. 190th St., Ste. 100
Gardena, CA 90248
Phone: 310-329-1425 Fax: 310-715-6633
CEO: Kosti Shirvanian
CFO: Lawrence F. McQuaide
1991 Sales: $200 million Employees: 1,580
Symbol: WW Exchange: NYSE
Industry: Pollution control equipment & services - solid waste management

Westfield Cos.
1 Park Circle
Westfield Center, OH 44251
Phone: 216-887-0101 Fax: 216-887-0840
CEO: Cary Blair
CFO: Cary Blair
1991 Sales: $484 million Employees: 1,512
Ownership: Privately held
Industry: Insurance - multiline & misc.

Westinghouse Electric Corp.
Westinghouse Bldg., Gateway Center
Pittsburgh, PA 15222
Phone: 412-244-2000 Fax: 412-642-3404
CEO: Gary M. Clark
CFO: Wayne H. Hollinshead
1992 Sales: $8,447 million Employees: 113,664
Symbol: WX Exchange: NYSE
Industry: Diversified operations - electronic systems, power systems, broadcasting

Westmoreland Coal Co.
200 S. Broad St., Ste. 700
Philadelphia, PA 19102
Phone: 215-545-2500 Fax: 215-735-7175
CEO: Pemberton Hutchinson
CFO: Larry Zalkin
1991 Sales: $568 million Employees: 1,226
Symbol: WCX Exchange: NYSE
Industry: Coal

Westport Bancorp, Inc.
87 Post Rd. East
Westport, CT 06880
Phone: 203-222-6911 Fax: —
CEO: Michael H. Flynn
CFO: Richard D. Silverman
1991 Sales: $26 million Employees: 164
Symbol: WBAT Exchange: NASDAQ
Industry: Banks - Northeast

Westvaco Corp.
299 Park Ave.
New York, NY 10171
Phone: 212-688-5000 Fax: 212-318-5050
CEO: John A. Luke
CFO: George E. Cruser
1992 Sales: $2,336 million Employees: 14,440
Symbol: W Exchange: NYSE
Industry: Paper & paper products

Westwood One, Inc.
9540 Washington Blvd.
Culver City, CA 90232
Phone: 310-204-5000 Fax: 310-836-1158
CEO: Norman J. Pattiz
CFO: William J. Battison
1991 Sales: $144 million Employees: —
Symbol: WONE Exchange: NASDAQ
Industry: Broadcasting - radio & TV

Wet Seal, Inc.
64 Fairbanks Rd.
Irvine, CA 92718
Phone: 714-583-9029 Fax: 714-583-0715
CEO: Kenneth C. Chilvers
CFO: Alan A. Weinstein
1991 Sales: $120 million Employees: 1,840
Symbol: WTSLA Exchange: NASDAQ
Industry: Retail - apparel & shoes

Wetterau Inc.
8920 Pershall Rd.
Hazelwood, MO 63042
Phone: 314-524-5000 Fax: 314-595-4097
CEO: Ted C. Wetterau
CFO: Kurt D. Blumenthal
1992 Sales: $5,740 million Employees: 15,500
Symbol: WETT Exchange: NASDAQ
Industry: Food - wholesale

Weyco Group, Inc.
234 E. Reservoir Ave.
Milwaukee, WI 53212
Phone: 414-263-8800 Fax: 414-263-8808
CEO: Thomas W. Florsheim
CFO: Robert Feitler
1991 Sales: $141 million Employees: 1,200
Symbol: WEYS Exchange: NASDAQ
Industry: Shoes & related apparel

Weyerhaeuser Co.
33663 Weyerhaeuser Way
Federal Way, WA 98003
Phone: 206-924-2345 Fax: 206-924-7407
CEO: John W. Creighton, Jr.
CFO: William C. Stivers
1992 Sales: $9,219 million Employees: 38,669
Symbol: WY Exchange: NYSE
Industry: Building products - wood, pulp & paper, financial services, real estate

Wheatley Gaso Inc.
6750 S. 57th W. Ave.
Tulsa, OK 74131
Phone: 918-446-4551 Fax: 918-582-5013
CEO: Gene J. Kaefer
CFO: David A. Moore
1992 Sales: $88 million Employees: 576
Symbol: WTXT Exchange: NASDAQ
Industry: Pumps and seals

indicates company is in *Hoover's Handbook of American Business.*

indicates company is in *Hoover's Handbook of World Business;* sales and employee numbers are for parent company.

Wheaton Inc.
1101 Wheaton Ave.
Millville, NJ 08332
Phone: 609-825-1400 Fax: 609-825-8461
CEO: Robert I. Veghte
CFO: Daniel M. Replogle, Jr.
1991 Sales: $490 million Employees: 8,000
Ownership: Privately held
Industry: Glass products & plastics

Wheelabrator Technologies Inc.
Liberty Lane
Hampton, NH 03842
Phone: 603-929-3000 Fax: 603-929-3139
CEO: Phillip B. Rooney
CFO: James E. Koenig
1992 Sales: $1,483 million Employees: 8,600
Symbol: WTI Exchange: NYSE
Industry: Energy - alternative sources

Wheeling-Pittsburgh Corp.
110 E. 59th St.
New York, NY 10022
Phone: 212-355-5200 Fax: —
CEO: Robin Chenery
CFO: Frederick G. Chbosky
1992 Sales: $930 million Employees: 5,811
Symbol: WHX Exchange: NYSE
Industry: Steel - production

Wherehouse Entertainment
19701 Hamilton Ave.
Torrance, CA 90502
Phone: 310-538-2314 Fax: 310-538-8698
CEO: Scott Young
CFO: John Hoffner
1991 Sales: $457 million Employees: 8,000
Ownership: Privately held
Industry: Retail - audio & video

Whirlpool Corp.
2000 M-63
Benton Harbor, MI 49022
Phone: 616-926-5000 Fax: 616-926-3568
CEO: David R. Whitwam
CFO: Michael J. Callahan
1992 Sales: $7,301 million Employees: 37,886
Symbol: WHR Exchange: NYSE
Industry: Appliances - household

White Swan Inc.
400 Fuller-Wiser Rd., Ste. 300
Euless, TX 76039
Phone: 817-283-5444 Fax: 817-283-1391
CEO: Ronald E. Elmquist
CFO: W. J. Beyer
1991 Sales: $780 million Employees: 2,000
Ownership: Privately held
Industry: Food - wholesale

Whitehall Corp.
2659 Nova Dr.
Dallas, TX 75229
Phone: 214-247-8747 Fax: 214-247-2024
CEO: George F. Baker
CFO: E. Forrest Campbell III
1991 Sales: $20 million Employees: 522
Symbol: WHT Exchange: NYSE
Industry: Electronics - military

Whiting-Turner Contracting Co.
300 E. Joppa Rd.
Towson, MD 21286
Phone: 410-821-1100 Fax: 410-337-5770
CEO: Willard Hackerman
CFO: Charles Meyers
1991 Sales: $509 million Employees: 900
Ownership: Privately held
Industry: Real estate operations - general contracting & construction management

Whitman Corp.
3501 Algonquin Rd.
Rolling Meadows, IL 60008
Phone: 708-818-5000 Fax: 708-818-5045
CEO: Bruce S. Chelberg
CFO: John P. Fagan
1992 Sales: $2,388 million Employees: 14,703
Symbol: WH Exchange: NYSE
Industry: Diversified operations - soft drink bottling, auto service, refrigeration equipment

Whitmire Distribution Corporation
81 Blue Ravine Rd.
Folsom, CA 95630
Phone: 916-985-5000 Fax: 916-985-5029
CEO: Melburn G. Whitmire
CFO: Peter McGurty
1992 Sales: $2,100 million Employees: 1,000
Ownership: Privately held
Industry: Drugs & health care products - wholesale

Whitney Holding Corp.
228 St. Charles Ave.
New Orleans, LA 70130
Phone: 504-586-7272 Fax: 504-586-3478
CEO: William L. Marks
CFO: Edward B. Grimball
1991 Sales: $251 million Employees: —
Symbol: WTNY Exchange: NASDAQ
Industry: Banks - Southeast

Whittaker Corp.
10880 Wilshire Blvd., 8th Fl.
Los Angeles, CA 90024
Phone: 310-475-9411 Fax: 310-879-9442
CEO: Joseph F. Alibrandi
CFO: Daniel Hofmann
1991 Sales: $158 million Employees: 1,000
Symbol: WKR Exchange: NYSE
Industry: Aerospace - aircraft equipment

Whittle Communications, L.P.
333 Main Ave.
Knoxville, TN 37902
Phone: 615-595-5000 Fax: 615-595-5898
CEO: Chris Whittle
CFO: Nick Glover
1992 Sales: $213 million Employees: 1,089
Ownership: Privately held
Industry: Diversified operations - publishing, cable TV & schools

Whole Foods Market, Inc.
2525 Wallingwood Dr., Ste. 1400
Austin, TX 78746
Phone: 512-328-7541 Fax: 512-328-5482
CEO: John Mackey
CFO: Glenda Flanagan
1992 Sales: $120 million Employees: 2,000
Symbol: WFMI Exchange: NASDAQ
Industry: Retail - natural food stores

Wichita River Oil Corp.
555 Seventeenth St., Ste. 905
Denver, CO 80202
Phone: 303-292-3300 Fax: 303-293-2263
CEO: Michael L. McDonald
CFO: Michael L. McDonald
1991 Sales: $3.9 million Employees: 41
Symbol: WRO Exchange: AMEX
Industry: Oil & gas - US exploration & production

Wickes Cos. Inc.
3340 Ocean Park Blvd., Ste. 2000
Santa Monica, CA 90405
Phone: 310-452-0161 Fax: 310-452-9509
CEO: James R. Birie
CFO: Wilhelm A. Mallory
1991 Sales: $2,360 million Employees: 25,200
Ownership: Privately held
Industry: Diversified operations - home improvement centers, textiles, automotive & industrial products

Wickes Lumber Co.
706 N. Deerpath Dr.
Vernon Hills, IL 60061
Phone: 708-367-6540 Fax: 708-367-3750
CEO: J. Steven Wilson
CFO: M. Benjet
1991 Sales: $746 million Employees: 4,057
Ownership: Privately held
Industry: Building products - retail

WICOR, Inc.
777 E. Wisconsin Ave.
Milwaukee, WI 53202
Phone: 414-291-7026 Fax: 414-291-7025
CEO: Stuart W. Tisdale
CFO: James C. Donnelly
1991 Sales: $682 million Employees: —
Symbol: WIC Exchange: NYSE
Industry: Utility - gas distribution

Wiener Enterprises, Inc.
5725 Powell St.
Harahan, LA 70123
Phone: 504-733-7055 Fax: Ext. 256
CEO: W. Wayne Foster
CFO: Lynn D. Malmstrom
1991 Sales: $50 million Employees: 551
Symbol: WPB Exchange: AMEX
Industry: Retail - apparel & shoes

Wilbur-Ellis Co.
320 California St.
San Francisco, CA 94104
Phone: 415-772-4000 Fax: 415-772-4011
CEO: Brayton Wilbur
CFO: Herb Tully
1991 Sales: $784 million Employees: 1,629
Ownership: Privately held
Industry: Chemicals - farm supplies & distribution

Willamette Industries, Inc.
1300 SW Fifth Ave., Ste. 3800
Portland, OR 97201
Phone: 503-227-5581 Fax: 503-273-5601
CEO: William Swindells
CFO: J. A. Parsons
1992 Sales: $2,372 million Employees: 11,350
Symbol: WMTT Exchange: NASDAQ
Industry: Paper & paper products

Willcox & Gibbs, Inc.
530 Fifth Ave.
New York, NY 10036
Phone: 212-869-1800 Fax: 212-764-3275
CEO: John K. Ziegler
CFO: Richard J. Mackey
1991 Sales: $600 million Employees: 2,655
Symbol: WG Exchange: NYSE
Industry: Machinery - general industrial

William Lyon Cos.
4490 Von Karman Ave.
Newport Beach, CA 92660
Phone: 714-833-3600 Fax: 714-476-8804
CEO: William Lyon
CFO: Paul Pfeiffer
1991 Sales: $772 million Employees: 263
Ownership: Privately held
Industry: Home building, apartment & real estate development

Williams Companies, Inc., The
One Willliams Center
Tulsa, OK 74172
Phone: 918-588-2000 Fax: 918-588-2296
CEO: Joseph H. Williams
CFO: Jack D. McCarthy
1992 Sales: $2,448 million Employees: 6,491
Symbol: WMB Exchange: NYSE
Industry: Oil & gas - production & pipeline

indicates company is in *Hoover's Handbook of American Business.*

indicates company is in *Hoover's Handbook of World Business;* sales and employee numbers are for parent company.

Williams Industries, Inc.
2849 Meadow View Rd.
Falls Church, VA 22042
Phone: 703-560-1505 Fax: 703-876-9443
CEO: Frank E. Williams, Jr.
CFO: Arthur V. Conover III
1991 Sales: $81 million Employees: 925
Symbol: WMSI Exchange: NASDAQ
Industry: Construction - heavy

Williams-Sonoma, Inc.
100 N. Point St.
San Francisco, CA 94133
Phone: 415-421-7900 Fax: 415-983-9887
CEO: W. Howard Lester
CFO: James E. Riley
1991 Sales: $313 million Employees: 4,500
Symbol: WSGC Exchange: NASDAQ
Industry: Retail - mail order & direct cookware & related housewares

Wilshire Oil Company of Texas
921 Bergen Ave.
Jersey City, NJ 07306
Phone: 201-420-2796 Fax: —
CEO: Sherry W. Izak
CFO: William Goldberg
1991 Sales: $7.3 million Employees: 16
Symbol: WOC Exchange: NYSE
Industry: Oil & gas - US exploration & production

Wind River Systems, Inc.
1010 Atlantic Ave.
Alameda, CA 94501
Phone: 510-748-4100 Fax: 510-814-2010
CEO: Dale Wilde
CFO: Dale Wilde
1991 Sales: $17 million Employees: 125
Ownership: Privately held
Industry: Computers - computer operating systems & development tools

Windmere Corp.
5980 Miami Lakes Dr.
Miami Lakes, FL 33014
Phone: 305-362-2611 Fax: 305-364-0635
CEO: David M. Friedson
CFO: Harry D. Schulman
1991 Sales: $142 million Employees: —
Symbol: WND Exchange: NYSE
Industry: Drugs & sundries - wholesale

Winn-Dixie Stores, Inc.
5050 Edgewood Court
Jacksonville, FL 32205
Phone: 904-783-5000 Fax: 904-783-5294
CEO: A. Dano Davis
CFO: Richard P. McCook
1992 Sales: $10,481 million Employees: 102,000
Symbol: WIN Exchange: NYSE
Industry: Retail - supermarkets

Winnebago Industries, Inc.
PO Box 152
Forest City, IA 50436
Phone: 515-582-3535 Fax: 515-582-6966
CEO: John K. Hanson
CFO: Edwin F. Barker
1991 Sales: $223 million Employees: 2,270
Symbol: WGO Exchange: NYSE
Industry: Building - mobile homes & RVs

Winston Resources, Inc.
535 Fifth Ave.
New York, NY 10017
Phone: 212-557-5000 Fax: —
CEO: Seymour Kugler
CFO: Reuben W. Abrams
1991 Sales: $16 million Employees: 92
Symbol: WRS Exchange: AMEX
Industry: Business services - personnel recruiting

Winthrop Resources Corp.
9900 Bren Rd. East
Minnetonka, MN 55343
Phone: 612-936-0226 Fax: —
CEO: John L. Morgan
CFO: Kirk A. MacKenzie
1991 Sales: $56 million Employees: 26
Symbol: WINR Exchange: NASDAQ
Industry: Computers - leasing services

Wisconsin Central Transportation Corp.
6250 N. River Rd.
Rosemont, IL 60017
Phone: 708-318-4600 Fax: —
CEO: Edward A. Burkhardt
CFO: Thomas F. Power, Jr.
1991 Sales: $114 million Employees: 929
Symbol: WCLX Exchange: NASDAQ
Industry: Transportation - rail

Wisconsin Energy Corp.
231 W. Michigan St.
Milwaukee, WI 53203
Phone: 414-221-2345 Fax: 414-221-2010
CEO: Richard A. Abdoo
CFO: Jerry G. Remmel
1992 Sales: $1,552 million Employees: 5,650
Symbol: WEC Exchange: NYSE
Industry: Utility - electric power

Wisconsin Public Service Corp.
700 N. Adams St.
Green Bay, WI 54301
Phone: 414-433-1598 Fax: 414-433-1297
CEO: Daniel A. Bollom
CFO: James H. Liethen
1991 Sales: $624 million Employees: 2,609
Symbol: WPS Exchange: NYSE
Industry: Utility - electric power

Wisconsin Southern Gas Co., Inc.
120 E. Sheridan Springs Rd.
Lake Geneva, WI 53147
Phone: 414-248-8861 Fax: 414-249-5423
CEO: Willard L. Decker
CFO: Richard E. Johnson
1991 Sales: $41 million Employees: 154
Symbol: WISC Exchange: NASDAQ
Industry: Utility - gas distribution

Wiser Oil Co.
210 Charles St.
Sistersville, WV 26175
Phone: 304-652-3861 Fax: 304-652-1314
CEO: Andrew J. Shoup, Jr.
CFO: Ronald D. Lee
1991 Sales: $37 million Employees: 99
Symbol: WISE Exchange: NASDAQ
Industry: Oil & gas - US exploration & production

Witco Corp.
520 Madison Ave.
New York, NY 10022
Phone: 212-605-3800 Fax: 212-605-3660
CEO: William R. Toller
CFO: Michael D. Fullwood
1992 Sales: $1,729 million Employees: 6,919
Symbol: WIT Exchange: NYSE
Industry: Chemicals - diversified

WL Gore & Associates Inc.
555 Papermill Rd.
Newark, DE 19711
Phone: 302-738-4880 Fax: 302-738-7710
CEO: Robert W. Gore
CFO: G. W. Gore
1991 Sales: $750 million Employees: 5,860
Ownership: Privately held
Industry: Diversified operations - fabrics, electronics, industrial & medical products

WLR Foods, Inc.
PO Box 228
Hinton, VA 22831
Phone: 703-867-4001 Fax: 703-867-4098
CEO: James L. Keeler
CFO: Delbert L. Seitz
1992 Sales: $514 million Employees: 5,350
Symbol: WLRF Exchange: NASDAQ
Industry: Food - meat products

Wm. Wrigley Jr. Co.
410 N. Michigan Ave.
Chicago, IL 60611
Phone: 312-644-2121 Fax: 312-644-2135
CEO: William Wrigley
CFO: John F. Bard
1992 Sales: $1,287 million Employees: 6,250
Symbol: WWY Exchange: NYSE
Industry: Food - gum

WMS Industries Inc.
3401 N. California Ave.
Chicago, IL 60618
Phone: 312-728-2300 Fax: 312-267-3747
CEO: Louis J. Nicastro
CFO: Harold H. Bach, Jr.
1992 Sales: $227 million Employees: 3,570
Symbol: WMS Exchange: NYSE
Industry: Leisure & recreational products - amusement games, hotels & casinos

Wolf FN & Co., Inc.
110 Wall St., 23rd Fl.
New York, NY 10005
Phone: 212-635-5666 Fax: 212-425-0119
CEO: Franklin N. Wolf
CFO: James Petrantis
1991 Sales: $23 million Employees: 60
Symbol: WOFG Exchange: NASDAQ
Industry: Financial - investment bankers

Wolohan Lumber Co.
1740 Midland Rd.
Saginaw, MI 48603
Phone: 517-793-4532 Fax: 517-793-4582
CEO: James L. Wolohan
CFO: Robert F. Anderson
1991 Sales: $304 million Employees: 1,700
Symbol: WLHN Exchange: NASDAQ
Industry: Building products - retail & wholesale

Wolverine Exploration Co.
201 Main St., Ste. 400
Ft. Worth, TX 76102
Phone: 817-335-4701 Fax: 817-332-8351
CEO: Glenn A. Adams
CFO: Jeffrey L. Stevens
1991 Sales: $22 million Employees: 8
Symbol: WEXC Exchange: NASDAQ
Industry: Oil & gas - US exploration & production

Wolverine World Wide, Inc.
9341 Courtland Dr.
Rockford, MI 49351
Phone: 616-866-5500 Fax: 616-866-0257
CEO: Thomas D. Gleason
CFO: George A. Andrews
1991 Sales: $314 million Employees: 4,747
Symbol: WWW Exchange: NYSE
Industry: Shoes & related apparel

Woodhead Industries, Inc.
3411 Woodhead Dr.
Northbrook, IL 60062
Phone: 708-272-7990 Fax: 708-272-8133
CEO: Alan Reed
CFO: Robert G. Jennings
1991 Sales: $74 million Employees: 816
Symbol: WDHD Exchange: NASDAQ
Industry: Electrical products - control & distribution devices

Woodward & Lothrop/John Wanamaker
1025 F St. NW
Washington, DC 20013
Phone: 202-879-8222 Fax: 202-879-8391
CEO: Arnold H. Aronson
CFO: Joseph F. Gallucci
1991 Sales: $838 million Employees: 11,500
Ownership: Privately held
Industry: Retail - regional department stores

Woolworth Corp.
233 Broadway
New York, NY 10279
Phone: 212-553-2000 Fax: 212-553-2042
CEO: Harold E. Sells
CFO: William K. Lavin
1992 Sales: $9,963 million Employees: 144,000
Symbol: Z Exchange: NYSE
Industry: Retail - discount & variety, athletic footwear

WordPerfect Corp.
1555 N. Technology Way
Orem, UT 84057
Phone: 801-225-5000 Fax: 801-222-5077
CEO: Bruce W. Bastian
CFO: Dan Campbell
1991 Sales: $533 million Employees: 5,000
Ownership: Privately held
Industry: Computers - word-processing software

WordStar International, Inc.
201 Alameda del Prado St.
Novato, CA 94949
Phone: 415-382-8000 Fax: 415-883-1617
CEO: Ron Posner
CFO: Jane Catelani
1992 Sales: $42 million Employees: 198
Symbol: WDST Exchange: NASDAQ
Industry: Computers - word-processing software

Workingmens Capital Holdings, Inc.
121 E. Kirkwood Ave.
Bloomington, IN 47408
Phone: 812-332-9465 Fax: —
CEO: Richard R. Haynes
CFO: Joseph A. Walker
1991 Sales: $15 million Employees: 41
Symbol: WCHI Exchange: NASDAQ
Industry: Financial - savings and loans

World Acceptance Corp.
1251 S. Pleasantburg Dr.
Greenville, SC 29605
Phone: 803-277-4570 Fax: —
CEO: Charles D. Walters
CFO: A. Alexander McLean III
1992 Sales: $40 million Employees: 690
Symbol: WRLD Exchange: NASDAQ
Industry: Financial - consumer loans

World Travel Partners
1055 Lenox Blvd., Ste. 420
Atlanta, GA 30319
Phone: 404-841-6600 Fax: 404-814-2983
CEO: Jack Alexander
CFO: Brian Learst
1992 Sales: $200 million Employees: 525
Ownership: Privately held
Industry: Business services - travel management

World-Wide Refinishing Systems
1020 N. University Parks Dr.
Waco, TX 76707
Phone: 817-776-4701 Fax: 817-772-7488
CEO: Donald Dwyer
CFO: Douglas Holsted
1991 Sales: $3 million Employees: 20
Ownership: Privately held
Industry: Building - bathtub & tile refinishing

WorldCorp, Inc.
13873 Park Center Rd., Ste. 490
Herndon, VA 22071
Phone: 703-834-9200 Fax: 703-834-9212
CEO: T. Coleman Andrews III
CFO: T. Coleman Andrews III
1991 Sales: $280 million Employees: 709
Symbol: WOA Exchange: NYSE
Industry: Transportation - airline

Worthen Bank & Trust Co.
200 W. Capitol Ave.
Little Rock, AR 72201
Phone: 501-378-1000 Fax: 501-378-1062
CEO: Curt Bradbury
CFO: Andrew T. Melton
1991 Sales: $218 million Employees: 1,626
Symbol: WOR Exchange: AMEX
Industry: Banks - Southeast

Worthington Foods, Inc.
900 Proprietors Rd.
Worthington, OH 43085
Phone: 614-885-9511 Fax: 614-885-2594
CEO: Dale E. Twomley
CFO: Dale E. Twomley
1991 Sales: $70 million Employees: 424
Symbol: WFDS Exchange: NASDAQ
Industry: Food

Worthington Industries, Inc.
1205 Dearborn Dr.
Columbus, OH 43085
Phone: 614-438-3210 Fax: 614-438-3136
CEO: John H. McConnell
CFO: Joseph H. Stegmayer
1992 Sales: $1,023 million Employees: 6,400
Symbol: WTHG Exchange: NASDAQ
Industry: Metal processing & fabrication

Worthington Voice Services
740 E. Lake View Plaza Blvd., Ste. E
Worthington, OH 43085
Phone: 614-431-9710 Fax: 614-431-5793
CEO: Eric Speicher
CFO: Eric Speicher
1991 Sales: $9.1 million Employees: 9
Ownership: Privately held
Industry: Telecommunications services - 900 number information

WPL Holdings, Inc.
222 W. Washington Ave.
Madison, WI 53703
Phone: 608-252-3311 Fax: 608-252-3397
CEO: Erroll B. Davis, Jr.
CFO: Edward M. Gleason
1991 Sales: $649 million Employees: 3,098
Symbol: WPH Exchange: NYSE
Industry: Utility - electric power

WSMP, Inc.
101 WSMP Dr.
Claremont, NC 28610
Phone: 704-459-7626 Fax: 704-459-0733
CEO: Cecil R. Hash
CFO: Richard F. Howard
1992 Sales: $68 million Employees: 1,834
Symbol: WSMP Exchange: NASDAQ
Industry: Retail - food & restaurants

WTD Industries
10260 SW Greenburg Rd.
Portland, OR 97223
Phone: 503-246-3440 Fax: 503-245-4229
CEO: Bruce L. Engel
CFO: K. Stanley Martin
1992 Sales: $214 million Employees: 1,300
Symbol: WTDQC Exchange: NASDAQ
Industry: Building products - wood

WWF Paper Corp.
Two Bala Plaza, 2nd Fl.
Bala Cynwyd, PA 19004
Phone: 215-667-9210 Fax: 215-667-1663
CEO: Edward V. Furlong, Jr.
CFO: George Sergio
1991 Sales: $650 million Employees: 400
Ownership: Privately held
Industry: Paper & paper products, fine paper converting & distributing

Wyle Laboratories
128 Maryland St.
El Segundo, CA 90245
Phone: 310-322-1763 Fax: 310-322-3603
CEO: Charles M. Clough
CFO: Theodore M. Freedman
1991 Sales: $453 million Employees: 1,910
Symbol: WYL Exchange: NYSE
Industry: Electronics - parts distribution

Wyman-Gordon Co.
244 Worcester St.
North Grafton, MA 01536
Phone: 508-756-5111 Fax: 508-839-7500
CEO: John M. Nelson
CFO: Luis E. Leon
1991 Sales: $355 million Employees: 3,000
Symbol: WYMN Exchange: NASDAQ
Industry: Aerospace - aircraft equipment

Wynns International, Inc.
500 N. State College Blvd., Ste. 700
Orange, CA 92668
Phone: 714-938-3700 Fax: 714-938-3739
CEO: James Carroll
CFO: Seymour A. Schlosser
1991 Sales: $274 million Employees: 1,924
Symbol: WN Exchange: NYSE
Industry: Automotive & trucking - replacement parts

X-Rite, Inc.
3100 44th St. SW
Grandville, MI 49418
Phone: 616-534-7663 Fax: 616-534-9212
CEO: D. Ted Thompson
CFO: Duane Kluting
1991 Sales: $29 million Employees: 260
Symbol: XRIT Exchange: NASDAQ
Industry: Instruments - control

Xerox Corp.
800 Long Ridge Rd.
Stamford, CT 06902
Phone: 203-968-3000 Fax: 203-968-4312
CEO: Paul A. Allaire
CFO: Alan Z. Senter
1992 Sales: $13,980 million Employees: 109,400
Symbol: XRX Exchange: NYSE
Industry: Office equipment & supplies - business machines, insurance

Xicor, Inc.
1511 Buckeye Dr.
Milpitas, CA 95035
Phone: 408-432-8888 Fax: 408-432-0640
CEO: Raphael Klein
CFO: Klaus G. Hendig
1991 Sales: $94 million Employees: 1,022
Symbol: XICO Exchange: NASDAQ
Industry: Electrical components - semiconductors

Xilinx, Inc.
2100 Logic Dr.
San Jose, CA 95124
Phone: 408-559-7778 Fax: 408-559-7114
CEO: Bernard V. Vonderschmitt
CFO: Gordon M. Steel
1992 Sales: $136 million Employees: 482
Symbol: XLNX Exchange: NASDAQ
Industry: Computers - system software

indicates company is in *Hoover's Handbook of American Business.*

indicates company is in *Hoover's Handbook of World Business;* sales and employee numbers are for parent company.

Xircom, Inc.
26025 Mureau Rd.
Calabasas, CA 91302
Phone: 818-878-7600 Fax: —
CEO: Dirk I. Gates
CFO: Wallace B. Jones
1991 Sales: $26 million Employees: 108
Symbol: XIRC Exchange: NASDAQ
Industry: Computers - peripheral equipment

XOMA Corp.
2910 Seventh St.
Berkeley, CA 94710
Phone: 510-644-1170 Fax: 510-644-0539
CEO: Steven C. Mendell
CFO: Larry J. Strauss
1991 Sales: $17 million Employees: 336
Symbol: XOMA Exchange: NASDAQ
Industry: Biomedical & genetic products

Xplor Corp.
20 Exchange Place
New York, NY 10005
Phone: 212-480-1050 Fax: —
CEO: Eric W. Goldman
CFO: William C. Kaltnecker
1991 Sales: $1.3 million Employees: 8
Symbol: XPLR Exchange: NASDAQ
Industry: Oil & gas - US exploration & production

Xscribe Corp.
6160 Cornerstone Ct. East
San Diego, CA 92121
Phone: 619-457-5091 Fax: 619-456-0671
CEO: Suren G. Dutia
CFO: Bruce C. Myers
1992 Sales: $7.8 million Employees: 50
Symbol: XSCR Exchange: NASDAQ
Industry: Computers - transcription software

XTRA Corp.
1105 N. Market St., Ste. 1300
Wilmington, DE 19801
Phone: 302-478-0705 Fax: —
CEO: Robert B. Goergen
CFO: Michael J. Soja
1991 Sales: $209 million Employees: 604
Symbol: XTR Exchange: NYSE
Industry: Transportation - equipment & leasing

Xylogics, Inc.
53 Third Ave.
Burlington, MA 01803
Phone: 617-272-8140 Fax: 617-273-5392
CEO: Bruce J. Bergman
CFO: Maurice L. Castonguay
1991 Sales: $25 million Employees: 153
Symbol: XLGX Exchange: NASDAQ
Industry: Electrical components - high-performance peripherals

Xyplex, Inc.
330 Codman Hill Rd.
Boxborough, MA 01719
Phone: 508-264-9900 Fax: —
CEO: Peter J. Nesbeda
CFO: Paul J. Murphy
1991 Sales: $42 million Employees: 233
Symbol: XPLX Exchange: NASDAQ
Industry: Telecommunications equipment

Xytronyx, Inc.
6555 Nancy Ridge Dr., Ste. 200
San Diego, CA 92121
Phone: 619-546-1114 Fax: 619-546-1170
CEO: Peter Baram
CFO: H. F. Pete Nelson
1992 Sales: $0.3 million Employees: 20
Symbol: XYX Exchange: AMEX
Industry: Biomedical & genetic products

Yamaha Corporation of America
6600 Orangethorpe Ave.
Buena Park, CA 90620
Phone: 714-522-9011 Fax: 714-522-9832
CEO: Masahiko Arimoto
CFO: —
1992 Sales: $4,103 million Employees: 11,647
Parent: Yamaha Corporation
Industry: Musical instruments, pianos, home furniture

Yankee Energy System, Inc.
999 West St.
Rocky Hill, CT 06067
Phone: 203-721-2000 Fax: —
CEO: Philip T. Ashton
CFO: Leonard A. O'Connor
1991 Sales: $234 million Employees: 680
Symbol: YES Exchange: NYSE
Industry: Utility - gas distribution

Yellow Freight System
10777 Barkley Ave.
Overland Park, KS 66211
Phone: 913-345-1020 Fax: 913-344-3433
CEO: George E. Powell III
CFO: David E. Loeffler
1992 Sales: $2,263 million Employees: 28,700
Symbol: YELL Exchange: NASDAQ
Industry: Transportation - trucks

Yes Clothing Co.
1360 E. 17th St.
Los Angeles, CA 90021
Phone: 213-742-0201 Fax: 213-742-0526
CEO: George W. Randall
CFO: Irving Rosenbluth
1992 Sales: $36 million Employees: 150
Symbol: YSCO Exchange: NASDAQ
Industry: Textiles - apparel

York Financial Corp.
101 S. George St.
York, PA 17401
Phone: 717-846-8777 Fax: 717-846-0913
CEO: Robert W. Pullo
CFO: James H. Moss
1991 Sales: $86 million Employees: 394
Symbol: YFED Exchange: NASDAQ
Industry: Financial - savings and loans

York International Corp.
631 S. Richland Ave.
York, PA 17403
Phone: 717-771-7890 Fax: 717-771-6476
CEO: Robert N. Pokelwaldt
CFO: Dean T. DuCray
1992 Sales: $1,939 million Employees: 11,500
Symbol: YRK Exchange: NYSE
Industry: Building products - a/c & heating

York Research Corp.
280 Park Ave., Ste. 2700W
New York, NY 10017
Phone: 212-557-6200 Fax: 212-557-5678
CEO: Robert M. Beningson
CFO: Michael Trachtenberg
1992 Sales: $1.2 million Employees: 25
Symbol: YORK Exchange: NASDAQ
Industry: Energy - cogeneration

Young & Rubicam Inc.
285 Madison Ave.
New York, NY 10017
Phone: 212-210-3000 Fax: 212-490-6397
CEO: Alexander S. Kroll
CFO: Dave Greene
1991 Sales: $1,057 million Employees: 10,324
Ownership: Privately held
Industry: Advertising & communications

Young's Market Co.
500 S. Central Ave.
Los Angeles, CA 90013
Phone: 213-629-5571 Fax: 213-612-1239
CEO: Vernon O. Underwood, Jr.
CFO: Dennis Hamann
1991 Sales: $850 million Employees: 1,500
Ownership: Privately held
Industry: Food, spirits & wine - wholesale

Younkers, Inc.
701 Walnut St.
Des Moines, IA 50397
Phone: 515-244-1112 Fax: 515-246-3170
CEO: Thomas Gould
CFO: Alan R. Raxter
1991 Sales: $341 million Employees: 4,300
Symbol: YONK Exchange: NASDAQ
Industry: Retail - apparel & shoes

Z-Barten Productions
8611 Hayden Place
Culver City, CA 90232
Phone: 310-202-7070 Fax: 310-202-9270
CEO: Maureen Barten
CFO: Dale Zable
1991 Sales: $1.4 million Employees: 25
Ownership: Privately held
Industry: Paper products - confetti, gifts & craft items

Zapata Corp.
711 Louisiana St., Zapata Tower
Houston, TX 77002
Phone: 713-226-6000 Fax: 713-226-6052
CEO: Ronald C. Lassiter
CFO: Marvin J. Migura
1991 Sales: $93 million Employees: 2,200
Symbol: ZOS Exchange: NYSE
Industry: Oil & gas - offshore drilling

Zebra Technologies Corp.
333 Corporate Woods Pkwy.
Vernon Hills, IL 60061
Phone: 708-634-6700 Fax: 708-913-8766
CEO: Edward L. Kaplan
CFO: Gerhard Cless
1991 Sales: $46 million Employees: 200
Symbol: ZBRA Exchange: NASDAQ
Industry: Machinery - bar code printing

Zeiders Enterprises, Inc.
3182 Golansky Blvd., Ste. 201
Woodbridge, VA 22192
Phone: 703-878-2007 Fax: 703-878-2703
CEO: Mike Zeiders
CFO: Cheryl Pettit
1991 Sales: $3.5 million Employees: 90
Ownership: Privately held
Industry: Business services - professional management services

Zeigler Coal Holding Company
50 Jerome Ln.
Fairview Heights, IL 62208
Phone: 618-394-2400 Fax: 618-394-2473
CEO: Michael K. Reilly
CFO: George Holway
1992 Sales: $1,100 million Employees: 4,000
Ownership: Privately held
Industry: Coal

Zemex Corp.
One W. Pack Square, Ste. 700
Asheville, NC 28801
Phone: 704-255-4900 Fax: 704-255-4934
CEO: Gerard E. Wood
CFO: Robert W. Morris
1991 Sales: $35 million Employees: 491
Symbol: ZMX Exchange: NYSE
Industry: Metals - nonferrous

indicates company is in *Hoover's Handbook of American Business.*

indicates company is in *Hoover's Handbook of World Business;* sales and employee numbers are for parent company.

Zenith Electronics Corp.
1000 Milwaukee Ave.
Glenview, IL 60025
Phone: 708-391-7000 Fax: 708-391-7253
CEO: Jerry K. Pearlman
CFO: Kell B. Benson
1991 Sales: $1,322 million Employees: 27,700
Symbol: ZE Exchange: NYSE
Industry: Audio & video home products

Zenith Laboratories, Inc.
140 Legrand Ave.
Northvale, NJ 07647
Phone: 201-767-1700 Fax: 201-784-1719
CEO: John H. Klein
CFO: Richard M. Shepperd
1991 Sales: $58 million Employees: 436
Symbol: ZENL Exchange: NASDAQ
Industry: Drugs - generic

Zenith National Insurance Corp.
21255 Califa St.
Woodland Hills, CA 91367
Phone: 818-713-1000 Fax: 818-713-0091
CEO: Stanley R. Zax
CFO: Fredricka Taubitz
1991 Sales: $546 million Employees: —
Symbol: ZNT Exchange: NYSE
Industry: Insurance - property & casualty

ZEOS International, Ltd.
530 Fifth Ave. NW
St. Paul, MN 55112
Phone: 612-633-4591 Fax: 612-633-0110
CEO: George E. Herrick
CFO: John K. Bakewell
1991 Sales: $231 million Employees: 744
Symbol: ZEOS Exchange: NASDAQ
Industry: Computers - mini & micro

Zero Corp.
444 S. Flower St., Ste. 2100
Los Angeles, CA 90071
Phone: 213-629-7000 Fax: 213-629-2366
CEO: Wilford D. Godbold, Jr.
CFO: George A. Daniels
1992 Sales: $160 million Employees: 1,715
Symbol: ZRO Exchange: NYSE
Industry: Electrical components - specialized electronic enclosures, card cages

Zeus Components, Inc.
100 Midland Ave.
Port Chester, NY 10573
Phone: 914-937-7400 Fax: 914-937-2553
CEO: Robert E. Schrader
CFO: Martin S. Fawer
1991 Sales: $96 million Employees: 373
Symbol: ZEUS Exchange: NASDAQ
Industry: Electronics - parts distribution

Zia Cosmetics
410 Townsend, 2nd Fl.
San Francisco, CA 94107
Phone: 415-543-7546 Fax: 415-543-7694
CEO: Franz Strachan
CFO: Zia Wesley-Hosford
1991 Sales: $1.2 million Employees: 16
Ownership: Privately held
Industry: Cosmetics & toiletries - natural skin care products

Ziegler BC & Co.
215 N. Main St.
West Bend, WI 53095
Phone: 414-334-5521 Fax: 414-334-0388
CEO: Peter D. Ziegler
CFO: V. C. Van Vooren
1991 Sales: $41 million Employees: 444
Symbol: ZCO Exchange: AMEX
Industry: Financial - investment bankers

Ziff Communications Co.
One Park Ave.
New York, NY 10016
Phone: 212-503-3500 Fax: 212-503-4599
CEO: William B. Ziff, Jr.
CFO: Patrick Burke
1991 Sales: $600 million Employees: 3,100
Ownership: Privately held
Industry: Publishing - magazines, direct marketing

Zilog, Inc.
210 Hacienda Ave.
Campbell, CA 95008
Phone: 408-370-8000 Fax: 408-370-8056
CEO: Edgar A. Sack
CFO: William R. Walker
1991 Sales: $110 million Employees: 1,308
Symbol: ZLOG Exchange: NASDAQ
Industry: Electrical components - integrated circuits

Zions Bancorporation
1380 Kennecott Bldg., Ste. 1380
Salt Lake City, UT 84133
Phone: 801-524-4787 Fax: 801-524-4659
CEO: Harris H. Simmons
CFO: Gary L. Anderson
1991 Sales: $344 million Employees: 2,405
Symbol: ZION Exchange: NASDAQ
Industry: Banks - West

Zitel Corp.
630 Alder Dr.
Milpitas, CA 95035
Phone: 408-321-9600 Fax: 408-321-9696
CEO: Jack H. King
CFO: Henry C. Harris
1991 Sales: $46 million Employees: 166
Symbol: ZITL Exchange: NASDAQ
Industry: Computers - solid state memory systems

Zoll Medical Corp.
500 W. Cummings Park
Woburn, MA 01801
Phone: 617-933-9150 Fax: —
CEO: Rolf S. Stutz
CFO: Duane M. Desisto
1991 Sales: $14 million Employees: —
Symbol: ZOLL Exchange: NASDAQ
Industry: Medical products

Zoom Telephonics, Inc.
207 South St.
Boston, MA 02111
Phone: 617-423-1072 Fax: 617-423-9231
CEO: Frank Manning
CFO: George H. Simmons
1991 Sales: $26 million Employees: 82
Symbol: ZOOMF Exchange: NASDAQ
Industry: Computers - modems

Zurn Industries, Inc.
One Zurn Place
Erie, PA 16505
Phone: 814-452-2111 Fax: 814-459-3535
CEO: George H. Schofield
CFO: Ronald A. Drapeau
1992 Sales: $596 million Employees: 3,900
Symbol: ZRN Exchange: NYSE
Industry: Pollution control equipment & services - environmental quality control systems

Zycad Corp.
1380 Willow Rd.
Menlo Park, CA 94025
Phone: 415-688-7400 Fax: 415-688-7550
CEO: Phillips W. Smith
CFO: Peter J. Cassidy
1991 Sales: $44 million Employees: 229
Symbol: ZCAD Exchange: NASDAQ
Industry: Computers - computer-aided engineering hardware for integrated circuit design

Zygo Corp.
Laurel Brook Rd.
Middlefield, CT 06455
Phone: 203-347-8506 Fax: 203-347-8372
CEO: Paul F. Forman
CFO: Clarence H. Thiesen
1992 Sales: $27 million Employees: 206
Symbol: ZIGO Exchange: NASDAQ
Industry: Electronics - measuring instruments

THE

INDEXES

Index of Companies by Headquarters Location

◆

Index of Companies by Industry

◆

Index of Companies by Stock Exchange Symbol

1993

INDEX OF COMPANIES BY HEADQUARTERS LOCATION

INDEX OF COMPANIES BY HEADQUARTERS LOCATION

INDEX OF COMPANIES BY HEADQUARTERS LOCATION

INDEX OF COMPANIES BY HEADQUARTERS LOCATION

INDEX OF COMPANIES BY HEADQUARTERS LOCATION

INDEX OF COMPANIES BY HEADQUARTERS LOCATION

INDEX OF COMPANIES BY HEADQUARTERS LOCATION

INDEX OF COMPANIES BY HEADQUARTERS LOCATION

INDEX OF COMPANIES BY HEADQUARTERS LOCATION

INDEX OF COMPANIES BY HEADQUARTERS LOCATION

GEORGIA

INDEX OF COMPANIES BY HEADQUARTERS LOCATION

INDEX OF COMPANIES BY HEADQUARTERS LOCATION

INDEX OF COMPANIES BY HEADQUARTERS LOCATION

INDEX OF COMPANIES BY HEADQUARTERS LOCATION

INDEX OF COMPANIES BY HEADQUARTERS LOCATION

INDEX OF COMPANIES BY HEADQUARTERS LOCATION

INDEX OF COMPANIES BY HEADQUARTERS LOCATION

INDEX OF COMPANIES BY HEADQUARTERS LOCATION

INDEX OF COMPANIES BY HEADQUARTERS LOCATION

INDEX OF COMPANIES BY HEADQUARTERS LOCATION

INDEX OF COMPANIES BY HEADQUARTERS LOCATION

INDEX OF COMPANIES BY HEADQUARTERS LOCATION

INDEX OF COMPANIES BY HEADQUARTERS LOCATION

INDEX OF COMPANIES BY HEADQUARTERS LOCATION

INDEX OF COMPANIES BY HEADQUARTERS LOCATION

INDEX OF COMPANIES BY HEADQUARTERS LOCATION

INDEX OF COMPANIES BY HEADQUARTERS LOCATION

INDEX OF COMPANIES BY HEADQUARTERS LOCATION

INDEX OF COMPANIES BY HEADQUARTERS LOCATION

INDEX OF COMPANIES BY HEADQUARTERS LOCATION

INDEX OF COMPANIES BY HEADQUARTERS LOCATION

INDEX OF COMPANIES BY HEADQUARTERS LOCATION

INDEX OF COMPANIES BY HEADQUARTERS LOCATION

INDEX OF COMPANIES BY HEADQUARTERS LOCATION

INDEX OF COMPANIES BY HEADQUARTERS LOCATION

INDEX OF COMPANIES BY HEADQUARTERS LOCATION

INDEX OF COMPANIES BY HEADQUARTERS LOCATION

INDEX OF COMPANIES BY HEADQUARTERS LOCATION

INDEX OF COMPANIES BY HEADQUARTERS LOCATION

INDEX OF COMPANIES BY INDUSTRY

INDEX OF COMPANIES BY INDUSTRY

INDEX OF COMPANIES BY INDUSTRY

Banks - Southeast

Banks - Southwest

Banks - West

INDEX OF COMPANIES BY INDUSTRY

INDEX OF COMPANIES BY INDUSTRY

INDEX OF COMPANIES BY INDUSTRY

INDEX OF COMPANIES BY INDUSTRY

INDEX OF COMPANIES BY INDUSTRY

INDEX OF COMPANIES BY INDUSTRY

INDEX OF COMPANIES BY INDUSTRY

Drugs

Drugs - generic

INDEX OF COMPANIES BY INDUSTRY

INDEX OF COMPANIES BY INDUSTRY

INDEX OF COMPANIES BY INDUSTRY

INDEX OF COMPANIES BY INDUSTRY

INDEX OF COMPANIES BY INDUSTRY

INDEX OF COMPANIES BY INDUSTRY

INDEX OF COMPANIES BY INDUSTRY

INDEX OF COMPANIES BY INDUSTRY

INDEX OF COMPANIES BY INDUSTRY

Medical products

Medical services

Metal ores - misc.

Metal processing & fabrication

INDEX OF COMPANIES BY INDUSTRY

INDEX OF COMPANIES BY INDUSTRY

INDEX OF COMPANIES BY INDUSTRY

INDEX OF COMPANIES BY INDUSTRY

INDEX OF COMPANIES BY INDUSTRY

INDEX OF COMPANIES BY INDUSTRY

INDEX OF COMPANIES BY INDUSTRY

INDEX OF COMPANIES BY INDUSTRY

INDEX OF COMPANIES BY INDUSTRY

INDEX OF COMPANIES BY INDUSTRY

INDEX OF COMPANIES BY STOCK EXCHANGE SYMBOL

INDEX OF COMPANIES BY STOCK EXCHANGE SYMBOL

INDEX OF COMPANIES BY STOCK EXCHANGE SYMBOL

INDEX OF COMPANIES BY STOCK EXCHANGE SYMBOL

INDEX OF COMPANIES BY STOCK EXCHANGE SYMBOL

INDEX OF COMPANIES BY STOCK EXCHANGE SYMBOL

INDEX OF COMPANIES BY STOCK EXCHANGE SYMBOL

INDEX OF COMPANIES BY STOCK EXCHANGE SYMBOL

INDEX OF COMPANIES BY STOCK EXCHANGE SYMBOL

INDEX OF COMPANIES BY STOCK EXCHANGE SYMBOL

INDEX OF COMPANIES BY STOCK EXCHANGE SYMBOL

INDEX OF COMPANIES BY STOCK EXCHANGE SYMBOL

INDEX OF COMPANIES BY STOCK EXCHANGE SYMBOL

INDEX OF COMPANIES BY STOCK EXCHANGE SYMBOL

INDEX OF COMPANIES BY STOCK EXCHANGE SYMBOL

INDEX OF COMPANIES BY STOCK EXCHANGE SYMBOL

INDEX OF COMPANIES BY STOCK EXCHANGE SYMBOL

INDEX OF COMPANIES BY STOCK EXCHANGE SYMBOL

INDEX OF COMPANIES BY STOCK EXCHANGE SYMBOL

INDEX OF COMPANIES BY STOCK EXCHANGE SYMBOL

INDEX OF COMPANIES BY STOCK EXCHANGE SYMBOL

INDEX OF COMPANIES BY STOCK EXCHANGE SYMBOL

INDEX OF COMPANIES BY STOCK EXCHANGE SYMBOL

INDEX OF COMPANIES BY STOCK EXCHANGE SYMBOL

INDEX OF COMPANIES BY STOCK EXCHANGE SYMBOL

INDEX OF COMPANIES BY STOCK EXCHANGE SYMBOL

INDEX OF COMPANIES BY STOCK EXCHANGE SYMBOL

INDEX OF COMPANIES BY STOCK EXCHANGE SYMBOL

INDEX OF COMPANIES BY STOCK EXCHANGE SYMBOL

INDEX OF COMPANIES BY STOCK EXCHANGE SYMBOL

INDEX OF COMPANIES BY STOCK EXCHANGE SYMBOL

INDEX OF COMPANIES BY STOCK EXCHANGE SYMBOL

INDEX OF COMPANIES BY STOCK EXCHANGE SYMBOL

INDEX OF COMPANIES BY STOCK EXCHANGE SYMBOL

INDEX OF COMPANIES BY STOCK EXCHANGE SYMBOL

INDEX OF COMPANIES BY STOCK EXCHANGE SYMBOL

INDEX OF COMPANIES BY STOCK EXCHANGE SYMBOL

INDEX OF COMPANIES BY STOCK EXCHANGE SYMBOL

INDEX OF COMPANIES BY STOCK EXCHANGE SYMBOL

INDEX OF COMPANIES BY STOCK EXCHANGE SYMBOL

INDEX OF COMPANIES BY STOCK EXCHANGE SYMBOL

ATTENTION SALES AND MARKETING EXECUTIVES, JOB HUNTERS, AND FUND RAISERS!

REACH YOUR PROSPECTS QUICKLY AND EASILY WITH HOOVER'S MASTERLIST ON DISK

The entire contents of *Hoover's MasterList of Major U.S. Companies 1993* is available on an IBM-compatible or Macintosh disk for only $129.95.

Use this data with your own software to:

- create prospect lists
- generate mailing labels
- merge personalized letters
- request company or product information

The disk contains approximately 12,000 executives' names from nearly 6,000 companies.

The data is available in tab-separated text (for use in word-processing programs), database, or spreadsheet format.

Save $30 when you order the book and disk combo for only $149.95.

To order, use the attached postage-paid reply card or call 800-486-8666. Please specify disk type and format when ordering.

OTHER VALUABLE RESOURCES FROM THE REFERENCE PRESS

Hoover's Handbook of American Business 1993
$34.95 hardcover, ISBN 1-878753-05-3
$24.95 trade paper, ISBN 1-878753-03-7
500 one-page profiles of the largest and most influential enterprises in America, including company histories and strategies, 10 years of key financial and employment data, lists of products, key officers, addresses, phone numbers, and fax numbers. Fully indexed.

Hoover's Handbook of World Business 1993
$32.95 hardcover, ISBN 1-878753-06-1
$21.95 trade paper, ISBN 1-878753-04-5
Profiles 191 non-U.S.–based companies that employ thousands of Americans in the U.S. and abroad. Includes a discussion of the world economy and business/economic profiles of 66 countries and 5 regions. The hardcover edition includes a combined index of this book and *Hoover's Handbook of American Business 1993.*

Hoover's Handbook of World Business 1993 on Disk
$49.95 computer disk
Executives' names, addresses, phone numbers, and fax numbers from *Hoover's Handbook of World Business 1993* on an IBM-compatible or Macintosh disk in tab-separated text, spreadsheet, or database format.

Hoover's Handbook of Emerging Companies 1993–1994
$32.95 hardcover, ISBN 1-878753-18-5
The first reasonably priced guide to 250 of America's most exciting growth enterprises. Company profiles include overviews and strategies, key financial data, lists of products and key competitors, names of key officers, addresses, and phone and fax numbers. Also included are lists of fast-growing and emerging companies from *Inc., Business Week, Forbes,* and other publications. Complete index. Available June 1993.

The Wilson Directory of Emerging Market Funds 1992–1993
$99.95 trade paper, ISBN 0-9696526-0-7
Profiles more than 400 equity funds with investments in developing countries. Profiles include country of domicile, closed or open-ended status, date operations commenced, fiscal year-end, stock exchange listing, contact details, size of fund, and more.

The Computer Industry Almanac 1993
$55.00 hardcover, ISBN 0-942107-04-7
Information and statistics on 2,500 companies and 6,000 people in the computer industry. This 816-page guide includes lists of over 400 periodicals in the industry; lists and rankings of companies, people, and products; and an overview of the industry. Available May 1993.

Access Nippon 1993: How to Succeed in Japan
$34.95 trade paper, ISBN 1-878753-13-4
The definitive guide to business in Japan, with general background information on how to enter this huge market and profiles of 29 key industries and nearly 300 Japanese corporate giants.

French Company Handbook 1992
$49.95 trade paper, ISBN 2-905437-07-3
Detailed profiles of France's largest companies, plus a wealth of information about the French economy. Profiles include company history; number of employees; sales by product line and geographic area; trademarks; international activities and exports; strategies, trends, and important developments; financial information in francs and dollars; and address, phone number, and fax number.

Brazil Company Handbook 1992, ISBN 1-878753-10-X
Mexico Company Handbook 1992, ISBN 1-878753-11-8
Venezuela Company Handbook 1992, ISBN 1-878753-12-6
$29.95 each, trade paper
Order all three for $79.85, ISBN 1-878753-16-9
Each handbook is updated annually and contains profiles of major public companies; a profile of the nation's economy; information on foreign investment opportunities and regulations; taxation and accounting principles and practices; vital data on each country's major bolsas (stock exchanges); and names of local mutual funds, money managers, and investment advisors. All financial information is in US$, for easy comparison. The 1990 and 1991 editions are also available.

Nordic Stock Guide 1992
$29.95 trade paper, ISBN 82-7353-015-9
This book contains financial profiles of 102 companies in Denmark, Finland, Norway, and Sweden, plus interest rate histories, exchange rates, commodity prices, and indexes for the Nordic countries. Also includes detailed financial data for each company.

Statistical Abstract of the United States 1992
$19.95 hardcover, ISBN 1-878753-08-8
The Bureau of the Census's annual compendium of who we are, where we live, what we do, and how we spend our national resources. Available from The Reference Press at 40% off the government price.

The 1993 National Directory of Addresses and Telephone Numbers
$79.95 trade paper, ISBN 1-55888-140-9
Contains addresses and phone numbers for top U.S. businesses in 500 industries, over 8,000 government agencies, colleges and universities, chambers of commerce, foreign embassies and consulates, and more. Listings are organized alphabetically and by business type, with more than 115,000 unique listings. All listings include full addresses and up-to-date telephone numbers. Most also have fax numbers.

The National Book of Lists 1992
$19.95 trade paper, ISBN 0-9632232-0-8
Identifies the top 40 companies or organizations in each of 50 categories, such as biotechnology, exporters, government agencies, private companies, SBA lenders, semiconductor manufacturers, and venture capital firms. Includes the company name, address, phone number, fax number, names and titles of top management, ranking criteria, and more.

TO ORDER, CALL 800-486-8666

I want to order the indicated quantities of the following publications:

Hoover's MasterList of Major U.S. Companies 1993
_______ $49.95 hardcover, ISBN 1-878753-14-2

Hoover's MasterList of Major U.S. Companies 1993 on Disk
_______ $129.95, ISBN 1-878753-32-0 Specify disk: PC❑ Mac❑ Format: tab text❑ spreadsheet❑ database❑

Hoover's MasterList of Major U.S. Companies 1993 book and disk combo
_______ $149.95, ISBN 1-878753-33-9 Specify disk: PC❑ Mac❑ Format: tab text❑ spreadsheet❑ database❑

Hoover's Handbook of World Business 1993
_______ $21.95 trade paper, ISBN 1-878753-04-5
_______ $32.95 library edition (hardcover with combined indexes from *Hoover's Handbook of World Business 1993* and *Hoover's Handbook of American Business 1993*), ISBN 1-878753-06-1

Hoover's Handbook of World Business 1993 on Disk
_______ $49.95, computer disk of all executive names and company addresses, phone numbers, and fax numbers

Hoover's Handbook of American Business 1993
_______ $24.95 trade paper, ISBN 1-878753-03-7 _______ $34.95 hardcover, ISBN 1-878753-05-3

Complete set of Hoover's Handbooks
Hoover's Handbook 1991, Hoover's Handbook of American Business 1992, Hoover's Handbook of World Business 1992, Hoover's Handbook of American Business 1993, Hoover's Handbook of World Business 1993
_______ $89.95 (a $113.75 value) plus $12.00 shipping and handling, all books trade paper

Hoover's Handbook of Emerging Companies 1993–1994 (available June 1993)
_______ $32.95 hardcover, ISBN 1-878753-18-5

The Computer Industry Almanac 1993
_______ $55.00 hardcover, ISBN 0-942107-04-7

Statistical Abstract of the United States 1992
_______ $19.95 hardcover, ISBN 1-878753-08-8

The Wilson Directory of Emerging Market Funds 1992–1993
_______ $99.95 trade paper, ISBN 0-9696526-0-7

Mexico Company Handbook 1992
_______ $29.95 trade paper, ISBN 1-878753-11-8

Brazil Company Handbook 1992
_______ $29.95 trade paper, ISBN 1-878753-10-X

Venezuela Company Handbook 1992
_______ $29.95 trade paper, ISBN 1-878753-12-6

Complete set of Latin American company handbooks
_______ $79.85 plus $6.00 shipping and handling, ISBN 1-878753-16-9

Access Nippon 1993
_______ $34.95 trade paper, ISBN 1-878753-13-4

Nordic Stock Guide 1992
_______ $29.95 trade paper, ISBN 82-7353-015-9

French Company Handbook 1992
_______ $49.95 trade paper, ISBN 2-905437-07-3

The 1993 National Directory of Addresses and Telephone Numbers
_______ $79.95 trade paper, ISBN 1-55888-140-9

The National Book of Lists 1992
_______ $19.95 trade paper, ISBN 0-9632232-0-8

SHIPPING & HANDLING

Unless otherwise indicated, shipping and handling to US addresses is $3.50 per item ordered for the first 3 items and $1.50 for each additional item.

MBRM93

❑ Make mine a standing order______(Y/N)
❑ Send me information about your other business reference products.
❑ I have the following suggestions for reference books: ______________________

❑ I bought this book from/at ______________________
Name ______________________ Telephone No. (______) ______________
Affiliation ______________________ Title ______________
Street Address ______________________
City ______________________ State ______________ Zip ______________

Credit card or prepayment required, except for public libraries and academic institutions.

❑ MasterCard ❑ Visa ❑ American Express Acct. No. ______________________
Signature ______________________ Expiration Date ______________
❑ Check for $______________ enclosed. ❑ Library /school PO# ______________

TO ORDER CALL 800-486-8666 OR FAX US AT 512-454-9401.

The Reference Press, Inc. • 6448 Highway 290 East, Ste. E-104, Austin, Texas 78723 • 512-454-7778

I want to order the indicated quantities of the following publications:

Hoover's MasterList of Major U.S. Companies 1993
_______ $49.95 hardcover, ISBN 1-878753-14-2

Hoover's MasterList of Major U.S. Companies 1993 on Disk
_______ $129.95, ISBN 1-878753-32-0 Specify disk: PC❑ Mac❑ Format: tab text❑ spreadsheet❑ database❑

Hoover's MasterList of Major U.S. Companies 1993 book and disk combo
_______ $149.95, ISBN 1-878753-33-9 Specify disk: PC❑ Mac❑ Format: tab text❑ spreadsheet❑ database❑

Hoover's Handbook of World Business 1993
_______ $21.95 trade paper, ISBN 1-878753-04-5
_______ $32.95 library edition (hardcover with combined indexes from *Hoover's Handbook of World Business 1993* and *Hoover's Handbook of American Business 1993*), ISBN 1-878753-06-1

Hoover's Handbook of World Business 1993 on Disk
_______ $49.95, computer disk of all executive names and company addresses, phone numbers, and fax numbers

Hoover's Handbook of American Business 1993
_______ $24.95 trade paper, ISBN 1-878753-03-7 _______ $34.95 hardcover, ISBN 1-878753-05-3

Complete set of Hoover's Handbooks
Hoover's Handbook 1991, Hoover's Handbook of American Business 1992, Hoover's Handbook of World Business 1992, Hoover's Handbook of American Business 1993, Hoover's Handbook of World Business 1993
_______ $89.95 (a $113.75 value) plus $12.00 shipping and handling, all books trade paper

Hoover's Handbook of Emerging Companies 1993–1994 (available June 1993)
_______ $32.95 hardcover, ISBN 1-878753-18-5

The Computer Industry Almanac 1993
_______ $55.00 hardcover, ISBN 0-942107-04-7

Statistical Abstract of the United States 1992
_______ $19.95 hardcover, ISBN 1-878753-08-8

The Wilson Directory of Emerging Market Funds 1992–1993
_______ $99.95 trade paper, ISBN 0-9696526-0-7

Mexico Company Handbook 1992
_______ $29.95 trade paper, ISBN 1-878753-11-8

Brazil Company Handbook 1992
_______ $29.95 trade paper, ISBN 1-878753-10-X

Venezuela Company Handbook 1992
_______ $29.95 trade paper, ISBN 1-878753-12-6

Complete set of Latin American company handbooks
_______ $79.85 plus $6.00 shipping and handling, ISBN 1-878753-16-9

Access Nippon 1993
_______ $34.95 trade paper, ISBN 1-878753-13-4

Nordic Stock Guide 1992
_______ $29.95 trade paper, ISBN 82-7353-015-9

French Company Handbook 1992
_______ $49.95 trade paper, ISBN 2-905437-07-3

The 1993 National Directory of Addresses and Telephone Numbers
_______ $79.95 trade paper, ISBN 1-55888-140-9

The National Book of Lists 1992
_______ $19.95 trade paper, ISBN 0-9632232-0-8

SHIPPING & HANDLING

Unless otherwise indicated, shipping and handling to US addresses is $3.50 per item ordered for the first 3 items and $1.50 for each additional item.

MBRM93

❑ Make mine a standing order______(Y/N)
❑ Send me information about your other business reference products.
❑ I have the following suggestions for reference books: ______________________

❑ I bought this book from/at ______________________
Name ______________________ Telephone No. (______) ______________
Affiliation ______________________ Title ______________
Street Address ______________________
City ______________________ State ______________ Zip ______________

Credit card or prepayment required, except for public libraries and academic institutions.

❑ MasterCard ❑ Visa ❑ American Express Acct. No. ______________________
Signature ______________________ Expiration Date ______________
❑ Check for $______________ enclosed. ❑ Library /school PO# ______________

TO ORDER CALL 800-486-8666 OR FAX US AT 512-454-9401.

The Reference Press, Inc. • 6448 Highway 290 East, Ste. E-104, Austin, Texas 78723 • 512-454-7778

Please tape along edge before mailing. Do NOT staple.

NO POSTAGE
NECESSARY
IF MAILED
IN THE
UNITED STATES

BUSINESS REPLY MAIL

FIRST-CLASS MAIL PERMIT NO. 7641 AUSTIN TX

POSTAGE WILL BE PAID BY ADDRESSEE

THE REFERENCE PRESS INC
6448 E HIGHWAY 290 STE E104
AUSTIN TX 78723-9965

Please tape along edge before mailing. Do NOT staple.

NO POSTAGE
NECESSARY
IF MAILED
IN THE
UNITED STATES

BUSINESS REPLY MAIL

FIRST-CLASS MAIL PERMIT NO. 7641 AUSTIN TX

POSTAGE WILL BE PAID BY ADDRESSEE

THE REFERENCE PRESS INC
6448 E HIGHWAY 290 STE E104
AUSTIN TX 78723-9965